MW01124693

Lost Books of the Bible: The Great Rejected Texts

By Joseph B. Lumpkin

The Lost Books of the Bible: The Rejected Texts
Copyright © 2009 Joseph B. Lumpkin.
All rights reserved.

Printed in the United States of America. No part of this book may be used or reproduced in any manner whatsoever without written permission except in the case of brief quotations embodied in critical articles and reviews.

First time or interested authors, contact Fifth Estate Publishers, Post Office Box 116, Blountsville, AL 35031.

First Printing February 2009

Cover Design by An Quigley

Printed on acid-free paper

Library of Congress Control No: 2009903201

ISBN: 9781936533572

Fifth Estate 2009

Table of Contents

Section One

Lost Scriptures of the Old Testament

Section Two

Apocalyptic Writings and the End of Days

Section Three

Lost Scriptures of the New Testament

INTRODUCTION

The study of scripture is a lifelong venture. Many times our search for deeper understanding of the holy book leads to questions beyond the Bible itself. As we encounter references to social conditions, cultural practices, and even other writings mentioned within the scriptures we are called to investigate and expand our knowledge in order to fully appreciate the context, knowledge base, and cultural significance of what is being taught. Thus, to fully understand the Bible, we are necessarily drawn to sources outside the Bible. These sources add to the historical, social, or theological understanding of Biblical times. As our view becomes more macrocosmic, we see the panoramic setting and further understand the full truth within the scriptures.

To point us to the sources we should be concerned with, we must know which books were popular and important at the time. There are several books mentioned in the Bible, which are not included in the Bible. They are not spiritual canon, either because they were not available at the time the canon was originally adopted, or at the time they were not considered "inspired." In cases when inspiration was questioned, one could argue that any book quoted or mentioned by a prophet or an apostle should be considered as spiritual canon, unfortunately this position would prove too simplistic.

Books and writings can fall under various categories such as civil records and laws, historical documents, or spiritual writings. A city or state census is not inspired, but it could add insight into certain areas of life. Spiritual writings which are directly quoted in the Bible serve as insights into the beliefs of the writer or what was considered acceptable by society at the time. As with any new discovery, invention, or belief, the new is interpreted based upon the structure of what came before. This was the way in the first century Christian church as beliefs were based upon the old Jewish understanding. Although, one should realize pagan beliefs were also added to the church as non-Jewish populations were converted, bringing with them the foundations of their beliefs on which they interpreted Christianity. In the case of Jude, James, Paul, and others, the Jewish past was giving way to the Christian present but their understanding and doctrine were still being influenced by what they had learned and experienced previously. It becomes obvious that to understand the Bible one should endeavor to investigate the books and doctrines that most influenced the writers of the Bible. Some of these doctrines evolved to become today's faith. Some diverged and competed as with orthodox doctrine, other simply faded away.

The Dead Sea Scrolls found in the caves of Qumran are of great interest in the venture of clarifying the history and doctrine in existence between biblical times and the fixing of canon. The scrolls were penned in the second century B.C. and were in use at least until the destruction of the second temple in 70 A.D. Similar scrolls to those found in the eleven caves of Qumran were also found at the Masada stronghold which fell in 73 A.D. Fragments of every book of the Old Testament except Esther were found in the caves of Qumran, but so were many other books.

Some of these books are considered to have been of equal importance and influence to the people of Qumran and to the writers and scholars of the time. Some of those studying the scrolls found in Qumran were the writers of the New Testament.

Knowing this, one might ask which of the dozens of non-canonical books most influenced the writers of the New Testament. It is possible to ascertain the existence of certain influences within the Bible context by using the Bible itself. The Bible can direct us to other works in three ways. The work can be mentioned by name, as is the Book of Jasher. The work can be quoted within the Bible text, as is the case with the Book of Enoch. The existence of the work can be alluded to, as is the case of the missing letter from the apostle Paul to the Corinthians.

In the case of those books named in the Bible, one can set a list as the titles are named. The list is lengthier than one might at first suspect. Most of these works have not been found. Some have been unearthed but their authenticity is questioned. Others have been found and the link between scripture and scroll is generally accepted. Following is a list of books mentioned in the Holy Bible.

The Book of Jasher: There are two references to the book in the Old Testament:

2 Samuel 1:18 - Behold, it is written in the Book of Jasher. "So the sun stood still, and the moon stopped, until the nations avenged themselves of their enemies."

Joshua 10:13 - Is it not written in the Book of Jasher? And the sun stopped in the middle of the sky and did not hasten to go down for about a whole day.

There are several books which have come to us entitled, "Book of Jasher." One is an ethical treatise from the Middle Ages. It begins with a section on the Mystery of the Creation of the World: It is clearly unrelated to the Biblical Book of Jasher.

Another was published in 1829 supposedly translated by Flaccus Albinus Alcuinus. It opens with the Chapter 1 Verse 1 reading: "While it was the beginning, darkness overspread the face of nature." It is now considered a fake.

The third and most important is by Midrash, first translated into English in 1840. It opens with Chapter 1 Verse 1 reading: "And God said, Let us make man in our image, after our likeness, and God created man in his own image." A comparison of Joshua 10:13 with Jasher 88:63-64 and 2Sam. 1:18 with Jasher 56:9 makes it clear that this Book of Jasher at least follows close enough with the Bible to be the Book of Jasher mentioned in the Bible.

Other books mentioned by name in the Bible are:

1. The Book of Wars of the Lord: "Therefore it is said in the Book of the Wars of the Lord." Num. 21:14

2. The Annals of Jehu: "Now the rest of the acts of Jehoshaphat, first to last, behold, they are written in the annals of Jehu the son of Hanani, which is recorded in the Book of the Kings of Israel." 2 Chronicles 20:34
3. The treatise of the Book of the Kings: "As to his sons and the many oracles against him and the rebuilding of the house of God, behold, they are written in the treatise of the Book of the Kings. Then Amaziah his son became king in his place." 2 Chronicles 24:27
4. The Book of Records, Book of the Chronicles of Ahasuerus: "Now when the plot was investigated and found to be so, they were both hanged on a gallows; and it was written in the Book of the Chronicles in the king's presence." ... "During that night the king could not sleep so he gave an order to bring the book of records, the chronicles, and they were read before the king." Esther 2:23; 6:1
5. The Acts of Solomon: "Now the rest of the acts of Solomon and whatever he did, and his wisdom, are they not written in the book of the Acts of Solomon?" 1 Kings 11:41
6. The Sayings of Hozai: "His prayer also and how God was entreated by him, and all his sin, his unfaithfulness, and the sites on which he built high places and erected the Asherim and the carved images, before he humbled himself, behold, they are written in the records of the Hozai." 2 Chronicles 33:19
7. The Chronicles of David: "Joab the son of Zeruiah had begun to count them, but did not finish; and because of this, wrath came upon Israel, and the number was not included in the account of the Chronicles of King David." 1 Chronicles 27:24
8. The Chronicles of Samuel, Nathan, Gad: "Now the acts of King David, from first to last, are written in the Chronicles of Samuel the seer, in the Chronicles of Nathan the prophet and in the Chronicles of Gad the seer." 1 Chronicles 29:29
9. Samuel's book: "Then Samuel told the people the ordinances of the kingdom, and wrote them in the book and placed it before the Lord." 1 Samuel 10:25
10. The Records of Nathan the prophet: "Now the rest of the acts of Solomon, from first to last, are they not written in the Records of Nathan the prophet, and in the prophecy of Ahijah the Shilonite, and in the visions of Iddo the seer concerning Jeroboam the son of Nebat?" 2 Chronicles 9:29
11. The Prophecy of Ahijah the Shilonite: "Now the rest of the acts of Solomon, from first to last, are they not written in the Records of Nathan the prophet, and in the prophecy of Ahijah the Shilonite, and in the visions of Iddo the seer concerning Jeroboam the son of Nebat?" 2 Chronicles 9:29
12. The Treatise of the Prophet Iddo: "Now the rest of the acts of Abijah, and his ways and his words are written in the treatise of the prophet Iddo." 2 Chronicles 13:22
13. The Book Of Jasher: "Is it not writeen in the book of Jasher? 2 Samuel 1:18 and Joshua 10:13

The existence of a book can be inferred as well, this is clearly seen with several missing epistles. Paul's letter to the church at Laodicea: "When this letter is read among you, have it also read in the church of the Laodiceans; and you, for your part read my letter that is coming from Laodicea." Colossians 4:16 (Since three earlier manuscripts do not contain the words "at Ephesus" in Eph 1:1, some have speculated that the letter coming from Laodicea was in fact the letter of Ephesians. Apostolic fathers also debated this possibility.) In Paul's first letter to Corinth, he predated that letter by saying: "I wrote you in my letter not to associate with immoral people" (1 Corinthians 5:9) (This could merely be a reference to the present letter of 1 Corinthians.)

Many books have been written containing the lost or apocryphal books. Thus, it is the purpose of this work to bring into light the treasures of books attributed to the Old Testament and New Testament. Here are those books written in the most ancient of times.

SECTION ONE

LOST SCRIPTURES OF THE OLD TESTAMENT

The First Book of Adam and Eve:

The Conflict With Satan

The First Book of Adam and Eve is an apocryphal story, written in a midrash style, detailing the life of Adam and Eve from the time God planted the Garden of Eden to the time that Cain killed his brother, Abel.

The story is a fanciful embellishment of the Genesis story up to the point of the cursing of Cain for the murder of Abel.

Of the numerous apocryphal works that were written regarding Adam and Eve this text seems to have most influenced early theologians. This is evident in the widespread popularity of the book from the third to the thirteenth century. Even though the book was widely read in the Middle Ages, and considered to shine light on what actually took place in the time of creation, today it is considered fiction and thus relegated to a collection of texts called the Pseudepigrapha, or "false writings."

The text shows some cobbling together of various works, combined into a single storyline. Although the foundation of the text can be traced to combined oral traditions thousands of years old, the primary story was likely created around two or three hundred years before Christ. Additions and details were added over many years, leading to this version being penned around the 3rd century A.D.

The text presented here is an embellishment of the Jewish storyline from Genesis that is "Christianized" by additions of allusions and references to the New Testament. Quite often the details of the story are made to foreshadow the birth, death, and resurrection of Jesus. The result is the text before you.

The central part of the text focuses on the conflict between Good and Evil in the form of Satan's endeavor to destroy God's creations, Adam and Eve. The story begs the eternal question, how does one know whether God or Satan guides the opportunity, situation, or person confronting us. The fight between good and evil, as well as the question of who is influencing our surroundings, are eternal, and the story attempts to answer in metaphor.

The creation story and the tale of Adam and Eve pervaded the thoughts of writers throughout the ancient world. Evidence is seen in the large number of versions that exist in various languages and cultures. Indeed, it is due to the amazing popularity of the text that it has survived in six languages: Greek, Latin, Armenian, Georgian, and Slavonic, as well as a fragment in Coptic. The stories may also be traced through the writings of Greeks, Syrians, Egyptians, Abyssinians, Hebrews, and other ancient peoples.

Most scholars agree that the text was written originally in Greek and that all of the six versions show evidence of Greek linguistic roots. Those Greek manuscripts we posses seem to be no more accurate to the original than any of the other translations, having been so many generations removed from the source document.

The foundation of our modern English translation began with the work of, Vicar of Broadwindsor, Dr. S. C. Malan, who worked from the Ethiopic edition edited by, Professor at the University of Munich. Dr. Trumpp, who had the advantage of having an older version at his disposal.

From an ancient oral tradition, to a 3rd century codex, through the hands of Dr. E. Trumpp and Dr. S. C. Malan, to this modern English version, the First Book of Adam and Eve has survived, just as mankind has survived the struggles written of in the book itself.

The Malan translation of the text was penned in a rather stilted and formal style of English resembling that of the King James Bible. The Malan translation was then taken and re-written with word choices and sentence structure altered to make it more palatable and understandable to the modern reader, while keeping the poetic flow of the text.

Notes and references are added in italicized font. Alternate words or phrases that may add more depth or possibilities in translation are place in parentheses.

The First Book of Adam and Eve

Chapter I

1 On the third day, God planted the garden in the east of the earth, on the border of
the world in the eastward direction toward and beyond the rising sun. There one
finds nothing but water that encompasses the whole world and reaches to the
borders of heaven. 2 And to the north of the garden there is a sea of water, clear and
pure to the taste, unlike anything else; so that, through the clearness one may look
into the depths of the earth. 3 And when a man washes himself in it, he becomes
perfectly clean and perfectly white, even if he were dark. 4 And God created that sea
of his own good pleasure, for He knew what would come of the man He would
make; so that after he had left the garden, because of his transgression, men should
be born in the earth. Among them are righteous ones who will die, whose souls God
would raise at the last day when all of them will return to their flesh, bathe in the
water of that sea, and repent of their sins. 5 But when God caused Adam go out of
the garden, He did not place him on the border of it northward. This was so that he
and Eve would not be able to go near to the sea of water where they could wash
themselves in it and be cleansed from their sins and erase the transgression they had
committed, so that they be no longer reminded of it in the thought of their
punishment. 6 As to the southern side of the garden, God did not want Adam to live
there either, because, when the wind blew from the north, it would bring to him, on
that southern side, the delicious smell of the trees of the garden. 7 So God did not
put Adam there. This was so that he would not be able to smell the sweet smell of
those trees and forget his transgression, and find consolation for what he had done
by taking delight in the smell of the trees and yet not be cleansed from his
transgression. 8 Also, because God is merciful and of great pity, and governs all
things in a way that He alone knows He made our father Adam to live in the
western border of the garden because on that side the land is very wide. 9 And God
commanded him to live there in a cave in a rock. This was the Cave of Treasures,
which is below the garden.

Chapter II

1 But when our father Adam, and Eve, went out of the garden, they walked the
ground on their feet, not knowing where they were going. 2 And when they came to
the opening of the gate of the garden and saw the land spread before them widely,
covered with stones large and small, and with sand, they feared and trembled, and
fell on their faces from the fear that came over them and they were as though they
were dead. 3 Until this time they had been in the garden land, beautifully planted
with all manner of trees and they now saw themselves in a strange land, which they
did not know and had never seen. 4 When they were in the garden they were filled
with the grace of a bright nature, and they had hearts not turned toward earthly
things. 5 Therefore God had pity on them; and when He saw them fallen before the
gate of the garden, He sent His Word to our father Adam, and to Eve, and raised
them from their fallen state.

Chapter III

1 God said to Adam, "I have ordained days and years on this earth, and you and your descendants shall live and walk in them until the days and years are fulfilled. Then I shall send the Word that created you and against which you have transgressed the Word that made you come out of the garden and that raised you when you were fallen. 2 Yes, this is the Word that will again save you when the five and a half days are fulfilled." 3 But when Adam heard these words from God, and of the great five and a half days he did not understand the meaning of them. 4 For Adam was thinking there would be only five and a half days for him until the end of the world. 5 And Adam cried and prayed to God to explain it to him. 6 Then God in his mercy for Adam who was made after His own image and likeness explained to him that these were 5,000 and 500 years and how (the) One would then come and save him and his descendants. 7 But before that, God had made this covenant with our father, Adam, in the same terms before he came out of the garden, when he was by the tree where Eve took of the fruit and gave it to him to eat. 8 Because, when our father, Adam, came out of the garden he passed by that tree and saw how God had changed the appearance of it into another form and how it had shriveled. 9 And as Adam went to it he feared, trembled, and fell down. But God in His mercy lifted him up and then made this covenant with him. 10 Also, when Adam was by the gate of the garden he saw the cherub with a sword of flashing fire in his hand, and the cherub grew angry and frowned at him. Both Adam and Eve became afraid of the cherub and thought he meant to put them to death. So they fell on their faces, trembling with fear. 11 But he had pity on them and showed them mercy. And turning from them, he went up to heaven and prayed to the Lord, and said; 12 "Lord, You sent me to watch at the gate of the garden, with a sword of fire. 13 But when Your servants, Adam and Eve, saw me, they fell on their faces, and were as dead. O my Lord, what shall we do to Your servants?" 14 Then God had pity on them, and showed them mercy, and sent His Angel to keep the garden. 15 And the Word of the Lord came to Adam and Eve, and raised them up. 16 And the Lord said to Adam, "I told you that at the end of the five and a half days I will send my Word and save you. 17 Therefore, strengthen your heart and stay in the Cave of Treasures, of which I have spoken to you before." 18 And when Adam heard this Word from God he was comforted with that which God had told him. For He had told him how He would save him.

Author's note: The year 1740 equates to the Hebrew year 5500. It was around this time the Great Revival or the Great Awakening began in the United States and lasted until around 1750. Some sources have the religious revival at 1678 – 1745 while other sources have 1740 – 1750. However, the time between creation and Adam's fall must be accounted for. The author is suggesting that the time between the fall of Adam and the death of Christ is 5500 years.

Chapter IV

1 But Adam and Eve cried for having come out of the garden, which was their first home. 2 And indeed, when Adam looked at his flesh he saw that it was altered, and he cried bitterly, he and Eve cried, over what they had done. And they walked and went gently down into the Cave of Treasures. 3 And as they came to it, Adam cried over himself and said to Eve, "Look at this cave that is to be our prison in this world,

and a place of punishment! 4 What is it compared with the garden? What is its narrowness compared with the space of the other? 5 What is this rock compared of those groves? What is the gloom of this cavern, compared with the light of the garden? 6 What is this overhanging ledge of rock that shelters us compared with the mercy of the Lord that overshadowed us? 7 What is the soil of this cave compared with the garden land? Does this earth, scattered with stones, compared to that garden planted with delicious fruit trees?" 8 And Adam said to Eve, "Look at your eyes, and at mine, which before beheld angels praising in heaven without ceasing. 9 Now we do not see as we did; our eyes have become of flesh; they cannot see like they saw before." 10 Adam said again to Eve, "What is our body today, compared to what it was in former days, when we lived in the garden?" 11 After this, Adam did not want to enter the cave under the overhanging rock. He never wanted to enter it again. 12 But he bowed to God's commands; and said to himself, "Unless I enter the cave, I shall again be a transgressor."

Chapter V

1 Then Adam and Eve entered the cave, and stood praying, in their own tongue, unknown to us, but which they knew well. 2 And as they prayed, Adam raised his eyes and saw the rock and the roof of the cave that covered him overhead. This prevented him from seeing either heaven or God's creatures. So he cried and beat his chest hard, until he dropped, and was as dead. 3 And Eve sat crying; for she believed he was dead. 4 Then she got up, spread her hands toward God, appealing to Him for mercy and pity, and said, "O God, forgive me my sin, the sin which I committed, and don't remember it against me. 5 For I alone caused Your servant to fall from the garden into this condemned land; from light into this darkness; and from the house of joy into this prison. 6 O God, look at this Your servant fallen in this manner, and bring him back to life, that he may cry and repent of his transgression which he committed through (because of) me. 7 Don't take away his soul at this time; but let him live so that he may stand after the measure of his repentance, and do Your will, as before his death. 8 But if You do not bring him back to life, then, O God, take away my own soul, so that I will be like him, and leave me not in this dungeon, alone; for I could not stand alone in this world, without him. 9 For You, O God, caused him to fall asleep, and took a bone from his side, and placed the flesh back in its place by Your divine power. 10 And You took me, the bone, and made me, a woman, bright like him, with heart, reason, and speech; and flesh like to his own; and You made me after the likeness of his looks, by Your mercy and power. 11 O Lord, I and he are one, and You, O God, are our Creator, You are He who made us both in one day. 12 Therefore, O God, give him life so that he may be with me in this strange land while we live in it due to our transgression. 13 But if You will not give him life, then take me, even me, like him; that we both may die the same day." 14 And Eve cried bitterly, and fell on our father, Adam, because of her great sorrow.

Chapter VI

1 But God looked at them, for they had killed themselves through great grief. 2 And He decided to raise them and comfort them. 3 Therefore, He sent His Word to them that they should stand and be raised immediately. 4 And the Lord said to Adam and Eve, "You transgressed of your own free will, until you came out of the garden in

which I had placed you. 5 Of your own free will have you transgressed through your desire for divinity, greatness, and an exalted state, such as I have; therefore I deprived you of the bright nature which you had then, and I made you come out of the garden to this land, rough and full of trouble. 6 If only you had not transgressed My commandment and had kept My law, and had not eaten of the fruit of the tree which I told you not to come near! And there were fruit trees in the garden better than that one. 7 But the wicked Satan did not keep his faith and had no good intent towards Me, and although I had created him he considered Me to be useless, and he sought the Godhead for himself. For this I hurled him down from heaven so that he could not remain in his first estate. It was he who made the tree appear pleasant to your eyes until you ate of it by believing his words. 8 Thus have you transgressed My commandment, and therefore I have brought on you all these sorrows. 9 For I am God the Creator, who, when I created My creatures, did not intend to destroy them. But after they had greatly roused My anger I punished them with grievous plagues until they repent. 10 But, if on the contrary they still continue hardened in their transgression they shall be under a curse forever."

Chapter VII

1 When Adam and Eve heard these words from God, they cried and sobbed even more, but they strengthened their hearts in God because they now felt that the Lord was to them like a father and a mother; and for this very reason, they cried before Him, and sought mercy from Him. 2 Then God had pity on them, and said: "O Adam, I have made My covenant with you, and I will not turn from it; neither will I let you return to the garden, until My covenant of the great five and a half days is fulfilled." 3 Then Adam said to God, "O Lord, You created us, and made us fit to be in the garden; and before I transgressed, You made all beasts come to me, that I should name them. 4 Your grace was then on me; and I named every one according to Your mind; and you made them all subject to me. 5 But now, O Lord God, that I have transgressed Your commandment, all beasts will rise against me and will devour me, and Eve Your handmaid; and will cut off our life from the face of the earth. 6 I therefore beg you, O God, that since You have made us come out of the garden, and have made us be in a strange land, You will not let the beasts hurt us." 7 When the Lord heard these words from Adam, He had pity on him, and felt that he had truly said that the beasts of the field would rise and devour him and Eve, because He, the Lord, was angry with the two of them because of their transgressions. 8 Then God commanded the beasts, and the birds, and all that moves on the earth, to come to Adam and to be familiar with him, and not to trouble him and Eve; nor any of the good and righteous among their offspring. 9 Then all the beasts paid homage to Adam, according to the commandment of God except the serpent, against which God was angry. It did not come to Adam, with the beasts.

Chapter VIII

1 Then Adam cried and said, "O God, when we lived in the garden, and our hearts were lifted up, we saw the angels that sang praises in heaven, but now we can't see like we once saw. No. When we entered the cave all creation became hidden from us." 2 Then God the Lord said to Adam, "When you were under subjection to Me, you had a bright nature within you and for that reason could you see distant things.

But after you transgressed your bright nature was taken out of you and it was not left in you to see distant things, but only things near to you, as is the ability of the flesh, for it is brutish." 3 When Adam and Eve had heard these words from God, they went their way, praising and worshipping Him with a sorrowful heart. 4 And God ceased communing with them.

Chapter IX

1 Then Adam and Eve came out of the Cave of Treasures, and came near to the garden gate. There they stood and looked at it and cried for having gone away from it. 2 And Adam and Eve went south of the gate of the garden to the side of it and found there the water that watered the garden, which came from the root of the Tree of Life, and they saw that the water was split from there into four rivers over the earth. 3 Then they came near to that water and looked at it and saw that it was the water that came up from under the root of the Tree of Life in the garden. 4 And Adam cried and wailed, and beat his chest for being cut out from the garden; and said to Eve: 5 "Why have you brought so many of these plagues and punishments on me, on yourself, and on our descendants?" 6 And Eve said to him, "What is it you have seen that has caused you to cry and to speak to me in this manner?" 7 And he said to Eve, "Do you not see this water that watered the trees of the garden, and flowed out from there that was with us in the garden? 8 And when we were in the garden we did not care about it, but since we came to this strange land we love it and turn it to use for our body." 9 But when Eve heard these words from him, she cried; and from the soreness of their crying, they fell into that water; and would have put an end to themselves in it so as never again to return and behold the creation for when they looked at the work of creation, they felt they must put an end to themselves.

Chapter X

1 Then God, merciful and gracious, looked at them as they were lying in the water, and close to death, and He sent an angel who brought them out of the water and laid them on the seashore as dead. 2 Then the angel went up to God and said, "O God, Your creatures have breathed their last breath." 3 Then God sent His Word to Adam and Eve, who raised them from their death. 4 And Adam said, after he was raised, "O God, while we were in the garden we did not require or care about this water, but since we came to this land we cannot do without it." 5 Then God said to Adam, "While you were under My command and were a bright angel you did not experience this water. 6 But now that you have transgressed My commandment, you can not do without water to wash your body and make it grow, for it is now like that of beasts, and is in want of water." 7 When Adam and Eve heard these words from God, they cried a bitter cry; and Adam entreated God to let him return into the garden and look at it a second time. 8 But God said to Adam, "I have made you a promise; when that promise is fulfilled, I will bring you back into the garden, you and your righteous descendants." 9 And God ceased to commune with Adam.

Authors note: Notice the text promises Adam and his righteous descendants will be returned to Eden after the 5,500 year term is completed. Thus, the righteous portion of mankind would be returned in the Hebrew year 5,500 plus the time between creation and Adam's fall.

Adam must be kept alive or transfigured since resurrection of the body was not part of Jewish doctrine.

Chapter XI

1 Adam and Eve then felt themselves burning with thirst, and heat, and sorrow. 2 And Adam said to Eve, "We shall not drink of this water even if we were to die. O Eve, when this water comes into our inner parts it will increase our punishments and that of our descendants." 3 Both Adam and Eve then went away from the water, and drank none of it at all but came and entered the Cave of Treasures. 4 But when in it Adam could not see Eve he only heard the noise she made. Neither could she see Adam, but heard the noise he made. 5 Then Adam cried in deep affliction and beat his chest, and he got up and said to Eve, "Where are you?" 6 And she said to him, "Look, I am standing here in this darkness." 7 He then said to her, "Remember the bright nature in which we lived, when we lived in the garden! 8 O Eve! Remember the glory that rested on us in the garden. O Eve! Remember the trees that overshadowed us in the garden while we moved among them. 9 O Eve! Remember that while we were in the garden, we knew neither night nor day. Think of the Tree of Life. From below it flowed the water and that shed splendor over us! Remember, O Eve, the land of the garden and the brightness of it. 10 Think, oh think of that garden in which there was no darkness while we lived in it. 11 But no sooner did we come into this Cave of Treasures than darkness surrounded us all around until we can no longer see each other, and all the pleasure of this life has come to an end."

Chapter XII

1 Then Adam beat his chest, he and Eve, and they mourned the whole night until the first light of dawn, and they sighed over the length of the night in Miyazia. 2 And Adam beat himself, and threw himself on the ground in the cave, from bitter grief, and because of the darkness and lay there as dead. 3 But Eve heard the noise he made in falling on the ground. And she felt about for him with her hands and found him like a corpse. 4 Then she was afraid, speechless, and she remained by him. 5 But the merciful Lord looked on the death of Adam, and on Eve's silence from fear of the darkness. 6 And the Word of God came to Adam and raised him from his death, and opened Eve's mouth that she might speak. 7 Then Adam stood up in the cave and said, "O God, why has light departed from us and darkness covered us? Why did you leave us in this extensive darkness? Why do you plague us like this? 8 And this darkness, O Lord, where was it before it covered us? It is because of this that we cannot see each other. 9 For so long as we were in the garden we neither saw nor even knew what darkness was. I was not hidden from Eve, neither was she hidden from me, until now that she cannot see me and no darkness came over us to separate us from each other. 10 But she and I were both in one bright light. I saw her and she saw me. Yet now since we came into this cave darkness has covered us and separated us from each other so that I do not see her, and she does not see me. 11 O Lord, will You then plague us with this darkness?"

Author's note: Miyazia equates to a particular month in the Ethiopian calendar.

Chapter XIII

1 Then when God, who is merciful and full of pity, heard Adam's voice, He said to him: 2 "O Adam, so long as the good angel was obedient to Me, a bright light rested on him and on his hosts. 3 But when he transgressed My commandment, I dispossessed him of that bright nature, and he became dark. 4 And when he was in the heavens, in the realms of light, he knew nothing of darkness. 5 But he transgressed, and I made him fall from the heaven onto the earth; and it was this darkness that came over him. 6 And, O Adam, while in My garden and obedient to Me that bright light rest also on you. 7 But when I heard of your transgression, I took from you that bright light. Yet, of My mercy, I did not turn you into darkness but I made your body a body of flesh over which I spread this skin in order that it may bear cold and heat. 8 If I had let My wrath fall heavily on you I should have destroyed you and had I turned you into darkness it would have been as if I had killed you. 9 But in My mercy I have made you as you are when you transgressed My commandment, O Adam, I drove you from the garden, and made you come forth into this land and commanded you to live in this cave and darkness covered you, as it did over him who transgressed My commandment. 10 Thus, O Adam, has this night deceived you. It is not to last forever but is only of twelve hours when it is over daylight will return. 11 Do not sigh or be moved and do not say in your heart that this darkness is long and drags on wearily. Do not say in your heart that I plague you with it. 12 Strengthen your heart and be not afraid. This darkness is not a punishment. Adam, I have made the day and have placed the sun in it to give light in order that you and your children should do your work. 13 For I knew you would sin and transgress and come out into this land. Yet I wouldn't force you nor ride heard over you, nor shut up, nor doom you through your fall, nor through your coming out from light into darkness, nor yet through your coming from the garden into this land. 14 For I made you of the light and I willed to bring out children of light from you that were like you. 15 But you did not keep My commandment one day until I had finished the creation and blessed everything in it. 16 Then, concerning the tree, I commanded you not to eat of it. Yet I knew that Satan, who deceived himself, would also deceive you. 17 So I made known to you by means of the tree, not to come near him. And I told you not to eat of the fruit thereof, nor to taste of it, nor yet to sit under it, nor to yield to it. 18 Had I not spoken to you, O Adam, concerning the tree and had I left you without a commandment and you had sinned it would have been an offence on My part, for not having given you any order you would turn around and blame Me for it. 19 But I commanded you, and warned you, and you fell. So that My creatures cannot blame Me; but the blame rests on them alone. 20 And, O Adam, I have made the day so that you and your descendants can work and toil in it. And I have made the night for them to rest in it from their work and for the beasts of the field to go forth by night and look for their food. 21 But little of darkness now remains, O Adam, and daylight will soon appear."

Chapter XIV

1 Then Adam said to God: "O Lord, take my soul and let me not see this gloom any more, or remove me to some place where there is no darkness." 2 But God the Lord

said to Adam, " I say to you, indeed, this darkness will pass from you every day, I have determined for you until the fulfillment of My covenant when I will save you and bring you back again into the garden and into the house of light you long for, in which there is no darkness. I will bring you to it in the kingdom of heaven." 3 Again God said to Adam, "All this misery that you have been made to take on yourself because of your transgression will not free you from the hand of Satan and it will not save you. 4 But I will. When I shall come down from heaven and shall become flesh of your descendants, and take on Myself the infirmity from which you suffer then the darkness that covered you in this cave shall cover Me in the grave, when I am in the flesh of your descendants. 5 And I, who am without years, shall be subject to the reckoning of years of times of months, and of days, and I shall be reckoned as one of the sons of men in order to save you." 6 And God ceased to commune with Adam.

Author's Note: John 1:14And the Word was made flesh, and dwelt among us, (and we beheld his glory, the glory as of the only begotten of the Father,) full of grace and truth.
John 12:46 American King James Version: I am come a light into the world, that whoever believes on me should not abide in darkness.

Chapter XV

1 Then Adam and Eve cried and was sorrowful because of God's word to them, that they should not return to the garden until the fulfillment of the days decreed on them, but mostly because God had told them that He should suffer for their salvation.

Chapter XVI

1 After this, Adam and Eve continued to stand in the cave, praying and crying, until the morning dawned on them. 2 And when they saw the light returned to them they refrained from being afraid and strengthened their hearts. 3 Then Adam came out of the cave. And when he came to the mouth of it and stood and turned his face towards the east and saw the sunrise in glowing rays and felt the heat thereof on his body, he was afraid of it and thought in his heart that this flame came forth to plague him. 4 He then cried and beat his chest and he fell on the ground on his face and made his appeal saying: 5 "O Lord, plague me not, neither consume me, nor yet take away my life from the earth." 6 For he thought the sun was God. 7 Because while he was in the garden and heard the voice of God and the sound He made in the garden, and feared Him, Adam never saw the brilliant light of the sun, neither did its flaming heat touch his body. 8 Therefore he was afraid of the sun when flaming rays of it reached him. He thought God meant to plague him with it all the days He had decreed for him. 9 For Adam also said in his thoughts, that God did not plague them with darkness but He had caused this sun to rise and to plague them with burning heat. 10 But while he was thinking like this in his heart the Word of God came to him and said: 11 " Adam, get up on your feet. This sun is not God, but it has been created to give light by day that I spoke to you about in the cave saying, 'The dawn would come, and there would be light by day.' 12 But I am God who comforted you in the night." 13 And God ceased to commune with Adam.

Chapter XVII

1 Then, Adam and Eve came out at the mouth of the cave and went toward the
garden. 2 But as they went near the western gate, from which Satan came when he
deceived Adam and Eve, they found the serpent that became Satan coming at the
gate, and it was sorrowfully licking the dust, and wiggling on its breast on the
ground because of the curse that fell on it from God. 3 Before the curse the serpent
was the most exalted of all beasts, now it was changed and become slippery and the
meanest of them all, and it crept on its breast and went on its belly. 4 Before, it was
the fairest of all beasts. It had been changed and became the most ugly of them all.
Instead of feeding on the best food, now it turned to eat the dust. Instead of living as
before, in the best places, now it lived in the dust. 5 It had been the most beautiful of
all beasts, and all stood speechless at its beauty, it was now abhorred of them. 6 And,
again, whereas it lived in a beautiful home, to which all other animals came from
everywhere; and where it drank, they drank also of the same; now, after it had
become venomous, by reason of God's curse, all beasts fled from its home and would
not drink of the water it drank, but fled from it.

Chapter XVIII

1 When the accursed serpent saw Adam and Eve it swelled its head, stood on its tail,
and with eyes blood- red, it acted like it would kill them. 2 It made straight for Eve
and ran after her while Adam stood by and yelled because he had no stick in his
hand with which to hit the serpent, and did not know how to put it to death. 3 But
with a heart burning for Eve, Adam approached the serpent and held it by the tail.
When it turned towards him and said to him: 4 "O Adam, because of you and Eve I
am slippery, and go on my belly." Then with its great strength it threw down Adam
and Eve and squeezed them, and tried to kill them. 5 But God sent an angel who
threw the serpent away from them, and raised them up. 6 Then the Word of God
came to the serpent, and said to it, "The first time I made you slick, and made you to
go on your belly but I did not deprive you of speech. 7 This time, however, you will
be mute, and you and your race will speak no more because, the first time My
creatures were ruined because of you, and this time you tried to kill them." 8 Then
the serpent was struck mute, and it was no longer able to speak. 9 And a wind blew
down from heaven by the command of God and carried away the serpent from
Adam and Eve and threw it on the seashore where it landed in India.

Chapter XIX

1 But Adam and Eve cried before God. And Adam said to Him: 2 "O Lord, when I
was in the cave I said this to you, my Lord, the beasts of the field would rise and
devour me and cut off my life from the earth." 3 Then Adam, because of what had
happened to him, beat his chest and fell on the ground like a corpse. Then the Word
of God came to him, who raised him, and said to him, 4 "O Adam, not one of these
beasts will be able to hurt you because I have made the beasts and other moving
things come to you in the cave. I did not let the serpent come with them because it
might have risen against you and made you tremble and the fear of it should fall into
your hearts. 5 I knew that the accursed one is wicked; therefore I would not let it
come near you with the other beasts. 6 But now strengthen your heart and fear not. I
am with you to the end of the days I have determined for you."

Chapter XX

1 Then Adam cried and said, "O God, take us away to some other place, where the serpent can not come near us again and rise against us. For I fear that it might find your handmaid Eve alone and kill her, for its eyes are hideous and evil." 2 But God said to Adam and Eve, " Don't be afraid. From now on, I will not let it come near you. I have driven it away from you and from this mountain. I will not leave in it the ability to hurt you." 3 Then Adam and Eve worshipped before God and gave Him thanks and praised Him for having delivered them from death.

Chapter XXI

1 Then Adam and Eve went in search of the garden. 2 And the heat beat like a flame on their faces and they sweated from the heat. And they cried before the Lord. 3 But the place where they cried was close to a high mountain (top) that faced the western gate of the garden. 4 Then Adam threw himself down from the top of that mountain. His face was torn and his flesh was ripped and he lost much of his blood and was close to death. 5 Meanwhile Eve remained standing on the mountain crying over him lying as he was. 6 And she said, "I don't wish to live after him, for all that he did to himself was because of me." 7 Then she threw herself after him; and was torn and ripped by stones and remained lying as dead. 8 But the merciful God, who looks over His creatures, looked at Adam and Eve as they lay dead, and He sent His Word to them and raised them. 9 And said to Adam, "O Adam, all this misery, which you have brought on yourself, will have no affect on My ruling, neither will it alter the covenant of the five thousand and five hundred (5,500) years."

Chapter XXII

1 Then Adam said to God, "I dry up in the heat, I am faint from walking, and I don't want to be in this world. And I don't know when You will let me rest and take me out of it." 2 Then the Lord God said to him, "O Adam, it cannot be now, not until you have ended your days. Then I shall bring you out of this miserable land." 3 And Adam said to God, "While I was in the garden I knew neither heat, nor fatigue, neither transience, nor trembling, nor fear; but now since I came to this land, all this affliction has come over me. 4 Then God said to Adam, "So long as you were keeping My commandment, My light and My grace rested on you. But when you transgressed My commandment, sorrow and misery came to you in this land." 5 And Adam cried and said, "O Lord, do not cut me off for this, neither punish me with heavy plagues, nor yet repay me according to my sin; for we, of our own will, transgressed Your commandment and ignored Your law and tried to become gods like you when Satan the enemy deceived us." 6 Then God said again to Adam, "Because you have endured fear and trembling in this land of fatigue and suffering, treading and walking about, going on this mountain, and dying from it, I will take all this on Myself in order to save you."

Author's note:
Isaiah 53
1 Who hath believed our report? and to whom is the arm of the LORD revealed?

2 For he shall grow up before him as a tender plant, and as a root out of a dry ground: he hath no form nor comeliness; and when we shall see him, there is no beauty that we should desire him.
3 He is despised and rejected of men; a man of sorrows, and acquainted with grief: and we hid as it were our faces from him; he was despised, and we esteemed him not.
4 Surely he hath borne our griefs, and carried our sorrows: yet we did esteem him stricken, smitten of God, and afflicted.
5 But he was wounded for our transgressions, he was bruised for our iniquities: the chastisement of our peace was upon him; and with his stripes we are healed.
6 All we like sheep have gone astray; we have turned every one to his own way; and the LORD hath laid on him the iniquity of us all.
7 He was oppressed, and he was afflicted, yet he opened not his mouth: he is brought as a lamb to the slaughter, and as a sheep before her shearers is dumb, so he openeth not his mouth.
8 He was taken from prison and from judgment: and who shall declare his generation? for he was cut off out of the land of the living: for the transgression of my people was he stricken.
9 And he made his grave with the wicked, and with the rich in his death; because he had done no violence, neither was any deceit in his mouth.
10 Yet it pleased the LORD to bruise him; he hath put him to grief: when thou shalt make his soul an offering for sin, he shall see his seed, he shall prolong his days, and the pleasure of the LORD shall prosper in his hand.
11 He shall see of the travail of his soul, and shall be satisfied: by his knowledge shall my righteous servant justify many; for he shall bear their iniquities.

Chapter XXIII

1 Then Adam cried more and said, "O God, have mercy on me and do not take on
yourself that which I will do." 2 But God withdrew His Word from Adam and Eve. 3
Then Adam and Eve stood on their feet and Adam said to Eve, "Strengthen yourself,
and I also will strengthen myself." And she strengthened herself as Adam told her. 4
Then Adam and Eve took stones and placed them in the shape of an altar and they
took leaves from the trees outside the garden, with which they wiped from the face
of the rock the blood they had spilled. 5 But that which had dropped on the sand
they took together with the dust with which it was mixed and offered it on the altar
as an offering to God. 6 Then Adam and Eve stood under the Altar and cried,
praying to God, "Forgive us our offense and our sin, and look at us with Your eye of
mercy. For when we were in the garden our praises and our hymns went up before
you without ceasing. 7 But when we came into this strange land, pure praise was no
longer ours, nor righteous prayer, nor understanding hearts, nor sweet thoughts, nor
wise judgment, nor long discernment, nor upright feelings, neither was our bright
nature left within us. But our body is changed from the likeness in which it was at
first when we were created. 8 Yet now look at our blood which is offered on these
stones and accept it at our hands as if it were the praise we used to sing to you at
first when we were in the garden." 9 And Adam began to make more requests of
God. Our Father, Who are in Heaven, be gracious unto us. O Lord, our God,
hallowed be Your Name and let the remembrance of You be glorified in Heaven
above and upon earth here below. Let Your kingdom reign over us now and forever.
The Holy Men of old said remit and forgive unto all men whatsoever they have done
unto me. And lead us not into temptation, but deliver us from the evil thing; for

Your is the kingdom and You shall reign in glory forever and forevermore, AMEN.

Author's note: Verse 4 and continuing to the end of the chapter contain and present ideas that are of an obviously Christian era. There would have been no "men of old" at the time of Adam and Eve. The text parallels the Lord's Prayer. This, and other references to Christian symbols, makes the dating of the text at about the 3rd century A.D. likely.

Matthew 6: 9
9 After this manner therefore pray ye: Our Father which art in heaven, Hallowed be your name.
10 Thy kingdom come, Thy will be done in earth, as it is in heaven.
11 Give us this day our daily bread.
12 And forgive us our debts, as we forgive our debtors.
13 And lead us not into temptation, but deliver us from evil: For thine is the kingdom, and the power, and the glory, for ever. Amen. 14 For if ye forgive men their trespasses, your heavenly Father will also forgive you: 15 But if ye forgive not men their trespasses, neither will your Father forgive your trespasses.

Chapter XXIV

1 Then the merciful God, who is good and a lover of men, looked at Adam and Eve
and at their blood, which they had held up as an offering to Him without an order
from Him for so doing. But He wondered at them and accepted their offering. 2 And
God sent from His presence a bright fire that consumed their offering. 3 He smelled
the sweet savor of their offering and showed them mercy. 4 Then the Word of God
came to Adam, and said to him, "O Adam, as you have shed your blood so will I
shed My own blood when I become flesh of your descendants. And as you died, O
Adam, so also will I die. And as you built an altar, so also will I make for you an
altar of the earth. And as you offered your blood on it, so also will I offer My blood
on an altar on the earth. 5 And as you appealed for forgiveness through that blood,
so also will I make My blood forgiveness of sins and erase transgressions in it. 6 And
now, behold, I have accepted your offering, O Adam, but the days of the covenant in
which I have bound you are not fulfilled. When they are fulfilled, then will I bring
you back into the garden. 7 Now, therefore, strengthen your heart. And when
sorrow comes over you make Me an offering and I will be favorable to you."

Chapter XXV

1 But God knew that Adam believed he would frequently kill himself and make an
offering to Him of his blood. 2 Therefore He said to him, "Adam, don't ever kill
yourself like this again, by throwing yourself down from that mountain." 3 But
Adam said to God, "I was thinking to put an end to myself right now for having
transgressed Your commandments and for my having come out of the beautiful
garden and for the bright light which You have taken from me, and for the praises
which poured out from my mouth without ceasing, and for the light that covered
me. 4 Yet because of Your goodness, O God, you did not get rid of me altogether, but
you have been favorable to me every time I die and you bring me to life. 5 And

thereby it will be made known that You are a merciful God who does not want anyone to perish, who would love it if no one should fall, and who does not condemn any one cruelly, badly, or by total destruction." 6 Then Adam remained silent. 7 And the Word of God came to him and blessed him and comforted him and covenanted with him that He would save him at the end of the days determined for him. 8 This, then, was the first offering Adam made to God and so it became his custom to do.

Chapter XXVI

1 Then Adam took Eve and they began to return to the Cave of Treasures where they lived. But when they got closer to it and saw it from a distance, heavy sorrow fell on Adam and Eve when they looked at it. 2 Then Adam said to Eve, "When we were on the mountain we were comforted by the Word of God that talked with us and the light that came from the east shown over us. 3 But now the Word of God is hidden from us and the light that shined over us has changed so much that it has disappeared and let darkness and sorrow cover us. 4 And we are forced to enter this cave that is like a prison, in which darkness covers us so that we are separated from each other. You cannot see me. I cannot see you." 5 When Adam had said these words, they cried and spread their hands before God because they were full of sorrow. 6 And they prayed to God to bring the sun for them to shine on them so that darkness would not return to them and that they wouldn't have to go under this covering of rock. They wanted to die rather than see the darkness. 7 Then God looked at Adam and Eve and at their great sorrow and all they had done with a fervent heart because of all the trouble they were in. When compared to their former state of well-being, all the misery that came over them did so in this strange land. 8 Therefore God was neither angry with them nor impatient, but he was patient and longsuffering toward them, as toward the children He had created. 9 Then the Word of God came to Adam and said to him, "Adam, regarding the sun, if I were to take it and bring it to you, days, hours, years and months would all stop and the covenant I have made with you, would never be fulfilled. 10 And you would be deserted and stuck in a perpetual plague and you would never be saved. 11 Yes, rather, bear up long, and calm your soul while you live night and day until the fulfillment of the days and the time of My covenant has come. 12 Then I shall come and save you, Adam. I do not wish for you to be afflicted. 13 And when I look at all the good things that you lived in before, and why you came out of them, then I am willing to show you mercy. 14 But I cannot alter the covenant that has gone out of My mouth, otherwise I would have brought you back into the garden. 15 However, when the covenant is fulfilled then I will show you and your descendants mercy, and bring you into a land of gladness where there is neither sorrow nor suffering but abiding joy and gladness, and light that never fails, and praises that never cease, and a beautiful garden that shall never pass away." 16 And God said again to Adam, "Be patient and enter the cave because of the darkness of which you were afraid shall only be twelve hours long. When it is over, light will come up." 17 Then when Adam heard these words from God, he and Eve worshipped before Him, and their hearts were comforted. They returned into the cave after their custom, while tears flowed from their eyes sorrow and wailing came from their hearts and they wished their soul would leave their body. 18 And Adam and Eve stood praying until the darkness of night covered them and Adam was hidden from Eve and she from him.

19 And they remained standing in prayer.

Chapter XXVII

1 Satan, the hater of all that is good, saw how they continued in prayer, and how God communed with them, and comforted them, and how He had accepted their offering. Then Satan made a phantasm. 2 He began by transforming his hosts. In his hands was a shining, glimmering fire, and they were in a huge light. 3 Then, he placed his throne near the mouth of the cave, because he could not enter it due to their prayers. And he shown light into the cave until the cave glistened over Adam and Eve while his hosts began to sing praises. 4 Satan did this so that when Adam saw the light he would think to himself that it was a heavenly light and that Satan's hosts were angels and that God had sent them to watch at the cave, and give him light in the darkness. 5 Satan planned that when Adam came out of the cave and saw them and Adam and Eve bowed to Satan, then he would overcome Adam and humble him before God a second time. 6 When, therefore, Adam and Eve saw the light, thinking it was real, they strengthened their hearts. Then, as they were trembling, Adam said to Eve: 7 "Look at that great light, and at those many songs of praise, and at that host standing outside who won't come into our cave. Why don't they tell us what they want or where they are from or what the meaning of this light is or what those praises are or why they have been sent to this place, and why they won't come in? 8 If they were from God, they would come into the cave with us and would tell us why they were sent." 9 Then Adam stood up and prayed to God with a burning heart and said: 10 "O Lord, is there in the world another god besides You who created angels and filled them with light, and sent them to keep us, who would come with them? 11 But, look, we see these hosts that stand at the mouth of the cave. They are in a great light and they sing loud praises. If they are of some other god(s) than You, tell me, and if they are sent by you, inform me of the reason for which You have sent them." 12 No sooner had Adam said this, than an angel from God appeared to him in the cave, who said to him, "O Adam, fear not. This is Satan and his hosts. He wishes to deceive you as he deceived you at first. For the first time, he was hidden in the serpent, but this time he is come to you in the likeness of an angel of light in order that, when you worshipped him, he might enslave you in the very presence of God." 13 Then the angel went from Adam and seized Satan at the opening of the cave, and stripped him of the false image (lie / pretense) he had assumed and brought him in his own hideous form to Adam and Eve who were afraid of him when they saw him. 14 And the angel said to Adam, "This hideous form has been his ever since God made him fall from heaven. He could not have come near you in it. Therefore, he transformed himself into an angel of light." 15 Then the angel drove Satan and his hosts away from Adam and Eve and said to them, "Fear not. God who created you will strengthen you." 16 And the angel left them. 17 But Adam and Eve remained standing in the cave and no consolation came to them as they were divided in their thoughts. 18 And when it was morning they prayed and then went out to seek the garden, for their hearts were seeking it, and they could get no consolation for having left it.

Chapter XXVIII

1 But when the crafty Satan saw that they were going to the garden he gathered

together his host and came in appearance on a cloud, intent on deceiving them. 2 But when Adam and Eve saw him in a vision, they thought they were angels of God come to comfort them about having left the garden, or to bring them back again into it. 3 And Adam spread his hands before God, begged Him to make him understand what they were. 4 Then Satan, the hater of all that is good, said to Adam, "O Adam, I am an angel of the great God and, behold the hosts that surround me. 5 God has sent us to take you and bring you to the northern border of the garden to the shore of the clear sea, and bathe you and Eve in it, and raise you to your former joy, that you return to the garden once again." 6 These words sank into the heart of Adam and Eve. 7 Yet God withheld His Word from Adam, and did not make him understand at once but waited to see his strength and whether he would be overcome as Eve was when in the garden, or whether he would win this battle. 8 Then Satan called to Adam and Eve and said, "Behold, we go to the sea of water," and they began to go. 9 And Adam and Eve followed them at little distance. 10 But when they came to the mountain to the north of the garden which was a very high mountain without any steps to the top of it, the Devil came near to Adam and Eve, and made them go up to the top in reality and not in a vision, because he wished to throw them down and kill them, and to wipe their names from the earth, so that this earth should belong to him and his hosts alone.

Chapter XXIX

1 But when the merciful God saw that Satan wished to kill Adam with his many tricks, and saw that Adam was meek and without guile, God spoke to Satan in a loud voice, and cursed him. 2 Then he and his hosts fled, and Adam and Eve remained standing on the top of the mountain, from there they saw below them the wide world, high above which they were. But they saw none of the host which time after time were by them. 3 They cried, both Adam and Eve, before God, and begged for forgiveness of Him. 4 Then the Word from God came to Adam, and said to him, "You must know and understand concerning this Satan, that he seeks to deceive you and your descendants after you." 5 And Adam cried before the Lord God, and begged and prayed to Him to give him something from the garden, as a token to him, wherein to be comforted. 6 And God considered Adam's thought, and sent the angel Michael as far as the sea that reaches India, to take from there golden rods and bring them to Adam. 7 This God did in His wisdom in order that these golden rods, being with Adam in the cave, should shine forth with light in the night around him, and put an end to his fear of the darkness. 8 Then the angel Michael went down by God's order, took golden rods, as God had commanded him, and brought them to God.

Author's note: God spoke to Adam concerning "this Satan," a turn of phrase that leads one to believe there are other Satans. Based on the meaning of the word satan, there is no limit to the number of satans one could have. Satan is derived from Hebrew, satan meaning "adversary". Satan, or the Devil, plays various evil roles in ancient and modern literature and in Jewish, Christian, Muslim and Zoroastrian religious traditions. Satan is an opponent of God and of those seeking to do God's will. He is often described as an angel named Lucifer who was cast out of heaven for rebelling against God, was condemned to roam the earth and rule hell, and who battles God for possession of souls and the earth. That legend is not found as such in the Bible but is based on interpretations of scattered Bible passages and later literary portrayals.

The English word "Satan" is from a Hebrew word meaning "to oppose" or "adversary." "Devil" is from the Greek diabolos , meaning "to slander or accuse." The name "Lucifer" appears in Isaiah 14 in the King James Version of the Bible

Chapter XXX

1 After these things, God commanded the angel Gabriel to go down to the garden
and say to the cherub who kept it, "Behold, God has commanded me to come into
the garden, and to take from it sweet smelling incense and give it to Adam." 2 Then
the angel Gabriel went down by God's order to the garden and told the cherub as
God had commanded him. 3 The cherub then said, "This is acceptable." And Gabriel
went in and took the incense. 4 Then God commanded his angel Raphael to go down
to the garden, and speak to the cherub about some myrrh to give to Adam. 5 And
the angel Raphael went down and told the cherub as God had commanded him, and
the cherub said, "This is acceptable." Then Raphael went in and took the myrrh. 6
The golden rods were from the Indian sea, where there are precious stones. The
incense was from the eastern border of the garden, and the myrrh from the western
border, from where bitterness came over Adam. 7 And the angels brought these
things to God, by the Tree of Life, in the garden. 8 Then God said to the angels, "Dip
them in the spring of water, then take them and sprinkle their water over Adam and
Eve, that they should be a little comforted in their sorrow, and give them to Adam
and Eve. 9 And the angels did as God had commanded them, and they gave all those
things to Adam and Eve on the top of the mountain on which Satan had placed
them, when he sought to make an end of them. 10 And when Adam saw the golden
rods, the incense and the myrrh, he rejoiced and cried because he thought that the
gold was a token of the kingdom from where he had come and the incense was a
token of the bright light which had been taken from him, and that the myrrh was a
token of the sorrow which he was in.

Chapter XXXI

1 After these things happened, God said to Adam, "You asked Me for something
from the garden to be comforted with, and I have given you these three tokens as a
consolation to you so that you trust in Me and in My covenant with you. 2 For I will
come and save you and when I am in the flesh, kings shall bring me gold, incense,
and myrrh. Gold is a token of My kingdom, incense is a token of My divinity, and
myrrh is a token of My suffering and of My death. 3 But, Adam, put these by you in
the cave, the gold so that it may shine light over you by night, the incense so that
you smell its sweet savor, and the myrrh to comfort you in your sorrow." 4 When
Adam heard these words from God, he worshipped before Him. He and Eve
worshipped Him and gave Him thanks because He had dealt mercifully with them.
5 Then God commanded the three angels, Michael, Gabriel and Raphael each to
bring what he had brought and give it to Adam. And they did so, one by one. 6 And
God commanded Suriyel and Salathiel to bear up Adam and Eve, and bring them
down from the top of the high mountain, and to take them to the Cave of Treasures.
7 There they laid the gold on the south side of the cave, the incense on the eastern
side, and the myrrh on the western side. For the mouth of the cave was on the north

side. 8 The angels then comforted Adam and Eve, and departed. 9 The gold was seventy rods. The incense was twelve pounds, and the myrrh was three pounds. 10 These remained by Adam in the Cave of Treasures, in the House of Treasures; therefore was it called 'Cave of Concealment.' And it was called the 'Cave of Treasures,' by reason of the bodies of righteous men that were in it. 11 God gave these three things to Adam on the third day after he had come out of the garden as a sign of the three days the Lord should remain in the heart of the earth. 12 And these three things, as they continued with Adam in the cave, gave him light by night, and by day they gave him a little relief from his sorrow.

Author's note: A rod is a unit of linear measure equal to approximately 5.5 yards and also a unit of area measure equivalent to approximately 30.25 square yards. Rod is also a description indicating a long, thin piece of unspecified size.

Author's note: Suriyel means "Command of God" and is one of the archangels from Judaic traditions. Other possible versions of his name are Suriel, Suriyel,(Some Dead Sea Scrolls translations), Esdreel, Sahariel, Juriel, Seriel, Sauriel, Surya, Jariel. The angel is mentioned in the Lost Book Of Enoch.
Salathiel means, "Whom I asked of God." The name is the son of Jeconiah (Matt. 1:12; 1 Chr. 3:17); also called the son of Neri (Luke 3:27) The probable explanation of the apparent discrepancy is that he was the son of Neri, the descendant of Nathan, and thus heir to the throne of David on the death of Jeconiah . See Jer. 22:30). The name acknowledges that the son is an answer to the parents' prayer to God (El) to help them conceive and birth a child. In 2 Esdras, the author claims to be "Ezra, who is also called Shealtiel" (3:1). For this reason, this work is also sometimes known as Ezra Shealtiel.

Chapter XXXII

1 And Adam and Eve remained in the Cave of Treasures until the seventh day. They neither ate of the fruit of the earth, nor drank water. 2 And on the eighth day, when it dawned, Adam said to Eve, " Eve, we prayed God to give us something from the garden and He sent his angels who brought us what we had desired. 3 But now, get up, and let us go to the sea of water we saw at first, and let us stand in it and pray that God will again be favorable to us and take us back to the garden, or give us something, or that He will give us comfort in some other land than this one we are in." 4 Then Adam and Eve came out of the cave and went and stood on the border of the sea in which they had thrown themselves before. 5 Then Adam said to Eve: "Come, go down into this place, and do not come out until the end of thirty days, when I shall come to you. And pray to God with burning heart and a sweet voice to forgive us. 6 And I will go to another place, and go down into it and do like you." 7 Then Eve went down into the water as Adam had commanded her. Adam also went down into the water, and they stood praying, and besought the Lord to forgive them their offense and to restore them to their former state. 8 And they stood like that praying until the end of the thirty-five days.

Author's note: There is a discrepancy between the 30 days mentioned first and the 35 days cited later in the chapter. The number 35 is a combination of 3, the number of spiritual completion, and 5, the number of grace.

Chapter XXXIII

1 But Satan, the hater of all that is good, sought them in the cave, but did not find them although he searched diligently for them. 2 But he found them standing in the water praying and thought within himself, "Adam and Eve are standing like that in that water praying to God to forgive them their transgression, and to restore them to their former state, and to take them from under my hand. 3 But I will deceive them so that they shall come out of the water, and not fulfill their vow." 4 Then the hater of all that is good, did not go to Adam, but he went to Eve, and took the form of an angel of God, praising and rejoicing, and he said to her: 5 "Peace be to you! Be glad and rejoice! God is favorable to you and He sent me to Adam. I have brought him the glad tidings of salvation and of his being filled with bright light as he was at first. 6 And Adam, in his joy for his restoration, has sent me to you so that you would come with me in order that I might crown you with light like him. 7 And he said to me, 'Speak to Eve; if she does not come with you, tell her of the sign when we were on the top of the mountain, how God sent his angels who took us and brought us to the Cave of Treasures; and laid the gold on the southern side, incense on the eastern side, and myrrh on the western side.' Now come to him." 8 When Eve heard these words from him, she rejoiced much. And thinking Satan's appearance was real; she came out of the sea. 9 He went first and she followed him until they came to Adam. Then Satan hid himself from her and she saw him no more. 10 She then came and stood before Adam, who was standing by the water and she rejoiced in God's forgiveness. 11 And as she called to him, he turned around and found her there and cried when he saw her and beat his chest from the bitterness of his grief. He sank into the water. 12 But God looked at him and at his misery and that he was about to breathe his last breath. And the Word of God came from heaven, raised him out of the water, and said to him, "Go up the high bank to Eve." And when he came up to Eve he said to her, "Who told you to come here?" 13 Then she told him the discourse of the angel who had appeared to her and had given her a sign. 14 But Adam grieved, and explained to her that it was Satan. He then took her and they both returned to the cave. 15 These things happened to them the second time they went down to the water seven days after their coming out of the garden. 16 They fasted in the water thirty-five days. It was altogether forty-two days since they had left the garden.

Chapter XXXIV

1 On the morning of the forty-third day, they came out of the cave, sorrowful and crying. Their bodies were lean, and they were parched from hunger and thirst, from fasting and praying, and from their heavy sorrow because of their transgression. 2 And when they had come out of the cave they went up the mountain to the west of the garden. 3 There they stood and prayed and asked God to grant them forgiveness of their sins. 4 And after their prayers Adam began to beg God, saying, "O my Lord, my God, and my Creator, You commanded the four elements to be gathered together, and they were gathered together by Your order. 5 Then You spread Your hand and created me out of one element, that of dust of the earth. You brought me into the garden at the third hour, on a Friday, and informed me of it in the cave. 6 Then, at first, I knew neither night nor day, because I had a bright nature so that the light in which I lived ever left me to know night or day. 7 Then, again, O Lord, in

that third hour in which You created me, You brought to me all beasts, and lions, and ostriches, and fowls of the air, and all things that move in the earth, which You had created at the first hour before me of the Friday. 8 And Your will was that I should name them all, one by one, with a suitable name. But You gave me understanding and knowledge and a pure heart and a right mind from you, that I should name them after Your own mind regarding the naming of them. 9 O God, You made them obedient to me and ordered that not one of them break from my control according to Your commandment and to the dominion which You had given me over them. But now they are all estranged from me. 10 Then it was in that third hour of Friday, in which You created me, and commanded me concerning the tree, to which I was neither to go near, nor to eat from; because You said to me in the garden, 'When you eat of it, from death you shall die.' 11 But if You had punished me as You said, with death, I should have died that very moment. 12 When You commanded me regarding the tree, that I was neither to approach nor to eat of it, Eve was not with me. You had not yet created her, neither had You yet taken her out of my side, so had she yet heard this order from you. 13 Then, at the end of the third hour of that Friday, O Lord, You caused a sleep to come over me, and I slept, and was overwhelmed in sleep. 14 Then You took a rib out of my side and You created her after my own likeness and image. Then I awoke and when I saw her and knew who she was, I said, 'This is bone of my bones, and flesh of my flesh. From now on she shall be called woman.' 15 It was of Your good will, O God, that You brought a sleep over me and that You quickly drew Eve out of my side until she was fully out, so that I did not see how she was made, neither could I witness. O my Lord, Your goodness and glory are awful and great. 16 And of Your goodwill, O Lord, You made us both with bodies of a bright nature, and You made the two of us one. You gave us Your grace and filled us with praises of the Holy Spirit that we should be neither hungry nor thirsty nor know what sorrow is, nor know faintness of heart, neither suffering, fasting nor weariness. 17 But now, O God, since we transgressed Your commandment and broke Your law, You have brought us out into a strange land, and have caused suffering, faintness, hunger and thirst to come over us. 18 Now, therefore, O God, we pray you, give us something to eat from the garden, to satisfy our hunger with it, and something wherewith to quench our thirst. 19 For, behold, many days, O God, we have tasted nothing and drunk nothing, and our flesh has dried up and our strength is wasted. Sleep is gone from our eyes from faintness and crying. 20 Then, O God, we dare not gather anything from the fruit of trees, from fear of you. For when we transgress the first time You spared us and did not make us die. 21 But now, we thought in our hearts that if we eat the fruit of the trees without God's order He will destroy us this time and will remove us from the earth. 22 And if we drink of this water without God's order He will make an end of us and root us up at once. 23 Now, therefore, O God, I have come to this place with Eve, and we beg You to give us some fruit from the garden so that we may be satisfied with it. 24 For we desire the fruit that is on the earth and all else that we lack in it."

Author's note: The four elements referred to are earth, air, fire, and water. Man was formed from dust, or earth.

Chapter XXXV

1 Then God looked again at Adam and his crying and groaning, and the Word of God came to him, and said to him: 2 "Adam, when you were in My garden, you knew neither eating nor drinking, faintness nor suffering, leanness of flesh, nor change; neither did sleep depart from your eyes. But since you transgressed and came into this strange land all these trials have come over you."

Author's note: It is unclear as to if this implies that Adam did not sleep or if he had no trouble sleeping while in the garden. Other verses seem to hint at the fact that his "bright nature and the perpetual glory of God shining in the garden provided no need nor place for sleep. While in the garden, Adam may not have needed sleep.

Chapter XXXVI

1 Then God commanded the cherub, who guarded the gate of the garden with a sword of fire in his hand, to take some of the fruit of the fig-tree and to give it to
Adam. 2 The cherub obeyed the command of the Lord God and went into the garden and brought two figs on two twigs, each fig hanging to its leaf. They were from two of the trees among which Adam and Eve hid themselves when God went to walk in the garden and the Word of God came to Adam and Eve and said to them, "Adam! Adam! Where are you?" 3 And Adam answered, "O God, here I am. When I heard
the sound of You and Your voice, I hid myself, because I am naked." 4 Then the
cherub took two figs and brought them to Adam and Eve. But he threw the figs to them from a distance because they would not come near the cherub, for their flesh
that could not come near the fire. 5 At first, angels trembled at the presence of Adam and were afraid of him. But now Adam trembled before the angels and was afraid of
them. 6 Then Adam came closer and took one fig, and Eve also came in turn and
took the other. 7 And as they took them up in their hands they looked at them and knew they were from the trees among which they had hidden themselves.

Chapter XXXVII

1 Then Adam said to Eve, "Do you not see these figs and their leaves with which we covered ourselves when we were stripped of our bright nature? But now, we do not know what misery and suffering may come to us from eating them. 2 Now,
therefore, Eve, let us restrain ourselves and not eat them. Let us ask God to give us of the fruit of the Tree of Life." 3 So Adam and Eve restrained themselves and did
not eat these figs. 4 But Adam began to pray to God and to beg Him to give him of the fruit of the Tree of Life, saying: "O God, when we transgressed Your commandment at the sixth hour of Friday, we were stripped of the bright nature we had, and did not continue in the garden after our transgression more than three
hours. 5 But in the evening You made us come out of it. O God, we transgressed against You one hour and all these trials and sorrows have come over us until this
day. 6 And those days together with this the forty-third days do not redeem that one
hour in which we transgressed! 7 O God, look at us with an eye of pity, and do not

avenge us according to our transgression of Your commandment in Your presence. 8
O God, give us of the fruit of the Tree of Life that we may eat it and live and turn not
to see sufferings and other trouble in this earth, for You are God. 9 When we
transgressed Your commandment You made us come out of the garden and sent a
cherub to keep the Tree of Life so that we should not eat thereof and live and know
nothing of faintness after we transgressed. 10 But now, O Lord, behold, we have
endured all these days and have borne sufferings. Make these forty-three days an
equivalent for the one hour in which we transgressed."

Author's note: The day begins at sundown, or about 6 P.M. This would mean that is the sin occurred in the sixth hour it would have been midnight in the garden. If Adam and Eve were removed three hours afterward it would have been 3 A.M.

Chapter XXXVIII

1 After these things the Word of God came to Adam, and said to him: 2 "Adam, as to
the fruit on the Tree of Life that you have asked for, I will not give it to you now, but
only when the 5,500 years are fulfilled. At that time I will give you fruit from the
Tree of Life and you will eat and live forever, both you and Eve, and also your
righteous descendants. 3 But these forty-three days cannot make amends for the
hour in which you transgressed My commandment. 4 Adam, I gave you the fruit of
the fig-tree in which you hid yourself for you to eat. So, you and Eve go and eat it. 5 I
will not deny your request; neither will I disappoint your hope. Therefore, endure
until the fulfillment of the covenant I made with you." 6 And God withdrew His
Word from Adam.

Chapter XXXIX

1 Then Adam returned to Eve and said to her, "Get up, and take a fig for yourself,
and I will take the other; and let us go to our cave." 2 Then Adam and Eve each took
a fig and went toward the cave. The time was about the setting of the sun and their
thoughts made them long to eat of the fruit. 3 But Adam said to Eve, "I am afraid to
eat of this fig. I do not know what may come over me from it." 4 So Adam cried and
stood praying before God saying, "Satisfy my hunger, without my having to eat this
fig because after I have eaten it, what will it profit me? And what shall I desire and
ask of you, O God, when it is gone?" 5 And he said again, "I am afraid to eat of it; for
I do not know what will befall me through it."

Chapter XL

1 Then the Word of God came to Adam and said to him, "Adam, why didn't you
have this trepidation, or this will to fast, or this care before now? And why didn't
you have this fear before you transgressed? 2 But when you came to live in this
strange land your animal body could not survive on earth without earthly food to
strengthen it and to restore its powers." 3 And God withdrew His Word for Adam.

Chapter XLI

1 Then Adam took the fig and laid it on the golden rods. Eve also took her fig and
put it on the incense. 2 And the weight of each fig was that of a water-melon; for the
fruit of the garden was much larger than the fruit of this land. 3 But Adam and Eve
remained standing and fasting the entirety of that night until the morning dawned. 4
When the sun rose they were still praying, but after they had finished praying Adam
said to Eve: 5 "Eve, come, let us go to the border of the garden looking south to the
place from where the river flows and is parted into four heads. There we will pray to
God and ask Him to give us some of the Water of Life to drink. 6 For God has not
fed us with the Tree of Life in order that we may not live. Therefore, we will ask him
to give us some of the Water of Life to quench our thirst with it, rather than with a
drink of water of this land." 7 When Eve heard these words from Adam she agreed,
and they both got up and came to the southern border of the garden, at the edge of
the river of water a short distance from the garden. 8 And they stood and prayed
before the Lord, and asked Him to look at them and for this one time to forgive
them, and to grant them their request. 9 After this prayer from both of them, Adam
began to pray with his voice before God, and said; 10 "O Lord, when I was in the
garden and saw the water that flowed from under the Tree of Life, my heart did not
desire, neither did my body require to drink of it. I did not know thirst, because I
was living, and above that which I am now. 11 So that in order to live I did not
require any Food of Life nor did I need to drink of the Water of Life. 12 But now, O
God, I am dead and my flesh is parched with thirst. Give me of the Water of Life that
I may drink of it and live. 13 O God, through Your mercy save me from these
plagues and trials, and bring me into another land different from this. Let me live in
Your garden."

Author's note: One could extrapolate the size of the fruit, knowing that the size of the fig leaves were large enough to fashion loincloths from them. (See Genesis 3:7) Later, we are told the size of a fig was that of a watermelon.

Chapter XLII

1 Then the Word of God came to Adam, and said to him: 2 "Adam, you said, 'Bring
me into a land where there is rest.' Another land than this will not bring you rest. It
is the kingdom of heaven alone where there is rest. 3 But you cannot enter into it at
present, but only after your judgment is past and fulfilled. 4 Then will I make you go
up into the kingdom of heaven, you and your righteous descendants; and I will give
you and them the rest you ask for now. 5 And if you said, 'Give me of the Water of
Life that I may drink and live,' it cannot be this day, but on the day that I shall
descend into hell, and break the gates of brass, and crush into pieces the kingdoms
of iron. 6 Then I will, through mercy, save your soul and the souls of the righteous,
and thus give them rest in My garden. That shall be when the end of the world is
come. 7 And the Water of Life you seek will not be granted you this day, but on the
day that I shall shed My blood on your head in the land of Golgotha. 8 For My blood
shall be the Water of Life to you at that time, and not to just you alone but to all your
descendants who shall believe in Me. This will be rest to them for forever." 9 The
Lord said again to Adam, "Adam, when you were in the garden these trials did not

come to you. 10 But since you transgressed My commandment, all these sufferings have covered you. 11 Now, also, your flesh requires food and drink. So drink then of that water that flows by you on the face of the earth. 12 Then God withdrew His Word from Adam. 13 And Adam and Eve worshipped the Lord, and returned from the river of water to the cave. It was noon when they drew near to the cave, they saw a large fire by it.

Author's note: The kingdom of iron refers to Rome.
Jesus was fixed to the cross above the ground and the people, (raised up so that all would be brought to Him) and the blood flowed from above and fell on the people below on Golgotha (goal-goth-uh), which was the hill outside the walls of Jerusalem where Jesus was crucified. See John 6:25 and 7:38

Chapter XLIII

1 Then Adam and Eve were afraid, and stood still. And Adam said to Eve, "What is that fire by our cave? We have done nothing in it to cause this fire. 2 We neither have bread to bake, nor broth to cook there. We have never known anything like this fire, and we do not know what to call it. 3 But ever since God sent the cherub with a sword of fire that flashed in his hand and had lightning coming from it we fell down and were like corpses from fear and we have not seen the like. 4 But now, Eve, look, this is the same fire that was in the cherub's hand, which God has sent to keep the cave in which we live. 5 O Eve, it is because God is angry with us and will drive us from it. 6 Eve, we have transgressed His commandment again in that cave, so that He had sent this fire to burn around it and prevent us from going into it. 7 If this is really the case, Eve, where shall we live? And where shall we flee to be away from the face of the Lord? Since, like it is with the garden, He will not let us live in it, and He has deprived us of the good things of it. But He has placed us in this cave, in which we have endured darkness, tests and hardships until at last we have found comfort in it. 8 But now that He has brought us out into another land, who knows what may happen in it? And who knows but that the darkness of that land may be far greater than the darkness of this land? 9 Who knows what may happen in that land by day or by night? And who knows whether it will be far or near, Eve? Do you think it will please God to put us far from the garden, Eve? Where will God put us to prevent us from beholding Him, because we have transgressed His commandment, and because we have made requests of Him all the time? 10 Eve, if God will bring us into a strange land other than this, in which we find consolation, it must be to put our souls to death, and blot out our name from the face of the earth. 11 O Eve, if we are further alienated from the garden and from God, where shall we find Him again, and ask Him to give us gold, incense, myrrh, and some fruit of the fig-tree? 12 Where shall we find Him to comfort us a second time? Where shall we find Him so that He may think of us regarding the covenant He has made on our behalf?" 13 Then Adam said nothing else more. And they kept looking, he and Eve, towards the cave, and at the fire that flared up around it. 14 But that fire was from Satan. For he had gathered trees and dry grasses, and had carried and brought them to the cave, and had set fire to them, in order to consume the cave and what was in it. 15 So that Adam and Eve should be left in sorrow, and he should cut off their trust in God, and make them deny Him. 16 But by the mercy of God he could not burn the cave because God sent His angel to the cave to guard it from this fire, until

it went out. 17 And this fire lasted from noon until the break of the next day. That was the forty-fifth day.

Chapter XLIV

1 Adam and Eve stood, looking at the fire and were unable to come near the cave from their fear of the fire. 2 And Satan kept on bringing trees and throwing them into the fire until the flames of the fire rose up very high and covered the entire cave, thinking in his mind, to consume the cave with the great fire. But the angel of the Lord was guarding it. 3 But he could not curse Satan nor wound him by word because he had no authority over him, neither did he attempt to do so with words from his mouth. 4 Therefore the angel tolerated him without uttering a bad word against him, until the Word of God came to Satan saying, "Go away from here at once before you deceive My servants, for this time you seek to destroy them. 5 Were it not for My mercy I would have destroyed you and your hosts from off the earth. But I have had patience with you until the end of the world." 6 Then Satan fled from before the Lord. But the fire went on burning around the cave like a coal-fire the entire day. This was the forty-sixth day that Adam and Eve had spent since they came out of the garden. 7 And when Adam and Eve saw that the heat of the fire had began to cool down, they started to walk toward the cave to get into it as they usually did but they could not because of the heat of the fire. 8 Then they both began crying because the fire separated them from the cave, and the fire came toward them, burning, and they were afraid. 9 Then Adam said to Eve, "See this fire of which we have a portion within us. It formerly obeyed us, but it no longer does so now, for we have violated the boundaries of creation and changed our condition and our nature has been altered. But the fire is not changed in its nature, nor altered from its creation. Therefore it now has power over us and when we come near it, it scorches our flesh."

Author's note: The Word of the Lord spoke to Satan stating, "I have had patience with you until the end of the world." This is a statement spoken in the future and recorded in the past. The precise meaning indicates that the statement was made at or after the end of the world.

Chapter XLV

1 Then Adam rose and prayed to God, saying, "This fire has separated us from the cave in which You have commanded us to live; and now, we cannot go into it." 2 Then God heard Adam, and sent him His Word, that said: 3 "Adam, see this fire! It is different from the flame and heat from the garden of delights and the good things in it! 4 When you were under My control all creatures yielded to you, but after you transgressed My commandment they all rose up over you." 5 God said again to him, "Adam, see how Satan has exalted you! He has deprived you of the Godhead and of an exalted state like Me, and has not kept his word to you but has ended up to become your enemy. He is the one who made this fire in which he meant to burn you and Eve. 6 Adam, why has he not kept his agreement with you even one day, but has deprived you of the glory that was on you when you obeyed his command? 7 Adam, do you think that he loved you when he made this agreement with you? Do you think that he loved you and wished to raise you on high? 8 No, Adam, he did not do anything out of love for you. He wished to force you to come out of light and

into darkness, and from an exalted state to degradation, and from glory to this humble state, from joy to sorrow, and from rest to hunger and fainting." 9 God also said to Adam, "See this fire kindled by Satan around your cave? See this curious thing that surrounds you? Know that it will surround both you and your descendants when you obey his command and he will plague you with fire and you will go down into hell after you are dead. 10 Then, you will experience the burning of his fire that will surround you and your descendants. You will not be delivered from it until My coming. Just as you cannot go into your cave right now because of the great fire around it, a way for you will not be made for you until My Word comes on the day My covenant is fulfilled. 11 There is no way for you at present to come from this life to rest until he who is My Word comes. Then He will make a way for you, and you shall have rest." Then God called to the fire that burned around the cave with His Word, that it split itself in half until Adam passed through it. Then the fire parted itself by God's order and a way was made for Adam. 12 And God withdrew His Word from Adam.

Author's note: By God's word His servants passed through the fire, just as the waters were parted.
The "WORD" is made flesh in the form of the Messiah.

Chapter XLVI

1 Then Adam and Eve began again to come into the cave. And when they came to the passage in the midst of the fire, Satan blew into the fire like a whirlwind and caused the burning coal-fire to cover Adam and Eve so that their bodies were singed and the coal-fire burned their skin. 2 Adam and Eve screamed from the burning of the fire, and said, "O Lord, save us! Do not leave us to be consumed and plagued by this burning fire. Do not require us as the payment for having transgressed Your commandment." 3 Then God looked at their bodies on which Satan had caused fire to burn. God sent His angel that held back the burning fire. But the wounds remained on their bodies. 4 Then God said to Adam, "See Satan's love for you. He pretended to give you the Godhead and greatness and, now look, he burns you with fire and seeks to destroy you from off the earth. 5 Then look at Me, Adam. I created you, and how many times have I delivered you out of his hand? If not, wouldn't he have destroyed you?" 6 God spoke again, this time to Eve and said, "He promised you in the garden, saying, 'As soon as you eat from the tree, your eyes will be opened, and you shall become like gods, knowing good and evil.' But look! He has burned your bodies with fire and has made you taste the taste of fire, in exchange for the taste of the garden. He has made you see the burning of fire, and the evil of it, and the power it has over you. 7 Your eyes have seen the good he has taken from you, and in truth he has opened your eyes. You have seen the garden in which you were with Me, and you have also seen the evil that has come over you from Satan. But as to the, Godhead he cannot give it to you, nor fulfill his promise to you. He was bitter against you and your descendants, that will come after you." 8 And God withdrew His Word form them.

Chapter XLVII

1 Then Adam and Eve came into the cave, still trembling because of the fire that had

scorched them. So Adam said to Eve: 2 "Look, in this world the fire burns our flesh. How will it be when we are dead and Satan shall punish our souls? Is not our deliverance far off unless God comes in His mercy and fulfills His promise to us?" 3 Then Adam and Eve stepped into the cave blessing themselves for coming into it once more. For they thought that they would never enter it, when they saw the fire around it. 4 But as the sun was setting the fire was still burning and coming closer to Adam and Eve in the cave, so that they could not sleep in it. After the sunset they went out of the cave. This was the forty-seventh day after they came out of the garden. 5 Adam and Eve then came under the top of hill by the garden to sleep, as they were accustomed. 6 And they stood and prayed God to forgive them their sins, and then fell asleep under the top of the mountain. 7 But Satan, the hater of all that is good, thought to himself: "God has promised salvation to Adam by covenant, and promised that He would deliver him from all the hardships that have befallen him, but God has not promised me by covenant, and will not deliver me out of my hardships. He has promised Adam that He should make him and his descendants live in the kingdom that I once lived in. I will kill Adam. 8 The earth shall be rid of him. The earth shall be left to me alone. When he is dead he will not have any descendants left to inherit the kingdom and it will remain my own realm. God will then be wanting me, and He will restore it to me and my hosts."

Chapter XLVIII

1 After this Satan called to his hosts, all of which came to him, and said to him: 2 "Our lord, what will you do?" 3 Then he said to them, "This Adam, whom God created out of the dust, is the one who has taken our kingdom from us. Come, let us gather together and kill him. Hurl a rock at him and at Eve, and crush them under it." 4 When Satan's hosts heard these words they came to the part of the mountain where Adam and Eve were asleep. 5 Then Satan and his host took a huge rock, broad and smooth, and without blemish. He thought to himself, "If there should be a hole in the rock, when it fell on them the hole in the rock might align over them so they would escape and not die." 6 He then said to his hosts, "Take up this stone and drop it flat on them so that it doesn't roll off them to somewhere else. And when you have hurled it at them get away from there quickly." 7 And they did as he told them. But as the rock fell down from the mountain toward Adam and Eve, God commanded the rock to become a covering over them so that it did them no harm. And so it was by God's order. 8 But when the rock fell, the whole earth quaked because of it, and was shaken from the size of the rock. 9 And as it quaked and shook Adam and Eve awoke from sleep and found themselves under a covering of rock. But they didn't know what had happened because when they fell asleep they were under the sky and not under a covering, and when they saw it they were afraid. 10 Then Adam said to Eve, "How has the mountain bent itself and the earth quaked and shaken on our account? And why has this rock spread itself over us like a tent? 11 Does God intend to plague us and to shut us up in this prison? Or will He close the earth over us? 12 He is angry with us for our having come out of the cave without His permission and for our having done so of our own accord without asking Him when we left the cave and came to this place." 13 Then Eve said, "Adam, if indeed the earth shook for our sake and this rock formed a tent over us because of our transgression we will be sorry, because our punishment will be long. 14 But get up and pray to God to let us know concerning this, and what this rock is that is

spread over us like a tent." 15 Then Adam stood up and prayed before the Lord to let him know what had brought about this difficult time. And Adam stood praying like that until the morning.

Chapter XLIX

1 Then the Word of God came and said: 2 "O Adam, who counseled you when you came out of the cave to come to this place?" 3 And Adam said to God, "Lord, we came to this place because of the heat of the fire that came over us inside the cave." 4 Then the Lord God said to Adam, "Adam, you dread the heat of fire for one night, but how will it be when you live in hell? 5 But Adam, do not be afraid and do not believe that I have placed this covering of rock over you to plague you. 6 It came from Satan, who had promised you the Godhead and majesty. It is he who threw down this rock to kill you under it, and Eve with you, and in this way to prevent you from living on the earth. 7 But, as that rock was falling down on you I was merciful. I commanded it to form a tent over you, and the rock under you to lower itself. 8 And this sign, O Adam, will happen to Me at My coming on earth: Satan will raise the people of the Jews to put Me to death and they will lay Me in a rock, and seal a large stone over Me, and I shall remain within that rock three days and three nights. 9 But on the third day I shall rise again, and it shall be salvation to you, O Adam, and to your descendants, so that you will believe in Me. But, Adam, I will not bring you from under this rock until three days and three nights have passed." 10 And God withdrew His Word from Adam. 11 But Adam and Eve lived under the rock three days and three nights, as God had told them. 12 And God did so to them because they had left their cave and had come to this same place without God's permission. 13 But, after three days and three nights, God created an opening in the covering of rock and allowed them to get out from under it. Their flesh was dried up, and their eyes and hearts were troubled from crying and sorrow.

Author's note: Some translations have the rock forming a dome, but the text gives no shape. If one reads the text closely, it becomes obvious that the shape of the falling rock may not be as important as the fact that the ground Adam and Eve were sleeping on was made to form a depression between the tent or dome shape and the depression of the ground. This formed a cave shape, which mimicked the cave in which Jesus would be buried. It is less obvious but implied that Adam and Eve had some amount of light inside the cave. The text gives no explanation, whether there were gaps, cracks, or holes for air and light.

Chapter L

1 Then Adam and Eve went out and came into the Cave of Treasures and stood praying in it the entire day until the evening. 2 And this took place at the end of the fifty days after they had left the garden. 3 But Adam and Eve rose again and prayed to God in the cave the whole of that night, and begged for mercy from Him. 4 And when the day dawned, Adam said to Eve, "Come! Let us go and do some work for our bodies." 5 So they went out of the cave, and came to the northern border of the garden, and they looked for something to cover their bodies with. But they found nothing, and did not know how to do the work. But their bodies were stained, and they could not speak from cold and heat. 6 Then Adam stood and asked God to

show him something with which to cover their bodies. 7 Then came the Word of God and said to him, "O Adam, take Eve and come to the seashore where you fasted before. There you will find skins of sheep that were left after lions ate the carcasses. Take them and make garments for yourselves, and clothe yourselves with them.

Author's Note: There is no direct explanation as to how Adam and Eve became naked again. One possibility is found in chapter XLVI, verse 1, which states that Satan blew into the fire and singed Adam and Eve. It is possible that the garments that the Lord had given them in Genesis 3:21 were burned away at this point, leaving Adam and Eve naked once more.

Chapter LI

1 When Adam heard these words from God, he took Eve and went from the northern side of the garden to the south of it, by the river of water where they once fasted. 2 But as they were on their way, and before they arrived, Satan, the wicked one, had heard the Word of God communing with Adam respecting his covering. 3 It distressed him, and he hurried to the place where the sheepskins were, with the intention of taking them and throwing them into the sea or of burning them so that Adam and Eve would not find them. 4 But as he was about to take them, the Word of God came from heaven and bound him by the side of those skins until Adam and Eve came near him. But as they got closer to him they were afraid of him and of his hideous appearance. 5 Then the Word of God came to Adam and Eve, and said to them, "This is he who was hidden in the serpent, who deceived you, and stripped from you your garment of light and glory. 6 This is he who promised you majesty and divinity. Where is the beauty that was on him? Where is his divinity? Where is his light? Where is the glory that rested on him? 7 Now his form is hideous. He has become abominable (offensive) among angels, and he has come to be called Satan. 8 Adam, he wished to steal from you this earthly garment of sheepskins so that he could destroy it not let you be covered with it. 9 What is his beauty that you should have followed him? And what have you gained by obeying him? See his evil works and then look at Me, your Creator. Look at the good deeds I do for you. 10 I bound him until you came and saw him and his weakness and that no power is left with him." 11 And God released him from his bonds.

Chapter LII

1 After this Adam and Eve said no more, but cried before God because of their creation, and their bodies that required an earthly covering. 2 Then Adam said to Eve, "Eve, this is the skin of beasts with which we shall be covered, but when we put it on we shall be wearing a sign of death on our bodies. Just as the owners of these skins have died and have decomposed, so also shall we die and pass away." 3 Then Adam and Eve took the skins and went back to the Cave of Treasures. When they were in it, they stood and prayed, as was their habit. 4 And they thought how they could make garments of those skins because they had no skill. 5 Then God sent to them His angel to show them how to accomplish this. And the angel said to Adam, "Go out and bring some palm-thorns." Then Adam went out, and brought some, as the angel had commanded him. 6 Then the angel began before them to work the skins, after the manner of one who prepares a shirt. And he took the thorns and stuck them into the skins before their eyes. 7 Then the angel again stood up and

prayed God that the thorns in those skins should be hidden, so as to be as if it were sewn with one thread. 8 And so it was, by God's order, and they became garments for Adam and Eve. And He clothed them with the skins. 9 From that time the nakedness of their bodies was covered from the sight of each other's eyes. 10 And this happened at the end of the fifty-first day. 11 Then when Adam's and Eve's bodies were covered they stood and prayed and sought mercy of the Lord and forgiveness, and gave Him thanks because He had mercy on them and had covered their nakedness. And they did not stop praying the entirety of that night. 12 Then, when the morning dawned at sunrise, they said their prayers, as was their custom, and then went out of the cave. 13 And Adam said to Eve, "Since we don't know what there is to the west of this cave, let us go out and see it today." Then they departed and went toward the western border.

Chapter LIII

1 They were not very far from the cave when Satan came toward them. He hid himself between them and the cave in the form of two ravenous lions that had been three days without food. And they came toward Adam and Eve as if to break them in pieces and devour them. 2 Then Adam and Eve cried out and begged God to deliver them from their paws. 3 Then the Word of God came to them and drove away the lions from them. 4 And God said to Adam, "Adam, what do you seek on the western border? And why have you left of your own will the eastern border which was your living place? 5 Now, turn back to your cave and remain in it, so that Satan won't deceive you or achieve his goal to overtake you. 6 In this western border, Adam, there will go from you a descendant that shall replenish it. And they will defile themselves with their sins, and with their yielding to the commands of Satan, and by following his works. 7 Therefore will I bring waters of a flood to cover them and overwhelm them all. But I will deliver what is left of the righteous among them and I will bring them to a distant land, but the land in which you live now shall remain desolate and without one inhabitant in it. 8 After God had spoken to them, they went back to the Cave of Treasures. But their flesh was dried up, and they were weak from fasting and praying, and from the sorrow they felt at having sinned against God.

Chapter LIV

1 Then Adam and Eve stood up in the cave and prayed the entire night until the morning dawned. And when the sun came up they both went out of the cave. Their minds were wandering from the heaviness of sorrow and they didn't know where they were going. 2 And they walked in that condition to the southern border of the garden. And they began to go up that border until they came to the eastern border, which was land's end. 3 And the cherub who guarded the garden was standing at the western gate to guard it from Adam and Eve in case they should attempt to suddenly come into the garden. 4 When Adam and Eve thought the cherub was not watching they came to the eastern border of the garden. But as they were standing by the gate, as if they desired to go in, the cherub turned around as if to put them to death according to the order God had given him. And the cherub suddenly came with a flashing sword of fire in his hand. When he saw them, he went toward them to kill them. For he was afraid that God would destroy him if they went into the

garden without God's order. 5 And the sword of the cherub seemed to shoot flames a distance away from it. But when he raised it over Adam and Eve, the flame of the sword did not flash out at them. 6 Because of this the cherub thought that God was approving to them and was bringing them back into the garden. And the cherub stood wondering. 7 He could not go up to Heaven to ascertain God's order regarding Adam and Eve's entering the garden so continued to stand by them, unable to leave them because he was afraid that if they should enter the garden without permission God would destroy him. 8 When Adam and Eve saw the cherub coming towards them with a flaming sword of fire in his hand they fell on their faces from fear, and were as dead. 9 Then, the heavens and the earth shook, and another cherubim came down from heaven to the cherub who guarded the garden, and saw him amazed and silent. 10 Then, again, other angels came down close to the place where Adam and Eve were. And the cherubs were split between joy and sorrow. 11 They were joyous because they thought that God was approving to Adam, and wished him to return to the garden and wished to return him to the gladness he once enjoyed. 12 But they were sorrowful over Adam because he was fallen like a dead man, he and Eve. And they said to themselves, "Adam has not died in this place, but God has put him to death for coming to this place and wishing to enter the garden without His permission."

Chapter LV

1 Then the Word of God came to Adam and Eve, and raised them up from their dead state, saying to them, "Why did you come up here? Do you intend to go into the garden from which I brought you out? You cannot return today but only when the covenant I have made with you is fulfilled." 2 Then Adam, when he heard the Word of God, and the fluttering of the angels, which he only heard and did not see, he and Eve cried and said to the angels: 3 "O Spirits, who wait on God, look at me and at my inability to see you! When I was in my former bright nature I could see you. I sang praises as you do and my heart was far above you. 4 But now that I have transgressed, that bright nature is gone from me and I have come to this miserable state in which I cannot see you. You do not serve me like you used to do. For my flesh has become like that of the animals. 5 O angels of God, ask God to restore me to the state I was in formerly and ask him to rescue me from this misery, and to remove the sentence of death He passed on me for having trespassed against Him. Ask Him, as I ask Him to do these things." 6 Then, when the angels heard these words they all grieved over him and cursed Satan who had misled Adam until he came from the garden to misery, and from life to death, and from peace to distress, and from gladness to a strange land. 7 Then the angels said to Adam, "You obeyed Satan and ignored the Word of God who created you. You believed that Satan would fulfill all he had promised you. 8 But now, Adam, we will make known to you what came over us though him, before his fall from heaven. 9 He gathered together his hosts and deceived them, promising to give them a great kingdom, a divine nature, and other promises he made them. 10 His hosts believed that his word was true, so they followed him, and renounced the glory of God. 11 He then ordered us, and some obeyed and under his command, and accepted his empty promises. But we would not obey and we did not take his orders. 12 Then, after he had fought with God and had dealt disrespectfully with Him, he gathered together his hosts and made war

with us. And if it had not been for God's strength that was with us we could not have prevailed against him to hurl him from heaven. 13 But when he fell from among us there was great joy in heaven because of his descent from us. If he had remained in heaven, nothing, not even one angel would have remained in it. 14 But God in His mercy drove him from among us to this dark earth because he had become darkness itself and a performer of unrighteousness. 15 And Adam, he has continued to make war against you until he tricked you and made you come out of the garden to this strange land, where all these trials have come to you. And death, which God brought to him, he has also brought to you because you obeyed him and sinned against God." 16 Then all the angels rejoiced and praised God and asked Him not to destroy Adam for his having sought to enter the garden at this time, but to bear with him until the fulfillment of the promise, and to help him in this world until he was free from Satan's hand.

Chapter LVI

1 Then the Word of God came to Adam, and said to him: 2 "Adam, look at that garden of joy and at this earth of toil, and see, the garden is full of angels, but look at yourself alone on this earth with Satan whom you obeyed. 3 If you had submitted and been obedient to Me and had kept My Word, you would be with My angels in My garden. 4 But when you sinned and obeyed Satan, you became his guests among his angels, that are full of wickedness, and you came to this earth that produces thorns and thistles for you. 5 O Adam, ask the one who deceived you to give you the divine nature he promised you, or to make you a garden as I had made for you, or to fill you with that same bright nature with which I had filled you. 6 Ask him to make you a body like the one I made you, or to give you a day of rest as I gave you, or to create within you a wise (intelligent, sound, reasonable) soul, as I created for you; or to take you from here to some other earth than this one which I gave you. But, Adam, he will not fulfill even one of the things he told you. 7 Acknowledge My favor toward you, and My mercy on you, My creature. Acknowledge that I have not shown vengeance on you for your transgression against Me, but in My pity for you I have promised you that at the end of the great five and a half days I will come and save you." 8 Then God said again to Adam and Eve, "Get up, go down from here before the cherub with a sword of fire in his hand destroys you." 9 But Adam's heart was comforted by God's words to him, and he worshipped before Him. 10 And God commanded His angels to escort Adam and Eve to the cave with joy instead of the fear that had come over them. 11 Then the angels took up Adam and Eve and brought them down the mountain by the garden, with songs and praises and hymns until they arrived at the cave. There the angels began to comfort and to strengthen them, and then departed from them towards heaven to their Creator, who had sent them. 12 But after the angels had departed from Adam and Eve, Satan came with shamefacedness and stood at the entrance of the cave in which were Adam and Eve. He then called to Adam, and said, "O Adam, come, let me speak to you." 13 Then Adam came out of the cave, thinking he was one of God's angels that had come to give him some good counsel.

Chapter LVII

1 But when Adam came out and saw his hideous figure he was afraid of him, and

said to him, "Who are you?" 2 Then Satan answered and said to him, "It is I, who hid myself within the serpent, and who spoke to Eve, and who enticed her until she obeyed my command. I am he who, using my deceitful speech, sent her to deceive you until you both ate of the fruit of the tree and rejected the command of God." 3 But when Adam heard these words from him, he said to him, "Can you make me a garden as God made for me? Or can you clothe me in the same bright nature in which God had clothed me? 4 Where is the divine nature you promised to give me? Where is that clever speech of yours that you had with us at first, when we were in the garden?" 5 Then Satan said to Adam, "Do you think that when I have promised someone something that I would actually deliver it to him or fulfill my word? Of course not. I myself have no hope of (never even thought of) obtaining what I promised. 6 Therefore I fell, and I made you fall for the same reason that I myself fell. Whoever accepts my counsel, falls. 7 But now, O Adam, because you fell you are under my rule and I am king over you because you have obeyed me and have sinned against your God. There will be no deliverance from my hands until the day promised you by your God." 8 Again he said, "Because we do not know the day agreed on with you by your God, nor the hour in which you shall be delivered, we will multiply wars and murders on you and your descendants after you. 9 This is our will and our good pleasure that we may not leave one of the sons of men to inherit our place in heaven. 10 Our home, Adam, is in burning fire and we will not stop our evil doing even a single day nor even a single hour. And I, O Adam, shall set you on fire when you come into the cave to live there." 11 When Adam heard these words he cried and mourned and said to Eve, "Did you hear what he said? He said that he would not fulfill any of what he promised you in the garden. Did he really, at that time, become king over us? 12 We will ask God, who created us, to deliver us out of his hands."

Chapter LVIII

1 Then Adam and Eve spread their hands before God, praying and begging Him to drive Satan away from them so that he could not harm them or force them to deny God. 2 Then, suddenly, God sent to them His angel who drove Satan away from them. This happened about sunset on the fifty-third day after they had come out of the garden. 3 Then Adam and Eve went into the cave, and stood up and lowered their faces to the ground to pray to God. 4 But before they prayed Adam said to Eve, "Look, you have seen what temptations have befallen us in this land. Come, let us get up and ask God to forgive us the sins we have committed and we will not come out until the end of the day before the fortieth day. And if we die in here He will save us." 5 Then Adam and Eve got up and joined together in entreating God. 6 They continued praying like this in the cave and did not come out of it in the night or day, until their prayers went up out of their mouths like a flame of fire.

Author's note: This little chapter has several details showing connections to customs of punishment and also to number symbolism. The day is the 53rd day. 5+3=8. Eight is the number of judgment. Adam and Eve elected to stay in the cave praying for 40 days minus 1. Forty is the number of testing and trails. The rains were to fall for 40 days. Jesus was in the desert for 40 days. The Israelites wondered in the desert for 40 years... However, when it came to punishment inflicted by the state, as was in the case of the flogging of Jesus, the punishment was 40 lashes minus 1.

Chapter LIX

1 But Satan, the hater of all that is good, did not allow them to finish their prayers.
He called to his hosts and they all came. Then he said to them, "Since Adam and Eve,
whom we deceived, have agreed together to pray to God night and day, and to beg
Him to deliver them, and since they will not come out of the cave until the end of the
fortieth day. 2 And since they will continue their prayers as they have both agreed to
do, that He will deliver them out of our hands and restore them to their former state,
let us see what we shall do to them." And his hosts said to him, "Power is yours, our
lord, to do what you command." 3 Then Satan, great in wickedness, took his hosts
and came into the cave on the thirtieth night of the forty day period, and he beat
Adam and Eve until he thought they were dead and he left them as dead. 4 Then the
Word of God came to Adam and Eve and raised them from their suffering, and God
said to Adam, "Be strong, and do not be afraid of him who has just come to you." 5
But Adam cried and said, "Where were you, my God, that they should punish me
with such blows and that this suffering should come over me and over Eve, your
handmaiden?" 6 Then God said to him, "Adam, see, he is lord and master of all you
have, he who said, he would give you divinity. Where is this love for you? And
where is the gift he promised? 7 Did it please him just once, Adam, to come to you,
comfort you, strengthen you, rejoice with you, or send his hosts to protect you,
because you have obeyed him and have obeyed his counsel and have followed his
commandment and transgressed Mine?" 8 Then Adam cried before the Lord, and
said, "Lord because I transgressed a little, You have severely punished me in return.
I ask You to deliver me out of his hands, or at least have pity on me and take my
soul out of my body now in this strange land." 9 Then God said to Adam, "If only
there had been this moaning and praying before you transgressed you would have
rest from the trouble in which you are now." 10 But God had patience with Adam,
and let him and Eve remain in the cave until they had fulfilled the forty days. 11 But
the strength and flesh withered on Adam and Eve from fasting and praying, from
hunger and thirst, because they had not tasted either food or drink since they left the
garden, and their bodies functioned erratically because they had no strength left to
continue in prayer from hunger until the end of the next day to the fortieth. They
were fallen down in the cave, yet what speech escaped from their mouths, was only
in praises.

Chapter LX

1 Then on the eighty-ninth day, Satan came to the cave, clad in a garment of light,
and belted with a bright girdle. 2 In his hands was a staff of light, and he looked
most frightening, but his face was pleasant and his speech was sweet. 3 He had
transformed himself like this in order to deceive Adam and Eve and to make them
come out of the cave before they had fulfilled the forty days. 4 He said to himself,
"When they had fulfilled the forty days' fasting and praying, God would restore
them to their former state but if He did not do this He would still be favorable to
them, and even if He had no mercy on them would He still give them something
from the garden to comfort them as He had already twice before." 5 Then Satan came
near the cave in beautiful appearance and said: 6 "Adam, you and Eve arise and
stand up and come along with me to a good land and don't be afraid. I am flesh and

bones like you and at first I was a creature that God created. 7 It was like this when He had created me, He placed me in a garden in the north on the border of the world. 8 And He said to me, 'Stay here!' And I remained there according to His word and I did not violate His commandment. 9 Then He made a sleep to come over me and then He brought you, Adam, out of my side, but He did not make you stay with me. 10 But God took you in His holy hand and placed you in a garden to the east. 11 Then I worried about you, because even though God had taken you out of my side, He had not allowed you to stay with me. 12 But God said to me: 'Do not worry about Adam, whom I brought out of your side, no harm will come to him. 13 For now I have brought out of his side a help-meet for him and I have given him joy by so doing.' " 14 Then Satan spoke again, saying, "I did not know how it is you came to be in this cave, nor anything about this trial that has come over you until God said to me, 'Behold, Adam has transgressed. He whom I had taken out of your side, and Eve also, whom I took out of his side have sinned and I have driven them out of the garden. I have made them live in a land of sorrow and misery because they transgressed against Me, and have obeyed Satan. And look, they are suffering to this day, the eightieth.' 15 Then God said to me, 'Get up, go to them, and make them come to your place, and do not permit Satan to come near them and afflict them. For they are now in great misery and lie helpless from hunger.' 16 He further said to me, 'When you have taken them to yourself, give them to eat of the fruit of the Tree of Life and give them to drink of the water of peace, and clothe them in a garment of light, and restore them to their former state of grace, and leave them not in misery, for they came from you. But grieve not over them, nor be sorry of that which has come over them. 17 But when I heard this, I was sorry and my heart could not bear it for your sake and I could not wait, my child. 18 But, Adam, when I heard the name of Satan I was afraid, and I said to myself, I will not come out because he might trap me as he did my children, Adam and Eve. 19 And I said, 'God, when I go to my children, Satan will meet me on the way and fight against me as he did against them.' 20 Then God said to me, 'Fear not; when you find him, hit him with the staff that is in your hand and don't be afraid of him, because you are old and established, and he shall not prevail against you.' 21 Then I said, 'O my Lord, I am old, and cannot go. Send Your angels to bring them.' 22 But God said to me, 'Angels are not like Adam and Eve; and they will not consent to come with them. But I have chosen you, because they are your offspring and are like you and they will listen to what you say.' 23 God said further to me, 'If you don't have enough strength to walk, I will send a cloud to carry you and set you down at the entrance of their cave, then the cloud will return and leave you there. 24 And if they will come with you, I will send a cloud to carry you and them.' 25 Then He commanded a cloud to carry me up and it brought me to you, and then it went back. 26 And now, my children, Adam and Eve, look at my old gray hair and at my feeble state, and at my coming from that distant place. Come with me to a place of rest." 27 Then he began to cry and to sob before Adam and Eve, and his tears poured on the ground like water. 28 And when Adam and Eve raised their eyes and saw his beard and heard his sweet talk, their hearts softened towards him and they obeyed him, because they believed he was true. 29 And it seemed to them that they were really his offspring when they saw that his face was like their own; and they trusted him.

Author note: This chapter is a cruel mockery. It represents the purpose of Christ turned upside down. Satan claims to be sent by God because he is in human form, in order to rescued

Adam and Eve because he was made like them and they would listen and obey him. Adam and Eve believed Satan. When Jesus came we rejected the true savior.

Later in the chapter the word "helpmeet" is used. Meet, in the archaic usage, means to be fit, suitable, or proper. Thus, in the King James usage, the word helpmeet means someone who is a fit or suitable helper. It was only in the 17th century that the two words help and meet were mistaken for one word, helpmeet, and came to mean a wife. Later, in the 18th century a mistake in spelling along with a misunderstanding of the broader meaning of the word produced the word "helpmate" to mean a wife or sexual mate.

Chapter LXI

1 Then Satan took Adam and Eve by the hand started to lead them out of the cave. 2
But when they had gone a little way out of it God knew that Satan had overcome
them and had brought them out before the forty days were ended in order to take
them to some distant place and to destroy them. 3 Then the Word of the Lord God
again came and cursed Satan and drove him away from them. 4 And God began to
speak to Adam and Eve, saying to them, "What made you come out of the cave to
this place?" 5 Then Adam said to God, "Did you create a man before us? Because,
when we were in the cave there suddenly came to us a friendly old man who said to
us, 'I am a messenger from God to you, to bring you back to some place of rest.' 6
And we believed that he was a messenger from you, O God, and we came out with
him. We did not know where we should go with him." 7 Then God said to Adam,
"This is the father of the evil arts who brought you and Eve out of the Garden of
Delights. And when he saw that you and Eve both joined together in fasting and
praying so that you did not come out of the cave before the end of the forty days, he
wished to make your efforts wasted and break your mutual bond in order to take
away all hope from you and to drive you to some place where he might destroy you.
8 Because he couldn't do anything to you unless he showed himself in the likeness of
you. 9 Therefore he came to you with a face like your own and began to give you
signs as if they were all true. 10 But because I am merciful and am favorable to you, I
did not allow him to destroy you. Instead, I drove him away from you. 11 Now,
Adam, take Eve and return to your cave and remain in it until the morning after the
fortieth day. And when you come out, go toward the eastern gate of the garden." 12
Then Adam and Eve worshipped God, and praised and blessed Him for the
deliverance that had come to them from Him. And they returned to the cave. This
happened in the evening of the thirty-ninth day. 13 Then Adam and Eve stood up
and with a fervent passion, prayed to God to give them strength, for they had
become weak because of hunger and thirst and prayer. But they watched the entire
night praying until morning. 14 Then Adam said to Eve, "Get up. Let us go toward
the eastern gate of the garden as God told us." 15 And they said their prayers as they
were accustomed to do every day, and they left the cave to go near to the eastern
gate of the garden. 16 Then Adam and Eve stood up and prayed and appealed to
God to strengthen them and to send them something to satisfy their hunger. 17 But
after they finished their prayers they were too weak to move. 18 Then the Word of
God came again, and said to them, "Adam, get up, go and bring the two figs here."
19 Then Adam and Eve got up, and went until they came near to the cave.

Chapter LXII

1 But Satan, the wicked one, was envious because of the consolation God had given them. 2 So he prevented them from getting the figs and went into the cave and took the two figs and buried them outside the cave so that Adam and Eve should not find them. He also had thought to destroy them. 3 But by God's mercy, as soon as those two figs were in the ground God defeated Satan's wishes regarding the figs and made them into two fruit trees that grew higher than the cave and shaded the cave because Satan had buried them on the eastern side of it. 4 Then when the two trees were grown, and were covered with fruit, Satan grieved and mourned, and said, "It would have been better to have left those figs where they were, because now they have become two fruit trees that Adam will eat from all the days of his life. But I had in my mind that when I buried them it would destroy them entirely and hide them forever. 5 But God has overturned my plan and would not let that sacred fruit perish, and He has made known my intention, and has defeated the plan I had formed against His servants." 6 Then Satan went away ashamed because he hadn't thought his plans all the way through.

Chapter LXIII

1 As they got closer to the cave Adam and Eve saw two fig trees covered with fruit, and giving shade to the cave. 2 Then Adam said to Eve, "It seems to me that we have gone the wrong way. When did these two trees grow here? It seems to me that the enemy wishes to lead us the wrong way. Do you suppose that there is another cave in the earth besides this one? 3 But, Eve let us go into the cave and find the two figs because this is our cave we were in. But if we do not find the two figs in it then it cannot be our cave." 4 Then they went into the cave and looked into the four corners of it but did not find the two figs. 5 And Adam cried and said to Eve, "Did we go to the wrong cave, Eve? It seems to me the two figs should have been in the cave." And Eve said, "I, do not know." 6 Then Adam stood up and prayed and said, "O God, You commanded us to come back to the cave to take the two figs and return to you. 7 But now, we cannot find them. God, have you taken them and planted these two trees, or have we lost our way (gotten lost) in the earth, or has the enemy deceived us? If this is real then, O God, reveal the secret of these two trees (outside) and figs to us." 8 Then the Word of God came to Adam, and said to him, "Adam, when I sent you to bring back the figs, Satan went ahead of you to the cave and took the figs, and buried them outside, east of the cave, thinking to destroy them, by not sowing them with good intent. 9 It wasn't because of him that these trees have immediately grown up but I had mercy on you and I commanded them to grow. And they grew to be two large trees, that would give you shade by their branches, and you should find rest, and by this I made you see My power and My marvelous works. 10 And, also I showed you Satan's cruelty and his evil works. Ever since you came out of the garden he has not ceased for a single day from doing you harm in some way. But I have not given him power over you." 11 And God said, "From now on, Adam, rejoice because of the trees that you and Eve can rest under when you feel weary. But do not eat any of their fruit or come near them." 12 Then Adam cried, and said, "God, will You kill us again, or will You drive us away from Your face, and cut off our life from the face of the earth? 13 O God, I beg you, if You know that these trees

bring either death or some other evil, as they did the first time, root them up from near our cave and leave us to die of the heat or hunger or thirst. 14 For we know Your marvelous works, O God, that they are great, and that by Your power You can bring one thing out of another without the thing's (person's) consent. For Your power can make rocks to become trees, and trees to become rocks."

Author's Note: They would have known it was their cave because the gold was still there. This verse brings up questions of Satan's power over Adam and Eve and the extent of any authority. In previous verses we were led to think Satan had gained power of them because of their sin. Now, in this verse we read," But I have not given him power over you." This seems to be a contradiction.

Chapter LXIV

1 Then God looked at Adam and at his strength of mind and at his ability to endure hunger, thirst, and heat. And He changed the two fig trees into two figs as they were at first. Then He said to Adam and Eve, "Each of you may take one fig." And they took them as the Lord commanded them. 2 And He said to them, "You must now go into the cave and eat the figs and satisfy your hunger or else you will die." 3 So, they went into the cave about sunset as God commanded them. And Adam and Eve stood up and prayed during the setting sun. 4 Then they sat down to eat the figs, but they did not know how to eat them because they were not accustomed to eating earthly food. They were afraid that if they ate, their stomach would become heavy and their flesh thickened, and their hearts would begin to crave earthly food. 5 But while they were seated, God sent them His angel, out of pity for them, so they wouldn't perish of hunger and thirst. 6 And the angel said to Adam and Eve, "God says to you that you do not have the strength that would be required to fast until death, so eat and strengthen your bodies, for you are now animal flesh and cannot subsist without food and drink." 7 Then Adam and Eve took the figs and began to eat of them. But God had put into them a mixture as of savory bread and blood. 8 Then, the angel left Adam and Eve as they ate of the figs until they had satisfied their hunger. Then they put aside what was left over, but by the power of God the figs became whole again, because God blessed them. 9 After this Adam and Eve got up and prayed with a joyful heart and renewed strength, and praised and rejoiced much for the entire night. And this was the end of the eighty-third day.

Author's not: The meaning of the phrase, "God says to you that you do not have the strength that would be required to fast until death…" is not clear. It is likely that it simply is somewhat inverted and should be, "If you fast, you will not have the required strength and you will die." Although one could look at it as a spiritual strength and a warning the one does not have the required determination to endure death by fasting. But God saw Adam had the will.

Chapter LXV

1 And when it was day, they got up and prayed, after their custom, and then went out of the cave. 2 But they became sick from the food they had eaten because they were not used to it, so they went about in the cave saying to each other: 3 "What has

our eating caused to happen to us, that we should be in such pain? We are in misery. We are going to die! It would have been better for us to have died keeping our bodies pure than to have eaten and defiled them with food." 4 Then Adam said to Eve, "This pain did not come to us in the garden, neither did we eat such bad food there. Eve, do you think that God will plague us through the food that is in us, or that our insides will come out, or that God intends to kill us with this pain before He has fulfilled His promise to us?" 5 Then Adam besought the Lord and said, "O Lord, let us not perish because of the food we have eaten. O Lord, don't punish us, but deal with us according to Your great mercy, and do not forsake us until the day of the promise You have made us." 6 Then God looked at them, and then equipped them to be able to eat (fitted them for eating) food at once, as it is to this day, so that they should not perish. 7 Then Adam and Eve came back into the cave sorrowful and crying because of the alteration of their bodies. And they both knew from that hour that they were altered beings and all hope of returning to the garden was now lost, and they could not enter it again. 8 For now their bodies had strange functions and all flesh that requires food and drink for its existence cannot be in the garden. 9 Then Adam said to Eve, "See, our hope is now lost and so is our faith that we will enter the garden. We no longer belong to the inhabitants of the garden but from now on we are earthy and of the dust, and of the inhabitants of the earth. We shall not return to the garden until the day in which God has promised to save us and to bring us again into the garden, as He promised us." 10 Then they prayed to God that He would have mercy on them. After this, their minds were quieted, their hearts were broken, and their longing was cooled down, and they were like strangers on earth. That night Adam and Eve spent in the cave, where they slept heavily because of the food they had eaten.

Chapter LXVI

1 When the morning of the day after they had eaten food came, Adam and Eve prayed in the cave, and Adam said to Eve, "Look, we asked God for food, and He gave it. But now let us also ask Him to give us a drink of water." 2 Then they got up, and went to the bank of the stream of water, that was on the south border of the garden, which they had thrown themselves in before. And they stood on the bank, and prayed to God that He would command them to drink the water. 3 Then the Word of God came to Adam, and said to him, "O Adam, your body has become brutish, and requires water to drink. Take some and drink it, you and Eve, then give thanks and praise." 4 Adam and Eve then went down to the stream and drank from it, until their bodies felt refreshed. After they drank, they praised God and then returned to their cave, as was their custom. This happened at the end of eighty-three days. 5 Then on the eighty-fourth day, they took the two figs and hung them in the cave together with the leaves of the figs. To them these were a sign and a blessing from God. And they placed them there so that if their descendants came there they would see the wonderful things God had done for them. 6 Then Adam and Eve stood outside the cave again and asked God to show them some food with which they could nourish their bodies. 7 Then the Word of God came and said to him, "Adam, go down west of the cave until you come to a land that has dark soil, and there you will find food." 8 And Adam obeyed the Word of God and took Eve, and went down to a land that had dark soil and found wheat growing ripe in the ear, and figs to eat; and Adam rejoiced over it. 9 Then the Word of God came again to

Adam, and said to him, "Take some of this wheat and make yourselves some bread with it, to nourish your body." And God gave Adam's heart wisdom to work the corn until it became bread. 10 Adam accomplished it all until he grew very faint and weak. He then returned to the cave rejoicing at what he had learned what he had done with the wheat, until it was made into bread.

The word, "corn" is used to mean a seed. However, the sentence indicates it is a seed of wheat that is used to make bread. The words for corn, meaning a seed, and wheat, are used to mean the same thing. In Egypt there is a type of wheat called Durra. The seed (corn) of wheat was likely Durra.

Chapter LXVII

1 When Adam and Eve went down to the land of black earth (mud) and came near to the wheat God had showed them and saw that it was ripe and ready for reaping, they did not have a sickle to reap it with. So they put themselves to the task and began to pull up the wheat by hand until the task was complete. 2 They then heaped it into a pile. They were weak from heat and from thirst and went under a shady tree where the breeze fanned them to sleep. 3 But Satan saw what Adam and Eve had done and he called his hosts, and said to them, "God has shown to Adam and Eve all about this wheat to strengthen their bodies, and, look, they have come and made a big pile of it. Now they are weak from the toil are now asleep. Come, let us set fire to this heap of corn (wheat seed), and burn it. Let us take that bottle of water that is by them and empty it out, so that they may find nothing to drink, and we kill them with hunger and thirst. 4 Then, when they wake up from their sleep and seek to return to the cave, we will come to them along the way and lead them in the wrong direction (get them lost) so that they die of hunger and thirst. Then perhaps they will reject God, and He may destroy them. So, in this way we can be rid of them." 5 Then Satan and his hosts set the wheat on fire and burned it up. 6 But from the heat of the flame Adam and Eve awoke from their sleep and saw the wheat burning and the bucket of water by them was poured out. 7 Then they cried and began to go back to the cave. 8 But as they were going up from below the mountain, Satan and his hosts met them in the form of angels, praising God. 9 Then Satan said to Adam, "Adam, why are you so pained with hunger and thirst? It seems to me that Satan has burnt up the wheat." And Adam said to him, "Yes." 10 Satan said to Adam, "Come back with us. We are angels of God. God sent us to you to show you another field of corn (wheat) better than that, and beyond it is a fountain of good water and many trees, near where you shall live. And you shall work the corn field and make it better than that which Satan has consumed." 11 Adam thought that he was true, and that they were angels who talked with him and so he went back with them. 12 Then Satan began to lead Adam and Eve in the wrong direction for eight days, until they both fell down as if dead, from hunger, thirst, and weakness. Then he fled with his hosts, and left them.

Author's note: In this recurring theme of deceit by Satan, we are confronted by the age-old question in life; is the circumstance that confronts us an opportunity from God or a detour and trap of Satan. How are we to know?

Chapter LXVIII

1 Then God looked at Adam and Eve, and at what had befallen them from Satan, and how he killed them. 2 So, God sent His Word and raised Adam and Eve from of death. 3 Then, when he was raised, Adam said, "O God, You have burnt and taken the seeds which You had given us. You have emptied out the bucket of water. And You have sent Your angels, who have caused us to lose our way from the corn (wheat) field. Will You kill us? If this is from you, O God, then take away our souls but stop punishing us." 4 Then God said to Adam, "I did not burn down the wheat, and I did not pour the water out of the bucket, and I did not send My angels to lead you astray. 5 But it is Satan, your master who did it. It was he to whom you have subjected yourself, while setting my commandment aside. It is He who burnt down the corn (wheat), and poured out the water, and who has led you astray. All the promises he has made you were just a trick, a deception, and a lie. 6 But now, Adam, you shall acknowledge My good deeds done to you." 7 And God told His angels to take Adam and Eve, and to lift them up to the field of wheat, which they found as before with the bucket full of water. 8 There they saw a tree and found on it solid manna, and they were astonished at God's power. And the angels commanded them to eat of the manna when they were hungry. 9 And God admonished Satan with a curse, not to come again and destroy the field of corn (wheat). 10 Then Adam and Eve took of the corn (wheat / seeds), and made an offering of it, and took it and offered it up on the mountain, at the place where they had offered up their first offering of blood. 11 And they offered this offering again on the altar they had built at first. And they stood up and prayed, and besought the Lord saying, "O God, when we were in the garden, our praises went up to you like this offering, and our innocence went up to you like incense. But now, O God, accept this offering from us, and don't turn us away or deprive us of Your mercy." 12 Then God said to Adam and Eve, "Since you have made this offering and have offered it to Me, I shall make it My flesh when I come down on earth to save you. I shall cause it to be offered continually on an altar for forgiveness and mercy for those who partake of it appropriately." 13 Then God sent a bright fire over the offering of Adam and Eve and filled it with brightness, grace, and light. And the Holy Spirit came down on that offering. 14 Then God commanded an angel to take fire tongs, like a spoon, and take an offering and bring it to Adam and Eve. And the angel did so as God had commanded him, and offered it to them. 15 And the souls of Adam and Eve were brightened, and their hearts were filled with joy and gladness and with the praises of God. 16 And God said to Adam, "This shall be a custom to you to perform when affliction and sorrow should come over you. But your deliverance and your entrance in to the garden, shall not be until the days are fulfilled as agreed between you and Me. If it were not for this, I would bring you back to My garden and to My favor and My mercy and pity for you, for the sake of the offering you have just made to My name." 17 Adam rejoiced at these words, which he heard from God. And Adam and Eve worshipped before the altar, to which they bowed, and then went back to the Cave of Treasures. 18 And this took place at the end of the twelfth day after the eightieth day (92 days), from the time Adam and Eve came out of the garden. 19 And they stood up the entire night praying until morning. Then they went out of the cave. 20 Then Adam said to Eve, with joy in his heart, because of the offering they had made to God that had been accepted by Him, "Let us do this three times every

week, on all the days of our life." 21 And as they agreed on these words and God was pleased with their thoughts and with the decision they made. 22 After this, the Word of God came to Adam, and said, "Adam, you have determined beforehand the days in which sufferings shall come over Me, when I am made flesh. They are the fourth day, which is Wednesday, and the preparation day, which is Friday. 23 But regarding the first day, I created all things in it, and I raised the heavens. Through My rising again on this day, will I create joy and raise them who believe in Me on high. Adam, make this offering all the days of your life." 24 Then the Word of God withdrew from Adam. 25 But Adam continued to make the offering as he had, every week, three times a week, until the end of seven weeks. And on the first day, which is the fiftieth, Adam made an offering as he was accustomed, and he and Eve took it and came to the altar before God, as He had taught them.

Author's note: The order and number of the days of the week are called out as follows, "the fourth day, Wednesday, on the preparation day Friday, and on the Sabbath Sunday." The Jewish Sabbath is from Friday at sundown to Saturday at sundown, wherein, Saturday is considered to be the Sabbath. The shift shows Christian influence and a dating later than the writer(s) would have us believe.

Chapter LXIX

1 Then Satan, the hater of all that is good, was envious of Adam the fact that his offering found favor with God. So Satan hurried and took a sharp stone from among the sharp ironstones, which were shaped in the form of a man. And Satan went and stood by Adam and Eve. 2 Adam was offering on the altar and had begun to pray with his hands spread before God. 3 Then Satan hurried with the sharp ironstone he had and pierced Adam on the right side, and blood and water flowed. Then Adam fell on the altar like a corpse, and Satan fled. 4 Then Eve came and took Adam and placed him below the altar. There she stayed, crying over him while a stream of blood flowed from Adam's side over his offering. 5 But God looked at the death of Adam. He then sent His Word and raised him up. And He said to him, "Fulfill your offering because, certainly Adam, it is worthy and there is no imperfection in it." 6 God continued speaking to Adam, "Thus will it also happen to Me while on the earth, when I shall be pierced and blood and water shall flow from My side and run over My body, which is the true offering, and which shall be offered on the altar as a perfect offering." 7 Then God commanded Adam to finish his offering. And when he had ended it he worshipped before God and praised Him for the signs He had showed him. 8 And God healed Adam in one day, which is the end of the seven weeks and is the fiftieth day. 9 Then Adam and Eve returned from the mountain and went into the Cave of Treasures, as they were used to do. This completed one hundred and forty days for Adam and Eve, since their coming out of the garden. 10 Then they both stood up that night and prayed to God. And when it was morning they went down to the west side of the cave, to the place where their wheat (corn) was, and there they rested under the shadow of a tree, as they were accustomed to do. 11 But when they were there, a multitude of beasts came all around them. It was Satan's wickedness and his way to wage war against Adam through marriage.

Author's note: The following chapter will explain how marriage fits into Satan's plan. The fact that Satan will use marriage against Adam and Eve indicates that the writer of this text viewed marriage in a less than positive light. It should also be stressed that the idea of a ceremony is not the point of marriage in this context. It is intercourse that establishes the state. The resulting children and complications were the point of Satan's plan.

Chapter LXX

1 After this Satan, the hater of all that is good, took the form of an angel, and two others with him. So, they looked like the three angels who had brought to Adam gold, incense, and myrrh. 2 They came to Adam and Eve while they were under the tree, and greeted Adam and Eve with friendly words that were full of deceit. 3 But when Adam and Eve saw their friendly countenance and heard their sweet speech, Adam rose, welcomed them, and brought them to Eve and they remained all together. Adam's heart was happy all the while because he thought that they were the same angels, who had brought him gold, incense, and myrrh. 4 This was because when they came to Adam the first time peace and joy came over him from them because they brought him good gifts. So Adam thought that they had come a second time to give him other gifts to make him rejoice. He did not know it was Satan, therefore he received them with joy and associated with them. 5 Then Satan, the tallest of them, said, "Rejoice, Adam, and be glad. Look, God has sent us to you to tell you something." 6 And Adam said, "What is it?" Then Satan said, "It is a simple thing, but it is the Word of God. Will you accept it from us and do it? If you will not accept it, we will return to God and tell Him that you would not receive His Word." 7 And Satan continued, saying to Adam, "Don't be afraid and don't shake. Don't you know us?" 8 But Adam said, "I do not know you." 9 Then Satan said to him, "I am the angel that brought you gold and took it to the cave. This other angel is the one that brought you incense. And that third angel is the one who brought you myrrh when you were on top of the mountain. It was he who carried you to the cave. 10 It was our other fellow angels who lifted you to the cave. God has not sent them with us this time because He said to us, 'You will be enough'. " 11 So when Adam heard these words he believed them, and said to the angels, "Speak the Word of God, and I will receive it." 12 And Satan said to him, "Swear and promise me that you will receive it." 13 Then Adam said, "I do not know how to swear and promise." 14 And Satan said to him, "Hold out your hand and put it inside my hand." 15 Then Adam held out his hand, and put it into Satan's hand. Satan said to him, "Now say this; As God who raised the stars in heaven, and established the dry ground on the waters, and has created me out of the four elements, and out of the dust of the earth, and is logical and true does speak, I will not break my promise, nor abandon my word." 16 And Adam swore. 17 Then Satan said to him, "Look, some time has passed since you came out of the garden, and you do not know wickedness or evil. But now God says to you, to take Eve who came out of your side, and marry her so that she will bear you children to comfort you and to drive from you trouble and sorrow. This thing is not difficult and there is nothing morally wrong in it for you.

Chapter LXXI

1 But when Adam heard these words from Satan, he sorrowed much, because of his oath and his promise. And he said, "Shall I commit adultery with my flesh and my bones, and shall I sin against myself, so that God will destroy me blot me out from the face of the earth? 2 First, I ate of the tree and He drove me out of the garden into

this strange land and deprived me of my bright nature, and brought my death. If I do this, He will cut off my life from the earth, and He will cast me into hell, and plague me there a long time. 3 But God never spoke the words that you have said and you are not God's angels. He did not send you. You are devils that have come to me under the false appearance of angels. Away from me, you cursed of God!" 4 Then the devils fled from Adam. And he and Eve got up and returned to the Cave of Treasures, and went into it. 5 Then Adam said to Eve, "If you saw what I did, don't tell anyone because I sinned against God in swearing by His great name, and I have placed my hand once again into that of Satan." Eve then held her peace as Adam told her. 6 Then Adam got up and spread his hands before God, beseeching and entreating Him with tears to forgive him of what he had done. And Adam remained standing and praying in that way for forty days and forty nights. He did not eat or drink until he dropped down on the ground from hunger and thirst. 7 Then God sent His Word to Adam, who raised him up from where he lay, and said to him, "Adam, why have you sworn by My name? Why have you made agreement with Satan again?" 8 But Adam cried and said, "O God, forgive me. I did this unwittingly because I believed they were God's angels." 9 And God forgave Adam and said to him, "Beware of Satan." 10 And He withdrew His Word from Adam. 11 Then Adam's heart was comforted, and he took Eve and they went out of the cave to prepare some food for their bodies. 12 But from that day Adam struggled in his mind about marrying Eve, because he was afraid that if he did it, God would be angry with him. 13 Then Adam and Eve went to the river of water, and sat on the bank, as people do when they enjoy themselves. 14 But Satan was jealous of them and planned to destroy them.

Author's note: Clearly, Adam viewed copulating with Eve as incest and therefore morally wrong, even though it was not yet law. The idea kindled his desire, which was in opposition to what Adam viewed as a moral issue. This issue will be visited again in other texts such as Jubliees and others as Cain's marriage to his sister is addressed.

Chapter LXXII

1 Then Satan, and ten from his hosts, transformed themselves into maidens, with more grace than any others in the entire world. 2 They came up out of the river in front of Adam and Eve, and they said among themselves, "Come, we will look at the faces of Adam and Eve who are of the men on earth. They are beautiful and their faces look different than ours." Then they came to Adam and Eve and greeted them, and they stood amazed at them. 3 Adam and Eve looked at them also, and wondered at their beauty, and said, "Is there another world under us with such beautiful creatures as these in it?" 4 And the maidens said to Adam and Eve, "Yes, indeed, many of us were created." 5 Then Adam said to them, "But how do you multiply?" 6 And they told him, "We have husbands who have married us and we bear them children, who grow up and in turn marry and are married and also bear children. Thus we increase. O Adam, you will not believe us, we will show you our husbands and our children." 7 Then they shouted over the river as if to call their husbands and their children. And men and children came up from the river, and every man came to his wife, and his children were with him. 8 But when Adam and Eve saw them, they stood speechless and were amazed at them. 9 Then they said to

Adam and Eve, "See all our husbands and our children? You should marry Eve as we have married our husbands so that you will have children as we have." This was the way Satan was to deceive Adam. 10 Satan also thought to himself, "God at first commanded Adam concerning the fruit of the tree, saying to him, 'Do not eat of it or else you shall die.' But Adam ate of it but God did not kill him. He only gave him by law death, plagues, and trials, until the day he shall leave his body. 11 But if I deceive him to do this thing and marry Eve without God's permission, God will kill him." 12 Therefore Satan worked this apparition before Adam and Eve, because he sought to kill him, and to make him disappear from off the face of the earth. 13 Meanwhile the fire of immorality came over Adam and he thought of committing transgression. But he restrained himself, fearing that if he followed the advice of Satan, God would put him to death. 14 Then Adam and Eve got up and prayed to God, while Satan and his hosts went down into the river in front of Adam and Eve so they would see them going back to their own world. 15 Then Adam and Eve went back to the Cave of Treasures, as they usually did around evening time. 16 And they both got up and prayed to God that night. Adam remained standing in prayer but did not know how to pray because of the thoughts in his heart about marrying Eve. And he continued this way until morning. 17 When light came up, Adam said to Eve, "Get up, let us go below the mountain where they brought us gold and let us ask the Lord concerning this matter." 18 Then Eve said, "What is that matter, Adam?" 19 And he answered her, "That I may request the Lord to inform me about marrying you because I will not do it without His permission or else He will kill you and me. For those devils have set my heart on fire with thoughts of what they showed us in their sinful visions. 20 Then Eve said to Adam, "Why do we need to go to the foot of the mountain? Let us rather stand up and pray in our cave to God to let us know whether this advice is good or not." 21 Then Adam rose up in prayer and said, "O God, you know that we transgressed against you, and from the moment we sinned we were stripped of our bright nature, and our body became brutish, requiring food and drink, and with animal desires. 22 Command us, O God, not to give way to them without Your permission, for fear that You will turn us into nothing. If you do not give us permission we will be overcome and follow that advice of Satan, and You will again kill us. 23 If not, then take our souls from us and let us be rid of this animal lust. And if You give us no order about this thing then separate Eve from me and me from her, and place us each far away from the other. 24 Then, O God, if You separate us from each other the devils will deceive us with their apparitions that resemble us, and destroy our hearts, and defile our thoughts towards each other. If our heart is not toward each other it will be toward them, through their appearance when the devils come to us in our likeness." Here Adam ended his prayer.

Chapter LXXIII

1 Then God considered the words of Adam that they were true, and that he could not wait long for His order, respecting the counsel of Satan. 2 And God approved Adam in what he had thought concerning this, and in the prayer he had offered in His presence; and the Word of God came to Adam and said to him, "O Adam, if only you had had this caution at first, before you came out of the garden into this land!" 3 After that, God sent His angel who had brought gold, and the angel who had brought incense, and the angel who had brought myrrh to Adam, that they should inform him respecting his marriage to Eve. 4 Then those angels said to Adam, "Take

the gold and give it to Eve as a wedding gift, and promise to marry her; then give her some incense and myrrh as a present; and be you both will be one flesh." 5 Adam obeyed the angels, and took the gold and put it into Eve's bosom in her garment; and promised to marry her with his hand. 6 Then the angels commanded Adam and Eve to get up and pray forty days and forty nights; when that was done, then Adam was to have sexual intercourse with his wife; for then this would be an act pure and undefiled; so that he would have children who would multiply, and replenish the face of the earth. 7 Then both Adam and Eve received the words of the angels; and the angels departed from them. 8 Then Adam and Eve began to fast and pray, until the end of the forty days; and then they had sexual intercourse, as the angels had told them. And from the time Adam left the garden until he wedded Eve, were two hundred and twenty-three days, that is seven months and thirteen days. 9 This was how Satan's war with Adam was won by Adam and Satan was defeated.

Author's note: In the apocryphal book of Tobit, the main character goes into his new bride after praying to still his lust and was thus pure.

The word "replenish" indicates that the earth was once full or "plenished" and was to be "replenished" or filled again. This is the same word used in Genesis, leading two the Second Creation Theory.

Chapter LXXIV

1 And they lived on the earth working so they could keep their bodies in good health. And they continued until the nine months of Eve's pregnancy were over and the time drew near when she would give birth. 2 Then she said to Adam, "The tokens placed in this cave since we left the garden show it to be a pure place. We will be praying in it again in a while. Because of this, it is not appropriate that I should give birth in it. Let us instead go to the sheltering rock cave that was formed by the command of God when Satan threw a big rock down on us in an attempt to kill us. 3 Adam then took Eve to that cave. When the time came for her to give birth she strained very much. Adam felt pity for her and he was very worried about her because she was close to death and the words of God to her were being fulfilled: " You shall bear a child in suffering, and in sorrow shall you bring forth a child." 4 But when Adam saw the distress Eve was in, he got up and prayed to God, and said, "O Lord, look at me with the eye of Your mercy, and deliver her out of her distress." 5 And God looked at His maid-servant Eve, and delivered her, and she gave birth to her first-born son, and with him a daughter. 6 Then Adam rejoiced at Eve's deliverance, and also over the children she had given him. And Adam ministered to Eve in the cave until the end of eight days, when they named the son Cain, and the daughter Luluwa. 7 The meaning of Cain is "hater," because he hated his sister in their mother's womb, before they were born. Because of this, Adam named him Cain. 8 But Luluwa means "beautiful," because she was more beautiful than her mother. 9 Then Adam and Eve waited until Cain and his sister were forty days old, when Adam said to Eve, "We will make an offering and offer it up in behalf of the children." 10 And Eve said, "We will first make one offering for the first-born son and then later we shall make one for the daughter."

Author's note: Jewish law says the woman is unclean for a time after giving birth. The act, having human blood present, makes the place unclean. The first cave served as home and temple. The second cave served as a place of safety and shelter.

It will be noted the each time Eve gave birth she did so with twins, symbolizing the replenishing or replacing of Adam and Eve.

Chapter LXXV

1 Then Adam prepared an offering. He and Eve brought it to the altar they had built
at first and offered it up for their children. 2 And Adam offered up the offering, and
asked God to accept his offering. 3 Then God accepted Adam's offering, and sent a
light from heaven that shined down on the offering. Adam and his son drew near to
the offering, but Eve and the daughter did not approach it. 4 Adam and his son were
joyful as they came down from the altar. Adam and Eve waited until the daughter
was eighty days old and then Adam prepared an offering and took it to Eve and to
the children. They went to the altar where Adam offered it up, as he was
accustomed, asking the Lord to accept his offering. 5 And the Lord accepted the
offering of Adam and Eve. Then Adam, Eve, and the children gathered together and
came down from the mountain, rejoicing. 6 But they did not return to the cave in
which they were born. Instead they went to the Cave of Treasures, so that the
children should live in it and be blessed with the tokens brought from the garden. 7
But after they had been blessed with the tokens they went back to the cave in which
they were born. 8 But, before Eve had offered up the offering, Adam had taken her
to the river of water in which they threw themselves at first. There they washed
themselves. Adam washed his body and Eve washed hers clean also, after the
suffering and distress that had come over them. 9 But after washing themselves in
the river of water, Adam and Eve returned every night to the Cave of Treasures,
where they prayed and were blessed, and then went back to their cave where their
children were born. 10 Adam and Eve did this until the children had been weaned.
After they were weaned, Adam made an offering for the souls of his children in
addition to the three times every week he made an offering for them. 11 When the
children were weaned, Eve conceived again, and when her pregnancy came to term,
she gave birth to another son and daughter. They named the son Abel and the
daughter Aklia. 12 Then at the end of forty days, Adam made an offering for the son,
and at the end of eighty days he made another offering for the daughter, and treated
them as he had previously treated Cain and his sister Luluwa. 13 He brought them
to the Cave of Treasures, where they received a blessing and then returned to the
cave where they were born. After these children were born, Eve stopped having
children.

Author's note: To compare the purification ritual recounted here to those of the Old Testament we look to the book of the law. Leviticus 12 (RSV) 1 The LORD said to Moses, 2 "Say to the people of Israel, If a woman conceives, and bears a male child, then she shall be unclean seven days; as at the time of her menstruation, she shall be unclean. 3 And on the eighth day the flesh of his foreskin shall be circumcised. 4 Then she shall continue for thirty-three days in the blood of her purifying; she shall not touch any hallowed thing, nor come into the sanctuary, until the days of her purifying are completed. 5 But if she bears a female child, then she shall be unclean two weeks, as in her menstruation; and she shall continue in the blood of her purifying for sixty-six days. 6 "And when the days of her purifying are completed, whether for a son or for a daughter, she shall bring to the priest at the door of the tent of meeting a lamb a year old for a burnt offering, and a young pigeon or a turtledove for a sin offering , 7 and he shall offer it before the LORD, and make atonement for her; then she shall be clean from the flow of her blood. This is the law for her who bears a child, either male or female. 8 And if she cannot afford a lamb, then she shall take two turtledoves or two young pigeons, one for a burnt offering and the other for a sin offering; and the priest shall make atonement for her, and she shall be clean."

Chapter LXXVI

1 As the children began to grow stronger and taller, Cain grew hard-hearted, and he ruled over his younger brother. 2 Often, when his father made an offering, Cain would remain behind and not go with them to make the offering. 3 But Abel had a meek heart, and was obedient to his father and mother. He frequently influenced them to make an offering because he loved it. He prayed and fasted much. 4 Then this sign came to Abel. As he was coming into the Cave of Treasures he saw the golden rods, the incense and the myrrh and he asked his parents, Adam and Eve, to tell him about them. Abel asked, "Where did you get these from?" 5 Then Adam told him all that had befallen them. And Abel felt deeply about what his father told him. 6 Then his father, Adam, told him about the works of God and of the garden. After hearing these things, Abel remained behind after his father left and stayed the entire of that night in the Cave of Treasures. 7 And that night, while he was praying, Satan appeared to him in the form of a man. And Satan said to him, "Often you have moved your father into making offerings, and to fast and pray. Because of this, I will kill you and make you perish from this world." 8 But Abel prayed to God and drove away Satan, and he did not believe the words of the devil. Then when it was day, an angel of God appeared to him, who said to him, "Do not stop your fasting, prayer, or offering to your God. For, look, the Lord has accepted your prayer. Be not afraid of the form which appeared to you in the night, and who cursed you to death." Then the angel departed from him. 9 Then Abel came to Adam and Eve when it was day, and told them about the vision he had seen. When they heard it they worried about it very much, but said nothing to him about it. They only comforted him. 10 But Satan came to the hard-hearted Cain by night and showed himself and said to him, "Since Adam and Eve love your brother Abel so much more than they love you, they wish to join him in marriage to your beautiful sister because they love him. However, they wish to join you in marriage to his ugly sister, because they hate you. 11 Now before they do that, I am telling you that you should kill your brother. That way your sister will be left for you and you can throw his sister away." 12 And Satan departed from him. But the devil remained behind in Cain's heart, and frequently prompted his ambition to kill his brother.

Author's note: Since the children were born in pairs, it seems more reasonable to have those that were not twins marry.

Note the word used in reference to Cain's heart. He was hard-hearted and the devil gave him ambition – or hope – or aspiration to kill. As if this were something to achieve as a noble end.

Chapter LXXVII

1 But when Adam saw that the older brother hated the younger brother, he attempted to soften their hearts. He said to Cain, "My son, take some of the fruits of

your sowing and make an offering to God, so that He might forgive you for your wickedness and your sin." 2 He said also to Abel, "Take some of the fruit of your sowing and make an offering and bring it to God, so that He might forgive you for your wickedness and your sin." 3 Then Abel obeyed his father and took some of his sowing, and made a good offering, and said to his father, Adam, "Come with me and show me how to offer it up." 4 And they went, Adam and Eve with him, and they showed him how to offer up his gift on the altar. Then after that they stood up and prayed that God would accept Abel's offering. 5 Then God looked at Abel and accepted his offering. And God was more pleased with Abel than He was with his offering, because of his good heart and pure body. There was no trace of guile in him. 6 Then they came down from the altar and went to the cave in which they lived. But because of his joy felt at making his offering, Abel repeated it three times a week, following the example of his father Adam. 7 But Cain did not want to make an offering, but after his father became very angry, he offered up a gift once. He took the smallest of his sheep for an offering and when he offered it up, his eyes were on the lamb. 8 Because of this, God did not accept his offering, because his heart was full of murderous thoughts. 9 And they all lived together like this in the cave in which Eve had given birth, until Cain was fifteen years old, and Abel twelve years old.

Chapter LXXVIII

1 Then Adam said to Eve, "The children have grown up. We must think of finding wives for them." 2 Then Eve answered, "How can we do that?" 3 Then Adam said to her, "We will join Abel's sister in marriage to Cain, and Cain's sister to Abel. 4 Then Eve said to Adam, "I do not like Cain because he is hard-hearted. So, let them stay with us until we offer up (an offering) to the Lord in their behalf." 5 And Adam said no more. 6 Meanwhile Satan came to Cain in the form of a man of the field, and said to him, "Look. Adam and Eve have discussed together about the marriage of you two, and they have agreed to marry Abel's sister to you, and your sister to Abel. 7 But if it were not that I love you, I would not have told you this thing. So, if you will take my advice and obey me, I will bring beautiful robes, plenty of gold and silver, and my relations will attend you on your wedding day." 8 Then Cain said with joy, "Where are your relations?" 9 And Satan answered, "My relations are in a garden in the north, where I once meant to bring your father Adam, but he would not accept my offer. 10 But if you will receive my words and if you will come to me after your wedding, you shall rest from the misery in which you are; and you shall rest and be better off than your father Adam." 11 At these words, Satan got Cain's attention (opened his ears), and Cain inclined toward Satan to listen (leaned towards his speech). 12 After this, he did not remain in the field, but he went to Eve, his mother, and beat her and cursed her, and said to her, "Why are you planning to take my sister to marry her to my brother? Am I dead?" 13 But his mother quieted him and sent him back to the field where he had been. 14 Then when Adam came, she told him of what Cain had done. 15 Adam was very worried, but held his peace, and did not say a word. 16 Then, the next morning Adam said to Cain his son, "Take of your young and good sheep and offer them up to your God, and I will speak to your brother and have him make an offering of corn to his God." 17 They both obeyed their father Adam, and they took their offerings, and offered them up on the mountain by the altar. 18 But Cain behaved arrogantly (haughtily) toward his

brother, and he shoved him from the altar, and would not let him offer up his gift on the altar, but he offered his own offering on it with a proud heart, full of guile and fraud. 19 But Abel set up stones that were near at hand and on that, he offered up his gift with a heart humble and free from guile. 20 Cain was then standing by the altar on which he had offered up his gift and he cried to God to accept his offering, but God did not accept it from Cain, nor did a divine fire come down to consume his offering. 21 But he remained standing over against the altar out of meanness, to make fun of his brother, and he glared at his brother Abel to see if God would accept his offering or not. 22 And Abel prayed to God to accept his offering. Then a divine fire came down and consumed his offering. And God smelled the sweet savor of his offering, because Abel loved Him and rejoice in Him. 23 And because God was well pleased with him, He sent him an angel of light in the form of a man to partake of his offering, because He had smelled the sweet savor of his offering, and he comforted Abel and strengthened his heart. 24 But Cain was looking on all that took place at his brother's offering, and was angry because of it. 25 Then he opened his mouth and blasphemed God because He had not accepted his offering. 26 But God said to Cain, "Why do you look sad? Be in right standing with Me so that I may accept your offering. You have not murmured against Me, but against yourself. 27 And God said this to Cain in rebuke, and because He hated him and his offering. 28 And Cain came down from the altar and his color changed and he had a sad face. And he came to his father and mother and told them all that had happened to him. And Adam grieved much because God had not accepted Cain's offering. 29 But Abel came down rejoicing, and with a glad heart, and told his father and mother how God had accepted his offering. And they rejoiced at it and kissed his face. 30 And Abel said to his father, "Because Cain shoved me from the altar, and would not allow me to offer my gift on it, I made an altar for myself and offered my gift on it."

31 But when Adam heard this he was very sorry because it was the altar he had built at first, and on which he had offered his own gifts. 32 Cain was so resentful and so angry that he went into the field. There, Satan came to him and said to him, "Your brother Abel has taken refuge with your father Adam, because you shoved him from the altar. They have kissed his face and they rejoice over him far more than over you." 33 When Cain heard these words of Satan he was filled with rage but he let no one know. But he was laying in wait to kill his brother, until he brought him into the cave, and then said to him: 34 "Brother, the country is so beautiful and there are such beautiful and pleasurable trees in it, and charming to look at! But brother, you have never been one day in the field to take your pleasure in that place. 35 Today, my brother, I wish very much that you would come into the field with me, to enjoy yourself and to bless our fields and our flocks, for you are righteous, and I love you much, O my brother! But you have alienated yourself from me." 36 Then Abel agreed to go with his brother Cain into the field. 37 But before going out, Cain said to Abel, "Wait for me and I will fetch a staff because of wild beasts." 38 Then Abel stood innocently waiting. But Cain, the presumptuous, got a staff and went out. 39 And Cain and his brother Abel began to walk in the path. Cain was talking to him, and comforting him, to make him forget everything.

Chapter LXXIX

1 And so they walked on until they came to a place they were alone where there were no sheep. Then Abel said to Cain, "Look, my brother, we are tired from

walking. We see none of the trees, or fruits, or the growing green plants, or the
sheep, or any of the things of which you told me. Where are those sheep of yours
that you told me to bless?" 2 Then Cain said to him, "Come on, and you shall see
many beautiful things very soon, but go before me until I catch up to you." 3 Then
Abel went on but Cain stayed behind him. 4 And Abel was innocently walking,
without suspecting any craftiness, not thinking that his brother would kill him. 5
Then Cain came up to him, comforted him with his words while walking a little
behind him. Then he ran up to him and beat him with the staff, blow after blow,
until he was dazed. 6 But when Abel fell down on the ground and saw that his
brother meant to kill him, he said to Cain, "O, my brother, have pity on me. By the
breasts we have sucked, do not hit me! By the womb that bore us and that brought
us into the world, do not beat me to death with that staff! If you are set on killing me,
take one of these large stones and kill me outright." 7 Then Cain, the hard-hearted,
and cruel murderer, took a large stone, and beat his brother's head with it until his
brains oozed out, and he wallowed in his blood, before him. 8 And Cain was not
sorry for what he had done. 9 But when the blood of righteous Abel fell on the earth,
it trembled as it drank his blood, and would have destroyed Cain because of it. 10
And the blood of Abel cried mysteriously to God to avenge him of his murderer. 11
Then Cain began to dig furiously at the ground to bury his brother, because he was
shaking from fear that came over him when he saw the earth tremble because of
him. 12 He then threw his brother into the hole he made, and covered him with dust.
But the ground would not receive him and it threw him up at once. 13 Again Cain
dug the ground and covered his brother in it, but again the ground threw him up.
Three times the ground threw up the body of Abel on itself. 14 The muddy ground
threw him up the first time because he was not the first creation. It threw him up the
second time and would not receive him because he was righteous and good and was
killed without a cause. The ground threw him up the third time and would not
receive him so that there might remain before his brother a witness against him. 15
And so the earth mocked Cain until the Word of God came to him concerning his
brother. 16 Then God was angry and very much displeased at Abel's death. And He
thundered from heaven, and lightning went out from Him, and the Word of the
Lord God came from heaven to Cain, and said to him, "Where is Abel, your
brother?" 17 Then Cain answered with a proud heart and a gruff voice, "How am I to
know, O God? Am I my brother's keeper?" 18 Then God said to Cain, "Cursed be the
earth that has drunk the blood of Abel, your brother. And as for you, you will
always be trembling and shaking, and this will be a mark on you so that whoever
finds you will kill you." 19 But Cain cried because God had said those words to him.
And Cain said to Him, "O God, whosoever finds me shall kill me, and I shall be
blotted out from the face of the earth." 20 Then God said to Cain, "Whoever finds
you will not kill you," because before this, God had been saying to Cain, "I shall put
seven punishments on anyone that kills Cain." For the word of God to Cain was,
"Where is your brother?" God said it in mercy to him, to try and make him repent. 21
And if Cain had repented at that time, and had said, "O God, forgive me my sin, and
the murder of my brother," God would then have forgiven him his sin. 22 But God
said to Cain, "Cursed be the ground that has drunk the blood of your brother" That
also, was God's mercy on Cain, because God did not curse him, but He cursed the
ground, although it was not the ground that had killed Abel, and committed a
wicked sin. 23 But it was fitting that the curse should fall on the murderer, and yet,
in mercy did God managed His thoughts so that no one should know the extent of

His anger for He turned it away from Cain.
24 And He said to him, "Where is your brother?" To which he answered and said, "I know not." Then the Creator said to him, "Be trembling and quaking."
25 Then Cain trembled and became terrified, and through this sign God made him an example before all the creation to show him as the murderer of his brother. Also God brought trembling and terror over him so that he might see the peace he had before and also see the trembling and terror he endured at the end, so that he might humble himself before God and repent of his sin, and seek the peace that he enjoyed at first.
26 The word of God said, "I will put seven punishments on anyone who kills Cain." So, God was not seeking to kill Cain with the sword, but He sought to make him die of fasting, and praying, and crying by His discipline, until the time that he was delivered from his sin.
27 And the seven punishments are the seven generations during which God awaited Cain for the murder of his brother.
28 But, ever since he had killed his brother, Cain could find no rest in any place, so he went back to Adam and Eve, trembling, terrified, and defiled with blood.

This ends The First Book of Adam and Eve

Author's note: Wallowing in the blood of a kill coveys an extreme in animal behavior and state.

What is amazing about this chapter is the limits explored to explain the thoughts, actions, and strategy of God toward Cain. We are told that the enigmatic mark left on Cain as a curse is actually the physical trait of shaking and trembling in fear. One may ask if this is the mark of cowardice exhibited by a bully.

The explanation of God's first statement to kill Cain, then cursing anyone who would kill Cain, then "waiting for Cain seven generations is wordy, convoluted, and odd. The author seems to be attempting to put all of the pieces together in some reasonable manner. This could be due to the knitting together of several sources with the last man left with the task of tying the story together into a cohesive conclusion.

The Second Book of Adam and Eve

The Second Book of Adam and Eve expands on the time from Cain's act of murder to the time Enoch was taken by God. It is, above all, a continuation of the story of ***The First Book of Adam and Eve.***

Like the first book, this book is also part of the "Pseudepigrapha", which is a collection of historical biblical works that are considered to be fiction. Although considered to be Pseudepigrapha, it carries significance in that it provides insight into what was considered acceptable religious writing and ideas of the time.

This book is a composite of oral versions of an account handed down by word of mouth, from generation to generation until an unknown author pieced the stories together into a written form.

This particular version is the work of unknown Egyptians. The lack of historical allusion makes it difficult to date the writing. Using other Pseudepigrapha works as a reference only slightly narrows the probable dates to a range of a few hundred years. Parts of the text were probably included in an oral tradition, two or three hundred years before the birth of Christ. Certainly, book two was written after book one.

Sections of the text are found in the Jewish Talmud, and the Islamic Koran. Although some think this shows how the books of Adam and Eve played a vital role in ancient literature, it could just as well expose the fact that the authors of the Adam and Eve stories borrowed heavily from accepted holy books.

The Egyptian author wrote in Arabic, but later translations were found written in Ethiopic. The present English translation was completed in the late 1800's by Dr. S. C. Malan and Dr. E. Trumpp. They translated the text into King James English from both the Arabic version and the Ethiopic version, which was then published in The Forgotten Books of Eden in 1927 by The World Publishing Company. The version presented here takes the 1927 version, written in King James style English, and renders it into wording more familiar to the modern reader. Tangled sentence structure and archaic words were replaced with a more clear, crisp, twenty-first century English.

Second Book of Adam and Eve

Chapter I.

1 When Luluwa heard Cain's words, she wept and went to call her father and mother, and told them how Cain had killed his brother Abel.
2 Then they all cried aloud and lifted up their voices, and slapped their faces, and threw dust upon their heads, and ripped their garments apart, and went out and came to the place where Abel was killed.
3 And they found him lying on the earth, killed, and beasts were around him. They wept and cried because he was a just person. Because his body was pure, from it went forth a smell of sweet spices.
4 And Adam carried him as Adam's tears streaming down his face; and he went to the Cave of Treasures, where he laid Abel, and Adam wound him up with sweet spices and myrrh.
5 And Adam and Eve continued in great grief by the burial site for a hundred and forty days. Abel was fifteen and a half years old, and Cain seventeen years and a half.
6 When the mourning for his brother was ended, Cain took his sister Luluwa and married her, without permission from his father and mother. Because of their heavy hearts they could not keep him from her.
7 He then went down to the foot of the mountain, away from the garden, near the place where he had killed his brother.
8 And in that place were many fruit trees and forest trees. His sister gave birth to his children, who in their turn began to multiply by degrees until they filled that place.
9 But Adam and Eve did not come together (have intercourse) for seven years after Abel's funeral. After this, however, Eve conceived. And while she was with child Adam said to her, "Come, let us take an offering and offer it up unto God and ask Him to give us a beautiful child in whom we may find comfort, and whom we may join in marriage to Abel's sister."
10 Then they prepared an offering and brought it up to the altar, and offered it before the Lord, and began to ask Him to accept their offering and to give them a good offspring.
11 And God heard Adam and accepted his offering. Then, Adam, Eve and their daughter worshipped, and came down to the Cave of Treasures and placed a lamp in it by the body of Abel to burn by the body, night and day.
12 Then Adam and Eve continued fasting and praying until Eve's time came that she should be delivered, when she said to Adam, "I wish to go to the cave in the rock, to give birth in it."
13 And he said, "Go, and take your daughter with you to wait on you; but I will remain in this Cave of Treasures before the body of my son Abel."
14 Then Eve listened to Adam, and she and her daughter left, but Adam remained by himself in the Cave of Treasures.

Chapter II.

1 And Eve gave birth to a son, perfectly beautiful in form and in demeanor. His

beauty was like that of his father Adam, yet more beautiful.
2 Then Eve was comforted when she saw him, and remained eight days in the cave;
then she sent her daughter unto Adam to tell him to come and see the child and
name him. But the daughter stayed in his place by the body of her brother, until
Adam returned.
3 But when Adam came and saw the child's good looks, his beauty, and his perfect
form, he rejoiced over him, and was comforted for Abel. Then he named the child
Seth, which means, "that God has heard my prayer, and has delivered me out of my
affliction." But it means also "power and strength."
4 Then after Adam had named the child, he returned to the Cave of Treasures; and
his daughter went back to her mother.
5 But Eve continued in her cave, until forty days were fulfilled, when she came to
Adam, and brought with her the child and her daughter.
6 And they came to a river of water, where Adam and his daughter washed
themselves, because of their sorrow for Abel; but Eve and the babe washed for
purification.
7 Then they returned, and took an offering, and went to the mountain and offered it
up for the babe; and God accepted their offering, and sent His blessing upon them,
and upon their son Seth; and they came back to the Cave of Treasures.
8 As for Adam, he did not have intercourse again with his wife Eve, all the days of
his life; neither was any more offspring born of them; but only those five, Cain,
Luluwa, Abel, Aklia, and Seth alone.
9 But Seth waxed in stature and in strength; and began to fast and pray, fervently.

Author's note: Abel was fifteen and a half years old, and Cain seventeen years and a half when Abel was killed. Cain and Luluwa were twins. Abel and Aklia were twins. Cain married his twin sister. Aklia was fifteen and a half when Abel died. Adam and Eve did not come together (have intercourse) for seven years after Abel's funeral. Aklia would now be twenty-two and a half. Eve carried Seth for nine months. At the time of Seth's birth, Aklia would have been twenty-three years old.

Chapter III.

1 At the end of seven years from the day Adam had been separated from his wife
Eve, Satan envied him, and when he saw Adam was separated from her, Satan
strove to make him live with her again.
2 Then Adam arose and went up above the Cave of Treasures and continued to sleep
there night by night. But every day as soon as it was light he came down to the cave
to pray there and to receive a blessing from it.
3 But when it was evening he went up on the top of the cave, where he slept by
himself, fearing that Satan could overcome him. And he continued apart in this way
for thirty-nine days.
4 Then when Satan, the hater of all that is good, saw Adam alone, fasting and
praying, he appeared unto him in the form of a beautiful woman who came and
stood in front of him in the night of the fortieth day, and said to him:
5 "Adam, from the time you have dwelt in this cave, we have experienced great
peace from you, and your prayers have reached us, and we have been comforted
because of you.
6 "But now, Adam, that you have gone up over the roof of the cave to sleep, we have

had doubts about you, and a great sorrow has come upon us because of your separation from Eve. Then again, when you are on the roof of this cave, your prayer is poured out, and your heart wanders from side to side.
7 "But when you were in the cave your prayer was like fire gathered together. It came down to us, and you found rest.
8 "Then I also worried over your children who are separated from you, and my sorrow is great about the murder of your son Abel because he was righteous, and over a righteous man every one will grieve.
9 "But I rejoiced over the birth of your son Seth. But after a little while I sorrowed greatly over Eve, because she is my sister. For when God sent a deep sleep over you, and drew her out of your side, He brought me out with her. But He raised her by placing her with you, while He lowered me.
10 "I rejoiced over my sister for her being with you. But God had made me a promise before, and said, 'Do not grieve; when Adam has gone up on the roof of the Cave of Treasures, and is separated from Eve his wife, I will send you to him and you shall join yourself to him in marriage, and bear five children for him, as Eve gave him five children.'
11 "And now, look! God's promise to me is fulfilled because it is He who has sent me to you for the wedding, because if you wed me I shall bear you finer and better children than those of Eve.
12 "You are still young. Do not end your youth in this world in sorrow. Spend the days of your youth in happiness and pleasure. Your days are few and your trials have been great. Be strong and end your days in this world in rejoicing. I shall take pleasure in you, and you shall rejoice with me in this way and without fear.
13 "Get up and fulfill the command of your God," she then came near Adam and embraced him.
14 But when Adam saw that he was going to be overcome by her, he prayed to God with a fervent heart to deliver him from her.
15 Then God sent His Word to Adam, saying, "Adam, that apparition is the one that promised you the Godhead, and majesty. He does not intend good for you, but shows himself to you at one time in the form of a woman and in another moment in the likeness of an angel, and on another occasions in the apparition of a serpent, and at another time in the semblance of a god. But he does all of this only to destroy your soul.
16 " Adam, now that you understand this in your heart you will see that I have delivered you many a time from his hands in order to show you that I am a merciful God. I wish you good and I do not wish your ruin."

Chapter IV.

1 Then God ordered Satan to show himself to Adam in his own hideous form, plainly.
2 But when Adam saw him he feared and trembled at the sight of him.
3 And God said to Adam, 'Look at this devil, and at his hideous sight, and know that he it is who made you fall from brightness into darkness, from peace and rest to toil and misery.
4 And look at him, Adam. He is the one who said that he is God! Can God be black? Would God take the form of a woman? Is there any one stronger than God? And can He be overpowered?

5 "See Adam. Look at him bound in your presence, in the air, unable to flee away! So, I say to you, do not be afraid of him. From now on, take care, and beware of him. He will try to do things to you."
6 Then God drove Satan away from Adam. And God strengthened Adam's heart and comforted him, saying, "Go down to the Cave of Treasures, and do not separate yourself from Eve. I will quiet all of your animal lust."
7 From that hour it left Adam and Eve, and they enjoyed rest by the commandment of God. But God did not do the same to any of Adam's seed (relations). God did this only to Adam and Eve.
8 Then Adam worshipped before the Lord for delivering him, and for having subdued his passions. And he came down from above the cave, and lived with Eve as had done before.
9 This ended the forty days of his separation from Eve.

Chapter V

1 When Seth was seven years old, he knew good and evil, and was consistent in fasting and praying, and spent all his nights in praying to God for mercy and forgiveness.
2 He also fasted when bringing up his offering every day. He fasted more than his father did because his demeanor was beautiful, like that of an angel of God. He also had a good heart, and his soul was precious; and for this reason he brought up his offering every day.
3 And God was pleased with his offering, but He was also pleased with his purity. And he continued doing the will of God, and of his father and mother until he was seven years old.
4 After that, as he was coming down from the altar after giving his offering, Satan appeared to him in the form of a beautiful angel, brilliant with light, with a staff of light in his hand, and wrapped with a girdle of light.
5 He greeted Seth with a beautiful smile, and began to beguile him with beautiful words, saying to him, "Seth, why do you live in this mountain? It is rough, full of stones and sand, and trees with no good fruit on them. It is a wilderness without houses or towns, no good place to live in. But everywhere there is heat, weariness, and trouble."
6 He said further, 'But we live in beautiful places, in a world other than this earth. Our world is one of light and we live in the best conditions. Our women are more beautiful than any others. Seth, I wish you to marry one of them, because I see that you are handsome to look at. In this land there is not one woman good enough for you and there are only five souls in it.
7 "But in our world there are many men and many young, unmarried women, all more beautiful one than the other. So, I wish to remove you from here so that you may see my relations and be wedded to which ever you like.
8 "You shall live by me and be at peace. You shall be filled with glory and light, just as we are.
9 "You shall remain in our world and rest from this world and its misery. You shall never again feel weak and weary. You shall never bring up an offering or appeal for mercy. You shall commit no more sin nor be swayed by passions.
10 "And if you will listen to what I say, you shall wed one of my daughters because to us it is not a sin and it is not considered animal lust.

11 "For in our world we have no God because we all are gods and we all are of the light and are heavenly, powerful, strong and glorious."

Chapter VI

1 When Seth heard these words he was amazed, and began to believe Satan's treacherous speech, and said to him, "You said there is another world created other than this one, and there are other creatures more beautiful than the creatures that are in this world?"
2 And Satan said, "Yes; you have heard me correctly, and I will tell you more good things about them and their ways."
3 But Seth said to him, "Your words have amazed me, and your beautiful description of it all."
4 "But I cannot go with you today, at least not until I have gone to my father Adam and to my mother Eve, and told them all you have said to me. Then if they give me permission to go with you, I will come."
5 Seth said, "I am afraid of doing any thing without my father's and mother's permission. I do not want to perish like my brother Cain, and like my father Adam, who transgressed the commandment of God. But, you know your way to this place, so come and meet me here tomorrow."
6 When Satan heard this, he said to Seth, "If you tell your father Adam what I have told you, he will not let you come with me.
7 But listen to me, do not tell your father and mother what I have said to you. Instead, come with me today. Come now to our world where you will see beautiful things and enjoy yourself there, and celebrate this day among my children, watching them and taking your fill of happiness; and have joy there. Then I shall bring you back to this place tomorrow. However, if you would rather stay there with me, so be it."
8 Then Seth answered, "The hope / love (spirit) of my father and of my mother, hangs on me and if I hide from them one day, they will die, and God will hold me guilty of sinning against them.
9 "And if they know that I have come to this place they assume it is to bring up my offering, and they would expect not to be separated from me one hour. Neither should I go to any other place unless they let me. But they treat me most kindly, because I always come back to them quickly."
10 Then Satan said to him, "What will happen to you if you were to disappear from them one night, and return to them at break of day?"

(Author's note: The assumption here is that he would sneak out after they fell asleep and not tell them.)

11 But Seth, when he saw how he kept on talking, and that he would not leave him alone, he ran and went up to the altar, and spread his hands to God, and sought deliverance from God.
12 Then God sent His Word, and cursed Satan, who fled from Him.
13 But Seth had gone up to the altar, saying in his heart. "The altar is the place of offering, and God is there. A divine fire shall consume what is on it and so Satan will be unable to hurt me, and shall not take me away from here."
14 Then Seth came down from the altar and went to his father and mother, whom he

found on his way and who were longing to hear his voice, because he had been missing a while.
15 He then began to tell them what had befallen him from Satan, under the form of an angel.
16 But when Adam heard his account, he kissed his face, and warned him against that angel, telling him it was Satan who appeared to him. Then Adam took Seth, and they went to the Cave of Treasures and rejoiced there.
17 But from that day on Adam and Eve were never separated from him wherever he went, whether for his offering or for any thing else.
18 This sign happened to Seth, when he was nine years old.

Chapter VII.

1 When our father Adam saw that Seth was of a perfect heart, he wished him to marry; lest the enemy should appear to him another time, and overcome him.
2 So Adam said to his son Seth, "I wish, 0 my son, that you wed your sister Aklia, Abel's sister, that she may bear you children, who shall replenish the earth, according to God's promise to us.
3 "Be not afraid, my son; there is no disgrace in it. I wish you to marry, from fear that if you do not the enemy could overcome you.'
4 Seth, however, did not wish to marry; but in obedience to his father and mother, he did not say a word.
5 So Adam married him to Aklia. And he was fifteen years old.
6 But when he was twenty years of age, he had a son, whom he called Enos (Enoch); and then had other children.
7 Then Enos grew up, married, and begat Cainan.
8 Cainan also grew up, married, and begat Mahalaleel.
9 Those fathers were born during Adam's lifetime, and dwelt by the Cave of Treasures.
10 Then were the days of Adam nine hundred and thirty years, and those of Mahalaleel one hundred. But Mahalaleel, when he was grown up, loved fasting, praying, and with hard work, until the end of our father Adam's days drew near.

Chapter VIII.

1 When our father Adam saw that his end was near, he called his son Seth, who came to him in the Cave of Treasures, and he said to him:
2 "Seth, my son, bring me your children and your children's children, so that I may shed my blessing on them before I die."
3 When Seth heard these words from his father Adam, he went from him, shed a flood of tears over his face, and gathered together his children and his children's children, and brought them to his father Adam.
4 But when our father Adam saw them around him, he wept at having to be separated from them.
5 And when they saw him weeping, they all wept together, and kissed his face saying, "How shall you be separated from us, father? And how shall the earth receive you and hide you from our eyes?" Thus they lamented with words like these.
6 Then our father Adam blessed them all, and said to Seth, after he had blessed them:

7 "Seth, my son, you know this world and that it is full of sorrow, and of weariness; and you know all that has come upon us from our trials in it. So, I command you in these words: I want you to keep being innocent, to be pure and just, and trusting in God; and do not believe the words of Satan, nor the apparitions in which he will show himself to you.
8 But keep the commandments that I give you this day; then give the same to your son Enos; and let Enos give it to his son Cainan; and Cainan to his son Mahalaleel; so that this commandment abide firm among all your children.
9 "Seth, my son, the moment I am dead take you my body and wrap it up with myrrh, aloes, and cassia, and leave me here in this Cave of Treasures in which are all the tokens which God gave us from the garden.
10 "My son, after a while a flood will come and overwhelm all creatures, and leave only eight souls out of it.
11 "But, my son, let those whom it will leave from among your children at that time, take my body with them out of this cave; and when they have taken it with them, let the oldest among them command his children to lay my body in a ship until the flood recedes, and they come out of the ship.
12 Then they shall take my body and lay it in the middle of the earth, shortly after they have been saved from the waters of the flood.
13 "The place where my body shall be laid is the middle of the earth and God shall come from that place and shall save all our kindred.
14 "But now, Seth, my son, place yourself at the head of your people. Tend to them and watch over them in the fear of God. Lead them in the good way. Command them to fast to God, and make them understand they should not to listen to Satan, or he will destroy them.
15 "I tell you again, separate your children and your children's children from Cain's children. Do not let them ever mix with them, nor come near them either to talk or to work."
16 Then Adam let his blessing descend upon Seth, and upon his children, and upon all his children's children.
17 He then turned to his son Seth, and to Eve his wife, and, said to them, "Preserve this gold, this incense, and this myrrh, that God has given us for a sign, because in days that are coming a flood will overwhelm the whole creation. But those who shall go into the ark shall take with them the gold, the incense, and the myrrh, together with my body, and will lay the gold, the incense, and the myrrh, with my body in the middle of the earth.
18 "Then, after a long time, the city in which the gold, the incense, and the myrrh are found with my body, shall be plundered. But when it is spoiled, the gold the incense, and the myrrh shall be taken care of with the spoil that is kept; and none of them shall perish, until the made man from the Word of God shall come. And kings shall take them, and shall offer to Him, gold in token of His being King; incense, in token of His being God of heaven and earth; and myrrh, in token of His passion.
19 "Gold also, as a token of His overcoming Satan, and all our foes; incense as a token that He will rise from the dead, and be exalted above things in heaven and things in the earth; and myrrh, in token that He will drink bitter gall; and feel the pains of hell from Satan.
20 "And now, Seth, my son, I have revealed to you hidden mysteries, which God had revealed to me. Keep my commandment for yourself and for your people."

Chapter IX

1 When Adam had ended his commandment to Seth, his limbs went limp, his hands and feet lost all strength, his voice became silent, and his tongue ceased to speak. He closed his eyes and gave up the ghost.
2 But when his children saw that he was dead, they threw themselves over him, men and women, old and young, weeping.
3 The death of Adam took place at the end of nine hundred and thirty years that he lived upon the earth; on the fifteenth day of Barmudeh, after the reckoning of an epact of the sun, at the ninth hour.

(Author's note: Barmudeh is the third month of the Egyptian calendar. The epact is the number of days into the moon's cycle that the solar calendar begins. Thus, it is the difference in days between the solar and lunar calendar.) (Adam had to die before his 1000th birthday so that he would fulfill the death curse from God. 1000 years is as one day.)

4 It was on a Friday, the very day on which he was created, and on which he rested. And the hour at which he died was the same as that at which he came out of the garden.
5 Then Seth wrapped him up well, and embalmed him with plenty of sweet spices, from sacred trees and from the Holy Mountain. And he laid his body on the eastern side of the inside of the cave, the side of the incense; and placed a lamp stand in front of him that kept burning.
6 Then his children stood before him weeping and wailing over him the entire night, until break of day.
7 Then Seth and his son Enos (Enoch), and Cainan, the son of Enos, went out and took good offerings to present to the Lord, and they came to the altar upon which Adam offered gifts to God.
8 But Eve said to them, "Wait until we have first asked God to accept our offering, and to keep the soul of Adam His servant by Him, and to take it up to rest."
9 And they all stood up and prayed.

Chapter X.

1 And when they had ended their prayer the Word of God came and comforted them concerning their father Adam.
2 After this, they offered their gifts for themselves and for their father.
3 And when they had ended their offering, the Word of God came to Seth, the eldest among them, saying to him, "Seth, Seth, Seth, three times. As I was with your father, so also shall I be with you, until the fulfillment of the promise I made your father saying, I will send My Word and save you and your seed.
4 "But as to your father Adam, keep you the commandment he gave you; and protect your seed (offspring) and keep them from that of Cain your brother."
5 And God withdrew His Word from Seth.
6 Then Seth, Eve, and their children, came down from the mountain to the Cave of Treasures.
7 But Adam was the first whose soul died in the land of Eden, in the Cave of Treasures; for no one died before him, but his son Abel, who died because he was murdered.

8 Then all the children of Adam rose up, and wept over their father Adam, and made offerings to him, one hundred and forty days.

Chapter XI.

1 After the death of Adam and of Eve, Seth separated his children, and his children's children, from Cain's children. Cain and his seed went down and lived to the west, below the place where he had killed his brother Abel.
2 But Seth and his children, lived to the north on the mountain of the Cave of Treasures, in order to be near to their father Adam.
3 And Seth the oldest (of his people), tall and good, with a worthy soul, and of a strong mind, stood at the head of his people; and tended to them in innocence, patience, and meekness, and did not allow even one of them to go down to Cain's children.
4 And because of their purity, they were named "Children of God," and they were with God instead of the hosts of angels who fell, for they continued in praises to God and in singing songs to Him in their cave, the Cave of Treasures.
5 Then Seth stood before the bodies of his father Adam and of his mother Eve, and he prayed night and day and asked for mercy for himself and his children, and that when he had some difficulty dealing with a child, God would give him counsel.
6 But Seth and his children did not like mundane work, but set themselves to do heavenly things, because they had no other thought other than praises, worship, and psalms to God.
7 Therefore did they at all times hear the voices of angels, praising and glorifying God; from within the garden, or when they were sent by God on an errand, or when they were going up to heaven.
8 Because of their own purity, Seth and his children heard and saw the angels. The garden was not far above them, only about fifteen spiritual (heavenly) cubits.
9 One spiritual cubit is equal to three cubits of man, altogether forty-five cubits.
10 Seth and his children lived on the mountain below the garden. They did not sow nor reap. They made no food for the body, not even wheat, but only enough for offerings. They ate the flavorful fruit of trees that grew on the mountain where they lived.
11 Seth often fasted for forty days, as did also his oldest children. The family of Seth smelled the smell of the trees in the garden when the wind blew that way.
12 They were happy, innocent, without sudden fear, there was no jealousy, no evil action, nor hatred among them. There was no animal passion. No one among them spoke either foul words or curse. There was neither evil intention nor fraud. The men of that time never swore, but when under hard circumstances, when men must swear, they swore by the blood of Abel the just.
13 But every day they compelled their children and their women to fast and pray, and to worship the most High God, in the cave. They blessed themselves by being near the body of their father Adam, and anointed themselves (with it).
14 And they did so until the end of Seth drew near.

(Author's note: It is unclear what the men anointed themselves with. It could be oil blessed by being left close to the body of Adam. To think that they anointed themselves with the oils from the dead body would violate religious laws that would be established latter than the story, yet far earlier than the writing of this 3rd century text.)

Chapter XII

1 Then Seth, the just, called his son Enos, and Cainan, the son of Enos, and Mahalaleel, the son of Cainan, and said he to them:
2 "My end is near, and I wish to build a roof over the altar on which gifts are offered."
3 They listened to his commandment and all of them, both old and young, went out and worked hard and built a beautiful roof over the altar.
4 And Seth's thought was that by doing this a blessing should come upon his children on the mountain. And he though he should present an offering for them before his death.
5 Then when the building of the roof was completed, he commanded them to make offerings. They worked diligently and brought them to Seth, their father, who took them and offered them upon the altar, and prayed God to accept their offerings, to have mercy on the souls of his children, and to keep them from the hand of Satan.
6 God accepted his offering and sent His blessing on him and on his children. Then God made a promise to Seth, saying, "At the end of the great five days and a half, which is the promise I have made to you and to your father, I will send My Word and save you and your seed." *(Author's note: A great day is 1000 years.)*
7 Then Seth and his children, and grandchildren met together and came down from the altar and went to the Cave of Treasures, where they prayed. And he blessed them in the body of our father Adam, and anointed them with it.
8 But Seth stayed in the Cave of Treasures, a few days, and then suffered - sufferings to death.
9 Then Enos, his first born son, came to him with Cainan, his son, and Mahalaleel, Cainan's son, and Jared, the son of Mahalaleel, and Enoch, Jared's son, and with their wives and children to receive a blessing from Seth.
10 Then Seth prayed over them, and blessed them, and earnestly requested them by the blood of Abel the just, saying, "I beg of you my children, not to let one of you go down from this Holy and pure Mountain.
11 Do not associate with the children of Cain the murderer and the sinner, who killed his brother. You know, my children, that we flee from him and from all his sin with all our might because he killed his brother Abel."
12 After having said this, Seth blessed Enos, his first-born son, and commanded him to minister continually in purity before the body of their father Adam, all the days of his life. He also made him promise to go at times to the altar, which he had built. And he commanded him to feed his people in righteousness, in judgment, and in purity all the days of his life.
13 Then Seth's limbs went limp. His hands and feet lost all strength. His voice became silent and unable to speak, and he gave up the ghost and died. Seth died the day after his nine hundred and twelfth year, on the twenty - seventh day of the month Abib; Enoch being then twenty years old.

(Author's note: There are three separate numbers of significance here. 27 is a gateway number to 9. 2+7=9. Nine is the number of endings. 912 reduces to the number 3, which is number of completeness. Abib is the seventh month of the year in the Hebrew calendar, corresponding to Nisan.)

14 Then they carefully wrapped up the body of Seth, and embalmed him with sweet spices, and laid him in the Cave Treasures, on the right side of our father Adam's body, and they mourned for him forty days. They offered gifts for him, as they had done for our father Adam.
15 After the death of Seth, Enos was raised to the head of his people, whom he fed in righteousness, and judgment, as his father had commanded him.
16 But by the time Enos was eight hundred and twenty years old, Cain had a very large number of offspring, because they had sex (married) often, being given to animal lusts, until the land below the mountain, was filled with them.

Chapter XIII

1 Lamech the blind lived in those days. He was one of the sons of Cain. He had a son whose name was Atun, and the two of them had many cattle.
2 Lamech was in the habit of sending them to graze with a young shepherd, who tended them. He was coming home in the evening when he went to his grandfather, his father Atun, and his mother Hazina, and he wept and he said to them, " I cannot feed those cattle alone, or someone may rob me of some of them, or kill me so they can take them." Because among the children of Cain there was a lot of robbery, murder, and sin.
3 Then Lamech pitied him, and he said, "You may be correct. When you are alone you might be overpowered by the men of this place."
4 So Lamech arose, took a bow he had kept ever since he was a youth, before he became blind, and he took large arrows, and smooth stones, and a sling, which he had, and he went to the field with the young shepherd, and placed himself behind the cattle while the young shepherd watched the cattle. Lamech did this for many days.
5 Meanwhile, ever since God had cast him off and had cursed him with trembling and fear, Cain could not be still (settle) nor find rest in any one place, so he wandered from place to place.
6 In his wanderings he came to Lamech's wives, and asked them about him. They said to him, "He is in the field with the cattle."
7 Then Cain went to look for him and as he came into the field, the young shepherd heard the noise he made, and the cattle herding together in front of him.
8 Then said he to Lamech, "My lord, is that a wild beast or a robber?"
9 And Lamech said to him, "Tell me where he is when he comes up."
10 Then Lamech bent his bow, placed an arrow on it, and fitted a stone in the sling, and when Cain came out from the open country, the shepherd said to Lamech, "Shoot, behold, he is coming."
11 Then Lamech shot at Cain with his arrow and hit him in his side. And Lamech struck him with a stone from his sling, and the stone struck his face and knocked out both his eyes. Then Cain fell dead instantly.
12 Then Lamech and the young shepherd came up to him and found him lying on the ground. And the young shepherd said to him, "It is Cain our grandfather, whom you have killed, my lord!"
18 Then Lamech grieved in bitterness and regret. And he clapped his hands together and struck the head of the youth with his flat palm, and the youth fell as if he were dead. But Lamech thought the youth was pretending, so he took up a stone and struck him, and smashed his head until he died.

Chapter XIV

1 When Enos was nine hundred years old, all the children of Seth, and of Cainan, and his first-born, with their wives and children, gathered around him, asking for a blessing from him.
2 Then he prayed over them and blessed them, and made them promise them by the blood of Abel the just, saying to them, "Do not let even one of your children go down from this Holy Mountain, and do not let them make friends with the children of Cain the murderer."
3 Then Enos called his son Cainan and said to him, "Look, my son, and set your heart on your people, and establish them in righteousness, and in innocence, and stand ministering before the body of our father Adam, all the days of your life."
4 After this Enos rested (died). He was nine hundred and eighty - five years old. Cainan wrapped him up, and laid him in the Cave of Treasures on the left of his father Adam, and made offerings for him, following the custom of his fathers.

Chapter XV

1 After the death of Enos, Cainan led his people in righteousness and innocence, as his father had commanded him. He also continued to minister before the body of Adam, in the Cave of Treasures.
2 Then when he had lived nine hundred and ten years, suffering and sickness came upon him. And when he was about to enter into rest (die), all the fathers with their wives and children came to him, and he blessed them, and earnestly urged them by the blood of Abel, the just, saying to them, "Let no one among you descend from this Holy Mountain; and do not make friends with the children of Cain the murderer."
3 Mahalaleel, his first - born son, received this commandment from his father, who blessed him and died.
4 Then Mahalaleel embalmed him with sweet spices, and laid him in the Cave of Treasures, with his fathers; and they made offerings for him, as was the custom of their fathers.

Chapter XVI

1 Then Mahalaleel led his people, and fed them in righteousness and innocence, and watched them to see they had no relationship with the children of Cain.
2 He also continued in the Cave of Treasures praying and ministering before the body of their father Adam, asking God for mercy on himself and on his people, until he was eight hundred and seventy years old, when he fell sick.
3 Then all his children gathered around him to see him, and to ask for his blessing on them all, before he left this world.
4 Then Mahalaleel arose and sat on his bed, his tears streaming down his face, and he called his eldest son Jared, who came to him.
5 He then kissed his face, and said to him, "Jared, my son, I solemnly urge you by Him who made heaven and earth, to watch over your people, and to feed them in righteousness and in innocence; and not to let even one of them go down from this Holy Mountain to the children of Cain, or he will perish with them.

6 "Hear, my son, there will come a great destruction upon this earth because of them. God will be angry with the world, and will destroy them with waters.
7 "But I also know that your children will not listen to you, and that they will go down from this mountain and have relations with the children of Cain, and that they shall perish with them.
8 " My son! Teach them, and watch over them, so that no guilt will be on you because of them."
9 Mahalaleel continued, saying to his son Jared, "When I die, embalm my body and lay it in the Cave of Treasures, by the bodies of my forefathers then stand by my body and pray to God, and take care of them, and fulfill your ministry before them, until you enter into rest yourself."
10 Mahalaleel then blessed all his children, then he laid down on his bed and entered into rest like his fathers.
11 But when Jared saw that his father Mahalaleel was dead, he wept and grieved, and embraced, and kissed his hands and his feet, and so did all his children.
12 And his children embalmed him carefully, and laid him by the bodies of his fathers. Then they stood and mourned for him forty days.

(Author's note: Mahalaleel's way of adjuring Jared, his son, was different in form from those before. He did not invoke the name of Abel, the just. The results were also different, in that it was at this time the children of Abel first began to have intercourse with the children of Cain.)

Chapter XVII

1 Then Jared kept his father's commandment, and arose like a lion over his people. He fed them in righteousness and innocence, and commanded them to do nothing without his consent. This was because he was afraid for them that they should go to the children of Cain.
2 He gave them orders repeatedly, and continued to do so until the end of the four hundred and eighty-fifth year of his life.
3 At the end of these years, there came to him a sign. As Jared was standing like a lion before the bodies of his fathers, praying and warning his people, Satan envied him and produced a beautiful specter because Jared would not let his children do anything without his counsel.
4 Satan appeared to him with thirty men of his hosts, in the form of handsome men. Satan himself was the oldest and tallest among them, with a fine beard.
5 They stood at the mouth of the cave, and called out Jared, who was in the cave.
6 He came out to them and found them looking like handsome men, full of light, and very beautiful. He was in awe of their beauty and their looks, and wondered to himself whether they might not be of the children of Cain.
7 He said also in his heart, " The children of Cain cannot come up to the height of this mountain, and none of them are this handsome as these appear to be, and among these men there is not one of my kindred, so they must be strangers."
8 Then Jared exchanged a greeting with them and he said to the oldest among them, " My father, tell me how you are so wonderful, and tell me who these are with you. They look to me like strange men."
9 Then the oldest began to weep and the rest wept with him, and he said to Jared, "I am Adam whom God made first, and this is Abel my son, who was killed by his

brother Cain, whose heart was influenced by Satan to murder.
10 "And this is my son Seth, whom I asked Lord to give me to comfort me when I no
longer had Abel.
11 "Then this one is my son Enos, son of Seth, and that other one is Cainan, son of
Enos, and that other one is Mahalaleel, son of Cainan, your father."
12 But Jared remained wondering at their appearance and at the words of the elder
to him.
13 Then the oldest said to him, "Do not stand there is awe, my son. We now live in
the land north of the garden, which God created before the world. He would not let
us live there, but placed us inside the garden, below which you are now living.
14 "After I transgressed, He made me come out of it and I was left to live in this cave.
That was when great and horrible troubles came on me. And when the time of my
death drew near, I commanded my son Seth to tend his people well. And my
commandment is to be handed from one to another, to the end of the generations to
come.
15 "But, Jared, my son, we live in beautiful regions while you live here in misery.
Your father Mahalaleel informed me that a great flood would come and overwhelm
the whole earth.
16 "Therefore, my son, fearing for your sakes, I rose and took my children with me,
and came here to visit you and your children. I found you standing in this cave
weeping, and your children scattered about this mountain in the heat and in misery.
17 "But, my son, as we missed our way, and came as far as this, we found other men
below this mountain; who inhabit a beautiful country, full of trees and of fruits, and
of all manner of lush, green vegetation. It is like a garden. When we found them we
thought they were you, until your father Mahalaleel told me they were no such
thing.
18 "Now, my son, listen to my advice, and go down to them, you and your children.
You will rest from all this suffering you are in. If you will not go down to them then
arise, take your children, and come with us to our garden. There, you shall live in
our beautiful land, and you shall rest from all this trouble which you and your
children are now living in."
19 But when he heard these words from the oldest, Jared was confused and went
here and there, but at that moment he found none of his children.
20 Then he answered and said to the old one, "Why have you hidden yourselves
until this day?"
21 And the oldest replied, "If your father had not told us, we would not have known
it."
22 Then Jared believed his words were true.
23 So that oldest said to Jared, "Wherefore did you turn about, so and so?" And he
said, "I was seeking one of my children, to tell him about my going with you, and
about their coming down to those about whom you have spoken to me."
24 When the old one heard Jared's intention, he said to him, "Do not worry about
that right now but come with us and you shall see our country. If the land in which
we live pleases you, we shall all return here and take your family with us. But if our
country does not please you, you shall come back to your own home."
25 And the old one urged Jared to go before one of his children came to talk him out
of his decision.
26 Jared, then, came out of the cave and went with them, and among them. And they
comforted him, until they came to the top of the mountain of the sons of Cain.

27 Then the old one said to one of his companions, "We have forgotten something by the mouth of the cave, and that is the chosen garment we had brought to clothe Jared with."
28 He then said to one of them, "One of you go back, and we will wait for you here until you come back. Then will we clothe Jared and he shall be like us, good, handsome, and fit to come with us into our country."
29 Then that one went back.
30 But when he was a short distance off, the old one called to him and said to him, "You stay there until I come up and speak to you."
31 Then he stood still and the old one went up to him and said to him, "One thing we forgot at the cave, it is this; we forgot to put out the lamp that burns inside the cave, above the bodies that are in there. Do it and come back to us, quickly."
32 That one went, and the old one came back to his fellows and to Jared. And they came down from the mountain, and Jared was with them. And they stayed by a fountain of water, near the houses of the children of Cain and waited for their companion until he brought the garment for Jared.
33 Then he who went back to the cave, put out the lamp, and came to them and brought an apparition with him and showed it them. And when Jared saw it he wondered at the beauty and grace thereof, and rejoiced in his heart believing it was all true.
34 But while they were staying there, three of them went into houses of the sons of Cain and said to them, "Bring us today some food by the fountain of water, for us and our companions to eat."
35 But when the sons of Cain saw them, they were in awe at them and thought: "These men are beautiful to look at. We have never seen such before." So they rose and came with them to the fountain of water, to see their companions.
36 They thought them so very handsome that they called aloud about their places for others to gather together and come and look at these beautiful beings. Then they gathered around them both men and women.
37 Then the old one said to them, "We are strangers in your land, bring us some good food and drink, and bring yourselves and your women, so we can entertain (refresh) ourselves with you."
38 When those men heard these words of the old one, every one of Cain's sons brought his wife, and another brought his daughter, and so, many women came to them; every one calling out to Jared either for himself or for his wife.
39 But when Jared saw what they did, his very soul wrenched itself from them and he would not taste their food or their drink.
40 The old one saw him as he wrenched himself from them, and said to him, "Do not be sad. I am the great elder, as you shall see me do, do yourself in like manner."
41 Then he spread his hands and took one of the women, and five of his companions did the same in front of Jared, that he should do as they did.
42 But when Jared saw them doing their wickedness he wept, and said in his mind, "My fathers never acted like this."
43 He then spread his hands and prayed with a fervent heart, and with much weeping, and begged God to deliver him from their hands.
44 No sooner did Jared begin to pray than the old one fled with his companions; for they could not abide in a place of prayer.
45 Then Jared turned round but could not see them, but found himself standing in the midst of the children of Cain.

46 He then wept and said, "0 God, do not destroy me with this race, concerning which my fathers have warned me. For now, my Lord God, I was thinking that those who appeared to me were my forefathers, but I have found them out to be devils, who lured me by way of this beautiful apparition, until I believed them.
47 "But now I ask You, 0 God, to deliver me from this race, among whom I am now staying, as You did deliver me from those devils. Send Your angel to pull me out of the middle of them. I do not have the power within myself to escape from among them."
48 When Jared had ended his prayer, God sent His angel into the middle of them and he took Jared and set him up on the mountain, and showed him the way, and he gave him wise advice, and then departed from him.

Chapter XVIII

1 The children of Jared were in the habit of visiting him hour after hour, to receive his blessing and to ask his advice for every thing they did, and when he had work to do, they did it for him.
2 But this time when they went into the cave they did not find Jared, but they found the lamp put out, and the bodies of the fathers thrown about, and voices came from them by the power of God, that said, "Satan in an apparition has deceived our son, wishing to destroy him, as he destroyed our son Cain."
3 They said also, "Lord God of heaven and earth, deliver our son from the hand of Satan, who produced such a great and false specter before him." They also spoke of other matters, by the power of God.
4 But when the children of Jared heard these voices they feared, and stood weeping for their father because they did not know what had happened to him.
5 And they wept for him that day until the setting of the sun.
6 Then Jared come with a mournful expression, miserable in mind and body, and sorrowful at having been separated from the bodies of his fathers.
7 But as he came near the cave, his children saw him and ran to the cave, and hugged his neck, crying, and saying to him, "0 father, where have you been, and why have you left us because we know you did not want to?" And they spoke again saying, "Father, when you disappeared the lamp over the bodies of our fathers went out, and the bodies were thrown about, and voices came from them"
8 When Jared heard this he was sorry, and went into the cave; and there found the bodies thrown about, the lamp put out, and the fathers themselves praying for his deliverance from the hand of Satan.
9 Then Jared fell upon the bodies and embraced them, and said, "My fathers, through your intercession, God delivered me from the hand of Satan! I beg you to ask God to keep me and to hide me from him to the day of my death."
10 Then all the voices ceased except the voice of our father Adam, who spoke to Jared by the power of God, just as one would speak to his friend, saying, "Jared, my son, offer gifts to God for having delivered you from the hand of Satan. And when you bring those offerings, offer them on the same altar on which I gave offerings. Even then you must beware of Satan, for he deluded me many a time with his specters, wishing to destroy me, but God delivered me out of his hand.
11 "Command your people that they be on their guard against him, and never cease to offer up gifts to God."
12 Then the voice of Adam also became silent; and Jared and his children wondered

at this. Then they laid the bodies as they were at first; and Jared and his children stood praying the entire night, until break of day.
13 Then Jared made an offering and offered it up on the altar, as Adam had commanded him. And as he went up to the altar, he prayed to God for mercy and for forgiveness of his sin concerning the lamp going out.
14 Then God appeared to Jared on the altar and blessed him and his children, and accepted their offerings; and commanded Jared to take of the sacred fire from the altar and light the lamp that shed light on the body of Adam.

Chapter XIX

1 Then God again revealed to him the promise He had made to Adam. He explained to him the 5500 years, and revealed to him the mystery of His coming to the earth.
2 And God said to Jared, "Let that fire you have taken from the altar to light the lamp abide with you to give light to the bodies. Do not let it come out of the cave until the body of Adam comes out.
3 But, Jared, take care of the fire, so that it burns brightly in the lamp. Do not go out of the cave again until you received an order through a vision, and not in an apparition, you see.

(Author's note: The distinction here is that a vision is internal and an apparition is external. Only God can guide us internally. Satan must entice and trick through external ploys.)

4 "Then command your people again not to have relations with the children of Cain, and not to learn their ways, for I am God who does not love hatred and works of iniquity."
5 God also gave many other commandments to Jared, and He blessed him. And then withdrew His Word from him.
6 Then Jared came near to his children, took some fire, and came down to the cave and lighted the lamp in front of the body of Adam. Then he gave his people the commandments just as God had told him to do.
7 This sign happened to Jared at the end of his four hundred and fiftieth year, as did many other wonders we did not record. But we record only this one for the sake of brevity to shorten our written account.
8 And Jared continued to teach his children eighty years, but after that they began to break the commandments he had given them, and to do many things without his permission. They began to go down from the Holy Mountain, one after another, and mix with the children of Cain, in obscene association.
9 Now the reason the children of Jared went down the Holy Mountain will now be revealed to you.

Chapter XX.

1 After Cain had gone down to the land of dark soil, and his children had multiplied, there was one of them, whose name was Genun, son of Lamech the blind who slew Cain.
2 Satan came to Genun in his childhood and made a variety trumpets and horns, and string instruments, cymbals and psalteries, and lyres and harps, and flutes. And Genun played them at all times and at every hour.

3 And when he played them, Satan came to them so that from among them were heard beautiful and sweet sounds that seized the heart with delight.
4 Then he gathered many crowds to play on them, and when they played it greatly pleased the children of Cain, who fanned themselves to flames of sin among themselves and they burned with fire while Satan inflamed their hearts with one another, and lust increased among them.
5 Satan also taught Genun to make strong drink out of corn. Genun used this to bring together crowd upon crowd in houses of drink, and brought into their hands all kinds of fruits and flowers, and they drank together.
6 Genun did this to multiply sin greatly. He also acted with pride, and taught the children of Cain to commit all manner of the grossest wickedness, which they did not know until then. And he put them up to all kinds of deeds, which they did not know of before.
7 Then, when Satan saw that they obeyed Genun and listened to him in every thing he told them, he rejoiced greatly, and he increased Genun's understanding until he took iron and with it made weapons of war.
8 Then when they were drunk, hatred and murder increased among them. One man would use violence against another and Satan would teach him evil in that one man would take the other man's children and defile them before him.
9 And when men saw they were vanquished and saw that others were not beaten, those who were beaten came to Genun and took refuge with him, and he made them part of his group.
10 Then sin increased among them greatly, until a man married his own sister, or daughter, or mother, and others, or the daughter of his father's sister (first cousin), so that there was no more distinction of relationship, and they could no longer discern what was sin and what was not, but always were wicked and the earth was defiled with sin. And they angered God the Judge, who had created them.
11 But Genun gathered together groups and groups, that played on horns and on all the other instruments we have already mentioned, at the foot of the Holy Mountain. They did that so the children of Seth who were on the Holy Mountain would hear it.
12 But when the children of Seth heard the noise, they wondered, and came by companies, and stood on the top of the mountain to look at those below. This went on an entire year.
13 At the end of that year, Genun saw that they were being won over to him little by little. Satan entered into him, and taught him to make the elements for dyeing garments of various patterns, and made him understand how to dye crimson and purple and what not.
14 And the sons of Cain who worked at all of this shone in beauty and gorgeous apparel. And they gathered together at the foot of the mountain in splendor, with horns and gorgeous dresses, and horse races, and they were committing all manner of disgusting acts.
15 Meanwhile the children of Seth, who were on the Holy Mountain, prayed and praised God in the place of the hosts of angels who had fallen. God had called them 'angels," because He rejoiced over them greatly.
16 But after this time they no longer kept His commandment, nor were held by the promise He had made to their fathers. But they relaxed from their fasting and praying, and from the counsel of Jared their father. And they kept on gathering together on the top of the mountain to watch the children of Cain, from morning until evening. And they watched what they did and they looked at their beautiful

dresses and ornaments.
17 Then the children of Cain looked up from below, and saw the children of Seth, standing in numbers on the top of the mountain, and they called to them to come down to them.
18 But from above them, the children of Seth said, "We don't know the way." Then Genun, the son of Lamech, heard them say they did not know the way, and he began to think to himself of ways he might bring them down.
19 Then Satan appeared to him by night, saying, "There is no way for them to come down from the part of the mountain on which they live, but when they come out tomorrow (to watch), say to them, 'Come to the western side of the mountain. There you will find a stream of water that comes down to the foot of the mountain, between two hills. That marks the way. Come down that way to us.'"
20 Then when it was day, Genun blew the horns and beat the drums below the mountain, as he was accustomed to do. The children of Seth heard it and came as they used to do.
21 Then Genun said to them from down below, "Go to the western side of the mountain, there you will find the way to come down."
22 But when the children of Seth heard these words from him, they went back into the cave to Jared to tell him all they had heard.
23 Then when Jared heard it, he was grieved because he knew that they would defy his wishes.
24 After this a hundred men of the children of Seth gathered together and said among themselves, "Come, let us go down to the children of Cain and see what they do, and enjoy ourselves with them."
25 But when Jared heard this of the hundred men his very soul was moved, and his heart was grieved. He then stood with great emotion in the middle of them, and earnestly compelled them by the blood of Abel the just and said, "Let no one of you go down from this holy and pure mountain, in which our fathers have ordered us to live."
26 But when Jared saw that they did not listen to his words, he said to them, "My good, innocent, and holy children, you must understand that once you go down from this holy mountain, God will not allow you to return to it again."
27 He again adjured them, saying, "I plead with you by the death of our father Adam, and by the blood of Abel, of Seth, of Enos, of Cainan, and of Mahalaleel, to listen to me. Do not go down from this holy mountain, because the moment you leave it, life and mercy will be taken from you; and you shall no longer be called 'children of God,' but 'children of the devil.'
28 But they would not listen to his words.
29 Enoch was already grown up at that time, and in his zeal for God, he stood and said, "Hear me, you large and small (young and old) sons of Seth! When you transgress the commandment of our fathers and go down from this holy mountain, you shall not come up here again for ever."
30 But they rose up against Enoch and would not listen to his words, but they went down from the Holy Mountain.
31 And when they looked at the daughters of Cain, at their beautiful figures, and at their hands and feet dyed with color, and the tattoos on their faces that ornamented them, the fire of sin was set ablaze in them.
32 Then Satan made them look most beautiful before the sons of Seth, as he also made the sons of Seth appear the most handsome in the eyes of the daughters of

Cain, so that the daughters of Cain lusted after the sons of Seth like ravenous beasts, and the sons of Seth lusted after the daughters of Cain until they committed disgusting and disgraceful acts with them.
33 But after they had fallen into this defilement they returned by the way they had come, and tried to ascend the Holy Mountain. But they could not because the stones of that holy mountain were on fire flashing before them, and prevented them so that they could not go up again.
34 And God was angry with them, and turned from them because they had come down from glory, and because of this had lost and forsaken their own purity and innocence, and were fallen into the defilement of sin.
35 Then God sent His Word to Jared, saying, "These of your children, whom you once called 'My children,' have broken My commandment, and have gone down to the house of damnation and sin. Send a messenger to those that are left so that they will not go down, and be lost."
36 Then Jared wept before the Lord, and asked Him for mercy and forgiveness. But he wished that his soul might depart from his body rather than hear these words from God about his children that went down from the Holy Mountain.
37 But he followed God's order and preached to them not to go down from that holy mountain, and not to hold relations with the children of Cain.
38 But they did not listen to his message, and they would not obey his advice.

Chapter XXI

1 After this, another group gathered together and went to look after their brothers but they perished with them as well. And so it was, company after company, until only a few of them remained.
2 Then Jared was sickened with grief. And his sickness was such that the day of his death was near.
3 Then he called Enoch his eldest son, and Methuselah Enoch's son, and Lamech the son of Methuselah, and Noah the son of Lamech.
4 And when they came to him he prayed over them and blessed them, and said to them, "You are righteous, innocent sons. Do not go down from this holy mountain, because you have seen your children and your children's children have gone down from this holy mountain, and have alienated themselves from this holy mountain through their reprehensible lust and transgression of God's commandment.
5 But I know, through the power of God, that He will not leave you on this holy mountain. Your children have transgressed His commandment and that of our fathers, which we had received from them.
6 But, my sons, God will take you to a strange land, and you never shall return to see this garden and this holy mountain with your own eyes once again.
7 Therefore, my sons, set your hearts on your own selves, and keep the commandment of God which is with you. And when you go from this holy mountain into a strange land which you do not know, take the body of our father Adam with you, and with it take these three precious gifts and offerings, namely, the gold, the incense, and the myrrh; and let them be in the place where the body of our father Adam shall lay.
8 And, my sons, of you who are left, the Word of God will come, and when he goes out of this land he shall take with him the body of our father Adam, and shall lay it in the middle of the earth, the place in which salvation shall be worked out."

9 Then Noah said to him, "Who is he of us that shall be left?"
10 And Jared answered, "You are he that shall be left. And you shall take the body of our father Adam from the cave, and place it with you in the ark when the flood comes.
11 "And your son Shem, who shall come out of your loins, it is he who shall lay the body of our father Adam in the middle of the earth, in the place where salvation shall come."
12 Then Jared turned to his son Enoch, and said to him "My son, abide in this cave, and minister diligently before the body of our father Adam all the days of your life, and feed your people in righteousness and innocence."
13 And Jared said no more. His hands went limp, his eyes closed, and he entered into rest like his fathers. His death took place in the three hundred and sixtieth year of Noah, and in the nine hundred and eighty-ninth year of his own life; on the twelfth of Takhsas on a Friday.

(Author's note: In this year, the month of Takhsas was likely to be December.)

14 But as Jared died, tears streamed down his face by reason of his great sorrow, for the children of Seth, who had fallen in his days.
15 Then Enoch, Methuselah, Lamech and Noah, these four, wept over him; embalmed him carefully, and then laid him in the Cave of Treasures. Then they rose and mourned for him forty days.
16 And when these days of mourning were ended, Enoch, Methuselah, Lamech and Noah remained in sorrow of heart because their father had departed from them and could not see him again.

Chapter XXII

1 Enoch kept the commandment of Jared his father, and continued to minister in the cave.
2 Many wonders happened to this man, Enoch, and he also wrote a celebrated book; but those wonders may not be told in this place.
3 Then after this, the children of Seth, as well as their children and their wives went astray and fell. And when Enoch, Methuselah, Lamech and Noah saw them, their hearts suffered because of their fall, which filled them with doubt and unbelief. And they wept and sought of God mercy to preserve them, and to bring them out of that wicked generation.
4 Enoch continued in his ministry before the Lord three hundred and eighty-five years, and at the end of that time he became aware through the grace of God, that God intended to remove him from the earth.
5 He then said to his son, "0 my son, I know that God intends to bring the waters of the Flood on the earth, and destroy our (His) creation.
6 "And you are the last rulers over the people on this mountain. And I know that not one (woman) will be left for you to have children on this holy mountain. Not one of you will rule over the children of his people. No great number of you will be left on this mountain."
7 Enoch also said to them, "Watch over your souls, and hold tight to your fear of God and your service to Him, and worship Him in righteous faith, and serve Him in righteousness, innocence and judgment. Worship Him in repentance and in purity."

8 When Enoch had ended his commandments to them, God transported him from that mountain to the land of life, to the mansions of the righteous and of the chosen ones, which is the abode of Paradise of joy, in light that reaches up to heaven. It is the light that is beyond the light of this world It is the light of God that fills the whole world and no place can contain.
9 Enoch was in the light of God and because of this he found himself out of the grasp of death, until God would have him die.
10 Altogether, not one of our fathers or of their children, remained on that holy mountain, except those three, Methuselah, Lamech, and Noah. All the rest went down from the mountain and fell into sin with the children of Cain. And they were forbidden to come back to that mountain. And none remained on it but those three men.
This completes The Second Book of Adam and Eve.

Author' Note:

In the preceding 171 pages we are confronted with the Genesis story, possibly embellished beyond recognition. Modern readers may find the story to be so fanciful as to be ridiculous. The story may appear to be repetitive and rife with storylines of Satanic deception and human frailty running in waves and cycles throughout the text. Yet, in this ancient script there is a central and universal question – and a singular answer.

How can we know if the circumstance, situation, or even the person in our life is an appointment of God or Satan?

If you are one of the millions of people who believe in an evil entity who is at war with God for the souls of mankind, this question is one of the most important of your life. It defines and clarifies if you are being obedient to God or being deceived by Satan.

Is it possible to know? According to the text, Satan has the power to produce apparitions, specters, and illusions, so believable that they cannot be distinguished from reality. Satan lies, and offers material enticements. Even these may be confused with the grace of God. After all,God gave Adam treasures to place in the cave for his comfort and consolation.

The answer to the eternal question is amazingly simple. Stop. Be still. Look within. Satan may be able to manipulate the material world, but he cannot touch the spirit. Satan may give apparitions and illusions, but God gives visions. The world is Satan's, but the soul is the domain of God. The mystical vision is the terrain of God to tread. Look there for the answer. He alone is there, waiting.

The Book of Enoch

Of all the books quoted, paraphrased, or referred to in the Bible, the Book of Enoch has influenced the writers of the Bible as few others have. Even more extensively than in the Old Testament, the writers of the New Testament were frequently influenced by other writings, including the Book of Enoch.

It is not the purpose of this work to make judgments as to the validity or worth of the Book of Enoch, but rather to simply put forth a meaningful question. Is not the non-canonical book that most influenced the thought and theology of the writers of the New Testament worth further research and contemplation?

Before we continue in our study of the Book of Enoch there are several questions we must keep in mind. If a book is mentioned or quoted in the Bible is it not worthy of further study? If it is worth investigating, is this the book of which the Bible speaks? What knowledge or insight does it add to our understanding of the Bible or the men who wrote it?

The Book of Enoch was once cherished by Jews and Christians alike. It is read in certain Coptic Christian Churches in Ethiopia. Two versions of the Book of Enoch exist today.

Most scholars date the Book of Enoch to sometime during the second century B.C. We do not know what earlier oral tradition, if any, the book contains. Enoch was considered inspired and authentic by certain Jewish sects of the first century B.C. and remained popular for at least five hundred years. The earliest Ethiopian text was apparently derived from a Greek manuscript of the Book of Enoch, which itself was a copy of an earlier text. The original was apparently written in the Semitic language, now thought to be Aramaic.

The Book of Enoch was discovered in the 18th century. It was assumed to have been penned after beginning of the Christian era. This theory was based upon the fact that it had quotes and paraphrases as well as concepts found in the New Testament. Thus, it was assumed that it was heavily influenced by writers such as Jude and Peter.

However, recent discoveries of copies of the book among the Dead Sea Scrolls found at Qumran prove the book was in existence before the time of Jesus Christ. These scrolls force a closer look and reconsideration. It becomes obvious that the New Testament did not influence the Book of Enoch; on the contrary, the Book of Enoch influenced the New Testament. The date of the original writing upon which the second century B.C. Qumran copies were based is shrouded in obscurity. Likewise lost are the sources of the oral traditions that came to be the Book of Enoch.

It has been largely the opinion of historians that the book does not really contain the authentic words of the ancient Enoch, since he would have lived several thousand years earlier than the first known appearance of the book attributed to him. However, the first century Christians accepted the Book of Enoch as inspired, if not authentic. They relied on it to understand the origin and purpose of many things, from angels to wind, sun, and stars. In fact, many of the key concepts used by Jesus Christ himself seem directly connected to terms and ideas in the Book of Enoch.

It is hard to avoid the evidence that Jesus not only studied the book, but also respected it highly enough to allude to its doctrine and content. Enoch is replete with mentions of the coming kingdom and other holy themes. It was not only Jesus who quoted phrases or ideas from Enoch, there are over one hundred comments in the New Testament which find precedence in the Book of Enoch.

Other evidence of the early Christians' acceptance of the Book of Enoch was for many years buried under the King James Bible's mistranslation of Luke 9:35, describing the transfiguration of Christ: "And there came a voice out of the cloud, saying, 'This is my beloved Son. Hear him.'" Apparently the translator here wished to make this verse agree with a similar verse in Matthew and Mark. But Luke's verse in the original Greek reads: "This is my Son, the Elect One (from the Greek ho eklelegmenos, lit., "This is mine, the elect one. Hear him."

The "Elect One" is a most significant term (found fourteen times) in the Book of Enoch. If the book was indeed known to the apostles of Christ, with its abundant descriptions of the Elect One who should "sit upon the throne of glory" and the Elect One who should "dwell in the midst of them;" then the great scriptural authenticity is justly accorded to the Book of Enoch when the "voice out of the cloud" tells the apostles, "This is my Son, the Elect One,"... the one promised in the Book of Enoch.

The Book of Jude tells us in Verse 14 that "Enoch, the seventh from Adam, prophesied." Jude also, in Verse 15, makes a direct reference to the Book of Enoch (2:1), where he writes, "to execute judgment on all, to convict all who are ungodly." As a matter of fact, it is a direct, word for word quote. Therefore, Jude's reference to the Enochian prophesies strongly leans toward the conclusion that these written prophesies were available to him at that time.

Fragments of ten Enoch manuscripts were found among the Dead Sea Scrolls. The number of scrolls indicate the Essenes (a Jewish commune or sect at the time of Christ) could well have used the Enochian writings as a community prayer book or teacher's manual and study text.

Many of the early church fathers also supported the Enochian writings. Justin Martyr ascribed all evil to demons whom he alleged to be the offspring of the angels who fell through lust for women; directly referencing the Enochian writings.

Athenagoras (170 A.D.), regarded Enoch as a true prophet. He describes the angels who "violated both their own nature and their office." In his writings, he goes into detail about the nature of fallen angels and the cause of their fall, which comes directly from the Enochian writings.

Since any book stands to be interpreted in many ways, Enoch posed problems for some theologians. Instead of reexamining their own theology, they sought to dispose of that which went counter to their beliefs. Some of the visions in Enoch are believed to point to the consummation of the age in conjunction with Christ's second coming which took place in A.D. 70 (in the destruction of Jerusalem).

This being the case, it should not surprise us that Enoch was declared a fake and was rejected by Hilary, Jerome, and Augustine. Enoch was subsequently lost to Western Christendom for over a thousand years.

Enoch's "seventy generations" was also a great problem. Many scholars thought it could not be made to stretch beyond the First Century. Copies of Enoch soon disappeared. Indeed, for almost two thousand years we knew only the references made to it in the Bible. Without having the book itself, we could not have known it was being quoted in the Bible, sometimes word for word by Peter and Jude.

"...the Lord, having saved a people out of the land of Egypt, afterward destroyed them that believed not. And angels that kept not their own principality, but left their proper habitation, he hath kept in everlasting bonds under darkness unto the judgment of the great day. Even as Sodom and Gomorrah, and the cities about them...in like manner...are set out as examples...." (Jude 5-7)

"For if God spared not the angels when they sinned, but cast them down into hell, and committed them to pits of darkness, to be reserved unto judgment." (2 Peter 2.4)

To what extent other New Testament writers regarded Enoch as scriptural canon may be determined by comparing their writings with those found in Enoch. A strong possibility of influence upon their thought and choice of wording is evidenced by a great many references found in Enoch which remind one of passages found in the New Testament.

The Book of Enoch had a profound impact on doctrines of both Jews and Christians. In short, the Book Of Enoch influenced and contributed to our modern day doctrine of angels, demons, hell, and jugement. Moreover, it set the stage for the Christology to come by expanding the reader's view of God's "Elect One." Later, the Enochian text (those books attributed to Enoch) spawned several divergent religions including the Order of Enochian Magick, The Hermetic Order of Sol, worship of the Enochian Angels, and others. These sects claim certain power derived by invoking the names and authority of the angels found in the Book Of Enoch.

The Book of Enoch seems to be a missing link between Jewish and Christian theology and is considered by many to be more Christian in its theology than Jewish.

It was considered scripture by many early Christians. The literature of the church fathers is filled with references to this book. The early second century apocryphal book of the Epistle of Barnabus makes many references and quotes from the Book of Enoch. Second and third century church fathers like Justin Martyr, Irenaeus, Origin and Clement of Alexandria all seemed to have accepted Enoch as authentic. Tertullian (160-230 A.D.) even called the Book of Enoch, "Holy Scripture". The Ethiopian Coptic Church holds the Book of Enoch as part of its official spiritual canon. It was widely known and read the first three centuries after Christ. This and many other books became discredited after the Council of Laodicea. And being under ban of the authorities, it gradually disappeared from circulation.

In 1773, rumors of a surviving copy of the book drew Scottish explorer James Bruce to distant Ethiopia. He found the Book of Enoch had been preserved by the Ethiopian church, which put it right alongside the other books of the Bible.

Bruce secured not one, but three Ethiopian copies of the book and brought them back to Europe and Britain. In 1773 Bruce returned from six years in Abyssinia. In 1821 Richard Laurence published the first English translation. The famous R.H. Charles edition was published in 1912. In the following years several portions of the Greek text surfaced. Then with the discovery of cave 4 at Qumran, seven fragmentary copies of the Aramaic text were discovered.

Even in its complete form, the Book of Enoch is not one manuscript. It is a composite of several manuscripts written by several authors. Enoch and Noah each have pieces of the book ascribed to them. Yet still today the most complete text of the multifaceted book is the Ethiopian copy.

Later, another "Book of Enoch" surfaced. This text, dubbed "2 Enoch" and commonly called "the Slavonic Enoch," was discovered in 1886 by Professor Sokolov in the archives of the Belgrade Public Library. It appears that just as the Ethiopian Enoch ("1 Enoch") escaped the sixth-century Church suppression of Enoch texts in the Mediterranean area, so a Slavonic Enoch survived far away, long after the originals from which it was copied were destroyed or hidden.

Specialists in the Enochian texts believe that the missing original from which the Slavonic was copied was probably a Greek manuscript, which itself may have been based on a Hebrew or Aramaic manuscript.

The Slavonic text is evidence of many later additions to the original manuscript. Unfortunately, later additions and the deletion of teachings considered "erroneous," rendered the text unreliable.

Because of certain references to dates and data regarding certain calendar systems in the Slavonic Enoch, some claim the text cannot be earlier than the seventh century A.D. Some see these passages not as evidence of Christian authorship, but as later Christian interpolations into an earlier manuscript. Enochian specialist R.H. Charles, for instance, believes that even the better of the two Slavonic manuscripts contains interpolations and is, in textual terms, "corrupt." It is for the reasons above; we will look only at the book referred to as 1 Enoch. We will leave the inferior manuscript of 2 Enoch for another day.

The translations used for this work are taken from both the Richard Laurence and R.H. Charles manuscripts in addition to numerous sources and commentaries. The texts were compared and, in some cases, transliterated for easier reading by the modern "American" English reader as some phrasing from the 18th and 19th centuries may seem somewhat clumsy to our 21st century eyes. When there are clear differences, a word is added in parentheses to show both paths of translations.

In addition to the translation notes there are Biblical references showing how the Book of Enoch contains various Old Testament sources or how the Book of Enoch was quoted, referenced, or was possibly used as a source document for New Testament writers. These Biblical references are italicized and the chapters and verses are noted. Author's notes and comments are noted and separated from the scripture text.

THE BOOK OF ENOCH

[Chapter 1]

1 The words of the blessing of Enoch, with which he blessed the elect and righteous, who will be living in the day of tribulation, when all the wicked and godless are to be removed.

2 And he began his story saying: Enoch a righteous man, whose eyes were opened by God, saw the vision of the Holy One in heaven, which the angels showed me, and I heard everything from them, and I saw and understood, but it was not for this generation, but for a remote one which is to come.

3 Concerning the elect I said, as I began my story concerning them: The Holy Great One will come out from His dwelling,

4 And the eternal God will tread on the earth, (even) on Mount Sinai, and appear in the strength of His might from heaven.

5 And all shall be very afraid, And the Watchers shall shake, And great fear and trembling shall seize them to the ends of the earth.

6 And the high mountains shall be shaken, and the high hills shall be laid low, and shall melt like wax in the flame.

7 And the earth shall be wholly torn apart, and all that is on the earth shall be destroyed, And there shall be a judgment on all.

8 But with the righteous He will make peace; and will protect the elect and mercy shall be on them. And they shall all belong to God, and they shall prosper, and they shall be blessed. And the light of God shall shine on them.

9 And behold! He comes with ten thousand of His holy ones (saints) to execute judgment on all, and to destroy all the ungodly (wicked); and to convict all flesh of all the works of their ungodliness, which they have ungodly committed, and of all the hard things which ungodly sinners have spoken against Him.

JUD 1:14 And Enoch also, the seventh from Adam, prophesied of these, saying, Behold, the Lord cometh with ten thousands of his saints, 15 To execute judgment upon all, and to convince all that are ungodly among them of all their ungodly deeds which they have ungodly committed, and of all their hard speeches which ungodly sinners have spoken against him.

[Chapter 2]

1 Observe everything that takes place in the sky, how the lights do not change their orbits, and the luminaries which are in heaven, how they all rise and set in order each in its season (proper time), and do not transgress against their appointed order.

2 Consider the earth, and give understanding to the things, which take place on it from start to finish, how steadfast they are, how none of the things on the earth change, but all the works of God appear to you.

3 Behold the summer and the winter, how the whole earth is filled with water, and clouds and dew and rain lie on it.

[Chapter 3]

1 Observe and see how (in the winter) all the trees seem as though they had withered and shed all their leaves, except fourteen trees, which do not lose their foliage but retain the old foliage from two to three years until the new comes.

[Chapter 4]

1 And again, observe the days of summer how the sun is above the earth. And you seek shade and shelter because of the heat of the sun, and the earth also burns with growing heat, and so you cannot walk on the earth, or on a rock because of its heat.

[Chapter 5]

1 Observe how the trees are covered with green leaves and how they bear fruit. Understand, know, and recognize that He that lives forever made them this way for you.

2 And all His works go on before Him from year to year forever, and all the work and the tasks which they accomplish for Him do not change, and so is it done.

3 Consider how the sea and the rivers in like manner accomplish their course do not change because of His commandments.

4 But you, you have neither held to nor have you done the commandments of the Lord, But you have turned away and spoken proud and hard words with your unclean mouths against His greatness. Oh, you hard-hearted, you shall find no peace.

5 Therefore shall you curse your days, and the years of your life shall perish, and the years of your destruction shall be multiplied and in an eternal curse you shall find no mercy.

6 In those days you shall make your names an eternal curse to all the righteous, and by you shall all who curse, curse, and all the sinners and godless shall curse you forever. And for you the godless there shall be a curse.

7 And all the elect shall rejoice, and there shall be forgiveness of sins, and mercy and peace and forbearance and joy. There shall be salvation for them, (like/and) a good light. And for all of you sinners there shall be no salvation, but on you all shall abide

a curse. But for the elect there shall be light and joy and peace, and they shall inherit the earth.

8 And then wisdom shall be given to the elect, and they shall all live and never again sin, either through forgetfulness or through pride: But those who are given wisdom shall be humble.

9 And they shall not again transgress, Nor shall they sin all the days of their life, Nor shall they die of the anger or wrath of God, But they shall complete the number of the days of their lives. And their lives shall be increased in peace, and their years will grow in joy and eternal gladness and peace, all the days of their lives.

[Chapter 6]

1 And it came to pass when the children of men had multiplied that in those days were born to them beautiful and fair daughters.

GEN 6:1 And it came to pass, when men began to multiply on the face of the earth, and daughters were born unto them, 2 That the sons of God saw the daughters of men that they were fair; and they took them wives of all which they chose. 3 And the LORD said, My spirit shall not always strive with man, for that he also is flesh: yet his days shall be an hundred and twenty years.

2 And the angels, the sons of heaven, saw and lusted after them, and said to one another: 'Come, let us choose us wives from among the children of men

3 And have children with them.' And Semjaza, who was their leader, said to them: 'I fear you will not agree to do this deed,

4 And I alone shall have to pay the penalty of this great sin.'

5 And they all answered him and said: 'Let us all swear an oath, and all bind ourselves by mutual curses so we will not abandon this plan but to do this thing.' Then they all swore together and bound themselves by mutual curses.

6 And they were in all two hundred who descended in the days of Jared in the summit of Mount Hermon, and they called it Mount Hermon, because they had sworn and bound themselves by mutual curses on the act.

JUD 1:5 I will therefore put you in remembrance, though ye once knew this, how that the Lord, having saved the people out of the land of Egypt, afterward destroyed them that believed not. 6 And the angels who kept not their first estate, but left their own habitation, he hath reserved in everlasting chains under darkness unto the judgment of the great day.

7 And these are the names of their leaders: Samlazaz, their leader, Araklba, Rameel, Kokablel, Tamlel, Ramlel, Danel, Ezeqeel, Baraqijal,

(Author's note: Samlazaz could be another spelling of Semjaza, and possibly be the same entity.)

8 Asael, Armaros, Batarel, Ananel, Zaqiel, Samsapeel, Satarel, Turel, Jomjael, Sariel. These are their chiefs of tens.

[Chapter 7]

1 And all of them together went and took wives for themselves, each choosing one for himself, and they began to go in to them and to defile themselves with sex with them,

GEN 5:32 And Noah was five hundred years old: and Noah begat Shem, Ham, and Japheth. 6:1 And it came to pass, when men began to multiply on the face of the earth, and daughters were born unto them, 2 That the sons of God saw the daughters of men that they were fair; and they took them wives of all which they chose. 3 And the LORD said, My spirit shall not always strive with man, for that he also is flesh: yet his days shall be an hundred and twenty years. 4 There were giants in the earth in those days; and also after that, when the sons of God came in unto the daughters of men, and they bare children to them, the same became mighty men which were of old, men of renown. 5 And GOD saw that the wickedness of man was great in the earth, and that every imagination of the thoughts of his heart was only evil continually. 6 And it repented the LORD that he had made man on the earth, and it grieved him at his heart.

2 And the angels taught them charms and spells, and the cutting of roots, and made them acquainted with plants.

3 And the women became pregnant, and they bare large giants, whose height was three thousand cubits (ells).

4 The giants consumed all the work and toil of men. And when men could no longer sustain them, the giants turned against them and devoured mankind.

5 And they began to sin against birds, and beasts, and reptiles, and fish, and to devour one another's flesh, and drank the blood.

6 Then the earth laid accusation against the lawless ones.

[Chapter 8]

1 And Azazel taught men to make swords, and knives, and shields, and breastplates, and taught them about metals of the earth and the art of working them, and bracelets, and ornaments, and the use of antimony, and the beautifying of the eyelids, and all kinds of precious stones, and all coloring and dyes.

2 And there was great impiety, they turned away from God, and committed fornication, and they were led astray, and became corrupt in all their ways.

3 Semjaza taught the casting of spells, and root-cuttings, Armaros taught counter-spells (release from spells), Baraqijal taught astrology, Kokabel taught the constellations (portents), Ezeqeel the knowledge of the clouds, Araqiel the signs of

the earth, Shamsiel the signs of the sun, and Sariel the course of the moon. And as men perished, they cried, and their cry went up to heaven.

[Chapter 9]

1 And then Michael, Uriel, Raphael, and Gabriel looked down from heaven and saw much blood being shed on the earth, and all lawlessness being done on the earth.

2 And they said to each other: 'Let the cries from the destruction of Earth ascend up to the gates of heaven.

3 And now to you, the holy ones of heaven, the souls of men make their petition, saying, "Bring our cause before the Most High."'

4 And they said to the Lord of the ages: 'Lord of lords, God of gods, King of kings, and God of the ages, the throne of your glory endures through all the generations of the ages, and your name holy and glorious and blessed to all the ages!

1TI 6:15 Which in his times he shall shew, who is the blessed and only Potentate, the King of kings, and Lord of lords; 16 Who only hath immortality, dwelling in the light which no man can approach unto; whom no man hath seen, nor can see: to whom be honour and power everlasting. Amen.

5 You have made all things, and you have power over all things: and all things are revealed and open in your sight, and you see all things, and nothing can hide itself from you.

6 Look at what Azazel has done, who hath taught all unrighteousness on earth and revealed the eternal secrets which were made and kept in heaven, which men were striving to learn:

7 And Semjaza, who taught spells, to whom you gave authority to rule over his associates.

8 And they have gone to the daughters of men on the earth, and have had sex with the women, and have defiled themselves, and revealed to them all kinds of sins.

GEN 6:4 There were giants in the earth in those days; and also after that, when the sons of God came in unto the daughters of men, and they bare children to them, the same became mighty men which were of old, men of renown.

9 And the women have borne giants, and the whole earth has thereby been filled with blood and unrighteousness.

GEN 6:5 And GOD saw that the wickedness of man was great in the earth, and that every imagination of the thoughts of his heart was only evil continually. 6 And it repented the LORD that he had made man on the earth, and it grieved him at his heart.

10 And now, behold, the souls of those who have died are crying out and making their petition to the gates of heaven, and their lament has ascended and cannot cease because of the lawless deeds which are done on the earth.

11 And you know all things before they come to pass, and you see these things and you have permitted them, and say nothing to us about these things. What are we to do with them about these things?'

[Chapter 10]

1 Then said the Most High, the Great and Holy One, Uriel go to the son of Lamech.

2 Say to him: 'Go to Noah and tell him in my name "Hide yourself!" and reveal to him the end that is approaching: that the whole earth will be destroyed, and a flood is about to come on the whole earth, and will destroy everything on it.'

GEN 7:4 For yet seven days, and I will cause it to rain upon the earth forty days and forty nights; and every living substance that I have made will I destroy from off the face of the earth.

3 'And now instruct him as to what he must do to escape that his offspring may be preserved for all the generations of the world.'

GEN 6:13 And God said unto Noah, The end of all flesh is come before me; for the earth is filled with violence through them; and, behold, I will destroy them with the earth. 14 Make thee an ark of gopher wood; rooms shalt thou make in the ark, and shalt pitch it within and without with pitch.

4 And again the Lord said to Raphael: 'Bind Azazel hand and foot, and cast him into the darkness and split open the desert, which is in Dudael, and cast him in.

5 And fill the hole by covering him rough and jagged rocks, and cover him with darkness, and let him live there for ever, and cover his face that he may not see the light.

6 And on the day of the great judgment he shall be hurled into the fire.

7 And heal the earth which the angels have ruined, and proclaim the healing of the earth, for I will restore the earth and heal the plague, that not all of the children of men may perish through all the secret things that the Watchers have disclosed and have taught their sons.

ROM 8:18 For I reckon that the sufferings of this present time are not worthy to be compared with the glory which shall be revealed in us. 19 For the earnest expectation of the creature waiteth for the manifestation of the sons of God. 20 For the creature was made subject to vanity, not willingly, but by reason of him who hath subjected the same in hope, 21 Because the creature itself also shall be delivered from the bondage of corruption into the glorious liberty of the children of God.

8 The whole earth has been corrupted through the works that were taught by Azazel: to him ascribe ALL SIN.'

9 To Gabriel said the Lord: 'Proceed against the bastards and the reprobates, and against the children of fornication and destroy the children of fornication and the children of the Watchers. Cause them to go against one another that they may destroy each other in battle: Shorten their days.

GEN 6:7 And the LORD said, I will destroy man whom I have created from the face of the earth; both man, and beast, and the creeping thing, and the fowls of the air; for it repenteth me that I have made them. 8 But Noah found grace in the eyes of the LORD.

10 No request that (the Watchers) their fathers make of you shall be granted them on their behalf; for they hope to live an eternal life, and that each one of them will live five hundred years.'

11 And the Lord said to Michael: 'Go, bind Semjaza and his team who have associated with women and have defiled themselves in all their uncleanness.

12 When their sons have slain one another, and they have seen the destruction of their beloved ones, bind them fast for seventy generations under the hills of the earth, until the day of the consummation of their judgment and until the eternal judgment is accomplished.

(Author's note: 70 generations of 500 years = 3500 years.)

13 In those days they shall be led off to the abyss of fire and to the torment and the prison in which they shall be confined for ever.'

14 Then Semjaza shall be burnt up with the condemned and they will be destroyed, having been bound together with them to the end of all generations.

15 Destroy all the spirits of lust and the children of the Watchers, because they have wronged mankind.

16 Destroy all wrong from the face of the earth and let every evil work come to an end and let (the earth be planted with righteousness) the plant of righteousness and truth appear; and it shall prove a blessing, the works of righteousness and truth shall be planted in truth and joy for evermore.

GEN 6:7 And the LORD said, I will destroy man whom I have created from the face of the earth; both man, and beast, and the creeping thing, and the fowls of the air; for it repenteth me that I have made them.

17 And then shall all the righteous survive, and shall live until they beget thousands of children, and all the days of their youth and their old age shall they complete in peace.

GEN 8:22 While the earth remaineth, seedtime and harvest, and cold and heat, and summer and winter, and day and night shall not cease.

GEN 9:1 And God blessed Noah and his sons, and said unto them, Be fruitful, and multiply, and replenish the earth.

18 And then shall the whole earth be untilled in righteousness and shall be planted with trees and be full of blessing. And all desirable trees shall be planted on it, and they shall plant vines on it.

19 And the vine which they plant shall yield fruit in abundance, and as for all the seed which is sown, each measurement (of it) shall bear a thousand, and each measurement of olives shall yield ten presses of oil.

20 You shall cleanse the earth from all oppression, and from all unrighteousness, and from all sin, and from all godlessness, and all the uncleanness that is brought on the earth you shall destroy from off the earth.

21 All the children of men shall become righteous, and all nations shall offer adoration and shall praise Me,

22 And all shall worship Me. And the earth shall be cleansed from all defilement, and from all sin, and from all punishment, and from all torment, and I will never again send another flood from this generation to all generations and for ever.

[Chapter 11]

1 And in those days I will open the storehouse of blessings in heaven, and rain down blessings on the earth and over the work and labor of the children of men.

2 Truth and peace shall be united throughout all the days of the world and throughout all the generations of men.'

[Chapter 12]

1 Then Enoch disappeared and no one of the children of men knew where he was hidden, and where he abode;

GEN 5:21 And Enoch lived sixty and five years, and begat Methuselah: 22 And Enoch walked with God after he begat Methuselah three hundred years, and begat sons and daughters: 23 And all the days of Enoch were three hundred sixty and five years: 24 And Enoch walked with God: and he was not; for God took him.

2 And what had become of him. And his activities were with the Holy Ones and the Watchers.

3 And I, Enoch, was blessing the Lord of majesty and the King of the ages, and lo! the Watchers called me, Enoch the scribe, and said to me:

4 'Enoch, you scribe of righteousness, go, tell the Watchers of heaven who have left the high heaven, the holy eternal place, and have defiled themselves with women, and have done as the children of earth do, and have taken to themselves wives:

5 "You have done great destruction on the earth: And you shall have no peace nor forgiveness of sin:

6 Since they delight themselves in their children, They shall see the murder of their beloved ones, and the destruction of their children shall and they shall lament, and shall make supplication forever, you will receive neither mercy or peace."

[Chapter 13]

1 And Enoch went and said: 'Azazel, you shall have no peace: a severe sentence has been passed against you that you should be bound:

2 And you shall not have rest or mercy (toleration nor request granted), because of the unrighteousness which you have taught, and because of all the works of godlessness,

3 And unrighteousness and sin which you have shown to men.

4 Then I went and spoke to them all together, and they were all afraid, and fear and trembling seized them.

5 And they asked me to write a petition for them that they might find forgiveness, and to read their petition in the presence of the Lord of heaven. They had been forbidden to speak (with Him) nor were they to lift up their eyes to heaven for shame of their sins because they had been condemned.

6 Then I wrote out their petition, and the prayer in regard to their spirits and their deeds individually and in regard to their requests that they should obtain forgiveness and forbearance.

7 And I went off and sat down at the waters of Dan, in the land of Dan, to the southwest of Hermon: I read their petition until I fell asleep.

8 And I had a dream, and I saw a vision of their chastisement, and a voice came to me that I would reprimand (reprove) them.

9 And when I awoke, I came to them, and they were all sitting gathered together, weeping in Abelsjail, which is between Lebanon and Seneser, with their faces covered.

10 And I recounted to them all the visions which I had seen when I was asleep, and I began to speak the words of righteousness, and to reprimand heavenly Watchers.

[Chapter 14]

1 This is the book of the words of righteousness, and of the reprimand of the eternal Watchers in accordance with the command of the Holy Great One in that vision I saw in my sleep.

2 What I will now say with a tongue of flesh and with the breath of my mouth: which the Great One has given to men to speak with it and to understand with the heart.

3 As He has created and given to man the power of understanding the word of wisdom, so has He created me also and given me the power of reprimanding the Watchers, the children of heaven.

4 I wrote out your petition, and in my vision it appeared that your petition will not be granted to you throughout all the days of eternity, and that judgment has been finally passed on you:

5 Your petition will not be granted. From here on you shall not ascend into heaven again for all eternity, and you will be bound on earth for all eternity.

6 Before this you will see the destruction of your beloved sons and you shall have no pleasure in them, but they shall fall before you by the sword.

7 Your petition shall not be granted on their behalf or on yours, even though you weep and pray and speak all the words contained in my writings.

8 In the vision I saw clouds that invited me and summoned me into a mist, and the course of the stars and the flashes of lightning and hurried me and drove me,

9 And the winds in the vision caused me to fly and lifted me up, and bore me into heaven. And I went in until I drew near to a wall which was built out of crystals and surrounded by tongues of fire, and it began to frighten me.

10 I went into the tongues of fire and drew near a large house which was built of crystals: and the walls of the house were like a mosaic of hailstones and the floor was made of crystals like snow.

11 Its ceiling was like the path of the stars and lightning flashes, and between them were fiery cherubim,

12 Their sky was clear as water. A flaming fire surrounded the walls, and its doors blazed with fire.

13 I entered that house, and it was hot as fire and cold as ice; there were no pleasures or life therein: fear covered me, and trembling got hold of me.

14 As I shook and trembled, I fell on my face.

15 And I saw a vision, And lo! there was a second house, greater than the first,

16 And the all the doors stood open before me, and it was built of flames of fire. And in every respect it was splendid and magnificent to the extent that I cannot describe it to you.

17 Its floor was of fire, and above it was lightning and the path of the stars, and its ceiling also was flaming fire.

18 And I looked and saw a throne set on high, its appearance was like crystal, and its wheels were like a shining sun, and there was the vision of cherubim.

1TI 6:16 Who only hath immortality, dwelling in the light which no man can approach unto; whom no man hath seen, nor can see: to whom be honour and power everlasting. Amen.

19 And from underneath the throne came rivers of fire so that I could not look at it.

20 And He who is Great in Glory sat on the throne, and His raiment shone more brightly than the sun and was whiter than any snow.

MAT 25:31 When the Son of man shall come in his glory, and all the holy angels with him, then shall he sit upon the throne of his glory:

21 None of the angels could enter or could behold His face because of the magnificence and glory and no flesh could behold Him.

22 The sea of fire surrounded Him, and a great fire stood in front of Him, and no one could draw close to Him: ten thousand times ten thousand stood before Him, but He needed no Holy council.

23 The most Holy Ones who were near to Him did not leave night or day.

24 And until then I had been prostrate on my face, trembling, and the Lord called me with His own mouth, and said to me:

25' Come here, Enoch, and hear my word.' And one of the Holy Ones came to me picked me up and brought me to the door: and I bowed down my face.

[Chapter 15]

1 And He answered and said to me, and I heard His voice: 'Do not be afraid, Enoch, you righteous man and scribe of righteousness.

2 Approach and hear my voice. Go and say to the Watchers of heaven, for whom you have come to intercede: "You should intercede for men, and not men for you."

3 Why and for what cause have you left the high, holy, and eternal heaven, and had sex with women, and defiled yourselves with the daughters of men and taken to yourselves wives, and done like the children of earth, and begotten giants (as your) sons?

4 Though you were holy, spiritual, living the eternal life, you have defiled yourselves with the blood of women, and have begotten children with the blood of flesh, and, as the children of men, you have lusted after flesh and blood like those who die and are killed.

5 This is why I have given men wives, that they might impregnate them, and have children by them, that deeds might continue on the earth.

6 But you were formerly spiritual, living the eternal life, and immortal for all generations of the world.

7 Therefore I have not appointed wives for you; you are spiritual beings of heaven, and in heaven was your dwelling place.

LUK 20:34 And Jesus answering said unto them, The children of this world marry, and are given in marriage: 35 But they which shall be accounted worthy to obtain that world, and the resurrection from the dead, neither marry, nor are given in marriage: 36 Neither can they die any more: for they are equal unto the angels; and are the children of God, being the children of the resurrection.

8 And now, the giants, who are produced from the spirits and flesh, shall be called evil spirits on the earth,

9 And shall live on the earth. Evil spirits have come out from their bodies because they are born from men and from the holy Watchers, their beginning is of primal origin;

10 They shall be evil spirits on earth, and evil spirits shall they be called spirits of the evil ones. [As for the spirits of heaven, in heaven shall be their dwelling, but as for the spirits of the earth which were born on the earth, on the earth shall be their dwelling.] And the spirits of the giants afflict, oppress, destroy, attack, war, destroy, and cause trouble on the earth.

11 They take no food, but do not hunger or thirst. They cause offences but are not observed.

12 And these spirits shall rise up against the children of men and against the women, because they have proceeded from them in the days of the slaughter and destruction.'

[Chapter 16]

1 'And at the death of the giants, spirits will go out and shall destroy without incurring judgment, coming from their bodies their flesh shall be destroyed until the

day of the consummation, the great judgment in which the age shall be consummated, over the Watchers and the godless, and shall be wholly consummated.'

MAT 8:28 And when he was come to the other side into the country of the Gergesenes, there met him two possessed with devils, coming out of the tombs, exceeding fierce, so that no man might pass by that way. 29 And, behold, they cried out, saying, What have we to do with thee, Jesus, thou Son of God? art thou come here to torment us before the time?

2 And now as to the Watchers who have sent you to intercede for them, who had been in heaven before,

3 (Say to them): "You were in heaven, but all the mysteries of heaven had not been revealed to you, and you knew worthless ones, and these in the hardness of your hearts you have made known to the women, and through these mysteries women and men work much evil on earth."

4 Say to them therefore: " You have no peace."'

[Chapter 17]

1 And they took me to a place in which those who were there were like flaming fire,

2 And, when they wished, they made themselves appear as men. They brought me to the place of darkness, and to a mountain the point of whose summit reached to heaven.

3 And I saw the lighted places and the treasuries of the stars and of the thunder and in the uttermost depths, where were a fiery bow and arrows and their quiver, and a fiery sword and all the lightning.

4 And they took me to the waters of life, and to the fire of the west, which receives every setting of the sun.

5 And I came to a river of fire in which the fire flows like water into the great sea towards the west.

6 I saw the great rivers and came to the great darkness, and went to the place where no flesh walks.

7 I saw the mountains of the darkness of winter and the place from where all the waters of the deep flow.

8 I saw the mouths of all the rivers of the earth and the mouth of the deep.

[Chapter 18]

1 I saw the storehouse of all the winds: I saw how He had adorned the whole creation with them and the firm foundations of the earth.

2 And I saw the corner-stone of the earth: I saw the four winds which support the earth and the firmament of the heaven.

3 I saw how the winds stretch out the height of heaven, and have their station between heaven and earth; these are the pillars of heaven.

4 I saw the winds of heaven which turn and bring the sky and the sun and all the stars to their setting place.

5 I saw the winds on the earth carrying the clouds: I saw the paths of the angels. I saw at the end of the earth the firmament of heaven above.

6 And I continued south and saw a place which burns day and night, where there are seven mountains of magnificent stones, three towards the east, and three towards the south.

7 And as for those towards the east, they were of colored stone, and one of pearl, and one of jacinth (a stone of healing), and those towards the south of red stone.

8 But the middle one reached to heaven like the throne of God, and was made of alabaster.

9 And the summit of the throne was of sapphire.

10 And I saw a great abyss of the earth, with pillars of heavenly fire, and I saw among them fiery pillars of Heaven, which were falling,

11 And as regards both height and depth, they were immeasurable.

12 And beyond that abyss I saw a place which had no firmament of heaven above, and no firmly founded earth beneath it: there was no water on it, and no birds,

13 But it was a desert and a horrible place. I saw there seven stars like great burning mountains,

14 And an angel questioned me regarding them. The angel said: 'This place is the end of heaven and earth.

15 This has become a prison for the stars and the host of heaven. And the stars which roll over the fire are they which have transgressed the commandment of the Lord in the beginning of their rising, because they did not come out at their proper times.

16 And He was angry with them, and bound them until the time when their guilt should be consummated even for ten thousand years.'

[Chapter 19]

1 And Uriel said to me: 'The angels who have had sex with women shall stand here, and their spirits, having assumed many different forms, are defiling mankind and shall lead them astray into sacrificing to demons as gods, here shall they stand, until the day of the great judgment in which they shall be judged and are made an end of.

2 And the women also of the angels who went astray shall become sirens (other versions read 'shall become peaceful' also, another version reads, 'shall salute them').'

3 And I, Enoch, alone saw the vision, the ends of all things: and no man shall see as I have seen.

1PE 4:7 But the end of all things is at hand: be ye therefore sober, and watch unto prayer.

[Chapter 20]

1 These are the names of the holy angels who watch.

2 Uriel, one of the holy angels, who is over the world, turmoil and terror.

3 Raphael, one of the holy angels, who is over the spirits of men.

4 Raguel, one of the holy angels who takes vengeance on the world of the luminaries.

5 Michael, one of the holy angels, set over the virtues of mankind and over chaos.

6 Saraqael, one of the holy angels, who is set over the spirits, who sin in the spirit.

7 Gabriel, one of the holy angels, who is over Paradise and the serpents and the Cherubim.

8 Remiel, one of the holy angels, whom God set over those who rise.

[Chapter 21]

1 Then, I proceeded to where things were chaotic and void.

2 And I saw there something horrible:

3 I saw neither a heaven above nor a firmly founded earth, but a place chaotic and horrible.

4 And there I saw seven stars of heaven bound together in it, like great mountains and burning with fire.

5 Then I said: 'For what sin are they bound, and on why have they been cast in here?' Then said Uriel, one of the holy angels, who was with me, and was chief over them: 'Enoch, why do you ask, and why art you eager for the truth?

6 These are some of the stars of heaven, which have transgressed the commandment of the Lord, and are bound here until ten thousand years, the time entailed by their sins, are consummated.'

7 And I went out from there to another place, which was still more horrible than the former, and I saw a terrible thing: a great fire there which burnt and blazed, and the place was cleft as far as the abyss, full of great falling columns of fire:

8 Neither its width or breadth could I see, nor could I see its source.

9 Then I said: 'I am afraid of this place and cannot stand to look at it.!' Then Uriel, one of the holy angels who was with me, answered and said to me: 'Enoch, why are you so afraid?'

10 And I answered: 'Because of this fearful place, and because of the spectacle of the pain.' And he said to me: 'This place is the prison of the angels, and here they will be imprisoned for ever.'

[Chapter 22]

1 And I went out to another place west where there was a mountain and hard rock.

2 And there was in it four hollow places, deep and wide and very smooth. How smooth are the hollow places and looked deep and dark.

3 Then Raphael answered, one of the holy angels who was with me, and said to me: 'These hollow places have been created for this very purpose, that the spirits of the souls of the dead should be gathered here, that all the souls of the children of men should brought together here. And these places have been made to receive them until the day of their judgment and until the period appointed, until the great judgment comes on them.'

4 I saw the spirit of a dead man, and his voice went out to heaven and made petitions.

5 And I asked Raphael the angel who was with me, and I said to him: 'This spirit which petitions,

6 Whose is it, whose voice goes up and petitions heaven?'

7 And he answered me saying: 'This is the spirit which went out from Abel, whom his brother Cain slew, and he makes his suit against him until his offspring is destroyed from the face of the earth, and his offspring are annihilated from among the children of men.'

GEN 4:8 And Cain talked with Abel his brother: and it came to pass, when they were in the field that Cain rose up against Abel his brother, and slew him. 9 And the LORD said unto Cain, Where is Abel thy brother? And he said, I know not: Am I my brother's keeper? 10 And he said, What hast thou done? the voice of thy brother's blood crieth unto me from the ground. 11 And now art thou cursed from the earth, which hath opened her mouth to receive thy brother's blood from thy hand; 12 When thou tillest the ground, it shall not henceforth yield unto thee her strength; a fugitive and a vagabond shalt thou be in the earth.

8 Then I asked, regarding all the hollow places: 'Why is one separated from the other?'

9 And he answered me and said to me: 'These three have been made that the spirits of the dead might be separated. Divisions have been made for the spirits of the righteous, in which there is the bright spring of water.

10 And one for sinners when they die and are buried in the earth and judgment has not been executed on them in their lifetime.

11 Here their spirits shall be set apart in this great pain until the great day of judgment and punishment and torment of those who curse for ever and retribution for their spirits.

12 There He shall bind them for ever. And such a division has been made for the spirits of those who make their petitions, who make disclosures concerning their destruction, when they were slain in the days of the sinners.

13 Such has been made for the spirits of men who were not righteous but sinners, who were complete in transgression, and of the transgressors they shall be companions, but their spirits shall not be destroyed in the day of judgment nor shall they be raised from here.'

14 Then I blessed the Lord of glory and said: 'Blessed be my Lord, the Lord of righteousness, who rules for ever.'

[Chapter 23]

1 From here I went to another place to the west of the ends of the earth.

2 And I saw a burning fire which ran without resting, and never stopped from its course day or night but flowed always in the same way.

3 And I asked saying: 'What is this which never stops?'

4 Then Raguel, one of the holy angels who was with me, answered me and said to me: 'This course of fire which you have seen is the fire in the west and is the fire of all the lights of heaven.'

[Chapter 24]

1 And from here I went to another place on the earth, and he showed me a mountain range of fire which burned day and night.

2 And I went beyond it and saw seven magnificent mountains, all differing from each other, and their stones were magnificent and beautiful, and their form was glorious: three towards the east, one founded on the other, and three towards the south, one on the other, and deep rough ravines, no one of which joined with any other.

3 And the seventh mountain was in the midst of these, and it was higher than them, resembling the seat of a throne.

4 And fragrant trees encircled the throne. And among them was a tree such as I had never smelled, nor was any among them or were others like it; it had a fragrance beyond all fragrance, and its leaves and blooms and wood would not ever wither:

5 And its fruit is beautiful, and its fruit resembles the dates of a palm. Then I said: 'How beautiful is this tree, and fragrant, and its leaves are fair, and its blooms very delightful in appearance.'

6 Then Michael, one of the holy and honored angels who was with me, and was their leader, spoke.

[Chapter 25]

1 And he said to me: 'Enoch, why do you ask me about the fragrance of the tree, and why do you wish to learn the truth?'

2 Then I answered him saying: 'I wish to know about everything, but especially about this tree.'

3 And he answered saying: 'This high mountain which you have seen, whose summit is like the throne of God, is His throne, where the Holy Great One, the Lord of Glory, the Eternal King, will sit, when He shall come down to visit the earth with goodness.

4 And as for this fragrant tree, no mortal is permitted to touch it until the great judgment, when He shall take vengeance on all and bring everything to its completion for ever.

5 It shall then be given to the righteous and holy. Its fruit shall be for food to the Elect: it shall be transplanted to the holy place, to the temple of the Lord, the Eternal King.

REV 22:1 And he shewed me a pure river of water of life, clear as crystal, proceeding out of the throne of God and of the Lamb. 2 In the midst of the street of it, and on either side of the river, was there the tree of life, which bare twelve manner of fruits, and yielded her fruit every month: and the leaves of the tree were for the healing of the nations. 3 And there shall be no more curses: but the throne of God and of the Lamb shall be in it; and his servants shall serve him.

6 Then they shall rejoice and be glad, and enter into the holy place; And its fragrance shall enter into their bones, And they shall live a long life on earth, as your fathers lived. And in their days there will be no sorrow or pain or torment or toil.'

7 Then I blessed the God of Glory, the Eternal King, who has prepared such things for the righteous, and has created them and promised to give to them.

[Chapter 26]

1 And I went from there to the middle of the earth, and I saw a blessed place in which there were trees with branches alive and blooming on a tree that had been cut down.

2 And there I saw a holy mountain,

3 And underneath the mountain to the east there was a stream and it flowed towards the south. And I saw towards the east another mountain higher than this, and between them a deep and narrow valley.

4 In it ran a stream underneath the mountain. And to the west of it there was another mountain, lower than the former and of small elevation, and a dry, deep valley between them; and another deep and dry valley was at the edge of the three mountains.

5 And all the valleys were deep and narrow, being formed from hard rock, and there were no trees planted on them.

6 And I was very amazed at the rocks in the valleys.

[Chapter 27]

1 Then I said: 'What is the purpose of this blessed land, which is entirely filled with trees, and what is the purpose of this accursed valley between them?'

2 Then Uriel, one of the holy angels who was with me, answered and said: 'This accursed valley is for those who are cursed for ever: Here shall all the accursed be gathered together who utter with their lips words against the Lord not befitting His glory or say hard things against Him. Here shall they be gathered together, and here shall be their place of judgment.

3 In the last days there shall be the spectacle of righteous judgment on them in the presence of the righteous for ever: here shall the merciful bless the Lord of glory, the Eternal King.

4 In the days of judgment they shall bless Him for the mercy in that He has shown them.'

5 Then I blessed the Lord of Glory and set out His glory and praised Him gloriously.

[Chapter 28]

1 Then, I went towards the east, into the midst of the mountain range in the desert, and I saw a wilderness.

2 And it was solitary, full of trees and plants. And water gushed out from above.

3 Rushing like a torrent which flowed towards the north-west it caused clouds and dew to fall on every side.

[Chapter 29]

1 Then I went to another place in the desert, and approached to the east of this mountain range.

2 And there I saw aromatic trees exuding the fragrance of frankincense and myrrh, and the trees also were similar to the almond tree.

[Chapter 30]

1 Beyond these, I went far to the east,

2 And I saw another place, a valley full of water like one that would not run dry.

3 And there was a tree, the color of fragrant trees was that of mastic. And on the sides of those valleys I saw fragrant cinnamon. And beyond these I proceeded to the east.

[Chapter 31]

1 And I saw other mountains, and among them were groves of trees, and there was nectar that flowed from them, which is named Sarara and Galbanum.

2 And beyond these mountains I saw another mountain to the east of the ends of the earth, on which there were aloe trees, and all the trees were full of fruit, being like almond trees.

3 And when it was burned it smelled sweeter than any fragrant odor.

[Chapter 32]

1 And after I had smelled these fragrant odors, I looked towards the north over the mountains I saw seven mountains full of fine nard and fragrant trees of cinnamon and pepper.

2 And then I went over the summits of all these mountains, far towards the east of the earth, and passed over the Red Sea and went far from it, and passed over the angel Zotiel.

3 And I came to the Garden of Righteousness. I saw far beyond those trees more trees and they were numerous and large. There were two trees there, very large, beautiful, glorious, and magnificent. The tree of knowledge, whose holy fruit they ate and acquired great wisdom.

4 That tree is in height like the fir, and its leaves are like those of the Carob tree,

5 And its fruit is like the clusters of the grapes, very beautiful: and the fragrance of the tree carries far.

6 Then I said: 'How beautiful is the tree, and how attractive is its look!' Then Raphael the holy angel, who was with me, answered me and said: 'This is the tree of wisdom, of which your father of old and your mother of old, who were your progenitors, have eaten, and they learned wisdom and their eyes were opened, and they knew that they were naked and they were driven out of the garden.'

[Chapter 33]

1 And from there I went to the ends of the earth and saw there large beasts, and each differed from the other; and I saw birds also differing in appearance and beauty and voice, the one differing from the other.

2 And to the east of those beasts I saw the ends of the earth where heaven rests on it, and the doors of heaven open. And I saw how the stars of heaven come out, and I counted the gates from which they came out,

3 And wrote down all their outlets, of each individual star by their number and their names, their courses and their positions, and their times and their months, as Uriel the holy angel who was with me showed me.

4 He showed me all things and wrote them down for me; also their names he wrote for me, and their laws and their functions.

[Chapter 34]

1 From there I went towards the north to the ends of the earth, and there I saw a great and glorious device at the ends of the whole earth.

2 And here I saw three gates of heaven open : through each of them proceed north winds: when they blow there is cold, hail, frost, snow, dew, and rain.

3 And out of one gate they blow for good: but when they blow through the other two gates, it is for violence and torment on the earth, and they blow with force.

[Chapter 35]

1 Then I went towards the west to the ends of the earth, and saw there three gates of heaven open such as I had seen in the east, the same number of gates, and the same number of outlets.

[Chapter 36]

1 And from there I went to the south to the ends of the earth, and saw there three open gates of heaven.

2 And from them come dew, rain, and wind. And from there I went to the east to the ends of heaven, and saw here the three eastern gates of heaven open and small gates above them.

3 Through each of these small gates pass the stars of heaven and they run their course to the west on the path which is shown to them.

4 And as often as I saw I blessed always the Lord of Glory, and I continued to bless the Lord of Glory who has done great and glorious wonders, who has shown the greatness of His work to the angels and to spirits and to men, that they might praise His work and all His creation: that they might see the power of His might and praise the great work of His hands and bless Him for ever.

[Chapter 37]

1 The second vision which he saw, the vision of wisdom which Enoch the son of Jared, the son of Mahalalel,

2 The son of Cainan, the son of Enos, the son of Seth, the son of Adam, saw. And this is the beginning of the words of wisdom which I lifted up my voice to speak and say to those which dwell on earth: Hear, you men of old time, and see, you that come after, the words of the Holy One which I will speak before the Lord of spirits.

3 The words are for the men of old time, and to those that come after. We will not withhold the beginning of wisdom from this present day. Such wisdom has never been given by the Lord of spirits as I have received according to my insight, according to the good pleasure of the Lord of spirits by whom the lot of eternal life has been given to me.

4 Now three Parables were imparted to me, and I lifted up my voice and recounted them to those that dwell on the earth.

[Chapter 38]

1 The first Parable: When the congregation of the righteous shall appear, and sinners shall be judged for their sins, and shall be driven from the face of the earth;

2 And when the Righteous One shall appear before the eyes of the elect righteous ones, whose works are weighed by the Lord of spirits, light shall appear to the righteous and the elect who dwell on the earth. Where will there be the dwelling for sinners, and where the will there be a resting-place for those who have denied the Lord of spirits? It had been good for them if they had not been born.

JOHN 1:1 In the beginning was the Word, and the Word was with God, and the Word was God. 2 The same was in the beginning with God. 3 All things were made by him; and without him was not any thing made that was made. 4 In him was life; and the life was the light of men. 5 And the light shineth in darkness; and the darkness comprehended it not.

3 When the secrets of the righteous shall be revealed and the sinners judged, and the godless driven from the presence of the righteous and elect,

4 From that time those that possess the earth shall no longer be powerful and mighty: And they shall not be able to look at the face of the holy ones, because the Lord of spirits has caused His light to appear on the face of the holy, righteous, and elect.

2CO 3:18 But we all, with open face beholding as in a glass the glory of the Lord, are changed into the same image from glory to glory, even as by the Spirit of the Lord.

5 Then the kings and the mighty shall be destroyed and be turned over into the hands of the righteous and holy.

6 And from then on none shall seek mercy from the Lord of spirits for themselves for their life is at an end.

[Chapter 39]

1 And it shall come to pass in those days that elect and holy children will descend from the high heaven, and their offspring will become one with the children of men.

2 And in those days Enoch received books of indignation and wrath, and books of turmoil and confusion. There will be no mercy for them, says the Lord of spirits.

3 And in those days a whirlwind carried me off from the earth, And set me down at the end of heaven.

4 There I saw another vision, the dwelling-places of the holy, and the resting-places of the righteous.

5 Here my eyes saw the dwelling places of His righteous angels, and the resting-places of the Holy Ones. And they petitioned and interceded and prayed for the children of men, and righteousness flowed before them like water, and mercy fell like dew on the earth: Thus it is among them for ever and ever.

6 And in that place my eyes saw the Elect One of righteousness and of faith,

7 And I saw his dwelling-place under the wings of the Lord of spirits.

6 And righteousness shall prevail in his days, and the righteous and elect shall be innumerable and will be before Him for ever and ever.

7 And all the righteous and elect ones before Him shall be as bright as fiery lights, and their mouth shall be full of blessing, and their lips shall praise the name of the Lord of spirits. Righteousness and truth before Him shall never fail.

8 There I wished to dwell, and my spirit longed for that dwelling-place; and thus it was decided and my portion was assigned and established by the Lord of spirits.

9 In those days I praised and exalted the name of the Lord of spirits with blessings and praises, because He had destined me for blessing and glory according to the good pleasure of the Lord of spirits.

10 For a long time my eyes looked at that place, and I blessed Him and praised Him, saying: 'Blessed is He, and may He be blessed from the beginning and for evermore. And in His presence there is no end.

11 He knows before the world was created what is for ever and what will be from generation to generation.

12 Those who do not sleep bless you, they stand before your glory and bless, praise, and exalt you, saying: "Holy, holy, holy, is the Lord of spirits: He fills the earth with spirits."'

13 And here my eyes saw all those who do not sleep: they stand before Him and bless Him saying: 'Blessed be you, and blessed be the name of the Lord for ever and ever.'

14 And my face was changed; for I could no longer see.

[Chapter 40]

1 And after that I saw thousands of thousands and ten thousand times ten thousand,

2 I saw a multitude beyond number and reckoning, who stood before the Lord of spirits. And on the four sides of the Lord of spirits I saw four figures, different from those that did not sleep, and I learned their names; for the angel that went with me told me their names, and showed me all the hidden things.

3 And I heard the voices of those four presences as they uttered praises before the Lord of glory.

4 The first voice blessed the Lord of spirits for ever and ever.

5 The second voice I heard blessing the Elect One and the elect ones who depend on the Lord of spirits.

6 And the third voice I heard pray and intercede for those who live on the earth and pray earnestly in the name of the Lord of spirits.

7 And I heard the fourth voice fending off the Satans (advisories or accusers) and forbidding them to come before the Lord of spirits to accuse them who dwell on the earth.

8 After that I asked the angel of peace who went with me, who showed me everything that is hidden: 'Who are these four figures which I have seen and whose words I have heard and written down?'

9 And he said to me: 'This first is Michael, the merciful and long-suffering; and the second, who is set over all the diseases and all the wounds of the children of men, is Raphael; and the third, who is set over all the powers, is Gabriel' and the fourth, who is set over the repentance and those who hope to inherit eternal life, is named Phanuel.'

10 And these are the four angels of the Lord of spirits and the four voices I heard in those days.

[Chapter 41]

1 And after that I saw all the secrets of heavens, and how the kingdom is divided, and how the actions of men are weighed in the balance.

2 And there I saw the mansions of the elect and the mansions of the holy, and my eyes saw all the sinners being driven from there which deny the name of the Lord of spirits, and they were being dragged off; and they could not live because of the punishment which proceeds from the Lord of spirits.

JOHN 14:2 In my Father's house are many mansions: if it were not so, I would have told you. I go to prepare a place for you. 3 And if I go and prepare a place for you, I will come again, and receive you unto myself; that where I am, there ye may be also.

3 And there my eyes saw the secrets of the lightning and of the thunder, and the secrets of the winds, how they are divided to blow over the earth, and the secrets of the clouds and dew,

4 And there I saw where they came from and how they saturate the dusty earth.

5 And there I saw closed storehouses out of which the winds are divided, the storehouse of the hail and winds, the storehouse of the mist, and of the clouds, and the cloud thereof hovers over the earth from the beginning of the world.

6 And I saw the storehouses of the sun and moon, where they go and where they come, and their glorious return, and how one is superior to the other, and their stately orbit, and how they do not leave their orbit, and they add nothing to their orbit and they take nothing from it, and they keep faith with each other, in accordance with the oath by which they are bound together.

7 And first the sun goes out and traverses his path according to the commandment of the Lord of spirits, and mighty is His name for ever and ever. And after that I saw the invisible and the visible path of the moon, and she accomplishes the course of her path in that place by day and by night-the one holding a position opposite to the other before the Lord of spirits. And they give thanks and praise and rest not; but their thanksgiving is for ever and ever.

8 For the sun makes many revolutions for a blessing or a curse, and the course of the path of the moon is light to the righteous and darkness to the sinners in the name of the Lord, who made a separation between the light and the darkness, and divided the spirits of men and strengthened the spirits of the righteous, in the name of His righteousness.

9 For no angel hinders and no power is able to hinder; for He appoints a judge for them all and He judges them all Himself.

[Chapter 42]

1 Wisdom found no place where she might dwell; then a dwelling-place was assigned her in heavens.

2 Wisdom went out to make her dwelling among the children of men, and found no dwelling-place. Wisdom returned to her place, and took her seat among the angels.

3 And unrighteousness went out from her storehouses. She found those she did not seek, and dwelt with them, (she sought no one in particular but found a place...); as rain in a desert and dew on a thirsty land.

[Chapter 43]

1 And I saw other lightning and the stars of heaven, and I saw how He called them all by their names and they obeyed Him.

2 And I saw how they are weighed in a righteous balance according to their proportions of light: I saw the width of their spaces and the day of their appearing, and how their revolution produces lightning:

3 And I saw their revolution according to the number of the angels, and how they keep faith with each other. And I asked the angel who went with me who showed me what was hidden:

4 'What are these?' And he said to me: 'The Lord of spirits has shown you their parable: these are the names of the holy who dwell on the earth and believe in the name of the Lord of spirits for ever and ever.'

[Chapter 44]

1 Also another phenomenon I saw in regard to the lightning: how some of the stars arise and become lightning and cannot part with their new form.

[Chapter 45]

1 And this is the second Parable: concerning those who deny the name of the dwelling of the holy ones and the Lord of spirits.

2 They shall not ascend to heaven, and they shall not come on the earth: Such shall be the lot of the sinners who have denied the name of the Lord of spirits, who are preserved for the day of suffering and tribulation.

3 On that day My Elect One shall sit on the throne of glory and shall try the works of the righteous, and their places of rest shall be innumerable. And their souls shall grow strong within them when they see My Elect One, And those who have called on My glorious name:

4 Then will I cause My Elect One to dwell among them. I will transform heaven and make it an eternal blessing and light,

5 And I will transform the earth and make it a blessing, and I will cause My elect ones to dwell on it. But the sinners and evil-doers shall not set foot on it.

6 For I have seen and satisfied My righteous ones with peace and have caused them to dwell before Me, but for the sinners there is judgment impending with Me, so that I shall destroy them from the face of the earth.

[Chapter 46]

1 And there I saw One whose face looked ancient. His head was white like wool, and with Him was another being whose countenance had the appearance of a man, and his face was full of graciousness, like one of the holy angels.

2 And I asked the angel who went with me and showed me all the hidden things, concerning that Son of Man, who he was, and where came from, and why he went with the Ancient One? And he answered and said to me:

3 "This is the son of Man who hath righteousness, with whom dwells righteousness, and who reveals all the treasures of that which is hidden, because the Lord of spirits

hath chosen him, and whose lot has preeminence before the Lord of spirits in righteousness and is for ever.

4 And this Son of Man whom you have seen shall raise up the kings and the mighty from their seats, and the strong from their thrones and shall loosen the reins of the strong, and break the teeth of the sinners.

5 And he shall put down the kings from their thrones and kingdoms because they do not exalt and praise Him, nor humbly acknowledge who bestowed their kingdom on them.

6 And he shall make the strong hang their heads, and shall fill them with shame. And darkness shall be their dwelling, and worms shall be their bed, and they shall have no hope of rising from their beds, because they do not exalt the name of the Lord of spirits."

7 They raise their hands against the Most High and tread on the earth and dwell on it and all their deeds manifest unrighteousness. Their power rests on their riches, and their faith is in the gods which they have made with their hands. They deny the name of the Lord of spirits,

8 And they persecute the houses of His congregations, and the faithful who depend on the name of the Lord of Spirits.

[Chapter 47]

1 In those days the prayer of the righteous shall have ascended, and the blood of the righteous from the earth shall be before the Lord of spirits.

2 In those days the holy ones who dwell above in heavens shall unite with one voice and supplicate and pray and praise, and give thanks and bless the name of the Lord of spirits on behalf of the blood of the righteous which has been shed, that the prayer of the righteous may not be in vain before the Lord of spirits, that they may have justice, and that they may not have to wait for ever.

3 In those days I saw the "Head of Days" when He seated himself on the throne of His glory, and the books of the living were opened before Him; and all His host which is in heaven above and His counselors stood before Him,

4 And the hearts of the holy were filled with joy because the number of the righteous had been offered, and the prayer of the righteous had been heard, and the blood of the righteous not been required before the Lord of spirits.

[Chapter 48]

1 And in that place I saw the spring of righteousness, which was inexhaustible. And around it were many springs of wisdom. And all the thirsty drank of them, and were filled with wisdom, and their dwellings were with the righteous and holy and elect.

2 And at that hour that Son of Man was named in the presence of the Lord of spirits. And his name was brought before the Head of Days.

3 Even before the sun and the signs were created, before the stars of heaven were made, His name was named before the Lord of spirits.

4 He shall be a staff to the righteous and they shall steady themselves and not fall. And he shall be the light of the Gentiles, and the hope of those who are troubled of heart.

5 All who dwell on earth shall fall down and worship before him, and will praise and bless and sing and celebrate the Lord of spirits.

6 And for this reason he has been chosen and hidden in front of (kept safe by) Him, before the creation of the world and for evermore.

7 And the wisdom of the Lord of spirits has revealed him to the holy and righteous; For he hath preserved the lot of the righteous, because they have hated and rejected this world of unrighteousness, and have hated all its works and ways in the name of the Lord of spirits. For in his name they are saved, and according to his good pleasure and it is He who has regard to their life.

8 In these days the kings of the earth and the strong who possess the land because of the works of their hands will be shamed, because on the day of their anguish and affliction they shall not be able to save themselves. And I will give them over into the hands of My elect.

9 As straw in the fire so shall they burn before the face of the holy; as lead in the water shall they sink before the face of the righteous, and no trace of them shall be found anymore.

10 And on the day of their affliction there shall be rest on the earth (because the evil ones will be destroyed), and before Him they shall fall down and not rise again, and there shall be no one to take them with his hands and raise them up; for they have denied the Lord of spirits and His Anointed. The name of the Lord of spirits be blessed.

[Chapter 49]

1 For wisdom is poured out like water, and glory will not fail before him ever.

2 For he is mighty in all the secrets of righteousness, and unrighteousness shall disappear like a shadow, and will no longer exist; because the Elect One stands before the Lord of spirits, and his glory is for ever and ever, and his might for all generations.

3 In him dwells the spirit of wisdom, and the spirit which gives insight, and the spirit of understanding and of might, and the spirit of those who have fallen asleep in righteousness.

4 And he shall judge the secret things, and no one shall be able to utter a lying or idle word before him, for he is the Elect One before the Lord of spirits according to His good pleasure.

[Chapter 50]

1 And in those days a change shall take place for the holy and elect, and the light of days shall abide on them, and glory and honor shall turn to the Holy.

2 On the day of trouble, affliction will be heaped on the evil. And the righteous shall be victorious in the name of the Lord of spirits. For He will do this to others that they may repent and turn away from the works of their hands.

3 They shall have no honor through the name of the Lord of spirits, but through His name they shall be saved, and the Lord of spirits will have compassion on them, for His mercy is great.

4 He is righteous also in His judgment, and in the presence of His glory unrighteousness also shall not stand: At His judgment the unrepentant shall perish before Him.

5 And from now on I will have no mercy on them, says the Lord of spirits.

[Chapter 51]

1 And in those days shall the earth also give back that which has been entrusted to it, and Sheol (the grave) also shall give back that which it has received, and hell shall give back that which it owes. For in those days the Elect One shall arise,

2 And he shall choose the righteous and holy from among them. For the day has drawn near that they should be saved.

3 And in those days the Elect One shall sit on His throne, and all the secrets of wisdom and counsel shall pour from His mouth, for the Lord of spirits hath given them to Him and has glorified Him.

4 In those days shall the mountains leap like rams, and the hills shall skip like lambs satisfied with milk, and the faces of all the angels in heaven shall be lighted up with joy.

5 And the earth shall rejoice, and the righteous shall dwell on it, and the elect shall walk on it.

[Chapter 52]

1 And after those days in that place where I had seen all the visions of that which is hidden, for I had been carried off in a whirlwind and they had borne me towards the west.

2 There my eyes saw all the secret things of heaven that shall be, a mountain of iron, and a mountain of copper, and a mountain of silver, and a mountain of gold, and a mountain of soft metal, and a mountain of lead.

3 And I asked the angel who went with me, saying, 'What things are these which I have seen in secret?'

4 And he said to me: 'All these things which you have seen shall serve the authority of His Messiah that he may be powerful and mighty on the earth.'

5 The angel of peace answered me saying: 'Wait a little while, and all secret things shall be revealed to you, things which surround the Lord of spirits.

6 And these mountains which your eyes have seen, the mountain of iron, and the mountain of copper, and the mountain of silver, and the mountain of gold, and the mountain of soft metal, and the mountain of lead, all of these shall be like wax before a fire in the presence of the Elect One. Like the water which streams down from above on those mountains, and they shall be weak under his feet.

7 And it shall come to pass in those days that none shall be saved, either by gold or by silver, and none will be able to save themselves or escape.

8 And there shall be no iron for war, nor materials for breastplates. Bronze shall be of no use, tin shall be worthless, and lead shall not be desired.

9 All these things shall be destroyed from the face of the earth, when the Elect One appears before the Lord of spirits.'

[Chapter 53]

1 There my eyes saw a deep valley with its mouth open, and all who dwell on the earth and sea and islands shall bring gifts and presents and tokens of homage to Him, but that deep valley shall not become full.

2 And their hands commit lawless deeds, and everything the righteous work at the sinners devour. The sinners shall be destroyed in front of the face of the Lord of spirits, and they shall be banished from off the face of His earth, and they shall perish for ever and ever.

3 For I saw all the angels of punishment abiding there and preparing all the instruments of Satan.

4 And I asked the angel of peace who went with me: 'For whom are they preparing these instruments?'

5 And he said to me: 'They prepare these for the kings and the powerful of this earth, that they may with them they be destroyed.

6 After this the Righteous and Elect One shall cause the house of His congregation to appear and from then on they shall hinder no more, in the name of the Lord of spirits.

7 And these mountains shall not stand as solid ground before His righteousness, but the hills shall be like springs of water, and the righteous shall have rest from the oppression of sinners.'

[Chapter 54]

1 And I looked and turned to another part of the earth, and saw there a deep valley with burning fire.

2 And they brought the kings and the powerful, and began to cast them into this deep valley.

3 And there my eyes saw how they made their instruments for them, iron chains of immeasurable weight.

4 And I asked the angel of peace who was with me, saying: 'For whom are these chains being prepared ?'

5 And he said to me: 'These are being prepared for the hosts of Azazel, so that they may take them and throw them into the bottom of the pit of hell, and they shall cover their jaws with rough stones as the Lord of spirits commanded.

6 And Michael, and Gabriel, and Raphael, and Phanuel shall take hold of them on that great day, and throw them into the burning furnace on that day, that the Lord of spirits may take vengeance on them for their unrighteousness in becoming servants to Satan and for leading astray those who live on the earth.'

7 And in those days, punishment will come from the Lord of spirits, and he will open all the storehouses of waters above heavens, and of the fountains which are under the surface of the earth.

8 And all the waters shall be come together (flow into or be joined) with the waters of heaven (above the sky), that which is above heavens is the masculine, and the water which is beneath the earth is the feminine.

9 And they shall destroy all who live on the dry land and those who live under the ends of heaven.

(Author's note: The previous verse refers to Noah's flood).

10 And when they have acknowledged the unrighteousness which they have done on the earth, by these they shall perish.

[Chapter 55]

1 And after that the Head of Days repented and said: 'I have destroyed all who dwell on the earth to no avail.'

2 And He swore by His great name: 'From now on I will not do this to all who dwell on the earth again, and I will set a sign in heaven: and this shall be a covenant of good faith between Me and them for ever, so long as heaven is above the earth. And this is in accordance with My command.

(Author's note: The previous verse refers to the rainbow).

3 When I have desired to take hold of them by the hand of the angels on the day of tribulation, anger, and pain because of this, I will cause My punishment and anger to abide on them, says God, the Lord of spirits.

4 You mighty kings who live on the earth, you shall have to watch My Elect One, sit on the throne of glory and judge Azazel, and all his associates, and all his hosts in the name of the Lord of spirits.'

[Chapter 56]

1 And I saw there the hosts of the angels of punishment going, and they held scourges and chains of iron and bronze.

2 And I asked the angel of peace who went with me, saying: 'To whom are these who hold the scourges going?'

3 And he said to me: 'Each one to the ones they have chosen and to their loved ones, that they may be cast into the chasm of the abyss in the valley.

4 And then that valley shall be filled with ones they chose and their loved ones, and the days of their lives shall be at an end, and the days of their leading astray shall no longer be remembered (counted).

5 In those days the angels shall return and gather together and throw themselves to the east on the Parthians and Medes. They shall stir up the kings, so that a spirit of unrest and disturbance will come on them, and they shall drive them from their thrones, that they may rush out like lions from their lairs, and as hungry wolves among their flocks.

(Author's note: The names of certain countries help set the date of the manuscript. Scholars believe, based on the names of the countries mentioned in Enoch that the book could not have been written prior to 250 B.C. since some countries did not exist before that date. One could add that the particular part of Enoch is the only thing dated, since the book consists of several disjointed parts.)

6 And they shall go up and trample the lands of My elect ones, and the land of His elect ones shall be before them a threshing-floor (trampled, barren ground and a highway).

7 But the city of my righteous ones shall be a hindrance to their horses, and they shall begin to fight among themselves, and their own right hand shall be strong against themselves, and a man shall not know his brother, nor a son his father or his mother, until there will be innumerable corpses because of their slaughter, and their punishment shall be not in vain.

8 In those days hell (Sheol) shall open its jaws, and they shall be swallowed up. Their destruction shall be final. Hell (Sheol) shall devour the sinners in the presence of the elect.'

REV 20:1 And I saw an angel come down from heaven, having the key of the bottomless pit and a great chain in his hand. 2 And he laid hold on the dragon, that old serpent, which is the Devil, and Satan, and bound him a thousand years.

[Chapter 57]

1 And it came to pass after this that I saw another host of chariots, and men riding on them. They were coming on the winds from the east, and from the west to the south.

2 The noise of their chariots was heard, and when this turmoil took place the holy ones from heaven watched it, and the pillars of the earth were shaken and moved, and the sound of it was heard from the one end of heaven to the other, in one day.

3 And all shall fall down and worship the Lord of spirits. This is the end of the second Parable.

[Chapter 58]

1 And I began to speak the third Parable concerning the righteous and elect.

2 Blessed are you, you righteous and elect, for glorious shall be your lot.

3 And the righteous shall be in the light of the sun, and the elect will be in the light of eternal life. The days of their life shall be unending, and the days of the holy will be without number.

4 And they shall seek the light and find righteousness with the Lord of spirits. Peace to the righteous in the name of the Eternal Lord!

5 And after this it shall be said to the holy in heaven that they should seek secrets of righteousness, and the destiny of faith. For it has become bright as the sun on earth, and the darkness is passed away.

6 And there shall be a light that never ends, and to a number of days they shall not come, for the darkness shall first have been destroyed, [And the light established before the Lord of spirits] and the light of righteousness established for ever before the Lord of spirits.

[Chapter 59]

1 In those days my eyes saw the secrets of the lightning, and of the lights, and they judge and execute their judgment, and they illuminate for a blessing or a curse as the Lord of spirits wills.

2 And there I saw the secrets of the thunder, and how when it resounds above in heaven, the sound thereof is heard, and he caused me to see the judgments executed on the earth, whether they are for well-being and blessing, or for a curse according to the word of the Lord of spirits.

3 And after that all the secrets of the lights and lightning were shown to me, and they lighten for blessing and for satisfying.

[Chapter 60] - Noah's Vision

1 In the year 500, in the seventh month, on the fourteenth day of the month in the life of Enoch, in that parable I saw how a mighty quaking made the heaven of heavens to quake, and the host of the Most High, and the angels, a thousand thousands and ten thousand times ten thousand, were disquieted with great foreboding.

2 And the Head of Days sat on the throne of His glory, and the angels and the righteous stood around Him.

3 And a great trembling seized me, and fear took hold of me, and my legs gave way, and I melted with weakness and I fell on my face.

4 And Michael sent another angel from among the holy ones and he raised me up, and when he had raised me up my spirit returned; for I had not been able to endure the look of this host, and the disturbance and the shaking of heaven.

5 And Michael said to me: 'Why are you upset with such a vision? Until this day, His mercy, and long-suffering has lasted toward those who dwell on the earth.'

6 And when the day, and the power, and the punishment, and the judgment come, which the Lord of spirits hath prepared for those who worship not the righteous law, and for those who deny the righteous judgment, and for those who take His name in vain, that day is prepared. It will be a covenant for the elect, but for sinners an inquisition. When the punishment of the Lord of spirits shall rest on them, it will

not come in vain, and it shall slay the children with their mothers and the children with their fathers.

7 And on that day two monsters were separated from one another, a female monster named Leviathan, to dwell in the abyss of the ocean over the fountains of the waters;

8 And the male is named Behemoth, who occupied with his breast a wasted wilderness named Duidain, on the east of the garden where the elect and righteous dwell, where my (great) grandfather was taken up, the seventh from Adam, the first man whom the Lord of spirits created.

9 And I asked the other angel to show me the might of those monsters, how they were separated on one day and thrown, the one into the abyss of the sea, and the other to the earth's desert.

10 And he said to me: ' Son of man, you wish to know what is kept secret.'

11 And the other angel who went with me and showed me what was kept secret; told me what is first and last in heaven in the sky, and beneath the earth in the depth, and at the ends of heaven, and on the foundation of heaven.

12 And the storehouse of the winds, and how the winds are divided, and how they are weighed, and how the doors of the winds are calculated for each according to the power of the wind, and the power of the lights of the moon according to the power that is fitting; and the divisions of the stars according to their names, and how all the divisions are divided.

13 And the thunder according to the places where they fall, and all the divisions that are made among the lightning that it may light, and their host that they may at once obey.

14 For the thunder has places of rest which are assigned while it is waiting for its peal; and the thunder and lightning are inseparable, and although not one and undivided, they both go together in spirit and are not separate.

15 For when the lightning flashes, the thunder utters its voice, and the spirit enforces a pause during the peal, and divides equally between them; for the treasury of their peals is like the sand (of an hourglass), and each one of them as it peals is held in with a bridle, and turned back by the power of the spirit, and pushed forward according to the many parts of the earth.

16 And the spirit of the sea is masculine and strong, and according to the might of His strength He draws it back with a rein, and in like manner it is driven forward and disperses in the midst of all the mountains of the earth.

17 And the spirit of the hoar-frost is his own angel, and the spirit of the hail is a good angel. And the spirit of the snow has forsaken his storehouse because of his strength.

18 There is a special spirit there, and that which ascends from it is like smoke, and its name is frost. And the spirit of the mist is not united with them in their storehouse, but it has a special storehouse; for its course is glorious both in light and in darkness, and in winter and in summer, and in its storehouse is an angel.

19 And the spirit of the dew has its dwelling at the ends of heaven, and is connected with the storehouse of the rain, and its course is in winter and summer; and its clouds and the clouds of the mist are connected, and the one gives to the other.

20 And when the spirit of the rain goes out from its storehouse, the angels come and open the storehouse and lead it out, and when it is diffused over the whole earth it unites with the water on the earth.

21 And whenever it unites with the water on the earth, (for the waters are for those who live on the earth), they are (become) nourishment for the earth from the Most High who is in heaven.

22 Therefore there is a measurement for the rain, and the angels are in charge of it. And these things I saw towards the Garden of the Righteous.

23 And the Angel of Peace who was with me, said to me:

24 'These two monsters, prepared in accordance with the greatness of the Lord, will feed them the punishment of the Lord. And children will be killed with their mothers, and sons with their fathers.'

[Chapter 61]

1 And I saw in those days that long cords were given to those angels, and they took to themselves wings and flew, and they went towards the north.

2 I asked the angel, saying to him: 'Why have those angels who have cords taken flight?' And he said to me: 'They have gone to take measurements.'

3 And the angel who went with me said to me: 'These shall bring the measurements of the righteous, and the cords of the righteous to the righteous, that they may rely on the name of the Lord of spirits for ever and ever.

4 The elect shall begin to dwell with the elect, and those are the measurements which shall be given to faith and which shall strengthen righteousness.

5 And these measurements shall reveal all the secrets of the depths of the earth, and those who have been destroyed by the desert, and those who have been devoured by the beasts, and those who have been devoured by the fish of the sea, that they may return and rely on the day of the Elect One. For none shall be destroyed before the Lord of spirits, and none can be destroyed.

6 And all who dwell in heaven received a command and power and one voice and one light like to fire.

7 And they blessed Him with their first words and exalted and praised Him in their wisdom. And they were wise in utterance and in the spirit of life.

8 And the Lord of spirits placed the Elect One on the throne of glory. And he shall judge all the works of the holy above in heaven, and in the balance their deeds shall be weighed.

9 And when he shall lift up his face to judge their secret ways according to the word of the name of the Lord of spirits, and their path according to the way of the righteous judgment of the Lord of spirits; then they shall all speak with one voice and bless and glorify and exalt the name of the Lord of spirits.

10 And He will summon all the host of heavens, and all the holy ones above, and the host of God, the cherubim, seraphim and ophannim, and all the angels of power, and all the angels of principalities (angels that rule over other angels), and the Elect One, and the other powers on the earth and over the water.

11 On that day shall raise one voice, and bless and glorify and exalt in the spirit of faith, and in the spirit of wisdom, and in the spirit of patience, and in the spirit of mercy, and in the spirit of judgment and of peace, and in the spirit of goodness, and shall all say with one voice: "Blessed is He, and may the name of the Lord of spirits be blessed for ever and ever."

12 All who do not sleep above in heaven shall bless Him. All the holy ones who are in heaven shall bless Him; and all the elect who dwell in the garden of life, and every spirit who is able to bless, and glorify, and exalt, and praise Your blessed name, and to the extent of its ability all flesh shall glorify and bless Your name for ever and ever.

13 For great is the mercy of the Lord of spirits. He is long-suffering, and all His works and all that He has created He has revealed to the righteous and elect, in the name of the Lord of spirits.

[Chapter 62]

1 Thus the Lord commanded the kings and the mighty and the exalted, and those who dwell on the earth, and said: 'Open your eyes and lift up your horns if you are able to recognize the Elect One.'

2 And the Lord of spirits seated Him on the throne of His glory, and the spirit of righteousness was poured out on Him, and the word of His mouth slays all the sinners, and all the unrighteous are destroyed from in front of His face.

REV 19:15 And out of his mouth goeth a sharp sword, that with it he should smite the nations: and he shall rule them with a rod of iron: and he treadeth the winepress of the fierceness and wrath of Almighty God. 16 And he hath on his vesture and on his thigh a name written, KING OF KINGS, AND LORD OF LORDS.

3 And in that day all the kings and the mighty, and the exalted and those who hold the earth shall stand up and shall see and recognize that He sits on the throne of His glory, and that righteousness is judged before Him, and no lying word is spoken before Him.

4 Then pain will come on them as on a woman in labor, and she has pain in giving birth when her child enters the mouth of the womb, and she has pain in childbirth.

5 And one portion of them shall look at the other, and they shall be terrified, and they shall look downcast, and pain shall seize them, when they see that Son of Man sitting on the throne of His glory.

MAT 25:31 When the Son of Man shall come in His glory, and all the holy angels with Him, then shall He sit upon the throne of His glory:

6 And the kings and the mighty and all who possess the earth shall bless and glorify and exalt Him who rules over all, who was hidden.

7 For from the beginning the Son of Man was hidden, and the Most High preserved Him in the presence of His might, and revealed Him to the elect.

8 And the congregation of the elect and holy shall be sown, and all the elect shall stand before Him on that day.

9 And all the kings and the mighty and the exalted and those who rule the earth shall fall down before Him on their faces, and worship and set their hope on that Son of Man, and petition Him and supplicate for mercy at His hands.

10 Nevertheless that Lord of spirits will so press them that they shall heavily go out from His presence, and their faces shall be filled with shame, and the darkness grows deeper on their faces.

11 And He will deliver them to the angels for punishment, to execute vengeance on them because they have oppressed His children and His elect.

12 And they shall be a spectacle for the righteous and for His elect. They shall rejoice over them, because the wrath of the Lord of spirits rests on them, and His sword is drunk with their blood.

13 The righteous and elect shall be saved on that day, and they shall never again see the face of the sinners and unrighteous.

14 And the Lord of spirits will abide over them, and they shall eat, lie down and rise up with the Son of Man for ever and ever.

15 The righteous and elect shall have risen from the earth, and ceased to be downcast and they will have been clothed with garments of life.

16 And these shall be the garments of life from the Lord of spirits; they shall not wear out nor will your glory pass away from before the Lord of spirits.

[Chapter 63]

1 In those days shall the mighty and the kings who possess the earth beg Him to grant them a little respite from His angels of punishment to whom they were delivered, that they might fall down and worship before the Lord of spirits, and confess their sins before Him.

2 And they shall bless and glorify the Lord of spirits, and say: 'Blessed is the Lord of spirits and the Lord of kings, and the Lord of the mighty and the Lord of the rich, and the Lord of glory and the Lord of wisdom,

3 And every secret is revealed in front of you. Your power is from generation to generation, and your glory for ever and ever. Deep and innumerable are all your secrets, and your righteousness is beyond reckoning.

4 We have now learned that we should glorify and bless the Lord of kings and Him who is King over all kings.'

5 And they shall say: 'Would that we had a respite to glorify and give thanks and confess our faith before His glory!

6 And now we long for a little respite but find it not. We are driven away and obtain it not: And light has vanished from before us, and darkness is our dwelling-place for ever and ever;

7 Because we have not believed in Him nor glorified the name of the Lord of spirits, but our hope was in the scepter of our kingdom, and in our own glory.

8 In the day of our suffering and tribulation He does not save and we find no respite for confession that our Lord is true in all His works, and in His judgments and His justice, and His judgments have no respect of persons. We pass away from before His face on account of our works, and all our sins are judged in (in comparison to) righteousness.'

10 Now they shall say to themselves: 'Our souls are full of unrighteous gain, but what we have gained does not prevent us from descending from the midst of our worldly gain into the torment (burden) of Hell (Sheol).'

11 And after that their faces shall be filled with darkness and shame before that Son of Man, and they shall be driven from His presence, and the sword shall abide before His face in their midst.

12 Thus spoke the Lord of spirits: 'This is the ordinance and judgment with respect to the mighty and the kings and the exalted and those who possess the earth before the Lord of spirits.'

[Chapter 64]

1 And other forms I saw hidden in that place.

2 I heard the voice of the angel saying: 'These are the angels who descended to the earth, and revealed what was hidden to the children of men and seduced the children of men into committing sin.'

[Chapter 65]

1 And in those days Noah saw the earth that it had sunk down and its destruction was near.

2 And he arose from there and went to the ends of the earth, and cried aloud to his grandfather, Enoch.

3 And Noah said three times with an embittered voice: "Hear me, hear me, hear me." And I said to him: 'Tell me what it is that is falling out on the earth that the earth is in such evil plight and shaken, lest perchance I shall perish with it?'

4 And there was a great disturbance on the earth, and a voice was heard from heaven, and I fell on my face. And Enoch my grandfather came and stood by me, and said to me: 'Why have you cried to me with a bitter cry and weeping?'

5 A command has gone out from the presence of the Lord concerning those who dwell on the earth that their ruin is accomplished because they have learned all the secrets of the angels, and all the violence of the Satans (deceivers, accusers);

6 And all their powers - the most secret ones - and all the power of those who practice sorcery, and the power of witchcraft, and the power of those who make molten images for the whole earth.

7 And how silver is produced from the dust of the earth, and how soft metal originates in the earth.

8 For lead and tin are not produced from the earth like the first; it is a fountain that produces them;

9 And an angel stands in it, and that angel is preeminent.' And after that my grandfather Enoch took hold of me by my hand and lifted me up, and said to me:

10 'Go, for I have asked the Lord of spirits about this disturbance on the earth.' And He said to me: "Because of their unrighteousness their judgment has been determined and shall not be withheld by Me for ever. Because of the sorceries which they have searched out and learned, the earth and those who dwell on it shall be destroyed."

11 And from these, they have no place of repentance for ever, because they have shown them what was hidden, and they are the damned. But as for you, my son, the Lord of spirits knows that you are pure and guiltless of this reproach concerning the secrets.

12 And He has destined your name to be among the holy, and will preserve you among those who dwell on the earth; and has destined your righteous seed both for kingship and for great honors, and from your seed shall proceed a fountain of the righteous and holy without number for ever.

[Chapter 66]

1 And after that he showed me the angels of punishment who are prepared to come and let loose all the powers of the waters which are beneath in the earth in order to bring judgment and destruction on all who dwell on the earth.

2 And the Lord of spirits gave commandment to the angels who were going out, that they should not cause the waters to rise but should hold them in check; for those angels were in charge of the forces of the waters.

3 And I went away from the presence of Enoch.

[Chapter 67]

1 And in those days the word of God came to me, and He said to me: 'Noah, your lot has come up before Me, a lot without blame, a lot of love and righteousness.

2 And now the angels are making a wooden structure, and when they have completed that task I will place My hand on it and preserve it (keep it safe), and there shall come out of it the seed of life, and a change shall set in so that the earth will not remain without inhabitants.

3 And I will establish your seed before me for ever and ever, and I will spread abroad those who dwell with you; and the face of the earth will be fruitful. They shall be blessed and multiply on the earth in the name of the Lord.'

4 And He will imprison those angels, who have shown unrighteousness, in that burning valley which my grandfather Enoch had formerly shown to me in the west among the mountains of gold and silver and iron and soft metal and tin.

5 And I saw that valley in which there was a great earth quake and a tidal waves of the waters.

6 And when all this took place, from that fiery molten metal and from the convulsion thereof in that place, there was a smell of sulfur produced, and it was connected with those waters, and that valley of the angels who had led mankind astray burned beneath that ground.

7 And there were streams of fire throughout the valley, where these angels are punished who had led astray those who dwell on the earth.

8 But those waters shall in those days serve for the kings and the mighty and the exalted, and those who dwell on the earth, for the healing of the body, but for the punishment of the spirit. Their spirit is full of lust, that they will be punished in their body, for they have denied the Lord of spirits. They will see their punishment daily, and yet, they believe not in His name.

9 There will be a relationship between the punishment and change. As their bodies burn, a change will take place in their spirit for ever and ever; for before the Lord of spirits none shall utter an idle word.

10 For the judgment shall come on them, because they believe in the lust of their body and deny the Spirit of the Lord.

11 And the waters will change in those days; for when those angels are punished in these waters, the springs shall change, and when the angels ascend, this water of the springs shall change their temperature and become cold.

12 And I heard Michael answering and saying: 'This judgment in which the angels are judged is a testimony for the kings and the mighty who possess the earth.'

13 Because these waters of judgment minister to the healing of the body of the kings and the lust of their bodies; therefore they will not see and will not believe that those waters will change and become a fire which burns for ever.

[Chapter 68]

1 And after that my grandfather Enoch gave me the explanations of all the secrets in the book of the Parables which had been given to him, and he put them together for me in the words of the book of the Parables.

2 And on that day Michael answered Raphael and said: 'The power of the spirit grips me and makes me tremble because of the severity of the judgment of the secrets, and the judgment of the angels. Who can endure the severe judgment which has been executed, and before which they melt away?'

3 And Michael answered again, and said to Raphael: 'Who would not have a softened heart concerning it, and whose mind would not be troubled by this judgment against them because of those who have led them out?'

4 And it came to pass when he stood before the Lord of spirits, Michael said thus to Raphael: 'I will not defend them under the eye of the Lord; for the Lord of spirits has been angry with them because they act as if they were the Lord.'

5 Therefore all that is hidden shall come on them for ever and ever; for no other angel or man shall have his portion in this judgment, but they alone have received their judgment for ever and ever.

[Chapter 69]

1 And after this judgment I will terrify and make them tremble because they have shown this to those who dwell on the earth.

2 And behold the names of those angels: the first of them is Samjaza; the second Artaqifa; and the third Armen, the fourth Kokabe, the fifth Turael; the sixth Rumjal; the seventh Danjal; the eighth Neqael; the ninth Baraqel; the tenth Azazel; the eleventh Armaros; the twelfth Batarjal; the thirteenth Busasejal; the fourteenth Hananel; the fifteenth Turel; and the sixteenth Simapesiel; the seventeenth Jetrel; the eighteenth Tumael; the nineteenth Turel; the twentieth Rumael; the twenty-first Azazyel;

3 And these are the chiefs of their angels and their names, and their leaders over hundreds, and leaders over fifties, and leaders over tens.

4 The name of the first Jeqon, that is, the one who led astray the sons of God, and brought them down to the earth, and led them astray through the daughters of men.

5 And the second was named Asbeel; he imparted to the holy sons of God evil counsel, and led them astray so that they defiled their bodies with the daughters of men.

6 And the third was named Gadreel; it is he who showed the children of men all the blows of death, and he led astray Eve, and showed the weapons of death to the sons of men; the shield and the coat of mail, and the sword for battle, and all the weapons of death to the children of men.

7 And from his hand they have proceeded against those who dwell on the earth from that day and for evermore.

8 And the fourth was named Penemue; he taught the children of men the bitter and the sweet, and he taught them all the secrets of their wisdom.

9 And he instructed mankind in writing with ink and paper, and thereby many sinned from eternity to eternity and until this day.

10 For men were not created for the purpose of confirming their good faith with pen and ink.

11 For men were created exactly like the angels, to the intent that they should continue pure and righteous; and death, which destroys everything, should not have taken hold of them, but through their knowledge they are perishing, and through this, the power of death consumes them.

12 And the fifth was named Kasdeja; this is he who showed the children of men all the wicked smitings (blows) of spirits and demons, and the smitings (blows) of the embryo in the womb, that it may pass away, and the smitings (blows) of the soul the bites of the serpent, and the smitings (blows) which befall through the midday heat, the son of the serpent named Taba'et.

13 And this is the task of Kasbeel, the chief of the oath which he showed to the holy ones when he dwelt high above in glory, and its name is Biqa.

14 This (angel) requested Michael to show him the hidden name, that he might enunciate it in the oath,

15 So that those might quake before that name and oath who revealed all that was in secret to the children of men. And this is the power of this oath, for it is powerful and strong, and he placed this oath Akae in the hand of (under the control of) Michael.

16 And these are the secrets of this oath (God's promise, word) that heaven was suspended before the world was created, and for ever, and they are strong through his oath (word, promise).

17 And through it the earth was founded on the water, and from the secret recesses of the mountains come beautiful waters, from the creation of the world and to eternity.

18 And through that oath the sea was created, and as its foundation He set for it the sand against the time of its anger (rage) that it dare not pass beyond it from the creation of the world to eternity.

19 And through that oath are the depths made fast, and abide and stir not from their place from eternity to eternity.

20 And through that oath the sun and moon complete their course, and deviate not from their ordinance from eternity to eternity.

21 And through that oath the stars complete their course, and He calls them by their names, and they answer Him from eternity to eternity.

22 [And in like manner the spirits of the water, and of the winds, and of all kinds of spirits, and (their) paths from all the quarters of the winds respond to His command.]

(Author's note: Verse 22 is not complete in some translations.)

23 And there are preserved the voices of the thunder and the light of the lightning: and there are preserved the storehouses of the hail and the storehouses of the hoarfrost,

24 And the storehouses of the mist, and the storehouses of the rain and the dew. And all these believe and give thanks before the Lord of spirits, and glorify (Him) with all their power, and their food is in every act of thanksgiving; they thank and glorify and exalt the name of the Lord of spirits for ever and ever.

25 And this oath is mighty over them and through it they are preserved and their paths are preserved, and their course is not destroyed.

26 And there was great joy among them, and they blessed and glorified and exalted because the name of that Son of Man had been revealed to them.

27 And he sat on the throne of his glory, and the sum of judgment was given to the Son of Man. And he caused the sinners and all those who led the world astray to pass away and be destroyed from off the face of the earth.

28 They shall be bound with chains, and shut up and imprisoned in their place of assembly, and all their works vanish from the face of the earth.

29 And from that time forward, there shall be nothing corruptible; for that Son of Man has appeared, and has seated himself on the throne of his glory. And all evil shall pass away before his face, and the word of that Son of Man shall go out and be strong before the Lord of spirits.

[Chapter 70]

1 And it came to pass after this that during His lifetime His name was raised up to the Son of Man,

2 And to the Lord of spirits from among those who dwell on the earth.

3 And He was raised aloft on the chariots of the spirit and His name vanished among them. And from that day I was no longer numbered among them; and He placed me between the two winds, between the North and the West, where the angels took the cords to measure the place for the elect and righteous for me.

4 And there I saw the first fathers and the righteous who dwell in that place from the beginning.

[Chapter 71]

1 And it came to pass after this that my spirit was translated (carried off) and it ascended into heaven; and I saw the sons of the holy angels (sons) of God. They were walking on flames of fire; their garments were white, and their faces shone like snow.

2 And I saw two rivers of fire, and the light of that fire shone like hyacinth, and I fell on my face before the Lord of spirits.

3 And the angel Michael, one of the archangels, seized me by my right hand, and lifted me up and led me out into all the secrets, and he showed me all the secrets of righteousness.

4 And he showed me all the secrets of the ends of heaven, and all the storehouses of all the stars, and all the lights, from where they proceed before the face of the holy ones.

5 And he translated (carried) my spirit into heaven of heavens, and I saw there as it were built of crystals, and between those crystals tongues of living fire.

REV 21:10 And he carried me away in the spirit to a great and high mountain, and shewed me that great city, the holy Jerusalem, descending out of heaven from God, 11 Having the glory of God: and her light was like unto a stone most precious, even like a jasper stone, clear as crystal.

6 My spirit saw circle of fire binding around the house of fire, and on its four sides were rivers full of living fire, and they encircled that house.

7 And round about were seraphim, cherubim, and ophannim; and these are they who sleep not and guard the throne of His glory.

8 And I saw angels who could not be counted, a thousand thousands, and ten thousand times ten thousand, encircling that house. And Michael, and Raphael, and Gabriel, and Phanuel, and the holy angels who are in heaven above, go in and out of that house.

9 And they came out from that house, and Michael and Gabriel, Raphael and Phanuel, and many holy angels without number.

10 And with them the Head of Days, His head white and pure as wool, and His raiment indescribable.

11 And I fell on my face, and my whole body melted, and my spirit was (transformed) transfigured. And I cried with a loud voice in the spirit of power, and I blessed and glorified and exalted.

12 And these blessings which came from my mouth were very pleasing before that Head of Days.

13 And the Head of Days came with Michael and Gabriel, Raphael and Phanuel, and thousands and ten thousands of angels without number.

14 And the angel came to me and greeted me with his voice, and said to me 'This is the Son of Man who is born to righteousness, and righteousness abides over him, and the righteousness of the Head of Days forsakes him not.'

15 And he said to me: 'He proclaims to you peace in the name of the world to come; for from there peace has proceeded since the creation of the world, and it shall be with you for ever and for ever and ever.

JOHN 17:24 Father, I will that they also, whom thou hast given me, be with me where I am; that they may behold my glory, which thou hast given me: for thou lovest me before the foundation of the world.

16 And all shall walk in His ways since righteousness never forsook Him. Their dwelling-place shall be with Him and it will be their heritage, and they shall not be separated from Him forever and ever and ever.

17 And so there shall be length of days with the Son of Man, and the righteous shall have peace and an upright way in the name of the Lord of spirits for ever and ever.'

HEB 4:3 For we which have believed do enter into rest, as he said, As I have sworn in my wrath, if they shall enter into my rest: although the works were finished from the foundation of the world.

[Chapter 72]

1 The book of the courses of the luminaries of heaven, the relations of each, according to their name, origin, and months (dominion and seasons) which Uriel, the holy angel who was with me, who is their guide, showed me; and he showed me all their laws (regulations) exactly as they are, and how it is with each of the years of the world and to eternity, until the new creation is accomplished which endures until eternity.

2 And this is the first law of the luminaries: the luminary the Sun has its rising in the eastern doors of heaven, and its setting in the western doors of heaven.

3 And I saw six doors in which the sun rises, and six doors in which the sun sets and the moon rises and sets in these doors, and the leaders of the stars and those whom they lead: six in the east and six in the west, and all following each other in accurately corresponding order.

4 There were also many windows to the right and left of these doors. And first there goes out the great luminary, named the Sun, and his sphere (orbit, disc) is like the sphere (orbit, disc) of heaven, and he is quite filled with illuminating and heating fire.

5 The chariot on which he ascends, the wind drives, and the sun goes down from heaven and returns through the north in order to reach the east, and is so guided that he comes to the appropriate door and shines in the face of heaven.

6 In this way he rises in the first month in the great door, which is the fourth.

7 And in that fourth door from which the sun rises in the first month are twelve windows, from which proceed a flame when they are opened in their season.

8 When the sun rises in heaven, he comes out through that fourth door, thirty mornings in succession, and sets accurately in the fourth door in the west of the heaven.

9 And during this period the day becomes daily longer and nights grow shorter to the thirtieth morning.

10 On that day the day is longer than the night by a ninth part, and the day amounts exactly to ten parts and the night to eight parts.

11 And the sun rises from that fourth door, and sets in the fourth and returns to the fifth door of the east thirty mornings, and rises from it and sets in the fifth door.

12 And then the day becomes longer by two parts and amounts to eleven parts, and the night becomes shorter and amounts to seven parts.

13 And it returns to the east and enters into the sixth door, and rises and sets in the sixth door one-and-thirty mornings on account of its sign.

14 On that day the day becomes longer than the night, and the day becomes double the night, and the day becomes twelve parts, and the night is shortened and becomes six parts.

15 And the sun mounts up to make the day shorter and the night longer, and the sun returns to the east and enters into the sixth door, and rises from it and sets thirty mornings.

16 And when thirty mornings are accomplished, the day decreases by exactly one part, and becomes eleven parts, and the night seven.

17 And the sun goes out from that sixth door in the west, and goes to the east and rises in the fifth door for thirty mornings, and sets in the west again in the fifth western door.

18 On that day the day decreases by two parts, and amounts to ten parts and the night to eight parts.

19 And the sun goes out from that fifth door and sets in the fifth door of the west, and rises in the fourth door for one-and-thirty mornings on account of its sign, and sets in the west.

20 On that day the day becomes equal with the night in length, and the night amounts to nine parts and the day to nine parts.

21 And the sun rises from that door and sets in the west, and returns to the east and rises thirty mornings in the third door and sets in the west in the third door.

22 And on that day the night becomes longer than the day, and night becomes longer than night, and day shorter than day until the thirtieth morning, and the night amounts exactly to ten parts and the day to eight parts.

23 And the sun rises from that third door and sets in the third door in the west and returns to the east, and for thirty mornings rises in the second door in the east, and in like manner sets in the second door in the west of heaven.

24 And on that day the night amounts to eleven parts and the day to seven parts.

25 And the sun rises on that day from that second door and sets in the west in the second door, and returns to the east into the first door for one-and-thirty mornings, and sets in the first door in the west of heaven.

26 And on that day the night becomes longer and amounts to the double of the day: and the night amounts exactly to twelve parts and the day to six.

(Author's note: The day is divided into 18 sections of 90 minutes each.)

27 And the sun has traversed the divisions of his orbit and turns again on those divisions of his orbit, and enters that door thirty mornings and sets also in the west opposite to it.

28 And on that night has the night decreased in length by a ninth part, and the night has become eleven parts and the day seven parts.

29 And the sun has returned and entered into the second door in the east, and returns on those his divisions of his orbit for thirty mornings, rising and setting.

30 And on that day the night decreases in length, and the night amounts to ten parts and the day to eight.

31 And on that day the sun rises from that door, and sets in the west, and returns to the east, and rises in the third door for one-and-thirty mornings, and sets in the west of heaven.

32 On that day the night decreases and amounts to nine parts, and the day to nine parts, and the night is equal to the day and the year is exactly as to its days three hundred and sixty-four.

33 And the length of the day and of the night, and the shortness of the day and of the night arise through the course of the sun these distinctions are separated.

34 So it comes that its course becomes daily longer, and its course nightly shorter.

35 And this is the law and the course of the great luminary which is named the sun, and his return as often as he returns sixty times and rises, for ever and ever.

36 And that which rises is the great luminary, and is so named according to its appearance, according as the Lord commanded.

37 As he rises, so he sets and decreases not, and rests not, but runs day and night, and his light is sevenfold brighter than that of the moon; but in regard to size, they are both equal.

[Chapter 73]

1 And after this law I saw another law dealing with the smaller luminary, which is named the Moon.

2 And her orbit is like the sphere (orbit, disc) of heaven, and her chariot in which she rides is driven by the wind, and light is given to her in measurement.

3 And her rising and setting change every month and her days are like the days of the sun, and when her light is uniformly (completely) full it amounts to the seventh part of the light of the sun.

4 And thus she rises. And her first phase in the east comes out on the thirtieth morning and on that day she becomes visible, and constitutes for you the first phase of the moon on the thirtieth day together with the sun in the door where the sun rises.

5 And the one half of her goes out by a seventh part, and her whole disc is empty, without light, with the exception of one-seventh part of it, and the fourteenth part of her light.

6 And when she receives one-seventh part of the half of her light, her light amounts to one-seventh part and the half thereof.

7 And she sets with the sun, and when the sun rises the moon rises with him and receives the half of one part of light, and in that night in the beginning of her morning in the beginning of the lunar day the moon sets with the sun, and is invisible that night with the fourteen parts and the half of one of them.

8 And she rises on that day with exactly a seventh part, and comes out and recedes from the rising of the sun, and in her remaining days she becomes bright in the remaining thirteen parts.

[Chapter 74]

1 And I saw another course, a law for her, and how according to that law she performs her monthly revolution.

2 And all these Uriel, the holy angel who is the leader of them all, showed to me, and their positions, and I wrote down their positions as he showed them to me, and I

wrote down their months as they were, and the appearance of their lights until fifteen days were accomplished.

3 In single seventh parts she accomplishes all her light in the east, and in single seventh parts accomplishes all her darkness in the west.

4 And in certain months she alters her settings, and in certain months she pursues her own peculiar course.

5 In two months the moon sets with the sun: in those two middle doors the third and the fourth.

6 She goes out for seven days, and turns about and returns again through the door where the sun rises, and all her light is full; and she recedes from the sun, and in eight days enters the sixth door from which the sun goes out.

7 And when the sun goes out from the fourth door she goes out seven days, until she goes out from the fifth and turns back again in seven days into the fourth door and accomplishes all her light; and she recedes and enters into the first door in eight days.

8 And she returns again in seven days into the fourth door from which the sun goes out.

9 Thus I saw their positions, how the moons rose and the sun set in those days.

10 And if five years are added together the sun has an excess of thirty days, and all the days which accrue to it for one of those five years, when they are full, amount to 364 days.

11 And an excess of the sun and of the stars amounts to six days; in five years six days every year come to 30 days, and the moon falls behind the sun and stars to the number of 30 days.

12 And the sun and the stars bring in all the years exactly, so that they do not advance or delay their position by a single day to eternity; but complete the years with perfect justice in 364 days.

13 In three years there are 1,092 days, and in five years 1,820 days, so that in eight years there are 2,912 days.

14 For the moon alone the days amount in three years to 1,062 days, and in five years she falls 50 days behind to the sum of 1,770 there is five to be added 1,000 and 62 days.

15 And in five years there are 1,770 days, so that for the moon the days six in eight years amount to 21,832 days.

16 For in eight years she falls behind to the amount of 80 days, all the days she falls behind in eight years are 80.

17 And the year is accurately completed in conformity with their world-stations and the stations of the sun, which rise from the doors through which the sun rises and sets 30 days.

[Chapter 75]

1 And the leaders of the heads of the (ten) thousands, who are in charge of the whole creation and over all the stars, have also to do with the four days of the year which are not counted in the yearly calendar, being not separated from their office, according to the reckoning of the year, and these render service on the four days which are not counted in the reckoning of the year.

2 And because of them men go wrong in them, for those luminaries truly render service to the stations of the world, one in the first door, one on the third door of heaven, one in the fourth door, and one in the sixth door, and the exactness of the year is accomplished through its separate three hundred and sixty-four stations.

3 For the signs and the times and the years and the days the angel Uriel showed to me, whom the Lord of glory hath set for ever over all the luminaries of heaven, in heaven and in the world, that they should rule on the face of heaven and be seen on the earth, and be leaders for the day via the sun and the night via the moon, and stars, and all the ministering creatures which make their revolution in all the chariots of heaven.

4 In like manner, twelve doors Uriel showed me, open in the sphere (disc) of the sun's chariot in heaven, through which the rays of the sun break out; and from them is warmth diffused over the earth, when they are opened at their appointed seasons.

5 And there are openings for the wind and the spirit of dew that when they are opened, stand open in heaven at the ends of the earth.

6 As for the twelve doors in the heaven, at the ends of the earth, out of which go out the sun, moon, and stars, and all the works of heaven in the east and in the west; there are many windows open to the left and right of them,

7 And one window at its appointed season produces warmth, corresponding to the doors from which the stars come out as He has commanded them; and in which they are set, corresponding to their number.

8 And I saw chariots in heaven, running in the world, above those doors in which the stars that never set.

9 And one is larger than all the rest, and it is that that makes its course through the entire world.

[Chapter 76]

1 At the ends of the earth I saw twelve doors open to all quarters of heaven, from which the winds go out and blow over the earth.

2 Three of them are open on the face of heaven, and three in the west; and three on the right of heaven, and three on the left.

3 And the three first are those of the east, and three are of the north, and three, after those on the left, of the south, and three of the west.

4 Through four of these come winds of blessing and prosperity (peace), and from those eight come hurtful winds; when they are sent, they bring destruction on all the earth and the water on it, and on all who dwell on it, and on everything which is in the water and on the land.

5 And the first wind from those doors, called the east wind, comes out through the first door which is in the east, inclining towards the south; from it desolation, drought, heat, and destruction come out .

6 And through the second door in the middle comes what is fitting (right, correct), and there come rain and fruitfulness and prosperity and dew. And through the third door which lies toward the north comes cold and drought.

7 And after these, comes out the south winds through three doors; through the first door of them inclining to the east comes out a hot wind.

8 And through the middle door next to it there comes out fragrant smells, and dew and rain, and prosperity and health.

9 And through the third door which lies to the west dew comes out and also rain, locusts and desolation.

10 And from the seventh door in the east comes the north winds, and dew, rain, locusts and desolation.

11 And from the center door come health and rain and dew and prosperity; and through the third door in the west come cloud and hoar-frost, and snow and rain, and dew and locusts.

12 And after these came the four west winds; through the first door adjoining the north come out dew and hoar-frost, and cold and snow and frost.

13 And from the center door come out dew and rain, and prosperity and blessing.

14 And through the last door which adjoins the south, come drought and desolation, and burning and destruction. And the twelve doors of the four quarters of heaven

are therewith completed, and all their laws and all their plagues and all their benefactions have I shown to you, my son Methuselah.

[Chapter 77]

1 And the first quarter is called the east, because it is the first; and the second, the south, because the Most High will descend there. From there will He who is blessed for ever descend.

2 And the west quarter is named the diminished, because there all the luminaries of the heaven wane and go down.

3 And the fourth quarter, named the north, is divided into three parts: the first of them is for the dwelling of men; and the second contains seas of water, and the abyss (deep) and forests and rivers, and darkness and clouds; and the third part contains the garden of righteousness.

4 I saw seven high mountains, higher than all the mountains which are on the earth: and from here comes hoar-frost, and days, seasons, and years pass away.

5 I saw seven rivers on the earth larger than all the rivers. One of them coming from the west pours its waters into the Great Sea.

6 And these two come from the north to the sea and pour their waters into the Erythraean Sea in the east.

7 And the remaining four come out on the side of the north to their own sea, two of them to the Erythraean Sea, and two into the Great Sea and some say they discharge themselves there into the desert.

8 I saw seven great islands in the sea and in the mainland, two in the mainland and five in the Great Sea.

[Chapter 78]

1 And the names of the sun are the following: the first Orjares, and the second Tomas.

2 And the moon has four names: the first name is Asonja, the second Ebla, the third Benase, and the fourth Erae.

3 These are the two great luminaries; their spheres (disc) are like the sphere (disc) of the heaven, and the size of the spheres (disc) of both is alike.

4 In the sphere (disc) of the sun there are seven portions of light which are added to it more than to the moon, and in fixed measurements it is transferred until the seventh portion of the sun is exhausted.

5 And they set and enter the doors of the west, and make their revolution by the north, and come out through the eastern doors on the face of heaven.

6 And when the moon rises one-fourteenth part appears in heaven, and on the fourteenth day the moon's light becomes full.

7 And fifteen parts of light are transferred to her until the fifteenth day when her light is full, according to the sign of the year, and she becomes fifteen parts, and the moon grows by an additional fourteenth parts.

8 And as the moon's waning decreases on the first day to fourteen parts of her light, on the second to thirteen parts of light, on the third to twelve, on the fourth to eleven, on the fifth to ten, on the sixth to nine, on the seventh to eight, on the eighth to seven, on the ninth to six, on the tenth to five, on the eleventh to four, on the twelfth to three, on the thirteenth to two, on the fourteenth to the half of a seventh, and all her remaining light disappears wholly on the fifteenth.

9 And in certain months the month has twenty-nine days and once twenty-eight.

10 And Uriel showed me another law: when light is transferred to the moon, and on which side it is transferred to her by the sun.

11 During all the period during which the moon is growing in her light, she is transferring it to herself when opposite to the sun during fourteen days her light is full in heaven, and when she is ablaze throughout, her light is full in heaven.

12 And on the first day she is called the new moon, for on that day the light rises on her.

13 She becomes full moon exactly on the day when the sun sets in the west, and from the east she rises at night, and the moon shines the whole night through until the sun rises over against her and the moon is seen over against the sun.

14 On the side whence the light of the moon comes out, there again she wanes until all the light vanishes and all the days of the month are at an end, and her sphere (disc) is empty, void of light.

15 And three months she makes of thirty days, and at her time she makes three months of twenty-nine days each, in which she accomplishes her waning in the first period of time, and in the first door for one hundred and seventy-seven days.

16 And in the time of her going out she appears for three months consisting of thirty days each, and she appears for three months consisting of twenty-nine each.

17 By night she looks like a man for twenty days each time, and by day she appears like heaven, and there is nothing else in her save her light.

[Chapter 79]

1 And now, my son Methuselah, I have shown you everything, and the law of all the stars of heaven is completed.

2 And he showed me all the laws of these for every day, and for every season of every rule, and for every year, and for its going out, and for the order prescribed to it every month and every week.

3 And the waning of the moon which takes place in the sixth door, for in this sixth door her light is accomplished, and after that there is the beginning of the waning.

4 And the waning which takes place in the first door in its season, until one hundred and seventy-seven days are accomplished, calculated according to weeks, twenty-five weeks and two days.

5 She falls behind the sun and the order of the stars exactly five days in the course of one period, and when this place which you see has been traversed.

6 Such is the picture and sketch of every luminary which Uriel the archangel, who is their leader, showed to me.

[Chapter 80]

1 And in those days the angel Uriel answered and said to me: 'Behold, I have shown you everything, Enoch, and I have revealed everything to you that you should see this sun and this moon, and the leaders of the stars of heaven and all those who turn them, their tasks and times and departures.

2 And in the days of the sinners the years shall be shortened, and their seed shall be tardy on their lands and fields, and all things on the earth shall alter, and shall not appear in their time. And the rain shall be kept back, and heaven shall withhold it.

3 And in those times the fruits of the earth shall be backward, and shall not grow in their time, and the fruits of the trees shall be withheld in their time.

4 And the moon shall alter her customs, and not appear at her time.

5 And in those days the sun shall be seen and he shall journey in the evening on the extremity of the great chariot in the west and shall shine more brightly than accords with the order of light.

6 And many rulers of the stars shall transgress their customary order. And these shall alter their orbits and tasks, and not appear at the seasons prescribed to them.

7 And the whole order of the stars shall be concealed from the sinners, and the thoughts of those on the earth shall err concerning them, and they shall be altered from all their ways, they shall err and take them to be gods.

8 And evil shall be multiplied on them, and punishment shall come on them so as to destroy all.'

[Chapter 81]

1 And he said to me: 'Enoch, look at these heavenly tablets and read what is written on them, and mark every individual fact.'

2 And I looked at the heavenly tablets, and read everything which was written on it and understood everything, and read the book of all the deeds of mankind, and of all the children of flesh; that shall be on the earth to the end of generations.

3 And I blessed the great Lord the King of glory for ever, in that He has made all the works of the world, and I exalted the Lord because of His patience, and blessed Him because of the children of men (sons of Abraham).

4 And then I said: 'Blessed is the man who dies in righteousness and goodness, concerning whom there is no book of unrighteousness written, and against whom no day of judgment shall be found.'

5 And the seven holy ones brought me and placed me on the earth before the door of my house, and said to me: 'Declare everything to your son Methuselah, and show to all your children that no flesh is righteous in the sight of the Lord, for He is their Creator.

6 For one year we will leave you with your son, until you give your last commands, that you may teach your children and record it for them, and testify to all your children; and in the second year they shall take you from their midst.

7 Let your heart be strong, for the good shall proclaim righteousness to the good; the righteous shall rejoice with the righteous, and shall wish one another well.

8 But the sinners shall die with the sinners, and the apostate shall go down with the apostate.

9 And those who practice righteousness shall die on account of the deeds of men, and be taken away on account of the deeds of the godless.'

10 And in those days they finished speaking to me, and I came to my people, blessing the Lord of the world.

[Chapter 82]

1 And now, my son Methuselah, all these things I am recounting to you and writing down for you! And I have revealed to you everything, and given you books

concerning all these; so, my son Methuselah, preserve the books from your father's hand, and see that you deliver them to the generations of the world.

2 I have given wisdom to you and to your children, and those children to come, that they may give it to their children for generations. This wisdom namely that passes their understanding.

3 And those who understand it shall not sleep, but shall listen that they may learn this wisdom, and it shall please those that eat thereof better than good food.

4 Blessed are all the righteous, blessed are all those who walk in the way of righteousness and sin not as the sinners, in the numbering of all their days in which the sun traverses heaven, entering into and departing from the doors for thirty days with the heads of thousands of the order of the stars, together with the four which are within the calendar which divide the four portions of the year, which lead them and enter with them four days.

5 Owing to them men shall be at fault and not count them in the whole number of days of the year. Men shall be at fault, and not recognize them accurately.

6 For they belong to the calculations of the year and are truly recorded therein for ever, one in the first door and one in the third, and one in the fourth and one in the sixth, and the year is completed in three hundred and sixty-four days.

7 And the account of it is accurate and the recorded counting thereof is exact; for the luminaries, and months and festivals, and years and days, has Uriel shown and revealed to me, to whom the Lord of the whole creation of the world hath subjected the host of heaven.

8 And he has power over night and day in heaven to cause the light to shine on men via the sun, moon, and stars, and all the powers of the heaven which revolve in their circular chariots.

9 And these are the orders of the stars, which set in their places, and in their seasons and festivals and months.

10 And these are the names of those who lead them, who watch that they enter at their times, in their orders, in their seasons, in their months, in their periods of dominion, and in their positions.

11 Their four leaders who divide the four parts of the year enter first; and after them the twelve leaders of the orders who divide the months; and for the three hundred and sixty days there are heads over thousands who divide the days; and for the four days in the calendar there are the leaders which divide the four parts of the year.

12 And these heads over thousands are interspersed between leader and leader, each behind a station, but their leaders make the division.

13 And these are the names of the leaders who divide the four parts of the year which are ordained:

14 Milki'el, Hel'emmelek, and Mel'ejal, and Narel. And the names of those who lead them: Adnar'el, and Ijasusa'el, and 'Elome'el.

15 These three follow the leaders of the orders, and there is one that follows the three leaders of the orders which follow those leaders of stations that divide the four parts of the year. In the beginning of the year Melkejal rises first and rules, who is named Tam'aini and sun, and all the days of his dominion while he bears rule are ninety-one days.

16 And these are the signs of the days which are to be seen on earth in the days of his dominion: sweat, and heat; and calms; and all the trees bear fruit, and leaves are produced on all the trees, and the harvest of wheat, and the rose-flowers, and all the flowers which come out in the field, but the trees of the winter season become withered.

17 And these are the names of the leaders which are under them: Berka'el, Zelebs'el, and another who is added a head of a thousand, called Hilujaseph: and the days of the dominion of this leader are at an end.

18 The next leader after him is Hel'emmelek, whom one names the shining sun, and all the days of his light are ninety-one days.

19 And these are the signs of his days on the earth: glowing heat and dryness, and the trees ripen their fruits and produce all their fruits ripe and ready, and the sheep pair and become pregnant, and all the fruits of the earth are gathered in, and everything that is in the fields, and the winepress: these things take place in the days of his dominion.

20 These are the names, and the orders, and the leaders of those heads of thousands: Gida'Ijal, Ke'el, and He'el, and the name of the head of a thousand which is added to them, Asfa'el: and the days of his dominion are at an end.

[Chapter 83]

1 And now, my son Methuselah, I will show you all my visions which I have seen, recounting them before you.

2 I saw two visions before I got married (took a wife), and the one was quite unlike the other: the first when I was learning to write: the second before I married (took) your mother, was when I saw a terrible vision.

3 And regarding them I prayed to the Lord. I had laid down in the house of my grandfather Mahalalel, when I saw in a vision how heaven collapsed and was carried off (removed, torn down) and fell to the earth.

4 And when it fell to the earth I saw how the earth was swallowed up in a great abyss, and mountains were suspended on mountains, and hills sank down on hills, and high trees were ripped from their stems, and hurled down and sunk in the abyss.

5 And then a word fell into my mouth, and I lifted up my voice to cry aloud, and said:

6 'The earth is destroyed.' And my grandfather Mahalalel woke me as I lay near him, and said to me: 'Why do you cry so, my son, and why do you make such moaning (lamentation)?'

7 And I recounted to him the whole vision which I had seen, and he said to me: 'You have seen a terrible thing , my son. Your dream (vision) is of a grave time and concerns the secrets of all the sin of the earth: it must sink into the abyss and be totally destroyed.

8 And now, my son, arise and pray to the Lord of glory, since you are a believer, that a remnant may remain on the earth, and that He may not destroy the whole earth.

9 My son, from heaven all this will come on the earth, and on the earth there will be great destruction.

10 After that I arose and prayed and implored and besought (God), and wrote down my prayer for the generations of the world, and I will show everything to you, my son Methuselah.

11 And when I had gone out below and seen the heaven, and the sun rising in the east, and the moon setting in the west, and a few stars, and the whole earth, and everything as He had known it in the beginning, then I blessed the Lord of judgment and exalted Him because He had made the sun to go out from the windows of the east, and he ascended and rose on the face of heaven, and set out and kept traversing the path shown to it.

[Chapter 84]

1 And I lifted up my hands in righteousness and blessed the Holy and Great One, and spoke with the breath of my mouth, and with the tongue of flesh, which God has made for the children of the flesh of men, that they should speak therewith, and He gave them breath and a tongue and a mouth that they should speak therewith:

2 Blessed be you, O Lord, King, Great and mighty in your greatness, Lord of the whole creation of heaven, King of kings and God of the whole world. And your power and kingship and greatness abide for ever and ever, and throughout all generations your dominion and all heavens are your throne for ever, and the whole earth your footstool for ever and ever.

3 For you have made and you rule all things, and nothing is too hard for you, wisdom never departs from the place of your throne, nor turns away from your presence. You know and see and hear everything, and there is nothing hidden from you for you see everything.

4 And now the angels of your heavens are guilty of trespass, and on the flesh of men abide your wrath until the great day of judgment.

5 And now, O God and Lord and Great King, I implore and beseech you to fulfill my prayer, to leave me a posterity on earth, and not destroy all the flesh of man, and make the earth without inhabitant, so that there should be an eternal destruction.

6 And now, my Lord, destroy from the earth the flesh which has aroused your wrath, but the flesh of righteousness and uprightness establish as an eternal plant bearing seed forever, and hide not your face from the prayer of your servant, O Lord.'

[Author's note: In chapter 85 and following, a series of animals is mentioned. These seem to refer to nations or ethnicities. For example, the eagles may refer to the Roman empire, the Islamic nation is represented by the asses, Abraham may be the white bull, Jacob is a sheep, Egyptians are wolves, and so on. See Daniel Chapter 10 for other like imagery.

Other writers have attempted to be more specific. Starting with the concept of Noah's three sons, Shem, Ham and Japheth, giving rise to all the animals or nations in Chapter 89, they link the white bull to Abraham; Abraham's son, Ishmael, to the wild ass; Isaac to the white bull; Esau to the wild boar; Jacob to the white sheep; the Assyrians to lions; The small lambs with open eyes to the Essenes; Jesus to the "sheep with the big horn"; and in 90.17, the final twelve shepherds represent the Christian era.]

[Chapter 85]

1 And after this I saw another dream, and I will show the whole dream to you, my son.

2 And Enoch lifted up his voice and spoke to his son Methuselah: 'I will speak to you, my son, hear my words. Incline your ear to the dream (vision) of your father.

3 Before I married (took) your mother Edna, I saw in a vision on my bed, and behold a bull came out from the earth, and that bull was white.

4 And after it came out a heifer, and along with this later came out two bulls, one of them black and the other red.

5 And that black bull gored the red one and pursued him over the earth, and then I could no longer see that red bull. But that black bull grew and that heifer went with him, and I saw that many oxen proceeded from him which resembled and followed him.

6 And that cow, that first one, went from the presence of that first bull in order to seek that red one, but found him not, and mourned with a great lamentation and sought him.

7 And I looked until that first bull came to her and quieted (calmed) her, and from that time onward she cried no more.

8 And after that she bore another white bull, and after him she bore many bulls and black cows.

9 And I saw in my sleep that white bull likewise grew and became a great white bull, and from him proceeded many white bulls, and they resembled him. And they began to father many white bulls, which resembled them, one following another.

[Chapter 86]

1 And again I looked with my eyes as I slept, and I saw the heaven above, and behold a star fell from heaven, and it arose and ate and pastured among those oxen (bulls).

2 And after that I saw the large and the black oxen (bulls), and behold they all changed their stalls and pastures and their heifers (cattle) , and began to live with each other.

3 And again I saw in the vision, and looked towards heaven, and behold I saw many stars descend and cast themselves down from heaven to that first star, and they became bulls among those cattle and pastured with them.

4 And I looked at them and saw they all let out their private (sexual) members, like horses, and began to mount the cows of the bulls (oxen), and they all became pregnant and bore elephants, camels, and asses.

5 And all the bulls (oxen) feared them and were frightened of them, and began to bite with their teeth and to devour, and to gore with their horns.

6 And, moreover, they began to devour those oxen; and behold all the children of the earth began to tremble and shake before them and to flee from them.

[Chapter 87]

1 And again I saw how they began to gore each other and to devour each other, and the earth began to cry aloud.

2 And I raised my eyes again to heaven, and I saw in the vision, and behold there came out from heaven beings who were like white men, and four went out from that place and three others with them.

3 And those three that had come out last grasped me by my hand and took me up, away from the generations of the earth, and raised me up to a high place, and showed me a tower raised high above the earth, and all the hills were lower.

4 And one said to me: 'Remain here until you see everything that befalls those elephants, camels, and asses, and the stars and the oxen, and all of them.'

[Chapter 88]

1 And I saw one of those four who had come out first, and he seized that first star which had fallen from heaven, and bound it hand and foot and cast it into an abyss; now that abyss was narrow and deep, and horrible and dark.

2PE 2:4 For if God spared not the angels that sinned, but cast them down to hell, and delivered them into chains of darkness, to be reserved unto judgment;

2 And one of them drew a sword, and gave it to those elephants and camels and asses then they began to smite each other, and the whole earth shook because of them.

3 And as I was beholding in the vision one of those four who had come out stoned them from heaven, and gathered and took all the great stars whose private (sexual) members were like those of horses, and bound them all hand and foot, and threw them in an abyss of the earth.

[Chapter 89]

1 And one of those four went to that white bull and instructed him in a secret, and he was terrified: he was born a bull and became a man, and built for himself a great vessel and dwelt on it.

2 And three bulls dwelt with him in the vessel and they were covered over. And again I raised my eyes towards heaven and saw a high roof, with seven water torrents on it, and those torrents flowed with much water into an enclosure.

3 And I looked again, and behold fountains were opened on the surface of that great enclosure, and the water began to bubble and swell and rise on the surface, and I saw that enclosure until all its surface was covered with water.

4 And the water, the darkness, and mist increased on it; and as I looked at the height of that water, the water had risen above the height of the enclosure, and was streaming over the enclosure, and it stood on the earth.

5 And all the cattle of the enclosure were gathered together until I saw how they sank and were swallowed up and perished in that water.

6 But that vessel floated on the water, while all the oxen (bulls) and elephants and camels and asses sank to the bottom with all the animals, so that I could no longer see them, and they were not able to escape, but perished and sank into the depths.

7 And again I watched in the vision until those water torrents were removed from that high roof, and the chasms of the earth were leveled up and other abysses were opened.

8 Then the water began to run down into these abysses, until the earth became visible; but that vessel settled on the earth, and the darkness retired and light appeared.

9 But that white bull which had become a man came out of that vessel, and the three bulls with him, and one of those three was white like that bull, and one of them was red as blood, and one black; and that white bull departed from them.

10 And they began to bring out beasts of the field and birds, so that there arose different genera: lions, tigers, wolves, dogs, hyenas, wild boars, foxes, squirrels, swine, falcons, vultures, kites, eagles, and ravens; and among them was born a white bull.

11 And they began to bite one another; but that white bull which was born among them fathered a wild ass and a white bull with it, and the wild asses multiplied.

12 But that bull which was born from him fathered a black wild boar and a white sheep; and the former fathered many boars, but the sheep gave birth to twelve sheep.

13 And when those twelve sheep had grown, they gave up one of them to the asses, and the asses again gave up that sheep to the wolves, and that sheep grew up among the wolves.

14 And the Lord brought the eleven sheep to live with it and to pasture with it among the wolves and they multiplied and became many flocks of sheep.

15 And the wolves began to fear them, and they oppressed them until they destroyed their little ones, and they threw their young into a deep river, but those sheep began to cry aloud on account of their little ones, and to complain to their Lord.

16 And a sheep which had been saved from the wolves fled and escaped to the wild asses; and I saw the sheep how they lamented and cried, and besought their Lord with all their might, until that Lord of the sheep descended at the voice of the sheep from a high abode, and came to them and pastured them.

17 And He called that sheep which had escaped the wolves, and spoke with it concerning the wolves that it should admonish them not to touch the sheep.

18 And the sheep went to the wolves according to the word of the Lord, and another sheep met it and went with it, and the two went and entered together into the assembly of those wolves, and spoke with them and admonished them not to touch the sheep from then on.

19 And on it I saw the wolves, and how they more harshly oppressed the sheep with all their power; and the sheep cried aloud.

20 And the Lord came to the sheep and they began to beat those wolves, and the wolves began to make lamentation; but the sheep became quiet and ceased to cry out.

21 And I saw the sheep until they departed from among the wolves; but the eyes of the wolves were blinded, and the wolves departed in pursuit of the sheep with all their power.

22 And the Lord of the sheep went with them, as their leader, and all His sheep followed Him.

23 And his face was dazzling and glorious and terrible to behold. But the wolves began to pursue those sheep until they reached a sea of water.

24 And that sea was divided, and the water stood on this side and on that before their face, and their Lord led them and placed Himself between them and the wolves.

25 And as those wolves had not yet seen the sheep, they proceeded into the midst of that sea, and the wolves followed the sheep, and those wolves ran after them into that sea.

26 And when they saw the Lord of the sheep, they turned to flee before His face, but that sea gathered itself together, and became as it had been created, and the water swelled and rose until it covered the wolves.

27 And I watched until all the wolves who pursued those sheep perished and were drowned.

28 But the sheep escaped from that water and went out into a wilderness, where there was no water and no grass; and they began to open their eyes and to see;

29 And I saw the Lord of the sheep pasturing them and giving them water and grass, and that sheep going and leading them.

30 And the sheep ascended to the summit of that high rock, and the Lord of the sheep sent it to them. And after that I saw the Lord of the sheep who stood before them, and His appearance was great and terrible and majestic, and all those sheep saw Him and were afraid before His face.

31 And they all feared and trembled because of Him, and they cried to that sheep which was among them:

32 'We are not able to stand before our Lord or to behold Him.' And that sheep which led them again ascended to the summit of that rock, but the sheep began to be

blinded and to wander from the way which he had showed them, but that sheep did not realize it.

34 And the Lord of the sheep was very angry with them, and that sheep discovered it, and went down from the summit of the rock, and came to the sheep, and found the greatest part of them blinded and fallen away.

35 And when they saw it they feared and trembled at its presence, and desired to return to their folds. And that sheep took other sheep with it, and came to those sheep which had fallen away, and began to slay them; and the sheep feared its presence, and thus that sheep brought back those sheep that had fallen away, and they returned to their folds.

36 And I saw in this vision until that sheep became a man and built a house for the Lord of the sheep, and placed all the sheep in that house.

37 And I saw until this sheep which had met that sheep which led them fell asleep (died); and I saw until all the great sheep perished and little ones arose in their place, and they came to a pasture, and approached a stream of water.

38 Then that sheep, their leader which had become a man, withdrew from them and fell asleep (died), and all the sheep looked for it (sought it) and cried over it with a great crying.

39 And I saw until they left off crying for that sheep and crossed that stream of water, and there arose the two sheep as leaders in the place of those which had led them and fallen asleep.

40 And I saw until the sheep came to a good place, and a pleasant and glorious land, and I saw until those sheep were satisfied; and that house stood among them in the (green) pleasant land.

41 And sometimes their eyes were opened, and sometimes blinded, until another sheep arose and led them and brought them all back, and their eyes were opened.

42 And the dogs and the foxes and the wild boars began to devour those sheep until the Lord of the sheep raised up another sheep, a ram from their midst, which led them.

43 And that ram began to butt on either side those dogs, foxes, and wild boars until he had destroyed them all.

44 And that sheep whose eyes were opened saw that ram, which was among the sheep, until it forsook its glory and began to butt those sheep, and trampled on them, and behaved itself unseemly.

45 And the Lord of the sheep sent the lamb to another lamb and raised it to being a ram and leader of the sheep instead of that ram which had forsaken its glory.

46 And it went to it and spoke to it alone, and raised it to being a ram, and made it the prince and leader of the sheep; but during all these things those dogs oppressed the sheep.

47 And the first ram pursued the second ram, and the second ram arose and fled before it; and I saw until those dogs pulled down the first ram.

48 And that second ram arose and led the little sheep. And those sheep grew and multiplied; but all the dogs, and foxes, and wild boars feared and fled before it, and that ram butted and killed the wild beasts, and those wild beasts had no longer any power among the sheep and robbed them no more of anything.

49 And that ram fathered many sheep and fell asleep; and a little sheep became ram in its place, and became prince and leader of those sheep.

50 And that house became great and broad, and it was built for those sheep: and a high and great tower was built on the house for the Lord of the sheep, and that house was low, but the tower was elevated and high, and the Lord of the sheep stood on that tower and they offered a full table before him.

51 And again I saw those sheep that they again erred and went many ways, and forsook that their house, and the Lord of the sheep called some from among the sheep and sent them to the sheep, but the sheep began to slay them.

52 And one of them was saved and was not slain, and it sped away and cried aloud over the sheep; and they sought to slay it, but the Lord of the sheep saved it from the sheep, and brought it up to me, and caused it to live there.

53 And many other sheep He sent to those sheep to testify to them and lament over them.

54 And after that I saw that when they forsook the house of the Lord and His tower they fell away entirely, and their eyes were blinded; and I saw the Lord of the sheep how He worked much slaughter among them in their herds until those sheep invited that slaughter and betrayed His place.

55 And He gave them over into the hands of the lions and tigers, and wolves and hyenas, and into the hand of the foxes, and to all the wild beasts, and those wild beasts began to tear in pieces those sheep.

56 And I saw that He forsook their house and their tower and gave them all into the hand of the lions, to tear and devour them, into the hand of all the wild beasts.

57 And I began to cry aloud with all my power, and to appeal to the Lord of the sheep, because the sheep were being devoured by all the wild beasts.

58 But He remained unmoved, though He saw it, and rejoiced that they were devoured and swallowed and robbed, and left them to be devoured in the hand of all the beasts.

59 And He called seventy shepherds, and gave those sheep to them that they might pasture them, and He spoke to the shepherds and their companions: 'Let each individual of you pasture the sheep from now on, and everything that I shall command you that do you.

60 And I will deliver them over to you duly numbered, and tell you which of them are to be destroyed-and them you will destroy.' And He gave over to them those sheep.

61 And He called another and spoke to him: 'Observe and mark everything that the shepherds will do to those sheep; for they will destroy more of them than I have commanded them.

62 And every excess and the destruction which will be done through the shepherds, record how many they destroy according to my command, and how many according to their own caprice; record against every individual shepherd all the destruction he effects.

63 And read out before me by number how many they destroy, and how many they deliver over for destruction, that I may have this as a testimony against them, and know every deed of the shepherds, that I may comprehend and see what they do, whether or not they abide by my command which I have commanded them.

64 But they shall not know it, and you shall not declare it to them, nor admonish them, but only record against each individual all the destruction which the shepherds effect each in his time and lay it all before me.'

65 And I saw until those shepherds pastured in their season, and they began to slay and to destroy more than they were bidden, and they delivered those sheep into the hand of the lions.

66 And the lions and tigers ate and devoured the greater part of those sheep, and the wild boars ate along with them; and they burned that tower and demolished that house.

67 And I became very sorrowful over that tower because that house of the sheep was demolished, and afterwards I was unable to see if those sheep entered that house.

68 And the shepherds and their associates delivered over those sheep to all the wild beasts, to devour them, and each one of them received in his time a definite number, it was written by the other in a book how many each one of them destroyed of them.

69 And each one slew and destroyed many more than was prescribed; and I began to weep and lament on account of those sheep.

70 And thus in the vision I saw that one who wrote, how he wrote down every one that was destroyed by those shepherds, day by day, and carried up and laid down and showed actually the whole book to the Lord of the sheep - everything that they

had done, and all that each one of them had made away with, and all that they had given over to destruction.

71 And the book was read before the Lord of the sheep, and He took the book from his hand and read it and sealed it and laid it down.

72 And I saw how the shepherds pastured for twelve hours, and behold three of those sheep turned back and came and entered and began to build up all that had fallen down of that house; but the wild boars tried to hinder them, but they were not able.

73 And they began again to build as before, and they raised up that tower, and it was named the high tower; and they began again to place a table before the tower, but all the bread on it was polluted and not pure.

74 And as touching all this the eyes of those sheep were blinded so that they saw not, and the eyes of their shepherds likewise were blinded; and they delivered them in large numbers to their shepherds for destruction, and they trampled the sheep with their feet and devoured them.

75 And the Lord of the sheep remained unmoved until all the sheep were dispersed over the field and mingled with the beasts, and the shepherds did not save them out of the hand of the beasts.

76 And this one who wrote the book carried it up, and showed it and read it before the Lord of the sheep, and implored Him on their account, and besought Him on their account as he showed Him all the doings of the shepherds, and gave testimony before Him against all the shepherds.

77 And he took the actual book and laid it down beside Him and departed.

[Chapter 90]

1 And I saw until that in this manner thirty-five shepherds undertook the pasturing of the sheep, and they completed their periods as did the first; and others received them into their hands, to pasture them for their period, each shepherd in his own period.

2 And after that I saw in my vision all the birds of heaven coming, the eagles, the vultures, the kites, the ravens; but the eagles led all the birds; and they began to devour those sheep, and to pick out their eyes and to devour their flesh.

3 And the sheep cried out because their flesh was being devoured by the birds, and as for me I looked and lamented in my sleep over that shepherd who pastured the sheep.

4 And I saw until those sheep were devoured by the dogs and eagles and kites, and they left neither flesh nor skin nor sinew remaining on them until only their bones stood there; and their bones too fell to the earth and the sheep became few.

5 And I saw until that twenty-three had undertaken the pasturing and completed in their many periods fifty-eight times.

6 But behold lambs were borne by those white sheep, and they began to open their eyes and to see, and to cry to the sheep.

7 They cried to them, but they did not hearken to what they said to them, but were very deaf, and their eyes were very blinded.

8 And I saw in the vision how the ravens flew on those lambs and took one of those lambs, and dashed the sheep in pieces and devoured them.

9 And I saw until horns grew on those lambs, and the ravens cast down their horns; and I saw until there sprouted a great horn of one of those sheep, and their eyes were opened.

10 And it looked at them and their eyes opened, and it cried to the sheep, and the rams saw it and all ran to it.

11 And notwithstanding all this, those eagles and vultures and ravens and kites kept on tearing the sheep and swooping down on them and devouring them until the sheep remained silent, but the rams lamented and cried out.

12 And those ravens fought and battled with it and sought to lay low its horn, but they had no power over it.

13 All the eagles and vultures and ravens and kites were gathered together, and there came with them all the sheep of the field, they all came together, and helped each other to break that horn of the ram.

14 And I saw that man, who wrote down the names of the shepherds and brought them up before the Lord of the sheep, came, and he helped that ram and showed it everything; its help was coming down.

15 And I looked until that Lord of the sheep came to them angry, all those who saw him ran, and they all fell into the shadow in front of Him.

16 All the eagles and vultures and ravens and kites, gathered together and brought with them all the wild sheep, and they all came together and helped one another in order to dash that horn of the ram in pieces.

17 And I looked at that man, who wrote the book at the command of the Lord, until he opened that book of the destruction that those last twelve shepherds had done. And he showed, in front of the Lord of the sheep, that they had destroyed even more than those before them had.

18 And I looked and the Lord of the sheep came to them and took the Staff of His Anger and struck the Earth. And the Earth was split. And all the animals, and the birds of the sky, fell from those sheep and sank in the earth, and it closed over them.

19 And I saw until a great sword was given to the sheep, and the sheep proceeded against all the beasts of the field to slay them, and all the beasts and the birds of the heaven fled before their face. And I saw that man, who wrote the book according to the command of the Lord, until he opened that book concerning the destruction which those twelve last shepherds had wrought, and showed that they had destroyed much more than their predecessors, before the Lord of the sheep. And I saw until the Lord of the sheep came to them and took in His hand the staff of His wrath, and smote the earth, and the earth clave asunder, and all the beasts and all the birds of heaven fell from among those sheep, and were swallowed up in the earth and it covered them.

20 And I saw until a throne was erected in the pleasant land, and the Lord of the sheep sat Himself on it, and the other took the sealed books and opened those books before the Lord of the sheep.

21 And the Lord called those men, the seven first white ones, and commanded that they should bring before Him, beginning with the first star which led the way, all the stars whose private members were like those of horses, and they brought them all before Him.

22 And He said to that man who wrote before Him, being one of those seven white ones, and said to him: 'Take those seventy shepherds to whom I delivered the sheep, and who taking them on their own authority slew more than I commanded them.'

23 And behold they were all bound, I saw, and they all stood before Him.

24 And the judgment was held first over the stars, and they were judged and found guilty, and went to the place of condemnation, and they were cast into an abyss, full of fire and flaming, and full of pillars of fire.

25 And those seventy shepherds were judged and found guilty, and they were cast into that fiery abyss.

26 And I saw at that time how a like abyss was opened in the midst of the earth, full of fire, and they brought those blinded sheep, and they were all judged and found guilty and cast into this fiery abyss, and they burned; now this abyss was to the right of that house.

27 And I saw those sheep burning and their bones burning.

28 And I stood up to see until they folded up that old house; and carried off all the pillars, and all the beams and ornaments of the house were at the same time folded up with it, and they carried it off and laid it in a place in the south of the land.

29 And I saw until the Lord of the sheep brought a new house greater and loftier than that first, and set it up in the place of the first which had been folded up; all its pillars were new, and its ornaments were new and larger than those of the first, the old one which He had taken away, and all the sheep were within it.

HEB 13:14 For here have we no continuing city, but we seek one to come.

30 And I saw all the sheep which had been left, and all the beasts on the earth, and all the birds of heaven, falling down and doing homage to those sheep and making petition to and obeying them in every thing.

31 And thereafter those three who were clothed in white and had seized me by my hand [who had taken me up before], and the hand of that ram also seizing hold of me, they took me up and set me down in the midst of those sheep before the judgment took place.

32 And those sheep were all white, and their wool was abundant and clean.

33 And all that had been destroyed and dispersed, and all the beasts of the field, and all the birds of heaven, assembled in that house, and the Lord of the sheep rejoiced with great joy because they were all good and had returned to His house.

34 And I saw until they laid down that sword, which had been given to the sheep, and they brought it back into the house, and it was sealed before the presence of the Lord, and all the sheep were invited into that house, but it held them not.

35 And the eyes of them all were opened, and they saw the good, and there was not one among them that did not see.

36 And I saw that the house was large and broad and very full.

37 And I saw that a white bull was born, with large horns and all the beasts of the field and all the birds of the air feared him and made petition to him all the time.

38 And I saw until all their generations were transformed, and they all became white bulls; and the first among them became a lamb, and that lamb became a great animal and had great black horns on its head; and the Lord of the sheep rejoiced over it and over all the oxen.

39 And I slept in their midst: And I awoke and saw everything.

40 This is the vision which I saw while I slept, and I awoke and blessed the Lord of righteousness and gave Him glory.

41 Then I wept greatly and my tears ceased not until I could no longer endure it; when I saw, they flowed on account of what I had seen; for everything shall come and be fulfilled, and all the deeds of men in their order were shown to me.

42 On that night I remembered the first dream, and because of it I wept and was troubled--because I had seen that vision.

[Author's note: As this section was interpreted from a Jewish point of reference, many have assumed the 'large horn' was Judas Maccabee. In the Christian frame of reference, the same symbol was Jesus Christ.]

[Author's note: At this point, the time frame and text flow becomes non sequitur. It appears the codex was not kept in sequence here. Thus, the translated pages are out of sequence. The flow of time and occurrences seems to follow the pattern listed:

91:6 to 92.1 through 92:5 then jumps to 93:1. The flow then continues from 93:1 to 93:10 and then jumps to 91:7. From 91:7 the text continues to 91:19. It then picks up again at 93:11 and continues.

If one were to attempt to put this section into a time line, the interval would link together in some fashion resembling the following:

Ten Weeks of Judgment

WEEK 1	Judgment & righteousness 93.3 Enoch's time Antediluvian
WEEK 2	Judgment & cleansing 93.4 Noah's time and the great flood
WEEK 3	Righteousness is planted 93.5 Abraham's time
WEEK 4	Law for all generations 93.6 Moses' time
WEEK 5	House of Glory 93.7 Solomon's time
WEEK 6	Jesus ascends, temple burned, elect scattered 93.8 Jesus' time
WEEK 7	Apostate generation Judgment of Fire 93.9 - 91.11 Our time
WEEK 8	A sword 91.12–13 New house, new heaven & earth Future time
WEEK 9	The righteous judgment revealed 91.14 The judgment time
WEEK 10	God's power is forever 91.15-16 Eternal time

When reading the text from this point to the end of chapter 93 one should keep this flow in mind.]

[Chapter 91]

1 And now, my son Methuselah, call to me all your brothers and gather together to me all the sons of your mother; for the word calls me, and the spirit is poured out on me, that I may show you everything that shall befall you for ever.'

2 And thereon Methuselah went and summoned to him all his brothers and assembled his relatives.

3 And he spoke to all the children of righteousness and said: 'Hear, you sons of Enoch, all the words of your father, and hearken, as you should, to the voice of my mouth; for I exhort you and say to you, beloved:

4 Love righteousness and walk in it, and draw near to righteousness without a double heart, and do not associate with those of a double heart, but walk in righteousness, my sons. And it shall guide you on good paths. And righteousness shall be your companion.'

JAM 1:6 But let him ask in faith, nothing wavering. For he that wavereth is like a wave of the sea driven with the wind and tossed. 7 For let not that man think that he shall receive any thing of the Lord. 8 A double minded man is unstable in all his ways.

5 'For I know that violence must increase on the earth, and a great punishment will be executed on the earth, it shall be cut off from its roots, and its whole construct will be destroyed.

6 And unrighteousness shall again be complete on the earth, and all the deeds of unrighteousness and of violence and sin shall prevail a second time.

7 And when sin and unrighteousness and blasphemy and violence in all kinds of deeds increase, and apostasy and transgression and uncleanness increase; a great chastisement shall come from heaven on all these, and the holy Lord will come out with wrath and chastisement to execute judgment on earth.

2TH 2:3 Let no man deceive you by any means: for that day shall not come, except there come a falling away first, and that man of sin be revealed, the son of perdition.

8 In those days violence shall be cut off from its roots, and the roots of unrighteousness together with deceit, and they shall be destroyed from under heaven.

9 And all the idols of the heathen shall be abandoned. And the temples burned with fire, and they shall remove them from the whole earth; and the heathen shall be cast into the judgment of fire, and shall perish in wrath and in grievous judgment for ever.

10 And the righteous shall arise from their sleep, and wisdom shall arise and be given to them.

11 And after that the roots of unrighteousness and those who plan violence and those who commit blasphemy shall be cut off, and the sinners shall be destroyed by the sword.

12 And after this there will be another week; the eighth, that of righteousness, and a sword will be given to it so that the Righteous Judgment may be executed on those who do wrong, and the sinners will be handed over into the hands of the righteous.

13 And, at its end, they will acquire Houses because of their righteousness, and a House will be built for the Great King in Glory, forever.

14 And after this, in the ninth week, the Righteous Judgment will be revealed to the whole world. And all the deeds of the impious will vanish from the whole Earth.

And the world will be written down for destruction and all men will look to the Path of Uprightness.

15 And, after this, in the tenth week, in the seventh part, there will be an Eternal Judgment that will be executed on the Watchers and the Great Eternal Heaven that will spring from the midst of the Angels.

16 And the First Heaven will vanish and pass away and a New Heaven will appear, and all the Powers of Heaven will shine forever, with light seven times as bright.

17 And after this, there will be many weeks without number, forever, in goodness and in righteousness. And from then on sin will never again be mentioned.

18 And now I tell you, my sons, and show you, the paths of righteousness and the paths of violence. I will show them to you again that you may know what will come to pass.

19 And now, hearken to me, my sons, and walk in the paths of righteousness, and walk not in the paths of violence; for all who walk in the paths of unrighteousness shall perish for ever.'

[Chapter 92]

1 The book written by Enoch {Enoch indeed wrote this complete doctrine of wisdom, (which is) praised of all men and a judge of all the earth} for all my children who shall live on the earth. And for the future generations who shall observe righteousness and peace.

2 Let not your spirit be troubled on account of the times; for the Holy and Great One has appointed days for all things.

3 And the righteous one shall arise from sleep, [Shall arise] and walk in the paths of righteousness, and all his path and conversation shall be in eternal goodness and grace.

4 He will be gracious to the righteous and give him eternal righteousness, and He will give him power so that he shall be (endowed) with goodness and righteousness. And he shall walk in eternal light.

5 And sin shall perish in darkness for ever, and shall no more be seen from that day for evermore.

[Chapter 93]

(Author's Note: Chapters 91 - 93 recount and expand on the events listed in the following weeks of prophecy. The explanation of the event are scattered in chapters 91 - 93, however, the list of events are stated clearly in the following list of weeks in chapter 93).

1 And after that Enoch both gave and began to recount from the books. And Enoch said:

2 'Concerning the children of righteousness and concerning the elect of the world, and concerning the plant of righteousness, I will speak these things. I Enoch will declare (them) to you, my sons, according to that which appeared to me in heavenly vision, and which I have known through the word of the holy angels, and have learned from heavenly tablets.'

3 And Enoch began to recount from the books and said: 'I was born the seventh in the first week, able judgment and righteousness still endured.

4 And after me there shall arise in the second week great wickedness, and deceit shall have sprung up; and in it there shall be the first end.

5 And in it a man shall be saved; and after it is ended unrighteousness shall grow up, and a law shall be made for the sinners. And after that in the third week at its close a man shall be elected as the plant of righteous judgment, and his posterity shall become the plant of righteousness for evermore.

6 And after that in the fourth week, at its close, visions of the holy and righteous shall be seen, and a law for all generations and an enclosure shall be made for them.

7 And after that in the fifth week, at its close, the house of glory and dominion shall be built for ever.

8 And after that in the sixth week, all who live in it shall be blinded, and the hearts of all of them shall godlessly forsake wisdom. And in it a man shall ascend; and at its close the house of dominion shall be burned with fire, and the whole race of the chosen root shall be dispersed.

9 And after that in the seventh week shall an apostate generation arise, and many shall be its deeds, and all its deeds shall be apostate.

10 And at its end shall be elected, the elect righteous of the eternal plant of righteousness shall be chosen to receive sevenfold instruction concerning all His creation.

11 For who is there of all the children of men that is able to hear the voice of the Holy One without being troubled? And who can think His thoughts? Who is there that can behold all the works of heaven?

12 And how should there be one who could behold heaven, and who is there that could understand the things of heaven and see a soul or a spirit and could tell of it, or ascend and see all their ends and think them or do like them?

13 And who is there of all men that could know what is the breadth and the length of the earth, and to whom has the measurement been shown of all of them?

14 Or is there any one who could discern the length of the heaven and how great is its height, and on what it is founded, and how great is the number of the stars, and where all the luminaries rest?

[Chapter 94]

1 And now I say to you, my sons, love righteousness and walk in it; because the paths of righteousness are worthy of acceptation, but the paths of unrighteousness shall suddenly be destroyed and vanish.

2 And to certain men of a generation shall the paths of violence and of death be revealed, and they shall hold themselves afar from them, and shall not follow them.

3 And now I say to you, the righteous, walk not in the paths of wickedness, nor in the paths of death, and draw not near to them, lest you be destroyed.

4 But seek and choose for yourselves righteousness and an elect life, and walk in the paths of peace, and you shall live and prosper.

5 And hold (keep) my words in the thoughts of your hearts, and permit them not to be erased from your hearts; for I know that sinners will tempt men to evilly entreat wisdom, so that no place may be found for her, and temptation will increase.

6 Woe to those who build unrighteousness and oppression and lay deceit as a foundation; for they shall be suddenly overthrown, and they shall have no peace.

7 Woe to those who build their houses with sin; for from all their foundations shall they be overthrown, and by the sword shall they fall. And those who acquire gold and silver shall suddenly perish in the judgment.

8 Woe to you, you rich, for you have trusted in your riches, and from your riches shall you depart, because you have not remembered the Most High in the days of your riches.

9 You have committed blasphemy and unrighteousness, and have become ready for the day of slaughter, and the day of darkness and the day of the great judgment.

10 Thus I speak and tell you: He who hath created you will overthrow you, and for your fall there shall be no compassion, and your Creator will rejoice at your destruction.

11 And your righteousness shall be a reproach to the sinners and the godless in those days.

JAM 5:1 Go to now, ye rich men, weep and howl for your miseries that shall come upon you. 2 Your riches are corrupted, and your garments are moth-eaten. 3 Your gold and silver is cankered; and the rust of them shall be a witness against you, and shall eat your flesh as it were fire. Ye have heaped treasure together for the last days. 4 Behold, the hire of the labourers who have reaped down your fields, which is of you kept back by fraud, crieth: and the cries of them which have reaped are entered into the ears of the Lord of sabaoth. 5 Ye have lived in pleasure on the earth, and been wanton; ye have nourished your hearts, as in a day of slaughter. 6 Ye have condemned and killed the just; and he doth not resist you.

(Author's note: In the above biblical verses from James, "sabaoth" is from the Hebrew, plural form of "host" or "army". The word is used almost exclusively in conjunction with the Divine name as a title of majesty: "the Lord of Hosts", or "the Lord God of Hosts".)

[Chapter 95]

1 Would that my eyes were rain clouds of water that I might weep over you, and pour down my tears as a cloud of water, that I might rest from my trouble of heart!

2 Who has permitted you to practice reproaches and wickedness? And so judgment shall overtake you, sinners.

3 You, righteous! Fear not the sinners, for again the Lord will deliver them into your hands, that you may execute judgment on them according to your desires.

4 Woe to you who speak against God (fulminate anathemas) which cannot be removed (reversed) - healing shall be far from you because of your sins.

5 Woe to you who repay your neighbor with evil; for you shall be repaid according to your works.

6 Woe to you, lying witnesses, and to those who weigh out injustice, for you shall suddenly perish.

7 Woe to you, sinners, for you persecute the righteous; for you shall be delivered up and persecuted because of injustice, and your yoke shall be heavy on you.

[Chapter 96]

1 Be hopeful, you righteous; for suddenly shall the sinners perish before you, and you shall have lordship over them, according to your desires.

2 And in the day of the tribulation of the sinners, your children shall mount and rise as eagles, and your nests shall be higher than the vultures'. You shall ascend as badgers and enter the crevices of the earth, and the clefts of the rock for ever before the unrighteous. And the satyrs (sirens) shall sigh and weep because of you.

3 Wherefore fear not, you that have suffered, for healing shall be your portion, and a bright light shall enlighten you, and the voice of rest you shall hear from heaven.

4 Woe to you, you sinners, for your riches make you appear like the righteous, but your hearts convict you of being sinners, and this fact shall be a testimony against you for a memorial of your evil deeds.

5 Woe to you who devour the finest of the wheat, and drink wine in large bowls (the best of waters), and tread under foot the lowly (humble) with your might.

6 Woe to you who drink water from every fountain (drink water all the time), for suddenly shall you be consumed and wither away, because you have forsaken the fountain of life.

(Author's note: The above reference is a euphemism for promiscuity.)

7 Woe to you who work unrighteousness and deceit and blasphemy; it shall be a memorial against you for evil.

8 Woe to you, you mighty, who with might oppress the righteous; for the day of your destruction is coming. Many and good days shall come to the righteous in those days - in the day of your judgment.

[Chapter 97]

1 Believe, you righteous, that the sinners will become a shame and perish in the day of unrighteousness.

2 Be it known to you, you sinners, that the Most High is mindful of your destruction, and the angels of heaven rejoice over your destruction.

3 What will you do, you sinners, and where shall you flee on that day of judgment, when you hear the voice of the prayer of the righteous?

4 You shall fare like to them, against whom these words shall be a testimony: "You have been companions of sinners."

5 And in those days the prayer of the righteous shall reach to the Lord, and for you the days of your judgment shall come.

6 And all the words of your unrighteousness shall be read out before the Great Holy One, and your faces shall be covered with shame, and He will reject every work which is grounded on unrighteousness.

7 Woe to you, you sinners, who live on the middle of the ocean and on the dry land, whose remembrance is evil against you.

8 Woe to you who acquire silver and gold in unrighteousness and say: "We have become rich with riches and have possessions; and have acquired everything we have desired.

9 And now let us do what we purposed, for we have gathered silver, and many are the servants in our houses and our granaries are full to the brim as if with water."

10 Yea, and like water your lies shall flow away; for your riches shall not abide but quickly depart (go up) from you, for you have acquired it all in unrighteousness, and you shall be given over to a great curse.

[Chapter 98]

1 And now I swear to you, to the wise and to the foolish, that you shall see (have) many experiences on the earth.

2 For you men shall put on more adornments than a woman, and colored garments more than a young woman, like royalty and in grandeur and in power, and in silver and in gold and in purple, and in splendor and in food they shall be poured out as water.

3 Therefore they shall have neither knowledge nor wisdom, and because of this they shall die together with their possessions; and with all their glory and their splendor, and in shame and in slaughter and in great destitution, their spirits shall be thrown into the furnace of fire.

4 I have sworn to you, you sinners, as a mountain has not become a slave, and a hill does not become the servant of a woman, even so sin has not been sent on the earth, but man of himself has created it, and they that commit it shall fall under a great curse.

5 And barrenness has not been given to the woman, but on account of the deeds of her own hands she dies without children.

6 I have sworn to you, you sinners, by the Holy Great One, that all your evil deeds are revealed in heaven, and that none of your wrong deeds (of oppression) are covered and hidden.

7 And do not think in your spirit nor say in your heart that you do not know and that you do not see that every sin is recorded every day in heaven in the presence of the Most High.

8 From now on, you know that all your wrongdoing that you do will be written down every day, until the day of your judgment.

9 Woe to you, you fools, for through your folly you shall perish; and you do not listen to the wise so no good will come to you against the wise,

10 And so and now, know you that you are prepared for the day of destruction. Therefore do not hope to live, you sinners, but you shall depart and die; for there will be no ransom for you; because you are prepared for the day of the great judgment, for the day of tribulation and great shame for your spirits.

11 Woe to you, you obstinate of heart, who work wickedness and eat blood. Where do you have good things to eat and to drink and to be filled? From all the good things which the Lord the Most High has placed in abundance on the earth; therefore you shall have no peace.

(Author's note: The above reference to eating blood may indicate cannibalism.)

GEN 9:3 Every moving thing that liveth shall be meat for you; even as the green herb have I given you all things. 4 But flesh with the life thereof, which is the blood thereof, shall ye not eat. 5 And surely your blood of your lives will I require; at the hand of every beast will I require it, and at the hand of man; at the hand of every man's brother will I require the life of man. 6 Whoso sheddeth man's blood, by man shall his blood be shed: for in the image of God made he man.

12 Woe to you who love the deeds of unrighteousness; wherefore do you hope for good for yourselves? You know that you shall be delivered into the hands of the righteous, and they shall cut off your necks and slay you, and have no mercy on you.

13 Woe to you who rejoice in the distress of the righteous; for no grave shall be dug for you.

14 Woe to you who say the words of the wise are empty; for you shall have no hope of life.

15 Woe to you who write down lying and godless words; for they write down their lies so that men may hear them and act godlessly towards their neighbor. Therefore they shall have no peace but die a sudden death.

[Chapter 99]

1 Woe to you who do godless acts, and praise and honor lies; you shall perish, and no happy life shall be yours.

2 Woe to them who pervert the words of righteousness, and transgress the eternal law, and count themselves as sinless. They shall be trodden under foot on the earth.

3 In those days make ready, you righteous, to raise your prayers as a memorial, and place them as a testimony before the angels, that they may place the sin of the sinners for a reminder before the Most High.

4 In those days the nations shall be stirred up, and the families of the nations shall arise on the day of destruction.

5 And in those days the destitute shall go and throw their children out, and they shall abandon them, so that their children shall perish because of them. They shall abandon their children that are still babies (sucklings), and not return to them, and shall have no pity on their loved ones.

6 Again, I swear to you, you sinners, that sin is prepared for a day of unceasing bloodshed.

MAT 24:6 And ye shall hear of wars and rumours of wars: see that ye be not troubled: for all these things must come to pass, but the end is not yet. 7 For nation shall rise against nation, and kingdom against kingdom: and there shall be famines, and pestilences, and earthquakes, in diverse places. 8 All these are the beginning of sorrows.

7 And they who worship stones, and carved images of gold and silver and wood and stone and clay, and those who worship impure spirits and demons, and all kinds of idols not according to knowledge, shall get no manner of help from them.

8 And they shall become godless by reason of the folly of their hearts, and their eyes shall be blinded through the fear of their hearts and through visions in their ambitions (dreams).

9 Through these they shall become godless and fearful; for they shall have done all their work with lies, and shall have worshiped a stone, therefore in an instant shall they perish.

10 But in those days blessed are all they who accept the words of wisdom, and understand them, and observe the paths of the Most High, and walk in the path of His righteousness, and become not godless with the godless, for they shall be saved.

11 Woe to you who spread evil to your neighbors, for you shall be slain in Hell.

12 Woe to you who make your foundation that of deceitful (sin) and lies, and who cause bitterness on the earth; for they shall thereby be utterly consumed.

13 Woe to you who build your houses through the hard labor of others, and all their building materials are the bricks and stones of sin; I tell you, you shall have no peace.

14 Woe to them who reject the measure and eternal inheritance of their fathers and whose souls follow after idols; for they shall have no rest.

15 Woe to them who do unrighteous acts and help oppression, and kill their neighbors until the day of the great judgment, for He will throw down your glory.

16 For He shall throw down your glory, and bring affliction on your hearts, and shall arouse His fierce anger, and destroy you all with the sword; and all the holy and righteous shall remember your sins.

[Chapter 100]

1 And in those days in one place the fathers together with their sons shall kill one another and brothers shall fall in death together until the streams flow with their blood.

2 For a man shall not withhold his hand from killing his sons and his sons' sons, and the sinner shall not withhold his hand from his honored brother, from dawn until sunset they shall kill one another.

MAR 13:12 Now the brother shall betray the brother to death, and the father the son; and children shall rise up against their parents, and shall cause them to be put to death.

3 And the horse shall walk up to the breast in the blood of sinners, and the chariot shall be submerged to its height.

REV 14:20 And the winepress was trodden without the city, and blood came out of the winepress, even unto the horse bridles, by the space of a thousand and six hundred furlongs.

4 In those days the angels shall descend into the secret places and gather together into one place all those who brought down sin and the Most High will arise on that day of judgment to execute great judgment among sinners.

5 And over all the righteous and holy He will appoint guardians from among the holy angels to guard them as the apple of an eye, until He makes an end of all wickedness and all sin, and even if the righteous sleep a long sleep, they have nothing to fear.

6 And the wise men will seek the truth and they and their sons will understand the words of this book, and recognize that their riches shall not be able to save them or overcome their sins.

7 Woe to you sinners, on the day of strong anguish, you who afflict the righteous and burn them with fire; you shall be requited according to your works.

8 Woe to you, you obstinate of heart, who watch in order to devise wickedness; therefore shall fear come on you and there shall be none to help you.

9 Woe to you, you sinners, on account of the words of your mouth, and on account of the deeds of your hands which your godlessness has caused, in blazing flames burning worse than fire shall you burn.

2TH 1:7 And to you who are troubled rest with us, when the Lord Jesus shall be revealed from heaven with his mighty angels, 8 In flaming fire taking vengeance on them that know not God, and that obey not the gospel of our Lord Jesus Christ: 9 Who shall be punished with everlasting destruction from the presence of the Lord, and from the glory of his power?

10 And now, know that the angels will ask Him in heaven about your deeds and from the sun and from the moon and from the stars they will ask about your sins because on the earth you execute judgment on the righteous.

11 And He will summon to testify against you every cloud and mist and dew and rain; for they shall all be withheld from falling on you, and they shall be mindful of your sins.

12 And now give gifts to the rain that it cease not from falling on you, nor the dew, when it has received gold and silver from you that it may fall. When the hoar-frost and snow with their chilliness, and all the snow storms with all their plagues fall on you, in those days you shall not be able to stand before them.

[Chapter 101]

1 Observe heaven, you children of heaven, and every work of the Most High, and fear Him and work no evil in His presence.

2 If He closes the windows of heaven, and withholds the rain and the dew from falling on the earth on your account, what will you do then?

3 And if He sends His anger on you because of your deeds, you cannot petition Him; for you spoke proud and arrogant words against His righteousness, therefore you shall have no peace.

4 Don't you see the sailors of the ships, how their ships are tossed back and forth by the waves, and are shaken by the winds, and are in great trouble?

5 And therefore they are afraid because all their nice possessions go on the sea with them, and they have bad feelings in their heart that the sea will swallow them and they will perish therein.

6 Are not the entire sea and all its waters, and all its movements, the work of the Most High, and has He not set limits to its actions, and confined it throughout by the sand?

7 And at His reproof it fears and dries up, and all its fish die and all that is in it; but you sinners that are on the earth fear Him not.

8 Has He not made heaven and the earth, and all that is in it? Who has given understanding and wisdom to everything that moves on the earth and in the sea?

9 Do not the sailors of the ships fear the sea? Yet you sinners do not fear the Most High.

[Chapter 102]

1 In those days if He sent a horrible fire on you, where will you flee, and where will you find deliverance? And when He launches out His Word against you will you not be shaken and afraid?

2 And all the luminaries shall be shaken with great fear, and all the earth shall be afraid and tremble and be alarmed.

3 And all the angels shall execute their commands and shall seek to hide themselves from the presence of He who is Great in Glory, and the children of earth shall tremble and shake; and you sinners shall be cursed for ever, and you shall have no peace.

4 Fear you not, you souls of the righteous, and fear not you who have died in righteousness.

5 And don't grieve if your soul has descended in to the grave in grief, and that in your life you were not rewarded according to your goodness, but wait for the day of the judgment of sinners and for the day of cursing and chastisement.

6 And when you die the sinners will say about you: "As we die, so die the righteous, and what benefit do they reap for their deeds?

7 See, even as we, so do they die in grief and darkness, and what have they more than we? From now on we are equal.

8 And what will they receive and what will they see for ever? Look, they too have died, and from now on for ever shall they see no light."

9 I tell you, you sinners, you are content to eat and drink, and rob and sin, and strip men naked, and acquire wealth and see good days.

10 Have you seen the righteous how their end was peace, that no violence is found in them until their death?

11 Nevertheless they died and became as though they had not been, and their spirits descended into Hell in tribulation.

[Chapter 103]

1 Now, therefore, I swear to the righteous, by the glory of the Great and Honored and Mighty One who reigns, I swear to you, I know this mystery.

2 I have read the heavenly tablets, and have seen the holy books, and have found written in it and inscribed regarding them.

3 That all goodness and joy and glory are prepared for them, and written down for the spirits of those who have died in righteousness, and that much good shall be given to you in reward for your labors, and that your lot is abundant beyond the lot of the living.

4 And the spirits of you who have died in righteousness shall live and rejoice, and your spirits shall not perish, nor shall your memory from before the face of the Great One to all the generations of the world, therefore no longer fear their abuse.

5 Woe to you, you sinners, when you have died, if you die in the abundance of your sins, and woe to those who are like you and say regarding you: "Blessed are the sinners, they have seen all their days.

6 And how they have died in prosperity and in wealth, and have not seen tribulation or murder in their life; and they have died in honor, and judgment has not been executed on them during their life."

7 You know that their souls will be made to descend into Hell and they shall be wracked in great tribulation.

8 And into darkness and chains and a burning flame where there is harsh judgment your spirits shall enter, and the great judgment shall be for all the generations of the world. Woe to you, for you shall have no peace.

9 The righteous and good who are alive, do not say: "In our troubled days we have worked hard and experienced every trouble, and met with much evil and been afflicted, and have become few and our spirit small.

10 And we have been destroyed and have not found any to help us even with a word. We have been tortured and destroyed, and not expect to live from day to day.

11 We hoped to be the head and have become the tail. We have worked hard and had no satisfaction in our labor; and we have become the food of the sinners and the unrighteous, and they have laid their yoke heavily on us.

12 They have ruled over us and hated us and hit us, and to those that hated us we have bowed our necks but they pitied us not.

13 We desired to get away from them that we might escape and be at rest, but found no place where we should flee and be safe from them.

14 We complained to the rulers in our tribulation, and cried out against those who devoured us, but they did not pay attention to our cries and would not listen to our voice.

15 And they helped those who robbed us and devoured us and those who made us few; and they concealed their oppression (wrongdoing), and they did not remove from us the yoke of those that devoured us and dispersed us and murdered us, and they concealed their murder, and did not remember that they had lifted up their hands against us."

[Chapter 104]

1 I swear to you, that in heaven the angels remember you for good before the glory of the Great One.

2 And your names are written before the glory of the Great One. Be hopeful; for before you were put to shame through sickness and affliction; but now you shall shine as the lights of heaven,

3 You shall shine and you shall be seen, and the doors of heaven shall be opened to you. And in your cry, cry for judgment, and it shall appear to you; for all your tribulation shall be visited on the rulers, and on all who helped those who plundered you.

4 Be hopeful, and do not throw away your hopes for you shall have great joy as the angels of heaven.

5 What will you have to do? You shall not have to hide on the day of the great judgment and you shall not be found as sinners, and the eternal judgment shall not come to you for all the generations, eternally.

6 And now fear not, you righteous, when you see the sinners growing strong and prospering in their ways; do not be their companions, but keep away from their violence.

7 For you shall become companions of the hosts of heaven. And, although you sinners say: "All our sins shall not be found out and be written down," nevertheless they shall write down all your sins every day.

8 And now I show to you that light and darkness, day and night, see all your sins.

9 Do not be godless in your hearts, and do not lie and do not change the words of righteousness, nor say that the words of the Holy Great One are lies, nor praise or rely on your idols; for all your lying and all your godlessness (leads not to) come not from righteousness but (leads to) from great sin.

10 And now I know this mystery, that sinners will alter and pervert the words of righteousness in many ways, and will speak wicked words, and lie, and practice great deceits, and write books concerning their words.

11 But when they write down all my words truthfully in their languages, and do not change or omit any of my words but write them all down truthfully - all that I first testified concerning them.

12 Then, I know another mystery, that books will be given to the righteous and the wise to produce joy and righteousness and much wisdom.

13 And to them the books shall be given, and they shall believe them and rejoice over them, and then all the righteous who have learned from them all the paths of righteousness shall be paid back.'

[Chapter 105]

1 In those days the Lord called them (the wise and righteous) to testify to the children of earth concerning their wisdom: Show it to them; for you are their guides, and a recompense over the whole earth.

2 For I and my son will be united with them for ever in the paths of righteousness in their lives; and you shall have peace: rejoice, you children of righteousness. Amen.

[Chapter 106]

Fragment of the Book of Noah

1 And after some days my son Methuselah took a wife for his son, Lamech, and she became pregnant by him and bore a son. And his body was white as snow and red as the blooming of a rose, and the hair of his head and his long curls were white as wool, and his eyes beautiful.

2 And when he opened his eyes, he lit up the whole house like the sun, and the whole house was very bright.

3 And on it he levitated (arose) in the hands of the midwife, opened his mouth, and conversed with the Lord of righteousness.

4 And his father, Lamech, was afraid of him and fled, and came to his father Methuselah. And he said to him: 'I have begotten a strange son, different and unlike man, and resembling the sons of the God of heaven; and his nature is different and he is not like us, and his eyes are as the rays of the sun, and his face is glorious.

6 And it seems to me that he did not spring from me but from the angels, and I fear that in his days a wonder may be performed on the earth.

7 And now, my father, I am here to ask you and beg you that you may go to Enoch, our father, and learn from him the truth, for his dwelling-place is among the angels."

8 And when Methuselah heard the words of his son, he came to me to the ends of the earth; for he had heard that I was there, and he cried aloud, and I heard his voice and I came to him. And I said to him: 'Behold, here am I, my son, why have you come to me? '

9 And he answered and said: 'Because of a great cause of anxiety have I come to you, and because of a disturbing vision have I approached.

10 And now, my father, hear me. To Lamech, my son, there has been born a son, the like of whom there is none other, and his nature is not like man's nature, and the color of his body is whiter than snow and redder than the bloom of a rose, and the

hair of his head is whiter than white wool, and his eyes are like the rays of the sun, and he opened his eyes and the whole house lit up.

11 And he levitated (arose) in the hands of the midwife, and opened his mouth and blessed the Lord of heaven.

12 And his father Lamech became afraid and fled to me, and did not believe that he was sprung from him, but that he was in the likeness of the angels of heaven; and now I have come to you that you may make known to me the truth.'

13 And I, Enoch, answered and said to him: 'The Lord will do a new thing on the earth, and this I have already seen in a vision, and make known to you that in the generation of my father Jared some of the angels of heaven violated the word of the Lord. And they commit sin and broke the law, and have had sex (united themselves) with women and committed sin with them, and have married some of them, and have had children by them.

14 And they shall produce on the earth giants not according to the spirit, but according to the flesh, and there shall be a great punishment on the earth, and the earth shall be cleansed from all impurity.

15 There shall come a great destruction over the whole earth, and there shall be a flood (deluge) and a great destruction for one year.

16 And this son who has been born to you shall be left on the earth, and his three children shall be saved with him: when all mankind that are on the earth shall die, he and his sons shall be saved.

17 And now make known to your son, Lamech, that he who has been born is in truth his son, and call his name Noah; for he shall be left to you, and he and his sons shall be saved from the destruction, which shall come on the earth on account of all the sin and all the unrighteousness, which shall be full (completed) on the earth in his days.

18 And after that (flood) there shall be more unrighteousness than that which was done before on the earth; for I know the mysteries of the holy ones; for He, the Lord, has showed me and informed me, and I have read (them) in heavenly tablets.

[Chapter 107]

1 And I saw written about them that generation after generation shall transgress, until a generation of righteousness arises, and transgression is destroyed and sin passes away from the earth, and all manner of good comes on it.

2 And now, my son, go and make known to your son Lamech that this son, which has been born, is in truth his son, and this is no lie.'

3 And when Methuselah had heard the words of his father Enoch, for he had shown to him everything in secret, he returned and showed those things to him and called the name of that son Noah; for he will comfort the earth after all the destruction.

[Chapter 108]

1 Another book which Enoch wrote for his son Methuselah and for those who will come after him, and keep the law in the last days.

2 You who have done good shall wait for those days until an end is made of those who work evil; and an end of the power of the wrongdoers.

3 And wait until sin has passed away indeed, for their names shall be blotted out of the book of life and out of the holy books, and their (children) seed shall be destroyed for ever, and their spirits shall be killed, and they shall cry and lament in a place that is a chaotic desert, and they shall be burned in the fire; for there is no earth there.

4 I saw something there like an invisible cloud; because it was so deep I could not look over it, and I saw a flame of fire blazing brightly, and things like shining mountains circling and sweeping back and forth.

5 And I asked one of the holy angels who was with me and said to him: 'What is this bright thing (shining)? For it is not heaven but there was only the flame of a blazing fire, and the voice of weeping and crying and moaning, lamenting, and agony.'

6 And he said to me: 'This place which you see are where the spirits of sinners and blasphemers, and of those who work wickedness, are cast and the spirits of those who pervert everything that the Lord hath spoken through the mouth of the prophets and even the prophecies (things that shall be).

7 For some of them are written and inscribed above in heaven, in order that the angels may read them and know that which shall befall the sinners, and the spirits of the humble, and of those who have afflicted their bodies, and been recompensed by God; and of those who have been abused (put to shame) by wicked men:

8 Who love God and loved neither gold nor silver nor any of the good things which are in the world, but gave over their bodies to torture.

9 Who, since they were born, longed not after earthly food, but regarded everything as a passing breath, and lived accordingly, and the Lord tried them much, and their spirits were found pure so that they should bless His name.

10 And all the blessings destined for them I have recounted in the books. And he has assigned them their reward, because they have been found to love heaven more than their life in the world, and though they were trodden under foot by wicked men, and experienced abuse and reviling from them and were put to shame, they blessed Me.

11 And now I will summon the spirits of the good who belong to the generation of light, and I will transform those who were born in darkness, who in the flesh were not rewarded with such honor as their faithfulness deserved.

12 And I will bring out in shining light those who have loved My holy name, and I will seat each on the throne of his honor.

MAT 19:28 And Jesus said unto them, Verily I say unto you, That ye which have followed me, in the regeneration when the Son of man shall sit in the throne of his glory, ye also shall sit upon twelve thrones, judging the twelve tribes of Israel.

13 And they shall shine for time without end; for righteousness is the judgment of God; because to the faithful He will give faithfulness in the habitation of upright paths.

14 And they shall see those who were born in darkness led into darkness, while the righteous shall shine. And the sinners shall cry aloud and see them shining, and they indeed will go where days and seasons are written down (prescribed) for them.'

The End

Introduction to The Second Book of Enoch: Slavonic Enoch

As part of the Enochian literature, The Second Book of Enoch is included in the pseudepigraphal corpus.

Pseudepigrapha : Spurious or pseudonymous writings, especially Jewish writings ascribed to various biblical patriarchs and prophets but composed within approximately 200 years of the birth of Jesus Christ.

In 1773, rumors of a surviving copy of an ancient book drew Scottish explorer James Bruce to distant Ethiopia. There, he found the "First Book of Enoch." Later, another "Book of Enoch" surfaced. The text, which is known as "Second Enoch," was discovered in 1886 by Professor Sokolov in the archives of the Belgrade Public Library. The Second Book of Enoch was written in the latter half of the first century A.D. The text was preserved only in Slavonic and consequently bears the designation, "Slavonic Enoch." The text has also been known by the titles of "2 Enoch", and "The Secrets of Enoch." 2 Enoch is basically an expansion of Genesis 5:21-32, taking the reader from the time of Enoch to the onset of the great flood of Noah's day.

The main theme of the book is the ascension of Enoch progressively through multiple heavens. During the ascension Enoch is transfigured into an angel and granted access to the secrets of creation. Enoch is then given a 30 day grace period to return to earth and instruct his sons and all the members of his household regarding everything God had revealed to him. The text reports that after period of grace an angel will then come to retrieve him to take him from the earth.

Many credible versions end with chapter 68, however there is a longer version of 2 Enoch, which we will examine. In this version the wisdom and insights given to the family of Enoch is passed from family members to Melchizedek, whom God raises up as an archpriest. Melchizedek then fulfills the function of a prophet-priest. To pave the way to Melchizedek, Methuselah functions as a priest for ten years and then passed his station on to Nir, Noah's younger brother. Nir's wife, Sopanim, miraculously conceives without human intercourse while about to die and posthumously gives birth to Melchizedek, who is born with the appearance and maturity of a three-year old child and the symbol of the priesthood on his chest.

The world is doomed to suffer the flood but Michael the archangel promises Melchizedek salvation. This establishes his priesthood for all of eternity. The text goes on to report that in the last generation, there will be another Melchizedek who will be "the head of all, a great archpriest, the Word and Power of God, who will perform miracles, greater and more glorious than all the previous ones".

The manuscripts, which contain and preserve this document, exist only in Old Slavonic. Of the twenty or more manuscripts dating from the 13th century A.D. no single one contains the complete text of 2 Enoch. When pieced together there appears to be two versions. These we will refer to as the long and short version.

The difference in length between the two is due to two quite different features. There are blocks of text found only in the longer manuscripts; but even when the passages are parallel, the longer manuscripts tend to be more full and detailed. At the same time there is so much verbal similarity when the passages correspond that a common source must be supposed.

The form of 2 Enoch is what one finds in Jewish Wisdom literature and Jewish Apocalyptic literature. It has been suggested that the longer version is characterized by editorial expansions and Christian interpolations. Hence, the shorter version contains fewer Christian elements. The author of 2 Enoch speaks much of the Creator and final judgment, but he speaks very little, about redemption, which seems to be absent from the thoughts of the author. Indeed, there seems to be a total lack of a Savior or Redeemer in 2 Enoch. What is noteworthy is that 2 Enoch has no reference to the mercy of God.

In the long version presented here, it appears that the last portion of the text was added as an afterthought. It contains the rise of Melchizedek. The appearance of Melchizedek ties 2 Enoch to several other texts forming a Melchizedkian tradition. The author of 2 Enoch follows a tradition in which an aged mother, who had been barren up to her deathbed, miraculously conceived Melchizedek without human intervention. Before she was able to give birth to the baby she died. The baby then emerged from her dead body with the maturity of a three-year-old boy. His priesthood will be perpetuated throughout the generations until "another Melchizedek" appears. If the last Melchizedek serves as the archpriest for the last generation, it indicates that in the mind of this Jewish writer, the Temple was to be rebuilt and would be the place were God would meet His people when the heathen nations were destroyed. The continuation and victory of the Jews as the selected and blessed people of God is implied. In this vein, 2 Enoch follows certain apocalyptic writings.

(For more information on apocalyptic writings see "End of Days" by Joseph Lumpkin.)

The Slavonic version is translated from a Greek source. Most scholars agree that there was either a Hebrew or Aramaic original lying behind the Greek source from which the Slavonic manuscripts were produced. The Hebrew origins are indicated by "Semitisms" in the work, but there are also Greek words and expressions, such as the names of the planets in chapter 30.

Proof that The Slavonic Enoch was written in Greek is shown by the derivation of Adam's name, and by several coincidences with the Septuagint. The origin of the story is perhaps based on Hebrew traditions and certain Semitic turns of language show up in the text. This tends to indicate that there was at one time a Hebrew or Aramaic text that preceded the Greek. From the Greek it was translated into Slavonic. Of this version there are five manuscripts or pieces thereof found.

The short version or the Slavonic Enoch was probably written by a single author in an attempt to bring all the current traditions about Enoch of his time into a central storyline and system. The schema to accomplish the unity of traditions implements Enoch's ascension through multiple heavens. This author was probably a Jew living in Egypt. There are several elements in the book, which betray Egyptian origin. The longer version of 2 Enoch was seeded with Christian elements and appended with an ending that does not fit well, illuminating the fact that there were several authors involved in the longer version.

Parts of the book was probably written in the late first century A.D. The first date is a limit set by the fact that Ethiopic Enoch, Ecclesiasticus, and Wisdom of Solomon are used as sources or references within the text; the second date is a limit set by the fact that the destruction of the Temple is not mentioned at all.

The Slavonic Enoch furnishes new material for the study of religious thought in the beginning of the Common Era. The ideas of the millennium and of the multiple heavens are the most important in this connection. Another very interesting feature is the presence of evil in heaven, the fallen angels in the second heaven, and hell in the third. The idea of evil in heaven may be a nod to the book of Job and the dialog between God and Satan, who was coming and going between heaven and earth. The idea of hell in the third heaven may have been derived from ideas expressed in the Old Testament book of Isaiah, which mentions that the sufferings of the wicked will be witnessed by the righteous in paradise.

Chapter 21 and forward for several chapters shows a heavy influence of Greek mythology. The Zodiac is mentioned along with celestial bodies with names such as Zeus, Cronus, Aphrodite, and others. The part of the text containing names and astrological descriptions could have been tampered with as late as the seventh century A.D.

By far, the most interesting and confusing section begins around chapter 25 and runs for several chapters. Here the text takes a turn toward Gnostic theology and cosmology. The Gnostics were a Christian sect, which formed and grew in the first century A.D. and thrived in the second century A.D.

Although Gnostic borrowed from Plato's (428 B.C. - 348 B.C.) creation myth, the maturity and construction of the story shows it to be of Gnostic Christian origin, placing it no earlier than the last part of the first century A.D. and no later than the end of the Second century. Add to the dating question the fact that the destruction of the Temple in Jerusalem is not mentioned, which leads to a date just before 70 A.D., if one assumes the Gnostic flavor was not added later.

The history of the text is obviously long and varied. It probably began as a Jewish oral tradition with pieces taken from several Enochian stories. It was first penned in Hebrew or Aramaic. The date of this incarnation of the text is unknown. Later, the story was expanded and embellished by Greek influences. Lastly, Christians and Gnostics commandeered the book and added their own matter. Thus 2 Enoch exhibits a kaleidoscope of cultural and religious contributions over a great scope of time from the first century B.C. (assuming it came after 1 Enoch) and ending as late as the seventh century A.D. These additions would allow any serious student insight into how ancient texts evolve.

Second Enoch was rediscovered and published in the early 19th century A.D The text before you uses the R. H. Charles and W. R. Morfill translation of 1896 with additions from other sources. Archaic terms and sentence structure were revised or explained to convey a more modern rendering for the twenty-first century readers.

2 Enoch
Slavonic Enoch
The Book of the Secrets of Enoch

Chapter 1
1 There was a wise man and a great craftsman, and the Lord formed a love for him and received him, so that he should see the highest dwellings and be an eye-witness of the wise and great and inconceivable and unchanging realm of God Almighty, and of the very wonderful and glorious and bright and manifold vision of the position of the Lord's servants, and of the inaccessible throne of the Lord, and of the degrees and manifestations of the spiritual (non-physical) hosts, and of the unspeakable ministration of the multitude of the elements, and of the various apparition and singing of the host of Cherubim which is beyond description, and of the limitless light.
2 At that time, he said, when my one hundred and sixty-fifth year was completed, I begat my son Methuselah.
3 After this I lived two hundred years and finished of all the years of my life three hundred and sixty-five years.
4 On the first day of the month I was in my house alone and was resting on my bed and slept.
5 And when I was asleep, great distress came up into my heart, and I was weeping with my eyes in sleep, and I could not understand what this distress was, or what was happening to me.
6 And there appeared to me two very large men, so big that I never saw such on earth. Their faces were shining like the sun, their eyes were like a burning light, and from their lips fire was coming out. They were singing. Their clothing was of various kinds in appearance and was purple. Their wings were brighter than gold, and their hands whiter than snow.
7 They were standing at the head of my bed and began to call me by my name.
8 And I arose from my sleep and clearly saw the two men standing in front of me.
9 And I greeted them and was seized with fear and the appearance of my face was changed to terror, and those men said to me:
10 Enoch, have courage and do not fear. The eternal God sent us to you, and you shall ascend today with us into heaven, and you shall tell your sons and all your household all that they shall do without you on earth in your house, and let no one seek you until the Lord returns you to them.
11 And I hurried to obey them and went out of my house, and went to the doors, as I was ordered, and I summoned my sons Methuselah and Regim and Gaidad and explained to them all the marvels the men had told me.

Chapter 2
1 Listen to me, my children, I do not know where I will go, or what will befall me. So now, my children, I tell you, do not turn from God in the face of that which is empty or prideful, which did not make heaven and earth, for these shall perish along with

those who worship them, and may the Lord make your hearts confident in the fear (respect) of him. And now, my children, let no one consider seeking me, until the Lord returns me to you.

Chapter 3
1 (It came to pass, when Enoch had finished speaking to his sons, that the angels took him on to their wings and lifted him up on to the first heaven and placed him on the clouds.)
And there I (Enoch) looked, and again I looked higher, and saw the ether, and they placed me on the first heaven and showed me a very large sea, bigger than the earthly sea.

Chapter 4
1 They brought the elders and rulers of the stellar orders in front of me, and showed me two hundred angels, who rule the stars and services of the stars to the heavens, and fly with their wings and come round all those who sail.

Chapter 5
1 And here I looked down and saw the storehouses of snow, and the angels who keep their amazing storehouses, and the clouds where they come out of and into which they go.

Chapter 6
1 They showed me the storehouse of the dew, like olive oil in its appearance and its form, as of all the flowers of the earth. And they also showed me many angels guarding the storehouses of these things, and how they are made to shut and open.

Chapter 7
1 And those men took me and led me up on to the second heaven, and showed me darkness, greater than earthly darkness, and there I saw prisoners hanging, watched, (guarded,) awaiting the great and limitless judgment, and the spirits were dark in appearance, more than earthly darkness, and perpetually weeping through all hours.
2 And I said to the men who were with me: Why are these being unceasingly tortured? They answered me: These are God's apostates, who did not obey God's commands, but took counsel with their own will, and turned away with their prince, who is also held captive in the fifth heaven.
3 And I felt great pity for them, and they greeted me, and said to me: Man of God, pray to the Lord for us. And I answered them: I am just a mortal man. Who am I that I should pray for spirits? Who knows where I go or what will become of me? Or who will pray for me?

Chapter 8
1 And those men took me from there and led me up on to the third heaven, and placed me there. I looked down and saw what this place produces and that it was so good that such as has never been known.
2 And I saw all the sweet, flowering trees and I saw their fruits, which were sweet smelling, and I saw all the foods that came from them and that the food was bubbling with fragrant vapors.

3 And in the middle of the trees was the tree of life, in that place where the Lord rests when he goes up into paradise. And this tree is of indescribable goodness and fragrance, and adorned more than anything existing. And all sides of its form were golden and brilliant red and fire-like and it was completely covered, and it produced all fruits.
4 Its root is in the garden at the earth's end.
5 And paradise resides between spiritual and physical.
6 And two springs come out which send forth honey and milk, and their springs send forth oil and wine, and they separate into four parts, and flow quietly around, and go down into the paradise of Eden, between the mutable and the eternal.
7 And there they go forth along the earth, and have a circular flow even as other elements.
8 And there is no unfruitful tree here, and every place is blessed.
9 Three hundred angels, which are very bright, are there to keep the garden, and with incessant sweet singing with voices, which are never silent, serve the Lord throughout all the hours of days.
10 And I said: How very sweet is this place, and those men said to me:

Chapter 9
1 This place, O Enoch, is prepared for the righteous, who endure all manner of offence from those that exasperate their souls, who avert their eyes from iniquity, and make righteous judgment, and give bread to the hungering, and cover the naked with clothing, and raise up the fallen, and help injured orphans, and who walk without fault before the face of the Lord, and serve him alone, and for them is prepared this place for eternal inheritance.

Chapter 10
1 And those two men led me up on to the Northern side, and showed me there a very terrible place, and there were every kind of tortures in that place: cruel darkness and gloom, and there was absolutely no light at all there, but murky fire constantly flaming above, and there is a fiery river coming out, and everywhere in that entire place is fire, and everywhere there is frost and ice, thirst and shivering, while the physical restraints are very cruel, and the spirits were fearsome and merciless, bearing angry weapons, torturing without mercy.
2 And I said: Woe, woe! This place is so terrible.
3 And those men said to me: This place, O Enoch, is prepared for those who dishonor God, who on earth practice sin against nature, which is sodomy of a child, corruption of children, performing magic, enchantments and devilish witchcrafts, and who boast of their wicked deeds, stealing, lying, slander, envy, resentment, fornication, murder, and who are accursed and steal the souls of men, and those who see the poor and still take away their goods so they grow rich, and injure them for other men's goods. And this is reserved for those who satisfy their own emptiness made the hungering die; those who clothe themselves by stripping the naked; and who did not know their creator, but instead bowed to lifeless gods who have no soul who cannot see nor hear, empty, who built carved images and bow down to unclean fashioning of useless gods, this place is prepared for these as an eternal inheritance.

Chapter 11
1 Those men took me, and led me up on to the fourth heaven, and showed me the entire succession of activities, and all the rays of the light of sun and moon.
2 And I measured their progression, and compared their light, and saw that the sun's light is greater than the moon's.
3 Its circle and the wheels on which it goes always is like the wind passing with very amazing speed with no rest day or night.
4 Its egress and ingress are accompanied by four huge stars, and each star has a thousand stars under it, to the right of the sun's wheel there are four thousand stars and to the left are four thousand, altogether eight thousand, going out with the sun continually.
5 And by day fifteen groups of ten thousand angels attend it, and by night there were a thousand.
6 And six-winged ones go fourth with the angels before the sun's wheel into the fiery flames, and a hundred angels kindle the sun and set it alight.

Chapter 12
1 And I looked and saw other flying elements of the sun, whose names are Phoenixes and Chalkydri, which are marvelous and wonderful, with feet and tails of a lion, and a crocodile's head, they appear to be purple in color like that in the rainbow; their size is nine hundred measures, their wings are like those of angels, each has twelve wings, and they attend and accompany the sun, bearing heat and dew, as it is ordered them from God.

(Note: The word CHALKYDRI means "serpents". It appears that the Slavonic translators rendered the Hebrew word SERAPHIM differently in various places in the text. The word was translated "Serpent" in some places and SERAPHIM in others.)

2 This is how the sun revolves and goes, and rises under the heaven, and its course goes under the earth with the light of its rays continually.

Chapter 13
1 Then those men carried me away to the east, and placed me at the sun's gates, where the sun has egress according to the seasons circuit and regulation of the months of the whole year, and the number of the hours day and night.
2 And I saw six gates open, each gate having sixty-one stadia (185 meters) and A quarter of one stadium (46.25 meters), and I measured them accurately, and knew their size. Through the gates the sun goes out, and goes to the west, and is made even, and rises throughout all the months, and turns back again from the six gates according to the succession of the seasons. In this way the period of the entire year is finished after the return of the four seasons.

(Note: 6 X 61=366 With the quarter day added, this is the length of the leap year.)

Chapter 14

1 And again those men led me away to the western parts, and showed me six great open gates corresponding to the eastern gates, opposite to where the sun sets, according to the number of the days three hundred and sixty-five and a quarter.

(Note that this is a solar calendar of the same length as our modern calendar.)

2 Again it goes down to the western gates, and diminishes (pulls away) its light with the prominent brightness, under the earth. The crown of its glory is in heaven with the Lord, and it is guarded by four hundred angels while the sun goes round on wheel under the earth. And it stands seven great hours in night, and spends half its course under the earth. And when it comes to the eastern approach in the eighth hour of the night it brings its lights and the crown of glory, and the sun burns (flames) outwardly more than fire.

Chapter 15
1 Then the elements of the sun, called Phoenixes and Chalkydri (Seraphim) break into song, therefore every bird flutters its wings, rejoicing at the giver of light, and they brake into song at the command of the Lord.
2 The giver of light comes to illuminate the entire world, and the morning guard takes shape, which is the rays of the sun, and the sun of the earth goes out, and receives its luminance to light up the entire face of the earth, and they showed me this calculation of the sun's going.
3 And the great gates, which it enters into, are for the calculation of the hours of the year. For this reason the sun is a great creation, whose circuit lasts twenty-eight years, and begins again from the beginning.

(Note: For 29 February, which is the leap year day, to fall on a particular weekday, there is a 28-year (2 x 14 year) cycle. This forms a type of perpetual calendar.)

Chapter 16
1 Those men showed me the great course of the moon. There are twelve great gates that are crowned from west to east, by which the moon comes and goes in its customary times.
2 It goes in at the first gate to the western places of the sun, by the first gates with thirty-one days exactly, by the second gates with thirty-one days exactly, by the third with thirty days exactly, by the fourth with thirty days exactly, by the fifth with thirty-one days exactly, by the sixth with thirty-one days exactly, by the seventh with thirty days exactly, by the eighth with thirty-one days perfectly, by the ninth with thirty-one days exactly, by the tenth with thirty days perfectly, by the eleventh with thirty-one days exactly, by the twelfth with twenty-eight days exactly.

(Note: The sum of the days total 365 with the year beginning in March.)

3 And it goes through the western gates in the order and number of the eastern, and accomplishes the three hundred and sixty-five and a quarter days of the solar year, while the lunar year has three hundred fifty-four, and there twelve days lacking of the solar circle, which are the lunar epacts of the whole year.

(Note: epact | The number of days by which the solar year differs from the lunar year.
• the number of days into the moon's phase cycle at the beginning of the solar (calendar) year.
Origin - mid 16th century. (Denoting the age of the moon in days at the beginning of the calendar year): from French épacte, via late Latin from Greek epaktai (h merai) 'intercalated (days).

4 The great circle also contains five hundred and thirty-two years.

(Note: The 532-year cycle is calculated from the creation of Adam, which, as we know, took place on Friday, March 1, 5508 B.C., which is the base date on which the entire calendar system of the Orthodox Church is founded. The final sections of the Typikon, which is the book that dictates the services, are the Paschalion Calendar sections. Here, there are tables reflecting the 532 year cycle of the Church services, which consists of 19-year solar cycles multiplied by 28-day lunar cycles. There is a table that consists of 19 columns by 28 rows, giving the Paschal Key number or letter for each of the years of the 532-year cycle. Once you know the Paschal Key, you look up the details in the following section, which consists of 35 brief calendar synopses, one for each possible day that Pascha can fall. Each of these synopses actually consists of two services; one for regular years, and one for leap years.

5 The quarter (of a day) is omitted for three years, the fourth fulfills it exactly.
6 Because of this, they are taken outside of heaven for three years and are not added to the number of days, because they change the time of the years to two new months toward completion, to two others toward the decrease.
7 And when the course through the western gates is finished, it returns and goes to the eastern to the lights, and goes this way day and night in its heavenly circles, below all circles, swifter than the heavenly winds, and spirits and elements and flying angels. Each angel has six wings.
8 In nineteen years it travels the course seven times.

Chapter 17
1 In the midst of the heavens I saw armed soldiers, serving the Lord, with drums and organs, with constant voice, with sweet voice, with sweet and unceasing voice and various singing, which it is impossible to describe, and which astonishes every mind, so wonderful and marvelous is the singing of those angels, and I was delighted listening to it.

Chapter 18
1 The men took me on to the fifth heaven and placed me, and there I saw many and countless soldiers, called Grigori, of human appearance, and their size (was) greater than that of great giants and their faces withered, and the silence of their mouths perpetual, and their was no service on the fifth heaven, and I said to the men who were with me:

(Note: The Greek transliteration egegoroi are the Watchers; a group of fallen angels who mated with mortal women and produced the Nephilim mentioned in the books of Jubilees, 1Enoch, and Genesis 6:4.)

2 Why are they so very withered and their faces melancholy, and their mouths silent,
and why is there no service in this heaven?
3 And they said to me: These are the Grigori, who with their prince Satanail (Satan)
rejected the Lord of Light. After them are those who are held in great darkness in the second heaven, and three of them went down on to earth from the Lord's throne, to the place Ermon, and broke through their vows on the shoulder of the hill Ermon and saw the daughters of men how good they are, and took to themselves wives, and fouled the earth with their deeds, who broke the law and mixing (with the women), giants are born and amazingly large men with great hatred.

(Note: The Hill of Ermon could be Mount Hermon, which is mentioned over a dozen times in the Bible.

4 And therefore God judged them with great judgment, and they weep for their brethren and they will be punished on the Lord's great day.
5 And I said to the Grigori: I saw your brethren and their works, and their great torments, and I prayed for them, but the Lord has condemned them to be under earth until this heaven and this earth shall end for ever.
6 And I said: Why do you stand there, brethren, and do not serve before the Lord's face, and have not put your services before the Lord's face? You could anger your Lord completely.
7 And they listened to my advice, and spoke to the four ranks in heaven. As I stood with those two men four trumpets sounded together with a loud voice, and the Grigori broke into song with one voice, and their voice went up before the Lord pitifully and touchingly.

Chapter 19
1 From there, those men took me and lifted me up on to the sixth heaven, and there I saw seven bands of angels, very bright and very glorious, and their faces shining more than the sun's shining, glistening, and there is no difference in their faces, or behavior, or manner of dress; and these make the orders, and learn the goings of the stars, and the alteration of the moon, or revolution of the sun, and the good administration of the world.
2 And when they see evildoing they make commandments and instruction, and make sweet and loud singing, and all (songs) of praise.
3 These are the archangels who are above angels, and they measure all life in heaven and on earth, and the angels who are (appointed) over seasons and years, the angels who are over rivers and sea, and who are over the fruits of the earth, and the angels who are over every grass, giving food to every and all living things, and the angels who write down all the souls of men, and all their deeds, and their lives before the Lord's face. In their midst are six Phoenixes and six Cherubim and six six-winged ones continually singing with one voice, and it is not possible to describe their singing, and they rejoice before the Lord at his footstool.

Chapter 20
1 And those two men lifted me up from there on to the seventh heaven, and I saw there a very great light, and fiery troops of great archangels, incorporeal forces, and dominions, orders and governments, Cherubim and Seraphim, thrones and many-eyed ones, nine regiments, the Ioanit stations of light, and I became afraid, and

began to tremble with great terror, and those men took me, and led me after them, and said to me:
2 Have courage, Enoch, do not fear, and showed me the Lord from afar, sitting on His very high throne. For what is there on the tenth heaven, since the Lord dwells there?
3 On the tenth heaven is God, in the Hebrew tongue he is called Aravat.

(Note: The meaning of Ioanit is not clear. However, it may be derived from the transliteration of the name John. John means, "The Lord is Gracious." The meaning of Aravat is equally unclear but seems to mean, "Father of Creation."
Each level of heaven represents or demonstrates a personality or part of the Godhead. One of the highest demonstrations of God's power and divinity is the power of Creation. It is found on the tenth level of heaven.)

4 And all the heavenly soldiers would come and stand on the ten steps according to their rank, and would bow down to the Lord, and would then return to their places in joy and bliss, singing songs in the unlimited light with soft and gentle voices, gloriously serving him.

(Note: Strong and fierce soldiers sing with soft, gentle voices, bowing and serving in bliss.)

Chapter 21
1 And the Cherubim and Seraphim standing around the throne, and the six-winged and many-eyed ones do not depart, standing before the Lord's face doing his will, and cover his whole throne, singing with gentle voice before the Lord's face: Holy, holy, holy, Lord Ruler of Sabaoth (Host / army), heavens and earth are full of Your glory.
2 When I saw all these things, the men said to me: Enoch, thus far we were commanded to journey with you, and those men went away from me and after that I did not see them.
3 And I remained alone at the end of the seventh heaven and became afraid, and fell on my face and said to myself: Woe is me. What has befallen me?
4 And the Lord sent one of his glorious ones, the archangel Gabriel, and he said to me: "Have courage, Enoch, do not fear, arise before the Lord's face into eternity, arise and come with me."
5 And I answered him, and said within myself: My Lord, my soul has departed from me from terror and trembling, and I called to the men who led me up to this place. I relied on them, and it is with them that I can go before the Lord's face.

(Note: When speaking to God, Enoch "said within himself." He did not have to speak aloud.)

6 And Gabriel lifted me up like a leaf caught up by the wind, and he placed me before the Lord's face.
7 And I saw the eighth heaven, which is called in the Hebrew tongue Muzaloth, (Zodiac) changer of the seasons, of drought, and of wet, and of the twelve constellations of the circle of the firmament, which are above the seventh heaven.
8 And I saw the ninth heaven, which is called in Hebrew Kuchavim, where are the heavenly homes of the twelve constellations of the circle of the firmament.

Chapter 22
1 On the tenth heaven, which is called Aravoth, I saw the appearance of the Lord's face, like iron made to glow in fire, and it shone forth and casted out, emitting sparks, and it burned.

(Note: One possible meaning of Aravoth is "three times holy" or "holy, holy, holy."

2 In a moment of eternity I saw the Lord's face, but the Lord's face is indescribable, marvelous and very amazing, and very, very terrible.
3 And who am I to tell of the Lord's unspeakable being, and of his very wonderful face? I cannot tell the amount of his instructions, and the variety of voices. The Lord's throne is very great and not made with hands, and I cannot tell the number of those standing around him. There were troops of Cherubim and Seraphim, and they sang unceasingly. I cannot tell of his unchanging beauty. Who shall tell of the unpronounceable greatness of his glory?
4 And I fell prone and bowed down to the Lord, and the Lord with his lips said to me:
5 Have courage, Enoch, do not fear, arise and stand before my face into eternity (stand before my face eternally / stand before my eternal face.)

(Note: Enoch is out of and above time-space. Eternity is now and he can feel the timelessness of where he is. The language struggles to convey this fact.)

6 And the archangel Michael lifted me up, and led me to the Lord's face.
7 And the Lord said to his servants, testing them: Let Enoch stand before my face into eternity, and the glorious ones bowed down to the Lord, and said: Let Enoch go according to Your word.
8 And the Lord said to Michael: Go and take Enoch and remove his earthly garments, and anoint him with my sweet ointment, and put him into the garments of My glory.
9 And Michael did as the Lord told him. He anointed me, and dressed me, and the appearance of that ointment is more than the great light, and his ointment is like sweet dew, and its smell mild, shining like the sun's ray, and I looked at myself, and I was transformed into one of his glorious ones.

(Note: The number symbolism of ten is that of new starts at a higher level, new beginnings, and re-creation.)

10 And the Lord summoned one of his archangels, whose name is Pravuil, whose knowledge was quicker in wisdom than the other archangels, who wrote all the deeds of the Lord; and the Lord said to Pravuil: Bring out the books from my store-houses, and a reed of quick-writing, and give it to Enoch, and deliver to him the best and comforting books out of your hand.

(Note: Enoch is now an angel. He now has access to the heavenly records and the understanding to use the knowledge. A reed was used in writing much like a quill was used.)

Chapter 23
1 And he was explaining to me all the works of heaven, earth and sea, and all the elements, their passages and goings, and the sounding of the thunders, the sun and moon, the progression and changes of the stars, the seasons, years, days, and hours, as well as the risings of the wind, the numbers of the angels, and the formation of their songs, and all human things, the tongue of every human song and life, the commandments, instructions, and sweet-voiced singings, and all things that are fitting to learn.
2 And Pravuil told me: All the things that I have told you, we have written. Sit and write all the souls of mankind, however many of them are born, and the places prepared for them to eternity. And he said, all souls are prepared for eternity, before the formation of the world.
3 And for both thirty days and thirty nights, and I wrote out all things exactly, and wrote three hundred and sixty-six books.

(Note: If all things were created in six days, then the souls of all people were created at that time. In Jewish mythology, the place that the souls were houses until birth was called the Guf. Each soul was created for a certain place, time, and destiny. According to one version of the myth, when the Guf is emptied of souls, time ceases. In another version, when the last soul dies and returns to God, time will end. Enoch wrote 366 book in a 720 hour period containing information on all things, including, "all souls (who) are prepared for eternity, before the formation of the world.")

Chapter 24
1 And the Lord summoned me, and said to me: Enoch, sit down on my left with Gabriel.
2 And I bowed down to the Lord, and the Lord spoke to me: Enoch, beloved, all that you see, all things that are standing finished, I tell you even before the very beginning, I created all things from non-being. I created the visible, physical things from the invisible, spiritual (world).
3 Hear, Enoch, and take in my words, for I have not told My angels My secret, and I have not told them their rise (beginnings), nor My endless realm, nor have they understood my creating, which I tell you today.
4 For before all things were visible, physical, I alone used to go about in the invisible, spiritual things, like the sun from east to west, and from west to east.
5 But even the sun has peace in itself, while I found no peace, because I was creating all things, and I conceived the thought of placing foundations, and of creating the visible, physical creation.

(Note: Overview of the heavens:
First heaven - , Enoch arrives on angel's wings. There are storehouses of snow and dew.
Second heaven - , Enoch finds a group of fallen angels. There is darkness and torture.
Third heaven - There are sweet flowers, trees, and fruit.
Fourth heaven – There are soldiers, heaven's army, and the progression of sun and moon.
Fifth heaven - The leaders of the fallen angels, the "Grigori" (Greek "Gregoroi," translating Mearim, the Hebrew word for watchers.) Three of them went down and had intercourse with the daughters of men, yielding giants, who became the source of enmity on earth.
Sixth heaven – Seven bands of angels and the ordering of the stars.
Seventh heaven, shows something unusual happening to Enoch when Gabriel puts Enoch in

front of the throne of the Lord.
The Eighth, Ninth, and Tenth Heavens are thought to be later additions and not part of the original text.
Eighth heaven - "Muzaloth" -- Zodiac
Ninth heaven - "Kuchavim" -- heavenly bodies (stars).
Tenth heaven - "Aravoth" -- descriptions of God's face like that of iron made to glow in fire.
Enoch sees the "appearance of the Lord's face," but describes it as indescribable.
Pravuil, the archangel, is commanded to write down secret information about astronomy, climate, and language and give it over to Enoch. In other Enochian writings the same angel, also spelled "Penemue", is criticized for teaching humans to write.

Chapter 25
1 I commanded in the very lowest parts, that the visible, physical things should come down from the invisible, spiritual (realm), and Adoil came down very great, and I beheld him, and he had a belly of great light.
2 And I said to him: Become undone, Adoil, and let the visible, physical (universe) come out of you.
3 And he came undone, and a great light came out. And I was in the midst of the great light, and as there is born light from light, there came forth a great age (eon / space of time), and showed all creation, which I had thought to create.
4 And I saw that it was good.
5 And I placed for myself a throne, and took my seat on it, and said to the light: Go up higher from here and station yourself high above the throne, and be a foundation to the highest things.
6 And above the light there is nothing else, and then I rose up and looked up from my throne.

(Note: Beginning with chapters 25 and 26, the book of 2 Enoch takes a rather Gnostic diversion. The Gnostics were a Christian sect that flourished around the 3rd century A.D. The Gnostic view of the Godhead borrowed heavily from the creation saga preached by Plato (circa 428 B.C. to 348 B.C.) The story of Adoil and the emanation of pure light from God, which brings about creation of the physical world, is similar to other Gnostic works. Gnosticism teaches that in the beginning a Supreme Being called The Father, The Divine All, The Origin, The Supreme God, or The Fullness, emanated the element of existence, both visible and invisible. His intent was not to create but, just as light emanates from a flame, so did creation shine forth from God. This manifested the primal element needed for creation.

This was the creation of Barbelo, who is the "Thought of God."
The Father's thought performed a deed and she was created from it. It is she who had appeared before him in the shining of his light. This is the first power which was before all of them and which was created from his mind. She is the Thought of the All and her light shines like his light. It is the perfect power, which is the visage of the invisible. She is the pure, undefiled Spirit who is perfect. She is the first power. Adoil has that place is this myth.

It could be said that Barbelo was the creative emanation and, like the Divine All, is both male and female. It was the "agreement" of Barbelo and the Divine All, representing the union of male and female,that created the Christ Spirit and all the Aeons. In some renderings the word "Aeon" is used to designate an ethereal realm or kingdom. In other versions "Aeon" indicates the ruler of the realm. The Aeons of this world are merely reflections of the Aeons of the eternal realm. The reflection is always inferior to real.

In several Gnostic cosmologies the "living" world is under the control of entities called Aeons, of which Sophia is head. This means the Aeons influence or control the soul, life force, intelligence, thought, and mind. Control of the mechanical or inorganic world is given to the Archons.

The Archons were created by Sophia. Sophia, probably out of pride, tried to emulate the creative force of God by created an image of herself. Meaning that she wanted to produce an offspring, without either consort or the approval of her Father, God. As an aeon, she did have the power to do so, but she wasn't perfect like the Great Spirit, or like the other two perfect aeons, Barbelo and the Autogenes. Nevertheless, in her arrogance, she attempted to create and failed. She was horrified when she saw her creation, imperfect, bruthish creature with a lion-faced serpent with eyes of fire, whom she called Yaldabaoth.
Sophia cast her offspring out of pleroma (heaven), and hid her child within a thick cloud from the other aeons, because of her embarrassment and shame.
Yaldabaoth was the first of the archon ("ruler") and he stole his mother's power, so that she wasn't able to escape from the cloud. Despite gaining Sophia's aeonic power, he was weak, but prideful, ambitious and power hungry.
Since the archons, including Yaldabaoth, were androgynous beings, Yaldabaoth fathered twelve archons, giving each a bit of his power. They were named Athoth, Harmas, Kalila-Oumbri, Yabel, Adonaiou (or Sabaoth), Cain, Abel, Abrisene, Yobel, Armoupieel, Melceir-Adonein and Belias. Seven archons would rule seven heavens and five in the abyss, which Yaldabaoth and the archons created. Each archon would rule a heaven (or the abyss), and created 365 angels to help them.

The archons rule the physical aspects of systems, regulation, limits, and order in the world. Both the ineptitude and cruelty of the Archons are reflected in the chaos and pain of the material realm.
(See the book, The Gnostic Scriptures, by Joseph Lumpkin, published by Fifth Estate.)

Although the above may be a digression from the text of 2 Enoch, it adds insight into the time frame and origins of its production. Gnostic influences were felt from the late first century to the early fourth century A.D. If the writer of this section of 2 Enoch was exposed to the Gnostic sect, it would conclusively make 2 Enoch a text with Christian influences.)

Chapter 26
1 And I summoned the very lowest a second time, and said: Let Archas come forth hard, and he came forth hard from the invisible, spiritual.
2 And Archas came forth, hard, heavy, and very red.
3 And I said: Be opened, Archas, and let there be born from you, and he came apart, and an age came forth, very great and very dark, bearing the creation of all lower things, and I saw that it was good and said to him:
4 Go down below, and make yourself solid, and be a foundation for the lower things, and it happened and he went down and stationed himself, and became the foundation for the lower things, and below the darkness there is nothing else.

(Note: Hard and heavy could be terms for "gravid" or pregnant, with birth being imminent. Archas could equate to "The Archons.")

Chapter 27
1 And I commanded that there should be taken from light and darkness, and I said: Be thick, and it became thick, and I spread it out with the light, and it became water, and I spread it out over the darkness, below the light, and then I made firm the waters, that is to say the bottomless (abyss), and I made foundation of light around the water, and created seven circles from inside, and made the water look like crystal, wet and dry, so it was like glass, and the circles were around the waters and the other elements, and I showed each one of them its path, and the seven stars each one of them in its heaven, that they go that way, and I saw that it was good.
2 And I made separations between light and darkness in the midst of the water here and there, and I said to the light, that it should be the day, and to the darkness, that it should be the night, and there was evening and there was morning on the first day.

(Note: The foundation of light around the water that is like crystal is likely a reference to the sky. One belief of the time was that the sky was an expanse of water like an endless sea.)

Chapter 28
1 And then I made firm the heavenly circle, and made that the lower water which is under heaven collect itself together into one whole, and that the chaos become dry, and it became so.
2 Out of the waves I created hard and large rock, and from the rock I piled up the dry (land), and the dry (land) I called earth, and the middle of the earth I called the abyss, or the bottomless. I collected the sea in one place and bound it together with a yoke. *(Note: This is the bank or shoreline.)*
3 And I said to the sea: Behold I give you eternal limits, and you shall not break loose from your integral parts.
4 Thus I made the firmament hold together. This day I called me the first-created, Sunday. (This, I call the first day of creation.)

Chapter 29
1 And for all the heavenly soldiers I made them the image and essence of fire, and my eye looked at the very hard, firm rock, and from the gleam of my eye the lightning received its wonderful nature, (which) is both fire in water and water in fire, and one does not put out the other, nor does the one dry up the other, therefore the lightning is brighter than the sun, softer than water and firmer than hard rock.

(Note: If the sky is made of water and lightning, which is fire, issues from the sky, then water and fire must exist together in a heavenly form.)

2 And from the rock I cut off a great fire, and from the fire I created the orders of the incorporeal (spiritual / non-physical) ten troops of angels, and their weapons are fiery and their raiment a burning flame, and I commanded that each one should stand in his order.

3 And one from out the order of angels, having violated the command he was given, conceived an impossible thought, to place his throne higher than the clouds above the earth so that he might become equal in rank to my power.
4 And I threw him out from the height with his angels, and he was flying in the air continuously above the bottomless (abyss).

(Note: We assume this ends the second day, although it is not mentioned.)

Chapter 30
1 On the third day I commanded the earth to make grow great and fruitful trees, and hills, and seed to sow, and I planted Paradise, and enclosed it, and placed armed guards in the form of my flaming angels, and in this way I created renewal.
2 Then came evening, and morning came of the fourth day.
3 On Wednesday, the fourth day, I commanded that there should be great lights on the heavenly circles.
4 On the first uppermost circle I placed the stars, Cronus, and on the second Aphrodite, on the third Ares, on the fifth Zeus, on the sixth Ermis (Hermes), on the seventh lesser the moon, and adorned it with the lesser stars.

(Note: The fourth heavenly circle is vacant. The Greek names for the heavenly bodies leave no doubt as to the influence of Greek words and ideas within this section of the text.)

5 And on the lower (parts) I placed the sun for the illumination of day, and the moon and stars for the illumination of night.
6 (And I set) the sun that it should go according to each of the twelve constellations , and I appointed the succession of the months and their names and lives, their thundering, and how they mark the hours, and how they should proceed.
7 Then evening came and morning came of the fifth day.
8 On Thursday, the fifth day, I commanded the sea, that it should bring forth fishes, and feathered birds of many varieties, and all animals creeping over the earth, going forth over the earth on four legs, and soaring in the air, of male and female sex, and every soul breathing the spirit of life.

(Note: Verse eight proclaims the creation of all souls breathing (inspired by) the spirit of life. The next verse proclaims the creation of man. This day filled the Guf and incarnation begins in next.)

9 And there came evening, and there came morning of the sixth day.
10 On Friday, the sixth day, I commanded my wisdom to create man from seven consistent applications: one, his flesh from the earth; two, his blood from the dew; three, his eyes from the sun; four, his bones from stone; five, his intelligence from the swiftness of the angels and cloud; six, his veins and his hair from the grass of the earth; seven, his soul from my breath and from the wind.
11 And I gave him seven natures: to the flesh - hearing, the eyes for sight, to the soul - smell, the veins for touch, the blood for taste, the bones for endurance, to the intelligence - enjoyment.
12 I created a saying (speech) from knowing. I created man from spiritual and from physical nature, from both come his death and life and appearance. He knows speech like some created thing. He is small in greatness and great in smallness, and I

placed him on earth, like a second angel, to be honorable, great and glorious. And I appointed him as ruler to rule on earth and to have my wisdom, and there was none like him on earth of all my existing creatures.
13 And I appointed him a name made from the four components, from east, from west, from south, and from north. And I appointed for him four special stars, and I called his name Adam, and showed him the two ways, the light and the darkness, and I told him:
14 This is good, and that bad, so that I should learn whether he has love towards me, or hatred, and so that it would be clear who in his race loves me.

(Note: The Hebrew name of Adam means "man.)

15 For I have seen his nature, but he has not seen his own nature, and therefore by not seeing it he will sin worse, and I said, "After sin is there nothing but death?"
16 And I put sleep into him and he fell asleep. And I took from him a rib, and created him a wife, so that death should come to him by his wife, and I took his last word and called her name mother, that is to say, Eve.

Chapter 31
1 Adam has life on earth, and I created a garden in Eden in the east, so that he should observe the testament and keep the command.
2 I made the heavens open to him, so that he would see the angels singing the song of victory, and the light without shadow.
3 And he was continuously in paradise, and the devil understood that I wanted to create another world, because Adam was lord on earth, to rule and control it.
4 The devil is the evil spirit of the lower places, he made himself a fugitive from the heavens as the devil and his name was Satan. Thus he became different from the angels, but his nature did not change his intelligence as it applied to his understanding of righteous and sinful things.
5 And he understood his condemnation and the sin that he had committed before. Therefore he devised a thought against Adam, in which he entered and seduced Eve, but did not touch Adam.
6 But I cursed ignorance. However, what I had blessed before I did not curse. I did not curse man, nor the earth, nor other creatures. But I cursed man's evil results, and his works.

Chapter 32
1 I said to him: You are earth (dirt), and into the earth from where I took you, you shall go, and I will not destroy you, but send you back from where I took you.
2 Then I can again receive you at My second presence.
3 And I blessed all my creatures, both physical and spiritual. And Adam was five and half hours in paradise.
4 And I blessed the seventh day, which is the Sabbath, on which he rested from all his works.

(Note: The five and a half hours is tied to the 5500 years of punishment mentioned in the Books of Adam and Eve. Se "The First and Second Books of Adam and Eve" by Joseph Lumpkin.)

Chapter 33

1 And I appointed the eighth day also, that the eighth day should be the first-created after my work, and that the first seven revolve in the form of the seventh thousand, and that at the beginning of the eighth thousand there should be a time of not-counting, endless, with neither years nor months nor weeks nor days nor hours.

(Note: A day is as a thousand years. This is a prophecy seems to indicate that after six thousand years there will be a thousand years of rest, then there will be timelessness.)

2 And now, Enoch, all that I have told you, all that you have understood, all that you have seen of heavenly things, all that you have seen on earth, all that I have written in books by my great wisdom, and all these things I have devised and created from the uppermost foundation to the lower and to the end, and there is no counselor nor inheritor to my creations.
3 I am eternal unto myself, not made with hands, and without change.
4 My thought is my own counselor, my wisdom and my word creates, and my eyes observe how all things stand here and tremble with terror.
5 If I turn away my face, then all things will be destroyed.
6 Apply your mind, Enoch, and know him who is speaking to you, and take the books there, which you yourself have written.
7 I give you Samuil and Raguil, who led you upward with the books, and go down to earth, and tell your sons all that I have told you, and all that you have seen, from the lower heaven up to my throne, and all the troops.
8 For I created all forces, and there is none that resists me and none that does not subject himself to me. For all subject themselves to my kingdom, and labor for my complete rule.
9 Give them the books of the handwriting, and they will read them and will know that I am the creator of all things, and will understand how there is no other God but me.
10 And let them distribute the books of your handwriting from children to children, generation to generation, nation to nation.
11 And Enoch, I will give you, my intercessor, the archangel Michael, for the writings of your fathers Adam, Seth, Enos, Cainan, Mahaleleel, and Jared your father.

Chapter 34

1 They have rejected my commandments and my yoke, therefore worthless seed has come up, not fearing God, and they would not bow down to me, but have begun to bow down to empty gods, and rejected my unity (oneness / sovereignty), and have piled the whole earth up with lies, offences, abominable lust with one another, and all manner of other unclean wickedness, which are disgusting to even mention.
2 And therefore I will bring down a deluge upon the earth and will destroy all men, and the whole earth will crumble together into great darkness.

Chapter 35

1 You will see that from their seed shall arise another generation, long afterward, but of them many will be full of very strong desires that are never satisfied.

2 He who raises that generation shall reveal the books of your writing of your fathers to them. And He must point out the guardianship of the world to the faithful men and workers of my pleasure, who do not acknowledge my name in empty words.
3 And they shall tell another generation, and those others who, having read, shall afterward be glorified more than the first.

Chapter 36
1 Now, Enoch, I give you a period of thirty days to spend in your house, and tell your sons and all your household, so that all may hear from you what was spoken by my face, so that they may read and understand that there is no other God but me.
2 And that they may always keep my commandments, and begin to read and absorb the books of your writing.
3 And after thirty days I shall send my angel for you, and he will take you from earth and from your sons and bring you to me.

Chapter 37
1 And the Lord called upon one of the older angels who was terrible and menacing, and He placed him by me. He appeared white as snow, and his hands were like ice, having the appearance of great frost, and he froze my face, because I could not endure the terror of the Lord, just as it is not possible to endure a stove's fire or the sun's heat, or the frost of the air.
2 And the Lord said to me: Enoch, if your face is not frozen here, no man will be able to look at your face.

Chapter 38
1 And the Lord said to those men who first led me up: "Let Enoch go down on to earth with you, and await him until the determined day."
2 And by night they placed me on my bed.
3 But Methuselah was expecting my return and was keeping watch at my bed by day and night. And he was filled with awe when he heard my return, and I told him, "Let all my household come together, so that I may tell them everything."

Chapter 39
1 Oh my children, my loved ones, hear the advice of your father, as much as is according to the Lord's will.
2 I have been allowed to come to you today, and preach to you, not from my lips, but from the Lord's lips, all that is now, and was, and all that will be until judgment day.
3 For the Lord has allowed me to come to you so that you could hear the words of my lips, of a man made great for you, but I am one who has seen the Lord's face, and it was like iron made to glow from fire it sends forth sparks and burns.
4 You look upon my eyes now. They are the eyes of a man enlarged with meaning for you, but I have seen the Lord's eyes, shining like the sun's rays and filling the eyes of man with awe.
5 You see now, my children, the right hand of a man that helps you, but I have seen the Lord's right hand filling heaven as he helped me.
6 You see the scope of my work is like your own, but I have seen the Lord's limitless and perfect scope, which has no end.

7 You hear the words of my lips, as I heard the words of the Lord, and they are like constant and great thunder with hurling of clouds.
8 And now, my children, hear the lecture of the father of the earth. I will tell you how fearful and awful it is to come before the face of the ruler of the earth, and how much more terrible and awful it is to come before the face of the ruler of heaven, who is the judge of the quick and the dead, and of the controller of the heavenly troops. Who (of us) can endure that endless pain?

Chapter 40
1 And now, my children, I know all things, for this is from the Lord's lips, and my eyes have seen this, from beginning to end.
2 I know all things, and have written all things in the books, the heavens and their end, and their abundance, and all the armies and their marching.
3 I have measured and described the stars, the great innumerable multitude of them.
4 What man has seen their revolutions and their entrances? For not even the angels see their number, but I have written all their names.
5 And I measured the sun's circumference, and measured its rays, and counted the hours. I also wrote down all things that go over the earth. I have written the things that are nourished, and all seed sown and unsown, which the earth produces, and all plants, and every grass and every flower, and their sweet smells, and their names, and the dwelling-places of the clouds, and their composition, and their wings, and how they carry rain and raindrops.
6 And I investigated all things, and described the road of the thunder and of the lightning, and they showed me the keys and their guardians, their rise, and the way they precede. They are let out gradually, in measure, by a chain. If they were not let out at a measured rate by a heavy chain their violence would hurl down the angry clouds and destroy all things on earth.
7 I described the treasure houses of the snow, and the storehouses of the cold and the frosty airs, and I observed the key-holders of the seasons. He fills the clouds with them, and it does not exhaust the treasure houses.
8 And I wrote down the resting places of the winds and observed and saw how their key-holders bear weighing-scales and measures. First, they put them in one side of the weighing-scale, then in the other side they place the weights and let them out according to measure skillfully, over the whole earth, to keep the heavy winds from making the earth rock.
9 And I measured out the whole earth, its mountains, and all hills, fields, trees, stones, rivers, all existing things I wrote down, the height from earth to the seventh heaven, and downwards to the very lowest hell, and the judgment-place, and the very great, open and weeping (gaping) hell.
10 And I saw how the prisoners are in pain, expecting the limitless judgment.
11 And I wrote down all those being judged by the judge, and all their judgment and sentences and all their works.

Chapter 41
1 And I saw throughout all time all the forefathers from Adam and Eve, and I sighed and broke into tears and spoke of the ruin and their dishonor.
2 And I sad, "Woe is me for my infirmity and for that of my forefathers," and thought in my heart and said:

3 "Blessed is the man who has not been born or who has been born and shall not sin before the Lord's face, because he will not come into this place, nor bear the yoke of this place on himself.

Chapter 42
1 I saw the key-holders and guards of the gates of hell standing like great serpents. And their faces were glowing like extinguishing lamps, and I saw their eyes of fire, and their sharp teeth. And I saw all of the Lord's works, how they are right, while some of the works of man are of limited good, and others bad, and in their works are those who are known to speak evil lies.

Chapter 43
1 My children, I measured and wrote out every work and every measure and every righteous judgment.
2 As one year is more honorable than another, so is one man more honorable than another. Some men are honored for great possessions, some for wisdom of heart, some for particular intellect, some for skillfulness, one for silence of lip, another for cleanliness, one for strength, another for beauty, one for youth, another for sharp wit, one for shape of body, another for sensibility, but let it be heard everywhere: There is none better than he who fears God. He shall be more glorious in time to come.

Chapter 44
1 The Lord created man with his hands in the likeness of his own face. The Lord made him small and great.
2 Whoever reviles the ruler's face hates the Lord's face, and has contempt for the Lord's face, and he who vents anger on any man without having been injured by him, the Lord's great anger will cut him down, he who spits on the face of man reproachfully will be cut down at the Lord's great judgment.
3 Blessed is the man who does not direct his heart with malice against any man, and helps the injured and condemned, and raises up the broken down, and shall do charity to the needy, because on the day of the great judgment every weight, every measure and every makeweight will be as in the market, so they are hung on scales and stand in the market, and every one shall learn his own measure, and according to his measure shall take his reward.

(Note: Makeweight is something put on a scale to make up the required weight for a more precise measurement.)

Chapter 45
1 Whoever hurries to make offerings before the Lord's face, the Lord will hasten that offering by giving of His work.
2 But whoever increases his lamp before the Lord's face and makes a judgment that is not true, the Lord will not increase his treasure in the realm of the highest.

(Note: Whoever makes himself out to be more than he is and whoever judges others without truth or cause, the Lord will not reward in heaven.)

3 When the Lord demands bread, or candles, or the flesh of beasts, or any other sacrifice, it is nothing; but God demands pure hearts, and with all He does it is only the tests of man's heart.

Chapter 46
1 Hear, my people, and take in the words of my lips.
2 If any one brings any gifts to an earthly ruler, and has disloyal thoughts in his heart, and the ruler know this, will the ruler not be angry with him, and refuse his gifts, and give him over to judgment?
3 Or if one man makes himself appear good to another by deceit of the tongue, but has evil in his heart, then will the other person not understand the treachery of his heart, and condemned him, since his lie was plain to all?
4 And when the Lord shall send a great light, then there will be judgment for the just and the unjust, and no one shall escape notice.

Chapter 47
1 And now, my children, with your minds and your hearts, mark well the words of your father, which all have come to you from the Lord's lips.
2 Take these books of your father's writing and read them.
3 For there are many books, and in them you will learn all the Lord's works, all that has been from the beginning of creation, and will be until the end of time.
4 And if you will observe my writing, you will not sin against the Lord; because there is no other except the Lord in heaven, nor in earth, nor in the very lowest places, nor in the foundation.
5 The Lord has placed the foundations in the unknown, and has spread out heavens, both physical and spiritual; he anchored the earth on the waters, and created countless creatures. Who has counted the water and the foundation of the mutable, or the dust of the earth, or the sand of the sea, or the drops of the rain, or the morning dew, or the wind's blowing (breathing)? Who has filled earth and sea, and the indestructible winter?
6 I (The Lord) cut the stars out of fire, and decorated heaven, and put it in their midst.

Chapter 48
1 The sun goes along the seven heavenly circles, which are the appointment of one hundred and eighty-two thrones. It goes down on a short day, and again one hundred and eighty-two. It goes down on a long day, and he has two thrones on which he rests, revolving here and there above the thrones of the months, from the seventeenth day of the month Tsivan it goes down to the month Thevan, from the seventeenth of Thevan it goes up.

(Note: The words Tsivan and Thevan refer to the summer and winter solstice, dividing the lengthening and shortening of days.
The sun goes in a sinusoidal wave, decreasing daylight time for 182 days and growing longer in daylight hours for 182 days, with an extra day, which is a long day. The total is 365 days.)

2 When it goes close to the earth, then the earth is glad and makes its fruits grow, and when it goes away, then the earth is sad, and trees and all fruits will not flower.

3 All this He measured, with good measurement of hours, and predetermined a measure by his wisdom, of the physical and the spiritual (realms).
4 From the spiritual realm he made all things that are physical, himself being spiritual.
5 So I teach you, my children, and tell you to distribute the books to your children, into all your generations, and among the nations who shall have the sense to fear God. Let them receive them, and may they come to love them more than any food or earthly sweets, and read them and apply themselves to them.
6 And those who do not understand the Lord, who do not fear God, who do not accept, but reject, who do not receive the books, a terrible judgment awaits these.
7 Blessed is the man who shall bear their yoke and shall drag them along, for he shall be released on the day of the great judgment.

Chapter 49
1 I swear to you, my children, but I do not swear by any oath, neither by heaven nor by earth, nor by any other creature created by God.
2 The Lord said: "There is no oath in Me, nor injustice, but only truth."
3 But there is no truth in men, so let them swear by the words, Yea, yea, or else, Nay, nay.
4 And I swear to you, yea, yea, that every man that has been in his mother's womb has had a place prepared for the repose of that soul, and a measure predetermined of how much it is intended that a man be tried (tested) in this world.
5 Yea, children, do not deceive yourselves, for there has been a place previously prepared for the soul of every man.

Chapter 50
1 I have put every man's work in writing and none born on earth can remain hidden nor his works remain concealed.
2 I see all things.
3 Therefore, my children, spend the number of your days in patience and meekness so that you may inherit eternal life.
4 For the sake of the Lord, endure every wound, every injury, every evil word, and every attack.
5 If your good deeds are not rewarded but returned for ill to you, do not repay them to neither neighbor nor enemy, because the Lord will return them for you and be your avenger on the day of great judgment, so that there should be no vengeance here among men.
6 Whoever of you spends gold or silver for his brother's sake, he will receive ample treasure in the world to come.
7 Do not injure widows or orphans or strangers, for if you do God's wrath will come upon you.

Chapter 51
1 Stretch out your hands to the poor according to your strength.
2 Do not hide your silver in the earth.
3 Help the faithful man in affliction, and affliction will not find you in the time of your trouble.
4 And bear every grievous and cruel yoke that comes upon you, for the sake of the Lord, and thus you will find your reward in the Day of Judgment.

5 It is good to go morning, midday, and evening into the Lord's house, for the glory of your creator.
6 Because every breathing thing glorifies him, and every creature, both physical and spiritual, gives him praise. (Gives His praise back to Him.)

Chapter 52
1 Blessed is the man who opens his lips in praise of God of Sabaoth (Host / army) and praises the Lord with his heart.
2 Cursed is every man who opens his lips for the purpose of bringing contempt and slander to (of) his neighbor, because he brings God into contempt.
3 Blessed is he who opens his lips blessing and praising God.
4 Cursed before the Lord all the days of his life, is he who opens his lips to curse and abuse.
5 Blessed is he who blesses all the Lord's works.
6 Cursed is he who brings the Lord's creation into contempt.
7 Blessed is he who looks down and raises the fallen.
8 Cursed is he who looks to and is eager for the destruction of what is not his.
9 Blessed is he who keeps the foundations of his fathers that were made firm from the beginning.
10 Cursed is he who corrupts the doctrine of his forefathers.
11 Blessed is he who imparts peace and love.
12 Cursed is he who disturbs those that love their neighbors.
13 Blessed is he who speaks with humble tongue and heart to all.
14 Cursed is he who speaks peace with his tongue, while in his heart there is no peace but a sword.
15 For all these things will be laid bare in the scales of balance and in the books, on the day of the great judgment.

Chapter 53
1 And now, my children, do not say: "Our father is standing before God, and is praying for our sins. For there is there no helper for any man who has sinned.
2 You see how I wrote down all of the works of every man, before his creation, all that is done among all men for all time, and none can tell or relate my writing, because the Lord sees all imaginings of man, and how they are empty and prideful, where they lie in the treasure houses of the heart.
3 And now, my children, mark well all the words of your father that I tell you, or you will be regretful, saying: Why did our father not tell us?

(Note: although chapters 51 and 52 seem similar to the Sermon on the Mount, Chapter 53 offers no balance between mercy and justice. "There is no helper for any man who has sinned," is a statement excluding a savior. Scholars point to this verse to conclude 2 Enoch is a Jewish text. As stated before, 2 Enoch seems to be a Jewish text that was Christianized by additions and embellishment of the core text. Chapter 53 is part of the core Jewish text, likely written before the Christian sect.)

Chapter 54
1 Let these books, which I have given you, be for an inheritance of your peace in that time that you do not understand this.

2 Hand them to all who want them, and instruct them, that they may see the Lord's very great and marvelous works.

Chapter 55
1 My children, behold, the day of my determined period (term and time) has approached.
2 For the angels who shall go with me are standing before me and urge me to my departure from you. They are standing here on earth, awaiting what has been told them.
3 For tomorrow I shall go up to heaven, to the uppermost Jerusalem, to my eternal inheritance.
4 Therefore I bid you to do the Lord's good pleasure before his face at all times.

(Note: The Jerusalem spoken of here is the spiritual Jerusalem, spoken of by John, coming down from heaven. The name, "Jerusalem" refers to the components of the actual name, which break down to mean "provision" and "peace".)

Chapter 56"
1 Methuselah answered his father Enoch, and said: What (food) is agreeable to your eyes, father, that I may prepare before your face, that you may bless our houses, and your sons, and that your people may be made glorious through you, and then that you may depart, as the Lord said?"
2 Enoch answered his son Methuselah and said: "Hear me, my child. From the time when the Lord anointed me with the ointment of his glory, there has been no food in me, and my soul remembers not earthly enjoyment, neither do I want anything earthly."

Chapter 57
1 My child Methuselah, summon all your brethren and all of your household and the elders of the people, that I may talk to them and depart, as is planned for me.
2 And Methuselah hurried, and summoned his brethren, Regim, Riman, Uchan, Chermion, Gaidad, and all the elders of the people before the face of his father Enoch; and he blessed them, and said to them:

Chapter 58
1 "Listen to me, my children, today.
2 In those days when the Lord came down to earth for Adam's sake, and visited all his creatures, which he created himself, after all these he created Adam, and the Lord called all the beasts of the earth, all the reptiles, and all the birds that soar in the air, and brought them all before the face of our father Adam.
3 And Adam gave names to all things living on earth.
4 And the Lord appointed him ruler over all, and subjected all things to him under his hands, and made them dumb and made them dull that they would be commanded by man, and be in subjection and obedience to him.
5 The Lord also created every man lord over all his possessions.
6 The Lord will not judge a single soul of beast for man's sake, but He judges the souls of men through their beasts in this world, for men have a special place.

7 And as every soul of man is according to number, similarly beasts will not perish, nor all souls of beasts which the Lord created, until the great judgment, and they will accuse man, if he did not feed them well.

Chapter 59
1 Whoever defiles the soul of beasts, defiles his own soul.
2 For man brings clean animals to make sacrifice for sin, that he may have cure for his soul.
3 And if they bring clean animals and birds for sacrifice, man has a cure. He cures his soul.
4 All is given you for food, bind it by the four feet, to make good the cure.
5 But whoever kills beast without wounds, kills his own souls and defiles his own flesh.
6 And he who does any beast any injury whatsoever, in secret, it is evil practice, and he defiles his own soul.

(Note: To kill without a wound is to inflict blunt force trauma - to beat them to death.)

Chapter 60
1 He who works the killing of a man's soul (he who murders), kills his own soul, and kills his own body, and there is no cure for him for all time.
2 He who puts a man in any snare (moral entrapment), shall stick himself in it, and there is no cure for him for all time.
3 He who puts a man in any vessel, his retribution will not be wanting at the great judgment for all time.
4 He who works dishonestly or speaks evil against any soul, will not make justice for himself for all time.

Chapter 61
1 And now, my children, keep your hearts from every injustice, which the Lord hates. Just as a man asks something for his own soul from God, so let him do the same to every living soul, because I know all things, how in the great time to come there is a great inheritance prepared for men, good for the good, and bad for the bad, no matter the number.
2 Blessed are those who enter the good houses, for in the bad houses there is no peace or return from them.
3 Hear, my children, small and great! When man puts a good thought in his heart, it brings gifts from his labors before the Lord's face. But if his hands did not make them, then the Lord will turn away his face from the labor of his hand, and (that) man cannot find the labor of his hands.
4 And if his hands made it, but his heart murmurs (complains), and his heart does not stop murmurs incessantly, he does not have (gain) any advantage.

Chapter 62
1 Blessed is the man who, in his patience, brings his gifts with faith before the Lord's face, because he will find forgiveness of sins.
2 But if he takes back his words before the time, there is no repentance for him; and if the time passes and he does not of his own will perform what is promised, there is no repentance after death.

3 Because every work which man does before the time (outside the time he has promised it), is all deceit before men, and sin before God.

Chapter 63
1 When man clothes the naked and fills the hungry, he will find reward from God.
2 But if his heart complains, he commits a double evil; ruin of himself and of that which he gives; and for him there will be no finding of reward because of that.
3 And if his own heart is filled with his food and his own flesh is clothed with his own clothing, he commits contempt, and will forfeit all his endurance of poverty, and will not find reward of his good deeds. (If he is selfish and does not add to the economy of others...)
4 Every proud and pontificating man is hateful to the Lord, and every false speech is clothed in lies. It will be cut with the blade of the sword of death, and thrown into the fire, and shall burn for all time.

Chapter 64
1 When Enoch had spoken these words to his sons, all people far and near heard how the Lord was calling Enoch. They took counsel together:
2 Let us go and kiss Enoch, and two thousand men came together and came to the place called Achuzan, where Enoch was with his sons.
3 And the elders of the people with the entire assembly came and bowed down and began to kiss Enoch and said to him:
4 "Our father Enoch, may you be blessed by the Lord, the eternal ruler, and now bless your sons and all the people, that we may be glorified today before your face.
5 For you shall be glorified before the Lord's face for eternity, since the Lord chose you from among all men on earth, and designated you as the writer of all his creation, both physical and spiritual, and you are redeemed from the sins of man, and are the helper of your household."

Chapter 65
1 And Enoch said to all his people: "Hear me, my children. Before all creatures were created, the Lord created the physical and spiritual things.
2 And then a long term passed. Then after all of that he created man in the likeness of his own form, and put eyes into him to see, and ears into him to hear, and a heart to reflect, and intellect to enable him to deliberate.
3 And the Lord saw all the works of man, and created all his creatures, and divided time. From time he determined the years, and from the years he appointed the months, and from the months he appointed the days, and of days he appointed seven.
4 And in those he appointed the hours, measured them out exactly, that man might reflect on time and count years, months, and hours, as they alternate from beginning to end, so that he might count his own life from the beginning until death, and reflect on his sin and write his works, both bad and good. No work is hidden from the Lord, so that every man might know his works and never transgress all his commandments, and keep my writing from generation to generation.
5 When all creation, both physical and spiritual, as the Lord created it, shall end, then every man goes to the great judgment, and then all time shall be destroyed

along with the years. And from then on there will be neither months nor days nor hours. They will run together and will not be counted.
6 There will be one eon, and all the righteous who shall escape the Lord's great judgment, shall be collected in the great eon. For the righteous the great eon will begin, and they will live eternally, and there will be no labor, nor sickness, nor humiliation, nor anxiety, nor need, nor brutality, nor night, nor darkness, but great light among them.
7 And they shall have a great indestructible wall, and a paradise that is bright and eternal, for all mortal things shall pass away, and there will be eternal life.

(Note: an eon is one billion years but is used to mean a very long but indefinite period of time. The word "eternal" means "unchanging, incorruptible, immortal." The word used for "mortal" is the opposite of "eternal", thus, "mortal, corruptible, changing.")

Chapter 66
1 And now, my children, keep your souls from all injustice the Lord hates.
2 Walk before his face with great fear (respect) and trembling and serve him only.
3 Bow down to the true God, not to dumb idols, but bow down to his likeness, and bring all just offerings before the Lord's face. The Lord hates what is unjust.

(Note: This is an odd command issued by Enoch, that the people are not to bow to dumb idols but are to bow to the likeness or similitude of God.)

4 For the Lord sees all things; when man takes thought in his heart, then he counsels the intellects, and every thought is always before the Lord, who made firm the earth and put all creatures on it.
5 If you look to heaven, the Lord is there; if you take thought of the sea's deep and all under the earth, the Lord is there.
6 For the Lord created all things. Bow not down to things made by man, leaving the Lord of all creation, because no work can remain hidden before the Lord's face.
7 Walk, my children, in long-suffering, in meekness, honesty, in thoughtfulness, in grief, in faith and in truth. Walk in (rely on) promises, in (times of) illness, in abuse, in wounds, in temptation, in nakedness, in privation, loving one another, until you go out from this age of ills, that you become inheritors of endless time.
8 Blessed are the just who shall escape the great judgment, for they shall shine forth more than the sun sevenfold, for in this world the seventh part is taken off from all, light, darkness, food, enjoyment, sorrow, paradise, torture, fire, frost, and other things; he put all down in writing, that you might read and understand.

Chapter 67
1 When Enoch had talked to the people, the Lord sent out darkness on to the earth, and there was darkness, and it covered those men standing with Enoch, and they took Enoch up on to the highest heaven, where the Lord is. And there God received him and placed him before His face, and the darkness went off from the earth, and light came again.
2 And the people saw and did not understand how Enoch had been taken, and they glorified God, and found a scroll in which was written "The God of the Spiritual." Then all went to their dwelling places.

Chapter 68
1 Enoch was born on the sixth day of the month Tsivan (the first month of the year), and lived three hundred and sixty-five years.
2 He was taken up to heaven on the first day of the month Tsivan and remained in heaven sixty days.
3 He wrote all these signs of all creation, which the Lord created, and wrote three hundred and sixty-six books, and handed them over to his sons and remained on earth thirty days, and was again taken up to heaven on the sixth day of the month Tsivan, on the very day and hour when he was born.
4 As every man's nature in this life is dark, so are also his conception, birth, and departure from this life.
5 At what hour he was conceived, at that hour he was born, and at that hour too he died.
6 Methuselah and his brethren, all the sons of Enoch, made haste, and erected an altar at that place called Achuzan, where Enoch had been taken up to heaven.
7 And they took sacrificial oxen and summoned all people and sacrificed the sacrifice before the Lord's face.
8 All people, the elders of the people and the whole assembly came to the feast and brought gifts to the sons of Enoch.
9 And they made a great feast, rejoicing and making merry three days, praising God, who had given them such a sign through Enoch, who had found favor with him, and that they should hand it on to their sons from generation to generation, from age to age. Amen.

(Note: Enoch was born on the 6th day of Tsivan. Tsivan is the first month of the year. The sum is seven, one of the holy numbers. He lived 365 years. One year of years. He remained in heaven 60 days. Six is the number of man, which always falls short of God.)

The Short Version Ends Here

The wife of Nir was Sopanim. She was sterile and never had at any time given birth to a child by Nir.
Sopanim was in her old age and in the last days (time) of her death. She conceived in her womb, but Nir the priest had not slept with her from the day that that the Lord had appointed him to conduct the liturgy in front of the face of the people.

When Sopanim saw her pregnancy, she was ashamed and embarrassed, and she hid herself during all the days until she gave birth. Not one of the people knew about it. When 282 days had been completed, and the day of birth had begun to approach, Nir thought about his wife, and he called her to come to him in his house, so that he might converse with her.

Sopanim came to Nir, her husband; and, behold, she was pregnant, and the day appointed for giving birth was drawing near. Nir saw her and became very ashamed. He said to her, "What is this that you have done, O wife? Why have you disgraced me in front of the face of these people? Now, depart from me and go back to where you began this disgrace of your womb, so that I might not defile my hands in front of The Face of The Lord on account of you and sin."

Sopanim spoke to her husband, Nir, saying, "O my lord! Look at me. It is the time of my old age, the day of my death has arrived. I do not understand how my menopause and the barrenness of my womb have been reversed." But Nir did not believe his wife, and for the second time he said to her, "Depart from me, or else I might assault you, and commit a sin in front of the face of The Lord."

And after Nir had spoken to his wife, Sopanim, she fell down at Nir's feet and died. Nir was extremely distressed and said to himself, "Could this have happened because of my words? And now, merciful is The Eternal Lord, because my hand was not upon her."

The archangel Gabriel appeared to Nir, and said to him, "Do not think that your wife Sopanim has died due to your error? This child, which is to be born from her, is a righteous fruit, and one whom I shall receive into paradise so that you will not be the father of a gift of God."

Nir hurried and shut the door of his house. He went to Noah, his brother, and he reported to him everything that had happened in connection with his wife. Noah hurried to the room of his brother. The appearance of his brother's wife was as if she were dead but her womb was at the same time giving birth.

Noah said to Nir, "Don't let yourself be sorrowful, Nir, my brother! Today the Lord has covered up our scandal, because nobody from the people knows this. Now let us go quickly and bury her, and the Lord will cover up the scandal of our shame." They placed Sopanim on the bed, wrapped her around with black garments, and shut the door. They dug a grave in secret.

When they had gone out toward the grave, a child came out from Sopanim's dead body and sat on the bed at her side. Noah and Nir came in to bury Sopanim and they saw the child sitting beside Sopanim's dead body and he was wiping his clothing. Noah and Nir were very terrified with a great fear, because the child was physically fully developed. The child spoke with his lips and blessed The Lord.
Noah and Nir looked at him closely, saying, "This is from the Lord, my brother." The badge of priesthood is on his chest, and it is glorious in appearance. Noah said to Nir, "God is renewing the priesthood from blood related to us, just as He pleases."

Noah and Nir hurried and washed the child, they dressed him in the garments of the priesthood, and they gave him bread to eat and he ate it. And they called him Melchizedek.

Noah and Nir lifted up the body of Sopanim, and took the black garment off of her and washed her. They clothed her in exceptionally bright garments and built a grave for her. Noah, Nir, and Melchizedek came and they buried her publicly. Then Noah said to his brother Nir, "Take care of this child in secret until the proper time comes, because all of the people on earth will become treacherous and they will begin to turn away from God. Having become completely ignorant (of God), when they see him, they will put him to death in some way."

Then Noah went away to his own place, and there came great lawlessness that began to become abundant over all the earth in the days of Nir. And Nir began to worry greatly about the child saying, "What will I do with him?" And stretching out his hands toward heaven, Nir called out to The Lord, saying, " It is miserable for me, Eternal Lord, that all of this lawlessness has begun to become abundant over all the earth in my lifetime! I realize how much nearer our end is because of the lawlessness of the people. And now, Lord, what is the vision about this child, and what is his destiny, or what will I do for him, so that he will not be joined along with us in this destruction?"

The Lord took notice of Nir and appeared to him in a night vision. And He said to him, "Nir, the great lawlessness which has come about on the earth I shall not tolerate anymore. I plan to send down a great destruction onto the earth. But do not worry about the child, Nir. In a short while I will send My archangel Gabriel and he will take the child and put him in the paradise of Edem. He will not perish along with those who must perish. As I have revealed it, Melchizedek will be My priest to all holy priests, I will sanctify him and I will establish him so that he will be the head of the priests of the future."

(Note: Edem means, "God will save." It is assumed Edem is Eden.)

Then Nir arose from his sleep and blessed The Lord, who had appeared to him saying: "Blessed be The Lord, The God of my fathers, who has approved of my priesthood and the priesthood of my fathers, because by His Word, He has created a great priest in the womb of Sopanim, my wife. For I have no descendants. So let this child take the place of my descendants and become as my own son. You will count him in the number of your servants."

"Therefore honor him together with your servants and great priests and me your servant, Nir. And behold, Melchizedek will be the head of priests in another generation. I know that great confusion has come and in confusion this generation will come to an end, and everyone will perish, except that Noah, my brother, will be preserved for procreation. From his tribe, there will arise numerous people, and Melchizedek will become the head of priests reigning over a royal people who will serve you, O Lord."

It happened when the child had completed 40 days in Nir's tent, The Lord said to the archangel Gabriel, "Go down to the earth to Nir the priest, and take the child Melchizedek, who is with him. Place him in the paradise of Edem for preservation. For the time is already approaching, and I will pour out all the water onto the earth, and everything that is on the earth will perish. And I will raise it up again, and Melchizedek will be the head of the priests in that generation." And Gabriel hurried, and came flying down when it was night when Nir was sleeping on his bed that night.

Gabriel appeared to him and said to him, "The Lord says: "Nir! Restore the child to me whom I entrusted to you." But Nir did not realize who was speaking to him and he was confused. And he said, "When the people find out about the child, they will seize him and kill him, because the heart of these people are deceitful before The

Lord." And he answered Gabriel and said, "The child is not with me, and I don't know who is speaking to me."

Gabriel answered him, " Nir, do not be afraid. I am the archangel Gabriel. The Lord sent me to take your child today. I will go with him and I will place him in the paradise of Edem." Then Nir remembered the first dream and believed it. He answered Gabriel, "Blessed be The Lord, who has sent you to me today! Now bless your servant Nir! Take the child and do to him all that has been said to you." And Gabriel took the child, Melchizedek on his wings in that same night, and he placed him in the paradise of Edem. Nir got up in the morning, and he went into his tent and did not find the child. There was great joy and grief for Nir because he felt the child had the place of a son.

The Lord said to Noah, "Make an ark that is 300 cubits in length, 50 cubits in width and in 30 cubits height. Put the entrance to the ark in its side; and make it with two stories in the middle" The Lord God opened the doors of heaven. Rain came onto the earth and all flesh died.

Noah fathered 3 sons: Shem, Ham and Japheth. He went into the ark in his six hundredth year. After the flood, he lived 350 years. He lived in all 950 years, according to The Lord our God.
To our God be Glory always, now and eternally. AMEN.

The Book of Jubilees
The Little Genesis, The Apocalypse of Moses

INTRODUCTION

The Book of Jubilees, also known as The Little Genesis and The Apocalypse of Moses, opens with an extraordinary claim of authorship. It is attributed to the very hand of Moses; penned while he was on Mount Sinai, as an angel of God dictated to him regarding those events that transpired from the beginning of the world. The story is written from the viewpoint of the angel. The angelic monolog takes place after the exodus of the children of Israel out of Egypt. The setting is atop Mount Sinai, where Moses was summoned by God. The text then unfolds as the angel reveals heaven's viewpoint of history. We are led through the creation of man, Adam's fall from grace, the union of fallen angels and earthly women, the birth of demonic offspring, the cleansing of the earth by flood, and the astonishing claim that man's very nature was somehow changed, bringing about a man with less sinful qualities than his antediluvian counterpart. The story goes on to fill in many details in Israel's history, ending at the point in time when the narrative itself takes place, after the exodus.

Scholars believe Jubilees was composed in the second century B.C. The Hebrew fragments found at Qumran are part of a Jewish library that contained other supporting literature such as the Book of Enoch and others. An analysis of the chronological development in the shapes of letters in the manuscripts confirms that Jubilees is pre-Christian in date and seems to have been penned between 100 and 200 B.C. Based on records of the High Priests of the time, the date of authorship is probably 140 – 100 B.C. The book of Jubilees is also cited in the Qumran Damascus Document in pre-Christian texts.

The Book of Jubilees was originally written in Hebrew. The author was a Pharisee (a doctor of the law), or someone very familiar with scripture and religious law. Since the scrolls were found in what is assumed to be an Essene library, and were dated to the time the Essene community was active, the author was probably a member of that particular religious group. Jubilees represents a hyper-legalistic and midrashic tendency, which was part of the Essene culture at the time.

"Midrash" – refers to writings containing extra-legal material of anecdotal or allegorical nature, designed either to clarify historical material, or to teach a moral point.

Jubilees represents a midrash on Genesis 1:1 through Exodus 12:50 which depicts the episodes from creation with the observance of the Sabbath by the angels and men to Israel's escape from Egyptian bondage.

Although originally written in Hebrew, the Hebrew texts were completely lost until the find at Qumran. Fragments of Jubilees were discovered among the Dead Sea Scrolls. At least fourteen copies of the Book of Jubilees have been identified from caves 1, 2, 3 and 11 at Qumran. This makes it clear that the Book of Jubilees was a popular and probably authoritative text for the community whose library was concealed in the caves. These fragments are actually generations closer to the original copies than many books in our accepted Bible. Unfortunately, the fragments found at Qumran were only pieces of the texts and offered the briefest of glimpses of the entire book. The only complete versions of the Book of Jubilees are in Ethiopic, which in turn were translations of a Greek version.

Four Ethiopian manuscripts of Jubilees were found to be hundreds of years old. Of these, the fifteenth and sixteenth century texts are the truest and least corrupted when compared to the fragments found at Qumran. There are also citations of Jubilees in Syriac literature that may reflect a lost translation from Hebrew. Pieces of Latin translations have also been found.

Other fragments of a Greek version are quoted or referenced by Justin Martyr, Origen, Diodorus of Antioch, Isidore of Alexandria, Isidore of Seville, Eutychius, Patriarch of Alexandria, John of Malala, and Syncellus. This amount of various information and translations is enough to allow us to reconstruct the original to a great degree. The internal evidence of Jubilees shows very little tampering by Christians during its transmission and subsequent translations, thus allowing a clear view of certain Jewish beliefs being propagated at the time of its origin. By removing certain variances, we can isolate Christian alterations and mistakes in translations with a reasonable degree of confidence. Due to the poor condition of the fragments of Qumran, we may never be able to confirm certain key phrases in Hebrew. Thus, as with many texts, including those of our own Bible, in the end we must trust in the accuracy of the ancient scribes and translators.

It should be noted that the books of Jubilees, Enoch, and Jasher present stories of "The Watchers"; a group of angels sent to earth to record and teach, but who fell by their own lust and pride into a demonic state. Both Enoch and Jubilees refer to a solar-based calendar. This may show a conflict or transition at the time of their penning since Judaism now uses a lunar-based calendar Laws, rites, and functions are observed and noted in Jubilees. Circumcision is emphasized in both humans and angels. Angelic observance of Sabbath laws as well as parts of Jewish religious laws are said to have been observed in heaven before they were revealed to Moses.

To the Qumran community, complete obedience to the Laws of Moses entailed observing a series of holy days and festivals at a particular time according to a specific calendar. The calendar described in Jubilees is one of 364 days, divided into four seasons of three months each with thirteen weeks to a season. Each month had 30 days with one day added at certain times for each of the four seasons. With 52 weeks in a year, the festival and holy days recur at the same point each year. This calendar became a hallmark of an orthodox Qumran community.

The adherence to a specific calendar is one of many ways the Book of Jubilees shows the devotion to religious law. The law had been placed at the pinnacle of importance in the lives of the community at Qumran. All aspects of life were driven by a seemingly obsessive compliance to every jot and tittle of the law. The Book Of Jubilees confirms what can only be inferred from the books of Ezra, Nehemiah, and Zechariah, that the law and those who carried it out were supreme.

As the law took hold, by its nature, it crystallized the society. Free expression died, smothered under a mantle of hyperorthodoxy. Since free thought invited accusations of violations of the law or claims of heresy, prudence, a closed mind, and a silent voice prevailed. Free thought was limited to religious or apocryphal writings, which upheld the orthodox positions of the day. The silent period between Malachi and Mark may be a reflection of this stasis. Jubilees, Enoch, and other apocryphal books found in the Qumran caves are a triumph over the unimaginative mindset brought on by making religious law supreme and human expression contrary to law punishable by death. It may be an odd manifestation that such a burst of creativity was fueled by the very search for order that suppressed free thought in the first place.

The Book of Jubilees seems to be an attempt to answer and explain all questions left unanswered in the Book of Genesis as well as to bolster the position of the religious law. It attempts to trace the source of religious laws back to an ancient beginning thereby adding weight and sanction.

In the Book of Jubilees, we discover the origin of the wife of Cain. There is information offered about angels and the beginnings of the human race, how demons came into existence, and the place of Satan in the plans of God. Information is offered in an attempt to make perfect sense of the vagaries left in Genesis. For the defense of order and law and to maintain religious law as the center point of Jewish life, Jubilees was written as an answer to both pagan Greeks and liberal Jews. From the divine placement of law and order to its explanation of times and events, Jubilees is a panorama of legalism.

The name "Jubilees" comes from the division of time into eras known as Jubilees. One Jubilee occurs after the equivalent of forty-nine years, or seven Sabbaths or weeks of years has passed. It is the numerical perfection of seven sevens. In a balance and symmetry of years, the Jubilee occurs after seven cycles of seven or forty-nine years have been completed. Thus, the fiftieth year is a Jubilee year. Time is told by referencing the number of Jubilees that have transpired from the time the festival was first kept. For example, Israel entered Canaan at the close of the fiftieth jubilee, which is about 2450 BCE.

The obsession with time, dates, and the strict observance of festivals are all evidence of legalism taken to the highest level.

Based on the approximate time of writing, Jubilees was created in the time of the Maccabees, in the high priesthood of Hyrcanus. In this period of time the appearance of the Messiah and the rise of the Messianic kingdom were viewed as imminent. Followers were preparing themselves for the arrival of the Messiah and the establishment of His eternal kingdom.

Judaism was in contact with the Greek culture at the time. The Greeks were known to be philosophers and were developing processes of critical thinking. One objective of Jubilees was to defend Judaism against the attacks of the Hellenists and to prove that the law was logical, consistent, and valid. Attacks against paganism and non-believers are embedded in the text along with defense of the law and its consistency through proclamations of the law being observed by the angels in heaven from the beginning of creation.

Moral lessons are taught by use of the juxtaposition of the "satans" and their attempts to test and lead mankind into sin against the warning and advice of scriptural wisdom from Moses and his angels.

Mastema is mentioned only in The Book of Jubilees and in the Fragments of a Zadokite Work. Mastema is Satan. The name Mastema is derived from the Hebrew, "Mastim," meaning "adversary." The word occurs as singular and plural. The word is equivalent to Satan (adversary or accuser). This is similar to the chief Satan and his class of "satans" in 1 Enoch 40:7.

Mastema is subservient to God. His task is to tempt men to sin and if they do, he accuses them in the presence of the Throne of God. He and his minions lead men into sin but do not cause the sin. Once men have chosen to sin, they lead them from sin to destruction. Since man is given free will, sin is a choice, with Mastema simply encouraging and facilitating the decision. The choice, we can assume, is our own and the destruction that follows is "self-destruction."

Beliar is also mentioned. Beliar is the Greek name for Belial or Beliaal. The name in its Hebrew equivalent means "without value." This was a demon known by the Jews as the chief of all the devils. Belial is the leader of the Sons of Darkness. Belial is mentioned in the Fragments of a Zadokite fragment along with Mastema, which states that at the time of the Antichrist, Belial shall be let loose against Israel, as God spoke through Isaiah the prophet. Belial is sometimes presented as an agent of God's punishment although he is considered a "satan."

Although it is impossible to explore here in any detail the ramification of superhuman entities and their culpability in man's sin, it is important to mention that Judaism had no doctrine of original sin. The fall of Adam and Eve may have removed man from the perfect environment and the curses that followed may have shortened his lifespan, but propagation of sin through the bloodline was not considered. Sin seemed to affect only man and the animals he was given dominion over. Yet, man continued to sin, and to increase in his capacity and modes of sin. The explanation offered for man's inability to resist is the existence of fallen angels; spiritual, superhuman creations whose task it was to teach us but who now tempt and mislead men. In the end, the world declines and crumbles under the evil influence of the fallen angels turned demons called, "The Watchers."

With the establishment of the covenant between Abraham and God, we are told that God had appointed spirits to "mislead" all the nations but would not assign a spirit to lead or mislead the children of Isaac but God himself would be leading them.

Within the text are recurring numbers. Seven, being the number of perfection, is the most common. The number three is cited, being the number of completion. However, the number twenty-two occurs in the accounts of creation and lineage. It is worth noting that there are twenty-two letters in the Hebrew alphabet. The number twenty-two represents a type of Godly assignment or appointment. It is also the number of the perfect foundation and of the God-given language. It is presented within the text as a reminder that God established the ways of the Jews and gave the Hebrew language and writing first and only to the Jews.

The angels converse in Hebrew and it is the heavenly tongue. The law is written by God using this alphabet thus the law is also holy. All men spoke Hebrew until the time of Babel when it was lost. However, when Abraham dedicated himself to God, his ears were opened and his tongue was sanctified and Hebrew was again spoken and understood.

Finally, the entire text is based on the numbers of forty-nine and fifty. Forty-nine represents the pinnacle of perfection, being made up of seven times seven. The number fifty, which is the number of the Jubilee, is the number of grace. In this year slaves were to be set free, debts were forgiven, and grace filled the land and people.

Drawing from the theology and myths at the time, the book of Jubilees expands and embellishes on the creation story, the fall of Adam and Eve, and the fall of the angels. The expanded detail written into the text may have been one reason it was eventually rejected. However, the effects of the book can still be seen throughout the Judeo-Christian beliefs of today. The theology espoused in Jubilees can be seen in the angelology and demonology taught in the Christian churches of today and widely held by many Jews.

In an attempt to answer questions left unaddressed in Genesis the writer confronts the origin and identification of Cain's wife. According to The Book Of Jubilees, Cain married his sister, as did all of the sons of Adam and Eve, except Abel, who was murdered. This seemed offensive to some, since it flies in the face of the very law it was written to defend. Yet, this seemed to the writer to be the lesser of evils, given the problematic questions. Inbreeding is dismissed with the observation that the law was not fully given and understood then. The effects of the act were mute due to the purity of the newly created race.

The seeming discrepancy between divine command of Adam's death decree and the timing of his death is addressed. Seeing that Adam continued to live even after he ate the fruit, which was supposed to bring on his death, the writer set about to clarify God's actions. The problem is explained away in a single sentence. Since a day in heaven is as a thousand years on earth and Adam died having lived less than a thousand years this meant he died in the same heavenly day. Dying within the same day of the crime was acceptable.

In an astonishing parallel to the Book Of Enoch, written at about the same time as Jubilees, the Watchers, or sons of God mentioned in Genesis 6, fell from grace when they descended to earth and had sex with the daughters of men. In the Book of Enoch, the angels descended for the purpose of seducing the women of earth. However, in The Book Of Jubilee the angels were sent to teach men, but after living on earth for a while, were tempted by their own lust and fell. The offspring of this unholy union were bloodthirsty and cannibalistic giants. The Book of Jubilees indicates that each of the offspring were somehow different, yet they are divided into categories of the Naphidim, (or Naphilim, depending on the transliteration), the Giants, and the Eljo. (Naphil are also mentioned, however, this word is the singular of Naphilim.)

As sin spread throughout the world and the minds of men were turned toward evil, God saw no alternative but to cleanse the earth with a flood and establish a "new nature" in man that does not have to sin. It is this new nature that the messiah will meet in mankind when He comes. As far as this author is aware, the re-creation of man's nature is mentioned in no other book. This idea of human nature being altered as it exited before the flood is found nowhere else but in Jubilees.

The angelic narrator tells us there were times in Israel's history when no evil existed and all men lived in accord. We are also told when and where the satans were allowed to attack and confound Israel. In this narrative, God uses his satans to harden the hearts of the Egyptians compelling them to pursue Israel and be destroyed.

The Book of Jubilees had other names throughout its history and propagation. "The Little Genesis" is another name given to this text. The description of "Little" does not refer to the size of the book, but to its canonical disposition.

"The Apocalypse of Moses" is another name denoting the same work. This title seems to have been used for only a short period of time. It refers to the revelation given to Moses as the recipient of all the knowledge disclosed in the book. The term "Apocalypse" means to make known or to reveal. With the exception of minor differences picked up through translation and copying, the three titles represent the same text.

About the Translation

The translation presented herein is based in part on that of R.H. Charles and his works of 1902 through 1913. Although the translation seems to be a faithful one, his scholarly tone, pedantry, and quasi-Elizabethan language made the text less than accessible. The pleonasm of the text as well as the ancient writer's tendency to repeat phrases for the sake of emphasis added to the general lack of readability. Furthermore, many of the verse breaks occurred in mid-sentence and certainly in mid-thought, adding confusion when viewing the text. All of these difficulties were corrected.

To aid in comprehension, it was decided that the text would be put through three phases of change. First, all verse breaks would be aligned with sentence breaks and with complete streams of thought when possible. Next, all archaic words and phrases would be replaced with their modern equivalent. Lastly, convoluted sentence structure would be clarified and rewritten. Notes of explanation and clarification are added in parentheses.

Due to the vast differences in societal structure and rules, certain phrases remained in their archaic form, seeing that they had no direct equivalence in our western culture. One such phrase is "uncovered the skirt." This phrase indicates the person was seen naked. In most cases it carries a connotation of intercourse. If one were to "uncover his father's skirt" it indicates the father's wife or concubine has been seen naked, usually with the intent of having sex with her.

When possible, the poetic flow of the text would be kept, but not at the expense of understanding. Various translations of each verse were referenced in order to compare and contrast differing viewpoints. The best rendering of the text was chosen and written into a more modern and readable format.

Since the book of Jubilees is written from the viewpoint of the angel narrating or dictating the text, when the words "I," "we," and "us" appear and the words are not readily connected to anyone within the sentence, it can be assumed the angel is referring to himself or the angelic host to which he belongs. When the narrator uses the word "you" he is referring to Moses, to whom the angel is speaking and dictating.

For simplicity's sake, it was decided to keep the word "soul" in the translation as related to the blood of animal and man. The phrase, "The soul is in the blood," will occur several times in the texts. It should be noted that the soul is the "life force," which came from God and belongs to God. It was considered sacred. It did not belong to man and was to be offered to God alone. Since blood represented life itself, it must be the centerpiece of any animal sacrifice. Sin or transgression of the law was punishable by death. Life must be offered as payment. The life force of an animal was offered in place of the life of the sinner. The blood of the animal represents this life.

Now, let us delve into this fascinating and illuminating book.

THE BOOK OF JUBILEES
THE LITTLE GENESIS, THE APOCALYPSE OF MOSES

This is the history of how the days were divided and of the days of the law and of the testimony, of the events of the years, and of the weeks of years, of their Jubilees throughout all the years of the world, as the Lord spoke to Moses on Mount Sinai when he went up to receive the tablets of the law and the commandment, according to the voice of God when he said to him, "Go up to the top of the Mount."

[Chapter 1]

1 It happened in the first year of the exodus of the children of Israel out of Egypt, in the third month, on the sixteenth day of the month, that God spoke to Moses, saying, "Come up to Me on the Mountain, and I will give you two tablets of stone of the law and the commandment, which I have written, that you may teach them."
2 Moses went up into the mountain of God, and the glory of the Lord rested on Mount Sinai, and a cloud overshadowed it six days.
3 He called to Moses on the seventh day out of the middle of the cloud, and the appearance of the glory of the Lord was like a flame on the top of the mountain.
4 Moses was on the mountain forty days and forty nights, and God taught him the earlier and the later history of the division of all the days of the law and of the testimony.
5 He said, "Open your heart to every word which I shall speak to you on this mountain, and write them in a book in order that their generations may see how I have not forsaken them for all the evil which they have committed when they transgressed the covenant which I establish between Me and you for their generations this day on Mount Sinai.
6 It will come to pass when all these things come on them, that they will recognize that I am more righteous than they in all their judgments and in all their actions, and they will recognize that I have truly been with them.
7 Write all these words for yourself which I speak to you today, for I know their rebellion and their stubbornness, before I brought them into the land of which I swore to their fathers, to Abraham and to Isaac and to Jacob, saying, " Unto your offspring will I give a land flowing with milk and honey.
8 They will eat and be satisfied, and they will turn to strange gods, to gods that cannot deliver them from any of their tribulation, and this witness shall be heard for a witness against them.
9 They will forget all My commandments, even all that I command them, and they will walk in the ways of the Gentiles, and after their uncleanness, and after their shame, and will serve their gods, and these will prove to them an offence and a tribulation and an sickness and a trap.
10 Many will perish and they will be taken captive, and will fall into the hands of the enemy, because they have forsaken My laws and My commandments, and the festivals of My covenant, and My sabbaths, and My holy place which I have made holy for Myself in their presence, and My tabernacle, and My sanctuary, which I have made holy for Myself in the midst of the land, that I should set My name on it, that it should reside there.

11 They will make themselves high places and places of worship and graven images. Each will worship graven images of his own making, Thus they will go astray. They will sacrifice their children to demons, and to all errors their hearts can work.
12 I will send witnesses to them that I may testify against them, but they will not hear. They will kill the witnesses. They will persecute those who seek the law, and they will abolish and change everything (in the Law) so as to work evil before My eyes.
13 I will hide My face from them. I will deliver them into the hand of the Gentiles. They will be captured like prey for their eating. I will remove them from the out of the land. I will scatter them among the Gentiles.
14 And they will forget My law and all My commandments and all My judgments. They will go astray regarding the observance of new moons, and sabbaths, and festivals, and jubilees, and laws.
15 After this they will turn to Me from among the Gentiles with all their heart and with all their soul and with all their strength, and I will gather them from among all the Gentiles, and they will seek me. I shall be found by them when they seek me with all their heart and with all their soul.
16 I will allow them to see abounding peace with righteousness. I will remove them, the plant of uprightness, with all My heart and with all My soul, and they shall be for a blessing and not for a curse, and they shall be the head and not the tail.
17 I will build My sanctuary among them, and I will dwell with them, and I will be their God and they shall be My people in truth and righteousness.
18 I will not forsake them nor fail them; for I am the Lord their God."
19 Moses fell on his face and prayed and said, 'O Lord my God, do not forsake Your people and Your inheritance, so that they should wander in the error of their hearts, and do not deliver them into the hands of their enemies, the Gentiles, so that they should rule over them and cause them to sin against You.
20 Let your mercy, O Lord, be lifted up on Your people, and create in them an upright spirit, and let not the spirit of Beliar rule over them to accuse them before You, and to ensnare them from all the paths of righteousness, so that they may perish from before Your face.
21 But they are Your people and Your inheritance, which You have delivered with Your great power from the hands of the Egyptians, create in them a clean heart and a holy spirit, and let them not be ensnared in their sins from now on until eternity."
22 The Lord said to Moses, "I know their contrariness and their thoughts and their stubbornness, and they will not be obedient until they confess their own sin and the sin of their fathers.
23 After this they will turn to Me in all uprightness and with all their heart and with all their soul, and I will circumcise the foreskin of their heart and the foreskin of the heart of their offspring, and I will create in them a holy spirit, and I will cleanse them so that they shall not turn away from Me from that day to eternity.
24 And their souls will cling to Me and to all My commandments, and they will fulfill My commandments, and I will be their Father and they shall be My children.
25 They all shall be called children of the living God, and every angel and every spirit shall know, yes, they shall know that these are My children, and that I am their Father in uprightness and righteousness, and that I love them.
26 Write down for yourself all these words which I say to you on this mountain, from the first to the last, which shall come to pass in all the divisions of the days in

the law and in the testimony and in the weeks and the jubilees to eternity, until I descend and dwell with them throughout eternity."
27 He said to the angel of the presence (of the Lord), "Write for Moses from the beginning of creation until My sanctuary has been built among them for all eternity.
28 The Lord will appear to the eyes of all, and all shall know that I am the God of Israel and the Father of all the children of Jacob, and King on Mount Zion for all eternity. And Zion and Jerusalem shall be holy."
29 The angel of the presence (of the Lord) who went before the camp of Israel took the tables of the divisions of the years, written from the time of the creation, concerning the law and the testimony of the weeks of the jubilees, according to the individual years, according to the numbering of all the jubilees, from the day of the new creation when the heavens and the earth shall be renewed and all their creation according to the powers of the heaven, and according to all the creation of the earth, until the sanctuary of the Lord shall be made in Jerusalem on Mount Zion, and all the stars and planets be renewed for healing, peace, and blessing for all the elect of Israel, and that this is the way it may be from that day and to all the days of the earth.

[Chapter 2]

1 The angel of the presence (of the Lord) spoke to Moses according to the word of the Lord, saying, "Write the complete history of the creation, how in six days the Lord God finished all His works and all that He created, and kept Sabbath on the seventh day and made it holy for all ages, and appointed it as a sign for all His works.
2 For on the first day He created the heavens which are above and the earth and the waters and all the spirits which serve before him which are the angels of the presence (of the Lord), and the angels of sanctification, and the angels of the spirit of fire, and the angels of the spirit of the winds, and the angels of the spirit of the clouds, and of darkness, and of snow and of hail and of white frost, and the angels of the voices and of the thunder and of the lightning, and the angels of the spirits of cold and of heat, and of winter and of spring and of autumn and of summer and of all the spirits of his creatures which are in the heavens and on the earth, He created the bottomless pit and the darkness, evening and night, and the light, dawn and day, which He has prepared in the knowledge of His heart.
3 When we saw His works, we praised Him, and worshiped before Him because of all His works; for seven great works did He create on the first day.
4 On the second day He created the sky between the waters (above and below), and the waters were divided on that day. Half of them went up above the sky and half of them went down below the sky that was in the middle over the face of the whole earth. And this was the only work God created on the second day.
5 On the third day He commanded the waters to pass from off the face of the whole earth into one place, and the dry land to appear.
6 The waters did as He commanded them, and they receded from off the face of the earth into one place, and the dry land appeared.
7 On that day He created for them all the seas according to their separate gathering-places, and all the rivers, and the gatherings of the waters in the mountains and on all the earth, and all the lakes, and all the dew of the earth, and the seed which is sown, and all sprouting things, and fruit-bearing trees, and trees of the wood, and

the garden of Eden, in Eden and throughout. These four great works God created on the third day.
8 On the fourth day He created the sun and the moon and the stars, and set them in the sky of the heaven, to give light on all the earth, and to rule over the day and the night, and divide the light from the darkness.
9 God appointed the sun to be a great sign on the earth for days and for sabbaths and for months and for feasts and for years and for sabbaths of years and for jubilees and for all seasons of the years.
10 And it divides the light from the darkness for prosperity that all things may prosper which sprout and grow on the earth. These three kinds He made on the fourth day.
11 On the fifth day He created great sea monsters in the depths of the waters, for these were the first things of flesh that were created by his hands, the fish and everything that moves in the waters, and everything that flies, the birds and all their kind.
12 And the sun rose above them to make them prosper, and the sun rose above everything that was on the earth, everything that sprouts out of the earth, and all fruit-bearing trees, and all flesh.
13 He created these three kinds on the fifth day. On the sixth day He created all the animals of the earth, and all cattle, and everything that moves on the earth.
14 After all this He created mankind. He created a man and a woman, and gave him dominion over all that is on the earth, and in the seas, and over everything that flies, and over beasts, and over cattle, and over everything that moves on the earth, and over the whole earth, and over all this He gave him dominion.
15 He created these four kinds on the sixth day. And there were altogether two and twenty kinds.
16 He finished all his work on the sixth day. That is all that is in the heavens and on the earth, and in the seas and in the abysses, and in the light and in the darkness, and in everything.
17 He gave us a great sign, the Sabbath day, that we should work six days, but keep Sabbath on the seventh day from all work.
18 All the angels of the presence (of the Lord), and all the angels of sanctification, these two great types of angels He has told to tell us to keep the Sabbath with Him in heaven and on earth.
19 And He said to us, "Look, I will separate to Myself a people from among all the peoples, and these shall keep the Sabbath day, and I will sanctify them to Myself as My people, and will bless them; as I have sanctified the Sabbath day and do sanctify it to Myself, even so will I bless them, and they shall be My people and I will be their God.
20 I have chosen the offspring of Jacob from among all that I have seen, and have written him down as My first-born son, and have sanctified him to Myself forever and ever; and I will teach them the Sabbath day, that they may keep Sabbath on it from all work."
21 He created in it a sign in accordance with which they should keep Sabbath with us on the seventh day, to eat and to drink, and to bless Him who has created all things as He has blessed and sanctified to Himself a particular, exclusive people above all peoples, and that they should keep Sabbath together with us.
22 He caused His commands to rise up as a sweet odor acceptable before Him all the days.

23 There were two and twenty heads (representatives) of mankind from Adam to Jacob, and two and twenty kinds of work (creation) were made until the seventh day; this is blessed and holy; and the former also is blessed and holy; and this one serves with that one for sanctification and blessing.
24 Jacob and his offspring were granted that they should always be the blessed and holy ones of the first testimony and law, even as He had sanctified and blessed the Sabbath day on the seventh day.
25 He created heaven and earth and everything that He created in six days, and God made the seventh day holy, for all His works; therefore He commanded on its behalf that, whoever does any work on it shall die, and that he who defiles it shall surely die.
26 Because of this, command the children of Israel to observe this day that they may keep it holy and not do on it any work, and not to defile it, as it is holier than all other days.
27 And whoever profanes it shall surely die, and whoever does any work on it shall surely die eternally, that the children of Israel may observe this day throughout their generations, and not be rooted out of the land; for it is a holy day and a blessed day.
28 Every one who observes it and keeps Sabbath on it from all his work will be holy and blessed throughout all days as we are blessed.
29 Declare and say to the children of Israel the law of this day that they should keep Sabbath on it, and that they should not forsake it in the error of their hearts; and that it is not lawful to do any work on it which is not suitable, to do their own pleasure on it, and that they should not prepare anything to be eaten or drunk on it, and that it is not lawful to draw water, or bring in or take out through their gates any burden which they had not prepared for themselves on the sixth day in their dwellings.
30 They shall not bring or take anything from house to house on that day; for that day is more holy and blessed than any jubilee day of the jubilees; on this we kept Sabbath in the heavens before it was made known to any flesh to keep Sabbath on the earth.
31 The Creator of all things blessed it, but He did not sanctify all peoples and nations to keep Sabbath, but Israel alone, them alone He permitted to eat and drink and to keep Sabbath on the earth.
32 And the Creator of all things blessed this day which He had created for blessing and holiness and glory above all days.
33 This law and testimony was given to the children of Israel as a law forever to their generations.

[Chapter 3]

1 On the sixth day of the second week, according to the word of God, we brought to Adam all the beasts, and all the cattle, and all the birds, and everything that moves on the earth, and everything that moves in the water, according to their kinds, and according to their types, the beasts on the first day; the cattle on the second day; the birds on the third day; and all that moves on the earth on the fourth day; and that moves in the water on the fifth day.
2 And Adam named them all by their respective names. As he called them, so was their name.
3 On these five days Adam saw all these, male and female, according to every kind that was on the earth, but he was alone and found no helpmate.

4 The Lord said to us, "It is not good that the man should be alone, let us make a helpmate for him."
5 And the Lord our God caused a deep sleep to fall on him, and he slept, and He took from Adam a rib from among his ribs for the woman, and this rib was the origin of the woman. And He built up the flesh in its place, and built the woman.
6 He awakened Adam out of his sleep and on awakening he rose on the sixth day, and He brought her to him, and he knew her, and said to her, "This is now bone of my bones and flesh of my flesh; she shall be called my wife; because she was taken from her husband."
7 Therefore shall man and wife become one and therefore shall a man leave his father and his mother, and cling to his wife, and they shall be one flesh.
8 In the first week Adam was created, and from his rib, his wife. In the second week God showed her to him, and for this reason the commandment was given to keep in their defilement. A male should be purified in seven days, and for a female twice seven days.
9 After Adam had completed forty days in the land where he had been created, we brought him into the garden of Eden to till and keep it, but his wife we brought in on the eightieth day, and after this she entered into the garden of Eden.
10 And for this reason the commandment is written on the heavenly tablets in regard to her that gives birth, "If she bears a male, she shall remain unclean for seven days according to the first week of days, and thirty-three days shall she remain in the blood of her purifying, and she shall not touch any holy thing, nor enter into the sanctuary, until she completes these days which are decreed in the case of a male child.
11 But in the case of a female child she shall remain unclean two weeks of days, according to the first two weeks, and sixty-six days in the blood of her purification, and they will be in all eighty days."
12 When she had completed these eighty days we brought her into the Garden of Eden, for it is holier than all the earth besides and every tree that is planted in it is holy.
13 Therefore, there was ordained regarding her who bears a male or a female child the statute of those days that she should touch no holy thing, nor enter into the sanctuary until these days for the male or female child are completed.
14 This is the law and testimony that was written down for Israel, in order that they should observe it all the days.
15 In the first week of the first jubilee, Adam and his wife were in the garden of Eden for seven years tilling and keeping it, and we gave him work and we instructed him to do everything that is suitable for tillage.
16 And he tilled the garden, and was naked and did not realize it, and was not ashamed. He protected the garden from the birds and beasts and cattle. He gathered its fruit, and ate, and put aside that which was left over for himself and for his wife.
17 After the completion of exactly seven years there, and in the second month, on the seventeenth day of the month, the serpent came and approached the woman, and the serpent said to the woman, "Has God commanded you saying, you shall not eat of every tree of the garden?"
18 She said to it, God said to us, of all the fruit of the trees of the garden, eat; but of the fruit of the tree which is in the middle of the garden God said to us, you shall not eat of it, neither shall you touch it, or you shall die."

19 The serpent said to the woman, "You shall not surely die. God does know that on the day you shall eat of it, your eyes will be opened, and you will be as gods, and you will know good and evil.

20 And the woman saw the tree that it was beautiful and pleasant to the eye, and that its fruit was good for food, and she took of it and ate.

21 First, she covered her shame with fig leaves and then she gave the fruit to Adam and he ate, and his eyes were opened, and he saw that he was naked.

22 He took fig leaves and sewed them together, and made an apron for himself, and covered his shame.

23 God cursed the serpent, and was very angry at it forever.

24 And He was very angry with the woman, because she listened to the voice of the serpent, and ate; and He said to her, "I will vastly multiply your sorrow and your pains, in sorrow you will bring forth children, and your master shall be your husband, and he will rule over you."

25 To Adam also he said, " Because you have listened to the voice of your wife, and have eaten of the tree of which I commanded you not to eat, cursed be the ground for your sake, thorns and thistles shall it produce for you, and you will eat your bread in the sweat of your face, untill you return to the earth from where you were taken; for earth you are, and to earth will you return."

26 And He made for them coats of skin, and clothed them, and sent them out from the Garden of Eden.

27 On that day on which Adam went out from the Garden, he offered as a sweet odor an offering, frankincense, incense, and sweet spice, and spices in the morning with the rising of the sun from the day when he covered his shame.

28 On that day was closed the mouth of all beasts, and of cattle, and of birds, and of whatever walks, and of whatever moves, so that they could no longer speak, for they had all spoken one with another with one dialect and with one language.

29 All flesh that was in the Garden of Eden He sent out of the Garden of Eden, and all flesh was scattered according to its kinds, and according to its types to the places that had been created for them.

30 Of all the beasts and cattle only to Adam alone He gave the ability to cover his shame.

31 Because of this, it is prescribed on the heavenly tablets as touching all those who know the judgment of the law, that they should cover their shame, and should not uncover themselves as the Gentiles uncover themselves.

32 On the new moon of the fourth month, Adam and his wife went out from the Garden of Eden, and they dwelt in the land of Elda in the land of their creation.

33 And Adam called the name of his wife Eve.

34 And they had no son until the first jubilee, and after this he knew her.

35 Now he tilled the land as he had been instructed in the Garden of Eden.

[Chapter 4]

1 In the third week in the second jubilee she gave birth to Cain, and in the fourth (week of the) jubilee she gave birth to Abel, and in the fifth(week of the) jubilee she gave birth to her daughter Awan. (A week is seven years.)

2 In the first year of the third jubilee, Cain killed Abel because God accepted the sacrifice of Abel, and did not accept the offering of Cain.

3 And he killed him in the field, and his blood cried from the ground to heaven, complaining because he had killed him.
4 The Lord blamed Cain, because he had killed Abel, and He made him a fugitive on the earth because of the blood of his brother, and He cursed him on the earth.
5 Because of this it is written on the heavenly tablets, "Cursed is he who kills his neighbor treacherously, and let all who have seen and heard say, 'So be it', and the man who has seen and not reported it, let him be accursed as the one committing it."
6 For this reason we announce when we come before the Lord our God all the sin that is committed in heaven and on earth, and in light and in darkness, and everywhere.
7 And Adam and his wife mourned for Abel four weeks of years, and in the fourth year of the fifth week they became joyful, and Adam knew his wife again, and she gave birth to a son, and he called his name Seth, for he said "God has raised up a second offspring to us on the earth instead of Abel; for Cain killed him."
8 In the sixth week he begat his daughter Azura.
9 And Cain took Awan his sister to be his wife and she gave birth to Enoch at the close of the fourth jubilee.
10 In the first year of the first week of the fifth jubilee, houses were built on the earth, and Cain built a city, and called its name after the name of his son Enoch.
11 Adam knew Eve his wife and she gave birth to a total of nine sons. In the fifth week of the fifth jubilee Seth took Azura his sister to be his wife, and in the fourth year of the sixth week she gave birth to Enos.
12 He began to call on the name of the Lord on the earth.
13 In the seventh jubilee in the third week Enos took Noam his sister to be his wife, and she gave birth to a son in the third year of the fifth week, and he called his name Kenan.
14 At the close of the eighth jubilee Kenan took Mualeleth his sister to be his wife, and she gave birth to a son in the ninth jubilee, in the first week in the third year of this week, and he called his name Mahalalel.
15 In the second week of the tenth jubilee Mahalalel took to him to wife Dinah, the daughter of Barakiel the daughter of his father's brother, and she gave birth to a son in the third week in the sixth year, and he called his name Jared, for in his days the angels of the Lord descended on the earth, those who are named the Watchers, that they should instruct the children of men, and that they should do judgment and uprightness on the earth.
16 In the eleventh jubilee Jared took to himself a wife, and her name was Baraka, the daughter of Rasujal, a daughter of his father's brother, in the fourth week of this jubilee, and she gave birth to a son in the fifth week, in the fourth year of the jubilee, and he called his name Enoch.
17 He was the first among men that are born on earth who learned writing and knowledge and wisdom and who wrote down the signs of heaven according to the order of their months in a book, that men might know the seasons of the years according to the order of their separate months.
18 He was the first to write a testimony and he testified to the sons of men among the generations of the earth, and recounted the weeks of the jubilees, and made known to them the days of the years, and set in order the months and recounted the Sabbaths of the years as we made them, known to him.
19 And what was and what will be he saw in a vision of his sleep, as it will happen to the children of men throughout their generations until the day of judgment; he

saw and understood everything, and wrote his testimony, and placed the testimony on earth for all the children of men and for their generations.

20 In the twelfth jubilee, in the seventh week of it, he took to himself a wife, and her name was Edna, the daughter of Danel, the daughter of his father's brother, and in the sixth year in this week she gave birth to a son and he called his name Methuselah.

21 He was with the angels of God these six jubilees of years, and they showed him everything that is on earth and in the heavens, the rule of the sun, and he wrote down everything.

22 And he testified to the Watchers, who had sinned with the daughters of men; for these had begun to unite themselves, so as to be defiled with the daughters of men, and Enoch testified against them all.

23 And he was taken from among the children of men, and we conducted him into the Garden of Eden in majesty and honor, and there he wrote down the condemnation and judgment of the world, and all the wickedness of the children of men.

24 Because of it God brought the waters of the flood on all the land of Eden; for there he was set as a sign and that he should testify against all the children of men, that he should recount all the deeds of the generations until the day of condemnation.

25 He burnt the incense of the sanctuary, even sweet spices acceptable before the Lord on the Mount.

26 For the Lord has four places on the earth, the Garden of Eden, and the Mount of the East, and this mountain on which you are this day, Mount Sinai, and Mount Zion which will be sanctified in the new creation for a sanctification of the earth; through it will the earth be sanctified from all its guilt and its uncleanness throughout the generations of the world.

27 In the fourteenth jubilee Methuselah took to himself a wife, Edna the daughter of Azrial, the daughter of his father's brother, in the third week, in the first year of this week, and he begat a son and called his name Lamech.

28 In the fifteenth jubilee in the third week Lamech took to himself a wife, and her name was Betenos the daughter of Baraki'il, the daughter of his father's brother, and in this week she gave birth to a son and he called his name Noah, saying, "This one will comfort me for my trouble and all my work, and for the ground which the Lord has cursed."

29 At the close of the nineteenth jubilee, in the seventh week in the sixth year of it, Adam died, and all his sons buried him in the land of his creation, and he was the first to be buried in the earth.

30 He lacked seventy years of one thousand years, because one thousand years are as one day in the testimony of the heavens. Therefore was it written concerning the tree of knowledge, "On the day that you eat of it you shall die." Because of this he did not complete the one thousand years but instead he died during it.

31 At the close of this jubilee Cain was killed after him in the same year; because his house fell on him and he died in the middle of his house, and he was killed by its stones. With a stone he had killed Abel, and by a stone he was killed in righteous judgment.

32 For this reason it was ordained on the heavenly tablets, with the instrument with which a man kills his neighbor with the same shall he be killed. In the same manner that he wounded him, in like manner shall they deal with him."

33 In the twenty-fifth jubilee Noah took to himself a wife, and her name was Emzara, the daughter of Rake'el, the daughter of his father's brother, in the first year in the fifth week, and in the third year of it she gave birth to Shem, in the fifth year of it she gave birth to Ham, and in the first year in the sixth week she gave birth to Japheth.

[Chapter 5]

1 When the children of men began to multiply on the face of the earth and daughters were born to them, and the angels of God saw them on a certain year of this jubilee, that they were beautiful, and they took themselves wives of all whom they chose, and they gave birth to their sons and they were giants.
2 Because of them lawlessness increased on the earth and all flesh corrupted its way. Men and cattle and beasts and birds and everything that walked on the earth were all corrupted in their ways and their orders, and they began to devour each other. Lawlessness increased on the earth and the imagination and thoughts of all men were continually, totally evil.
3 God looked on the earth, and saw it was corrupt, and all flesh had corrupted its orders, and all that were on the earth had committed all manner of evil before His eyes.
4 He said that He would destroy man and all flesh on the face of the earth that He had created.
5 But Noah found grace before the eyes of the Lord.
6 And against the angels whom He had sent on the earth, He had boiling anger, and He gave commandment to root them out of all their dominion, and He commanded us to bind them in the depths of the earth, and look, they are bound in the middle of the earth, and are kept separate.
7 And against their sons went out a command from His mouth that they should be killed with the sword, and be left under heaven.
8 He said, "My spirit shall not always abide on man; for they also are flesh and their days shall be one hundred and twenty years."
9 He sent His sword into their presence that each should kill his neighbor, and they began to kill each other until they all fell by the sword and were destroyed from the earth.
10 And their fathers were witnesses of their destruction, and after this they were bound in the depths of the earth forever, until the day of the great condemnation, when judgment is executed on all those who have corrupted their ways and their works before the Lord.
11 He destroyed all wherever they were, and there was not one left of them whom He judged according to all their wickedness.
12 Through His work He made a new and righteous nature, so that they should not sin in their whole nature forever, but should be all righteous each in his own way always.
13 The judgment of all is ordained and written on the heavenly tablets in righteousness, even the judgment of all who depart from the path that is ordained for them to walk; and if they do not walk it, judgment is written down for every creature and for every kind.

14 There is nothing in heaven or on earth, or in light or in darkness, or in the abode of the dead or in the depth, or in the place of darkness that is not judged. All their judgments are ordained and written and engraved.
15 He will judge all, the great according to his greatness, and the small according to his smallness, and each according to his way.
16 He is not one who will regard the position of any person, nor is He one who will receive gifts, if He says that He will execute judgment on each.
17 If one gave everything that is on the earth, He will not regard the gifts or the person of any, nor accept anything at his hands, for He is a righteous judge.
18 Of the children of Israel it has been written and ordained, if they turn to him in righteousness He will forgive all their transgressions and pardon all their sins. It is written and ordained that He will show mercy to all who turn from all their guilt once each year.
19 And as for all those who corrupted their ways and their thoughts before the flood, no person was acceptable to God except Noah. His sons were saved in deference to him, and these God kept from the waters of the flood on his account; for Noah's heart was righteous in all his ways. He upheld the laws and did as God commanded him and he had not departed from anything that was ordained for him.
20 The Lord said that he would destroy everything on the earth, both men and cattle, and beasts, and birds of the air, and that which moves on the earth.
21 And He commanded Noah to make an ark, so that he might save himself from the waters of the flood.
22 And Noah made the ark in all respects as He commanded him, in the twenty-seventh jubilee of years, in the fifth week in the fifth year on the new moon of the first month.
23 He entered in the sixth year of it, in the second month, on the new moon of the second month, until the sixteenth; and he entered, and all that we brought to him, into the ark, and the Lord closed it from the outside on the seventeenth evening.
24 And the Lord opened seven floodgates of heaven, and He opened the mouths of the fountains of the great deep, seven mouths in number.
25 And the floodgates began to pour down water from the heaven forty days and forty closets, And the fountains of the deep also sent up waters, until the whole world was full of water.
26 The waters increased on the earth, by fifteen cubits (a cubit is about 18 inches) the waters rose above all the high mountains. And the ark was lift up from the earth. And it moved on the face of the waters.
27 And the water covered the face of the earth five months, which is one hundred and fifty days.
28 And the ark went and rested on the top of Lubar, one of the mountains of Ararat.
29 On the new moon in the fourth month the fountains of the great deep were closed and the floodgates of heaven were restrained; and on the new moon of the seventh month all the mouths of the bottomless gulfs of the earth were opened, and the water began to flow down into the deep below.
30 On the new moon of the tenth month the tops of the mountains were seen, and on the new moon of the first month the earth became visible.
31 The waters disappeared from the earth in the fifth week in the seventh year of it, and on the seventeenth day in the second month the earth was dry.
32 On the twenty-seventh of it he opened the ark, and sent out beasts, and cattle, and birds, and every moving thing.

[Chapter 6]

1 On the new moon of the third month he went out of the ark, and built an altar on that mountain.
2 And he made atonement for the earth, and took a kid and made atonement by its blood for all the guilt of the earth; for every thing that had been on it had been destroyed, except those that were in the ark with Noah.
3 He placed the fat of it on the altar, and he took an ox, and a goat, and a sheep and kids, and salt, and a turtle-dove, and the young of a dove, and placed a burnt sacrifice on the altar, and poured on it an offering mingled with oil, and sprinkled wine and sprinkled frankincense over everything, and caused a good and pleasing odor to arise, acceptable before the Lord.
4 And the Lord smelled the good and pleasing odor, and He made a covenant with Noah that there should not be any more floods to destroy the earth; that all the days of the earth seed-time and harvest should never cease; cold and heat, and summer and winter, and day and night should not change their order, nor cease forever.
5 "Increase and multiply on the earth, and become many, and be a blessing on it. I will inspire the fear of you and the dread of you in everything that is on earth and in the sea.
6 Look, I have given you all beasts, and all winged things, and everything that moves on the earth, and the fish in the waters, and all things for food; as the green herbs, I have given you all things to eat.
7 But you shall not eat anything live or with blood in it, for the life of all flesh is in the blood, or your blood of your lives will be required. At the hand of every man, at the hand of every beast will I require the blood of man.
8 Whoever sheds man's blood by man shall his blood be shed, for in the image of God He made man.
9 Increase, and multiply on the earth."
10 Noah and his sons swore that they would not eat any blood that was in any flesh, and he made a covenant before the Lord God forever throughout all the generations of the earth in this month.
11 Because of this He spoke to you that you should make a covenant with the children of Israel with an oath. In this month, on the mountain you should sprinkle blood on them because of all the words of the covenant, which the Lord made with them forever.
12 This testimony is written concerning you that you should observe it continually, so that you should not eat on any day any blood of beasts or birds or cattle during all the days of the earth, and the man who eats the blood of beast or of cattle or of birds during all the days of the earth, he and his offspring shall be rooted out of the land.
13 And you will command the children of Israel to eat no blood, so that their names and their offspring may be before the Lord our God continually.
14 There is no limit of days, for this law. It is forever. They shall observe it throughout their generations, so that they may continue supplicating on your behalf with blood before the altar; every day and at the time of morning and evening they shall seek forgiveness on your behalf perpetually before the Lord that they may keep it and not be rooted out.

15 And He gave to Noah and his sons a sign that there should not again be a flood on the earth.
16 He set His bow (a rainbow) in the cloud as a sign of the eternal covenant that there should never again be a flood on the earth to destroy it for all the days of the earth.
17 For this reason it is ordained and written on the heavenly tablets, that they should celebrate the feast of weeks in this month once a year, to renew the covenant every year.
18 This whole festival was celebrated in heaven from the day of creation until the days of Noah, which were twenty-six jubilees and five weeks of years. Noah and his sons observed it for seven jubilees and one week of years, until the day of Noah's death. From the day of Noah's death his sons did away with it until the days of Abraham, and they ate blood.
19 But Abraham observed it, and Isaac and Jacob and his children observed it up to your days, and in your days the children of Israel forgot it until you celebrated it anew on this mountain.
20 Command the children of Israel to observe this festival in all their generations for a commandment to them, one day in the year in this month they shall celebrate the festival.
21 For it is the feast of weeks and the feast of first-fruits, this feast is twofold and of a double nature, according to what is written and engraved concerning it, celebrate it.
22 For I have written in the book of the first law, in that which I have written for you, that you should celebrate it in its season, one day in the year, and I explained to you its sacrifices that the children of Israel should remember and should celebrate it throughout their generations in this month, the same day in every year.
23 On the new moon of the first month, and on the new moon of the fourth month, and on the new moon of the seventh month, and on the new moon of the tenth month are the days of remembrance, and the days of the seasons in the four divisions of the year. These are written and ordained as a testimony forever.
24 Noah ordained them for himself as feasts for the generations forever, so that they have become a memorial to him.
25 On the new moon of the first month he was told to make for himself an ark, and on that day the earth was dry and he saw from the opened ark, the earth. On the new moon of the fourth month the mouths of the depths of the bottomless pit beneath were closed.
26 On the new moon of the seventh month all the mouths of the abysses of the earth were opened, and the waters began to descend into them.
27 On the new moon of the tenth month the tops of the mountains were seen, and Noah was glad.
28 Because of this he ordained them for himself as feasts for a memorial forever, and thus are they ordained.
29 And they placed them on the heavenly tablets, each had thirteen weeks; from one to another passed their memorial, from the first to the second, and from the second to the third, and from the third to the fourth.
30 All the days of the commandment will be two and fifty weeks of days, and these will make the entire year complete. Thus it is engraved and ordained on the heavenly tablets.
31 And there is no neglecting this commandment for a single year or from year to year.

32 Command you the children of Israel that they observe the years according to this counting, three hundred and sixty-four days, and these will constitute a complete year, and they will not disturb its time from its days and from its feasts; for every thing will fall out in them according to their testimony, and they will not leave out any day nor disturb any feasts.
33 But if they neglect and do not observe them according to His commandment, then they will disturb all their seasons and the years will be dislodged from this order, and they will neglect their established rules.
34 And all the children of Israel will forget and will not find the path of the years, and will forget the new moons, and seasons, and sabbaths and they will wrongly determine all the order of the years.
35 For I know and from now on will I declare it to you, and it is not of my own devising; for the book lies written in the presence of me, and on the heavenly tablets the division of days is ordained, or they forget the feasts of the covenant and walk according to the feasts of the Gentiles after their error and after their ignorance.
36 For there will be those who will assuredly make observations of the moon and how it disturbs the seasons and comes in from year to year ten days too soon.
37 For this reason the years will come upon them when they disturb (misinterpret) the order, and make an abominable day the day of testimony, and an unclean day a feast day, and they will confound all the days, the holy with the unclean, and the unclean day with the holy; for they will go wrong as to the months and sabbaths and feasts and jubilees.
38 For this reason I command and testify to you that you may testify to them; for after your death your children will disturb them, so that they will not make the year three hundred and sixty-four days only, and for this reason they will go wrong as to the new moons and seasons and sabbaths and festivals, and they will eat all kinds of blood with all kinds of flesh.

[Chapter 7]

1 In the seventh week in the first year of it, in this jubilee, Noah planted vines on the mountain on which the ark had rested, named Lubar, one of the Ararat Mountains, and they produced fruit in the fourth year, and he guarded their fruit, and gathered it in that year in the seventh month.
2 He made wine from it and put it into a vessel, and kept it until the fifth year, until the first day, on the new moon of the first month.
3 And he celebrated with joy the day of this feast, and he made a burnt sacrifice to the Lord, one young ox and one ram, and seven sheep, each a year old, and a kid of the goats, that he might make atonement thereby for himself and his sons.
4 He prepared the kid first, and placed some of its blood on the flesh that was on the altar that he had made, and all the fat he laid on the altar where he made the burnt sacrifice, and the ox and the ram and the sheep, and he laid all their flesh on the altar.
5 He placed all their offerings mingled with oil on it, and afterwards he sprinkled wine on the fire which had previously been made on the altar, and he placed incense on the altar and caused a sweet odor to rise up which was acceptable before the Lord his God.
6 And he rejoiced and he and his children drank the wine with joy.

7 It was evening, and he went into his tent, and being drunken he lay down and slept, and was uncovered in his tent as he slept.
8 And Ham saw Noah his father naked, and went out and told his two brothers (ridiculed his father to his two brothers) who were outside.
9 Shem took his garment and arose, he and Japheth, and they placed the garment on their shoulders and went backward and covered the shame of their father, and their faces were backward.
10 Noah awoke from his sleep and knew all that his younger son had done to him, and he cursed his son and said, "Cursed be Canaan; an enslaved servant shall he be to his brothers."
11 And he blessed Shem, and said, "Blessed be the Lord God of Shem, and Canaan shall be his servant.
12 God shall enlarge Japheth, and God shall dwell in the dwelling of Shem, and Canaan shall be his servant."
13 Ham knew that his father had cursed, him, his younger son, and he was displeased that he had cursed him, his son. And Ham parted from his father, he and his sons with him, Cush and Mizraim and Put and Canaan.
14 And he built for himself a city and called its name after the name of his wife Ne'elatama'uk.
15 Japheth saw it, and became envious of his brother, and he too built for himself a city, and he called its name after the name of his wife Adataneses.
16 Shem dwelt with his father Noah, and he built a city close to his father on the mountain, and he too called its name after the name of his wife Sedeqetelebab.
17 These three cities are near Mount Lubar; Sedeqetelebab in front of the mountain on its east; and Na'eltama'uk on the south; Adatan'eses towards the west.
18 These are the sons of Shem, Elam, and Asshur, and Arpachshad who was born two years after the flood, and Lud, and Aram.
19 The sons of Japheth, Gomer, Magog, Madai , Javan, Tubal and Meshech and Tiras, these are the descendants of Noah.
20 In the twenty-eighth jubilee Noah began to direct his sons in the ordinances and commandments, and all the judgments that he knew, and he exhorted his sons to observe righteousness, and to cover the shame of their flesh, and to bless their Creator, and honor father and mother, and love their neighbor, and guard their souls from fornication and uncleanness and all iniquity.
21 Because of these three things came the flood on the earth, namely, the fornication that the Watchers committed against the law of their ordinances when they went whoring after the daughters of men, and took themselves wives of all they chose, and they made the beginning of uncleanness.
22 And they begat sons, the naphilim (Naphidim), and they were all dissimilar, and they devoured one another, and the Giants killed the Naphil, and the Naphil killed the Eljo, and the Eljo killed mankind, and one man killed one another.
23 Every one committed himself to crime and injustice and to shed much blood, and the earth was filled with sin.
24 After this they sinned against the beasts and birds, and all that moved and walked on the earth, and much blood was shed on the earth, and men continually desired only what was useless and evil.
25 And the Lord destroyed everything from the face of the earth. Because of the wickedness of their deeds, and because of the blood they had shed over all the earth, He destroyed everything. "

26 We were left, I and you, my sons, and everything that entered with us into the ark, and behold I see your works before me that you do not walk in righteousness, for in the path of destruction you have begun to walk, and you are turning one against another, and are envious one of another, and so it comes that you are not in harmony, my sons, each with his brother.
27 For I see the demons have begun their seductions against you and against your children and now I fear on your behalf, that after my death you will shed the blood of men on the earth, and that you, too, will be destroyed from the face of the earth.
28 For whoever sheds man's blood, and who ever eats the blood of any flesh, shall all be destroyed from the earth.
29 There shall be no man left that eats blood, or that sheds the blood of man on the earth, nor shall there be left to him any offspring or descendants living under heaven. Into the abode of the dead shall they go, and into the place of condemnation shall they descend, and into the darkness of the deep shall they all be removed by a violent death.
30 Do not smear blood on yourself or let it remain on you. Out of all the blood there shall be shed and out of all the days in which you have killed any beasts or cattle or whatever flies on the earth you must do a good work to your souls by covering that which has been shed on the face of the earth.
31 You shall not be like him who eats blood, but guard yourselves that none may eat blood before you, cover the blood, for thus have I been commanded to testify to you and your children, together with all flesh.
32 Do not permit the soul (life) to be eaten with the flesh, that your blood, which is your life, may not be required at the hand of any flesh that sheds it on the earth.
33 For the earth will not be clean from the blood that has been shed on it, for only through the blood of him that shed it will the earth be purified throughout all its generations.
34 Now, my children, listen, have judgment and righteousness that you maybe planted in righteousness over the face of the whole earth, and your glory lifted up in the presence of my God, who spared me from the waters of the flood.
35 Look, you will go and build for yourselves cities, and plant in them all the plants that are on the earth, and moreover all fruit-bearing trees.
36 For three years the fruit of everything that is eaten will not be gathered, and in the fourth year its fruit will be accounted holy, offered as first fruit, acceptable before the Most High God, who created heaven and earth and all things.
37 Let them offer in abundance the first of the wine and oil as first-fruits on the altar of the Lord, who receives it, and what is left let the servants of the house of the Lord eat before the altar which receives it.
38 In the fifth year make the release so that you release it in righteousness and uprightness, and you shall be righteous, and all that you plant shall prosper. For this is how Enoch did it, the father of your father commanded Methuselah, his son, and Methuselah commanded his son Lamech, and Lamech commanded me all the things that his fathers commanded him.
39 I also will give you commandment, my sons, as Enoch commanded his son in the first jubilees, while still living, the seventh in his generation, he commanded and testified to his son and to his son's sons until the day of his death.

[Chapter 8]

1 In the twenty-ninth jubilee, in the beginning of first week, Arpachshad took to himself a wife and her name was Rasu'eja, the daughter of Susan, the daughter of Elam, and she gave birth to a son in the third year in this week, and he called his name Kainam.
2 The son grew, and his father taught him writing, and he went to seek for himself a place where he might seize a city for himself.
3 He found writing which former generations had carved on a rock, and he read what was on it, and he transcribed it and sinned because of it, for it contained the teaching of the Watchers, which they had used to observe the omens of the sun and moon and stars in all the signs of heaven.
4 He wrote it down and said nothing of it, for he was afraid to speak to Noah about it or he would be angry with him because of it.
5 In the thirtieth jubilee, in the second week, in the first year of it, he took to himself a wife, and her name was Melka, the daughter of Madai, the son of Japheth, and in the fourth year he begat a son, and called his name Shelah; for he said, "Truly I have been sent."
6 Shelah grew up and took to himself a wife, and her name was Mu'ak, the daughter of Kesed, his father's brother, in the one and thirtieth jubilee, in the fifth week, in the first year of it.
7 And she gave birth to a son in the fifth year of it, and he called his name Eber, and he took to himself a wife, and her name was Azurad, the daughter of Nebrod, in the thirty-second jubilee, in the seventh week, in the third year of it.
8 In the sixth year of it, she gave birth to a son, and he called his name Peleg, for in the days when he was born the children of Noah began to divide the earth among themselves, for this reason he called his name Peleg.
9 They divided it secretly among themselves, and told it to Noah.
10 In the beginning of the thirty-third jubilee they divided the earth into three parts, for Shem and Ham and Japheth, according to the inheritance of each, in the first year in the first week, when one of us (angels) who had been sent, was with them.
11 He called his sons, and they drew close to him, they and their children, and he divided the earth into the lots, which his three sons were to take in possession, and they reached out their hands, and took the writing out of the arms of Noah, their father.
12 There came out on the writing as Shem's lot the middle of the earth that he should take as an inheritance for himself and for his sons for the generations of eternity. From the middle of the mountain range of Rafa, from the mouth of the water from the river Tina, and his portion goes towards the west through the middle of this river, and it extends until it reaches the water of the abysses, out of which this river goes out and pours its waters into the sea Me'at, and this river flows into the great sea.
13 All that is towards the north is Japheth's, and all that is towards the south belongs to Shem. And it extends until it reaches Karaso, this is in the center of the tongue of land that looks towards the south.
14 His portion extends along the great sea, and it extends in a straight line until it reaches the west of the tongue that looks towards the south, for this sea is named the tongue of the Egyptian Sea.

15 And it turns from here towards the south towards the mouth of the great sea on the shore of its waters, and it extends to the west to Afra, and it extends until it reaches the waters of the river Gihon, and to the south of the waters of Gihon, to the banks of this river.
16 It extends towards the east, until it reaches the Garden of Eden, to the south of it and from the east of the whole land of Eden and of the whole east, it turns to the east and proceeds until it reaches the east of the mountain named Rafa, and it descends to the bank of the mouth of the river Tina.
17 This portion came out by lot for Shem and his sons, that they should possess it forever to his generations forever.
18 Noah rejoiced that this portion came out for Shem and for his sons, and he remembered all that he had spoken with his mouth in prophecy; for he had said, "Blessed be the Lord God of Shem and may the Lord dwell in the dwelling of Shem."
19 He knew that the Garden of Eden is the holy of holies, and the dwelling of the Lord, and Mount Sinai the center of the desert, and Mount Zion which is the center of the navel of the earth, these three were created as holy places facing each other.
20 And he blessed the God of gods, who had put the word of the Lord into his mouth, and the Lord forever.
21 And he knew that a blessed portion and a blessing had come to Shem and his sons and to their generations forever which was the whole land of Eden and the whole land of the Red Sea, and the whole land of the east and India, and on the Red Sea and the mountains of it, and all the land of Bashan, and all the land of Lebanon and the islands of Kaftur, and all the mountains of Sanir and Amana, and the mountains of Asshur in the north, and all the land of Elam, Asshur, and Babel, and Susan and Ma'edai, and all the mountains of Ararat, and all the region beyond the sea, which is beyond the mountains of Asshur towards the north, a blessed and spacious land, and all that is in it is very good.
22 Ham received the second portion, beyond the Gihon towards the south to the right of the Garden, and it extends towards the south and it extends to all the mountains of fire, and it extends towards the west to the sea of 'atel and it extends towards the west until it reaches the sea of Ma'uk which was that sea into which everything that is not destroyed descends.
23 It goes out towards the north to the limits of Gadir, and it goes out to the coast of the waters of the sea to the waters of the great sea until it draws near to the river Gihon, and goes along the river Gihon until it reaches the right of the Garden of Eden.
24 This is the land that came out for Ham as the portion which he was to occupy forever for himself and his sons to their generations forever.
25 Japheth received the third portion beyond the river Tina to the north of the outflow of its waters, and it extends north-easterly to the whole region of Gog, and to all the country east of it.
26 It extends northerly, and it extends to the mountains of Qelt towards the north, and towards the sea of Ma'uk, and it goes out to the east of Gadir as far as the region of the waters of the sea.
27 It extends until it approaches the west of Fara and it returns towards Aferag, and it extends easterly to the waters of the sea of Me'at.

28 It extends to the region of the river Tina in a northeasterly direction until it approaches the boundary of its waters towards the mountain Rafa, and it turns round towards the north.
29 This is the land that came out for Japheth and his sons as the portion of his inheritance that he should possess five great islands, and a great land in the north, for himself and his sons, for their generations forever.
30 But it is cold, and the land of Ham is hot, and the land of Shem is neither hot nor cold, but it is of blended cold and heat.

[Chapter 9]

1 Ham divided among his sons, and the first portion came out for Cush towards the east, and to the west of him for Mizraim, and to the west of him for Put, and to the west of him on the sea for Canaan.
2 Shem also divided among his sons, and the first portion came out for Elam and his sons, to the east of the river Tigris until it approaches the east, the whole land of India, and on the Red Sea on its coast, and the waters of Dedan, and all the mountains of Mebri and Ela, and all the land of Susan and all that is on the side of Pharnak to the Red Sea and the river Tina.
3 Asshur received the second Portion, all the land of Asshur and Nineveh and Shinar and to the border of India, and it ascends and skirts the river.
4 Arpachshad received the third portion, all the land of the region of the Chaldees to the east of the Euphrates, bordering on the Red Sea, and all the waters of the desert close to the tongue of the sea which looks towards Egypt, all the land of Lebanon and Sanir and Amana to the border of the Euphrates.
5 Aram received the fourth portion, all the land of Mesopotamia between the Tigris and the Euphrates to the north of the Chaldees to the border of the mountains of Asshur and the land of Arara.
6 Lud got the fifth portion, the mountains of Asshur and all surrounding to them until it reaches the Great Sea, and until it reaches the east of Asshur his brother.
7 Japheth also divided the land of his inheritance among his sons.
8 The first portion came out for Gomer to the east from the north side to the river Tina, and in the north there came out for Magog all the inner portions of the north until it reaches to the sea of Me'at.
9 Madai received as his portion that he should possess from the west of his two brothers to the islands, and to the coasts of the islands.
10 Javan got the fourth portion, every island and the islands that are towards the border of Lud.
11 For Tubal there came out the fifth portion in the middle of the tongue that approaches towards the border of the portion of Lud to the second tongue, to the region beyond the second tongue to the third tongue.
12 Meshech received the sixth portion, that is the entire region beyond the third tongue until it approaches the east of Gadir.
13 Tiras got the seventh portion, four great islands in the middle of the sea, which reach to the portion of Ham, and the islands of Kamaturi came out by lot for the sons of Arpachshad as his inheritance.

14 Thus the sons of Noah divided to their sons in the presence of Noah their father, and he bound them all by an oath, and invoked a curse on every one that sought to seize any portion which had not fallen to him by his lot.
15 They all said, 'so be it; so be it " (amen and amen) for themselves and their sons forever throughout their generations until the day of judgment, on which the Lord God shall judge them with a sword and with fire for all the unclean wickedness of their errors, that they have filled the earth with, which are transgression, uncleanness and fornication and sin.

[Chapter 10]

1 In the third week of this jubilee the unclean demons began to lead astray the children of the sons of Noah, and to make them sin and to destroy them.
2 The sons of Noah came to Noah their father, and they told him about the demons that were leading astray and blinding and slaying his sons' sons.
3 And he prayed before the Lord his God, and said,
"God of the spirits of all flesh, who have shown mercy to me and have spared me and my sons from the waters of the flood,
and have not caused me to die as You did the sons of perdition; For Your grace has been great toward me,
and great has been Your mercy to my soul. Let Your grace be lifted up on my sons, and do not let the wicked spirits rule over them or they will destroy them from the earth.
4 But bless me and my sons, so that we may increase and multiply and replenish the earth.
5 You know how Your Watchers, the fathers of these spirits, acted in my day, and as for these spirits which are living, imprison them and hold them fast in the place of condemnation, and let them not bring destruction on the sons of your servant, my God; for these are like cancer and are created in order to destroy.
6 Let them not rule over the spirits of the living; for You alone can exercise dominion over them. And let them not have power over the sons of the righteous from now and forever."
7 And the Lord our God commanded us (angels) to bind all of them.
8 The chief of the spirits, Mastema, came and said, "Lord, Creator, let some of them remain before me, and let them listen to my voice, and do all that I shall say to them; for if some of them are not left to me, I shall not be able to execute the power of my will on the sons of men, for these are for corruption and leading astray before my judgment, for great is the wickedness of the sons of men."
9 He said, "Let one-tenth of them remain before him, and let nine-tenths of them descend into the place of condemnation."
10 He commanded one of us to teach Noah all their medicines, for He knew that they would not walk in uprightness, nor strive in righteousness.
11 We did according to all His words, all the malignant evil ones we bound in the place of condemnation and a tenth part of them we left that they might be subject in the presence of Satan on the earth.
12 We explained to Noah all the medicines of their diseases, together with their seductions, how he might heal them with herbs of the earth.

13 Noah wrote down all things in a book as we instructed him concerning every kind of medicine. Thus the evil spirits were precluded from hurting the sons of Noah.
14 He gave all that he had written to Shem, his eldest son, for he loved him greatly above all his sons.
15 And Noah slept with his fathers, and was buried on Mount Lubar in the land of Ararat.
16 Nine hundred and fifty years he completed in his life, nineteen jubilees and two weeks and five years.
17 In his life on earth he was greater than all the children of men except Enoch because of his righteousness he was perfect. For Enoch's office was ordained for a testimony to the generations of the world, so that he should recount all the deeds of generation to generation, until the day of judgment.
18 In the three and thirtieth jubilee, in the first year in the second week, Peleg took to himself a wife, whose name was Lomna the daughter of Sina'ar, and she gave birth to a son for him in the fourth year of this week, and he called his name Reu, for he said, "Look the children of men have become evil because the building a city and a tower in the land of Shinar was for an evil purpose."
19 For they departed from the land of Ararat eastward to Shinar, for in his days they built the city and the tower, saying, "Go to, let us rise up thereby into heaven."
20 They began to build, and in the fourth week they made brick with fire, and the bricks served them for stone,

and the clay with which they cemented them together was asphalt which comes out of the sea, and out of the fountains of water in the land of Shinar.
21 They built it, forty-three years were they building it. Its breadth was 203 bricks, and the height of a brick was the third of one; its height amounted to 5433 cubits and 2 palms, and the extent of one wall was thirteen times 600 feet and of the other thirty times 600 feet.
22 And the Lord our God said to us, "Look, they are one people, and they begin to do this, and now nothing will be withheld from them. Let us go down and confound their language, that they may not understand one another's speech, and they may be dispersed into cities and nations, and they will not be in agreement together with one purpose until the day of judgment."
23 And the Lord descended, and we descended with him to see the city and the tower that the children of men had built.
24 He confounded their language, and they no longer understood one another's speech, and they then ceased to build the city and the tower.
25 For this reason the whole land of Shinar is called Babel, because the Lord confounded all the language of the children of men there, and from that place they were dispersed into their cities, each according to his language and his nation.
26 Then, the Lord sent a mighty wind against the tower and it fell to the earth, and behold it was between Asshur and Babylon in the land of Shinar, and they called its name "Overthrow."
27 In the fourth week in the first year in the beginning of it in the four and thirtieth jubilee, were they dispersed from the land of Shinar.
28 Ham and his sons went into the land that he was to occupy, which he acquired as his portion in the land of the south.
29 Canaan saw the land of Lebanon to the river of Egypt was very good, and he did not go into the land of his inheritance to the west that is to the sea, and he dwelt in

the land of Lebanon, eastward and westward from the border of Jordan and from the border of the sea.
30 Ham, his father, and Cush and Mizraim, his brothers, said to him, "You have settled in a land which is not yours, and which did not fall to us by lot, do not do so. If you do you and your sons will be conquered in the land and be accursed through a war. By war you have settled, and by war will your children fall, and you will be rooted out forever.
31 Do not live in the land of Shem, for to Shem and to his sons did it come by their lot.
32 Cursed are you, and cursed will you be beyond all the sons of Noah, by the curse by which we bound ourselves by an oath in the presence of the holy judge, and in the presence of Noah our father."
33 But he did not listen to them, and settled in the land of Lebanon from Hamath to the border of Egypt, he and his sons until this day. For this reason that land is named Canaan. And Japheth and his sons went towards the sea and settled in the land of their portion, and Madai saw the land of the sea and it did not please him, and he begged Ham and Asshur and Arpachshad, his wife's brother for a portion, and he dwelt in the land of Media, near to his wife's brother until this day.
34 And he called his and his son's dwelling-place, Media, after the name of their father Madai.

[Chapter 11]

1 In the thirty-fifth jubilee, in the third week, in the first year of it, Reu took to himself a wife, and her name was 'Ora, the daughter of 'Ur, the son of Kesed, and she gave birth to a son, and he called his name Seroh, in the seventh year of this week in this jubilee.
2 The sons of Noah began to war with each other, to take captives and kill each other, and to shed the blood of men on the earth, and to eat blood, and to build strong cities, and walls, and towers, and individuals began to exalt themselves above the nation, and to establish kingdoms, and to go to war, people against people, and nation against nation, and city against city, and all began to do evil, and to acquire arms, and to teach their sons war, and they began to capture cities, and to sell male and female slaves.
3 Ur, the son of Kesed, built the city of Ara of the Chaldees, and called its name after his own name and the name of his father.
4 And they made themselves molten images, and they worshipped the idols and the molten image they had made for themselves, and they began to make graven images and unclean and shadowy presence, and malevolent and malicious spirits assisted and seduced them into committing transgression and uncleanness.
5 Prince Mastema exerted himself to do all this, and he sent out other spirits, which were put under his control, to do all manner of wrong and sin, and all manner of transgression, to corrupt and destroy, and to shed blood on the earth.
6 For this reason he called the name of Seroh, Serug, for every one turned to do all manner of sin and transgression.
7 He grew up, and dwelt in Ur of the Chaldees, near to the father of his wife's mother, and he worshipped idols, and he took to himself a wife in the thirty-sixth

jubilee, in the fifth week, in the first year of it, and her name was Melka, the daughter of Kaber, the daughter of his father's brother.

8 She gave birth to Nahor, in the first year of this week, and he grew and dwelt in Ur of the Chaldees, and his father taught him the sciences of the Chaldees to divine and conjure, according to the signs of heaven.

9 In the thirty-seventh jubilee in the sixth week, in the first year of it, he took to himself a wife, and her name was 'Ijaska, the daughter of Nestag of the Chaldees.

10 And she gave birth to Terah in the seventh year of this week.

11 Prince Mastema sent ravens and birds to devour the seed that was sown in the land, in order to destroy the land, and rob the children of men of their labors. Before they could plow in the seed, the ravens picked it from the surface of the ground.

12 This is why he called his name Terah because the ravens and the birds reduced them to destitution and devoured their seed.

13 The years began to be barren, because of the birds, and they devoured all the fruit of the trees from the trees, it was only with great effort that they could harvest a little fruit from the earth in their days.

14 In this thirty-ninth jubilee, in the second week in the first year, Terah took to himself a wife, and her name was 'Edna, the daughter of Abram, the daughter of his father's sister.

15 In the seventh year of this week she gave birth to a son, and he called his name Abram, by the name of the father of his mother, for he had died before his daughter had conceived a son.

16 And the child began to understand the errors of the earth that all went astray after graven images and after uncleanness,

and his father taught him writing, and he was two weeks of years old, and he separated himself from his father, that he might not worship idols with him.

17 He began to pray to the Creator of all things that He might spare him from the errors of the children of men, and that his portion should not fall into error after uncleanness and vileness.

18 The time came for the sowing of seed in the land, and they all went out together to protect their seed against the ravens, and Abram went out with those that went, and the child was a lad of fourteen years.

19 A cloud of ravens came to devour the seed, and Abram ran to meet them before they settled on the ground, and cried to them before they settled on the ground to devour the seed, and said, "Descend not, return to the place from where you came," and they began to turn back.

20 And he caused the clouds of ravens to turn back that day seventy times, and of all the ravens throughout all the land where Abram was there settled not so much as one.

21 All who were with him throughout all the land saw him cry out, and all the ravens turn back, and his name became great in all the land of the Chaldees.

22 There came to him this year all those that wished to sow, and he went with them until the time of sowing ceased, and they sowed their land, and that year they brought enough grain home to eat and they were satisfied.

23 In the first year of the fifth week Abram taught those who made implements for oxen, the artificers in wood, and they made a vessel above the ground, facing the frame of the plow, in order to put the seed in it, and the seed fell down from it on the share of the plow, and was hidden in the earth, and they no longer feared the ravens.

24 After this manner they made vessels above the ground on all the frames of the plows, and they sowed and tilled all the land, according as Abram commanded them, and they no longer feared the birds.

[Chapter 12]

1 In the sixth week, in the seventh year of it, that Abram said to Terah his father, saying, "Father!"
2 He said, "Look, here am I, my son." He said, "What help and profit have we from those idols which you worship, and in the presence of which you bow yourself?
3 For there is no spirit in them. They are dumb forms, and they mislead the heart.
4 Do not worship them, Worship the God of heaven, who causes the rain and the dew to fall on the earth and does everything on the earth, and has created everything by His word, and all life is from His presence.
5 Why do you worship things that have no spirit in them?
For they are the work of men's hands, and you bear them on your shoulders, and you have no help from them, but they are a great cause of shame to those who make them, and they mislead the heart of those who worship them. Do not worship them."
6 His father said to him, "I also know it, my son, but what shall I do with a people who have made me serve them?
7 If I tell them the truth, they will kill me, because their soul clings to them so they worship them and honor them.
8 Keep silent, my son, or they will kill you." And these words he spoke to his two brothers, and they were angry with him and he kept silent.
9 In the fortieth jubilee, in the second week, in the seventh year of it, Abram took to himself a wife, and her name was Sarai, the daughter of his father, and she became his wife.
10 Haran, his brother, took to himself a wife in the third year of the third week, and she gave birth to a son in the seventh year of this week, and he called his name Lot.
11 Nahor, his brother, took to himself a wife.
12 In the sixtieth year of the life of Abram, that is, in the fourth week, in the fourth year of it, Abram arose in the night and burned the house of the idols, and he burned all that was in the house and no man knew it.
13 And they arose and sought to save their gods from the fire.
14 Haran hasted to save them, but the fire flamed over him, and he was burnt in the fire, and he died in Ur of the Chaldees before Terah his father, and they buried him in Ur of the Chaldees.
15 Terah went out from Ur of the Chaldees, he and his sons, to go into the land of Lebanon and into the land of Canaan, and he dwelt in the land of Haran, and Abram dwelt with Terah his father in Haran two weeks of years.
16 In the sixth week, in the fifth year of it, Abram sat up all night on the new moon of the seventh month to observe the stars from the evening to the morning, in order to see what would be the character of the year with regard to the rains, and he was alone as he sat and observed.
17 And a word came into his heart and he said, "All the signs of the stars, and the signs of the moon and of the sun are all in the hand of the Lord. Why do I search them out?

18 If He desires, He causes it to rain, morning and evening, and if He desires, He withholds it, and all things are in his hand."
19 He prayed in the night and said, "My God, God Most High, You alone are my God, and You and Your dominion have I chosen. And You have created all things, and all things that are the work of Your hands.
20 Deliver me from the hands of evil spirits who have dominion over the thoughts of men's hearts, and let them not lead me astray from You, my God. And establish me and my offspring forever so that we do not go astray from now and forever."
21 He said, "Shall I return to Ur of the Chaldees who are trying to find me? Should I return to them? Am I to remain here in this place? The right path is before You. Make it prosper in the hands of your servant that he may fulfill it and that I may not walk in the deceitfulness of my heart, O my God."
22 He stopped speaking and stopped praying, and then the word of the Lord was sent to him through me, saying, "Get out of your country, and from your kindred and from the house of your father and go to a land which I will show you, and I shall make you a great and numerous nation.
23 And I will bless you and I will make your name great,
and you will be blessed in the earth, and in You shall all families of the earth be blessed, and I will bless them that bless you, and curse them that curse you.
24 I will be a God to you and your son, and to your son's son, and to all your offspring, fear not, from now on and to all generations of the earth I am your God."
25 The Lord God said, "Open his mouth and his ears, that he may hear and speak with his mouth, with the language which has been revealed," for it had ceased from the mouths of all the children of men from the day of the overthrow of Babel.
26 And I opened his mouth, and his ears and his lips, and I began to speak with him in Hebrew in the tongue of the creation.
27 He took the books of his fathers, and these were written in Hebrew, and he transcribed them, and he began from then on to study them, and I made known to him that which he could not understand, and he studied them during the six rainy months.
28 In the seventh year of the sixth week he spoke to his father and informed him, that he would leave Haran to go into the land of Canaan to see it and return to him.
29 Terah his father said to him; "Go in peace. May the eternal God make your path straight. And the Lord be with you, and protect you from all evil, and grant to you grace, mercy and favor before those who see you, and may none of the children of men have power over you to harm you. Go in peace.
30 If you see a land pleasant to your eyes to dwell in, then arise and take me with you and take Lot with you, the son of Haran your brother as your own son, the Lord be with you.
31 Nahor your brother leave with me until you return in peace, and we go with you all together."

[Chapter 13]

1 Abram journeyed from Haran, and he took Sarai, his wife, and Lot, his brother Haran's son and they went to the land of Canaan, and he came into Asshur, and proceeded to Shechem, and dwelt near a tall oak.
2 He saw the land was very pleasant from the border of Hamath to the tall oak.

3 The Lord said to him, "To you and to your offspring I will give this land."
4 He built an altar there, and he offered on it a burnt sacrifice to the Lord, who had appeared to him.
5 He left from that place and went to the mountain Bethel on the west and Ai on the east, and pitched his tent there.
6 He saw the land was very wide and good, and everything grew on it, vines, and figs, and pomegranates, oaks, and ilexes, and turpentine and oil trees, and cedars and cypresses, and date trees, and all trees of the field, and there was water on the mountains.
7 And he blessed the Lord who had led him out of Ur of the Chaldees, and had brought him to this land.
8 In the first year, in the seventh week, on the new moon of the first month, he built an altar on this mountain, and called on the name of the Lord and said, "You, the eternal God, are my God."
9 He offered on the altar a burnt sacrifice to the Lord that He should be with him and not forsake him all the days of his life.
10 He left that place and went toward the south, and he came to Hebron and Hebron was built at that time, and he lived there two years, and he went from that place into the land of the south, to Bealoth, and there was a famine in the land.
11Abram went into Egypt in the third year of the week, and he dwelt in Egypt five years before his wife was torn away from him.
12 Now, Tanais in Egypt was built seven years after Hebron.
13 When Pharaoh seized Sarai, the wife of Abram the Lord plagued Pharaoh and his house with great plagues because of Sarai, Abram's wife.
14 Abram was celebrated and admired because of his great possessions of sheep, and cattle, and donkeys, and horses, and camels, and menservants, and maidservants, and in silver and gold. Lot and his brother's son were also wealthy.
15 Pharaoh gave back Sarai, the wife of Abram, and he sent him out of the land of Egypt, and he journeyed to the place where he had pitched his tent at the beginning, to the place of the altar, with Ai on the east, and Bethel on the west, and he blessed the Lord his God who had brought him back in peace.
16 In the forty-first jubilee in the third year of the first week, that he returned to this place and offered on it a burnt sacrifice, and called on the name of the Lord, and said, "You, the most high God, are my God forever and ever."
17 In the fourth year of this week Lot parted from him, and Lot lived in Sodom, and the men of Sodom sinned greatly.
18 It grieved him in his heart that his brother's son had parted from him because Abram had no children.
19 After Lot had parted from him, in the fourth year of this week. In that year when Lot was taken captive, the Lord said to Abram, "Lift up your eyes from the place where you are dwelling, northward and southward, and westward and eastward.
20 All the land that you see I will give to you and to your offspring forever, and I will make your offspring as the sand of the sea, though a man may number the dust of the earth, yet your offspring shall not be numbered.
21 Arise, walk through the land in the length of it and the breadth of it, and see it all. To your offspring will I give it." And Abram went to Hebron, and lived there.
22 And in this year came Chedorlaomer, king of Elam, and Amraphel, king of Shinar, and Arioch king of Sellasar, and Tergal, king of nations, and killed the king

of Gomorrah, and the king of Sodom fled, and many fell through wounds in the valley of Siddim, by the Salt Sea.
23 They took captive Sodom and Adam and Zeboim, and they took Lot captive, the son of Abram's brother, and all his possessions, and they went to Dan.
24 One who had escaped came and told Abram that his brother's son had been taken captive.
25 And Abram equipped his household servants for Abram, and for his offspring, a tenth of the first-fruits to the Lord, and the Lord ordained it as a law forever that they should give it to the priests who served before Him, that they should possess it forever.
26 There is no limit of days to this law, for He has ordained it for the generations forever that they should give to the Lord the tenth of everything, of the seed and of the wine and of the oil and of the cattle and of the sheep.
27 He gave it to His priests to eat and to drink with joy before Him.
28 The king of Sodom came and bowed down to him, and said, "Our Lord Abram, give to us the souls which you have rescued, but let the booty be yours."
29 And Abram said to him, "I lift up my hands to the Most High God, that from a thread to a shoe-latchet I shall not take anything that is yours so that you could never say, I have made Abram rich, except only what the young men, Aner and Eschol, and Mamre have eaten, and the portion of the men who went with me. These shall take their portion."

[Chapter 14]

1 After these things, in the fourth year of this week, on the new moon of the third month, the word of the Lord came to Abram
in a dream, saying, "Fear not, Abram, I am your defender, and your reward will be very great."
2 He said, "Lord, Lord, what will you give me, seeing I go from here childless, and the son of Maseq, the son of my handmaid, Eliezer of Damascus, he will be my heir, and to me you have given no offspring."
3 He said to him, "This man will not be your heir, but one that will come out of your own bowels. He will be your heir."
4 And He brought him out abroad, and said to him, "Look toward heaven and number the stars if you are able to number them."
5 He looked toward heaven, and beheld the stars. And He said to him, "so shall your offspring be."
6 And he believed in the Lord, and it was counted to him as righteousness.
7 God said to him, "I am the Lord that brought you out of Ur of the Chaldees, to give you the land of the Canaanites to possess it forever, and I will be God to you and to your offspring after you."
8 He said, "Lord, Lord, how shall I know that I shall inherit it?"
9 God said to him, "Take Me a heifer of three years, and a goat of three years, and a sheep of three years, and a turtle-dove, and a pigeon."
10 And he took all these in the middle of the month and he dwelt at the oak of Mamre, which is near Hebron.

11 He built an altar there, and sacrificed all these. He poured their blood on the altar, and divided them in half, and laid them over against each other, but the birds he did not divide.
12 Birds came down on the pieces, and Abram drove them away, and did not permit the birds to touch them.
13 It happened, when the sun had set, that an ecstasy fell on Abram, and such a horror of great darkness fell on him, and it was said to Abram, "Know of a surety that your offspring shall be a stranger in a land that is not theirs, and they shall be brought into bondage, and afflicted for four hundred years.
14 The nation also to whom they will be in bondage will I judge, and after that they shall come out from that place with many possessions.
15 You will go to your fathers in peace, and be buried in a good old age.
16 But in the fourth generation they shall return here, for the iniquity of the Amorites is not yet full."
17 And he awoke from his sleep, and he arose, and the sun had set; and there was a flame, and a furnace was smoking, and a flame of fire passed between the pieces.
18 On that day the Lord made a covenant with Abram, saying, "To your offspring will I give this land, from the river of Egypt to the great river, the river Euphrates, the Kenites, the Kenizzites, the Kadmonites, the Perizzites, and the Rephaim, the Phakorites, and the Hivites, and the Amorites, and the Canaanites, and the Girgashites, and the Jebusites.
19 The day passed, and Abram offered the pieces, and the birds, and their fruit offerings, and their drink offerings, and the fire devoured them.
20 On that day we made a covenant with Abram, in the same way we had covenanted with Noah in this month; and Abram renewed the festival and laws for himself forever.
21Abram rejoiced, and made all these things known to Sarai his wife. He believed that he would have offspring, but she did not bear.
22 Sarai advised her husband Abram, and said to him, "Go in to Hagar, my Egyptian maid, it may be that I shall build up offspring to you by her."
23Abram listened to the voice of Sarai his wife, and said to her, "Do so." And Sarai took Hagar, her maid, the Egyptian, and gave her to Abram, her husband, to be his wife.
24 He went in to her, and she conceived and gave birth to a son, and he called his name Ishmael, in the fifth year of this week; and this was the eighty-sixth year in the life of Abram.

[Chapter 15]

1 In the fifth year of the fourth week of this jubilee, in the third month, in the middle of the month, Abram celebrated the feast of the first-fruits of the grain harvest.
2 And he made new offerings on the altar, the first-fruits of the produce to the Lord, a heifer, and a goat, and a sheep on the altar as a burnt sacrifice to the Lord; their fruit offerings and their drink offerings he offered on the altar with frankincense.
3 The Lord appeared to Abram, and said to him, "I am God Almighty. Examine yourself and demonstrate yourself before me and be perfect.
4 I will make My covenant between Me and you, and I will multiply you greatly."

5 Abram fell on his face, and God talked with him, and said, "My law is with you, and you will be the father of many nations.
6 Neither shall your name any more be called Abram, but your name from now on, even forever, shall be Abraham.
7 For I have made you the father of many nations.
8 I will make you very great, and I will make you into nations, and kings shall come forth from you.
9 I shall establish My covenant between Me and you, and your offspring after you, throughout their generations, for an eternal covenant, so that I may be a God to you, and to your offspring after you.
10 You may possess the land where you have been a sojourner, the land of Canaan, and you will possess it forever, and I will be their God."
11 The Lord said to Abraham, "Keep my covenant, you and your offspring after you, and circumcise every male among you, and circumcise your foreskins, and it shall be a token of an eternal covenant between Me and you.
12 And the eighth day you shall circumcise the child, every male throughout your generations, him that is born in the house, or whom you have bought with money from any stranger, whom you have acquired who is not of your offspring.
13 He that is born in your house shall surely be circumcised, and those whom you have bought with money shall be circumcised, and My covenant shall be in your flesh for an eternal ordinance.
14 The uncircumcised male who is not circumcised in the flesh of his foreskin on the eighth day, that soul shall be cut off from his people, for he has broken My covenant."
15 God said to Abraham, "As for Sarai your wife, her name shall no more be called Sarai, but Sarah shall be her name.
16 I will bless her, and give you a son by her, and I will bless him, and he shall become a nation, and kings of nations shall proceed from him."
17 Abraham fell on his face, and rejoiced, and said in his heart, "Shall a son be born to him that is a hundred years old, and shall Sarah, who is ninety years old, bring forth?"
18 Abraham said to God, "Oh, that Ishmael might live before you!"
19 God said, "Yea, and Sarah also shall bear you a son, and you will call his name Isaac, and I will establish My covenant with him, an everlasting covenant, and for his offspring after him.
20 And as for Ishmael also have I heard you, and behold I will bless him, and make him great, and multiply him greatly, and he shall beget twelve princes, and I will make him a great nation.
21 But My covenant will I establish with Isaac, whom Sarah shall bear to you this time next year."
22 God ceased speaking with him, and God went up from Abraham.
23 Abraham did according as God had said to him, and he took Ishmael his son, and all that were born in his house, and whom he had bought with his money, every male in his house, and circumcised the flesh of their foreskin.
24 On that same day was Abraham circumcised, and all the men of his house, and all those whom he had bought with money from the children of the stranger were circumcised with him.

25 This law is for all the generations forever, and there is no variance of days, and no omission of one day out of the eight days, for it is an eternal law, ordained and written on the heavenly tablets.
26 Every one that is born, the flesh of whose foreskin is not circumcised on the eighth day, does not belong to the children of the covenant which the Lord made with Abraham, but instead they belong to the children of destruction; nor is there any other sign on him that he is the Lord's, but he is destined to be destroyed and killed from the earth, and to be rooted out of the earth, for he has broken the covenant of the Lord our God.
27 All the angels of the presence (of the Lord) and all the angels of sanctification have been created already circumcised from the day of their creation, and before the angels of the presence (of the Lord) and the angels of sanctification He has sanctified Israel, that they should be with Him and with His holy angels.
28 Command the children of Israel and let them observe the sign of this covenant for their generations as an eternal law, and they will not be rooted out of the land.
29 For the command is ordained for a covenant, that they should observe it forever among all the children of Israel.
30 For Ishmael and his sons and his brothers, and Esau, the Lord did not cause them to come to Him, and he did not choose them. Although they are the children of Abraham, He knew them, but He chose Israel to be His people.
31 He sanctified them, and gathered them from among all the children of men; for there are many nations and many peoples, and all are His, and over all nations He has placed spirits in authority to lead them astray from Him.
32 But over Israel He did not appoint any angel or spirit, for He alone is their ruler, and He will preserve them and require them at the hand of His angels and His spirits, and at the hand of all His powers in order that He may preserve them and bless them, that they may be His and He may be theirs from now on forever.
33 I announce to you that the children of Israel will not keep true to this law, and they will not circumcise their sons according to all this law; for in the flesh of their circumcision they will omit this circumcision of their sons, and all of the sons of Beliar will leave their sons uncircumcised as they were born.
34 There will be great wrath from the Lord against the children of Israel because they have forsaken His covenant and turned aside from His word, and provoked (God) and blasphemed, because they do not observe the ordinance of this law; for they have treated their genitalia like the Gentiles, so that they may be removed and rooted out of the land. And there will no more be pardon or forgiveness to them for all the sin of this eternal error.

[Chapter 16]

1 On the new moon of the fourth month we appeared to Abraham, at the oak of Mamre, and we talked with him, and we announced to him that Sarah, his wife, would give him a son.
2 And Sarah laughed, for she heard that we had spoken these words to Abraham. We warned her, and she became afraid, and denied that she had laughed because of the words.
3 We told her the name of her son, as his name is ordained and written in the heavenly tablets and it is Isaac.

4 We told her that when we returned to her at a set time, she would have conceived a son.

5 In this month the Lord executed his judgments on Sodom, and Gomorrah, and Zeboim, and all the region of the Jordan, and He burned them with fire and brimstone, and destroyed them and they are destroyed until this day, because of all their works. They are wicked and vast sinners, and they defile themselves and commit fornication in their flesh, and work uncleanness on the earth as I have told you.

6 In like manner, God will execute judgment on the places where they have done similar to the uncleanness of the Sodomites, and they will suffer a judgment like that of Sodom.

7 But for Lot, we made an exception, for God remembered Abraham, and sent him out from the place of the overthrow.

8 And he and his daughters committed sin on the earth, such as had not been on the earth since the days of Adam until his time, for the man had sex with his daughters.

9 It was commanded and engraved concerning all his offspring, on the heavenly tablets, to remove them and root them out, and to execute judgment on them like the judgment of Sodom, and to leave no offspring of that man on earth on the day of condemnation.

10 In this month Abraham moved from Hebron, and departed and lived between Kadesh and Shur in the mountains of Gerar.

11 In the middle of the fifth month he moved from that place, and lived at the Well of the Oath.

12 In the middle of the sixth month the Lord visited Sarah and did to her as He had spoken and she conceived.

13 And she gave birth to a son in the third month. In the middle of the month, at the time of which the Lord had spoken to Abraham, on the festival of the first-fruits of the harvest, Isaac was born.

14 Abraham circumcised his son on the eighth day, he was the first that was circumcised according to the covenant that is ordained forever.

15 In the sixth year of the fourth week we came to Abraham at the Well of the Oath, and we appeared to him.

16 We returned in the seventh month, and found Sarah with child before us and we blessed him, and we announced to him all the things that had been decreed concerning him, so that he should not die until he should beget six more sons and saw them before he died.

17 But in Isaac should his name and offspring be called, and that all the offspring of his sons should be Gentiles, and be counted with the Gentiles; but from the sons of Isaac one should become a holy offspring, and should not be counted among the Gentiles.

18 For he should become the portion (dowry) of the Most High, and all his offspring had fallen into the possession of God, that they should be to the Lord a people for His possession above all nations and that they should become a kingdom and priests and a holy nation.

19 We went our way, and we announced to Sarah all that we had told him, and they both rejoiced with very great joy.

20 He built there an altar to the Lord who had delivered him, and who was causing him to rejoice in the land of his sojourning, and he celebrated a festival of joy in this month for seven days, near the altar which he had built at the Well of the Oath.

21 He built tents for himself and for his servants on this festival, and he was the first to celebrate the feast of tabernacles on the earth.
22 During these seven days he brought a burnt offering to the Lord each day to the altar consisting of two oxen, two rams, seven sheep, one male goat, for a sin offering that he might atone thereby for himself and for his offspring.
23 As an offering of thanks he brought, seven rams, seven kids, seven sheep, and seven male goats, and their fruit offerings and their drink offerings; and he burnt all the fat of it on the altar, a chosen offering to the Lord for a sweet smelling odor.
24 Morning and evening he burnt fragrant substances, frankincense and incense, and sweet spice, and nard, and myrrh, and spice, and aromatic plants; all these seven he offered, crushed, mixed together in equal parts and pure.
25 And he celebrated this feast during seven days, rejoicing with all his heart and with all his soul, he and all those who were in his house, and there was no stranger with him, nor any that was uncircumcised.
26 He blessed his Creator who had created him in his generation, for He had created him according to His good pleasure. God knew and perceived that from him would arise the plant of righteousness for the eternal generations, and from him a holy offspring, so that it should become like Him who had made all things.
27 He blessed and rejoiced, and he called the name of this festival the festival of the Lord, a joy acceptable to the Most High God.
28 And we blessed him forever, and all his offspring after him throughout all the generations of the earth, because he celebrated this festival in its season, according to the testimony of the heavenly tablets.
29 For this reason it is ordained on the heavenly tablets concerning Israel, that they shall celebrate the feast of tabernacles seven days with joy, in the seventh month, acceptable before the Lord as a statute forever throughout their generations every year.
30 To this there is no limit of days; for it is ordained forever regarding Israel that they should celebrate it and dwell in tents, and set wreaths on their heads, and take leafy boughs, and willows from the brook.
31Abraham took branches of palm trees, and the fruit of good and pleasing trees, and every day going round the altar with the branches seven times a day in the morning, he praised and gave thanks to his God for all things in joy.

[Chapter 17]

1 In the first year of the fifth week Isaac was weaned in this jubilee, and Abraham made a great banquet in the third month, on the day his son Isaac was weaned.
2 Ishmael, the son of Hagar, the Egyptian, was in front of Abraham, his father, in his place, and Abraham rejoiced and blessed God because he had seen his sons and had not died childless.
3 He remembered the words which He had spoken to him on the day that Lot had departed from him, and he rejoiced because the Lord had given him offspring on the earth to inherit the earth, and he blessed with all his mouth the Creator of all things.
4 Sarah saw Ishmael playing and dancing, and Abraham rejoicing with great joy, and she became jealous of Ishmael and said to Abraham, "Throw out this bondwoman and her son. The son of this bondwoman will not be heir with my son, Isaac."

5 And the situation was troubling to Abraham, because of his maidservant and because of his son, because he did not want to drive them from him.
6 God said to Abraham "Let it not be troubling in your sight, because of the child and because of the bondwoman. Listen to Sarah and to all her words and do them, for in Isaac shall your name and offspring be called.
7 But as for the son of this bondwoman I will make him a great nation, because he is of your offspring."
8 Abraham got up early in the morning, and took bread and a bottle of water, and placed them on the shoulders of Hagar and the child, and sent her away.
9 And she departed and wandered in the wilderness of Beersheba, and the water in the bottle was spent, and the child was thirsty, and was not able to go on, and fell down.
10 His mother took him and laid him under an olive tree, and went and sat her down over away from him at the distance of a bow-shot; for she said, "Let me not see the death of my child," and she sat and wept.
11 An angel of God, one of the holy ones, said to her, "Why do you weep, Hagar? Stand. Take the child, and hold him in your hand, for God has heard your voice, and has seen the child."
12 She opened her eyes, and she saw a well of water, and she went and filled her bottle with water, and she gave her child a drink, and she arose and went towards the wilderness of Paran.
13 And the child grew and became an archer, and God was with him, and his mother took him a wife from among the daughters of Egypt.
14 She (the wife) gave birth to a son, and he called his name Nebaioth; for she said, "The Lord was close to me when I called on him."
15 In the seventh week, in the first year of it, in the first month in this jubilee, on the twelfth of this month, there were voices in heaven regarding Abraham, that he was faithful in all that He told him, and that he loved the Lord, and that in every affliction he was faithful.
16 Prince Mastema came and said before God, "Look, Abraham loves Isaac his son, and he delights in him above all things, tell him to offer him as a burnt-offering on the altar, and You will see if he will do this command, and You will know if he is faithful in everyway that You test him.
17 The Lord knew that Abraham was faithful throughout all his afflictions, for He had tried him through his country and with famine, and had tried him with the wealth of kings, and had tried him again through his wife, when she was torn from him, and with circumcision; and had tried him through Ishmael and Hagar, his maid-servant, when he sent them away.
18 In everything that He had tried him, he was found faithful, and his soul was not impatient, and he was not slow to act, because he was faithful and a lover of the Lord.

[Chapter 18]

1 God said to him, "Abraham. Abraham." and he said, "Look, here am I."
2 He said, "Take your beloved son, Isaac, whom you love, and go to the high country, and offer him on one of the mountains which I will point out to you."

3 He got early in the morning and saddled his donkey, and took two young men with him, and Isaac his son, and split the wood of the burnt offering, and he went to the place on the third day, and he saw the place afar off.
4 He came to a well of water (near Mount Moriah), and he said to his young men, "You stay here with the donkey, and I and the lad shall go yonder, and when we have worshipped we shall come back to you."
5 He took the wood of the burnt-offering and laid it on Isaac his son, and he took the fire and the knife, and they went both of them together to that place.
6 Isaac said to his father, "Father" and he said, "Here am I, my son." He said to him, "Look, we have the fire, and the knife, and the wood, but where is the sheep for the burnt-offering, father?"
7 He said, "God will provide for himself a sheep for a burnt-offering, my son." And he neared the place of the mountain of God.
8 He built an altar, and he placed the wood on the altar, and bound Isaac his son, and placed him on the wood that was on the altar, and stretched out his hand to take the knife to kill Isaac, his son.
9 I stood in the presence of him, and before prince Mastema, (and the holy angels stood and wept over the altar as prince Mastema and his angels rejoiced and said "Isaac will be destroyed and we will see if Abraham is faithful), and the Lord said, "Command him not to lay his hand on the lad, nor to do anything to him, for I have shown that he fears the Lord."
10 I called to him from heaven, and said to him, "Abraham, Abraham." and he was terrified and said, "Here am I."
11 I said to him, "Lay not your hand on the lad, neither do anything to him; for now I have shown that you fear the Lord, and have not withheld your son, your first-born son, from me."
12 Prince Mastema was put to shame (and was bound by the angels); and Abraham lifted up his eyes and looked and saw a ram caught by his horns, and Abraham went and took the ram and offered it as a burnt-offering in place of his son.
13 Abraham called that place "The Lord has seen," so that it is said the Lord has seen. This is Mount Zion.
14 The Lord called Abraham by his name a second time from heaven, as he caused us to appear to speak to him in the name of the Lord.
15 He said, "By Myself have I sworn," said the Lord, "Because you have done this thing, and have not withheld your son, your beloved son, from Me, that in blessing I will bless you, and in multiplying I will multiply your offspring as the stars of heaven, and as the sand which is on the seashore.
16 Your offspring shall inherit the cities of its enemies, and in your offspring shall all nations of the earth be blessed. Because you have obeyed My voice, and I have shown to all that you are faithful to Me in all that I have said to you, "Go in peace."
17 Abraham went back to his young men, and they stood and went back together to Beersheba, and Abraham lived by the Well of the Oath.
18 And he celebrated this festival every year, seven days with joy, and he called it the festival of the Lord according to the seven days during which he went and returned in peace.
19 Accordingly, it has been ordained and written on the heavenly tablets regarding Israel and its children that they should observe this festival seven days with the joy of festival.

[Chapter 19]

1 In the first year of the first week in the forty-second jubilee, Abraham returned and lived across from Hebron, in Kirjath Arba for two weeks of years.
2 In the first year of the third week of this jubilee the days of the life of Sarah were completed, and she died in Hebron.
3 Abraham went to mourn over her and bury her, and we tested him to see if his spirit was patient and he had neither anger nor contempt in the words of his mouth, and he was found patient in this and was not disturbed.
4 In patience of spirit he discussed with the children of Heth that they should give him a place in which to bury his dead.
5 And the Lord gave him grace before all who saw him, and he asked the sons of Heth in gentleness, and they gave him the land of the double cave over beside Mamre, that is Hebron, for four hundred pieces of silver.
6 They said to him, "We shall give it to you for nothing," but he would not take it from them for nothing, for he gave the price of the place and paid the money in full. And he bowed down before them twice, and after this he buried his dead in the double cave.
7 All the days of the life of Sarah were one hundred and twenty-seven years, that is, two jubilees and four weeks and one year, these are the days of the years of the life of Sarah.
8 This is the tenth trial with which Abraham was tested, and he was found faithful and patient in spirit.
9 He did not say a single word regarding the rumor in the land of how God had said that He would give it to him and to his offspring after him, but instead he begged for a place there to bury his dead. Because he was found faithful, it was recorded on the heavenly tablets that he was the friend of God.
10 In the fourth year of it (this jubilee) he took a wife for his son Isaac and her name was Rebecca the daughter of Bethuel, the son of Nahor, the brother of Abraham the sister of Laban and daughter of Bethuel; and Bethuel was the son of Melca, who was the wife of Nahor, the brother of Abraham.
11 Abraham took to himself a third wife from among the daughters of his household servants, for Hagar had died before Sarah, and her name was Keturah,. And she gave birth to six sons, Zimram, and Jokshan, and Medan, and Midian, and Ishbak, and Shuah, in the two weeks of years.
12 In the sixth week, in the second year of it, Rebecca gave birth to two sons of Isaac, Jacob and Esau.
13 And Jacob had no beard and was a straight and tall man who dwelt in tents, and Esau was a powerful a man of the field, and was hairy.
14 The youths grew, and Jacob learned to write, but Esau did not learn, for he was a man of the field and a hunter, and he learned war, and all his deeds were fierce.
15Abraham loved Jacob, but Isaac loved Esau.
16 And Abraham saw the deeds of Esau, and he knew that in Jacob should his name and offspring be called. He called Rebecca and gave commandment regarding Jacob, for he knew that she too loved Jacob much more than Esau.

17 He said to her, "My daughter, watch over my son Jacob, for he shall take my place on the earth. He shall be a blessing throughout the children of men and for the glory of all the offspring of Shem.
18 I know that the Lord will choose him to be a people (nation) and a possession to Himself, above all peoples that are on the face of the earth.
19 Isaac, my son, loves Esau more than Jacob, but I see that you truly love Jacob.
20 Add still further to your kindness to him, and regard him in love, for he shall be a blessing to us on the earth from now on to all generations of the earth.
21 Let your hands be strong and let your heart rejoice in your son Jacob, for I have loved him far beyond all my sons. He shall be blessed forever, and his offspring shall fill the whole earth.
22 If a man can number the sand of the earth, his offspring also shall be numbered.
23 And all the blessings with which the Lord has blessed me and my offspring shall belong to Jacob and his offspring always.
24 In his offspring shall my name be blessed, and the name of my fathers, Shem, Noah, Enoch, Mahalalel, Enos, Seth, and Adam. And these shall serve to lay the foundations of the heaven, and to strengthen the earth, and to renew all the stars and planets which are in the sky.
27 He called Jacob and kissed him in front of Rebecca, his mother, and blessed him, and said, "Jacob, my beloved son, whom my soul loves, may God bless you from above the sky, and may He give you all the blessings with which He blessed Adam, Enoch, Noah, and Shem; and all the things of which He told me, and all the things which He promised to give me, may He cause to be yours and your offspring forever, according to the days of heaven above the earth.
28 And the Spirits of Mastema shall not rule over you or over your offspring or turn you from the Lord, who is your God from now on forever.
29 May the Lord God be a father to you and may you be like His first-born son, and to the people always. Go in peace, my son."
30 And they both went out together from Abraham.
31 Rebecca loved Jacob, with all her heart and with all her soul, very much more than Esau, but Isaac loved Esau much more than Jacob.

[Chapter 20]

1 In the forty-second jubilee, in the first year of the seventh week, Abraham called Ishmael, and his twelve sons, and Isaac and his two sons, and the six sons of Keturah, and their sons.
2 And he commanded them that they should observe the way of the Lord, that they should work righteousness, and love each his neighbor, and act in this manner among all men, that they should each walk with regard to the ways of the Lord to do judgment and righteousness on the earth.
3 He also commanded them that they should circumcise their sons, according to the covenant, which God had made with them, and not deviate to the right or the left of all the paths which the Lord had commanded us, and that we should keep ourselves from all fornication and uncleanness.
4 He said, "If any woman or maid commits fornication among you, burn her with fire. And do not let them commit fornication with her with their eyes or their heart;

and do not let them take to themselves wives from the daughters of Canaan, because the offspring of Canaan will be rooted out of the land."
5 He told them about the judgment on the giants, and the judgment on the Sodomites, how they had been judged because of their wickedness, and had died because of their fornication and uncleanness, and corruption through fornication together.
6 He said, "Guard yourselves from all fornication and uncleanness, and from all pollution of sin, or you will make our name a curse, and your whole life a shame, and all your sons to be destroyed by the sword, and you will become accursed like Sodom, and all that is left of you shall be as the sons of Gomorrah.
7 I implore you, my sons, love the God of heaven and cling to all His commandments.
8 Do not walk after their idols and after their ways of uncleanness, and do not make yourselves molten or graven gods. They are empty, and there is no spirit in them, for they are work of men's hands, and all who trust in them, trust in nothing.
9 Do not serve them, nor worship them, but serve the most high God, and worship Him continually, and hope for His presence always, and work uprightness and righteousness before Him, that He may have pleasure in you and grant you His mercy, and send rain on you morning and evening, and bless all your works which you have performed on the earth, and bless your bread and your water, and bless the fruit of your womb and the fruit of your land, and the herds of your cattle, and the flocks of your sheep.
10 You will be for a blessing on the earth, and all nations of the earth will desire you, and bless your sons in my name, that they may be blessed as I am."
11 He gave to Ishmael and to his sons, and to the sons of Keturah, gifts, and sent them away from Isaac his son, and he gave everything to Isaac his son.
12 Ishmael and his sons, and the sons of Keturah and their sons, went together and settled from Paran to the border of Babylon in all the land that is toward the East facing the desert.
13 These mingled (intermarried) with each other, and their names were called Arabs, and Ishmaelites.

[Chapter 21]

1 In the sixth year of the seventh week of this jubilee Abraham called Isaac his son, and commanded him, saying, "I have become old. I do not know the day of my death but I am full of my days.
2 I am one hundred and seventy-five years old, and throughout all the days of my life I have remembered the Lord, and sought with all my heart to do His will, and to walk uprightly in all His ways.
3 My soul has hated idols. I have given my heart and spirit to the observance of the will of Him who created me.
4 For He is the living God, and He is holy and faithful, and He is righteous beyond all, and He is no respecter of men or of their gifts, for God is righteous, and executes judgment on all those who transgress His commandments and despise His covenant.
5 My son, observe His commandments and His law and His judgments, and do not walk after the abominations and after the graven images and after the molten images.

6 And eat no blood at all of animals or cattle, or of any bird that flies in the heaven.
7 If you kill a sacrificial animal as an acceptable peace offering, kill it, and pour out its blood on the altar. Place all the fat of the offering on the altar with fine flour and the meat offering mingled with oil with its drink offering. Place them all together on the altar of burnt offering. It is a sweet odor before the Lord.
8 You will offer the fat of the sacrifice of thanks offerings on the fire which is on the altar, and the fat which is on the belly, and all the fat on the inside, behind the two kidneys, and all the fat that is on them, and lobes of the liver you will remove, together with the kidneys.
9 Offer all these for a sweet odor acceptable before the Lord, with its meat-offering and with its drink-offering, and the bread of the offering to the Lord.
10 Eat its meat on that day and on the second day, but do not let the sun go down on it until it is eaten. Let nothing be left over for the third day, for it is not acceptable. Let it no longer be eaten, and all who eat of it will bring sin on themselves, for thus I have found it written in the books of my forefathers, and in the words of Enoch, and in the words of Noah.
11 On all your offerings you will scatter salt, and do not let the salt of the covenant be lacking in all your offerings before the Lord.
12 As regards the wood of the sacrifices, beware to bring only these and no other wood to the altar in addition to these, cypress, bay, almond, fir, pine, cedar, savin, fig, olive, myrrh, laurel, aspalathus.
13 Of these kinds of wood lay on the altar under the sacrifice, such as have been tested as to their appearance, and do not lay on it any split or dark wood, but hard and clean, without fault, a healthy and new growth. Do not lay old wood on it, because there is no longer fragrance in it as before.
14 Besides these kinds of wood there is none other that you will place on the altar, for the fragrance is dispersed, and the smell of its fragrance will not go up to heaven.
15 Observe this commandment and do it, my son, that you may be upright in all your deeds.
16 Be clean in your body at all times. Wash yourself with water before you approach to offer on the altar. Wash your hands and your feet before you draw near to the altar, and when you are done sacrificing, wash your hands and your feet again.
17 Let no blood appear on you or on your clothes. Be on your guard against blood, my son. Be on your guard continually and cover it with dust.
18 Do not eat any blood for it is the soul. Eat no blood whatsoever.
19 Take no payment for shedding the blood of man, or it will cause it to be shed without fear of punishment, without judgment. It is the blood that is shed that causes the earth to sin, and the earth cannot be cleansed from the blood of man except by the blood of he who shed it.
20 Take no present or gift for the blood of man, blood for blood, that you may be accepted before the Lord, the Most High God. He is the defense of the good, so that you may be preserved from all evil, and that He may withhold you from every kind of death.
21 I see, my son, all the works of the children of men are sin and wickedness, and all their deeds are uncleanness and an abomination and a pollution, and there is no righteousness in them.
22 Beware, or you will walk in their ways and tread in their paths, and commit a sin worthy of death before the Most High God. He will hide His face from you and give you back into the hands of your transgression, and root you out of the land, and

your offspring likewise from under heaven, and your name and your offspring shall perish from the whole earth.
23 Turn away from all their deeds and all their uncleanness, and observe the laws of the Most High God, and do His will and be upright in all things.
24 If you do this, He will bless you in all your deeds, and will raise up from you a plant of righteousness through all the earth, throughout all generations of the earth, and my name and your name shall not be forgotten under heaven forever.
25 Go, my son in peace. May the Most High God, my God and your God, strengthen you to do His will, and may He bless all your offspring and the remainder of your offspring for the generations forever, with all righteous blessings, that you may be a blessing on all the earth."
26 And he went out from him rejoicing.

[Chapter 22]

1 In the first week in the forty-fourth jubilee, in the second year, that is, the year in which Abraham died, Isaac and Ishmael came from the Well of the Oath to celebrate the feast of weeks which is the feast of the first-fruits of the harvest to Abraham, their father, and Abraham rejoiced because his two sons had come.
2 Isaac had many possessions in Beersheba, and Isaac desired to go and see his possessions and to return to his father.
3 In those days Ishmael came to see his father, and they both came together, and Isaac offered a sacrifice for a burnt offering, and presented it on the altar of his father that he had made in Hebron.
4 He offered a thanks offering and made a feast of joy in the presence of Ishmael, his brother, and Rebecca made new cakes from the new grain, and gave them to Jacob, her son, to take them to Abraham, his father, from the first-fruits of the land, that he might eat and bless the Creator of all things before he died.
5 Isaac, also, sent Jacob to Abraham with an offering of his best for thanks so that he might eat and drink.
6 He ate and drank, and blessed the Most High God, who has created heaven and earth, who has made all the fat things of the earth, and given them to the children of men that they might eat and drink and bless their Creator.
7 "And now I give thanks to You, my God, because you have caused me to see this day, behold, I am one hundred three score and fifteen years, an old man and full of days, and all my days have been peace to me.
8 The sword of the adversary has not overcome me in all that You have given me and my children all the days of my life until this day.
9 My God, may Your mercy and Your peace be on Your servant, and on the offspring of his sons, that they may be to You a chosen nation and an inheritance from among all the nations of the earth from now on to all the days of the generations of the earth, to all the ages."
10 He called Jacob and said, "My son Jacob, may the God of all bless you and strengthen you to do righteousness, and His will before Him, and may He choose you and your offspring that you may become a people for His inheritance according to His will always.
11 My son, Jacob, draw near and kiss me." And he drew near and kissed him, and he said, "Blessed be my son Jacob and all the sons of God Most High, to all the ages.

May God give to you an offspring of righteousness; and some of your sons may He sanctify throughout the whole earth. May nations serve you, and all the nations bow themselves before your offspring.
12 Be strong in the presence of men, and exercise authority over all the offspring of Seth. Then your ways and the ways of your sons will be justified, so that they shall become a holy nation.
13 May the Most High God give you all the blessings with which He has blessed me and He blessed Noah and Adam. May they rest on the sacred head of your offspring from generation to generation forever.
14 May He cleanse you from all unrighteousness and impurity so that you may be forgiven all the transgressions, which you have committed ignorantly. May He strengthen you, and bless you.
15 May you inherit the whole earth, and may He renew His covenant with you so that you may be to Him a nation for His inheritance for all the ages, and so that He may be to you and to your offspring a God in truth and righteousness throughout all the days of the earth.
16 My son Jacob, remember my words. Observe the commandments of Abraham, your father, separate yourself from the nations (gentiles), and do not eat with them. Do not emulate their works, and do not associate with them because their works are unclean, and all their ways are a pollution and an abomination and uncleanness.
17 They offer their sacrifices to the dead and they worship evil spirits, and they eat over the graves, and all their works are empty and nothingness.
18 They have no heart to understand and their eyes do not see what their works are, and how they go astray by saying to a piece of wood, "You are my God," and to a stone, "You are my Lord and you are my deliverer," because the stone and wood have no heart.
19 And as for you, my son Jacob, may the Most High God help you and the God of heaven bless you and remove you from their uncleanness and from all their error.
20 Jacob, be warned. Do not take a wife from any offspring of the daughters of Canaan, for all his offspring are to be rooted out of the earth.
21 Because of the transgression of Ham, Canaan erred, and all his offspring shall be destroyed from the earth including any remnant of it, and none springing from him shall exist except on the day of judgment.
22 And as for all the worshippers of idols and the profane, there shall be no hope for them in the land of the living, and no one on earth will remember them, for they shall descend into the abode of the dead, and they shall go into the place of condemnation. As the children of Sodom were taken away from the earth, so will all those who worship idols be taken away.
23 Fear not, my son Jacob. Be not dismayed, son of Abraham. May the Most High God preserve you from destruction, and may He deliver you from all the paths of error.
24 This house have I built for myself that I might put my name on it in the earth. It is given to you and to your offspring forever, and it will be named the house of Abraham. It is given to you and your offspring forever, for you will build my house and establish my name before God forever. Your offspring and your name will stand throughout all generations of the earth."
25 He ceased commanding him and blessing him.

26 The two lay together on one bed, and Jacob slept in the embracing arms of Abraham, his father's father, and he kissed him seven times, and his affection and his heart rejoiced over him.
27 He blessed him with all his heart and said, "The Most High God, the God of all, and Creator of all, who brought me out from Ur of the Chaldees that He might give me this land to inherit forever, that I might establish a holy offspring.
28 Blessed be the Most High forever."
29 And he blessed Jacob and said, "May Your grace and Your mercy be lift up on my son, over whom I rejoice with all my heart and my affection and on his offspring always.
30 Do not forsake him, nor diminish him from now to the days of eternity, and may Your eyes be opened on him and on his offspring, that You may preserve him, and bless him, and may sanctify him as a nation for Your inheritance. Bless him with all Your blessings from now to all the days of eternity, and renew Your covenant and Your grace with him and with his offspring according to all Your good pleasure to all the generations of the earth."

[Chapter 23]

1 He placed Jacob's two fingers on his eyes, and he blessed the God of gods, and he covered his face and stretched out his feet and slept the sleep of eternity, and was gathered to his fathers.
2 In spite of all this, Jacob was lying in his embracing arms, and knew not that Abraham, his father's father, was dead.
3 Jacob awoke from his sleep, and realized Abraham was cold as ice, and he said, "Father, father," but there was no answer, and he knew that he was dead.
4 He arose from his embracing arms and ran and told Rebecca, his mother, and Rebecca went to Isaac in the night, and told him and they went together, and Jacob with them, and a lamp was in his hand, and when they had gone in they found Abraham lying dead.
5 Isaac fell on the face of his father and wept and kissed him.
6 Ishmael, his son, heard the voices in the house of Abraham, and he arose, and went to Abraham his father, and wept over Abraham his father, he and all the house of Abraham, and they wept greatly.
7 His sons, Isaac and Ishmael, buried him in the double cave, near Sarah his wife, and all the men of his house, and Isaac and Ishmael, and all their sons, and all the sons of Keturah in their places wept for him forty days and then the days of weeping for Abraham were ended.
8 He lived three jubilees and four weeks of years, one hundred and seventy-five years, and completed the days of his life, being old and full of days.
9 For the days of the lives of their forefathers were nineteen jubilees; and after the Flood they began to grow less than nineteen jubilees, and to decrease in jubilees, and to grow old quickly, and to be full of their days because of the many types of hardships and the wickedness of their ways, with the exception of Abraham.
10 For Abraham was perfect in all his deeds with the Lord, and well-pleasing in righteousness all the days of his life. Yet, he did not complete four jubilees in his life, when he had grown old because of the wickedness in the world, and was full of his days.

11 All the generations which shall arise from this time until the day of the great judgment shall grow old quickly, before they complete two jubilees, and their knowledge shall forsake them because of their old age and all their knowledge shall vanish away.
12 In those days, if a man lives a jubilee and a-half of years, they shall say regarding him, "He has lived long," and the greater part of his days are pain and sorrow and hardship, and there is no peace. For calamity follows on calamity, and wound on wound, and hardship on hardship, and evil deeds on evil deeds, and illness on illness, and all judgments of destruction such as these, piled one on another, illness and overthrow, and snow and frost and ice, and fever, and chills, and mental and physical incapacity, and famine, and death, and sword, and captivity, and all kinds of calamities and pains.
13 All of these shall come on an evil generation, which transgresses on the earth. Their works are uncleanness and fornication, and pollution and abominations.
14 Then they shall say, "The days of the forefathers were many, lasting a thousand years, and were good; but the days of our lives, if a man lives a long life are three score years and ten, and, if he is strong, four score years, and those evil, and there is no peace in the days of this evil generation."
15 In that generation the sons shall convict their fathers and their elders of sin and unrighteousness, and of the words of their mouths and the great wickedness which they perform, and concerning their forsaking the covenant which the Lord made between them and Him. They should observe and do all His commandments and His ordinances and all His laws, without departing either to the right hand or the left.
16 For all have done evil, and every mouth speaks sinfully and all their works are unclean and an abomination, and all their ways are pollution, uncleanness, and destruction.
17 The earth shall be destroyed because of all their works, and there shall be no fruit (seed) of the vine, and no oil; for their actions are altogether faithless, and they shall all perish together, beasts and cattle and birds, and all the fish of the sea, because of the children of men.
18 They shall quarrel with one another, the young with the old, and the old with the young, the poor with the rich, the lowly with the great, and the beggar with the prince, because of the law and the covenant; for they have forgotten the commandments, and covenant, and feasts, and months, and Sabbaths, and jubilees, and all judgments.
19 They shall use swords and war to turn them back to the way, but they shall not return until much blood has been shed on the earth, one by another.
20 Those who have escaped shall not return from their wickedness to the way of righteousness, but they shall all raise themselves to a high status through deceit and wealth, that they may each steal all that belongs of his neighbor, and they shall name the great name (of God), but not in truth and not in righteousness, and they shall defile the holy of holies with their uncleanness and the corruption of their pollution.
21 A great punishment shall come because of the deeds of this generation, and the Lord will give them over to the sword and to judgment and to slavery, and to be plundered and consumed.
22 And He will arouse the Gentile sinners against them, who have neither mercy nor compassion, and who shall respect no one, neither old nor young, nor any one, for they are more wicked, strong, and evil than all the children of men.

23 They shall use violence against Israel and shall violate Jacob, and much blood shall be shed on the earth, and there shall be none to gather the dead and none to bury them.
24 In those days they shall cry aloud, and call and pray that they may be saved from the hand of the sinners, the Gentiles. But none shall be excluded (none shall be saved).
25 The heads of the children shall be white with grey hair, and a child of three weeks shall appear old like a man of one hundred years, and their work and worth shall be destroyed by hardship and oppression.
26 In those days the children shall begin to study the laws, and to seek the commandments, and to return to the path of righteousness.
27 The days shall begin to grow many and increase among those children of men until their days draw close to one thousand years, and to a greater number of years than before age was recorded.
28 There shall be neither old man nor one who is aged, for all shall be as children and youths.
29 All their days shall be full and they shall live in peace and in joy, and there shall be neither Satan nor any evil destroyer because all their days shall be days of blessing and healing.
30 And at that time the Lord will heal His servants, and they shall rise up and see great peace, and drive out their adversaries. The righteous shall understand and be thankful, and rejoice with joy forever and ever, and they shall see all their judgments and all their curses enacted on their enemies.
31 Their bones shall rest in the earth, and their spirits shall have much joy, and they shall know that it is the Lord who executes judgment, and shows mercy to hundreds and thousands and to all that love Him.
32 Moses, write down these words. Write them and record them on the heavenly tablets for a testimony for the generations forever.

[Chapter 24]

1 It happened after the death of Abraham, that the Lord blessed Isaac his son, who arose from Hebron and went and dwelt at the Well of the Vision in the first year of the third week of this jubilee, seven years.
2 In the first year of the fourth week a famine began in the land, besides the first famine, which had been in the days of Abraham.
3 Jacob made lentil soup, and Esau came from the field hungry. He said to Jacob his brother, "Give me some of this red soup."
4 Jacob said to him, "Sell to me your birthright and I will give you bread, and also some of this lentil soup." And Esau said in his heart, "If I shall die what good is my birthright to me?"
5 He said to Jacob, "I give it to you." And Jacob said, "Swear to me, this day," and he swore to him.
6 And Jacob gave his brother Esau bread and soup, and he ate until he was satisfied, and Esau despised his birthright. For this reason was Esau's name called Edom (red), because of the red soup which Jacob gave him for his birthright.
7 And Jacob became the elder, and Esau was brought down from his dignity.

8 The famine covered the land, and Isaac departed to go down into Egypt in the
second year of this week, and went to the king of the Philistines to Gerar, into the
presence of Abimelech.
9 The Lord appeared to him and said to him, "Do not go down into Egypt. Dwell in
the land that I shall tell you of, and sojourn in this land, and I will be with you and
bless you.
10 For to you and to your offspring will I give all this land, and I will establish My
oath which I swore to Abraham your father, and I will multiply your offspring as the
stars of heaven, and will give to your offspring all this land.
11 And in your offspring shall all the nations of the earth be blessed, because your
father obeyed My voice, and kept My ways and My commandments, and My laws,
and My ordinances, and My covenant; and now do as you are told and dwell in this
land."
12 And he dwelt in Gelar three weeks of years. And Abimelech commanded
concerning him, and concerning all that was his, saying, "Any man that shall touch
him or anything that is his shall surely die."
13 Isaac grew strong among the Philistines, and he got many possessions, oxen and
sheep and camels and donkeys and a great household.
14 He sowed in the land of the Philistines and brought in a hundred-fold, and Isaac
became very great, and the Philistines envied him.
15 Now all the wells that the servants of Abraham had dug during the life of
Abraham, the Philistines had stopped them after the death of Abraham, and filled
them with dirt.
16 Abimelech said to Isaac, "Go from us, for you are much mightier than we." Isaac
departed from that place in the first year of the seventh week, and sojourned in the
valleys of Gerar.
17 And they dug the wells of water again which the servants of Abraham, his father,
had dug, and which the Philistines had filled after the death of Abraham his father,
and he called their names as Abraham his father had named them.
18 The servants of Isaac dug a well in the valley, and found fresh, flowing water, and
the shepherds of Gerar bickered with the shepherds of Isaac, saying, "The water is
ours." Isaac called the name of the well "Perversity," because they had been perverse
with us.
19 And they dug a second well, and they fought for that also, and he called its name
"Enmity."
20 He left that place and they dug another well, and for that they did not fight, and
he called the name of it "Room," and Isaac said, "Now the Lord has made room for
us, and we have increased in the land."
21 And he went up from that place to the Well of the Oath in the first year of the first
week in the forty-fourth jubilee.
22 The Lord appeared to him in the night of the new moon of the first month, and
said to him, "I am the God of Abraham your father; fear not, for I am with you, and
shall bless you and shall surely multiply your offspring as the sand of the earth, for
the sake of Abraham my servant."
23 And he built an altar there, which Abraham his father had first built, and he
called on the name of the Lord, and he offered sacrifice to the God of Abraham his
father.
24 They dug a well and they found fresh, flowing water.

25 The servants of Isaac dug another well and did not find water, and they went and told Isaac that they had not found water, and Isaac said, "I have sworn this day to the Philistines and this thing has been announced to us."
26 And he called the name of that place the Well of the Oath, because there he had sworn to Abimelech and Ahuzzath ,his friend, and also to Phicol, who was the commander and his host.
27 Isaac knew that day that he had sworn to them under pressure to make peace with them.
28 On that day Isaac cursed the Philistines and said, "Cursed be the Philistines to the day of wrath and indignation from among all nations. May God make them a disdain and a curse and an object of anger and indignation in the hands of the Gentile sinners and in the hands of the Kittim.
29 Whoever escapes the sword of the enemy and the Kittim, may the righteous nation root them out in judgment from under heaven. They shall be the enemies and foes of my children throughout their generations on the earth.
30 No part of them will remain. Not even one shall be spared on the day of the wrath of judgment. The offspring of the Philistines will experience destruction, rooting out, and expulsion from the earth and this is all that is in store for them. There shall not be a name or an offspring left on the earth for these Caphtorim (the seat of the Philistine state).
31 For though he rises up to heaven, he shall be brought down, and though he makes himself strong on earth, from there shall he be dragged out, and though he hide himself among the nations, even from that place shall he be rooted out.
32 Though he descends into the abode of the dead, his condemnation shall be great, and he shall have no peace there.
33 If he goes into captivity by the hands of those that seek his life they shall kill him on the way (to his imprisonment), and neither his name nor offspring shall be left on all the earth. Into an eternal curse shall he depart."
34 It is written and engraved concerning him on the heavenly tablets, that on the day of judgment he will be rooted out of the earth.

[Chapter 25]

1 In the second year of this week in this jubilee, Rebecca called Jacob her son, and spoke to him, saying, "My son, do not take a wife from the daughters of Canaan as Esau, your brother, who took two wives of the daughters of Canaan, and they have made my soul bitter with all their unclean acts, for all their actions are fornication and lust, and there is no righteousness in them, because their deeds are evil.
2 I love you greatly, my son, and my heart and my affection bless you every hour of the day and in every night.
3 Now, my son, listen to my voice, and do the will of your mother, and do not take a wife of the daughters of this land, but only from the house of my father, and of those related to my father.
4 If you will take you a wife of the house of my father, the Most High God will bless you, and your children shall be a righteous generation and a holy offspring." And then spoke Jacob to Rebecca, his mother, and said to her, "Look, mother, I am nine weeks of years old, and I have neither been with nor have I touched any woman, nor

have I engaged myself to any, nor I have even thought of taking me wife of the daughters of Canaan.
5 For I remember, mother, the words of Abraham, our father, for he commanded me not to take a wife of the daughters of Canaan, but to take me a wife from the offspring of my father's house and from my kind folks.
6 I have heard before that daughters have been born to Laban, your brother, and I have set my heart on them to take a wife from among them.
7 For this reason I have guarded myself in my spirit against sinning or being corrupted in any way throughout all the days of my life; for with regard to lust and fornication, Abraham, my father, gave me many commands.
8 Despite all that he has commanded me, these two and twenty years my brother has argued with me, and spoken frequently to me and said, "My brother, take a wife that is a sister of my two wives," but I refused to do as he has done.
9 I swear before you mother, that all the days of my life I will not take me a wife from the daughters of the offspring of Canaan, and I will not act wickedly as my brother has done.
10 Do not be afraid mother, be assured that I shall do your will and walk in uprightness, and not corrupt my ways forever."
11 When she heard this, she lifted up her face to heaven and extended the fingers of her hands, and opened her mouth and blessed the Most High God, who had created the heaven and the earth, and she gave Him thanks and praise.
12 She said, "Blessed be the Lord God, and may His holy name be blessed forever and ever. He has given me Jacob as a pure son and a holy offspring; for he is Yours, and Yours shall his offspring be continually, throughout all the generations forever.
13 Bless him, O Lord, and place in my mouth the blessing of righteousness, that I may bless him."
14 At that hour, when the spirit of righteousness descended into her mouth, she placed both her hands on the head of Jacob, and said, "Blessed are You, Lord of righteousness and God of the ages, and may You bless him beyond all the generations of men.
15 My Son, may He give you the path of righteousness, and reveal righteousness to your offspring.
16 May He make your sons many during your life, and may they arise according to the number of the months of the year. And may their sons become many and great beyond the stars of heaven, and may their numbers be more than the sand of the sea.
17 May He give them this good and pleasing land, as He said He would give it to Abraham and to his offspring after him always, and may they hold it as a possession forever.
18 My son, may I see blessed children born to you during my life, and may all your offspring be blessed and holy.
19 And as you have refreshed your mother's spirit during her life, the womb of her that gave birth to you blesses you now. My affection and my heart (breasts) bless you and my mouth and my tongue greatly praise you.
20 Increase and spread over the earth. May your offspring be perfect in the joy of heaven and earth forever. May your offspring rejoice, and on the great day of peace may they have peace.
21 May your name and your offspring endure to all the ages, and may the Most High God be their God, and may the God of righteousness dwell with them, and may His sanctuary be built by you all the ages.

22 Blessed be he that blesses you, and all flesh that curses you falsely, may it be cursed."
23 And she kissed him, and said to him, "May the Lord of the world love you as the heart of your mother and her affection rejoice in you and bless you." And she ceased from blessing.

[Chapter 26]

1 In the seventh year of this week Isaac called Esau, his elder son, and said to him, " I am old, my son, and my sight is dim, and I do not know the day of my death.
2 Now, take your hunting weapons, your quiver, and your bow, and go out to the field, and hunt and catch me venison, my son, and make me flavorful meat, like my soul loves, and bring it to me that I may eat, and that my soul may bless you before I die."
3 But Rebecca heard Isaac speaking to Esau.
4 Esau went out early to the field to hunt and catch and bring home meat to his father.
5 Rebecca called Jacob, her son, and said to him, "Look, I heard Isaac, your father, speak to Esau, your brother, saying, "Hunt for me, and make me flavorful meat, and bring it to me that I may eat and bless you before the Lord before I die."
6 Now, my son, do as you are told and do as I command you. Go to your flock and fetch me two good kids of the goats, and I will make them good tasting meat for your father, like he loves, and you will bring it to your father that he may eat and bless you to the Lord before he dies."
7 Jacob said to Rebecca his mother, "Mother, I shall not withhold anything which my father would eat and which would please him, but I am afraid that he will recognize my voice and wish to touch me.
8 And you know that I am smooth, and Esau, my brother, is hairy, and I he will see me an evildoer because I am doing something that he has not told me to do and he will be very angry with me, and I shall bring on myself a curse, and not a blessing."
9 Rebecca, his mother, said to him, "Your curse be on me, my son, just do as you are told."
10 Jacob obeyed the voice of Rebecca, his mother, and went and brought back two good and fat goat kids, and brought them to his mother, and his mother made them tasty meat like he loved.
11 Rebecca took the good and pleasing clothes of Esau, her elder son, which was with her in the house, and she clothed Jacob, her younger son, with them, and she put the skins of the kids on his hands and on the exposed parts of his neck.
12 And she gave the meat and the bread, which she had prepared, to her son Jacob.
13 Jacob went in to his father and said, "I am your son. I have done as you asked me. Arise and sit and eat of that which I have caught, father, that your soul may bless me."
14 Isaac said to his son, "How have you found game so quickly, my son?"
15 Jacob said, "Because the Lord your God caused me to find."
16 Isaac said to him, "Come closer, that I may feel you, my son, and know if you are my son Esau or not."
17 Jacob went near to Isaac, his father, and he felt him and said, "The voice is Jacob's voice, but the hands are the hands of Esau," and he did not recognize him, because it

was a decision from heaven to remove his power of perception and Isaac discerned
not, because his hands were hairy as his brother Esau's, so Isaac blessed him.
18 He said, "Are you my son Esau? " and Jacob said, "I am your son," and Isaac said,
"Bring it to me that I may eat of that which you have caught, my son, that my soul
may bless you."
19 And Jacob brought it to him, and he ate, and Jacob brought him wine and he
drank.
20 Isaac, his father, said to him, "Come close and kiss me, my son."
21 He came close and kissed Isaac. And he smelled the smell of his raiment, and he
blessed Jacob and said, "Look, the smell of my son is as the smell of a full field which
the Lord has blessed.
22 May the Lord give you of the dew of heaven and of the dew of the earth, and
plenty of corn and oil. Let nations serve you and peoples bow down to you.
23 Be ruler over your brothers, and let your mother's sons bow down to you; and
may all the blessings that the Lord has blessed me and blessed Abraham, my father
be imparted to you and to your offspring forever. Cursed be he that curses you, and
blessed be he that blesses you."
24 It happened as soon as Isaac had made an end of blessing his son Jacob, that Jacob
had went away from Isaac his father and hid himself.
25 Esau, his brother, came in from his hunting. And he also made flavorful meat,
and brought it to his father and Esau said to his father, "Let my father arise, and eat
of my venison that your soul may bless me."
26 Isaac, his father, said to him, "Who are you?" Esau said to him, "I am your first
born, your son Esau. I have done as you have commanded me."
27 Isaac was very greatly surprised, and said, "Who is he that has hunted and caught
and brought it to me, and I have eaten of all before you came, and have blessed him,
and he shall be blessed, and all his offspring forever."
28 It happened when Esau heard the words of his father Isaac that he cried with a
very loud and bitter cry, and said to his father, "Bless me also, father!"
29 Isaac said to him, "Your brother came with trickery, and has taken away your
blessing."
30 He said, "Now I know why his name is Jacob. Behold, he has supplanted me
these two times, he took away my birth-right, and now he has taken away my
blessing."
31 Esau said, "Have you not reserved a blessing for me, father?" and Isaac answered
and said to Esau, "Look, I have made him your lord, and all his brothers have I
given to him for servants. I have strengthened him with plenty of corn and wine and
oil. Now what shall I do for you, my son?"
32 Esau said to Isaac, his father, "Have you only one blessing, father? Please. Bless
me, also, father. "
33 Esau lifted up his voice and wept. And Isaac answered and said to him, "Far from
the dew of the earth shall be your dwelling, and far from the dew of heaven from
above.
34 By your sword will you live, and you will serve your brother.
35 It shall happen that when you become great, and do shake his yoke from off your
neck, you will sin completely and commit a sin worthy of death, and your offspring
shall be rooted out from under heaven."

36 Esau kept threatening Jacob because of the blessing his father blessed him with, and he said in his heart, "May the days of mourning for my father come now, so that I may kill my brother Jacob."

[Chapter 27]

1 Rebecca was told Esau's words in a dream, and Rebecca sent for Jacob her younger son, and said to him, "Look Esau, your brother, will take vengeance on you and kill you.
2 Now, therefore, my son, do as you are told, and get up and flee to Laban, my brother, to Haran, and stay with him a few days until your brother's anger fades away, and he removes his anger from you, and forgets all that you have done. Then I will send for you to come from that place."
3 Jacob said, "I am not afraid. If he wishes to kill me, I will kill him."
4 But she said to him, "Let me not be bereft of both my sons on one day."
5 Jacob said to Rebecca, his mother, "Look, you know that my father has become old, and does not see because his eyes are dull. If I leave him he will think it is wrong. If I leave him and go away from you, my father will be angry and will curse me.
6 I will not go. When he sends me, only then will I go."
7 Rebecca said to Jacob, "I will go in and speak to him, and he will send you away."
8 Rebecca went in and said to Isaac, "I hate my life because of the two daughters of Heth, whom Esau has taken as wives. If Jacob take a wife from among the daughters of the land such as these, I could not live with it, because the daughters of Canaan are evil."
9 Isaac called Jacob and blessed him, and warned him and said to him, "Do not take you a wife of any of the daughters of Canaan. Arise and go to Mesopotamia, to the house of Bethuel, your mother's father, and take a wife from that place of the daughters of Laban, your mother's brother.
10 And God Almighty bless you and increase and multiply you that you may become a company of nations, and give you the blessings of my father, Abraham, to you and to your offspring after you, that you may inherit the land that you travel in and all the land which God gave to Abraham. Go in peace, my son."
11 Isaac sent Jacob away, and he went to Mesopotamia, to Laban the son of Bethuel the Syrian, the brother of Rebecca, Jacob's mother.
12 It happened after Jacob had departed to Mesopotamia that the spirit of Rebecca was grieved for her son, and she wept.
13 Isaac said to Rebecca, "My sister, weep not because of Jacob, my son, for he goes in peace, and in peace will he return.
14 The Most High God will preserve him from all evil and will be with him. He will not forsake him all his days, for I know that his ways will be made to prosper in all things wherever he goes, until he return in peace to us, and we see him in peace. Fear not on his account, my sister, for he is on the upright path and he is a perfect man, and he is faithful and will not perish. Weep not."
15 Isaac comforted Rebecca because of her son Jacob, and blessed him.
16 Jacob went from the Well of the Oath to go to Haran on the first year of the second week in the forty-fourth jubilee, and he came to Luz on the mountains, that is, Bethel, on the new moon of the first month of this week, and he came to the place

at dusk and turned from the way to the west of the road that is close, and that night he slept there, for the sun had set.
17 He took one of the stones of that place (as a pillow) and laid down under the tree, and he was journeying alone, and he slept.
18 Jacob dreamt that night, and saw a ladder set up on the earth, and the top of it reached to heaven, and he saw the angels of the Lord ascended and descended on it, and behold, the Lord stood on it.
19 And He spoke to Jacob and said, "I am the Lord God of Abraham, your father, and the God of Isaac. The land you are sleeping on I will give to you and to your offspring after you.
20 Your offspring shall be as the dust of the earth, and you will increase to the west and to the east, to the north and the south, and in you and in your offspring shall all the families of the nations be blessed.
21 Behold, I will be with you, and will keep you wherever you go. I will bring you into this land again in peace. I will not leave you until I do everything that I told you."
22 Jacob awoke from his sleep and said, "Truly this place is the house of the Lord, and I did not know it."
23 He was afraid and said, "I am afraid because this place is none other than the house of God, and this is the gate of heaven, and I did not know it."
24 Jacob got up early in the morning, and took the stone that he had placed under his head and set it up as a pillar for a sign. And he poured oil on the top of it. And he called the name of that place Bethel, but the name of the place was previously Luz.
25 And Jacob vowed a vow to the Lord, saying, "If the Lord will be with me, and will keep me in the way that I go, and give me bread to eat and clothes to put on, so that I come again to my father's house in peace, then the Lord shall be my God, and this stone which I have set up as a pillar for a sign in this place shall be the Lord's house, and of all that you gave me, I shall give the tenth to you, my God."

[Chapter 28]

1 He went on his journey, and came to the land of the east, to Laban, the brother of Rebecca, and he was with him, and Jacob served Laban for Rachel his daughter one week of years. In the first year of the third week of years he said to him, "Give me my wife, for whom I have served you seven years ," and Laban said to Jacob, "I will give you your wife."
2 Laban made a feast, and took Leah his elder daughter, and gave her to Jacob as a wife, and gave Leah Zilpah for a handmaid; and Jacob did not know, for he thought that she was Rachel.
3 He went in to her, and saw she was Leah; and Jacob was angry with Laban, and said to him, "Why have you done this to me?
4 Did I not serve you for Rachel and not for Leah? Why have you wronged me?
5 Take your daughter, and I will go. You have done evil to me." For Jacob loved Rachel more than Leah because Leah's eyes were weak, but her form was very beautiful. Rachel had beautiful eyes and a beautiful and very voluptuous form.
6 Laban said to Jacob, "It is not done that way in our country, we do not to give the younger before the elder." And it is not right to do this; for thus it is ordained and written in the heavenly tablets, that no one should give his younger daughter before

the elder; but the elder one is given first and after her the younger. The man who does so will have guilt placed against him in heaven, and none is righteous that does this thing, for this deed is evil before the Lord.
7 Command the children of Israel that they not do this thing. Let them neither take nor give the younger before they have given the elder, for it is very wicked.
8 And Laban said to Jacob, "Let the seven days of the feast pass by, and I shall give you Rachel, that you may serve me another seven years, that you may pasture my sheep as you did in the former week (of years)."
9 On the day when the seven days of the feast of Leah had passed, Laban gave Rachel to Jacob, that he might serve him another seven years, and he gave Rachel, Bilhah, the sister of Zilpah, as a handmaid.
10 He served yet other seven years for Rachel, for Leah had been given to him for nothing, since it was Rachel he wanted.
11 And the Lord opened the womb of Leah, and she conceived and gave birth to a son for Jacob, and he called his name Reuben, on the fourteenth day of the ninth month, in the first year of the third week.
12 But the womb of Rachel was closed, for the Lord saw that Leah was hated and Rachel loved.
13 Again Jacob went in to Leah, and she conceived, and gave birth to a second son for Jacob, and he called his name Simeon, on the twenty-first of the tenth month, and in the third year of this week.
14 Again Jacob went in to Leah, and she conceived, and gave birth to a third son, and he called his name Levi, in the new moon of the first month in the sixth year of this week.
15 Again Jacob went in to her, and she conceived, and gave birth to a fourth son, and he called his name Judah, on the fifteenth of the third month, in the first year of the fourth week.
16 Because of all this Rachel envied Leah, for she did not bear a child, and she said to Jacob, "Give me children;" and Jacob said, "Have I withheld from you the fruits of your womb? Have I left you?"
17 And when Rachel saw that Leah had given birth to four sons for Jacob: Reuben and Simeon and Levi and Judah, she said to him, "Go in to Bilhah my handmaid, and she will conceive, and bear a son for me."
18 She gave him Bilhah, her handmaid, to wife. And he went in to her, and she conceived, and gave birth to a son, and he called his name Dan, on the ninth of the sixth month, in the sixth year of the third week.
19 Jacob went in again to Bilhah a second time, and she conceived, and gave birth to another son for Jacob, and Rachel called his name Napthali, on the fifth of the seventh month, in the second year of the fourth week.
20 When Leah saw that she had become sterile and could no longer have children, she envied Rachel, and she also gave her handmaid Zilpah to Jacob to wife, and she conceived, and gave birth to a son, and Leah called his name Gad, on the twelfth of the eighth month, in the third year of the fourth week.
21 He went in to her again, and she conceived and gave birth to a second son, and Leah called his name Asher, on the second of the eleventh month, in the fifth year of the fourth week.
22 Jacob went in to Leah, and she conceived, and gave birth to a son, and she called his name Issachar, on the fourth of the fifth month, in the fourth year of the fourth week, and she gave him to a nurse.

23 Jacob went in again to her, and she conceived, and gave birth to two children, a son and a daughter, and she called the name of the son Zabulon, and the name of the daughter Dinah, in the seventh day of the seventh month, in the sixth year of the fourth week.
24 The Lord was gracious to Rachel, and opened her womb, and she conceived, and gave birth to a son, and she called his name Joseph, on the new moon of the fourth month, in the sixth year in this fourth week.
25 In the days when Joseph was born, Jacob said to Laban, "Give me my wives and sons, and let me go to my father Isaac, and let me make household for myself; for I have completed the years in which I have served you for your two daughters, and I will go to the house of my father."
26 Laban said to Jacob, "Stay with me and I will pay you wages, and pasture my flock for me again, and take your wages."
27 They agreed with one another that he should give him as his wages those of the lambs and kids which were born spotted black and white, these were to be his wages.
28 All the sheep brought out spotted and speckled and black, variously marked, and they brought out again lambs like themselves, and all that were spotted were Jacob's and those which were not spotted were Laban's.
29 Jacob's possessions multiplied greatly, and he possessed oxen and sheep and donkeys and camels, and men-servants and maid-servants.
30 Laban and his sons envied Jacob, and Laban took back his sheep from him, and he envied him and watched him for an opportunity to do evil.

[Chapter 29]

1 It happened when Rachel had given birth to Joseph, that Laban went to shear his sheep; for they were distant from him, a three-day journey.
2 Jacob saw that Laban was going to shear his sheep, and Jacob called Leah and Rachel, and spoke sweetly to them in order to convince them to come with him to the land of Canaan.
3 For he told them how he had seen everything in a dream. All that God had spoken to him that he should return to his father's house, and they said, "To every place where you go we will go with you."
4 Jacob blessed the God of Isaac his father, and the God of Abraham his father's father, and he arose and placed his wives and his children on donkeys, and took all his possessions and crossed the river, and came to the land of Gilead, and Jacob hid his intention from Laban and did not tell him.
5 In the seventh year of the fourth week Jacob turned his face toward Gilead in the first month, on the twenty-first of it.
6 Laban pursued and overtook Jacob in the mountain of Gilead in the third month, on the thirteenth of it. And the Lord did not permit him to injure Jacob for he appeared to him in a dream by night.
7 Laban spoke to Jacob. On the fifteenth of those days Jacob made a feast for Laban, and for all who came with him, and Jacob swore to Laban that day, and Laban also swore to Jacob, that neither should cross the mountain of Gilead to do evil to the other.

8 He made a heap (of stones) for a witness there; wherefore the name of that place is called, "The Heap of Witness," after this heap.
9 But before they used to call the land of Gilead the land of the Rephaim. The Rephaim were born giants whose height was ten, nine, eight, down to seven cubits.
10 Their dwelling place was from the land of the children of Ammon to Mount Hermon, and the seats of their kingdom were Karnaim and Ashtaroth, and Edrei, and Misur, and Beon.
11 The Lord destroyed them because of the evil of their deeds, for they were malevolent, and the Amorites were wicked and sinful. There is no people today which has committed the full range of their sins, and their life on the earth was shortened.
12 Jacob sent Laban away, and he departed into Mesopotamia, the land of the East, and Jacob returned to the land of Gilead.
13 He passed over the Jabbok in the ninth month, on the eleventh of it. On that day Esau, his brother, came to him, and he was reconciled to him, and departed from him to the land of Seir, but Jacob dwelt in tents.
14 In the first year of the fifth week in this jubilee he crossed the Jordan, and dwelt beyond the Jordan. He pastured his sheep from the sea of the heap to Bethshan, and to Dothan and to the forest of Akrabbim.
15 He sent his father Isaac all of his possessions such as clothing, and food, and meat, and drink, and milk, and butter, and cheese, and some dates of the valley.
16 Four times a year, he sent gifts to his mother Rebecca who was living at the tower of Abraham. He sent the gifts between the times of the months between plowing and reaping, and between autumn and the rain season, and between winter and spring.
17 For Isaac had returned from the Well of the Oath and gone up to the tower of his father Abraham, and he dwelt there apart from his son Esau.
18 For in the days when Jacob went to Mesopotamia, Esau took to himself a wife Mahalath, the daughter of Ishmael,
and he gathered together all the flocks of his father and his wives, and went up and dwelt on Mount Seir, and left Isaac his father at the Well of the Oath alone.
19 And Isaac went up from the Well of the Oath and dwelt in the tower of Abraham his father on the mountains of Hebron, and that is where Jacob sent all that he did send to his father and his mother from time to time, all they needed, and they blessed Jacob with all their heart and with all their soul.

[Chapter 30]

1 In the first year of the sixth week he went up to Salem, to the east of Shechem, in the fourth month, and he went in peace. Shechem, the son of Hamor, the Hivite, the prince of the land carried off Dinah, the daughter of Jacob, into the house, and he had sex with her and defiled her. She was a little girl, a child of twelve years.
2 He begged his father and her brothers that she might be given to him as a wife.
3 Jacob and his sons were very angry because of the men of Shechem, for they had defiled Dinah, their sister. They spoke to them while planning evil acts and they dealt deceitfully with them and tricked them.
4 Simeon and Levi came unexpectedly to Shechem and executed judgment on all the men of Shechem, and killed all the men whom they found in it. They did not leave a

single one remaining in it. They killed all in hand to hand battle because they had dishonored their sister Dinah.
5 Let it not again be done from now on that a daughter of Israel be defiled. Judgment is ordained in heaven against them that they should destroy all the men of the Shechemites with the sword because they had committed shame in Israel.
6 The Lord delivered them into the hands of the sons of Jacob that they might exterminate them with the sword and execute judgment on them. That it might not again be done in Israel that a virgin of Israel should be defiled.
7 If there is any man in Israel who wishes to give his daughter or his sister to any man who is of the offspring of the Gentiles he shall surely die. They shall stone him, for he has committed shame in Israel. They shall burn the woman with fire, because she has dishonored the name of the house of her father, and she shall be rooted out of Israel.
8 Do not let an adulteress and let no uncleanness be found in Israel throughout all the days of the generations of the earth. For Israel is holy to the Lord, and every man who has defiled it shall surely die. They shall stone him.
9 For it has been ordained and written in the heavenly tablets regarding all the offspring of Israel. He who defiles it shall surely die. He shall be killed by stoning. There is no limit of days for this law. There is no remission, and no atonement.
10 The man who has defiled his daughter shall be rooted out from every corner of all Israel, because he has given of his offspring to Moloch (a pagan God, the worship of which involved burning the child alive), and committed impurity and defiled his child.
11 Moses, command the children of Israel and exhort them not to give their daughters to the Gentiles, and not to take for their sons any of the daughters of the Gentiles, for this is abominable before the Lord.
12 It is because of this that I have written all the deeds of the Shechemites, which they committed against Dinah, and placed them in the words of the Law for you. I have also written how the sons of Jacob spoke, saying, "We will not give our daughter to a man who is uncircumcised, for that is a reproach to us."
13 It is a reproach to Israel that anyone take the daughters of the Gentiles, for this is unclean and abominable to Israel.
14 Israel will not be free from this uncleanness if it has a wife of the daughters of the Gentiles, or has given any of its daughters to a man who is of any of the Gentiles.
15 There will be plague upon plague, and curse upon curse, and every judgment and plague and curse will come if he does this thing, or if they ignore those who commit uncleanness, or defile the sanctuary of the Lord, or those who profane His holy name. If any of these happen the whole nation together will be judged for all the uncleanness and profanation of this man.
16 There will be no judging people by their position and no receiving fruits, or offerings, or burnt-offerings, or fat, or the fragrance of sweet odor from his hands. It will be unacceptable and so warn every man and woman in Israel who defiles the sanctuary.
17 For this reason I have commanded you, saying, "Give this testimony to Israel, see how the Shechemites and their sons fared? See how they were delivered into the hands of two sons of Jacob, and they killed them under torture? It was counted to them for righteousness, and it is written down to them for righteousness.
18 The offspring of Levi were chosen for the priesthood, and to be Levites, that they might minister before the Lord, as we do, continually. Levi and his sons will be

blessed forever, for he was zealous to execute righteousness and judgment and vengeance on all those who arose against Israel.
19 So they wrote a testimony in his favor of blessing and righteousness on the heavenly tablets in the presence of the God of all.
20 We remember the righteousness that the man fulfilled during his life, throughout the years, until a thousand generations they will record it. It will come to him and to his descendants after him, and he has been recorded on the heavenly tablets as a friend and a righteous man.
21 All this account I have written for you, and have commanded you to tell the children of Israel, so that they will not commit sin nor transgress the laws nor break the covenant which has been ordained for them. They should fulfill it and be recorded as friends (of God).
22 But if they transgress and work uncleanness in any way, they will be recorded on the heavenly tablets as adversaries (of God), and they will be blotted out of the book of life. Instead, they will be recorded in the book of those who will be destroyed and with those who will be rooted out of the earth.
23 On the day when the sons of Jacob killed Shechem it was written in the record in their favor in heaven that they had executed righteousness and uprightness and vengeance on the sinners, and it was written for a blessing.
24 They brought Dinah, their sister, out of the house of Shechem. They took everything that was in Shechem captive. They took their sheep and their oxen and their donkeys, and all their wealth, and all their flocks, and brought them all to Jacob their father.
25 He reproached them because they had put the city to the sword for he feared those who dwelt in the land, the Canaanites and the Perizzites.
26 The dread of the Lord was on all the cities that are near Shechem. They did not fight or chase after the sons of Jacob, for terror had fallen on them.

[Chapter 31]

1 On the new moon of the month, Jacob spoke to all the people of his house, saying, "Purify yourselves and change your clothes, and let us get up and go to Bethel where I vowed a vow to Him on the day when I fled from Esau my brother. Let us do this because God has been with me and brought me into this land in peace. You must put away the strange gods that you raise among you."
2 They gave up the strange gods and that which was in their ears and which was on their necks and the idols which Rachel stole from Laban her father she gave wholly to Jacob. And he burnt and broke them to pieces and destroyed them, and hid them under an oak, which is in the land of Shechem.
3 He went up on the new moon of the seventh month to Bethel. And he built an altar at the place where he had slept, and he set up a pillar there, and he sent word to his father, Isaac, and his mother, Rebecca. He asked to come to Isaac. There, Jacob wished to offer his sacrifice.
4 Isaac said, "Let my son, Jacob, come, and let me see him before I die."
5 Jacob went to his father, Isaac, and his mother, Rebecca, to the house of his father Abraham, and he took two of his sons with him, Levi and Judah.

6 Rebecca came out from the tower to the front of it to kiss Jacob and embrace him, for her spirit had revived when she heard, "Look Jacob your son has come," and she kissed him.
7 She saw his two sons and she recognized them. She said to him, "Are these your sons, my son?" and she embraced them and kissed them, and blessed them, saying, "In you shall the offspring of Abraham become illustrious, and you shall prove a blessing on the earth."
8 Jacob went in to Isaac his father, to the room where he lay, and his two sons were with him. He took his father's hand, stooped down, he kissed him. Isaac held on to the neck of Jacob his son, and wept on his neck.
9 The darkness left the eyes of Isaac, and he saw the two sons of Jacob, Levi, and Judah. And he said, "Are these your sons, my son? Because they look like you."
10 He said to Isaac, "They were truly my sons, and you have clearly seen that they are truly my sons."
11 They came near to him, and he turned and kissed them and embraced them both together.
12 The spirit of prophecy came down into his mouth, and he took Levi by his right hand and Judah by his left.
13 He turned to Levi first, and began to bless him first, and said to him, "May the God of all, the very Lord of all the ages, bless you and your children throughout all the ages.
14 May the Lord give to you and your offspring greatness and great glory from among all flesh. May the Lord cause you and your offspring to draw near to Him to serve in His sanctuary like the angels of the presence (of the Lord) and as the holy ones. The offspring of your sons shall be for the glory and greatness and holiness of God. May He make them great throughout all the ages. They shall be judges and princes, and chiefs of all the offspring of the sons of Jacob. They shall speak the word of the Lord in righteousness, and they shall judge all His judgments in righteousness.
15 They shall declare My ways to Jacob and My paths to Israel. The blessing of the Lord shall be given in their mouths to bless all the offspring of the beloved.
16 Your mother has called your name Levi, and rightly has she called your name. You will be joined to the Lord and be the companion of all the sons of Jacob. Let His table be your table, and let your sons eat from it. May your table be full throughout all generations, and let your food not fail in all the ages.
17 Let all who hate you fall down before you, and let all your adversaries be rooted out and perish. Blessed be he that blesses you, and cursed be every nation that curses you."
18 To Judah he said, "May the Lord give you strength and power to put all that hate you under your feet. You and one of your sons will be a prince over the sons of Jacob. May your name and the name of your sons go out across every land and region.
19 Then shall the Gentiles fear you, and all the nations and people shall shake (with fear of you). In you will be the help of Jacob, and in you will be found the salvation of Israel.
20 When you sit on the throne, which honors of your righteousness, there shall be great peace for all the offspring of the sons of the beloved. Blessed be he that blesses you, and cursed be all that hate you, afflict you, or curse you. They shall be rooted out and destroyed from the earth."

21 He turned, kissed him again, and embraced him, and rejoiced greatly because he had seen the sons of his son, Jacob, clearly and truly.
22 He stepped out from between his feet and fell down. He bowed down to him, and blessed them. He rested there with Isaac, his father, that night, and they ate and drank with joy.
23 He made the two sons of Jacob sleep, the one on his right hand and the other on his left. It was counted to him for righteousness.
24 Jacob told his father everything during the night about how the Lord had shown him great mercy, and how he had caused him to prosper in all his ways, and how he protected him from all evil.
25 Isaac blessed the God of his father Abraham, who had not withdrawn his mercy and his righteousness from the sons of his servant Isaac.
26 In the morning, Jacob told his father, Isaac, the vow, which he had vowed to the Lord. He told him of the vision which he had seen, and that he had built an altar. He told him that everything was ready for the sacrifice to be made before the Lord as he had vowed. He had come to set him on a donkey.
27 Isaac said to Jacob his son, "I am not able to go with you, for I am old and not able to endure the way. Go in peace, my son. I am one hundred and sixty-five years this day. I am no longer able to journey. Set your mother on a donkey and let her go with you.
28 I know that you have come on my account, my son. May this day be blessed on which you have seen me alive, and I also have seen you, my son.
29 May you prosper and fulfill the vow that you have vowed. Do not put off your vow, for you will be called to account for the vow. Now hurry to perform it, and may He who has made all things be pleased. It is to Him you have vowed the vow."
30 He said to Rebecca, "Go with Jacob your son," and Rebecca went with Jacob her son, and Deborah with her, and they came to Bethel.
31 Jacob remembered the prayer with which his father had blessed him and his two sons, Levi and Judah. He rejoiced and blessed the God of his fathers, Abraham and Isaac.
32 He said, "Now I know that my sons and I have an eternal hope in the God of all." Thus is it ordained concerning the two. They recorded it as an eternal testimony to them on the heavenly tablets how Isaac blessed his sons.

[Chapter 32]

1 That night he stayed at Bethel, and Levi dreamed that they had ordained and made his sons and him the priests of the Most High God forever. Then he awoke from his sleep and blessed the Lord.
2 Jacob rose early in the morning, on the fourteenth of this month, and he gave a tithe for all that came with him, both of men and cattle, both of gold and every vessel and garment. Yes, he gave tithes of all.
3 In those days Rachel became pregnant with her son Benjamin. Jacob counted his sons starting from him and going to the oldest and Levi fell to the portion of the Lord. (Levi was the third son – three is the number of spiritual completeness.) His father clothed him in the garments of the priesthood and filled his hands.
4 On the fifteenth of this month, he brought fourteen oxen from among the cattle, and twenty-eight rams, and forty-nine sheep, and seven lambs, and twenty-one kids

of the goats to the altar as a burnt-offering on the altar of sacrifice. The offering was well pleasing and a sweet odor before God.
5 This was his offering, done in acknowledgement of the vow in which he had promised that he would give a tenth, with their fruit-offerings and their drink-offerings.
6 When the fire had consumed it, he burnt incense over the fire, and for a thank-offering he sacrificed two oxen and four rams and four sheep, four male goats, and two sheep of a year old, and two kids of the goats. This he did daily for seven days.
7 He, his men, and all his sons were eating this with joy during seven days and blessing and thanking the Lord, who had delivered him out of all his tribulation and had given him His promise.
8 He tithed all the clean animals, and made a burnt sacrifice, but he did not give the unclean animals to Levi his son. He gave him (responsibility for) all the souls of the men. Levi acted in the priestly office at Bethel in the presence of Jacob his father, in preference to his ten brothers. He was a priest there, and Jacob gave his vow, and he gave a tithe to the Lord again and sanctified it, and it became holy to Him.
9 For this reason it is ordained on the heavenly tablets as a law for the offering of the tithe should be eaten in the presence of the Lord every year, in the place where it is chosen that His name should live and reside. This law has no limit of days forever.
10 This law is written so that it may be fulfilled every year. The second tithe should be eaten in the presence of the Lord, in the place where it has been chosen, and nothing shall be left over from it from this year to the following year.
11 In its year shall the seed be eaten until the days of the gathering of the seed of the year. The wine shall be consumed until the days of the wine, and the oil until the days of its season.
12 All that is left of it and all that becomes old will be regarded as spoiled, let it be burnt with fire, for it is unclean.
13 Let them eat it together in the sanctuary, and let them not permit it to become old.
14 All the tithes of the oxen and sheep shall be holy to the Lord, and shall belong to his priests. They will eat before Him from year to year, for thus is it ordained and written on the heavenly tablets regarding the tithe.
15 On the following night, on the twenty-second day of this month, Jacob resolved to build that place and to surround the court with a wall, and to sanctify it and make it holy forever, for himself and his children after him.
16 The Lord appeared to him by night and blessed him and said to him, "Your name shall not be called Jacob, but they will call your name Israel."
17 And He said to him again, "I am the Lord who created the heaven and the earth, and I will increase you and multiply you greatly, and kings shall come forth from you, and they shall be judges everywhere the foot of the sons of men have walked.
18 I will give to your offspring all the earth that is under heaven. They shall judge all the nations, as they desire. After that they shall possess the entire earth and inherit it forever."
19 And He finished speaking with him, and He went up from him.
20 Jacob watched until He had ascended into heaven.
21 In a vision at night he saw an angel descend from heaven with seven tablets in his hands, and he gave them to Jacob, and he read them and knew all that was written on it that would happen to him and his sons throughout all the ages.
22 He showed him all that was written on the tablets, and said to him, "Do not build on this place, and do not make it an eternal sanctuary, and do not live here. This is

not the place. Go to the house of Abraham your father and live with Isaac, your father, until the day he dies.
23 For in Egypt you will die in peace, and in this land you will be buried with honor in the sepulcher of your fathers, with Abraham and Isaac.
24 Do not fear. As you have seen and read it shall all be. Write down everything that you have seen and read."
25 Jacob said, "Lord, how can I remember all that I have read and seen?" He said to him, "I will bring all things to your remembrance."
26 He ascended from Jacob, and Jacob awoke from his sleep. He remembered everything that he had read and seen, and he wrote down all the words.
27 He celebrated there yet another day, and he sacrificed on that day as he had sacrificed on all the former days. He called its name "Addition," because this day was added, and the former days he called "The Feast."
28 It was made known and revealed to him and it is written on the heavenly tablets that he should celebrate the day, and add it to the seven days of the feast.
29 Its name was called "Addition," because that it was recorded among the days of the feast days, according to the number of the days of the year.
30 In the night, on the twenty-third of this month, Deborah, Rebecca's nurse died, and they buried her beneath the city under the oak of the river. He called the name of this place, "The river of Deborah," and he called the oak, "The oak of the mourning of Deborah."
31 Rebecca departed and returned to her house, to his father Isaac. Jacob sent rams and sheep and male goats by her so that she should prepare a meal for his father such as he desired.
32 He followed his mother until he came to the land of Kabratan, and he lived there.
33 Rachel gave birth to a son in the night, and called his name "son of my sorrow", for she broke down while giving birth to him, but his father called his name Benjamin. This happened on the eleventh day of the eighth month in the first of the sixth week of this jubilee.
34 Rachel died there and she was buried in the land of Ephrath, the same is Bethlehem, and Jacob built a pillar on the grave of Rachel, on the road above her grave.

[Chapter 33]

1 Jacob went and lived to the south of Magdaladra'ef. He and Leah, his wife, went to his father, Isaac, on the new moon of the tenth month.
2 Reuben saw Bilhah, Rachel's maid, the concubine of his father, bathing in water in a secret place, and he loved her.
3 He hid himself at night, and he entered the house of Bilhah at night. He found her sleeping alone on a bed in her house.
4 He had sex with her. She awoke and saw that is was Reuben lying with her in the bed. She uncovered the border of her covering and grabbed him and cried out when she discovered that it was Reuben.
5 She was ashamed because of him and released her hand from him, and he fled.
6 Because of this, she mourned greatly and did not tell it to any one.
7 When Jacob returned and sought her, she said to him, "I am not clean for you. I have been defiled in regard to you. Reuben has defiled me, and has had sex with me

in the night. I was asleep and did not realize he was there until he uncovered my skirt and had sex with me."
8 Jacob was very angry with Reuben because he had sex with Bilhah, because he had uncovered his father's skirt.
9 Jacob did not approach her again because Reuben had defiled her. And as for any man who uncovers his father's skirt his deed is wicked greatly, for he is disgusting to the Lord.
10 For this reason it is written and ordained on the heavenly tablets that a man should not lie with his father's wife,
and should not uncover his father's skirt. This is unclean and they shall surely die together, the man who lies with his father's wife and the woman also, for they have committed uncleanness on the earth.
11 There shall be nothing unclean before our God in the nation that He has chosen for Himself as a possession.
12 Again, it is written a second time, "Cursed be he who lies with the wife of his father, for he has uncovered his father's shame." All the holy ones of the Lord said, "So be it. So be it."
13 "Moses, command the children of Israel so that they observe this word. It entails a punishment of death. It is unclean, and there is no atonement forever for the man who has committed this. He is to be put to death. Kill him by stoning. Root him out from among the people of our God.
14 No man who does so in Israel will be permitted to remain alive a single day on the earth. He is abominable and unclean.
15 Do not let them say, "Reuben was granted life and forgiveness after he had sex with his father's concubine, although she had a husband, and her husband, Jacob, his father, was still alive."
16 Until that time the ordinance and judgment and law had not been revealed in its completeness for all. In your days it has been revealed as a law of seasons and of days. It is an everlasting law for all generations forever. For this law has no limit of days, and no atonement for it.
17 They must both be rooted out of the entire nation. On the day they committed it they shall be killed.
18 Moses, write it down for Israel that they may observe it, and do according to these words, and not commit a sin punishable by death. The Lord our God is judge, who does not respect persons (position) and accepts no gifts.
19 Tell them these words of the covenant, that they may hear and observe, and be on their guard with respect to them, and not be destroyed and rooted out of the land; for an uncleanness, and an abomination, and a contamination, and a pollution are all they who commit it on the earth before our God.
20 There is no greater sin on earth than fornication that they commit. Israel is a holy nation to the Lord its God, and a nation of inheritance. It is a priestly and royal nation and for His own possession. There shall appear no such uncleanness among the holy nation.
21 In the third year of this sixth week, Jacob and all his sons went and lived in the house of Abraham, near Isaac his father and Rebecca his mother.
22 These were the names of the sons of Jacob, the first-born
Reuben, Simeon, Levi, Judah, Issachar, Zebulon, which are the sons of Leah. The sons of Rachel are Joseph and Benjamin. The

sons of Bilhah are Dan and Naphtali; and the sons of Zilpah, Gad and Asher. Dinah is the daughter of Leah, the only daughter of Jacob.

23 They came and bowed themselves to Isaac and Rebecca. When they saw them they blessed Jacob and all his sons, and Isaac rejoiced greatly, for he saw the sons of Jacob, his younger son and he blessed them.

[Chapter 34]

1 In the sixth year of this week of the forty-fourth jubilee Jacob sent his sons and his servants to pasture their sheep in the pastures of Shechem.

2 The seven kings of the Amorites assembled themselves together (to fight) against them and kill them. They hid themselves under the trees, to take their cattle as booty.

3 Jacob, Levi, Judah and Joseph were in the house with Isaac their father, for his spirit was sorrowful, and they could not leave him. Benjamin was the youngest, and for this reason he remained with his father.

4 The king of Taphu, the king of Aresa, the king of Seragan, the king of Selo, the king of Ga'as, the king of Bethoron, the king of Ma'anisakir, and all those who dwell in these mountains and who dwell in the woods in the land of Canaan came.

5 They announced to Jacob saying, "Look, the kings of the Amorites have surrounded your sons, and plundered their herds."

6 And he left his house, he and his three sons and all the servants of his father, and his own servants, and he went against them with six thousand men, who carried swords.

7 He killed them in the pastures of Shechem, and pursued those who fled, and he killed them with the edge of the sword, and he killed Aresa and Taphu and Saregan and Selo and Amani sakir and Gaga'as, and he recovered his herds.

8 He conquered them, and imposed tribute on them that they should pay him five fruit products of their land. He built (the cities of) Robel and Tamnatares.

9 He returned in peace, and made peace with them, and they became his servants until the day that he and his sons went down into Egypt.

10 In the seventh year of this week he sent Joseph from his house to the land of Shechem to learn about the welfare of his brothers. He found them in the land of Dothan.

11 They dealt treacherously with him, and formed a plot against him to kill him, but they changed their minds and sold him to Ishmaelite merchants. They brought him down into Egypt, and they sold him to Potiphar, the eunuch of Pharaoh, the chief of the cooks and priest of the city of Elew."

12 The sons of Jacob slaughtered a kid, and dipped Joseph's coat in the blood and sent it to Jacob their father on the tenth of the seventh month.

13 They brought it to him in the evening and he mourned all that night. He became feverish with mourning for Joseph's death, and he said, "An evil beast has devoured Joseph". All the members of his house mourned and grieved with him that day.

14 His sons and his daughter got up to comfort him, but he refused to be comforted for his son.

15 On that day Bilhah heard that Joseph had perished, and she died mourning him. She was living in Qafratef, and Dinah his daughter, died after Joseph had perished.

16 There were now three reasons for Israel to mourn in one month. They buried Bilhah next to the tomb of Rachel, and Dinah his daughter. They were (all) buried there.
17 He mourned for Joseph one year, and did not cease, for he said, "Let me go down to my grave mourning for my son."
18 For this reason it is ordained for the children of Israel that they should remember and mourn on the tenth of the seventh month. On that day the news came which made Jacob weep for Joseph. On this day they should make atonement for their sins for themselves with a young goat on the tenth of the seventh month, once a year, for they had grieved the sorrow of their father regarding Joseph his son.
19 This day, once a year, has been ordained that they should grieve on it for their sins, and for all their transgressions and for all their errors, so that they might cleanse themselves.
20 After Joseph perished, the sons of Jacob took to themselves wives. The name of Reuben's wife is Ada; and the name of Simeon's wife is Adlba'a, a Canaanite. The name of Levi's wife is Melka, of the daughters of Aram, of the offspring of the sons of Terah. The name of Judah's wife is Betasu'el, a Canaanite. The name of Issachar's wife is Hezaqa, and the name of Zabulon's wife is Ni'iman. The name of Dan's wife is Egla. The name of Naphtali's wife is Rasu'u, of Mesopotamia. The name of Gad's wife is Maka. The name of Asher's wife is Ijona. The name of Joseph's wife is Asenath, the Egyptian. The name of Benjamin's wife is Ijasaka.
21 And Simeon repented, and took a second wife from Mesopotamia as his brothers had done.

[Chapter 35]

1 In the first year of the first week of the forty-fifth jubilee Rebecca called Jacob, her son, and commanded him regarding his father and regarding his brother, that he should honor them all the days of his life.
2 Jacob said, "I will do everything you have commanded. I will honor them. This will be honor and greatness to me, and righteousness before the Lord.
3 Mother, you know from the time I was born until this day, all my deeds and all that is in my heart. I always think good concerning all.
4 Why should I not do this thing which you have commanded me, that I should honor my father and my brother?
5 Tell me, mother, what perversity have you seen in me and I shall turn away from it, and mercy will be on me."
6 She said to him, "My son, in all my days I have not seen any perverseness in you, but only upright deeds. Yet, I will tell you the truth, my son, I shall die this year. I shall not survive this year in my life. I have seen the day of my death in a dream. I should not live beyond a hundred and fifty-five years. I have completed all the days that I am to live my life."
7 Jacob laughed at the words of his mother because his mother had said she should die. She was sitting across from him in possession of her strength, and she was still strong. She came and went (as she wished). She could see well, and her teeth were strong. No sickness had touched her all the days of her life.

8 Jacob said to her, "If my days of life are close to yours and my strength remain with me as your strength I would be blessed, mother. You will not die. You are simply joking with me regarding your death."

9 She went in to Isaac and said to him, " I make one request of you. Make Esau swear that he will not injure Jacob, nor pursue him with intent to harm him. You know Esau's thoughts have been perverse from his youth, and there is no goodness in him. He desires to kill him after you die.

10 You know all that he has done since the day Jacob, his brother, went to Haran until this day. He has forsaken us with his whole heart, and has done evil to us. He has stolen your flocks and carried off all your possessions while you watched.

11 When we asked him and begged him for what was our own, he did as a man (stranger) who was taking pity on us (giving a token like one giving alms to a beggar).

12 He is bitter against you because you blessed Jacob, your perfect and upright son. There is no evil but only goodness in Jacob. Since he came from Haran to this day he has not robbed us of anything. He always brings us everything in its season. He rejoices and blesses us with all his heart when we take his hands. He has not parted from us since he came from Haran until this day, and he remains with us continually at home honoring us."

13 Isaac said to her, "I also know and see the deeds of Jacob who is with us, how he honors us with all his heart. Before, I loved Esau more than Jacob because he was the first-born, but now I love Jacob more than Esau, for Esau has done many evil deeds, and there is no righteousness in him. All his ways are unrighteousness and violence.

14 My heart is troubled because of all his deeds. Neither he nor his offspring will be exempt because they are those who will be destroyed from the earth and who will be rooted out from under heaven. He and his children have forsaken the God of Abraham and gone after his wives (wives' gods) and after their uncleanness and after their error.

15 You told me to make him swear that he will not kill Jacob his brother, but even if he swears, he will not abide by his oath. He will not do good but evil only.

16 If he desires to kill Jacob, his brother, then into Jacob's hands he will be given. He will not escape from Jacob's hands.

17 Do not be afraid for Jacob, for the guardian of Jacob is great, powerful, honored, and praised more than the guardian of Esau."

18 Rebecca called for Esau and he came to her, and she said to him, "I have a request of you, my son. Promise to do it, my son."

19 He said, "I will do everything that you say to me, and I will not refuse your request."

20 She said to him, "I ask you that the day I die, you will take me in and bury me near Sarah, your father's mother, and that you and Jacob will love each other and that neither will desire evil against the other, but (have) mutual love only. Do this so you will prosper, my son, and be honored in the all of the land, and no enemy will rejoice over you. You will be a blessing and a mercy in the eyes of all those that love you."

21 He said, "I will do all that you have told me. I shall bury you on the day you die near Sarah, my father's mother, as you have desired that her bones may be near your bones.

22 Jacob, my brother, I shall love above all flesh. I have only one brother in all the earth but him. It is only what is expected of me. It is no great thing if I love him, for he is my brother, and we were sown together in your body, and together came we out from your womb. If I do not love my brother, whom shall I love?
23 I beg you to exhort Jacob concerning me and concerning my sons, for I know that he will assuredly be king over me and my sons, for on the day my father blessed him he made him the higher and me the lower.
24 I swear to you that I shall love him, and not desire evil against him all the days of my life but good only."
25 And he swore to her regarding all this matter. While Esau was there, she called Jacob and gave him her orders according to the words that she had spoken to Esau.
26 He said, "I shall do your pleasure, believe me that no evil will proceed from me or from my sons against Esau. I shall be first in nothing except in love only."
27 She and her sons ate and drank that night, and she died, three jubilees and one week and one year old on that night. Her two sons, Esau and Jacob, buried her in the double cave near Sarah, their father's mother.

[Chapter 36]

1 In the sixth year of this week Isaac called his two sons Esau and Jacob, and they came to him, and he said to them, "My sons, I am going the way of my fathers, to the eternal house where my fathers are.
2 Bury me near Abraham my father, in the double cave in the field of Ephron the Hittite, where Abraham purchased a sepulcher to bury in. Bury me in the sepulcher I dug for myself.
3 I command you, my sons, to practice righteousness and uprightness on the earth, so that the Lord may do to you what he said he would do to Abraham and to his offspring.
4 Love one another. Love your brothers as a man who loves his own soul. Let each seek how he may benefit his brother, and act together on the earth. Let them love each other as their own souls.
5 I command and warn you to reject idols. Hate them, and do not love them. They are fully deceptive to those that worship them and for those that bow down to them.
6 Remember the Lord God of Abraham, your father, and how I worshipped Him and served Him in righteousness and in joy, that God might multiply you and increase your offspring as the multitude of stars in heaven, and establish you on the earth as the plant of righteousness, which will not be rooted out to all the generations forever.
7 And now I shall make you swear a great oath, for there is no oath which is greater than that which is by the name glorious, honored, great, splendid, wonderful and mighty, which created the heavens and the earth and all things together, that you will fear Him and worship Him.
8 Each will love his brother with affection and righteousness. Neither will desire to do evil against his brother from now on forever all the days of your life so that you may prosper in all your deeds and not be destroyed.
9 If either of you plans evil against his brother, know that he that plans evil shall fall into his brother's hand, and shall be rooted out of the land of the living, and his offspring shall be destroyed from under heaven.

10 But on that day there will be turbulence, curses, wrath, anger, and will He burn his land and his city and all that is his with a devouring fire like the fire He sent to burn Sodom and he shall be blotted out of the book of the discipline of the children of men, and he will not be recorded in the book of life. He shall be added in the book of destruction. He shall depart into eternal curses. Their condemnation may be always renewed in hate and in curses and in wrath and in torment and in anger and in plagues and in disease forever.

11 My sons, this, I say and testify to you, will be the result according to the judgment which shall come on the man who wishes to injure his brother."

12 Then he divided all his possessions between the two on that day, and he gave the larger portion to him that was the first-born, and the tower and all that was around it, and all that Abraham possessed at the Well of the Oath.

13 He said, "This larger portion I will give to the first-born."

14 Esau said, "I have sold and relinquished my birthright to Jacob. Let it be given to him. I have nothing to say regarding it, for it is his."

15 Isaac said, "May a blessing rest on you, my sons, and on your offspring this day. You have given me rest, and my heart is not pained concerning the birthright, or that you should work wickedness because of it.

16 May the Most High God bless the man and his offspring forever that does righteousness."

17 He stopped commanding them and blessing them, and they ate and drank together in front of him, and he rejoiced because there was one mind between them, and they went out from him and rested that day and slept.

18 Isaac slept on his bed that day rejoicing. He slept the eternal sleep, and died one hundred and eighty years old. He lived twenty-five weeks and five years; and his two sons, Esau and Jacob, buried him.

19 After that Esau went to the land of Edom, to the mountains of Seir, and lived there.

20 Jacob lived in the mountains of Hebron, in the high place of the land in which his father Abraham had journeyed. He worshipped the Lord with all his heart. He had divided the days of his generations according to the commands he had seen.

21 Leah, his wife, died in the fourth year of the second week of the forty-fifth jubilee, and he buried her in the double cave near Rebecca his mother to the left of the grave of Sarah, his father's mother. All her sons and his sons came to mourn over Leah, his wife, with him and to comfort him regarding her. He was lamenting her for he loved her greatly after Rachel, her sister, died. She was perfect and upright in all her ways and she honored Jacob. All the days that she lived with him he did not hear from her mouth a harsh word, for she was gentle, peaceable, upright and honorable.

22 And he remembered all the deeds she had done during her life and he lamented her greatly. He loved her with all his heart and with all his soul.

[Chapter 37]

1 On the day that Isaac, the father of Jacob and Esau died, the sons of Esau heard that Isaac had given the elder's portion to his younger son, Jacob, and they were very angry.

2 They argued with their father, saying, "Why has your father given Jacob the portion of the elder and passed you over even though you are the elder and Jacob the younger?"

3 He said to them, "Because I sold my birthright to Jacob for a small portion of lentils (lentil soup), and on the day my father sent me to hunt, catch, and bring him something that he should eat and bless me, Jacob came with deceit and brought my father food and drink. My father blessed him and put me under his hand.

4 Now our father has caused Jacob and me to swear that we shall not devise evil plans against his brother (each other), and that we shall continue in love and in peace each with his brother and not make our ways corrupt."

5 They said to him, "We shall not listen to you to make peace with him. We are stronger than him and we are more powerful than he is. We shall depose him and kill him, and destroy him and his sons. If you will not go with us, we shall hurt you also.

6 Listen! Let us send to Aram, Philistia, Moab, and Ammon. Let us take chosen men who are trained in battle, and let us go against him and do battle with him. Let us exterminate him from the earth before he grows strong."

7 Their father said to them, "Do not go and do not make war with him or you shall fall before him."

8 They said to him, "This is how you have acted from your youth until this day. You have continued to put your neck under his yoke. We shall not listen to these words."

9 Then they sent to Aram, and to Aduram to the friend of their father, and they also hired one thousand chosen men of war.

10 And there came to them from Moab and from the children of Ammon, those who were hired, one thousand chosen men, and from Philistia, one thousand chosen warriors, and from Edom and from the Horites one thousand chosen warriors, and from the Kittim mighty warriors.

11 They said to their father, "Go out with them and lead them or else we shall kill you."

12 And he was filled with boiling anger on seeing that his sons were forcing him to go before them to lead them against Jacob, his brother.

13 But afterward he remembered all the evil that lay hidden in his heart against Jacob his brother, and he did not remember the oath he had sworn to his father and to his mother that he would plan no evil against Jacob, his brother, all his days.

14 Because Jacob was in mourning for his wife Leah, he did not know they were coming to battle against him until they approached the tower with four thousand soldiers and chosen warriors. The men of Hebron sent to him saying, "Look your brother has come against you to fight. He has with him four thousand men carrying swords, shields, and weapons." They told him this because they loved Jacob more than Esau.

15 So they told him, for Jacob was a more gracious and merciful man than Esau.

16 But Jacob would not believe until they came very near to the tower.

17 He closed the gates of the tower; and he stood on the battlements and spoke to his brother Esau and said, "Noble is the comfort you have come to give me concerning the death of my wife. Is this the oath that you swore to your father and again to your mother before they died? You have broken the oath, and on the moment that you swore to your father you were condemned."

18 Then Esau answered and said to him, "Neither the children of men nor the beasts of the earth have sworn an oath of righteousness and kept it forever. Every day they

lay evil plans one against another regarding how they might kill their adversary or foe.
19 You will hate my children and me forever, so there is no observing the tie of brotherhood with you.
20 Hear these words that I declare to you. If the boar can change its skin and make its bristles as soft as wool, or if it can cause horns to sprout out on its head like the horns of a stag or of a sheep, then will I observe the tie of brotherhood with you. Like breasts separate themselves from their mother (and fight), you and I have never been brothers.
21 If the wolves make peace with the lambs and not devour or do them violence, and if their hearts are towards them for good, then there shall be peace in my heart towards you. If the lion becomes the friend of the ox and makes peace with him and if he is bound under one yoke with him and plows with him, then will I make peace with you.
22 When the raven becomes white as the raza (a white bird?), then know that I have loved you and shall make peace with you. You will be rooted out, and your sons shall be rooted out, and there shall be no peace for you."
23 Jacob saw that Esau had decided in his heart to do evil toward him, and that he desired with all his soul to kill him. Jacob saw that Esau had come pouncing like the wild boar which charges the spear that is set to pierce and kills it, and yet does not even slow down. Then he spoke to his own people and to his servants and told them that Esau and his men were going to attack him and all his companions.

[Chapter 38]

1 After that Judah spoke to Jacob, his father, and said to him, "Bend your bow, father, and send forth your arrows and bring down the adversary and kill the enemy. You have the power to do it. We will not kill your brother because he is your kin and he is like you, so we will honor his life."
2 Then Jacob bent his bow and sent forth the arrow and struck Esau, his brother, on the right side of his chest and killed him.
3 And again he sent forth an arrow and struck Adoran the Aramaean, on the left side of his chest, and it drove him backward and killed him. Then the sons of Jacob and their servants went out, dividing themselves into companies on the four sides of the tower.
4 Judah went out in front. Naphtali and Gad along with fifty servants went to the south side of the tower, and they killed all they found before them. Not one individual escaped.
5 Levi, Dan, and Asher went out on the east side of the tower along with fifty men, and they killed the warriors of Moab and Ammon.
6 Reuben, Issachar, and Zebulon went out on the north side of the tower along with fifty men and they killed the warriors of the Philistines.
7 Reuben's son, Simeon, Benjamin, and Enoch went out on the west side of the tower along with fifty men and they killed four hundred men, stout warriors of Edom and of the Horites. Six hundred fled, and four of the sons of Esau fled with them, and left their father lying killed, as he had fallen on the hill that is in Aduram.
8 And the sons of Jacob pursued them to the mountains of Seir. And Jacob buried his brother on the hill that is in Aduram, and he returned to his house.

9 The sons of Jacob crushed the sons of Esau in the mountains of Seir, and made them bow their necks so that they became servants of the sons of Jacob.
10 They sent a message to their father to inquire whether they should make peace with them or kill them.
11 Jacob sent word to his sons that they should make peace. They made peace with them but also placed the yoke of servitude on them, so that they paid tribute to Jacob and to his sons always.
12 And they continued to pay tribute to Jacob until the day that he went down to Egypt.
13 The sons of Edom have not escaped the yoke of servitude imposed by the twelve sons of Jacob until this day.
14 These are the kings that reigned in Edom before there was any king over the children of Israel (until this day) in the land of Edom.
15 And Balaq, the son of Beor, reigned in Edom, and the name of his city was Danaba. Balaq died, and Jobab, the son of Zara of Boser, ruled in his place.
16 Jobab died, and Asam, of the land of Teman, ruled in his place.
17 Asam died, and Adath, the son of Barad, who killed Midian in the field of Moab, ruled in his place, and the name of his city was Avith.
18 Adath died, and Salman, from Amaseqa, ruled in his place.
19 Salman died, and Saul of Ra'aboth by the river, ruled in his place. Saul died, and Ba'elunan, the son of Achbor, ruled in his place.
20 Ba'elunan, the son of Achbor died, and Adath ruled in his place, and the name of his wife was Maitabith, the daughter of Matarat, the daughter of Metabedza'ab. These are the kings who reigned in the land of Edom.

[Chapter 39]

1 Jacob lived in the land that his father journeyed in, which is the land of Canaan.
2 These are the generations of Jacob. Joseph was seventeen years old when they took him down into the land of Egypt, and Potiphar, a eunuch of Pharaoh, the chief cook, bought him.
3 He made Joseph the manager over Potiphar's entire house and the blessing of the Lord came on the house of the Egyptian because of Joseph. And the Lord caused him to prosper in all that he did.
4 The Egyptian turned everything over to the hands of Joseph because he saw that the Lord was with him, and that the Lord caused him to prosper him in all that he did.
5 Joseph's appearance was beautiful, and his master's wife watched Joseph, and she loved him and wanted him to have sex with her.
6 But he did not surrender his soul because he remembered the Lord and the words which Jacob, his father, used to read to him from the writings of Abraham, that no man should commit fornication with a woman who has a husband. For him the punishment of death has been ordained in the heavens before the Most High God, and the sin will be recorded against him in the eternal books, which are always in the presence of the Lord.
7 Joseph remembered these words and refused to have sex with her.
8 And she begged him for a year, but he refused and would not listen.

9 But while he was in the house she embraced him and held him tightly in order to force him to sleep with her. She closed the doors of the house and held on to him, but he left his garment in her hands and broke through the door and ran out from her presence.
10 The woman saw that he would not sleep with her, and she slandered him in the presence of his master, saying "Your Hebrew servant, whom you love, sought to force me to have sex with him. When I shouted for help he fled and left his garment in my hands. I tried to stop him but he broke through the door."
11 When the Egyptian saw Joseph's garment and the broken door, and heard the words of his wife, he threw Joseph into prison and put him in the place where the prisoners of the king were kept.
12 He was there in the prison, and the Lord gave Joseph favor in the sight of the chief of the prison guards and caused him to have compassion for Joseph, because he saw that the Lord was with him, and that the Lord made all that he did to prosper.
13 He turned over all things into his hands, and the chief of the prison guards knew of nothing that was going on in the prison, because Joseph did everything for him, and the Lord perfected it. He remained there two years.
14 In those days Pharaoh, king of Egypt, was very angry at his two eunuchs, the chief butler, and the chief baker. He put them in the prison facility of the house of the chief cook, where Joseph was kept.
15 The chief of the prison guards appointed Joseph to serve them, and he served them.
16 They both dreamed a dream, the chief butler and the chief baker, and they told it to Joseph.
17 As he interpreted to them so it happened to them, and Pharaoh restored the chief butler to his office and he killed the chief baker as Joseph had interpreted to them.
18 But the chief butler forgot Joseph was in the prison, although he had informed him of what would happen to him. He did not remember to inform Pharaoh of how Joseph had told him (about his dream), because he forgot.

[Chapter 40]

1 In those days Pharaoh dreamed two dreams in one night concerning a famine that was to be in all the land, and he awoke from his sleep and called all the magicians and interpreters of dreams that were in Egypt. He told them his two dreams but they were not able to tell him what they meant.
2 Then the chief butler remembered Joseph and told the king of him, and he brought him out from the prison, and the king told his two dreams to him.
3 He said before Pharaoh that his two dreams were one, and he said to him, "Seven years shall come in which there shall be plenty in all the land of Egypt, but after that, seven years of famine. Such a famine as has not been in all the land.
4 Now, let Pharaoh appoint administrators in all the land of Egypt, and let them store up food in every city throughout all the years of plenty, and there will be food for the seven years of famine, and those of the land will not perish through the famine, even though it will be very severe."

5 The Lord gave Joseph favor and mercy in the eyes of Pharaoh. Pharaoh said to his servants, "We shall not find such a wise and prudent man like this man, because the spirit of the Lord is with him."
6 And he appointed Joseph the second in command in his entire kingdom and gave him authority over all Egypt, and placed him on the second chariot of Pharaoh to ride.
7 And he clothed him with fine linen clothes, and he put a gold chain around his neck, and a crier proclaimed before him "El" "El wa Abirer," and he placed a ring on his hand and made him ruler over all his house, and lifted him up before the people, and said to him, "Only on the throne shall I be greater than you."
8 Joseph ruled over all the land of Egypt, and all the governors of Pharaoh, and all his servants, and all those who did the king's business loved him because he walked in uprightness, because he was without pride and arrogance. He did not judge people by their position, and did not accept gifts, but he judged all the people of the land in uprightness.
9 The land of Egypt was at peace before Pharaoh because of Joseph, because the Lord was with him, and the Lord gave him favor and mercy for all his generations before all those who knew him and those who heard of him, and Pharaoh's kingdom was run efficiently, and there was no Satan (adversary) and no evil person in it.
10 And the king called Joseph's name Sephantiphans, and gave Joseph the daughter of Potiphar, the daughter of the priest of Heliopolis, the chief cook to marry.
11 On the day that Joseph stood before Pharaoh he was thirty years old.
12 In that year Isaac died. Things transpired as Joseph had said in the interpretation of Pharaoh's dream and there were seven years of plenty over all the land of Egypt, and the land of Egypt abundantly produced, one measure producing eighteen hundred measures.
13 Joseph gathered food into every city until they were full of grain and they could no longer count or measure it because of its multitude.

[Chapter 41]

1 In the forty-fifth jubilee, in the second week, and in the second year, Judah took his first-born Er, a wife from the daughters of Aram, named Tamar.
2 But he hated her, and did not have sex with her, because her mother was of the daughters of Canaan, and he wished to take him a wife of the lineage of his mother, but Judah, his father, would not permit him to do that.
3 Er, the first-born of Judah, was wicked, and the Lord killed him.
4 And Judah said to Onan, his brother, "Go in to your brother's wife and perform the duty of a husband's brother to her, and raise up offspring to your brother."
5 Onan knew that the offspring would not be his, but his brother's only, and he went into the house of his brother's wife, and spilt his seed (ejaculates) on the ground, and he was wicked in the eyes of the Lord, and He killed him.
6 Judah said to Tamar, his daughter-in-law, "Remain in your father's house as a widow until Shelah, my son has grown up, and I shall give you to him to wife."
7 He grew up, but Bedsu'el, the wife of Judah, did not permit her son Shelah to marry. Bedsu'el, Judah's wife, died in the fifth year of this week.
8 In the sixth year Judah went up to shear his sheep at Timnah.

9 And they told Tamar, "Look, your father-in-law is going up to Timnah to shear his sheep." And she took off her widow's clothes, and put on a veil, and adorned herself, and sat in the gate connecting the road to Timnah.
10 As Judah was going along he saw her, and thought she was a prostitute, and he said to her, "Let me come in to you," and she said to him, "Come in," and he went in.
11 She said to him, "Give me my pay," and he said to her, "I have nothing with me except my ring that is on my finger, my necklace, and my staff which is in my hand."
12 She said to him, "Give them to me until you send me my pay." And he said to her, "I will send to you a kid of the goats", and he gave her his ring, necklace, and staff, and she conceived by him.
13 Judah went to his sheep, and she went to her father's house.
14 Judah sent a kid of the goats by the hand of his shepherd, an Adullamite, but he could not find her, so he asked the people of the place, saying, "Where is the prostitute who was here?"
15 They said to him, "There is no prostitute here with us." And he returned and informed Judah that he had not found her, "I asked the people of the place, and they said to me, "There is no prostitute here." "
16 He said, "If you see her give the kids to her or we become a cause of ridicule." And when she had completed three months, it was revealed that she was with child, and they told Judah, saying, "Look Tamar, your daughter-in-law, is with child by whoredom."
17 And Judah went to the house of her father, and said to her father and her brothers, "Bring her out, and let them burn her, for she has committed uncleanness in Israel."
18 It happened when they brought her out to burn her that she sent to her father-in-law the ring and the necklace, and the staff, saying, "Tell us whose are these, because by him am I with child."
19 Judah acknowledged, and said, "Tamar is more righteous than I am.
20 Do not let them burn her." And for that reason she was not given to Shelah, and he did not again approach her and after that she gave birth to two sons, Perez and Zerah, in the seventh year of this second week.
21 At this time the seven years of fruitfulness were completed, of which Joseph spoke to Pharaoh.
22 Judah acknowledged the evil deed that he had done because he had sex with his daughter-in-law, and he hated himself for it.
23 He acknowledged that he had transgressed and gone astray, because he had uncovered the skirt of his son, and he began to lament and to supplicate before the Lord because of his transgression.
24 We told him in a dream that it was forgiven him because he supplicated earnestly, and lamented, and did not commit the act again.
25 And he received forgiveness because he turned from his sin and from his ignorance, because he transgressed greatly before our God. Every one that acts like this, every one who has sex with his mother-in-law, let them burn him alive with fire. Because there is uncleanness and pollution on them, let them burn them alive.
26 Command the children of Israel that there should be no uncleanness among them, because every one who has sex with his daughter-in-law or with his mother-in-law has committed

uncleanness. Let them burn the man who has had sex with her with fire, and likewise burn the woman, so that God will turn away wrath and punishment from Israel.
27 We told Judah that his two sons had not had sex with her, and for this reason his offspring was established for a second generation, and would not be rooted out.
28 For in single-mindedness he had gone and sought for punishment, namely, according to the judgment of Abraham, which he had commanded his sons. Judah had sought to burn her alive.

[Chapter 42]

1 In the first year of the third week of the forty-fifth jubilee the famine began to come into the land, and the rain refused to be given to the earth. None whatsoever fell.
2 The earth became barren, but in the land of Egypt there was food, because Joseph had gathered the seed of the land in the seven years of plenty and had preserved it.
3 The Egyptians came to Joseph that he might give them food, and he opened the storehouses where the grain of the first year was stored, and he sold it to the people of the land for gold.
4 Jacob heard there was food in Egypt, and he sent his ten sons that they should procure food for him in Egypt, and they arrived among those that went there, but Benjamin he did not send.
5 Joseph recognized them, but they did not recognize him. He spoke to them and questioned them, and he said to them, "Are you not spies and have you not come to explore ways to enter this land?"
6 And he put them in custody.
7 After that, he set them free again, and detained Simeon alone and sent his nine brothers away.
8 He filled their sacks with corn, and he put their gold back in their sacks, and they did not know it. Joseph then commanded them to bring their younger brother, because they had told him their father was living and also their younger brother.
9 They went up from the land of Egypt and they came to the land of Canaan. There they told their father all that had happened to them, and how the ruler of the country had spoken rudely to them, and had seized Simeon until they should bring Benjamin.
10 Jacob said, "You have taken my children from me! Joseph is gone and Simeon also is gone, and now you will take Benjamin away. I am the victim of your wickedness."
11 He said, "My son will not go down with you because fate may have it that he would fall sick. Their mother gave birth to two sons, and one has died, and this one also you will take from me. If, by fate, he took a fever on the road, you would turn my old age to sorrow and death."
12 He saw that every man's money had been returned to him in his sack, and for this reason he feared to send him.
13 The famine increased and became grievous in the land of Canaan, and in all lands except in the land of Egypt. Egypt had food because many of the children of the Egyptians had stored up their seed for food from the time when they saw Joseph gathering seed together and putting it in storehouses and preserving it for the years of famine.

14 The people of Egypt fed themselves on it during the first year of their famine but when Israel saw that the famine was very serious in the land, and that there was no deliverance, he said to his sons, "Go again, and procure food for us so that we will not die."
15 They said, "We shall not go unless our youngest brother go with us!"
16 Israel saw that if he did not send Benjamin with them, they would all perish because of the famine.
17 Reuben said, "Give him to me, and if I do not bring him back to you, kill my two sons in payment for his soul." Israel said to Reuben, "He shall not go with you."
18 Judah came near and said, "Send him with me, and if I do not bring him back to you, let me bear your blame all the days of my life."
19 He sent him with them in the second year of this week on the first day of the month.
20 They all came to the land of Egypt, and they had presents in their hands of sweet spice, almonds, turpentine nuts, and pure honey.
21 And they went and stood before Joseph, and he saw Benjamin his brother, and he knew him, and said to them, "Is this your youngest brother?" They said to him, "It is he."
22 He said, "The Lord be gracious to you, my son!" And he sent Benjamin into his house and he brought out Simeon to them. Joseph made a feast for them, and they presented to him the gifts that they had brought in their hands.
23 They ate before Joseph and he gave them all a portion of food, but the portion of food given to Benjamin was seven times larger than any of theirs.
24 And they ate and drank and got up and remained with their donkeys.
25 Joseph devised a plan whereby he might learn their thoughts as to whether they desired peace or not. He said to the steward who was over his house, "Fill all their sacks with food. Place their money back in their vessels. Put my cup, the silver cup out of which I drink, in the sack of the youngest and send them away."

[Chapter 43]

1 He did as Joseph had told him, and filled all their sacks with food for them and put their money back into their sacks, and put the cup in Benjamin's sack.
2 Early in the morning they departed, and it happened that when they had gone from that place, Joseph said to the steward of his house, "Pursue them, run and seize them, and say, 'You have repaid my kindness with evil. You have stolen from me the silver cup out of which my lord drinks.'
3 Bring me back their youngest brother. Go! Get him quickly before I go to my seat of judgment (judge you guilt of disobeying an order). "
4 He ran after them and said the words as he was told. They said to him, "God forbid that your servants should do this thing, and steal any utensil or money from the house of your lord, like the things we found in our sacks the first time we, your servants, came back from the land of Canaan.
5 We have not stolen any utensil. How could we? Look here in our sacks and search, and wherever you find the cup in the sack of any man among us, let him be killed, and we and our donkeys will serve your lord."
6 He said to them, "Not so. If I find it, the man whose sack I find it in I shall take as a servant, and the rest of you shall return in peace to your house."

7 He was searching in their vessels, beginning with the eldest and ending with the youngest, when it was found in Benjamin's sack.
8 They ripped their garments in frustration, and placed their belongings back on their donkeys, and returned to the city and came to the house of Joseph. They all bowed themselves with their faces to the ground in front of him.
9 Joseph said to them, "You have done evil." They said, "What shall we say and how shall we defend ourselves? Our lord has discovered the transgression of his servants; and now we and our donkeys are the servants of our lord."
10 Joseph said to them, "I too fear the Lord. As for you, go to your homes and let your brother be my servant, because you have done evil. I delight in this cup as no one else delights in his cup and yet you have stolen it from me."
11 Judah said, "O my lord, I pray you to let your servant speak a word in my lord's ear. Your servant's mother had two sons for our father. One went away and was lost, and has not been found since. This one alone is left of his mother, and your servant our father loves him. He would die if the lad were lost to him.
12 When we go to your servant our father, and the lad is not with us, it will happen that he will die. We will have brought so much sorrow on our father it will bring his death.
13 Now rather let me, your servant, stay here as a bondsman to my lord instead of the boy. Let the lad go with his brothers, because I will stand in for him at the hand of your servant our father. If I do not bring him back, your servant will bear the blame of our father forever."
14 Joseph saw that they were all in accord in doing good to one another. Then, he could not refrain himself, and he told them that he was Joseph.
15 And he conversed with them in the Hebrew tongue and hugged their necks and wept.
16 At first they did not recognize him and then they began to weep. He said to them, "Do not weep for me, but hurry and bring my father to me. See, it is my mouth that speaks and the eyes of my brother Benjamin see me.
17 Pay attention. This is the second year of the famine, and there are still five years to come without harvest or fruit of trees or plowing.
18 You and your households come down quickly, so that you won't die because of the famine. Do not be grieved for your possessions, because the Lord sent me before you to set things in order that many people might live.
19 Tell my father that I am still alive. You see that the Lord has made me as a father to Pharaoh, and ruler over his house and over all the land of Egypt.
20 Tell my father of all my glory, and all the riches and glory that the Lord has given me."
21 By the command of Pharaoh's mouth, he gave them chariots and provisions for the way, and he gave them all multi-colored raiment and silver.
22 He sent corn, raiment, silver, and ten donkeys that carried all of this to his father, and he sent them away.
23 They went up and told their father that Joseph was alive, and was measuring out corn to all the nations of the earth, and that he was ruler over all the land of Egypt.
24 But their father did not believe it, because he was not in his right mind. But when he saw the wagons, which Joseph had sent, the life of his spirit revived, and he said, "It is enough for me if Joseph lives. I will go down and see him before I die."

[Chapter 44]

1 Israel took his journey from Haran's house on the new moon of the third month,
and he stopped at the Well of the Oath on the way and he offered a sacrifice to the
God of his father Isaac on the seventh of this month.
2 Jacob remembered the dream that he had at Bethel, and he feared to go down into
Egypt.
3 He was thinking of sending word to Joseph to come to him because he did not
want to go down. He remained there seven days, hoping fate would permit him to
see a vision as to whether he should remain or go down.
4 He celebrated the harvest festival of the first-fruits with old grain, because in all
the land of Canaan there was not a handful of seed in the ground because the famine
was affecting all the beasts, and cattle, and birds, and all men.
5 On the sixteenth the Lord appeared to him, and said to him, "Jacob, Jacob," and he
said, "Here I am."
6 And He said to him, "I am the God of your fathers, the God of Abraham and Isaac.
Do not be afraid to go down into Egypt, because I will be there to make you a great
nation. I will go down with you, and I will bring you up again. You will be buried in
this land and Joseph will put his hands on your eyes (to close them in death). Do not
be afraid. Go down into Egypt."
7 And his sons got up and placed their father and their possessions on wagons.
8 Israel got up from the Well of the Oath on the sixteenth of this third month, and he
went to the land of Egypt.
9 Israel sent Judah before him to his son Joseph to examine the Land of Goshen,
because Joseph had told his brothers that they should come and live there so they
could be near him.
10 This was the best land in Egypt. It was near to him and suitable for all of the cattle
they had.
11 These are the names of the sons of Jacob who went into Egypt with Jacob their
father; Reuben, the First-born of Israel and his sons Enoch, and Pallu, and Hezron
and Carmi, making five.
12 Simeon and his sons Jemuel, and Jamin, and Ohad, and Jachin, and Zohar, and
Shaul, the son of the Zephathite woman, making seven.
13 Levi and his sons Gershon, and Kohath, and Merari, making four.
14 Judah and his sons Shela, and Perez, and Zerah, making four.
15 Issachar and his sons Tola, and Phua, and Jasub, and Shimron, making five.
16 Zebulon and his sons Sered, and Elon, and Jahleel, making four.
17 These are the sons of Jacob and their sons whom Leah bore to Jacob in
Mesopotamia, six, and their one sister, Dinah and all the souls of the sons of Leah,
and their sons, who went with Jacob their father into Egypt. Twenty-nine souls, and
Jacob, making thirty, were the number of people that went into Egypt.
18 And the sons of Zilpah, Leah's handmaid, the wife of Jacob, who bore to Jacob
Gad and Ashur and their sons who went with him into Egypt.

19 The sons of Gad are Ziphion, and Haggi, and Shuni, and Ezbon, and Eri, and Areli, and Arodi, which make eight souls in total. The sons of Asher are Imnah, and Ishvah, and Ishvi, and Beriah, and Serah, and their one sister, which makes six in total.
20 All the souls were fourteen, and all those of Leah were forty-four.
21 The sons of Rachel, the wife of Jacob are Joseph and Benjamin.
22 There were born to Joseph in Egypt before his father came into Egypt, those whom Asenath, daughter of Potiphar, priest of Heliopolis gave birth to him, Manasseh, and Ephraim. The wife and children of Joseph totaled three.
23 The sons of Benjamin, Bela and Becher and Ashbel, Gera, and Naaman, and Ehi, and Rosh, and Muppim, and Huppim, and Ard with Benjamin totaled eleven.
24 And all the souls of Rachel were fourteen.
25 And the sons of Bilhah, the handmaid of Rachel, the wife of Jacob, whom she gave birth to Jacob, were Dan and Naphtali. These are the names of their sons who went with them into Egypt.
26 The sons of Dan were Hushim, and Samon, and Asudi. and "Ijaka, and Salomon, all totaling six.
27 All but one died the year in which they entered into Egypt, and there was left to Dan only Hushim.
28 These are the names of the sons of Naphtali: Jahziel, and Guni and Jezer, and Shallum, and 'Iv.
29 And 'Iv, who was born after the years of famine, died in Egypt.
30 All the souls (offspring) of Rachel were twenty-six.
31 All the souls (offspring) of Jacob, which went into Egypt, were seventy souls.
32 These are his children and his children's children, in all seventy, but five died in Egypt in the time of Joseph's rule and they had no children.
33 In the land of Canaan two sons of Judah died, Er and Onan, and they had no children, and the children of Israel buried those who died, and they were counted among the seventy Gentile nations.

[Chapter 45]

1 On the new moon of the fourth month, in the second year of the third week of the forty-fifth jubilee, Israel went into the country of Egypt, to the land of Goshen.
2 Joseph went to meet his father, Jacob, in the land of Goshen, and he hugged his father's neck and wept.
3 Israel said to Joseph, "Now that I have seen you let me die and may the Lord God of Israel, the God of Abraham, and the God of Isaac, who has not withheld His mercy and His grace from His servant Jacob, be blessed.
4 It is enough for me to have seen your face while I am yet alive. Yes, this is the true vision which I saw at Bethel.
5 Blessed be the Lord my God forever and ever, and blessed be His name."
6 Joseph and his brothers ate bread in the presence of their father and drank wine, and Jacob rejoiced with very great joy because he saw Joseph eating with his brothers and drinking in the presence of him, and he blessed the Creator of all things who had preserved him, and had preserved for him his twelve sons.

7 Joseph had given his father and his brothers as a gift the right of dwelling in the land of Goshen and in Rameses and all of the region around it, which he ruled over in the presence of Pharaoh.
8 Israel and his sons dwelt in the land of Goshen, the best part of the land of Egypt, and Israel was one hundred and thirty years old when he came into Egypt. Joseph nourished his father and his brothers and also their possessions (servants) with bread as much as they needed for the seven years of the famine.
9 The land of Egypt became available for purchase because of the famine, and Joseph acquired all the land of Egypt for Pharaoh in return for food, and he got possession of the people and their cattle and everything for Pharaoh.
10 The years of the famine were completed, and Joseph gave the people in the land seed and food that they might sow the land in the eighth year, because the river had overflowed all the land of Egypt.
11 For in the seven years of the famine it had not overflowed and had irrigated only a few places on the banks of the river, but now it overflowed and the Egyptians sowed the land, and it produced much corn that year.
12 This was the first year of the fourth week of the forty-fifth jubilee. Joseph took one-fifth of the corn of the harvest for the king and left four parts for them for food and for seed, and Joseph made it a law for Egypt until this day.
13 Israel lived in the land of Egypt seventeen years, and all the days which he lived were three jubilees, one hundred and forty-seven years, and he died in the fourth year of the fifth week of the forty-fifth jubilee.
14 Israel blessed his sons before he died and told them everything that they would go through in the land of Egypt. He revealed to them what they would live through in the last days, and he blessed them and gave Joseph two portions of the land.
15 He slept with his fathers, and he was buried in the double cave in the land of Canaan, near Abraham his father, in the grave which he dug for himself in the land of Hebron.
16 And he gave all his books and the books of his fathers to Levi, his son so that he might preserve them and replicate them for his children until this day.

[Chapter 46]

1 It happened that after the death of Jacob the children of Israel continued to multiply in the land of Egypt, and they became a great nation, and they were in one accord of heart, so that brother loved brother and every man helped his brother. They increased abundantly and multiplied greatly, ten weeks of years, all the days of the life of Joseph.
2 There was neither Satan nor any evil in all the days of the life of Joseph after his father, Jacob (had died), because all the Egyptians respected the children of Israel all the days of the life of Joseph.
3 Joseph died, being a hundred and ten years old. He lived seventeen years in the land of Canaan, and ten years he was a servant, and three years in prison, and eighty years he was under the king, ruling all the land of Egypt.
4 He died and so did all his brothers and all of that generation. But, he commanded the children of Israel before he died that they should carry his bones with them when they went out from the land of Egypt.

5 And he made them swear regarding his bones, because he knew that the Egyptians would not bring his bones out of Egypt or bury him in the land of Canaan, because while dwelling in the land of Assyria, king Makamaron, the king of Canaan, fought against Egypt in the valley and killed the king of Egypt there, and pursued the Egyptians to the gates of "Ermon.
6 But he was not able to enter, because another king, a new king, had become king of Egypt, and he was stronger than he (Makamaron), and he returned to the land of Canaan, and the gates of Egypt were closed so that none came or went from Egypt.
7 Joseph died in the forty-sixth jubilee, in the sixth week, in the second year, and they buried him in the land of Egypt, and all his brothers died after him.
8 The king of Egypt went to war against the king of Canaan in the forty-seventh jubilee, in the second week in the second year, and the children of Israel brought out all the bones of the children of Jacob except the bones of Joseph, and they buried them in the field in the double cave in the mountain.
9 Then, most of them returned to Egypt, but a few of them remained in the mountains of Hebron, and Amram your father remained with them.
10 The king of Canaan was victorious over the king of Egypt, and he closed the gates of Egypt.
11 He devised an evil plan against the children of Israel to afflict them. He said to the people of Egypt, "Look, the people of the children of Israel have increased and multiplied more than we.
12 Let us use wisdom and deal with them before they become too many. Let us make them our slaves before we go to war and they rise up against us on the side of our enemies. Before they leave and fight against us let us do this because their hearts and faces (allegiances) are towards the land of Canaan."
13 He set over them taskmasters to enforce slavery, and they built strong cities for Pharaoh, Pithom, and Raamses and they built all the walls and all the fortifications, which had fallen in the cities of Egypt.
14 They enslaved them with harshness, and the more they were evil toward them, the more they increased and multiplied.
15 And the people of Egypt despised the children of Israel.

[Chapter 47]

1 In the seventh week, in the seventh year, in the forty-seventh jubilee, your father went out from the land of Canaan, and you (Moses) were born in the fourth week, in the sixth year of it, in the forty-eighth jubilee; this was the time of tribulation for the children of Israel.
2 Pharaoh, the king of Egypt, issued a command ordering them to throw all their newborn male children into the river.
3 And they threw them into the river for seven months until the day that you were born. It is said that your mother hid you for three months.
4 She made an ark for you, and covered it with pitch and tar, and placed it in the reeds on the bank of the river. She placed you in it seven days. Your mother came by night and nursed you. By day Miriam, your sister, guarded you from the birds.
5 In those days Tharmuth, the daughter of Pharaoh, came to bathe in the river, and she heard you crying. She told her maids to bring you out, and they brought you to her.

6 She took you out of the ark, and she had compassion on you.
7 Your sister said to her, "Shall I go and call to you one of the Hebrew women to nurse this baby for you?" And she said to her, "Go."
8 Your sister went and called your mother, Jochebed, and Pharaoh's daughter gave her wages (employed her), and she nursed you.
9 Afterwards, when you grew up, they brought you to the daughter of Pharaoh, and you became her son. Amram, your father, taught you writing. After you had completed three weeks (twenty-seven years) they brought you into the royal court.
10 You were three weeks of years at court until the time when you went out from the royal court and saw an Egyptian beating your friend who was of the children of Israel, and you killed him and hid him in the sand.
11 On the second day you came across two children of Israel quarreling together, and you asked the one who was doing wrong, "Why did you hit your brother?"
12 He was angry and indignant, and said, "Who made you a prince and a judge over us?
13 Do you want to kill me like you killed the Egyptian yesterday?" You were afraid and you fled on because of these words.

[Chapter 48]

1 In the sixth year of the third week of the forty-ninth jubilee you fled and went to live in the land of Midian for five weeks and one year. You returned to Egypt in the second week in the second year in the fiftieth jubilee.
2 You know what He said to you on Mount Sinai, and what prince Mastema desired to do with you when you returned to Egypt.
3 Did he (Mastema) not seek to kill you with all his power and to deliver the Egyptians from your hand when he saw that you were sent to execute judgment and to take revenge on the Egyptians?
4 But I delivered you out of his hand, and you performed the signs and wonders which you were sent to perform in Egypt against Pharaoh, and against all of his household, and against his servants and his people.
5 The Lord exacted a great vengeance on them for Israel's sake, and struck them through the plagues of blood, frogs, lice, dog-flies, malignant boils, breaking out in pustules, the death of their cattle, and the plague of hailstones. He destroyed everything that grew from them by plagues of locusts, which devoured the remainder left by the hail, and by darkness, and by the death of the first-born of men and animals. The Lord took vengeance on all of their idols and burned them with fire.
6 Everything was sent through your hand, that you should declare these things before they were done. You spoke with the king of Egypt in the presence of all his servants and in the presence of his people and everything took place according to your words. Ten great and terrible judgments came on the land of Egypt so that you might execute vengeance on Egypt for Israel.
7 And the Lord did everything for Israel's sake according to His covenant, which he had ordained with Abraham. He took vengeance on them because they had brought them by force into bondage.
8 Prince Mastema stood against you, and sought to deliver you into the hands of Pharaoh. He helped the Egyptian sorcerers when they stood up and committed the

evil acts they did in your presence. Indeed, we permitted them to work, but the remedies we did not allow to be worked by their hands.
9 The Lord struck them with malignant ulcers (hemorrhoids?), and they were not able to stand. They could not perform a single sign because we destroyed them.
10 Even after all of these signs and wonders, prince Mastema was not put to shame because he took courage and cried to the Egyptians to pursue you with all the power the Egyptians had, with their chariots, and with their horses, and with all the hosts of the peoples of Egypt.
11 But I stood between the Egyptians and Israel, and we delivered Israel out of his hand, and out of the hand of his people. The Lord brought them through the middle of the sea as if it were dry land.
12 The Lord our God threw all the people whom he (Mastema) brought to pursue Israel into the middle of the sea, into the depths of the bottomless pit, beneath the children of Israel, even as the people of Egypt had thrown their (Israel's) children into the river. He took vengeance on one million of them. In addition to one thousand strong and energetic men were destroyed because of the death of the suckling children of your people, which they had thrown into the river.
13 On the fourteenth day and on the fifteenth and on the sixteenth and on the seventeenth and on the eighteenth days, prince Mastema was bound and imprisoned and placed behind the children of Israel so that he might not accuse them.
14 On the nineteenth day we let them (Mastema and his demons) loose so that they might help the Egyptians pursue the children of Israel.
15 He hardened their hearts and made them stubborn, and the plan was devised by the Lord our God that He might strike the Egyptians and throw them into the sea.
16 On the fourteenth day we bound him that he might not accuse the children of Israel on the day when they asked the Egyptians for vessels and garments, vessels of silver, and vessels of gold, and vessels of bronze, in order to exact from the Egyptians a price in return for the bondage they had been forced to serve.
17 We did not lead the children of Israel from Egypt empty handed.

[Chapter 49]

1 Remember the commandment which the Lord commanded you concerning the Passover. You should celebrate it in its season on the fourteenth day of the first month. You should kill the sacrifice before evening. They should eat it by night on the evening of the fifteenth from the time of the setting of the sun.
2 Because on this night, at the beginning of the festival and the beginning of the joy, you were eating the passover in Egypt, when all the powers of Mastema had been let loose to kill all the first-born in the land of Egypt, from the first-born of Pharaoh to the first-born of the captive maid-servant in the mill, and even the first-born of the cattle.
3 This is the sign that the Lord gave them, in every house on the door post on which they saw the blood of a lamb of the first year they should not enter to kill, but should pass by it, that all those should be exempt that were in the house because the sign of the blood was on its door posts.
4 And the powers of the Lord did everything as the Lord commanded them, and they passed by all the children of Israel, and the plague did not come on them to destroy them, cattle, man, or dog.

5 The plague was oppressive in Egypt, and there was no house in Egypt where there was not one dead, and weeping, and lamentation.
6 All Israel was eating the flesh of the paschal lamb, and drinking the wine, and was praising, and blessing, and giving thanks to the Lord God of their fathers, and they were ready to get out from under the yoke of Egypt and the evil bondage.
7 Remember this day all the days of your life. Observe it from year to year all the days of your life, once a year, on its day, according to all the law of it. Do not forsake it from day to day, or from month to month.
8 It is an eternal law, and engraved on the heavenly tablets regarding all the children of Israel that they should observe it on its day once a year, every year, throughout all their generations. There is no limit of days, for this is a law forever.
9 The man who is free from uncleanness, and does not come to observe Passover on the occasion of its day and does not bring an acceptable offering before the Lord to eat and to drink before the Lord on the day of its festival will be guilty. If he is clean and close at hand (near the temple) and does not come, he shall be cut off because he did not offer the offering of the Lord in its appointed season. He shall take the guilt on himself.
10 Let the children of Israel come and observe the passover on the day of its fixed time, on the fourteenth day of the first month, between the evenings, from the third part of the day to the third part of the night, for two portions of the day are given to the light, and a third part to the evening.
11 The Lord commanded you to observe it between the evenings.
12 And it is not permissible to kill the sacrifice during any period of light, but only during the period bordering on the evening, and let them eat it at the time of the evening, until the third part of the night. Whatever is left over of all its flesh from the third part of the night and onwards is to be burned with fire.
13 They shall not cook it with water (boil or seethe it), nor shall they eat it raw, but roast it on the fire. They shall eat it with care, making sure its head with the inwards and its feet are roasted with fire, and they shall not break any bone of it, for of the children of Israel no bone shall be crushed.
14 For this reason the Lord commanded the children of Israel to observe the passover on the day of its fixed time, and they shall not break a bone of it, because it is a festival day He commanded. There was no passing over from any other day or any other month, but on the exact day let the festival be observed.
15 Command the children of Israel to observe the passover throughout their days, every year, once a year on the day of its fixed time, and it shall be a memorial well pleasing in the presence of the Lord, and no plague shall come on them to kill or to strike in that year in which they celebrate the passover in its season in every respect according to His command.
16 And they shall not eat it outside the sanctuary of the Lord, but before the sanctuary of the Lord, and all the people of the congregation of Israel shall celebrate it in its appointed season.
17 Every man twenty years of age and upward, who has come on the day of the Passover shall eat it in the sanctuary of your God before the Lord. This is how it is written and ordained. They should eat it in the sanctuary of the Lord.
18 When the children of Israel come into the land of Canaan that they are to possess, set up the tabernacle (tent) of the Lord within the land occupied by one of their tribes until the sanctuary of the Lord has been built in the land. There, let them come

and celebrate the passover at tabernacle of the Lord, and let them kill it before the Lord from year to year.
19 When the house of the Lord has been built in the land of their inheritance, they shall go there and kill the passover in the evening, at sunset, at the third part of the day.
20 They shall offer its blood on the threshold of the altar, and shall place its fat on the fire, which is on the altar, and they shall eat its flesh roasted with fire in the yard of the house, which has been sanctified in the name of the Lord.
21 They may not celebrate the passover in their cities, nor in any place except at the tabernacle of the Lord, or before His house where His name has dwelt. They shall not stray from the Lord.
22 Moses, command the children of Israel to observe the ordinances of the passover, as it was commanded to you. Declare to them every year the purpose and time of the festival of unleavened bread. They should eat unleavened bread seven days. They should observe its festival and bring an offering every day during those seven days of joy before the Lord on the altar of your God.
23 Celebrate this festival with haste as when you went out from Egypt and you entered into the wilderness of Shur, because on the shore of the sea you completed it (the exodus).

[Chapter 50]

1 I made this law known to you the days of the Sabbaths in the desert of Sinai, between Elim and Sinai.
2 I told you of the Sabbaths of the land on Mount Sinai, and I told you of the jubilee years in the sabbaths of years, but have I not told you the year of it until you enter the land which you are to possess.
3 Keep the sabbaths of the land while they live on it, and they shall know the jubilee year.
4 I have ordained for you the year of weeks and the years and the jubilees. There are forty-nine jubilees from the days of Adam until this day, and one week and two years, and there are forty years yet to come for learning the commandments of the Lord, until they pass over into the land of Canaan, crossing the Jordan to the west.
5 The jubilees shall pass by until Israel is cleansed from all guilt of fornication, and uncleanness, and pollution, and sin, and error, and it dwells with confidence in all the land. There shall be no more Satan or any evil one, and the land shall be clean from that time forever.
6 I have written down the commandment for them regarding the Sabbaths and all the judgments of its laws for you.
7 Six days will you labor, but the seventh day is the Sabbath of the Lord your God.
8 You shall do no manner of work in it, you and your sons, and your menservants and your maidservants, and all your cattle and travelers also who lodge with you. The man that does any work on it shall die. Whoever desecrates that day, whoever has sex with his wife, whoever says he will do something on it, or he that will set out on a journey on it in regard to any buying or selling, or whoever draws water on it which he had not prepared for himself on the sixth day, and whoever takes up any burden to carry it out of his tent or out of his house shall die.

9 You shall do no work whatsoever on the Sabbath day except what you have prepared for yourselves on the sixth day, so as to eat, and drink, and rest. Keep Sabbath free from all work on that day. It is to bless the Lord your God, who has given you a day of festival and a holy day, and a day of the holy kingdom. This is a day for Israel among all their days forever.
10 Great is the honor which the Lord has given to Israel that they should eat, drink, and be satisfied on this festival day. Rest on it from all labor, which belongs to the labor of the children of men, except burning frankincense and bringing offerings and sacrifices before the Lord for days and for Sabbaths.
11 Only this work shall be done on the Sabbath days in the sanctuary of the Lord your God so that they may atone for Israel with sacrifice continually from day to day for a memorial pleasing before the Lord, so that He may always receive them from day to day according to what you have been commanded.
12 Every man who does any work on it, or takes a trip, or tills his farm, whether in his house or any other place, and whoever lights a fire, or rides a beast, or travels by ship on the sea shall die. And whoever strikes or kills anything, or slaughters a beast or a bird, or whoever catches an animal or a bird or a fish, or whoever fasts or makes war on the Sabbaths, the man who does any of these things on the Sabbath shall die. This is done so that the children of Israel will observe the Sabbaths according to the commandments regarding the Sabbaths of the land. It is written in the tablets, which He gave into my hands that I should write out for you the laws of the seasons, and the seasons according to the division of their days.

This completes the account of the division of the days.

The History Of The Book Of Jasher

The Book Of Jasher, or Sefer Ha Yashar, is referred to in the books of Joshua and Second Samuel of the Holy Bible.

"Behold it is written in the Book of Jasher."--II Samuel, i. 18
"Is not this written in the Book of Jasher?"--Joshua, x. 13.

Jasher (Yashar) is a Hebrew word meaning "upright". Jasher is not the name of the author or any prophet or judge of Israel, as scholars had previously thought. The name refers to the fact that the record, facts, and history are upright, correct, and thus, trustworthy.

The value of The Book of Jasher is seen in the large quantity of additional detail revealed in the period between divine creation and the time of Joshua's leadership over Israel when the Israelites enter into the land of Canaan.

The Book of Jasher includes details about the antediluvian patriarchs, angels, watchers, the flood, the tower of Babel, and many other events mentioned in the Bible. The tales are expanded and infused with detail not previously available.

This means we receive insight into the lives of Abraham, Noah, Enoch, Joseph, and many other biblical figures. We come to understand how they became great and why they acted as they did. We are also given hitherto unknown knowledge of historical events. We are shown how God's hand shaped history through his love and anger. We see how his disappointment with men and angels ended in earth's near total destruction.

We learn how the power of Nimrod, the great hunter, arose. We are told how all animals were guided to the ark of Noah, and why the tower of Babel was attacked by God and angels. Such detailed accounts bring the Old Testament into an understandable focus.

According to the Encyclopedia Judaica, Volume 14, p. 1099, Jasher was "probably written in the 13th century A.D." However, some scholars have proposed various dates between the 9th century and 16th century A.D.

There are three separate and different books named Jasher, however the Mormon Church, otherwise known as The Church of Jesus Christ of Latter-day Saints, considers this rendition of Jasher to be the book referenced in the Old Testament. The belief of the church leadership is bolstered by the preface in the 1625 version, which claims its original source came from the ruins of Jerusalem in 70 A.D.

Jasher is held in high repute by many Mormons but is not officially endorsed by the Mormon Church. The official stance of the Mormon Church falls short of making Jasher part of their Holy Scriptures but does endorse the book as being valid and authentic. The Mormon Church places the book of Jasher on the same level as other apocryphal writings and states in the church magazine, The Ensign, After reviewing the standard scholarly analysis of how the book appears to have been composed of old Jewish legends, the book of Jasher is considered to be of great benefit to the reader. The article concluded with an injunction to treat it according to the Lord's advice on how to study the Apocrypha. The article goes on to quote the church stance on the Apocrypha.

"Verily, thus saith the Lord unto you concerning the Apocrypha — There are many things contained therein that are true, and it is mostly translated correctly; There are many things contained therein that are not true, which are interpolations by the hands of men. Verily, I say unto you, that it is not needful that the Apocrypha should be translated. Therefore, whoso readeth it, let him understand, for the Spirit manifesteth truth; And whoso is enlightened by the Spirit shall obtain benefit And whoso receiveth not by the Spirit, cannot be benefitted. Therefore it is not needful that it should be translated. Amen." (D.&C. 91:1-6)

In the early 1800s, Moses Samuel of Liverpool, England, was given a copy of the 1625 A.D. Hebrew work. Jasher, he found, was written in a theological or Rabbinical type of Hebrew, which is a more classical Hebrew. Samuel translated the text into English and in 1839 sold it to Mordecai Manuel Noah, a Jewish New York publisher, who published it in 1840.

Copyright of the translation was obtained by J. H. Parry & Company in Salt Lake City, who published it in 1887.

Samuel's translation was written in "Elizabethan or King James" English and contained archaic words, phrases, and idioms.

The translation offered here is taken from the J. H. Parry translation with all archaic language and idioms edited and restated in modern English.

According to Bernard Wasserstein, in the Transactions of the Jewish Historical Society of England Vol. XXXV, Samuel translated into English the pseudo-biblical Book of Jasher, a supposedly ancient Hebrew text which Samuel convinced himself was authentic. After failing to persuade the Royal Asiatic Society to publish it, he sold his translation for £150 in 1839 to the American Jewish newspaper-owner and philanthropist Mordecai M. Noah. It appeared in New York the following year but with Noah's name and not Samuel's on the title page. "I did not put my name to it as my Patron and myself differed about its authenticity", Samuel later explained. This was odd since Noah seems to have had a lower opinion of the work's authenticity than Samuel. The translation was accepted as accurate, but the publication provoked criticism by scholars who rejected the claims made on behalf of the text. It won acceptance, however, by the Mormon prophet Joseph Smith. (p. 2)

The prophet, Joseph Smith's attraction to the book was due in part to the history contained in the preface of the book.

According to the history documented in the preface of the Book of Jasher, Titus destroyed Jerusalem in 70 A.D. but the book was miraculously rescued at that time. During the destruction of the Jewish temple a Roman officer named Sidrus discovered a Hebrew scholar hiding in a library. The officer took the scholar and all the books safely back to his estates in Seville, Spain. The manuscript was transferred to the Jewish college in Cordova, Spain. The book was kept there until its printings in Venice in 1625.

There is no evidence to substantiate these claims, but there is nothing to conclusively dismiss the claims either.

In reality, it is possible that a Jew living in Spain or Italy may have penned the book, but we have no way to be definite regarding the date of writing of the original book. Part of the confusion arises from the fact that Jasher seems to be a compilation of several stories gathered by priests over many generations. Most of the stories and history contain reliable, authentic Jewish terms and traditions. It is the weight of these correct facts and references that lend credence to the authenticity of the seed literature that formed Jasher.

Scholars view Jasher with much skepticism due to the absence of any evidence or mention of the book prior to 1625. The basis of the stories contained in Jasher are mythically old, but the book itself has not been found in its present form prior to the printing in the 1600s. However, it is the opinion of the editor that Jasher will offer some insight into the murky and sometimes sparse historical landscape of Genesis. At the least, we may state that the book reflects what the priestly scholars who wrote the book believed.

The texts presented here represents an accurate version of the Book of Jasher rendered in modern English. Although the book was translated in the 1800s, the translator chose to use the more stilted and less accessible Elizabethan or King James style of English in order to add weight and religious authority to the text. This made the book less than pleasant to read for the modern audience. In the translation before you archaic words and expressions were replaced with their modern counterparts. A word for word replacement was not attempted. When an archaic word needed to be replaced with a phrase for the purpose of clarity this technique was embraced so as to render the text readily understandable. It is our sincere hope our goal was accomplished and the reader will find this version interesting and easy to read.

The Book of Jasher

THIS IS THE BOOK OF THE GENERATIONS OF MAN WHOM GOD CREATED ON THE EARTH ON THE DAY WHEN THE LORD GOD MADE HEAVEN AND EARTH.

CHAPTER 1
1 God said, Let us make man in our image, in our likeness, and God created man in his own image.
2 God formed man from the dirt, and he blew into his nostrils the breath of life, and man became a living soul with the capacity of speech.
3 And the Lord said, It is not good for man to be alone; I will make him a helper and a mate.
4 The Lord caused a deep sleep to come on Adam, and he slept. God took away one of his ribs, and he fashioned flesh on it, and formed it and brought it to Adam. Adam awoke from his sleep, and saw a woman was standing in front of him.
5 He said, This is bone of my bones and it shall be called woman, because it has been taken from man. Adam named her Eve, because she was the mother of all living (mankind).
6 God blessed them and on the day he created them he called their names Adam and Eve. The Lord God said, Be prolific and reproduce and fill the earth.
7 The Lord God took Adam and his wife, and he placed them in the garden of Eden to farm it and to keep it. He commanded them and said, "You may eat from every tree of the garden, but you may never eat from the tree of the knowledge of good and evil. On the day that you eat thereof you will certainly die.
8 When God had blessed and commanded them, he departed from them. Adam and his wife lived in the garden according to the command which the Lord had commanded them.
9 The serpent, which God had created with them in the earth, came to them to incite them to go contrary to the command of God which he had commanded them.
10 And the serpent enticed and persuaded the woman to eat from the tree of knowledge, and the woman listened to the voice of the serpent, and she went contrary to the word of God, and took from the tree of the knowledge of good and evil, and she ate, and she took from it and gave also to her husband and he ate.
11 And Adam and his wife went contrary to the command of God which he commanded them, and God knew it, and his anger was set ablaze against them and he cursed them.
12 And the Lord God drove them that day from the garden of Eden, to till the ground from which they were taken, and they went and lived at the east of the garden of Eden; and Adam had sex with his wife Eve and she bore two sons and three daughters.
13 She called the name of the first born Cain, saying, I have obtained a man from the Lord, and the name of the other she called Abel, for she said, Empty we came into the earth, and empty we shall be taken from it.
14 And the boys grew up and their father gave them a possession in the land; and Cain was a farmer of the ground, and Abel a keeper of sheep.
15 And it was at the expiration of a few years, that they brought a first-fruit offering

to the Lord, and Cain brought from the fruit of the ground, and Abel brought from the firstlings of his flock from the fat thereof, and God turned and inclined to Abel and his offering, and a fire came down from the Lord from heaven and consumed it.
16 And to Cain and his offering the Lord did not turn, and he did not incline to it, for he had brought from the inferior fruit of the ground before the Lord, and Cain was jealous against his brother Abel on account of this, and he sought an opportunity to kill him.
17 Some time after, Cain and Abel his brother went one day into the field to do their work; and they were both in the field, Cain farming and plowing his ground, and Abel feeding his flock; and the flock passed that part which Cain had plowed in the ground, and it sorely grieved Cain on this account.
18 And Cain approached his brother Abel in anger, and he said to him, What gives you the right to come and live here and bring your flock to feed in my land?
19 And Abel answered his brother Cain and said to him, What gives you the right to eat the flesh of my flock and clothe yourself with their wool?
20 Take off the wool of my sheep with which you have clothed yourself, and pay me for their resources you have used and flesh which you have eaten, and when you shall have done this, I will then go from your land as you have said.
21 Cain said to his brother Abel, Certainly if I kill you this day, who will require your blood from me?
22 And Abel answered Cain, saying, Certainly God who has made us in the earth, he will avenge my cause, and he will require my blood from you should you kill me, for the Lord is the judge and arbiter, and it is he who will repay man according to his evil, and the wicked man according to the wickedness that he may do on earth.
23 And now, if you should kill me here, certainly God knows your secret views, and will judge you for the evil which you did declare to do to me this day.
24 When Cain heard the words which Abel his brother had spoken, the anger of Cain was set ablaze against his brother Abel for declaring this thing.
25 Cain hurried and rose up, and took the iron part of his plowing instrument, with which he suddenly struck his brother and he killed him, and Cain spilt the blood of his brother Abel on the earth, and the blood of Abel streamed on the earth before the flock.
26 And after this Cain repented having slain his brother, and he was sadly grieved, and he wept over him and it troubled him greatly.
27 Cain rose up and dug a hole in the field, wherein he put his brother's body, and he turned the dust over it.
28 And the Lord knew what Cain had done to his brother, and the Lord appeared to Cain and said to him, Where is Abel your brother that was with you?
29 And Cain lied, and said, I do not know. Am I my brother's keeper? And the Lord said to him, What have you done? The voice of your brother's blood cries to me from the ground where you have slain him.
30 For you have slain your brother and have lied before me, and imagined in your heart that I saw you not, nor knew all your actions.
31 But you did this thing and did kill your brother for naught and because he spoke rightly to you, and now, therefore, cursed be you from the ground which opened its mouth to receive your brother's blood from your hand, and wherein you did bury him.
32 It shall be when you shall till it, the land will no longer give you its strength as in the beginning, for thorns and thistles shall the ground produce, and you shall be

moving and wandering in the earth until the day of your death.
33 And at that time Cain went out from the presence of the Lord, from the place where he was, and he went moving and wandering in the land toward the east of Eden, he and all those belonging to him.
34 Cain had sex with his wife in those days, and she conceived and gave birth to a son, and he called his name Enoch, saying, In that time the Lord began to give him rest and quiet in the earth.
35 At that time Cain also began to build a city: and he built the city and he called the name of the city Enoch, according to the name of his son; for in those days the Lord had given him rest on the earth, and he did not move about and wander as in the beginning.
36 And Irad was born to Enoch, and Irad had Mechuyael and Mechuyael had Methusael.

CHAPTER 2

1 It was in the hundred and thirtieth year of the life of Adam on the earth, that he again had sex with Eve his wife, and she conceived and gave birth to a son and he looked like Adam, and she called his name Seth, saying, Because God has appointed me another offspring in the place of Abel, for Cain has slain him.
2 And Seth lived one hundred and five years, and he had a son; and Seth called the name of his son Enosh, saying, Because in that time the sons of men began to reproduce, and to afflict their souls and hearts by disobeying and rebelling against God.
3 It was in the days of Enosh that the sons of men continued to rebel and go contrary to God, to increase the anger of the Lord against the sons of men.
4 And the sons of men went and they served other gods, and they forgot the Lord who had created them in the earth: and in those days the sons of men made images of brass and iron, wood and stone, and they bowed down and served them.
5 Every man made his god and they bowed down to them, and the sons of men turned away from the Lord all the days of Enosh and his children; and the anger of the Lord was set ablaze on account of their works and abominations which they did in the earth.
6 The Lord caused the waters of the river Gihon to overwhelm them, and he destroyed and consumed them, and he destroyed the third part of the earth. Notwithstanding this, the sons of men did not turn from their evil ways, and their hands were yet extended to do evil in the sight of the Lord.
7 In those days there was neither sowing nor reaping in the earth; and there was no food for the sons of men and the famine was very great in those days.
8 And the seed which they sowed in those days in the ground became thorns, thistles and briers; for from the days of Adam was this declaration concerning the earth, of the curse of God, which he cursed the earth, on account of the sin which Adam sinned before the Lord.
9 And it was when men continued to rebel and go contrary to God, and to corrupt their ways, that the earth also became corrupt.
10 And Enosh lived ninety years and he had Cainan.
11 Cainan grew up and he was forty years old, and he became wise and had knowledge and skill in all wisdom, and he reigned over all the sons of men, and he

led the sons of men to wisdom and knowledge; for Cainan was a very wise man and had understanding in all wisdom, and with his wisdom he ruled over spirits and demons.
12 Cainan knew by his wisdom that God would destroy the sons of men for having sinned on earth, and that the Lord would in the latter days bring on them the waters of the flood.
13 And in those days Cainan wrote on tablets of stone what was to take place in time to come, and he put them in his treasure troves.
14 Cainan reigned over the whole earth, and he turned some of the sons of men to the service of God.
15 When Cainan was seventy years old, he had three sons and two daughters.
16 These are the names of the children of Cainan; the name of the first born was Mahlallel, the second was Enan, and the third was Mered, and their sisters were Adah and Zillah; these are the five children of Cainan that were born to him.
17 Lamech, the son of Methusael, became related to Cainan by marriage, and he took his two daughters for his wives, and Adah conceived and gave birth to a son to Lamech, and she called his name Jabal.
18 And she again conceived and gave birth to a son, and called his name Jubal; and Zillah, her sister, was unable to conceive in those days and had no offspring.
19 For in those days the sons of men began to trespass against God, and to go contrary to the commandments which he had given Adam, to be prolific and reproduce in the earth.
20 Some of the sons of men caused their wives to drink a mixture that would render them unable to conceive, in order that they might retain their figures and their beautiful appearance might not fade.
21 And when the sons of men caused some of their wives to drink, Zillah drank with them.
22 The child-bearing women appeared abominable in the sight of their husbands and they treated them as widows, while their husbands lived with those unable to conceive and to those women they were attached.
23 And in the end of days and years, when Zillah became old, the Lord opened her womb.
24 She conceived and gave birth to a son and she called his name Tubal Cain, saying, After I had withered away have I obtained him from the Almighty God.
25 And she conceived again and gave birth to a daughter, and she called her name Naamah, for she said, After I had withered away have I obtained pleasure and delight.
26 Lamech was old and advanced in years, and his eyes were dim that he could not see, and Tubal Cain, his son, was leading him and it was one day that Lamech went into the field and Tubal Cain his son was with him, and while they were walking in the field, Cain the son of Adam advanced towards them; for Lamech was very old and could not see much, and Tubal Cain his son was very young.
27Tubal Cain told his father to draw his bow, and with the arrows he struck Cain, who was yet far off, and he killed him, because he appeared be an animal to them.
28 And the arrows entered Cain's body although he was at a distance from them, and he fell to the ground and died.
29 The Lord rewarded Cain's evil according to his wickedness, which he had done to his brother Abel, according to the word of the Lord which he had spoken.
30 And it came to pass when Cain had died, that Lamech and Tubal went to see the

animal which they had slain, and they saw, and behold Cain their grandfather was fallen dead on the earth.
31 Lamech was very much grieved at having done this, and in clapping his hands together (in grief) he struck his son and caused his death.
32 And the wives of Lamech heard what Lamech had done, and they sought to kill him.
33 The wives of Lamech hated him from that day, because he killed Cain and Tubal Cain, and the wives of Lamech separated from him, and would not listen to him in those days.
34 And Lamech came to his wives, and he begged them to listen to him about this matter.
35 He said to his wives Adah and Zillah, Hear my voice O wives of Lamech, attend to my words, for now you have imagined and said that I killed a man with my wounds, and a child with my stripes for they did no violence, but certainly know that I am old and grey-headed, and that my eyes are heavy through age, and I did this thing unknowingly.
36 And the wives of Lamech listened to him in this matter, and they returned to him with the advice of their father Adam, but they bore no children to him from that time, knowing that God's anger was increasing in those days against the sons of men, to destroy them with the waters of the flood for their evil acts.
37 Mahlallel the son of Cainan lived sixty-five years and he had Jared; and Jared lived sixty-two years and he had Enoch.

CHAPTER 3

1 Enoch lived sixty-five years and he had Methuselah; and Enoch walked with God after having a son, Methuselah, and he served the Lord, and despised the evil ways of men.
2 And the soul of Enoch was wrapped up in the instruction of the Lord, in knowledge and in understanding; and he wisely retired from the sons of men, and cloistered himself from them for many days.
3 It was at the expiration of many years, while he was serving the Lord, and praying before him in his house, that an angel of the Lord called to him from Heaven, and he said, Here am I.
4 And he said, Rise, go forth from your house and from the place where you hide yourself, and appear to the sons of men, in order that you may teach them the way in which they should go and the work which they must accomplish in order to enter into the ways of God.
5 Enoch rose up according to the word of the Lord, and went forth from his house, from his place and from the chamber in which he was concealed; and he went to the sons of men and taught them the ways of the Lord, and at that time assembled the sons of men and acquainted them with the instruction of the Lord.
6 He ordered it to be proclaimed in all places where the sons of men lived, saying, Where is the man who wishes to know the ways of the Lord and good works? Let him come to Enoch.
7 And all the sons of men then assembled to him, for all who desired this thing went to Enoch, and Enoch reigned over the sons of men according to the word of the Lord, and they came and bowed to him and they heard his word.

8 The spirit of God was on Enoch, and he taught all his men the wisdom of God and his ways, and the sons of men served the Lord all the days of Enoch, and they came to hear his wisdom.
9 And all the kings of the sons of men, both greatest and least, together with their princes and judges, came to Enoch when they heard of his wisdom, and they bowed down to him, and they also required of Enoch to reign over them, to which he consented.
10 They assembled in all, one hundred and thirty kings and princes, and they made Enoch king over them and they were all under his power and command.
11 And Enoch taught them wisdom, knowledge, and the ways of the Lord; and he made peace among them, and peace was throughout the earth during the life of Enoch.
12 Enoch reigned over the sons of men two hundred and forty-three years, and he did justice and righteousness with all his people, and he led them in the ways of the Lord.
13 These are the generations of Enoch, Methuselah, Elisha, and Elimelech, three sons; and their sisters were Melca and Nahmah, and Methuselah lived eighty-seven years and he had Lamech.
14 It was in the fifty-sixth year of the life of Lamech when Adam died. Nine hundred and thirty years old was he at his death. His two sons, with Enoch and Methuselah his son, buried him with great grandeur, as at the burial of kings, in the cave which God had told him.
15 And in that place all the sons of men mourned and wept greatly on account of Adam; it has therefore become a custom among the sons of men to this day.
16 Adam died because he ate of the tree of knowledge; he and his children after him, as the Lord God had spoken.
17 And it was in the year of Adam's death which was the two hundred and forty-third year of the reign of Enoch, in that time Enoch resolved to separate himself from the sons of men and to cloister himself as at first in order to serve the Lord.
18 Enoch did so, but did not entirely cloister himself from them, but kept away from the sons of men three days and then went to them for one day.
19 During the three days that he was in his chamber, he prayed to, and praised the Lord his God, and the day on which he went and appeared to his subjects he taught them the ways of the Lord, and all they asked him about the Lord he told them.
20 And he did in this manner for many years, and he afterward concealed himself for six days, and appeared to his people one day in seven; and after that once in a month, and then once in a year, until all the kings, princes and sons of men sought for him, and desired again to see the face of Enoch, and to hear his word; but they could not, as all the sons of men were greatly afraid of Enoch, and they feared to approach him on account of the Godlike awe that was seated on his countenance; therefore no man could look at him, fearing he might be punished and die.
21 All the kings and princes resolved to assemble the sons of men, and to come to Enoch, thinking that they might all speak to him at the time when he should come forth among them, and they did so.
22 The day came when Enoch went forth and they all assembled and came to him, and Enoch spoke to them the words of the Lord and he taught them wisdom and knowledge, and they bowed down before him and they said, May the king live! May the king live!
23 Some time after, when the kings and princes and the sons of men were speaking

to Enoch, and Enoch was teaching them the ways of God, an angel of the Lord then called to Enoch from heaven, and wished to bring him up to heaven to make him reign there over the sons of God, as he had reigned over the sons of men on earth.
24 When at that time Enoch heard this he went and assembled all the inhabitants of the earth, and taught them wisdom and knowledge and gave them divine instructions, and he said to them, I have been required to ascend into heaven; but I do not know the day of my going.
25 And now therefore I will teach you wisdom and knowledge and will give you instruction before I leave you, how to act on earth so that you may live (as you should); and he did so.
26 He taught them wisdom and knowledge, and gave them instruction, and he rebuked them, and he placed before them statutes and judgments to do on earth, and he made peace among them, and he taught them everlasting life, and lived with them some time teaching them all these things.
27 At that time the sons of men were with Enoch, and Enoch was speaking to them, and they lifted up their eyes and the likeness of a great horse descended from heaven, and the horse paced in the air.
28 And they told Enoch what they had seen, and Enoch said to them, On my account does this horse descend on earth; the time is come when I must go from you and I shall no more be seen by you.
29 The horse descended at that time and stood before Enoch, and all the sons of men that were with Enoch saw him.
30 Enoch then again ordered a voice to be proclaimed, saying, Where is the man who delights to know the ways of the Lord his God, let him come this day to Enoch before he is taken from us.
31 All the sons of men assembled and came to Enoch that day; and all the kings of the earth with their princes and counselors remained with him that day; and Enoch then taught the sons of men wisdom and knowledge, and gave them divine instruction; and he bade them serve the Lord and walk in his ways all the days of their lives, and he continued to make peace among them.
32 It was after this that he rose up and rode on the horse; and he went forth and all the sons of men went after him, about eight hundred thousand men; and they went with him one day's journey.
33 And the second day he said to them, Return home to your tents, why will you go? Perhaps you may die; and some of them went from him, and those that remained went with him six day's journey; and Enoch said to them every day, Return to your tents, that you may die; but they were not willing to return, and they went with him.
34 And on the sixth day some of the men remained and clung to him, and they said to him, We will go with you to the place where you go; as the Lord lives, only death shall separate us.
35 They urged so much to go with him that he ceased speaking to them; and they went after him and would not return.
36 When the kings returned they caused a census to be taken, in order to know the number of remaining men that went with Enoch; and it was on the seventh day that Enoch ascended into heaven in a whirlwind, with horses and chariots of fire.
37 And on the eighth day all the kings that had been with Enoch sent to bring back the number of men that were with Enoch, in that place from which he ascended into heaven.
38 All those kings went to the place and they found the earth there filled with snow,

and on the snow were large stones of snow, and one said to the other, Come, let us break through the snow and see, perhaps the men that remained with Enoch are dead, and are now under the stones of snow, and they searched but could not find Enoch, for he had ascended into heaven.

CHAPTER 4

1 All the days that Enoch lived on earth, were three hundred and sixty-five years.
2 And when Enoch had ascended into heaven, all the kings of the earth rose and took Methuselah his son and anointed him, and they caused him to reign over them in the place of his father.
3 Methuselah acted uprightly in the sight of God, as his father Enoch had taught him, and he likewise during the whole of his life taught the sons of men wisdom, knowledge and the fear of God, and he did not turn from the good way either to the right or to the left.
4 But in the latter days of Methuselah, the sons of men turned from the Lord; they corrupted the earth, they robbed and plundered each other, and they rebelled against God; they went contrary to, they corrupted their ways, and would not listen to the voice of Methuselah, but rebelled against him.
5 And the Lord was greatly wroth against them, and the Lord continued to destroy the offspring in those days, so that there was neither sowing nor reaping in the earth.
6 For when they sowed the ground in order that they might obtain food for their support, behold, thorns and thistles were produced which they did not sow.
7 And still the sons of men did not turn from their evil ways, and their hands were still extended to do evil in the sight of God, and they provoked the Lord with their evil ways, and the Lord was very wroth, and repented that he had made man.
8 He thought to destroy and annihilate them and he did so.
9 In those days when Lamech the son of Methuselah was one hundred and sixty years old, Seth the son of Adam died.
10 And all the days that Seth lived were nine hundred and twelve years, and he died.
11 Lamech was one hundred and eighty years old when he took Ashmua, the daughter of Elishaa the son of Enoch his uncle, and she conceived.
12 And at that time the sons of men sowed the ground, and a little food was produced, yet the sons of men did not turn from their evil ways, and they trespassed and rebelled against God.
13 The wife of Lamech conceived and gave birth to a son at that time, at the revolution of the year.
14 And Methuselah called his name Noah, saying, The earth was in his days at rest and free from corruption, and Lamech his father called his name Menachem, saying, This one shall comfort us in our works and miserable toil in the earth, which God had cursed.
15 The child grew up and was weaned, and he went in the ways of his father Methuselah, perfect and upright with God.
16 And all the sons of men departed from the ways of the Lord in those days as they multiplied on the face of the earth with sons and daughters, and they taught one another their evil practices and they continued sinning against the Lord.
17 Every man made to himself a god, and they robbed and plundered every man his

neighbor as well as his relative, and they corrupted the earth, and the earth was filled with violence.
18 And their judges and rulers went to the daughters of men and took their wives by force from their husbands according to their choice, and the sons of men in those days took from the cattle of the earth, the beasts of the field and the fowls of the air, and taught the mixture of animals of one species with the other, in order therewith to provoke the Lord; and God saw the whole earth and it was corrupt, for all flesh had corrupted its ways on earth, all men and all animals.
19 And the Lord said, I will blot out man that I created from the face of the earth, yea from man to the birds of the air together with cattle and beasts that are in the field, for I repent that I made them.
20 All men who walked in the ways of the Lord died in those days, before the Lord brought the evil on man which he had declared, for this was from the Lord that they should not see the evil which the Lord spoke of concerning the sons of men.
21 And Noah found grace in the sight of the Lord, and the Lord chose him and his children to raise up offspring on the face of the whole earth.

CHAPTER 5

1 It was in the eighty-fourth year of the life of Noah that Enoch the son of Seth died; he was nine hundred and five years old at his death.
2 In the one hundred and seventy ninth year of the life of Noah, Cainan the son of Enosh died, and the age of Cainan was nine hundred and ten years, and he died.
3 And in the two hundred and thirty fourth year of the life of Noah, Mahlallel the son of Cainan died, and the days of Mahlallel were eight hundred and ninety-five years, and he died.
4 Jared the son of Mahlallel died in those days, in the three hundred and thirty-sixth year of the life of Noah; and all the days of Jared were nine hundred and sixty-two years, and he died.
5 And all who followed the Lord died in those days, before they saw the evil which God declared to do on earth.
6 After the lapse of many years, in the four hundred and eightieth year of the life of Noah, when all those men who followed the Lord had died away from among the

7 Speak ye, and proclaim to the sons of men, saying, Thus says the Lord, return from your evil ways and turn away from your works, and the Lord will repent of the evil that he declared to do to you, so that it shall not come to pass.
8 For thus says the Lord, Behold I give you a period of one hundred and twenty years; if you will turn to me and turn away from your evil ways, then will I also turn away from the evil which I told you, and it shall not exist, says the Lord.
9 And Noah and Methuselah spoke all the words of the Lord to the sons of men, day after day, constantly speaking to them.
10 But the sons of men would not listen to them, nor incline their ears to their words, and they were stubborn.
11 And the Lord granted them a period of one hundred and twenty years, saying, If they will return, then will God repent of the evil, so as not to destroy the earth.
12 Noah the son of Lamech refrained from taking a wife in those days to beget children, for he said, Certainly now God will destroy the earth, wherefore then shall I beget children?
13 Noah was a just man, he was perfect in his generation, and the Lord chose him to raise up offspring from his offspring on the face of the earth.
14 And the Lord said to Noah, Take to you a wife, and beget children, for I have seen you righteous before me in this generation.
15 You shall raise up offspring, and your children with you, in the midst of the earth; and Noah went and took a wife, and he chose Naamah the daughter of Enoch, and she was five hundred and eighty years old.
16 And Noah was four hundred and ninety-eight years old, when he took Naamah for a wife.
17 Naamah conceived and gave birth to a son, and he called his name Japheth, saying, God has enlarged me in the earth; and she conceived again and gave birth to a son, and he called his name Shem, saying, God has made me a remnant, to raise up descendants the midst of the earth.
18 And Noah was five hundred and two years old when Naamah gave birth to Shem, and the boys grew up and went in the ways of the Lord, in all that Methuselah and Noah their father taught them.
19 Lamech the father of Noah, died in those days; yet verily he did not go with all his heart in the ways of his father, and he died in the hundred and ninety-fifth year of the life of Noah.
20 And all the days of Lamech were seven hundred and seventy years, and he died.
21 All the sons of men who knew the Lord, died in that year before the Lord brought evil on them; for the Lord willed them to die, so as not to behold the evil that God would bring on their brothers and relatives, as he had so declared to do.
22 In that time, the Lord said to Noah and Methuselah, Stand forth and proclaim to the sons of men all the words that I spoke to you in those days, perchance they may turn from their evil ways, and I will then repent of the evil and will not bring it.
23 And Noah and Methuselah stood forth, and said in the ears of the sons of men, all that God had spoken concerning them.
24 But the sons of men would not listen, neither would they incline their ears to all their declarations.
25 It was after this that the Lord said to Noah, The end of all flesh is come before me on account of their evil deeds, and behold I will destroy the earth.
26 And take with you gopher wood, and go to a certain place and make a large ark,

and place it in that spot.
27 Thus shall you make it; three hundred cubits in length, fifty cubits broad and thirty cubits high.
28 And you shall make a door, open at its side, and to a cubit you shall finish above, and cover it within and without with pitch.
29 And behold I will bring the flood of waters on the earth, and all flesh will be destroyed; from under the heavens all that is on earth shall perish.
30 You and your household shall go and gather two couple of all living things, male and female, and shall bring them to the ark, to raise up offspring from them on earth.
31 Gather to you all food that is eaten by all the animals, that there may be food for you and for them.
32 You shall choose for your sons three maidens from the daughters of men, and they shall be wives to your sons.
33 And Noah rose up, and he made the ark, in the place where God had commanded him, and Noah did as God had ordered him.
34 In his five hundred and ninety-fifth year Noah commenced to make the ark, and he made the ark in five years, as the Lord had commanded.
35 Then Noah took the three daughters of Eliakim, son of Methuselah, for wives for his sons, as the Lord had commanded Noah.
36 It was at that time Methuselah the son of Enoch died; he was nine hundred and sixty years old at his death.

CHAPTER 6

1 At that time, after the death of Methuselah, the Lord said to Noah, Go with your household into the ark; behold I will gather to you all the animals of the earth, the beasts of the field and the fowls of the air, and they shall all come and surround the ark.
2 You shall go and seat yourself by the doors of the ark, and all the beasts, the animals, and the fowls, shall assemble and place themselves before you, and such of them as will come and crouch before you, you shall take and deliver into the hands of your sons, who will bring them to the ark, and all that will stand before you you shall leave.
3 And the Lord brought this about on the next day, and animals, beasts and fowls came in great multitudes and surrounded the ark.
4 Noah went and seated himself by the door of the ark, and of all flesh that crouched before him he brought into the ark, and all that stood before him he left on earth.
5 A lioness came with her two whelps, male and female, and the three crouched before Noah; the two whelps rose up against the lioness and struck her, and made her flee from her place, and she went away, and they returned to their places and crouched on the earth before Noah.
6 And the lioness ran away, and stood in the place of the lions.
7 And Noah saw this and wondered greatly, and he rose and took the two whelps and brought them into the ark.
8 Noah brought into the ark from all living creatures that were on earth, so that there was none left but those which Noah brought into the ark.

9 Two and two came to Noah into the ark, but from the clean animals and clean fowls, he brought seven couples as God had commanded him.
10 And all the animals, and beasts, and fowls were still there, and they surrounded the ark at every place, and the rain had not descended till seven days after.
11 On that day the Lord caused the whole earth to shake, and the sun darkened, and the foundations of the world raged, and the whole earth was moved violently, and the lightning flashed, and the thunder roared, and all the fountains in the earth were broken up, such as was not known to the inhabitants before; and God did this mighty act in order to terrify the sons of men, that there might be no more evil on earth.
12 And still the sons of men would not return from their evil ways, and they increased the anger of the Lord at that time, and did not even direct their hearts to all this.
13 At the end of seven days, in the six hundredth year of the life of Noah, the waters of the flood were on the earth.
14 All the fountains of the deep were broken up, and the windows of heaven were opened, and the rain was on the earth forty days and forty nights.
15 And Noah and his household, and all the living creatures that were with him, came into the ark on account of the waters of the flood, and the Lord shut him in.
16 All the sons of men that were left on the earth became exhausted through evil on account of the rain, for the waters were coming more violently on the earth, and the animals and beasts were still surrounding the ark.
17 And the sons of men assembled together, about seven hundred thousand men and women, and they came to Noah to the ark.
18 They called to Noah, saying, Open for us that we may come to you in the ark--and wherefore shall we die?
19 And Noah, with a loud voice answered them from the ark, saying, Have you not all rebelled against the Lord, and said that he does not exist? Therefore the Lord brought on you this evil, to destroy and cut you off from the face of the earth.
20 Is not this the thing that I spoke to you of one hundred and twenty years back, and you would not listen to the voice of the Lord, and now do you desire to live on earth?
21 They said to Noah, We are ready to return to the Lord; only open for us that we may live and not die.
22 And Noah answered them, saying, Behold now that you see the trouble of your souls, you wish to return to the Lord; why did you not return during these hundred and twenty years, which the Lord granted you as the determined period?
23 But now you come and tell me this on account of the troubles of your souls, now also the Lord will not listen to you, neither will he give ear to you on this day, so that you will not now succeed in your wishes.
24 The sons of men approached in order to break into the ark, to come in on account of the rain, for they could not bear the rain on them.
25 And the Lord sent all the beasts and animals that stood around the ark. And the beasts overpowered them and drove them from that place, and every man went his way and they again scattered themselves on the face of the earth.
26 The rain was still descending on the earth, and it descended forty days and forty nights, and the waters prevailed greatly on the earth; all flesh that was on the earth or in the waters died, whether men, animals, beasts, creeping things or birds of the air, and there only remained Noah and those that were with him in the ark.

27 The waters prevailed and they greatly increased on the earth, and they lifted up the ark and it was raised from the earth.
28 And the ark floated on the face of the waters; it was tossed on the waters so that all the living creatures within were turned about like pottage in a cauldron.
29 Great anxiety seized all the living creatures that were in the ark, and the ark was like to be broken.
30 And all the living creatures that were in the ark were terrified: the lions roared, and the oxen lowed, and the wolves howled, and every living creature in the ark spoke and lamented in its own language, so that their voices reached to a great distance, and Noah and his sons cried and wept in their troubles; they were greatly afraid that they had reached the gates of death.
31 And Noah prayed to the Lord, and cried to him on account of this, and he said, O Lord help us, for we have no strength to bear this evil that has encompassed us, for the waves of the waters have surrounded us, mischievous torrents have terrified us, the snares of death have come before us; answer us, O Lord, answer us, light up your countenance toward us and be gracious to us, redeem us and deliver us.
32 The Lord listened to the voice of Noah, and the Lord remembered him.
33 And a wind passed over the earth; the waters were still and the ark rested.
34 The fountains of the deep and the windows of heaven were stopped, and the rain from heaven was restrained.
35 And the waters decreased in those days, and the ark rested on the mountains of Ararat.
36 Noah then opened the windows of the ark, and Noah still called out to the Lord at that time and he said, O Lord, who did form the earth and the heavens and all that are therein, bring forth our souls from this confinement, and from the prison wherein you have placed us, for I am much wearied with sighing.
37 And the Lord listened to the voice of Noah, and said to him, When you have completed a full year you shall then go forth.
38 And at the revolution of the year, when a full year was completed to Noah's dwelling in the ark, the waters were dried from off the earth, and Noah put off the covering of the ark.
39 At that time, on the twenty-seventh day of the second month, the earth was dry, but Noah and his sons and those that were with him did not go out from the ark until the Lord told them.
40 And the day came that the Lord told them to go out, and they all went out from the ark.
41 They went and returned every one to his way and to his place, and Noah and his sons lived in the land that God had told them; they served the Lord all their days, and the Lord blessed Noah and his sons on their going out from the ark.
42 And he said to them, Be prolific and fill all the earth; become strong and increase abundantly in the earth and reproduce therein.

CHAPTER 7

1 And these are the names of the sons of Noah: Japheth, Ham and Shem; and children were born to them after the flood, for they had taken wives before the flood.
2 These are the sons of Japheth: Gomer, Magog, Madai, Javan, Tubal, Meshech, and Tiras, seven sons.

3 And the sons of Gomer were Askinaz, Rephath and Tegarmah.
4 And the sons of Magog were Elichanaf and Lubal.
5 And the children of Madai were Achon, Zeelo, Chazoni and Lot.
6 And the sons of Javan were Elisha, Tarshish, Chittim and Dudonim.
7 And the sons of Tubal were Ariphi, Kesed and Taari.
8 And the sons of Meshech were Dedon, Zaron and Shebashni.
9 And the sons of Tiras were Benib, Gera, Lupirion and Gilak; these are the sons of Japheth according to their families, and their numbers in those days were about four hundred and sixty men.
10 And these are the sons of Ham: Cush, Mitzraim, Phut and Canaan, four sons; and the sons of Cush were Seba, Havilah, Sabta, Raama and Satecha, and the sons of Raama were Sheba and Dedan.
11 And the sons of Mitzraim were Lud, Anom and Pathros, Chasloth and Chaphtor.
12 And the sons of Phut were Gebul, Hadan, Benah and Adan.
13 And the sons of Canaan were Zidon, Heth, Amori, Gergashi, Hivi, Arkee, Seni, Arodi, Zimodi and Chamothi.
14 These are the sons of Ham, according to their families, and their numbers in those days were about seven hundred and thirty men.
15 And these are the sons of Shem: Elam, Ashur, Arpachshad, Lud and Aram, five sons; and the sons of Elam were Shushan, Machul and Harmon.
16 And the sons of Ashar were Mirus and Mokil, and the sons of Arpachshad were Shelach, Anar and Ashcol.
17 And the sons of Lud were Pethor and Bizayon, and the sons of Aram were Uz, Chul, Gather and Mash.
18 These are the sons of Shem, according to their families; and their numbers in those days were about three hundred men.
19 These are the generations of Shem: Shem had Arpachshad and Arpachshad had Shelach, and Shelach had Eber and to Eber were born two children, the name of one was Peleg, for in his days the sons of men were divided, and in the latter days the earth was divided.
20 And the name of the second was Yoktan, meaning that in his day the lives of the sons of men were diminished and lessened.
21 These are the sons of Yoktan: Almodad, Shelaf, Chazarmoveth, Yerach, Hadurom, Ozel, Diklah, Obal, Abimael, Sheba, Ophir, Havilah and Jobab; all these are the sons of Yoktan.
22 And Peleg his brother had Yen, and Yen had Serug, and Serug had Nahor and Nahor had Terah, and Terah was thirty-eight years old, and he had Haran and Nahor.
23 And Cush the son of Ham, the son of Noah, took a wife in those days in his old age, and she gave birth to a son, and they called his name Nimrod, saying, At that time the sons of men again began to rebel and go contrary to God; the child grew up, and his father loved him greatly, for he was the son of his old age.
24 The garments of skin which God made for Adam and his wife, when they went out of the garden, were given to Cush.
25 For after the death of Adam and his wife, the garments were given to Enoch, the son of Jared, and when Enoch was taken up to God, he gave them to Methuselah, his son.
26 At the death of Methuselah, Noah took them and brought them to the ark, and they were with him until he went out of the ark.

27 And in their going out, Ham stole those garments from Noah his father; he took them and hid them from his brothers.
28 When Ham had his first born Cush, he gave him the garments in secret, and they were with Cush many days.
29 Cush also concealed them from his sons and brothers, and when Cush had begotten Nimrod, he gave him those garments through his love for him, and Nimrod grew up, and when he was twenty years old he put on those garments.
30 Nimrod became strong when he put on the garments, and God gave him might and strength, and he was a mighty hunter in the earth. He was a mighty hunter in the field, and he hunted the animals and he built altars, and he offered on them the animals before the Lord.
31 Nimrod strengthened himself, and he rose up from among his brothers, and he fought the battles of his brothers against all their enemies round about.
32 The Lord delivered all the enemies of his brothers in his hands, and God prospered him from time to time in his battles, and he reigned on earth.
33 Therefore it became current in those days, when a man ushered forth those that he had trained up for battle, he would say to them, like God did to Nimrod who was a mighty hunter in the earth and who succeeded in the battles that prevailed against his brothers, that he delivered them from the hands of their enemies: so may God strengthen us and deliver us this day.
34 And when Nimrod was forty years old, there was a war between his brothers and the children of Japheth, so that they were in the power of their enemies.
35 Nimrod went forth at that time, and he assembled all the sons of Cush and their families, about four hundred and sixty men; he hired also from some of his friends and acquaintances about eighty men, and he gave them their hire; he went with them to battle, and when he was on the road, Nimrod strengthened the hearts of the people that went with him.
36 And he said to them, Do not fear, neither be alarmed, for all our enemies will be delivered into our hands, and you may do with them as you please.
37 All the men that went were about five hundred, and they fought against their enemies; they destroyed them, and subdued them, and Nimrod placed standing officers over them in their respective places.
38 He took some of their children as security, and they were all servants to Nimrod and to his brothers, and Nimrod and all the people that were with him turned homeward.
39 When Nimrod had joyfully returned from battle, after having conquered his enemies, all his brothers, together with those who knew him before, assembled to make him king over them and they placed the regal crown on his head.
40 He set over his subjects and people, princes, judges, and rulers, as is the custom among kings.
41 He placed Terah the son of Nahor the prince of his host, and he dignified him and elevated him above all his princes.
42 And while he was reigning according to his heart's desire, after having conquered all his enemies around, he advised with his counselors to build a city for his palace, and they did so.
43 They found a large valley opposite to the east, and they built him a large and extensive city, and Nimrod called the name of the city that he built Shinar, for the Lord had vehemently shaken his enemies and destroyed them.
44 Nimrod lived in Shinar, and he reigned securely, and he fought with his enemies

and he subdued them; he prospered in all his battles, and his kingdom became very great.
45 All nations and tongues heard of his fame, and they gathered themselves to him, and they bowed down to the earth; they brought him offerings, and he became their lord and king, and they all lived with him in the city at Shinar; Nimrod reigned in the earth over all the sons of Noah, and they were all under his power and counsel.
46 And all the earth was of one tongue and words of union, but Nimrod did not go in the ways of the Lord; he was more wicked than all the men that were before him, from the days of the flood until those days.
47 He made gods of wood and stone, he bowed down to them, he rebelled against the Lord, and taught all his subjects and the people of the earth his wicked ways; Mardon his son was more wicked than his father.
48 And every one that heard of the acts of Mardon the son of Nimrod would say, concerning him, From the wicked goes forth wickedness. Therefore it became a proverb in the whole earth, saying, From the wicked goes forth wickedness, and it was current in the words of men from that time to this.
49 Terah the son of Nahor, prince of Nimrod's host, was in those days very great in the sight of the king and his subjects, and the king and princes loved him, and they elevated him very high.
50 And Terah took a wife and her name was Amthelo the daughter of Cornebo; the wife of Terah conceived and gave birth to a son in those days.
51 Terah was seventy years old when he had him, and Terah called the name of his son Abram, because the king had raised him in those days, and dignified him above all his princes that were with him.

CHAPTER 8

1 It was in the night that Abram was born, that all the servants of Terah, and all the wise men of Nimrod and his conjurors came and ate and drank in the house of Terah, and they rejoiced with him on that night.
2 When all the wise men and conjurors went out from the house of Terah, they lifted up their eyes toward heaven that night to look at the stars; they saw, and behold, one very large star came from the east and ran in the heavens; he swallowed up the four stars from the four sides of the heavens.
3 And all the wise men of the king and his conjurors were astonished at the sight, and the sages understood this matter, and they knew its import.
4 They said to each other, This only betokens the child that has been born to Terah this night, who will grow up and be prolific, and reproduce, and possess all the earth, he and his children for ever, and he and his descendants will kill great kings, and inherit their lands.
5 The wise men and conjurors went home that night; in the morning all these wise men and conjurors rose up early, and assembled in an appointed house.
6 And they spoke and said to each other, Behold the sight that we saw last night is hidden from the king; it has not been made known to him.
7 And should this thing get known to the king in the latter days, he will say to us, Why have you concealed this matter from me, and then we shall all suffer death; therefore, now let us go and tell the king the sight which we saw, and the interpretation thereof, and we shall then remain clear.

8 And they did so; they all went to the king and bowed down to him to the ground,
and they said, May the king live, may the king live.
9 We heard that a son was born to Terah the son of Nahor, the prince of your host,
and we last night came to his house, and we ate and drank and rejoiced with him
that night.
10 And when your servants went out from the house of Terah, to go to our
respective homes to abide there for the night, we lifted up our eyes to heaven and
we saw a great star coming from the east, and the same star ran with great speed
and swallowed up four great stars, from the four sides of the heavens.
11 And your servants were astonished at the sight which we saw, and were greatly
terrified; we made our judgment on the sight and knew by our wisdom the proper
interpretation thereof, that this thing applies to the child that is born to Terah, who
will grow up and reproduce greatly, and become powerful and kill all the kings of
the earth, and inherit all their lands, he and his offspring forever.
12 Now our lord and king, behold we have truly acquainted you with what we have
seen concerning this child.
13 If it seems good to the king to give his father value for this child, we will kill him
before he shall grow up and increase in the land, and his evil increase against us,
that we and our children perish through his evil.
14 And the king heard their words and they seemed good in his sight, and he sent
and called for Terah, and Terah came before the king.
15 And the king said to Terah, I have been told that a son was last night born to you,
and after this manner was observed in the heavens at his birth.
16 And now therefore give me the child, that we may kill him before his evil springs
up against us, and I will give you for his value, your house full of silver and gold.
17Terah answered the king and said to him: My Lord and king, I have heard your
words, and your servant shall do all that his king desires.
18 But my lord and king, I will tell you what happened to me last night, that I may
see what advice the king will give his servant, and then I will answer the king on
what he has just spoken. The king said, Speak.
19 And Terah said to the king, Ayon, son of Mored, came to me last night, saying,
20 Give to me the great and beautiful horse that the king gave you, and I will give
you silver and gold, and straw and provender for its value; and I said to him, Wait
till I see the king concerning your words, and behold whatever the king says, that
will I do.
21 And now my lord and king, behold I have made this thing known to you, and the
advice which my king will give to his servant, that will I follow.
22 The king heard the words of Terah, and his anger was set ablaze and he
considered him in the light of a fool.
23 And the king answered Terah and said to him, Are you so silly, ignorant, or
deficient in understanding to do this thing, to give your beautiful horse for silver
and gold or even for straw and provender?
24 Are you so short of silver and gold that you should do this thing, because you
cannot obtain straw and provender to feed your horse? And what is silver and gold
to you, or straw and provender, that you should give away that fine horse which I
gave you, like which there is none to be had on the whole earth?
25 The king left off speaking, and Terah answered the king, saying, Like to this has
the king spoken to his servant;
26 I beseech you, my lord and king, what is this which you did say to me, Give your

son that we may kill him, and I will give you silver and gold for his value; what shall I do with silver and gold after the death of my son? Who shall inherit me? Certainly then at my death, the silver and gold will return to my king who gave it.
27 And when the king heard the words of Terah, and the parable which he brought concerning the king, it grieved him greatly and he was troubled at this thing, and his anger burned within him.
28 And Terah saw that the anger of the king was set ablaze against him, and he answered the king, saying, All that I have is in the king's power; whatever the king desires to do to his servant, that let him do, yea, even my son, he is in the king's power, without value in exchange, he and his two brothers that are older than he.
29 And the king said to Terah, No, but I will purchase your younger son for a price.
30 Terah answered the king, saying, I beseech you my lord and king to let your servant speak a word before you, and let the king hear the word of his servant, and Terah said, Let my king give me three days' time till I consider this matter within myself, and consult with my family concerning the words of my king; and he pressed the king greatly to agree to this.
31 The king listened to Terah, and he did so and he gave him three days' time. Terah went out from the king's presence, and he came home to his family and spoke to them all the words of the king; and the people were greatly afraid.
32 And it was in the third day that the king sent to Terah, saying, Send me your son for a price as I spoke to you; and should you not do this, I will send and kill all you have in your house, so that you shall not even have a dog remaining.
33 And Terah hurried (as the thing was urgent from the king), and he took a child from one of his servants, which his handmaid had born to him that day, and Terah brought the child to the king and received value for him.
34 And the Lord was with Terah in this matter, that Nimrod might not cause Abram's death. The king took the child from Terah and with all his might dashed his head to the ground, for he thought it had been Abram; this was concealed from him from that day, and it was forgotten by the king, as it was the will of Providence not to suffer Abram's death.
35 And Terah took Abram his son secretly, together with his mother and nurse, and he concealed them in a cave, and he brought them their provisions monthly.
36 The Lord was with Abram in the cave and he grew up, and Abram was in the cave ten years, and the king and his princes, soothsayers and sages, thought that the king had killed Abram.

CHAPTER 9

1 And Haran, the son of Terah, Abram's oldest brother, took a wife in those days.
2 Haran was thirty-nine years old when he took her; and the wife of Haran conceived and gave birth to a son, and he called his name Lot.
3 She conceived again and gave birth to a daughter, and called her name Milca; and she again conceived and gave birth to a daughter and called her name Sarai.
4 Haran was forty-two years old when he had Sarai, which was in the tenth year of the life of Abram; and in those days Abram and his mother and nurse went out from the cave, as the king and his subjects had forgotten the affair of Abram.
5 When Abram came out from the cave, he went to Noah and his son Shem, and he remained with them to learn the instruction of the Lord and his ways; no man knew

where Abram was, and Abram served Noah and Shem his son for a long time.
6 Abram was in Noah's house thirty-nine years, and Abram knew the Lord from three years old; he went in the ways of the Lord until the day of his death, as Noah and his son Shem had taught him, and all the sons of the earth in those days greatly went contrary to the Lord, and they rebelled against him and they served other gods. They forgot the Lord who had created them in the earth; and the inhabitants of the earth made to themselves, at that time, every man his god; gods of wood and stone which could neither speak, hear, nor deliver, and the sons of men served them and they became their gods.
7 The king and all his servants, and Terah with all his household were then the first of those that served gods of wood and stone.
8 And Terah had twelve gods of large size, made of wood and stone, after the twelve months of the year, and he served each one monthly, and every month Terah would bring his meat offering and drink offering to his gods; thus did Terah all the days.
9 All that generation were wicked in the sight of the Lord, and they thus made every man his god, but they turned away from the Lord who had created them.
10 And there was not a man found in those days in the whole earth who knew the Lord (for they served each man his own god) except Noah and his household; and all those who were under his counsel knew the Lord in those days.
11 Abram the son of Terah was becoming great in those days in the house of Noah, and no man knew it, and the Lord was with him.
12 The Lord gave Abram an understanding heart, and he knew all the works of that generation were vain, and that all their gods were vain and were of no avail.
13 And Abram saw the sun shining on the earth, and Abram said to himself, Certainly now this sun that shines on the earth is God, and him will I serve.
14 And Abram served the sun in that day and he prayed to him, and when evening came the sun set as usual, and Abram said within himself, Certainly this cannot be God?
15 And Abram still continued to speak within himself, Who is he who made the heavens and the earth? Who created on earth? Where is he?
16 And night darkened over him; he lifted up his eyes toward the west, north, south, and east, and he saw that the sun had vanished from the earth, and the day became dark.
17 And Abram saw the stars and moon before him, and he said, Certainly this is the God who created the whole earth as well as man, and behold these his servants are gods around him: and Abram served the moon and prayed to it all that night.
18 And in the morning when it was light and the sun shone on the earth as usual, Abram saw all the things that the Lord God had made on earth.
19 And Abram said to himself, Certainly these are not gods that made the earth and all mankind, but these are the servants of God. And Abram remained in the house of Noah and there knew the Lord and his ways. He served the Lord all the days of his life, and all that generation forgot the Lord, and served other gods of wood and stone, and rebelled all their days.
20 And king Nimrod reigned securely, and all the earth was under his control, and all the earth was of one tongue and words of union.
21 And all the princes of Nimrod and his great men took counsel together: Phut, Mitzraim, Cush and Canaan with their families, and they said to each other, Come let us build ourselves a city and in it a strong tower and its top reaching heaven, and we will make ourselves famed so that we may reign on the whole world, in order

that the evil of our enemies may cease from us; that we may reign mightily over them, and that we may not become scattered over the earth on account of their wars.
22 They all went before the king, and they told the king these words, and the king agreed with them in this affair, and he did so.
23 All the families assembled consisting of about six hundred thousand men, and they went to seek an extensive piece of ground to build the city and the tower, and they sought in the whole earth and they found none like one valley at the east of the land of Shinar, about two days' walk, and they journeyed there and they lived there.
24 And they began to make bricks and burn fires to build the city and the tower that they had imagined to complete.
25 And the building of the tower was to them a transgression and a sin, and they began to build it While they were building against the Lord God of heaven, they imagined in their hearts to war against him and to ascend into heaven.
26 And all these people and all the families divided themselves in three parts; the first said, We will ascend into heaven and fight against him; the second said, We will ascend to heaven and place our own gods there and serve them; and the third part said, We will ascend to heaven and strike him with bows and spears. And God knew all their works and all their evil thoughts, and he saw the city and the tower which they were building.
27 They built themselves a great city and a very high and strong tower; on account of its height, the mortar and bricks did not reach the builders in their ascent to it until those who went up had completed a full year, and after that, they reached the builders and gave them the mortar and the bricks; thus was it done daily.
28 And behold these ascended and others descended the whole day; and if a brick should fall from their hands and get broken, they would all weep over it; if a man fell and died, none of them would look at him.
29 The Lord knew their thoughts, and it came to pass when they were building they cast the arrows toward the heavens, and all the arrows fell on them filled with blood; when they saw them they said to each other, Certainly we have slain all those that are in heaven.
30 For this was from the Lord in order to cause them to err, and in order to destroy them from off the face of the ground.
31 They built the tower and the city, and they did this thing daily until many days and years were elapsed.
32 And God said to the seventy angels who stood foremost before him, to those who were near to him, saying, Come let us descend and confuse their tongues, that one man shall not understand the language of his neighbor, and they did so to them.
33 From that day following, they forgot each man his neighbor's tongue, and they could not understand to speak in one tongue; when the builder took from the hands of his neighbor lime or stone which he did not order, the builder would cast it away and throw it on his neighbor, that he would die.
34 And they did so many days, and they killed many of them in this manner.
35 The Lord struck the three divisions that were there, and he punished them according to their works and designs; those who said, We will ascend to heaven and serve our gods, became like apes and elephants; those who said, We will strike the heaven with arrows, the Lord killed them, one man through the hand of his neighbor; and the third division of those who said, We will ascend to heaven and fight against him, the Lord scattered them throughout the earth.
36 Those who were left among them, when they knew and understood the evil

which was coming on them, turned away from the building, and they also became scattered on the face of the whole earth.
37 And they ceased building the city and the tower; therefore he called that place Babel, for there the Lord confounded the Language of the whole earth; behold it was at the east of the land of Shinar.
38 As to the tower which the sons of men built, the earth opened its mouth and swallowed up one third part thereof, and a fire also descended from heaven and burned another third, and the other third is left to this day; it is of that part which was aloft, and its circumference is three days' walk.
39 Many of the sons of men died in that tower, a people without number.

CHAPTER 10

1 Peleg the son of Eber died in those days, in the forty-eighth year of the life of Abram son of Terah, and all the days of Peleg were two hundred and thirty-nine years.
2 When the Lord had scattered the sons of men on account of their sin at the tower, behold they spread forth into many divisions, and all the sons of men were dispersed into the four corners of the earth.
3 And all the families became each according to its language, its land, or its city.
4 And the sons of men built many cities according to their families, in all the places where they went, and throughout the earth where the Lord had scattered them.
5 Some of them built cities in places from which they later abandoned, and they called these cities after their own names, or the names of their children, or after their particular occurrences.
6 The sons of Japheth, the son of Noah went and built themselves cities in the places where they were scattered; they called all their cities after their names, and the sons of Japheth were divided on the face of the earth into many divisions and languages.
7 And these are the sons of Japheth according to their families: Gomer, Magog, Medai, Javan, Tubal, Meshech and Tiras; these are the children of Japheth according to their generations.
8 Tthe children of Gomer, according to their cities, were the Francum, who dwell in the land of Franza, by the river Franza, by the river Senah.
9 And the children of Rephath are the Bartonim, who dwell in the land of Bartonia by the river Ledah, which empties its waters in the great sea Gihon, that is, Oceanus.
10 The children of Tugarma are ten families, and these are their names: Buzar, Parzunac, Balgar, Elicanum, Ragbib, Tarki, Bid, Zebuc, Ongal and Tilmaz; all these spread and rested in the north and built themselves cities.
11 And they called their cities after their own names; those are they who abide by the rivers Hithlah and Italac to this day.
12 But the families of Angoli, Balgar and Parzunac, they dwelll by the great river Dubnee; and the names of their cities are also according to their own names.
13 The children of Javan are the Javanim who dwell in the land of Makdonia, and the children of Medaiare are the Orelum that dwell in the land of Curson, and the children of Tubal are those that dwell in the land of Tuskanah by the river Pashiah.
14 The children of Meshech are the Shibashni and the children of Tiras are Rushash, Cushni, and Ongolis; all these went and built themselves cities; those are the cities that are situated by the sea Jabus by the river Cura, which empties itself into the river Tragan.

15 And the children of Elishah are the Almanim, and they also went and built themselves cities; those are the cities situated between the mountains of Job and Shibathmo; and of them were the people of Lumbardi who dwell opposite the mountains of Job and Shibathmo, and they conquered the land of Italia and remained there to this day.
16 The children of Chittim are the Romim who dwell in the valley of Canopia by the river Tibreu.
17 The children of Dudonim are those who dwell in the cities of the sea Gihon, in the land of Bordna.
18 These are the families of the children of Japheth according to their cities and languages when they were scattered after the tower; they called their cities after their names and occurrences; and these are the names of all their cities according to their families which they built in those days after the tower.
19 And the children of Ham were Cush, Mitzraim, Phut and Canaan according to their generation and cities.
20 All these went and built themselves cities as they found fit places for them, and they called their cities after the names of their fathers Cush, Mitzraim, Phut and Canaan.
21 The children of Mitzraim are the Ludim, Anamim, Lehabim, Naphtuchim, Pathrusim, Casluchim and Caphturim, seven families.
22 All these dwell by the river Sihor, that is the brook of Egypt, and they built themselves cities and called them after their own names.
23 The children of Pathros and Casloch intermarried together, and from them went forth the Pelishtim, the Azathim, and the Gerarim, the Githim and the Ekronim, in all five families; these also built themselves cities, and they called their cities after the names of their fathers to this day.
24 The children of Canaan also built themselves cities, and they called their cities after their names, eleven cities and others without number.
25 Four men from the family of Ham went to the land of the plain; these are the names of the four men: Sodom, Gomorrah, Admah and Zeboyim.
26 And these men built themselves four cities in the land of the plain, and they called the names of their cities after their own names.
27 They and their children and all belonging to them lived in those cities, and they were prolific and multiplied greatly and lived peaceably.
28 Seir the son of Hur, son of Hivi, son of Canaan, went and found a valley opposite to Mount Paran, and he built a city there; he and his seven sons and his household lived there, and he called the city which he built Seir, according to his name; that is the land of Seir to this day.
29 These are the families of the children of Ham, according to their languages and cities, when they were scattered to their countries after the tower.
30 Some of the children of Shem, son of Noah, father of all the children of Eber, also went and built themselves cities in the places wherein they were scattered, and they called their cities after their names.
31 The sons of Shem were Elam, Ashur, Arpachshad, Lud and Aram, and they built themselves cities and called the names of all their cities after their names.
32 Ashur, son of Shem, and his children and household went forth at that time, a very large body of them, and they went to a distant land that they found; they met with a very extensive valley in the land that they went to, and they built themselves four cities, and they called them after their own names and occurrences.

33 And these are the names of the cities which the children of Ashur built: Ninevah,
Resen, Calach and Rehobother; the children of Ashur dwell there to this day.
34 The children of Aram also went and built themselves a city, and they called the
name of the city Uz after their eldest brother; they dwell therein. That is the land of
Uz to this day.
35 And in the second year after the tower a man from the house of Ashur, whose
name was Bela, went from the land of Ninevah to sojourn with his household
wherever he could find a place; they came until opposite the cities of the plain
against Sodom, and they lived there.
36 And the man rose up and built there a small city, and called its name Bela, after
his name; that is the land of Zoar to this day.
37 These are the families of the children of Shem according to their language and
cities, after they were scattered on the earth after the tower.
38 And every kingdom, city, and family of the families of the children of Noah built
themselves many cities after this.
39 And they established governments in all their cities in order to be regulated by
their orders; so did all the families of the children of Noah forever.

CHAPTER 11

1 Nimrod son of Cush was still in the land of Shinar, and he reigned over it and
lived there, and he built cities in the land of Shinar.
2 These are the names of the four cities which he built, and he called their names
after the occurrences that happened to them in the building of the tower:
3 He called the first Babel, saying, Because the Lord there confounded the language
of the whole earth. The name of the second he called Erech, because from there God
dispersed them.
4 And the third he called Eched, saying there was a great battle at that place; the
fourth he called Calnah, because his princes and mighty men were consumed there,
and they troubled the Lord; they rebelled and went contrary to him.
5 When Nimrod had built these cities in the land of Shinar, he placed in them the
remainder of his people, his princes and his mighty men that were left in his
kingdom.
6 Nimrod lived in Babel, and there he renewed his reign over the rest of his subjects,
and he reigned securely, and the subjects and princes of Nimrod called his name
Amraphel, saying that at the tower his princes and men fell through his means.
7 Notwithstanding this, Nimrod did not return to the Lord, and he continued in
wickedness and teaching wickedness to the sons of men; and Mardon, his son, was
worse than his father and continued to add to the abominations of his father.
8 And he caused the sons of men to sin; therefore it is said, From the wicked goes
forth wickedness.
9 At that time there was war between the families of the children of Ham, as they
were dwelling in the cities which they had built.
10 And Chedorlaomer, king of Elam, went away from the families of the children of
Ham; he fought with them and he subdued them, and he went to the five cities of
the plain; he fought against them and he subdued them, and they were under his
control.
11 And they served him twelve years and gave him a yearly tax.

12 At that time Nahor, son of Serug died, in the forty-ninth year of the life of Abram, son of Terah.
13 In the fiftieth year of the life of Abram, son of Terah, Abram came forth from the house of Noah, and went to his father's house.
14 And Abram knew the Lord, and he followed in his ways and instructions, and the Lord his God was with him.
15Terah his father was in those days still captain of the host of king Nimrod, and he still followed strange gods.
16 And Abram came to his father's house and saw twelve gods standing there in their temples, and the anger of Abram was set ablaze when he saw these images in his father's house.
17 And Abram said, As the Lord lives these images shall not remain in my father's house; so shall the Lord who created me do to me if in three days' time I do not break them all.
18 Abram went from them, and his anger burned within him. And Abram hurried and went from the chamber to his father's outer court, and he found his father sitting in the court, and all his servants with him, and Abram came and sat before him.
19 Abram asked his father, saying, Father, tell me where is God who created heaven and earth, and all the sons of men on earth, and who created you and me. And Terah answered his son Abram and said, Behold those who created us are all with us in the house.
20 And Abram said to his father, My lord, show them to me I pray you. And Terah brought Abram into the chamber of the inner court, and Abram saw, and behold the whole room was full of gods of wood and stone, twelve great images and others less than they without number.
21 And Terah said to his son, Behold these are they which made all you see on earth, and which created me and you, and all mankind.
22 Terah bowed down to his gods, and he then went away from them, and Abram, his son, went away with him.
23 When Abram had gone from them he went to his mother and sat before her, and he said to his mother, Behold, my father has shown me those who made heaven and earth, and all the sons of men.
24 Now, therefore, hurry and fetch a kid from the flock, and make of it savory meat, that I may bring it to my father's gods as an offering for them to eat; perhaps I may thereby become acceptable to them.
25 And his mother did so; she fetched a kid, and made savory meat thereof, and brought it to Abram, and Abram took the savory meat from his mother and brought it before his father's gods, and he drew nigh to them that they might eat; and Terah his father, did not know of it.
26 Abram saw on the day when he was sitting among them, that they had no voice, no hearing, no motion, and not one of them could stretch forth his hand to eat.
27 And Abram mocked them, and said, Certainly the savory meat that I prepared has not pleased them, or perhaps it was too little for them, and for that reason they would not eat; therefore tomorrow I will prepare fresh savory meat, better and more plentiful than this, in order that I may see the result.
28 It was on the next day that Abram directed his mother concerning the savory meat, and his mother rose and fetched three fine kids from the flock; she made of them some excellent savory meat, such as her son was fond of, and she gave it to her son Abram, and Terah his father did not know of it.

29 Abram took the savory meat from his mother and brought it before his father's gods into the chamber; he came nigh to them that they might eat, and he placed it before them, and Abram sat before them all day thinking perhaps they might eat.
30 Abram viewed them, and behold they had neither voice nor hearing, nor did one of them stretch forth his hand to the meat to eat.
31 And in the evening of that day in that house Abram was clothed with the spirit of God.
32 He called out and said, Woe to my father and this wicked generation, whose hearts are all inclined to vanity, who serve these idols of wood and stone which can neither eat, smell, hear nor speak, who have mouths without speech, eyes without sight, ears without hearing, hands without feeling, and legs which cannot move; like them are those that made them and that trust in them.
33 When Abram saw all these things his anger was set ablaze against his father, and he hurried and took a hatchet in his hand, and came to the chamber of the gods; he broke all his father's gods.
34 And when he was done breaking the images, he placed the hatchet in the hand of the great god which was there before them, and he went out; and Terah his father came home, for he had heard at the door the sound of the striking of the hatchet; so Terah came into the house to know what this was about.
35 Terah, having heard the noise of the hatchet in the room of images, ran to the room to the images, and he met Abram going out.
36 And Terah entered the room and found all the idols fallen down and broken, and the hatchet in the hand of the largest, which was not broken, and the savory meat which Abram his son had made was still before them.
37 When Terah saw this his anger was greatly set ablaze, and he hurried and went from the room to Abram.
38 And he found Abram his son still sitting in the house; and he said to him, What is this work you have done to my gods?
39 Abram answered Terah his father and he said, Not so my lord, for I brought savory meat before them, and when I came near to them with the meat that they might eat, they all at once stretched forth their hands to eat before the great one had put forth his hand to eat.
40 And the large one saw their works that they did before him, and his anger was violently set ablaze against them, and he went and took the hatchet that was in the house and came to them and broke them all, and behold the hatchet is yet in his hand as you see.
41 And Terah's anger was set ablaze against his son Abram, when he spoke this; and Terah said to Abram his son in his anger, What is this tale that you have told? You speak lies to me.
42 Is there in these gods spirit, soul or power to do all you have told me? Are they not wood and stone, and have I not myself made them, and can you speak such lies, saying that the large god that was with them struck them? It is you that did place the hatchet in his hands, and then said he struck them all.
43 Abram answered his father and said to him, And how can you then serve these idols in whom there is no power to do any thing? Can those idols in which you trust deliver you? Can they hear your prayers when you call on them? Can they deliver you from the hands of your enemies, or will they fight your battles for you against your enemies, that you should serve wood and stone which can neither speak nor hear?

44 And now certainly it is not good for you nor for the sons of men that are connected with you, to do these things; are you so silly, so foolish or so short of understanding that you will serve wood and stone, and do after this manner?
45 And forget the Lord God who made heaven and earth, and who created you in the earth, and thereby bring a great evil on your souls in this matter by serving stone and wood?
46 Did not our fathers in days of old sin in this manner, and the Lord God of the universe brought the waters of the flood on them and destroyed the whole earth?
47 And how can you continue to do this and serve gods of wood and stone, who cannot hear, or speak, or deliver you from oppression, thereby bringing down the anger of the God of the universe on you?
48 Now therefore my father refrain from this, and bring not evil on your soul and the souls of your household.
49 And Abram hurried and sprang from before his father, and took the hatchet from his father's largest idol, with which Abram broke it and ran away.
50 Terah, seeing all that Abram had done, hurried to go from his house; he went to the king and he came before Nimrod and stood before him, and he bowed down to the king and the king said, What do you want?
51 And he said, I beseech you my lord, to hear me--Now fifty years back a child was born to me, and thus has he done to my gods and thus has he spoken; and now therefore, my lord and king, send for him that he may come before you, and judge him according to the law, that we may be delivered from his evil.
52 The king sent three men of his servants, and they went and brought Abram before the king. And Nimrod and all his princes and servants were that day sitting before him, and Terah also sat before them.
53 And the king said to Abram, What is this that you have done to your father and to his gods? And Abram answered the king in the words that he spoke to his father, and he said, The large god that was with them in the house did to them what you have heard.
54 And the king said to Abram, Had they power to speak and eat and do as you have said? And Abram answered the king, saying, And if there be no power in them why do you serve them and cause the sons of men to err through your follies?
55 Do you imagine that they can deliver you or do anything small or great, that you should serve them? And why will you not sense the God of the whole universe, who created you and in whose power it is to kill and keep alive?
56 0 foolish, simple, and ignorant king, woe to you forever.
57 I thought you would teach your servants the upright way, but you have not done this; you have filled the whole earth with your sins and the sins of your people who have followed your ways.
58 Do you not know, or have you not heard, that this evil which you do, our ancestors sinned therein in days of old, and the eternal God brought the waters of the flood on them and destroyed them all, and also destroyed the whole earth on their account? And will you and your people rise up now and do like this work, in order to bring down the anger of the Lord God of the universe, and to bring evil on you and the whole earth?
59 Now therefore put away this evil deed which you did, and serve the God of the universe, as your soul is in his hands, and then it will be well with you.
60 And if your wicked heart will not listen to my words to cause you to turn away from your evil ways, and to serve the eternal God, then you will die in shame in the

latter days, you, your people and all who are connected with you, hearing your words or walking in your evil ways.
61 When Abram had ceased speaking before the king and princes, Abram lifted up his eyes to the heavens, and he said, The Lord sees all the wicked, and he will judge them.

CHAPTER 12

1 When the king heard the words of Abram he ordered him to be put into prison; and Abram was ten days in prison.
2 At the end of those days the king ordered that all the kings, princes and governors of different provinces and the sages should come before him, and they sat before him, and Abram was still in the house of confinement.
3 The king said to the princes and sages, Have you heard what Abram, the son of Terah, has done to his father? Thus has he done to him, and I ordered him to be brought before me, and thus has he spoken; his heart did not misgive him, neither did he stir in my presence, and behold now he is confined in the prison.
4 Therefore decide what judgment is due to this man who reviled the king; who spoke and did all the things that you heard.
5 And they all answered the king saying, The man who reviles the king should be hanged on a tree; but having done all the things that he said and having despised our gods, he must therefore be burned to death, for this is the law in this matter.
6 If it pleases the king to do this, let him order his servants to kindle a fire both night and day in your brick furnace, and then we will cast this man into it. And the king did so, and he commanded his servants that they should prepare a fire for three days and three nights in the king's furnace, that is in Casdim; and the king ordered them to take Abram from prison and bring him out to be burned.
7 And all the king's servants, princes, lords, governors, and judges, and all the inhabitants of the land, about nine hundred thousand men, stood opposite the furnace to see Abram.
8 And all the women and little ones crowded on the roofs and towers to see what was going on with Abram, and they all stood together at a distance; and there was not a man left that did not come that day to behold the scene.
9 When Abram was come, the conjurors of the king and the sages saw Abram, and they cried out to the king, saying, Our sovereign lord, certainly this is the man whom we know to have been the child at whose birth the great star swallowed the four stars, which we declared to the king fifty years ago.
10 And behold now his father has also gone contrary to your commands, and mocked you by bringing you another child, which you did kill.
11 And when the king heard their words, he was greatly angered, and he ordered Terah to be brought before him.
12 And the king said, Have you heard what the conjurors have spoken? Now tell me truly, how did you? If you shall speak truth you shall be acquitted.
13 Seeing that the king's anger was so much set ablaze, Terah said to the king, My lord and king, you have heard the truth, and what the sages have spoken is right. And the king said, How could you do this thing, to go contrary to my orders and to give me a child that you did not beget, and to take value for him?
14 Terah answered the king, Because my tender feelings were excited for my son, at

that time, I took a son of my handmaid, and I brought him to the king.
15 And the king said, Who advised you to do this? Tell me, do not hide anything from me, and then you shall not die.
16 And Terah was greatly terrified in the king's presence, and he said to the king, It was Haran my eldest son who advised me to do this. Haran was in those days that Abram was born, two and thirty years old.
17 But Haran did not advise his father to do anything, for Terah said this to the king in order to deliver his soul from the king, for he feared greatly. The king said to Terah, Haran your son who advised you to do this shall die through fire with Abram; for the sentence of death is on him for having rebelled against the king's desire in doing this thing.
18 Haran at that time felt inclined to follow the ways of Abram, but he kept it within himself.
19 And Haran said in his heart, Behold now the king has seized Abram on account of these things which Abram did, and it shall come to pass, that if Abram prevail over the king I will follow him, but if the king prevail I will go after the king.
20 When Terah had spoken this to the king concerning Haran his son, the king ordered Haran to be seized with Abram.
21 And they brought them both, Abram and Haran his brother, to cast them into the fire; and all the inhabitants of the land and the king's servants and princes and all the women and little ones were there standing over them that day.
22 And the king's servants took Abram and his brother, and they stripped them of all their clothes excepting their lower garments which were on them.
23 And they bound their hands and feet with linen cords, and the servants of the king lifted them up and cast them both into the furnace.
24 The Lord loved Abram and he had compassion over him, and the Lord came down and delivered Abram from the fire and he was not burned.
25 But all the cords with which they bound him were burned, while Abram remained and walked about in the fire.
26 Haran died when they had cast him into the fire, and he was burned to ashes, for his heart was not perfect with the Lord; and those men who cast him into the fire, the flame of the fire spread over them, and they were burned, and twelve of them died.
27 Abram walked in the midst of the fire three days and three nights, and all the servants of the king saw him walking in the fire, and they came and told the king, saying, Behold we have seen Abram walking about in the midst of the fire, and even the lower garments which are on him are not burned, but the cord with which he was bound is burned.
28 When the king heard their words his heart fainted and he would not believe them; so he sent other faithful princes to see this matter, and they went and saw it and told it to the king. And the king rose to go and see it, and he saw Abram walking to and fro in the midst of the fire, and he saw Haran's body burned, and the king wondered greatly.
29 The king ordered Abram to be taken out from the fire; and his servants approached to take him out and they could not, for the fire was round about and the flame ascending toward them from the furnace.
30 The king's servants fled from it, and the king rebuked them, saying, Make haste and bring Abram out of the fire that you shall not die.
31 The servants of the king again approached to bring Abram out, and the flames

came on them and burned their faces so that eight of them died.
32 When the king saw that his servants could not approach the fire that would burn them,, the king called to Abram, O servant of the God who is in heaven, go forth from amidst the fire and come here before me. And Abram listened to the voice of the king, and he went forth from the fire and came and stood before the king.
33 When Abram came out, the king and all his servants saw Abram coming before the king with his lower garments on him that were not burned, but the cord with which he was bound was burned.
34 And the king said to Abram, How is it that you were not burned in the fire?
35 Abram said to the king, The God of heaven and earth in whom I trust and who has all in his power, he delivered me from the fire into which you did cast me.
36 Haran the brother of Abram was burned to ashes, and they sought for his body; they found it consumed.
37 Haran was eighty-two years old when he died in the fire of Casdim. And the king, princes, and inhabitants of the land, seeing that Abram was delivered from the fire, came and bowed down to Abram.
38 And Abram said to them, Do not bow down to me, but bow down to the God of the world who made you, and serve him, and go in his ways for it is he who delivered me from out of this fire; it is he who created the souls and spirits of all men, and formed man in his mother's womb, and brought him forth into the world; it is he who will deliver those who trust in him from all pain.
39 This thing seemed very wonderful in the eyes of the king and princes, that Abram was saved from the fire and that Haran was burned. And the king gave Abram many presents and he gave him his two head servants from the king's house; the name of one was Oni and the name of the other was Eliezer.
40 All the kings, princes and servants gave Abram many gifts of silver and gold and pearl, and the king and his princes sent him away, and he went in peace.
41 Abram went forth from the king in peace, and many of the king's servants followed him, and about three hundred men joined him.
42 And Abram returned on that day and went to his father's house, he and the men that followed him, and Abram served the Lord his God all the days of his life; he walked in his ways and followed his law.
43 From that day forward Abram inclined the hearts of the sons of men to serve the Lord.
44 At that time Nahor and Abram took to themselves wives, the daughters of their brother Haran; the wife of Nahor was Milca and the name of Abram's wife was Sarai. And Sarai, wife of Abram, was unable to conceive; she had no children in those days.
45 At the expiration of two years from Abram's going out of the fire, that is in the fifty-second year of his life, behold king Nimrod sat in Babel on the throne, and the king fell asleep and dreamed that he was standing with his troops and hosts in a valley opposite the king's furnace.
46 And he lifted up his eyes and saw a man in the likeness of Abram coming forth from the furnace; he came and stood before the king with his drawn sword, and then sprang to the king with his sword, when the king fled from the man, for he was afraid; while he was running, the man threw an egg on the king's head, and the egg became a great river.
47 And the king dreamed that all his troops sank in that river and died, and the king took flight with three men who were before him and he escaped.

48 The king looked at these men and they were clothed in princely dresses as the garments of kings, and had the appearance and majesty of kings.
49 And while they were running, the river again turned to an egg before the king; there came forth from the egg a young bird which came before the king, and flew at his head and plucked out the king's eye.
50 The king was grieved at the sight, and he awoke out of his sleep and his spirit was agitated; he felt a great terror.
51 In the morning the king rose from his couch in fear, and he ordered all the wise men and magicians to come before him, when the king related his dream to them.
52 And a wise servant of the king, whose name was Anuki, answered the king, saying, This is nothing else but the evil of Abram and his offspring which will spring up against my Lord and king in the latter days.
53 And behold the day will come when Abram and his offspring and the children of his household will war with my king, and they will strike all the king's hosts and his troops.
54 And as to what you have said concerning three men which you did see like yourself, and which did escape, this means that only you will escape with three kings from the kings of the earth who will be with you in battle.
55 And that which you saw of the river which turned to an egg as at first, and the young bird plucking out your eye, this means nothing else but the offspring of Abram which will kill the king in latter days.
56 This is my king's dream, and this is its interpretation, and the dream is true, and the interpretation which your servant has given you is right.
57 Now therefore my king, certainly you know that it is now fifty-two years since your sages saw this at the birth of Abram, and if my king will suffer Abram to live in the earth it will be to the injury of my lord and king, for all the days that Abram lives neither you nor your kingdom will be established, for this was known formerly at his birth; and why will not my king kill him, that his evil may be kept from you in latter days?
58 And Nimrod listened to the voice of Anuki; he sent some of his servants in secret to go and seize Abram and bring him before the king to suffer death.
59 Eliezer, Abram's servant whom the king had given him, was at that time in the presence of the king, and he heard what Anuki had advised the king, and what the king had said to cause Abram's death.
60 Eliezer said to Abram, Hasten, rise up and save your soul, that you may not die through the hands of the king, for thus did he see in a dream concerning you, and thus did Anuki interpret it, and thus also did Anuki advise the king concerning you.
61 Abram listened to the voice of Eliezer, and Abram hurried and ran for safety to the house of Noah and his son Shem, and he concealed himself there and found a place of safety; and the king's servants came to Abram's house to seek him, but they could not find him, and they searched throughout the country and he was not to be found; they went and searched in every direction and he was not to be met with.
62 And when the king's servants could not find Abram they returned to the king, but the king's anger against Abram was stilled, as they did not find him, and the king drove from his mind this matter concerning Abram.
63 Abram was concealed in Noah's house for one month, until the king had forgotten this matter, but Abram was still afraid of the king; and Terah came to see Abram his son secretly in the house of Noah, and Terah was very great in the eyes of the king.

64 Abram said to his father, Do you not know that the king thinks to kill me, and to annihilate my name from the earth by the advice of his wicked counselors?
65 Now whom have you here and what have you in this land? Arise, let us go together to the land of Canaan, that we may be delivered from his hand, that you not perish also through him in the latter days.
66 Do you not know or have you not heard, that it is not through love that Nimrod gives you all this honor, but it is only for his benefit that he bestows all this good on you?
67 And if he does to you greater good than this, certainly these are only vanities of the world, for wealth and riches cannot avail in the day of wrath and anger.
68 Now therefore listen to my voice, and let us arise and go to the land of Canaan, out of the reach of injury from Nimrod; and serve the Lord who created you in the earth and it will be well with you; and cast away all the vain things which you pursue.
69 And Abram ceased to speak when Noah and his son Shem answered Terah, saying, True is the word which Abram hath said to you.
70 And Terah listened to the voice of his son Abram, and Terah did all that Abram said, for this was from the Lord that the king should not cause Abram's death.

CHAPTER 13

1 Terah took his son Abram and his grandson Lot, the son of Haran, and Sarai his daughter-in-law, the wife of his son Abram, and all the souls of his household and went with them from Ur Casdim to go to the land of Canaan. And when they came as far as the land of Haran they remained there, for it was very good land for pasture, and of sufficient territory for those who accompanied them.
2 And the people of the land of Haran saw that Abram was good and upright with God and men, and that the Lord his God was with him. Some of the people of the land of Haran came and joined Abram, and he taught them the instruction of the Lord and his ways; these men remained with Abram in his house and they adhered to him.
3 Abram remained in the land three years, and at the expiration of three years the Lord appeared to Abram and said to him; I am the Lord who brought you forth from Ur Casdim, and delivered you from the hands of all your enemies.
4 Now therefore if you will listen to my voice and keep my commandments, my statutes and my laws, I will cause your enemies to fall before you. I will reproduce your descendants like the stars of heaven, and I will send my blessing on all the works of your hands, and you shall lack nothing.
5 Arise now, take your wife and all belonging to you and go to the land of Canaan and remain there. And I, God, will be there for you and I will bless you. And Abram rose and took his wife and all belonging to him, and he went to the land of Canaan as the Lord had told him; and Abram was fifty years old when he went from Haran.
6 Abram came to the land of Canaan and lived in the midst of the city, and there he pitched his tent among the children of Canaan, inhabitants of the land.
7 The Lord appeared to Abram when he came to the land of Canaan, and said to him, This is the land which I gave to you and to your descendants after you forever, and I will make them like the stars of heaven, and I will give to your descendants all the lands which you see for an inheritance.

8 And Abram built an altar in the place where God had spoken to him, and there Abram called on the name of the Lord.
9 At that time, at the end of three years of Abram's dwelling in the land of Canaan, in that year Noah died, which was the fifty-eighth year of the life of Abram; all the days that Noah lived were nine hundred and fifty years and he died.
10 Abram lived in the land of Canaan, he, his wife, and all belonging to him, and all those that accompanied him, together with those that joined him from the people of the land; but Nahor, Abram's brother, and Terah his father, and Lot the son of Haran and all belonging to them lived in Haran.
11 In the fifth year of Abram's dwelling in the land of Canaan the people of Sodom and Gomorrah and all the cities of the plain revolted from the power of Chedorlaomer, king of Elam; for all the kings of the cities of the plain had served Chedorlaomer for twelve years, and given him a yearly tax, but in those days in the thirteenth year, they rebelled against him.
12 In the tenth year of Abram's dwelling in the land of Canaan there was war between Nimrod king of Shinar and Chedorlaomer king of Elam, and Nimrod came to fight with Chedorlaomer and to subdue him.
13 For Chedorlaomer was at that time one of the princes of the hosts of Nimrod, and when all the people at the tower were dispersed and those that remained were also scattered on the face of the earth, Chedorlaomer went to the land of Elam and reigned over it and rebelled against his lord.
14 In those days when Nimrod saw that the cities of the plain had rebelled, he came with pride and anger to war with Chedorlaomer, and Nimrod assembled all his princes and subjects, about seven hundred thousand men, and went against Chedorlaomer, and Chedorlaomer went out to meet him with five thousand men, and they prepared for battle in the valley of Babel which is between Elam and Shinar.
15 All those kings fought there, and Nimrod and his people were smitten before the people of Chedorlaomer, and there fell from Nimrod's men about six hundred thousand, and Mardon the king's son fell among them.
16 And Nimrod fled and returned in shame and disgrace to his land, and he was under subjection to Chedorlaomer for a long time, and Chedorlaomer returned to his land and sent princes of his host to the kings that lived around him, to Arioch king of Elasar, and to Tidal king of Goyim, and made a covenant with them, and they were all obedient to his commands.
17 It was in the fifteenth year of Abram's dwelling in the land of Canaan, which is the seventieth year of the life of Abram, the Lord appeared to Abram in that year and said to him, I am the Lord who brought you out from Ur Casdim to give you this land for an inheritance.
18 Now therefore walk before me and be perfect and keep my commands, for to you and to your descendants I will give this land for an inheritance, from the river Mitzraim to the great river Euphrates.
19 And you shall come to your fathers in peace and in good age, and the fourth generation shall return here in this land and shall inherit it forever. And Abram built an altar, and he called on the name of the Lord who appeared to him, and he brought up sacrifices on the altar to the Lord.
20 At that time Abram returned and went to Haran to see his father and mother, and his father's household, and Abram and his wife and all belonging to him returned to Haran; Abram lived in Haran five years.

21 And many of the people of Haran, about seventy-two men, followed Abram and Abram taught them the instruction of the Lord and his ways, and he taught them to know the Lord.
22 In those days the Lord appeared to Abram in Haran, and he said to him, Behold, I spoke to you twenty years ago saying,
23 Go forth from your land, from your birth-place and from your father's house, to the land which I have shown you to give it to you and to your children, for there in that land I will bless you, and make you a great nation, and make your name great, and in you shall the families of the earth be blessed.
24 Now therefore arise, go forth from this place, you, your wife, and all belonging to you, also every one born in your house and all the souls you have made in Haran, and bring them out with you from here, and rise to return to the land of Canaan.
25 And Abram arose and took his wife Sarai and all belonging to him and all that were born to him in his house and the souls which they had made in Haran, and they came out to go to the land of Canaan.
26 Abram went and returned to the land of Canaan, according to the word of the Lord. And Lot the son of his brother Haran went with him; Abram was seventy-five years old when he went forth from Haran to return to the land of Canaan.
27 And he came to the land of Canaan according to the word of the Lord to Abram, and he pitched his tent and he lived in the plain of Mamre, and with him was Lot his brother's son, and all belonging to him.
28 And the Lord again appeared to Abram and said, To your offspring I will give this land; there he built an altar to the Lord who appeared to him, which is still to this day in the plains of Mamre.

CHAPTER 14

1 In those days there was in the land of Shinar a wise man who had understanding in all wisdom, and of a beautiful appearance, but he was poor and indigent; his name was Rikayon and he was hard set to support himself.
2 And he resolved to go to Egypt, to Oswiris the son of Anom king of Egypt, to show the king his wisdom; for perhaps he might find grace in his sight, to raise him up and give him maintenance; and Rikayon did so.
3 When Rikayon came to Egypt he asked the inhabitants of Egypt concerning the king, and the inhabitants of Egypt told him the custom of the king of Egypt, for it was then the custom of the king of Egypt that he went from his royal palace and was seen abroad only one day in the year, and after that the king would return to his palace to remain there.
4 On the day when the king went forth he passed judgment in the land, and every one having a suit came before the king that day to obtain his request.
5 When Rikayon heard of the custom in Egypt and that he could not come into the presence of the king, he grieved greatly and was very sorrowful.
6 In the evening Rikayon went out and found a house in ruins, formerly a bake house in Egypt, and he abode there all night in bitterness of soul and pinched with hunger, and sleep was removed from his eyes.
7 And Rikayon considered within himself what he should do in the town until the king made his appearance, and how he might maintain himself there.
8 And he rose in the morning and walked about, and met in his way those who sold

vegetables and various sorts of offspring with which they supplied the inhabitants.
9 Rikayon wished to do the same in order to get a maintenance in the city, but he
was unacquainted with the custom of the people, and he was like a blind man
among them.
10 And he went and obtained vegetables to sell for his support, and the crowd
assembled about him and ridiculed him, and took his vegetables from him and left
him nothing.
11 He rose up from there in bitterness of soul, and went sighing to the bake house in
which he had remained all the night before, and he slept there the second night.
12 On that night again he reasoned within himself how he could save himself from
starvation, and he devised a scheme how to act.
13 And he rose up in the morning and acted ingeniously, and went and hired thirty
strong men of the crowd, carrying their war instruments in their hands, and he led
them to the top of the Egyptian sepulchre, and he placed them there.
14 He commanded them, saying, Thus says the king, Strengthen yourselves and be
valiant men, and let no man be buried here until two hundred pieces of silver be
given, and then he may be buried; and those men did according to the order of
Rikayon to the people of Egypt the whole of that year.
15 In eight months time Rikayon and his men gathered great riches of silver and
gold, and Rikayon took a great quantity of horses and other animals, and he hired
more men, and he gave them horses and they remained with him.
16 When the year came round, at the time the king went forth into the town, all the
inhabitants of Egypt assembled together to speak to him concerning the work of
Rikayon and his men.
17 The king went forth on the appointed day, and all the Egyptians came before him
and cried to him, saying,
18 May the king live forever. What is this thing you do in the town to your servants,
not to allow a dead body buried until so much silver and gold be given? Was there
ever the like to this done in the whole earth, from the days of former kings, yes even
from the days of Adam, to this day, that the dead should be buried only for a set
price?
19 We know it to be the custom of kings to take a yearly tax from the living, but you
do not only do this, but from the dead also you exact a tax day by day.
20 Now, O king, we can no more bear this, for the whole city is ruined on this
account, and do you not know it?
21 When the king heard all that they had spoken he was very angry, and his anger
burned within him at this affair, for he had known nothing of it.
22 And the king said, Who and where is he that dares to do this wicked thing in my
land without my command? Certainly you will tell me.
23 They told him all the works of Rikayon and his men, and the king's anger was
aroused, and he ordered Rikayon and his men to be brought before him.
24 And Rikayon took about a thousand children, sons and daughters, and clothed
them in silk and embroidery, and he set them on horses and sent them to the king by
means of his men, and he also took a great quantity of silver and gold and precious
stones, and a strong and beautiful horse, as a present for the king, with which he
came before the king and bowed down to the earth before him; the king, his
servants and all the inhabitants of Egypt wondered at the work of Rikayon; they saw
his riches and the presents that he had brought to the king.
25 It greatly pleased the king and he wondered at it; and when Rikayon sat before

him the king asked him concerning all his works, and Rikayon spoke all his words wisely before the king, his servants and all the inhabitants of Egypt.
26 When the king heard the words of Rikayon and his wisdom, Rikayon found grace in his sight, and he met with grace and kindness from all the servants of the king and from all the inhabitants of Egypt, on account of his wisdom and excellent speeches, and from that time they loved him greatly.
27 And the king answered and said to Rikayon, Thy name shall no more be called Rikayon but Pharaoh shall be your name, since you did exact a tax from the dead; and he called his name Pharaoh.
28 The king and his subjects loved Rikayon for his wisdom, and they consulted with all the inhabitants of Egypt to make him prefect under the king.
29 All the inhabitants of Egypt and its wise men did so, and it was made a law in Egypt.
30 They made Rikayon Pharaoh prefect under Oswiris king of Egypt, and Rikayon Pharaoh governed over Egypt, daily administering justice to the whole city, but Oswiris the king would judge the people of the land one day in the year, when he went out to make his appearance.
31 And Rikayon Pharaoh cunningly usurped the government of Egypt, and he exacted a tax from all the inhabitants of Egypt.
32 And all the inhabitants of Egypt greatly loved Rikayon Pharaoh, and they made a decree to call every king that should reign over them and their descendants in Egypt, Pharaoh.
33 Therefore all the kings that reigned in Egypt from that time forward were called Pharaoh to this day.

CHAPTER 15

1 In that year there was a heavy famine throughout the land of Canaan, and the inhabitants of the land could not remain on account of the famine for it was very severe.
2 Abram and all belonging to him rose and went down to Egypt on account of the famine, and when they were at the brook Mitzraim they remained there some time to rest from the fatigue of the road.
3 Abram and Sarai were walking at the border of the brook Mitzraim, and Abram beheld his wife Sarai that she was very beautiful.
4 And Abram said to his wife Sarai, Since God has created you with such a beautiful countenance, I am afraid of the Egyptians that they will kill me and take you away, for the fear of God is not in these places.
5 Certainly then you shall do this, Say you are my sister to all that may ask you, in order that it may be well with me, and that we may live and not be put to death.
6 And Abram commanded the same to all those that came with him to Egypt on account of the famine; also his nephew Lot he commanded, saying, If the Egyptians ask you concerning Sarai say she is the sister of Abram.
7 And yet with all these orders Abram did not put confidence in them, but he took Sarai and placed her in a chest and concealed it among their vessels, for Abram was greatly concerned about Sarai on account of the wickedness of the Egyptians.
8 Abram and all belonging to him rose up from the brook Mitzraim and came to Egypt; and they had scarcely entered the gates of the city when the guards stood up

to them saying, Give tithe to the king from what you have, and then you may come into the town; Abram and those that were with him did so.
9 Abram and the people that were with him came to Egypt and they brought the chest in which Sarai was concealed, and the Egyptians saw the chest.
10 And the king's servants approached Abram, saying, What have you here in this chest which we have not seen? Now open the chest and give tithe to the king of all that it contains.
11 Abram said, This chest I will not open, but all you demand on it I will give. And Pharaoh's officers answered Abram, saying, It is a chest of precious stones, give us the tenth of its value.
12 Abram said, All that you desire I will give, but you must not open the chest.
13 And the king's officers pressed Abram; they reached the chest and opened it with force, and they saw a beautiful woman was in the chest.
14 When the officers of the king saw Sarai they were struck with admiration at her beauty, and all the princes and servants of Pharaoh assembled to see Sarai, for she was very beautiful. The king's officers ran and told Pharaoh all that they had seen, and they praised Sarai to the king; Pharaoh ordered her to be brought, and the woman came before the king.
15 Pharaoh observed Sarai and she pleased him greatly, and he was struck with her beauty; the king rejoiced greatly on her account, and made presents to those who brought him the news concerning her.
16 The woman was then brought to Pharaoh's house, and Abram grieved on account of his wife; he prayed to the Lord to deliver her from the hands of Pharaoh.
17 And Sarai also prayed at that time and said, O Lord God you did tell my Lord Abram to go from his land and from his father's house to the land of Canaan, and you did promise to do well with him if he would perform your commands; now behold we have done that which you commanded us; we left our land and our families, and we went to a strange land and to a people whom we have not known before.
18 We came to this land to avoid the famine, and this evil accident has befallen me; now therefore, O Lord God, deliver us and save us from the hand of this oppressor, and do well with me for the sake of your mercy.
19 The Lord listened to the voice of Sarai, and the Lord sent an angel to deliver Sarai from the power of Pharaoh.
20The king came and sat before Sarai and behold an angel of the Lord was standing over them, and he appeared to Sarai and said to her, Do not fear, for the Lord has heard your prayer.
21 The king approached Sarai and said to her, What is that man to you who brought you here? and she said, He is my brother.
22 The king said, It is incumbent on us to make him great, to elevate him and to do to him all the good which you shall command us. At that time the king sent to Abram silver and gold and precious stones in abundance, together with cattle, men servants and maid servants; and the king ordered Abram to be brought and he sat in the court of the king's house, and the king greatly exalted Abram on that night.
23 The king approached to speak to Sarai and he reached out his hand to touch her when the angel struck him heavily; he was terrified and he refrained from reaching to her.
24 And when the king came near to Sarai, the angel struck him to the ground, and acted thus to him the whole night, and the king was terrified.

25 The angel on that night struck heavily all the servants of the king, and his whole household, on account of Sarai, and there was a great lamentation that night among the people of Pharaoh's house.
26 And Pharaoh, seeing the evil that befell him, said, Certainly on account of this woman has this thing happened to me, and he removed himself at some distance from her and spoke pleasing words to her.
27 The king said to Sarai, Tell me I pray you concerning the man with whom you came here; and Sarai said, This man is my husband, and I said to you that he was my brother for I was afraid that you would put him to death through wickedness.
28 And the king kept away from Sarai, and the plagues of the angel of the Lord ceased from him and his household; Pharaoh knew that he was smitten on account of Sarai, and the king was greatly astonished at this.
29 In the morning the king called for Abram and said to him, What is this you have done to me? Why did you say, She is my sister, since I wanted to take her as a wife, and this heavy plague has therefore come on me and my household.
30 Now therefore here is your wife, take her and go from our land so we don't all die on her account. And Pharaoh took more cattle, men servants and maid servants, and silver and gold, to give to Abram, and he returned to him Sarai his wife.
31 And the king took a maiden whom he had by his concubines, and he gave her to Sarai for a handmaid.
32 The king said to his daughter, It is better for you my daughter to be a handmaid in this man's house than to be mistress in my house, after we have seen the evil that came upon us on account of this woman.
33 Abram arose, and he and all belonging to him went away from Egypt; and Pharaoh ordered some of his men to accompany him and all that went with him.
34 And Abram returned to the land of Canaan, to the place where he had made the altar, where he at first had pitched his tent.
35 Lot the son of Haran, Abram's brother, had a heavy stock of cattle, flocks and herds and tents, for the Lord was bountiful to them on account of Abram.
36 When Abram was dwelling in the land the herdsmen of Lot quarrelled with the herdsmen of Abram, for their property was too great for them to remain together in the land, and the land could not bear them on account of their cattle.
37 When Abram's herdsmen went to feed their flock they would not go into the fields of the people of the land, but the cattle of Lot's herdsmen did otherwise, for they were allowed to feed in the fields of the people of the land.
38 And the people of the land saw this occurrence daily, and they came to Abram and quarrelled with him on account of Lot's herdsmen.
39 And Abram said to Lot, What is this you are doing to me, to make me despicable to the inhabitants of the land, that you ordered your herdsman to feed your cattle in the fields of other people? Do you not know that I am a stranger in this land among the children of Canaan, and why will you do this to me?
40 Abram quarrelled daily with Lot on account of this, but Lot would not listen to Abram; he continued to do the same and the inhabitants of the land came and told Abram.
41 And Abram said to Lot, How long will you be to me a stumbling block with the inhabitants of the land? Now I petition you let there be no more quarrelling between us, for we are kinsmen.
42 I request you to separate from me, go and choose a place where you may dwell with your cattle and all belonging to you, but keep yourself at a distance from me,

you and your household.
43 And don't be afraid in going from me, for if any one does an injury to you, let me know and I will avenge your cause from him, only remove from me.
44 When Abram had spoken all these words to Lot, then Lot arose and lifted up his eyes toward the plain of Jordan.
45 And he saw that all of this place was well watered, and good for man as well as affording pasture for the cattle.
46 Lot went from Abram to that place, and he there pitched his tent and he lived in Sodom, and they were separated from each other.
47 And Abram lived in the plain of Mamre, which is in Hebron, and he pitched his tent there, and Abram remained in that place many years.

CHAPTER 16

1 At that time Chedorlaomer king of Elam sent to all the neighboring kings, to Nimrod, king of Shinar who was then under his power, and to Tidal, king of Goyim, and to Arioch, king of Elasar, with whom he made a covenant, saying, Come up to me and assist me, that we may strike all the towns of Sodom and its inhabitants, for they have rebelled against me these thirteen years.
2 These four kings went up with all their camps, about eight hundred thousand men, and they went as they were, and struck every man they found in their road.
3 And the five kings of Sodom and Gomorrah, Shinab king of Admah, Shemeber king of Zeboyim, Bera king of Sodom, Bersha king of Gomorrah, and Bela king of Zoar, went out to meet them, and they all joined together in the valley of Siddim.
4 These nine kings made war in the valley of Siddim; and the kings of Sodom and Gomorrah were smitten before the kings of Elam.
5 The valley of Siddim was full of lime pits and the kings of Elam pursued the kings of Sodom, and the kings of Sodom with their camps fled and fell into the lime pits; all that remained went to the mountain for safety. The five kings of Elam came after them and pursued them to the gates of Sodom, and they took all that there was in Sodom.
6 They plundered all the cities of Sodom and Gomorrah, and they also took Lot, Abram's brother's son, and his property; they seized all the goods of the cities of Sodom, and they went away. Unic, Abram's servant, who was in the battle, saw this, and told Abram all that the kings had done to the cities of Sodom, and that Lot was taken captive by them.
7 Abram heard this, and he rose up with about three hundred and eighteen men that were with him, and that night he pursued these kings and struck them; they all fell before Abram and his men, and there was none remaining but the four kings who fled, and they each went his own road.
8 Abram recovered all the property of Sodom, and he also recovered Lot and his property, his wives and little ones and all belonging to him, so that Lot lacked nothing.
9 And when he returned from smiting these kings, he and his men passed the valley of Siddim where the kings had made war together.
10 Bera king of Sodom, and the rest of his men that were with him, went out from

the lime pits into which they had fallen, to meet Abram and his men.
11 And Adonizedek king of Jerusalem, the same was Shem, went out with his men to meet Abram and his people, with bread and wine, and they remained together in the valley of Melech.
12 Adonizedek blessed Abram, and Abram gave him a tenth from all that he had brought from the spoil of his enemies, for Adonizedek was a priest before God.
13 And all the kings of Sodom and Gomorrah who were there, with their servants, approached Abram and begged him to return their servants whom he had made captive, and to take to himself all the property.
14 Abram answered the kings of Sodom, saying, As the Lord lives who created heaven and earth, and who redeemed my soul from all affliction, and who delivered me this day from my enemies and gave them into my hand, I will not take anything belonging to you, that you may not boast tomorrow, saying, Abram became rich from our property that he saved.
15 For the Lord my God in whom I trust said to me, You shall lack nothing, for I will bless you in all the works of your hands.
16 Now here is all belonging to you, take it and go; as the Lord lives I will not take from a living soul down to a shoetie or thread, excepting the expense of the food of those who went out with me to battle, as also the portions of the men who went with me, Anar, Ashcol, and Mamre, they and their men, as well as those also who had remained to watch the baggage, they shall take their portion of the spoil.
17 And the kings of Sodom gave Abram according to all that he had said; they pressed him to take of whatever he chose, but he would not.
18 He sent away the kings of Sodom and the remainder of their men, and he gave them orders about Lot, and they went to their respective places.
19 And Lot, his brother's son, he also sent away with his property, and he went with them, and Lot returned to his home, to Sodom, and Abram and his people returned to their home to the plains of Mamre, which is in Hebron.
20 At that time the Lord again appeared to Abram in Hebron, and he said to him, Do not fear, your reward is very great before me, for I will not leave you until I shall have multiplied you and blessed you and made your offspring like the stars in heaven, which cannot be measured nor numbered.
21 And I will give to your descendants all these lands that you see with your eyes, I will give them for an inheritance forever, only be strong and do not fear, walk before me and be perfect.
22 In the seventy-eighth year of the life of Abram, in that year Reu died, the son of Peleg, and all the days of Reu were two hundred and thirty-nine years, and he died.
23 And Sarai, the daughter of Haran, Abram's wife, was still unable to conceive in those days; she did not bear to Abram either son or daughter.
24 When she saw that she gave birth to no children she took her handmaid Hagar, whom Pharaoh had given her, and she gave her to Abram her husband for a wife.
25 For Hagar learned all the ways of Sarai as Sarai taught her; she was not in any way deficient in following her good ways.
26 Sarai said to Abram, Behold here is my handmaid Hagar, go to her that she may bring forth on my knees, that I may also obtain children through her.
27 At the end of ten years of Abram's dwelling in the land of Canaan, which is the eighty-fifth year of Abram's life, Sarai gave Hagar to him.
28 And Abram listened to the voice of his wife Sarai; he took his handmaid Hagar and Abram came to her and she conceived.

29 When Hagar saw that she had conceived she rejoiced greatly, and her mistress was despised in her eyes; she said within herself, This can only be that I am better before God than Sarai my mistress, for all the days that my mistress has been with my lord, she did not conceive, but me the Lord has caused in so short a time to conceive by him.
30 And when Sarai saw that Hagar had conceived by Abram, Sarai was jealous of her handmaid, and Sarai said within herself, This is certainly nothing else but that she must be better than I am.
31 Sarai said to Abram, My wrong be on you, for at the time when you prayed before the Lord for children why did you not pray on my account, that the Lord should give me offspring from you?
32 When I speak to Hagar in your presence she hates my word because she has conceived so you will say nothing to her; may the Lord judge between me and you for what you have done to me.
33 And Abram said to Sarai, Behold your handmaid is in your hand, do to her as it may seem good in your eyes; and Sarai afflicted her, and Hagar fled from her to the wilderness.
34 An angel of the Lord found her in the place where she had fled, by a well, and he said to her, Do not fear, for I will reproduce your offspring, for you shall bear a son and you shall call his name Ishmael; now then return to Sarai your mistress, and submit yourself under her hands.
35 And Hagar called the place of that well Beer-lahai-roi; it is between Kadesh and the wilderness of Bered.
36 And Hagar at that time returned to her master's house, and at the end of days Hagar gave birth to a son to Abram, and Abram called his name Ishmael; and Abram was eighty-six years old when he had him.

CHAPTER 17

1 In those days, in the ninety-first year of the life of Abram, the children of Chittim made war with the children of Tubal, for when the Lord had scattered the sons of men on the face of the earth, the children of Chittim went and settled in the plain of Canopia, and they built themselves cities there and lived by the river Tibreu.
2 The children of Tubal lived in Tuscanah, and their boundaries reached the river Tibreu, and the children of Tubal built a city in Tuscanan, and they called the name Sabinah, after the name of Sabinah son of Tubal their father, and they lived there to this day.
3 It was at that time the children of Chittim made war with the children of Tubal, and the children of Tubal were smitten before the children of Chittim; the children of Chittim caused three hundred and seventy men to fall from the children of Tubal.
4 At that time the children of Tubal swore to the children of Chittim, saying, You shall not intermarry among us, and no man shall give his daughter to any of the sons of Chittim.
5 For all the daughters of Tubal were in those days fair, for no women were then found in the whole earth so fair as the daughters of Tubal.
6 And all who delighted in the beauty of women went to the daughters of Tubal and took wives from them, and the sons of men, kings and princes, who greatly delighted in the beauty of women, took wives in those days from the daughters of Tubal.

7 At the end of three years after the children of Tubal had sworn to the children of Chittim not to give them their daughters for wives, about twenty men of the children of Chittim went to take some of the daughters of Tubal, but they found none.
8 For the children of Tubal kept their oaths not to intermarry with them, and they would not break their oaths.
9 In the days of harvest the children of Tubal went into their fields to get in their harvest, when the young men of Chittim assembled and went to the city of Sabinah, and each man took a young woman from the daughters of Tubal, and they came to their cities.
10 And the children of Tubal heard of it and they went to make war with them; they could not prevail over them, for the mountain was very high; when they saw they could not prevail over them they returned to their land.
11 And at the revolution of the year the children of Tubal went and hired about ten thousand men from those cities that were near them, and they went to war with the children of Chittim.
12 And the children of Tubal went to war with the children of Chittim, to destroy their land and to distress them. In this engagement the children of Tubal prevailed over the children of Chittim, and the children of Chittim, seeing that they were greatly distressed, lifted up the children which they had had by the daughters of Tubal, on the wall which had been built, to be before the eyes of the children of Tubal.
13 And the children of Chittim said to them, Have you come to make war with your own sons and daughters, and have we not been considered your flesh and bones from that time till now?
14 When the children of Tubal heard this they ceased to make war with the children of Chittim, and they went away.
15 They returned to their cities and the children of Chittim at that time assembled and built two cities by the sea; they called one Purtu and the other Ariza.
16 And Abram the son of Terah was then ninety-nine years old.
17 At that time the Lord appeared to him and said, I will make my covenant between me and you, and I will greatly reproduce your offspring, and this is the covenant which I make between me and you, that every male child be circumcised, you and your descendants after you.
18 At eight days old shall it be circumcised, and this covenant shall be in your flesh for an everlasting covenant.
19 And now therefore your name shall no more be called Abram but Abraham, and your wife shall no more be called Sarai but Sarah.
20 For I will bless you both, and I will reproduce your descendants, that you shall become a great nation, and kings shall come forth from you.

CHAPTER 18

1 Abraham rose and did all that God had ordered him; he took the men of his household and those bought with his money, and he circumcised them as the Lord had commanded him.
2 There was not one left whom he did not circumcise, and Abraham and his son Ishmael were circumcised in the flesh of their foreskin; Ishmael was thirteen years old when he was circumcised in the flesh of his foreskin.

3 And in the third day Abraham went out of his tent and sat at the door to enjoy the heat of the sun, during the pain of his flesh.
4 The Lord appeared to him in the plain of Mamre and sent three of his ministering angels to visit him, and he was sitting at the door of the tent. He lifted his eyes and saw three men were coming from a distance; he rose up and ran to meet them, and he bowed down to them and brought them into his house.
5 And he said to them, If now I have found favor in your sight, turn in and eat a morsel of bread. He urged them, they turned in and he gave them water and they washed their feet, and he placed them under a tree at the door of the tent.
6 Abraham ran and took a calf, tender and good, and he hurried to kill it, and gave it to his servant Eliezer to dress.
7 And Abraham came to Sarah into the tent, and said to her, Make ready quickly three measures of fine meal, knead it and make cakes to cover the pot containing the meat, and she did so.
8 Abraham hurried and brought before them butter and milk, beef and mutton, and put it before them to eat, before the flesh of the calf was sufficiently done, and they ate.
9 When they were done eating one of them said to him, I will return to you according to the time of life, and Sarah your wife shall have a son.
10 And the men afterward departed and went their ways, to the places to which they were sent.
11 In those days all the people of Sodom and Gomorrah, and of the whole five cities, were greatly wicked and sinful against the Lord. They provoked the Lord with their abominations, and they grew worse as they aged abominably and scornfully before the Lord, and their wickedness and crimes were in those days great before the Lord.
12 They had in their land a very extensive valley, about half a day's walk, and in it there were fountains of water and a great deal of herbage surrounding the water.
13 All the people of Sodom and Gomorrah went there four times a year, with their wives and children and all belonging to them, and they rejoiced there with timbrels and dances.
14 In the time of rejoicing they would all rise and lay hold of their neighbor's wives, and some, the virgin daughters of their neighbors, and they enjoyed them; each man saw his wife and daughter in the hands of his neighbor and did not say a word.
15 And they did so from morning to night; afterward they returned home each man to his house and each woman to her tent; so they always did four times in the year.
16 Also when a stranger came into their cities and brought goods which he had purchased with a view to dispose of there, the people of these cities would assemble, men, women and children, young and old, and go to the man and take his goods by force, giving a little to each man until there was an end to all the goods of the owner which he had brought into the land.
17 And if the owner of the goods quarreled with them, saying, What is this work which you have done to me, then they would approach him one by one, and each would show him the little which he took and taunt him, saying, I only took that little which you did give me; when he heard this from them all, he would arise and go from them in sorrow and bitterness of soul. Then they would all arise and go after him, and drive him out of the city with great noise and tumult.
18 There was a man from the country of Elam who was leisurely going on the road, seated on his ass, which carried a fine mantle of varied colors, and the mantle was bound with a cord on the ass.

19 The man was on his journey passing through the street of Sodom when the sun set in the evening; he remained there in order to abide during the night, but no one would let him into his house. At that time there was in Sodom a wicked and mischievous man, one skillful to do evil, and his name was Hedad.
20 And he lifted up his eyes and saw the traveler in the street of the city, and he came to him and said, Whence come you and where do you go?
21 The man said to him, I am traveling from Hebron to Elam where I belong, and as I passed the sun set and no one would invite me to enter his house; you have bread and water and also straw and feed for my ass, and I am short of nothing.
22 And Hedad answered and said to him, All that you shall want shall be supplied by me, but in the street you shall not abide all night.
23 Hedad brought him to his house, and he took off the mantle from the ass with the cord, and brought them to his house. He gave the ass straw and feed while the traveler ate and drank in Hedad's house, and he abode there that night.
24 And in the morning the traveler rose up early to continue his journey, when Hedad said to him, Wait, comfort your heart with a morsel of bread and then go, and the man did so; and he remained with him, and they both ate and drank together during the day, then the man rose up to go.
25 And Hedad said to him, Behold now the day is declining, you had better remain all night that your heart may be comforted; and he pressed him so that he tarried there all night, and on the second day he rose up early to go away, when Hedad pressed him, saying, Comfort your heart with a morsel of bread and then go, and he remained and ate with him also the second day. Then the man rose up to continue his journey.
26 And Hedad said to him, Behold now the day is declining, remain with me to comfort your heart and in the morning rise up early and go your way.
27 The man would not remain, but rose and saddled his ass, and while he was saddling his ass the wife of Hedad said to her husband, Behold this man has remained with us for two days eating and drinking and he has given us nothing, and now shall he go away from us without giving anything? Hedad said to her, Be silent.
28 And the man saddled his ass to go, and he asked Hedad to give him the cord and mantle to tie it on the ass.
29 And Hedad said to him, What do you say? And he said to him, That you my lord shall give me the cord and the mantle made with varied colors which you concealed in your house to take care of it.
30 And Hedad answered the man, saying, This is the interpretation of your dream, the cord which you did see means that your life will be lengthened out like a cord, and having seen the mantle colored with all sorts of colors, means that you shall have a vineyard in which you will plant trees of all fruits.
31 And the traveler answered, saying, Not so my lord, for I was awake when I gave you the cord and also a mantle woven with different colors, which you took off the ass to put by for me; and Hedad answered and said, Certainly I have told you the interpretation of your dream and it is a good dream, and this is the interpretation of it.
32 Now the sons of men give me four pieces of silver, which is my charge for interpreting dreams, and of you only I require three pieces of silver.
33 And the man was provoked at the words of Hedad, and he cried bitterly, and he brought Hedad to Serak judge of Sodom.
34 And the man laid his cause before Serak the judge, when Hedad replied, saying,

It is not so, but thus the matter stands. And the judge said to the traveler, This man Hedad tells you truth, for he is famed in the cities for the accurate interpretation of dreams.
35 And the man cried at the word of the judge, and he said, Not so my Lord, for it was in the day that I gave him the cord and mantle which was on the ass, in order to put them by in his house; they both disputed before the judge, the one saying, Thus the matter was, and the other declaring otherwise.
36 Hedad said to the man, Give me four pieces of silver that I charge for my interpretations of dreams; I will not make any allowance; give me the expense of the four meals that you ate in my house.
37 And the man said to Hedad, Truly I will pay you for what I ate in your house, only give me the cord and mantle which you did conceal in your house.
38 Hedad replied before the judge and said to the man, Did I not tell you the interpretation of your dream? The cord means that your days shall be prolonged like a cord, and the mantle, that you will have a vineyard in which you will plant all kinds of fruit trees.
39 This is the proper interpretation of your dream, now give me the four pieces of silver that I require as a compensation, for I will make you no allowance.
40 And the man cried at the words of Hedad and they both quarreled before the judge; the judge gave orders to his servants, who drove them rashly from the house.
41 And they went away quarreling from the judge. When the people of Sodom heard them, they gathered about them and spoke harshly against the stranger, and they drove him rashly from the city.
42 And the man continued his journey on his ass with bitterness of soul, lamenting and weeping.
43 And while he was on his way he wept at what had happened to him in the corrupt city of Sodom.

CHAPTER 19

1 The cities of Sodom had four judges to four cities, and these were their names, Serak in the city of Sodom, Sharkad in Gomorrah, Zabnac in Admah, and Menon in Zeboyim.
2 Eliezer Abraham's servant applied to them different names, and he converted Serak to Shakra, Sharkad to Shakrura, Zebnac to Kezobim, and Menon to Matzlodin.
3 By desire of their four judges the people of Sodom and Gomorrah had beds erected in the streets of the cities and if a man came to these places, they laid hold of him and brought him to one of their beds and by force made him to lie in them.
4 As he lay down, three men would stand at his head and three at his feet, and measure him by the length of the bed; if the man was less than the bed, these six men would stretch him at each end, and when he cried out to them they would not answer him.
5 If he was longer than the bed, they would draw together the two sides of the bed at each end, until the man had reached the gates of death.
6 And if he continued to cry out to them, they would answer him, saying, Thus it shall be done to a man that comes into our land.
7 When men heard all these things that the people of the cities of Sodom did, they refrained from coming there.

8 And when a poor man came to their land they would give him silver and gold, and cause a proclamation in the whole city not to give him a morsel of bread to eat. If the stranger should remain there some days and die from hunger, not having been able to obtain a morsel of bread, then at his death all the people of the city would come and take their silver and gold which they had given to him.
9 Those that could recognize the silver or gold which they had given him took it back, and at his death they also stripped him of his garments, and they would fight about them; he that prevailed over his neighbor took them.
10 After that they would carry him and bury him under some of the shrubs in the desert; so they did all the days to any one that came to them and died in their land.
11 And in the course of time Sarah sent Eliezer to Sodom, to see Lot and inquire after his welfare.
12 Eliezer went to Sodom, and he met a man of Sodom fighting with a stranger, and the man of Sodom stripped the poor man of all his clothes and went away.
13 And this poor man cried to Eliezer and begged his favor on account of what the man of Sodom had done to him.
14 He said to him, Why do you act thus to the poor man who came to your land?
15 The man of Sodom answered Eliezer, saying, Is this man your brother, or have the people of Sodom made you a judge this day, that you speak about this man?
16 Eliezer strove with the man of Sodom on account of the poor man, and when Eliezer approached to recover the poor man's clothes from the man of Sodom, he hurried and with a stone struck Eliezer in the forehead.
17 The blood flowed copiously from Eliezer's forehead, and when the man saw the blood he caught hold of Eliezer, saying, Give me my wage for having rid you of this bad blood that was in your forehead, for such is the custom and the law in our land.
18 And Eliezer said to him, You have wounded me and require me to pay you your wage? Eliezer would not listen to the words of the man of Sodom.
19 And the man laid hold of Eliezer and brought him to Shakra the judge of Sodom for judgment.
20 The man spoke to the judge, saying, I beseech you my lord, thus has this man done, for I struck him with a stone that the blood flowed from his forehead, and he is unwilling to give me my wage.
21 And the judge said to Eliezer, This man speaks truth to you, give him his wage, for this is the custom in our land. Eliezer heard the words of the judge, and he lifted up a stone and struck the judge; the stone struck on his forehead, and the blood flowed copiously from the forehead of the judge, and Eliezer said, If this then is the custom in your land give to this man what I should have given him, for this has been your decision; you did decree it.
22 And Eliezer left the man of Sodom with the judge, and he went away.
23 When the kings of Elam had made war with the kings of Sodom, the kings of Elam captured all the property of Sodom and they took Lot captive with his property, and when it was told to Abraham he went and made war with the kings of Elam. He recovered from their hands all the property of Lot as well as the property of Sodom.
24 At that time the wife of Lot gave birth to a daughter, and he called her name Paltith, saying, Because God had delivered him and his whole household from the kings of Elam. Paltith daughter of Lot grew up, and one of the men of Sodom took her for a wife.
25 And a poor man came into the city to seek a maintenance, and he remained in the

city some days, and all the people of Sodom caused a proclamation of their custom not to give this man a morsel of bread to eat until he dropped dead on the earth, and they did so.
26 And Paltith the daughter of Lot saw this man lying in the streets starved with hunger and no one would give him any thing to keep him alive; he was just on the point of death.
27 And her soul was filled with pity on account of the man and she fed him secretly with bread for many days, and the soul of this man was revived.
28 For when she went forth to fetch water she would put the bread in the water pitcher, and when she came to the place where the poor man was, she took the bread from the pitcher and gave it him to eat; so she did many days.
29 And all the people of Sodom and Gomorrah wondered how this man could bear starvation for so many days.
30 And they said to each other, This can only be because he eats and drinks, for no man can bear starvation for so many days or live as this man has, without even his countenance changing. Three men concealed themselves in a place where the poor man was stationed to know who it was that brought him bread to eat.
31 Paltith daughter of Lot went forth that day to fetch water and she put bread into her pitcher of water; she went to draw water by the poor man's place and took out the bread from the pitcher and gave it to the poor man and he ate it.
32 And the three men saw what Paltith did to the poor man, and they said to her, It is you then who have supported him, and therefore he has not starved, nor changed in appearance nor died like the rest.
33 The three men went out of the place in which they were concealed, and they seized Paltith and the bread which was in the poor man's hand.
34 They took Paltith and brought her before their judges, and they said to them, Thus did she do, and it is she who supplied the poor man with bread, therefore he did not die all this time; now therefore declare to us the punishment due to this woman for having gone contrary to our law.
35 And the people of Sodom and Gomorrah assembled and set ablaze a fire in the street of the city, and they took the woman and cast her into the fire and she was burned to ashes.
36 In the city of Admah there was a woman to whom they did the same.
37 For a traveler came into the city of Admah to stay there all night, with the intention of going home in the morning. He sat opposite the door of the house of the young woman's father, to remain there, as the sun had set when he had reached that place; the young woman saw him sitting by the door of the house.
38 He asked her for a drink of water and she said to him, Who art you? And he said to her, I was this day going on the road, and reached here when the sun set, so I will stay here all night, and in the morning I will arise early and continue my journey.
39 And the young woman went into the house and fetched the man bread and water to eat and drink.
40 This affair became known to the people of Admah, and they assembled and brought the young woman before the judges, that they should judge her for this act.
41 And the judge said, The judgment of death must pass on this woman because she went contrary to our law, and this therefore is the decision concerning her.
42 The people of those cities assembled and brought out the young woman, and anointed her with honey from head to foot, as the judge had decreed, and they placed her before a swarm of bees which were then in their hives, and the bees flew

on her and stung her that her whole body was swelled.
43 The young woman cried out on account of the bees, but no one took notice of her or pitied her, and her cries ascended to heaven.
44 And the Lord was provoked at this and at all the works of the cities of Sodom, for they had abundance of food, and had tranquility among them, and still would not sustain the poor and the needy. In those days their evil doings and sins became great before the Lord.
45 The Lord sent for two of the angels that had come to Abraham's house, to destroy Sodom and its cities.
46 And the angels rose up from the door of Abraham's tent, after they had eaten and drunk, and they reached Sodom in the evening, and Lot was then sitting in the gate of Sodom. When he saw them he rose to meet them, and he bowed down to the ground.
47 He welcomed them greatly and brought them into his house, and he gave them food which they ate, and they stayed all night in his house.
48 And the angels said to Lot, Arise, go forth from this place, you and all belonging to you, that you not be consumed in the iniquity of this city, for the Lord will destroy this place.
49 The angels laid hold on the hand of Lot and on the hand of his wife, and on the hands of his children, and all belonging to him, and they brought him forth and set him outside of the cities.
50 And they said to Lot, Escape for your life. He fled and all belonging to him.
51 Then the Lord rained on Sodom and on Gomorrah and on all these cities brimstone and fire from the Lord out of heaven.
52 And he overthrew these cities, all the plain and all the inhabitants of the cities, and that which grew on the ground; Ado the wife of Lot looked back to see the destruction of the cities, for her compassion was moved on account of her daughters who remained in Sodom, for they did not go with her.
53 And when she looked back she became a pillar of salt, and it is yet in that place to this day.
54 The oxen which stood in that place daily licked up the salt to the extremities of their feet, and in the morning it would spring forth afresh, and they again licked it up to this day.
55 Lot and two of his daughters that remained with him fled and escaped to the cave of Adullam, and they remained there for some time.
56 And Abraham rose up early in the morning to see what had been done to the cities of Sodom; and he looked and beheld the smoke of the cities going up like the smoke of a furnace.
57 Lot and his two daughters remained in the cave, and they made their father drink wine, and they lay with him, for they said there was no man on earth that could produce descendants from them, for they thought that the whole earth was destroyed.
58 They both lay with their father and conceived and gave birth to sons. The first born called the name of her son Moab, saying, From my father did I conceive him; he is the father of the Moabites to this day.
59 And the younger also called her son Benami; he is the father of the children of Ammon to this day.
60 After this Lot and his two daughters went away from there, and he lived on the other side of the Jordan with his two daughters and their sons, and the sons of Lot

grew up, and they went and took themselves wives from the land of Canaan, and they had children and they were prolific and multiplied.

CHAPTER 20

1 At that time Abraham journeyed from the plain of Mamre and he went to the land of the Philistines, and he lived in Gerar; it was in the twenty-fifth year of Abraham's being in the land of Canaan, and the hundredth year of the life of Abraham, that he came to Gerar in the land of the Philistines.
2 And when they entered the land he said to Sarah his wife, Say you are my sister, to any one that shall ask you, in order that we may escape the evil of the inhabitants of the land.
3 As Abraham was dwelling in the land of the Philistines, the servants of Abimelech, king of the Philistines, saw that Sarah was greatly beautiful, and they asked Abraham concerning her, and he said, She is my sister.
4 And the servants of Abimelech went to Abimelech, saying, A man from the land of Canaan is come to dwell in the land, and he has a sister that is exceeding fair.
5 Abimelech heard the words of his servants who praised Sarah to him, and Abimelech sent his officers, and they brought Sarah to the king.
6 And Sarah came to the house of Abimelech; the king saw that Sarah was beautiful, and she pleased him greatly.
7 And he approached her and said to her, What is that man to you with whom you did come to our land? And Sarah answered and said, He is my brother, and we came from the land of Canaan to dwell wherever we could find a place.
8 Abimelech said to Sarah, Behold my land is before you, place your brother in any part of this land that pleases you, and it will be our duty to exalt and elevate him above all the people of the land since he is your brother.
9 And Abimelech sent for Abraham, and Abraham came to Abimelech.
10 Abimelech said to Abraham, Behold I have given orders that you shall be honored as you desire on account of your sister Sarah.
11 And Abraham went forth from the king, and the king's present followed him.
12 As at evening time, before men laid down to rest, the king was sitting on his throne, and a deep sleep fell on him, and he lay on the throne and slept till morning.
13 He dreamed that an angel of the Lord came to him with a drawn sword in his hand, and the angel stood over Abimelech and wished to kill him with the sword; the king was terrified in his dream and said to the angel, In what have I sinned against you that you come to kill me with your sword?
14 And the angel answered and said to Abimelech, Behold you die on account of the woman which last night you brought to your house, for she is a married woman, the wife of Abraham who came to your house; now therefore return that man his wife, for she is his wife; should you not return her, know that you will certainly die, you and all belonging to you.
15 On that night there was a great outcry in the land of the Philistines, and the inhabitants of the land saw the figure of a man standing with a drawn sword in his hand, and he struck the inhabitants of the land with the sword, yes, he continued to strike them.
16 And the angel of the Lord struck the whole land of the Philistines on that night,

and there was a great confusion on that night and on the following morning.
17 Every womb was closed, and all their issues, and the hand of the Lord was on them on account of Sarah, wife of Abraham, whom Abimelech had taken.
18 And in the morning Abimelech rose with terror and confusion and with a great dread; he sent and had his servants called in; he related his dream to them, and the people were greatly afraid.
19 One man standing among the servants of the king answered the king, saying, O sovereign king, restore this woman to her husband, for he is her husband, for the same happened to the king of Egypt when this man came to Egypt.
20 He said concerning his wife, She is my sister, for such is his manner of doing when he comes to dwell in the land in which he is a stranger.
21 Pharaoh sent and took this woman for a wife and the Lord brought on him grievous plagues until he returned the woman to her husband.
22 Now therefore, O sovereign king, know what happened last night to the whole land, for there was a very great consternation and great pain and lamentation, and we know that it was on account of the woman which you did take.
23 Now, therefore, restore this woman to her husband, that it should not happen to us as it did to Pharaoh king of Egypt and his subjects, and that we may not die. Abimelech hurried and had Sarah called for, and she came before him, and he had Abraham called for, and he came before him.
24 Abimelech said to them, What is this work you have been doing in saying you are brother and sister, and I took this woman for a wife?
25 And Abraham said, Because I thought I would suffer death on account of my wife; and Abimelech took flocks and herds, and men servants and maid servants, and a thousand pieces of silver, and he gave them to Abraham, and he returned Sarah to him.
26 Abimelech said to Abraham, Behold the whole land is before you, dwell in it wherever you shall choose.
27 And Abraham and Sarah, his wife, went forth from the king's presence with honor and respect, and they lived in the land, even in Gerar.
28 All the inhabitants of the land of the Philistines and the king's servants were still in pain through the plague which the angel had inflicted on them the whole night on account of Sarah.
29 Abimelech sent for Abraham, saying, Pray now for your servants to the Lord your God, that he may put away this mortality from among us.
30 And Abraham prayed on account of Abimelech and his subjects, and the Lord heard the prayer of Abraham, and he healed Abimelech and all his subjects.

CHAPTER 21

1 It was at that time the end of a year and four months of Abraham's dwelling in the land of the Philistines in Gerar, that God visited Sarah, and the Lord remembered her and she conceived and gave birth to a son to Abraham.
2 Abraham called the name of the son which Sarah gave birth to him, Isaac.
3 And Abraham circumcised his son Isaac at eight days old, as God had commanded Abraham to do to his descendants after him; Abraham was one hundred and Sarah ninety years old when Isaac was born to them.
4 The child grew up and was weaned, and Abraham made a great feast on the day

that Isaac was weaned.
5 Shem and Eber and all the great people of the land, and Abimelech king of the Philistines and his servants, and Phicol, the captain of his host, came to eat and drink and rejoice at the feast which Abraham made on the day of his son Isaac's being weaned.
6 Also Terah, the father of Abraham, and Nahor his brother, came from Haran, they and all belonging to them, for they greatly rejoiced on hearing that a son had been born to Sarah.
7 They came to Abraham, and they ate and drank at the feast which Abraham made on the day of Isaac's being weaned.
8 Terah and Nahor rejoiced with Abraham, and they remained with him many days in the land of the Philistines.
9 At that time Serug the son of Reu died, in the first year of the birth of Isaac son of Abraham.
10 And all the days of Serug were two hundred and thirty-nine years, and he died.
11 Ishmael the son of Abraham was grown up in those days; he was fourteen years old when Sarah gave birth to Isaac to Abraham.
12 And God was with Ishmael the son of Abraham, and he grew up, and he learned to use the bow and became an archer.
13 When Isaac was five years old he was sitting with Ishmael at the door of the tent.
14 Ishmael came to Isaac and seated himself opposite to him, and he took the bow and drew it and put the arrow in it, and intended to kill Isaac.
15 Sarah saw the act which Ishmael desired to do to her son Isaac, and it grieved her greatly on account of her son; she sent for Abraham, and said to him, Cast out this bondwoman and her son, for her son shall not be heir with my son, for thus did he seek to do to him this day.
16 Abraham listened to the voice of Sarah, and he rose up early in the morning. He took twelve loaves and a bottle of water which he gave to Hagar, and sent her away with her son, and Hagar went with her son to the wilderness. They lived in the wilderness of Paran with the inhabitants of the wilderness; Ishmael was an archer, and he lived in the wilderness a long time.
17 He and his mother afterward went to the land of Egypt, and they lived there; Hagar took a wife for her son from Egypt, and her name was Meribah.
18 And the wife of Ishmael conceived and gave birth to four sons and two daughters. Ishmael and his mother and his wife and children afterward went and returned to the wilderness.
19 They made themselves tents in the wilderness, in which they lived, and they continued to travel and then to rest monthly and yearly.
20 And God gave Ishmael flocks and herds and tents on account of Abraham his father, and the man increased in cattle.
21 Ishmael lived in deserts and in tents, traveling and resting for a long time, and he did not see the face of his father.
22 Some time later, Abraham said to Sarah his wife, I will go and see my son Ishmael, for I have a desire to see him, for I have not seen him for a long time.
23 Abraham rode on one of his camels to the wilderness to seek his son Ishmael, for he heard that he was dwelling in a tent in the wilderness with all belonging to him.
24 Abraham went to the wilderness and reached the tent of Ishmael about noon, and he asked after Ishmael; he found the wife of Ishmael sitting in the tent with her children, and Ishmael her husband and his mother were not with them.

25 Abraham asked the wife of Ishmael, saying, Where has Ishmael gone? And she said, He has gone to the field to hunt. Abraham was still mounted on the camel, for he would not get off to the ground as he had sworn to his wife Sarah that he would not get off from the camel.
26 And Abraham said to Ishmael's wife, My daughter, give me a little water that I may drink, for I am fatigued from the journey.
27 And Ishmael's wife answered and said to Abraham, We have neither water nor bread. She continued sitting in the tent and did not notice Abraham, neither did she ask him who he was.
28 But she was beating her children in the tent, and she was cursing them, and she also cursed her husband Ishmael and reproached him. Abraham heard the words of Ishmael's wife to her children, and he was very angry and displeased.
29 Abraham called to the woman to come out to him from the tent, and the woman came and stood opposite to Abraham, for Abraham was still mounted on the camel.
30 And Abraham said to Ishmael's wife, When your husband Ishmael returns home say these words to him,
31 A very old man from the land of the Philistines came here to seek you, and thus was his appearance and figure; I did not ask him who he was, and seeing you were not here he spoke to me and said, When Ishmael your husband returns tell him thus did this man say, When you come home put away this nail of the tent which you have placed here, and place another nail in its stead.
32 Abraham finished his instructions to the woman, and he turned and went off on the camel homeward.
33 After that Ishmael came from the hunt by him and his mother, and returned to the tent, and his wife spoke these words to him,
34 A very old man from the land of the Philistines came to seek you, and thus was his appearance and figure; I did not ask him who he was, and seeing you were not at home he said to me, When your husband comes home tell him, thus says the old man, Put away the nail of the tent which you have placed here and place another nail in its stead.
35 Ishmael heard the words of his wife, and he knew that it was his father, and that his wife did not honor him.
36 And Ishmael understood his father's words that he had spoken to his wife, and Ishmael listened to the voice of his father; Ishmael cast off that woman and she went away.
37 Ishmael afterward went to the land of Canaan, and he took another wife and he brought her to his tent to the place where he then lived.
38 And at the end of three years Abraham said, I will go again and see Ishmael my son, for I have not seen him for a long time.
39 He rode on his camel and went to the wilderness, and he reached the tent of Ishmael about noon.
40 He asked after Ishmael, and his wife came out of the tent and said, He is not here my lord, for he has gone to hunt in the fields, and to feed the camels. And the woman said to Abraham, Turn in my lord into the tent, and eat a morsel of bread, for your soul must be wearied on account of the journey.
41 And Abraham said to her, I will not stop for I am in haste to continue my journey, but give me a little water to drink, for I have thirst; the woman hurried and ran into the tent and she brought out water and bread to Abraham, which she placed before him and she urged him to eat; he ate and drank and his heart was comforted and he

blessed his son Ishmael.
42 He finished his meal and he blessed the Lord, and he said to Ishmael's wife, When Ishmael comes home say these words to him,
43 A very old man from the land of the Philistines came here and asked after you, and you were not here; and I brought out bread and water and he ate and drank and his heart was comforted.
44 And he spoke these words to me: When Ishmael your husband comes home, say to him, The nail of the tent which you have is very good, do not put it away from the tent.
45 Abraham finished commanding the woman, and he rode off to his home to the land of the Philistines; and when Ishmael came to his tent his wife went forth to meet him with joy and a cheerful heart.
46 And she said to him, An old man came here from the land of the Philistines and thus was his appearance, and he asked after you and you were not here, so I brought out bread and water, and he ate and drank and his heart was comforted.
47 And he spoke these words to me, When Ishmael your husband comes home say to him, The nail of the tent which you have is very good, do not put it away from the tent.
48 Ishmael knew that it was his father, and that his wife had honored him, and the Lord blessed Ishmael.

CHAPTER 22

1 Ishmael then rose up and took his wife and his children and his cattle and all belonging to him, and he journeyed from there and he went to his father in the land of the Philistines.
2 Abraham related to Ishmael his son the transaction with the first wife that Ishmael took, according to what she did.
3 Ishmael and his children lived with Abraham many days in that land, and Abraham lived in the land of the Philistines a long time.
4 And the days increased and reached twenty six years; after that Abraham with his servants and all belonging to him went from the land of the Philistines and removed to a great distance, and they came near to Hebron and remained there. The servants of Abraham dug wells of water, and Abraham and all belonging to him lived by the water. The servants of Abimelech king of the Philistines heard the report that Abraham's servants had dug wells of water in borders of the land.
5 They came and quarreled with the servants of Abraham and robbed them of the great well which they had dug.
6 Abimelech king of the Philistines heard of this affair; he with Phicol the captain of his host and twenty of his men came to Abraham, and Abimelech spoke to Abraham concerning his servants; Abraham rebuked Abimelech concerning the well of which his servants had robbed him.
7 Abimelech said to Abraham, As the Lord lives who created the whole earth, I did not hear of the act which my servants did to your servants until this day.
8 And Abraham took seven ewe lambs and gave them to Abimelech, saying, Take these, I pray you, from my hands that it may be a testimony for me that I dug this well.

9 Abimelech took the seven ewe lambs which Abraham had given to him, for he had also given him cattle and herds in abundance; Abimelech swore to Abraham concerning the well, therefore he called that well Beersheba, for there they both swore concerning it.
10 And they both made a covenant in Beersheba, and Abimelech rose up with Phicol the captain of his host and all his men; they returned to the land of the Philistines, and Abraham and all belonging to him lived in Beersheba and he was in that land a long time.
11 Abraham planted a large grove in Beersheba, and he made to it four gates facing the four sides of the earth; he planted a vineyard in it, so that if a traveler came to Abraham he entered any gate which was in his road, and remained there and ate and drank and satisfied himself and then departed.
12 For the house of Abraham was always open to the sons of men that passed and returned, who came daily to eat and drink in the house of Abraham.
13 Any man who had hunger and came to Abraham's house, Abraham would give him bread that he might eat and drink and be satisfied; any one that came naked to his house he would clothe with garments as he might choose and give him silver and gold, and make known to him the Lord who had created him in the earth; this did Abraham all his life.
14 Abraham and his children and all belonging to him lived in Beersheba, and he pitched his tent as far as Hebron.
15 And Abraham's brother Nahor and his father and all belonging to them lived in Haran, for they did not come with Abraham to the land of Canaan.
16 And children were born to Nahor which Milca the daughter of Haran, and sister to Sarah, Abraham's wife, gave birth to, to him.
17 These are the names of those that were born to him: Uz, Buz, Kemuel, Kesed, Chazo, Pildash, Tidlaf, and Bethuel, being eight sons; these are the children of Milca which she gave birth to, to Nahor, Abraham's brother.
18 And Nahor had a concubine and her name was Reumah, and she also gave birth to, to Nahor: Zebach, Gachash, Tachash and Maacha, being four sons.
19 The children that were born to Nahor were twelve sons besides his daughters, and they also had children born to them in Haran.
20 And the children of Uz the first born of Nahor were Abi, Cheref, Gadin, Melus, and Deborah their sister.
21 And the sons of Buz were Berachel, Naamath, Sheva, and Madonu.
22 And the sons of Kemuel were Aram and Rechob.
23 And the sons of Kesed were Anamlech, Meshai, Benon and Yifi; the sons of Chazo were Pildash, Mechi and Opher.
24 And the sons of Pildash were Arud, Chamum, Mered and Moloch.
25 And the sons of Tidlaf were Mushan, Cushan and Mutzi.
26 And the children of Bethuel were Sechar, Laban and their sister Rebecca.
27 These are the families of the children of Nahor, that were born to them in Haran; and Aram the son of Kemuel and Rechob his brother went away from Haran, and they found a valley in the land by the river Euphrates.
28 And they built a city there, and they called the name of the city after the name of Pethor the son of Aram, that is Aram Naherayim to this day.
29 The children of Kesed also went to dwell where they could find a place, and they found a valley opposite to the land of Shinar, and they lived there.
30 There they built themselves a city, and they called the name of the city Kesed after

the name of their father; that is the land Kasdim to this day, and the Kasdim lived in that land and they were prolific and multiplied greatly.
31 Terah, father of Nahor and Abraham, went and took another wife in his old age, and her name was Pelilah, and she conceived and gave birth to him a son and he called his name Zoba.
32 Terah lived twenty-five years after he had Zoba.
33 And Terah died in that year, that is in the thirty-fifth year of the birth of Isaac son of Abraham.
34 The days of Terah were two hundred and five years, and he was buried in Haran.
35 Zoba the son of Terah lived thirty years and he had Aram, Achlis and Merik.
36 Aram, son of Zoba son of Terah, had three wives and he had twelve sons and three daughters; the Lord gave to Aram the son of Zoba, riches and possessions, and abundance of cattle, and flocks and herds, and the man increased greatly.
37 Aram the son of Zoba and his brother and all his household journeyed from Haran, and they went to dwell where they should find a place, for their property was too great to remain in Haran; for they could not stop in Haran together with their brothers the children of Nahor.
38 Aram the son of Zoba went with his brothers, and they found a valley at a distance toward the eastern country and they lived there.
39 They also built a city there, and they called the name thereof Aram, after the name of their eldest brother; that is Aram Zoba to this day.
40 Isaac the son of Abraham was growing up in those days, and Abraham his father taught him the way of the Lord to know the Lord, and the Lord was with him.
41 When Isaac was thirty-seven years old, Ishmael his brother was going about with him in the tent.
42 And Ishmael boasted of himself to Isaac, saying, I was thirteen years old when the Lord spoke to my father to circumcise us, and I did according to the word of the Lord which he spoke to my father, and I gave my soul to the Lord, and I did not go contrary to his word which he commanded my father.
43 Isaac answered Ishmael, saying, Why do you boast to me about this, about a little bit of your flesh which you did take from your body, concerning which the Lord commanded you?
44 As the Lord lives, the God of my father Abraham, if the Lord should say to my father, Take now your son Isaac and bring him up an offering before me, I would not refrain but I would joyfully accede to it.
45 And the Lord heard the word that Isaac spoke to Ishmael, and it seemed good in the sight of the Lord, and he thought to try Abraham in this matter.
46 The day arrived when the sons of God came and placed themselves before the Lord, and Satan also came with the sons of God before the Lord.
47 And the Lord said to Satan, Wherefore do you come? Satan answered the Lord and said, From going to and fro in the earth, and from walking up and down in it.
48 And the Lord said to Satan, What is your word to me concerning all the children of the earth? Satan answered the Lord and said, I have seen all the children of the earth who serve you and remember you when they require anything from you.
49 When you give them the thing which they require from you, they sit at their ease and turn away from you, and they remember you no more.
50 Have you seen Abraham the son of Terah, who at first had no children? He served you and erected altars to you wherever he came, and he brought up offerings on them, and he proclaimed your name continually to all the children of the earth.

51 And now that his son Isaac is born to him, he has forsaken you, he has made a great feast for all the inhabitants of the land, and the Lord he has forgotten.
52 For amidst all that he has done he brought you no offering; neither burnt offering nor peace offering, neither ox, lamb nor goat of all that he killed on the day that his son was weaned.
53 Even from the time of his son's birth till now, being thirty-seven years, he built no altar before you, nor brought any offering to you, for he saw that you did give what he requested before you, and he therefore turned away from you.
54 And the Lord said to Satan, Have you thus considered my servant Abraham? for there is none like him on earth, a perfect and an upright man before me, one that fears God and avoids evil; as I live, were I to say to him, Bring up Isaac your son before me, he would not withhold him from me, much more if I told him to bring up a burnt offering before me from his flock or herds.
55 Satan answered the Lord and said, Speak then now to Abraham as you have said, and you will see whether he will not this day go contrary to and cast aside your words.

CHAPTER 23

1 At that time the word of the Lord came to Abraham, and said to him, Abraham. And Abraham said, Here I am.
2 He said to him, Take now your son, your only son whom you love, even Isaac, and go to the land of Moriah, and offer him there for a burnt offering on one of the mountains which shall be shown to you, for there you will see a cloud and the glory of the Lord.
3 And Abraham said within himself, How shall I separate my son Isaac from Sarah his mother, in order to bring him up for a burnt offering before the Lord?
4 Abraham came into the tent, and he sat before Sarah his wife, and he spoke these words to her,
5 My son Isaac is grown up and he has not for some time studied the service of his God; tomorrow I will go and bring him to Shem, and Eber his son, and there he will learn the ways of the Lord. For they will teach him to know the Lord as well as to know that when he prays continually before the Lord, he will answer him; there he will know the way of serving the Lord his God.
6 And Sarah said, You have spoken well, go my lord and do to him as you have said, but remove him not at a great distance from me, neither let him remain there too long, for my soul is bound within his soul.
7 Abraham said to Sarah, My daughter, let us pray to the Lord our God that he may do good with us.
8 And Sarah took her son Isaac and he abode all that night with her, and she kissed and embraced him, and gave him instructions till morning.
9 She said to him, O my son, how can my soul separate itself from you? And she still kissed him and embraced him, and she gave Abraham instructions concerning him.
10 Sarah said to Abraham, O my lord, I pray you take care of your son, and watch over him, for I have no other son or daughter but him.
11 Turn not away from him. If he is hungry give him bread, and if he is thirsty give him water to drink; do not let him go on foot, neither let him sit in the sun.
12 Neither let him go by himself in the road, neither force him from whatever he

may desire, but do to him as he may say to you.
13 Sarah wept bitterly the whole night on account of Isaac, and she gave him instructions till morning.
14 In the morning Sarah selected a very fine and beautiful garment from those garments which she had in the house, that Abimelech had given to her.
15 She dressed Isaac her son with them, and she put a turban on his head; she enclosed a precious stone in the top of the turban, and gave them provision for the road. They went forth, and Isaac went with his father Abraham, and some of their servants accompanied them to see them on their way.
16 Sarah went out with them, and she accompanied them on the road to see them off; they said to her, Return to the tent.
17 When Sarah heard the words of her son Isaac she wept bitterly, and Abraham her husband wept with her, and their son wept with them a great weeping; also those who went with them wept greatly.
18 And Sarah caught hold of her son Isaac, and she held him in her arms, and she embraced him and continued to weep with him. And Sarah said, Who knows if after this day I shall ever see you again?
19 They still wept together, Abraham, Sarah and Isaac, and all those that accompanied them on the road wept with them, and Sarah afterward turned away from her son, weeping bitterly; then all her men servants and maid servants returned with her to the tent.
20 And Abraham went with Isaac his son to bring him up as an offering before the Lord, as He had commanded him.
21 Abraham took two of his young men with him, Ishmael the son of Hagar and Eliezer his servant, and they went together with them. While they were walking in the road the young men spoke these words to themselves,
22 Ishmael said to Eliezer, Now my father Abraham is going with Isaac to bring him up for a burnt offering to the Lord, as He commanded him.
23 When he returns he will give to me all he possesses, to inherit after him, for I am his firstborn.
24 And Eliezer answered Ishmael and said, Certainly Abraham did cast you away with your mother, and swear that you should not inherit any thing of all he possesses. To whom will he give all that he has, with all his treasures, but to me his servant, who has been faithful in his house, who has served him night and day, and has done all he desired me? To me he will bequeath at his death all he possesses.
25 While Abraham was proceeding with his son Isaac along the road, Satan came and appeared to Abraham in the figure of a very aged man, humble and of contrite spirit; he approached Abraham and said to him, Are you silly or brutish, that you go to do this thing today to your only son?
26 For God gave you a son in your latter days, in your old age, and will you go and slaughter him today because he committed no violence, and will you cause the soul of your only son to perish from the earth?
27 Do you not know and understand that this thing cannot be from the Lord? For the Lord cannot do to man such evil on earth to say to him, Go slaughter your child.
28 Abraham heard this and knew that it was the word of Satan who endeavored to draw him aside from the way of the Lord, but Abraham would not listen to the voice of Satan, and Abraham rebuked him so that he went away.
29 Satan returned and came to Isaac; he appeared to Isaac in the figure of a young man comely and well favored.

30 He approached Isaac and said to him, Do you not know and understand that your old silly father brings you to the slaughter today for nothing?
31 Now therefore, my son, do not listen or attend to him, for he is a silly old man; let not your precious soul and beautiful figure be lost from the earth.
32 And Isaac heard this, and said to Abraham, Have you heard, my father, that which this man has spoken? Even thus has he spoken.
33 And Abraham answered his son Isaac and said to him, Take heed of him and do not listen to his words, nor attend to him, for he is Satan, endeavoring to draw us aside this day from the commands of God.
34 Abraham still rebuked Satan, and Satan went from them; seeing he could not prevail over them he hid himself from them, and he went and passed before them in the road; he transformed himself to a large brook of water in the road. Abraham and Isaac and his two young men reached that place, and they saw a brook large and powerful as the mighty waters.
35 They entered the brook and passed through it, and the waters at first reached their legs.
36 And they went deeper in the brook and the waters reached up to their necks. They were all terrified on account of the water and while they were going over the brook Abraham recognized that place, and he knew that there was no water there before.
37 Abraham said to his son Isaac, I know this place in which there was no brook or water, now therefore it is Satan who does all this to us, to draw us aside on this day from the commands of God.
38 And Abraham rebuked him and said to him, The Lord rebuke you, O Satan, begone from us for we go by the commands of God.
39 And Satan was terrified at the voice of Abraham, and he went away from them; the place again became dry land as it was at first.
40 Abraham went with Isaac toward the place that God had told him.
41 And on the third day Abraham lifted up his eyes and saw the place at a distance which God had told him of.
42 A pillar of fire appeared to him that reached from the earth to heaven, and a cloud of glory on the mountain, and the glory of the Lord was seen in the cloud.
43 And Abraham said to Isaac, My son, do you see in that mountain, which we perceive at a distance, that which I see on it?
44 And Isaac answered and said to his father, I see and there is a pillar of fire and a cloud, and the glory of the Lord is seen on the cloud.
45 And Abraham knew that his son Isaac was accepted before the Lord for a burnt offering.
46 Abraham said to Eliezer and to Ishmael his son, Do you also see that which we see on the mountain which is at a distance?
47 And they answered and said, We see nothing more than like the other mountains of the earth. Abraham knew that they were not accepted before the Lord to go with them, and Abraham said to them, Stay here with the ass while I and Isaac my son will go to yonder mount and worship there before the Lord and then return to you.
48 Eliezer and Ishmael remained in that place, as Abraham had commanded.
49 And Abraham took wood for a burnt offering and placed it on his son Isaac, and he took the fire and the knife, and they both went to that place.
50 When they were on the way Isaac said to his father, Behold, I see here the fire and wood, and where then is the lamb that is to be the burnt offering before the Lord?

51 And Abraham answered his son Isaac, saying, The Lord has made choice of you my son, to be a perfect burnt offering instead of the lamb.
52 And Isaac said to his father, I will do all that the Lord spoke to you with joy and cheerfulness of heart.
53 Abraham again said to Isaac his son, Is there in your heart any thought or counsel concerning this, which is not proper? Tell me my son, I pray you, O my son conceal it not from me.
54 And Isaac answered his father Abraham and said to him, O my father, as the Lord lives and as your soul lives, there is nothing in my heart to cause me to deviate either to the right or to the left from the word that he has spoken to you.
55 Neither limb nor muscle has moved or stirred at this, nor is there in my heart any thought or evil counsel concerning this.
56 But I am of joyful and cheerful heart in this matter, and I say, Blessed is the Lord who has this day chosen me to be a burnt offering before Him.
57 Abraham greatly rejoiced at the words of Isaac, and they went on and came together to that place that the Lord had spoken of.
58 Abraham approached to build the altar in that place, and Abraham was weeping. Isaac took stones and mortar until they had finished building the altar.
59 And Abraham took the wood and placed it in order on the altar which he had built.
60 He took his son Isaac and bound him in order to place him on the wood which was on the altar, to kill him for a burnt offering before the Lord.
61 Isaac said to his father, Bind me securely and then place me on the altar that I should not turn and move, and break loose from the force of the knife on my flesh and thereof profane the burnt offering; and Abraham did so.
62 Isaac still said to his father, O my father, when you have slain me and burnt me for an offering, take with you that which remains of my ashes to bring to Sarah my mother, and say to her, This is the sweet smelling savor of Isaac. But do not tell her this if she should sit near a well or on any high place, that she would cast her soul after me and die.
63 And Abraham heard the words of Isaac, and he lifted up his voice and wept when Isaac spake these words. Abraham's tears gushed down on Isaac his son, and Isaac wept bitterly; he said to his father, Hasten, O my father, and do with me the will of the Lord our God as He has commanded you.
64 The hearts of Abraham and Isaac rejoiced at this thing which the Lord had commanded them; but the eye wept bitterly while the heart rejoiced.
65 And Abraham bound his son Isaac and placed him on the altar on the wood, and Isaac stretched forth his neck on the altar before his father. Abraham stretched forth his hand to take the knife to kill his son as a burnt offering before the Lord.
66 At that time the angels of mercy came before the Lord and spoke to him concerning Isaac, saying,
67 0 Lord, you are a merciful and compassionate King over all that you have created in heaven and in earth, and you support them all; give therefore ransom and redemption instead of your servant Isaac, and pity and have compassion on Abraham and Isaac his son who are this day performing your commands.
68 Have you seen, O Lord, how Isaac the son of Abraham your servant is bound down to the slaughter like an animal? Now therefore let your pity be roused for them, O Lord.
69 At that time the Lord appeared to Abraham and called to him from heaven, and

said to him, Lay not your hand on the lad, neither do anything to him, for now I know that you fear God in performing this act, and in not withholding your son, your only son, from me.
70 And Abraham lifted up his eyes and looked, and behold, a ram was caught in a thicket by his horns; that was the ram which the Lord God had created in the earth in the day that he made earth and heaven.
71 For the Lord had prepared this ram from that day, to be a burnt offering instead of Isaac.
72 This ram was advancing to Abraham when Satan caught hold of him and entangled his horns in the thicket, so that he might not advance to Abraham, in order that Abraham might kill his son.
73 And Abraham, seeing the ram advancing to him and Satan withholding him, fetched him and brought him before the altar; he loosened his son Isaac from his binding, and he put the ram in his stead. Abraham killed the ram on the altar, and brought it up as an offering in the place of his son Isaac.
74 Abraham sprinkled some of the blood of the ram on the altar, and he exclaimed and said, This is in the place of my son, and may it be considered this day as the blood of my son before the Lord.
75 And all that Abraham did on this occasion by the altar, he would exclaim and say, This is in place of my son, and may it this day be considered before the Lord in the place of my son; and Abraham finished the whole service by the altar, and the service was accepted before the Lord, and was accounted as if it had been Isaac; and the Lord blessed Abraham and his descendants on that day.
76 Satan went to Sarah, and he appeared to her in the figure of an old man very humble and meek, and Abraham was yet engaged in the burnt offering before the Lord.
77 And he said to her, Do you not know all the work that Abraham has made with your only son this day? For he took Isaac and built an altar, and killed him, and brought him up as a sacrifice on the altar; Isaac cried and wept before his father, but he looked not at him, neither did he have compassion over him.
78 Satan repeated these words, and he went away from her. Sarah heard all the words of Satan, and she imagined him to be an old man from among the sons of men who had been with her son, and had come and told her these things.
79 And Sarah lifted up her voice and wept and cried out bitterly on account of her son; she threw herself on the ground and she cast dust on her head, and she said, O my son, Isaac my son, O that I had this day died instead of you. And she continued to weep and said, It grieves me for you, O my son, my son Isaac, O that I had died this day in your stead.
80 She still continued to weep, and said, It grieves me for you after I have reared you and have brought you up; now my joy is turned into mourning over you; I who had a longing for you, and cried and prayed to God till I gave birth to you at ninety years old. And now you have served this day for the knife and the fire, to be made an offering.
81 But I console myself with you, my son, in its being the word of the Lord, for you did perform the command of your God. Who can go contrary to the word of our God, in whose hands is the soul of every living creature?
82 You are just, O Lord our God, for all your works are good and righteous; for I also am rejoiced with your word which you did command; while my eye weeps bitterly my heart rejoices.

83 Sarah laid her head on the bosom of one of her handmaids, and she became as still as a stone.
84 Afterward she rose up and went about making inquiries till she came to Hebron; she inquired of all those whom she met walking in the road and no one could tell her what had happened to her son.
85 She came with her maid servants and men servants to Kireath-arba, which is Hebron, and she asked concerning her son; she remained there while she sent some of her servants to seek where Abraham had gone with Isaac. They went to seek him in the house of Shem and Eber, and they could not find him, and they sought throughout the land and he was not there.
86 And then Satan came to Sarah in the shape of an old man; he came and stood before her, and said to her, I spoke falsely to you, for Abraham did not kill his son and he is not dead. When she heard the word her joy was so greatly violent on account of her son, that her soul went out through joy; she died and was gathered to her people.
87 When Abraham had finished his service he returned with his son Isaac to his young men, and they rose up and went together to Beersheba, and they came home.
88 And Abraham sought for Sarah, and could not find her, and he made inquiries concerning her. They said to him, She went as far as Hebron to seek you both where you had gone, for thus was she informed.
89 Abraham and Isaac went to her to Hebron, and when they found that she was dead they lifted up their voices and wept bitterly over her; Isaac fell on his mother's face and wept over her, and he said, O my mother, my mother, how have you left me, and where have you gone? O how, how have you left me!
90 And Abraham and Isaac wept greatly and all their servants wept with them on account of Sarah, and they mourned over her a great and heavy mourning.

CHAPTER 24

1 The life of Sarah was one hundred and twenty-seven years, and Sarah died; and Abraham rose up from before his dead to seek a burial place to bury his wife Sarah. He went and spoke to the children of Heth, the inhabitants of the land, saying,
2 I am a stranger and a sojourner with you in your land; give me possession of a burial place in your land, that I may bury my dead from before me.
3 And the children of Heth said to Abraham, Behold the land is before you, in the choice of our sepulchers bury your dead, for no man shall withhold you from burying your dead.
4 Abraham said to them, If you are agreeable to this, go and entreat Ephron the son of Zochar for me, requesting that he may give me the cave of Machpelah which is in the end of his field, and I will purchase it of him for whatever he desires for it.
5 And Ephron lived among the children of Heth, and they went and called for him, and he came before Abraham. Ephron said to Abraham, Behold all you require your servant will do; Abraham said, No, but I will buy the cave and the field which you have for value, in order that it may be for possession of a burial place forever.
6 And Ephron answered and said, Behold the field and the cave are before you, give whatever you desire. Abraham said, Only at full value will I buy it from your hand, and from the hands of those that go in at the gate of your city, and from the hand of your descendants forever.

7 Ephron and all his brothers heard this, and Abraham weighed to Ephron four hundred shekels of silver in the hands of Ephron and in the hands of all his brothers. Abraham wrote this transaction; he wrote it and testified it with four witnesses.
8 And these are the names of the witnesses: Amigal son of Abishna the Hittite, Adichorom son of Ashunach the Hivite, Abdon son of Achiram the Gomerite, Bakdil the son of Abudish the Zidonite.
9 Abraham took the book of the purchase and placed it in his treasures, and these are the words that Abraham wrote in the book, namely:
10 That the cave and the field Abraham bought from Ephron the Hittite and from his descendants, and from those that go out of his city, and from their descendants forever, are to be a purchase to Abraham and to his descendants and to those that go forth from his loins, for a possession of a burial place forever. And he put a signet to it and testified it with witnesses.
11 The field and the cave that was in it and all that place were made sure to belong to Abraham and to his descendants after him, from the children of Heth; behold it is before Mamre in Hebron which is in the land of Canaan.
12 After this Abraham buried his wife Sarah there, and that place and all its boundary became to Abraham and to his descendants for a possession of a burial place.
13 And Abraham buried Sarah with pomp as observed at the interment of kings, and she was buried in very fine and beautiful garments.
14 At her bier was Shem, his sons Eber and Abimelech, together with Anar, Ashcol and Mamre, and all the grandees of the land followed her bier.
15 The days of Sarah were one hundred and twenty-seven years and she died, and Abraham made a great and heavy mourning, and he performed the rites of mourning for seven days.
16 And all the inhabitants of the land comforted Abraham and Isaac his son on account of Sarah.
17 When the days of their mourning passed by Abraham sent away his son Isaac. He went to the house of Shem and Eber, to learn the ways of the Lord and his instructions, and Abraham remained there three years.
18 At that time Abraham rose up with all his servants, and they went and returned homeward to Beersheba, and Abraham and all his servants remained in Beersheba.
19 At the revolution of the year Abimelech king of the Philistines died in that year; he was one hundred and ninety-three years old at his death. Abraham went with his people to the land of the Philistines, and they comforted the whole household and all his servants, and then he turned and went home.
20 It was after the death of Abimelech that the people of Gerar took Benmalich his son, and he was only twelve years old, and they made him lay the place of his father.
21 And they called his name Abimelech after the name of his father, for thus it was their custom to do in Gerar. Abimelech reigned instead of Abimelech his father, and he sat on his throne.
22 And Lot the son of Haran also died in those days, in the thirty-ninth year of the life of Isaac; all the days that Lot lived were one hundred and forty years and he died.
23 And these are the children of Lot, that were born to him by his daughters; the name of the first born was Moab, and the name of the second was Benami.
24 The two sons of Lot went and took themselves wives from the land of Canaan,

and they gave birth to children to them. The children of Moab were Ed, Mayon, Tarsus, and Kanvil, four sons; these are fathers to the children of Moab to this day.
25 And all the families of the children of Lot went to dwell wherever they should light on, for they were prolific and increased abundantly.
26 And they went and built themselves cities in the land where they lived, and they called the names of the cities which they built after their own names.
27 Nahor the son of Terah, brother to Abraham, died in those days in the fortieth year of the life of Isaac. All the days of Nahor were one hundred and seventy-two years; he died and was buried in Haran.
28 And when Abraham heard that his brother was dead he grieved sadly, and he mourned over his brother many days.
29 Abraham called for Eliezer his head servant to give him orders concerning his house, and he came and stood before him.
30 And Abraham said to him, Behold I am old, I do not know the day of my death; for I am advanced in days; now therefore rise up, go forth and do not take a wife for my son from this place and from this land, from the daughters of the Canaanites among whom we dwell.
31 But go to my land and to my birthplace, and take from there a wife for my son. The Lord God of Heaven and earth who took me from my father's house and brought me to this place, and said to me, To your offspring will I give this land for an inheritance forever, he will send his angel before you and prosper your way, that you may obtain a wife for my son from my family and from my father's house.
32 The servant answered his master Abraham and said, Behold I go to your birthplace and to your father's house, and take a wife for your son from there; but if the woman be not willing to follow me to this land, shall I take your son back to the land of your birthplace?
33 And Abraham said to him, See that you do not bring my son here again, for the Lord before whom I have walked will send his angel before you and prosper your way.
34 Eliezer did as Abraham ordered him, and Eliezer swore to Abraham his master on this matter; and Eliezer rose up and took ten camels of the camels of his master, and ten men from his master's servants with him, and they rose up and went to Haran, the city of Abraham and Nahor, in order to fetch a wife for Isaac the son of Abraham. While they were gone Abraham sent to the house of Shem and Eber, and they brought from there his son Isaac.
35 Isaac came home to his father's house to Beersheba, while Eliezer and his men came to Haran; and they stopped in the city by the watering place, and he made his camels to kneel down by the water and they remained there.
36 Eliezer, Abraham's servant, prayed and said, O God of Abraham my master; send me I pray you good speed this day and show kindness to my master, that you shall appoint this day a wife for my master's son from his family.
37 And the Lord listened to the voice of Eliezer, for the sake of his servant Abraham, and he happened to meet with the daughter of Bethuel, the son of Milcah, the wife of Nahor, brother to Abraham, and Eliezer came to her house.
38 Eliezer related to them all his concerns, and that he was Abraham's servant; they greatly rejoiced at him.
39 And they all blessed the Lord who brought this thing about; they gave him Rebecca, the daughter of Bethuel, for a wife for Isaac.
40 The young woman was of a beautiful appearance; she was a virgin, and Rebecca

was ten years old in those days.
41 And Bethuel and Laban and his children made a feast on that night, and Eliezer and his men came and ate and drank and rejoiced there on that night.
42 Eliezer rose up in the morning, he and the men that were with him, and he called to the whole household of Bethuel, saying, Send me away that I may go to my master; they rose up and sent away Rebecca and her nurse Deborah, the daughter of Uz, and they gave her silver and gold, men servants and maid servants, and they blessed her.
43 And they sent Eliezer away with his men and the servants took Rebecca; he went and returned to his master to the land of Canaan.
44 Isaac took Rebecca and she became his wife, and he brought her into the tent.
45 And Isaac was forty years old when he took Rebecca, the daughter of his uncle Bethuel, for a wife.

CHAPTER 25

1 It was at that time that Abraham again took a wife in his old age, and her name was Keturah, from the land of Canaan.
2 She gave birth to, to him: Zimran, Jokshan, Medan, Midian, Ishbak and Shuach, being six sons. And the children of Zimran were Abihen, Molich and Narim.
3 The sons of Jokshan were Sheba and Dedan, and the sons of Medan were Amida, Joab, Gochi, Elisha and Nothach; and the sons of Midian were Ephah, Epher, Chanoch, Abida and Eldaah.
4 The sons of Ishbak were Makiro, Beyodua and Tator.
5 The sons of Shuach were Bildad, Mamdad, Munan and Meban; all these are the families of the children of Keturah the Canaanitish woman which she gave birth to, to Abraham the Hebrew.
6 And Abraham sent all these away, and he gave them gifts; they went away from his son Isaac to dwell wherever they would find a place.
7 And all these went to the mountain at the east, and they built themselves six cities in which they lived to this day.
8 But the children of Sheba and Dedan, children of Jokshan, with their children, did not dwell with their brothers in their cities; they journeyed and encamped in the countries and wildernesses to this day.
9 And the children of Midian, son of Abraham, went to the east of the land of Cush. There they found a large valley in the eastern country, and remained there and built a city. They lived therein; that is the land of Midian to this day.
10 Midian lived in the city which he built, he and his five sons and all belonging to him.
11 And these are the names of the sons of Midian according to their names in their cities: Ephah, Epher, Chanoch, Abida and Eldaah.
12 And the sons of Ephah were Methach, Meshar, Avi and Tzanua, and the sons of Epher were Ephron, Zur, Alirun and Medin; the sons of Chanoch were Reuel, Rekem, Azi, Alyoshub and Alad.
13 The sons of Abida were Chur, Melud, Kerury, Molchi; and the sons of Eldaah were Miker, and Reba, and Malchiyah and Gabol. These are the names of the Midianites according to their families, and afterward the families of Midian spread throughout the land of Midian.

14 These are the generations of Ishmael the son of Abraham, whom Hagar, Sarah's handmaid, gave birth to, to Abraham.
15 And Ishmael took a wife from the land of Egypt, and her name was Ribah, the same is Meribah.
16 And Ribah gave birth to, to Ishmael: Nebayoth, Kedar, Adbeel, Mibsam and their sister Bosmath.
17 And Ishmael cast away his wife Ribah, and she went from him and returned to Egypt to the house of her father. She lived there, for she had been very bad in the sight of Ishmael, and in the sight of his father Abraham.
18 And Ishmael afterward took a wife from the land of Canaan, and her name was Malchuth, and she gave birth to, to him: Nishma, Dumah, Masa, Chadad, Tema, Yetur, Naphish and Kedma.
19 These are the sons of Ishmael, and these are their names, being twelve princes according to their nations. And the families of Ishmael afterward spread forth, and Ishmael took his children and all the property that he had gained, together with the souls of his household and all belonging to him, and they went to dwell where they should find a place.
20 They went and lived near the wilderness of Paran, and their dwelling was from Havilah to Shur, that is before Egypt as you come toward Assyria.
21 Ishmael and his sons lived in the land, and they had children born to them, and they were prolific and increased abundantly.
22 These are the names of the sons of Nebayoth the first born of Ishmael: Mend, Send, Mayon; and the sons of Kedar were Alyon, Kezem, Chamad and Eli.
23 The sons of Adbeel were Chamad and Jabin; and the sons of Mibsam were Obadiah, Ebedmelech and Yeush; these are the families of the children of Ribah the wife of Ishmael.
24 The sons of Mishma the son of Ishmael were Shamua, Zecaryon and Obed; and the sons of Dumah were Kezed, Eli, Machmad and Amed.
25 The sons of Masa were Melon, Mula and Ebidadon; and the sons of Chadad were Azur, Minzar and Ebedmelech; and the sons of Tema were Seir, Sadon and Yakol.
26 The sons of Yetur were Merith, Yaish, Alyo, and Pachoth; and the sons of Naphish were Ebed-Tamed, Abiyasaph and Mir; and the sons of Kedma were Calip, Tachti, and Omir; these were the children of Malchuth the wife of Ishmael according to their families.
27 All these are the families of Ishmael according to their generations, and they lived in those lands wherein they had built themselves cities to this day.
28 Rebecca the daughter of Bethuel, the wife of Abraham's son Isaac, was unable to conceive in those days, she had no children. Isaac lived with his father in the land of Canaan, and the Lord was with Isaac. Arpachshad the son of Shem the son of Noah died in those days, in the forty-eighth year of the life of Isaac, and all the days that Arpachshad lived were four hundred and thirty-eight years, and he died.

CHAPTER 26

1 In the fifty-ninth year of the life of Isaac the son of Abraham, Rebecca his wife was still unable to conceive in those days.
2 And Rebecca said to Isaac, Truly I have heard, my lord, that your mother Sarah was unable to conceive in her days until my Lord Abraham, your father, prayed for

her and she conceived by him.
3 Now therefore stand up, you also pray to God and he will hear your prayer and remember us through his mercies.
4 And Isaac answered his wife Rebecca, saying, Abraham has already prayed for me to God to reproduce his descendants, now therefore this barrenness must proceed to us from you.
5 And Rebecca said to him, But arise now you also and pray, that the Lord may hear your prayer and grant me children. Isaac listened to the words of his wife, and Isaac and his wife rose up and went to the land of Moriah to pray there and to seek the Lord, and when they had reached that place Isaac stood up and prayed to the Lord on account of his wife because she was unable to conceive.
6 And Isaac said, O Lord God of heaven and earth, whose goodness and mercies fill the earth, you who did take my father from his father's house and from his birthplace, and brought him to this land, and did say to him, To your descendants I will give the land, and you did promise him and did declare to him, I will reproduce your descendants as the stars of heaven and as the sand of the sea, now may your words be verified which you did speak to my father.
7 For you are the Lord our God, our eyes are toward you to give us descendants of men, as you did promise us, for you are the Lord our God and our eyes are directed toward you only.
8 And the Lord heard the prayer of Isaac the son of Abraham; the Lord was entreated of him and Rebecca his wife conceived.
9 And in about seven months after the children struggled together within her, it pained her greatly and she was wearied on account of them. She said to all the women who were then in the land, Did such a thing happen to you as it has to me? And they said to her, No.
10 And she said to them, Why am I alone in this among all the women that were on earth? And she went to the land of Moriah to seek the Lord on account of this; she went to Shem and Eber his son to make inquiries of them in this matter, that they should seek the Lord in this thing respecting her.
11 She also asked Abraham to seek and inquire of the Lord about all that had befallen her.
12 They all inquired of the Lord concerning this matter, and they brought her word from the Lord and told her, Two children are in your womb, and two nations shall rise from them; one nation shall be stronger than the other, and the greater shall serve the younger.
13 When her days to be delivered were completed, she knelt down, and behold there were twins in her womb, as the Lord had spoken to her.
14 The first came out red all over like a hairy garment, and all the people of the land called his name Esau, saying, This one was made complete from the womb.
15 And after that came his brother, and his hand took hold of Esau's heel, therefore they called his name Jacob.
16 Isaac, the son of Abraham, was sixty years old when he had them.
17 The boys grew up to their fifteenth year, and they came among the society of men. Esau was a designing and deceitful man, and an expert hunter in the field; Jacob was a man perfect and wise, dwelling in tents, feeding flocks and learning the instructions of the Lord and the commands of his father and mother.
18 Isaac and the children of his household lived with his father Abraham in the land of Canaan, as God had commanded them.

19 Ishmael the son of Abraham went with his children and all belonging to them; they returned there to the land of Havilah, and they lived there.
20 And all the children of Abraham's concubines went to dwell in the land of the east, for Abraham had sent them away from his son and had given them presents, and they went away.
21 Abraham gave all that he had to his son Isaac, and he also gave him all his treasures.
22 And he commanded him saying, Do you not know and understand the Lord is God in heaven and in earth, and there is no other beside him?
23 It was he who took me from my father's house, and from my birthplace, and gave me all the delights on earth; who delivered me from the counsel of the wicked, for in him I did trust.
24 He brought me to this place, and delivered me from Ur Casdim, and said to me, To your descendants I will give all these land and they shall inherit them when they keep my commandments, my statutes and my judgments that I have commanded you, and which I shall command them.
25 Now therefore my son, listen to my voice, and keep the commandments of the Lord your God, which I commanded you. Do not turn from the right way either to the right or to the left, in order that it may be well with you and your children after you forever.
26 And remember the wonderful works of the Lord and his kindness that he has shown toward us, in having delivered us from the hands of our enemies; the Lord our God caused them to fall into our hands; now therefore keep all that I have commanded you and turn not away from the commandments of your God; serve none beside him, in order that it may be well with you and your descendants after you.
27 Teach your children and your descendants the instructions of the Lord and his commandments, and teach them the upright way in which they should go, in order that it may be well with them forever.
28 Isaac answered his father and said to him, That which my Lord has commanded thatI will do, and I will not depart from the commands of the Lord my God; I will keep all that he commanded me. And Abraham blessed his son Isaac, and also his children, and Abraham taught Jacob the instruction of the Lord and his ways.
29 It was at that time that Abraham died, in the fifteenth year of the life of Jacob and Esau, the sons of Isaac, and all the days of Abraham were one hundred and seventy-five years. He died and was gathered to his people in good old age, old and satisfied with days, and Isaac and Ishmael his sons buried him.
30 When the inhabitants of Canaan heard that Abraham was dead, they all came with their kings and princes and all their men to bury Abraham.
31 All the inhabitants of the land of Haran, all the families of the house of Abraham, all the princes and grandees, and the sons of Abraham by the concubines, all came when they heard of Abraham's death. They rewarded Abraham's kindness, and comforted Isaac his son, and they buried Abraham in the cave which he bought from Ephron the Hittite and his children, for the possession of a burial place.
32 All the inhabitants of Canaan, and all those who had known Abraham, wept for Abraham a whole year; men and women mourned over him.
33 Alll the little children, and all the inhabitants of the land wept on account of Abraham, for Abraham had been good to them all, because he had been upright with God and men.

34 There arose not a man who feared God like Abraham, for he had feared his God from his youth, and had served the Lord, and had gone in all his ways during his life from his childhood to the day of his death.
35 And the Lord was with him and delivered him from the counsel of Nimrod and his people; when he made war with the four kings of Elam he conquered them.
36 He brought all the children of the earth to the service of God and he taught them the ways of the Lord, and caused them to know the Lord.
37 He formed a grove and planted a vineyard therein, and he had always prepared in his tent meat and drink to those that passed through the land, that they might satisfy themselves in his house.
38 The Lord God delivered the whole earth on account of Abraham.
39 It was after the death of Abraham that God blessed his son Isaac and his children, and the Lord was with Isaac as he had been with his father Abraham, for Isaac kept all the commandments of the Lord as Abraham his father had commanded him; he did not turn to the right or to the left from the right path which his father had commanded him.

CHAPTER 27

1 Esau at that time, after the death of Abraham, frequently went in the field to hunt.
2 Nimrod king of Babel, the same was Amraphel, also frequently went with his mighty men to hunt in the field, and to walk about with his men in the cool of the day.
3 Nimrod was observing Esau all those days, for jealousy was formed in the heart of Nimrod against Esau.
4 On a certain day Esau went in the field to hunt, and he found Nimrod walking in the wilderness with his two men.
5 All his mighty men and his people were with him in the wilderness, but they kept at a distance; they went from him in different directions to hunt, and Esau concealed himself from Nimrod, and he lurked for him in the wilderness.
6 And Nimrod and his men that were with him did not know him. Nimrod and his men frequently walked about in the field at the cool of the day, and to know where his men were hunting in the field.
7 Nimrod and two of his men that were with him came to the place where they were, when Esau appeared suddenly from his lurking place, drew his sword, and hurriedly ran to Nimrod and cut off his head.
8 Esau fought a desperate fight with the two men that were with Nimrod, and when they called out to him, Esau turned to them and struck them to death with his sword.
9 All the mighty men of Nimrod, who had left him to go to the wilderness, heard the cry at a distance, and they knew the voices of those two men; they ran to know the cause of it and they found their king and the two men that were with him lying dead in the wilderness.
10 When Esau saw the mighty men of Nimrod coming at a distance, he fled, and thereby escaped. Esau took the valuable garments of Nimrod which Nimrod's father had bequeathed to Nimrod, with which Nimrod prevailed over the whole land; he ran and concealed them in his house.
11 Esau took those garments and ran into the city on account of Nimrod's men, and

he came to his father's house wearied and exhausted from fight, and he was ready to die through grief when he approached his brother Jacob and sat before him.
12 And he said to his brother Jacob, Behold I shall die this day; wherefore then do I want the birthright? And Jacob acted wisely with Esau in this matter, and Esau sold his birthright to Jacob, for it was so brought about by the Lord.
13 Esau's portion in the cave of the field of Machpelah, which Abraham had bought from the children of Heth for the possession of a burial ground, Esau also sold to Jacob, and Jacob bought all this from his brother Esau for value given.
14 Jacob wrote all of this in a book and he testified the same with witnesses, and sealed it, and the book remained in the hands of Jacob.
15 When Nimrod the son of Cush died, his men lifted him up and brought him in consternation, and buried him in his city, and all the days that Nimrod lived were two hundred and fifteen years and he died.
16 The days that Nimrod reigned on the people of the land were one hundred and eighty-five years; and Nimrod died by the sword of Esau in shame and contempt, and the descendants of Abraham caused his death as he had seen in his dream.
17 At the death of Nimrod his kingdom became divided into many divisions, and all those parts that Nimrod reigned over were restored to the respective kings of the land, who recovered them after the death of Nimrod. All the people of the house of Nimrod were for a long time enslaved to all the other kings of the land.

CHAPTER 28

1 In those days, after the death of Abraham, in that year the Lord brought a heavy famine in the land. While the famine was raging in the land of Canaan, Isaac rose up to go down to Egypt on account of the famine, as his father Abraham had done.
2 And the Lord appeared that night to Isaac and said to him, Do not go down to Egypt but rise and go to Gerar, to Abimelech king of the Philistines, and remain there till the famine shall cease.
3 Isaac rose up and went to Gerar, as the Lord commanded him, and he remained there a full year.
4 And when Isaac came to Gerar, the people of the land saw that Rebecca his wife was of a beautiful appearance, and the people of Gerar asked Isaac concerning his wife, and he said, She is my sister, for he was afraid to say she was his wife that the people of the land should kill him on account of her.
5 The princes of Abimelech went and praised the woman to the king, but he answered them not, neither did he give attention to their words.
6 But he heard them say that Isaac declared her to be his sister, so the king reserved this within himself.
7 And when Isaac had remained three months in the land, Abimelech looked out the window, and he saw Isaac was sporting with Rebecca his wife, for Isaac lived in the outer house belonging to the king, so that the house of Isaac was opposite the house of the king.
8 And the king said to Isaac, What is this you have done to us in saying of your wife, She is my sister? How easily might one of the great men of the people have lain with her, and you would then have brought guilt on us.
9 And Isaac said to Abimelech, Because I was afraid that I die on account of my wife, therefore I said, She is my sister.
10 At that time Abimelech gave orders to all his princes and great men, and they

took Isaac and Rebecca his wife and brought them before the king.
11 The king commanded that they should dress them in princely garments, and make them ride through the streets of the city, and proclaim before them throughout the land, saying, This is the man and this is his wife; whoever touches this man or his wife shall certainly die. And Isaac returned with his wife to the king's house, and the Lord was with Isaac and he continued to become great and lacked nothing.
12 And the Lord caused Isaac to find favor in the sight of Abimelech, and in the sight of all his subjects, and Abimelech acted well with Isaac, for Abimelech remembered the oath and the covenant that existed between his father and Abraham.
13 Abimelech said to Isaac, Behold the whole earth is before you; dwell wherever it may seem good in your sight until you shall return to your land. Abimelech gave Isaac fields and vineyards and the best part of the land of Gerar, to sow and reap and eat the fruits of the ground until the days of the famine would have passed by.
14 And Isaac sowed in that land, and received a hundred-fold in the same year, and the Lord blessed him.
15 The man became great, and he had possession of flocks and possession of herds and a great store of servants.
16 When the days of the famine had passed away the Lord appeared to Isaac and said to him, Rise up, go forth from this place and return to your land, to the land of Canaan; Isaac rose up and returned to Hebron which is in the land of Canaan, he and all belonging to him as the Lord commanded him.
17 Ater this Shelach the son at Arpachshad died in that year, which is the eighteenth year of the lives of Jacob and Esau; all the days that Shelach lived were four hundred and thirty-three years and he died.
18 At that time Isaac sent his younger son Jacob to the house of Shem and Eber, and he learned the instructions of the Lord; Jacob remained in the house of Shem and Eber for thirty-two years; Esau his brother did not go for he was not willing to go, and he remained in his father's house in the land of Canaan.
19 Esau was continually hunting in the fields to bring home what he could get, so did Esau all the days.
20 Esau was a designing and deceitful man, one who hunted after the hearts of men and inveigled them, and Esau was a valiant man in the field; in the course of time he went as usual to hunt and came as far as the field of Seir, the same is Edom.
21 And he remained in the land of Seir hunting in the field a year and four months.
22 Esau there saw in the land of Seir the daughter of a man of Canaan, and her name was Jehudith, the daughter of Beeri, son of Epher, from the families of Heth the son of Canaan.
23 Esau took her for a wife, and he came to her; forty years old was Esau when he took her, and he brought her to Hebron, the land of his father's dwelling place, and he lived there.
24 It came to pass in those days, in the hundred and tenth year of the life of Isaac, that is in the fiftieth year of the life of Jacob, in that year Shem the son of Noah died; Shem was six hundred years old at his death.
25 And when Shem died Jacob returned to his father to Hebron which is in the land of Canaan.
26 And in the fifty-sixth year of the life of Jacob, people came from Haran, and Rebecca was told concerning her brother Laban the son of Bethuel.
27 The wife of Laban was unable to conceive in those days, and gave birth to no children, and also all his handmaids gave birth to none, to him.

28 And the Lord afterward remembered Adinah the wife of Laban, and she conceived and gave birth to twin daughters, and Laban named his daughters: the name of the elder Leah, and the name of the younger Rachel.
29 And those people came and told these things to Rebecca, and Rebecca rejoiced greatly that the Lord had visited her brother and that he had gotten children.

CHAPTER 29

1 Isaac the son of Abraham became old and advanced in days, and his eyes became heavy through age; they were dim and could not see.
2 At that time Isaac called to Esau his son, saying, Get I pray you your weapons, your quiver and your bow; rise up and go forth into the field and get me some venison, make me savory meat and bring it to me that I may eat in order that I may bless you before my death, as I have now become old and gray-headed.
3 And Esau did so; he took his weapon and went forth into the field to hunt for venison, as usual, to bring to his father as he had ordered him, so that he might bless him.
4 And Rebecca heard all the words that Isaac had spoken to Esau, and she hurried and called her son Jacob, saying, Thus did your father speak to your brother Esau, and thus did I hear, now therefore hurry and make that which I shall tell you.
5 Rise up and go, I pray you, to the flock and fetch me two fine kids of the goats; I will get the savory meat for your father and you shall bring the savory meat that he may eat before your brother will have come from the hunt, in order that your father may bless you.
6 And Jacob hurried and did as his mother had commanded him, and he made the savory meat and brought it before his father before Esau had come from his hunt.
7 And Isaac said to Jacob, Who are you, my son? And he said, I am your first born Esau. I have done as you did order me, now therefore rise up I pray you and eat of my hunt, in order that your soul may bless me as you did speak to me.
8 And Isaac rose up and he ate and drank, and his heart was comforted; he blessed Jacob and Jacob went away from his father. As soon as Isaac had blessed Jacob and had gone away from him, behold Esau came from his hunt in the field, and he also made savory meat and brought it to his father to eat thereof and to bless him.
9 And Isaac said to Esau, And who was he that has taken venison and brought it me before you came and whom I did bless? And Esau knew that his brother Jacob had done this, and the anger of Esau was set ablaze against his brother Jacob that he had acted thus toward him.
10 And Esau said, Is he not rightly called Jacob? For he has supplanted me twice, he took away my birthright and now he has taken away my blessing. And Esau wept greatly. When Isaac heard the voice of his son Esau weeping, Isaac said to Esau, What can I do, my son, your brother came with subtlety and took away your blessing? Esau hated his brother Jacob on account of the blessing that his father had given him, and his anger was greatly roused against him.
11 And Jacob was very much afraid of his brother Esau; he rose up and fled to the house of Eber the son of Shem, and he concealed himself there on account of his brother. Jacob was sixty-three years old when he went forth from the land of Canaan from Hebron, and Jacob was concealed in Eber's house fourteen years on account of his brother Esau, and he continued there to learn the ways of the Lord

and his commandments.
12 When Esau saw that Jacob had fled and escaped from him, and that Jacob had cunningly obtained the blessing, then Esau grieved greatly. He was also troubled at his father and mother; he rose up and took his wife and went away from his father and mother to the land of Seir, and he lived there. Esau saw there a woman from among the daughters of Heth whose name was Bosmath, the daughter of Elon the Hittite, and he took her for a wife in addition to his first wife, and Esau called her name Adah, saying the blessing had in that time passed from him.
13 And Esau lived in the land of Seir six months without seeing his father and mother, and afterward Esau took his wives and rose up and returned to the land of Canaan. And Esau placed his two wives in his father's house in Hebron.
14 The wives of Esau troubled and provoked Isaac and Rebecca with their works, for they walked not in the ways of the Lord, but served their father's gods of wood and stone as their father had taught them; they were more wicked than their father.
15 They went according to the evil desires of their hearts, and they sacrificed and burnt incense to the Baalim, and Isaac and Rebecca became weary of them.
16 And Rebecca said, I am weary of my life because of the daughters of Heth; if Jacob took a wife of the daughters of Heth, such as these which are of the daughters of the land, what good then is life to me?
17 In those days Adah the wife of Esau conceived and gave birth to him a son, and Esau called the name of the son that was born to him Eliphaz, and Esau was sixty-five years old when she gave birth to him.
18 Ishmael the son of Abraham died in those days, in the sixty-fourth year of the life of Jacob, and all the days that Ishmael lived were one hundred and thirty-seven years and he died.
19 And when Isaac heard that Ishmael was dead he mourned for him, and Isaac lamented over him many days.
20 At the end of fourteen years of Jacob's residing in the house of Eber, Jacob desired to see his father and mother, and Jacob came to the house of his father and mother to Hebron, and Esau had in those days forgotten what Jacob had done to him in having taken the blessing from him.
21 And when Esau saw Jacob coming to his father and mother he remembered what Jacob had done to him, and he was greatly incensed against him and he sought to kill him.
22 And Isaac the son of Abraham was old and advanced in days, and Esau said, Now my father's time is drawing nigh that he must die, and when he shall die I will kill my brother Jacob.
23 This was told to Rebecca, and she hurried and sent and called for Jacob her son, and she said to him, Arise, go and flee to Haran to my brother Laban and remain there for some time, until your brother's anger be turned from you and then shall you come back.
24 And Isaac called to Jacob and said to him, Take not a wife from the daughters of Canaan, for thus did our father Abraham command us according to the word of the Lord which he had commanded him, saying, Unto your offspring will I give this land; if your children keep my covenant that I have made with you, then I will also perform to your children that which I have spoken to you and I will not turn away from them.
25 Now therefore my son listen to my voice, to all that I shall command you, and refrain from taking a wife from among the daughters of Canaan; arise, go to Haran

to the house of Bethuel your mother's father, and take to you a wife from there from the daughters of Laban your mother's brother.
26 Therefore be careful that you should not forget the Lord your God and all his ways in the land to which you go, and should get connected with the people of the land and pursue vanity and turn away from the Lord your God.
27 But when you come to the land there serve the Lord, do not turn to the right or to the left from the way which I commanded you and which you did learn.
28 And may the Almighty God grant you favor in the sight of the people of the earth, that you may take there a wife according to your choice; one who is good and upright in the ways of the Lord.
29 May God give to you and your descendants the blessing of your father Abraham, and make you prolific and reproduce, and may you become a multitude of people in the land where you go; may God cause you to return to this land, the land of your father's dwelling, with children and with great riches, with joy and with pleasure.
30 And Isaac finished commanding Jacob and blessing him, and he gave him many gifts, together with silver and gold, and he sent him away. Jacob listened to his father and mother; he kissed them and arose and went to Padan-aram, and Jacob was seventy-seven years old when he went out from the land of Canaan from Beersheba.
31 When Jacob went away to go to Haran Esau called to his son Eliphaz, and secretly spoke to him, saying, Now hurry, take your sword in your hand and pursue Jacob and pass before him in the road, and lurk for him; kill him with your sword in one of the mountains, and take all belonging to him and come back.
32 Eliphaz the son of Esau was an active man and expert with the bow as his father had taught him, and he was a noted hunter in the field and a valiant man.
33 Eliphaz did as his father had commanded him, and Eliphaz was at that time thirteen years old; Eliphaz rose up and went and took ten of his mother's brothers with him and pursued Jacob.
34 He closely followed Jacob, and he lurked for him in the border of the land of Canaan opposite to the city of Shechem.
35 And Jacob saw Eliphaz and his men pursuing him; Jacob stood still in the place in which he was going, in order to know what this was, for he did not know the thing. Eliphaz drew his sword and he went on advancing, he and his men, toward Jacob. And Jacob said to them, Why have you come here, and what does it mean that you pursue with your swords?
36 And Eliphaz came near to Jacob and he answered and said to him, Thus did my father command me, and now therefore I will not deviate from the orders which my father gave me. When Jacob saw that Esau had spoken to Eliphaz to employ force, Jacob then approached and supplicated Eliphaz and his men, saying to him,
37 Behold all that I have and which my father and mother gave to me, that you should take and go from me, and do not kill me; may this thing be accounted to you a righteousness.
38 And the Lord caused Jacob to find favor in the sight of Eliphaz the son of Esau, and his men, and they listened to the voice of Jacob, and they did not put him to death; Eliphaz and his men took all belonging to Jacob together with the silver and gold that he had brought with him from Beersheba; they left him nothing.
39 Eliphaz and his men went away from him and they returned to Esau to Beersheba, and they told him all that had occurred to them with Jacob, and they gave him all that they had taken from Jacob.

40 Esau was indignant at Eliphaz his son, and at his men that were with him, because they had not put Jacob to death.
41 And they answered and said to Esau, Because Jacob supplicated us in this matter not to kill him, our pity was increased toward him, and we took all belonging to him and brought it to you. Esau took all the silver and gold which Eliphaz had taken from Jacob and he put them by in his house.
42 At that time when Esau saw that Isaac had blessed Jacob, and had commanded him, saying, You shall not take a wife from among the daughters of Canaan, and that the daughters of Canaan were bad in the sight of Isaac and Rebecca,
43 Then he went to the house of Ishmael his uncle, and in addition to his older wives he took Machlath the daughter of Ishmael, the sister of Nebayoth, for a wife.

CHAPTER 30

1 Jacob went forth continuing his road to Haran, and he came as far as mount Moriah, and he stayed there all night near the city of Luz. The Lord appeared there to Jacob on that night and said to him, I am the Lord God of Abraham and the God of Isaac your father; the land on which you dwell I will give to you and your descendants.
2 Behold I am with you and will keep you wherever you go, and I will reproduce your descendants as the stars of Heaven, and I will cause all your enemies to fall before you; when they make war with you they shall not prevail over you, and I will bring you again to this land with joy, with children, and with great riches.
3 Jacob awoke from his sleep and he rejoiced greatly at the vision which he had seen, and he called the name of that place Bethel.
4 Jacob rose up from that place quite jubilant, and when he walked his feet felt light to him for joy, and he went from there to the land of the children of the East, and returned to Haran and sat by the shepherd's well.
5 There he found some men going from Haran to feed their flocks, and Jacob made inquiries of them, and they said, We are from Haran.
6 And he said to them, Do you know Laban, the son of Nahor? And they said, We know him and look, his daughter Rachel is coming along to feed her father's flock.
7 While he was yet speaking with them, Rachel the daughter of Laban came to feed her father's sheep, for she was a shepherdess.
8 When Jacob saw Rachel, the daughter of Laban, his mother's brother, he ran and kissed her and lifted up his voice and wept.
9 Jacob told Rachel that he was the son of Rebecca, her father's sister, and Rachel ran and told her father; Jacob continued to cry because he had nothing with him to bring to the house of Laban.
10 When Laban heard that his sister's son Jacob had come, he ran, kissed him and embraced him, brought him into the house and gave him bread, and he ate.
11 And Jacob related to Laban what his brother Esau had done to him, and what his son Eliphaz had done to him in the road.
12 Jacob resided in Laban's house for one month, and Jacob ate and drank in the house of Laban, and afterward Laban said to Jacob, Tell me what shall be your

wages, for how can you serve me for nothing?
13 Laban had no sons but only daughters; his other wives and handmaids were still unable to conceive in those days. These are the names of Laban's daughters which his wife Adinah had borne to him: the name of the elder was Leah and the name of the younger was Rachel. Leah was tender-eyed, but Rachel was beautiful and well favored, and Jacob loved her.
14 And Jacob said to Laban, I will serve you seven years for Rachel your younger daughter; and Laban consented to this and Jacob served Laban seven years for his daughter Rachel.
15 In the second year of Jacob's dwelling in Haran, that is in the seventy ninth year of the life of Jacob, Eber the son of Shem died; he was four hundred and sixty-four years old at his death.
16 And when Jacob heard that Eber was dead he grieved greatly; he lamented and mourned over him many days.
17 In the third year of Jacob's dwelling in Haran, Bosmath, the daughter of Ishmael, the wife of Esau, gave birth to him a son, and Esau called his name Reuel.
18 And in the fourth year of Jacob's residence in the house of Laban, the Lord visited Laban and remembered him on account of Jacob, and sons were born to him: his first born was Beor, his second was Alib, and the third was Chorash.
19 The Lord gave Laban riches and honor, sons and daughters, and the man increased greatly on account of Jacob.
20 In those days Jacob served Laban in all manner of work, in the house and in the field, and the blessing of the Lord was in all that belonged to Laban in the house and in the field.
21 In the fifth year Jehudith died, the daughter of Beeri, the wife of Esau, in the land of Canaan, and she had no sons but daughters only.
22 These are the names of her daughters which she gave birth to, to Esau: the name of the elder was Marzith, and the name of the younger was Puith.
23 And when Jehudith died, Esau rose up and went to Seir to hunt in the field, as usual, and Esau lived in the land of Seir for a long time.
24 In the sixth year Esau took for a wife, in addition to his other wives, Ahlibamah, the daughter of Zebeon the Hivite, and Esau brought her to the land of Canaan.
25 And Ahlibamah conceived and gave birth to, to Esau, three sons: Yeush, Yaalan, and Korah.
26 In those days, in the land of Canaan, there was a quarrel between the herdsmen of Esau and the herdsmen of the inhabitants of the land of Canaan, for Esau's cattle and goods were too abundant for him to remain in the land of Canaan, in his father's house; the land of Canaan could not bear him on account of his cattle.
27 And when Esau saw that his quarreling increased with the inhabitants of the land of Canaan, he rose up and took his wives and his sons and his daughters, and all belonging to him, and the cattle which he possessed, and all his property that he had acquired in the land of Canaan; he went away from the inhabitants of the land to the land of Seir, and Esau and all belonging to him lived in the land of Seir.
28 But from time to time Esau would go and see his father and mother in the land of Canaan, and Esau intermarried with the Horites, and he gave his daughters to the sons of Seir, the Horite.
29 He gave his elder daughter Marzith to Anah, the son of Zebeon, his wife's brother, and Puith he gave to Azar, the son of Bilhan the Horite; Esau lived in the mountain, he and his children, and they were prolific and multiplied.

CHAPTER 31

1 In the seventh year, Jacob's service to Laban was completed, and Jacob said to Laban, Give me my wife, for the days of my service are fulfilled; Laban did so, and Laban and Jacob assembled all the people of that place and they made a feast.
2 In the evening Laban came to the house, and afterward Jacob came there with the people of the feast, and Laban extinguished all the lights that were there in the house.
3 Jacob said to Laban, Why do you do this thing to us? And Laban answered, Such is our custom to act in this land.
4 Afterward Laban took his daughter Leah, and he brought her to Jacob, and he came to her and Jacob did not know that she was Leah.
5 And Laban gave his daughter Leah his maid Zilpah for a handmaid.
6 All the people at the feast knew what Laban had done to Jacob, but they didn't tell a thing to Jacob.
7 All the neighbors came that night to Jacob's house, and they ate and drank and rejoiced, and played before Leah on timbrels, and with dances, and they responded before Jacob, Heleah, Heleah.
8 Jacob heard their words but did not understand their meaning, but he thought such might be their custom in this land.
9 And the neighbors spoke these words before Jacob during the night, and all the lights that were in the house Laban had that night been extinguished.
10 In the morning, when daylight appeared, Jacob turned to his wife and he saw it was Leah that had been lying in his bosom, and Jacob said, So now I know what the neighbors said last night, Heleah, they said, and I knew it not.
11 Jacob called to Laban, and said to him, What is this that you did to me? Certainly I served you for Rachel; why did you deceive me and give me Leah?
12 Laban answered Jacob, saying, Not so is it done in our place to give the younger before the elder; therefore if you desire to take her sister likewise, take her to you for the service which you will serve me for another seven years.
13 Jacob did so, and he also took Rachel for a wife; he served Laban seven years more, and Jacob also came to Rachel, and he loved Rachel more than Leah; Laban gave her his maid Bilhah for a handmaid.
14 When the Lord saw that Leah was hated, the Lord opened her womb and she conceived and gave birth to Jacob four sons in those days.
15 And these are their names: Reuben, Simeon, Levi, and Judah, and afterward she ceased bearing.
16 At that time Rachel was unable to conceive and had no children, and Rachel envied her sister Leah. When Rachel saw that she gave birth to no children to Jacob, she took her handmaid Bilhah, and she gave birth to Jacob two sons, Dan and Naphtali.
17 When Leah saw that she had ceased bearing, she also took her handmaid Zilpah, and she gave her to Jacob for a wife. Jacob also came to Zilpah, and she gave birth to Jacob two sons, Gad and Asher.
18 Leah again conceived and gave birth to Jacob in those days two sons and one daughter, and these are their names: Issachar, Zebulon, and their sister Dinah.
19 Rachel was still unable to conceive in those days and Rachel prayed to the Lord at

that time, and she said, O Lord God remember me and visit me, I beg you, for now my husband will cast me off, for I have borne him no children.
20 Now O Lord God, hear my supplication before you, and see my affliction, and give me children like one of the handmaids, that I may no more bear my reproach.
21 God heard her and opened her womb, and Rachel conceived and gave birth to a son, and she said, The Lord has taken away my reproach. She called his name Joseph, saying, May the Lord add to me another son; Jacob was ninety-one years old when she gave birth to him.
22 At that time Jacob's mother, Rebecca, sent her nurse Deborah the daughter of Uz, and two of Isaac's servants to Jacob.
23 They came to Jacob to Haran and said to him, Rebecca has sent us to you that you shall return to your father's house to the land of Canaan; Jacob listened to them of this which his mother had spoken.
24 At that time, the other seven years which Jacob served Laban for Rachel were completed, and it was at the end of fourteen years that he had lived in Haran, Jacob said to Laban, Give me my wives and send me away that I may go to my land, for behold my mother did send to me from the land at Canaan that I should return to my father's house.
25 And Laban said to him, Not so I pray you; if I have found favor in your sight do not leave me; tell me your wages and I will give them, and remain with me.
26 Jacob said to him, This is what you shall give me for wages, that I shall this day pass through all your flock and take away from them every lamb that is speckled and spotted and such as are brown among the sheep, and among the goats, and if you will do this thing for me I will return and feed your flock and keep them as at first.
27 Laban did so, and Laban removed from his flock all that Jacob had said and gave them to him.
28 And Jacob placed all that he had removed from Laban's flock in the hands of his sons, and Jacob was feeding the remainder of Laban's flock.
29 When the servants of Isaac which he had sent to Jacob saw that Jacob would not return with them to the land of Canaan to his father, they went away from him and returned home to the land of Canaan.
30 And Deborah remained with Jacob in Haran; she did not return with the servants of Isaac to the land of Canaan, and Deborah resided with Jacob's wives and children in Haran.
31 Jacob served Laban six years longer, and when the sheep brought forth, Jacob removed from them such as were speckled and spotted, as he had determined with Laban; Jacob did so at Laban's for six years, and the man increased abundantly. He had cattle and maid servants and men servants, camels, and asses.
32Jacob had two hundred drove of cattle, and his cattle were of large size and of beautiful appearance and were very productive; all the families of the sons of men desired to get some of the cattle of Jacob, for they were greatly prosperous.
33 Many of the sons of men came to procure some of Jacob's flock, and Jacob gave them a sheep for a man servant or a maid servant or for an ass or a camel, or whatever Jacob desired from them they gave him.
34 Jacob obtained riches and honor and possessions by means of these transactions with the sons of men, and the children of Laban envied him of this honor.
35 In the course of time he heard the words of Laban's sons, saying, Jacob has taken away all that was our father's, and of that which was our father's has he acquired all

this glory.
36 And Jacob observed the countenance of Laban and of his children, and it was not toward him in those days as it had been before.
37 The Lord appeared to Jacob at the expiration of the six years, and said to him, Arise, go forth out of this land, and return to the land of your birthplace and I will be with you.
38 And Jacob rose up at that time and he mounted his children and wives and all belonging to him on camels, and he went forth to go to the land of Canaan to his father Isaac.
39 Laban did not know that Jacob had gone from him, for Laban had been sheep-shearing that day.
40 Rachel stole her father's images, and she took them and concealed them on the camel on which she sat, and she went on.
41 And this is the manner of the images: in taking a man who is the firstborn and slaying him and taking the hair off his head; taking salt and salting the head and anointing it in oil, then taking a small tablet of copper or a tablet of gold and writing the name on it and placing the tablet under his tongue; taking the head with the tablet under the tongue and putting it in the house and lighting up lights before it and bowing down to it.
42 And at the time when they bow down to it, it speaks to them in all matters that they ask of it, through the power of the name which is written in it.
43 And some make them in the figures of men, of gold and silver, and go to them in times known to them, and the figures receive the influence of the stars, and tell them future things; in this manner were the images which Rachel stole from her father.
44 Rachel stole these images which were her father's in order that Laban might not know through them where Jacob had gone.
45 Laban came home and he asked concerning Jacob and his household, and he was not to be found; Laban sought his images to know where Jacob had gone, and could not find them. He went to some other images, and he inquired of them and they told him that Jacob had fled from him to his father's, to the land of Canaan.
46 Laban then rose up and took his brothers and all his servants, and he went forth and pursued Jacob, and he overtook him in mount Gilead.
47 And Laban said to Jacob, What is this you have done to me to flee and deceive me, and lead my daughters and their children as captives taken by the sword?
48 You did not suffer me to kiss them and send them away with joy, and you did steal my gods and did go away.
49 And Jacob answered Laban, saying, Because I was afraid that you would take your daughters by force from me; and now with whomsoever you find your gods he shall die.
50 And Laban searched for the images and he examined in all Jacob's tents and furniture, but could not find them.
51 And Laban said to Jacob, We will make a covenant together and it shall be a testimony between me and you; if you shall afflict my daughters, or shall take other wives besides my daughters, even God shall be a witness between me and you in this matter.
52 And they took stones and made a heap, and Laban said, This heap is a witness between me and you. He called the name thereof Gilead.
53 Jacob and Laban offered sacrifice on the mount, and they ate there by the heap, and they stayed in the mount all night. Laban rose up early in the morning; he

wept with his daughters and he kissed them, and he returned to his place.
54 He hurried and sent off his son Beor, who was seventeen years old, with Abichorof the son of Uz, the son of Nahor, and with them were ten men.
55 They hurried and went and passed on the road before Jacob, and they came by another road to the land of Seir.
56 They came to Esau and said to him, Thus says your brother and relative, your mother's brother Laban, the son of Bethuel, saying,
57 Have you heard what Jacob your brother has done to me, who first came to me naked and gave birth to? I went to meet him and brought him to my house with honor; I made him great, and I gave him my two daughters for wives and also two of my maids.
58 And God blessed him on my account; he increased abundantly, and had sons, daughters and maid servants.
59 He has also an immense stock of flocks and herds, camels and asses, also silver and gold in abundance; when he saw that his wealth increased, he left me while I went to shear my sheep, and he rose up and fled in secrecy.
60 He lifted his wives and children on camels, and he led away all his cattle and property which he acquired in my land, and he lifted up his countenance to go to his father Isaac, to the land of Canaan.
61 He did not let me kiss my daughters and their children; he led my daughters as captives taken by the sword, and he also stole my gods and he fled.
62 And now I have left him in the mountain of the brook of Jabuk, him and all belonging to him; he lacks nothing.
63 If it be your wish to go to him, go then and there you will find him, and you can do to him as your soul desires; and Laban's messengers came and told Esau all these things.
64 Esau heard all the words of Laban's messengers, and his anger was greatly set ablaze against Jacob, and he remembered his hatred, and his anger burned within him.
65 Esau hurried and took his children and servants and the souls of his household, being sixty men; he went and assembled all the children of Seir the Horite and their people, being three hundred and forty men. He took all this number of four hundred men with drawn swords, and he went to Jacob to strike him.
66 Esau divided this number into several parts, and he took the sixty men of his children and servants and the souls of his household as one head, and gave them in care of Eliphaz his eldest son.
67 The remaining heads he gave to the care of the six sons of Seir the Horite, and he placed every man over his generations and children.
68 The whole of this camp went as it was, and Esau went among them toward Jacob, and he conducted them with speed.
69 And Laban's messengers departed from Esau and went to the land of Canaan, and they came to the house of Rebecca the mother of Jacob and Esau.
70 They told her saying, Behold your son Esau has gone against his brother Jacob with four hundred men, for he heard that he was coming, and he is gone to make war with him, and to strike him and to take all that he has.
71 Rebecca hurried and sent seventy two men from the servants of Isaac to meet Jacob on the road; for she said, Perhaps Esau may make war in the road when he meets him.
72 These messengers went on the road to meet Jacob, and they met him in the road

of the brook on the opposite side of the brook Jabuk. Jacob said when he saw them, This camp is destined to me from God. And Jacob called the name of that place Machnayim.
73 And Jacob knew all his father's people, and he kissed them and embraced them and came with them. Jacob asked them concerning his father and mother, and they said, They were well.
74 These messengers said to Jacob, Rebecca your mother has sent us to you, saying, I have heard, my son, that your brother Esau has gone forth against you on the road with men from the children of Seir the Horite.
75 Therefore, my son, listen to my voice and see with your counsel what you will do; when he comes up to you, supplicate him, and do not speak rashly to him, and give him a present from what you possess, and from what God has favored you with.
76 And when he asks you concerning your affairs, conceal nothing from him, perhaps he may turn from his anger against you and you will thereby save your soul, you and all belonging to you, for it is your duty to honor him, for he is your elder brother.
77 When Jacob heard the words of his mother which the messengers had spoken to him, Jacob lifted up his voice and wept bitterly, and did as his mother then commanded him.

CHAPTER 32

1 At that time Jacob sent messengers to his brother Esau toward the land of Seir, and he spoke to him words of supplication.
2 He commanded them, saying, Thus shall you say to my lord, to Esau, Thus says your servant Jacob, Let not my lord imagine that my father's blessing with which he did bless me has proved beneficial to me.
3 For I have been these twenty years with Laban, and he deceived me and changed my wages ten times, as it has all been already told to my lord.
4 And I served him in his house very laboriously, and God afterward saw my affliction, my labor and the work of my hands, and he caused me to find grace and favor in his sight.
5 And afterward through God's great mercy and kindness I acquired oxen and asses and cattle, and men servants and maid servants.
6 And now I am coming to my land and my home to my father and mother, who are in the land of Canaan; I have sent to let my lord know all this in order to find favor in the sight of my lord, so that he may not imagine that I have of myself obtained wealth, or that the blessing with which my father blessed me has benefited me.
7 Those messengers went to Esau, and found him on the borders of the land of Edom going toward Jacob, and four hundred men of the children of Seir the Horite were standing with drawn swords.
8 And the messengers of Jacob told Esau all the words that Jacob had spoken to them concerning Esau.
9 Esau answered them with pride and contempt and said to them, Certainly I have heard and truly it has been told to me what Jacob has done to Laban, who exalted him in his house and gave him his daughters for wives, and he had sons and daughters, and abundantly increased in wealth and riches in Laban's house through his means.

10 When he saw that his wealth was abundant and his riches great he fled with all belonging to him, from Laban's house, and he led Laban's daughters away from the face of their father, as captives taken by the sword without telling him of it.
11 And not only to Laban has Jacob done thus but also to me has he done so and has twice supplanted me, and shall I be silent?
12 Now therefore I have this day come with my camps to meet him, and I will do to him according to the desire of my heart.
13 And the messengers returned and came to Jacob and said to him, We came to your brother, to Esau, and we told him all your words, and thus has he answered us; behold he comes to meet you with four hundred men.
14 Now then know and see what you shall do, and pray before God to deliver you from him.
15 And when he heard the words of his brother which he had spoken to the messengers of Jacob, Jacob was greatly afraid and he was distressed.
16 And Jacob prayed to the Lord his God, and he said, O Lord God of my fathers, Abraham and Isaac, you did say to me when I went away from my father's house, saying,
17 I am the Lord God of your father Abraham and the God of Isaac, to you do I give this land and your descendants after you, and I will make your descendants as the stars of heaven, and you shall spread forth to the four sides of heaven, and in you and in your offspring shall all the families of the earth be blessed.
18 You did establish your words, and did give to me riches and children and cattle, as the utmost wishes of my heart did you give to your servant; you gave to me all that I asked from you, so that I lacked nothing.
19 Afterward you said to me, Return to your parents and to your birth place and I will still do well with you.
20 And now that I have come, and you did deliver me from Laban, I shall fall in the hands of Esau who will kill me, yea, together with the mothers of my children.
21 Now therefore, O Lord God, deliver me, I pray you, also from the hands of my brother Esau, for I am greatly afraid of him.
22 And if there is no righteousness in me, do it for the sake of Abraham and my father Isaac.
23 For I know that through kindness and mercy I have acquired this wealth; now therefore I beseech you to deliver me this day with your kindness and to answer me.
24 And Jacob ceased praying to the Lord; he divided the people that were with him with the flocks and cattle into two camps, and he gave the half to the care of Damesek, the son of Eliezer, Abraham's servant, for a camp, with his children; the other half he gave to the care of his brother Elianus the son of Eliezer, to be for a camp with his children.
25 And he commanded them, saying, Keep yourselves at a distance with your camps, and do not come too near each other, and if Esau comes to one camp and kills it, the other camp at a distance from it will escape him.
26 Jacob tarried there that night, and during the whole night he gave his servants instructions concerning the forces and his children.
27 The Lord heard the prayer of Jacob on that day, and the Lord then delivered Jacob from the hands of his brother Esau.
28 The Lord sent three angels of the angels of heaven, and they went before Esau and came to him.
29 And these angels appeared to Esau and his people as two thousand men, riding

on horses furnished with all sorts of war instruments, and they appeared in the sight of Esau and all his men to be divided into four camps, with four chiefs to them.
30 And one camp went on and they found Esau coming with four hundred men toward his brother Jacob, and this camp ran toward Esau and his people and terrified them. Esau fell off the horse in alarm, and all his men separated from him in that place, for they were greatly afraid.
31 And the whole camp shouted after them when they fled from Esau, and all the warlike men answered, saying,
32 Certainly we are the servants of Jacob, who is the servant of God, and who then can stand against us? And Esau said to them, O then, my lord and brother Jacob is your lord, whom I have not seen for these twenty years, and now that I have this day come to see him, do you treat me in this manner?
33 And the angels answered him saying, As the Lord lives, were not Jacob of whom you speak your brother, we would not let one remain from you and your people, but only on account of Jacob we will do nothing to them.
34 And this camp passed from Esau and his men and it went away, and Esau and his men had gone from them about a league when the second camp came toward him with all sorts of weapons, and they also did to Esau and his men as the first camp had done to them.
35 And when they had left it to go on, behold the third camp came toward him and they were all terrified, and Esau fell off the horse, and the whole camp cried out, and said, Certainly we are the servants of Jacob, who is the servant of God, and who can stand against us?
36 Esau again answered them saying, O then, Jacob my lord and your lord is my brother, and for twenty years I have not seen his countenance and hearing this day that he was coming, I went this day to meet him, and do you treat me in this manner?
37 They answered him, and said to him, As the Lord lives, were not Jacob your brother as you did say, we would not leave a remnant from you and your men, but on account of Jacob of whom you speak being your brother, we will not meddle with you or your men.
38 And the third camp also passed from them, and he still continued his road with his men toward Jacob, when the fourth camp came toward him, and they also did to him and his men as the others had done.
39 When Esau beheld the evil which the four angels had done to him and to his men, he became greatly afraid of his brother Jacob, and he went to meet him in peace.
40 And Esau concealed his hatred against Jacob, because he was afraid for his life on account of his brother Jacob, and because he imagined that the four camps that he had lighted on were Jacob's servants.
41 And Jacob tarried that night with his servants in their camps, and he resolved with his servants to give to Esau a present from all that he had with him, and from all his property; Jacob rose up in the morning, he and his men, and they chose from among the cattle a present for Esau.
42 And this is the amount of the present which Jacob chose from his flock to give to his brother Esau: he selected two hundred and forty head from the flocks, and he selected from the camels and asses thirty each, and of the herds he chose fifty kine.
43 He put them all in ten droves, and he placed each sort by itself; he delivered them into the hands of ten of his servants, each drove by itself.
44 He commanded them, and said to them, Keep yourselves at a distance from each

other, and put a space between the droves, and when Esau and those who are with him shall meet you and ask you, saying, Whose are you, and where do you go, and to whom belongs all this before you, you shall say to them, We are the servants of Jacob, and we come to meet Esau in peace, and behold Jacob comes behind us.
45 And that which is before us is a present sent from Jacob to his brother Esau.
46 And if they shall say to you, Why does he delay behind you, from coming to meet his brother and to see his face, then you shall say to them, Certainly he comes joyfully behind us to meet his brother, for he said, I will appease him with the present that goes to him, and after this I will see his face; per chance he will accept me.
47 So the whole present passed on in the hands of his servants, and went before him on that day, and he lodged that night with his camps by the border of the brook of Jabuk. He rose up in the middle of the night and took his wives and his maid servants and all belonging to him, and that night he passed them over the ford Jabuk.
48 When he passed all belonging to him over the brook, Jacob was left by himself; a man met him, and he wrestled with him that night until the breaking of the day, and the hollow of Jacob's thigh was out of joint through wrestling with him.
49 At the break of day the man left Jacob there, and he blessed him and went away; Jacob passed the brook at the break of day, and he rested on his thigh.
50 And the sun rose on him when he had passed the brook, and he came up to the place of his cattle and children.
51 They went on till midday, and while they were going the present was passing on before them.
52 And Jacob lifted up his eyes and looked, and behold Esau was at a distance, coming along with many men, about four hundred, and Jacob was greatly afraid of his brother.
53 Jacob hurried and divided his children to his wives and his handmaids, and his daughter Dinah he put in a chest, and delivered her into the hands of his servants.
54 He passed before his children and wives to meet his brother, and he bowed down to the ground, yes, he bowed down seven times until he approached his brother. And God caused Jacob to find grace and favor in the sight of Esau and his men, for God had heard the prayer of Jacob.
55 The fear of Jacob and his terror fell on his brother Esau, for Esau was greatly afraid of Jacob for what the angels of God had done to Esau, and Esau's anger against Jacob was turned into kindness.
56 And when Esau saw Jacob running toward him, he also ran toward him and he embraced him, and he fell on his neck, and they kissed and they wept.
57 And God put fear and kindness toward Jacob in the hearts of the men that came with Esau, and they also kissed Jacob and embraced him.
58 Also Eliphaz, the son of Esau, with his four brothers, sons of Esau, wept with Jacob, and they kissed him and embraced him, for the fear of Jacob had fallen on them all.
59 And Esau lifted up his eyes and saw the women with their children, the children of Jacob, walking behind Jacob and bowing along the road to Esau.
60 And Esau said to Jacob, Who are these with you, my brother? Are they your children or your servants? And Jacob answered Esau and said, They are my children which God hath graciously given to your servant.
61 While Jacob was speaking to Esau and his men, Esau beheld the whole camp, and

he said to Jacob, How did you get the whole camp that I met last night? And Jacob said, To find favor in the sight of my lord, it is that which God graciously gave to your servant.
62 The present came before Esau, and Jacob pressed Esau, saying, Take I pray you the present that I have brought to my lord. And Esau said, Why should I? Keep that which you have to yourself.
63 And Jacob said, It is incumbent on me to give all this, since I have seen your face, that you still live in peace.
64 Esau refused to take the present, and Jacob said to him, I beseech you my lord, if now I have found favor in your sight, then receive my present at my hand, for I have therefore seen your face, as you I had seen a god-like face, because you were pleased with me.
65 And Esau took the present, and Jacob also gave to Esau silver and gold and bdellium, for he pressed him so much that he took them.
66 Esau divided the cattle that were in the camp, and he gave half to the men who had come with him, for they had come on hire, and the other half he delivered to the hands of his children.
67 The silver and gold and bdellium he gave in the hands of Eliphaz his eldest son, and Esau said to Jacob, Let us remain with you, and we will go slowly along with you until you come to my place with me, that we may dwell there together.
68 And Jacob answered his brother and said, I would do as my lord speaks to me, but my lord knows that the children are tender, and the flocks and herds with their young who are with me go but slowly, for if they went swiftly they would all die, for you know their burdens and their fatigue.
69 Therefore let my lord pass on before his servant, and I will go on slowly for the sake of the children and the flock until I come to my lord's place to Seir.
70 And Esau said to Jacob, I will place with you some of the people that are with me to take care of you in the road, and to bear your fatigue and burden, and he said, I will do so, my lord, if I may find grace in your sight?
71 Behold I will come to you to Seir to dwell there together as you have spoken, go then with your people for I will follow you.
72 Jacob said this to Esau in order to remove Esau and his men from him, so that Jacob might afterward go to his father's house to the land of Canaan.
73 Esau listened to the voice of Jacob, and Esau returned with the four hundred men that were with him on their road to Seir, and Jacob and all belonging to him went that day as far as the extremity of the land of Canaan in its borders, and he remained there some time.

CHAPTER 33

1 Some time after Jacob went away from the borders of the land, he came to the land of Shalem, that is the city of Shechem, which is in the land of Canaan, and he rested in front of the city.
2 And he bought a parcel of the field which was there from the children of Hamor, the people of the land, for five shekels.
3 Jacob there built himself a house and pitched his tent there, and he made booths for his cattle; therefore he called the name of that place Succoth.

4 And Jacob remained in Succoth a year and six months.
5 At that time some of the women of the inhabitants of the land went to the city of
Shechem to dance and rejoice with the daughters of the people of the city, and when
they went forth then Rachel and Leah the wives of Jacob with their families also
went to behold the rejoicing of the daughters of the city.
6 And Dinah the daughter of Jacob also went along with them and saw the
daughters of the city, and they remained there before these daughters while all the
people of the city were standing by them to behold their rejoicings, and all the great
people of the city were there.
7 Shechem the son of Hamor, the prince of the land was also standing there to see
them.
8 Shechem saw Dinah the daughter of Jacob sitting with her mother before the
daughters of the city, and the damsel pleased him greatly, and he asked his friends
and his people, saying, Whose daughter is that sitting among the women whom I do
not know in this city?
9 And they said to him, Certainly this is the daughter of Jacob the son of Isaac the
Hebrew, who has lived in this city for some time, and when it was reported that the
daughters of the land were going forth to rejoice she went with her mother and maid
servants to sit among them as you see.
10 Shechem saw Dinah the daughter of Jacob, and when he looked at her his soul
became fixed on Dinah.
11 And he sent and had her taken by force, and Dinah came to the house of
Shechem; he seized her forcibly and lay with her and humbled her, and he loved her
greatly and placed her in his house.
12 And they came and told the thing to Jacob, and when Jacob heard that Shechem
had defiled his daughter Dinah, Jacob sent twelve of his servants to fetch Dinah from
the house of Shechem, and they went and came to the house of Shechem to take
away Dinah from there.
13 When they came Shechem went out to them with his men and drove them from
his house, and he would not let them come before Dinah, but Shechem was sitting
with Dinah kissing and embracing her before their eyes.
14 The servants of Jacob came back and told him, saying, When we came, he and his
men drove us away, and thus did Shechem do to Dinah before our eyes.
15 Jacob knew moreover that Shechem had defiled his daughter, but he said nothing;
his sons were feeding his cattle in the field, and Jacob remained silent till their
return.
16 Before his sons came home Jacob sent two maidens from his servants' daughters
to take care of Dinah in the house of Shechem, and to remain with her, and Shechem
sent three of his friends to his father Hamor the son of Chiddekem, the son of Pered,
saying, Get me this damsel for a wife.
17 Hamor the son of Chiddekem the Hivite came to the house of Shechem his son,
and he sat before him, and Hamor said to his son, Shechem, Is there not a woman
among the daughters of your people, that you will take an Hebrew woman who is
not of your people?
18 And Shechem said to him, Her only must you get for me, for she is delightful in
my sight. Hamor did according to the word of his son, for he was greatly beloved
by him.
19 And Hamor went forth to Jacob to commune with him concerning this matter,
and when he had gone from the house of his son Shechem, before he came to Jacob

to speak to him, the sons of Jacob had come from the field as soon as they heard the thing that Shechem the son of Hamor had done.
20 And the men were very much grieved concerning their sister, and they all came home fired with anger, before the time of gathering in their cattle.
21 They came and sat before their father and they spoke to him set ablaze with wrath, saying, Certainly death is due to this man and to his household, because the Lord God of the whole earth commanded Noah and his children that man shall never rob, nor commit adultery; now behold Shechem has both ravaged and committed fornication with our sister, and not one of all the people of the city spoke a word to him.
22 Certainly you know and understand that the judgment of death is due to Shechem, and to his father, and to the whole city on account of the thing which he has done.
23 And while they were speaking before their father in this matter, Hamor the father of Shechem came to speak to Jacob the words of his son concerning Dinah, and he sat before Jacob and before his sons.
24 And Hamor spoke to them, saying, The soul of my son Shechem longs for your daughter; I pray you give her to him for a wife and intermarry with us; give us your daughters and we will give you our daughters, and you shall dwell with us in our land and we will be as one people in the land.
25 For our land is very extensive, so dwell and trade therein and get possessions in it, and do therein as you desire, and no one shall prevent you by saying a word to you.
26 And Hamor ceased speaking to Jacob and his sons, and behold Shechem his son had come after him, and he sat before them.
27 And Shechem spoke before Jacob and his sons, saying, May I find favor in your sight that you will give me your daughter, and whatever you say to me that will I do for her.
28 Ask me for abundance of dowry and gift, and I will give it, and whatever you say to me that will I do, and whoever he be that will rebel against your orders, he shall die; only give me the damsel for a wife.
29 And Simeon and Levi answered Hamor and Shechem his son deceitfully, saying, All you have spoken to us we will do for you.
30 And behold our sister is in your house, but keep away from her until we send to our father Isaac concerning this matter, for we can do nothing without his consent.
31 For he knows the ways of our father Abraham, and whatever he says to us we will tell you; we will conceal nothing from you.
32 And Simeon and Levi spoke this to Shechem and his father in order to find a pretext, and to seek counsel what was to be done to Shechem and to his city in this matter.
33 And when Shechem and his father heard the words of Simeon and Levi, it seemed good in their sight, and Shechem and his father rose to go home.
34 And when they had gone, the sons of Jacob said to their father, Behold, we know that death is due to these wicked ones and to their city, because they went contrary to that which God had commanded to Noah and his children and his descendants after them.
35 And also because Shechem did this thing to our sister Dinah in defiling her, for such vileness shall never be done among us.
36 Now therefore know and see what you will do, and seek counsel and pretext

what is to be done to them, in order to kill all the inhabitants of this city.
37 Simeon said to them, Here is a proper advice for you: tell them to circumcise every male among them as we are circumcised, and if they do not wish to do this, we shall take our daughter from them and go away.
38 And if they consent to do this and will do it, then when they are sunk down with pain, we will attack them with our swords, as on one who is quiet and peaceable, and we will kill every male person among them.
39 Simeon's advice pleased them, and Simeon and Levi resolved to do to them as it was proposed.
40 And on the next morning Shechem and Hamor his father came again to Jacob and his sons, to speak concerning Dinah, and to hear what answer the sons of Jacob would give to their words.
41 And the sons of Jacob spoke deceitfully to them, saying, We told our father Isaac all your words, and your words pleased him.
42 But he spoke to us, saying, Thus did Abraham his father command him from God the Lord of the whole earth, that any man who is not of his descendants that should wish to take one of his daughters, shall cause every male belonging to him to be circumcised, as we are circumcised, and then we may give him our daughter for a wife.
43 Now we have made known to you all our ways that our father spoke to us, for we cannot do this of which you spoke to us, to give our daughter to an uncircumcised man, for it is a disgrace to us.
44 But herein we will consent to you, to give you our daughter, and we will also take to ourselves your daughters, and will dwell among you and be one people as you have spoken, if you will listen to us and consent to be like us, to circumcise every male belonging to you as we are circumcised.
45 And if you will not listen to us, to have every male circumcised as we are circumcised, as we have commanded, then we will come to you, and take our daughter from you and go away.
46 Shechem and his father Hamor heard the words of the sons of Jacob, and the thing pleased them greatly, and Shechem and his father Hamor hurried to do the wishes of the sons of Jacob, for Shechem was very fond of Dinah, and his soul was riveted to her.
47 Shechem and his father Hamor hurried to the gate of the city, and they assembled all the men of their city and spoke to them the words of the sons of Jacob, saying,
48 We came to these men, the sons of Jacob, and we spoke to them concerning their daughter, and these men will consent to do according to our wishes, and behold our land is of great extent for them, and they will dwell in it, and trade in it, and we shall be one people; we will take their daughters, and our daughters we will give to them for wives.
49 But only on this condition will these men consent to do this thing, that every male among us be circumcised as they are circumcised, as their God commanded them, and when we shall have done according to their instructions to be circumcised, then they will dwell among us, together with their cattle and possessions, and we shall be as one people with them.
50 When all the men of the city heard the words of Shechem and his father Hamor, then all the men of their city were agreeable to this proposal, and they obeyed to be circumcised; for Shechem and his father Hamor were greatly esteemed by them, being the princes of the land.

51 On the next day, Shechem and Hamor his father rose up early in the morning, and they assembled all the men of their city into the middle of the city, and they called for the sons of Jacob, who circumcised every male belonging to them on that day and the next.
52 And they circumcised Shechem and Hamor his father, and the five brothers of Shechem, and then every one rose up and went home; for this thing was from the Lord against the city of Shechem, and from the Lord was Simeon's counsel in this matter, in order that the Lord might deliver the city of Shechem into the hands of Jacob's two sons.

CHAPTER 34

1 The number of all the males that were circumcised were six hundred and forty-five men, and two hundred and forty-six children.
2 But Chiddekem, son of Pered, the father of Hamor, and his six brothers, would not listen to Shechem and his father Hamor; they would not be circumcised, for the proposal of the sons of Jacob was loathsome in their sight, and their anger was greatly roused at this, that the people of the city had not listened to them.
3 In the evening of the second day, they found eight small children who had not been circumcised, for their mothers had concealed them from Shechem and his father Hamor, and from the men of the city.
4 And Shechem and his father Hamor sent to have them brought before them to be circumcised, when Chiddekem and his six brothers sprang at them with their swords, and sought to kill them.
5 And they sought to kill also Shechem and his father Hamor and they sought to kill Dinah with them on account of this matter.
6 They said to them, What is this thing that you have done? Are there no women among the daughters of your brothers the Canaanites, that you wish to take to yourselves daughters of the Hebrews, whom ye knew not before, and will do this act which your fathers never commanded you?
7 Do you imagine that you will succeed through this act which you have done? And what will you answer in this affair to your brothers the Canaanites who will come tomorrow and ask you concerning this thing?
8 If your act shall not appear just and good in their sight, what will you do for your lives, and me for our lives, in your not having listened to our voices?
9 And if the inhabitants of the land and all your brothers the children of Ham, shall hear of your act, saying,
10 On account of a Hebrew woman did Shechem and Hamor his father, and all the inhabitants of their city, do that with which they had been unacquainted and which their ancestors never commanded them, where then will you fly or where conceal your shame all your days before your brothers, the inhabitants of the land of Canaan?
11 Now therefore we cannot bear up against this thing which you have done, neither can we be burdened with this yoke on us which our ancestors did not command us.
12 Behold tomorrow we will go and assemble all our brothers, the Canaanitish brothers who dwell in the land, and we will all come and strike you and all those who trust in you, that there shall not be a remnant left from you or them.
13 And when Hamor and his son Shechem and all the people of the city heard the

words of Chiddekem and his brothers, they were terribly afraid of their lives at their words, and they repented of what they had done.
14 And Shechem and his father Hamor answered their father Chiddekem and his brothers, and they said to them, All the words which you spoke to us are true.
15 Now do not say, nor imagine in your hearts that on account of the love of the Hebrews we did this thing that our ancestors did not command us.
16 But because we saw that it was not their intention and desire to accede to our wishes concerning their daughter as to our taking her, except on this condition, so we listened to their voices and did this act which you saw in order to obtain our desire from them.
17 And when we shall have obtained our request from them, we will then return to them and do to them that which you say to us.
18 We petition you then to wait and tarry until our flesh will be healed and we again become strong, and we will then go together against them, and do to them that which is in your hearts and in ours.
19 And Dinah the daughter of Jacob heard all these words which Chiddekem and his brothers had spoken, and what Hamor and his son Shechem and the people of their city had answered them.
20 She hurried and sent one of her maidens, that her father had sent to take care of her in the house of Shechem, to Jacob her father and to her brothers, saying:
21 Thus did Chiddekem and his brothers advise concerning you, and thus did Hamor and Shechem and the people of the city answer them.
22 And when Jacob heard these words he was filled with wrath, and he was indignant at them, and his anger was set ablaze against them.
23 And Simeon and Levi swore and said, As the Lord lives, the God of the whole earth, by this time tomorrow, there shall not be a remnant left in the whole city.
24 Twenty young men had concealed themselves who were not circumcised, and these young men fought against Simeon and Levi, and Simeon and Levi killed eighteen of them, and two fled from them and escaped to some lime pits that were in the city, and Simeon and Levi sought for them, but could not find them.
25 And Simeon and Levi continued to go about in the city, and they killed all the people of the city at the edge of the sword, and they left none remaining.
26 There was a great consternation in the midst of the city, and the cry of the people of the city ascended to heaven, and all the women and children cried aloud.
27 And Simeon and Levi killed all the city; they left not a male remaining in the whole city.
28 And they killed Hamor and Shechem his son at the edge of the sword, and they brought away Dinah from the house of Shechem and they went from there.
29 The sons of Jacob went and returned, and came on the slain, and spoiled all their property which was in the city and the field.
30 And while they were taking the spoil, three hundred men stood up and threw dust at them and struck them with stones. Then Simeon turned to them and he killed them all with the edge of the sword, and Simeon turned before Levi and came into the city.
31 They took away their sheep and their oxen and their cattle, and also the remainder of the women and little ones, and they led all these away; they opened a gate and went out and came to their father Jacob with vigor.
32 When Jacob saw all that they had done to the city, and saw the spoil that they took from them, Jacob was very angry at them, and Jacob said to them, What is this

that you have done to me? I had obtained rest among the Canaanitish inhabitants of the land; none of them meddled with me.
33 And now you have done this to make me obnoxious to the inhabitants of the land, among the Canaanites and the Perizzites, and I am but of a small number; they will all assemble against me and kill me when they hear of your work with their brothers, and I and my household will be destroyed.
34 Simeon and Levi and all their brothers with them answered their father Jacob and said to him, Behold we live in the land, and shall Shechem do this to our sister? Why are you silent at all that Shechem has done? And shall he deal with our sister as with a harlot in the streets?
35 The number of women whom Simeon and Levi took captives from the city of Shechem, whom they did not kill, was eighty-five who had not known man.
36 And among them was a young damsel of beautiful appearance and well favored, whose name was Bunah, and Simeon took her for a wife, and the number of the males which they took captives and did not kill was forty-seven men, and the rest they killed.
37 All the young men and women that Simeon and Levi had taken captives from the city of Shechem were servants to the sons of Jacob and to their children after them, until the day of the sons of Jacob going forth from the land of Egypt.
38 And when Simeon and Levi had gone forth from the city, the two young men that were left, who had concealed themselves in the city and did not die among the people of the city, rose up; these young men went into the city and walked about in it, and found the city desolate without man, and only women weeping, and these young men cried out and said, Behold, this is the evil which the sons of Jacob the Hebrew did to this city in their having this day destroyed one of the Canaanitish cities, and were not afraid of their lives of all the land of Canaan.
39 These men left the city and went to the city of Tapnach, and they came there and told the inhabitants of Tapnach all that had befallen them, and all that the sons of Jacob had done to the city of Shechem.
40 The information reached Jashub king of Tapnach, and he sent men to the city of Shechem to see those young men, for the king did not believe them in this account, saying, How could two men lay waste such a large town as Shechem?
41 The messengers of Jashub came back and told him, saying, We came to the city, and it is destroyed, there is not a man there; only weeping women; neither is any flock or cattle there, for all that was in the city the sons of Jacob took away.
42 Jashub wondered at this, saying, How could two men do this thing to destroy so large a city, and not one man able to stand against them?
43 For the like has not been from the days of Nimrod, and not even from the remotest time, has the like taken place; and Jashub, king of Tapnach, said to his people, Be courageous and we will go and fight against these Hebrews, and do to them as they did to the city; we will avenge the cause of the people of the city.
44 Jashub, king of Tapnach, consulted with his counselors about this matter, and his advisers said to him, Alone you will not prevail over the Hebrews, for they must be powerful to do this work to the whole city.
45 If two of them laid waste the whole city, and no one stood against them, certainly if you will go against them, they will all rise against us and destroy us likewise.
46 But if you will send to all the kings that surround us, and let them come together, then we will go with them and fight against the sons of Jacob; then you will prevail against them.

47 Jashub heard the words of his counselors, and their words pleased him and his people, and he did so; Jashub king of Tapnach sent to all the kings of the Amorites that surrounded Shechem and Tapnach, saying,
48 Go up with me and assist me, and we will strike Jacob the Hebrew and all his sons, and destroy them from the earth, for thus did he do to the city of Shechem, and do you not know of it?
49 And all the kings of the Amorites heard the evil that the sons of Jacob had done to the city of Shechem, and they were greatly astonished at them.
50 The seven kings of the Amorites assembled with all their armies about ten thousand men with drawn swords, and they came to fight against the sons of Jacob; Jacob heard that the kings of the Amorites had assembled to fight against his sons, and Jacob was greatly afraid; it distressed him.
51 And Jacob exclaimed against Simeon and Levi, saying, What is this act that you did? Why have you injured me, to bring against me all the children of Canaan to destroy me and my household? For I was at rest, even I and my household, and you have done this thing to me and provoked the inhabitants of the land against me by your proceedings.
52 Judah answered his father, saying, Was it for naught my brothers Simeon and Levi killed all the inhabitants of Shechem? Certainly it was because Shechem had humbled our sister, and went contrary to the command of our God to Noah and his children, for Shechem took our sister away by force, and committed fornication with her.
53 Shechem did all this evil and not one of the inhabitants of his city interfered with him, to say, Why will you do this? Certainly for this my brothers went and struck the city, and the Lord delivered it into their hands, because its inhabitants had gone contrary to the commands of our God. Is it then for naught that they have done all this?
54 Now why are you afraid or distressed, and why are you displeased at my brothers, and why is your anger set ablaze against them?
55 Certainly our God who delivered into their hand the city of Shechem and its people, he will also deliver into our hands all the Canaanitish kings who are coming against us, and we will do to them as my brothers did to Shechem.
56 Now be tranquil about them and cast away your fears, but trust in the Lord our God, and pray to him to assist us and deliver us, and deliver our enemies into our hands.
57 Judah called to one of his father's servants, Go now and see where those kings who are coming against us are situated with their armies.
58 And the servant went and looked far off, and went up opposite Mount Sihon, and saw all the camps of the kings standing in the fields, and he returned to Judah and said, Behold the kings are situated in the field with all their camps, a people greatly numerous like the sand on the seashore.
59 And Judah said to Simeon and Levi, and to all his brothers, Strengthen yourselves and be sons of valor, for the Lord our God is with us, do not fear them.
60 Stand forth each man, equipped with his weapons of war, his bow and his sword, and we will go and fight against these uncircumcised men; the Lord is our God, He will save us.
61 They rose up, and each put on his weapons of war, great and small, eleven sons of Jacob, and all the servants of Jacob with them.
62 All the servants of Isaac who were with Isaac in Hebron, all came to them

equipped in all sorts of war instruments, and the sons of Jacob and their servants, being one hundred and twelve men, went towards these kings, and Jacob also went with them.
63 And the sons of Jacob sent to their father Isaac the son of Abraham to Hebron, the same is Kireath-arba, saying,
64 Pray we beseech you for us to the Lord our God, to protect us from the hands of the Canaanites who are coming against us, and to deliver them into our hands.
65 Isaac the son of Abraham prayed to the Lord for his sons, and he said, O Lord God, you did promise my father, saying, I will reproduce your descendants as the stars of heaven, and you did also promise me, and establish you your word, now that the kings of Canaan are coming together, to make war with my children because they committed no violence.
66 Now therefore, O Lord God, God of the whole earth, pervert, I pray you, the counsel of these kings that they may not fight against my sons.
67 And impress the hearts of these kings and their people with the terror of my sons and bring down their pride, that they may turn away from my sons.
68 With your strong hand and outstretched arm deliver my sons and their servants from them, for power and might are in your hands to do all this.
69 And the sons of Jacob and their servants went toward these kings, and they trusted in the Lord their God, and while they were going, Jacob their father also prayed to the Lord and said, O Lord God, powerful and exalted God, who has reigned from days of old, from thence till now and forever;
70 You are He who stirs up wars and causes them to cease, in your hand are power and might to exalt and to bring down; O may my prayer be acceptable before you that you may turn to me with your mercies, to impress the hearts of these kings and their people with the terror of my sons, and terrify them and their camps, and with your great kindness deliver all those that trust in you, for it is you who can bring people under us and reduce nations under our power.

CHAPTER 35

1 All the kings of the Amorites came and took their stand in the field to consult with their counselors what was to be done with the sons of Jacob, for they were still afraid of them, saying, Take notice that two of them killed the whole city of Shechem.
2 And the Lord heard the prayers of Isaac and Jacob, and he filled the hearts of all these kings' advisers with great fear and terror that they unanimously exclaimed,
3 Are you silly or is there no understanding in you, that you will fight with the Hebrews; why will you take delight in your own destruction this day?
4 See, two of them came to the city of Shechem without fear or terror, and they killed all the inhabitants of the city, that no man stood up against them, and how will you be able to fight with them all?
5 Certainly you know that their God is greatly fond of them and has done mighty things for them, such as have not been done from days of old and among all the gods of nations; there is none can do like his mighty deeds.
6 Certainly he delivered their father Abraham, the Hebrew, from the hand of Nimrod, and from the hand of all his people who had many times sought to kill him.
7 He delivered him also from the fire in which king Nimrod had cast him, and his

God delivered him from it.
8 And who else can do like this? Certainly it was Abraham who killed the five kings of Elam when they had touched his brother's son who in those days lived in Sodom.
9 And took his servant that was faithful in his house and a few of his men, and they pursued the kings of Elam in one night and killed them; then restored to his brother's son all his property which they had taken from him.
10 Certainly you know the God of these Hebrews is much delighted with them, and they are also delighted with him, for they know that he delivered them from all their enemies.
11 And consider this, through his love toward his God, Abraham took his only and precious son and intended to bring him up as a burnt offering to his God; had it not been for God who prevented him from doing this, he would then have done it through his love to his God.
12 God saw all his works and swore to him, and promised him that he would deliver his sons and all his descendants from every trouble that would befall them, because he had done this thing and through his love to his God stifled his compassion for his child.
13 And have you not heard what their God did to Pharaoh king of Egypt and to Abimelech king of Gerar through taking Abraham's wife, who said of her, She is my sister; that they might kill him on account of her and think of taking her for a wife? And God did to them and their people all that you heard of.
14 And then, we ourselves saw with our own eyes that Esau, the brother of Jacob, came to him with four hundred men with the intention of slaying him, for he remembered that he had taken away from him his father's blessing.
15 And he went to meet him when he came from Syria to strike the mother with the children, and who delivered him from his hands but his God in whom he trusted? He delivered him from the hand of his brother and also from the hands of his enemies, and certainly he again will protect them.
16 Who does not know that it was their God who inspired them with strength to do to the town of Shechem the evil which you heard of?
17 Could it then be with their own strength that two men could destroy such a large city as Shechem had it not been for their God in whom they trusted? He spoke and did to them all this to kill the inhabitants of the city in their city.
18 And can you then prevail over them who have come forth together from your city to fight with all of them, even if a thousand times as many more should come to your assistance?
19 Certainly you know and understand that you do not come to fight with them, but you come to war with their God who chose them, and you have therefore all come this day to be destroyed.
20 So refrain from this evil which you are endeavoring to bring on yourselves, and it will be better for you not to go to battle with them, although they are but few in numbers, because their God is with them.
21 When the kings of the Amorites heard all the words of their advisers, their hearts were filled with terror; they were afraid of the sons of Jacob and would not fight against them.
22 They inclined to believe the words of their advisers and they listened to all their words. The words of the counselors greatly pleased the kings, and they did so.
23 And the kings turned and refrained from the sons of Jacob, for they dared not approach them to make war with them; they were greatly afraid of them, and their

hearts melted within them from their fear.
24 For this proceeded from the Lord to them; he heard the prayers of his servants Isaac and Jacob, for they trusted in him. And all these kings returned with their camps on that day, each to his own city, and they did not at that time fight with the sons of Jacob.
25 The sons of Jacob kept their station that day till evening opposite mount Sihon, and seeing that these kings did not come to fight against them, the sons of Jacob returned home.

CHAPTER 36

1 At that time the Lord appeared to Jacob saying, Arise, go to Bethel and remain there; make there an altar to the Lord who appears to you, who delivered you and your sons from affliction.
2 And Jacob rose up with his sons and all belonging to him; they went and came to Bethel according to the word of the Lord.
3 Jacob was ninety-nine years old when he went up to Bethel, and Jacob and his sons and all the people that were with him remained in Bethel in Luz; he built an altar there to the Lord who appeared to him, and Jacob and his sons remained in Bethel six months.
4 At that time Deborah the daughter of Uz, the nurse of Rebecca, who had been with Jacob died and Jacob buried her beneath Bethel under an oak that was there.
5 And Rebecca the daughter of Bethuel, the mother of Jacob, also died at that time in Hebron, the same is Kireath-arba. She was buried in the cave of Machpelah which Abraham had bought from the children of Heth.
6 And the life of Rebecca was one hundred and thirty-three years, and she died. When Jacob heard that his mother Rebecca was dead he wept bitterly for his mother, and made a great mourning for her and for Deborah her nurse beneath the oak. He called the name of that place Allon-bachuth.
7 Laban the Syrian died in those days, for God struck him because he went contrary to the covenant that existed between him and Jacob.
8 Jacob was a hundred years old when the Lord appeared to him and blessed him and called his name Israel, and Rachel the wife of Jacob conceived in those days.
9 At that time Jacob and all belonging to him journeyed from Bethel to go to his father's house, to Hebron.
10 And while they were going on the road, and there was yet but a little way to come to Ephrath, Rachel gave birth to a son; she had hard labor and died.
11 Jacob buried her on the way to Ephrath, which is Bethlehem, and he set a pillar on her grave which is there to this day; the days of Rachel were forty-five years when she died.
12 Jacob called the name of his son that was born to him, which Rachel gave birth to, Benjamin, for he was born to him in the land on the right hand.
13 It was after the death of Rachel that Jacob pitched his tent in the tent of her handmaid Bilhah.
14 And Reuben was jealous for his mother Leah on account of this; he was filled with anger, and he rose up in his anger and went and entered the tent of Bilhah and then removed his father's bed.

15 At that time the portion of birthright, together with the kingly and priestly offices, was removed from the sons of Reuben for he had profaned his father's bed; the birthright was given to Joseph, the kingly office to Judah, and the priesthood to Levi, because Reuben had defiled his father's bed.
16 These are the generations of Jacob who were born to him in Padan-aram, and the sons of Jacob were twelve:
17 The sons of Leah were Reuben the first born, and Simeon, Levi, Judah, Issachar, Zebulun, and their sister Dinah; and the sons of Rachel were Joseph and Benjamin.
18 The sons of Zilpah, Leah's handmaid, were Gad and Asher, and the sons of Bilhah, Rachel's handmaid, were Dan and Naphtali; these are the sons of Jacob which were born to him in Padan-aram.
19 Jacob and his sons and all belonging to him journeyed and came to Mamre, which is Kireath-arba, that is in Hebron, where Abraham and Isaac sojourned; Jacob with his sons and all belonging to him lived with his father in Hebron.
20 His brother Esau, his sons and all belonging to him went to the land of Seir and lived there and had possessions in the land of Seir, and the children of Esau were prolific and multiplied greatly in the land of Seir.
21 These are the generations of Esau that were born to him in the land of Canaan, and the sons of Esau were five:
22 And Adah gave birth to, to Esau, his first born Eliphaz, and she also gave birth to, to him, Reuel, and Ahlibamah gave birth to, to him, Jeush, Yaalam and Korah.
23 These are the children of Esau who were born to him in the land of Canaan; the sons of Eliphaz the son of Esau were: Teman, Omar, Zepho, Gatam, Kenaz and Amalex; the sons of Reuel were Nachath, Zerach, Shamah and Mizzah.
24 The sons of Jeush were Timnah, Alvah, Jetheth; the sons of Yaalam were Alah, Phinor and Kenaz.
25 And the sons of Korah were Teman, Mibzar, Magdiel and Eram; these are the families of the sons of Esau according to their territories in the land of Seir.
26 These are the names of the sons of Seir the Horite, inhabitants of the land of Seir: Lotan, Shobal, Zibeon, Anah, Dishan, Ezer and Dishon, being seven sons.
27 The children of Lotan were Hori, Heman and their sister Timna, that is Timna who came to Jacob and his sons; they would not give ear to her and she became a concubine to Eliphaz the son of Esau; she gave birth to, to him, Amalek.
28 And the sons of Shobal were Alvan, Manahath, Ebal, Shepho, and Onam, and the sons of Zibeon were Ajah, and Anah; this was that Anah who found the Yemim in the wilderness when he fed the asses of Zibeon his father.
29 And while he was feeding his father's asses he led them to the wilderness at different times to feed them.
30 There was a day that he brought them to one of the deserts on the seashore, opposite the wilderness of the people, and while he was feeding them, suddenly a very heavy storm came from the other side of the sea and rested on the asses that were feeding there, and they all stood still.
31 Afterward about one hundred and twenty great and terrible animals came out from the wilderness at the other side of the sea; they all came to the place where the asses were, and they placed themselves there.
32 And those animals, from their middle downward, were in the shape of the children of men; from their middle upward, some had the likeness of bears, and some the likeness of the keephas, with tails behind them from between their shoulders reaching down to the earth, like the tails of the ducheephath. These

animals came and mounted and rode on these asses, and led them away, and they went away to this day.
33 One of these animals approached Anah, struck him with his tail, and then fled from that place.
34 And when he saw this work he was greatly afraid of his life, and he fled and escaped to the city.
35 He related to his sons and brothers all that had happened to him, and many men went to seek the asses but could not find them. Anah and his brothers went no more to that place from that day on for they were greatly afraid for their lives.
36 The children of Anah the son of Seir, were Dishon and his sister Ahlibamah; the children of Dishon were Hemdan, Eshban, Ithran and Cheran; the children of Ezer were Bilhan, Zaavan and Akan, and the children of Dishon were Uz and Aran.
37 These are the families of the children of Seir the Horite, according to their dukedoms in the land of Seir.
38 Esau and his children lived in the land of Seir the Horite, the inhabitant of the land, and they had possessions in it and were prolific and multiplied greatly. Jacob and his children and all belonging to them lived with their father Isaac in the land of Canaan, as the Lord had commanded Abraham their father.

CHAPTER 37

1 In the one hundred and fifth year of the life of Jacob, that is the ninth year of Jacob's dwelling with his children in the land of Canaan, he came from Padan-aram.
2 And in those days Jacob journeyed with his children from Hebron; they went and returned to the city of Shechem, they and all belonging to them and they lived there, for the children of Jacob obtained good and fattening pasture land for their cattle in the city of Shechem, the city of Shechem having then been rebuilt; there were in it about three hundred men and women.
3 Jacob and his children and all belonging to him lived in the part of the field which Jacob had bought from Hamor the father of Shechem, when he came from Padan-aram before Simeon and Levi had smitten the city.
4 And all those kings of the Canaanites and Amorites that surrounded the city of Shechem heard that the sons of Jacob had again come to Shechem and lived there.
5 They said, Shall the sons of Jacob the Hebrew again come to the city and dwell therein, after that they have smitten its inhabitants and driven them out? Shall they now return and also drive out those who are dwelling in the city or kill them?
6 And all the kings of Canaan again assembled, and they came together to make war with Jacob and his sons.
7 Jashub king of Tapnach sent also to all his neighboring kings, to Elan king of Gaash, and to Ihuri king of Shiloh, and to Parathon king of Chazar, and to Susi king of Sarton, and to Laban king of Bethchoran, and to Shabir king of Othnay-mah, saying,
8 Come up to me and assist me, and let us strike Jacob the Hebrew and his sons and all belonging to him, for they are again come to Shechem to possess it and to kill its inhabitants as before.
9 And all these kings assembled together and came with all their camps, a people greatly plentiful like the sand on the seashore, and they were all opposite to Tapnach.

10 Jashub king of Tapnach went forth to them with all his army, and he encamped with them opposite to Tapnach outside the city; all these kings they divided into seven divisions, being seven camps against the sons of Jacob.
11 And they sent a declaration to Jacob and his son, saying, All of you come forth to us that we may have an interview together in the plain, and revenge the cause of the men of Shechem whom you killed in their city; you will now again return to the city of Shechem and dwell therein, and kill its inhabitants as before.
12 The sons of Jacob heard this and their anger was set ablaze greatly at the words of the kings of Canaan, and ten of the sons of Jacob hurried and rose up, and each of them put on his weapons of war; and there were one hundred and two of their servants with them equipped in battle array.
13 And all these men, the sons of Jacob with their servants, went toward these kings and Jacob their father was with them; they all stood on the heap of Shechem.
14 Jacob prayed to the Lord for his sons, and he spread forth his hands to the Lord, and said, O God, you are an Almighty God, you are our father; you did form us and we are the works of your hands; I pray you deliver my sons through your mercy from the hand of their enemies who are this day coming to fight with them and save them from their hand, for in your hand is power and might to save the few from the many.
15 And give to my sons, your servants, strength of heart and might to fight with their enemies, to subdue them, and to make their enemies fall before them. Let not my sons and their servants die through the hands of the children of Canaan.
16 But if it seems good in your eyes to take away the lives of my sons and their servants, take them in your great mercy through the hands of your ministers, that they may not perish this day by the hands of the kings of the Amorites.
17 When Jacob ceased praying to the Lord the earth shook from its place, and the sun darkened, and all these kings were terrified and a great consternation seized them.
18 The Lord listened to the prayer of Jacob, and the Lord impressed the hearts of all the kings and their hosts with the terror and awe of the sons of Jacob.
19 For the Lord caused them to hear the voice of chariots, and the voice of mighty horses from the sons of Jacob, and the voice of a great army accompanying them.
20 And these kings were seized with great terror at the sons of Jacob; while they were standing in their quarters, behold the sons of Jacob advanced on them with one hundred and twelve men, with a great and tremendous shouting.
21 And when the kings saw the sons of Jacob advancing toward them, they were still more panic stricken; they were inclined to retreat from before the sons of Jacob as at first and not to fight with them.
22 But they did not retreat, saying, It would be a disgrace to us to retreat twice from before the Hebrews.
23 The sons of Jacob came near and advanced against all these kings and their armies, and what they saw was a very mighty people, numerous as the sand of the sea.
24 And the sons of Jacob called to the Lord and said, Help us O Lord, help us and answer us, for we trust in you, and let us not die by the hands of these uncircumcised men who this day have come against us.
25 The sons of Jacob put on their weapons of war and they took in their hands each man his shield and his javelin, and they approached to do battle.
26 And Judah, the son of Jacob, ran first before his brothers and ten of his servants

with him, and he went toward these kings.
27 Jashub, king of Tapnach, also came forth first with his army before Judah, and Judah saw Jashub and his army coming toward him, and Judah's wrath was set ablaze; his anger burned within him, and he approached to the fight in which Judah ventured his life.
28 Jashub and all his army were advancing toward Judah and he was riding on a very strong and powerful horse; Jashub was a very valiant man, and covered with iron and brass from head to foot.
29 And while he was on the horse, he shot arrows with both hands from before and behind, as was his manner in all his battles; he never missed the place to which he aimed his arrows.
30 When Jashub came to fight with Judah and was darting many arrows against Judah, the Lord bound the hand of Jashub and all the arrows that he shot rebounded on his own men.
31 And in spite of this Jashub kept advancing toward Judah, to challenge him with the arrows, but the distance between them was about thirty cubits. When Judah saw Jashub darting forth his arrows against him, he ran to him with his wrath-excited strength.
32 Judah took up a large stone from the ground, its weight was sixty shekels, and Judah ran toward Jashub and with the stone struck him on his shield, so that Jashub was stunned with the blow and fell off his horse to the ground.
33 The shield burst asunder out of the hand of Jashub, and through the force of the blow sprang to the distance of about fifteen cubits, and the shield fell before the second camp.
34 The kings that came with Jashub saw at a distance the strength of Judah, the son of Jacob, and what he had done to Jashub; they were terribly afraid of Judah.
35 And they assembled near Jashub's camp, seeing his confusion, and Judah drew his sword and struck forty-two men of the camp of Jashub, and the whole of Jashub's camp fled before Judah. No man stood against him and they left Jashub and fled from him, and Jashub was still prostrate on the ground.
36 Jashub, seeing that all the men of his camp had fled from him, hurried and rose up with terror against Judah and stood on his legs opposite Judah.
37 And Jashub had a single combat with Judah, placing shield toward shield, and Jashub's men all fled for they were greatly afraid of Judah.
38 Jashub took his spear in his hand to strike Judah on his head, but Judah had quickly placed his shield to his head against Jashub's spear so that the shield of Judah received the blow from Jashub's spear, and the shield was split in two.
39 And when Judah saw that his shield was split, he hastily drew his sword and struck Jashub at his ankles and cut off his feet, so that Jashub fell on the ground and the spear fell from his hand.
40 Judah hastily picked up Jashub's spear with which he severed his head and cast it next to his feet.
41 When the sons of Jacob saw what Judah had done to Jashub, they all ran into the ranks of the other kings and the sons of Jacob fought with the army of Jashub and the armies of all the kings that were there.
42 The sons of Jacob caused fifteen thousand of their men to fall, and they struck them as if smiting at gourds, and the rest fled for their lives.
43 Judah was still standing by the body of Jashub and stripped Jashub of his coat of mail.

44 Judah also took off the iron and brass that were around Jashub, and then nine men of the captains of Jashub came along to fight against Judah.
45 Judah hurried and took up a stone from the ground, and with it struck one of them on the head; his skull was fractured and the body also fell from the horse to the ground.
46 And the eight captains that remained, seeing the strength of Judah, were greatly afraid and they fled; Judah with his ten men pursued them and they overtook them and killed them.
47 The sons of Jacob were still smiting the armies of the kings, and they killed many of them, but those kings daringly kept their stand with their captains and did not retreat from their places; they shouted against those of their armies that fled from before the sons of Jacob, but none would listen to them, for they were afraid for their lives that they should die.
48 And all the sons of Jacob, after having smitten the armies of the kings, returned and came before Judah; Judah was still slaying the eight captains of Jashub and stripping off their garments.
49 And Levi saw Elon, king of Gaash, advancing toward him with his fourteen captains to strike him, but Levi did not know it for certain.
50 Elon with his captains approached nearer, and Levi looked back and saw that battle was coming to him from the rear. Levi ran with twelve of his servants, and they went and killed Elon and his captains with the edge of the sword.

CHAPTER 38

1 Ihuri king of Shiloh came up to assist Elon and he approached Jacob, when Jacob drew his bow that was in his hand and with an arrow struck Ihuri, which caused his death.
2 And when Ihuri king of Shiloh was dead, the four remaining kings fled from their station with the rest of the captains; they endeavored to retreat, saying, We have no more strength with the Hebrews after their having killed the three kings and their captains who were more powerful than we are.
3 When the sons of Jacob saw that the remaining kings had left their station, they pursued them and Jacob also came from the heap of Shechem from the place where he was standing; they went after the kings and they approached them with their servants.
4 And the kings and the captains with the rest of their armies, seeing that the sons of Jacob approached them, were afraid for their lives and fled till they reached the city of Chazar.
5 The sons of Jacob pursued them to the gate of the city of Chazar, and they struck a great smiting among the kings and their armies, about four thousand men. While they were smiting the army of the kings, Jacob was occupied with his bow, confining himself to smiting the kings and killed them all.
6 And he killed Parathon king of Chazar at the gate of the city of Chazar and afterward struck Susi king of Sarton, and Laban king of Bethchorin, and Shabir king of Machnaymah; he killed them all with arrows, an arrow to each of them, and they died.
7 The sons of Jacob, seeing that all the kings were dead and that they were broken up and retreating, continued to carry on the battle with the armies of the kings opposite

the gate of Chazar, and they still struck about four hundred of their men.
8 Three men of the servants of Jacob fell in that battle and when Judah saw that three of his servants had died, it grieved him greatly and his anger burned within him against the Amorites.
9 And all the men that remained of the armies of the kings were greatly afraid for their lives, and they ran and broke the gate of the walls of the city of Chazar; they all entered the city for safety.
10 They concealed themselves in the midst of the city of Chazar, for the city of Chazar was very large and extensive, and when all these armies had entered the city, the sons of Jacob ran after them to the city.
11 Four mighty men, experienced in battle, went forth from the city and stood against the entrance of the city with drawn swords and spears in their hands; they placed themselves opposite the sons of Jacob and would not let them enter the city.
12 Naphtali ran and came between them and with his sword struck two of them, and cut off their heads at one stroke.
13 He turned to the other two and saw that they had fled; he pursued them, overtook them, struck them and killed them.
14 When the sons of Jacob came to the city and saw there was another wall to the city, they sought for the gate of the wall and could not find it; Judah sprang on the top of the wall and Simeon and Levi followed him, and they all three descended from the wall into the city.
15 Simeon and Levi killed all the men who ran for safety into the city and also the inhabitants of the city with their wives and little ones they killed with the edge of the sword, and the cries of the city ascended up to heaven.
16 And Dan and Naphtali sprang on the wall to see what caused the noise of the wailing, for the sons of Jacob felt anxious about their brothers; they heard the inhabitants of the city speaking with weeping and pleas, saying, Take all that we possess in the city and go away, only do not put us to death.
17 When Judah, Simeon, and Levi had ceased smiting the inhabitants of the city, they ascended the wall and called to Dan and Naphtali, who were on the wall, and to the rest of their brothers; Simeon and Levi informed them of the entrance into the city, and all the sons of Jacob came to gather the spoil.
18 And the sons of Jacob took the spoil of the city of Chazar, the flocks and herds, and the property, and they took all that could be captured, and went away that day from the city.
19 On the next day the sons of Jacob went to Sarton, for they heard that the men of Sarton who had remained in the city were assembling to fight with them for having slain their king. Sarton was a very high and fortified city, and it had a deep rampart surrounding the city.
20 And the pillar of the rampart was about fifty cubits and its breadth forty cubits; there was no place for a man to enter the city on account of the rampart. The sons of Jacob saw the rampart of the city, and they sought an entrance in it but could not find it.
21 For the entrance to the city was at the rear, and every man that wished to come into the city came by that road and went around the whole city, and afterwards entered the city.
22 The sons of Jacob seeing they could not find the way into the city, their anger was set ablaze greatly, and the inhabitants of the city seeing that the sons of Jacob were coming to them were greatly afraid of them, for they had heard of their strength and

what they had done to Chazar.
23 And the inhabitants of the city of Sarton could not go out toward the sons of Jacob after having assembled in the city to fight against them, that they might thereby not get into the city. But when they saw that they were coming toward them, they were greatly afraid of them, for they had heard of their strength and what they had done to Chazar.
24 So the inhabitants of Sarton speedily took away the bridge of the road of the city from its place, before the sons of Jacob came, and they brought it into the city.
25 The sons of Jacob came and sought the way into the city, and could not find it and the inhabitants of the city went up to the top of the wall, and saw that the sons of Jacob were seeking an entrance into the city.
26 The inhabitants of the city reproached the sons of Jacob from the top of the wall and they cursed them, and the sons of Jacob heard the reproaches and they were greatly incensed; their anger burned within them.
27 The sons of Jacob were provoked at them, and they all rose and sprang over the rampart with the force of their strength, and through their might passed the forty cubits' breadth of the rampart.
28 And when they had passed the rampart they stood under the wall of the city, and they found all the gates of the city enclosed with iron doors.
29 The sons of Jacob came near to break open the doors of the gates of the city, and the inhabitants did not let them, for from the top of the wall they were casting stones and arrows on them.
30 And the number of the people that were on the wall was about four hundred men, and when the sons of Jacob saw that the men of the city would not let them open the gates of the city, they sprang and ascended the top of the wall, and Judah went up first to the east part of the city.
31 And Gad and Asher went up after him to the west corner of the city, and Simeon and Levi to the north, and Dan and Reuben to the south.
32 The men who were on the top of the wall, the inhabitants of the city, seeing that the sons of Jacob were coming up to them, all fled from the wall, descended into the city and concealed themselves in the middle of the city.
33 Issachar and Naphtali that remained under the wall approached and broke the gates of the city, and set ablaze a fire at the gates of the city that the iron melted, and all the sons of Jacob came into the city, they and all their men; they fought with the inhabitants of the city of Sarton and struck them with the edge of the sword, and no man stood up before them.
34 About two hundred men fled from the city and they all went and hid themselves in a certain tower in the city; Judah pursued them to the tower and broke down the tower which fell on the men, and they all died.
35 The sons of Jacob went up the road of the roof of that tower, and they looked and there was another strong and high tower at a distance in the city, and the top of it reached to heaven. The sons of Jacob hurried and descended and went with all their men to that tower, and found it filled with about three hundred men, women and little ones.
36 The sons of Jacob struck a great smiting among those men in the tower and they ran away and fled from them.
37 And Simeon and Levi pursued them when twelve mighty and valiant men came out to them from the place where they had concealed themselves.
38 And those twelve men maintained a strong battle against Simeon and Levi, and

Simeon and Levi could not prevail over them; those valiant men broke the shields of Simeon and Levi, and one of them struck at Levi's head with his sword when Levi hastily placed his hand to his head, for he was afraid of the sword. The sword struck Levi's hand, and the hand of Levi was nearly cut off.
39 Levi seized the sword of the valiant man in his hand and took it forcibly from the man; with it he struck at the head of the powerful man and he severed his head.
40 Eleven men approached to fight with Levi, for they saw that one of them was killed; the sons of Jacob fought but the sons of Jacob could not defeat them, for those men were very powerful.
41 And the sons of Jacob seeing that they could not win over them, Simeon gave a loud and tremendous shriek, and the eleven powerful men were stunned at the voice of Simeon's shrieking.
42 Judah at a distance knew the voice of Simeon's shouting, and Naphtali and Judah ran with their shields to Simeon and Levi and found them fighting with those powerful men, unable to defeat them as their shields were broken.
43 Naphtali saw that the shields of Simeon and Levi were broken and he took two shields from his servants and brought them to Simeon and Levi.
44 And Simeon, Levi and Judah on that day fought all three against the eleven mighty men until the time of sunset, but they could not win over them.
45 This was told to Jacob, and he was very grieved; he prayed to the Lord, and he and Naphtali his son went against these mighty men.
46 Jacob approached, drew his bow, and came near to the mighty men, and killed three of their men with the bow; the remaining eight turned back and then the war waged against them in the front and rear. They were greatly afraid for their lives and could not stand before the sons of Jacob, and they fled from before them.
47 In their flight they met Dan and Asher coming toward them, and they suddenly fell on them and fought with them, and killed two of them; Judah and his brothers pursued them and struck the remainder of them, and killed them.
48 All the sons of Jacob returned and walked through the city searching if they could find any men; they found about twenty young men in a cave in the city; Gad and Asher struck them all and Dan and Naphtali lighted on the rest of the men who had fled and escaped from the second tower, and they struck them all.
49 The sons of Jacob struck all the inhabitants of the city of Sarton, but the women and little ones they left in the city and did not kill them.
50 And all the inhabitants of the city of Sarton were powerful men; one of them would pursue a thousand, and two of them would not flee from ten thousand of the rest of men.
51 The sons of Jacob killed all the inhabitants of the city of Sarton with the edge of the sword; no man stood up against them, and they left the women in the city.
52 The sons of Jacob took all the spoil of the city and captured what they desired, and they took flocks and herds and property from the city; the sons of Jacob did to Sarton and its inhabitants as they had done to Chazar and its inhabitants, and they turned and went away.

CHAPTER 39

1 When the sons of Jacob went from the city of Sarton, they had gone about two hundred cubits when they met the inhabitants of Tapnach coming toward them, for

they went out to fight with them because they had smitten the king of Tapnach and all his men.
2 So all that remained in the city of Tapnach came out to fight with the sons of Jacob and they thought to retake from them the booty and the spoil which they had captured from Chazar and Sarton.
3 The rest of the men of Tapnach fought with the sons of Jacob in that place, and the sons of Jacob struck them and they fled before them. They pursued them to the city of Arbelan and they all fell before the sons of Jacob.
4 The sons of Jacob returned and came to Tapnach to take away the spoil of Tapnach; when they came to Tapnach they heard that the people of Arbelan had gone out to meet them to save the spoil of their brothers. The sons of Jacob left ten of their men in Tapnach to plunder the city, and they went out toward the people of Arbelan.
5 The men of Arbelan went out with their wives to fight with the sons of Jacob, for their wives were experienced in battle; they went out, about four hundred men and women.
6 And all the sons of Jacob shouted with a loud voice; they all ran toward the inhabitants of Arbelan with a great and tremendous voice.
7 The inhabitants of Arbelan heard the noise of the shouting of the sons of Jacob and their roaring like the noise of lions and like the roaring of the sea and its waves.
8 And fear and terror possessed their hearts on account of the sons of Jacob; they were terribly afraid of them and they retreated and fled before them into the city. The sons of Jacob pursued them to the gate of the city and they came on them in the city.
9 The sons of Jacob fought with them in the city, and all their women were engaged in slinging against the sons of Jacob; the combat was very severe among them all of that day till evening.
10 And the sons of Jacob could not prevail over them; the sons of Jacob had almost perished in that battle. The sons of Jacob cried to the Lord and greatly gained strength toward evening; the sons of Jacob struck all the inhabitants of Arbelan by the edge of the sword, men, women and little ones.
11 Also the remainder of the people who had fled from Sarton, the sons of Jacob struck them in Arbelan, and the sons of Jacob did to Arbelan and Tapnach as they had done to Chazar and Sarton. When the women saw that all the men were dead, they went on the roofs of the city and struck the sons of Jacob by showering down stones like rain.
12 And the sons of Jacob hurried and came into the city and seized all the women and struck them with the edge of the sword. The sons of Jacob captured all the spoil and booty, flocks and herds and cattle.
13 The sons of Jacob did to Machnaymah as they had done to Tapnach, to Chazar and to Shiloh, and they turned from there and went away.
14 On the fifth day the sons of Jacob heard that the people of Gaash had gathered against them to battle, because they had slain their king and their captains, for there had been fourteen captains in the city of Gaash, and the sons of Jacob had slain them all in the first battle.
15 And the sons of Jacob that day put on their weapons of war, and they marched to battle against the inhabitants of Gaash. In Gaash there was a strong and mighty people of the people of the Amorites; Gaash was the strongest and best fortified city of all the cities of the Amorites, and it had three walls.
16 The sons of Jacob came to Gaash and they found the gates of the city locked and

about five hundred men standing at the top of the outer-most wall; a people numerous as the sand on the sea shore were in ambush for the sons of Jacob from outside the city at the rear.
17 And the sons of Jacob approached to open the gates of the city, and while they were drawing near to it, those who were in ambush at the rear of the city came forth from their places and surrounded the sons of Jacob.
18 The sons of Jacob were enclosed between the people of Gaash, and the battle was both to their front and rear; all the men that were on the wall were casting from the wall on them, arrows and stones.
19 And Judah, seeing that the men of Gaash were getting too strong for them, gave a most piercing and tremendous shriek and all the men of Gaash were terrified at the voice of Judah's cry; men fell from the wall at his powerful shriek and all those that were from without and within the city were greatly afraid of their lives.
20 And the sons of Jacob still came closer to break the doors of the city when the men of Gaash threw stones and arrows on them from the top of the wall, and made them flee from the gate.
21 The sons of Jacob returned against the men of Gaash who were with them from outside the city and they struck them terribly, as striking against gourds, and they could not stand against the sons of Jacob for fright and terror had seized them at the shriek of Judah.
22 The sons of Jacob killed all those men who were outside the city, and the sons of Jacob still drew nearer to make an entrance into the city and to fight under the city walls, but they could not for all the inhabitants of Gaash who remained in the city had surrounded the walls of Gaash in every direction; the sons of Jacob were unable to approach the city to fight with them.
23 The sons of Jacob came near to one corner to fight under the wall; the inhabitants of Gaash threw arrows and stones on them like showers of rain, and they fled from under the wall.
24 And the people of Gaash who were on the wall, seeing that the sons of Jacob could not prevail over them from under the wall, reproached the sons of Jacob in these words, saying,
25 What is the matter with you in the battle that you cannot prevail? Can you then do to the mighty city of Gaash and its inhabitants as you did to the cities of the Amorites that were not so powerful? Certainly to those weak ones among us you did those things and killed them in the entrance of the city, for they had no strength when they were terrified at the sound of your shouting.
26 And will you now then be able to fight in this place? Certainly here you will all die, and we will avenge the cause of those cities that you have laid waste.
27 And the inhabitants of Gaash greatly reproached the sons of Jacob and reviled them with their gods, and continued to cast arrows and stones on them from the wall.
28 Judah and his brothers heard the words of the inhabitants of Gaash and their anger was greatly roused, and Judah was zealous of his God in this matter, and he called out and said, O Lord, help, send help to us and our brothers.
29 And he ran at a distance with all his might with his drawn sword in his hand, and he sprang from the earth and by dint of his strength mounted the wall, and his sword fell from his hand.
30 And Judah shouted on the wall, and all the men that were on the wall were terrified; some of them fell from the wall into the city and died, and those who were

yet on the wall, when they saw Judah's strength were greatly afraid and fled for their lives into the city for safety.
31 And some were emboldened to fight with Judah on the wall; they came close to kill him when they saw there was no sword in Judah's hand and they thought of casting him from the wall to his brothers; twenty men of the city came up to assist them, they surrounded Judah and all shouted over him, and approached him with drawn swords; they terrified Judah, and Judah cried out to his brothers from the wall.
32 And Jacob and his sons drew the bow from under the wall, and struck three of the men that were on the top of the wall, and Judah continued to cry and he exclaimed, O Lord help us, O Lord deliver us, and he cried out with a loud voice on the wall, and the cry was heard at a great distance.
33 After this cry he again repeated a shout, and all the men who surrounded Judah on the top of the wall were terrified; they each threw his sword from his hand at the sound of Judah's shouting and his tremor and fled.
34 Judah took the swords which had fallen from their hands and he fought with them and killed twenty of their men on the wall.
35 About eighty men and women still ascended the wall from the city and they all surrounded Judah, and the Lord impressed the fear of Judah in their hearts so that they were unable to approach him.
36 And Jacob and all who were with him drew the bow from under the wall, and they killed ten men on the wall; they fell below the wall in front of Jacob and his sons.
37 And the people on the wall seeing that twenty of their men had fallen still ran toward Judah with drawn swords, but they could not approach him for they were greatly terrified at Judah's strength.
38 And one of their mighty men whose name was Arud approached to strike Judah on the head with his sword, when Judah hastily put his shield to his head; the sword hit the shield and it was split in two.
39 This mighty man after he had struck Judah ran for his life at the fear of Judah, and his feet slipped on the wall and he fell among the sons of Jacob who were below the wall, and the sons of Jacob struck him and killed him.
40 And Judah's head pained him from the blow of the powerful man; Judah had nearly died from it.
41 And Judah cried out on the wall owing to the pain produced by the blow, when Dan heard him, and his anger burned within him; he also rose up and went a distance and ran and sprang from the earth and mounted the wall with his wrath-excited strength.
42 And when Dan came on the wall near to Judah, all the men on the wall fled who had stood against Judah; they went up to the second wall and they threw arrows and stones on Dan and Judah from the second wall and endeavored to drive them from the wall.
43 And the arrows and stones struck Dan and Judah and they had nearly been killed on the wall; wherever Dan and Judah fled from the wall they were attacked with arrows and stones from the second wall.
44 Jacob and his sons were still at the entrance of the city below the first wall, and they were not able to draw their bow against the inhabitants of the city as they could not be seen by them, being on the second wall.
45 Dan and Judah, when they could no longer bear the stones and arrows that fell

on them from the second wall, both sprang onto the second wall near the people of the city; when the people of the city who were on the second wall saw that Dan and Judah had come to them on the second wall, they all cried out and descended below between the walls.
46 Jacob and his sons heard the noise of the shouting from the people of the city and they were still at the entrance of the city; they were anxious about Dan and Judah who were not seen by them, they being on the second wall.
47 Naphtali went up with his wrath-excited might and sprang on the first wall to see what caused the noise of shouting which they had heard in the city; Issachar and Zebulun came near to break the doors of the city, and they opened the gates of the city and came into the city.
48 Naphtali leaped from the first wall to the second and came to assist his brothers; the inhabitants of Gaash who were on the wall, seeing that Naphtali was the third who had come up to assist his brothers, all fled and descended into the city, and Jacob and all his sons and all their young men came into the city to them.
49 Judah and Dan and Naphtali descended from the wall into the city and pursued the inhabitants of the city, and Simeon and Levi were from outside the city and didn't know that the gate was opened; they went up from there to the wall and came down to their brothers into the city.
50 The inhabitants of the city had all descended into the city and the sons of Jacob came to them from different directions; the battle waged against them from the front and the rear, and the sons of Jacob struck them terribly and killed about twenty thousand of them men and women; not one of them could stand up against the sons of Jacob.
51 And the blood flowed plentifully in the city, and it was like a brook of water; the blood flowed like a brook to the outer part of the city, and reached the desert of Bethchorin.
52 And the people of Bethchorin saw at a distance the blood flowing from the city of Gaash and about seventy men from among them ran to see the blood, and they came to the place where the blood was.
53 They followed the track of the blood and came to the wall of the city of Gaash, and they saw the blood issue from the city. They heard the voice of crying from the inhabitants of Gaash, for it ascended to heaven, and the blood was continuing to flow abundantly like a brook of water.
54 And all the sons of Jacob were still smiting the inhabitants of Gaash, and were engaged in slaying them till evening, about twenty thousand men and women. And the people of Chorin said, Certainly this is the work of the Hebrews, for they are still carrying on war in all the cities of the Amorites.
55 And those people hurried and ran to Bethchorin, and each took his weapons of war; they cried out to all the inhabitants of Bethchorin, who also put on their weapons of war to go and fight with the sons of Jacob.
56 When the sons of Jacob had done smiting the inhabitants of Gaash, they walked about the city to strip all the slain. Coming into the innermost part of the city and farther on they met three very powerful men, and there was no sword in their hand.
57 The sons of Jacob came up to the place where they were and the powerful men ran away; one of them had taken Zebulun, who he saw was a young lad and of short stature, and with his might dashed him to the ground.
58 And Jacob ran to him with his sword and Jacob struck him below his loins with the sword and cut him in two, and the body fell on Zebulun.

59 The second one approached and seized Jacob to fell him to the ground; Jacob turned to him and shouted to him, while Simeon and Levi ran and struck him on the hips with the sword and felled him to the ground.
60 And the powerful man rose up from the ground with wrath-excited might; Judah came to him before he had gained his footing and struck him on the head with the sword, and his head was split and he died.
61 The third powerful man, seeing that his companions were killed, ran from before the sons of Jacob and the sons of Jacob pursued him into the city; while the powerful man was fleeing he found one of the swords of the inhabitants of the city, he picked it up and turned to the sons of Jacob and fought them with that sword.
62 The powerful man ran to Judah to strike him on the head with the sword, and there was no shield in the hand of Judah; while he was aiming to strike him, Naphtali hastily took his shield and put it to Judah's head and the sword of the powerful man hit the shield of Naphtali, and Judah escaped the sword.
63 Simeon and Levi ran onto the powerful man with their swords and struck at him forcibly with their swords, and the two swords entered the body of the powerful man and divided it in two, length-wise.
64 And the sons of Jacob struck the three mighty men at that time, together with all the inhabitants of Gaash, and the day was about to decline.
65 And the sons of Jacob walked about Gaash and took all the spoil of the city, even the little ones and women they did not allow to live, and the sons of Jacob did to Gaash as they had done to Sarton and Shiloh.

CHAPTER 40

1 And the sons of Jacob led away all the spoil of Gaash, and went out of the city by night.
2 They were going out marching toward the castle of Bethchorin, and the inhabitants of Bethchorin were going to the castle to meet them; on that night the sons of Jacob fought with the inhabitants of Bethchorin, in the castle of Bethchorin.
3 And all the inhabitants of Bethchorin were mighty men; one of them would not flee from before a thousand men, and they fought on that night on the castle; their shouts were heard on that night from afar and the earth quaked at their shouting.
4 And all the sons of Jacob were afraid of those men as they were not accustomed to fight in the dark, and they were greatly perplexed. The sons of Jacob cried to the Lord, saying, Give help to us O Lord, deliver us that we may not die by the hands of these uncircumcised men.
5 And the Lord listened to the voice of the sons of Jacob, and the Lord caused great terror and confusion to seize the people of Bethchorin; they fought among themselves with one another in the darkness of night, and struck each other in great numbers.
6 The sons of Jacob, knowing that the Lord had brought a spirit of perverseness among those men, and that they fought each man with his neighbor, went forth from among the bands of the people of Bethchorin and went as far as the descent of the castle of Bethchorin, and farther. They stayed there securely with their young men on that night.
7 And the people of Bethchorin fought the whole night, one man with his brother, and the other with his neighbor; they cried out in every direction on the castle and

their cry was heard at a distance, and the whole earth shook at their voice for they were powerful above all the people of the earth.
8 And all the inhabitants of the cities of the Canaanites, the Hittites, the Amorites, the Hivites and all the kings of Canaan, and also those who were on the other side of the Jordan heard the noise of the shouting that night.
9 They said, Certainly these are the battles of the Hebrews who are fighting against the seven cities, who came near to them; who can stand against those Hebrews?
10 All the inhabitants of the cities of the Canaanites and all those who were on the other side of the Jordan were greatly afraid of the sons of Jacob, for they said, Behold the same will be done to us as was done to those cities, for who can stand against their mighty strength?
11 And the cries of the Chorinites were very great on that night and continued to increase; they struck each other till morning, and numbers of them were killed.
12 And the morning appeared; all the sons of Jacob rose up at daybreak and went up to the castle, and they struck those who remained of the Chorinites in a terrible manner and they were all killed in the castle.
13 And the sixth day appeared, and all the inhabitants of Canaan saw at a distance all the people of Bethchorin lying dead in the castle of Bethchorin, and scattered about as the carcasses of lambs and goats.
14 And the sons of Jacob led all the spoil which they had captured from Gaash and went to Bethchorin; they found the city full of people like the sand of the sea, and they fought with them, and the sons of Jacob struck them there till evening time.
15 And the sons of Jacob did to Bethchorin as they had done to Gaash and Tapnach, and as they had done to Chazar, to Sarton and to Shiloh.
16 The sons of Jacob took with them the spoil of Bethchorin and all the spoil of the cities, and on that day they went home to Shechem.
17 And the sons of Jacob came home to the city of Shechem and they remained outside the city, and then rested there from the war, and stayed there all night.
18 And all their servants together with all the spoil that they had taken from the cities, were left outside the city, and they did not enter the city, for they said, Perhaps there may yet be more fighting against us, and they may come to besiege us in Shechem.
19 Jacob and his sons and their servants remained that night and the next day in the portion of the field which Jacob had purchased from Hamor for five shekels, and all that they had captured was with them.
20 All the booty which the sons of Jacob had captured was in the portion of the field, immense as the sand on the seashore.
21 The inhabitants of the land observed them from afar, and they all were afraid of the sons of Jacob who had done this thing, for no king from the days of old had ever done the like.
22 The seven kings of the Canaanites resolved to make peace with the sons of Jacob, for they were greatly afraid for their lives on account of the sons of Jacob.
23 And on that day, being the seventh day, Japhia king of Hebron sent secretly to the king of Ai, and to the king of Gibeon, and to the king of Shalem, and to the king of Adulam, and to the king of Lachish, and to the king of Chazar, and to all the Canaanitish kings who were under their subjection, saying,
24 Go up with me, and come to me that we may go to the sons of Jacob, and I will make peace with them and form a treaty with them, that all your lands not be destroyed by the swords of the sons of Jacob as they did to Shechem and the cities

around it, as you have heard and seen.
25 And when you come to me, do not come with many men, but let every king bring his three head captains and every captain bring three of his officers.
26 And come all of you to Hebron; we will go together to the sons of Jacob and request them to form a treaty of peace with us.
27 And all those kings did as the king of Hebron had sent to them, for they were all under his counsel and command, and all the kings of Canaan assembled to go to the sons of Jacob to make peace with them; the sons of Jacob returned and went to the portion of the field that was in Shechem, for they did not put confidence in the kings of the land.
28 And the sons of Jacob returned and remained in the portion of the field ten days, and no one came to make war with them.
29 When the sons of Jacob saw that there was no appearance of war, they all assembled and went to the city of Shechem, and the sons of Jacob remained in Shechem.
30 And at the expiration of forty days, all the kings of the Amorites assembled from all their places and came to Hebron, to Japhia, king of Hebron.
31 The number of kings that came to Hebron to make peace with the sons of Jacob was twenty-one kings, and the number of captains that came with them was sixty-nine, and their men were one hundred and eighty-nine; all these kings and their men rested by Mount Hebron.
32 And the king of Hebron went out with his three captains and nine men, and these kings resolved to go to the sons of Jacob to make peace.
33 They said to the king of Hebron, Go before us with your men, speak for us to the sons of Jacob, and we will come after you and confirm your words, and the king of Hebron did so.
34 The sons of Jacob heard that all the kings of Canaan had gathered together and rested in Hebron, and the sons of Jacob sent four of their servants as spies, saying, Go and spy these kings, and search and examine their men whether they are few or many, and if they are but few in number, count them all and come back.
35 And the servants of Jacob went secretly to these kings, and did as the sons of Jacob had commanded them. On that day they came back to the sons of Jacob, and said to them, We came to those kings, and they are few in number; we counted them all, and surely there were two hundred and eighty-eight, kings and men.
36 The sons of Jacob said, They are but few in number, therefore we will not all go out to them. In the morning the sons of Jacob rose up and chose sixty-two of their men, and ten of the sons of Jacob went with them; and they put on their weapons of war, for they said, They are coming to make war with us. For they didn't know that they were coming to make peace with them.
37 And the sons of Jacob went with their servants to the gate of Shechem, toward those kings, and their father Jacob was with them.
38 And when they had come forth, there the king of Hebron and his three captains and nine men with him were coming along the road toward the sons of Jacob; the sons of Jacob lifted up their eyes, and saw at a distance Japhia, king of Hebron, with his captains, coming toward them, And the sons of Jacob took their stand at the place of the gate of Shechem, and did not proceed.
39 The king of Hebron continued to advance, he and his captains, until he came near to the sons of Jacob; he and his captains bowed down to them to the ground, and the king of Hebron sat with his captains in front of Jacob and his sons.

40 The sons of Jacob said to him, What has happened to you, O king of Hebron? Why have you come to us this day? What do you require from us? And the king of Hebron said to Jacob, I petition you my lord, all the kings of the Canaanites have this day come to make peace with you.
41 And the sons of Jacob heard the words of the king of Hebron; they would not consent to his proposals; the sons of Jacob had no faith in him, for they imagined that the king of Hebron had spoken deceitfully to them.
42 The king of Hebron knew from the words of the sons of Jacob that they did not believe his words, and the king of Hebron approached nearer to Jacob, and said to him, I beg you, my lord, to be assured that all these kings have come to you on peaceable terms, for they have not come with all their men, neither did they bring their weapons of war with them, for they have come to seek peace from my lord and his sons.
43 The sons of Jacob answered the king of Hebron, saying, Go to all these kings and if you speak truth to us, let them each come singly before us; if they come to us unarmed, we shall then know that they seek peace from us.
44 And Japhia, king of Hebron, sent one of his men to the kings and they all came before the sons of Jacob, and bowed down to them to the ground; these kings sat before Jacob and his sons and spoke to them, saying,
45 We have heard all that you did to the kings of the Amorites with your sword and greatly mighty arm, so that no man could stand up before you; we were afraid of you for the sake of our lives, that it would happen to us as it did to them.
46 So we have come to you to form a treaty of peace between us, and now therefore contract with us a covenant of peace and truth, that you will not meddle with us, inasmuch as we have not meddled with you.
47 And the sons of Jacob knew that they had really come to seek peace from them. And the sons of Jacob listened to them, and formed a covenant with them.
48 The sons of Jacob swore to them that they would not meddle with them, and all the kings of the Canaanites swore also to them, and the sons of Jacob made them pay tribute from that day forward.
49 And after this all the captains of these kings came with their men before Jacob, with presents in their hands for Jacob and his sons, and they bowed down to him to the ground.
50 These kings then urged the sons of Jacob and begged of them to return all the spoil they had captured from the seven cities of the Amorites, and the sons of Jacob did so; they returned all that they had captured, the women, the little ones, the cattle and all the spoil which they had taken, and they sent them off; they went away each to his city.
51 And all these kings again bowed down to the sons of Jacob, and they sent or brought them many gifts in those days; the sons of Jacob sent off these kings and their men, and they went peaceably away from them to their cities, and the sons of Jacob also returned to their home, to Shechem.
52 And there was peace from that day forward between the sons of Jacob and the kings of the Canaanites, until the children of Israel came to inherit the land of Canaan.

CHAPTER 41

1 At the revolution of the year the sons of Jacob journeyed from Shechem, and they came to Hebron, to their father Isaac; they lived there, but their flocks and herds they fed daily in Shechem, for there was there in those days good and fattening pasture. Jacob and his sons and all their household lived in the valley of Hebron.
2 It was in those days, in that year, being the hundred and sixth year of the life of Jacob, in the tenth year of Jacob's coming from Padan-aram, that Leah the wife of Jacob died; she was fifty-one years old when she died in Hebron.
3 Jacob and his sons buried her in the cave of the field of Machpelah, which is in Hebron, which Abraham had bought from the children of Heth for the possession of a burial place.
4 The sons of Jacob lived with their father in the valley of Hebron; all the inhabitants of the land knew their strength and their fame went throughout the land.
5 Joseph the son of Jacob and his brother Benjamin, the sons of Rachel, the wife of Jacob, were yet young in those days, and did not go out with their brothers during their battles in all the cities of the Amorites.
6 And when Joseph saw the strength of his brothers and their greatness, he praised them and extolled them, but he ranked himself greater than them and extolled himself above them; Jacob, his father, also loved him more than any of his sons for he was a son of his old age, and through his love toward him he made him a coat of many colors.
7 And when Joseph saw that his father loved him more than his brothers, he continued to elevate himself above his brothers, and he brought to his father evil reports concerning them.
8 The sons of Jacob seeing all of Joseph's conduct toward them, and that their father loved him more than any of them, hated him and could not ever speak peaceably to him.
9 Joseph was seventeen years old, and he was still magnifying himself above his brothers, and thought of raising himself above them.
10 At that time he dreamed a dream, and he came to his brothers and told them his dream, and he said to them, I dreamed a dream, and behold we were all binding sheaves in the field, and my sheaf rose and placed itself on the ground and your sheaves surrounded it and bowed down to it.
11 And his brothers answered him and said to him, What means this dream that you did dream? Do you imagine in your heart to reign or rule over us?
12 And he still came and told the thing to his father Jacob, and Jacob kissed Joseph when he heard these words from his mouth, and Jacob blessed Joseph.
13 When the sons of Jacob saw that their father had blessed Joseph and had kissed him, and that he loved him greatly, they became jealous of him and hated him all the more.
14 After this Joseph dreamed another dream and related the dream to his father in the presence of his brothers, and Joseph said to his father and brothers, Behold I have again dreamed a dream, and behold the sun and the moon and the eleven stars bowed down to me.
15 And his father heard the words of Joseph and his dream, and seeing that his brothers hated Joseph on account of this matter, Jacob therefore rebuked Joseph before his brothers on account of this thing, saying, What does this dream mean which you have dreamed, and this magnifying yourself before your brothers who are older than you are?
16 Do you imagine in your heart that I and your mother and your eleven brothers

will come and bow down to you, that you speak these things?
17 And his brothers were jealous of him on account of his words and dreams; they continued to hate him, and Jacob reserved the dreams in his heart.
18 The sons of Jacob went one day to feed their father's flock in Shechem, for they were still herdsmen in those days; while the sons of Jacob were that day feeding in Shechem they delayed, and the time of gathering in the cattle was passed, and they had not arrived.
19 And Jacob saw that his sons were delayed in Shechem, and Jacob said within himself, Perhhaps the people of Shechem have risen up to fight against them, therefore they have delayed coming today.
20 And Jacob called Joseph his son and commanded him, saying, Behold your brothers are feeding in Shechem this day and look, they have not yet come back; therefore go and see where they are, and bring back word to me concerning the welfare of your brothers and the welfare of the flock.
21 And Jacob sent his son Joseph to the valley of Hebron; Joseph came for his brothers to Shechem, and could not find them, and Joseph went toward the field which was near Shechem to see where his brothers had turned. But he missed his road in the wilderness and didn't know which way he should go.
22 And an angel of the Lord found him wandering in the road toward the field, and Joseph said to the angel of the Lord, I seek my brothers; have you not heard where they are feeding? And the angel of the Lord said to Joseph, I saw your brothers feeding here, and I heard them say they would go to feed in Dothan.
23 Joseph listened to the voice of the angel of the Lord, and he went to his brothers in Dothan and he found them in Dothan feeding the flock.
24 Joseph advanced to his brothers but before he had come near them, they had resolved to kill him.
25 Simeon said to his brothers, Behold the man of dreams is coming to us this day, so now come and let us kill him and cast him into one of the pits that are in the wilderness; when his father shall seek him from us, we will say an evil beast has devoured him.
26 Reuben heard the words of his brothers concerning Joseph and said to them, You should not do this thing, for how can we look up to our father Jacob? Cast him into this pit to die there, but do not put forth a hand on him to spill his blood. Reuben said this in order to deliver him from their hand, to bring him back to his father.
27 When Joseph came to his brothers he sat before them, and they rose upon him and seized him and struck him to the earth, and stripped the coat of many colors which he had on.
28 They took him and cast him into a pit and in the pit there was no water, but serpents and scorpions. And Joseph was afraid of the serpents and scorpions that were in the pit. Joseph cried out with a loud voice and the Lord hid the serpents and scorpions in the sides of the pit, and they did no harm to Joseph.
29 And Joseph called out from the pit to his brothers, and said to them, What have I done to you, and in what have I sinned? Why do you not fear the Lord concerning me? Am I not of your bones and flesh, and is not Jacob your father, my father? Why do you do this thing to me this day, and how will you be able to look up to our father Jacob?
30 And he continued to cry out and call to his brothers from the pit, and he said, O Judah, Simeon, and Levi, my brothers, lift me up from the place of darkness in which you have placed me, and come this day to have compassion on me, you children of

the Lord and sons of Jacob my father. And if I have sinned to you, are you not the
sons of Abraham, Isaac, and Jacob? If they saw an orphan they had compassion over
him, or one that was hungry, they gave him bread to eat, or one that was thirsty,
they gave him water to drink, or one that was naked, they covered him with
garments!
31 And how then can you withhold your pity from your brother, for I am of your
flesh and bones, and if I have sinned to you, certainly you will do this on account of
my father!
32 Joseph spoke these words from the pit, and his brothers could not listen to him,
nor incline their ears to the words of Joseph, and Joseph was crying and weeping in
the pit.
33 And Joseph said, O that my father knew this day, the act which my brothers have
done to me and the words which they have this day spoken to me.
34 All his brothers heard his cries and weeping in the pit, and his brothers went and
removed themselves from the pit, so that they might not hear the cries of Joseph and
his weeping in the pit.

CHAPTER 42

1 They went and sat on the opposite side, about the distance of a bow-shot, and they
sat there to eat bread; while they were eating they held counsel together what was to
be done with him, whether to kill him or to bring him back to his father.
2 They were holding the counsel when they lifted up their eyes, and saw at once
there was a company of Ishmaelites coming at a distance by the road of Gilead,
going down to Egypt.
3 And Judah said to them, What gain will it be to us if we kill our brother? Perhaps
God will require him from us; this then is the counsel proposed concerning him,
which you shall do to him: Look at this company of Ishmaelites going down to
Egypt,
4 So now let us dispose of him to them and let not our hand be on him; they will lead
him along with them and he will be lost among the people of the land and we will
not put him to death with our own hands. And the proposal pleased his brothers
and they did according to the word of Judah.
5 While they were discussing this matter and before the company of Ishmaelites had
come up to them, seven trading men of Midian passed by them; as they passed they
were thirsty and they lifted up their eyes and saw the same pit in which Joseph was
held, and they looked and saw every species of bird was on him.
6 These Midianites ran to the pit to drink water for they thought that it contained
water, and on coming to the pit they heard the voice of Joseph crying and weeping
in there, and they looked down into the pit, and they saw there was a youth of good-
looking appearance and well-favored.
7 They called to him and said, Who are you and who brought you here, and who
placed you in this pit in the wilderness? And they all assisted to raise up Joseph and
they drew him out and brought him up from the pit, and took him and went away
on their journey and passed by his brothers.
8 And these said to them, Why do you do this, to take our servant from us and to go
away? Certainly we placed this youth in the pit because he rebelled against us, and

you come and bring him up and lead him away; now then give us back our servant.
9 And the Midianites answered and said to the sons of Jacob, Is this your servant, or does this man attend you? Perhaps you are all his servants, for he is more handsome and well-favored than any of you, and why do you all speak falsely to us?
10 So we will not listen to your words nor give you our attention, for we found the youth in the pit in the wilderness and we took him; we will therefore go on.
11 And all the sons of Jacob approached them and rose up to them and said to them, Give us back our servant, and why will you all die by the edge of the sword? And the Midianites cried out against them and they drew their swords and approached to fight with the sons of Jacob.
12 Then Simeon rose up from his seat against them, and sprang on the ground and drew his sword and approached the Midianites and he gave a terrible shout before them, so that his shouting was heard at a distance, and the earth shook at Simeon's shouting.
13 The Midianites were terrified on account of Simeon and the noise of his shouting, and they fell on their faces and were excessively alarmed.
14 Simeon said to them, Surely I am Simeon, the son of Jacob the Hebrew, who have only with my brothers destroyed the city of Shechem and the cities of the Amorites; so shall God moreover do to me if all your brothers, the people of Midian, and also the kings of Canaan, were to come with you; they could not fight against me.
15 Now therefore give us back the youth whom you have taken, or I'll give your flesh to the birds of the skies and the beasts of the earth.
16 The Midianites were more afraid of Simeon, and they approached the sons of Jacob with terror and fright, and with pathetic words, saying,
17 Certainly you have said that the young man is your servant and that he rebelled against you, and therefore you placed him in the pit; what then will you do with a servant who rebels against his master? So now sell him to us, and we will give you all that you require for him. The Lord was pleased to do this in order that the sons of Jacob should not kill their brother.
18 And the Midianites saw that Joseph was of a good-looking appearance and well-favored; they desired him in their hearts and were urgent to purchase him from his brothers.
19 The sons of Jacob listened to the Midianites and they sold their brother Joseph to them for twenty pieces of silver. Reuben their brother was not with them, and the Midianites took Joseph and continued their journey to Gilead.
20 They were going along the road, and the Midianites repented of what they had done, in having purchased the young man, and one said to the other, What is this thing that we have done, in taking this youth from the Hebrews who is of good-looking appearance and well-favored?
21 Perhaps this youth is stolen from the land of the Hebrews, and why then have we done this thing? If he should be sought for and found in our hands we shall die through him.
22 Now certainly hardy and powerful men have sold him to us, the strength of one of whom you saw this day; perhaps they stole him from his land with their might and with their powerful arm, and have therefore sold him to us for the small value which we gave to them.
23 While they were thus discussing together, they looked and saw the company of Ishmaelites which was coming at first, and which the sons of Jacob saw, was advancing toward the Midianites; the Midianites said to each other, Come let us sell

this youth to the company of Ishmaelites who are coming toward us. We will take for him the little that we gave for him, and we will be delivered from his evil.
24 And they did so, and they reached the Ishmaelites, and the Midianites sold Joseph to the Ishmaelites for twenty pieces of silver which they had given for him to his brothers.
25 And the Midianites went on their road to Gilead, and the Ishmaelites took Joseph and they let him ride on one of the camels, and they were leading him to Egypt.
26 When Joseph heard that the Ishmaelites were proceeding to Egypt, Joseph lamented and wept at this thing that he was to be so far removed from the land of Canaan, from his father, and he wept bitterly while he was riding on the camel. One of their men observed him, and made him go down from the camel and walk on foot, and still Joseph continued to cry and weep, and he said, O my father, my father.
27 One of the Ishmaelites rose up and struck Joseph on the cheek, and still he continued to weep; and Joseph was fatigued in the road, and was unable to proceed on account of the bitterness of his soul; they all struck him and afflicted him in the road, and they terrified him in order that he might cease from weeping.
28 And the Lord saw the condition of Joseph and his trouble, and the Lord brought down on those men darkness and confusion, and the hand of everyone that struck him became withered.
29 And they said to each other, What is this thing that God has done to us in the road? And they knew not that this befell them on account of Joseph. And the men proceeded on the road, and they passed along the road of Ephrath where Rachel was buried.
30 Joseph reached his mother's grave, and Joseph hurried and ran to his mother's grave, and fell on the grave and wept.
31 Joseph cried aloud on his mother's grave and said, O my mother, my mother, O you who did give me birth, awake now, and rise and see your son, how he has been sold for a slave, and no one to pity him.
32 O rise and see your son, weep with me on account of my troubles, and see the heart of my brothers.
33 Arouse my mother, arouse, awake from your sleep for me, and direct your battles against my brothers. O how have they stripped me of my coat and sold me already twice for a slave, and separated me from my father, and there is no one to pity me.
34 Arouse and lay your cause against them before God, and see whom God will justify in the judgment, and whom he will condemn.
35 Rise, O my mother, rise, awake from your sleep and see my father how his soul is with me this day, and comfort him and ease his heart.
36 And Joseph continued to speak these words, and Joseph cried aloud and wept bitterly on his mother's grave; and he ceased speaking, and from bitterness of heart he became still as a stone on the grave.
37 And Joseph heard a voice speaking to him from beneath the ground, which answered him with bitterness of heart, and with a voice of weeping and praying in these words:
38 My son, my son Joseph, I have heard the voice of your weeping and the voice of your lamentation; I have seen your tears; I know your troubles, my son, and it grieves me for your sake, and abundant grief is added to my grief.
39 Now therefore my son, Joseph my son, hope in the Lord, and wait for him and do not fear, for the Lord is with you, he will deliver you from all trouble.
40 Rise my son, go down to Egypt with your masters and do not fear, for the Lord is

with you, my son. And she continued to speak like these words to Joseph, and she was still.
41 And Joseph heard this, and he wondered greatly at this, and he continued to weep. After this one of the Ishmaelites observed him crying and weeping on the grave, and his anger was set ablaze against him, and he drove him from there, and he struck him and cursed him.
42 And Joseph said to the men, May I find grace in your sight to take me back to my father's house, and he will give you abundance of riches.
43 And they answered him, saying, Are you not a slave, and where is your father? And if you had a father you would not already twice have been sold for a slave for so little value; their anger was still roused against him, and they continued to strike him and to chastise him, and Joseph wept bitterly.
44 The Lord saw Joseph's affliction, and the Lord again struck these men, and chastised them, and the Lord caused darkness to envelope them on the earth, and the lightning flashed and the thunder roared, and the earth shook at the voice of the thunder and of the mighty wind; the men were terrified and knew not where they should go.
45 The beasts and camels stood still, and they led them, but they would not go, they struck them, and they crouched on the ground; the men said to each other, What is this that God has done to us? What are our transgressions and what are our sins that this thing has thus befallen us?
46 One of them answered and said to them, Perhaps on account of the sin of afflicting this slave has this thing happened this day to us; now we should implore him strongly to forgive us and then we shall know on whose account this evil befalls us; if God willl have compassion over us, then we shall know that all this comes to us on account of the sin of afflicting this slave.
47 And the men did so, and they supplicated Joseph and pressed him to forgive them; and they said, We have sinned to the Lord and to you, now therefore vouchsafe to request of your God that he shall put away this death from among us, for we have sinned to him.
48 Joseph did according to their words and the Lord listened to Joseph, and the Lord put away the plague which he had inflicted on those men on account of Joseph; the beasts rose up from the ground and they conducted them, and they went on; the raging storm abated and the earth became tranquilized and the men proceeded on their journey to go down to Egypt. The men knew that this evil had befallen them on account of Joseph.
49 And they said to each other, We now know that it was on account of his affliction that this evil befell us; now why shall we bring this death on our souls? Let us hold counsel what to do to this slave.
50 And one answered and said, Certainly he told us to bring him back to his father; so come, let us take him back and we will go to the place that he will tell us, and take from his family the price that we gave for him and we will then go away.
51 One answered again and said, Behold this counsel is very good, but we cannot do so for the way is very far from us, and we cannot leave our road.
52 One more answered and said to them, This is the counsel to be adopted, we will not swerve from it; behold we are this day going to Egypt and when we shall have come to Egypt, we will sell him there at a high price, and we will be delivered from his evil.
53 And this thing pleased the men and they did so; they continued their journey to

Egypt with Joseph.

CHAPTER 43

1 When the sons of Jacob had sold their brother Joseph to the Midianites, their hearts were smitten on account of him and they repented of their acts, and they sought for him to bring him back but could not find him.
2 Reuben returned to the pit in which Joseph had been put in order to lift him out and restore him to his father; Reuben stood by the pit and heard not a word. He called out Joseph! Joseph! and no one answered or uttered a word.
3 And Reuben said, Joseph has died through fright, or some serpent has caused his death. Reuben descended into the pit, searched for Joseph and could not find him in the pit, and he came out again.
4 And Reuben tore his garments and he said, The child is not there, and how shall I reconcile my father about him if he is dead? He went to his brothers and found them grieving on account of Joseph, and counseling together how to appease their father about him. Reuben said to his brothers, I came to the pit and behold Joseph was not there, what then shall we say to our father, for my father will only seek the lad from me.
5 His brothers answered him saying, Thus and thus we did, and our hearts afterward struck us on account of this act, and we now sit to seek a pretext how we shall appease our father to it.
6 And Reuben said to them, What is this you have done to bring down the grey hairs of our father in sorrow to the grave? This thing is not good that you have done.
7 And Reuben sat with them, and they all rose up and swore to each other not to tell this thing to Jacob. They all said, The man who will tell this to our father or his household, or who will report this to any of the children of the land, we will all rise up against him and kill him with the sword.
8 And the sons of Jacob feared each other in this matter, from the youngest to the oldest; no one spoke a word, and they concealed the thing in their hearts.
9 Afterward they sat down to determine and invent something to say to their father Jacob concerning all these things.
10 Issachar said to them, Here is advice for you if it seems good in your eyes to do this thing. Take the coat which belongs to Joseph and tear it, and kill a kid of the goats and dip it in its blood.
11 And send it to our father and when he sees it he will say an evil beast has devoured him, therefore tear his coat and behold his blood will be on his coat, and by your doing this we shall be free of our father's murmurings.
12 Issachar's advice pleased them and they listened to him, and they did according to the word of Issachar which he had counselled them.
13 They hurried and took Joseph's coat and tore it, and they killed a kid of the goats and dipped the coat in the blood of the kid, and then trampled it into the dust. They sent the coat to their father Jacob by the hand of Naphtali, and they commanded him to say these words:
14 We had gathered in the cattle and had come as far as the road to Shechem and farther, when we found this coat on the road in the wilderness dipped in blood and in dust; now therefore know whether it is your son's coat or not.
15 And Naphtali went and he came to his father and he gave him the coat, and he

spoke to him all the words which his brothers had commanded him.
16 Jacob saw Joseph's coat and he knew it and he fell on his face to the ground, and became as still as a stone Afterward he rose up and cried out with a loud and weeping voice and said, It is the coat of my son Joseph!
17 Jacob hurried and sent one of his servants to his sons, who went to them and found them coming along the road with the flock.
18 The sons of Jacob came to their father about evening, and behold their garments were torn and dust was on their heads, and they found their father crying out and weeping with a loud voice.
19 Jacob said to his sons, Tell me truly what evil have you this day suddenly brought on me? They answered their father Jacob, saying, We were coming along this day after the flock had been gathered in, and we came as far as the city of Shechem by the road in the wilderness; we found this coat filled with blood on the ground, and we knew it and we sent it to you so you could know it.
20 Jacob heard the words of his sons and he cried out with a loud voice, and he said, It is the coat of my son; an evil beast has devoured him. Joseph is rent in pieces, for I sent him this day to see whether it was well with you and well with the flocks and to bring me word again from you; he went as I commanded him, and this has happened to him today while I thought my son was with you.
21 And the sons of Jacob answered and said, He did not come to us, neither have we seen him from the time of our going out from you until now.
22 When Jacob heard their words he again cried out aloud, and he rose up and tore his garments; he put sackcloth on his loins and he wept bitterly; he mourned and lifted up his voice in weeping and exclaimed and said these words,
23 Joseph my son, O my son Joseph, I sent you this day after the welfare of your brothers, and behold you have been torn in pieces; through my hand has this happened to my son.
24 It grieves me for you Joseph my son, it grieves me for you; how sweet you were to me during life, and now how greatly bitter is your death to me.
25 0 that I had died in your stead Joseph my son, for it grieves me sadly for you my son, O my son, my son. Joseph my son, where are you, and where have you been drawn? Arouse, arouse from your place, and come and see my grief for you, O my son Joseph.
26 Come now and number the tears gushing from my eyes down my cheeks, and bring them up before the Lord, that his anger may turn from me.
27 0 Joseph my son, how did you fall, by the hand of one by whom no one had fallen from the beginning of the world to this day; for you have been put to death by the smiting of an enemy, inflicted with cruelty, but certainly I know that this has happened to you on account of the multitude of my sins.
28 Arise now and see how bitter is my trouble for you my son, although I did not rear you nor fashion you nor give you breath and soul, but it was God who formed you and built your bones and covered them with flesh and breathed in your nostrils the breath of life, and then he gave you to me.
29 Now truly God who gave you to me, he has taken you from me; such then has happened to you.
30 And Jacob continued to speak like these words concerning Joseph, and he wept bitterly; he fell to the ground and became still.
31 All the sons of Jacob seeing their father's trouble repented of what they had done, and they also wept bitterly.

32 And Judah rose up and lifted his father's head from the ground, and placed it on his lap; he wiped his father's tears from his cheeks, and Judah wept a very great weeping while his father's head was reclining on his lap, still as a stone.
33 The sons of Jacob saw their father's trouble, and they lifted up their voices and continued to weep; Jacob was yet lying on the ground still as a stone.
34 And all his sons and his servants and his servant's children rose up and stood round him to comfort him, and he refused to be comforted.
35 The whole household of Jacob rose up and mourned a great mourning on account of Joseph and their father's trouble, and the sad news reached Isaac, the son of Abraham, the father of Jacob, and he wept bitterly on account of Joseph, he and all his household. He went from the place where he lived in Hebron, and his men with him, and he comforted Jacob his son but he refused to be comforted.
36 And after this, Jacob rose up from the ground, and his tears were running down his cheeks, and he said to his sons, Rise up and take your swords and your bows, and go forth into the field, and seek whether you can find my son's body and bring it to me that I may bury it.
37 Seek also, I pray you, among the beasts and hunt them, and that which shall come the first before you seize and bring it to me; perhaps the Lord will this day pity my affliction, and prepare before you that which tore my son in pieces; bring it to me, and I will avenge the cause of my son.
38 And his sons did as their father had commanded them, and they rose up early in the morning, and each took his sword and his bow in his hand, and they went forth into the field to hunt the beasts.
39 And Jacob was still crying aloud and weeping and walking to and fro in the house, and smiting his hands together, saying, Joseph my son, Joseph my son.
40 The sons of Jacob went into the wilderness to seize the beasts, and there a wolf came toward them; they seized him and brought him to their father and said to him, This is the first we have found, and we have brought him to you as you did command us, and your son's body we could not find.
41 And Jacob took the beast from the hands of his sons, and he cried out with a loud and weeping voice, holding the beast in his hand, and he spoke with a bitter heart to the beast, Why did you devour my son Joseph, and how did you have no fear of the God of the earth, or of my trouble for my son Joseph?
42 You did devour my son for nothing. He committed no violence. I was responsible for him. God will require him that is persecuted.
43 And the Lord opened the mouth of the beast in order to comfort Jacob with its words, and it answered Jacob and spoke these words to him,
44 As God lives who created us in the earth, and as your soul lives, my lord, I did not see your son, neither did I tear him to pieces, but from a distant land I also came to seek my son who went from me this day, and I know not whether he is living or dead.
45 And I came this day into the field to seek my son, and your sons found me, and seized me and increased my grief, and have this day brought me before you, and I have now spoken all my words to you.
46 Now therefore, O son of man, I am in your hands, and do to me this day as it may seem good in your sight, but by the life of God who created me, I did not see your son nor did I tear him to pieces, neither has the flesh of man entered my mouth all the days of my life.
47 When Jacob heard the words of the beast he was greatly astonished, and sent

forth the beast from his hand, and she went her way.
48 And Jacob was still crying aloud and weeping for Joseph day after day, and he mourned for his son many days.

CHAPTER 44

1 The sons of Ishmael who had bought Joseph from the Midianites, who had bought him from his brothers, went to Egypt with Joseph. They came on the borders of Egypt and when they came near to Egypt, they met four men of the sons of Medan the son of Abraham, who had gone forth from the land of Egypt on their journey.
2 The Ishmaelites said to them, Do you desire to purchase this slave from us? And they said, Deliver him over to us, and they delivered Joseph over to them; they observed him that he was a very good-looking youth and they purchased him for twenty shekels.
3 The Ishmaelites continued their journey to Egypt and the Medanim also returned that day to Egypt. The Medanim said to each other, Look, we have heard that Potiphar, an officer of Pharaoh, captain of the guard, seeks a good servant who willl stand before him to attend him, and to make him overseer over his house and all belonging to him.
4 So let us sell him for what we may desire, if he is able to give us that which we shall require for him.
5 And these Medanim came to the house of Potiphar, and said to him, We have heard that you seek a good servant to attend you; here we have a servant that will please you, if you can give to us that which we may desire and we will sell him to you.
6 And Potiphar said, Bring him before me, and I will see him; if he please me I will give to you that which you may require for him.
7 And the Medanim went and brought Joseph and placed him before Potiphar, and he observed him, and he pleased him greatly and Potiphar said to them, Tell me what you require for this youth.
8 And they said, Four hundred pieces of silver we desire for him. Potiphar said, I will give it if you bring me the record of his sale to you and will tell me his history for perhaps he may be stolen, for this youth is neither a slave nor the son of a slave, but I observe in him the appearance of a goodly and handsome person.
9 And the Medanim went and brought to him the Ishmaelites who had sold him to them, and they told him, saying, He is a slave and we sold him to them.
10 And Potiphar heard the words of the Ishmaelites in his giving the silver to the Medanim, and the Medanim took the silver and went on their journey; the Ishmaelites also returned home.
11 Potiphar took Joseph and brought him to his house that he might serve him, and Joseph found favor in the sight of Potiphar; he placed confidence in him and made him overseer over his house, and all that belonged to him he delivered over into his hand.
12 And the Lord was with Joseph and he became a prosperous man; the Lord blessed the house of Potiphar for the sake of Joseph.
13 And Potiphar left all that he had in the hands of Joseph; Joseph was one that caused things to come in and go out, and everything was regulated by his wish in the house of Potiphar.

14 And Joseph was eighteen years old, a youth with beautiful eyes and of very good appearance, and no one was like him in all the land of Egypt.

15 At that time while he was in his master's house, going in and out of the house and attending his master, Zelicah, his master's wife lifted up her eyes toward Joseph and she looked at him, and behold he was a youth handsome and well-favored.

16 And she coveted his beauty in her heart, and her soul was fixed on Joseph, and she enticed him day after day, and Zelicah persuaded Joseph daily, but Joseph did not lift up his eyes to give attention to his master's wife.

17 And Zelicah said to him, How goodly are your appearance and form, truly I have looked at all the slaves and have not seen so beautiful a slave as you are. Joseph said to her, Certainly he who created me in my mother's womb created all mankind.

18 She said to him, How beautiful are your eyes, with which you have dazzled all the inhabitants of Egypt, men and women. He said to her, How beautiful they are while we are alive, but should you behold them in the grave, certainly you would move away from them.

19 And she said to him, How beautiful and pleasing are all your words; take now, I pray you, the harp which is in the house, and play with your hands and let us hear your words.

20 And he said to her, How beautiful and pleasing are my words when I speak the praise of my God and his glory. She said to him, How very beautiful is the hair of your head, find the golden comb which is in the house, take it I pray you, and curl the hair of your head.

21 And he said to her, How long will you speak these words? Stop uttering these words to me, and rise and attend to your domestic affairs.

22 And she said to him, There is no one in my house, and there is nothing to attend to but to your words and to your wish. Yet in spite of all this, she could not bring Joseph to her, neither did he place his eyes on her, but directed his eyes below to the ground.

23 Zelicah desired Joseph in her heart that he should lie with her; at the time that Joseph was sitting in the house doing his work, Zelicah came and sat before him, and she enticed him daily with her discourse to lie with her, or even to look at her, but Joseph would not listen to her.

24 And she said to him, If you will not do according to my words, I will treat you with the punishment of death, and put an iron yoke on you.

25 And Joseph said to her, Certainly God who created man loosens the fetters of prisoners, and it is he who will deliver me from your prison and from your judgment.

26 When she could not persuade him and her soul being still fixed on him, her desire threw her into a grave sickness.

27 All the women of Egypt came to visit her and said to her, Why are you in this declining state? You lack nothing; certainly your husband is a great and esteemed prince in the sight of the king, should you lack anything of what your heart desires?

28 Zelicah answered them, saying, This day it shall be made known to you from where this disorder comes which you see in me, and she commanded her maid servants to prepare food for all the women; she made a banquet for them, and all the women ate in the house of Zelicah.

29 And she gave them knives to peel the citrons to eat them, and she commanded that they should dress Joseph in costly garments, that he should appear before them, and Joseph came before their eyes and all the women looked on Joseph and could

not take their eyes from off him; they all cut their hands with the knives that they had in their hands, and all the citrons that were in their hands were filled with blood.
30 And they knew not what they had done but they continued to look at the beauty of Joseph, and did not turn their eyelids from him.
31 Zelicah saw what they had done, and she said to them, What is this work that you have done? Look, I gave you citrons to eat and you have all cut your hands.
32 And all the women saw their hands, and truly they were full of blood, and their blood flowed down on their garments. They said to her, This slave in your house has overcome us, and we could not turn our eyelids from him on account of his beauty.
33 She said to them, Certainly this happened to you in the moment that you looked at him, and you could not contain yourselves from him; how then can I refrain when he is constantly in my house, and I see him day after day going in and out of my house? How then can I keep from declining or even from perishing on account of this?
34 And they said to her, The words are true, for who can see this beautiful form in the house and refrain from him, and is he not your slave and attendant in your house, and why do you not tell him that which is in your heart, but allow your soul to perish through this matter?
35 And she said to them, I am daily endeavoring to persuade him, and he will not consent to my wishes; I promised him everything that is good, and yet I could meet with no return from him; I am therefore in a declining state as you see.
36 Zelicah became very ill on account of her desire toward Joseph, and she was desperately lovesick on account of him; but all the people of the house of Zelicah and her husband knew nothing of this matter, that Zelicah was ill on account of her love to Joseph.
37 All the people of her house asked her, saying, Why are you ill and declining, and lack nothing? And she said to them, I know not this thing which daily is increasing on me.
38 All the women and her friends came daily to see her, and they spoke with her, and she said to them, This can only be through the love of Joseph. They said to her, Entice him and seize him secretly; perhaps he may listen to you and put off this death from you.
39 And Zelicah became worse from her love to Joseph, and she continued to decline, till she scarcely had strength to stand.
40 On a certain day Joseph was doing his master's work in the house, and Zelicah came secretly and fell suddenly on him; Joseph rose up against her, he was more powerful than she, and he brought her down to the ground.
41 And Zelicah wept on account of the desire of her heart toward him, and she begged him with weeping, and her tears flowed down her cheeks; she spoke to him in a voice of pleading and in bitterness of soul, saying,
42 Have you ever heard, seen or known of so beautiful a woman as I am, or better than myself, who speaks daily to you, falls into a decline through love for you, confers all this honor on you, and still you will not listen to my voice?
43 If it be through fear of your master that he punish you, as the king lives no harm shall come to you from your master through this thing; now, therefore do listen to me, and consent for the sake of the honor which I have conferred on you, and put off this death from me, for why should I die for your sake? And she ceased to speak.

44 And Joseph answered her, saying, Keep away from me, and leave this matter to my master; behold my master knows not what there is with me in the house, for all that belongs to him he has delivered into my hands, and how shall I do these things in my master's house?
45 For he has also greatly honored me in his house, and he has also made me overseer over his house, and he has exalted me, and there is no one greater in this house than I am, and my master has refrained nothing from me, excepting you who are his wife. How then can you speak these words to me, and how can I do this great evil and sin to God and to your husband?
46 Now therefore keep away from me, and speak no more such words as these, for I will not listen to your words. But Zelicah would not listen to Joseph when he spoke these words to her; she daily enticed him to listen to her.
47 It was after this that the brook of Egypt was filled above all its sides, and all the inhabitants of Egypt went forth, and also the king and princes went forth with timbrels and dances, for it was a great rejoicing in Egypt and a holiday at the time of the overflow of the sea Sihor, and they went there to rejoice all the day.
48 And when the Egyptians went out to the river to rejoice, as was their custom, all the people of the house of Potiphar went with them. But Zelicah would not go with them for she said, I am unable to. She remained alone in the house, and no other person was with her in the house.
49 And she rose up and ascended to her temple in the house, and dressed herself in princely garments, and she placed on her head precious stones of onyx stones, inlaid with silver and gold, and she beautified her face and skin with all sorts of women's purifying liquids, and she perfumed the temple and the house with cassia and frankincense, and she spread myrrh and aloes. Afterward she sat in the entrance of the temple, in the passage of the house, through which Joseph passed to do his work, and then Joseph came from the field and entered the house to do his master's work.
50 He came to the place through which he had to pass and saw all the work of Zelicah, and he turned back.
51 Zelicah saw Joseph turning back from her; she called out to him, saying What ails you Joseph? Come to your work, and look, I will make room for you until you will have passed to your seat.
52 And Joseph returned and came to the house, and passed from there to the place of his seat, and he sat down to do his master's work as usual and behold Zelicah came to him and stood before him in princely garments, and the scent from her clothes was spread some distance.
53 She hurried and caught hold of Joseph and his garments, and said to him, As the king lives if you will not perform my request you shall die this day. And she hurried and stretched forth her other hand and drew a sword from beneath her garments, and she placed it on Joseph's neck; she said, Rise and perform my request, and if not you will die this day.
54 Joseph was afraid of her doing this thing, and he rose up to flee from her; she seized the front of his garments, and in the terror of his flight the garment which Zelicah seized was torn; Joseph left the garment in the hand of Zelicah and he fled and got out, for he was afraid.
55 When Zelicah saw that Joseph's garment was torn and that he had left it in her hand, and had fled, she was afraid for her life, that the report should spread concerning her. She rose up and acted with cunning and put off the garments in which she was dressed, and she put on her other garments.

56 She took Joseph's garment and laid it beside her, and she went and seated herself in the place where she had sat in her illness, before the people of her house had gone out to the river. She called a young lad who was then in the house, and she ordered him to call the people of the house to her.
57 And when she saw them she said to them with a loud voice and lamentation, See what a Hebrew your master has brought to me in the house, for he came this day to lie with me.
58 For when you had gone out he came to the house, and seeing that there was no person in the house, he came to me and caught hold of me with intent to lie with me.
59 And I seized his garments and tore them and called out against him with a loud voice, and when I had lifted up my voice he was afraid for his life and left his garment before me, and fled.
60 The people of her house spoke nothing, but their wrath was very much set ablaze against Joseph, and they went to his master and told him the words of his wife.
61 Potiphar came home enraged, and his wife cried out to him, saying, What is this thing that you have done to me in bringing a Hebrew servant into my house, for he came to me this day to sport with me; thus did he do to me this day.
62 Potiphar heard the words of his wife and ordered Joseph to be punished with severe stripes, and they did so to him.
63 While they were smiting him, Joseph called out with a loud voice, and he lifted up his eyes to heaven, and he said, O Lord God, you know that I am innocent of all these things, and why shall I die this day through falsehood, by the hand of these uncircumcised wicked men whom you know?
64 And while Potiphar's men were beating Joseph, he continued to cry out and weep, and there was a child there eleven months old, and the Lord opened the mouth of the child, and he spake these words before Potiphar's men, who were smiting Joseph, saying,
65 What do you want of this man, and why do you do this evil to him? My mother speaks falsely and utters lies; thus was the transaction.
66 And the child told them accurately all that happened, and all the words of Zelicah to Joseph day after day did he relate to them.
67 And all the men heard the words of the child and they wondered greatly at the child's words, and the child ceased to speak and became still.
68 Potiphar was very much ashamed at the words of his son, and he commanded his men not to beat Joseph anymore, and the men ceased beating Joseph.
69 Potiphar took Joseph and ordered him to be brought to justice before the priests, who were judges belonging to the king, in order to judge him concerning this affair.
70 Potiphar and Joseph came before the priests who were the king's judges, and he said to them, Decide I beg you, what judgment is due to a servant, for thus has he done.
71 And the priests said to Joseph, Why did you do this thing to your master? and Joseph answered them, saying, Not so my lords, thus was the matter; and Potiphar said to Joseph, Certainly I entrusted in your hands all that belonged to me, and I withheld nothing from you but my wife, and how could you do this evil?
72 And Joseph answered saying, Not so my lord, as the Lord lives, and as your soul lives, my lord, the word which you did hear from your wife is untrue, for thus was the affair this day.
73 A year has elapsed to me since I have come to your house; have you seen any iniquity in me, or any thing which might cause you to demand my life?

74 The priests said to Potiphar, Send, we pray you, and let them bring before us Joseph's torn garment, and let us see the tear in it, and if it shall be that the tear is in front of the garment, then his face must have been opposite to her and she must have caught hold of him to come to her, and with deceit did your wife do all that she has spoken.
75 They brought Joseph's garment before the priests who were judges, and they saw and behold the tear was in front of Joseph, and all the judging priests knew that she had pressed him, and they said, The judgment of death is not due to this slave for he has done nothing, but his judgment is that he be placed in the prison house on account of the report, which through him has gone forth against your wife.
76 Potiphar heard their words and he placed him in the prison house, the place where the king's prisoners are confined, and Joseph was in the house of confinement twelve years.
77 And in spite of this, his master's wife did not turn from him, and she did not cease from speaking to him day after day to listen to her, and at the end of three months Zelicah continued going to Joseph to the house of confinement day by day, and she enticed him to listen to her, and Zelicah said to Joseph, How long will you remain in this house? But listen now to my voice, and I will bring you out of this house.
78 And Joseph answered her, saying, It is better for me to remain in this house than to listen to your words, to sin against God; she said to him, If you will not perform my wish, I will pluck out your eyes, add fetters to your feet, and will deliver you into the hands of them whom you did not know before.
79 Joseph answered her and said, Behold the God of the whole earth is able to deliver me from all that you can do to me, for he opens the eyes of the blind, and loosens those that are bound, and preserves all strangers who are unacquainted with the land.
80 And when Zelicah was unable to persuade Joseph to listen to her, she ceased going to entice him; Joseph was still confined in the house of confinement. And Jacob the father of Joseph, and all his brothers who were in the land of Canaan still mourned and wept in those days on account of Joseph, for Jacob refused to be comforted for his son Joseph, and Jacob cried aloud and wept and mourned all those days.

CHAPTER 45

1 It was in that year, which is the year of Joseph's going down to Egypt after his brothers had sold him, that Reuben the son of Jacob went to Timnah and took a wife Eliuram, the daughter of Avi the Canaanite, and he came to her.
2 And Eliuram the wife of Reuben conceived and gave birth, to him: Hanoch, Palu, Chetzron and Carmi, four sons; and Simeon his brother took his sister Dinah for a wife, and she gave birth to, to him: Memuel, Yamin, Ohad, Jachin and Zochar, five sons.
3 Afterward he came to Bunah the Canaanitish woman, the same is Bunah whom Simeon took captive from the city of Shechem, and Bunah was before Dinah and attended to her; Simeon came to her, and she gave birth to him, Saul.
4 And Judah went at that time to Adulam, and he came to a man of Adulam, and his name was Hirah; Judah saw there the daughter of a man from Canaan, and her name was Aliyath, the daughter of Shua. He took her and came to her, and Aliyath

gave birth to, to Judah: Er, Onan and Shiloh, three sons.
5 Levi and Issachar went to the land of the east, and they took to themselves for wives the daughters of Jobab the son of Yoktan, the son of Eber; Jobab the son of Yoktan had two daughters; the name of the elder was Adinah, and the name of the younger was Aridah.
6 And Levi took Adinah, and Issachar took Aridah, and they came to the land of Canaan, to their father's house; Adinah gave birth to, to Levi: Gershon, Kehath and Merari, three sons.
7 And Aridah gave birth to, to Issachar: Tola, Puvah, Job and Shomron, four sons; Dan went to the land of Moab and took for a wife Aphlaleth, the daughter of Chamudan the Moabite, and he brought her to the land of Canaan.
8 Aphlaleth was unable to conceive, she had no children, and God afterward remembered Aphlaleth the wife of Dan, and she conceived and gave birth to a son; she called his name Chushim.
9 And Gad and Naphtali went to Haran and took from there the daughters of Amuram the son of Uz, the son of Nahor, for wives.
10 And these are the names of the daughters of Amuram: the name of the elder was Merimah, and the name of the younger Uzith; Naphtali took Merimah, and Gad took Uzith and brought them to the land of Canaan, to their father's house.
11 And Merimah gave birth to, to Naphtali: Yachzeel, Guni, Jazer and Shalem, four sons; and Uzith gave birth to, to Gad: Zephion, Chagi, Shuni, Ezbon, Eri, Arodi and Arali, seven sons.
12 Asher went forth and took Adon the daughter of Aphlal, the son of Hadad, the son of Ishmael, for a wife and he brought her to the land of Canaan.
13 And Adon the wife of Asher died in those days, she had no children; it was after the death of Adon that Asher went to the other side of the river and took for a wife Hadurah the daughter of Abimael, the son of Eber, the son of Shem.
14 The young woman was of a beautiful appearance and a woman of sense, and she had been the wife of Malkiel the son of Elam, the son of Shem.
15 Hadurah gave birth to a daughter to Malkiel, and he called her name Serach, and Malkiel died after this and Hadurah went and remained in her father's house.
16 After the death of the wife at Asher he went and took Hadurah for a wife, and brought her to the land of Canaan, and Serach her daughter he also brought with them; she was three years old and the child was brought up in Jacob's house.
17 And the girl was of a beautiful appearance and she went in the holy ways of the children of Jacob; she lacked nothing, and the Lord gave her wisdom and understanding.
18 Hadurah the wife of Asher conceived and gave birth to, to him: Yimnah, Yishvah, Yishvi and Beriah, four sons.
19 Zebulun went to Midian and took for a wife Merishah the daughter of Molad, the son of Abida, the son of Midian, and brought her to the land of Canaan.
20 And Merushah gave birth to, to Zebulun: Sered, Elon and Yachleel, three sons.
21 Jacob sent to Aram, the son of Zoba, the son of Terah, and he took for his son Benjamin Mechalia the daughter of Aram, and she came to the land of Canaan to the house of Jacob; Benjamin was ten years old when he took Mechalia the daughter of Aram for a wife.
22 And Mechalia conceived and gave birth to, to Benjamin: Bela, Becher, Ashbel, Gera and Naaman, five sons; Benjamin afterward went and took for a wife Aribath, the daughter of Shomron, the son of Abraham, in addition to his first wife, and he

was eighteen years old; Aribath gave birth to, to Benjamin: Achi, Vosh, Mupim, Chupim, and Ord, five sons.
23 In those days Judah went to the house of Shem and took Tamar the daughter of Elam, the son of Shem, for a wife for his first born Er.
24 And Er came to his wife Tamar, and she became his wife; when he came to her he outwardly destroyed his offspring, and his work was evil in the sight of the Lord, and the Lord killed him.
25 It was after the death of Er, Judah's first born, that Judah said to Onan, Go to your brother's wife and marry her as the next of kin and raise up children to your brother.
26 And Onan took Tamar for a wife and he came to her; Onan also did like the work of his brother, and his work was evil in the sight of the Lord, and he killed him also.
27 When Onan died, Judah said to Tamar, Remain in your father's house until my son Shiloh will have grown up; Judah had no more delight in Tamar, to give her to Shiloh, for he said, Perhaps he will also die like his brothers.
28 And Tamar rose up and went and remained in her father's house, and Tamar was in her father's house for some time.
29 At the revolution of the year, Aliyath the wife of Judah died; Judah was comforted for his wife, and after the death of Aliyath, Judah went up with his friend Hirah to Timnah to shear their sheep.
30 Tamar heard that Judah had gone up to Timnah to shear the sheep, and that Shiloh was grown up, and Judah did not delight in her.
31 And Tamar rose up and put off the garments of her widowhood; she put on a veil and entirely covered herself; she went and sat in the public thoroughfare which is on the road to Timnah.
32 Judah passed and saw her and took her and he came to her, and she conceived by him; at the time of being delivered there were twins in her womb, and he called the name of the first Perez and the name of the second Zarah.

CHAPTER 46

1 In those days Joseph was still confined in the prison house in the land of Egypt.
2 At that time the attendants of Pharaoh were standing before him, the chief of the butlers and the chief of the bakers which belonged to the king of Egypt.
3 And the butler took wine and placed it before the king to drink, and the baker placed bread before the king to eat, and the king drank of the wine and ate of the bread; he and his servants and ministers that ate at the king's table.
4 And while they were eating and drinking, the butler and the baker remained there, and Pharaoh's ministers found many flies in the wine which the butler had brought, and stones of nitre were found in the baker's bread.
5 And the captain of the guard placed Joseph as an attendant on Pharaoh's officers, and Pharaoh's officers were in confinement one year.
6 At the end of the year, they both dreamed dreams in one night, in the place of confinement where they were, and in the morning Joseph came to them to attend on them as usual. He saw them and their countenances were dejected and sad.
7 And Joseph asked them, Why are your countenances sad? They said, we dreamed a dream and there was no one here to interpret it. Joseph said to them, Relate, I pray you, your dream to me, and God shall give you an answer of peace as you desire.
8 The butler related his dream to Joseph and said, I saw in my dream there was a

large vine before me and on that vine I saw three branches; the vine speedily blossomed and reached a great height, and its clusters were ripened and became grapes.
9 And I took the grapes and pressed them in a cup, and placed it in Pharaoh's hand and he drank; and Joseph said to him, The three branches that were on the vine are three days.
10 Yet within three days, the king will order you to be brought out and he will restore you to your office; you shall give the king his wine to drink as at first when you were his butler; but let me find favor in your sight, so that you shall remember me to Pharaoh when it will be well with you; do this kindness to me and get me brought forth from this prison, for I was stolen away from the land of Canaan and was sold for a slave in this place.
11 Also that which was told you concerning my master's wife is false, for they placed me in this dungeon for nothing. The butler answered Joseph, saying, If the king deals well with me as at first, as you last interpreted to me, I will do all that you desire and get you brought out of this dungeon.
12 And the baker, seeing that Joseph had accurately interpreted the butler's dream, also approached and related the whole of his dream to Joseph.
13 He said to him, In my dream I looked and there were three white baskets on my head; I looked again and then there were in the upper-most basket all manner of baked meats for Pharaoh; there the birds were eating them from off my head.
14 And Joseph said to him, The three baskets which you saw are three days, yet within three days Pharaoh will take off your head and hang you on a tree, and the birds will eat your flesh from off you, as you saw in your dream.
15 In those days the queen was about to be delivered, and on that day she gave birth to a son to the king of Egypt; they announced that the king had gotten his firstborn son and all the people of Egypt together with the officers and servants of Pharaoh rejoiced greatly.
16 On the third day of his birth Pharaoh made a feast for his officers and servants, for the hosts of the land of Zoar and of the land of Egypt.
17 And all the people of Egypt and the servants of Pharaoh came to eat and drink with the king at the feast of his son, and to rejoice at the king's rejoicing.
18 All the officers of the king and his servants were rejoicing at that time for eight days at the feast, and they made merry with all sorts of musical instruments, with timbrels and with dances in the king's house for eight days.
19 And the butler, to whom Joseph had interpreted his dream, forgot Joseph and did not mention him to the king as he had promised, for this thing was from the Lord in order to punish Joseph because he had trusted in man.
20 And Joseph remained after this in the prison house two years, until he had completed twelve years.

CHAPTER 47

1 Isaac the son of Abraham was still living in those days in the land of Canaan; he was very aged, one hundred and eighty years old, and Esau his son, the brother of Jacob, was in the land of Edom; he and his sons had possessions in it among the children of Seir.
2 And Esau heard that his father's time was drawing near to die, and he and his sons

and household came to the land of Canaan to his father's house. Jacob and his sons went forth from the place where they lived in Hebron and they all came to their father Isaac, and they found Esau and his sons in the tent.
3 And Jacob and his sons sat before his father Isaac, and Jacob was still mourning for his son Joseph.
4 And Isaac said to Jacob, Bring your sons here to me and I will bless them; and Jacob brought his eleven children before his father Isaac.
5 And Isaac placed his hands on all the sons of Jacob, and he took hold of them and embraced them, and kissed them one by one. Isaac blessed them on that day and he said to them, May the God of your fathers bless you and increase your offspring like the stars of heaven for number.
6 Isaac also blessed the sons of Esau, saying, May God cause you to be a dread and a terror to all that will behold you, and to all your enemies.
7 Isaac called Jacob and his sons and they all came and sat before Isaac, and Isaac said to Jacob, The Lord God of the whole earth said to me, Unto your offspring I will give this land for an inheritance if your children keep my statutes and my ways, and I will perform to them the oath which I swore to your father Abraham.
8 Now therefore my son, teach your children and your children's children to fear the Lord, and to go in the good way which will please the Lord your God, for if you keep the ways of the Lord and his statutes the Lord will also keep to you his covenant with Abraham, and will do well with you and your descendants always.
9 When Isaac had finished commanding Jacob and his children, he gave up the ghost and died, and was gathered to his people.
10 And Jacob and Esau fell on the face of their father Isaac, and they wept, and Isaac was one hundred and eighty years old when he died in the land of Canaan, in Hebron. His sons carried him to the cave of Machpelah, which Abraham had bought from the children of Heth for a possession of a burial place.
11 And all the kings of the land of Canaan went with Jacob and Esau to bury Isaac, and all the kings of Canaan showed Isaac great honor at his death.
12 The sons of Jacob and the sons of Esau went barefooted round about, walking and lamenting until they reached Kireath-arba.
13 And Jacob and Esau buried their father Isaac in the cave of Machpelah, which is in Kireath-arba in Hebron; they buried him with very great honor, as at the funeral of kings.
14 Jacob and his sons, and Esau and his sons, and all the kings of Canaan made a great and heavy mourning, and they buried him and mourned for him many days.
15 At the death of Isaac, he left his cattle and his possessions and all belonging to him to his sons; and Esau said to Jacob, Behold I pray you, all that our father has left we will divide into two parts, and I will have the choice; Jacob said, We will do so.
16 Jacob took all that Isaac had left in the land of Canaan, the cattle and the property, and he placed them in two parts before Esau and his sons, and he said to Esau, Behold all this is before you, choose to yourself the half which you will take.
17 And Jacob said to Esau, Hear I pray you what I will speak to you, saying, The Lord God of heaven and earth spoke to our fathers Abraham and Isaac, saying, Unto your descendants will I give this land for an inheritance forever.
18 Now therefore all that our father has left is before you, and behold all the land is before you; choose from them what you desire.
19 If you desire the whole land take it for you and your children forever, and I will take these riches, and if you desire the riches take them with you, and I will take this

land for me and for my children to inherit forever.
20 Nebayoth, the son of Ishmael, was then in the land with his children, and Esau went on that day and consulted with him, saying,
21 Thus has Jacob spoken to me; thus has he answered me, now give your advice and we will listen.
22 And Nebayoth said, What is this that Jacob hath spoken to you? Behold all the children of Canaan are dwelling securely in their land, and Jacob says he will inherit it with his descendants all the days.
23 Go now therefore and take all your father's riches and leave Jacob your brother in the land, as he has spoken.
24 And Esau rose up and returned to Jacob, and did all that Nebayoth the son of Ishmael had advised; and Esau took all the riches that Isaac had left, the souls, the beasts, the cattle and the property, and all the riches; he gave nothing to his brother Jacob, and Jacob took all the land of Canaan, from the brook of Egypt to the river Euphrates, and he took it for an everlasting possession, and for his children and for his descendants after him forever.
25 Jacob also took from his brother Esau the cave of Machpelah, which is in Hebron, which Abraham had bought from Ephron for a possession of a burial place for him and his descendants forever.
26 And Jacob wrote all these things in the book of purchase, and he signed it, and testified all this with four faithful witnesses.
27 These are the words which Jacob wrote in the book, saying: The land of Canaan and all the cities of the Hittites, the Hivites, the Jebusites, the Amorites, the Perizzites, and the Gergashites, all the seven nations from the river of Egypt to the river Euphrates.
28 And the city of Hebron Kireath-arba, and the cave which is in it, the whole did Jacob buy from his brother Esau for value, for a possession and for an inheritance for his descendants after him forever.
29 And Jacob took the book of purchase and the signature, the command and the statutes and the revealed book, and he placed them in an earthen vessel in order that they should remain for a long time, and he delivered them into the hands of his children.
30 Esau took all that his father had left him after his death from his brother Jacob, and he took all the property, from man and beast, camel and ass, ox and lamb, silver and gold, stones and bdellium, and all the riches which had belonged to Isaac the son of Abraham; there was nothing left which Esau did not take to himself from all that Isaac had left after his death.
31 Esau took all this and he and his children went home to the land of Seir the Horite, away from his brother Jacob and his children.
32 And Esau had possessions among the children of Seir, and Esau returned not to the land of Canaan from that day forward.
33 The whole land of Canaan became an inheritance to the children of Israel for an everlasting inheritance, and Esau with all his children inherited the mountain of Seir.

CHAPTER 48

1 In those days, after the death of Isaac, the Lord commanded and caused a famine on the whole earth.

2 At that time Pharaoh, king of Egypt, was sitting on his throne in the land of Egypt; he lay in his bed and dreamed dreams and Pharaoh saw in his dream that he was standing by the side of the river of Egypt.
3 While he was standing he saw seven fat fleshed and well favored cattle come up out of the river.
4 And seven other cattle, lean fleshed and ill favored, came up after them, and the seven ill favored ones swallowed up the well favored ones, and still their appearance was ill as at first.
5 And he awoke; he slept again and he dreamed a second time, and he saw seven ears of corn come up on one stalk, full and good, and seven thin ears blasted with the east wind sprang up after them, and the thin ears swallowed up the full ones, then Pharaoh awoke out of his dream.
6 In the morning the king remembered his dreams and his spirit was sadly troubled on account of his dreams, and the king hurried, sent and called for all the magicians of Egypt and the wise men, and they came and stood before Pharaoh.
7 And the king said to them, I have dreamed dreams, and there is none to interpret them; they said to the king, relate your dreams to your servants and let us hear them.
8 And the king related his dreams to them, and they all answered and said with one voice to the king, May the king live forever; this is the interpretation of your dreams.
9 The seven good cattle which you saw denotes seven daughters that will be born to you in the latter days, and the seven cattle which you saw come up after them and swallowed them up, are for a sign that the daughters which will be born to you will all die in the lifetime of the king.
10 And that which you saw in the second dream of seven full good ears of corn coming up on one stalk, this is their interpretation: that you will build to yourself in the latter days seven cities throughout the land of Egypt; that which you saw of the seven poor ears of corn springing up after them and swallowing them up while you saw them with your eyes, is for a sign that the cities which you will build will all be destroyed in the latter days, in the lifetime of the king.
11 And when they spoken these words the king did not incline his ear to their words, neither did he fix his heart on them, for the king knew in his wisdom that they did not give a proper interpretation of the dreams; when they had finished speaking before the king, he answered them, saying, What is this thing that you have spoken to me? Certainly you have uttered falsely and spoken lies; therefore now give the proper interpretation of my dreams, that you may not die.
12 The king commanded after this, and he sent and called again for other wise men, and they came and stood before the king. The king related his dreams to them, and they all answered him according to the first interpretation; the king's anger was set ablaze and he was very upset. A nd the king said to them, Certainly you speak lies and utter falsehood in what you have said.
13 The king commanded that a proclamation should be issued throughout the land of Egypt, saying, It is determined by the king and his great men, that any wise man who knows and understands the interpretation of dreams, and will not come this day before the king, shall die.
14 The man that will declare to the king the proper interpretation of his dreams, there shall be given to him all that he will require from the king. And all the wise men of the land of Egypt came before the king, together with all the magicians and sorcerers that were in Egypt and in Goshen, in Rameses, in Tachpanches, in Zoar,

and in all the places on the borders of Egypt; they all stood before the king.
15 And all the nobles and the princes, and the attendants belonging to the king, came together from all the cities of Egypt and they all sat before the king, and the king related his dreams before the wise men and the princes; all that sat before the king were astonished at the vision.
16 And all the wise men who were before the king were greatly divided in their interpretation of his dreams; some of them interpreted them to the king, saying, The seven good cattle are seven kings, who from the king's lineage will be raised over Egypt.
17 And the seven bad cattle are seven princes who will stand up against them in the latter days and destroy them; the seven ears of corn are the seven great princes belonging to Egypt, who will fall in the hands of the seven less powerful princes of their enemies, in the wars of our lord the king.
18 And some of them interpreted to the king in this manner, saying, The seven good cattle are the strong cities of Egypt, and the seven bad cattle are the seven nations of the land of Canaan, who will come against the seven cities of Egypt in the latter days and destroy them.
19 And that which you saw in the second dream, of seven good and bad ears of corn, is a sign that the government of Egypt will again return to your descendants as at first.
20 And in this reign the people of the cities of Egypt will turn against the seven cities of Canaan who are stronger than they are and will destroy them, and the government of Egypt will return to your descendants.
21 Some of them said to the king, This is the interpretation of your dreams; the seven good cattle are seven queens, whom you will take for wives in the latter days, and the seven bad cattle denote that those women will all die in the lifetime of the king.
22 And the seven good and bad ears of corn which you did see in the second dream are fourteen children, and it will be in the latter days that they will stand up and fight among themselves, and seven of them will strike the seven that are more powerful.
23 Some of them said these words to the king, The seven good cattle denote that seven children will be born to you, and they will kill seven of your children's children in the latter days; and the seven good ears of corn which you saw in the second dream are those princes against whom seven other less powerful princes will fight and destroy them in the latter days, and avenge your children's cause, and the government will again return to your offspring.
24 The king heard all the words of the wise men of Egypt and their interpretation of his dreams, and none of them pleased the king.
25 And the king knew in his wisdom that they did not altogether speak correctly in all these words, for this was from the Lord to frustrate the words of the wise men of Egypt in order that Joseph might go forth from the house of confinement, and in order that he should become great in Egypt.
26 The king saw that none among all the wise men and magicians of Egypt spoke correctly to him, and the king's wrath was set ablaze, and his anger burned within him.
27 And the king commanded that all the wise men and magicians should go out from before him, and they all went out from before the king with shame and disgrace.
28 Then the king commanded that a proclamation be sent throughout Egypt to kill

all the magicians that were in Egypt, and not one of them should be allowed to live.
29 And the captains of the guards belonging to the king rose up, and each man drew his sword; they began to strike the magicians of Egypt and the wise men.
30 After this Merod, chief butler to the king, came and bowed down before the king and sat before him.
31 The butler said to the king, May the king live forever, and his government be honored in the land.
32 You were angry with your servant in those days now two years past and did place me in the ward, and I was for some time in the ward, I and the chief of the bakers.
33 And there was with us a Hebrew servant belonging to the captain of the guard, his name was Joseph, for his master had been angry with him and placed him in the house of confinement, and he attended us there.
34 Some time after when we were in the ward, we dreamed dreams in one night, I and the chief of the bakers; we dreamed, each man according to the interpretation of his dream.
35 And we came in the morning and told them to that servant, and he interpreted to us our dreams, to each man according to his dream he correctly interpreted.
36 And it came to pass as he interpreted to us, so was the event; there fell not to the ground any of his words.
37 Now therefore my lord and king do not kill the people of Egypt for nothing; consider that the slave is still confined in the house by the captain of the guard his master, in the house of confinement.
38 If it pleases the king let him send for him that he may come before you and he will make known to you the correct interpretation of the dream which you did dream.
39 The king heard the words of the chief butler, and the king ordered that the wise men of Egypt should not be slain.
40 And the king ordered his servants to bring Joseph before him, and the king said to them, Go to him and do not terrify him that he be confused and will not know to speak properly.
41 The servants of the king went to Joseph, and they brought him hastily out of the dungeon; the king's servants shaved him, and he changed his prison garment and came before the king.
42 The king was sitting on his royal throne in a princely dress surrounded with a golden ephod, and the fine gold which was on it sparkled, and the gem and the ruby and the emerald, together with all the precious stones that were on the king's head dazzled the eye, and Joseph wondered greatly at the king.
43 And the throne on which the king sat was covered with gold and silver and with onyx stones, and it had seventy steps.
44 It was their custom throughout the land of Egypt that every man who came to speak to the king, if he was a prince or one that was respected in the sight of the king, he ascended to the king's throne as far as the thirty-first step, and the king would descend to the thirty-sixth step and speak with him.
45 If he was one of the common people, he ascended to the third step, and the king would descend to the fourth and speak to him, as their custom was. Also any man who understood to speak in all the seventy languages, he ascended the seventy steps, and went up and spoke till he reached the king.
46 And any man who could not complete the seventy, he ascended as many steps as

the languages which he knew to speak in.
47 It was customary in those days in Egypt that no one should reign over them, but one who understood to speak in the seventy languages.
48 When Joseph came before the king he bowed down to the ground before the king, and he ascended to the third step, and the king sat on the fourth step and spoke with Joseph.
49 The king said to Joseph, I dreamed a dream, and there is no interpreter to interpret it properly, and I commanded that all the magicians of Egypt and the wise men thereof should come before me; I related my dreams to them, and no one has properly interpreted them to me.
50 After this I heard about you, that you are a wise man, and can correctly interpret every dream that you hear.
51 And Joseph answered Pharaoh, saying, Let Pharaoh relate his dreams that he dreamed; certainly the interpretations belong to God. And Pharaoh related his dreams to Joseph, the dream of the cattle, and the dream of the ears of corn, and the king ceased speaking.
52 Joseph was then clothed with the spirit of God before the king, and he knew all the things that would befall the king from that day forward; he knew the proper interpretation of the king's dream, and he spoke before the king.
53 Joseph found favor in the sight of the king, and the king listened carefully and with his heart, and he heard all the words of Joseph. And Joseph said to the king, Do not imagine that they are two dreams, for it is only one dream, for that which God has chosen to do throughout the land he has shown to the king in his dream, and this is the proper interpretation of your dream:
54 The seven good cattle and ears of corn are seven years, and the seven bad cattle and ears of corn are also seven years; it is one dream.
55 Know this, the seven years that are coming there will be a great plenty throughout the land, and after that the seven years of famine will follow them, a very severe famine; all the plenty will be forgotten from the land, and the famine will consume the inhabitants of the land.
56 The king dreamed one dream, and the dream was therefore repeated to Pharaoh because the thing is established by God, and God will shortly bring it to pass.
57 Now therefore I will give you counsel and deliver your soul and the souls of the inhabitants of the land from the evil of the famine, that you search throughout your kingdom for a man very discreet and wise, who knows all the affairs of government, and appoint him to superintend over the land of Egypt.
58 And let the man whom you place over Egypt appoint officers under him, that they gather in all the food of the good years that are coming, and let them lay up corn and deposit it in your appointed stores.
59 And let them keep that food for the seven years of famine, that it may be available for you and your people and your whole land, and that you and your land be not cut off by the famine.
60 Let all the inhabitants of the land also be ordered that they gather in, every man the produce of his field, of all sorts of food, during the seven good years, and that they place it in their stores; that it may be available for them in the days of the famine and that they may live on it.
61 This is the proper interpretation of your dream, and this is the counsel given to save your soul and the souls of all your subjects.
62 The king answered and said to Joseph, Who says and who knows that your words

are correct? And he said to the king, This shall be a sign for you respecting all my words, that they are true and that my advice is good for you.
63 Behold your wife sits this day on the stool of delivery, and she will bear you a son and you will rejoice with him; when your child shall have gone forth from his mother's womb, your firstborn son that has been born two years ago shall die, and you will be comforted in the child that will be born to you this day.
64 Joseph finished speaking these words to the king, and he bowed down to the king and he went out, and when Joseph had gone out from the king's presence, those signs which Joseph had spoken to the king came to pass on that day.
65 The queen gave birth to a son on that day and the king heard the glad tidings about his son, and he rejoiced, and when the reporter had gone forth from the king's presence, the king's servants found the firstborn son of the king fallen dead on the ground.
66 There was great lamentation and noise in the king's house, and the king heard it and said, What is the noise and lamentation that I have heard in the house? They told the king that his firstborn son had died, then the king knew that all Joseph's words that he had spoken were correct; the king was consoled for his son by the child that was born to him on that day as Joseph had said.

CHAPTER 49

1 After these things the king sent and assembled all his officers and servants, and all the princes and nobles belonging to the king, and they all came before the king.
2 And the king said to them, Behold you have seen and heard all the words of this Hebrew man, and all the signs which he declared would come to pass, and not any of his words have fallen to the ground.
3 You know that he has given a proper interpretation of the dream, and it will certainly come to pass; now therefore take counsel, and know what you will do and how the land will be delivered from the famine.
4 Search now and see whether the likes of him can be found, in whose heart there is wisdom and knowledge, and I will appoint him over the land.
5 For you have heard what the Hebrew man has advised concerning this to save the land from the famine, and I know that the land will not be delivered from the famine but with the advice of the Hebrew man, him that advised me.
6 And they all answered the king and said, The counsel which the Hebrew has given concerning this is good; now therefore, our lord and king, behold the whole land is in your hand, do that which seems good in your sight.
7 Him whom you choose, and whom you in your wisdom know to be wise and capable of delivering the land with his wisdom, him shall the king appoint to be under him over the land.
8 And the king said to all the officers: I have thought that since God has made known to the Hebrew man all that he has spoken, there is none so discreet and wise in the whole land as he is; if it seems good in your sight I will place him over the land, for he will save the land with his wisdom.
9 All the officers answered the king and said, But certainly it is written in the laws of Egypt, and it should not be violated, that no man shall reign over Egypt, nor be the second to the king, but one who has knowledge in all the languages of the sons of men.

10 Now therefore our lord and king, behold this Hebrew man can only speak the Hebrew language; how then can he be over us as the second under government, a man who not even knows our language?
11 Now we pray you send for him, and let him come before you, and prove him in all things, and do as you see fit.
12 And the king said, It shall be done tomorrow, and the thing that you have spoken is good. All the officers came on that day before the king.
13 But that night the Lord sent one of his ministering angels and he came into the land of Egypt to Joseph, and the angel of the Lord stood over Joseph; there Joseph was lying in the bed at night in his master's house in the dungeon, for his master had put him back into the dungeon on account of his wife.
14 The angel roused him from his sleep, and Joseph rose up and stood on his legs, and there the angel of the Lord was standing opposite to him; the angel of the Lord spoke with Joseph and he taught him all the languages of man in that night, and he called his name Jehoseph.
15 The angel of the Lord went from him and Joseph returned and lay on his bed, and Joseph was astonished at the vision which he saw.
16 It came to pass in the morning that the king sent for all his officers and servants and they all came and sat before the king, and the king ordered Joseph to be brought; the king's servants went and brought Joseph before Pharaoh.
17 And the king came forth and ascended the steps of the throne and Joseph spoke to the king in all languages; Joseph went up to him and spoke to the king until he arrived before the king in the seventieth step, and he sat before the king.
18 And the king greatly rejoiced on account of Joseph, and all the king's officers rejoiced greatly with the king when they heard all the words of Joseph.
19 That thing seemed good in the sight of the king and the officers, to appoint Joseph to be second to the king over the whole land of Egypt, and the king spoke to Joseph, saying,
20 Now you did give me counsel to appoint a wise man over the land of Egypt, in order with his wisdom to save the land from the famine. Now therefore, since God has made all this known to you, and all the words which you have spoken, there is not throughout the land a discreet and wise man like to you.
21 And your name no more shall be called Joseph, but Zaphnath Paaneah shall be your name; you shall be second to me, and according to your word shall be all the affairs of my government; at your word shall my people go out and come in.
22 Also from under your hand shall my servants and officers receive their salary which is given to them monthly, and to you shall all the people of the land bow down; only in my throne will I be greater than you.
23 And the king took off his ring from his hand and put it on the hand of Joseph, and the king dressed Joseph in a princely garment; he put a golden crown on his head, and he put a golden chain on his neck.
24 The king commanded his servants and they made him ride in the second chariot belonging to the king, that went opposite to the king's chariot. He caused him to ride on a great and strong horse from the king's horses, and to be conducted through the streets of the land of Egypt.
25 And the king commanded that all those that played on timbrels, harps and other musical instruments should go forth with Joseph; one thousand timbrels, one thousand mecholoth, and one thousand nebalim went after him.
26 And five thousand men, with drawn swords glittering in their hands, went

marching and playing before Joseph; twenty thousand of the great men of the king, with girdles of skin covered with gold, marched at the right hand of Joseph, and twenty thousand at his left. All the women and girls went on the roofs or stood in the streets playing and rejoicing at Joseph, and gazed at the appearance of Joseph and at his beauty.
27 And the king's people went before him and behind him, perfuming the road with frankincense and with cassia and with all sorts of fine perfume, and scattered myrrh and aloes along the road. Twenty men proclaimed these words before him throughout the land in a loud voice:
28 Do you see this man whom the king has chosen to be his second? All the affairs of government shall be regulated by him, and he that disobeys his orders, or that does not bow down before him to the ground, shall die, for he would be rebelling against the king and his second person in command.
29 And when the heralds had ceased announcing, all the people of Egypt bowed down to the ground before Joseph and said, May the king live, also may his second one live; all the inhabitants of Egypt bowed down along the road, and when the heralds approached them, they bowed down; they rejoiced with all sorts of timbrels, pipes and harps before Joseph.
30 And Joseph on his horse lifted up his eyes to heaven, and called out and said, He raises the poor man from the dust. He lifts up the needy from the dunghill. O Lord of Hosts, happy is the man who trusts in you.
31 And Joseph passed throughout the land of Egypt with Pharaoh's servants and officers, and they showed him the whole land of Egypt and all the king's treasures.
32 Joseph returned and came that day before Pharaoh, and the king gave to Joseph a possession in the land of Egypt, a possession of fields and vineyards. And the king gave to Joseph three thousand talents of silver and one thousand talents of gold, and onyx stones and bdellium and many gifts.
33 On the next day the king commanded all the people of Egypt to bring to Joseph offerings and gifts, and said that he that violated the command of the king should die; they made a high place in the street of the city and spread out garments there, and whoever brought anything to Joseph put it into the high place.
34 And all the people of Egypt cast something into the high place, one man a golden earring, and the other rings and earrings, and different vessels of gold and silver work, and onyx stones and bdellium he put on the high place; every one gave something of what he possessed.
35 And Joseph took all these and placed them in his treasuries, and all the officers and nobles belonging to the king exalted Joseph. They gave him many gifts, seeing that the king had chosen him to be his second in leadership.
36 The king sent to Potiphera, the son of Ahiram priest of On, and he took his young daughter Osnath and gave her to Joseph for a wife.
37 And the girl was very beautiful, a virgin, one whom man had not known, and Joseph took her for a wife; the king said to Joseph, I am Pharaoh, and beside you none shall dare to lift up his hand or his foot to regulate my people throughout the land of Egypt.
38 Joseph was thirty years old when he stood before Pharaoh, and Joseph went out from before the king and became the king's second in command in Egypt.
39 The king gave Joseph a hundred servants to attend him in his house, and Joseph also sent and purchased many servants and they remained in the house of Joseph.
40 Joseph then built for himself a very magnificent house like to the houses of kings,

before the court of the king's palace, and he made in the house a large temple, very elegant in appearance and convenient for his residence; three years Joseph spent in erecting his house.
41 And Joseph made for himself a very elegant throne of an abundance of gold and silver, and he covered it with onyx stones and bdellium; he made on it the likeness of the whole land of Egypt, and the likeness of the river of Egypt that waters the whole land of Egypt. Joseph sat securely on his throne in his house and the Lord increased Joseph's wisdom.
42 And all the inhabitants of Egypt and Pharaoh's servants and his princes loved Joseph greatly, for this thing was from the Lord to Joseph.
43 And Joseph had an army that made war, going out in hosts and troops to the number of forty thousand six hundred men, capable of bearing arms to assist the king and Joseph against the enemy, besides the king's officers and his servants and inhabitants of Egypt without number.
44 And Joseph gave to his mighty men, and to all his army, shields and javelins, and caps and coats of mail and stones for slinging.

CHAPTER 50

1 At that time the children of Tarshish came against the sons of Ishmael, and made war with them, and the children of Tarshish fought the Ishmaelites for a long time.
2 The children of Ishmael were small in number in those days, and they could not succeed over the children of Tarshish, and they were extremely oppressed.
3 And the old men of the Ishmaelites sent a record to the king of Egypt, saying, Send I pray you to your servants: officers and army to help us to fight against the children of Tarshish, for we have been diminishing away for a long time.
4 And Pharaoh sent Joseph with the mighty men and army which were with him, and also his mighty men from the king's house.
5 They went to the land of Havilah to the children of Ishmael to assist them against the children of Tarshish, and the children of Ishmael fought with the children of Tarshish. Joseph struck the Tarshishites and he subdued all their land, and the children of Ishmael lived there to this day.
6 And when the land of Tarshish was subdued, all the Tarshishites ran away, and came to the border of their brothers the children of Javan; Joseph with all his mighty men and army returned to Egypt, not one man of them missing.
7 At the revolution of the year, in the second year of Joseph's reigning over Egypt, the Lord gave great plenty throughout the land for seven years as Joseph had spoken, for the Lord blessed all the produce of the earth in those days for seven years; they ate and were greatly satisfied.
8 And Joseph at that time had officers under him, and they collected all the food of the good years, and heaped corn year by year, and they placed it in the treasuries of Joseph.
9 At any time when they gathered the food, Joseph commanded that they should bring the corn in the ears, and also bring with it some of the soil of the field, so that it would not spoil.
10 And Joseph did according to this year by year, and he heaped up corn like the sand of the sea for abundance, for his stores were immense and could not be numbered for abundance.

11 Also all the inhabitants of Egypt gathered all sorts of food in their stores in great abundance during the seven good years, but they did not do to it as Joseph did.
12 All the food which Joseph and the Egyptians had gathered during the seven years of plenty was secured for the land in stores for the seven years of famine, for the support of the whole land.
13 And the inhabitants of Egypt filled each man his store and his concealed place with corn, to be for support during the famine.
14 And Joseph placed all the food that he had gathered in all the cities of Egypt, and he closed all the stores and placed sentinels over them.
15 Joseph's wife Osnath the daughter of Potiphera gave birth to him two sons, Manasseh and Ephraim, and Joseph was thirty-four years old when he had them.
16 And the lads grew up and they followed in his ways and in his instructions; they did not deviate from the way which their father taught them, either to the right or left.
17 And the Lord was with the lads, and they grew up and had understanding and skill in all wisdom and in all the affairs of government. All the king's officers and his great men of the inhabitants of Egypt honored the lads, and they were brought up among the king's children.
18 The seven years of plenty that were throughout the land were at an end; the seven years of famine came after them as Joseph had spoken, and the famine spread throughout the land.
19 All the people of Egypt saw that the famine had begun in the land of Egypt, and all the people of Egypt opened their stores of corn for the famine hung over them.
20 And they found all the food that was in their stores full of vermin and not fit to eat, and the famine stayed throughout the land; all the inhabitants of Egypt came and cried before Pharaoh, for the famine was heavy on them.
21 And they said to Pharaoh, Give food to your servants; why shall we die through hunger before your eyes, even we and our little ones?
22 And Pharaoh answered them, saying, And why do you cry to me? Did not Joseph command that the corn should be laid up during the seven years of plenty for the years of famine? Why did you not listen to his voice?
23 And the people of Egypt answered the king, saying, As your soul lives, our lord, your servants have done all that Joseph ordered, for your servants also gathered in all the produce of their fields during the seven years of plenty and laid it in the stores to this day.
24 And when the famine prevailed over your servants we opened our stores, and behold all our produce was filled with vermin and was not fit for food.
25 When the king heard all that had befallen the inhabitants of Egypt, the king was greatly afraid on account of the famine, and he was much terrified; the king answered the people of Egypt, saying, Since all this has happened to you, go to Joseph, do whatever he shall say to you; do not go contrary to his commands.
26 And all the people of Egypt went forth and came to Joseph, and said to him, Give to us food, for why shall we die before you through hunger? We gathered in our produce during the seven years as you did command, and we put it in store, and thus has it happened to us.
27 And when Joseph heard all the words of the people of Egypt and what had happened to them, Joseph opened all his stores of the produce and he sold it to the people of Egypt.
28 And the famine stayed throughout the land, and the famine was in all countries,

but in the land of Egypt there was produce for sale.
29 All the inhabitants of Egypt came to Joseph to buy corn, for the famine hung over them, and all their corn was spoiled, and Joseph daily sold it to all the people of Egypt.
30 And all the inhabitants of the land of Canaan and the Philistines, and those beyond the Jordan, and the children of the east and all the cities of the lands far and near heard that there was corn in Egypt, and they all came to Egypt to buy corn, for the famine hung over them.
31 Joseph opened the stores of corn and placed officers over them, and they daily stood and sold to all that came.
32 Joseph knew that his brothers also would come to Egypt to buy corn, for the famine spread throughout the earth. And Joseph commanded all his people that they should cause it to be announced throughout the land of Egypt, saying,
33 It is the pleasure of the king, of his second and of their great men, that any person who wishes to buy corn in Egypt shall not send his servants to Egypt to purchase, but his sons; also any Egyptian or Canaanite who shall come from any of the stores from buying corn in Egypt, if he goes and sells it throughout the land, he shall die, for no one shall buy but for the support of his household.
34 And any man leading two or three beasts shall die, for a man shall only lead his own beast.
35 Joseph placed sentinels at the gates of Egypt, and commanded them, saying, Any person who may come to buy corn, permit him not to enter until his name and the name of his father, and the name of his father's father be written down; whatever is written by day, send their names to me in the evening that I may know their names.
36 And Joseph placed officers throughout the land of Egypt; he commanded them to do all these things.
37 Joseph did all these things, and made these standards in order that he might know when his brothers would come to Egypt to buy corn; Joseph's people caused it daily to be announced in Egypt according to these words and standards which Joseph had commanded.
38 And all the inhabitants of the east and west country, and of all the earth, heard of the rules and regulations which Joseph had enacted in Egypt, and the inhabitants of the extreme parts of the earth came and they bought corn in Egypt day after day, and then went away.
39 All the officers of Egypt did as Joseph had commanded, and all that came to Egypt to buy corn, the gate keepers would write their names, and their fathers' names, and daily bring them in the evening to Joseph.

CHAPTER 51

1 Jacob afterward heard that there was corn in Egypt, and he called to his sons to go to Egypt to buy corn, for on them also did the famine occur, and he called to his sons, saying,
2 Behold I hear that there is corn in Egypt, and all the people of the earth go there to purchase; now therefore why will you show yourselves (pretend to be) satisfied before the whole earth? You go also down to Egypt and buy us a little corn among those that come there, that we may not die.
3 And the sons of Jacob listened to the voice of their father, and they rose up to go

down to Egypt in order to buy corn among the rest that came there.
4 And Jacob their father commanded them, saying, When you come into the city do not enter together in one gate, on account of the inhabitants of the land.
5 And the sons of Jacob went forth and they went to Egypt, and the sons of Jacob did all as their father had commanded them; Jacob did not send Benjamin, for he said, Lest an accident might happen to him on the road like his brother. Ten of Jacob's sons went forth.
6 While the sons of Jacob were going on the road, they repented of what they had done to Joseph, and they spoke to each other, saying, We know that our brother Joseph went down to Egypt, and now we will seek him where we go, and if we find him we will take him from his master for a ransom, and if not, by force, and we will die for him.
7 And the sons of Jacob agreed to this thing and strengthened themselves on account of Joseph, to deliver him from the hand of his master, and the sons of Jacob went to Egypt; when they came near to Egypt they separated from each other, and they came through ten gates of Egypt, and the gate keepers wrote their names that day, and brought them to Joseph in the evening.
8 And Joseph read the names from the hand of the gatekeepers of the city, and he found that his brothers had entered at the ten gates of the city, and Joseph at once commanded that it should be proclaimed throughout the land of Egypt, saying,
9 Go forth all you store guards, close all the corn stores and let only one remain open, that those who come may purchase from it.
10 And all the officers of Joseph did so at that time, and they closed all the stores and left only one open.
11 Joseph gave the written names of his brothers to him that was set over the open store, and he said to him, Whosoever shall come to you to buy corn, ask his name, and when men of these names shall come before you, seize them and send them, and they did so.
12 And when the sons of Jacob came into the city, they joined together in the city to search for Joseph before they bought themselves corn.
13 And they went to the walls of the harlots and they sought Joseph there for three days, for they thought that Joseph would come in the walls of the harlots, for Joseph was very handsome and well favored; the sons of Jacob sought Joseph for three days and they could not find him.
14 The man who was set over the open store sought for those names which Joseph had given him, and he did not find them.
15 And he sent to Joseph, saying, These three days have passed, and those men whose names you gave to me have not come, so Joseph sent servants to search for the men in all Egypt, and to bring them before Joseph.
16 Joseph's servants went and came into Egypt and could not find them, and went to Goshen and they were not there, and then went to the city of Rameses and could not find them.
17 Joseph continued to send sixteen servants to seek his brothers, and they went and spread themselves in the four corners of the city; four of the servants went into the house of the harlots, and they found the ten men there searching for their brother.
18 Those four men took them and brought them before Joseph, and they bowed down to him to the ground. Joseph was sitting on his throne in his temple, clothed with princely garments, and on his head was a large crown of gold, and all the mighty men were sitting around him.

19 And the sons of Jacob saw Joseph, and his figure and good-looks and dignity of
countenance seemed wonderful in their eyes, and they again bowed down to him to
the ground.
20 Joseph saw his brothers and he knew them, but they knew him not, for Joseph
was very great in their eyes, therefore they knew him not.
21 And Joseph spoke to them, saying, From where did you come? And they all
answered and said, Thy servants have come from the land of Canaan to buy corn,
for the famine prevails throughout the earth, and your servants heard that there was
corn in Egypt, so they have come among the other comers to buy corn for their
support.
22 And Joseph answered them, saying, If you have come to purchase as you say,
why do you come through ten gates of the city? It can only be that you have come to
spy through the land.
23 And they all together answered Joseph, and said, Not so my lord, we are right,
your servants are not spies, but we have come to buy corn, for your servants are all
brothers, the sons of one man in the land of Canaan, and our father commanded us,
saying, When you come to the city do not enter together at one gate on account of
the inhabitants of the land.
24 And Joseph again answered them and said, That is the thing which I spoke to
you, you have come to spy through the land, therefore you all came through ten
gates of the city; you have come to see how barren the land has become.
25 Certainly every one that comes to buy corn goes his way, and you are already
three days in the land; what do you do in the walls of harlots in which you have
been for these three days? Certainly spies do these things.
26 And they said to Joseph, Far be it from our lord to speak thus, for we are twelve
brothers, the sons of our father Jacob, in the land of Canaan, the son of Isaac, the son
of Abraham, the Hebrew; behold the youngest is with our father this day in the land
of Canaan, and one is not, for he was lost from us, and we thought perhaps he might
be in this land, so we are seeking him throughout the land, and have come even to
the houses of harlots to seek him there.
27 And Joseph said to them, And have you then sought him throughout the earth,
that there only remained Egypt for you to seek him in? And what also should your
brother do in the houses of harlots, if he were in Egypt? Have you not said, that you
are from the sons of Isaac, the son of Abraham, and what shall the sons of Jacob do
then in the houses of harlots?
28 And they said to him, Because we heard that Ishmaelites stole him from us, and it
was told to us that they sold him in Egypt, and your servant, our brother, is very
handsome and well favored, so we thought he would certainly be in the houses of
harlots, therefore your servants went there to seek him and give ransom for him.
29 Joseph still answered them, saying, Certainly you speak falsely and utter lies, to
say of yourselves that you are the sons of Abraham; as Pharaoh lives you are spies,
therefore you have come to the houses of harlots that you should not be known.
30 Joseph said to them, And now if you find him, and his master requires of you a
great price, will you give it for him? And they said, It shall be given.
31 And he said to them, And if his master will not consent to part with him for a
great price, what will you do to him on his account? And they answered him,
saying, If he will not give him to us we will kill him, and take our brother and go
away.
32 And Joseph said to them, That is the thing which I have spoken to you; you are

spies, for you are come to kill the inhabitants of the land, for we heard that two of your brothers struck all the inhabitants of Shechem, in the land of Canaan, on account of your sister, and you now come to do the same in Egypt on account of your brother.
33 Only hereby shall I know that you are true men; if you will send home one from among you to fetch your youngest brother from your father, and bring him here to me, and by doing this thing I will know that you are right.
34 And Joseph called to seventy of his mighty men, and he said to them, Take these men and bring them into the ward.
35 And the mighty men took the ten men, they laid hold of them and put them into the ward, and they were in the ward three days.
36 And on the third day Joseph had them brought out of the ward, and he said to them, Do this for yourselves if you be true men, so that you may live: one of your brothers shall be confined in the ward while you go and take home the corn for your household to the land of Canaan, and get your youngest brother, and bring him here to me, that I may know that you are true men when you do this thing.
37 And Joseph went out from them and came into the chamber, and wept a great weeping, for his pity was enlarged for them; he washed his face, and returned to them again, and he took Simeon from them and ordered him to be bound, but Simeon was not willing to be done so, for he was a very powerful man and they could not bind him.
38 And Joseph called to his mighty men and seventy valiant men came before him with drawn swords in their hands, and the sons of Jacob were terrified at them.
39 Joseph said to them, Seize this man and confine him in prison until his brothers come to him, and Joseph's valiant men hurried and they all laid hold of Simeon to bind him, and Simeon gave a loud and terrible shriek and the cry was heard at a distance.
40 All the valiant men of Joseph were so terrified at the sound of the shriek that they fell on their faces, and they were greatly afraid and fled.
41 And all the men that were with Joseph fled, for they were greatly afraid for their lives, and only Joseph and Manasseh his son remained there; Manassah the son of Joseph saw the strength of Simeon, and he was greatly angered.
42 And Manassah the son of Joseph rose up to Simeon, and Manassah struck Simeon a heavy blow with his fist against the back of his neck, and Simeon was stilled of his rage.
43 Manassah laid hold of Simeon and he seized him violently and he bound him and brought him into the house of confinement, and all the sons of Jacob were astonished at the act of the youth.
44 And Simeon said to his brothers, None of you must say that this is the smiting of an Egyptian, but it is the smiting of the house of my father.
45 After this Joseph ordered him to be called who was in charge of the storehouse, to fill their sacks with corn as much as they could carry, and to restore every man's money into his sack, and to give them provision for the road, and thus he did to them.
46 And Joseph commanded them, saying, Take care that you not go contrary to my orders to bring your brother as I have told you, and it shall be when you bring your brother here to me, then will I know that you are true men, and you shall traffic in the land, and I will restore to you your brother, and you shall return in peace to your father.

47 And they all answered and said, According as our lord speaks so will we do, and they bowed down to him to the ground.
48 Every man lifted his corn on his ass, and they went out to go to the land of Canaan to their father; and they came to the inn and Levi spread his sack to give feed to his ass, when he saw and there his money in full weight was still in his sack.
49 And the man was greatly afraid, and he said to his brothers, My money is returned, and look, it is even in my sack; the men were greatly afraid, and they said, What is this that God has done to us?
50 And they all said, And where is the Lord's kindness with our fathers, with Abraham, Isaac, and Jacob, that the Lord has this day delivered us into the hands of the king of Egypt to contrive against us?
51 Judah said to them, Certainly we are guilty sinners before the Lord our God in having sold our brother, our own flesh, and wherefore do you say, Where is the Lord's kindness with our fathers?
52 Reuben said to them, Said I not to you, do not sin against the lad, and you would not listen to me? Now God requires him from us, and how dare you say, Where is the Lord's kindness with our fathers, while you have sinned to the Lord?
53 They stayed overnight in that place, and they rose up early in the morning and loaded their asses with their corn; they led them and went on and came to their father's house in the land of Canaan.
54 And Jacob and his household went out to meet his sons, and Jacob saw and behold their brother Simeon was not with them; Jacob said to his sons, Where is your brother Simeon, whom I do not see? And his sons told him all that had befallen them in Egypt.

CHAPTER 52

1 They entered their house, and every man opened his sack and they looked and there every man's bundle of money was there, at which they and their father were greatly terrified.
2 And Jacob said to them, What is this that you have done to me? I sent your brother Joseph to inquire after your welfare and you said to me: A wild beast did devour him.
3 And Simeon went with you to buy food and you say the king of Egypt hath confined him in prison, and you wish to take Benjamin to cause his death also, and bring down my grey hairs with sorrow to the grave on account of Benjamin and his brother Joseph.
4 Now therefore my son shall not go down with you, for his brother is dead and he is left alone, and mischief may befall him by the way in which you go, as it befell his brother.
5 Reuben said to his father, You shall kill my two sons if I do not bring your son and place him before you. Jacob said to his sons, Abide ye here and do not go down to Egypt, for my son shall not go down with you to Egypt, nor die like his brother.
6 And Judah said to them, Refrain from him until the corn is finished, and he will then say, Take down your brother, when he finds his own life and the life of his household in danger from the famine.
7 In those days the famine was severe throughout the land, and all the people of the

earth went and came to Egypt to buy food, for the famine continued greatly among them, and the sons of Jacob remained in Canaan a year and two months until their corn was finished.
8 And it came to pass after their corn was finished, the whole household of Jacob was pinched with hunger, and all the infants of the sons of Jacob came together and they approached Jacob; they all surrounded him, and said to him, Give to us bread, for why shall we all perish through hunger in your presence?
9 Jacob heard the words of his son's children, and he wept a great weeping, and his pity was roused for them. Jacob called to his sons and they all came and sat before him.
10 And Jacob said to them, Have you not seen how your children have been weeping over me this day, saying, Give to us bread, and there is none? Now therefore return and buy for us a little food.
11 And Judah answered and said to his father, If you will send our brother with us we will go down and buy corn for you, and if you will not send him then we will not go down, for certainly the king of Egypt particularly requested us, saying, You shall not see my face unless your brother is with you. The king of Egypt is a strong and mighty king, and behold if we shall go to him without our brother we shall all be put to death.
12 Do you not know and have you not heard that this king is very powerful and wise, and there is no one like him in all the earth? Behold we have seen all the kings of the earth and we have not seen one like that king, the king of Egypt; certainly among all the kings of the earth there is none greater than Abimelech king of the Philistines, yet the king of Egypt is greater and mightier than he, and Abimelech can only be compared to one of his officers.
13 Father, you have not seen his palace and his throne, and all his servants standing before him; you have not seen that king on his throne in his pomp and royal appearance, dressed in his kingly robes with a large golden crown on his head; you have not seen the honor and glory which God has given to him, for there is no one like him in all the earth.
14 Father, you have not seen the wisdom, the understanding and the knowledge which God has given in his heart, nor heard his sweet voice when he spoke to us.
15 We know not, father, who made him acquainted with our names and all that happened to us, yet he asked also after you, saying, Is your father still living, and is it well with him?
16 You have not seen the affairs of the government of Egypt regulated by him, without inquiring of Pharaoh his lord; you have not seen the awe and fear which he impressed on all the Egyptians.
17 And also when we went from him, we were threatened of doing to Egypt like to the rest of the cities of the Amorites, and we were greatly angered against all his words which he spoke concerning us as spies; now when we shall again come before him his terror will fall on us all, and not one of us will be able to speak to him either a little or a great thing.
18 Now therefore father, send we pray you the lad with us, and we will go down and buy you food for our support, and not die through hunger. And Jacob said, Why have you dealt so ill with me to tell the king you had a brother? What is this thing that you have done to me?
19 And Judah said to Jacob his father, Give the lad into my care and we will rise up and go down to Egypt and buy corn, and then return, and it shall be when we return

if the lad is not with us, then let me bear your blame forever.
20 Have you seen all our infants weeping over you through hunger and there is no power in your hand to satisfy them? Now let your pity be roused for them and send our brother with us and we will go.
21 For how will the Lord's kindness to our ancestors be manifested to you when you say that the king of Egypt will take away your son? As the Lord lives I will not leave him until I bring him and place him before you; but pray for us to the Lord, that he may deal kindly with us, to cause us to be received favorably and kindly before the king of Egypt and his men, for had we not delayed certainly by now we had returned a second time with your son.
22 And Jacob said to his sons, I trust in the Lord God that he may deliver you and give you favor in the sight of the king of Egypt, and in the sight of all his men.
23 Now therefore rise up and go to the man, and take for him in your hands a present from what can be obtained in the land and bring it before him, and may the Almighty God give you mercy before him that he may send Benjamin and Simeon your brothers with you.
24 And all the men rose up, and they took their brother Benjamin, and they took in their hands a large present of the best of the land, and they also took a double portion of silver.
25 And Jacob strictly commanded his sons concerning Benjamin, saying, Take care of him in the way in which you are going, and do not separate yourselves from him in the road, neither in Egypt.
26 And Jacob rose up from his sons and spread forth his hands and he prayed to the Lord on account of his sons, saying, O Lord God of heaven and earth, remember your covenant with our father Abraham, remember it with my father Isaac and deal kindly with my sons and deliver them not into the hands of the king of Egypt; do it I pray you O God for the sake of your mercies and redeem all my children and rescue them from Egyptian power, and send them their two brothers.
27 And all the wives of the sons of Jacob and their children lifted up their eyes to heaven and they all wept before the Lord, and cried to him to deliver their fathers from the hand of the king of Egypt.
28 Jacob wrote a record to the king of Egypt and gave it into the hand of Judah and into the hands of his sons for the king of Egypt, saying,
29 From your servant Jacob, son of Isaac, son of Abraham the Hebrew, the prince of God, to the powerful and wise king, the revealer of secrets, king of Egypt, greeting.
30 Be it known to my lord the king of Egypt, the famine was heavy on us in the land of Canaan, and I sent my sons to you to buy us a little food from you for our support.
31 For my sons surrounded me and I being very old cannot see with my eyes, for my eyes have become very dim through age, as well as with daily weeping for my son, for Joseph who was lost from before me; I commanded my sons that they should not enter the gates of the city when they came to Egypt, on account of the inhabitants of the land.
32 And I also commanded them to go about Egypt to seek for my son Joseph, perhaps they might find him there, and they did so, and you did consider them as spies of the land.
33 Have we not heard concerning you that you did interpret Pharaoh's dream and did speak truly to him? How then do you not know in your wisdom whether my sons are spies or not?

34 Now therefore, my lord and king, behold I have sent my son before you, as you did speak to my sons; I beg you to put your eyes on him until he is returned to me in peace with his brothers.
35 For do you not know, or have you not heard that which our God did to Pharaoh when he took my mother Sarah, and what he did to Abimelech king of the Philistines on account of her, and also what our father Abraham did to the nine kings of Elam, how he struck them all with a few men that were with him?
36 And also what my two sons Simeon and Levi did to the eight cities of the Amorites, how they destroyed them on account of their sister Dinah?
37 And also on account of their brother Benjamin they consoled themselves for the loss of his brother Joseph; what will they then do for him when they see the hand of any people prevailing over them, for his sake?
38 Do you not know, O king of Egypt, that the power of God is with us, and that also God ever hears our prayers and forsakes us not all the days?
39 And when my sons told me of your dealings with them, I called not to the Lord on account of you, for then you would have perished with your men before my son Benjamin came before you, but I thought that as Simeon my son was in your house, perhaps you might deal kindly with him, therefore I did not do this thing to you.
40 Now therefore behold Benjamin my son comes to you with my sons, take care of him and put your eyes on him, and then will God place his eyes over you and throughout your kingdom.
41 Now I have told you all that is in my heart, and behold my sons are coming to you with their brother; examine the face of the whole earth for their sake and send them back in peace with their brothers.
42 And Jacob gave the record to his sons into the care of Judah to give it to the king of Egypt.

CHAPTER 53

1 The sons of Jacob rose up and took Benjamin and all of the presents; they went and came to Egypt and they stood before Joseph.
2 And Joseph beheld his brother Benjamin with them and he saluted them, and these men came to Joseph's house.
3 Joseph commanded the superintendent of his house to give food to his brothers to eat, and he did so to them.
4 At noon time Joseph sent for the men to come before him with Benjamin, and the men told the superintendent of Joseph's house concerning the silver that was returned in their sacks; he said to them, It will be well with you, fear not. And he brought their brother Simeon to them.
5 And Simeon said to his brothers, The lord of the Egyptians has acted very kindly to me; he did not keep me bound, as you saw with your eyes, for when you went out from the city he let me free and dealt kindly with me in his house.
6 And Judah took Benjamin by the hand, and they came before Joseph, and they bowed down to him to the ground.
7 The men gave the present to Joseph and they all sat before him, and Joseph said to them, Is it well with you, is it well with your children, is it well with your aged father? And they said, It is well. And Judah took the record which Jacob had sent and gave it into the hand of Joseph.

8 Joseph read the letter and knew his father's writing, and he wished to weep; he went into an inner room and he wept a great weeping, and he came out.
9 He lifted up his eyes and observed his brother Benjamin and said, Is this your brother of whom you spoke to me? Benjamin approached Joseph, and Joseph placed his hand on his head and he said to him, May God be gracious to you my son.
10 And when Joseph saw his brother, the son of his mother, he again wished to weep, and he entered the chamber, and he wept there; he washed his face and came out and refrained from weeping; he said, Prepare food.
11 Joseph had a cup from which he drank; it was of silver beautifully inlaid with onyx stones and bdellium, and Joseph struck the cup in the sight of his brothers while they were sitting to eat with him.
12 Joseph said to the men, I know by this cup that Reuben the first born, Simeon and Levi and Judah, Issachar and Zebulun are children from one mother; seat yourselves to eat according to your births.
13 He also placed the others according to their births and said, I know that this your youngest brother has no brother; I, like him, have no brother; he shall therefore sit down to eat with me.
14 Benjamin went up before Joseph and sat on the throne and the men beheld the acts of Joseph, and they were astonished at them; the men ate and drank at that time with Joseph, and he then gave presents to them. Joseph gave one gift to Benjamin, and Manasseh and Ephraim saw the acts of their father, and they also gave presents to him, and Osnath gave him one present, and there were five presents in the hands of Benjamin.
15 Joseph brought out wine to drink, and they would not drink; they said, From the day in which Joseph was lost we have not drunk wine, nor eaten any delicacies.
16 And Joseph swore to them, and he pressed them hard; they drank plentifully with him on that day, and Joseph afterward turned to his brother Benjamin to speak with him, and Benjamin was still sitting on the throne before Joseph.
17 Joseph said to him, Have you had any children? And he said, Your servant has ten sons, and these are their names: Bela, Becher, Ashbal, Gera, Naaman, Achi, Rosh, Mupim, Chupim, and Ord, and I called their names after my brother whom I have not seen.
18 He ordered them to bring before him his map of the stars, whereby Joseph knew all the times, and Joseph said to Benjamin, I have heard that the Hebrews are acquainted with all wisdom, do you know anything of this?
19 And Benjamin said, Thy servant knows all the wisdom which my father taught me. Joseph said to Benjamin, Look now at this instrument and understand where your brother Joseph is in Egypt, who you said went down to Egypt.
20 And Benjamin observed that instrument with the map of the stars of heaven, and he was wise and looked therein to know where his brother was. Benjamin divided the whole land of Egypt into four divisions, and he found that he who was sitting on the throne before him was his brother Joseph; Benjamin wondered greatly, and when Joseph saw that his brother Benjamin was so much astonished, he said to Benjamin, What have you seen, and why are you astonished?
21 Benjamin said to Joseph, I can see by this that Joseph my brother sits here with me on the throne, and Joseph said to him, I am Joseph your brother; reveal not this thing to your brothers. I will send you with them when they go away and I will command them to be brought back again into the city, and I will take you away from them.
22 And if they risk their lives and fight for you, then shall I know that they have

repented of what they did to me; I will make myself known to them and if they turn away from you when I take you, then shall you remain with me, and I will fight with them, and they shall go away. I will not become known to them.
23 At that time Joseph commanded his officer to fill their sacks with food and to put each man's money into his sack, and to put the cup in the sack of Benjamin and give them provision for the road, and they did so to them.
24 On the next day the men rose up early in the morning and loaded their asses with their corn; they went forth with Benjamin, and went to the land of Canaan with their brother Benjamin.
25 They had not gone far from Egypt when Joseph commanded him that was set over his house, saying, Rise, pursue these men before they get too far from Egypt, and say to them, Why have you stolen my master's cup?
26 Joseph's officer rose up and he reached them, and he spoke to them all the words of Joseph; when they heard this thing they became greatly angry, and they said, He with whom your master's cup shall be found shall die, and we will also become slaves.
27 They hurried and each man brought down his sack from his ass, and they looked in their bags and the cup was found in Benjamin's bag; they all tore their garments and they returned to the city, and they struck Benjamin in the road, continually smiting him until he came into the city, and they stood before Joseph.
28 Judah's anger was set ablaze, and he said, This man has only brought me back to destroy Egypt this day.
29 The men came to Joseph's house, and they found Joseph sitting on his throne, and all the mighty men standing at his right and left.
30 And Joseph said to them, What is this act that you have done, that you took away my silver cup and went away? But I know that you took my cup in order to know thereby in what part of the land your brother was.
31 Judah said, What shall we say to our lord, what shall we speak and how shall we justify ourselves; God has this day found the iniquity of all your servants, therefore has he done this thing to us this day.
32 Joseph rose up and caught hold of Benjamin and took him from his brothers with violence, and he came to the house and locked the door at them; Joseph commanded him that was set over his house that he should say to them, Thus says the king, Go in peace to your father, behold I have taken the man in whose hand my cup was found.

CHAPTER 54

1 When Judah saw the dealings of Joseph with them, Judah approached him and broke open the door, and came with his brothers before Joseph.
2 And Judah said to Joseph, Let it not seem bothersome in the sight of my lord, may your servant I pray you speak a word before you? And Joseph said to him, Speak.
3 Judah spoke before Joseph and his brothers were there standing before them; Judah said to Joseph, Certainly when we first came to our lord to buy food, you did consider us as spies of the land, and we brought Benjamin before you, and you still make sport of us this day.
4 Now therefore let the king hear my words and send I pray you our brother that he may go along with us to our father, that your son not perish this day with all the souls of the inhabitants of Egypt.

5 Do you not know what two of my brothers, Simeon and Levi, did to the city of Shechem and to seven cities of the Amorites on account of our sister Dinah, and also what they would do for the sake of their brother Benjamin?
6 I with my strength, who am greater and mightier than both of them, come this day on you and your land if you are unwilling to send our brother.
7 Have you not heard what our God who made choice of us did to Pharaoh on account of Sarah our mother, whom he took away from our father, that he struck him and his household with heavy plagues; even to this day the Egyptians relate this wonder to each other? So will our God do to you on account of Benjamin whom you have this day taken from his father, and on account of the evils which you this day heap over us in your land; for our God will remember his covenant with our father Abraham and bring evil on you because you have grieved the soul of our father this day.
8 Now hear my words that I have this day spoken to you, and send our brother that he may go away that you and the people of your land not die by the sword, for you cannot all prevail over me.
9 Joseph answered Judah, saying, Why have you opened wide your mouth and why do you boast over us, saying, Strength is with you? As Pharaoh lives, if I command all my valiant men to fight with you, certainly you and these your brothers would sink into the mud.
10 Judah said to Joseph, Certainly it becomes you and your people to fear me; as the Lord lives if I once draw my sword I shall not sheathe it again until I shall this day have slain all Egypt, and I will begin with you and finish with Pharaoh your master.
11 And Joseph answered and said to him, Certainly strength belongs not alone to you; I am stronger and mightier than you; certainly if you draw your sword I will put it to your neck and the necks of all your brothers.
12 Judah said to him, Certainly if I this day open my mouth against you I would swallow you up that you be destroyed from off the earth and perish this day from your kingdom. And Joseph said, Certainly if you open your mouth I have power and might to close your mouth with a stone until you shall not be able to utter a word; see how many stones are before us, truly I can take a stone and force it into your mouth and break your jaws.
13 And Judah said, God is witness between us, that we have not hereto desired to battle with you, only give us our brother and we will go from you. Joseph answered and said, As Pharaoh lives, if all the kings of Canaan came together with you, you should not take him from my hand.
14 Now therefore go your way to your father, and your brother shall be to me a slave, for he has robbed the king's house. And Judah said, What is it to you or to the character of the king, certainly the king sends forth from his house, throughout the land, silver and gold either in gifts or expenses, and you still talk about your cup which you did place in our brother's bag and say that he has stolen it from you?
15 God forbid that our brother Benjamin or any of the offspring of Abraham should do this thing to steal from you, or from any one else, whether king, prince, or any man.
16 Now therefore cease this accusation that the whole earth not hear your words, saying, For a little silver the king of Egypt argued with the men, and he accused them and took their brother for a slave.
17 And Joseph answered and said, Take this cup and go from me and leave your brother for a slave, for it is the judgment of a thief to be a slave.

18 And Judah said, Why are you not ashamed of your words, to leave our brother and to take your cup? Certainly if you give us your cup, or a thousand times as much, we will not leave our brother for the silver which is found in the hand of any man, that we will not die over him.
19 Joseph answered, And why did you turn away from your brother and sell him for twenty pieces of silver to this day; why then will you not do the same to this your brother?
20 And Judah said, The Lord is witness between me and you that we desire not your battles; now therefore give us our brother and we will go from you without quarreling.
21 And Joseph answered and said, If all the kings of the land should assemble they will not be able to take your brother from my hand. Judah said, What shall we say to our father, when he sees that our brother comes not with us, and will grieve over him?
22 Joseph answered and said, This is the thing which you shall tell to your father, saying, The rope has gone after the bucket.
23 Judah said, Certainly you are a king, and why speak you these things, giving a false judgment? Woe to the king who is like you.
24 Joseph answered and said, There is no false judgment in the word that I spoke on account of your brother Joseph, for all of you sold him to the Midianites for twenty pieces of silver. And you all denied it to your father and said to him, An evil beast has devoured him; Joseph has been torn to pieces.
25 And Judah said, Behold the fire of Shem burns in my heart, now I will burn all your land with fire; Joseph answered and said, Certainly your sister-in-law Tamar, who killed your sons, extinguished the fire of Shechem.
26 Judah said, If I pluck out a single hair from my flesh, I will fill all Egypt with its blood.
27 Joseph answered and said, Such is your custom to do as you did to your brother whom you sold, and you dipped his coat in blood and brought it to your father in order that he might say an evil beast devoured him and here is his blood.
28 When Judah heard this thing he was greatly enraged and his anger burned within him, and there was before him in that place a stone, the weight of which was about four hundred shekels; Judah's anger was set ablaze and he took the stone in one hand and cast it to the heavens and caught it with his left hand.
29 He placed it afterward under his legs, and he sat on it with all his strength and the stone was turned into dust from the force of Judah.
30 Joseph saw the act of Judah and he was very much afraid, but he commanded Manassah his son and he also did with another stone like to the act of Judah, and Judah said to his brothers, Let not any of you say this man is an Egyptian, but by his doing this thing he is of our father's family.
31 And Joseph said, Not to you only is strength given, for we are also powerful men, and why will you boast over us all? Judah said to Joseph, Send I pray you our brother and ruin not your country this day.
32 And Joseph answered and said to them, Go and tell your father an evil beast has devoured him as you said concerning your brother Joseph.
33 Judah spoke to his brother Naphtali, and said to him, Hurry, go now and number all the streets of Egypt and come and tell me; Simeon said to him, Let not this thing be a trouble to you; now I will go to the mount and take up one large stone from the mount and level it at every one in Egypt, and kill all that are in it.

34 Joseph heard all these words that his brothers spoke before him, and they did not know that Joseph understood them for they imagined that he knew not to speak Hebrew.
35 Joseph was greatly afraid at the words of his brothers that they should destroy Egypt, and he commanded his son Manasseh, saying, Go now, hurry and gather to me all the inhabitants of Egypt, and all the valiant men together, and let them come to me now on horseback and on foot and with all sorts of musical instruments, and Manasseh went and did so.
36 Naphtali went as Judah had commanded him, for Naphtali was lightfooted as one of the swift stags, and he could walk on the ears of corn and they would not break under him.
37 He went and numbered all the streets of Egypt and found them to be twelve, and he came quickly and told Judah, and Judah said to his brothers, Hurry and put on every man his sword on his loins and we will come over Egypt and strike them all, and let not a remnant remain.
38 Judah said, Behold, I will destroy three of the streets with my strength, and you shall each destroy one street; when Judah was speaking this thing, then the inhabitants of Egypt and all the mighty men came toward them with all sorts of musical instruments and with loud shouting.
39 And their number was five hundred cavalry and ten thousand infantry, and four hundred men who could fight without sword or spear, only with their hands and strength.
40 And all the mighty men came with great storming and shouting, and they all surrounded the sons of Jacob and terrified them, and the ground quaked at the sound of their shouting.
41 When the sons of Jacob saw these troops they were greatly afraid of their lives, and Joseph did so in order to terrify the sons of Jacob to become tranquilized.
42 Judah, seeing some of his brothers terrified, said to them, Why are you afraid while the grace of God is with us? Judah saw all the people of Egypt surrounding them at the command of Joseph to terrify them, only Joseph commanded them, saying, Do not touch any of them.
43 Then Judah hurried and drew his sword and uttered a loud and bitter scream, and he struck with his sword, and he stomped on the ground and he still continued to shout against all the people.
44 When he did this thing the Lord caused the terror of Judah and his brothers to fall on the valiant men and all the people that surrounded them.
45 They all fled at the sound of the shouting, and they were terrified and fell one on the other, and many of them died as they fell, and they all fled from before Judah and his brothers and from before Joseph.
46 While they were fleeing, Judah and his brothers pursued them to the house of Pharaoh and they all escaped; Judah again sat before Joseph and roared at him like a lion, and gave a great and tremendous shriek at him.
47 The shriek was heard at a distance, and all the inhabitants of Succoth heard it, and all Egypt quaked at the sound of the shriek; also the walls of Egypt and of the land of Goshen fell in from the shaking of the earth, and Pharaoh also fell from his throne on the ground; also all the pregnant women of Egypt and Goshen miscarried when they heard the noise of the shaking, for they were terribly afraid.
48 And Pharaoh sent word, saying, What is this thing that has this day happened in the land of Egypt? They came and told him all the things from beginning to end,

and Pharaoh was alarmed and he wondered and was greatly afraid.

49 His fright increased when he heard all these things, and he sent to Joseph, saying, You have brought to me the Hebrews to destroy all Egypt; what will you do with that thievish slave? Send him away and let him go with his brothers, and let us not perish through their evil, even we, you and all Egypt.

50 And if you desire not to do this thing, cast off from you all my valuable things, and go with them to their land if you delightest in it, for they will this day destroy my whole country and kill all my people; even all the women of Egypt have miscarried through their scream. See what they have done merely by their shouting and speaking? And if they fight with the sword, they will destroy the land; now therefore choose that which you desire, whether me or the Hebrews, whether Egypt or the land of the Hebrews.

51 They came and told Joseph all the words of Pharaoh that he had said concerning him, and Joseph was greatly afraid at the words of Pharaoh and Judah and his brothers were still standing before Joseph indignant and enraged, and all the sons of Jacob roared at Joseph, like the roaring of the sea and its waves.

52 Joseph was greatly afraid of his brothers and on account of Pharaoh, and Joseph sought a way to make himself known to his brothers, that they should not destroy all Egypt.

53 Joseph commanded his son Manasseh, and Manasseh went and approached Judah and placed his hand on his shoulder, and the anger of Judah was stilled.

54 And Judah said to his brothers, Let no one of you say that this is the act of an Egyptian youth for this is the work of my father's house.

55 Joseph seeing and knowing that Judah's anger was stilled, he approached to speak to Judah in the language of mildness.

56 And Joseph said to Judah, Certainly you speak truth and have this day verified your assertions concerning your strength, and may your God who delights in you, increase your welfare; but tell me truly why from among all your brothers do you argue with me on account of the lad, as none of them have spoken one word to me concerning him.

57 And Judah answered Joseph, saying, Certainly you must know that I was security for the lad to his father, saying, If I brought him not to him I should bear his blame forever.

58 So I have approached you from among all my brothers, for I saw that you were unwilling to allow him to go from you; now therefore may I find grace in your sight that you shall send him to go with us and then I will remain as a substitute for him, to serve you in whatever you desire, for whereever you shall send me I will go to serve you with great energy.

59 Send me now to a mighty king who has rebelled against you, and you shall know what I will do to him and to his land; although he may have cavalry and infantry or an exceeding mighty people, I will kill them all and bring the king's head before you.

60 Do you not know or have you not heard that our father Abraham with his servant Eliezer struck all the kings of Elam with their hosts in one night, they left not one remaining? And ever since that day our father's strength was given to us for an inheritance, for us and our descendants forever.

61 Joseph answered and said, You speak truth, and falsehood is not in your mouth, for it was also told to us that the Hebrews have power and that the Lord their God delights much in them, and who then can stand before them?

62 However, on this condition will I send your brother, if you will bring before me

his brother the son of his mother, of whom you said that he had gone from you down to Egypt; it shall come to pass when you bring to me his brother I will take him in his stead, because not one of you was security for him to your father. When he shall come to me, I will then send with you his brother for whom you have been security.
63 And Judah's anger was set ablaze against Joseph when he spoke this thing, and his eyes dropped blood with anger, and he said to his brothers, How does this man this day seek his own destruction and that of all Egypt!
64 And Simeon answered Joseph, saying, Did we not tell you at first that we knew not the particular spot to which he went, and whether he be dead or alive, and why does my lord speak these things?
65 Joseph, observing the countenance of Judah discerned that his anger began to kindle when he spoke to him, saying, Bring to me your other brother instead of this brother.
66 And Joseph said to his brothers, Certainly you said that your brother was either dead or lost, now if I should call him this day and he should come before you, would you give him to me instead of his brother?
67 And Joseph began to speak and call out, Joseph, Joseph, come this day before me, and appear to your brothers and sit before them.
68 When Joseph spoke this thing before them, they looked each a different way to see from where Joseph would come before them.
69 And Joseph observed all their acts, and said to them, Why do you look here and there? I am Joseph whom you sold to Egypt, now therefore let it not grieve you that you sold me, for as a support during the famine did God send me from you.
70 And his brothers were terrified at him when they heard the words of Joseph, and Judah was greatly terrified at him.
71 When Benjamin heard the words of Joseph he was before them in the inner part of the house, and Benjamin ran to Joseph his brother and embraced him and fell on his neck, and they wept.
72 When Joseph's brothers saw that Benjamin had fallen on his brother's neck and wept with him, they also fell on Joseph and embraced him, and they wept a great weeping with Joseph.
73 And the voice was heard in the house of Joseph that they were Joseph's brothers, and it pleased Pharaoh greatly, for he was afraid of them that they should destroy Egypt.
74 Pharaoh sent his servants to Joseph to congratulate him concerning his brothers who had come to him, and all the captains of the armies and troops that were in Egypt came to rejoice with Joseph, and all Egypt rejoiced greatly about Joseph's brothers.
75 And Pharaoh sent his servants to Joseph, saying, Tell your brothers to fetch all belonging to them and let them come to me, and I will place them in the best part of the land of Egypt, and they did so.
76 Joseph commanded him that was set over his house to bring out to his brothers gifts and garments, and he brought out to them many garments being robes of royalty and many gifts, and Joseph divided them among his brothers.
77 And he gave to each of his brothers a change of garments of gold and silver, and three hundred pieces of silver, and Joseph commanded them all to be dressed in these garments, and to be brought before Pharaoh.
78 And Pharaoh, seeing that all Joseph's brothers were valiant men, and of beautiful

appearance, greatly rejoiced.
79 And afterward they went out from the presence of Pharaoh to go to the land of Canaan, to their father, and their brother Benjamin was with them.
80 Joseph rose up and gave to them eleven chariots from Pharaoh, and Joseph gave to them his chariot on which he rode on the day of his being crowned in Egypt, to fetch his father to Egypt; Joseph sent to all his brothers' children, garments according to their numbers, and a hundred pieces of silver to each of them, and he also sent garments to the wives of his brothers from the garments of the king's wives, and he sent them.
81 He gave to each of his brothers ten men to go with them to the land of Canaan to serve them, to serve their children and all belonging to them in coming to Egypt.
82 Joseph sent by the hand of his brother Benjamin ten suits of garments for his ten sons, a portion above the rest of the children of the sons of Jacob.
83 And he sent to each fifty pieces of silver, and ten chariots on the account of Pharaoh; he sent to his father ten asses laden with all the luxuries of Egypt, and ten female asses laden with corn and bread and nourishment for his father and to all that were with him as provisions for the road.
84 And he sent to his sister Dinah garments of silver and gold, and frankincense and myrrh, and aloes and women's ornaments in great plenty; he sent the same from the wives of Pharaoh to the wives of Benjamin.
85 He gave to all his brothers, also to their wives, all sorts of onyx stones and bdellium, and from all the valuable things among the great people of Egypt, nothing of all the costly things was left but what Joseph sent of to his father's household.
86 He sent his brothers away, and they went, and he sent his brother Benjamin with them.
87 And Joseph went out with them to accompany them on the road to the borders of Egypt, and he commanded them concerning his father and his household to come to Egypt.
88 And he said to them, Do not quarrel on the road, for this thing was from the Lord to keep a great people from starvation, for there will be yet five years of famine in the land.
89 And he commanded them, saying, When you come to the land of Canaan, do not come suddenly before my father about this affair, but act in your wisdom.
90 And Joseph ceased to command them, and he turned and went back to Egypt, and the sons of Jacob went to the land of Canaan with joy and cheerfulness to their father Jacob.
91 Tthey came to the borders of the land, and they said to each other, What shall we do in this matter before our father, for if we come suddenly to him and tell him the matter, he will be greatly alarmed at our words and will not believe us.
92 They went along until they came near to their houses and they found Serach, the daughter of Asher, going forth to meet them; the damsel was very good and subtle, and knew how to play on the harp.
93 They called to her and she came before them and kissed them, and they took her and gave her a harp, saying, Go now before our father and sit before him; strike on the harp and speak these words.
94 And they commanded her to go to their house, and she took the harp and hurried before them, and she came and sat near Jacob.
95 She played well and sang, and uttered in the sweetness of her words: Joseph my uncle is living and he rules throughout the land of Egypt, and is not dead.

96 She continued to repeat and utter these words, and Jacob heard her words and they were agreeable to him.
97 He listened while she repeated them twice and three times, and joy entered the heart of Jacob at the sweetness of her words, and the spirit of God was on him and he knew all her words to be true.
98 Jacob blessed Serach when she spoke these words before him, and he said to her, My daughter, may death never prevail over you, for you have revived my spirit; only speak again before me as you have spoken, for you have uplifted me with all your words.
99 And she continued to sing these words and Jacob listened and it pleased him, and he rejoiced, and the spirit of God was on him.
100 While he was yet speaking with her, he saw his sons come to him with horses and chariots and royal garments and servants running before them.
101 Jacob rose up to meet them and saw his sons dressed in royal garments and he saw all the treasures that Joseph had sent to them.
102 They said to him, Be informed that our brother Joseph is living, and it is he who rules throughout the land of Egypt, and it is he who spoke to us as we told you.
103 Jacob heard all the words of his sons, and his heart palpitated at their words, for he could not believe them until he saw all that Joseph had given them and what he had sent him, and all the signs which Joseph had spoken to them.
104 They opened all before him, and showed him all that Joseph had sent; they gave to each what Joseph had sent him and he knew that they had spoken the truth, and he rejoiced greatly an account of his son.
105 Jacob said, It is enough for me that my son Joseph is still living; I will go and see him before I die.
106 And his sons told him all that had happened to them, and Jacob said, I will go down to Egypt to see my son and his children.
107 Jacob rose up and put on the garments which Joseph had sent him, and after he had washed and shaved his hair, he put on his head the turban which Joseph had sent him.
108 All the people of Jacob's house and their wives put on the garments which Joseph had sent to them, and they greatly rejoiced at Joseph that he was still living and that he was ruling in Egypt.
109 And all the inhabitants of Canaan heard of this thing, and they came and rejoiced much with Jacob that he was still living.
110 Jacob made a feast for them for three days, and all the kings of Canaan and nobles of the land ate and drank and rejoiced in the house of Jacob.

CHAPTER 55

1 It came to pass after this that Jacob said, I will go and see my son in Egypt and then come back to the land of Canaan of which God had spoken to Abraham, for I cannot leave the land of my birth-place.
2 Then the word of the Lord came to him, saying, Go down to Egypt with all your household and remain there; fear not to go down to Egypt for I will there make you a great nation.
3 Jacob said within himself, I will go and see my son whether the fear of his God is yet in his heart among all the inhabitants of Egypt.

4 And the Lord said to Jacob, Fear not about Joseph, for he still retains his integrity to serve me, as will seem good in your sight. Jacob rejoiced greatly concerning his son.
5 At that time Jacob commanded his sons and household to go to Egypt according to the word of the Lord to him, and Jacob rose up with his sons and all his household, and he went out from the land of Canaan from Beersheba with joy and gladness of heart; they went to the land of Egypt.
6 It came to pass when they came near Egypt, Jacob sent Judah before him to Joseph that he might show him a situation in Egypt, and Judah did according to the word of his father; he hurried and ran and came to Joseph and they assigned for them a place in the land of Goshen for all his household, and Judah returned and came along the road to his father.
7 Joseph harnessed the chariot and assembled all his mighty men and his servants and all the officers of Egypt in order to go and meet his father Jacob, and Joseph's mandate was proclaimed in Egypt, saying, All that do not go to meet Jacob shall die.
8 On the next day Joseph went forth with all Egypt a great and mighty host, all dressed in garments of fine linen and purple and with instruments of silver and gold and with their instruments of war with them.
9 And they all went to meet Jacob with all sorts of musical instruments, with drums and timbrels, strewing myrrh and aloes all along the road; they all went after this fashion and the earth shook at their shouting.
10 All the women of Egypt went on the roofs of Egypt and on the walls to meet Jacob, and on the head of Joseph was Pharaoh's regal crown, for Pharaoh had sent it to him to put on at the time of his going to meet his father.
11 When Joseph came within fifty cubits of his father, he alighted from the chariot and he walked toward his father; when all the officers of Egypt and her nobles saw that Joseph had gone on foot toward his father, they also alighted and walked on foot toward Jacob.
12 And when Jacob approached the camp of Joseph, Jacob observed the camp that was coming toward him with Joseph and it gratified him, and Jacob was astonished at it.
13 Jacob said to Judah, Who is that man whom I see in the camp of Egypt dressed in kingly robes with a very red garment on him and a royal crown on his head, who has alighted from his chariot and is coming toward us? And Judah answered his father, saying, He is your son Joseph the king; and Jacob rejoiced in seeing the glory of his son.
14 Joseph came near to his father and he bowed to his father, and all the men of the camp bowed to the ground with him before Jacob.
15 And behold Jacob ran and hurried to his son Joseph and fell on his neck and kissed him, and they wept; Joseph also embraced his father and kissed him and they wept, and all the people of Egypt wept with them.
16 Jacob said to Joseph, Now I will die cheerfully after I have seen your face, that you are still living and with glory.
17 The sons of Jacob and their wives and their children and their servants, and all the household of Jacob wept greatly with Joseph and they kissed him and wept greatly with him.
18 Joseph and all his people returned home afterward to Egypt, and Jacob and his sons and all the children of his household came with Joseph to Egypt; Joseph placed them in the best part of Egypt, in the land of Goshen.

19 Joseph said to his father and his brothers, I will go up and tell Pharaoh, saying, My brothers and my father's household and all belonging to them have come to me, and now they are in the land of Goshen.
20 And Joseph did so and took from his brothers Reuben, Issachar, Zebulun and his brother Benjamin and he placed them before Pharaoh.
21 And Joseph spoke to Pharaoh, saying, My brothers and my father's household and all belonging to them, together with their flocks and cattle have come to me from the land of Canaan, to sojourn in Egypt; for the famine was severely on them.
22 And Pharaoh said to Joseph, Place your father and brothers in the best part of the land; withhold not from them all that is good, and cause them to eat of the best of the land.
23 And Joseph answered, saying, Yes, I have stationed them in the land of Goshen for they are shepherds, therefore let them remain in Goshen to feed their flocks, apart from the Egyptians.
24 And Pharaoh said to Joseph, Do with your brothers all that they shall say to you. And the sons of Jacob bowed down to Pharaoh, and they went forth from him in peace, and Joseph afterward brought his father before Pharaoh.
25 And Jacob came and bowed down to Pharaoh, and Jacob blessed Pharaoh, and he then went out; Jacob and all his sons and all his household lived in the land of Goshen.
26 In the second year, that is in the hundred and thirtieth year of the life of Jacob, Joseph maintained his father and his brothers and all his father's household with bread according to their little ones; all the days of the famine they lacked nothing.
27 And Joseph gave to them the best part of the whole land; the best of Egypt they had, all the days of Joseph, and Joseph also gave to them and to all his father's household, clothes and garments year by year; the sons of Jacob remained securely in Egypt all the days of their brother.
28 And Jacob always ate at Joseph's table, Jacob and his sons did not leave Joseph's table day or night, besides what Jacob's children consumed in their houses.
29 And all Egypt ate bread during the days of the famine from the house of Joseph, for all the Egyptians sold all belonging to them on account of the famine.
30 Joseph purchased all the lands and fields of Egypt for bread on the account of Pharaoh, and Joseph supplied all Egypt with bread all the days of the famine; Joseph collected all the silver and gold that came to him for the corn which they bought throughout the land, and he accumulated much gold and silver, besides an immense quantity of onyx stones, bdellium and valuable garments which they brought to Joseph from every part of the land when their money was gone.
31 And Joseph took all the silver and gold that came into his hand, about seventy two talents of gold and silver, and also onyx stones and bdellium in great abundance, and Joseph went and concealed them in four parts; he concealed one part in the wilderness near the Red sea, and one part by the river Perath, and the third and fourth parts he concealed in the desert opposite to the wilderness of Persia and Media.
32 He took part of the gold and silver that was left and gave it to all his brothers, to all his father's household, and to all the women of his father's household; the rest he brought to the house of Pharaoh, about twenty talents of gold and silver.
33 Joseph gave all the gold and silver that was left to Pharaoh, and Pharaoh placed it in the treasury, and the days of the famine ceased after that in the land. They sowed and reaped in the whole land, and they obtained their usual quantity year by year;

they lacked nothing.
34 And Joseph lived securely in Egypt and the whole land was under his advice, and his father and all his brothers lived in the land of Goshen and took possession of it.
35 Joseph was very aged, advanced in days, and his two sons Ephraim and Manasseh remained constantly in the house of Jacob, together with the children of the sons of Jacob their brothers, to learn the ways of the Lord and his law.
36 And Jacob and his sons lived in the land of Egypt in the land of Goshen, and they took possession of it, and they were prolific and multiplied in it.

CHAPTER 56

1 Jacob lived in the land of Egypt seventeen years, and the days of Jacob, and the years of his life were a hundred and forty seven years.
2 At that time Jacob was attacked with that illness of which he died and he sent and called for his son Joseph from Egypt, and Joseph his son came from Egypt and came to his father.
3 Jacob said to Joseph and to his sons, Behold I die, and the God of your ancestors will visit you and bring you back to the land which the Lord swore to give to you and to your children after you; now therefore when I am dead, bury me in the cave which is in Machpelah in Hebron in the land of Canaan, near my ancestors.
4 Jacob made his sons swear to bury him in Machpelah, in Hebron, and his sons swore to him concerning this thing.
5 And he commanded them, saying, Serve the Lord your God, for he who delivered your fathers will also deliver you from all trouble.
6 And Jacob said, Call all your children to me, and all the children of Jacob's sons came and sat before him, and Jacob blessed them, and he said to them, The Lord God of your fathers shall grant you a thousand times as much and bless you, and may he give you the blessing of your father Abraham. And all the children of Jacob's sons went forth on that day after he had blessed them.
7 On the next day Jacob again called for his sons and they all assembled and came to him and sat before him, and Jacob on that day blessed his sons before his death; each man did he bless according to his blessing. So it is written in the book of the law of the Lord pertaining to Israel.
8 And Jacob said to Judah, I know my son that you are a mighty man for your brothers; reign over them, and your sons shall reign over their sons forever.
9 Only teach your sons the bow and all the weapons of war, in order that they may fight the battles of their brother who will rule over his enemies.
10 And Jacob again commanded his sons on that day, saying, Behold I shall this day be gathered to my people; carry me up from Egypt and bury me in the cave of Machpelah as I have commanded you.
11 But take care I pray you that none of your sons carry me, only yourselves, and this is the manner you shall do to me, when you carry my body to go with it to the land of Canaan to bury me:
12 Judah, Issachar and Zebulun shall carry my bier at the eastern side; Reuben, Simeon and Gad at the south; Ephraim, Manasseh and Benjamin at the west; Dan, Asher and Naphtali at the north.
13 Let not Levi carry with you, for he and his sons will carry the ark of the covenant of the Lord with the Israelites in the camp, neither let Joseph my son carry, for as a

king so let his glory be; but Ephraim and Manasseh shall be in their stead.
14 Thus shall you do to me when you carry me away; do not neglect anything of all that I command you and it shall come to pass when you do this to me, that the Lord will remember you favorably and your children after you forever.
15 And you my sons, honor each his brother and his relative, and command your children and your children's children after you to serve the Lord God of your ancestors always,
16 In order that you may prolong your days in the land, you and your children and your children's children forever, when you do what is good and upright in the sight of the Lord your God, to follow in all his ways.
17 And you, Joseph my son, forgive I pray you the prongs of your brothers and all their wrongdoings in the injury that they heaped on you, for God intended it for you and your children's benefit.
18 And O my son leave not your brothers to the inhabitants of Egypt, neither hurt their feelings, for behold I consign them to the hand of God and in your hand to guard them from the Egyptians; the sons of Jacob answered their father saying, O, our father, all that you have commanded us, so will we do; may God only be with us.
19 Jacob said to his sons, So may God be with you when you keep all his ways; turn not from his ways either to the right or the left in performing what is good and upright in his sight.
20 For I know that many and severe troubles will befall you in the latter days in the land, yes, your children and children's children; only serve the Lord and he will save you from all trouble.
21 It shall come to pass when you shall go after God to serve him and will teach your children after you, and your children's children, to know the Lord, then will the Lord raise up to you and your children a servant from among your children; the Lord will deliver you through his hand from all affliction, and bring you out of Egypt and bring you back to the land of your fathers to inherit it securely.
22 Jacob ceased commanding his sons, and he drew his feet into the bed. He died and was gathered to his people.
23 And Joseph fell on his father and he cried out and wept over him and he kissed him, and he called out in a bitter voice, and he said, O my father, my father.
24 His son's wives and all his household came and fell on Jacob, and they wept over him and cried in a very loud voice concerning Jacob.
25 All the sons of Jacob rose up together, and they tore their garments, and they all put sackcloth on their loins; they fell on their faces, and they cast dust on their heads toward the heavens.
26 And the thing was told to Osnath Joseph's wife; she rose up and put on a sack and she with all the Egyptian women came and mourned and wept for Jacob.
27 Also all the people of Egypt who knew Jacob came all on that day when they heard this thing, and all Egypt wept for many days.
28 Also from the land of Canaan the women came to Egypt when they heard that Jacob was dead, and they wept for him in Egypt for seventy days.
29 It came to pass after this that Joseph commanded his servants the doctors to embalm his father with myrrh and frankincense and all manner of incense and perfume, and the doctors embalmed Jacob as Joseph had commanded them.
30 And all the people of Egypt and the elders and all the inhabitants of the land of Goshen wept and mourned over Jacob, and all his sons and the children of his

household lamented and mourned over their father Jacob many days.
31 After the days of his weeping had passed away, at the end of seventy days,
Joseph said to Pharaoh, I will go up and bury my father in the land of Canaan as he
made me swear, and then I will return.
32 Pharaoh sent Joseph, saying, Go up and bury your father as he said, and as he
made you swear; Joseph rose up with all his brothers to go to the land of Canaan to
bury their father Jacob as he had commanded them.
33 And Pharaoh commanded that it should be announced throughout Egypt, saying,
Whoever goes not up with Joseph and his brothers to the land of Canaan to bury
Jacob, shall die.
34 And all Egypt heard of Pharaoh's proclamation, and they all rose up together, and
all the servants of Pharaoh, and the elders of his house, and all the elders of the land
of Egypt went up with Joseph, and all the officers and nobles of Pharaoh went up as
the servants of Joseph; they went to bury Jacob in the land of Canaan.
35 And the sons of Jacob carried the bier on which he lay; according to all that their
father commanded them, so did his sons to him.
36 The bier was of pure gold, and it was inlaid round about with onyx stones and
bdellium; and the covering of the bier was gold woven work, joined with threads,
and over them were hooks of onyx stones and bdellium.
37 And Joseph placed on the head of his father Jacob a large golden crown, and he
put a golden rod in his hand, and they surrounded the bier as was the custom of
kings during their lives.
38 And all the troops of Egypt went before him in this array; at first all the mighty
men of Pharaoh and the mighty men of Joseph, and after them the rest of the
inhabitants of Egypt; they were all girded with swords and equipped with coats of
mail, and the trappings of war were on them.
39 All the weepers and mourners went at a distance opposite to the bier, going and
weeping and lamenting, and the rest of the people went after the bier.
40 Joseph and his household went together near the bier barefooted and weeping,
and the rest of Joseph's servants went around him; each man had his ornaments on
him and they were all armed with their weapons of war.
41 Fifty of Jacob's servants went in front of the bier and they scattered along the road
myrrh and aloes, and all manner of perfume, and all the sons of Jacob that carried
the bier walked on the perfumery; the servants of Jacob went before them spreading
the perfume along the road.
42 And Joseph went up with a heavy camp, and they did after this manner every
day until they reached the land of Canaan. They came to the threshing floor of Atad,
which was on the other side of Jordan, and they mourned an extremely great and
heavy mourning in that place.
43 And all the kings of Canaan heard of this thing and they all went forth, each man
from his house, thirty-one kings of Canaan; they all came with their men to mourn
and weep over Jacob.
44 All these kings observed Jacob's bier, and there Joseph's crown was on it; they
also put their crowns on the bier and encircled it with crowns.
45 All these kings made in that place a great and heavy mourning with the sons of
Jacob and Egypt over Jacob, for all the kings of Canaan knew the valor of Jacob and
his sons.
46 And the report reached Esau, saying, Jacob died in Egypt, and his sons and all
Egypt are conveying him to the land of Canaan to bury him.

47 Esau heard this thing, and he was dwelling in mount Seir; he rose up with his sons and all his people and all his household, a people greatly great, and they came to mourn and weep over Jacob.
48 And it came to pass, when Esau came he mourned for his brother Jacob, and all Egypt and all Canaan again rose up and mourned a great mourning with Esau over Jacob in that place
49 Joseph and his brothers brought their father Jacob from that place, and they went to Hebron to bury Jacob in the cave by his fathers.
50 They came to Kireath-arba, to the cave, and as they came Esau stood with his sons against Joseph and his brothers as a hindrance in the cave, saying, Jacob shall not be buried in here, for it belongs to us and to our father.
51 Joseph and his brothers heard the words of Esau's sons, and they were greatly angered, and Joseph approached Esau, saying, What is this thing which they have spoken? Certainly my father Jacob bought it from you for great riches after the death of Isaac, now five and twenty years ago, and also all the land of Canaan he bought from you and from your sons, and your descendants after you.
52 Jacob bought it for his sons and his descendants after him for an inheritance for ever, and why do you speak these things this day?
53 And Esau answered, saying, You speak falsely and utter lies, for I sold not anything belonging to me in all this land, as you say, neither did my brother Jacob buy what belonged to me in this land.
54 Esau spoke these things in order to deceive Joseph with his words, for Esau knew that Joseph was not present in those days when Esau sold all belonging to him in the land of Canaan to Jacob.
55 Joseph said to Esau, Certainly my father inserted these things with you in the record of purchase, and testified the record with witnesses, and behold it is with us in Egypt.
56 Esau answered, saying to him, Bring the record; all that you will find in the record, so we will do.
57 Joseph called to Naphtali his brother and said, Hurry quickly, stay not, and run I pray you to Egypt and bring all the records; the record of the purchase, the sealed record and the open record, and also all the first records in which all the transactions of the birthright are written, bring with you.
58 You shall bring them to us here, that we may know from them all the words of Esau and his sons which they spoke this day.
59 And Naphtali listened to the voice of Joseph and he hurried and ran to go down to Egypt, and Naphtali was lighter on foot than any of the stags that were on the wilderness, for he could go on ears of corn without crushing them.
60 When Esau saw that Naphtali had gone to fetch the records, he and his sons increased their resistance against the cave, and Esau and all his people rose up against Joseph and his brothers to battle.
61 All the sons of Jacob and the people of Egypt fought with Esau and his men, and the sons of Esau and his people were smitten before the sons of Jacob, and the sons of Jacob killed of Esau's people forty men.
62 Chushim the son of Dan, the son of Jacob, was at that time with Jacob's sons, but he was about a hundred cubits distant from the place of battle, for he remained with the children of Jacob's sons by Jacob's bier to guard it.
63 And Chushim was dumb and deaf, still he understood the voice of consternation among men.

64 And he asked, saying, Why do you not bury the dead, and what is this great consternation? They answered him the words of Esau and his sons and he ran to Esau in the midst of the battle; he killed Esau with a sword; he cut off his head and it sprang to a distance, and Esau fell among the people of the battle.
65 When Chushim did this thing the sons of Jacob prevailed over the sons of Esau, and the sons of Jacob buried their father Jacob by force in the cave, and the sons of Esau watched it.
66 Jacob was buried in Hebron, in the cave of Machpelah which Abraham had bought from the sons of Heth for the possession of a burial place, and he was buried in very costly garments.
67 No king had such honor paid him as Joseph paid to his father at his death, for he buried him with great honor like the burial of kings.
68 And Joseph and his brothers made a mourning of seven days for their father.

CHAPTER 57

1 It was after this that the sons of Esau waged war with the sons of Jacob, and the sons of Esau fought with the sons of Jacob in Hebron, and Esau was still lying dead and not buried.
2 The battle was heavy between them, and the sons of Esau were smitten before the sons of Jacob, and the sons of Jacob killed of the sons of Esau eighty men, and not one died of the people of the sons of Jacob; the hand of Joseph prevailed over all the people of the sons of Esau, and he took Zepho, the son of Eliphaz, the son of Esau, and fifty of his men captive; he bound them with chains of iron, and gave them into the hands of his servants to bring them to Egypt.
3 It came to pass when the sons of Jacob had taken Zepho and his people captive, all those that remained were greatly afraid for their lives from the house of Esau, that they should also be taken captive; they all fled with Eliphaz the son of Esau and his people, with Esau's body, and they went on their road to Mount Seir.
4 They came to Mount Seir and they buried Esau in Seir, but they had not brought his head with them to Seir, for it was buried in that place where the battle had been in Hebron.
5 And it came to pass when the sons of Esau had fled from before the sons of Jacob, the sons of Jacob pursued them to the borders of Seir, but they did not kill a single man from among them when they pursued them, for Esau's body which they carried with them increased their confusion. So they fled and the sons of Jacob turned back from them and came up to the place where their brothers were in Hebron, and they remained there on that day, and on the next day until they rested from the battle.
6 It came to pass on the third day they assembled all the sons of Seir the Horite, and they assembled all the children of the east, a multitude of people like the sand of the sea, and they went and came down to Egypt to fight with Joseph and his brothers in order to deliver their brothers.
7 Joseph and all the sons of Jacob heard that the sons of Esau and the children of the east had come on them to do battle in order to deliver their brothers.
8 Joseph and his brothers and the strong men of Egypt went forth and fought in the city of Rameses, and Joseph and his brothers dealt out a tremendous blow among the sons of Esau and the children of the east.
9 They killed of them six hundred thousand men, and they killed among them all the

mighty men of the children of Seir the Horite; there were only a few of them left, and they killed also a great many of the children of the east, and of the children of Esau; Eliphaz the son of Esau, and the children of the east all fled before Joseph and his brothers.
10 Joseph and his brothers pursued them until they came to Succoth, and they yet killed of them in Succoth thirty men, and the rest escaped and they fled each to his city.
11 And Joseph and his brothers and the mighty men of Egypt turned back from them with joy and cheerfulness of heart, for they had smitten all their enemies.
12 Zepho the son of Eliphaz and his men were still slaves in Egypt to the sons of Jacob, and their pains increased.
13 When the sons of Esau and the sons of Seir returned to their land, the sons of Seir saw that they had all fallen into the hands of the sons of Jacob and the people of Egypt, on account of the battle of the sons of Esau.
14 And the sons of Seir said to the sons of Esau, You have seen and therefore you know that this camp was on your account, and not one mighty man or an adept one in war remaineth.
15 So now go forth from our land, go from us to the land of Canaan to the land of the dwelling of your fathers; wherefore shall your children inherit the effects of our children in latter days?
16 And the children of Esau would not listen to the children of Seir, and the children of Seir considered to make war with them.
17 The children of Esau sent secretly to Angeas king of Africa, the same is Dinhabah, saying,
18 Send to us some of your men and let them come to us, and we will fight together with the children of Seir the Horite, for they have resolved to fight with us to drive us away from the land.
19 And Angeas king of Dinhabah did so, for he was in those days friendly to the children of Esau, and Angeas sent five hundred valiant infantry to the children of Esau, and eight hundred cavalry.
20 The children of Seir sent to the children of the east and to the children of Midian, saying, You have seen what the children of Esau have done to us, on whose account we are almost all destroyed in their battle with the sons of Jacob.
21 So now come to us and assist us, and we will fight them together; we will drive them from the land and be avenged of the cause of our brothers who died for their sakes in their battle with their brothers the sons of Jacob.
22 And all the children of the east listened to the children of Seir, and they came to them about eight hundred men with drawn swords, and the children of Esau fought with the children of Seir at that time in the wilderness of Paran.
23 The children of Seir won over the sons of Esau, and the children of Seir killed on that day of the children of Esau in that battle about two hundred men of the people of Angeas king of Dinhabah.
24 And on the second day the children of Esau came again to fight a second time with the children of Seir, and the battle was severe on the children of Esau this second time, and it troubled them greatly on account of the children of Seir.
25 And when the children of Esau saw that the children of Seir were more powerful than they were, some men of the children of Esau turned and assisted the children of Seir their enemies.
26 And there fell yet of the people of the children of Esau in the second battle fifty-

eight men of the people at Angeas king of Dinhabah.
27 And on the third day the children of Esau heard that some of their brothers had turned from them to fight against them in the second battle; and the children of Esau mourned when they heard this thing.
28 They said, What shall we do to our brothers who turned from us to assist the children of Seir our enemies? And the children of Esau again sent to Angeas king of Dinhabah, saying,
29 Send to us again other men that with them we may fight with the children of Seir, for they have already twice been stronger than we were.
30 And Angeas again sent to the children of Esau about six hundred valiant men, and they came to assist the children of Esau.
31 In ten days' time the children of Esau again waged war with the children of Seir in the wilderness of Paran, and the battle was very severe on the children of Seir; the children of Esau won this time over the children of Seir, and the children of Seir were smitten before the children of Esau; the children of Esau killed from them about two thousand men.
32 And all the mighty men of the children of Seir died in this battle, and there only remained their young children that were left in their cities.
33 All Midian and the children of the east went themselves in flight from the battle, and they left the children of Seir and fled when they saw that the battle was severe on them; the children of Esau pursued all the children of the east until they reached their land.
34 And the children of Esau killed yet of them about two hundred and fifty men and from the people of the children of Esau there fell in that battle about thirty men, but this evil came on them through their brothers turning from them to assist the children of Seir the Horite; the children of Esau again heard of the evil doings of their brothers, and they again mourned on account of this thing.
35 It came to pass after the battle, the children of Esau turned back and came home to Seir, and the children of Esau killed those who had remained in the land of the children of Seir; they killed also their wives and little ones, they left not a soul alive except fifty young boys and girls whom they allowed to live; the children of Esau did not put them to death, and the boys became their slaves, and the girls they took for wives.
36 The children of Esau lived in Seir in the place of the children of Seir, and they inherited their land and took possession of it.
37 And the children of Esau took all belonging in the land to the children of Seir, also their flocks, their bullocks and their goods, and all belonging to the children of Seir did the children of Esau take. And the children of Esau lived in Seir in the place of the children of Seir to this day, and the children of Esau divided the land into divisions to the five sons of Esau, according to their families.
38 It came to pass in those days that the children of Esau resolved to crown a king over them in the land of which they possessed. And they said to each other, Not so, for he shall reign over us in our land; we shall be under his counsel and he shall fight our battles against our enemies, and they did so.
39 And all the children of Esau swore, saying, that none of their brothers should ever reign over them, but a strange man who is not of their brothers; for the souls of all the children of Esau were embittered every man against his son, brother and friend, on account of the evil they sustained from their brothers when they fought with the children of Seir.

40 So then the sons of Esau swore, saying, from that day forward they would not choose a king from their brothers, but one from a strange land to this day.
41 There was a man there from the people of Angeas king of Dinhabah; his name was Bela the son of Beor, who was a very valiant man, beautiful and admired and wise in all wisdom, and a man of sense and counsel; and there was none of the people of Angeas like him.
42 And all the children of Esau took him and anointed him and they crowned him for a king; they bowed down to him, and said, May the king live, may the king live.
43 They spread out the sheet, and they brought him each man earrings of gold and silver or rings or bracelets, and they made him very rich in silver and in gold, in onyx stones and bdellium, and they made him a royal throne; they placed a regal crown on his head and they built a palace for him and he lived therein, and he became king over all the children of Esau.
44 And the people of Angeas took their wages for their battle from the children of Esau, and they went and returned at that time to their master in Dinhabah.
45 And Bela reigned over the children of Esau thirty years, and the children of Esau lived in the land instead of the children of Seir, and they lived securely in their stead to this day.

CHAPTER 58

1 It came to pass in the thirty-second year of the Israelites going down to Egypt, that is in the seventy-first year of the life of Joseph, in that year died Pharaoh king of Egypt, and Magron his son reigned in his stead.
2 And Pharaoh commanded Joseph before his death to be a father to his son, Magron, and that Magron should be under the care of Joseph and under his counsel.
3 All Egypt consented to this thing that Joseph should be king over them, for all the Egyptians loved Joseph as before, only Magron the son of Pharaoh sat on his father's throne, and he became king in those days in his father's stead.
4 Magron was forty-one years old when he began to reign, and forty years he reigned in Egypt, and all Egypt called his name Pharaoh after the name of his father, as it was their custom to do in Egypt to every king that reigned over them.
5 And it came to pass when Pharaoh reigned in his father's stead, he placed the laws of Egypt and all the affairs of government in the hand of Joseph, as his father had commanded him.
6 Joseph became king over Egypt, for he superintended over all Egypt, and all Egypt was under his care and under his counsel, for all Egypt inclined to Joseph after the death of Pharaoh; they loved him greatly to reign over them.
7 But there were some people among them who did not like him, saying, No stranger shall reign over us. Still the whole government of Egypt was passed in those days onto Joseph, after the death of Pharaoh, he being the regulator, doing as he liked throughout the land without anyone interfering.
8 And all Egypt was under the care of Joseph, and Joseph made war with all his surrounding enemies, and he subdued them; also all the land and all the Philistines, to the borders of Canaan, did Joseph subdue; they were all under his power and they gave a yearly tax to Joseph.
9 Pharaoh king of Egypt sat on his throne in his father's stead, but he was under the control and counsel of Joseph, as he was at first under the control of his father.

10 Neither did he reign but in the land of Egypt only, under the counsel of Joseph, but Joseph reigned over the whole country at that time, from Egypt to the great river Perath.

11 And Joseph was successful in all his ways and the Lord was with him, and the Lord gave Joseph additional wisdom, and honor, and glory, and love toward him in the hearts of the Egyptians and throughout the land; Joseph reigned over the whole country forty years.

12 And all the countries of the Philistines and Canaan and Zidon, and on the other side of Jordan, brought presents to Joseph all his days, and the whole country was in the hands of Joseph, and they brought to him a yearly tribute as it was regulated, for Joseph had fought against all his surrounding enemies and subdued them; the whole country was in the hands of Joseph, and Joseph sat securely on his throne in Egypt.

13 Also all his brothers the sons of Jacob lived securely in the land, all the days of Joseph, and they were prolific and multiplied greatly in the land; they served the Lord all their days as their father Jacob had commanded them.

14 It came to pass at the end of many days and years, when the children of Esau were dwelling quietly in their land with Bela their king, that the children of Esau were prolific and multiplied in the land; they resolved to go and fight with the sons of Jacob and all Egypt, and to deliver their brother Zepho, the son of Eliphaz, and his men, for they were yet in those days slaves to Joseph.

15 The children of Esau sent to all the children of the east and they made peace with them, and all the children of the east came to them to go with the children of Esau to Egypt to battle.

16 There came also to them of the people of Angeas, king of Dinhabah; they also sent to the children of Ishmael and they also came to them.

17 And all this people assembled and came to Seir to assist the children of Esau in their battle, and this camp was very large and strong with people, numerous as the sand of the sea, about eight hundred thousand men, infantry and cavalry, and all these troops went down to Egypt to fight with the sons of Jacob; they encamped by Rameses.

18 And Joseph went forth with his brothers with the mighty men of Egypt, about six hundred men, and they fought with them in the land of Rameses; the sons of Jacob at that time again fought with the children of Esau, in the fiftieth year of the sons of Jacob going down to Egypt, that is the thirtieth year of the reign of Bela over the children of Esau in Seir.

19 And the Lord gave all the mighty men of Esau and the children of the east into the hand of Joseph and his brothers, and the people of the children of Esau and the children of the east were smitten before Joseph.

20 Of the people of Esau and the children of the east that were slain, there fell before the sons of Jacob about two hundred thousand men, and their king Bela the son of Beor fell with them in the battle. When the children of Esau saw that their king had fallen in battle and was dead, their hands became weak in the combat.

21 Joseph and his brothers and all Egypt were still smiting the people of the house of Esau, and all Esau's people were afraid of the sons of Jacob and fled from before them.

22 Joseph and his brothers and all Egypt pursued them a day's journey, and they killed yet from them about three hundred men, continuing to strike them in the road; they afterward turned back from them.

23 Joseph and all his brothers returned to Egypt, not one man was missing from

them, but of the Egyptians there fell twelve men.
24 And when Joseph returned to Egypt he ordered Zepho and his men to be additionally bound, and they bound them in irons and they increased their grief.
25 All the people of the children of Esau, and the children of the east, returned in shame each to his city, for all the mighty men that were with them had fallen in battle.
26 When the children of Esau saw that their king had died in battle they hurried and took a man from the people of the children of the east; his name was Jobab the son of Zarach, from the land of Botzrah, and they caused him to reign over them instead of Bela their king.
27 Jobab sat on the throne of Bela as king in his stead, and Jobab reigned in Edom over all the children of Esau ten years; the children of Esau went no more to fight with the sons of Jacob from that day forward, for the sons of Esau knew the courage of the sons of Jacob, and they were greatly afraid of them.
28 But from that day forward the children of Esau hated the sons of Jacob, and the hatred and enmity were very strong between them all the days, to this day.
29 And it came to pass after this, at the end of ten years, Jobab, the son of Zarach, from Botzrah, died, and the children of Esau took a man whose name was Chusham, from the land of Teman, and they made him king over them instead of Jobab; Chusham reigned in Edom over all the children of Esau for twenty years.
30 And Joseph, king of Egypt, and his brothers, and all the children of Israel lived securely in Egypt in those days, together with all the children of Joseph and his brothers, having no hindrance or evil accident and the land of Egypt was at that time at rest from war in the days of Joseph and his brothers.

CHAPTER 59

1 These are the names of the sons of Israel who lived in Egypt, who had come with Jacob; all the sons of Jacob came to Egypt, every man with his household.
2 The children of Leah were Reuben, Simeon, Levi, Judah, Issachar and Zebulun, and their sister Dinah.
3 And the sons of Rachel were Joseph and Benjamin.
4 And the sons of Zilpah, the handmaid of Leah, were Gad and Asher.
5 And the sons of Bilhah, the handmaid of Rachel, were Dan and Naphtali.
6 And these were their descendants that were born to them in the land of Canaan, before they came to Egypt with their father Jacob:
7 The sons of Reuben were Chanoch, Pallu, Chetzron and Carmi.
8 And the sons of Simeon were Jemuel, Jamin, Ohad, Jachin, Zochar and Saul, the son of the Canaanitish woman.
9 And the children of Levi were Gershon, Kehath and Merari, and their sister Jochebed, who was born to them in their going down to Egypt.
10 And the sons of Judah were Er, Onan, Shelah, Perez and Zarach.
11 And Er and Onan died in the land of Canaan; and the sons of Perez were Chezron and Chamul.
12 And the sons of Issachar were Tola, Puvah, Job and Shomron.
13 And the sons of Zebulun were Sered, Elon and Jachleel, and the son of Dan was Chushim.
14 And the sons of Naphtali were Jachzeel, Guni, Jetzer and Shilam.

15 And the sons of Gad were Ziphion, Chaggi, Shuni, Ezbon, Eri, Arodi and Areli.
16 And the children of Asher were Jimnah, Jishvah, Jishvi, Beriah and their sister Serach; and the sons of Beriah were Cheber and Malchiel.
17 And the sons of Benjamin were Bela, Becher, Ashbel, Gera, Naaman, Achi, Rosh, Mupim, Chupim and Ord.
18 And the sons of Joseph that were born to him in Egypt were Manasseh and Ephraim.
19 All the souls that went forth from the loins of Jacob were seventy souls; these are they who came with Jacob their father to Egypt to dwell there: and Joseph and all his brothers lived securely in Egypt, and they ate of the best of Egypt all the days of the life of Joseph.
20 And Joseph lived in the land of Egypt ninety-three years, and Joseph reigned over all Egypt eighty years.
21 When the days of Joseph drew near that he should die, he sent and called for his brothers and all his father's household, and they all came together and sat before him.
22 Joseph said to his brothers and all of his father's household, Behold I die, and God will certainly visit you and bring you up from this land to the land which he swore to your fathers to give to them.
23 And it shall be when God shall visit you to bring you up from here to the land of your fathers, then bring up my bones with you from here.
24 Joseph made the sons of Israel to swear for their descendants after them, saying, God will certainly visit you and you shall bring up my bones with you from here.
25 And it came to pass after this that Joseph died in that year, the seventy-first year of the Israelites going down to Egypt.
26 And Joseph was one hundred and ten years old when he died in the land of Egypt, and all his brothers and all his servants rose up and they embalmed Joseph, as was their custom, and his brothers and all Egypt mourned over him for seventy days.
27 And they put Joseph in a coffin filled with spices and all sorts of perfume; they buried him by the side of the river, that is Sihor, and his sons and all his brothers, and the whole of his father's household made a seven day's mourning for him.
28 It came to pass after the death of Joseph, all the Egyptians began in those days to rule over the children of Israel; Pharaoh, king of Egypt, who reigned in his father's stead, took all the laws of Egypt and conducted the whole government of Egypt under his counsel, and he reigned securely over his people.

CHAPTER 60

1 And when the year came round, being the seventy-second year from the Israelites going down to Egypt, after the death of Joseph, Zepho the son of Eliphaz, the son of Esau, fled from Egypt, he and his men, and they went away.
2 And he came to Africa, which is Dinhabah, to Angeas king of Africa; Angeas received them with great honor, and he made Zepho the captain of his host.
3 And Zepho found favor in the sight of Angeas and in the sight of his people, and Zepho was captain of the host to Angeas king of Africa for many days.
4 Zepho enticed Angeas king of Africa to collect all his army to go and fight with the Egyptians, and with the sons of Jacob, and to avenge of them the cause of his

brothers.
5 But Angeas would not listen to Zepho to do this thing, for Angeas knew the strength of the sons of Jacob, and what they had done to his army in their warfare with the children of Esau.
6 And Zepho was in those days very great in the sight of Angeas and in the sight of all his people, and he continually enticed them to make war against Egypt, but they would not.
7 It came to pass in those days there was in the land of Chittim a man in the city of Puzimna, whose name was Uzu, and he became degenerately deified by the children of Chittim; the man died and had no son, only one daughter whose name was Jania.
8 And the girl was greatly beautiful, admired and intelligent, there was none seen like her for beauty and wisdom throughout the land.
9 And the people of Angeas king of Africa saw her and they came and praised her to him; Angeas sent to the children of Chittim, and he requested to take her to himself for a wife, and the people of Chittim consented to give her to him for a wife.
10 When the messengers of Angeas were going forth from the land of Chittim to take their journey, behold the messengers of Turnus king of Bibentu came to Chittim, for Turnus king of Bibentu also sent his messengers to request Jania for him, to take to himself for a wife, for all his men had also praised her to him, therefore he sent all his servants to her.
11 The servants of Turnus came to Chittim, and they asked for Jania, to be taken to Turnus their king for a wife.
12 The people of Chittim said to them, We cannot give her, because Angeas king of Africa desired her to take her to him for a wife before you came, and that we should give her to him; now therefore we cannot do this thing to deprive Angeas of the girl in order to give her to Turnus.
13 For we are greatly afraid of Angeas that he come in battle against us and destroy us, and Turnus your master will not be able to deliver us from his hands.
14 When the messengers of Turnus heard all the words of the children of Chittim, they turned back to their master and told him all the words of the children of Chittim.
15 And the children of Chittim sent a memorial to Angeas, saying, Behold Turnus has sent for Jania to take her to him for a wife, and thus have we answered him; we heard that he has collected his whole army to go to war against you, and he intends to pass by the road of Sardunia to fight against your brother Lucus, and after that he will come to fight against you.
16 Angeas heard the words of the children of Chittim which they sent to him in the record, and his anger was set ablaze and he rose up and assembled his whole army and came through the islands of the sea, the road to Sardunia, to his brother Lucus king of Sardunia.
17 Niblos, the son of Lucus, heard that his uncle Angeas was coming, and he went out to meet him with a heavy army, and he kissed him and embraced him, and Niblos said to Angeas, When you ask my father after his welfare, when I shall go with you to fight with Turnus, ask of him to make me captain of his host. Angeas did so, and he came to his brother and his brother came to meet him, and he asked him after his welfare.
18 And Angeas asked his brother Lucus after his welfare, and to make his son Niblos captain of his host, and Lucus did so; Angeas and his brother Lucus rose up and they went toward Turnus to battle, and there was with them a great army and a

strong people.
19 And he came in ships, and they came into the province of Ashtorash, and behold
Turnus came toward them, for he went forth to Sardunia, and intended to destroy it
and afterward to pass on from there to Angeas to fight with him.
20 Angeas and Lucus his brother met Turnus in the valley of Canopia, and the battle
was strong and mighty between them in that place.
21 And the battle was severe on Lucus king of Sardunia, and all his army fell, and
Niblos his son fell also in that battle.
22 And his uncle Angeas commanded his servants and they made a golden coffin for
Niblos and they put him into it, and Angeas again waged battle toward Turnus;
Angeas was stronger than he, and he killed him, and he struck all his people with
the edge of the sword, and Angeas avenged the cause of Niblos his brother's son and
the cause of the army of his brother Lucus.
23 And when Turnus died, the hands of those that survived the battle became weak,
and they fled from before Angeas and Lucus his brother.
24 Angeas and his brother Lucus pursued them to the highroad, which is between
Alphanu and Romah, and they killed the whole army of Turnus with the edge of the
sword.
25 Lucus king of Sardunia commanded his servants that they should make a coffin
of brass, and that they should place therein the body of his son Niblos, and they
buried him in that place.
26 And they built on it a high tower there on the highroad, and they called its name
after the name of Niblos to this day; they also buried Turnus king of Bibentu there in
that place with Niblos.
27 And so on the highroad between Alphanu and Romah the grave of Niblos is on
one side and the grave of Turnus on the other, and a pavement is between them to
this day.
28 When Niblos was buried, Lucus his father returned with his army to his land
Sardunia, and Angeas his brother king of Africa went with his people to the city of
Bibentu, that is the city of Turnus.
29 And the inhabitants of Bibentu heard of his fame and they were greatly afraid of
him; they went forth to meet him with weeping and supplication, and the
inhabitants of Bibentu entreated of Angeas not to kill them nor destroy their city; he
did so, for Bibentu was in those days reckoned as one of the cities of the children of
Chittim; so he did not destroy the city.
30 But from that day forward the troops of the king of Africa would go to Chittim to
wreck and rob it, and whenever they went, Zepho the captain of the host of Angeas
would go with them.
31 It was after this that Angeas turned with his army and they came to the city of
Puzimna, and Angeas then took Jania the daughter of Uzu for a wife and brought
her to his city to Africa.

CHAPTER 61

1 It came to pass at that time Pharaoh king of Egypt commanded all his people to
make for him a strong palace in Egypt.
2 And he also commanded the sons of Jacob to assist the Egyptians in the building,
and the Egyptians made a beautiful and elegant palace for a royal habitation; he

lived there and he renewed his government and he reigned securely.
3 And Zebulun the son of Jacob died in that year, that is the seventy-second year of the going down of the Israelites to Egypt; Zebulun died a hundred and fourteen years old and was put into a coffin and given into the hands of his children.
4 And in the seventy-fifth year his brother Simeon died; he was a hundred and twenty years old at his death, and he was also put into a coffin and given into the hands of his children.
5 Zepho the son of Eliphaz the son of Esau, captain of the host to Angeas king of Dinhabah, was still daily enticing Angeas to prepare for battle to fight with the sons of Jacob in Egypt; Angeas was unwilling to do this thing, for his servants had related to him all the might of the sons of Jacob, what they had done to them in their battle with the children of Esau.
6 And Zepho was in those days daily enticing Angeas to fight with the sons of Jacob.
7 After some time Angeas listened to the words of Zepho and consented to him to fight with the sons of Jacob in Egypt, and Angeas got all his people in order, a people numerous as the sand which is on the seashore, and he formed his resolution to go to Egypt to battle.
8 Among the servants of Angeas was a youth fifteen years old, Balaam the son of Beor was his name and the youth was very wise and understood the art of witchcraft.
9 And Angeas said to Balaam, Summon for us, I pray you, with the witchcraft, that we may know who will succeed in this battle to which we are now proceeding.
10 And Balaam ordered that they should bring him wax, and he made thereof the likeness of chariots and horsemen representing the army of Angeas and the army of Egypt; he put them in the cunningly prepared waters that he had for that purpose, and he took in his hand the boughs of myrtle trees, and he exercised his cunning; he joined them over the water, and there appeared to him in the water the resembling images of the hosts of Angeas falling before the resembling images of the Egyptians and the sons of Jacob.
11 Balaam told this thing to Angeas, and Angeas despaired and did not arm himself to go down to Egypt to battle, and he remained in his city.
12 And when Zepho the son of Eliphaz saw that Angeas despaired of going forth to battle with the Egyptians, Zepho fled from Angeas from Africa, and he went and came to Chittim.
13 And all the people of Chittim received him with great honor, and they hired him to fight their battles all the days; Zepho became greatly rich in those days, and the troops of the king of Africa still spread themselves in those days; the children of Chittim assembled and went to Mount Cuptizia on account of the troops of Angeas king of Africa who were advancing on them.
14 It was one day that Zepho lost a young heifer and he went to seek it, and he heard it lowing round about the mountain.
15 Zepho went and he saw that there was a large cave at the bottom of the mountain, and there was a great stone there at the entrance of the cave; Zepho split the stone and he came into the cave and he looked and there a large animal was devouring the ox; from the middle upward it resembled a man, and from the middle downward it resembled an animal, and Zepho rose up against the animal and killed it with his swords.
16 The inhabitants of Chittim heard of this thing, and they rejoiced greatly, and said, What shall we do to this man who has slain this animal that devoured our cattle?

17 And they all assembled to consecrate one day in the year to him, and they called the name thereof Zepho after his name; they brought to him drink offerings year after year on that day, and they brought to him gifts.
18 At that time Jania the daughter of Uzu wife of king Angeas became ill, and her illness was heavily felt by Angeas and his officers, and Angeas said to his wise men, What shall I do to Jania and how shall I heal her from her illness? And his wise men said to him, Because the air of our country is not like the air of the land of Chittim, and our water is not like their water, therefore from this has the queen become ill.
19 For through the change of air and water she became ill, and also because in her country she drank only the water which came from Purmah, which her ancestors had brought up with bridges.
20 And Angeas commanded his servants, and they brought to him in vessels of the waters of Purmah belonging to Chittim, and they weighed those waters with all the waters of the land of Africa, and they found those waters lighter than the waters of Africa.
21 Angeas saw this thing, and he commanded all his officers to assemble the hewers of stone in thousands and tens of thousands, and they hewed stone without number; the builders came and they built a greatly strong bridge and they conveyed the spring of water from the land of Chittim to Africa, and those waters were for Jania the queen and for all her concerns, to drink from and to bake, wash and bathe with, and also to water all offspring from which food can be obtained, and all fruit of the ground.
22 And the king commanded that they should bring of the soil of Chittim in large ships, and they also brought stones to build there; the builders built palaces for Jania the queen, and the queen became healed of her illness.
23 And at the revolution of the year the troops of Africa continued coming to the land of Chittim to rob as usual, and Zepho son of Eliphaz heard their report; he gave orders concerning them and he fought with them and they fled before him, and he delivered the land of Chittim from them.
24 And the children of Chittim saw the bravery of Zepho, and the children of Chittim resolved and made Zepho king over them; he became king over them and while he reigned they went to subdue the children of Tubal, and all the surrounding islands.
25 Their king Zepho led them and they made war with Tubal and the islands, and they subdued them; when they returned from the battle they renewed his government for him, and they built for him a very large palace for his royal habitation and seat, and they made a large throne for him; Zepho reigned over the whole land of Chittim and over the land of Italia fifty years.

CHAPTER 62

1 In that year, being the seventy-ninth year of the Israelites going down to Egypt, Reuben the son of Jacob died, in the land of Egypt; Reuben was a hundred and twenty-five years old when he died and they put him into a coffin, and he was given into the hands of his children.
2 In the eightieth year his brother Dan died; he was a hundred and twenty years at his death, and he was also put into a coffin and given into the hands of his children.
3 In that year Chusham king of Edom died, and after him reigned Hadad the son of

Bedad, for thirty-five years; in the eighty-first year Issachar the son of Jacob died in Egypt, and Issachar was a hundred and twenty-two years old at his death; he was put into a coffin in Egypt, and given into the hands of his children.
4 In the eighty-second year Asher his brother died, he was a hundred and twenty-three years old at his death, and he was placed in a coffin in Egypt and given into the hands of his children.
5 In the eighty-third year Gad died; he was a hundred and twenty-five years old at his death, and he was put into a coffin in Egypt and given into the hands of his children.
6 And it came to pass in the eighty-fourth year, that is the fiftieth year of the reign of Hadad, son of Bedad, king of Edom, that Hadad assembled all the children of Esau; he got his whole army in readiness, about four hundred thousand men, and he directed his way to the land of Moab; he went to fight with Moab and to make them subordinate to him.
7 The children of Moab heard this thing, and they were very much afraid; they sent to the children of Midian to assist them in fighting with Hadad, son of Bedad, king of Edom.
8 And Hadad came to the land of Moab, and Moab and the children of Midian went out to meet him; they placed themselves in battle array against him in the field of Moab.
9 Hadad fought with Moab, and there fell of the children of Moab and the children of Midian many slain ones, about two hundred thousand men.
10 The battle was very severe on Moab, and when the children of Moab saw that the battle was so severe, they weakened their hands and turned their backs, and left the children of Midian to carry on the battle.
11 And the children of Midian knew not the intentions of Moab, but they strengthened themselves in battle and fought with Hadad and all his army, and all Midian fell before him.
12 Hadad struck all Midian with a heavy smiting, and he killed them with the edge of the sword, he left none remaining of those who came to assist Moab.
13 When all the children of Midian had perished in battle, and the children at Moab had escaped, Hadad made all Moab at that time subservient to him, and they became under his hand; they gave a yearly tax as it was ordered, and Hadad turned and went back to his land.
14 At the revolution of the year, when the rest of the people of Midian that were in the land heard that all their brothers had fallen in battle with Hadad for the sake of Moab, because the children of Moab had turned their backs in battle and left Midian to fight, then five of the princes of Midian resolved with the rest of their brothers who remained in their land to fight with Moab to avenge the cause of their brothers.
15 The children of Midian sent to all their brothers the children of the east, and all their brothers, all the children of Keturah came to assist Midian to fight with Moab.
16 The children of Moab heard this thing, and they were greatly afraid that all the children of the east had assembled together against them for battle, and they the children of Moab sent a memorial to the land of Edom to Hadad the son of Bedad, saying,
17 Come now to us and assist us and we will strike Midian, for they all assembled together and have come against us with all their brothers the children of the east to battle, to avenge the cause of Midian that fell in battle.
18 Hadad, son of Bedad, king of Edom, went forth with his whole army and went to

the land of Moab to fight with Midian, and Midian and the children of the east fought with Moab in the field of Moab, and the battle was very fierce between them.
19 Hadad struck all the children of Midian and the children of the east with the edge of the sword, and Hadad at that time delivered Moab from the hand of Midian; those that remained of Midian and of the children of the east fled before Hadad and his army, and Hadad pursued them to their land and struck them with a very heavy slaughter, and the slain fell in the road.
20 Hadad delivered Moab from the hand of Midian, for all the children of Midian had fallen by the edge of the sword, and Hadad turned and went back to his land.
21 And from that day forth, the children of Midian hated the children of Moab because they had fallen in battle for their sake, and there was a great and mighty enmity between them all the days.
22 And all that were found of Midian in the road of the land of Moab perished by the sword of Moab, and all that were found of Moab in the road of the land of Midian, perished by the sword of Midian; thus did Midian to Moab and Moab to Midian for many days.
23 It came to pass at that time that Judah the son of Jacob died in Egypt, in the eighty-sixth year of Jacob's going down to Egypt, and Judah was a hundred and twenty-nine years old at his death, and they embalmed him and put him into a coffin, and he was given into the hands of his children.
24 And in the eighty-ninth year Naphtali died; he was a hundred and thirty-two years old, and he was put into a coffin and given into the hands of his children.
25 It came to pass in the ninety-first year of the Israelites going down to Egypt, that is in the thirtieth year of the reign of Zepho the son of Eliphaz, the son of Esau, over the children of Chittim, the children of Africa came upon the children of Chittim to rob them as usual, but they had not come on them for these thirteen years.
26 They came to them in that year, and Zepho the son of Eliphaz went out to them with some of his men and struck them desperately, and the troops of Africa fled from before Zepho and the slain fell before him, and Zepho and his men pursued them, going on and smiting them until they were near to Africa.
27 And Angeas king of Africa heard the thing which Zepho had done, and it troubled him greatly, and Angeas was afraid of Zepho all the days.

CHAPTER 63

1 In the ninety-third year Levi, the son of Jacob, died in Egypt, and Levi was a hundred and thirty-seven years old when he died; they put him into a coffin and he was given into the hands of his children.
2 It came to pass after the death of Levi, when all Egypt saw that the sons of Jacob the brothers of Joseph were dead, all the Egyptians began to afflict the children of Jacob, and to embitter their lives from that day to the day of their going forth from Egypt. They took from their hands all the vineyards and fields which Joseph had given to them, and all the elegant houses in which the people of Israel lived, and all the valuables of Egypt, the Egyptians took all from the sons of Jacob in those days.
3 And the hand of all Egypt became more heavy in those days against the children of Israel, and the Egyptians injured the Israelites until the children of Israel were wearied of their lives on account of the Egyptians.
4 It came to pass in those days, in the hundred and second year of Israel's going

down to Egypt, that Pharaoh king of Egypt died, and Melol his son reigned in his stead; all the mighty men of Egypt and all that generation which knew Joseph and his brothers died in those days.
5 And another generation rose up in their stead, which had not known the sons of Jacob and all the good which they had done to them, and all their might in Egypt.
6 And so all Egypt began from that day on to embitter the lives of the sons of Jacob, and to afflict them with all manner of hard labor, because they had not known their ancestors who had delivered them in the days of the famine.
7 This was also from the Lord for the children of Israel, to benefit them in their latter days in order that all the children of Israel might know the Lord their God.
8 And in order to know the signs and mighty wonders which the Lord would do in Egypt on account of his people Israel, in order that the children of Israel might fear the Lord God of their ancestors, and walk in all his ways, they and their descendants after them all the days.
9 Melol was twenty years old when he began to reign, and he reigned ninety-four years, and all Egypt called his name Pharaoh after the name of his father, as it was their custom to do to every king who reigned over them in Egypt.
10 At that time all the troops of Angeas king of Africa went forth to scatter along the land of Chittim as usual for robbery.
11 Zepho the son of Eliphaz the son of Esau heard their report, and he went forth to meet them with his army, and he fought them there in the road.
12 Zepho struck the troops of the king of Africa with the edge of the sword, and left none remaining of them, and not even one returned to his master in Africa.
13 Angeas heard of this which Zepho the son of Eliphaz had done to all his troops, that he had destroyed them, and Angeas assembled all his troops, all the men of the land of Africa, a people numerous like the sand by the seashore.
14 And Angeas sent to Lucus his brother, saying, Come to me with all your men and help me to strike Zepho and all the children of Chittim who have destroyed my men; Lucus came with his whole army, a very great force, to assist Angeas his brother to fight with Zepho and the children of Chittim.
15 Zepho and the children of Chittim heard this thing, and they were greatly afraid and a great terror fell on their hearts.
16 Zepho also sent a letter to the land of Edom to Hadad the son of Bedad king of Edom and to all the children of Esau, saying,
17 I have heard that Angeas king of Africa is coming to us with his brother for battle against us, and we are greatly afraid of him, for his army is very great, particularly as he comes against us with his brother and his army likewise.
18 Now therefore come up also with me and help me, and we will fight together against Angeas and his brother Lucus, and you will save us out of their hands, but if not, know that we shall all die.
19 And the children of Esau sent a letter to the children of Chittim and to Zepho their king, saying, We cannot fight against Angeas and his people for a covenant of peace has been between us these many years, from the days of Bela the first king, and from the days of Joseph the son of Jacob king of Egypt with whom we fought on the other side of Jordan when he buried his father.
20 When Zepho heard the words of his brothers the children of Esau, he refrained from them, and Zepho was greatly afraid of Angeas.
21 And Angeas and Lucus his brother arrayed all their forces, about eight hundred thousand men, against the children of Chittim.

22 And all the children of Chittim said to Zepho, Pray for us to the God of your
ancestors, perhaps he may deliver us from the hand of Angeas and his army, for we
have heard that he is a great God and that he delivers all who trust in him.
23 Zepho heard their words, and Zepho sought the Lord and he said,
24 0 Lord God of Abraham and Isaac my ancestors, this day I know that you are a
true God, and all the gods of the nations are vain and useless.
25 Remember now this day to me your covenant with Abraham our father, which
our ancestors related to us, and do graciously with me this day for the sake of
Abraham and Isaac our fathers; save me and the children of Chittim from the hand
of the king of Africa who comes against us for battle.
26 And the Lord listened to the voice of Zepho, and he had regard for him on
account of Abraham and Isaac, and the Lord delivered Zepho and the children of
Chittim from the hand of Angeas and his people.
27 Zepho fought Angeas king of Africa and all his people on that day, and the Lord
gave all the people of Angeas into the hands of the children of Chittim.
28 The battle was severe on Angeas, and Zepho struck all the men of Angeas and
Lucus his brother with the edge of the sword, and there fell from them to the
evening of that day about four hundred thousand men.
29 When Angeas saw that all his men perished, he sent a letter to all the inhabitants
of Africa to come to him, to assist him in the battle, and he wrote in the letter, saying,
All who are found in Africa let them come to me from ten years old and upward; let
them all come to me, and behold if he comes not he shall die; all that he has, with his
whole household, the king will take.
30 All the rest of the inhabitants of Africa were terrified at the words of Angeas, and
there went out of the city about three hundred thousand men and boys, from ten
years upward, and they came to Angeas.
31 And at the end of ten days Angeas renewed the battle against Zepho and the
children of Chittim, and the battle was very great and strong between them.
32 And from the army of Angeas and Lucus, Zepho sent many of the wounded to
him about two thousand men, and Sosiphtar the captain of the host of Angeas fell in
that battle.
33 And when Sosiphtar had fallen, the African troops turned their backs to flee; they
fled, and Angeas and Lucus his brother were with them.
34 Zepho and the children of Chittim pursued them, and they struck them still
heavily on the road, about two hundred men; they pursued Azdrubal the son of
Angeas who had fled with his father, and they struck twenty of his men in the road,
and Azdrubal escaped from the children of Chittim, and they did not kill him.
35 Angeas and Lucus his brother fled with the rest of their men, and they escaped
and came into Africa with terror and consternation, and Angeas feared all the days
that Zepho the son of Eliphaz would go to war with him.

CHAPTER 64

1 Balaam the son of Beor was at that time with Angeas in the battle, and when he
saw that Zepho conquered over Angeas, he fled from there and came to Chittim.
2 And Zepho and the children of Chittim received him with great honor, for Zepho
knew Balaam's wisdom, and Zepho gave to Balaam many gifts and he remained
with him.

3 When Zepho had returned from the war, he commanded all the children of Chittim to be numbered who had gone into battle with him, and there not one was missing.
4 Zepho rejoiced at this thing, and he renewed his kingdom, and he made a feast to all his subjects.
5 But Zepho remembered not the Lord and considered not that the Lord had helped him in battle, and that he had delivered him and his people from the hand of the king of Africa; he still walked in the ways of the children of Chittim and the wicked children of Esau to serve other gods which his brothers the children of Esau had taught him; it is therefore said, From the wicked goes forth wickedness.
6 Zepho reigned over all the children of Chittim securely, but knew not the Lord who had delivered him and all his people from the hand of the king of Africa; the troops of Africa came no more to Chittim to rob as usual, for they knew the power of Zepho who had smitten them all at the edge of the sword, so Angeas was afraid of Zepho the son of Eliphaz and the children of Chittim all the days.
7 At that time when Zepho had returned from the war, and when Zepho had seen how he conquered over all the people of Africa and had smitten them in battle at the edge of the sword, then Zepho advised with the children of Chittim to go to Egypt to fight with the sons of Jacob and with Pharaoh king of Egypt.
8 For Zepho heard that the mighty men of Egypt were dead and that Joseph and his brothers the sons of Jacob were dead, and that all their children, the children of Israel, remained in Egypt.
9 Zepho considered to go to fight against them and all Egypt to avenge the cause of his brothers the children of Esau, whom Joseph with his brothers and all Egypt had smitten in the land of Canaan, when they went up to bury Jacob in Hebron.
10 And Zepho sent messengers to Hadad, son of Bedad, king of Edom, and to all his brothers the children of Esau, saying,
11 Did you say that you would not fight against the king of Africa for he is a member of your covenant? Consider that I fought with him and struck him and all his people.
12 Now therefore I have resolved to fight against Egypt and the children of Jacob who are there, and I will be revenged of them for what Joseph, his brothers and ancestors did to us in the land of Canaan when they went up to bury their father in Hebron.
13 Now then if you are willing to come to me to assist me in fighting against them and Egypt, we shall avenge the cause of our brothers.
14 And the children of Esau listened to the words of Zepho, and the children of Esau gathered themselves together, a very great people; they went to assist Zepho and the children of Chittim in battle.
15 Zepho sent to all the children of the east and to all the children of Ishmael with words like these, and they gathered themselves and came to the assistance of Zepho and the children of Chittim in the war on Egypt.
16 And all these kings, the king of Edom and the children of the east, and all the children of Ishmael, and Zepho the king of Chittim went forth and arrayed all their hosts in Hebron.
17 The camp was very large, extending in length a distance of three days' journey, a people numerous as the sand on the seashore which cannot be counted.
18 And all these kings and their hosts went down and came against all Egypt in battle, and encamped together in the valley of Pathros.

19 All Egypt heard their report and they also gathered themselves together, all the people of the land of Egypt, and of all the cities belonging to Egypt about three hundred thousand men.
20 The men of Egypt sent also to the children of Israel who were in those days in the land of Goshen, to come to them in order to go and fight with these kings.
21 The men of Israel assembled and were about one hundred and fifty men, and they went into battle to assist the Egyptians.
22 The men of Israel and of Egypt went forth, about three hundred thousand men and one hundred and fifty men, and they went toward these kings to battle; they placed themselves outside the land of Goshen opposite Pathros.
23 The Egyptians believed not in Israel to go with them in their camps together for battle, for all the Egyptians said, Perhaps the children of Israel will deliver us into the hand of the children of Esau and Ishmael, for they are their brothers.
24 And all the Egyptians said to the children of Israel, Remain here together in your stand and we will go and fight against the children of Esau and Ishmael; if these kings should gain over us, then you all come together on them and assist us, and the children of Israel did so.
25 Zepho the son of Eliphaz the son of Esau king of Chittim and Hadad the son of Bedad king of Edom and all their camps, and all the children of the east, and children of Ishmael, a people numerous as sand, encamped together in the valley of Pathros opposite Tachpanches.
26 Balaam the son of Beor the Syrian was there in the camp of Zepho, for he came with the children of Chittim to the battle, and Balaam was a man highly honored in the eyes of Zepho and his men.
27 Zepho said to Balaam, Try by divination for us that we may know who will win the battle, we or the Egyptians.
28 And Balaam rose up and tried the art of divination, and he was skillful in the knowledge of it, but he was confused and the work was destroyed in his hand.
29 And he tried it again but it did not succeed; Balaam despaired of it and left it and did not complete it, for this was from the Lord in order to cause Zepho and his people to fall into the hand of the children of Israel, who had trusted in the Lord, the God of their ancestors, in their war.
30 Zepho and Hadad put their forces in battle array, and all the Egyptians went alone against them, about three hundred thousand men, and not one man of Israel was with them.
31 All the Egyptians fought with these kings opposite Pathros and Tachpanches, and the battle was severe against the Egyptians.
32 The kings were stronger than the Egyptians in that battle, and about one hundred and eighty men of Egypt fell on that day, and about thirty men of the forces of the kings, and all the men of Egypt fled from before the king; so the children of Esau and Ishmael pursued the Egyptians, continuing to strike them to the place where the camp of the children of Israel was.
33 And all the Egyptians cried to the children of Israel, saying, Hurry to us and assist us and save us from the hand of Esau, Ishmael and the children of Chittim.
34 The hundred and fifty men of the children of Israel ran from their station to the camps of these kings, and the children of Israel cried to the Lord their God to deliver them.
35 And the Lord listened to Israel, and the Lord gave all the men of the kings into their hands, and the children of Israel fought against these kings; the children of

Israel struck about four thousand of the kings' men.
36 The Lord threw a great consternation into the camp of the kings, so that the fear of the children of Israel fell on them.
37 And all the hosts of the kings fled from before the children of Israel and the children of Israel pursued them continuing to strike them to the borders of the land of Cush.
38 The children of Israel killed of them in the road two thousand men, and of the children of Israel not one fell.
39 When the Egyptians saw that the children of Israel had fought with such few men with the kings, and that the battle was so very severe against them,
40 All the Egyptians were greatly afraid of their lives on account of the strong battle, and all Egypt fled, every man hiding himself from the arrayed forces; they hid themselves in the road, and they left the Israelites to fight alone.
41 And the children of Israel inflicted a terrible blow on the kings' men, and they returned from them after they had driven them to the border of the land of Cush.
42 All Israel knew the thing which the men of Egypt had done to them, that they had fled from them in battle, and had left them to fight alone.
43 So the children of Israel also acted with cunning, and as the children of Israel returned from battle, they found some of the Egyptians in the road and struck them there.
44 And while they killed them, they said to them these words:
45 Why did you go from us and leave us, being a few people to fight against these kings who had many people to strike us, that you might thereby save your own souls?
46 And of some which the Israelites met on the road, the children of Israel spoke to each other, saying, Smite, strike, for he is an Ishmaelite, or an Edomite, or from the children of Chittim; they stood over him and killed him, and they knew that he was an Egyptian.
47 The children of Israel did these things cunningly against the Egyptians because they had deserted in battle and had fled from them.
48 And the children of Israel killed of the men of Egypt in the road in this manner about two hundred men.
49 All the men of Egypt saw the evil which the children of Israel had done to them, so all Egypt feared greatly the children of Israel, for they had seen their great power and that not one man of them had fallen.
50 So all the children of Israel returned with joy on their road to Goshen, and the rest of Egypt returned each man to his place.

CHAPTER 65

1 It came to pass after these things that all the counselors of Pharaoh, king of Egypt, and all the elders of Egypt assembled and came before the king and bowed down to the ground, and they sat before him.
2 And the counselors and elders of Egypt spoke to the king, saying,
3 Behold the people of the children of Israel is greater and mightier than we are, and you know all the evil which they did to us in the road when we returned from battle.
4 And you have also seen their strong power, for this power is to them from their fathers, for only a few men stood up against a people numerous as the sand, and

struck them at the edge of the sword; of themselves not one has fallen, so that if they had been numerous they would then have utterly destroyed them.
5 Now therefore give us counsel what to do with them, until we gradually destroy them from among us so they don't become too numerous for us in the land.
6 For if the children of Israel should increase in the land, they will become an obstacle to us; if any war should happen to take place, they with their great strength will join our enemy against us, and fight against us, destroy us from the land and go away from it.
7 So the king answered the elders of Egypt and said to them, This is the plan advised against Israel, from which we will not depart,
8 Consider in the land are Pithom and Rameses, cities unfortified against battle; it's best for you and us to build them, and to fortify them.
9 Now go also and act cunningly toward them, and proclaim a voice in Egypt and in Goshen at the command of the king, saying,
10 All ye men of Egypt, Goshen, Pathros and all their inhabitants! The king has commanded us to build Pithom and Rameses and to fortify them for battle; those among you of all Egypt, of the children of Israel and of all the inhabitants of the cities who are willing to build with us, you shall each have his wages given to him daily at the king's order. So go first and do cunningly and gather yourselves to come to Pithom and Rameses to build.
11 And while you are building, cause an announcement of this kind to be made throughout Egypt every day at the command of the king.
12 When some of the children of Israel shall come to build with you, you shall give them their wages daily for a few days.
13 And after they have built with you for their daily hire, drag yourselves away from them daily one by one in secret, and then you shall rise up and become their taskmasters and officers; you shall leave them afterward to build without wages; should they refuse, then force them with all your might to build.
14 And if you do this it will be well with us to strengthen our land against the children of Israel, for on account of the fatigue of the building and the work, the children of Israel will decrease, because you will deprive them of their wives day by day.
15 And all the elders of Egypt heard the counsel of the king, and the counsel seemed good in their eyes and in the eyes of the servants of Pharaoh, and in the eyes of all Egypt; they did according to the word of the king.
16 And all the servants went away from the king; they caused an announcement to be made in all Egypt, in Tachpanches and in Goshen, and in all the cities which surrounded Egypt, saying,
17 You have seen what the children of Esau and Ishmael did to us, who came to war against us and wished to destroy us.
18 Now therefore the king commanded us to fortify the land, to build the cities Pithom and Rameses, and to fortify them for battle, if they should again come against us.
19 Whoever of you from all Egypt and from the children of Israel will come to build with us, he shall have his daily wages given by the king, as his command is to us.
20 And when Egypt and all the children of Israel heard all that the servants of Pharaoh had spoken, there came persons from the Egyptians and the children of Israel to build with the servants of Pharaoh, Pithom and Rameses, but none of the children of Levi came with their brothers to build.

21 All the servants of Pharaoh and his princes came at first with deceit to build with all Israel as daily hired laborers, and they gave to Israel their daily hire at the beginning.
22 And the servants of Pharaoh built with all Israel, and were employed in that work with Israel for a month.
23 And at the end of the month, all the servants of Pharaoh began to withdraw secretly from the people of Israel daily.
24 And Israel went on with the work at that time, but they then received their daily wage, because some of the men of Egypt were yet carrying on the work with Israel at that time; therefore the Egyptians gave Israel their wage in those days in order that they, the Egyptians their fellow-workmen, might also take the pay for their labor.
25 At the end of a year and four months all the Egyptians had withdrawn from the children of Israel, so that the children of Israel were left alone engaged in the work.
26 And after all the Egyptians had withdrawn from the children of Israel they returned and became oppressors and officers over them, and some of them stood over the children of Israel as task masters, to receive from them all that they gave them for the pay of their labor.
27 And the Egyptians did in this manner to the children of Israel day by day, in order to afflict them in their work.
28 And all the children of Israel were alone engaged in the labor, and the Egyptians refrained from giving any pay to the children of Israel from that time forward.
29 When some of the men of Israel refused to work on account of the wages not being given to them, the exactors and the servants of Pharaoh oppressed them and struck them with heavy blows, and made them return by force to labor with their brothers; thus did all the Egyptians to the children of Israel all the days.
30 And all the children of Israel were greatly afraid of the Egyptians in this matter, and all the children of Israel returned and worked alone without pay.
31 The children of Israel built Pithom and Rameses; all the children of Israel did the work, some making bricks, and some building, and the children of Israel built and fortified all the land of Egypt and its walls. The children of Israel were engaged in work for many years, until the time came when the Lord remembered them and brought them out of Egypt.
32 But the children of Levi were not employed in the work with their brothers of Israel from the beginning to the day of their going forth from Egypt.
33 For all the children of Levi knew that the Egyptians had spoken all these words with deceit to the Israelites, therefore the children of Levi refrained from approaching the work with their brothers.
34 The Egyptians did not direct their attention to make the children of Levi work afterward, since they had not been with their brothers at the beginning, therefore the Egyptians left them alone.
35 And the hands of the men of Egypt were directed with continued severity against the children of Israel in that work, and the Egyptians made the children of Israel work with rigor.
36 The Egyptians embittered the lives of the children of Israel with hard work in mortar and bricks, and also in all manner of work in the field.
37 The children of Israel called Melol the king of Egypt "Meror, king of Egypt," because in his days the Egyptians had embittered their lives with all manner of work.
38 And all the work wherein the Egyptians made the children of Israel labor, they

exacted with rigor, in order to afflict the children of Israel. But the more they afflicted them, the more they increased and grew, and the Egyptians were grieved because of the children of Israel.

CHAPTER 66

1 At that time Hadad the son of Bedad king of Edom died; Samlah from Mesrekah,
from the country of the children of the east, reigned in his place.
2 In the thirteenth year of the reign of Pharaoh king of Egypt, which was the
hundred and twenty-fifth year of the Israelites going down into Egypt, Samlah had
reigned over Edom eighteen years.
3 And when he reigned, he brought forth his army to go and fight against Zepho the
son of Eliphaz and the children of Chittim, because they had made war against
Angeas king of Africa, and they destroyed his whole army.
4 But he did not engage with him, for the children of Esau prevented him, saying, he
was their brother; so Samlah listened to the voice of the children of Esau and turned
back with all his forces to the land of Edom, and did not proceed to fight against
Zepho the son of Eliphaz.
5 And Pharaoh king of Egypt heard this thing, saying, Samlah king of Edom has
resolved to fight the children of Chittim, and afterward he will come to fight against
Egypt.
6 When the Egyptians heard this matter, they increased the labor on the children of
Israel, that the Israelites should do to them as they did to them in their war with the
children of Esau in the days of Hadad.
7 So the Egyptians said to the children of Israel, Hurry and do your work, and finish
your task, and strengthen the land, should the children of Esau your brothers come
to fight against us, for on your account will they come against us.
8 And the children of Israel did the work of the men of Egypt day by day, and the
Egyptians afflicted the children of Israel in order to lessen them in the land.
9 But as the Egyptians increased the labor on the children of Israel, so did the
children of Israel increase and reproduce, and all Egypt was filled with the children
of Israel.
10 And in the hundred and twenty-fifth year of Israel's going down into Egypt, all
the Egyptians saw that their counsel did not succeed against Israel, but that they
increased and grew and the land of Egypt and the land of Goshen were filled with
the children of Israel.
11 So all the elders of Egypt and its wise men came before the king and bowed down
to him and sat before him.
12 And all the elders of Egypt and the wise men there said to the king, May the king
live forever; you did counsel us the counsel against the children of Israel, and we did
to them according to the word of the king.
13 But in proportion to the increase of the labor so do they increase and grow in the
land, and look the whole country is filled with them.
14 So now our lord and king, the eyes of all Egypt are on you to give them advice
with your wisdom, by which they may rule over Israel to destroy them, or to
diminish them from the land; the king answered them saying, Give your counsel in
this matter that we may know what to do to them.
15 And an officer, one of the king's counselors, whose name was Job, from

Mesopotamia, in the land of Uz, answered the king, saying,
16 If it please the king, let him hear the counsel of his servant; the king said to him, Speak.
17 And Job spoke before the king, the princes, and before all the elders of Egypt, saying,
18 Behold the counsel of the king which he advised formerly respecting the labor of the children of Israel is very good, and you must not remove from them that labor forever.
19 But this is the advice counselled by which you may lessen them, if it seems good to the king to afflict them.
20 Behold we have feared war for a long time, and we said, When Israel becomes prolific in the land, they will drive us from the land if a war would take place.
21 If it please the king, let a royal decree go forth, and let it be written in the laws of Egypt which shall not be revoked, that every male child born to the Israelites, his blood shall be spilled on the ground.
22 And by your doing this, when all the male children of Israel will have died, the evil of their wars will cease; let the king do so and send for all the Hebrew midwives and order them in this matter to execute it. So the thing pleased the king and the prince; the king did according to the word of Job.
23 The king sent for the Hebrew midwives to be called, of which the name of one was Shephrah, and the name of the other Puah.
24 And the midwives came before the king, and stood in his presence.
25 the king said to them, When you do the office of a midwife to the Hebrew women, and see them on the stools, if it be a son then you shall kill him, but if it be a daughter then she shall live.
26 But if you will not do this thing, then will I burn you up and all your houses with fire.
27 But the midwives feared God and did not listen to the king of Egypt nor to his words; when the Hebrew women brought forth to the midwife son or daughter, then did the midwife do all that was necessary to the child and let it live; thus did the midwives all the days.
28 And this thing was told to the king, and he sent and called for the midwives and he said to them, Why have you done this thing and have saved the children alive?
29 And the midwives answered and spoke together before the king, saying,
30 Let not the king think that the Hebrew women are as the Egyptian women, for all the children of Israel are vigorous, and before the midwife comes to them they are delivered, and as for us your handmaids, for many days no Hebrew woman has brought forth on us, for all the Hebrew women are their own midwives, because they are vigorous.
31 And Pharaoh heard their words and believed them in this matter, and the midwives went away from the king, and God dealt well with them; the people multiplied and increased greatly.

CHAPTER 67

1 There was a man in the land of Egypt of the children of Levi, whose name was Amram, the son of Kehath, the son of Levi, the son of Israel.
2 And this man went and took a wife, namely Jochebed the daughter of Levi his

father's sister, and she was one hundred and twenty-six years old, and he came to her.
3 And the woman conceived and gave birth to a daughter, and she called her name Miriam, because in those days the Egyptians had embittered the lives of the children of Israel.
4 She conceived again and gave birth to a son and she called his name Aaron, for in the days of her conception, Pharaoh began to spill the blood of the male children of Israel.
5 In those days Zepho died, the son of Eliphaz, son of Esau, king of Chittim; Janeas reigned in his stead.
6 And the time that Zepho reigned over the children of Chittim was fifty years, and he died and was buried in the city of Nabna in the land of Chittim.
7 And Janeas, one of the mighty men of the children of Chittim, reigned after him for fifty years.
8 It was after the death of the king of Chittim that Balaam the son of Beor fled from the land of Chittim, and he went and came to Egypt to Pharaoh king of Egypt.
9 Pharaoh received him with great honor for he had heard of his wisdom, and he gave him presents and made him a counsellor and praised him.
10 Balaam lived in Egypt, in honor with all the nobles of the king, and the nobles exalted him, because they all coveted to learn his wisdom.
11 And in the hundred and thirtieth year of Israel's going down to Egypt, Pharaoh dreamed that he was sitting on his kingly throne, and lifted up his eyes and saw an old man standing before him; there were scales in the hands of the old man, such scales as are used by merchants.
12 And the old man took the scales and hung them before Pharaoh.
13 And the old man took all the elders of Egypt and all its nobles and great men, and he tied them together and put them in one scale.
14 And he took a milk kid and put it into the other scale, and the kid's weight surpassed all.
15 And Pharaoh was astonished at this dreadful vision, why the kid should surpass all, and Pharaoh awoke and behold it was a dream.
16 Pharaoh rose up early in the morning and called all his servants and related to them the dream, and the men were greatly afraid.
17 And the king said to all his wise men, Interpret I pray you the dream which I dreamed, that I may know it.
18 Balaam the son of Beor answered the king and said to him, This means nothing else but a great evil that will spring up against Egypt in the latter days.
19 For a son will be born to Israel who will destroy all Egypt and its inhabitants, and bring forth the Israelites from Egypt with a mighty hand.
20 Now therefore, O king, take counsel on this matter, that you may destroy the hope of the children of Israel and their expectation, before this evil arises against Egypt.
21 And the king said to Balaam, And what shall we do to Israel? Certainly after a certain manner did we at first counsel against them and could not succeed over them.
22 So now you also give advice against them by which we may succeed over them.
23 Balaam answered the king, saying, Send now and call your two counselors, and we will see what their advice is on this matter and afterward your servant will speak.

24 And the king sent and called his two counselors Reuel the Midianite and Job the
Uzite, and they came and sat before the king.
25 And the king said to them, Behold you have both heard the dream which I have
dreamed, and the interpretation thereof; so now give counsel and know and see
what is to be done to the children of Israel, whereby we may succeed over them,
before their evil will spring up against us.
26 And Reuel the Midianite answered the king and said, May the king live, may the
king live forever.
27 If it seems good to the king, let him desist from the Hebrews and leave them, and
let him not stretch forth his hand against them.
28 For these are they whom the Lord chose in days of old, and took as the lot of his
inheritance from among all the nations of the earth and the kings of the earth; and
who is there that stretched his hand against them with punishment, of whom their
God was not avenged?
29 Certainly you know that when Abraham went down to Egypt, Pharaoh, the
former king of Egypt, saw Sarah his wife, and took her for a wife, because Abraham
said, She is my sister, for he was afraid that the men of Egypt should kill him on
account of his wife.
30 And when the king of Egypt had taken Sarah then God struck him and his
household with heavy plagues, until he restored to Abraham his wife Sarah, then
was he healed.
31 And Abimelech the Gerarite, king of the Philistines, God punished on account of
Sarah wife of Abraham, in stopping up every womb from man to beast.
32 When their God came to Abimelech in the dream of night and terrified him in
order that he might restore to Abraham Sarah whom he had taken, afterward all the
people of Gerar were punished on account of Sarah, and Abraham prayed to his God
for them, and he was entreated of him, and he healed them.
33 And Abimelech feared all this evil that came on him and his people, and he
returned to Abraham his wife Sarah, and gave him many gifts with her.
34 He did so also to Isaac when he had driven him from Gerar, and God had done
wonderful things to him, that all the water courses of Gerar were dried up and their
productive trees did not bring forth.
35 Until Abimelech of Gerar, and Ahuzzath one of his friends, and Pichol the captain
of his host, went to him and they bent and bowed down before him to the ground.
36 They requested of him to petition for them, and he prayed to the Lord for them,
and the Lord was entreated of him and he healed them.
37 Jacob also, the plain man, was delivered through his integrity from the hand of
his brother Esau, and the hand of Laban the Syrian his mother's brother, who had
sought his life; likewise from the hand of all the kings of Canaan who had come
together against him and his children to destroy them, the Lord delivered them out
of their hands, that they turned on them and struck them, for who had ever stretched
forth his hand against them without penalty?
38 Certainly Pharaoh the former, your father's father, raised Joseph the son of Jacob
above all the princes of the land of Egypt when he saw his wisdom, for through his
wisdom he rescued all the inhabitants of the land from the famine.
39 After which he ordered Jacob and his children to come down to Egypt in order
that through their virtue, the land of Egypt and the land of Goshen might be
delivered from the famine.
40 So now if it seems good in your eyes, cease from destroying the children of Israel,

but if it be not your will that they shall dwell in Egypt, send them forth from here that they may go to the land of Canaan, the land where their ancestors sojourned.
41 And when Pharaoh heard the words of Jethro he was very angry with him, so that he rose with shame from the king's presence and went to Midian, his land, and took Joseph's stick with him.
42 And the king said to Job the Uzite, What do you say Job, and what is your advice respecting the Hebrews?
43 So Job said to the king, Behold all the inhabitants of the land are in your power, let the king do as it seems good in his eyes.
44 And the king said to Balaam, What do you say, Balaam? Speak your word that we may hear it.
45 And Balaam said to the king, Of all that the king has counselled against the Hebrews will they be delivered, and the king will not be able to prevail over them with any counsel.
46 For if you think to lessen them by the flaming fire, you cannot prevail over them, for certainly their God delivered Abraham their father from Ur of the Chaldeans; if you think to destroy them with a sword, certainly Isaac their father was delivered from it and a ram was placed in his stead.
47 And if with hard and rigorous labor you think to lessen them, you will not prevail even in this, for their father Jacob served Laban in all manner of hard work and prospered.
48 Now therefore, O King, hear my words, for this is the counsel which is counselled against them, by which you will prevail over them, and from which you should not depart:
49 If it please the king let him order all their children which shall be born from this day forward to be thrown into the water, for by this can you wipe away their name, for none of them nor of their fathers were tried in this manner.
50 And the king heard the words of Balaam, and the thing pleased the king and the princes, and the king did according to the word of Balaam.
51 The king ordered an announcement to be issued and a law to be made throughout the land of Egypt, saying, Every male child born to the Hebrews from this day forward shall be thrown into the water.
52 Pharaoh called to all his servants, saying, Go now and search throughout the land of Goshen where the children of Israel are, and see that every son born to the Hebrews will be cast into the river, but every daughter you shall let live.
53 And when the children of Israel heard this thing which Pharaoh had commanded, to cast their male children into the river, some of the people separated from their wives and others adhered to them.
54 And from that day forward, when the time of delivery arrived to those women of Israel who had remained with their husbands, they went to the field to bring forth there, and they brought forth in the field and left their children on the field and returned home.
55 And the Lord who had sworn to their ancestors to reproduce them sent one of his ministering angels which are in heaven to wash each child in water, to anoint and swathe it and to put into its hands two smooth stones from one of which it sucked milk and from the other honey, and he caused its hair to grow to its knees, by which it might cover itself; to comfort it and to cleave to it through his compassion for it.
56 And when God had compassion over them and had desired to reproduce them on the face of the land, he ordered his earth to receive them to be preserved therein till

the time of their growing up, after which the earth opened its mouth and vomited them forth and they sprouted forth from the city like the herb of the earth, and the grass of the forest, and they returned each to his family and to his father's house, and they remained with them.
57 And the babes of the children of Israel were on the earth like the herb of the field, through God's grace to them.
58 And when all the Egyptians saw this thing, they went forth, each to his field with his yoke of oxen and his ploughshare, and they plowed it up as one ploughs the earth at offspring time.
59 And when they plowed they were unable to hurt the infants of the children of Israel, so the people increased and thrived greatly.
60 And Pharaoh ordered his officers daily to go to Goshen to seek for the babes of the children of Israel.
61 And when they had sought and found one, they took it from its mother's bosom by force, and threw it into the river, but the female child they left with its mother; thus did the Egyptians do to the Israelites all the days.

CHAPTER 68

1 It was at that time the spirit of God was on Miriam the daughter of Amram the sister of Aaron, and she went forth and prophesied about the house, saying, Behold a son will be born to us from my father and mother this time, and he will save Israel from the hands of Egypt.
2 And when Amram heard the words of his daughter, he went and took his wife back to the house, after he had driven her away at the time when Pharaoh ordered every male child of the house of Jacob to be thrown into the water.
3 So Amram took Jochebed his wife, three years after he had driven her away, and he came to her and she conceived.
4 At the end of seven months from her conception she brought forth a son, and the whole house was filled with great light as of the light of the sun and moon at the time of their shining.
5 And when the woman saw the child that it was good and pleasing to the sight, she hid him for three months in an inner room.
6 In those days the Egyptians conspired to destroy all the Hebrews there.
7 And the Egyptian women went to Goshen where the children of Israel were, and they carried their young ones on their shoulders, their babes who could not yet speak.
8 And in those days, when the women of the children of Israel brought forth, each woman had hidden her son from the Egyptians, that the Egyptians might not know of their bringing forth, and might not destroy them from the land.
9 And the Egyptian women came to Goshen and their children who could not speak were on their shoulders, and when an Egyptian woman came into the house of a Hebrew woman her babe began to cry.
10 And when it cried the child that was in the inner room answered it, so the Egyptian women went and told it at the house of Pharaoh.
11 And Pharaoh sent his officers to take the children and kill them; thus did the Egyptians to the Hebrew women all the days.
12 And it was at that time, about three months from Jochebed's concealment of her

son, that the thing was known in Pharaoh's house.
13 And the woman hurried to take away her son before the officers came, and she took for him an ark of bulrushes, and daubed it with slime and with pitch and put the child therein, and she laid it in the flags by the river's brink.
14 And his sister Miriam stood afar off to learn what would be done to him, and what would become of her words.
15 And God sent forth at that time a terrible heat in the land of Egypt, which burned up the flesh of man like the sun in his circuit, and it greatly oppressed the Egyptians.
16 And all the Egyptians went down to bathe in the river on account of the consuming heat which burned up their flesh.
17 And Bathia, the daughter of Pharaoh, went also to bathe in the river, owing to the consuming heat; her maidens walked at the riverside, and all the women of Egypt as well.
18 Bathia lifted up her eyes to the river and she saw the ark on the water, and sent her maid to
fetch it.
19 She opened it and saw the child, and then the babe wept, and she had compassion on him and said, This is one of the Hebrew children.
20 And all the women of Egypt walking on the riverside desired to give him suck, but he would not suck, for this thing was from the Lord in order to restore him to his mother's breast.
21 And Miriam his sister was at that time among the Egyptian women at the riverside, and she saw this thing and said to Pharaoh's daughter, Shall I go and fetch a nurse of the Hebrew women, that she may nurse the child for you?
22 And Pharaoh's daughter said to her, Go, and the young woman went and called the child's mother.
23 And Pharaoh's daughter said to Jochebed, Take this child away and suckle it for me, and I will pay you your wages, two bits of silver daily; and the woman took the child and nursed it.
24 At the end of two years, when the child grew up, she brought him to the daughter of Pharaoh, and he was to her as a son; she called his name Moses, for she said, Because I drew him out of the water.
25 And Amram his father called his name Chabar, for he said, It was for him that he associated with his wife whom he had turned away.
26 And Jochebed his mother called his name Jekuthiel, Because, she said, I have hoped for him to the Almighty, and God restored him to me.
27 And Miriam his sister called him Jered, for she descended after him to the river to learn what would happen to him.
28 And Aaron his brother called his name Abi Zanuch, saying, My father left my mother and returned to her on his account.
29 And Kehath the father of Amram called his name Abigdor, because on his account did God repair the breach of the house of Jacob, that they could no longer throw their male children into the water.
30 And their nurse called him Abi Socho, saying, In his tabernacle was he hidden for three months, on account of the children of Ham.
31 And all Israel called his name Shemaiah, son of Nethanel, for they said, In his days has God heard their cries and rescued them from their oppressors.
32 And Moses was in Pharaoh's house and was to Bathia, Pharaoh's daughter, as a son, and Moses grew up among the king's children.

CHAPTER 69

1 The king of Edom died in those days, in the eighteenth year of his reign, and was buried in his temple which he had built for himself as his royal residence in the land of Edom.
2 The children of Esau sent to Pethor, which is on the river, and they fetched from there a young man of beautiful eyes and handsome, whose name was Saul; they made him king over them in the place of Samlah.
3 And Saul reigned over all the children of Esau in the land of Edom for forty years.
4 When Pharaoh king of Egypt saw that the counsel which Balaam had advised respecting the children of Israel did not succeed, but that still they were prolific, multiplied and increased throughout the land of Egypt,
5 Then Pharaoh commanded in those days that a proclamation should be issued throughout Egypt to the children of Israel, saying, No man shall lessen anything of his daily labor.
6 And the man who shall be found deficient in his labor which he performs daily, whether in mortar or in bricks, then his youngest son shall be put in their place.
7 And the labor of Egypt strengthened on the children of Israel in those days, and if one brick was deficient in any man's daily labor, the Egyptians took his youngest boy by force from his mother and put him into the building in the place of the brick which his father had left wanting.
8 And the men of Egypt did so to all the children of Israel day by day, all the days for a long period.
9 But the tribe of Levi did not at that time work with the Israelites their brothers from the beginning, for the children of Levi knew the cunning of the Egyptians which they exercised at first toward the Israelites.

CHAPTER 70

1 In the third year from the birth of Moses, Pharaoh was sitting at a banquet when Alparanith the queen was sitting at his right and Bathia at his left, and the lad Moses was lying on her bosom, and Balaam the son of Beor with his two sons, and all the princes of the kingdom were sitting at table in the king's presence.
2 And the lad stretched forth his hand on the king's head, and took the crown from the king's head and placed it on his own head.
3 When the king and princes saw the work which the boy had done, the king and princes were terrified, and one man to his neighbor expressed astonishment.
4 And the king said to the princes who were before him at table, What speak you and what say you, O ye princes, in this matter, and what is to be the judgment against the boy on account of this act?
5 And Balaam the son of Beor the magician answered before the king and princes and said, Remember now, O my lord and king, the dream which you did dream many days ago, and that which your servant interpreted to you.
6 Now therefore this is a child from the Hebrew children in whom is the spirit of God, and let not my lord the king imagine that this youngster did this thing without knowledge.

7 For he is a Hebrew boy, and wisdom and understanding are with him, although he is yet a child; with wisdom has he done this and chosen to himself the kingdom of Egypt.
8 For this is the manner of all the Hebrews to deceive kings and their nobles, to do all these things cunningly, in order to make the kings of the earth and their men tremble.
9 Certainly you know that Abraham their father acted thus, who deceived the army of Nimrod king of Babel and Abimelech king of Gerar, and that he possessed himself of the land of the children of Heth and all the kingdoms of Canaan.
10 And that he descended into Egypt and said of Sarah his wife, she is my sister, in order to mislead Egypt and her king.
11 His son Isaac also did so when he went to Gerar and lived there, and his strength prevailed over the army of Abimelech king of the Philistines.
12 He also thought of making the kingdom of the Philistines stumble, in saying that Rebecca his wife was his sister.
13 Jacob also dealt treacherously with his brother and took from his hand his birthright and his blessing.
14 He went then to Padan-aram to the house of Laban his mother's brother, and cunningly obtained from him his daughter, his cattle and all belonging to him, and fled away and returned to the land of Canaan to his father.
15 His sons sold their brother Joseph, who went down into Egypt and became a slave, and was placed in the prison house for twelve years.
16 Until the former Pharaoh dreamed dreams and withdrew him from the prison house, and magnified him above all the princes in Egypt on account of his interpreting his dreams to him.
17 And when God caused a famine throughout the land he sent for and brought his father and all his brothers, and all of his father's household, and supported them without price or reward, and bought the Egyptians for slaves.
18 Now therefore my lord king behold this child has risen up in their stead in Egypt, to do according to their deeds and to trifle with every king, prince and judge.
19 If it please the king, let us now spill his blood on the ground, that he shall not grow up and take away the government from your hand, and then the hope of Egypt perish after he shall have reigned.
20 And Balaam said to the king, Let us moreover call for all the judges of Egypt and the wise men thereof, and let us know if the judgment of death is due to this boy as you did say; then we will kill him.
21 Pharaoh sent and called for all the wise men of Egypt and they came before the king; an angel of the Lord came among them, and he was like one of the wise men of Egypt.
22 And the king said to the wise men, Certainly you have heard what this Hebrew boy who is in the house has done, and thus has Balaam judged in the matter.
23 Now you judge also and see what is due to the boy for the act he has committed.
24 And the angel, who seemed like one of the wise men of Pharaoh, answered and said as follows, before all the wise men of Egypt and before the king and the princes:
25 If it please the king let the king send for men who shall bring before him an onyx stone and a coal of fire, and place them before the child; if the child shall stretch forth his hand and take the onyx stone, then shall we know that with wisdom has the youth done all that he has done, and we must kill him.
26 But if he stretches forth his hand on the coal, then shall we know that it was not

with knowledge that he did this thing, and he shall live.
27 The thing seemed good in the eyes of the king and the princes, so the king did according to the word of the angel of the Lord.
28 The king ordered the onyx stone and coal to be brought and placed before Moses.
29 They placed the boy before them, and the lad endeavored to stretch forth his hand to the onyx stone, but the angel of the Lord took his hand and placed it on the coal, and the coal became extinguished in his hand; he lifted it up and put it into his mouth, and burned part of his lips and part of his tongue, and he became swollen in mouth and tongue.
30 And when the king and princes saw this, they knew that Moses had not acted with wisdom in taking off the crown from the king's head.
31 So the king and princes refrained from slaying the child. Moses remained in Pharaoh's house, growing up, and the Lord was with him.
32 And while the boy was in the king's house, he was robed in purple and he grew among the children of the king.
33 And when Moses grew up in the king's house, Bathia the daughter of Pharaoh considered him as a son, and all the household of Pharaoh honored him, and all the men of Egypt were afraid of him.
34 And he daily went forth and came into the land of Goshen where his brothers the children of Israel were, and Moses saw them daily in shortness of breath and hard labor.
35 And Moses asked them, saying, How is this labor assigned to you day by day?
36 And they told him all that had befallen them, and all the injunctions which Pharaoh had put on them before his birth.
37 And they told him all the counsels which Balaam the son of Beor had counselled against them, and what he had also counselled against him in order to kill him when he had taken the king's crown from off his head.
38 And when Moses heard these things his anger was set ablaze against Balaam, and he sought to kill him, and he was in ambush for him day by day.
39 Balaam was afraid of Moses, and he and his two sons rose up and went forth from Egypt, and they fled and delivered their souls and took themselves to the land of Cush to Kikianus, king of Cush.
40 And Moses was in the king's house going out and coming in; the Lord gave him favor in the eyes of Pharaoh and in the eyes of all his servants, and in the eyes of all the people of Egypt, and they loved Moses greatly.
41 The day arrived when Moses went to Goshen to see his brothers that he saw the children of Israel in their burdens and hard labor, and Moses was grieved on their account.
42 And Moses returned to Egypt and came to the house of Pharaoh, and came before the king, and Moses bowed down before the king.
43 And Moses said to Pharaoh, I pray you my lord, I have come to seek a small request from you, turn not away my face empty; and Pharaoh said to him, Speak.
44 And Moses said to Pharaoh, Let there be given to your servants the children of Israel who are in Goshen, one day to rest therein from their labor.
45 And the king answered Moses and said, Behold I have lifted up your face in this thing to grant your request.
46 And Pharaoh ordered an announcement to be issued throughout Egypt and Goshen, saying,
47 To you, all the children of Israel, thus says the king, for six days you shall do your

work and labor, but on the seventh day you shall rest and shall not preform any work, thus shall you do all the days as the king and Moses the son of Bathia have commanded.
48 And Moses rejoiced at this thing which the king had granted to him, and all the children of Israel did as Moses ordered them.
49 For this thing was from the Lord to the children of Israel, for the Lord had begun to remember the children of Israel to save them for the sake of their fathers.
50 And the Lord was with Moses and his fame went throughout Egypt.
51 And Moses became great in the eyes of all the Egyptians, and in the eyes of all the children of Israel, seeking good for his people Israel and speaking words of peace regarding them to the king.

CHAPTER 71

1 When Moses was eighteen years old he desired to see his father and mother and he went to them at Goshen, and when Moses had come near Goshen he came to the place where the children of Israel were engaged in work, and he observed their burdens, and he saw an Egyptian smiting one of his Hebrew brothers.
2 When the man who was beaten saw Moses he ran to him for help, for the man Moses was greatly respected in the house of Pharaoh, and he said to him, My lord attend to me; this Egyptian came to my house in the night, bound me, and came to my wife in my presence, and now he seeks to take my life away.
3 And when Moses heard this wicked thing, his anger was set ablaze against the Egyptian, and he turned this way and the other, and when he saw there was no man there he struck the Egyptian and hid him in the sand, and delivered the Hebrew from the hand of him that struck him.
4 And the Hebrew went to his house, and Moses returned to his home, and went forth and came back to the king's house.
5 And when the man had returned home, he thought of leaving his wife, for it was not right in the house of Jacob for any man to come to his wife after she had been defiled.
6 The woman went and told her brothers, and the woman's brothers sought to kill him, and he fled to his house and escaped.
7 On the second day Moses went forth to his brothers, and looked and saw two men were quarreling; he said to the wicked one, Why do you strike your neighbor?
8 And he answered him and said to him, Who has set you for a prince and judge over us? Do you think to kill me as you did kill the Egyptian? And Moses was afraid and said, Certainly the thing is known?
9 And Pharaoh heard of this affair, and he ordered Moses to be slain, so God sent his angel and he appeared to Pharaoh in the likeness of a captain of the guard.
10 And the angel of the Lord took the sword from the hand of the captain of the guard, and took his head off with it, for the likeness of the captain of the guard was turned into the likeness of Moses.
11 And the angel of the Lord took hold of the right hand of Moses, and brought him forth from Egypt, and placed him outside the borders of Egypt, a distance of forty

days' journey.
12 And Aaron his brother alone remained in the land of Egypt, and he prophesied to the children of Israel, saying,
13 Thus says the Lord God of your ancestors, Throw away, each man, the abominations of his eyes, and do not defile yourselves with the idols of Egypt.
14 And the children of Israel rebelled and would not listen to Aaron at that time.
15 And the Lord thought to destroy them, were it not that the Lord remembered the covenant which he had made with Abraham, Isaac and Jacob.
16 In those days the hand of Pharaoh continued to be severe against the children of Israel, and he crushed and oppressed them until the time when God sent forth his word and took notice of them.

CHAPTER 72

1 It was in those days that there was a great war between the children of Cush and the children of the east and Aram, and they rebelled against the king of Cush in whose hands they were.
2 So Kikianus king of Cush went forth with all the children of Cush, a people numerous as the sand, and he went to fight against Aram and the children of the east, to bring them under subjection.
3 When Kikianus went out, he left Balaam the magician with his two sons, to guard the city and the lowest sort of the people of the land.
4 So Kikianus went forth to Aram and the children of the east, and he fought against them and struck them; they all fell down wounded before Kikianus and his people.
5 He took many of them captives and he brought them under subjection as at first, and he encamped on their land to take tax from them as usual.
6 Balaam the son of Beor, when the king of Cush had left him to guard the city and the poor of the city, rose up and advised with the people of the land to rebel against king Kikianus, not to let him enter the city when he would come home.
7 And the people of the land listened to him and they swore to him and made him king over them, and his two sons for captains of the army.
8 So they rose up and raised the walls of the city at the two corners, and they built an exceedingly strong building.
9 At the third corner they dug ditches without number, between the city and the river which surrounded the whole land of Cush, and they made the waters of the river burst forth there.
10 At the fourth corner they collected numerous serpents by their incantations and enchantments, and they fortified the city and lived therein; no one went out or in before them.
11 Kikianus fought against Aram and the children of the east and he subdued them as before; they gave him their usual tax and he went and returned to his land.
12 When Kikianus the king of Cush approached his city and all the captains of the forces with him, they lifted up their eyes and saw that the walls of the city were built up and greatly elevated, so the men were astonished at this.
13 They said one to the other, It is because they saw that we were delayed, in battle, and were greatly afraid of us; therefore have they done this thing and raised the city walls and fortified them so that the kings of Canaan might not come in battle against them.

14 So the king and the troops approached the city door and they looked up and behold, all the gates of the city were closed; they called out to the sentinels, saying, Open to us, that we may enter the city.
15 But the sentinels refused to open to them by the order of Balaam the magician, their king; they did not allow them enter their city.
16 So they raised a battle with them opposite the city gate, and one hundred and thirty men of the army at Kikianus fell on that day.
17 On the next day they continued to fight and they fought at the side of the river; they endeavored to pass but were not able, so some of them sank in the pits and died.
18 The king ordered them to cut down trees to make rafts, on which they might pass to them, and they did so.
19 When they came to the place of the ditches, the waters revolved by mills, and two hundred men on ten rafts were drowned.
20 On the third day they came to fight at the side where the serpents were, but they could not approach there, for the serpents killed of them one hundred and seventy men; then they ceased fighting against Cush, and they besieged Cush for nine years; no person came out or in.
21 At the time that the war and the siege were against Cush, Moses fled from Egypt from Pharaoh who sought to kill him for having slain the Egyptian.
22 Moses was eighteen years old when he fled from Egypt from the presence of Pharaoh, and he fled and escaped to the camp of Kikianus, which at that time was besieging Cush.
23 Moses was nine years in the camp of Kikianus king of Cush, all the time that they were besieging Cush, and Moses went out and came in with them.
24 And the king and princes and all the fighting men loved Moses, for he was great and worthy, his stature was like a noble lion, his face was like the sun and his strength was like that of a lion, and he was counsellor to the king.
25 And at the end of nine years, Kikianus was seized with a mortal disease, and his illness consumed him, and he died on the seventh day.
26 So his servants embalmed him, carried him and buried him opposite the city gate to the north of the land of Egypt.
27 They built over him an elegant strong and high building, and they placed great stones below.
28 And the king's scribes engraved on those stones all the might of their king Kikianus, and all his battles which he had fought; they are written there at this day.
29 After the death of Kikianus king of Cush it grieved his men and troops greatly on account of the war.
30 So they said one to the other, Give us counsel what we are to do at this time, as we have resided in the wilderness nine years away from our homes.
31 If we say we will fight against the city many of us will fall wounded or killed, and if we remain here in the siege we shall also die.
32 For now all the kings of Aram and of the children of the east will hear that our king is dead, and they will attack us suddenly in a hostile manner; they will fight against us and leave no remnant of us.
33 So now let us go and make a king over us, and let us remain in the siege until the city is delivered up to us.
34 And they wished to choose on that day a man for king from the army of Kikianus, and they found no person of their choice like Moses to reign over them.

35 They hurried and stripped off each man his garments and cast them on the ground, and they made a great heap and placed Moses thereon.
36 And they rose up and blew with trumpets and called out before him, and said, May the king live, may the king live!
37 And all the people and nobles swore to him to give him for a wife Adoniah the queen, the Cushite, wife of Kikianus, and they made Moses king over them on that day.
38 And all the people of Cush issued an announcement on that day, saying, Every man must give something to Moses of what is in his possession.
39 They spread out a sheet on the heap, and every man cast into it something of what he had, one a gold earring and the other a coin.
40 Also of onyx stones, bdellium, pearls and marble did the children of Cush cast to Moses on the heap, also silver and gold in great abundance.
41 And Moses took all the silver and gold, all the vessels, and the bdellium and onyx stones, which all the children of Cush had given to him, and he placed them among his treasures.
42 And Moses reigned over the children of Cush on that day, in the place of Kikianus king of Cush.

CHAPTER 73

1 In the fifty-fifth year of the reign of Pharaoh king of Egypt, that is in the hundred and fifty-seventh year of the Israelites going down into Egypt, Moses reigned in Cush.
2 Moses was twenty-seven years old when he began to reign over Cush, and forty years he did reign.
3 And the Lord granted Moses favor and grace in the eyes of all the children of Cush; the children of Cush loved him greatly, so Moses was favored by the Lord and by men.
4 In the seventh day of his reign, all the children of Cush assembled and came before Moses and bowed down to him to the ground.
5 And all the children spoke together in the presence of the king, saying, Give us counsel that we may see what is to be done to this city.
6 For it is now nine years that we have been besieging round about the city and have not seen our children and our wives.
7 So the king answered them, saying, If you will listen to my voice in all that I shall command you, then the Lord will give the city into our hands and we shall subdue it.
8 For if we fight with them as in the former battle which we had with them before the death of Kikianus, many of us will fall down wounded as before.
9 Now therefore hear this counsel for you in this matter; if you will listen to my voice, then will the city be delivered into our hands.
10 So all the forces answered the king, saying, All that our lord shall command that we will do.
11 And Moses said to them, Pass through and proclaim a voice in the whole camp to all the people, saying,
12 Thus says the king, Go into the forest and bring with you of the young ones of the stork, each man a young one in his hand.

13 And any person disobeying the word of the king, who shall not bring his young one, shall die and the king will take all belonging to him.
14 And when you bring them they shall be in your keeping; you shall rear them until they grow up, and you shall teach them to strike their prey, as is the way of the young ones of the hawk.
15 So all the children of Cush heard the words of Moses, and they rose up and caused announcement to be issued throughout the camp, saying,
16 To you, all the children of Cush, the king's order is that you all go together to the forest and catch there the young stork; each man his young one in his hand and you shall bring them home.
17 Any person violating the order of the king shall die and the king will take all that belongs to him.
18 And all the people did so, and they went out to the wood and they climbed the fir trees and each man caught a young one in his hand, all the young of the storks; they brought them into the desert and reared them by order of the king; they taught them to strike similar to the young hawks.
19 And after the young storks were reared, the king ordered them to be hungry for three days, and all the people did so.
20 On the third day the king said to them, Strengthen yourselves and become courageous men; put on each man his armor and gird on his sword, and each man ride his horse and each take his young stork in his hand.
21 And we will rise up and fight against the city at the place where the serpents are, and all the people did as the king had ordered.
22 And each man took his young one in his hand and they went away; when they came to the place of the serpents the king said to them, Send forth each man his young stork on the serpents.
23 And they sent forth each man his young stork at the king's order, and the young storks ran on the serpents and they devoured them all and destroyed them out of that place.
24 When the king and people had seen that all the serpents were destroyed in that place, all the people sent up a great shout.
25 And they approached and fought against the city and took and subdued it, and they entered the city.
26 There died on that day one thousand and one hundred men of the people of the city, all that inhabited the city, but of the people besieging not one died.
27 So all the children of Cush each went to his home, to his wife and children and to all belonging to him.
28 And Balaam the magician, when he saw that the city was taken, opened the gate and he and his two sons and eight brothers fled and returned to Egyp,to Pharaoh king of Egypt.
29 They are the sorcerers and magicians who are mentioned in the book of the law, standing against Moses when the Lord brought the plagues on Egypt.
30 So Moses took the city by his wisdom, and the children of Cush placed him on the throne instead of Kikianus king of Cush.
31 They placed the royal crown on his head and they gave him a wife Adoniah the Cushite queen, wife of Kikianus.
32 Moses feared the Lord God of his fathers so that he came not to her, nor did he turn his eyes to her.
33 For Moses remembered how Abraham had made his servant Eliezer swear,

saying to him, You shall not take a woman from the daughters of Canaan for my son Isaac.
34 Also what Isaac did when Jacob had fled from his brother, when he commanded him saying, You shall not take a wife from the daughters of Canaan, nor make alliance with any of the children of Ham.
35 For the Lord our God gave Ham the son of Noah, and his children and all his descendants as slaves to the children of Shem and to the children of Japheth, and to their descendants after them for slaves forever.
36 Therefore Moses turned not his heart nor his eyes to the wife of Kikianus all the days that he reigned over Cush.
37 Moses feared the Lord his God all his life, and Moses walked before the Lord in truth with all his heart and soul; he turned not from the right way all the days of his life; he declined not from the way either to the right or to the left, in which Abraham, Isaac and Jacob had walked.
38 Moses strengthened himself in the kingdom of the children of Cush; he guided the children of Cush with his usual wisdom, and Moses prospered in his kingdom.
39 At that time Aram and the children of the east heard that Kikianus king of Cush had died, so Aram and the children of the east rebelled against Cush in those days.
40 Moses gathered all the children of Cush, a people very mighty, about thirty thousand men and he went forth to fight with Aram and the children of the east.
41 They went at first to the children of the east and when the children of the east heard their report, they went to meet them, and engaged in battle with them.
42 And the war was severe against the children of the east, so the Lord gave all the children of the east into the hand of Moses; about three hundred men fell down slain.
43 All the children of the east turned back and retreated, so Moses and the children of Cush followed them and subdued them, and put a tax on them as was their custom.
44 So Moses and all the people with him passed from there to the land of Aram for battle.
45 And the people of Aram also went to meet them; they fought against them and the Lord delivered them into the hand of Moses, and many of the men of Aram fell down wounded.
46 Aram also was subdued by Moses and the people of Cush, and also gave their usual tax.
47 And Moses brought Aram and the children of the east under subjection to the children of Cush; Moses and all the people who were with him turned to the land of Cush.
48 Moses strengthened himself in the kingdom of the children of Cush and the Lord was with him, and all the children of Cush were afraid of him.

CHAPTER 74

1 In the end of years Saul king of Edom died, and Baal Chanan the son of Achbor reigned in his place.
2 In the sixteenth year of the reign of Moses over Cush, Baal Chanan the son of Achbor reigned in the land of Edom over all the children of Edom for thirty-eight years.

3 In his days Moab rebelled against the power of Edom, having been under Edom since the days of Hadad the son of Bedad, who struck them and Midian, and brought Moab under subjection to Edom.

4 And when Baal Chanan the son of Achbor reigned over Edom, all the children of Moab withdrew their allegiance from Edom.

5 Angeas king of Africa died in those days, and Azdrubal his son reigned in his stead.

6 And in those days Janeas king of the children of Chittim died, and they buried him in his temple which he had built for himself in the plain of Canopia for a residence; Latinus reigned in his stead.

7 In the twenty-second year of the reign of Moses over the children of Cush, Latinus reigned over the children of Chittim forty-five years.

8 And he also built for himself a great and mighty tower; he built therein an elegant temple for his residence, to conduct his government as was the custom.

9 In the third year of his reign he caused an announcement to be made to all his skilful men who made many ships for him.

10 And Latinus assembled all his forces, and they came in ships, and went there to fight with Azdrubal son of Angeas king of Africa; they came to Africa and engaged in battle with Azdrubal and his army.

11 And Latinus won over Azdrubal, and Latinus took from Azdrubal the aqueduct which his father had brought from the children of Chittim, when he took Janiah the daughter of Uzi for a wife; so Latinus overthrew the bridge of the aqueduct and struck the whole army of Azdrubal a severe blow.

12 The remaining strong men of Azdrubal strengthened themselves, and their hearts were filled with envy; they courted death, and again engaged in battle with Latinus king of Chittim.

13 The battle was severe on all the men of Africa and they all fell wounded before Latinus and his people, and Azdrubal the king also fell in that battle.

14 The king Azdrubal had a very beautiful daughter whose name was Ushpezena, and all the men of Africa embroidered her likeness on their garment on account of her great beauty and attractive appearance.

15 The men of Latinus saw Ushpezena, the daughter of Azdrubal, and praised her to Latinus their king.

16 And Latinus ordered her to be brought to him; Latinus took Ushpezena for a wife and he turned back on his way to Chittim.

17 It was after the death of Azdrubal son of Angeas, when Latinus had turned back to his land from the battle, that all the inhabitants of Africa rose up and took Anibal the son of Angeas, the younger brother of Azdrubal, and made him king instead of his brother over the whole land at Africa.

18 And when he reigned he resolved to go to Chittim to fight with the children of Chittim, to avenge the cause of Azdrubal his brother and the cause of the inhabitants of Africa, and he did so.

19 He made many ships and he came there with his whole army, and he went to Chittim.

20 So Anibal fought with the children of Chittim, and the children of Chittim fell wounded before Anibal and his army, and Anibal avenged his brother's cause.

21 And Anibal continued the war for eighteen years with the children of Chittim, and Anibal lived in the land of Chittim and encamped there for a long time.

22 Anibal struck the children of Chittim very severely and he killed their great men

and princes, and of the rest of the people he struck about eighty thousand men.
23 And at the end of days and years, Anibal returned to his land of Africa, and he reigned securely in the place of Azdrubal his brother.

CHAPTER 75

1 At that time in the hundred and eightieth year of the Israelites going down into Egypt, there went forth from Egypt courageous men, thirty thousand on foot, from the children of Israel who were all of the tribe of Joseph, of the children of Ephraim the son of Joseph.
2 For they said the period was completed which the Lord had appointed to the children of Israel in the times of old, which he had spoken to Abraham.
3 And these men prepared themselves, and each man put his sword at his side, and every man his armor on him, and they trusted to their strength; they went out together from Egypt with a mighty hand.
4 But they brought no provision for the road, only silver and gold, not even did they bring bread for that day in their hands, for they thought of getting their provision for pay from the Philistines; if not they would take it by force.
5 These men were very mighty and bold men; one man could pursue a thousand and two could rout ten thousand, so they trusted their strength and went together as they were.
6 They directed their course toward the land of Gath, and they went down and found the shepherds of Gath feeding the cattle of the children of Gath.
7 They said to the shepherds, Give us some of the sheep for pay that we may eat, for we are hungry; we have eaten no bread this day.
8 And the shepherds said, Are they our sheep or cattle that we should give them to you even for pay? So the children of Ephraim approached to take them by force.
9 And the shepherds of Gath shouted over them so their cry was heard at a distance; all the children of Gath went out to them.
10 When the children of Gath saw the evil doings of the children of Ephraim, they returned and assembled the men of Gath; they put on each man his armor and came forth to the children of Ephraim for battle.
11 And they engaged with them in the valley of Gath, and the battle was severe; they struck from each other a great many on that day.
12 And on the second day the children of Gath sent to all the cities of the Philistines that they should come to their help, saying,
13 Come up to us and help us, that we may strike the children of Ephraim who have come forth from Egypt to take our cattle, and to fight against us without cause.
14 And the souls of the children of Ephraim were exhausted with hunger and thirst, for they had eaten no bread for three days. Forty thousand men went out from the cities of the Philistines to the assistance of the men of Gath.
15 These men were engaged in battle with the children of Ephraim, and the Lord delivered the children of Ephraim into the hands of the Philistines.
16 They struck all the children of Ephraim, all who had gone forth from Egypt, none were remaining but ten men who had run away from the engagement.
17 This evil was from the Lord against the children of Ephraim for they went contrary to the word of the Lord in going forth from Egypt, before the period had arrived which the Lord in the days of old had appointed to Israel.

18 And of the Philistines also there fell a great many, about twenty thousand men, and their brothers carried them and buried them in their cities.
19 And the slain of the children of Ephraim remained forsaken in the valley of Gath for many days and years and were not brought to burial, and the valley was filled with men's bones.
20 The men who had escaped from the battle came to Egypt and told all the children of Israel all that had happened to them.
21 Their father Ephraim mourned over them for many days, and his brothers came to console him.
22 And he came to his wife and she gave birth to a son, and he called his name Beriah, for she was unfortunate in his house.

CHAPTER 76

1 Moses the son of Amram was still king in the land of Cush in those days, and he prospered in his kingdom; he conducted the government of the children of Cush in justice, in righteousness and integrity.
2 And all the children of Cush loved Moses all the days that he reigned over them, and all the inhabitants of the land of Cush were greatly afraid of him.
3 In the fortieth year of the reign of Moses over Cush, Moses was sitting on the royal throne while Adoniah the queen was before him, and all the nobles were sitting around him.
4 And Adoniah the queen said before the king and the princes, What is this thing which you, the children of Cush, have done for this long time?
5 Certainly you know that for forty years that this man has reigned over Cush he has not approached me, nor has he served the gods of the children of Cush.
6 Now therefore hear, O ye children of Cush, and let this man no more reign over you as he is not of our people.
7 Behold Menacrus my son is grown up, let him reign over you for it is better for you to serve the son of your lord than to serve a stranger, slave of the king of Egypt.
8 And all the people and nobles of the children of Cush heard the words which Adoniah the queen had spoken in their ears.
9 All the people were preparing until the evening, and in the morning they rose up early and made Menacrus, son of Kikianus, king over them.
10 All the children of Cush were afraid to stretch forth their hand against Moses, for the Lord was with Moses, and the children of Cush remembered the oath which they swore to Moses, therefore they did no harm to him.
11 But the children of Cush gave many presents to Moses, and sent him from them with great honor.
12 So Moses went forth from the land of Cush and went home and ceased to reign over Cush; Moses was sixty-six years old when he went out of the land of Cush, for the thing was from the Lord. For the period had arrived which he had appointed in the days of old, to bring forth Israel from the affliction of the children of Ham.
13 So Moses went to Midian, for he was afraid to return to Egypt on account of Pharaoh, and he went and sat at a well of water in Midian.

14 And the seven daughters of Reuel the Midianite went out to feed their father's flock.
15 And they came to the well and drew water to water their father's flock.
16 But the shepherds of Midian came and drove them away, and Moses rose up and helped them and watered the flock.
17 And they came home to their father Reuel, and told him what Moses did for them.
18 They said, An Egyptian man has delivered us from the hands of the shepherds; he drew up water for us and watered the flock.
19 And Reuel said to his daughters, And where is he? Why have you left the man?
20 And Reuel sent for him and fetched him and brought him home, and he ate bread with him.
21 And Moses related to Reuel that he had fled from Egypt and that he reigned forty years over Cush, and that they afterward had taken the government from him and had sent him away in peace with honor and with presents.
22 And when Reuel had heard the words of Moses, Reuel said within himself, I will put this man into the prison house, whereby I shall win over the children of Cush, for he has fled from them.
23 They took and put him into the prison house, and Moses was in prison ten years; while Moses was in the prison house, Zipporah the daughter of Reuel took pity on him, and supported him with bread and water all the time.
24 All the children of Israel were yet in the land of Egypt serving the Egyptians in all manner of hard work, and the hand of Egypt continued in severity over the children of Israel in those days.
25 At that time the Lord struck Pharaoh king of Egypt, and he was afflicted with the plague of leprosy from the sole of his foot to the crown of his head; owing to the cruel treatment of the children of Israel this plague at that time was from the Lord on Pharaoh king of Egypt.
26 For the Lord had listened to the prayer of his people the children of Israel, and their cry reached him on account of their hard work.
27 Still his anger did not turn from them, and the hand of Pharaoh was still stretched out against the children of Israel. Pharaoh hardened his neck before the Lord, he increased his yoke over the children of Israel, and embittered their lives with all manner of hard work.
28 When the Lord had inflicted the plague on Pharaoh king of Egypt, he asked his wise men and sorcerers to cure him.
29 And his wise men and sorcerers said to him that if the blood of little children were put into the wounds he would be healed.
30 Pharaoh listened to them, and sent his ministers to Goshen to the children of Israel to take their little children.
31 And Pharaoh's ministers went and took the infants of the children of Israel from the bosoms of their mothers by force, and they brought them to Pharaoh daily, a child each day, and the physicians killed them and applied them to the plague; thus they did all the days.
32 And the number of the children which Pharaoh killed was three hundred and seventy-five.
33 But the Lord listened not to the physicians of the king of Egypt, and the plague went on increasing mightily.
34 Pharaoh was ten years afflicted with that plague, still the heart of Pharaoh was

more hardened against the children of Israel.
35 At the end of ten years the Lord continued to afflict Pharaoh with destructive plagues.
36 And the Lord struck him with a bad tumor and sickness in the stomach, and that plague turned to a severe boil.
37 At that time the two ministers of Pharaoh came from the land of Goshen where all the children of Israel were, and went to the house of Pharaoh and said to him, We have seen the children of Israel slacken in their work and negligent in their labor.
38 And when Pharaoh heard the words of his ministers, his anger was set ablaze against the children of Israel greatly, for he was greatly grieved at his bodily pain.
39 And he answered and said, Now that the children of Israel know that I am ill, they turn and scoff at us. Now therefore harness my chariot for me, and I will take myself to Goshen and will see the scoff of the children of Israel with which they are deriding me. So his servants harnessed the chariot for him.
40 And they took and made him ride on a horse, for he was not able to ride of himself.
41 He took with him ten horsemen and ten footmen, and went to the children of Israel to Goshen.
42 When they had come to the border of Egypt, the king's horse passed into a narrow place, elevated in the hollow part of the vineyard, fenced on both sides, the low plain country being on the other side.
43 The horses ran rapidly in that place and pressed each other, and the other horses pressed the king's horse.
44 And the king's horse fell into the low plain while the king was riding on it; he fell and the chariot turned over the king's face and the horse lay on the king, and the king cried out for his flesh was very sore.
45 And the flesh of the king was torn from him, and his bones were broken and he could not ride; this thing was from the Lord to him, for the Lord had heard the cries of his people the children of Israel and their affliction.
46 And his servants carried him on their shoulders,slowly and carefully, and they brought him back to Egypt, and the horsemen who were with him also came back to Egypt.
47 They placed him in his bed and the king knew that his end was come to die, so Aparanith the queen his wife came and cried before the king, and the king wept a great weeping with her.
48 And all his nobles and servants came on that day and saw the king in that affliction, and wept a great weeping with him.
49 The princes of the king and all his counselors advised the king to cause one to reign in his stead in the land, whomever he would choose from his sons.
50 The king had three sons and two daughters which Aparanith the queen his wife had borne to him, besides the king's children of concubines.
51 And these were their names: the firstborn Othri, the second Adikam, and the third Morion, and their sisters: the name of the elder Bathia and of the other Acuzi.
52 Othri the first born of the king was an idiot, impetuous and hurried in his words.
53 But Adikam was a cunning and wise man and knowing in all the wisdom of Egypt, but of unseemly appearance, thick in flesh and very short in stature; his height was one cubit.
54 And when the king saw Adikam his son intelligent and wise in all things, the king resolved that he should be king in his stead after his death.

55 He took for him a wife Gedudah daughter of Abilot, and he was ten years old; she gave birth to, to him, four sons.
56 And afterward he went and took three wives and had eight sons and three daughters.
57 And the disorder greatly consumed the king, and his flesh stank like the flesh of a carcass cast on the field in summer time, during the heat of the sun.
58 And when the king saw that his sickness had greatly strengthened itself over him, he ordered his son Adikam to be brought to him, and they made him king over the land in his place.
59 At the end of three years the king died, in shame, disgrace, and disgust, and his servants carried him and buried him in the sepulcher of the kings of Egypt in Zoan Mizraim.
60 But they embalmed him not as was usual with kings, for his flesh was putrid, and they could not approach to embalm him on account of the stench, so they buried him in haste.
61 For this evil was from the Lord to him, for the Lord had rewarded him evil for the evil which in his days he had done to Israel.
62 And he died with terror and with shame, and his son Adikam reigned in his place.

CHAPTER 77

1 Adikam was twenty years old when he reigned over Egypt, he reigned four years.
2 In the two hundred and sixth year of Israel's going down to Egypt did Adikam reign over Egypt, but he continued not so long in his reign over Egypt as his fathers had continued their reigns.
3 For Melol his father reigned ninety-four years in Egypt, but he was sick ten years and died, for he had been wicked before the Lord.
4 And all the Egyptians called the name of Adikam Pharaoh like the name of his fathers, as was their custom to do in Egypt.
5 And all the wise men of Pharaoh called the name of Adikam Ahuz, for short it's called Ahuz in the Egyptian language.
6 Adikam was greatly ugly, and he was a cubit and a span and he had a great beard which reached to the soles of his feet.
7 And Pharaoh sat on his father's throne to reign over Egypt, and he conducted the government of Egypt in his wisdom.
8 While he reigned he exceeded his father and all the preceding kings in wickedness, and he increased his yoke over the children of Israel.
9 He went with his servants to Goshen to the children of Israel, and he strengthened the labor over them and he said to them, Complete your work, each day's task, and let not your hands slacken from our work from this day forward as you did in the days of my father.
10 He placed officers over them from among the children of Israel, and over these officers he placed taskmasters from among his servants.
11 And he placed over them a measure of bricks for them to do according to that number, day by day, and he turned back and went to Egypt.
12 At that time the taskmasters of Pharaoh ordered the officers of the children of Israel according to the command of Pharaoh, saying,

13 Thus says Pharaoh, Do your work each day, and finish your task, and observe the daily measure of bricks; diminish not anything.

14 And it shall come to pass that if you are deficient in your daily bricks, I will put your young children in their stead.

15 And the taskmasters of Egypt did so in those days as Pharaoh had ordered them.

16 And whenever any deficiency was found in the children of Israel's measure of their daily bricks, the taskmasters of Pharaoh would go to the wives of the children of Israel and take infants of the children of Israel to the number of bricks deficient, they would take them by force from their mother's laps, and put them in the building instead of the bricks;

17 While their fathers and mothers were crying over them and weeping when they heard the weeping voices of their infants in the wall of the building.

18 And the taskmasters prevailed over Israel, that the Israelites should place their children in the building, so that a man placed his son in the wall and put mortar over him, while his eyes wept over him, and his tears ran down on his child.

19 And the taskmasters of Egypt did so to the babes of Israel for many days, and no one pitied or had compassion over the babes of the children of Israel.

20 And the number of all the children killed in the building was two hundred and seventy, some whom they had built on instead of the bricks which had been left deficient by their fathers, and some whom they had drawn out dead from the building.

21 And the labor imposed on the children of Israel in the days of Adikam exceeded in hardship that which they performed in the days of his father.

22 The children of Israel sighed every day on account of their heavy work, for they had said to themselves, Certainly when Pharaoh dies, his son will rise up and lighten our work!

23 But they increased the latter work more than the former, and the children of Israel sighed at this and their cry ascended to God on account of their labor.

24 God heard the voice of the children of Israel and their cry in those days, and God remembered to them his covenant which he had made with Abraham, Isaac and Jacob.

25 And God saw the burden of the children of Israel and their heavy work in those days, and he determined to deliver them.

26 Moses the son of Amram was still confined in the dungeon in those days, in the house of Reuel the Midianite, and Zipporah the daughter of Reuel supported him with food secretly day by day.

27 Moses was confined in the dungeon in the house of Reuel for ten years.

28 And at the end of ten years which was the first year of the reign of Pharaoh over Egypt, in the place of his father,

29 Zipporah said to her father Reuel, No person inquires or seeks after the Hebrew man, whom you bound in prison now ten years.

30 So therefore, if it seems good in your sight, let us send and see whether he is living or dead. But her father knew not that she had supported him.

31 And Reuel her father answered and said to her, Has ever such a thing happened that a man would be shut up in a prison without food for ten years, and that he should live?

32 And Zipporah answered her father, saying, Certainly you have heard that the God of the Hebrews is great and mighty, and does wonders for them at all times.

33 He it was who delivered Abraham from the Chaldeans, and Isaac from the sword

of his father, and Jacob from the angel of the Lord who wrestled with him at the ford of Jabbuk.
34 Also with this man he has done many things; he delivered him from the river in Egypt and from the sword of Pharaoh, and from the children of Cush, so also he can deliver him from famine and make him live.
35 And the thing seemed good in the sight of Reuel, and he did according to the word of his daughter, and sent to the dungeon to ascertain what became of Moses.
36 He saw, and behold the man Moses was living in the dungeon, standing on his feet, praising and praying to the God of his ancestors.
37 And Reuel commanded Moses to be brought out of the dungeon, so they shaved him and he changed his prison garments and ate bread.
38 And afterward Moses went into the garden of Reuel which was behind the house, and he there prayed to the Lord his God, who had done mighty wonders for him.
39 It was while he prayed he looked opposite to him, and there a sapphire stick was placed in the ground, which was planted in the midst of the garden.
40 He approached the stick and looked, and saw the name of the Lord God of hosts was engraved on it, written and developed on the stick.
41 And he read it and stretched forth his hand and he plucked it like a forest tree from the thicket, and the stick was in his hand.
42 This is the stick with which all the works of our God were performed, after he had created heaven and earth and all the host of them, seas, rivers and all their fish.
43 And when God had driven Adam from the garden of Eden, he took the stick in his hand and went and tilled the ground from which he was taken.
44 The stick came down to Noah and was given to Shem and his descendants, until it came into the hand of Abraham the Hebrew.
45 And when Abraham had given all he had to his son Isaac, he also gave to him this stick.
46 When Jacob had fled to Padan-aram, he took it into his hand, and when he returned to his father he had not left it behind him.
47 Also when he went down to Egypt he took it into his hand and gave it to Joseph, one portion above his brothers, for Jacob had taken it by force from his brother Esau.
48 After the death of Joseph, the nobles of Egypt came into the house of Joseph, and the stick came into the hand of Reuel the Midianite; when he went out of Egypt, he took it in his hand and planted it in his garden.
49 And all the mighty men of the Kinites tried to pluck it when they endeavored to get Zipporah his daughter, but they were unsuccessful.
50 That stick remained planted in the garden of Reuel until he who had a right to it came and took it.
51 And when Reuel saw the stick in the hand of Moses, he wondered at it, and he gave him his daughter Zipporah for a wife.

CHAPTER 78

1 At that time Baal Channan son of Achbor, king of Edom, died and was buried in his house in the land of Edom.
2 After his death the children of Esau sent to the land of Edom, and took from there a man who was in Edom, whose name was Hadad, and they made him king over them in the place of Baal Channan, their king.

3 And Hadad reigned over the children of Edom forty-eight years.
4 When he reigned he resolved to fight against the children of Moab to bring them under the power of the children of Esau as they were before, but he was not able to because the children of Moab heard this thing, and they rose up and hurried to elect a king over them from among their brothers.
5 Afterward they gathered together a large crowd, and sent them to the children of Ammon their brothers for help to fight against Hadad king of Edom.
6 And Hadad heard the thing which the children of Moab had done, and was greatly afraid of them, and refrained from fighting against them.
7 In those days Moses, the son of Amram, in Midian, took Zipporah, the daughter of Reuel the Midianite, for a wife.
8 And Zipporah walked in the ways of the daughters of Jacob, she was nothing short of the righteousness of Sarah, Rebecca, Rachel and Leah.
9 And Zipporah conceived and gave birth to a son and he called his name Gershom, for he said, I was a stranger in a foreign land; but he circumcised not his foreskin, at the command of Reuel his father-in-law.
10 And she conceived again and gave birth to a son, but circumcised his foreskin, and called his name Eliezer, for Moses said, Because the God of my fathers was my help and delivered me from the sword of Pharaoh.
11 And Pharaoh king of Egypt greatly increased the labor of the children of Israel in those days, and continued to make his yoke heavier on the children of Israel.
12 And he ordered an announcement to be made in Egypt, saying, Give no more straw to the people to make bricks with, let them go and gather themselves straw as they can find it.
13 Also the number of bricks which they shall make let them give each day, and diminish nothing from them, for they are idle in their work.
14 And the children of Israel heard this, and they mourned and sighed, and they cried to the Lord on account of the bitterness of their souls.
15 And the Lord heard the cries of the children of Israel, and saw the oppression with which the Egyptians oppressed them.
16 And the Lord was zealous for his people and his inheritance, and heard their voice, and he resolved to take them out of the affliction of Egypt, to give them the land of Canaan for a possession.

CHAPTER 79

1 Iin those days Moses was feeding the flock of Reuel the Midianite his father-in-law, beyond the wilderness of Sin, and the stick which he took from his father-in-law was in his hand.
2 And it came to pass one day that a kid of goats strayed from the flock, and Moses pursued it and it came to the mountain of God to Horeb.
3 When he came to Horeb the Lord appeared there to him in the bush, and he found the bush burning with fire, but the fire had no power over the bush to consume it.
4 Moses was greatly astonished at this sight because the bush was not consumed, and he approached to see this mighty thing; the Lord called to Moses out of the fire and commanded him to go down to Egypt to Pharaoh king of Egypt, to send the children of Israel from his service.
5 And the Lord said to Moses, Go, return to Egypt for all those men who sought your life are dead, and you shall speak to Pharaoh to send forth the children of Israel

from his land.
6 The Lord showed him to do signs and wonders in Egypt before the eyes of Pharaoh and the eyes of his subjects, in order that they might believe that the Lord had sent him.
7 Moses listened to all that the Lord had commanded him, and he returned to his father-in-law and told him these things, and Reuel said to him, Go in peace.
8 Moses rose up to go to Egypt and took his wife and sons with him; he was at an inn in the road, and an angel of God came down, and sought an occasion against him.
9 He wished to kill him on account of his firstborn son because he had not circumcised him and had gone contrary to the covenant which the Lord had made with Abraham.
10 For Moses had listened to the words of his father-in-law which he had spoken to him, not to circumcise his first born son, so he did not circumcise him.
11 Zipporah saw the angel of the Lord seeking an occasion against Moses, and she knew that this thing was because of his not having circumcised her son Gershom.
12 Zipporah hurried and took some of the sharp rock stones that were there, and circumcised her son, and delivered her husband and her son from the hand of the angel of the Lord.
13 Aaron the son of Amram, the brother of Moses, was in Egypt walking at the river side on that day.
14 And the Lord appeared to him in that place; he said to him, Go now toward Moses in the wilderness. And he went and met him in the mountain of God, and he kissed him.
15 Aaron lifted up his eyes and saw Zipporah the wife of Moses and her children, and he said to Moses, Who are these to you?
16 And Moses said to him, They are my wife and sons which God gave to me in Midian; the thing grieved Aaron on account of the woman and her children.
17 Aaron said to Moses, Send away the woman and her children that they may go to her father's house, and Moses listened to the words of Aaron, and did so.
18 Zipporah returned with her children and they went to the house of Reuel, and remained there until the time arrived when the Lord had visited his people and brought them forth from Egypt from the hand at Pharaoh.
19 Moses and Aaron came to Egypt to the community of the children of Israel and spoke to them all the words of the Lord, and the people rejoiced a very great rejoicing.
20 Moses and Aaron rose up early the next day and went to the house of Pharaoh, and they took in their hands the stick of God.
21 When they came to the king's gate, two young lions were confined there with iron instruments; no person went out or came in from before them, unless those whom the king ordered to come, when the conjurors came and withdrew the lions by their incantations, and this brought them to the king.
22 Moses hurried and lifted up the stick on the lions and loosed them, and Moses and Aaron came into the king's house.
23 The lions also came with them in joy, and they followed them and rejoiced as a dog rejoices over his master when he comes from the field.
24 When Pharaoh saw this thing he was astonished at it and was greatly terrified at the report, for their appearance was like the appearance of the children of God.
25 And Pharaoh said to Moses, What do you require? And they answered him

saying, The Lord God of the Hebrews has sent us to you, to say, Send forth my people that they may serve me.
26 When Pharaoh heard their words he was greatly terrified before them, and he said to them, Go today and come back to me tomorrow. And they did according to the word of the king.
27 When they had gone Pharaoh sent for Balaam the magician and to Jannes and Jambres his sons and to all the magicians and conjurors and counselors which belonged to the king; they all came and sat before the king.
28 And the king told them all the words which Moses and his brother Aaron had spoken to him; the magicians said to the king, But how could the men come to you, on account of the lions which were confined at the gate?
29 The king said, Because they lifted up their rod against the lions and loosed them, and came to me, and the lions also rejoiced at them as a dog rejoices to meet his master.
30 Balaam the son of Beor the magician answered the king saying, These are none other than magicians like ourselves.
31 So now send for them and let them come and we will try them, and the king did so.
32 In the morning Pharaoh sent for Moses and Aaron to come before the king, and they took the rod of God and came to the king and spoke to him saying,
33 Thus said the Lord God of the Hebrews, Send away my people that they may serve me.
34 And the king said to them, But who will believe you that you are the messengers of God and that you come to me by his order?
35 Now therefore give a wonder or sign in this matter, and then the words which you speak will be believed.
36 Aaron hurried and threw the rod out of his hand before Pharaoh and before his servants, and the rod turned into a serpent.
37 The sorcerers saw this and each man cast his rod on the ground and they became serpents.
38 The serpent of Aaron's rod lifted up its head and opened its mouth to swallow the rods of the magicians.
39 Balaam the magician answered and said, This thing has been from the days of old that a serpent should swallow its fellow, and that living things devour each other.
40 So now restore it to a rod as it was at first and we will also restore our rods as they were at first; if your rod shall swallow our rods we will know that the spirit of God is in you, and if not, you are only a magician like ourselves.
41 Aaron hurried and stretched forth his hand and caught hold of the serpent's tail and it became a rod in his hand; the sorcerers did the same with their rod and got hold each man of the tail of his serpent, and they became rods as at first.
42 When they were restored to rods, the rod of Aaron swallowed up their rods.
43 And when the king saw this thing, he ordered the book of records that related to the kings of Egypt to be brought; they brought the book of records, the chronicles of the kings of Egypt in which all the idols of Egypt were inscribed, for they thought they would find there the name of Jehovah, but they found it not.
44 And Pharaoh said to Moses and Aaron, Behold I have not found the name of your God written in this book, and his name I do not know.
45 The counselors and wise men answered the king, We have heard that the God of the Hebrews is a son of the wise, the son of ancient kings.

46 Pharaoh turned to Moses and Aaron and said to them, I know not the Lord whom you have declared, neither will I send his people away.
47 And they answered and said to the king, The Lord God of Gods is his name; he proclaimed his name over us from the days of our ancestors and sent us, saying, Go to Pharaoh and say to him, Send my people away that they may serve me.
48 Now therefore send us, that we may take a journey for three days in the wilderness and there may sacrifice to him, for from the days of our going down to Egypt, he has not taken from our hands either burnt offering, oblation or sacrifice; if you will not send us, his anger will be set ablaze against you and he will strike Egypt either with the plague or with the sword.
49 And Pharaoh said to them, Tell me now his power and his might. They said to him, He created the heaven and the earth, the seas and all their fish; he formed the light, created the darkness, caused rain on the earth and watered it, and made the herbage and grass to sprout; he created man and beast and the animals of the forest, the birds of the air and the fish of the sea, and by his mouth they live and die.
50 Certainly he created you in your mother's womb and put into you the breath of life, and reared you and placed you on the royal throne of Egypt, and he will take your breath and soul from you and return you to the ground from where you were taken.
51 And the anger of the king was set ablaze at their words and he said to them, But who among all the Gods of nations can do this? My river is my own, and I have made it for myself.
52 And he drove them from him; he ordered the labor on Israel to be more severe than it was yesterday and before.
53 Moses and Aaron went out from the king's presence, and they saw the children of Israel in an evil condition for the taskmasters had made their labor extremely heavy.
54 Moses returned to the Lord and said, Why have you ill-treated your people? For since I came to speak to Pharaoh what you sent me for, he has greatly ill-used the children of Israel.
55 The Lord said to Moses, Look and you will see that with an outstretched hand and heavy plagues, Pharaoh will send the children of Israel from his land.
56 And Moses and Aaron lived among their brothers the children of Israel in Egypt.
57 As for the children of Israel the Egyptians embittered their lives with the heavy work which they imposed on them.

CHAPTER 80

1 And at the end of two years, the Lord again sent Moses to Pharaoh to bring forth the children of Israel, and to send them out of the land of Egypt.
2 Moses went and came to the house of Pharaoh, and he spoke to him the words of the Lord who had sent him, but Pharaoh would not listen to the voice of the Lord; God roused his might in Egypt on Pharaoh and his subjects, and God struck Pharaoh and his people with very great and severe plagues.
3 The Lord sent by the hand of Aaron and turned all the waters of Egypt into blood, with all their streams and rivers.
4 And when an Egyptian came to drink and draw water, he looked into his pitcher, and behold all the water was turned into blood; when he came to drink from his cup the water in the cup became blood.

5 And when a woman kneaded her dough and cooked her food, their appearance was turned to that of blood.
6 The Lord sent again and caused all their waters to bring forth frogs and all the frogs came into the houses of the Egyptians.
7 And when the Egyptians drank, their bellies were filled with frogs and they danced in their bellies as they dance when in the river.
8 All their drinking water and cooking water turned to frogs, also when they lay in their beds their perspiration bred frogs.
9 In spite of all this the anger of the Lord did not turn from them, and his hand was stretched out against all the Egyptians to strike them with every heavy plague.
10 He sent and changed their dust to lice, and the lice became in Egypt to the height of two cubits on the earth.
11 The lice were also very numerous in the flesh of man and beast, in all the inhabitants of Egypt; also on the king and queen the Lord sent the lice, and it grieved Egypt greatly on account of the lice.
12 Still the anger of the Lord did not turn away, and his hand was still stretched out over Egypt.
13 And the Lord sent all kinds of beasts of the field into Egypt, and they came and destroyed all Egypt, man and beast, and trees and all things that were in Egypt.
14 And the Lord sent fiery serpents, scorpions, mice, weasels, toads, together with others creeping in dust.
15 Flies, hornets, fleas, bugs and gnats, each swarm according to its kind.
16 And all reptiles and winged animals according to their kind came to Egypt and upset the Egyptians greatly.
17 The fleas and flies came into the eyes and ears of the Egyptians.
18 The hornet came on them and drove them away, and they removed from it into their inner rooms, and it pursued them.
19 When the Egyptians hid themselves on account of the swarm of animals, they locked their doors after them, and God ordered the Sulanuth which was in the sea to come up and go into Egypt.
20 She had long arms, ten cubits in length of the cubit of a man.
21 And she went on the roofs and uncovered the raftering and flooring and cut them, and stretched forth her arm into the house and removed the lock and the bolt, and opened the houses of Egypt.
22 Afterward came the swarm of animals into the houses of Egypt, and the swarm of animals destroyed the Egyptians, and it upset them greatly.
23 Still the anger of the Lord did not turn away from the Egyptians, and his hand was yet stretched forth against them.
24 God sent the pestilence and the pestilence pervaded Egypt, in the horses and asses and in the camels, in herds of oxen and sheep and in man.
25 When the Egyptians rose up early in the morning to take their cattle to pasture they found all their cattle dead.
26 There remained of the cattle of the Egyptians only one in ten, and of the cattle belonging to Israel in Goshen not one died.
27 And God sent a burning inflammation in the flesh of the Egyptians, which burst their skins; it became a severe itch in all the Egyptians from the soles of their feet to the crowns of their heads.
28 And many boils were in their flesh, that their flesh wasted away until they became rotten and putrid.

29 Still the anger of the Lord did not turn away, and his hand was still stretched out over all Egypt.
30 And the Lord sent a very heavy hail, which struck their vines and broke their fruit trees and dried them up that they fell on them.
31 Also every green herb became dry and perished, for a mingling fire descended with the hail, therefore the hail and the fire consumed all things.
32 Also men and beasts that were found abroad perished of the flames of fire and of the hail, and all the young lions were exhausted.
33 And the Lord sent and brought numerous locusts into Egypt, the Chasel, Salom, Chargol, and Chagole, locusts each of its kind, which devoured all that the hail had left remaining.
34 Then the Egyptians rejoiced at the locusts, although they consumed the produce of the field, and they caught them in abundance and salted them for food.
35 And the Lord turned a mighty wind of the sea which took away all the locusts, even those that were salted, and thrust them into the Red Sea; not one locust remained within the boundaries of Egypt.
36 God sent darkness on Egypt, that the whole land of Egypt and Pathros became dark for three days so that a man could not see his hand when he lifted it to his mouth.
37 At that time many of the people of Israel died who had rebelled against the Lord and who would not listen to Moses and Aaron, and believed not in them that God had sent them.
38 And who had said, We will not go forth from Egypt because we'll perish with hunger in a desolate wilderness. They were those who would not listen to the voice of Moses.
39 The Lord plagued them in the three days of darkness, and the Israelites buried them in those days without the Egyptians knowing of them or rejoicing over them.
40 The darkness was very great in Egypt for three days, and any person who was standing when the darkness came remained standing in his place; he that was sitting remained sitting, and he that was lying continued lying in the same state; he that was walking remained sitting on the ground in the same spot; and this thing happened to all the Egyptians until the darkness had passed away.
41 The days of darkness passed away and the Lord sent Moses and Aaron to the children of Israel saying, Celebrate your feast and make your Passover, for behold I come in the middle of the night among all the Egyptians; I will strike all their firstborn, from the firstborn of a man to the first born of a beast, and when I see your Passover, I will pass over you.
42 And the children of Israel did according to all that the Lord had commanded Moses and Aaron, thus did they in that night.
43 It came to pass in the middle of the night that the Lord went forth in the midst of Egypt and struck all the firstborn of the Egyptians, from the firstborn of man to the firstborn of beast.
44 And Pharaoh rose up in the night, he and all his servants and all the Egyptians, and there was a great cry throughout Egypt in that night for there was not a house in which there was not a corpse.
45 Also the likenesses of the firstborn of Egypt which were carved in the walls at their houses were destroyed and fell to the ground.
46 Even the bones of their firstborn who had died before this and whom they had buried in their houses were raked up by the dogs of Egypt on that night and

dragged before the Egyptians and cast before them.
47 And all the Egyptians saw this evil which had suddenly come on them, and all the Egyptians cried out with a loud voice.
48 And all the families of Egypt wept on that night, each man for his son and each man for his daughter, being the firstborn, and the tumult of Egypt was heard at a distance on that night.
49 Bathia the daughter of Pharaoh went forth with the king on that night to seek Moses and Aaron in their houses; they found them in their houses eating and drinking and rejoicing with all Israel.
50 And Bathia said to Moses, Is this the reward for the good which I have done to you, who have reared you and made you grow and prosper and you have brought this evil on me and my father's house?
51 And Moses said to her, Certainly ten plagues did the Lord bring on Egypt; did any evil accrue to you from any of them? Did one of them affect you? And she said, No.
52 And Moses said to her, Although you are the firstborn to your mother, you shall not die and no evil shall reach you in the midst of Egypt.
53 And she said, What advantage is it to me when I see the king, my brother, and all his household and subjects in this evil, whose firstborn perish with all the firstborn of Egypt?
54 And Moses said to her, Certainly your brother and his household and subjects, the families of Egypt, would not listen to the words of the Lord, therefore did this evil come on them.
55 Pharaoh king of Egypt approached Moses and Aaron and some of the children of Israel who were with them in that place, and he prayed to them saying,
56 Rise up and take your brothers, all the children of Israel who are in the land with their sheep and oxen, and all belonging to them; they shall leave nothing remaining, only pray for me to the Lord your God.
57 And Moses said to Pharaoh, Behold you are your mother's firstborn, yet fear not for you will not die, for the Lord has commanded that you shall live in order to show you his great might and strong stretched out arm.
58 Pharaoh ordered the children of Israel to be sent away, and all the Egyptians strengthened themselves to send them, for they said, We are all perishing.
59 And all the Egyptians sent the Israelites forth with great riches, sheep and oxen and precious things according to the oath of the Lord between him and our Father Abraham.
60 And the children of Israel delayed going away until night, and when the Egyptians came to them to bring them out, they said to them, Are we thieves, that we should go forth at night?
61 And the children of Israel asked of the Egyptians, vessels of silver and vessels of gold, and garments, and the children of Israel stripped the Egyptians.
62 Moses hurried and rose up and went to the river of Egypt and brought up from there the coffin of Joseph and took it with him.
63 The children of Israel also brought up each man his father's coffin with him, and each man the coffins of his tribe.

CHAPTER 81

1 The children of Israel journeyed from Rameses to Succoth, about six hundred thousand men on foot besides the little ones and their wives.
2 Also a mixed multitude went up with them, flocks and herds, even much cattle.
3 The temporary time of the children of Israel who lived in the land of Egypt in hard labor was two hundred and ten years.
4 And at the end of two hundred and ten years, the Lord brought forth the children of Israel from Egypt with a strong hand.
5 The children of Israel traveled from Egypt and from Goshen and from Rameses, and encamped in Succoth on the fifteenth day of the first month.
6 The Egyptians buried all their firstborn whom the Lord had smitten, and all the Egyptians buried their slain for three days.
7 The children of Israel traveled from Succoth and encamped in Ethom, at the end of the wilderness.
8 On the third day after the Egyptians had buried their firstborn, many men rose up from Egypt and went after Israel to make them return to Egypt, for they regretted that they had sent the Israelites away from serving them.
9 One man said to his neighbor, Certainly Moses and Aaron spoke to Pharaoh saying, We will go a three days' journey in the wilderness and sacrifice to the Lord our God.
10 So now let us rise up early in the morning and make them return; it shall be that if they return with us to Egypt to their masters, then we will know that there is faith in them, but if they will not return then will we fight with them, and make them come back with great power and a strong hand.
11 All the nobles of Pharaoh rose up in the morning, and with them about seven hundred thousand men; they went forth from Egypt on that day and came to the place where the children of Israel were.
12 And all the Egyptians looked and saw Moses and Aaron and all the children of Israel were sitting before Pi-hahiroth, eating and drinking and celebrating the feast of the Lord.
13 All the Egyptians said to the children of Israel, Certainly you said, We will go a journey for three days in the wilderness and sacrifice to our God and return.
14 So now this day makes five days since you went; why do you not return to your masters?
15 Moses and Aaron answered them, saying, Because the Lord our God has testified in us saying, You shall no more return to Egypt, but take yourselves to a land flowing with milk and honey; as the Lord our God had sworn to our ancestors to give to us.
16 And when the nobles of Egypt saw that the children of Israel did not listen to them to return to Egypt, they prepared themselves to fight with Israel.
17 The Lord strengthened the hearts of the children of Israel over the Egyptians so that they gave them a severe beating; the battle was severe on the Egyptians and all the Egyptians fled from before the children of Israel; many of them perished by the hand of Israel.
18 And the nobles of Pharaoh went to Egypt and told Pharaoh, saying, The children of Israel have fled and will no more return to Egypt, and in this manner did Moses and Aaron speak to us.
19 Pharaoh heard this thing, and his heart and the hearts of all his subjects were turned against Israel; they repented that they had sent Israel, and all the Egyptians advised Pharaoh to pursue the children of Israel to make them come back to their

burdens.
20 They said each man to his brother, What is this which we have done, that we have sent Israel from our service?
21 The Lord strengthened the hearts of all the Egyptians to pursue the Israelites, for the Lord desired to overthrow the Egyptians in the Red Sea.
22 Pharaoh rose up and harnessed his chariot; he ordered all the Egyptians to assemble, not one man was left excepting the little ones and the women.
23 And all the Egyptians went forth with Pharaoh to pursue the children of Israel, and the camp of Egypt was a very large and strong camp, about ten hundred thousand men.
24 All of this camp went and pursued the children of Israel to bring them back to Egypt, and they reached them encamping by the Red Sea.
25 The children of Israel lifted up their eyes, and saw all the Egyptians pursuing them; the children of Israel were greatly terrified at them and the children of Israel cried to the Lord.
26 On account of the Egyptians, the children of Israel divided themselves into four divisions and they were divided in their opinions for they were afraid of the Egyptians, and Moses spoke to each of them.
27 The first division was of the children of Reuben, Simeon, and Issachar, and they decided to cast themselves into the sea, for they were greatly afraid of the Egyptians.
28 And Moses said to them, Fear not, stand still and see the salvation of the Lord which He will effect this day for you.
29 The second division was of the children of Zebulun, Benjamin and Naphtali, and they resolved to go back to Egypt with the Egyptians.
30 And Moses said to them, Fear not, for as you have seen the Egyptians this day, so shall you see them no more for ever.
31 The third division was of the children of Judah and Joseph, and they resolved to go to meet the Egyptians to fight with them.
32 And Moses said to them, Stand in your places for the Lord will fight for you, and you shall remain silent.
33 And the fourth division was of the children of Levi, Gad, and Asher, and they resolved to go into the midst of the Egyptians to confound them. Moses said to them, Remain in your stations and fear not, only call to the Lord that he may save you out of their hands.
34 After this Moses rose up from among the people and prayed to the Lord and said,
35 O Lord God of the whole earth, save now your people whom you brought forth from Egypt, and let not the Egyptians boast that power and might are theirs.
36 So the Lord said to Moses, Why do you cry to me? Speak to the children of Israel that they shall proceed, and stretch out your rod on the sea and divide it and the children of Israel shall pass through it.
37 And Moses did so; he lifted up his rod on the sea and divided it.
38 And the waters of the sea were divided into twelve parts, and the children of Israel passed through on foot with shoes, as a man would pass through a prepared road.
39 The Lord displayed to the children of Israel his wonders in Egypt and in the sea by the hand of Moses and Aaron.
40 When the children of Israel had entered the sea the Egyptians came after them, and the waters of the sea covered them and they all sank in the water; not one man was left except Pharaoh, who gave thanks to the Lord and believed in him, therefore

the Lord did not cause him to perish at that time with the Egyptians.
41 The Lord ordered an angel to take him from among the Egyptians, who cast him on the land of Ninevah and he reigned over it for a long time.
42 On that day the Lord saved Israel from the hand of Egypt, and all the children of Israel saw that the Egyptians had perished; they beheld the great hand of the Lord in what he had performed in Egypt and in the sea.
43 Then sang Moses and the children of Israel this song to the Lord, on the day when the Lord caused the Egyptians to fall before them.
44 And all Israel sang in concert saying, I will sing to the Lord for He is greatly exalted, the horse and his rider has he cast into the sea, consider that it is written in the book of the law of God.
45 After this the children of Israel proceeded on their journey and encamped in Marah; the Lord gave to the children of Israel statutes and judgments in that place in Marah, and the Lord commanded the children of Israel to walk in all his ways and to serve him.
46 They journeyed from Marah and came to Elim; in Elim were twelve springs of water and seventy date trees and the children encamped there by the waters.
47 They journeyed from Elim and came to the wilderness of Sin, on the fifteenth day of the second month after their departure from Egypt.
48 At that time the Lord gave manna to the children of Israel to eat, and the Lord caused food to rain from heaven for the children of Israel day by day.
49 And the children of Israel ate the manna for forty years, all the days that they were in the wilderness, until they came to the land of Canaan to possess it.
50 They proceeded from the wilderness of Sin and encamped in Alush.
51 And they proceeded from Alush and encamped in Rephidim.
52 When the children of Israel were in Rephidim, Amalek the son of Eliphaz, the son of Esau, the brother of Zepho, came to fight with Israel.
53 And he brought with him eight hundred and one thousand men, magicians and conjurers, and he prepared for battle with Israel in Rephidim.
54 They carried on a great and severe battle against Israel, and the Lord delivered Amalek and his people into the hands of Moses and the children of Israel, and into the hand of Joshua, the son of Nun, the Ephrathite, the servant of Moses.
55 The children of Israel struck Amalek and his people at the edge of the sword, but the battle was very severe on the children of Israel.
56 And the Lord said to Moses, Write this thing as a memorial for you in a book, and place it in the hand of Joshua, the son of Nun your servant; you shall command the children of Israel, saying, When you come to the land of Canaan, you shall utterly wipe out the remembrance of Amalek from under heaven.
57 And Moses did so, and he took the book and wrote on it these words, saying,
58 Remember what Amalek has done to you in the road when you went forth from Egypt.
59 He met you in the road and struck your rear, even those that were feeble behind you when you were faint and weary.
60 Therefore it shall be when the Lord your God shall have given you rest from all your enemies round about in the land which the Lord your God gives you for an inheritance, to possess it, that you shall blot out the remembrance of Amalek from under heaven, you shall not forget it.
61 The king who shall have pity on Amalek or on his memory or on his offspring, behold I will blame him, and I will cut him off from among his people.

62 And Moses wrote all these things in a book, and he advised the children of Israel respecting all these matters.

CHAPTER 82

1 The children of Israel proceeded from Rephidim and camped in the wilderness of Sinai, in the third month from their going forth from Egypt.
2 At that time Reuel the Midianite, the father-in-law of Moses, came with Zipporah his daughter and her two sons for he had heard of the wonders of the Lord which he had done to Israel, that he had delivered them from the hand of Egypt.
3 Reuel came to Moses in the wilderness where he was camped, where the mountain of God was.
4 And Moses went forth to meet his father-in-law with great honor, and all Israel was with him.
5 Reuel and his children remained among the Israelites for many days, and Reuel knew the Lord from that day forward.
6 In the third month from the children of Israel's departure from Egypt, on the sixth day, the Lord gave to Israel the ten commandments on Mount Sinai.
7 All Israel heard all these commandments, and all Israel rejoiced greatly in the Lord on that day.
8 And the glory of the Lord rested on Mount Sinai; he called to Moses and Moses came in the midst of a cloud and ascended the mountain.
9 Moses was on the mount forty days and forty nights; he ate no bread and drank no water, and the Lord instructed him in the standards and judgments in order to teach the children of Israel.
10 And the Lord wrote the ten commandments which he had commanded the children of Israel on two tablets of stone, which he gave to Moses to command the children of Israel.
11 At the end of forty days and forty nights, when the Lord had finished speaking to Moses on Mount Sinai, the Lord gave to Moses the tablets of stone written with the finger of God.
12 When the children of Israel saw that Moses delayed coming down from the mount, they gathered round Aaron and said, As for this man Moses, we know not what has become of him.
13 Now therefore rise up, make to us a god who shall go before us, so that you shall not die.
14 Aaron was greatly afraid of the people, and he ordered them to bring him gold and he made it into a molten calf for the people.
15 The Lord said to Moses, before he had come down from the mount, Go down, for your people whom you brought forth from Egypt have corrupted themselves.
16 They have made to themselves a molten calf and have bowed down to it; now therefore leave me, that I may consume them from off the earth for they are a stubborn people.
17 And Moses sought the countenance of the Lord, and he prayed to the Lord for the people on account of the calf which they had made; afterward he descended from the mount and in his hands were the two tablets of stone which God had given him to command the Israelites.
18 When Moses approached the camp and saw the calf which the people had made,

the anger of Moses was set ablaze and he broke the tablets under the mount.
19 Moses came to the camp; he took the calf and burned it with fire, and ground it till it became fine dust and scattered it on the water, and gave it to the Israelites to drink.
20 There died of the people by the swords of each other about three thousand men who had made the calf.
21 The next morning Moses said to the people, I will go up to the Lord, perhaps I may make atonement for your sins which you have sinned to the Lord.
22 And Moses again went up to the Lord, and he remained with the Lord forty days and forty nights.
23 And during the forty days Moses entreaed the Lord on behalf of the children of Israel, and the Lord listened to the prayer of Moses, and the Lord was begged of him on behalf of Israel.
24 Then spoke the Lord to Moses to cut out two stone tablets and to bring them up to the Lord, who would write on them the ten commandments.
25 Moses did so, and he came down and fashioned the two tablets and went up to Mount Sinai to the Lord, and the Lord wrote the ten commandments on the tablets.
26 Moses remained yet with the Lord forty days and forty nights, and the Lord instructed him in standards and judgments to give to Israel.
27 The Lord commanded him respecting the children of Israel that they should make a sanctuary for the Lord that his name might rest therein, and the Lord showed him the likeness of the sanctuary and the likeness of all its vessels.
28 And at the end of the forty days, Moses came down from the mount and the two tablets were in his hand.
29 And Moses came to the children of Israel and spoke to them all the words of the Lord, and he taught them laws, rules and judgments which the Lord had taught him.
30 Moses told the children of Israel the word of the Lord, that a sanctuary should be made for him to dwell among the children of Israel.
31 And the people rejoiced greatly at all the good which the Lord had spoken to them through Moses, and they said, We will do all that the Lord has spoken to you.
32 And the people rose up like one man and they made generous offerings to the sanctuary of the Lord; each man brought the offering of the Lord for the work of the sanctuary and for all its service.
33 All the children of Israel brought each man of all that was found in his possession for the work of the sanctuary of the Lord, gold, silver and brass, and every thing that was serviceable for the sanctuary.
34 All the wise men who were practiced in work came and made the sanctuary of the Lord, according to all that the Lord had commanded, every man in the work in which he had skill; all the wise men in heart made the sanctuary and its furniture and all the vessels for the holy service as the Lord had commanded Moses.
35 And the work of the sanctuary of the tabernacle was completed at the end of five months; the children of Israel did all that the Lord had commanded Moses.
36 And they brought the sanctuary and all its furniture to Moses; like to the representation which the Lord had shown to Moses, so did the children of Israel.
37 And Moses saw the work, and behold they did it as the Lord had commanded him, so Moses blessed them.

CHAPTER 83

1 In the twelfth month, in the twenty-third day of the month, Moses took Aaron and
his sons and dressed them in their garments and anointed them, and did to them as
the Lord had commanded him, and Moses brought up all the offerings which the
Lord had on that day commanded him.
2 Moses afterward took Aaron and his sons and said to them, For seven days you
shall remain at the door of the tabernacle, for thus am I commanded.
3 And Aaron and his sons did all that the Lord had commanded them through
Moses, and they remained for seven days at the door of the tabernacle.
4 On the eighth day, being the first day of the first month, in the second year from
the Israelites' departure from Egypt, Moses erected the sanctuary and put in all the
furniture of the tabernacle and all the furniture of the sanctuary, and he did all that
the Lord had commanded him.
5 Moses called to Aaron and his sons, and they brought the burnt offering and the
sin offering for themselves and the children of Israel, as the Lord had commanded
Moses.
6 On that day the two sons of Aaron, Nadab and Abihu, took strange fire and
brought it before the Lord who had not commanded them to do it, and a fire went
forth from before the Lord and consumed them, and they died before the Lord on
that day.
7 Then on the day when Moses had completed erecting the sanctuary, the princes of
the children of Israel began to bring their offerings before the Lord for the dedication
of the altar.
8 And they brought up their offerings each prince for one day, a prince each day for
twelve days.
9 And all the offerings which they brought, each man in his day, one silver charger
weighing one hundred and thirty shekels, one silver bowl of seventy shekels after
the shekel of the sanctuary, both of them full of fine flour mingled with oil for a meat
offering;
10 One spoon, weighing ten shekels of gold, full of incense;
11 One young bullock, one ram, one lamb of the first year for a burnt offering;
12 And one kid of the goats for a sin offering.
13 For a sacrifice of peace offering: two oxen, five rams, five male goats, five lambs
of a year old.
14 Thus did the twelve princes of Israel day by day, each man in his day.
15 It was after this in the thirteenth day of the month, that Moses commanded the
children of Israel to observe the Passover.
16 And the children of Israel kept the Passover in its season in the fourteenth day of
the month; as the Lord had commanded Moses, so did the children of Israel.
17 And in the second month, on the first day thereof, the Lord spoke to Moses
saying,
18 Number the heads of all the males of the children of Israel from twenty years old
and upward, you and your brother Aaron and the twelve princes of Israel.
19 And Moses did so, and Aaron came with the twelve princes of Israel, and they
counted the children of Israel in the wilderness of Sinai.
20 And the number of the children of Israel by the houses of their fathers, from
twenty years old and upward, were six hundred and three thousand, five hundred
and fifty.
21 But the children of Levi were not numbered among their brothers the children of

Israel.
22 And the number of all the males of the children of Israel from one month old and upward, was twenty-two thousand, two hundred and seventy-three.
23 And the number of the children of Levi from one month old and above, was twenty-two thousand.
24 Moses placed the priests and the Levites each man to his service and to his burden to serve the sanctuary of the tabernacle, as the Lord had commanded Moses.
25 And on the twentieth day of the month, the cloud was taken away from the tabernacle of testimony.
26 At that time the children of Israel continued their journey from the wilderness of Sinai, they took a journey of three days and the cloud rested on the wilderness of Paran; there the anger of the Lord was set ablaze against Israel, for they had provoked the Lord in asking him for meat to eat.
27 And the Lord listened to their voice, and gave them meat which they ate for one month.
28 But after this the anger of the Lord was set ablaze against them, and he struck them with a great slaughter, and they were buried there in that place.
29 The children of Israel called that place Kebroth Hattaavah, because there they buried the people that lusted flesh.
30 And they departed from Kebroth Hattaavah and pitched in Hazeroth, which is in the wilderness of Paran.
31 And while the children of Israel were in Hazeroth, the anger of the Lord was set ablaze against Miriam on account of Moses, and she became leprous, white as snow.
32 She was confined outside the camp for seven days until she had been received again after her leprosy.
33 The children of Israel afterward departed from Hazeroth and camped in the end of the wilderness of Paran.
34 At that time, the Lord spoke to Moses to send twelve men from the children of Israel, one man to a tribe, to go and explore the land of Canaan.
35 Moses sent the twelve men and they came to the land of Canaan to search and examine it, and they explored the whole land from the wilderness of Sin to Rechob as you come to Chamoth.
36 At the end of forty days they came to Moses and Aaron, and they brought him word as it was in their hearts; ten of the men brought up an evil report to the children of Israel, of the land which they had explored saying, It is better for us to return to Egypt than to go to this land, a land that consumes its inhabitants.
37 But Joshua the son of Nun and Caleb the son of Jephuneh, who were of those that explored the land said, The land is very good.
38 If the Lord delights in us, then he will bring us to this land and give it to us for it is a land flowing with milk and honey.
39 But the children of Israel would not listen to them, and they listened to the words of the ten men who had brought up an evil report of the land.
40 The Lord heard the murmurings of the children of Israel and he was angry and swore, saying,
41 Certainly not one man of this wicked generation shall see the land from twenty years old and upward except Caleb the son of Jephuneh and Joshua the son of Nun.
42 But certainly this wicked generation shall perish in this wilderness, and their children shall come to the land and they shall possess it. So the anger of the Lord was set ablaze against Israel and he made them wander in the wilderness for forty

years until the end of that wicked generation because they did not follow the Lord.
43 And the people lived in the wilderness of Paran a long time, and they afterward proceeded to the wilderness by the way of the Red Sea.

CHAPTER 84

1 At that time Korah the son of Jetzer the son of Kehath the son of Levi, took many men of the children of Israel and they rose up and quarreled with Moses and Aaron and the whole congregation.
2 And the Lord was angry with them and the earth opened its mouth and swallowed them up, with their houses and all belonging to them, and all the men belonging to Korah.
3 After this God made the people go round by the way of Mount Seir for a long time.
4 At that time the Lord said to Moses, Provoke not a war against the children of Esau, for I will not give to you of any thing belonging to them, as much as the sole of the foot could tread on, for I have given Mount Seir for an inheritance to Esau.
5 Therefore did the children of Esau fight against the children of Seir in former times, and the Lord had delivered the children of Seir into the hands of the children of Esau, and destroyed them from before them and the children of Esau lived in their stead to this day.
6 So the Lord said to the children of Israel, Fight not against the children of Esau your brothers for nothing in their land belongs to you, but you may buy food of them for money and eat it, and you may buy water of them for money and drink it.
7 And the children of Israel did according to the word of the Lord.
8 The children of Israel wandered in the wilderness, going round by the way of Mount Sinai for a long time, and touched not the children of Esau; they continued in that district for nineteen years.
9 At that time Latinus king of the children of Chittim died, in the forty-fifth year of his reign, which is the fourteenth year of the children of Israel's departure from Egypt.
10 They buried him in his place which he had built for himself in the land of Chittim, and Abimnas reigned in his place for thirty-eight years.
11 The children of Israel passed the boundary of the children of Esau in those days, at the end of nineteen years, and they came and passed the road of the wilderness of Moab.
12 And the Lord said to Moses, Besiege not Moab, and do not fight against them, for I will give you nothing of their land.
13 And the children of Israel passed the road of the wilderness of Moab for nineteen years, and they did not fight against them.
14 In the thirty-sixth year of the children of Israel's departing from Egypt the Lord struck the heart of Sihon, king of the Amorites; he waged war and went forth to fight against the children of Moab.
15 And Sihon sent messengers to Beor the son of Janeas, the son of Balaam, counsellor to the king of Egypt and to Balaam his son, to curse Moab in order that it might be delivered into the hand of Sihon.
16 And the messengers went and brought Beor the son of Janeas, and Balaam his son, from Pethor in Mesopotamia; so Beor and Balaam his son came to the city of Sihon and they cursed Moab and their king in the presence of Sihon king of the

Amorites.
17 So Sihon went out with his whole army and he went to Moab and fought against them; he subdued them and the Lord delivered them into his hands, and Sihon killed the king of Moab.
18 Sihon took all the cities of Moab in the battle; he also took Heshbon from them, for Heshbon was one of the cities of Moab, and Sihon placed his princes and his nobles in Heshbon, and Heshbon belonged to Sihon in those days.
19 Therefore the parable speakers (wise men), Beor and Balaam his son, uttered these words, saying, Come to Heshbon, the city of Sihon will be built and established.
20 Woe to you Moab! You are lost, O people of Kemosh! Behold it is written on the book of the law of God.
21 And when Sihon had conquered Moab, he placed guards in the cities which he had taken from Moab, and a considerable number of the children of Moab fell in battle into the hand of Sihon; he made a great capture of them, sons and daughters, and he killed their king; so Sihon turned back to his own land.
22 And Sihon gave numerous presents of silver and gold to Beor and Balaam his son, and he dismissed them, and they went to Mesopotamia to their home and country.
23 At that time all the children of Israel passed from the road of the wilderness of Moab, and returned and surrounded the wilderness of Edom.
24 So the whole congregation came to the wilderness of Sin in the first month of the fortieth year from their departure from Egypt, and the children of Israel lived there in Kadesh of the wilderness of Sin, and Miriam died there and she was buried there.
25 At that time Moses sent messengers to Hadad king of Edom, saying, Thus says your brother Israel, Let me pass I pray you through your land, we will not pass through field or vineyard, we will not drink the water of the well; we will walk in the king's road.
26 And Edom said to him, You shall not pass through my country. And Edom went forth to meet the children of Israel with a mighty people.
27 And the children of Esau refused to let the children of Israel pass through their land, so the Israelites left them and did not fight against them.
28 For before this the Lord had commanded the children of Israel, saying, You shall not fight against the children of Esau. Therefore the Israelites went away from them and did not fight against them.
29 So the children of Israel departed from Kadesh, and all the people came to Mount Hor.
30 At that time the Lord said to Moses, Tell your brother Aaron that he shall die there, for he shall not come to the land which I have given to the children of Israel.
31 And Aaron went up at the command of the Lord to Mount Hor, in the fortieth year, in the fifth month, in the first day of the month.
32 And Aaron was one hundred and twenty-three years old when he died in Mount Hor.

CHAPTER 85

1 The king Arad the Canaanite, who lived in the south, heard that the Israelites had come by the way of the spies, and he arranged his forces to fight against the Israelites.

2 And the children of Israel were greatly afraid of him, for he had a great and courageous army, so the children of Israel resolved to return to Egypt.

3 The children of Israel turned back about the distance of three days' journey to Maserath Beni Jaakon, for they were greatly afraid on account of the king Arad.

4 And the children of Israel would not get back to their places, so they remained in Beni Jaakon for thirty days.

5 When the children of Levi saw that the children of Israel would not turn back, they were zealous for the sake of the Lord; they rose up and fought against the Israelites their brothers, and killed of them a great many and forced them to turn back to their place, Mount Hor.

6 And when they returned, king Arad was still arranging his host for battle against the Israelites.

7 Israel vowed a vow saying, If you will deliver this people into my hand, then I will utterly destroy their cities.

8 The Lord listened to the voice of Israel, and he delivered the Canaanites into their hands; he utterly destroyed them and their cities, and he called the name of the place Hormah.

9 The children of Israel journeyed from Mount Hor and camped in Oboth, and they journeyed from Oboth and they camped at Ije-abarim, in the border of Moab.

10 And the children of Israel sent to Moab, saying, Let us pass now through your land into our place, but the children of Moab would not allow the children of Israel to pass through their land, for the children of Moab were greatly afraid that the children of Israel should do to them as Sihon king of the Amorites had done to them, who had taken their land and had slain many of them.

11 Therefore Moab would not permit the Israelites to pass through his land, and the Lord commanded the children of Israel, saying that they should not fight against Moab, so the Israelites removed themselves from Moab.

12 And the children of Israel journeyed from the border of Moab; they came to the other side of Arnon, the border of Moab, between Moab and the Amorites, and they camped on the border of Sihon, king of the Amorites, in the wilderness of Kedemoth.

13 The children of Israel sent messengers to Sihon, king of the Amorites, saying,

14 Let us pass through your land; we will not turn into the fields or into the vineyards; we will go along by the king's highway until we shall have passed your border. But Sihon would not let the Israelites pass.

15 So Sihon collected all the people of the Amorites and went forth into the wilderness to meet the children of Israel, and he fought against Israel in Jahaz.

16 The Lord delivered Sihon king of the Amorites into the hands of the children of Israel, and Israel struck all the people of Sihon with the edge of the sword and avenged the cause of Moab.

17 The children of Israel took possession of the land of Sihon from Aram to Jabuk, to the children of Ammon, and they took all the booty of the cities.

18 Israel took all these cities, and Israel lived in all the cities of the Amorites.

19 All the children of Israel resolved to fight against the children of Ammon, to take their land also.

20 So the Lord said to the children of Israel, Do not besiege the children of Ammon, neither stir up battle against them, for I will give nothing to you of their land; the children of Israel listened to the word of the Lord, and did not fight against the children of Ammon.

21 The children of Israel turned and went up by the way of Bashan to the land of Og, king of Bashan, and Og the king of Bashan went out to meet the Israelites in battle; he had with him many courageous men, and a very strong force from the people of the Amorites.
22 And Og king of Bashan was a very powerful man, but Naaron his son was greatly powerful, even stronger than he was.
23 And Og said in his heart, Behold now the whole camp of Israel takes up a space of several miles. Now will I strike them at once without sword or spear.
24 Og went up Mount Jahaz and took from there one large stone, the length of which was three parsa, and he placed it on his head, and resolved to throw it on the camp of the children of Israel to strike all the Israelites with that stone.
25 And the angel of the Lord came and pierced the stone on the head of Og, and the stone fell on the neck of Og so that Og fell to the earth on account of the weight of the stone on his neck.
26 At that time the Lord said to the children of Israel, Be not afraid of him for I have given him and all his people and all his land into your hands, and you shall do to him as you did to Sihon.
27 Moses went down to him with a small number of the children of Israel, and Moses struck Og with a stick at the ankles of his feet and killed him.
28 The children of Israel afterward pursued the children of Og and all his people; they beat and destroyed them till there was no remnant left of them.
29 Moses afterward sent some of the children of Israel to spy out Jaazer, for Jaazer was a very famous city.
30 The spies went to Jaazer and explored it, and the spies trusted in the Lord; they fought against the men of Jaazer.
31 These men took Jaazer and its villages and the Lord delivered them into their hands, and they drove out the Amorites who had been there.
32 And the children of Israel took the land of the two kings of the Amorites, sixty cities which were on the other side of Jordan, from the brook of Arnon to Mount Herman.
33 The children of Israel journeyed and came into the plain of Moab which is on this side of Jordan, by Jericho.
34 And the children of Moab heard all the evil which the children of Israel had done to the two kings of the Amorites, to Sihon and Og; so all the men of Moab were greatly afraid of the Israelites.
35 The elders of Moab said, Behold the two kings of the Amorites, Sihon and Og, who were more powerful than all the kings of the earth, if they could not stand against the children of Israel how then can we stand before them?
36 Certainly they sent us a message before now to pass through our land on their way, and we would not allow them; now they will turn on us with their heavy swords and destroy us. Moab was distressed on account of the children of Israel and they were greatly afraid of them, and they counselled together what was to be done to the children of Israel.
37 The elders of Moab decided and took one of their men, Balak the son of Zippor the Moabite, and made him king over them at that time, and Balak was a very wise man.
38 And the elders of Moab rose up and sent to the children of Midian to make peace with them, for a great battle and enmity had been in those days between Moab and Midian, from the days of Hadad the son of Bedad king of Edom, who struck Midian

in the field of Moab, to these days.
39 The children of Moab sent to the children of Midian and made peace with them, and the elders of Midian came to the land of Moab to make peace on behalf of the children of Midian.
40 And the elders of Moab counselled with the elders of Midian what to do in order to save their lives from Israel.
41 All the children of Moab said to the elders of Midian, The children of Israel shall lick up all that are round about us, as the ox licks up the grass of the field, for thus did they do to the two kings of the Amorites who are stronger than we are.
42 The elders of Midian said to Moab, We have heard that at the time when Sihon king of the Amorites fought against you, when he prevailed over you and took your land, he had sent to Beor the son of Janeas and to Balaam his son from Mesopotamia, and they came and cursed you; therefore did the hand of Sihon prevail over you, that he took your land.
43 Now therefore you send also to Balaam his son for he still remains in his land and give him his wage, that he may come and curse all the people of whom you are afraid; so the elders of Moab heard this thing, and it pleased them to send to Balaam the son of Beor.
44 So Balak the son of Zippor king of Moab sent messengers to Balaam, saying,
45 Behold there is a people come out from Egypt, see how they cover the face of the earth and they are against me.
46 So now come and curse this people for me for they are too mighty for me; perhaps I shall succeed to fight against them and drive them out, for I heard that he whom you bless is blessed, and whom you curse is cursed.
47 So the messengers of Balak went to Balaam and brought Balaam to curse the people to fight against Moab.
48 And Balaam came to Balak to curse Israel, and the Lord said to Balaam, Curse not this people for they are blessed.
49 And Balak urged Balaam day by day to curse Israel, but Balaam did not listen to Balak on account of the word of the Lord which he had spoken to Balaam.
50 And when Balak saw that Balaam would not accede to his wish, he rose up and went home; Balaam also returned to his land and he went from there to Midian.
51 The children of Israel journeyed from the plain of Moab and camped by Jordan from Beth-jesimoth even to Abel-shittim, at the end of the plains of Moab.
52 When the children of Israel stayed in the plain of Shittim, they began to commit prostitution with the daughters of Moab.
53 The children of Israel approached Moab, and the children of Moab pitched their tents opposite to the camp of the children of Israel.
54 The children of Moab were afraid of the children of Israel, and the children of Moab took all their daughters and their wives of beauty and attractive appearance, and dressed them in gold and silver and costly garments.
55 The children of Moab seated those women at the door of their tents in order that the children of Israel might see them and turn to them, and not fight against Moab.
56 All the children of Moab did this thing to the children of Israel, and every man placed his wife and daughter at the door of his tent; all the children of Israel saw the act of the children of Moab, and the children of Israel turned to the daughters of Moab and coveted them, and they went to them.
57 It came to pass that when a Hebrew came to the door of the tent of Moab and saw a daughter of Moab, and desired her in his heart and spoke with her at the door of

the tent that which he desired, while they were speaking together the men of the tent would come out and speak to the Hebrew like these words:
58 Certainly you know that we are brothers, we are all the descendants of Lot and the descendants of Abraham his brother, why then will you not remain with us, and why will you not eat our bread and our sacrifice?
59 When the children of Moab had thus overwhelmed him with their speeches and enticed him by their flattering words, they seated him in the tent and cooked and sacrificed for him, and he ate of their sacrifice and of their bread.
60 They then gave him wine and he drank and became intoxicated; they placed before him a beautiful damsel and he did with her as he liked, for he knew not what he was doing, as he had drunk plentifully of wine.
61 Thus did the children of Moab to Israel in that place, in the plain of Shittim, and the anger of the Lord was set ablaze against Israel on account of this matter; he sent a pestilence among them and there of the Israelites twenty-four thousand men died.
62 Then there was a man of the children of Simeon whose name was Zimri, the son of Salu, who connected himself with the Midianite Cosbi, the daughter of Zur, king of Midian, in the sight of all the children of Israel.
63 And Phineas the son of Elazer, the son of Aaron the priest, saw this wicked thing which Zimri had done; he took a spear and rose up and went after them, pierced them both and killed them, and the pestilence ceased from the children of Israel.

CHAPTER 86

1 At that time after the pestilence, the Lord said to Moses and to Elazer the son of Aaron the priest,
2 Count the heads of the whole community of the children of Israel, from twenty years old and upward, all that went forth in the army.
3 And Moses and Elazer numbered the children of Israel after their families, and the number of all Israel was seven hundred thousand, seven hundred and thirty.
4 The number of the children of Levi, from one month old and upward, was twenty-three thousand, and among these there was not a man of those numbered by Moses and Aaron in the wilderness of Sinai.
5 For the Lord had told them that they would die in the wilderness, so they all died, and not one had been left of them excepting Caleb the son of Jephuneh, and Joshua the son of Nun.
6 And it was after this that the Lord said to Moses, Say to the children of Israel to avenge on Midian the cause of their brothers the children of Israel.
7 Moses did so, and the children of Israel chose from among them twelve thousand men, being one thousand to a tribe, and they went to Midian.
8 And the children of Israel warred against Midian, and they killed every male, also the five princes of
Midian, and Balaam the son of Beor they killed with the sword.
9 And the children of Israel took the wives of Midian captive, with their little ones and their cattle, and all belonging to them.
10 They took all the booty and all the valuables, and they brought it to Moses and to Elazer to the plains of Moab.
11 Moses and Elazer and all the princes of the congregation went forth to meet them with joy.

12 And they divided all the goods of Midian, and the children of Israel had been revenged on Midian for the cause of their brothers the children of Israel.

CHAPTER 87

1 At that time the Lord said to Moses, Behold your days are approaching to an end, take now Joshua the son of Nun your servant and place him in the tabernacle and I will command him, and Moses did so.
2 The Lord appeared in the tabernacle in a pillar of cloud, and the pillar of cloud stood at the entrance of the tabernacle.
3 The Lord commanded Joshua the son of Nun and said to him, Be strong and courageous, for you shall bring the children of Israel to the land which I swore to give them, and I will be with you.
4 And Moses said to Joshua, Be strong and courageous, for you will make the children of Israel inherit the land, and the Lord will be with you; he will not leave you nor turn away from you, be not afraid or disheartened.
5 Moses called to all the children of Israel and said to them, You have seen all the good which the Lord your God has done for you in the wilderness.
6 Now therefore observe all the words of this law and walk in the way of the Lord your God, turn not from the way which the Lord has commanded you, either to the right or to the left.
7 And Moses taught the children of Israel rules and judgments and laws to do in the land as the Lord had commanded him.
8 And he taught them the way of the Lord and his laws; behold they are written on the book of the law of God which he gave to the children of Israel by the hand of Moses.
9 And Moses finished commanding the children of Israel, and the Lord said to him, Go up to the Mount Abarim and die there, and be gathered to your people as Aaron your brother was gathered.
10 And Moses went up as the Lord had commanded him, and he died there in the land of Moab by the order of the Lord, in the fortieth year from the Israelites going forth from the land of Egypt.
11 And the children of Israel wept for Moses in the plains of Moab for thirty days, and the days of weeping and mourning for Moses were completed.

CHAPTER 88

1 It was after the death of Moses that the Lord said to Joshua the son of Nun,
2 Rise up and pass the Jordan to the land which I have given to the children of Israel, and you shall make the children of Israel inherit the land.
3 Every place on which the sole of your feet treads shall belong to you; from the wilderness of Lebanon to the great river, the river of Perath, shall be your boundary.
4 No man shall stand up against you all the days of your life; as I was with Moses, so will I be with you, only be strong and of good courage to observe all the law which Moses commanded you; turn not from the way either to the right or to the left, in order that you may prosper in all that you do.
5 And Joshua commanded the officers of Israel, saying, Pass through the camp and

command the people, saying, Prepare for yourselves provisions, for in three days
more you will pass the Jordan to possess the land.
6 The officers of the children of Israel did so, and they commanded the people and
they did all that Joshua had commanded.
7 Joshua sent two men to spy out the land of Jericho, and the men went and spied
out Jericho.
8 And at the end of seven days they came to Joshua in the camp and said to him, The
Lord has delivered the whole land into our hands; the inhabitants thereof are melted
with fear because of us.
9 And it came to pass after that, that Joshua rose up in the morning and all Israel
with him, and they journeyed from Shittim; Joshua and all Israel with him passed
the Jordan, and Joshua was eighty-two years old when he passed the Jordan with
Israel.
10 The people went up from Jordan on the tenth day of the first month, and they
camped in Gilgal at the eastern corner of Jericho.
11 And the children of Israel kept the Passover in Gilgal in the plains of Jericho, on
the fourteenth day of the month, as it is written in the law of Moses.
12 The manna ceased at that time on the morning of the Passover, and there was no
more manna for the children of Israel and they ate of the produce of the land of
Canaan.
13 Jericho was entirely closed against the children of Israel, no one came out or went
in.
14 And it was in the second month, on the first day of the month, that the Lord said
to Joshua, Rise up, behold I have given Jericho into your hand with all the people
there; all your fighting men shall go round the city, once each day, thus shall you do
for six days.
15 And the priests shall blow on trumpets; when you hear the sound of the trumpet,
all the people shall give a great shouting, that the walls of the city shall fall down; all
the people shall go up every man against his opponent.
16 And Joshua did so according to all that the Lord had commanded him.
17 On the seventh day they went round the city seven times, and the priests blew on
trumpets.
18 At the seventh round, Joshua said to the people, Shout, for the Lord has delivered
the whole city into our hands.
19 Only the city and all that it contains shall be accursed to the Lord, and keep
yourselves from the accursed thing, that you make the camp of Israel accursed and
trouble it.
20 But all the silver and gold and brass and iron shall be consecrated to the Lord,
they shall come into the treasury of the Lord.
21 And the people blew on trumpets and made a great shouting, and the walls of
Jericho fell down; all the people went up, every man straight before him, and they
took the city and utterly destroyed all that was in it, both man and woman, young
and old, ox and sheep and ass, with the edge of the sword.
22 And they burned the whole city with fire; only the vessels of silver and gold,
brass and iron, they put into the treasury of the Lord.
23 Joshua swore at that time, saying, Cursed be the man who builds Jericho; he shall
lay the foundation thereof in his firstborn, and in his youngest son he shall set up the
gates of it.
24 And Achan the son of Carmi, the son of Zabdi, the son of Zerah, son of Judah,

dealt treacherously in the accursed thing, and he took of the accursed thing and hid it in the tent, and the anger of the Lord was set ablaze against Israel.
25 It was after this when the children of Israel had returned from burning Jericho, Joshua sent men to spy out also Ai, and to fight against it.
26 And the men went up and spied out Ai, and they returned and said, Let not all the people go up with you to Ai, only let about three thousand men go up and strike the city, for the men there are few.
27 And Joshua did so; there went up with him of the children of Israel about three thousand men, and they fought against the men of Ai.
28 And the battle was severe against Israel, and the men of Ai struck thirty-six men of Israel, and the children of Israel fled from before the men of Ai.
29 When Joshua saw this thing, he tore his garments and fell on his face to the ground before the Lord, he with the elders of Israel, and they put dust on their heads.
30 And Joshua said, Why O Lord did you bring this people over the Jordan? What shall I say after the Israelites have turned their backs against their enemies?
31 So now all the Canaanites, inhabitants of the land, will hear this thing and surround us and cut off our name.
32 And the Lord said to Joshua, Why do you fall on your face? Rise, get up, for the Israelites have sinned and taken of the accursed thing; I will no more be with them unless they destroy the accursed thing from among them.
33 And Joshua rose up and assembled the people, and brought the Urim by the order of the Lord, and the tribe of Judah was taken, and Achan the son of Carmi was taken.
34 Joshua said to Achan, Tell me my son, what have you done, and Achan said, I saw among the spoil a goodly garment of Shinar and two hundred shekels of silver, and a wedge of gold of fifty shekels weight; I coveted them and took them, and behold they are all hid in the earth in the middle of the tent.
35 And Joshua sent men who went and took them from the tent of Achan, and they brought them to Joshua.
36 Joshua took Achan and these utensils, and his sons and daughters and all belonging to him, and they brought them into the valley of Achor.
37Joshua burned them there with fire, and all the Israelites stoned Achan with stones; they raised over him a heap of stones, therefore he called that place the valley of Achor. So the Lord's anger was appeased, and Joshua afterward came to the city and fought against it.
38 And the Lord said to Joshua, Fear not, neither be dismayed, behold I have given into your hand Ai, her king and her people, and you shall do to them as you did to Jericho and her king, only the goods and the cattle there you shall take for yourselves; lay an ambush for the city behind it.
39 So Joshua did according to the word of the Lord, and he chose from among the sons of war thirty thousand courageous men; he sent them and they lay in ambush for the city.
40 And he commanded them, saying, When you shall see us we will flee before them with cunning, and they will pursue us; you shall then rise out of the ambush and take the city, and they did so.
41 Joshua fought, and the men of the city went out toward Israel, not knowing that they were lying in ambush for them behind the city.
42 Joshua and all the Israelites pretended to be wearied out before them, and they

fled by the way of the wilderness with cunning.
43 The men of Ai gathered all the people who were in the city to pursue the Israelites; they went out and were drawn away from the city; not one remained and they left the city open and pursued the Israelites.
44 Those who were lying in ambush rose up out of their places, hurried to come to the city and took it and set it on fire; the men of Ai turned back, and there the smoke of the city ascended to the skies, and they had no means of retreating either one way or the other.
45 All the men of Ai were in the midst of Israel, some on this side and some on that side, and they struck them so that not one of them remained.
46 The children of Israel took Melosh king of Ai alive and they brought him to Joshua, and Joshua hanged him on a tree and he died.
47 And the children of Israel returned to the city after having burned it; they struck all those that were in it with the edge of the sword.
48 The number of those that had fallen of the men of Ai, both man and woman, was twelve thousand; only the cattle and the goods of the city they took to themselves, according to the word of the Lord to Joshua.
49 And all the kings on this side Jordan, all the kings of Canaan, heard of the evil which the children of Israel had done to Jericho and to Ai, and they gathered themselves together to fight against Israel.
50 Only the inhabitants of Gibeon were greatly afraid of fighting against the Israelites that they should perish, so they acted cunningly; they came to Joshua and to all Israel and said to them, We have come from a distant land, so now make a covenant with us.
51 And the inhabitants of Gibeon over-reached the children of Israel, and the children of Israel made a covenant with them, and they made peace with them; the princes of the congregation swore to them, but afterward the children of Israel knew that they were neighbors to them and were dwelling among them.
52 But the children of Israel killed them not; for they had sworn to them by the Lord, and they became hewers of wood and drawers of water.
53 Joshua said to them, Why did you deceive me, to do this thing to us? And they answered him, Because it was told to your servants all that you had done to all the kings of the Amorites, and we were greatly afraid of our lives, and we did this thing.
54 Joshua appointed them on that day to hew wood and to draw water, and he divided them for slaves to all the tribes of Israel.
55 And when Adonizedek king of Jerusalem heard all that the children of Israel had done to Jericho and to Ai, he sent to Hoham king of Hebron and to Piram king at Jarmuth, and to Japhia king of Lachish and to Deber king of Eglon, saying,
56 Come up to me and help me, that we may strike the children of Israel and the inhabitants of Gibeon who have made peace with the children of Israel.
57 And they gathered themselves together and the five kings of the Amorites went up with all their camps, a mighty people numerous as the sand of the seashore.
58 All these kings came and camped before Gibeon, and they began to fight against the inhabitants of Gibeon, and all the men of Gibeon sent to Joshua, saying, Come up quickly to us and help us, for all the kings of the Amorites have gathered together to fight against us.
59 Joshua and all the fighting people went up from Gilgal, and Joshua came suddenly to them and struck these five kings with a great slaughter.
60 And the Lord confounded them before the children at Israel, who struck them

with a terrible slaughter in Gibeon, and pursued them along the way that goes up to Beth Horon to Makkedah; they fled from before the children of Israel.
61 And while they were fleeing, the Lord sent on them hailstones from heaven, and more of them died by the hailstones than by the slaughter of the children of Israel.
62 The children of Israel pursued them, and they still struck them in the road, going on and smiting them.
63 And when they were smiting, the day was declining toward evening and Joshua said in the sight of all the people, Sun, stand still on Gibeon, and you moon in the valley of Ajalon, until the nation shall have revenged itself on its enemies.
64 The Lord listened to the voice of Joshua, and the sun stood still in the midst of the heavens, and it stood still six and thirty moments, and the moon also stood still and hurried not to go down a whole day.
65 And there was no day like that, before it or after it that the Lord listened to the voice of a man, for the Lord fought for Israel.

CHAPTER 89

1 Then Joshua spoke this song on the day that the Lord had given the Amorites into the hand of Joshua and the children of Israel, and he said it in the sight of all Israel,
2 You have done mighty things, O Lord, you have performed great deeds; who is like you? My lips shall sing to your name.
3 My goodness and my fortress, my high tower, I will sing a new song to you; with thanksgiving I will sing to you, you are the strength of my salvation.
4 All the kings of the earth shall praise you, the princes of the world shall sing to you, the children of Israel shall rejoice in your salvation; they shall sing and praise your power.
5 To you, O Lord, we confided; we said you are our God, for you were our shelter and strong tower against our enemies.
6 To you we cried and were not ashamed, in you we trusted and were delivered; when we cried to you, you heard our voice, you delivered our souls from the sword, you showed to us your grace, you gave to us your salvation, you rejoiced our hearts with your strength.
7 You went forth for our salvation, with your arm you redeemed your people; you answered us from the heavens of your holiness, you saved us from ten thousands of people.
8 The sun and moon stood still in heaven, and you stood in your wrath against our oppressors and commanded your judgments over them.
9 All the princes of the earth stood up, the kings of the nations had gathered themselves together, they were not moved at your presence; they desired your battles.
10 You rose against them in your anger, and brought down your wrath on them; you destroyed them in your anger, and cut them off in your heart.
11 Nations have been consumed with your fury, kingdoms have declined because of your wrath, you wounded kings in the day of your anger.
12 You poured out your fury on them, your wrathful anger took hold of them; you turned their iniquity on them, and cut them off in their wickedness.
13 They spread a trap and fell therein; in the net they hid, their foot was caught.
14 Your hand was ready for all your enemies who said, Through their sword they

possessed the land, through their arm they lived in the city; you filled their faces with shame, you brought their horns down to the ground, you terrified them in your wrath and destroyed them in your anger.
15 The earth trembled and shook at the sound of your storm over them, you did not withhold their souls from death, and brought down their lives to the grave.
16 You pursued them in your storm, you concumed them in your whirlwind, you turned their rain into hail, they fell in deep pits so that they could not rise.
17 Their carcasses were like rubbish cast out in the middle of the streets.
18 They were consumed and destroyed in your anger, you saved your people with your might.
19 Therefore our hearts rejoice in you, our souls exalt in your salvation.
20 Our tongues shall relate your might, we will sing and praise your wondrous works.
21 For you did save us from our enemies, you did deliver us from those who rose up against us, you did destroy them from before us and depress them beneath our feet.
22 Thus shall all your enemies perish O Lord, and the wicked shall be like chaff driven by the wind, and your beloved shall be like trees planted by the waters.
23 So Joshua and all Israel with him returned to the camp in Gilgal, after having smitten all the kings, so that not a remnant was left of them.
24 And the five kings fled alone on foot from battle and hid themselves in a cave, and Joshua sought for them in the field of battle and did not find them.
25 And it was afterward told to Joshua, saying, The kings are found and there, they are hidden in a cave.
26 And Joshua said, Appoint men to be at the mouth of the cave to guard them, that they not take themselves away. And the children of Israel did so.
27 And Joshua called to all Israel and said to the officers of battle, Place your feet on the necks of these kings, and Joshua said, So shall the Lord do to all your enemies.
28 Joshua commanded afterward that they should kill the kings and cast them into the cave, and put great stones at the mouth of the cave.
29 Joshua went afterward with all the people that were with him on that day to Makkedah, and he struck it with the edge of the sword.
30 He utterly destroyed the souls and all belonging to the city, and he did to the king and people there as he had done to Jericho.
31 He passed from there to Libnah and he fought against it; the Lord delivered it into his hands and Joshua struck it with the edge of the sword, and all the souls there and he did it and to the king there as he had done to Jericho.
32 From there he passed on to Lachish to fight against it, and Horam king of Gaza went up to assist the men of Lachish, and Joshua struck him and his people until there was none left to him.
33 Joshua took Lachish and all the people there, and he did to it as he had done to Libnah.
34 Joshua passed from there to Eglon, and he took that also; he struck it and all the people there with the edge of the sword.
35 From there he passed to Hebron and fought against it and took it and utterly destroyed it; he returned from there with all Israel to Debir and fought against it and struck it with the edge of the sword.
36 And he destroyed every soul in it, he left none remaining; he did to it and the king thereof as he had done to Jericho.
37 Joshua struck all the kings of the Amorites from Kadesh-barnea to Azah; he took

their country at once, for the Lord had fought for Israel.
38 And Joshua with all Israel came to the camp to Gilgal.
39 When at that time Jabin king of Chazor heard all that Joshua had done to the
kings of the Amorites, Jabin sent to Jobat king of Midian, and to Laban king of
Shimron, to Jephal king of Achshaph, and to all the kings of the Amorites, saying,
40 Come quickly to us and help us, that we may strike the children of Israel before
they come on us and do to us as they have done to the other kings of the Amorites.
41 And all these kings listened to the words of Jabin, king of Chazor, and they went
forth with all their camps, seventeen kings, and their people were as numerous as
the sand on the seashore, together with horses and chariots innumerable; they came
and camped together at the waters of Merom, and they were met together to fight
against Israel.
42 The Lord said to Joshua, Fear them not, for tomorrow about this time I will
deliver them up all slain before you, you shall cripple their horses and burn their
chariots with fire.
43 And Joshua with all the men of war came suddenly on them and struck them, and
they fell into their hands, for the Lord had delivered them into the hands of the
children of Israel.
44 So the children of Israel pursued all these kings with their camps and struck them
until there was none left of them, and Joshua did to them as the Lord had spoken to
him.
45 Joshua returned at that time to Chazor and struck it with the sword and
destroyed every soul in it and burned it with fire; from Chazor, Joshua passed to
Shimron and struck it and utterly destroyed it.
46 From there he passed to Achshaph and he did to it as he had done to Shimron.
47 From there he passed to Adulam and he struck all the people in it, and he did to
Adulam as he had done to Achshaph and to Shimron.
48 He passed from them to all the cities of the kings which he had smitten, and he
struck all the people that were left of them and he utterly destroyed them.
49 Only their booty and cattle the Israelites took to themselves as a prey, but every
human being they struck; they permitted not a soul to live.
50 As the Lord had commanded Moses so did Joshua and all Israel, they failed not in
anything.
51 So Joshua and all the children of Israel struck the whole land of Canaan as the
Lord had commanded them, and struck all their kings, being thirty and one kings,
and the children of Israel took their whole country.
52 Besides the kingdoms of Sihon and Og which are on the other side Jordan, of
which Moses had smitten many cities, Moses gave them to the Reubenites and the
Gadites and to half the tribe of Manasseh.
53 And Joshua struck all the kings that were on this side of Jordan to the west, and
gave them for an inheritance to the nine tribes and to the half tribe of Israel.
54 For five years Joshua carried on the war with these kings, and he gave their cities
to the Israelites, and the land became tranquil from battle throughout the cities of the
Amorites and the Canaanites.

CHAPTER 90

1 At that time in the fifth year after the children of Israel had passed over Jordan,

after the children of Israel had rested from their war with the Canaanites, great and severe battles arose between Edom and the children of Chittim, and the children of Chittim fought against Edom.
2 Abianus king of Chittim went forth in that year, that is in the thirty-first year of his reign, and a great force with him of the mighty men of the children of Chittim, and he went to Seir to fight against the children of Esau.
3 Hadad the king of Edom heard of his report, and he went forth to meet him with many people and a strong force, and engaged in battle with him in the field of Edom.
4 And the hand of Chittim prevailed over the children of Esau, and the children of Chittim killed of the children of Esau two and twenty thousand men, and all the children of Esau fled from before them.
5 The children of Chittim pursued them and they reached Hadad king of Edom, who was running before them and they caught him alive, and brought him to Abianus king of Chittim.
6 And Abianus ordered him to be slain; Hadad king of Edom died in the forty-eighth year of his reign.
7 And the children of Chittim continued their pursuit of Edom; they struck them with a great slaughter and Edom became subject to the children of Chittim.
8 And the children of Chittim ruled over Edom, and Edom came under the hands of the children of Chittim and became one kingdom from that day.
9 From that time they could no more lift up their heads, and their kingdom became one with the children of Chittim.
10 Abianus placed officers in Edom and all the children of Edom became subject to Abianus, and Abianus turned back to his own land, Chittim.
11 When he returned he renewed his government and built for himself a spacious and fortified palace for a royal residence, and reigned securely over the children of Chittim and over Edom.
12 In those days, after the children of Israel had driven away all the Canaanites and the Amorites, Joshua was old and advanced in years.
13 And the Lord said to Joshua, You are old, advanced in life, and a great part of the land remains to be possessed.
14 Now therefore divide this land for an inheritance to the nine tribes and to the half tribe of Manasseh, and Joshua rose up and did as the Lord had spoken to him.
15 And he divided the whole land to the tribes of Israel as an inheritance according to their divisions.
16 But to the tribe at Levi he gave no inheritance. The offerings of the Lord are their inheritance as the Lord had spoken of them by the hand of Moses.
17 Joshua gave Mount Hebron to Caleb the son of Jephuneh, one portion above his brothers, as the Lord had spoken through Moses.
18 Therefore Hebron became an inheritance to Caleb and his children to this day.
19 Joshua divided the whole land by lots to all Israel for an inheritance, as the Lord had commanded him.
20 And the children of Israel gave cities to the Levites from their own inheritance, and suburbs for their cattle, and property; as the Lord had commanded Moses so did the children of Israel, and they divided the land by lot whether great or small.
21 They went to inherit the land according to their boundaries, and the children of Israel gave to Joshua the son of Nun an inheritance among them.
22 By the word of the Lord they gave to him the city which he required, Timnath-

serach in Mount Ephraim, and he built the city and lived therein.
23 These are the inheritances which Elazer the priest and Joshua the son of Nun and
the heads of the fathers of the tribes portioned out to the children of Israel by lot in
Shiloh, before the Lord, at the door of the tabernacle, and they left off dividing the
land.
24 And the Lord gave the land to the Israelites, and they possessed it as the Lord had
spoken to them, and as the Lord had sworn to their ancestors.
25 And the Lord gave to the Israelites rest from all their enemies around them, and
no man stood up against them; the Lord delivered all their enemies into their hands,
and not one thing failed of all the good which the Lord had spoken to the children of
Israel, yes, the Lord performed everything.
26 Joshua called to all the children of Israel and he blessed them, and commanded
them to serve
the Lord, and afterward sent them away; they went each man to his city, and each
man to his inheritance.
27 And the children of Israel served the Lord all the days of Joshua, and the Lord
gave them rest from all around them, and they lived securely in their cities.
28 It came to pass in those days, that Abianus king of Chittim died, in the thirty-
eighth year of his reign, that is the seventh year of his reign over Edom; they buried
him in his place which he had built for himself, and Latinus reigned in his stead fifty
years.
29 During his reign he brought forth an army, and he went and fought against the
inhabitants of Britannia and Kernania, the children of Elisha son of Javan, and he
succeeded over them and made them subjects.
30 He then heard that Edom had revolted from under the hand of Chittim, and
Latinus went to them and struck them and subdued them, and placed them under
the hand of the children of Chittim; Edom became one kingdom with the children of
Chittim all the days.
31 And for many years there was no king in Edom, and their government was with
the children of Chittim and their king.
32 It was in the twenty-sixth year after the children of Israel had passed the Jordan,
that is the sixty-sixth year after the children of Israel had departed from Egypt, that
Joshua was old, advanced in years, being one hundred and eight years old in those
days.
33 Joshua called to all Israel, to their elders, their judges and officers, after the Lord
had given to all the Israelites rest from all their enemies round about; Joshua said to
the elders of Israel and to their judges, Behold I am old, advanced in years, and you
have seen what the Lord has done to all the nations whom he has driven away from
before you, for it is the Lord who has fought for you.
34 Now therefore strengthen yourselves to keep and to do all the words of the law of
Moses, not to deviate from it to the right or to the left, and not to come among those
nations who are left in the land; neither shall you make mention of the name of their
gods, but you shall cleave to the Lord your God, as you have done to this day.
35 Joshua greatly encouraged the children of Israel to serve the Lord all their days.
36 And all the Israelites said, We will serve the Lord our God all our days, we and
our children, and our children's children, and our offspring forever.
37 Joshua made a covenant with the people on that day and he sent away the
children of Israel, and they went each man to his inheritance and to his city.
38 And it was in those days, when the children of Israel were dwelling securely in

their cities, that they buried the coffins of the tribes of their ancestors which they had brought up from Egypt, each man in the inheritance of his children; the twelve sons of Jacob did the children of Israel bury, each man in the possession of his children.
39 And these are the names of the cities where they buried the twelve sons of Jacob, whom the children of Israel had brought up from Egypt:
40 They buried Reuben and Gad on this side of Jordan, in Romia, which Moses had given to their children.
41 And Simeon and Levi they buried in the city Mauda, which he had given to the children of Simeon, and the suburb of the city was for the children of Levi.
42 And Judah they buried in the city of Benjamin opposite Bethlehem.
43 And the bones of Issachar and Zebulun they buried in Zidon, in the portion which fell to their children.
44 Dan was buried in the city of his children in Eshtael, and Naphtali and Asher they buried in Kadesh-naphtali, each man in his place which he had given to his children.
45 And the bones of Joseph they buried in Shechem in the part of the field which Jacob had purchased from Hamor, and which became to Joseph for an inheritance.
46 And they buried Benjamin in Jerusalem opposite the Jebusite, which was given to the children of Benjamin; the children of Israel buried their fathers each man in the city of his children.
47 And at the end of two years, Joshua the son of Nun died, one hundred and ten years old, and the time which Joshua judged Israel was twenty-eight years; Israel served the Lord all the days of his life.
48 And the other affairs of Joshua and his battles and his reproofs with which he reproved Israel, and all which he had commanded them, and the names of the cities which the children of Israel possessed in his days, they are written in the book of the words of Joshua to the children of Israel and in the book of the wars of the Lord, which Moses and Joshua and the children of Israel had written.
49 And the children of Israel buried Joshua in the border of his inheritance, in Timnath-serach which was given to him in Mount Ephraim.
50 And Elazer the son of Aaron died in those days; they buried him in a hill belonging to Phineas his son, which was given him in Mount Ephraim.

CHAPTER 91

1 At that time, after the death of Joshua, the children of the Canaanites were still in the land, and the Israelites resolved to drive them out.
2 And the children of Israel asked of the Lord, saying, Who shall first go up for us to the Canaanites to fight against them? And the Lord said, Judah shall go up.
3 And the children of Judah said to Simeon, Go up with us into our lot, and we will fight against the Canaanites and we likewise will go up with you in your lot; so the children of Simeon went with the children of Judah.
4 The children of Judah went up and fought against the Canaanites, so the Lord delivered the Canaanites into the hands of the children of Judah; they struck in Bezek ten thousand men.
5 They fought with Adonibezek in Bezek, he fled from before them, and they pursued him and caught him; they took hold of him and cut off his thumbs and great toes.
6 And Adonibezek said, Three score and ten kings having their thumbs and great

toes cut off, gathered their meat under my table, as I have done, so God has rewarded me; they brought him to Jerusalem and he died there.
7 And the children of Simeon went with the children of Judah, and they struck the Canaanites with the edge of the sword.
8 The Lord was with the children of Judah, and they possessed the mountain, and the children of Joseph went up to Bethel, the same is Luz, and the Lord was with them.
9 And the children of Joseph spied out Bethel, and the watchmen saw a man going forth from the city, and they caught him and said to him, Show us now the entrance of the city and we will show kindness to you.
10 And that man showed them the entrance of the city, and the children of Joseph came and struck the city with the edge of the sword.
11 The man with his family they sent away, and he went to the Hittites and he built a city; he called the name there Luz, so all the Israelites lived in their cities, and the children at Israel lived in their cities; the children of Israel served the Lord all the days of Joshua, and all the days of the elders, who had lengthened their days after Joshua, and saw the great work of the Lord which he had performed for Israel.
12 And the elders judged Israel after the death of Joshua for seventeen years.
13 All the elders also fought the battles of Israel against the Canaanites and the Lord drove the Canaanites from before the children of Israel in order to place the Israelites in their land.
14 And he accomplished all the words which he had spoken to Abraham, Isaac, and Jacob, and the oath which he had sworn, to give to them and to their children the land of the Canaanites.
15 The Lord gave to the children of Israel the whole land of Canaan as he had sworn to their ancestors, and the Lord gave them rest from those around them, and the children of Israel lived securely in their cities.
16 Blessed be the Lord forever, amen, and amen.
17 Strengthen yourselves, and let the hearts of all you that trust in the Lord. Be of good courage.

THE STORY OF AHIKAR

History and Introduction

The Story of Ahikar is one of the oldest sources of wisdom literature. Its influence can be traced through the Koran, as well as the Old and New Testaments. The oldest version, which we can only assume to be the original Papyrus, appears to have been produced circa 500 B. C. It is written in Aramaic and was discovered among the ruins of Elephantine.

The earliest mention of Ahikar is in the Book of Tobit in the form of the name "Achiacharus". According to the book of Tobit, Ahikar was a relative and friend to Tobit. He was the chief counselor of the Assyrian ruler, Sennacherib. The book of Tobit mentions Nadab, Ahiker's nephew, whom Ahikar adopted, and who sought to repay the kindness by attempting to kill his uncle. Tobit concludes, "but God made good his dishonor in His sight and Ahikar returned to the light, but Nadab went into darkness everlasting" (Tobit, xiv. 10, 11, according to the Codex Sinaiticus).

In the Old Testament we see Ahikar was the chancellor of the Assyrian king Sennacherib, son of Esar-haddon (II Kings, xix. 37).

The basic story of Ahikar contains four divisions: (1) The Narrative; (2) The Teaching; (3) The Journey to Egypt; (4) The Similitudes or Parables. Parts of the story are found in various forms in Greek, Rumanian, Slavonic, and Syriac, to name a few versions. The versions differ widely in number of parables and content.

The story may be fiction, although it may be based on a real individual. It is written in a narrative, which has action and intrigue, and holds the attention to the end.

The story opens with the statement that Ahikar had sixty wives. The number should not be taken literally. It symbolizes a vague but large amount of something. The impetus of the story is that although Ahiker had many, many wives, he had no son. Lacking an heir, her decides to adopt his nephew, Nadan, who grows into a treacherous and despicable person. Ahikar attempts to educate the boy in wisdom and knowledge, but this is twisted into Machiavellian intrigue. We, however, get the benefit of the deeper teaching in the form of sayings and parables. Even though Ahikar has trained his nephew and has gone as far as to ask the king to accept Nadan as his replacement, the nephew still turns on Ahikar and attempts of put an end to his uncle. With the help of God and a friend, Ahikar escapes. In time the nephew fails and his true nature shows through, to the dismay of the king.

The storyline proves that no good deed goes unpunished, but in the end, if you are a good and wise person you will be remembered and missed. Truth, being like cream, will rise to the surface and be revealed. If God is on your side and you are still alive, you will be reinstated and exonerated.

Commentary for this section is placed in parentheses within the body of the text, to aid in clarification or to bring out alternate meanings in translation.

CHAP. I.

1. *The story of Ahikar the* Wise, Vizier of Sennacherib the King, and of Nadan, sister's son to Ahikar the Sage.

2 There was a Vizier (counselor) in the days of King Sennacherib, son of Sarhadum, King of Assyria and Nineveh, a wise man named Ahikar, and he was counselor of the king Sennacherib.

3 He had a vast fortune and many possessions, and he was a skilful and wise philosopher, in knowledge, opinion and in government. He had married sixty women, and had built a castle for each of them.

4 But with it all of this, he had no child by any of these women, who might be his heir. (He had no son.)

5 Because of this he was very sad. One day he assembled the astrologers and the learned men and the magicians and explained to them his condition about how he was barren (of a son).

6And they said to him, 'Go, sacrifice to the gods and beg them that perchance they may provide you with a boy.'

7And he did as they told him and offered sacrifices to the idols, and earnestly and desperately entreated them.

8And they answered him not one word. And he went away sorrowful and dejected, and he left them with a pain in his heart.

9And he returned, and earnestly pleaded to the Most High God, and believed, and sought Him with a burning heart, saying, ' Most High God, Creator of Heavens and earth, Creator of all created things!

10 I beg You to give me a boy, that I may be consoled by him, that he may be present at my death, that he may close my eyes, and that he may bury me.'

11 Then a voice came to him saying, 'because you have relied first (predominately) on graven images (idols), and have offered sacrifices to them, you shall remain childless all of your life.

12 But take Nadan your sister's son, and make him your child and teach him your

learning and your good breeding (manners), and at your death he shall bury you.'

13 Thereupon he took Nadan his sister's son, who was a little suckling. And he handed him over to eight wet-nurses (lactating women who function as nannies), that they might suckle him and bring him up.

14 And they brought him up with good food and gentle training and silken clothing, and purple and crimson. And he was seated upon couches of silk.

15 And when Nadan grew big and walked, shooting up, like a tall cedar, Ahikar taught him good manners along with writing, science, and philosophy.

16 And after many days King Sennacherib looked at Ahikar and saw that he had grown very old, and moreover he said to him.

17 ' my honored friend, the skilful, the trusty, the wise, the governor, my secretary, my vizier, my Chancellor and director; truly you are grown very old and are weighted down with years; and your departure from this world must be near.

18 Tell me who shall replace you in my service after you are gone.' And Ahikar said to him, ' my lord, may your head live forever (may your dynasty endure)! There is Nadan, my sister's son. I have made him my child.

19 And I have raised and taught him my wisdom and my knowledge.'

20 And the king said to him, 'Ahikar, bring him to me here, so that I may see him, and if I find him suitable, I will put him in your place; and you shall go your way, to take a rest and to live the remainder of your life in sweet repose.'

21 Then Ahikar went and presented Nadan his sister's son. And he did homage and wished him power and honor.

22 And he looked at him and admired him and rejoiced in him and said to Ahikar: 'Is this your son, Ahikar? I pray that God may preserve him. And as you have served me and my father Sarhadum so may this boy of yours serve me and fulfill my undertakings, my needs, and my business, so that I may honor him and make him powerful for your sake.'

23 And Ahikar did obeisance to the king and said to him 'May your head live forever, my lord the king! I seek from you that you may be patient with my boy Nadan and forgive his mistakes that he may serve you as it is fitting.'

24 Then the king swore to him that he would make him the greatest of his favorites, and the most powerful of his friends, and that he should be with him in all honor

and respect. And he kissed his hands and bade him farewell.

25 And he took Nadan his sister's son with him and seated him in a parlor and set about teaching him night and day till he had crammed him with wisdom and knowledge more than with bread and water.

CHAP. II.

1. Thus he taught him, saying: 'my son, hear my words and follow my advice and remember what I say.

2 If you hear a word, let it die in your heart, and reveal it not to another, lest it becomes a live coal and burn your tongue and cause a pain in your body, and you bring reproach on yourself, and you are shamed before God and man. (If you cannot keep a secret, you will never be trusted.)

3 My son, if you have heard a report, spread it not; and if you have seen something, tell it not. (Do not gossip.)

4 My son, make your eloquence easy to the listener, and be not hasty to return an answer. (Do not pontificate or be a know-it-all.)

5 My son, when you have heard anything, hide it not. (Do not keep secrets.)

6 My son, loose not a sealed knot, nor untie it, and seal not a loosened knot. (A wax seal was placed over a knot that tied a box or document closed to show that it was meant to be opened only by a particular person.)

7 My son, covet not outward beauty, for it wanes and passes away, but an honorable remembrance lasts for ever. (Beauty fades. Integrity remains.)

8 My son, let not a silly (foolish) woman deceive you with her speech, lest you die the most miserable of deaths, and she entangle you in the net until you are trapped.

9 My son, desire not a woman decorated with gaudy dress and ointments, who is despicable and silly (foolish) in her soul. Woe to you if you bestow on her anything that is yours, or promise her what is in your hand and, she entice you into sin, and God be angry with you.

10 My son, be not like the almond-tree, for it brings forth leaves before all the trees, and edible fruit after them all, but be like the mulberry - tree, which brings forth

edible fruit before all the trees, and leaves after them all. (The word for "almond-tree" is the same word for "haste.")

11 My son, bend your head low down, and soften your voice, and be courteous, and walk in the straight path, and be not foolish. And raise not your voice when you laugh, for if it were by a loud voice that a house was built, the ass would build many houses every day; and if it were by means of strength that the plough were driven, the plough would never be removed from under the shoulders of the camels. (Do not be loud, showy, or a braggart. Be solemn, humble, and courteous. Don't be an ass.)

12 My son, the removing of stones with a wise man is better than the drinking of wine with a sorry man. (Better to work with the wise than play with the fools.)

13 My son, pour out your wine on the tombs of the just, and drink not with ignorant, contemptible people. (Honor the righteous, even if they are dead, but stay away from the ignorant, even if they are the only people around.)

14 My son, stay close (hold on) to wise men who fear God and be like them, and go not near the ignorant, or you will become like him and learn his ways.

15 My son, when you think you have found a comrade or a friend, try (test) him, and afterwards make him a comrade and a friend; and do not praise him without a trial; and do not waste your speech on a man who lacks wisdom.

16 My son, while a shoe stays on your foot, walk with it on the thorns, and make a road for your son, and for your household and your children, and make your ship taut before she goes on the sea and its waves and sinks and cannot be saved. (Prepare yourself before you venture out, and as you go, forge a path for your people.)

17 My son, if the rich man eats a snake, they say, "It is by his wisdom," and if a poor man eats it, the people say, "It is from his hunger."

18 My son, be content with your daily bread and your goods, and covet not what is another's. (Do not be envious.)

19 My son, be not neighbor to the fool, and eat not bread with him, and rejoice not in the misfortune of your neighbors. If your enemy wrongs you, show him kindness.

20 My son, respect and honor a man who fears God.

21 My son, the ignorant man falls and stumbles, and the wise man, even if he stumbles, he is not shaken, and even if he falls he gets up quickly, and if he is sick,

he can take care of his life. But as for the ignorant, stupid man, for his disease there is no drug.

22 My son, if a man approach you who is inferior (of lower status) to yourself, go forward to meet him, and remain standing, and if he cannot recompense (pay you back) you, his Lord will recompense you for him.

23 My son, do not spare your son from a beating, for the thrashing of your son is like manure to the garden, and like tying the mouth of a purse, and like the tethering of beasts, and like the bolting of the door.

24 My son, keep your son from wickedness, and teach him manners before he rebels against you and brings you into contempt amongst the people and you hang your head (in shame) in the streets and the assemblies and you be punished for the evil of his wicked deeds.

25 My son, get you a fat ox with a foreskin, and an ass great with its hoofs, and get not an ox with large horns, nor make friends with a tricky man, nor get a quarrelsome slave, nor a thievish handmaid, for everything which you commit to them they will ruin. (Chose utility and not looks. Choose only those who you can trust.)

26 My son, let not your parents curse you, and the Lord be pleased with them; for it has been said, "He who despise his father or his mother let him die the death (I mean the death of sin); and he who honors his parents shall prolong his days and his life and shall see all that is good."

27 My son, walk not on the road without weapons, for you know not when the foe may meet you, so that you may be ready for him. (Be prepared to defend yourself.)

28 My son, be not like a bare, leafless tree that does not grow, but be like a tree covered with its leaves and its boughs; for the man who has neither wife nor children is disgraced in the world and is hated by them, like a leafless and fruitless tree. (Marry, have children, produce good things in the world.)

29 My son, be like a fruitful tree on the roadside, whose fruit is eaten by all who pass by, and the beasts of the desert rest under its shade and eat of its leaves.

30 My son, every sheep that wanders from its path and its companions becomes food for the wolf.

31 My son, say not, "My lord is a fool and I am wise,' and do not repeat words of ignorance and folly, or you will be despised by him.

32 My son, be not one of those servants, to whom their lords say, "Get away from us," but be one of those to whom they say, "Approach and come near to us."

33 My son, caress not your slave in the presence of his companion, for you know not which of them shall be of most value to you in the end. (It was common to have sex with a slave. It is best not to divide or make even a slave jealous so both will continue to serve well.)

34 My son, be not afraid of your Lord who created you, lest He be silent to you.

35 My son, make your speech fair and sweeten your tongue; but do not permit your companion to tread on your foot, lest he tread at another time on your breast.

36 My son, if you beat a wise man with a word of wisdom, it will lurk in his breast like a subtle sense of shame; but if you beat the ignorant with a stick he will neither understand nor hear,

37 My son, if you send a wise man for your needs, do not give him many orders, for he will do your business as you desire: and if you send a fool, do not order him, but go thyself and do your business, for if you order him, he, will not do what you desire. If they send you on business, hurry to fulfill it quickly,

38 My son, do not make an enemy of a man stronger than yourself, for he will take your measure, and his revenge on you.

39 My son, make trial of your son, and of your servant, before you commit your belongings to them, or they will make away with them; for he who has a full hand is called wise, even if he is stupid and ignorant, and he who has an empty hand is called poor and ignorant, even if he is the prince of sages.

40 My son, I have eaten a colocynth, (Also called bitter apple. Used as a purgative) and swallowed aloes (bitter succulent used as a strong laxative), and I have found nothing more bitter than poverty and scarcity.

41 My son, teach your son frugality and hunger, so that he may do well in the management of his household.

42 My son, teach not to the ignorant the language of wise men, for it will be burdensome to him.

43 My son, display not your condition to your friend, or he will despise you.

44 My son, the blindness of the heart is more grievous than the blindness of the eyes, for the blindness of the eyes may be guided little by little, but the blindness of the

heart is not guided, and it leaves the straight path, and goes in a crooked way.

45 My son, the stumbling of a man with his foot is better than the stumbling of a man with his tongue.

46 My son, a friend who is near is better than a more excellent brother who is far away.

47 My son, beauty fades but learning lasts, and the world wanes and becomes vain (empty), but a good name neither becomes vain (empty) nor wanes.

48 My son, the man who has no rest, his death would be better than his life; and the sound of weeping is better than the sound of singing; for sorrow and weeping, if the fear of God is in them, are better than the sound of singing and rejoicing.

49 My child! The thigh of a frog in your hand is better than a goose in the pot of your neighbor; and a sheep near you is better than an ox far away; and a sparrow in your hand is better than a thousand sparrows flying; and poverty which gathers is better than the scattering of much provision; and a living fox is better than a dead lion; and a pound of wool is better than a pound of wealth. What I mean is that gold and silver are hidden and covered up in the earth, and not seen; but the wool stays in the markets and it is seen, and it is a beauty to him who wears it.

50 My son, a small fortune is better than a scattered fortune.

51 My son, a living dog is better than a dead poor man.

52 My son, a poor man who does right is better than a rich man who is dead in sins.

53 My son, keep a word in your heart, and it shall be much to you, and beware or you will reveal the secret of your friend.

54 My son, let not a word issue from your mouth until you have taken counsel with your heart. And do not stand between quarrelling persons, because from a bad word there comes a quarrel, and from a quarrel there comes war, and from war there comes fighting, and you will be forced to be a witness (take sides); so run from there and rest yourself.

55 My son, do not stand up against a man stronger than yourself, but get you a patient spirit, and endurance and an upright conduct, for there is nothing better than that.

56 My son, do not hate your first friend, for the second one may not last.

57 My son, visit the poor in his affliction, and speak of him in the Sultan's presence, and do your diligence to save him from the mouth of the lion.

58 My son, do not rejoice in the death of your enemy, for after a little while you shall be his neighbor, but him who mocks you, respect and honor and be quick to greet him.

59 My son, if water would stand still in heaven, and a black crow becomes white, and myrrh grow sweet as honey, then ignorant men and fools might understand and become wise.

60 My son, if you desire to be wise, restrain your tongue from lying, and your hand from stealing, and your eyes from observing evil; then you will be called wise.

61 My son, let the wise man beat you with a rod, but do not even let the fool anoint you with sweet salve. Be humble in your youth and you shall be honored in your old age.

62 My son, do not stand against a man in his days of power, or a river in the days of its flood. (Everything and everyone has his season.)

63 My son, be not hasty in wedding a wife, for if it turns out well, she will say, 'My lord, make provision for me'; and if it turns out ill, she will rant at him who was the cause of it.

64 My son, whosoever is elegant in his dress, he is the same in his speech; and he who has a mean appearance in his dress, he also is the same in his speech. (Dress for success. The wardrobe makes the man. You can discern the man by his wardrobe.)

65 My son, if you have committed a theft, make it known to the Sultan, and give him a share of it, that you may be delivered from him, for otherwise you will endure bitterness. (Mutual culpability is implied, however, confession and recompense is also suggested.)

66 My son, make a friend of the man whose hand is satisfied and filled, and make no friend of the man whose hand is closed and hungry.

67 There are four things in which neither the king nor his army can be secure: oppression by the chancellor, and bad government, and perversion of the will, and tyranny over the subject; and four things which cannot be hidden: the prudent, and the foolish, and the rich, and the poor.

CHAP. III

Thus spoke Ahikar, and when he had finished these injunctions and proverbs to Nadan, his sister's son, he thought that he would keep them all. Ahikar did not know that instead Nadan was displaying weariness and contempt and mockery to him.

2 After that, Ahikar sat still in his house and delivered over to Nadan all his goods, and the slaves, and the handmaidens, and horses, and cattle, and everything else that he had possessed and gained; and the power of granting permission and of forbidding remained in the hand of Nadan.

3 And Ahikar sat at rest is his house, and every now and then Ahikar went and paid his respects to the king, and returned home.

4 Now when Nadan understood that the power of granting permission and of forbidding was in his own hand, he despised the position of Ahikar and scoffed at him, and set about blaming him whenever he appeared, saying, 'My uncle Ahikar is senile, and he knows nothing now.'

5 And he began to beat the slaves and the handmaidens, and to sell the horses and the camels and spend extravagantly with all that his uncle Ahikar had owned.

6 And when Ahikar saw that he had no compassion on his servants nor on his household, he arose and chased him from his house, and sent to inform the king that he had thrown away his possessions and his provision.

7 And the king arose and called Nadan and said to him: 'While Ahikar remains in health, no one shall rule over his goods, nor over his household, nor over his possessions.'

8 And the hand of Nadan was lifted off from his uncle Ahikar and from all his goods, and in the meantime he went neither in nor out, nor did he greet him. (Nadan's lordship of the household was countermanded by the king.)

9 Thereupon Ahikar was sorry for all of his toil with Nadan his sister's son, and he continued to be very sorrowful.

10 And Nadan had a younger brother named Benuzardan, so Ahikar took him to himself in place of Nadan, and brought him up and honored him with the utmost honor. And he delivered over to him all that he possessed, and made him governor of his house.

11 Now when Nadan found out what had happened he was seized with envy and

jealousy, and he began to complain to every one who questioned him, and to mock his uncle Ahikar, saying: 'My uncle has chased me from his house, and has preferred my brother to me, but if the Most High God give me the power, I shall bring upon him the misfortune of being killed.'

12 And Nadan continued to meditate as to the stumbling block he might contrive for him. And after a while Nadan turned it over in his mind, and wrote a letter to Achish, son of Shah the Wise, king of Persia, saying thus:

13 'Peace and health and might and honor from Sennacherib king of Assyria and Nineveh, and from his chancellor and his secretary Ahikar unto you, great king! Let there be peace between you and me.

14 And when this letter reaches you, if you will arise and go quickly to the plain of Nisrin, and to Assyria and Nineveh, I will deliver up the kingdom to you without war and without battle-array.'

15 And he wrote also another letter in the name of Ahikar to Pharaoh king of Egypt. 'Let there be peace between you and me, mighty king!

16 If at the time of this letter reaching you, you will arise and go to Assyria and Nineveh to the plain of Nisrin, I will deliver up to you the kingdom without war and without fighting.'

17 And the writing of Nadan was like to the writing of his uncle Ahikar.

18 Then he folded the two letters, and sealed them with the seal of his uncle Ahikar; they were nevertheless in the king's palace.

19 Then he went and wrote a letter likewise from the king to his uncle Ahikar: 'Peace and health to my Vizier, my Secretary, my Chancellor, Ahikar.

20 Ahikar, when this letter reaches you, assemble all the soldiers who are with you, and let them be perfect in clothing and in numbers, and bring them to me on the fifth day in the plain of Nisrin.

21 And when you shall see me there coming towards you, haste and make the army move against me as an enemy who would fight with me, for I have with me the ambassadors of Pharaoh king of Egypt, that they may see the strength of our army and may fear us, for they are our enemies and they hate us.'

22 Then he sealed the letter and sent it to Ahikar by one of the king's servants. And he took the other letter, which he had written and spread it before the king and read it to him and showed him the seal.

23 And when the king heard what was in the letter he was perplexed with a great perplexity and was angry with a great and fierce rage, and said, 'Ah, I have shown my wisdom! What have I done to Ahikar that he has written these letters to my enemies? Is this the way he pays me back for my benefits to him?'

24 And Nadan said to him, 'Be not grieved, king, nor be angry, but let us go to the plain of Nisrin and see if the tale be true or not.'

25 Then Nadan arose on the fifth day and took the king and the soldiers and the vizier, and they went to the desert to the plain of Nisrin. And the king looked, and Ahikar and the army were set in array.

26 And when Ahikar saw that the king was there, he approached and signaled to the army to move as if in war and to fight in array against the king as it had been found in the letter, he not knowing what a pit Nadan had dug for him.

27 And when the king saw the act of Ahikar he was seized with anxiety and terror and perplexity, and was angry with a great rage.

28 And Nadan said to him, 'Have you seen, my lord the king! What this contemptible person has done? But do not be angry or grieved or pained, but go to your house and sit on your throne, and I will bring Ahikar to you bound and chained with chains, and I will chase away your enemy from you without toil.'

29 And the king returned to his throne, being provoked about Ahikar, and did nothing concerning him. And Nadan went to Ahikar and said to him, 'W'allah, (By God) my uncle! The king truly rejoiced in you with great joy and thanks you for having done what he commanded you.

30 And now he has sent me to you that you may dismiss the soldiers to their duties and come yourself to him with your hands bound behind you, and your feet chained, that the ambassadors of Pharaoh may see this, and that the king may be feared by them and by their king.'

31 Then Ahikar and said answered, 'To hear is to obey.' And he arose right away and bound his hands behind him, and chained his feet.

32 And Nadan took him and went with him to the king. And when Ahikar entered the king's presence he did obeisance before him on the ground, and wished for power and perpetual life to the king.

33 Then said the king, ' Ahikar, my Secretary, the Governor of my affairs, my Chancellor, the ruler of my State, tell me what evil have I done to you that you have rewarded me by this ugly deed.'

34 Then they showed him the letters in his writing and with his seal. And when Ahikar saw this, his limbs trembled and his tongue was tied at once, and he was unable to speak a word from fear; but he hung his head towards the earth and was speechless.

35 And when the king saw this, he felt certain that the thing was from him, and he arose at once and commanded them to kill Ahikar, and to strike his neck with the sword outside of the city.

86 Then Nadan screamed and said, ' Ahikar, blackface! What good did your meditation or your power bring you in the doing of this deed to the king?' This is what that storyteller said.

37 And the name of the swordsman was Abu Samik. And the king said to him, 'swordsman arise, and go, sever the neck of Ahikar at the door of his house, and cast away his head from his body a hundred cubits.' (A cubit is about 18 inches. 100 cubits is about 150 feet.)

38 Then Ahikar knelt before the king, and said, 'Let my lord the king live forever! And if you desire to kill me, let your wish be fulfilled, but I know that I am not guilty. The wicked man has to give an account of his wickedness; nevertheless, my lord the king, I beg of you and of your friendship, permit the swordsman to give my body to my slaves, that they may bury me, and let your slave be your sacrifice.'

39 The king arose and commanded the swordsman to do with him according to his desire.

40 And then and there he commanded his servants to take Ahikar and the swordsman and for Ahikar to go with him naked that they might kill him.

41 And when Ahikar knew for certain that he was to be killed he sent to his wife, and said to her, 'Come out and meet me, and let there be with you a thousand young virgins, and dress them in gowns of purple and silk that they may weep for me fore my death.

42 And prepare a table for the swordsman and for his servants. And mingle plenty of wine, that they may drink.'

43 And she did all that he commanded her. And she was very wise, clever, and prudent. And she brought into action all of her possible courtesy and learning.

44 And when the army of the king and the swordsman arrived they found the table set in order, and the wine and the luxurious foods and they began eating and drinking until they were gorged and drunken.

45 Then Ahikar took the swordsman aside apart from the company and said, ' Abu Samik, do you not know that when Sarhadum the king, the father of Sennacherib, wanted to kill you, I took you and hid you in a certain place until the king's anger subsided and he asked for you?

46 And when I brought you into his presence he rejoiced in you. Now remember the kindness I did you.

47 And I know that the king will change his mind about me and will be angry with a great rage about my execution.

48 Because I am not guilty, and it shall he when you shall present me before him in his palace, you shall meet with great good fortune, and know that Nadan, my sister's son, has deceived me and has done this bad deed to me, and the king will be sorry for having slain me. Now, I have a cellar in the garden of my house, and no one knows of it.

49 Hide me in it with the knowledge of my wife. And I have a slave in prison whom deserves to be killed.

50 Bring him out and dress him in my clothes, and command the servants when they are drunk to slay him. They will not know whom it is they are killing.

51 And cast away his head a hundred cubits from his body, and give his body to my slaves that they may bury it. And you shall have laid up a great treasure with me. (I will owe you greatly.)

52 And then the swordsman did as Ahikar had commanded him, and he went to the king and said to him, 'May your head live for ever!' (This is a wicked pun, but refers to the continuation of the king's dynasty through his wisdom.)

53 Then Ahikar's wife let down to him in the hiding-place every week what sufficed for him and no one knew of it but herself.

54 And the story was reported and repeated and spread abroad in every place of how Ahikar the Sage had been killed and was dead, and all the people of that city mourned for him.

55 And they wept and said: 'Pity for you, Ahikar! And for your learning and your courtesy! How sad about you and about your knowledge! Where can another like you be found? And where can there be a man so intelligent, so learned, so skilled in ruling as to resemble you that he may fill your place?'

56 But the king was repenting about Ahikar, and his repentance brought him

nothing.

57 Then he called for Nadan and said to him, 'Go and take your friends with you and make a mourning and a weeping for your uncle Ahikar, and lament for him as the custom is, doing honor to his memory.'

58 But when Nadan, the foolish, the ignorant, the hardhearted, went to the house of his uncle, he neither wept nor sorrowed nor wailed, but assembled heartless and dissolute people and set about eating and drinking.

59 And Nadan began to seize the maidservants and the slaves belonging to Ahikar, and bound them and tortured them and beat them with a harsh beating.

60 And he did not respect the wife of his uncle, she who had brought him up like her own boy, but wanted her to fall into sin with him.

61 But Ahikar had been cast into the hiding-place, and he heard the weeping of his slaves and his neighbors, and he praised the Most High God, the Merciful One, and gave thanks, and he always prayed and besought the Most High God.

62 And the swordsman came from time to time to Ahikar while he was within the hiding-place: and Ahikar met and encouraged him. And the swordsman comforted him and wished his deliverance.

63 And when the story was reported in other countries that Ahikar the Sage had been killed all the kings were grieved and despised king Sennacherib, and they lamented over Ahikar the solver of riddles.

CHAP. IV.

And when the king of Egypt had made sure that Ahikar was slain, he began right away to write a letter to king Sennacherib, saying to him in it of the peace and the health and the might and the honor which we wish specially for you, my beloved brother, king Sennacherib.

2 I have been desiring to build a castle between the heaven and the earth, and I want you to send me a wise, clever man from yourself (your realm) to build it for me, and to answer me all my questions, and that I may have the taxes and the custom duties of Assyria for three years.'

3 Then he sealed the letter and sent it to Sennacherib.

4 He took it and read it and gave it to his chancellors and to the nobles of his kingdom, and they were perplexed and ashamed, and he was angry with a great rage, and was puzzled about how he should act.

5 Then he assembled the old men and the learned men and the wise men and the philosophers, and the diviners and the astrologers, and every one who was in his country, and read them the letter and said to them, Who among you will go to Pharaoh king of Egypt and answer him his questions?'

6 And they said to him, ' our lord the king, you know that there is none in your kingdom who is acquainted with these questions except Ahikar, your vizier and secretary.

7 But as for us, we have no skill in this, unless Nadan his sister's son does, for he taught him all his wisdom and learning and knowledge. Call him to you, possibly he can untie this hard knot.'

8 Then the king called Nadan and said to him, 'Look at this letter and understand what is in it.' And when Nadan read it, he said, ' my lord, who is able to build a castle between the heaven and the earth?'

9 And when the king heard the words of Nadan he was sorry with a great and harsh sorrow, and stepped down from his throne and sat in the ashes, and began to weep and wail over Ahikar

10 Saying, 'I am in grief. Ahikar, knew the secrets and the riddles! Woe is me for you, Ahikar, teacher of my country and ruler of my kingdom, where shall I find anyone like you? Ahikar, teacher of my country, where shall I turn for you? Woe is me for you! How did I destroy you! And I listened to the talk of a stupid, ignorant boy without knowledge, without religion, and without manliness.

11 Oh, Oh, I say to myself! Who can give you to me just for one more time, or bring me word that Ahikar is alive? And I would give him the half of my kingdom.

12 Where is this to me? Ah, Ahikar! That I might see you just for once, that I might take my fill of gazing at you, and delighting in you.

13 Oh! My grief for you is to all time! Ahikar, how could I have killed you? I was impulsive in your case and so I had not seen the end of the matter.'

14 And the king went on weeping night and day. Now when the swordsman saw the anger and sorrow of the king on account of Ahikar, his heart was softened towards him, and he approached into his presence and said to him:

15 My lord! Command your servants to cut off my head.' Then said the king to him: 'Woe to you, Abu Samik, 'what is your fault?'

16 And the swordsman said unto him, ' my master, every slave who acts contrary to the word of his master is killed, and I have acted contrary to your command.'

17 Then the king said unto him. 'Woe unto you, Abu Samik, in what way have you acted contrary to my command?'

18 And the swordsman said unto him, ' my lord, you commanded me to kill Ahikar, and I knew that you would change your mind concerning him, and that he had been wronged, and I hid him in a certain place, and I killed one of his slaves, and he is now safe in the cistern, and if you command me I will bring him to you.'

19 And the king said unto him. 'Woe to you, Abu Samik, you have mocked me and I am your lord.'

20 And the swordsman said unto him, 'No, but by the life of your head, my lord! Ahikar safe and alive.'

21 And when the king heard what he was saying, he felt sure of the matter, and his head swam, and he fainted from joy, and he commanded them to bring Ahikar.

22 And he said to the swordsman, ' trusty servant, if your speech is true, I would pleased and obliged to enrich you, and exalt your dignity above that of all your friends.'

23 And the swordsman went along rejoicing until he came to Ahikar's house. And he opened the door of the hiding-place, and went down and found Ahikar sitting, praising God, and thanking Him.

24 And he shouted to him, saying, ' Ahikar, I bring the greatest of joy, and happiness, and delight!'

25 And Ahikar said to him, 'What is the news, Abu Samik?' And he told him all about Pharaoh from the beginning to the end. Then he took him and went to the king.

26 And when the king looked at him, he saw him in a state of need, being bereft, and that his hair had grown long like that of the wild beasts' and his nails were like the claws of an eagle, and that his body was dirty with dust, and the color of his face had changed and faded and was now like ashes.

27 And when the king saw him he sorrowed over him and rose at once and

embraced him and kissed him, and wept over him and said: 'Praise be to God, who has brought you back to me.'

28 Then he consoled him and comforted him. And he stripped off his robe, and put it on the swordsman, and was very gracious to him, and gave him great wealth, and made Ahikar rest (recuperate).

29 Then Ahikar said to the king, 'Let my lord the king live forever! These are the deeds of the children of the world. I have raised me a palm - tree that I might lean on it, and it bent sideways, and threw me down.

30 But, my lord, I am in your presence and do not want to make you sad.' And the king said to him: 'Blessed be God, who showed you mercy, and knew that you were wronged, and saved you and rescued you from being killed.

31 But go to the warm bath, and shave your head, and cut your nails, and change your clothes and amuse yourself for the space of forty days, that you may do good to yourself and improve your condition and so the color of your face may come back to you.

32 Then the king stripped off his costly robe, and put it on Ahikar, and Ahikar thanked God and bowed to the king, and departed to his home glad and happy, praising the Most High God.

33 And the people of his household rejoiced with him, and his friends and every one who heard that he was alive rejoiced also.

CHAP. V.

1 And he did as the king commanded him, and took a rest for forty days.

2 Then he dressed himself in his gayest dress, and went riding to the king, with his slaves behind him and before him, rejoicing and delighted.

3 But when Nadan, his sister's son, found out what was happening, fear took hold of him and terror, and he was confused, not knowing what to do.

4 And when Ahikar saw it he entered into the king's presence and greeted him, and he returned the greeting, and made him sit down at his side, saying to him, 'my beloved Ahikar, look at these letters which the king of Egypt sent to us, after he had heard that you were dead.

5 They have provoked us and overcome us, and many of the people of our country have fled to Egypt for fear of the taxes that the king of Egypt has sent to demand from us.'

6 Then Ahikar took the letter and read it and understood all that was in it.

7 Then he said to the king, do not be angry, my lord! I will go to Egypt, and I will give the answers to Pharaoh, and I will display this letter to him, and I will reply to him about the taxes, and I will send back all those who have run away; and I will put your enemies to shame with the help of the Most High God, and for the Happiness of your kingdom.'

8 And when the king heard these word from Ahikar, he rejoiced with a great joy, and his heart was expanded and he showed him favor.

9 And Ahikar said to the king: 'Grant me a delay of forty days that I may consider this question and manage it.' And the king permitted this.

10 And Ahikar went to his home, and he commanded the huntsmen to capture two young eaglets for him, and they captured them and brought them to him: and he commanded the weavers of ropes to weave two cables of cotton for him, each of them two thousand cubits long (about 3000 ft.), and he had the carpenters brought and ordered them to make two great boxes, and they did this.

11 Then he took two little lads, and spent every day sacrificing lambs and feeding the eagles and the boys, and making the boys ride on the backs of the eagles, and he bound them with a firm knot, and tied the cable to the feet of the eagles and let them soar upwards little by little every day, to a distance of ten cubits, till they grew accustomed and were educated to it; and they rose all the length of the rope until they reached the sky; the boys being on their backs. Then he drew them to himself.

12 And when Ahikar saw that his desire was fulfilled he charged the boys that when they were borne aloft to the sky they were to shout, saying:

13 Bring us clay and stone that we may build a castle for king Pharaoh, for we are idle.'

14 And Ahikar was never done training them and exercising them until they had reached the greatest possible point of skill.

15 Then leaving them he went to the king and said to him, ' my lord, the work you desired is finished. Come with me that I may show you the wonder.'

16 So the king sprang up and sat with Ahikar and went to a wide place and sent to

bring the eagles and the boys, and Ahikar tied them and let them off into the air all the length of the ropes and they began to shout as he had taught them. Then he drew them to himself and put them in their places.

17 And the king and those who were with him wondered with a great wonder: and the king kissed Ahikar between his eyes and said to him, 'Go in peace, to Egypt and answer the questions of Pharaoh and overcome him by the strength of the Most High God. You are my beloved and the pride of my kingdom.'

18 Then he said his farewell to the king, and took his troops and his army and the young men and the eagles, and went toward the dwellings of Egypt; and when he had arrived, he turned towards the country of the king.

19 And when the people of Egypt knew that Sennacherib had sent a man of his Private Council to talk with Pharaoh and to answer his questions, they carried the news to king Pharaoh, and he sent a party of his Private Councilors to bring Ahikar before him.

20 And he came and entered into the presence of Pharaoh, and bowed to him as it is fitting to do to kings.

21 And he said to him: ' my lord the king! Sennacherib the king hails you with abundance of peace, and might, and honor.

22 And he has sent me, who am one of his servants, that I may answer your questions, and may fulfill all your desire: for you have sent to seek from my lord the king a man who will build you a castle between the heaven and the earth.

23 And I by the help of the Most High God and your noble favor and the power of my lord the king will build it for you as you desire.

24 But, my lord the king, what you have said in it about the taxes of Egypt for three years - now the stability of a kingdom is strict justice, and if you win and my hand has no skill in replying to you, then my lord the king will send you the taxes which you have mentioned.

25 And if I shall have answered you in your questions, it shall remain for you to send whatever you have mentioned to my lord the king.'

26 And when Pharaoh heard that speech, he wondered and was perplexed by the freedom of his tongue and the pleasantness of his speech.

27 And king Pharaoh said to him, 'Man, what is your name?' And he said, 'Your servant is Abiqam, and I a little ant of the ants of king Sennacherib.'

28 And Pharaoh said to him, 'Had your lord no one of higher dignity than you, that he has sent me a little ant to reply to me, and to converse with me?'

29 And Ahikar said to him, 'My lord the king! I would to God Most High that I may fulfill what is on your mind, for God is with the weak that He may confound the strong.'

30 Then Pharaoh commanded that they should prepare a place to live for Abiqam and supply him with provisions of meat, and drink, and all that he needed.

31 And when it was finished, three days afterwards Pharaoh clothed himself in purple and red and sat on his throne, and all his counselors and the magnates of his kingdom were standing with their hands crossed, their feet close together, and their heads bowed.

32 And Pharaoh sent to fetch Abiqam, and when he was presented to him, he did bowed before him and kissed the ground in front of him.

33 And king Pharaoh said to him, 'Abiqam, whom am I like, and the nobles of my kingdom, to whom are they like?'

34 And Ahikar said to him ' my lord the king, you are like the idol Bel, and the nobles of your kingdom are like his servants.'

35 He said to him, 'Go, and come back here tomorrow.' So Ahikar went as king Pharaoh had commanded him.

36 And the next day Ahikar went into the presence of Pharaoh, and bowed and stood before the king. And Pharaoh was dressed in a red color, and the nobles were dressed in white.

37 And Pharaoh said to him ' Abiqam, whom am I like, and the nobles of my kingdom, to whom are they like?'

35 And Abiqam said to him, ' my lord, you are like the sun, and your servants are like its beams.' And Pharaoh said to him, 'Go to your house, and come here tomorrow.'

39 Then Pharaoh commanded his Court to wear pure white, and Pharaoh was dressed like them and sat upon his throne and he commanded them to fetch Ahikar. And he entered and sat down before him.

40 And Pharaoh said to him, ' Abiqam, whom am I like, and my nobles, to whom are they like?'

41 And Abiqam said to him, ' my lord, you are like the moon, and your nobles are like the planets and the stars.' And Pharaoh said to him, 'Go, and tomorrow be here.'

42 Then Pharaoh commanded his servants to wear robes of various colors, and Pharaoh wore a red velvet dress, and sat on his throne, and commanded them to fetch Abiqam. And he entered and bowed before him.

43 And he said, ' Abiqam, whom am I like, and my armies, to whom are they like?' And he said, ' my lord, you are like the month of April, and your armies are like its flowers.'

44 And when the king heard It he rejoiced with a great joy, and said, ' Abiqam, the first time you compared me to the idol Bel, and my nobles to his servants.

45 And the second time you compared me to the sun, and my nobles to the sunbeam'.

46 And the third time you compared me to the moon, and my nobles to the planets and the stars.

47 And the fourth time you compared me to the month of April, and my nobles to its flowers. But now, Abiqam, tell me, your lord, king Sennacherib, whom is he like, and his nobles, to whom are they like?'

48 And Ahikar shouted with a loud voice and said: 'Be it far from me to make mention of my lord the king and you seated on your throne. But get up on your feet that I may tell you whom my lord the king is like and to whom his nobles are like.'

49 And Pharaoh was perplexed by the freedom of his tongue and his boldness in answering. Then Pharaoh arose from his throne, and stood before Ahikar, and said to him, 'Tell me now, that I may understand whom your lord the king is like, and his nobles, to whom they are like.'

50 And Ahikar said to him: 'My lord is the God of heaven, and his nobles are the lightning and the thunder, and when he wills the winds blow and the rain falls.

51 And he commands the thunder, and it lightens and rains, and he holds the sun, and it gives not its light, and the moon and the stars, and they do not circle.

52 And he commands the tempest, and it blows and the rain falls and it tramples on April and destroys its flowers and its houses.'

53 And when Pharaoh heard this speech, he was greatly confused and was angry with a great rage, and said to him: 'Tell me the truth, oh man, and let me know who

you really are!'

54 And he told him the truth. 'I am Ahikar the scribe, greatest of the Private Councilors of king Sennacherib and I am his vizier and the Governor of his kingdom, and his Chancellor.'

55 And he said to him, 'You have told the truth in this saying. But we have heard of Ahikar, that king Sennacherib has killed him, yet you seem to be alive and well.'

56 And Ahikar said to him, 'Yes, so it was, but praise be to God, who knows what is hidden, for my lord the king commanded me to be killed, and he believed the word of licentious men, but the Lord delivered me, and blessed is he who trusts in Him.'

57 And Pharaoh said to Ahikar, 'Go, and tomorrow be you here, and tell me a word that I have never heard from my nobles nor from the people of my kingdom and my country.'

CHAP. VI.

1 And Ahikar went to his dwelling, and wrote a letter, saying in it the following:

2 'From Sennacherib king of Assyria and Nineveh to Pharaoh king of Egypt.

3 'Peace be to you, my brother and what we make known to you by this is that a brother has need of his brother, and kings of each other, and my hope from you is that you would lend me nine hundred talents of gold, for I need it for the feeding of some of the soldiers, that I may spend it upon them. And after a little while I will send it you.'

4 Then he folded the letter, and presented it to Pharaoh the next day.

5 And when he saw it, he was perplexed and said to him, 'Truly I have never heard anything like this language from any one.'

6 Then Ahikar said to him, 'Truly this is a debt which you owe to my lord the king.'

7 And Pharaoh accepted this, saying, ' Ahikar, it is people like you who are honest in the service of kings.

8 Blessed be God who has made you perfect in wisdom and has adorned you with philosophy and knowledge.

9 And now, Ahikar, there remains what we desire from you, that you should build

us a castle between heaven and earth.'

10 Then said Ahikar, 'To hear is to obey. I will build you a castle according to your wish and choice; but, my lord, prepare us lime (calcium hydroxide) and stone and clay and workmen, and I have skilled builders who will build for you as you desire.'

11 And the king prepared all that for him, and they went to a wide place. Ahikar and his boys came to it, and he took the eagles and the young men with him; and the king and all his nobles went and the whole city assembled, that they might see what Ahikar would do.

12 Then Ahikar let the eagles out of the boxes, and tied the young men on their backs, and tied the ropes to the eagles' feet, and let them go in the air. And they soared upwards, until they remained between heaven and earth.

13 And the boys began to shout, saying, 'Bring bricks, bring clay, that we may build the king's castle, for we are standing idle!'

14 And the crowd was astonished and amazed and they wondered. And the king and his nobles wondered.

15 And Ahikar and his servants began to beat the workmen and they shouted for the king's troops, saying to them, 'Bring to the skilled workmen what they want and do not hinder them from their work.'

16 And the king said to him, 'You are mad. Who can bring anything up to that distance?'

17 And Ahikar said to him, ' my lord, how shall we build a castle in the air? And if my lord the king were here, he would have built several castles in a single day.'

18 And Pharaoh said to him, 'Go to your dwelling Ahikar, , and rest, for we have given up building the castle, and tomorrow come to me.'

19 Then Ahikar went to his dwelling and the next day he appeared before Phanaoh. And Pharaoh said, ' Ahikar, what news is there of the horse of your lord? For when he neighs in the country of Assyria and Nineveb, and our mares hear his voice, they cast their young.' (Give birth before time and lose their young.)

20 And when Ahikar heard this speech he went and took a cat, and bound her and began to flog her with a violent flogging until the Egyptians heard it, and they went and told the king about it. (Cats were sacred to the Egyprians.)

21 And Pharaoh sent to bring back Ahikar, and said to him, ' Ahikar, why do you

flog and beat that dumb beast like you do?'

22 And Ahikar said to him, ' my lord the king, truly she has done an ugly deed to me, and has deserved this beating and flogging, for my lord king Sennacherib had given me a fine cock, and he had a strong true voice and knew the hours of the day and the night.

23 And the cat got up this very night and cut off its head and went away, and because of this deed I have treated her to this beating.'

24 And Pharaoh said to him, ' Ahikar, I see from all this that you are growing old and are senile, for between Egypt and Nineveh there are sixty-eight parasangs (around 10,000 paces), and how did she go this very night and cut off the head of your cock and come back?'

25 And Ahikar said to him, ' my lord! if there were such a distance between Egypt and Nineveh, how could your mares hear when my lord the king's horse neighs and cast their young? And how could the voice of the horse reach to Egypt?'

26 And when Pharaoh heard he knew that Ahikar had answered his questions.

27 And Pharaoh said, ' Ahikar, I want you to make me ropes from the sands of the sea.'

28 And Ahikar said to him, ' my lord the king, order them to bring me a rope out of the treasury that I may make one like it.'

29 Then Ahikar went to the back of the house, and bored holes in the rough shore of the sea, and took a handful of sand of the sea in his hand and when the sun rose, and penetrated into the holes, he spread the sand in the sun till it became as if woven like ropes.

30 And Ahikar said, 'Command your servants to take these ropes, and whenever you desire it, I will weave you some like them.'

31 And Pharaoh said, ' Ahikar, we have a millstone here and it has been broken and I want you to sew it up.'

32 Then Ahikar looked at it and found another stone.

33 And he said to Pharaoh. ' My lord! I am a foreigner and I have no tool for sewing.

34 But I want you to command your faithful shoemakers to cut awls from this stone,

that I may sew that millstone.'

35 Then Pharaoh and all his nobles laughed. And he said, 'Blessed be the Most High God, who gave you this wit and knowledge.'

36 And when Pharaoh saw that Ahikar had overcome him, and returned him his answers, he at once became excited, and commanded them to collect for him three years' taxes, and to bring them to Ahikar.

37 And he stripped off his robes and put them upon Ahikar, and his soldiers, and his servants, and gave him the expenses of his journey.

38 And he said to him, 'Go in peace, strength of his lord and pride of his Doctors. Do any of the Sultans have a man like you? Give my greetings to your lord king Sennacherib, and tell him how we have sent him gifts, for kings are content with little.'

39 Then Ahikar arose, and kissed king Pharaoh's hands and kissed the ground in front of him, and wished him strength and continuance, and abundance in his treasury, and said to him, ' my lord! I desire from you that not one of our countrymen may remain in Egypt.'

40 And Pharaoh arose and sent heralds to proclaim in the streets of Egypt that not one of the people of Assyria or Nineveh should remain in the land of Egypt, but that they should go with Ahikar.

41 Then Ahikar went and took leave of king Pharaoh, and journeyed, seeking the land of Assyria and Nineveh; and he had some treasures and a great deal of wealth.

42 And when the news reached king Sennacherib that Ahikar was coming, he went out to meet him and rejoiced over him exceedingly with great joy and embraced him and kissed him, and said to him, 'Welcome home, kinsman, my brother Ahikar, the strength of my kingdom, and pride of my realm.

43 Ask what you would have from me, even if you desire the half of my kingdom and of my possessions.

44 Then said Ahikar unto him, ' my lord the king, live forever! Show favor, my lord the king, to Abu Samik on my behalf, for my life was in the hands of God and in his.'

45 Then Sennacherib the king said, 'Honor be to you, my beloved Ahikar! I will make the station of Abu Samik the swordsman higher than all my Private Councilors and my favorites.'

46 Then the king began to ask him how he had got on with Pharaoh from his first arrival until he had come away from his presence, and how he had answered all his questions, and how he had received the taxes from him, and the changes of raiment and the gifts.

47 And Sennacherib the king rejoiced with a great joy, and said to Ahikar, 'Take what you would desire to have of this tribute, for it is all within the grasp of your hand.'

48 And Ahikar said: 'Let the king live forever! I desire nothing but the safety of my lord the king and the continuance of his greatness.

49 My lord! What can I do with wealth and its like? But if you will show me favor, give me Nadan, my sister's son, that I may repay him for what he has done to me, and grant me his blood and hold me guiltless of it.'

50 And Sennacherib the king said, 'Take him, I have given him to you,' And Ahikar took Nadan, his sister's son, and bound his hands with chains of iron, and took him to his home, and put a heavy fetter on his feet, and tied it with a tight knot, and after binding him like this, he cast him into a dark room, beside the retiring place (bed room), and appointed Nebu - hal as sentinel (guard) over him and commanded him to give him a loaf of bread and a little water every day.

CHAP. VII,

1 And whenever Ahikar went in or out he scolded Nadan, his sister's son, saying to him wisely:

2 Nadan, my boy, I have done to you all that is good and kind. And you have rewarded me for it with what is ugly and bad and with killing.

3 'My son, it is said in the proverbs: He who does not listen with his ear, they will make him listen with the scruff of his neck.'

4 And Nadan said, 'For what cause are you angry with me?'

5 And Ahikar said to him, 'Because I brought you up, and taught you, and gave you honor and respect and made you great, and raised you with the best of etiquette and manners, and seated you in my place that you might be my heir in the world, and you treated me with killing and repaid me with my ruin.

6 But the Lord knew that I was wronged, and He saved me from the snare, which

you had for me, for the Lord heals the broken hearts and hinders the envious and the arrogant.

7 My boy, you have been to me like the scorpion which, when it strikes on brass, pierces it.

8 My boy, you are like the gazelle who was eating the roots of the madder (the Rubia Peregrina plant yields a red dye - wild madder), and it said to her, "Eat of me today and take your fill, and tomorrow they will tan your hide in my roots."

9 My boy, you have been to me like a man who saw his comrade naked in the chilly time of winter; and he took cold water and poured it upon him.

10 My boy, you have been to me like a man who took a stone, and threw it up to heaven to stone his Lord with it. And the stone did not hit, and did not reach high enough, but it became the cause of guilt and sin.

11 My boy, if you had honored me and respected me and had listened to my words you would have been my heir, and would have reigned over my dominions.

12 My son, know you that if the tail of the dog or the pig were ten cubits long it would not approach to the worth of the horse's even if it were like silk.

13 My boy, I thought that you would have been my heir at my death; and you through your envy and your insolence desired to kill me. But the Lord delivered me from your cunning.

14 My son, you have been to me like a trap which was set up on the dunghill, and there came a sparrow and found the trap set up. And the sparrow said to the trap, "What are you doing here?" Said the trap, "I am praying here to God."

15 And the lark asked it also, "What is the piece of wood that you hold?" Said the trap, "That is a young oak-tree on which I lean at the time of prayer.

16 The lark said: "And what is that thing in your mouth?" Said the trap: "That is bread and food which I carry for all the hungry and the poor who come near me."

17 The lark said: "Now then may I come forward and eat, for I am hungry?" And the trap said to him, "Come forward." And the lark approached that it might eat.

18 But the trap sprang up and seized the lark by its neck

19 And the lark said to the trap, "If that is your bread for the hungry, God does not

accept your alms or your kind deeds.

20 And if that is your fasting and your prayers, God does not accept your fast nor your prayer, and God will not bring to fruition what is good concerning you."

21 My boy, you have been to me as a lion who made friends with an ass, and the ass kept walking in front of the lion for a time; and one day the lion sprang upon the ass and ate it up.

22 My boy, you have been to me like a weevil in the wheat. It is good for nothing but to spoil the wheat and chew at it.

23 My boy, you have been like a man who sowed ten measures of wheat, and when it was harvest time, he arose and reaped it, and gathered it, and threshed it, and toiled over it to the very end, and it turned out to be ten measures, and its master said to it: " you lazy thing! You have not grown and you have not shrunk."

24 My boy, you have been to me like the quail that had been hurled into the net. She could not save herself, but she called out to the quails, so that she might throw (lure) them into the net with her.

25 My son, you have been to me like the dog that was cold and it went into the potter's house to get warm.

26 And when it had gotten warm, it began to bark at them, and they chased it out and beat it, so that it would not bite them.

27 My son, you have been to me like the pig who went into the hot bath with people of quality, and when it came out of the hot bath, it saw a filthy hole and it went down and, wallowed in it.

28 My son, you have been to me like the goat, which joined its comrades on their way to the sacrifice, and it was unable to save itself.

29 My boy, the dog which is not fed from its hunting becomes food for flies.

30 My son, the hand which does not labor and plough but is greedy and deceitful shall be cut off from its shoulder.

31 My son, the eye in which light is not seen, the ravens shall pick at it and pluck it out.

32 My boy, you have been to me like a tree, and men were cutting its branches, and

the tree said to them, "If something of me were not in your hands, you would not be able to cut me."

33 My boy, you are like the cat to which they said: "cease thieving until we make a chain of gold for you and feed you with sugar and almonds."

34 And she said, "I cannot forget the craft of my father and my mother."

35 My son, you have been like the serpent riding on a thorn-bush when he was in the middle of a river, and a wolf saw them and said, "bad behavior upon bad behavior, let him who is more of a troublemaker than they lead both of us."

36 And the serpent said to the wolf, "The lambs and the goats and the sheep which you have eaten all your life, will you return them to their fathers and to their parents or not?"

37 Said the wolf, "No." And the serpent said to him, "I think that after myself (between the two of us) you are the worst of us."

38 My boy, I fed you with good food and you did not feed me with dry bread.

39 My boy, I gave you sugared water to drink and good syrup, and you did not give me water from the well to drink.

40 My boy, I taught you, and brought you up, and you dug a (pit for a) hiding-place for me and did conceal me.

41 My boy, I brought you up with the best upbringing and trained you like a tall cedar; and you have twisted and bent me.

42 My boy, it was my hope for you that you would build me a fortified castle, that I might be concealed from my enemies in it, and you became to me like one burying (me) in the depth of the earth; but the Lord took pity on me and delivered me from your deceit.

43 My boy, I wished you well, but you rewarded me with evil and hatefulness, and now I would desire tears from your eyes, and make you food for dogs, and cut out your tongue, and take off your head with the edge of the sword, and reward you for your abominable deeds.'

44 And when Nadan heard this speech from his uncle Ahikar, he said: ' my uncle! Deal with me according to your knowledge, and forgive me my sins, for who is there who has sinned like me, or who is there who forgives like you?

45 Accept me, my uncle! Now I will serve in your house, and groom your horses and sweep up the dung of your cattle, and feed your sheep, for I am the wicked and you are the righteous: I am the guilty and you the (one) forgiving.'

46 And Ahikar said to him, 'My boy, you are like the tree which was fruitless beside the water, and its master was desirous to cut it down, and it said to him, "Remove me to another place, and if I do not bear fruit, cut me down."

47 And its master said to it, "You have been beside the water and have not borne fruit. How shall you bear fruit when you are in another place?"

48 My boy, the old age of the eagle is better than the youth of the crow.

49 My boy, they said to the wolf, "Keep away from the sheep or their dust will harm you." And the wolf said, "The dregs of the sheep's milk are good for my eyes."

50 My boy, they made the wolf go to school that he might learn to read, and they said to him, "Say A, B." He said, "Lamb and goat in my belly."

51 My boy, they set the ass down at the table and he fell, and began to roll himself in the dust, and one said, "Let him roll himself, for it is his nature, he will not change."

52 My boy, the saying has been confirmed which goes like this: "If you beget a boy, call him your son, and if you raise a boy, call him your slave."

53 My boy, he who does good shall meet with good; and he who does evil shall meet with evil, for the Lord rewards a man according to the measure of his work.

54 My boy, what shall I say more to you than these sayings, for the Lord knows what is hidden, and is acquainted with the mysteries and the secrets.

55 And He will avenge you and will judge between you and me, and will reward you according to your (evil) desires.

56 And when Nadan heard that speech from his uncle Ahikar, he swelled up immediately and became like a blown-out bladder.

57 And his limbs swelled and his legs and his feet and his side, and he was ripped apart and his belly burst apart and his guts were scattered, and he perished, and died.

58 And his end was destruction, and he went to hell. For he who digs a pit for his brother shall fall into it; and he who sets up traps shall be caught in them.

59 This is what happened and what we discovered about the tale of Ahikar, and praise be to God for ever.

Amen, and peace.

60 This chronicle is finished with the help of God, may He be exalted:

Amen, Amen, Amen.

SECTION TWO
APOCALYPTIC WRITINGS AND THE END OF DAYS

End of Days
The Apocalyptic Writings

Introduction

Is mankind headed for destruction? How will it all end? When will it happen? What is man's destiny? Will we die by our own hand or by the hand of God?

For thousands of years the questions have been the same. Millions of souls have searched for the answers to no avail; nevertheless, some believed they knew. We call them prophets. They saw the end of our world and they believed their visions were true. Are we to believe their God-given insights into the End Of Days?

Perhaps God did pull back the curtain that blinds man to his future. Maybe these writers did see the end and how it would come upon us.

The prophets of doom revealed a scenario of global cataclysm. They tell the story of rulers bankrupting nations to fund tremendous wars. They tell of weather gone awry; of ice and snow, rain and floods, hurricanes and earthquakes where seldom they occurred. They tell us of what is happening all around us today.

Most scholars agree that many of the apocalyptic texts written between 70 and 200 A.D. were produced out of a national dismay and confusion following the destruction of the temple of the Jews in Israel in 70 A.D. The texts are attempts of a people, who believed themselves to be God's chosen, to explain why pagans were allowed by the God of the Jews to overthrow the way of worship, and of life of His chosen ones. Other apocalyptic books were written to explain and expand various biblical ideas linked to judgment and the end of days. The date, background, and purpose of each text will be discussed in more detail later.

The apocalyptic literature presented here allows us a rare glimpse into the ancient mindset and visions of how mankind may end. Most writings of this kind took place between 200 B.C. and 200 A.D, although a few were later and dated to the third century. The common thread was the moral and spiritual decline of man leading to his destruction. One could argue that the annihilation of the human race was to be brought about by our own hands due to our evil and sinful ways; however, it is the power unleashed by the wrath of God that gives way to the cleansing of the earth as all evil is destroyed and divine order is re-established. Only those who followed God and kept his laws would be spared.

Books written by those claiming to be Abraham, Thomas, Ezra, Baruch, and other giants of faith come down to us in ancient scrolls proclaiming the exact sequence of events leading to mankind's termination. Every society possesses apocalyptic texts. Every race and every nation carries in its literature and religion the implicit reiterating and unrelenting question; is the end near? The answer…yes, it is and here are its signs.

Presented in this book are four great apocalyptic works. "The Apocalypse of Abraham," "The Apocalypse Of Thomas" which is also called "The Revelation of

Thomas," 2 Baruch, which is also known as the Syriac Apocalypse of Baruch, and 4 Ezra, sometimes also referred to as 2 Esdras or the Apocalypse of Ezra.

These books represent the greatest among the apocalyptic writings of the era. Each gives its own unique insights into the End Of Days and yet, they all proclaim the same message; Follow God, turn from evil, or be destroyed.

The Apocalypse of Abraham

"The Apocalypse of Abraham" is part of a body of writings called "Abrahamic Writings," which flourished around and just after the time of Christ.

The manuscript dates from A.D. 80-170 with most scholars placing it between 80 and 100 A.D. The original text was written in a Semitic language, however it has survived only in Old Slavonic renditions.

Many of the Jewish non-canonical and extra-biblical materials that circulated in the Slavic lands came from Byzantium. They greatly influenced the development of Slavic literature. Non-canonical books brought from Byzantium were translated and became sections (pieces) of various Slavonic traditions. The Eastern Orthodox church nurtured an environment in which the apocryphal texts were encouraged toward the view of providing additional information as a secondary source to the canonical mainstream texts. Pseudepigraphical (certain writings other than the canonical books and the Apocrypha, professing to be Biblical in character) texts attributed to Adam, Enoch, Noah, Jacob, Abraham, Moses, and other patriarchs survived in this environment and were incorporated in hagiographical (the writing and critical study of the lives of the saints) and historical volumes.

An English translation of "The Apocalypse of Abraham" was produced by G. H. Box and J. I. Landsman in 1918 (The Apocalypse of Abraham, London: Society for Promoting Christian Knowledge) but that translation does not read well for the modern English audience. Thus arises the need to have the Box and other mainstream translations combined and updated into a more readable and accessible mode for today's reader.

It should be noted here that there are two versions of the "Apocalypse of Abraham," a long and a short version. The text in the book before you contains a combination of these two versions. When the two versions agree, which was more often than not the case, the clearest and best wording was chosen to express both in a single phrase.

When there were variations in meaning, alternate translations are shown in parentheses. When one version covered information not contained in the other translation, the additional lines were added, making this book the most complete body of information available as a single text.

"The Apocalypse of Abraham" is written in an haggadic midrash tradition. (Haggadic - embracing the interpretation of the non-legal portions of the Hebrew Bible. These midrashim are sometimes referred to as *haggadah,* a term that refers to all non-legal discourse in classical rabbinic literature). (Midrash – a Hebrew word referring to a method of exegesis of a Biblical text and teachings in the form of legal or exegetical commentaries on the Jewish Bible).

As with much of the Haaadic literature, the writings are an expansion and detailed explanation of existent biblical texts. That is to say, the writer took a section of an Old Testament canonical text and expanded it into a larger, more detailed story in order to explain in further detail the moral and religious implications of the original text.

Apocalyptic writings abound in the same time frame in the first century. It is thought they were spurred into creative existence by the utter destruction of the Jewish Temple in 70 A.D. and the attempted annihilation of Christians, many of whom were converted Jews, at the same time.

"The Apocalypse of Abraham" is based on Genesis 15:9-17 and concludes with the apocalypse. The book is of Jewish origin with features which might suggest that it had its beginning in the Essene community. This is seen clearly in the references to the "Elect One," a term that also appears in the Lost Book Of Enoch." (See "The Lost Book Of Enoch" by Joseph Lumpkin.)

Approximately one-third of the "Apocalypse of Abraham" contains an account of Abraham's conversion from polytheism to henotheism. Whereas polytheism believes in and worships many gods, each according to his or her dominion and special power; monotheism is the belief in one god; and henotheism focuses on one god but does not deny the existence of the other gods. The Amarna period of Egyptian history is an example a society that held to the henotheistic belief system.

The apocalyptic section of the Abraham text begins with the search for the God that made all things and the rejection of god's (idols) made by men. He (Abraham) reasons that if man made the gods with his own hands that man must therefore be greater than the gods he made.

Abraham's prayers are answered and he is told how to sacrifice to God. The preparation and sacrifice follows the biblical account, except that instead of birds of prey appearing and consuming the sacrifice, it is Azazel who does so. The angel Jaoel (Iaoel or Joel), guides Abraham into heaven and teaches him a song that is to be sung only on that realm or sphere of heaven.

While in heaven, Abraham sees a vision of the sin and degradation of his own progeny. As their sin increases, God withdraws his protection and the great temple is overrun by "heathen nations" and the progeny is killed and enslaved.

The five main characters in the book are El (God), Jaoel, Azazel, Abraham, and a powerful figure simply known as "The Man." There are also minor characters such as Abraham's father and merchants who travel in the area in which Abraham lived.

We learn in the first chapter of the Apocalypse of Abraham that Abraham is the son of Terah and the brother of Nahor.

Chapter 1

1. I was standing guard one day over the gods of my father Terah and my brother Nahor…

We also know Abraham's family were polytheists who worshipped idols that their father made. We learn that Terah sold his idols to others as well. Abraham is depicted as a precocious and sassy youth who questions things taken for granted by others.

He asked a question that seems most insightful for its time; If you carve an idol to worship as a god, does not that make you greater than the god you made? If that is true, why worship that which is lesser? This simple question puts him on the path of searching for the God who made all things including man.

Jaoel is the angel assigned to guide Abraham on his search. Jaoel takes him to heaven and leads him into visions, instructing him along the way.

Since Jaoel is allowed to come and go from the seventh heaven, we must assume him to be an angel of very high rank, though not found mentioned by this name elsewhere.

The name Jaoel consists of two parts, Jah and El both names of God in the Old Testament. Jaoel shows and explains a universal duality.

The duality of the universe is seen in the "right handed" and "left handed" principle. The Lord Himself used this principle when speaking of the 'sheep and the goats" in Matthew 25.

Here in the Abrahamic writings there are people coming out of a temple on the left side and on the right side. The deities in the story are the God El, who in this writing assumes the name of Azazel, a name that appears a great deal in the Books of Enoch, and is used in the Old Testament in the account of the Day of Atonement, where one goat is slain in the Tabernacle, whilst the other is set free, and the Hebrew text reads it is "for Azazel."

Azazel is portrayed as an unclean bird which came down upon the sacrifice Abraham, the Biblical patriarch, prepared. This is in reference to Genesis 15:11 Birds of prey came down upon the carcasses, and Abram drove them away.

Azazel is also associated with Hell. Abraham tells Azazel he will burn in hell and be in the underworld or Hades.

Azazel appears four times in Old Testament: Leviticus 16 :8, 10, and 26, where the ritual for the Day of Atonement is described. After the priest has made atonement for himself, he is to take two goats on behalf of Israel. One is to be a sacrifice to the Lord, the other is to be the 'scape goat,' which is the goat for Azazel.

This word has been understood to mean the "goat that departs," considering it to be derived from two Hebrew words: "ez" (goat) and "azal" (turn off). It is also associated with the Arabic word, "azala" (banish), or (remove), It has been rendered "for entire removal." Refer to Leviticus 16:22. However, in I Chronicles 5:8, the father of Bela, a Reubenite, is named "Azaz," which means strong.

This name comes from the Hebrew verb "azaz", a which means "to be strong." Azazel is also seen as an evil spirit in Enoch 8:1; 10:4; II Chroncicles 11:15; Isaiah 34:14; and Revelations 18:2. In this way Azazel can be seen as the opponent or antithesis to the Lord and a precursor to Satan.

The figure of "The Man" is rather ambiguous. He is not fully messianic, yet he is endowed with power from God.

He may have come from the Essene idea of the Teacher of Righteousness and his connection with the coming, expected messiah.

Another explanation of the figure may come from an early Christian idea originating in a Judeo-Christian sect, which saw Jesus as precursor of the real and awaited Messiah, or it may simply be a Jewish text being badly interpreted and biased by an early Christian editor.

The evolution of El and his origin has drawn debate and acrimony since the beginning of theological study.

The people of Aramean and Canaanite origin seem to have contributed to the religion of El. Both religions place El as the highest god of a pantheon. Yet, because there is a pantheon of gods there is polytheism.

The clearest example of this adoption of the Israelite Elism comes from Deuteronomy 32 and related texts. El rules over his sons, and assigns each of them a people or tribe to govern. Here, to our surprise, we find Yahweh (the Lord) portrayed as one of El Elyon's divine sons.

Psalm 29 shows Yahweh as one of the sons of El, but a powerful god who is less subordinate than the others and more like an elder son.

Psalm 29 introduces the Canaanite cosmology which was more simple and familial; El being the father image and king.

We find within the Israelite religion two variations of the same high god. These different versions of Elism (the belief in a god called El) show that this god was variously worshipped depending upon location. Locations north of Palestine would have brought the worship of Yahweh in contact with Canaanite religion and that may explain its distinctly Canaanite quality.

Continuing the relationship between El and his sons, Psalm 82 has El stripping all his sons of authority and condemning them to mortality.

From this viewpoint, the Aramean god, El, seems to be related Canaanite mythology. Both likely descended from a Mesopotamian religion. Yet now, after being failed and disappointed by all others gods, whom we presume are his sons, El is forced to rule alone. Now we have the pathway set between polytheism and monotheism.

This last steps between the idea of a ruling court of gods and the singular god, El, can be seen clearly in the following translation and study by John Gray, Near Eastern Mythology:

"God has taken His place in the assembly of the gods (lit. 'sons of El"),
He declares His judgment among the gods: "
How long will you give crooked judgment,
and favor the wicked?
You ought to sustain the case of the weak and the orphan;
You ought to vindicate the destitute and down-trodden
You ought to rescue the weak and the poor,
To deliver them from the power of the wicked
You (Hebrew "they") walk in darkness
While all earth's foundations are giving away.
I declare "Gods you may be,
Sons of the Most high, all of you;
Yet you will die as men,
You will fall as one of the bright ones."

Psalm 82:1-7

"In the final line we read sharim for sarim ("princes"), from which it is indistinguishable in the Hebrew manuscripts, and find another reference to the fall of Athtar, the bright Venus star in Isaiah 14:12 ff and in the myth of Baal." (John Gray, Near Eastern Mythology)

Now, having introduced the cast of characters and set the historical and theological stage, let us proceed to the "Apocalypse of Abraham."

The Apocalypse of Abraham

Chapter 1

1. I was standing guard one day over the gods of my father Terah and my brother Nahor.
2. While I was testing them to find out which god was really the strongest and I was completing the services, I, Abraham, received my chance.
3. My father Terah was sacrificing to his gods of wood, stone, gold, silver, copper, and of iron and I entered their temple for the service, and found a god named Marumath, carved from stone, which had fallen at the feet of the iron god, Nakhin.
4. At that point my heart was perplexed (troubled) and I thought that I could not put it back in its place by myself because of its weight, since it was made of large stones.
5. So, I went and told my father, and he came in with me. When we both lifted it to put it in its place, its head fell off while I was holding it by its head.
6. Then when my father saw that the head of his god Marumath had fallen.
7. He yelled at me, saying, "Abraham!"
8. And I said, "Here I am!" And he told me to bring me the axes and chisels from the house. So, I brought them to him from the house.
9. Then he cut another Marumath without a head from another stone. He then smashed the head that had fallen off Marumath. He then crushed the rest of that (broken) Marumath.

Chapter 2

1. He created five more gods and gave them to me. He ordered me to sell them outside on the road to town.
2. I saddled my father's ass and loaded the gods on it and went out on the highway to sell them.
3. The merchants from Phandana of Syria were coming with their camels, on their way to Egypt to buy kokonil from the Nile.
4. I questioned them and they answered me. I walked along with them and talked with them. Then, one of their camels screamed and the ass was frightened and fled, throwing off the gods. Three of them were broken and two remained intact.
5. Then the Syrians saw that I had gods, they said to me: "Why did you not tell us that you had gods? We would have bought them before the ass. heard the camel's cry. You would had lost nothing."
6. Then they said, "Give us the gods that remain and we will give you a suitable price."
7. I considered this and grieved. But they paid both for the smashed gods and the gods which remained. I had been worried how I would bring payment to my father.
8. I threw the three broken gods into the water of the river Gur, which was in this place. And they sank deeply into the river Gur and were not seen again.

Chapter 3

1. As I was still walking on the road, my heart was disturbed and my mind was distracted.
2. I thought, "What is this deed of inequality my father is doing?

3. Is it not he who is god because his gods come into being through his sculpting, planning, and his skill (workmanship)?
4. They ought to honor my father because the gods are his work. What reward does my father received for his works?
5. Marumath fell and could not stand up in his (own) sanctuary, and could not I lift him myself until my father came and we stood him up (together). Even then we were not able to do it and his head fell off of him.
7. Then he put another stone on it from another god, which he (my father) had made without a head. The other five gods which got smashed when they fell from the ass could not save themselves. They did not harm the ass (to avenge themselves) because it smashed them. Nor did their broken pieces come up out of the river.
8. And I thought to myself, "If this is so, how can my father's god Marumath, which has the head of one stone and is made from another stone, save a man, or hear a man's prayer, or grant him any gift?"

Chapter 4
1. Thinking this way, I came to my father's house. I watered the ass and fed the ass with hay. I took out the silver and placed it in my father Terah's hand.
2. And when he saw it, he was happy, and he said, "You are blessed, Abraham, by the god of my gods, since you have brought me the price for the gods, so that my labor was not empty (for nothing)."
3. I answered and said to him, "Listen, father Terah! In you is the blessing of your gods, because you are the god of them, since you created them because their blessing is their hell and their power is empty.
4. They did not help themselves; how then can they help you or bless me?
5. I did well for you in this transaction, because through my good sense I brought you the silver for the broken gods."
6. When he heard what I had to say he became violently angry with me, since I had spoken words harshly contrary to his gods.

Chapter 5
1. Having thought about my father's anger, I left.
2. And afterward when I had left, he called me saying, "Abraham!" I answered, "Here I am!"
3. He said, " Gather these wood chips. I was making gods from fir before you came.
4. I will use the chips to cook food when I prepared my midday meal."
5. Then, when I was picking up the wooden chips, I found a small god among them which would fit in my left hand.
6. On its forehead was written: god Barisat. Then, I put the chips on the fire in to prepare food for my father, and went out to ask him about the food, I put Barisat near the kindling for the fire.
7. I spoke to him as if to threaten him. I said, "Barisat, watch that the fire does not go out before I come back!
8. If the fire goes out, blow on it so it flares up." I went out and said nothing of this to anyone.
9. When I returned I found Barisat fallen on his back. His feet were enveloped by fire and burning fiercely.

10. When I saw it, I laughed and I said to myself, "Barisat, truly you know how to light a fire and cook food!"
11. Then, while saying this in my laughter, I saw that he had burned up slowly with fire and turned to ashes.
12. I carried the food to my father to eat.
13. I gave him wine and milk, and he drank and he enjoyed himself and he thanked and spoke praise to Marumath his god.
14. Then I said to him, "Father Terah, do not bless Marumath your god, do not praise him!
15 Instead, praise your god Barisat, because he loved you enough that he threw himself into the fire in order to cook your food."
16. Then my father said to me said, "Where is he now?" And I said, "He has burned in the flames of the fire and become dust." And he said, "Great is the power of Barisat! I will make another today, and tomorrow he will prepare my food."

Chapter 6
1. When I, Abraham, heard these words from my father, I laughed to myself and I groaned from the disgust and anger in my heart.
2. I said, "How can a piece of a body made (by Terah) help my father, Terah?
3. How can he have enslaved his body to his soul (will or desire), and allowed his soul (will or desire) to be enslaved by a spirit (not his spirit but "a" spirit), when the spirit is stupid and ignorant?"
4. And I said, "It is only proper to withstand this evil that I may compel my mind toward purity. I will lay my thoughts out before him clearly.
5. " I answered and said, "Father Terah, no matter which of these gods you praise, your thoughts err.
6. Don't you see that the gods of my brother Nahor which stand in the holy sanctuary are more worthy than yours?
7. Look! Zouchaios, my brother Nahor's god is more worthy than your god Marumath because he is made of gold, which is valued by man.
8. And if Zouchaios grows old with time, he will be remolded, whereas, if Marumath deteriorates or is broken, he will not be renewed, because he is made of stone.
9. What about Ioav, the other god who stands with Zouchaios? He is also more worthy than the god Barisat.
10. He, Ioay, is carved from wood and then forged from silver; because he too is made of something that is given with love (comparison), and is valued by man according to their outward experience.
11. But Barisat, your god, is rooted in the earth. When he was large (great) it is a wonder because he had branches and flowers and was worth praise when he was still not carved.
12. But then you shaped him with an axe and you created (him as) a god by your skill.
13. Look! He has already dried up.
14. His substance (fruit/fatness) has perished.
15. From the height he has fallen to the earth.
16. He descended from greatness to a lowly state, and his face and appearance has wasted (withered) away.
17. He was burned up by the fire and he turned into ashes and disappeared.

18. Then you say, "Let me make another and tomorrow he will prepare my food for me." He was destroyed and no power (strength) was left in him (because of or to prevent) his own destruction.

Chapter 7
1. This I say: Fire is more valuable in the formation of things because even the untamable things are subdued in (by) it, and it laughs at those things which are destroyed easily by its burning.
3. But neither is it worthy (valuable), because it is subject to the water.
4. But water is more worthy (venerable/powerful) than fire because water overcomes fire and sweetens the earth with fruit.
5. But I would not call water a god either because water is taken under the earth and water is subject to the earth.
6. I will not call earth a goddess either because it is dried by the sun and was made for man for his work.
7. I think the sun is more worthy among the gods, because with its rays it illuminates the entire universe and all the air.
8. But I will would not place the sun among the gods because there are those who obscure his course. They are the moon and the clouds.
9. I will not call the moon or the stars gods, because at times during the night they also dim their light.
10. Listen, Terah my father, I will seek the God who created all the other gods we have thought exist.
11. I seek who or what is it that made the heavens red and the sun golden and who has given light to the moon and the stars and who has dried the earth in the midst of the many waters. I will seek who it is that has set you yourself among the things and who has sought me out in the of my thoughts of questioning.
12. God will reveal himself by himself to us!"

Chapter 8
1. Then, I was thinking about my father Terah being in the court of my house when the voice of the Mighty One came down from the heavens in a stream of fire and it called to me saying, "Abraham, Abraham!"
2. And I said, "Here I am."
3. Then he said, "You are searching in the wisdom of your heart for the God of gods, the Creator? I am he.
4. Get out from Terah, your father, and go away from the house, that you too may not be killed because of the sins of your father's house."
5. Then, as I went out and I was not outside the entrance of the court yet, the sound of a tremendous thunder came and burned him and his house and everything in his house to the ground for a space of forty cubits.

Chapter 9
1. Then a voice spoke to me twice: "Abraham, Abraham!"
2 I said, "Here I am!" And He said, "Look! It is I, fear not for I am with you because I AM before the ages, I am the Mighty God who created the first light of the world. I am your protection (shield) and your helper."

3. He continued and said, "Behold, it is I, Fear not because I am Before the World Was, I Am Mighty, the God who has created all, I am the light of the age.
4. I am your protector and your helper.
5. Go, get me a three-year-old heifer, a three-year-old female goat, a three-year-old ram, a turtledove, and a pigeon.
6. Go, take me a young heifer of three years, and a female goat of three years, and a ram of three years, a turtledove and a pigeon, and bring me a pure sacrifice.
7. In this sacrifice I will lay before (make known to) you the ages to come, and tell you what is in store, and you will see great things which you have not seen before.
8. I will tell you things kept guarded and you will see great things which you have not seen, because you desired me and searched for me, and so I called you my beloved.
9. But for forty days abstain from every kind of food cooked by fire, and from drinking because you have loved to search me out, and I have named you "my friend."
10 And also abstain from anointing yourself with oil for forty days, and then give me the sacrifice which I have commanded you, in a place which I will show you high on a mountain, and there I will reveal to you the ages which have been created and established by my word.
11. (And there I will show you the things which were made in the ages and by my word that affirmed and created, and renewed.) I will make known to you what will come to pass for them who have done evil and for those who have done righteousness (just deeds) in the generations of men."

Chapter 10
1. Then, I heard the voice telling me such things.
2. And I heard the voice of Him who spoke these words to me, and I looked around (for Him).
3. I found I could not breathe, and fear seized my spirit. My soul seemed to leave me and I fell down like a stone, like a dead man falls to the earth, and I had no strength to stand.
4. I was laying with my face down to the earth when I heard the voice of the Holy One speaking, "Go, Jaoel, and by the power of my ineffable name raise up man, that man over there and strengthen him , so that he recovers from his trembling.
5. Consecrate this man for me and strengthen him against his trembling."
6. The angel he sent to me in the likeness of a man came, and he took me by my right (hand) and set me up upon my feet and said to me, "Stand up Abraham, friend of God who loves you. Do not let your trembling seize you! For look! I have been sent to you to strengthen you and bless you in the name of God, who loves you. He is the Creator of the heaven and the Earth. Do not fear but and run to Him.
7. I am called Jaoel by Him who gives life to those who exist with me on the seventh level of heaven. It is done by the power of the goodness of the ineffable name that is dwelling in me.
8. I am the one who has been given (the authority) to restrain the threats and attacks of the Living One's Cherubim against one another, and to teach those who have Him within them, the song of the seventh hour of the night of man, according to His commandment. (I teach those who carry the song through man's night of the seventh hour.)

9. I am the one who ordered your father's house to be burned with him because he honored the dead (gods).
10. I am given authority to restrain the Leviathan (serpent/reptiles) because every attack and menace of every Leviathan (serpent/reptile) are subject to me.
11. I am he who has been given power to loosen Hades, and destroy him who watches over the dead.
12. I have been sent to bless you and your land now, for the Eternal One whom you have invoked has prepared for you. For your sake I have ventured my way upon earth.
13. Stand up, Abraham, go boldly, be very joyful and rejoice. And I (also rejoice) with you because you are venerable and I am with you! For everlasting honor has been prepared for you by the Eternal One.
14. Go, and do the sacrifices commanded. For I, and with me Michael, blesses you forever.
15. I have been commanded to be with you, and with the generations that will spring from you, Be of good cheer and go!"

Chapter 11
1.. And I stood up and saw him who had grasped me by the right hand and set me on my feet.
2. The appearance of his body was like sapphire, and the look of his appearance was like peridot, and the hair of his head was like snow.
3. A kidaris (a Scythian hat with long flaps usually worn by kings) was on his head and its look was like that of a rainbow.
4. His garments were purple and a golden staff was in his right hand.
5. And he said to me, "Abraham," And I said, "Here is your servant!"
6. He said, "Do not let my appearance frighten you. Nor should you let my speech trouble your soul.
7. Come with me, and I will be with you visibly until the sacrifice, but after the sacrifice I will be invisible forever more.
8. Be of good cheer, and come!"

Chapter 12
1. The two of us went together for forty days and nights, and I ate no bread and drank no water because my food and my drink was to see the angel who was with me, and to hear his voice.
2. We came to the Mount of God, Mount Horeb, and I said to the angel, "Singer to the Eternal One! I have no sacrifice and I do not know of a place with an altar on the mountain.
3. How can I bring a sacrifice?"
4. And he said to me, "Look around you." And when I looked around, there following us were all the required animals, the young heifer, the female goat, the ram, the turtle dove and the pigeon.
5. And the angel said to me, "Abraham!" And I said, "Here am I."
6. And he said, "Slaughter all these animals, and divide them into halves, place the one half against (across from/facing) the other, but do not divide (sever) the birds.
7. Give these to the men whom I will show you (that are) standing by you because these are the altar upon the Mountain, to offer a sacrifice to the Eternal (One).

8. But, the turtledove and the pigeon you will give to me because I will ascend on the wings of the birds to show you what is in the heavens, on the earth, in the sea, in the abyss, in the lower depths, in the garden of Eden, in its rivers, and in the fullness of the universe. And you will see its circles in all."

Chapter 13
1. I did everything commanded me by the angel, and I gave the angels who had come to us the divided animals, but the angel Jaoel took the birds.
2. Then I waited until the evening sacrifice. Then and there an unclean bird flew down upon the carcasses, and I drove it away.
3. The unclean bird spoke to me and said, "Abraham, what are you doing upon these holy heights where no man eats or drinks and there is no food for man here but these heavenly beings consume everything with fire and will burn you up?
4. Forsake the man who is with you and run away because if you ascend into the heights they will destroy (kill/make an end of) you."
5. Then, when I saw the bird speaking I said to the angel: "What is this, my lord?"
6. And he said, "This is ungodliness; this is Azazel."
7. And he said to it (the bird), "Disgrace upon you, Azazel! For Abraham's portion is in heaven, but yours is upon the earth because you have chosen this for the dwelling place of your uncleanness and you have loved it.
8. Therefore the Eternal Mighty Lord forced you to dwell upon the earth, and through you every evil spirit of lies, rage, and trials came forth for the generations of ungodly men.
9. God, the Eternal and Mighty One, has not permitted the bodies of the righteous to be (end up) in your hands so that the life of the righteous and the destruction of the unclean may be assured.
10. Listen! You have no permission to tempt the righteous at all.
11. Leave this man! You cannot deceive him, because he is the enemy of you and of those who follow you and those who love what you want.
12. Behold, the garment which is heaven was formerly yours has been set aside for him, and the mortality which was his has been given over to you."

Chapter 14
1. And the angel said to me, "Abraham!"
2. And I said, "Here I am." And the angel said to me, "Know that from now on and forever the Eternal One has chosen you.
3. Be bold! I command you to use this authority against him who reviles the truth.
4. Will I not be able to revile him who has scattered about the earth the secrets of heaven and who has taken counsel against the Mighty One?
5. Say to him, "May you stoke (be kindling in) the fires of the earth's furnace!
6. Go, Azazel, into the deserted parts of the earth.
7. Your inheritance is over those who are with you, with the stars and with the men born by the clouds, whose reward you are. They exist because of you (through your being).
8. Hate is your pious act.
9.Therefore you will destroy yourself and be gone from me!"
10. And I spoke the words that the angel taught me. But the angel said to me, "Do not answer him! For God has given him power over those who answer him."

11. And the angel spoke to me again saying, "However much he speaks to you, do not answer him so that he may not get to you easily (freely).
12. The Eternal One gave him the gravity and the will. Do not answer him."
13. I did what the angel commanded me. And whatever he said to me about the fall (descent), I did not answered him.

Chapter 15
1. As the sun was setting, I beheld smoke like that of a furnace, and the angels who had the divided portions of the sacrifice came down from the top of the smoking furnace.
2. And the angel lifted me with his right hand and set me upon the right wing of the pigeon, and he sat on the left wing of the turtle dove. Neither birds had been slaughtered.
3. He flew me to the borders of the flaming fire, and we rose on many winds to the heavens which were above the firmament (sky/ theater of stars/ the sphere where the stars are stationed).
4. In the air, we ascended to a height that I could see a strong (bright) light impossible to describe.
5. In the light of a fiercely burning fire (Gehenna?), I saw many people, male in appearance. All of them were constantly changing their appearance and form. They were running as they were being changed, and they were worshipping and crying out with a sound of words that I could not recognize.

Chapter 16
1. And I said to the angel, "Why have you now brought me here?
2. I can no longer see clearly, and I am growing weak. My spirit is leaving me?"
3. And he said, "Remain close to me and do not fear.
3. He, the One you cannot see, is coming toward us now with a tremendous voice of holiness.
4. He is the Eternal One who loves you. But you yourself cannot see (look at) Him.
5. But you may find your spirit growing faint on account of the choirs of those who cry out because I am with you to strengthen you (fight against the weakness for I am here to strengthen you)."

Chapter 17
1. While he was still speaking, the fire coming toward us surrounded us and there was a voice amidst the fire like a voice of many waters, like the sound of a violent sea. And I wanted to fall down and worship. And the angel knelt down with me and worshipped.
2. However, the surface of the high place where we were standing changed constantly, inclining, rolling high and low.
3. And the angel said, "Worship, Abraham, and sing the song which I now will teach you.
4. Never stop signing it. Sing it in continuously from beginning to end. "
5. And the song which he taught me to sing had words that were appropriate to the area of heaven (sphere) we were standing in.
6. Each area (sphere) in heaven has its own song of praise, and only those who live there know how to sign it, and those on earth cannot know it or sing it.

7. They could know it only if they were taught by the messengers of heaven. And the words of that song were of a type and meaning.
8. So I bowed down since there was no solid ground on which to prostrate myself and I recited the song which he had taught me.
9. And he said, "Recite it without ceasing." And I recited, and he himself recited the song along with me.

"Eternal, Mighty, Holy God (El), God of unlimited power, Self-originated, Incorruptible, Immaculate, Without beginning, having no mother or father, Spotless, Immortal, Self-Created, Illuminated with your own light, without mother or father, self-begotten, High, radiant, Wise, Lover Of Men, Favorable, Generous, Bountiful, Jealous Over Me, Patient (compassionate), Most Merciful, Eli (my God), Eternal, Mighty, Holy Sabbath, Most Glorious El, El, El, El, (God) Jaoel (Yahoel/Joel) (Ja El/Lord God). You are he whom my soul has loved, the Guardian, Eternal, Radiant, Shining, Made of light, Voice of thunder. You appear as lightning, All seeing, you receive the prayers of those who honor you and turn away from the prayers of those who besiege you with their provoking ways. You redeem (free) those who are in the midst of the unrighteous and those who are confused among the wicked one who inhabited world in the corruptible life. You renew the life of the righteous. Before the morning light shines, you make the light shine upon your creation from the light of your face in order to bring the day on the earth. And in your heavenly dwellings there is an inexhaustible light of another kind. It is the inexpressible splendor from the lights of your face. Accept my prayer, and let it be sweet to you, and also the sacrifice which you yourself made to yourself through me who searched for you. Receive me favorably and show to me, and teach me, and make known to your servant what you have promised me."

Chapter 18
1. While I was still reciting the song, the mouth of the fire on the surface rose high in the air.
2. And I heard a voice like a roaring sea. It was not stopped by even the plethora of fire. And as the fire rose up very high I saw under the fire a throne of fire, and around it were many eyes watching.
3. They were the all-seeing ones and they were singing their song.
4. Under the throne were four radiant (on fire) Living Ones singing but they looked as if they were one creature but each one had four faces.
5. This is how they appeared and how they looked to me; each one had the face of a lion, a man, an ox and an eagle, and because of their four heads upon their bodies, they had sixteen faces.
6. Each one had three pairs of wings coming out of their shoulders, their sides, and their hips. With the wings from the shoulders they covered their faces. With the wings from their hips they covered their feet. The two middle wings were spread out and they flew erect as if standing up (straight forward).
7. Then, when they had ended their singing they looked at one another and threatened one another.
8. Then, when the angel who was with me saw that they were threatening each other he left me and went running to them. He turned the face of each living creature from the face which was opposite it so that they could not see each other's faces
9. And he taught them the song of peace which the Eternal One has in himself.

10. And while I stood alone and watched, I saw a chariot with wheels of fire behind the Living Ones.
11. Each wheel had eyes around it and it was full of eyes. Above the wheels was the throne which I had seen before. It was covered with fire, and the fire encircled it.
12. An indescribable fire contained a mighty fiery host, and I heard its holy voice like the voice of a man.

Chapter 19
1. And a voice came to me out of the middle of the fire, saying, "Abraham, "Abraham!" and I answered saying "Here am I!" And he said, "Look at the wide places (areas/expanses) which are under the firmament (sky/theater of stars) on which you now stand.
2. Notice that no other place (area/expanse) has yielded the one for whom you have searched or who has loved you."
3. While he was still talking, the areas opened up. Below me were the heavens and I saw a fire which was wide-spread. There was a light, which is the storehouse (vault) of life.
4. There was the dew that God will use to awaken the dead, the spirits of the righteous, those that had gone on before, and the spirits of those souls who are yet to be born. Judgment and righteousness, peace and blessing, and an innumerable host of angels, and the Living Ones, and the Power of the Invisible Glory sat above the Living Ones.
5. All of these were in the seventh firmament, on which I stood.
6. And I looked down from the high mountain on which I stood on to the sixth firmament, and there I saw a host of angels of pure spirit (incorporeal) without bodies, whose duty was to carry out the commands of the fiery angels who were upon the seventh firmament (some translations have the eighth firmament) , as I was standing suspended over them.
7. And I looked down on the sixth firmament and there were no other powers of any form, only the angels of pure spirit.
8. I was standing on its elevation. And on this firmament there was nothing in any form and no other host, but only the spiritual angels.
9. I saw a host on the seventh firmament and He commanded that the sixth firmament should be removed from my sight, and I saw there on the fifth firmament the powers of the stars which carry out the commands laid upon them, and the elements of the earth obeyed them.

Chapter 20
1. And the Eternal, Mighty One said to me, "Abraham, Abraham!" And I said, “Here I am!"
2. And He said to me, "Look at the stars which are beneath you, and number them for me, and then tell me their number."
3. And I said, "How can I? I am just a man made of the dust of the earth." And He said to me, " I will make your progeny a nation as large as the number of the stars and as powerful the power of the stars, and I will set these people a section (piece) for me as my own inheritance.
4. They will be distinct from those of Azazel. And yet I include Azazel in my house."
5. And I said, "Eternal and Mighty One. Let your servant speak before you and do not let your fury ignite (burn/rage) against your chosen (selected/elect) one.

6. "Look!, before you led me up, Azazel insulted (railed against/reproached) me. Since he is now not before you how can you establish (constitute/count) yourself with them?"

Chapter 21
1. Then He said to me, "Look beneath your feet at the firmament and understand the creation represented and foretold in this expanse, the creatures who exist in it, and the ages prepared after it."
2. And I looked beneath my feet and beneath the sixth heaven and saw the earth and its fruits, and what moved upon it and its beings that moved, and the host of its men, and the ungodliness of some of their souls and the righteous deeds of other souls. I saw the lower regions and the torment (perdition) in the abyss.
3. And I saw the sea and its islands, its monsters (Leviathan) and its fishes, and Leviathan and his lair, his realm (caves), and the world which lay above him, and his movements and the destructions he caused the world.
4. I saw there the streams and the rivers with their waters rising, and their winding courses. And I saw there the Garden of Eden and its fruits, the source of the river that issues from it, the trees and their blossoms, and the men (ones) who did good deeds (behaved righteously/ justly). And I saw in it (the garden) their foods and their restfulness (blessedness).
5. And I saw there a tremendous multitude of men and women and children, half of them on the right side of the door (vision), and half of them on the left side of the door (vision).

Chapter 22
1. And I said, "Eternal, Mighty One! What is this vision of creation?"
2. And he said to me, "This is my will for what is in the light and it was good before my face.
3. After this I gave them a command and by my word and they came into existence.
4. Whatever I had decreed was to exist had already been decided (outlined in this) and all things created, which you see, had stood in front of me (in my sight) before it was created.
5. And I said, "Lord, Mighty and Eternal! Who are the people in this vision on this side and on that side?"
6. And He said to me, "Those who are on the left side are all those who existed (were born) before and after your day, some destined for judgment and restoration, and others for vengeance and estrangement at the end of the age.
7. Those on the right side of the vision are the people set a section (piece) for me. These are the ones I have prepared to be born of your lineage and to be called "my people." Some of these even come from Azazel.

Chapter 23
1. Now look again in the vision and see who it is that seduced Eve and what the fruit of the Tree was, and you will know what is to be, and how it will be for your progeny among the people at the end of the days of the age.

3. And all that you cannot understand I will make known to you for you are well-pleasing in my sight, and I will tell you of those things which are kept in my heart.
4. Then I looked into the vision, and my eyes looked at the side of the Garden of Eden, and I saw there a man of imposing height and he was great (powerful) in stature, incomparable in appearance.
5. He was embracing (entwined with) a woman who looked like his size and stature. They were standing under a tree of the Garden of Eden, and the fruit of this tree was like a bunch of grapes on a vine. Standing behind the tree was one who had the appearance of a serpent (dragon) but it had the hands and feet of a man and it had wings on its shoulders.
6. There were six pairs of wings, so that there were six wings on the right shoulder and six on the left shoulder.
7. As I continued looking, I saw the man and the woman eating the fruit from the tree. And the serpent (dragon) was holding the grapes of the tree and feeding them to the two I saw embracing each other.
8. And I said, "Who are these two that embrace, and who is this between them, and what is the fruit which they are eating, Oh, Mighty, Eternal One?"
9. And He said, "This is the world of men (this is humanity). This (one) is Adam (man), and that one, who is their desire upon the earth, is Eve.
10. But he who is between them is the ungodliness of their behavior that is sending them on the way to perdition. It is Azazel."
11. And I said, "Eternal Mighty One! Why have you given the likes of him (Azazel) the power to destroy mankind (children or generations of men) and their works upon the earth?"
12. And He said to me, " I gave him power over them who want do evil and those whom I have already hated and they will even come to love him."
13. And I said. "Eternal, Mighty One! Why did you want to bring into existence an evil that men would desire in their heart since you are angered at what was chosen by those who do useless (vain/unprofitable) things in your light (counsel/presence)?"

Chapter 24
1. He said to me, "I am angered by mankind on your account, and on account of those who will be of your family to come, because as you can see in the vision, the burden of destiny is placed upon them, and I will tell you what will be, and how much will take place in the last days. Now look at everything in the vision."
2. I looked and saw the created beings that had come into existence before me.
3. And I saw Adam and Eve and the cunning adversary who was with them; the crafty Cain, who had been influenced (led) by the adversary to break the law; and I saw the murdered (slaughtered) Abel and the destruction (lawlessness/perdition) brought on him that was caused through the lawless one.
4. And I saw there fornication and those who desired it, and its defilement and their jealousness; and the fire of the corruption in the lower depths of the earth.
5. And I saw theft and those who run after it, and the means and ways of their punishment (retribution) at the judgment of the Great Court (Assize).
6. And I saw naked men with their foreheads against each other, and their disgrace, and the passions which they had for each other, and their retribution (and the shame and harm they worked against one another).

7. And I saw Desire, and in her hand was the head of every kind of lawlessness, and her scorn and contempt and waste was assigned to destruction (perdition).

Chapter 25

1. Then I saw something that looked like an idol. It was the idol of jealousy.
2. It was carved in wood like father used to make. Its body was made of glittering bronze that covered the wood.
3. And in front of it I saw a man who was worshipping the idol, and in front of him there was an altar, and upon the altar a boy was killed as a sacrifice in the presence of the idol.
4. And I said to him, "What is this idol, and what is the altar, and who are those being sacrificed, and who is the one who performs the sacrifice, and what is the beautiful temple which I see, the are and beauty of your glory like that which lies beneath Your throne?"
5. And he said, "Hear, Abraham! This temple which you have seen, the altar and the works are my idea of the priesthood performing in the name of my glory, where every prayer (request/petition) of man will enter and live, they include the praise of kings and prophets and whatever sacrifice I decree to be made for me.
6. And He said, "Abraham, listen! What you see is the Temple, it is a copy of that which is in the heavens. It is glorious in its appearance and beauty. I will give it to the sons of men to ordain a priesthood for my glorious name. In it the prayers of man will be spoken, and sacrifices offered.)
7. I have ordained this for your people, especially those who will arise out of your lineage.
8. But the idol which you saw is the image of jealousy that will be set up by some of those who will come out of your own loins in later days.
9. And the man who sacrifices in murder is he who pollutes my Temple. These are witnesses to the final judgment, and their appointment (reward) has been set from the beginning of creation."

Chapter 26

1.. And I said, "Eternal Mighty One! Why did you establish it like this, and then proclaim the knowledge (testify) of it?" And He said to me, "Listen Abraham, and understand what I am about to say to you, and answer my question. Why did your father Terah not listen to you, and why did he not cease his idolatrous (demonic worship) practices, together with his entire house?"
2. And I said, "Eternal Mighty One, certainly because he did not want to obey me because I did not follow his (ways/deeds) works."
3. And He said to me, "The will of your father is in him (up to him), and your will is in you (up to you), and likewise the counsel of my own will is within me (up to me/in my control), and it is prepared for (has prepared) the coming days before you have any knowledge of them or can see the future with your own eyes. Now look again into the vision, and see how it will be with your children (progeny/generations)."

Chapter 27

1. And I looked and I saw the vision sway. From its left side a crowd of unbelievers (ungodly people) ran out and they captured the men, women, and children and they murdered (slaughtered like animals) most of them and others they kept as slaves.

And I saw them (the killers) run towards them (the slaves) through four doors which were high with stairs and they burned the Temple with fire, and they took and broke the holy things that were in the temple.
2. And I said, " Eternal One! Behold, my progeny, whom you have accepted, are robbed by these ungodly men. Some are killed, and others they enslave. The Temple they have burned with fire, and the beautiful things in it they have robbed and destroyed. If this is to be, why have you ripped my heart like this?"
3. And he said to me, "Listen, Abraham, all that you have seen will happen because of your progeny who will continually provoke me because of the idols that you saw, and because of the human sacrifice in the vision, through their drive and desire to do evil and there schemes in the Temple. You saw it and that is how it will be."
4. And I said, "Eternal, Mighty One! Allow these works of evil brought about by ungodliness pass by, and instead show me those who fulfilled the commandments, show me the works of righteousness. I know in truth you can do this."
5. And He said to me, "The days of the righteous (will arrive) are seen symbolized by the lives of righteous rulers who will arise, and whom I have created to rule at the appointed times. But you must know that out of them will arise others who care only for their own interests. These are symbolized by those (killers) I have already shown you.

Chapter 28
1. And I answered and said, "Mighty, Eternal One, you who are holy by your power, show mercy, I pray. Since you have brought me up here to your high place and you have showed your beloved the things about which I asked, please tell me now: Will what I saw be their lot for long?"
2. And He showed me a multitude of His people and said to me, "Because of them, I will be provoked by them through the four high doorways you saw, and my retribution for their deeds will be accomplished. But in the fourth descent of one hundred years, which is the same as one hour of the age, the same is a hundred years, there will be evil (misfortune) among the (heathen) nations, but also for one hour there will be mercy and honor (in) among those nations.

Chapter 29
1.. And I said, " Eternal One! How long are the hours of the age?" And He said, "Twelve hours have I ordained for this present ungodly age to rule among the (heathen) nations and within your progeny, and until the end of the times it will be even as you saw. And now reckon (calculate) and understand and look again into the vision.
2. And he said, "I decreed to keep twelve periods of the impious age among the heathens and among your progeny, and what you have seen will be until the end of time."
3. And I looked and saw a Man going out from the left side of the (heathen) nations.
4. And there went men and women and children out from the side of (heathen) nations like many multitudes and they worshipped Him.
6. And while I still looked, there came many from the right side, and some of these insulted Him, and some of them even struck Him, but others worshipped Him.
7. As I watched, I saw Azazel come up to Him and he kissed Him on the face and then turned and stood behind Him.

8. Then I said, "Eternal, Mighty One! Who is this Man who is insulted and beaten, who is worshipped by the nations and kissed by Azazel?"
9. And He answered and said, "Hear Me Abraham! The Man you saw insulted and beaten and yet worshipped by many, He is the Relief/Liberty/Freedom granted for (by) the nations of people who will be born from (out of) you in the last days, in the twelfth hour of the age of ungodliness.
10. But in the twelfth hour of my last (final) age of my fulfillment will I set up this Man from your tribe (generation), whom you saw issue from among my people, and all who follow will become like (imitate) this Man, and they will be called by me (and they will consider Him to be called by Me) and they will join the others, even those who desire to change within themselves.
11. Regarding those who emerge from the left side of the vision, the meaning is this; there will be many from the (heathen) nations who will set their hopes on (trust in) Him. But those whom you saw from your progeny on the right of the vision who insulted Him and struck Him, many will be offended because of Him, but some will worship Him. And He will test those of your progeny who have worshipped Him in the twelfth hour at the end in order to shorten the age of ungodliness.
12. Before the age of the righteous begins to grow, my judgment will come upon the (nations/heathen) lawless (wicked) peoples through the people of your progeny who have been separated to me.
13. And in those days I will bring upon all creatures of the earth ten plagues, through misfortune and disease and the groans of their bitter grief. And this will be brought upon the generations of men because of the provocation and the corruption of mankind, because they provoke me. And then the righteous men of your progeny will survive in the number (amount/count) which is kept secret by me, and will hasten the coming of the glory of My Name to that place prepared before for those you saw destroyed in the vision.
14. And they will live and be established by the sacrifices of righteousness in the age of the godly, and they will rejoice in me continually, and receive those who return to me in repentance because their inner torment will be great for those who have wrongfully misused (mocked) them in this world.
15. And they will see the honor bestowed on those who are mine in the day of glory. Abraham, see what you have seen and hear what you have heard, and take knowledge of all that you have come to know.
16. Go to your inheritance for behold, I am with you to the age."

Chapter 30

1. While He was still speaking to me, I found myself on the earth again, and I said, " Eternal One! I am no longer in the glory on high.
2. Still there is one matter which my soul longs to know and understand that was not revealed to me."
3. And he said to me, "I will explain to you the things you desired in your heart to know which are the ten plagues that I prepared against the heathen nations, and which have been destined to begin at the passing of the twelfth hour of the age of the earth.
4. Hear therefore what I tell you because it will come to pass. The first is the sorrow and pain of (need) sickness;
5. The second, the massive burning and destruction of many cities;
6. The third, the destruction and pestilence (sickness) of animals (cattle);

7. The fourth, hunger of the whole world and its people;
8. The fifth, among the rulers, destruction by means of earthquake and the sword;
9. The sixth, the increase of hail and snow;
10. The seventh, wild bests will be their grave (animals will kill them);
11. The eighth, hunger and pestilence will change their course of destruction (alternate with destruction);
12. The ninth, punishment (execution) by the sword and flight in distress;
13. The tenth, thunder and voices and destructive earthquake.

Chapter 31
1. And then I will sound the trumpet in the air, and I will send my ELECT ONE (chosen one), and He will have all measure of my power (He will have one measure of all my power).
2. He will summon my people (who were despised) from all nations, and I will send fire upon those who have insulted them and who have ruled over them in this age. And those who have chosen my desire and kept my commandments will rejoice with celebrations (parties) over the downfall of the men who continued to followed after the idols.
3. And I will take those who have covered me with mockery and give them over to the scorn of the coming age.
4. I have prepared them to be food for the fires of Hades, and be in perpetual flight through the air of the depths of Hades (the underworld). And they will be the contents of a worm's belly (Azazel).
5. For they joined (a marital or sexual term) one to whom they had not been given to, and they abandoned the Lord who gave them strength.

Chapter 32
1. "Hear Me, Abraham, because you will see that in the seventh generation from you will go out into a strange land and the heathen will enslave and oppress them. And they leave the land of their slavery, after they have been mistreated for an hour of the age of ungodliness, and the heathen nation whom they will serve I will judge.
2. And the Lord said this too, "Have you heard, Abraham, what I told you, what your tribe will encounter in the last days?"
3. Abraham heard and accepted the words of God in his heart.

Apocalypse of Thomas

"The Apocalypse Of Thomas" is also called "The Revelation of Thomas." The differing names come from the fact that the word rendered "Apocalypse" means to reveal or make known. This is the same title given to the last book of the New Testament. Its title in Greek is best interpreted as "The Apocalypse of John," however the English book carries the title of "The Revelation of John," or simply, "Revelation."

Very little of the history of the Apocalypse of Thomas is known. The only reference to it in ancient writings seems to be a single citation by Jerome in his chronicles written in the eighth to ninth century A.D.

Two versions of the Apocalypse exist in Latin, the longer version seems to be a later development. The longer text makes use of metaphors and symbols similar to those used in the Book of Revelation. Both texts describe how the Earth will be destroyed and the dead will come back to life in the final days.

The composition of the Apocalypse of Thomas has two distinct streams of thought. It is akin to Daniel in its form of prophecy, which describes events contemporary with the author and continues them into the future; yet it is also akin to John when the text describes the signs of the end.

Historical references in the long text suggest a fifth-century date. The text speaks of a king who is a "lover of the law." The text refers to his two sons whose names begin with A and H. King Theodosius fits the bill and his sons have Latin names corresponding to the letters as follows: "The first is named with the first letter A (as in Arcadius,) the second with the eighth letter H, (as in Honorius.) The first will die before the second."

The reference to the Latin alphabet would suggest that it was the original language of composition. This would place the earliest possible date of writing (and most scholars agree) at about 300 - 400 A.D.

Several manuscripts and fragments of the Apocalypse of Thomas have been found. The text presented here is the best combination of many texts. Since some are shorter than others and many are fragments, it was thought that by combining all of the better known texts a complete, longer and more complete version could be presented.

The version presented here is based on a combination of the best manuscripts and translations found. They include the F. Wilhelm text of 1907, the E. Hauler work on the fifth century Vienna fragment, the Verona manuscript of eighth century, the 1755 Dionisi work, 1911 Dom Bihlmeyer text from Munich, and the Anglo-Saxon Old English version at Vercelli.

End Times

THE APOCALYPSE OF THOMAS

Chapter 1
1. This begins the letter of (from) the Lord to Thomas.
2. "Hear about the things that must happen in the last times. The world will be shared between kings, then after that when the hour of the end draws near there will be seven days of great signs in heaven, and the powers of the heavens will be moved.
3. There will be famine, war and earthquakes in various places, snow, ice, and tremendous drought. There will be many open conflicts among the peoples, blasphemy, unrighteousness, envy, evil, laziness, pride and excess, and everyone will speak in the manner that he wishes.
4. And my priests will fight among themselves, and will sacrifice to me with minds of deceit. Because of this I will not look upon them. The priests will see the people forsaking the house of the Lord and turning to the world.
5. They will venture into restricted places in the house of God. And they will claim many things and places for themselves that were lost and those things and places will become subject to Caesar in the way they were given before as poll-taxes in the cities, as it is with gold and silver.
6. And the chief men of the cities will be condemned and their possessions will be brought to the treasury of the kings, and it will be filled.
7. There will be disturbances throughout all the people, and there will be death. The house of the Lord will be forsaken, and their altars will be despised, so that spiders weave their webs on them.
8. The place of holiness will be dishonored and violated, the priesthood contaminated. Distress will increase and righteousness will be overcome.
9. Happiness will die and gladness will leave. In those days evil will abound. People will cater to those of status and wealth. Hymns will stop coming from the house of the Lord. Truth will cease. Greed will abound among the priests. No upright man nor an upright priesthood will be found.

Chapter 2
1. Near the last days a king will arise. He will be a lover of the law who will not hold office for long but he will leave two sons.
2. The first is named with the first letter A (as in Arcadius,) the second with the eighth letter H, (as in Honorius.) The first will die before the second.

(Arcadius died in 408 A.D.- Honorius in 423 A.D. The somewhat uneventful life of Arcadius is of less importance than the significant developments that occurred during his reign. Born around 377 A.D. to General Theodosius, Arcadius and his younger brother, Honorius, ruled the eastern and western halves of the Roman Empire respectively from 395. Arcadius was proclaimed Augustus in January of 383 at the age of five or six. In the following year, his younger brother was born. Honorius achieved the office of consul posterior in 386. The chance for having his own two sons ruling both halves of Rome not only seemed practical and feasible, but such an arrangement would establish their father as the head of a new dynasty. With thoughts in that direction, Honorius was made Augustus in 393 and accompanied his father west in the summer of 394. Even though Arcadius was nearing maturity and the age of consent he was placed again under the guardianship of the Prefect of the East. In January of 395, Theodosius the Great died and his two sons took theoretical

control of the two halves of the Roman Empire.).

3. After this, two princes will arise to oppress the nations. Under their hands a very great famine will occur. The famine will take place in the right-hand section of the east and that nation will rise up against another nation and be driven out from their own borders.
4. Again another king will arise. He will be a deceitful man. He will order a golden image of Caesar to be made, set up, and worshipped in the house of God. Martyrdoms will be widespread.
5. Then the faith will return to the servants of the Lord, and holiness will greatly increase but so will distress and pain increase.
6. The mountains will be comforted (will comfort them?) and will drop down the sweetness of fire from its face, so that the (predestined) number of the saints may be completed.
7. After a little space of time a king will arise out of the east. He will be a lover of the law. He will cause all good and necessary things to be in supply within the house of the Lord. He will show mercy to the widows and the needy.
8. He will order that a royal gift to be given to the priests. In his days (the days of the king) there will be abundance of all things.
9. After that a king will arise, this time in the southern section of the world, and will rule for only a short time. In his days the economy will bankrupt (treasury will fail) because of the wages of the Roman soldiers. And he will order the substance of all the older citizens be taken and given to the king so it could be distributed.

Chapter 3

1. After that there will be plenty of corn and wine and oil, but a tremendous lack of money, so that it would take the substances of gold and silver to buy corn, and there will be tremendous hunger (dearth). (Hyper-inflation is indicated here.)
2. At that time the sea level will rise greatly and communications will be cut off from man to man. The kings, princes and the captains of the earth will be nervous (troubled/ fearful), and no man will speak freely.
3. Grey hairs will be seen upon boys, and the young men will not respect or listen to the aged.
4. After that will arise another king, a deceitful man, who will rule for a short time. In his days there will be all manner of evils. There will be genocide of the race of men living in the east to Babylon (the death of the race of men from the east to Babylon).
5. Famine and death by the sword will follow from Chanaan (Canaan) to Rome. Then all the springs of water and all the wells will dry up (boil over) and be turned into dust and blood.

Chapter 4

1. The heaven will be moved and the stars will fall upon the earth. The sun will be cut in half like the moon, and the moon will not give light.
2. There will be great signs and wonders in those days when Antichrist draws near. These are the signs for those that live on the earth. In those days the pains of great and hard work like those of a woman in labor will come upon them.
3. Woe to them that build because they will not live in there buildings.
4. Woe to them that plow the ground because they labor for no cause (no results).

Woe to them that marry because they will bring forth sons in the famine.
5. Woe to them that join house to house or field to field because all things will be consumed with fire. Woe to them that are not introspective (examine themselves and their actions) while time allows because after this they will be condemned forever.
6. Woe to them that turn away from the poor when he asks.
7. You will know that I am the Father most high and I am the Father of all spirits. As you will see, this is the beginning of the latter age.

Chapter 5
1. These are the seven signs of the ending of this world. There will be in all the earth famine and tremendous disease and sicknesses of vast proportions.
2. All nations will take captives and men will fall by the edge of the sword.
3. The beginning of the days of judgment will make you wonder greatly.
4. At the third hour (The Jewish day starts around 6:00 P.M.) of the first day will be a loud and powerful voice in the firmament (sky/theater of stars) of heaven, and a large cloud of blood will come down out of the north, and loud thunder and powerful lightning will follow the cloud.
5. Blood will rain down on all the earth. These are the signs of the first day. *(There is some dispute as to whether this is a literal Sunday or Monday. It is assumed by the editor that Sunday is the first day.)*
6. And on the second day there will be a loud voice in the firmament of heaven, and the earth will be moved out of its place and the portals of the eastern part of heaven will be and a great power will be sent forth as if it were belched by the portals of heaven themselves and the power will cover all the heaven even until evening and there will be fear and trembling in the world.
7. These are the signs of the second day. In the third day at about the second hour, there will be a voice in heaven, and the vast depths of the earth will sound their voices from the four corners of the earth.
8. The first heaven will be rolled up like a scroll and will vanish quickly in an instant.
9. Smoke and stench of the brimstone in the chasms will darken the day until the tenth hour. Then all men will say, "I think the end draws near, that we will die." These are the signs of the third day.
10. And on the fourth day at the first hour, the eastern section of the earth will sound, the abyss will roar and all the earth be moved by a strong earthquake.
11. In that day all the idols of the heathen will fall along with all the buildings on earth. These are the signs of the fourth day.
12. And on the fifth day, at the sixth hour the thunder will be loud and sudden in the sky, and the stars (powers of light) and the sphere of the sun will be snatched away, and there will be total (vast) darkness over the world until evening, and the stars will be sent off their course.
13. In that day all nations will hate the world and all men will despise his life on the world. These are the signs of the fifth day.
14. On the sixth day there will be signs in heaven. At the fourth hour the firmament of heaven will be split from east to west. And the angels of the heavens will be looking out on the earth and they will open the heavens.
15. And all men will see the host of the angels above the earth looking out of heaven. Then all men will flee.

16. All men will flee to the mountains and hide themselves from the face of the righteous angels, and will say, "I wish the earth would open and swallow us!" These things will happen like this world has never seen since it was created.
17. Then they will see me coming from above in the light of my Father with the power and honor of the holy angels.
18. At my coming, the fires that border/restrain paradise will be removed because paradise is encompassed with fire.
19. And this is a perpetual fire that will consume the earth and all the elements of the world. Then they will be clothed, and be carried by the hand of the holy angels as I have told you before.
20. They will be lifted up in the air on a cloud of light, and will go with me into heaven rejoicing. They will continue in the light and honor of my Father.
21. There be gladness abounding with my Father and before the holy angels. These are the signs of the sixth day.

Chapter 6
1. Then will the spirits and souls of all men come out of paradise and will come on all the earth and every one of them will go to his own body where it is laid up, and every one of them will say, "My body lies here."
2. And when the loud voices of those spirits will be heard, like a huge earthquake (there will be a large earthquake) all over the world.
3. The mountains will be split in two from above and the rocks from beneath. Then every spirit will return into his own vessel and the bodies of the saints who have died (which have fallen asleep) will rise.
4. Then will their bodies be changed into the image and likeness and the honor of the holy angels, and into the power of the image of my holy Father.
5. Then will they be clothed with the garments of life eternal made from the cloud of light which has never been seen in this world, because that cloud came down out of the highest realm of the heaven from the power of my Father.
6. And that cloud will contain the beauty of all the spirits that have believed in me.
7. And on the seventh day at the eighth hour there will be voices in the four corners of the heaven. And all the air will be shaken, and filled with holy angels, and they will make war among the heathen all the day long. And in that day my elect will be sought out by the holy angels and saved from the destruction of the world. Then all men (unbelievers) will see that the hour of their destruction draws near.
8. These are the signs of the seventh day. And when the seven days are passed by, on the eighth day at the sixth hour there will be a sweet and tender voice in heaven from the east. Then that angel will be revealed which has power over all the holy angels and all the angels will go out with him who is sitting upon a chariot made of the clouds of my holy Father and they will rejoice, running upon the air beneath the heaven to deliver the elect that have believed in me.
9. And they will rejoice that the destruction of this world has come.
10. Thomas, you must hear because I am the Son of God the Father and I am the father of all spirits. You must hear my signs that will come to pass at the end of this world.
11. The end of the world will come and the world will pass away before my elect depart out of the world. I will tell (have told) you openly (plainly) what will come,

but when these things will come to pass even the princes of the angels do not know. It is now hidden from their sight as to what day the end will come."

12. The words of the Savior to Thomas are ended, concerning the end of this world.

4 Ezra - History

2 Esdras, also referred to as 4 Ezra or the Apocalypse of Ezra, was written toward the end of the first century A.D. to explain the destruction of the temple in 70 A.D. It is listed among the Apocrypha by the Catholic Church and most Protestant churches, however the Ethiopian and Russian Orthodox churches consider it to be canon.

In the years of the Renaissance and afterward heated arguments over this book inflamed emotions. Discussion regarding the book has evoked high tension and responses from the beginning. The French intelligentsia were among the most verbal. The French mystic Antoinette Bourignon said it was "the finest book in the Bible." John Floyer said it was "the best Key to all the Old and New Prophecies". Saint Jerome included the book in his Latin version of the Bible but assigned it to the apocryphal section. There were opponents also. Humphrey Prideaux considered it "a Book too absurd for the Romanists themselves to receive into their Canon."

Within the Old Testament apocrypha, 2 Esdras or 4 Ezra occupies a special place because it is dated from approximately A.D. 90, well into the New Testament era. The Vulgate version, written by Jerome, contains second and third century texts. These contain additions made by Christian writers, which made the book more acceptable to the Christian audience. 4 Ezra 7:28-9,: "For my son Jesus will be revealed with those that are with him, and they that remain will rejoice for four hundred years. After these years will my son Christ die, and all men that have life."

This makes it the only book in the Old Testament to name Jesus as the Christ. Even though many scholars believe this portion of text to be an addition made around the third to fourth century, it makes Ezra the perfect bridge between the Old Testament and New Testament.

4 EZRA / 2 ESDRAS

4 Ezra Chapter 1

1: The second book of the prophet Esdras, the son of Saraias, the son of Azarias, the son of Helchias, the son of Sadamias, the son of Sadoc, the son of Achitob,
2: The son of Achias, the son of Phinees, the son of Heli, the son of Amarias, the son of Aziei, the son of Marimoth, the son of Ama, son of Uzzi, son of Borith, the son of Abishua, the son of Phinehas, the son of Eleazar,
3: The son of Aaron, of the tribe of Levi; which was captive in the land of the Medes, in the reign of Areexerxes, King of the Persians.
4: And the word of the Lord came to me, saying,
5: "Go your way, and show my people their sinful deeds, and their children their wickedness which they have done against me; that they may tell their children's children:
6: Because the sins of their fathers are increased in them for they have forgotten me, and have offered (sacrificed) to strange gods.
7: Am not I even he that brought them out of the land of Egypt, from the house of bondage? But they have provoked me to rage, and despised my counsels.
8: Pull out the hair of your head, and cast all evil upon them, for they have not been obedient to my law, but they are a rebellious people.
9: How long will I forbear them, unto whom I have done so much good?
10: Many kings have I destroyed for their sakes; Pharaoh with his servants and all his power have I beaten down.
11: All the nations have I destroyed before them, and in the east I have scattered the people of two provinces, even of Tyrus and Sidon, and have killed all their enemies.
12: Speak therefore to them, saying, Thus says the Lord,
13: I led you through the sea and in the beginning gave you a large and safe passage; I gave you Moses for a leader, and Aaron for a priest.
14: I gave you light in a pillar of fire, and great wonders have I done among you; yet you have forgotten me, says the Lord.
15: Thus, says the Almighty Lord, The quails were a gift to you; I gave you tents for your safeguard; nevertheless you murmured there,
16: And did not triumph in my name for the destruction of your enemies, but even to this day you continue to complain.
17: Where are the benefits that I have done for you? When you were hungry and thirsty in the wilderness, did you not cry to me,
18: Saying, Why have you brought us into this wilderness to kill us? It had been better for us to have served the Egyptians, than to die in this wilderness.
19: Then had I pity upon your mourning, and gave you manna to eat; so you ate angels' bread.
20: When you were thirsty, did I not cleave the rock, and waters flowed out to fill you? For the heat I covered you with the leaves of the trees.
21: I divided among you a fruitful land, I cast out the Canaanites, the Pherezites, and the Philistines, before you: what will I yet do more for you? says the Lord.
22: Thus says the Almighty Lord, When you were in the wilderness, in the river of the Amorites, being thirsty, and blaspheming my name,

23: I did not give you fire for your blasphemies, but cast a tree in the water, and made the river sweet.
24: What will I do to you, O Jacob, O Judah, who would not obey me? I will turn to other nations, and to those will I give my name, that they may keep my statutes.
25: Seeing you have forsaken me, I will forsake you also; when you desire me to be gracious to you, I will have no mercy upon you.
26: When ever you will call upon me, I will not hear you, for you have defiled your hands with blood, and your feet are swift to commit murder of men.
27: You have not forsaken me, but your own selves, says the Lord.
28: Thus says the Almighty Lord, Have I not prayed for (whished blessings on) you as a father his sons, as a mother her daughters, and a nurse her young babes,
29: That you would be my people, and I should be your God; that you would be my children, and I should be your father?
30: I gathered you together, as a hen gathers her chickens under her wings, but now, what will I do to you? I will cast you away from my face.
31: When you offer to me, I will turn my face from you for your solemn feast days, your new moons, and your circumcisions, have I forsaken.
32: I sent to you my servants the prophets, whom you have taken and slain, and torn their bodies in pieces, whose blood I will require of your hands, says the Lord.
33: Thus says the Almighty Lord, Your house is desolate, I will cast you out as the wind does the stubble (of hay).
34: And your children will not be fruitful; for they have despised my commandment, and have done the thing that is an evil before me.
35: Your houses will I give to a people that will come; which not having heard of me yet will believe me; to whom I have showed no signs, yet they will do that I have commanded them.
36: They have seen no prophets, yet they will call their sins to remembrance, and acknowledge them.
37: I take to witness the grace of the people to come, whose little ones rejoice in gladness: and though they have not seen me with bodily eyes, yet in spirit they believe the thing that I say.
38: And now, brother, behold what glory; and see the people that come from the east:
39: To whom I will give for leaders, Abraham, Isaac, and Jacob, Oseas, Amos, and Micheas, Joel, Abdias, and Jonas,
40: Nahum, and Abacuc, Sophonias, Aggeus, Zachary, and Malachy, which is called also an angel of the Lord.

4 Ezra Chapter 2

1: Thus says the Lord, I brought this people out of bondage, and I gave them my commandments by (my) menservants, the prophets; whom they would not hear, but (they) despised my counsels.
2: The mother that bare them says to them, Go your way, you children; for I am a widow and forsaken.
3: I brought you up with gladness; but with sorrow and heaviness have I lost you, for you have sinned before the Lord your God, and done that thing that is evil before him.
4: But what will I now do to you? I am a widow and forsaken; go your way, O my children, and ask mercy of the Lord.

5: As for me, O father, I call upon you for a witness over the mother of these children, which would not keep my covenant,
6: That you bring them to confusion, and their mother to a spoil, that there may be no offspring of them.
7: Let them be scattered abroad among the heathen, let their names be put out of the earth for they have despised my covenant.
8: Woe be to you, Assur, you that hide the unrighteous in you! O you wicked people, remember what I did to Sodom and Gomorrha;
9: Whose land lies in clods of pitch (clumps of tar) and heaps of ashes; even so also will I do to them that hear me not, says the Almighty Lord.
10: Thus says the Lord to Esdras, Tell my people that I will give them the Kingdom of Jerusalem, which I would have given to Israel.
11: Their glory also will I take to me, and give these the everlasting tabernacles, which I had prepared for them.
12: They will have the tree of life for an ointment of sweet savor; they will neither labor, nor be weary.
13: Go, and you will receive: pray for few days to you, that they may be shortened: the kingdom is already prepared for you: watch.
14: Take heaven and earth to witness; for I have broken the evil in pieces, and created the good; for I live, says the Lord.
15: Mother, embrace your children, and bring them up with gladness, make their feet as fast as a pillar, for I have chosen you, says the Lord.
16: And those that are dead will I raise up again from their places, and bring them out of the graves, for I have known my name in Israel.
17: Fear not, you mother of the children for I have chosen you, says the Lord.
18: For your help will I send my servants Esau and Jeremy, after whose counsel I have sanctified and prepared for you twelve trees laden with various fruits,
19: And as many fountains flowing with milk and honey, and seven mighty mountains, whereupon there grow roses and lilies, whereby I will fill your children with joy.
20: Do right to the widow, judge for (protect) the fatherless, give to the poor, defend the orphan, clothe the naked,
21: Heal the broken and the weak, do not mock the lame to scorn, defend the maimed, and let the blind man come into the clearness of my sight.
22: Keep the old and young within your walls.
23: Where ever you find the dead, take them and bury them, and I will give you the first place in my resurrection.
24: Abide still, my people, and take your rest, for your quietness still comes.
25: Nourish your children, you good nurse; establish their feet.
26: As for the servants whom I have given you, there will not one of them perish; for I will require them from among your number.
27: Do not weary: for when the day of trouble and heaviness comes, others will weep and be sorrowful, but you will be merry and have abundance.
28: The heathen will envy you, but they will be able to do nothing against you, says the Lord.
29: My hands will cover you, so that your children will not see hell.
30: Be joyful, you mother, with your children; for I will deliver you, says the Lord.

31: Remember your children that sleep (that died), for I will bring them out of the sides of the earth, and show mercy to them: for I am merciful, says the Lord Almighty.
32: Embrace your children until I come and show mercy to them: for my wells run over, and my grace will not fail.
33: I Esdras received a charge of the Lord upon the mount Oreb, that I should go to Israel; but when I came to them, they treated me as nothing and despised the commandment of the Lord.
34: Therefore I say to you, O you heathen, that hear and understand, look for your Shepherd, he will give you everlasting rest; for he is near at hand, that will come in the end of the world.
35: Be ready to receive the reward of the kingdom, for the everlasting light will shine upon you for evermore.
36: Flee the shadow of this world, receive the joyfulness of your glory: I testify of my Savior openly.
37: Receive the gift that is given to you, and be glad, giving thanks to him that has led you to the heavenly kingdom.
38: Arise up and stand, Look at the number of those that are sealed in the feast of the Lord;
39: Which have left the shadow of the world, and have received glorious garments of the Lord.
40: Take your number, O Sion, and shut up those of yours that are clothed in white, which have fulfilled the law of the Lord.
41: The number of your children, whom you longed for, is fulfilled: call on the power of the Lord, that your people, which have been called from the beginning, may be made holy.
42: I Esdras saw upon Mount Sion a great people, whom I could not number, and they all praised the Lord with songs.
43: In the midst of them there was a young man of a high stature, taller than all the rest, and upon every one of their heads he set crowns, and was more exalted; which I marveled at greatly.
44: So I asked the angel, and said, Sir, what are these?
45: He answered and said to me, These are they that have put off the mortal clothing, and put on the immortal, and have confessed the name of God: now are they crowned, and receive palms.
46: Then said I to the angel, What young person is it that crowns them, and gives them palms in their hands?
47: So he answered and said to me, It is the Son of God, whom they have confessed in the world. Then I began greatly to laud them that stood so solidly for the name of the Lord.
48: Then the angel said to me, Go your way, and tell my people what manner of things, and how great wonders of the Lord your God, you have seen.

4 Ezra Chapter 3
1: In the thirtieth year after the ruin of the city I was in Babylon, and lay troubled upon my bed, and my thoughts came up over my heart:
2: I saw the desolation of Sion, and the wealth of those dwelling at Babylon.
3: And my spirit was disturbed, so that I began to speak words full of fear to the most High, and said,

4: O Lord, who upholds rule, you spoke at the beginning, when you did plant the earth, and that yourself alone, and commanded the people,
5: And gave a body to Adam without soul, which was the workmanship of yours hands, and did breathe into him the breath of life, and he was made living before you.
6: And you lead him into paradise, which your right hand had planted, before ever the earth came forward.
7: You gave him the commandment to love your way: which he transgressed, and immediately you appointed death in him and in his generations, of whom came numberless nations, tribes, people, and kindred.
8: And every people walked after their own will, and did awful things before you, and despised your commandments.
9: And again in process of time you brought the flood upon those that dwelt in the world, and destroyed them.
10: And it came to pass in every of them, that as death was to Adam, so was the flood to these.
11: Nevertheless, you left one of them , namely, Noah with his household, from who came all righteous men.
12: And it happened, that when they that dwelt upon the earth began to multiply, and had gotten them many children, and were a great people, they began again to be more ungodly than the first.
13: Now when they lived so wickedly before you, you chose a man from among them, whose name was Abraham.
14: Him you loved, and to him only you showed your will:
15: And made an everlasting covenant with him, promising him that you would never forsake his seed.
16: And to him you gave Isaac, and to Isaac also you gave Jacob and Esau. You chose Jacob for your own, and put Esau away: and so Jacob became a great multitude.
17: And when you led his seed out of Egypt, you brought them up to Mount Sinai.
18: And bowing the heavens, you set fast the earth, moved the whole world, and made the depths to tremble, and troubled the men of that age.
19: And your glory went through four gates, of fire, and of earthquake, and of wind, and of cold; that you might give the law to the seed of Jacob, and diligence to the generation of Israel.
20: And yet you did not take away from them a wicked heart, that your law might bring forth fruit in them.
21: For the first Adam (man) bearing a wicked heart transgressed, and was overcome; and so be all that are born of him.
22: Thus infirmity was made permanent; and the law (also) in the heart of the people with the malignity of the root; so that the good departed away, and the evil still lived there.
23: So the times passed away, and the years were brought to an end: then you raised you up a servant, called David:
24: Whom you commanded to build a city to your name, and there to offer incense and offerings to you.
25: When this was done many years, then they that inhabited the city forsook you,
26: And in all things did as Adam and all his generations had done for they also had a wicked heart:
27: And so you gave your city over into the hands of yours enemies.

28: Are their deeds then any better that inhabit Babylon, that they should therefore have the dominion over Sion?
29: For when I came there, and had seen sins without number, then my soul saw many evildoers in this thirtieth year, so that my heart failed me.
30: For I have seen how you allow them sinning, and have spared wicked doers: and have destroyed your people, and have preserved yours enemies, and have not signified it.
31: I do not remember how this way may be left: Are they then of Babylon better than they of Sion?
32: Or is there any other people that knows you beside Israel? Or what generation has so believed your covenants like Jacob has?
33: And yet their reward does not appear, and their labor has no fruit: for I have gone here and there through the heathen, and I see that they flow in wealth, and think not upon your commandments.
34: Weigh our wickedness now in the balance, and theirs also that dwell the world; and so will your name no where be found but in Israel.
35: Or when was it that they which dwell upon the earth have not sinned in your sight? Or what people have so kept your commandments?
36: You will find that Israel by name has kept your precepts; but not the heathen.

4 Ezra Chapter 4

1: And the angel, whose name was Uriel, was sent to me and gave me an answer,
2: And said, Your heart has gone to far in this world, and you think to understand the way of the most High?
3: Then I said, Yea, my lord. And he answered me, and said, I am sent to show you three ways, and to set forth three comparisons before you:
4: Whereof if you can answer one, I will show you also the way that you desire to see, and I will show you from where the wicked heart came.
5: And I said, Tell on, my lord. Then said he to me, Go your way, weigh me the weight of the fire, or measure me the blast of the wind, or call me again the day that is past.
6: Then I answered and said, What man is able to do that, that you should ask such things of me?
7: And he said to me, If I should ask you how great dwellings are in the midst of the sea, or how many springs are in the beginning of the deep, or how many springs are above the firmament, or which are the outgoings of paradise:
8: I would expect you would say to me, I never went down into the deep, nor as yet into hell, neither did I ever climb up into heaven.
9: Nevertheless now have I asked you but only of the fire and wind, and of the day through which you have passed, and of things from which you can not be separated, and yet you can give me no answer.
10: He said moreover to me, Your own things, and such as are grown up with you, you do not know;
11: How should your vessel (body /mind) then be able to comprehend the way of the Highest, and the world being now outwardly corrupted to understand the corruption that is evident in my sight?
12: Then I said to him, It were better that we were not at all, than that we should live still in wickedness, and to suffer, and not to know wherefore.

13: He answered me, and said, I went into a forest into a plain, and the trees took counsel,
14: And said, Come, let us go and make war against the sea that it may depart away before us, and that we may make us more woods.
15: The floods of the sea also in like manner took counsel, and said, Come, let us go up and subdue the woods of the plain, that there also we may make us another country.
16: The thought of the wood was in vain, for the fire came and consumed it.
17: The thought of the floods of the sea came likewise to naught, for the sand stood up and stopped them.
18: If you wert judge now betwixt these two, whom would you begin to justify? Or whom would you condemn?
19: I answered and said, Verily it is a foolish thought that they both have devised, for the ground is given to the wood, and the sea also has his place to bear his floods.
20: Then he answered me, and said, You have given a right judgment, but why not judge yourself also?
21: Like the ground is given to the wood, and the sea to his floods: even so they that dwell upon the earth may understand nothing but that which is upon the earth: and he that dwells above the heavens may only understand the things that are above the height of the heavens.
22: Then I answered and said, I beseech you, O Lord, let me have understanding:
23: It was not my mind to be curious of the high things, but of such as pass by us daily, namely, wherefore Israel is given up as a criticism for the heathen, and for what cause the people whom you have loved is given over to ungodly nations, and why the law of our forefathers is brought to nothing, and the written covenants come to no effect,
24: And we pass away out of the world like grasshoppers, and our life is aw and fear, and we are not worthy to obtain mercy.
25: What will he do to his name whereby we are called? Of these things have I asked.
26: Then he answered me, and said, The more you search, the more you will marvel; for the world hastens fast to pass away,
27: And cannot comprehend the things that are promised to the righteous in time to come: for this world is full of unrighteousness and sickness.
28: But as concerning the things whereof you ask me, I will tell you. Evil is sown, but the destruction has not yet come.
29: If therefore that which is sown is not turned upside down, and if the place where the evil is sown does not pass away, then that which is sown with good cannot come.
30: For the grain of evil seed has been sown in the heart of Adam from the beginning, and how much ungodliness has it brought up to this time? And how much will it yet bring forth until the time of threshing come?
31: Ponder now by yourself, how much wicked fruit the grain of evil seed has brought forth.
32: And when the ears will be cut down, which are without number, how large of a floor will they fill?
33: Then I answered and said, How, and when will these things come to pass? Are our years few and evil?
34: And he answered me, saying, Do not try to be above the most Highest your hurry is in vain to be above him, for you have much exceeded yourself.

35: Did not the souls of the righteous also ask questions of these things in their chambers, saying, How long will I hope in this way? When comes the fruit of the floor of our reward?
36: And to these things Uriel the archangel gave them answer, and said, When the number of seeds is filled in you: for he has weighed the world in the balance.
37: By measure he has measured the times; and by number has he numbered the times; and he does not move nor stir them, until the said measure be fulfilled.
38: Then I answered and said, O Lord that upholds rule, even we all are full of sin,.
39: For our sakes peradventure it is that the floors of the righteous are not filled, because of the sins of them that dwell upon the earth.
40: So he answered me, and said, Go your way to a woman with child, and ask of her when she has fulfilled her nine months, if her womb may keep the birth any longer within her.
41: Then said I, No, Lord, she cannot. And he said to me, In the grave the chambers of souls are like the womb of a woman:
42: Like a woman that labors makes haste to escape the necessity of the travail: even so do these places haste to deliver those things that are committed to them.
43: From the beginning, look what you desire to see, it will be showed you.
44: Then I answered and said, If I have found favor in your sight, and if it is possible, and if I am worthy,
45: Show me then whether there is more to come than is past, or more past than is to come.
46: What is past I know, but what is for to come I know not.
47: And he said to me, Stand up upon the right side, and I will explain the illustration to you.
48: So I stood, and saw, and, behold, a hot burning oven passed by before me; and it when the flame was gone by I looked, and, behold, the smoke remained still.
49: After this there passed by before me a watery cloud, and sent down much rain with a storm; and when the stormy rain was past, the drops remained still.
50: Then he said to me, Think about this; as the rain is more than the drops, and as the fire is greater than the smoke; but the drops and the smoke remain behind; so the quantity which is past is greater.
51: Then I prayed, and said, I will live until that time? Or what will happen in those days?
52: He answered me, and said, As for the tokens whereof you ask me, I may tell you of them in pieces: but as touching your life, I am not sent to show you; for I do not know it.

4 Ezra Chapter 5

1: However, to share a small part with you, the days will come, that they which dwell upon earth will be taken in a great number, and the way of truth will be hidden, and the land will be barren of faith.
2: But iniquity will be increased above that which now you see, or that you have heard long ago.
3: And the land, that you see now supporting plants, will you see wasted suddenly.
4: But if the most High grants you to live, you will see after the third trumpet that the sun will suddenly shine again in the night, and the moon three time in the day:
5: And blood will drop out of wood, and the stone will have a voice, and the people will be troubled:

6: He will rule, whom they do not look for that dwell upon the earth, and the fowls will take their flight away together:
7: And the Sodomitish sea will cast out fish and make a noise at night, which many have not known: but they will all hear the voice of it.
8: There will be a confusion in many places, and the fire will be sent out again often, and the wild beasts will change their places, and women having their periods will give birth to monsters:
9: And salt waters will be found in the sweet, and all friends will destroy one another; then common sense will hide itself, and understanding withdraw itself into his secret rooms,
10: And will be sought of many, and yet not be found: then will unrighteousness and sexual passion be multiplied upon earth.
11: One land also will ask another, and say, Is righteousness that makes a man righteous gone through you? And it will say, No.
12: At the same time men will hope, but nothing will be obtain: they will labor, but their ways will not prosper.
13: I have permission to show you such things; and if you will pray again, and weep as now, and fast even days, you will hear yet greater things.
14: Then I awoke, and an extreme fearfulness went through all my body, and my mind was troubled, so that it fainted.
15: So the angel that was come to talk with me held me, comforted me, and set me up upon my feet.
16: And in the second night Salathiel the captain of the people came to me, saying, Where have you been? and why do you look so worried?
17: Do you not know that Israel is committed to you in the land of their captivity?
18: Get up then, and eat bread, and do not forsake us, as the shepherd that leaves his flock in the hands of cruel wolves.
19: Then said I to him, Go your way from me, and come not near me. And he heard what I said, and went from me.
20: And so I fasted seven days, mourning and weeping, as Uriel the angel commanded me.
21: And after seven days so it was, that the thoughts of my heart were very grievous to me again,
22: And my soul recovered the spirit of understanding, and I began to talk with the most High again,
23: And said, O Lord that upholds rule, of every wood of the earth, and of all the trees thereof, you have chosen your one and only vine:
24: And of all lands of the whole world you have chosen your one pit; and of all the flowers thereof one lily:
25: And of all the depths of the sea you have filled you one river: and of all built cities you have hallowed Sion to yourself:
26: And of all the fowls that are created you have named you one dove: and of all the cattle that are made you have provided you one sheep:
27: And among all the multitudes of people you have gotten you one people: and to this people, whom you loved, you gave a law that is approved of all.
28: And now, O Lord, why have you given this one people over to many? On this one root have you prepared others so why have you scattered your only one people among many?

29: And they who preached your promises for money, and believed not your covenants, have trodden them down.
30: If you hated your people this much, should you not punish them with your own hands?
31: Now when I had spoken these words, the angel that came to me the night before was sent to me,
32: And said to me, Hear me, and I will instruct you; hearken to the thing that I say, and I will tell you more.
33: And I said, Speak on, my Lord. Then said he to me, You are very troubled in mind for Israel's sake. Do you love that people better than he that made them?
34: And I said, No, Lord: but of very grief have I spoken: for my restraints pain me every hour, while I labor to comprehend the way of the most High, and to seek out part of his judgment.
35: And he said to me, You cannot. And I said, Why, Lord? Why was I born then? Why was my mother's womb not my grave, that I might not have seen the travail of Jacob, and the wearisome toil of the stock of Israel?
36: And he said to me, Number me the things that are not yet come, gather me together the dross that are scattered abroad, make me the flowers green again that are withered,
37: Open me the places that are closed, and bring out the winds to me that are shut up in them, show me the image of a voice: and then I will declare to you the thing that you labor to know.
38: And I said, O Lord that upholds rule, who may know these things, but he that has not his dwelling with men?
39: I am unwise: how may I then speak of these things whereof you ask me?
40: Then he said to me, Like you cannot do these things that I have spoken of, neither can you find out my judgment, or in the end the love that I have promised to my people.
41: And I said, Behold, O Lord, yet are you near to them that be reserved till the end: and what will they do that have been before me, or we that be now, or they that will come after us?
42: And he said to me, I will liken my judgment to a ring: like as there is no slackness (slowness) of the last, even so there is no swiftness of the first.
43: So I answered and said, Could you not make those that have been made, and be now, and that are to come, at once; that you might show your judgment sooner?
44: Then he answered me, and said, The creature may not rise above the maker; neither may the world hold them at once that will be created therein.
45: And I said, As you have said to your servant, that you, which gives life to all, have given life at once to the creature that you have created, and the creature bare it: even so it might now also bear them that now be present at once.
46: And he said to me, Ask the womb of a woman, and say to her, If you bring forth children, why do you it not together, but one after another? pray her therefore to bring forth ten children at once.
47: And I said, She cannot: but must do it by (its) distance (duration) of time.
48: Then said he to me, Even so have I given the womb of the earth to those that be sown in it in their times.
49: For like as a young child may not bring forth the things that belong to the aged, even so have I disposed the world which I created.

50: And I asked, and said, Seeing you have now given me the way, I will proceed to speak before you: for our mother, of whom you have told me that she is young, now draws near to age.
51: He answered me, and said, Ask a woman that bears children, and she will tell you.
52: Say to her, Why are they whom you have now brought forth like those that were before, but smaller?
53: And she will answer you, They that are born in the strength of youth are of one fashion, and they that are born in the (her) time of age, when the womb fails, are otherwise.
54: Consider therefore also, how that you are smaller than those that were before you.
55: And so are they that come after you less than you, as the creatures which now begin to be old, and have passed over the strength of youth.
56: Then I said, Lord, I beg you, if I have found favor in your sight, show your servant by whom you visit your creature.

4 Ezra Chapter 6
1: And he said to me, In the beginning, when the earth was made, before the borders of the world stood, or ever the winds blew,
2: Before it thundered and lightened, or ever the foundations of paradise were laid,
3: Before the fair flowers were seen, or ever the moveable powers were established, before the innumerable multitude of angels were gathered together,
4: Or ever the heights of the air were lifted up, before the measures of the firmament were named, or ever the chimneys in Sion were hot,
5: And in the event the present years were sought out, and or if ever the inventions of them that now sin were turned, before they were sealed that have gathered faith for a treasure:
6: I then considered these things, and they all were made through me alone, and through none other: by me also they will be ended, and by none other.
7: Then I answered and said, What will be the splitting apart of the times and when will the end of the first, and the beginning of it that follows be ?
8: And he said to me, From Abraham to Isaac, when Jacob and Esau were born of him, Jacob's hand held first the heel of Esau.
9: For Esau is the end of the world, and Jacob is the beginning of it that follows.
10: The hand of man is between the heel and the hand. Now, Esdras, do not ask any more questions.
11: I answered then and said, O Lord that upholds rule, if I have found favor in your sight,
12: I beg of you to show your servant the end of your tokens, that you showed me in part the last night.
13: So he answered and said to me, Stand up upon your feet, and hear a mighty sounding voice.
14: And it will be as it were a great motion; but the place where you stand will not be moved.
15: And therefore when it speaks be not afraid: for the word is of the end, and the foundation of the earth is understood.
16: And why? because the speech of these things trembles and is moved: for it knows that the end of these things must be changed.

17: And it happened, that when I had heard it I stood up upon my feet, and hearkened, and, behold, there was a voice that spoke, and the sound of it was like the sound of many waters.
18: And it said, Behold, the days come, that I will begin to draw near, and to visit them that dwell upon the earth,
19: And will begin to make inquisition of them, what they be that have hurt unjustly with their unrighteousness, and when the affliction of Sion will be fulfilled;
20: And when the world, that will begin to vanish away, will be finished, then will I show these tokens: the books will be opened before the firmament, and they will see all together:
21: And the children of a year old will speak with their voices, the women with child will bring forth untimely children of three or four months old, and they will live, and be raised up.
22: And suddenly will the sown places appear unsown, the full storehouses will suddenly be found empty:
23: And that trumpet will give a sound, which when every man hears, they will be suddenly afraid.
24: At that time will friends fight one against another like enemies, and the earth will stand in fear with those that dwell therein, the springs of the fountains will stand still, and in (for) three hours they will not run.
25: Whoever remains from all these that I have told you will escape, and see my salvation, and the end of your world.
26: And the men that are received will see it, who have not tasted death from their birth and the heart of the inhabitants will be changed, and turned into another meaning.
27: For evil will be put out, and deceit will be quenched.
28: As for faith, it will flourish, corruption will be overcome, and the truth, which has been so long without fruit, will be declared.
29: And when he talked with me, behold, I looked by little and little upon him before whom I stood.
30: And these words said he to me; I am come to show you the time of the night to come.
31: If you will pray even more, and fast seven days again, I will tell you greater things by day than I have heard.
32: For your voice is heard before the most High: for the Mighty has seen your righteous dealing, he has seen also your purity, which you have had ever since your youth.
33: And therefore has he sent me to show you all these things, and to say to you, "Be of good comfort and fear not
34: Do not be quick to think vain thoughts concerning the former times, or you will be hasty concerning the last times."
35: And after this I wept again, and fasted seven days in like manner, that I might fulfill the three weeks which he told me.
36: And in the eighth night was my heart vexed within me again, and I began to speak before the most High.
37: For my spirit was set on fire, and my soul was in distress.
38: And I said, O Lord, you spoke from the beginning of the creation on the first day and said; Let heaven and earth be made; and your word was a perfect work.

39: And then was the spirit, and darkness and silence were on every side; the sound of man's voice was not yet formed.
40: Then you commanded a beautiful light to come out of your treasures, that your work might appear.
41: On the second day you made the spirit of the firmament, and commanded it to section (piece) asunder, and to make a division betwixt the waters, that the one section (piece) might go up, and the other remain beneath.
42: On the third day you commanded that the waters should be gathered in the seventh part of the earth; six areas you dried up, and kept them, so that these being planted of God and tilled might serve you.
43: As soon as your word went forth the work was made.
44: For immediately there was great and innumerable fruit, and many and various pleasures for the taste, and flowers of unchangeable color, and odors of wonderful smell: and this was done the third day.
45: On the fourth day you commanded that the sun should shine, and the moon give her light, and the stars should be in order:
46: And gave them a order to do service to man that was going to be made.
47: On the fifth day you said to the seventh section, where the waters were gathered that it should bring forth living creatures, fowls and fishes: and so it came to pass.
48: For the dumb lifeless water brought forth living things at the commandment of God, that all people might praise your wondrous works.
49: Then you ordained two living creatures, one you called Behemoth, and the other (you called) Leviathan;
50: And did separate the one from the other: for the seventh section, namely, where the water was gathered together, might not hold them both.
51: To Behemoth you gave one section, which was dried up the third day, that he should dwell in the same place, where there are a thousand hills:
52: But to Leviathan you gave the seventh sections, namely, the moist; and have kept him to be devoured of whom you will, and when.
53: On the sixth day you gave commandment to the earth, that before you it should bring forth beasts, cattle, and creeping things.
54: And after these, Adam also, whom you made lord of all your creatures: of (from) him we all come, and also the people whom you have chosen.
55: All this have I spoken before you, O Lord, because you made the world for our sakes.
56: As for the other people, which also come of Adam, you have said that they are nothing, but are like to spittle: and have likened the abundance of them to a drip that falls from a vessel.
57: And now, O Lord, behold, these heathen, which have been reputed as nothing, have begun to be lords over us, and to devour us.
58: But we your people, whom you have called your firstborn, your only begotten, and your fervent lover, are given into their hands.
59: If the world now is made for our sakes, why do we not possess an inheritance with the world? How long will this last?

4 Ezra Chapter 7

1: And when I had ended speaking these words, there was sent to me the angel which had been sent to me the nights before.

2: And he said to me, Get up, Esdras, and hear the words that I have come to tell you.
3: And I said, Speak on, my God. Then said he to me, The sea is set in a wide place, that it might be deep and great.
4: But the entrance way is narrow and like a river;
5: Who then could go into the sea to look on it to rule it? If he did not go through the narrow, how could he come into the broad place?
6: There is also another thing; A city is built, and set upon a broad field, and is full of all good things.
7: The entrance of it is narrow, and is set in a dangerous place to fall, like as if there were a fire on the right hand, and on the left a deep water.
8: And one only path is between them both, even between the fire and the water, so small that there could but one man go there at once.
9: If this city now were given to a man for an inheritance, if he never will pass the danger set before it, how will he receive this inheritance?
10: And I said, Lord, that is true. Then he said to me, Even so also is Israel's portion.
11: Because for their sakes I made the world: and when Adam transgressed my statutes, then I decreed what was done.
12: Then were the entrances of this world made narrow, full of sorrow and travail: they are few and evil, full of dangers, and very painful.
13: For the entrances of the greater world were wide and safe, and brought immortal fruit.
14: Unless the living labors to enter these strait and vain things, they can never receive those things that are stored up for them.
15: Why disquiet yourself, seeing you are but a corruptible man? Why are you disturbed? You are only mortal?
16: Why have you not considered in your mind this thing that is to come, rather than that which is present?
17: Then I answered and said, O Lord that upholds rule, you have ordained in your law, that the righteous should inherit these things, but that the ungodly should perish.
18: Therefore, the righteous can endure difficult circumstances while hoping for better ones; but those who have done wickedly have suffered the difficult circumstances and will not see the easier.
19: And he said to me. There is no judge above God, and none that has understanding above the Highest.
20: For there are many that perish in this life, because they despise the law of God that is set before them. (Let many perish rather than the law…)
21: For God has plainly stated his commandment so that they that came should live, and what they should observe to avoid punishment.
22: Nevertheless they were not obedient to him; but spoke against him, and imagined vain things,
23: Deceived themselves by their wicked deeds; and said of the most High, that he does not exist; and ignore his ways:
24: But they despised His law, and denied his covenants; his statutes they have not been faithful, and have not performed his works.
25: And therefore, Esdras, for the empty are empty things, and for the full are the full things.

26: The time will come, that these tokens which I have told you will come to pass, and the bride (city) will appear, and her coming forth will be seen, that now is withdrawn from the earth.
27: And whosoever is delivered from these evils will see my wonders.
28: For my son Jesus will be revealed with those that are with him, and they that remain will rejoice for four hundred years.
29: After these years will my son Christ die, so that all men may have life.
30: And the world will be turned into the primal silence seven days, like as in the judgments of before so that no man will remain.
31: And after seven days the world that still sleeps, will be raised up, and that which is corrupt will die.
32: The earth will restore those that are asleep in her, and so will the dust those that dwell in silence, and the secret places will deliver those souls that were committed to them.
33: And the most High will appear on the seat of judgment, and misery will pass away, and the long suffering will have an end:
34: But only judgment will remain, truth will stand, and faith will grow strong.
35: And the recompense will follow, and the reward will be showed, and the good deeds will be of force, and wicked deeds will bear no rule.
36: Then I said, Abraham prayed first for the Sodomites; and Moses for the fathers that sinned in the wilderness;
37: And Jesus after him for Israel in the time of Achan;
38: And Samuel and David for the destruction: and Solomon for them that should come to the sanctuary;
39: And Helias for those that received rain and for the dead, that he might live;
40: And Ezechias for the people in the time of Sennacherib; and many pray for many.
41: Now, seeing corruption is matured, and wickedness increased, and the righteous have prayed for the ungodly; will it not be so now also?
42: He answered me, and said, This present life is not the end where much glory abides; therefore have they prayed for the weak.
43: But the day of doom will be the end of this time, and the beginning of the immortality to come, where corruption is past,
44: Hedonism is at an end, infidelity is cut off, righteousness is increased, and truth is sprung up.
45: No man are able to save him that is destroyed, nor to oppress him that has gotten the victory.
46: I answered then and said, This is my first and last saying, that it had been better not to have given the earth to Adam: or else, when it was given him, to have restrained him from sinning.
47: For what profit is it for men now in this present time to live in heaviness, and after death to look for punishment?
48: O Adam, what have you done? For though it was you that sinned, you are not fallen alone, but we all that come from you.
49: For what profit is it to us, if there be promised us an immortal time, whereas we have done the works that bring death?
50: And that there is promised us an everlasting hope, whereas ourselves being most wicked are made vain?
51: And that there are laid up for us dwellings of health and safety, whereas we have lived wickedly?

52: And that the glory of the most High is kept to defend them which have led a wary life, whereas we have walked in the most wicked ways of all?
53: And that there should be showed a paradise, whose fruit endures for ever, wherein is security and medicine, since we will not enter into it?
54: (For we have walked in unpleasant places.)
55: And that the faces of them which have used abstinence will shine above the stars, whereas our faces will be blacker than darkness?
56: For while we lived and committed sin, we did not considered that we should begin to suffer for it after death.
57: He answered me, and said, This is the condition of the battle, which man that is born upon the earth will fight;
58: That, if he is overcome, he will suffer as you have said: but if he gains victory, he will receive the thing that I say.
59: For this is the life whereof Moses spoke to the people while he lived, saying, Choose you life, that you may live.
60: Nevertheless they did not believe him, nor yet the prophets after him, no nor me which have spoken to them,
61: That there should not be such heaviness in their destruction, as will be joy over them that are persuaded to salvation.
62: I answered then, and said, I know, Lord, that the most High is called merciful, in that he has mercy upon them which are not yet come into the world,
63: And upon those also that turn to his law;
64: And that he is patient, and long suffers those that have sinned, as his creatures;
65: And that he is bountiful, for he is ready to give where it needs;
66: And that he is of great mercy, for he multiplies more and more mercies to them that are present, and that are past, and also to them which are to come.
67: For if he will not multiply his mercies, the world would not continue with them that inherit therein.
68: He forgives for if he did not do so out of his goodness so that they which have committed sin might be relieved of them, the ten thousandth part of men should not remain living.
69: And being judge, if he should not forgive them that are cured with his word, and put out the multitude of contentions,
70: There should be very few left out of an innumerable multitude.

4 Ezra Chapter 8
1: And he answered me, saying, The most High has made this world for many, but the world to come for few.
2: I will illustrate this to you, Esdras; When you ask the earth, it will say to you, that it gives much mold (rotten earth) that earthen vessels are made, but little dust that gold comes of: this is the course of this present world.
3: There are many created, but few will be saved.
4: So I said, Swallow then down, O my soul, understanding, and devour wisdom.
5: For you have agreed to give ear, and are willing to prophesy: for you have only space enough to live.
6: O Lord, if you do not permit your servant, that we may pray before you, and you give us seed to our heart, and the beginnings to our understanding, that there may come fruit of it; how will each man live that is corrupt, who bears the place of a man?

7: For you are alone, and we all one workmanship of your hands, as you have said.
8: For when the body is fashioned now in the mother's womb, and you gives it members, your creature is preserved in fire and water, and nine months your workmanship endures your creature which is created in her.
9: But that which keeps and is kept will both be preserved: and when the time comes, the womb preserved delivers up the things that grew in it.
10: For you have commanded out of the parts of the body, that is to say, out of the breasts, milk to is given, which is the fruit of the breasts,
11: That the thing which is fashioned may be nourished for a time, till you dispose it to your mercy.
12: You brought it up with your righteousness, and nurtured it in your law, and reformed it with your judgment.
13: And you will give it life as your creature, and quicken it as your work.
14: If therefore you will destroy him which with so great labor was fashioned, it is an easy thing to be ordained by your commandment, that the thing which was made might be preserved.
15: Now therefore, Lord, I will speak; touching man in general, you know best; but touching your people, for whose sake I am sorry;
16: And for yours inheritance, for whose cause I mourn; and for Israel, for whom I am heavy; and for Jacob, for whose sake I am troubled;
17: Therefore will I begin to pray before you for myself and for them: for I see the fall (failure) of us that dwell in the land.
18: But I have heard the swiftness of the judge which is to come.
19: Therefore hear my voice, and understand my words, and I will speak before you.
20: This is the beginning of the words of Esdras, before he was taken up: and I said, O Lord, you that dwell in everlastingness which watches all things from above in the heaven and in the air;
21: Whose throne is inestimable; whose glory may not be comprehended; before whom the hosts of angels stand with trembling,
22: Whose service is as knowledge of wind and fire; whose word is true, and sayings constant; whose commandment is strong, and ordinance fearful;
23: Whose look dries up the depths, and indignation makes the mountains to melt away; which are the truth witnesses.
24: O hear the prayer of your servant, and give ear to the petition of your creature.
25: For while I live I will speak, and so long as I have understanding I will answer.
26: Look not upon the sins of your people; but on them which serve you in truth.
27: Pay no attention to the devising of the wicked of the heathen, but the desire of those that keep your testimonies in afflictions.
28: Think not about those that have pretended to walk before you: but remember them, which according to your will have known your fear.
29: Let it not be your will to destroy them which have lived like beasts; but to look upon them that have clearly taught your law.
30: Take no indignation at them which are deemed worse than beasts; but love them that always put their trust in your righteousness and glory.
31: For we and our fathers do languish of such diseases but because of us sinners you will be called merciful.
32: For if you have a desire to have mercy upon us, you will be called merciful, to us namely, that have no works of righteousness.

33: For the just, which have many good works laid up with you, will out of their own deeds receive reward.
34: For what is man, that you should take displeasure at him? or what is a corruptible generation, that you should be so bitter toward it?
35: For in truth there is no man among them that is born that has not acted wickedly; and among the faithful there is none which has not acted wrongly.
36: For in this, O Lord, your righteousness and your goodness will be declared, if you be merciful to them which have not the confidence of good works.
37: Then he answered me, and said, Some things have you spoken aright, and according to your words it will be.
38: For indeed I will not think on the disposition of them which have sinned before death, before judgment, before destruction:
39: But I will rejoice over the disposition of the righteous, and I will remember also their pilgrimage, and the salvation, and the reward, that they will have.
40: Like as I have spoken now, so will it come to pass.
41: For as the husbandman sows much seed upon the ground, and plants many trees, and yet the thing that is sown good in his season cometh not up, neither doth all that is planted take root; even so is it of them that are sown in the world; they will not all be saved.
42: I answered then and said, If I have found grace, let me speak.
43: Like as the husbandman's seed perishes, if it come not up, and receive not your rain in due season; or if there come too much rain, and corrupt it:
44: Even so perishes man also, which is formed with your hands, and is called yours own image, because you are like to him, for whose sake you have made all things, and likened him to the husbandman's seed.
45: Be not wroth with us but spare your people, and have mercy upon yours own inheritance: for you are merciful to your creature.
46: Then he answered me, and said, Things present are for the present, and things to cometh for such as be to come.
47: For you come far short that you should be able to love my creature more than I. But I have often times drawn near to you, and to it, but never to the unrighteous.
48: In this also you are marvelous before the most High:
49: In that you have humbled yourself, as it becomes you, and have not judged yourself worthy to be much glorified among the righteous.
50: For many great miseries will be done to them that in the latter time will dwell in the world, because they have walked in great pride.
51: But understand you for yourself, and seek out the glory for such as be like you.
52: For to you is paradise opened, the tree of life is planted, the time to come is prepared, plenteousness is made ready, a city is built, and rest is allowed, yea, perfect goodness and wisdom.
53: The root of evil is sealed up from you, weakness and the moth is hid from you, and corruption is fled into hell to be forgotten:
54: Sorrows are passed, and in the end is showed the treasure of immortality.
55: And therefore ask no more questions concerning the multitude of them that perish.
56: For when they had taken liberty, they despised the most High, thought scorn of his law, and forsook his ways.
57: Moreover they have trodden down his righteous,
58: And said in their heart, that there is no God; even knowing they must die.

59: For as the things said before will receive you, so thirst and pain are prepared for them, for it was not his will that men should come to nothing:
60: But they which be created have defiled the name of him that made them, and were unthankful to him which prepared life for them.
61: And therefore is my judgment now at hand.
62: These things have I not showed to all men, but to you, and a few like you. Then I answered and said,
63: Look Lord, now you showed me the multitude of wonders, which you will begin to do in the last times; but at what time, you have not showed me.

4 Ezra Chapter 9
1: He answered me then, and said, Measure the time diligently in itself and when you see some of the signs past, which I have told you before,
2: Then will you understand, that it is the very same time, wherein the Highest will begin to visit the world which he made.
3: Therefore when there will be seen earthquakes and uproars of the people in the world:
4: Then will you well understand, that the most High spoke of those things from the days that were before you, even from the beginning.
5: For like as all that is made in the world has a beginning and an end, and the end is manifest:
6: Even so the times also of the Highest have plain beginnings in wonder and powerful works, and endings in effects and signs.
7: And every one that will be saved, and will be able to escape by his works, and by faith, whereby you have believed,
8: Will be preserved from the said perils, and will see my salvation in my land, and within my borders for I have sanctified them for me from the beginning.
9: Then will they be in pitiful case, which now have abused my ways and they that have cast them away despitefully will dwell in torments.
10: For such as in their life have received benefits, and have not known me;
11: And they that have hated my law while they had yet liberty, and, when as yet place of repentance was open to them, understood not, but despised it;
12: The same must know it after death by pain.
13: And therefore be you not curious how the ungodly will be punished, and when, but enquire how the righteous will be saved, whose the world is, and for whom the world is created.
14: Then I answered and said,
15: I have said before, and now do speak, and will speak it also hereafter, that there be many more of them which perish, than of them which will be saved.
16: Like as a wave is greater than a drop.
17: And he answered me, saying, As the field is, so is also the seed; as the flowers be, such are the colors also; such as the workman is, such also is the work; and as the husbandman is himself, so is his husbandry also; for it was the time of the world.
18: And now when I prepared the world, which was not yet made, even for them to dwell in that now live, no man spoke against me.
19: For then every one obeyed but now the manners of them which are created in this world that is made are corrupted by a perpetual seed, and rid themselves by a law which is unsearchable.

20: So I considered the world, and, behold, there was peril because of the schemes and actions that were come into it.
21: And I saw, and heartily spared it, and have kept me a grape of the cluster, and a plant of a great people.
22: Let the multitude perish then which was born in vain; and let my grape be kept, and my plant; for with great labor have I made it perfect.
23: Nevertheless, if you will cease yet seven days more, (but you will not fast in them,
24: But go into a field of flowers, where no house is built, and eat only the flowers of the field; taste no flesh, drink no wine, but eat flowers only);
25: And pray to the Highest continually, then will I come and talk with you.
26: So I went my way into the field which is called Ardath, as he commanded me; and there I sat among the flowers, and did eat of the herbs of the field, and the meat of the same satisfied me.
27: After seven days I sat upon the grass, and my heart was vexed within me, like as before;
28: And I opened my mouth, and began to talk before the most High, and said,
29: O Lord, you that show yourself to us, you was showed to our fathers in the wilderness, in a place where no man walks, in a barren place, when they came out of Egypt.
30: And you spoke saying, Hear me, O Israel; and mark my words, you seed of Jacob.
31: For, behold, I sow my law in you, and it will bring fruit in you, and you will be honored in it for ever.
32: But our fathers, who received the law, kept it not, and observed not your ordinances; and though the fruit of your law did not perish, neither could it, for it was yours;
33: Yet they that received it perished, because they kept not the thing that was sown in them.
34: And, lo, it is a custom, when the ground has received seed, or the sea a ship, or any vessel meat or drink, that, that being perished wherein it was sown or cast into,
35: That thing also which was sown, or cast therein, or received, doth perish, and remains not with us but with us it has not happened so.
36: For we that have received the law perish by sin, and our heart also which received it
37: Notwithstanding the law perishes not, but remains in his force.
38: And when I spoke these things in my heart, I looked back with mine eyes, and upon the right side I saw a woman, and, behold, she mourned and wept with a loud voice, and was much grieved in heart, and her clothes were rent, and she had ashes upon her head.
39: Then let I my thoughts go that I was in, and turned me to her,
40: And said to her, Why do you weep? Why are you so grieved in your mind?
41: And she said to me, Sir, let me alone, that I may bewail myself and add to my sorrow, for I am sore vexed in my mind, and brought very low.
42: And I said to her, What ails you? Tell me.
43: She said to me, I, your servant, have been barren and had no child, though I had an husband thirty years,
44: And those thirty years I did nothing else day and night, and every hour, but make my, prayer to the Highest.

45: After thirty years God heard me, your handmaid, looked upon my misery, considered my trouble, and gave me a son; and I was very glad of him, so was my husband also, and all my neighbors: and we gave great honor to the Almighty.
46: And I nourished him with great travail.
47: So when he grew up, and came to the time that he should have a wife, I made a feast.

4 Ezra Chapter 10
1: And it so came to pass, that when my son was entered into his wedding chamber, he fell down, and died.
2: Then we all overthrew the lights, and all my neighbors rose up to comfort me so I took my rest to the second day at night.
3: And when they had all left off to comfort me, to the end I might be quiet; then rose I up by night and fled, and came hither into this field, as you see.
4: And I do now purpose not to return into the city but here to stay, and neither to eat nor drink, but continually to mourn and to fast until I die.
5: Then I left the meditations wherein I was, and spoke to her in anger, saying,
6: You foolish woman above all other, see you not our mourning, and what happens to us?
7: How that Sion, our mother, is full of all heaviness and much humbled, mourning very sore?
8: And now, seeing we all mourn and are sad, for we are all in heaviness, are you grieved for one son?
9: For ask the earth, and she will tell you, that it is she which ought to mourn for the fall of so many that grow upon her.
10: For out of her came all at the first, and out of her will all others come, and, behold, they walk almost all into destruction, and a multitude of them is utterly pulled up by the roots.
11: Who then should make more mourning than she, that has lost so great a multitude; and not you, which are sorry but for one?
12: But if you say to me, My lamentation is not like the earth's, because I have lost the fruit of my womb, which I brought forth with pains, and bare with sorrows;
13: But the earth not so for the multitude present in it according to the course of the earth is gone, as it came:
14: Then say I to you, Like as you have brought forth with labor; even so the earth also has given her fruit, namely man, ever since the beginning to him that made her.
15: Now therefore keep your sorrow to yourself, and bear with a good courage that which has befallen you.
16: For if you will acknowledge the determination of God to be just, you will both receive your son in time, and will be commended among women.
17: Go your way then into the city to your husband.
18: And she said to me, That will I not do, I will not go into the city, but here will I die.
19: So I proceeded to speak further to her, and said,
20: Do not so, but be counseled by me; for how many are the adversities of Sion? Be comforted in regard of the sorrow of Jerusalem.
21: For you see that our sanctuary is laid waste, our altar broken down, our temple destroyed;

22: Our psaltery is laid on the ground, our song is put to silence, our rejoicing is at an end, the light of our candlestick is put out, the ark of our covenant is spoiled, our holy things are defiled, and the name that is called upon us is almost profaned. Our children are put to shame, our priests are burnt, our Levites are gone into captivity, our virgins are defiled, and our wives ravished; our righteous men carried away, our little ones destroyed, our young men are brought in bondage, and our strong men are become weak;
23: And, which is the greatest of all, the seal of Sion has now lost her honor; for she is delivered into the hands of them that hate us.
24: And therefore shake off your great heaviness, and put away the multitude of sorrows, that the Mighty may be merciful to you again, and the Highest will give you rest and ease from your labor.
25: And while I was talking with her, behold, her face upon a sudden shined exceedingly, and her countenance glistered, so that I was afraid of her, and mused what it might be.
26: And, behold, suddenly she made a great cry very fearful: so that the earth shook at the noise of the woman.
27: And I looked, and, behold, the woman appeared to me no more, but there was a city built, and a large place showed itself from the foundations: then was I afraid, and cried with a loud voice, and said,
28: Where is Uriel the angel, who came to me at the first, for he has caused me to fall into many trances, and mine end is turned into corruption, and my prayer to rebuke?
29: And as I was speaking these words behold, he came to me, and looked upon me.
30: And, lo, I lay as one that was dead, and mine understanding was taken from me and he took me by the right hand, and comforted me, and set me upon my feet, and said to me,
31: What ails you? And why are you so disquieted? And why is your understanding troubled, and the thoughts of your heart?
32: And I said, Because you have forsaken me, and yet I did according to your words, and I went into the field, and, lo, I have seen, and yet see, that I am not able to express.
33: And he said to me, Stand up manfully, and I will advise you.
34: Then said I, Speak on, my lord, in me; only forsake me not, lest I die frustrated of my hope.
35: For I have seen that I knew not, and hear that I do not know.
36: Or is my sense deceived, or my soul in a dream?
37: Now therefore I beseech you that you will show your servant of this vision.
38: He answered me then, and said, Hear me, and I will inform you, and tell you wherefore you are afraid; for the Highest will reveal many secret things to you.
39: He has seen that your way is right; for that you sorrow continually for your people, and make great lamentation for Sion.
40: This therefore is the meaning of the vision which you lately saw:
41: You saw a woman mourning and you began to comfort her:
42: But now see you the likeness of the woman no more, but there appeared to you a city built.
43: And whereas she told you of the death of her son, this is the solution:
44: This woman, whom you saw is Sion and whereas she said to you, even she whom you see as a city built,

45: Whereas, I say, she said to you, that she has been thirty years barren, those are the thirty years wherein there was no offering made in her.
46: But after thirty years Solomon built the city and offered offerings: and then bare the barren a son.
47: And whereas she told you that she nourished him with labor: that was the dwelling in Jerusalem.
48: But whereas she said to you, That my son coming into his marriage chamber happened to have a fail, and died: this was the destruction that came to Jerusalem.
49: And, behold, you saw her likeness, and because she mourned for her son, you began to comfort her: and of these things which have chanced, these are to be opened to you.
50: For now the most High sees that you are truly grieved, and allow from your whole heart for her, so has he showed you the brightness of her glory, and the pleasantness of her beauty:
51: And therefore I asked you to remain in the field where no house was built:
52: For I knew that the Highest would show this to you.
53: Therefore I commanded you to go into the field, where no foundation of any building was.
54: For in the place wherein the Highest begins to show his city, there can no man's building be able to stand.
55: And therefore fear not, let not yours heart be affrighted, but go your way in, and see the beauty and greatness of the building, as much as yours eyes be able to see:
56: And then will you hear as much as yours ears may comprehend.
57: For you are blessed above many other, and are called with the Highest; and so are but few.
58: But tomorrow at night you will remain here;
59: And so will the Highest show you visions of the high things, which the most High will do to them that dwell upon the earth in the last days. So I slept that night and another, like as he commanded me.

4 Ezra Chapter 11
1: Then saw I a dream, and, behold, there came up from the sea an eagle, which had twelve feathered wings and three heads.
2: And I saw, and, behold, she spread her wings over all the earth, and all the winds of the air blew on her, and were gathered together.
3: And I beheld, and out of her feathers there grew other contrary feathers; and they became little feathers and small.
4: But her heads were at rest; the head in the midst was greater than the other, yet rested it with the residue.
5: Moreover I beheld, and lo, the eagle flew with her feathers, and reigned upon earth, and over them that dwelt therein.
6: And I saw that all things under heaven were subject to her, and no man spoke against her, no, not one creature upon earth.
7: And I beheld, and, lo, the eagle rose upon her talons, and spoke to her feathers, saying,
8: Watch not all at once, sleep every one in his own place, and watch by course:
9: But let the heads be preserved for the last.
10: And I beheld, and, lo, the voice went not out of her heads, but from the midst of her body.

11: And I numbered her contrary feathers, and, behold, there were eight of them.
12: And I looked, and, behold, on the right side there arose one feather, and reigned over all the earth;
13: And so it was, that when it reigned, the end of it came, and the place thereof appeared no more: so the next following stood up. and reigned, and had a great time;
14: And it happened, that when it reigned, the end of it came also, like as the first, so that it appeared no more.
15: Then came there a voice to it, and said,
16: Hear you that have borne rule over the earth so long, this I say to you, before you begin to appear no more,
17: There will none after you attain to your time, neither to the half thereof.
18: Then arose the third, and reigned as the others before, and appeared no more also.
19: So went it with all the residue one after another, as that every one reigned, and then appeared no more.
20: Then I beheld, and, lo, in process of time the feathers that followed stood up upon the right side, that they might rule also; and some of them ruled, but within a while they appeared no more:
21: For some of them were set up, but ruled not.
22: After this I looked, and, behold, the twelve feathers appeared no more, nor the two little feathers:
23: And there was no more upon the eagle's body, but three heads that rested, and six little wings.
24: Then saw I also that two little feathers divided themselves from the six, and remained under the head that was upon the right side; for the four continued in their place.
25: And I beheld, and, lo, the feathers that were under the wing thought to set up themselves and to have the rule.
26: And I beheld, and, lo, there was one set up, but shortly it appeared no more.
27: And the second was sooner away than the first.
28: And I beheld, and, lo, the two that remained thought also in themselves to reign.
29: And when they so thought, behold, there awaked one of the heads that were at rest, namely, it that was in the midst; for that was greater than the two other heads.
30: And then I saw that the two other heads were joined with it.
31: And, behold, the head was turned with them that were with it, and did eat up the two feathers under the wing that would have reigned.
32: But this head put the whole earth in fear, and bare rule in it over all those that dwelt upon the earth with much oppression; and it had the governance of the world more than all the wings that had been.
33: And after this I beheld, and, lo, the head that was in the midst suddenly appeared no more, like as the wings.
34: But there remained the two heads, which also in like sort ruled upon the earth, and over those that dwelt therein.
35: And I beheld, and, lo, the head upon the right side devoured it that was upon the left side.
36: Then I head a voice, which said to me, Look before you, and consider the thing that you see.

37: And I beheld, and lo, as it were a roaring lion chased out of the wood: and I saw that he sent out a man's voice to the eagle, and said,
38: Hear you, I will talk with you, and the Highest will say to you,
39: Are not you it that remain of the four beasts, whom I made to reign in my world, that the end of their times might come through them?
40: And the fourth came, and overcame all the beasts that were past, and had power over the world with great fearfulness, and over the whole compass of the earth with much wicked oppression; and so long time dwelt he upon the earth with deceit.
41: For the earth have you not judged with truth.
42: For you have afflicted the meek, you have hurt the peaceable, you have loved liars, and destroyed the dwellings of them that brought forth fruit, and have cast down the walls of such as did you no harm.
43: Therefore is your wrongful dealing come up to the Highest, and your pride to the Mighty.
44: The Highest also has looked upon the proud times, and, behold, they are ended, and his abominations are fulfilled.
45: And therefore appear no more, you eagle, nor your horrible wings, nor your wicked feathers nor your malicious heads, nor your hurtful claws, nor all your vain body:
46: That all the earth may be refreshed, and may return, being delivered from your violence, and that she may hope for the judgment and mercy of him that made her.

4 Ezra Chapter 12

1: And while the lion spoke these words to the eagle, I saw,
2: And, behold, the head that remained and the four wings appeared no more, and the two went to it and set themselves up to reign, and their kingdom was small, and fill of uproar.
3: And I saw, and, behold, they appeared no more, and the whole body of the eagle was burnt so that the earth was in great fear: then awaked I out of the trouble and trance of my mind, and from great fear, and said to my spirit,
4: Lo, this have you done to me, in that you search out the ways of the Highest.
5: Lo, yet am I weary in my mind, and very weak in my spirit; and little strength is there in me, for the great fear wherewith I was afflicted this night.
6: Therefore will I now beseech the Highest, that he will comfort me to the end.
7: And I said, Lord that upholds rule, if I have found grace before your sight, and if I am justified with you before many others, and if my prayer indeed be come up before your face;
8: Comfort me then, and show me your servant the interpretation and plain difference of this fearful vision, that you may perfectly comfort my soul.
9: For you have judged me worthy to show me the last times.
10: And he said to me, This is the interpretation of the vision:
11: The eagle, whom you saw come up from the sea, is the kingdom which was seen in the vision of your brother Daniel.
12: But it was not expounded to him, therefore now I declare it to you.
13: Behold, the days will come, that there will rise up a kingdom upon earth, and it will be feared above all the kingdoms that were before it.
14: In the same will twelve kings reign, one after another:

15: Whereof the second will begin to reign, and will have more time than any of the twelve.
16: And this do the twelve wings signify, which you saw.
17: As for the voice which you heard speak, and that you saw not to go out from the heads but from the midst of the body thereof, this is the interpretation:
18: That after the time of that kingdom there will arise great strivings, and it will stand in peril of failing: nevertheless it will not then fall, but will be restored again to his beginning.
19: And whereas you saw the eight small under feathers sticking to her wings, this is the interpretation:
20: That in him there will arise eight kings, whose times will be but small, and their years swift.
21: And two of them will perish, the middle time approaching: four will be kept until their end begin to approach: but two will be kept to the end.
22: And whereas you saw three heads resting, this is the interpretation:
23: In his last days will the most High raise up three kingdoms, and renew many things therein, and they will have the dominion of the earth,
24: And of those that dwell therein, with much oppression, above all those that were before them: therefore are they called the heads of the eagle.
25: For these are they that will accomplish his wickedness, and that will finish his last end.
26: And whereas you saw that the great head appeared no more, it signifies that one of them will die upon his bed, and yet with pain.
27: For the two that remain will be slain with the sword.
28: For the sword of the one will devour the other but at the last will he fall through the sword himself.
29: And whereas you saw two feathers under the wings passing over the head that is on the right side;
30: It signifies that these are they, whom the Highest has kept to their end: this is the small kingdom and full of trouble, as you saw.
31: And the lion, whom you saw rising up out of the wood, and roaring, and speaking to the eagle, and rebuking her for her unrighteousness with all the words which you have heard;
32: This is the anointed, which the Highest has kept for them and for their wickedness to the end: he will reprove them, and will upbraid them with their cruelty.
33: For he will set them before him alive in judgment, and will rebuke them, and correct them.
34: For the rest of my people will he deliver with mercy, those that have been pressed upon my borders, and he will make them joyful until the coming of the day of judgment, whereof I have spoken to you from the beginning.
35: This is the dream that you saw, and these are the interpretations.
36: You only have been meet to know this secret of the Highest.
37: Therefore write all these things that you have seen in a book, and hide them.
38: And teach them to the wise of the people, whose hearts you know may comprehend and keep these secrets.
39: But wait you here yourself yet seven days more, that it may be showed you, whatsoever it pleases the Highest to declare to you. And with that he went his way.

40: And when all the people saw that the seven days were past, and I had not come again into the city, they gathered them all together, from the least to the greatest, and came to me, and said,
41: What have we offended you? And what evil have we done against you, that you forsake us, and sit here in this place?
42: For of all the prophets you only are left us, as a cluster of the vintage, and as a candle in a dark place, and as a haven or ship preserved from the tempest.
43: Are not the evils which are come to us sufficient?
44: If you will forsake us, how much better had it been for us, if we also had been burned in the midst of Sion?
45: For we are not better than they that died there. And they wept with a loud voice. Then I answered them, and said,
46: Be of good comfort, O Israel; and be not heavy, you house of Jacob:
47: For the Highest has you in remembrance, and the Mighty has not forgotten you in temptation.
48: As for me, I have not forsaken you, neither am I left you; but am come into this place, to pray for the desolation of Sion, and that I might seek mercy for the low estate of your sanctuary.
49: And now go your way home every man, and after these days will I come to you.
50: So the people went their way into the city, like as I commanded them:
51: But I remained still in the field seven days, as the angel commanded me; and did eat only in those days of the flowers of the field, and had my meat of the herbs

4 Ezra Chapter 13
1: And it came to pass after seven days, I dreamed a dream by night.
2: And, lo, there arose a wind from the sea, that it moved all the waves thereof.
3: And I beheld, and, lo, that man waxed strong with the thousands of heaven and when he turned his countenance to look, all the things trembled that were seen under him.
4: And when the voice went out of his mouth, all they burned that heard his voice, like as the earth fails when it feels the fire.
5: And after this I beheld, and, lo, there was gathered together a multitude of men, out of number, from the four winds of the heaven, to subdue the man that came out of the sea
6: But I beheld, and, lo, he had graved himself a great mountain, and flew up upon it.
7: But I would have seen the region or place throughout the hill was graven, and I could not.
8: And after this I beheld, and, lo, all they which were gathered together to subdue him were sore afraid, and yet did fight.
9: And, lo, as he saw the violence of the multitude that came, he neither lifted up his hand, nor held sword, nor any instrument of war:
10: But only I saw that he sent out of his mouth as it had been a blast of fire, and out of his lips a flaming breath, and out of his tongue he cast out sparks and tempests.
11: And they were all mixed together; the blast of fire, the flaming breath, and the great tempest; and fell with violence upon the multitude which was prepared to fight, and burned them up every one, so that upon a sudden of an innumerable multitude nothing was to be perceived, but only dust and smell of smoke; when I saw this I was afraid.

12: Afterward saw I the same man come down from the mountain, and call to him another peaceable Multitude.
13: And there came much people to him, whereof some were glad, some were sorry, and some of them were bound, and other some brought of them that were offered. Then was I sick through great fear, and I awakened, and said,
14: You have showed your servant these wonders from the beginning, and have counted me worthy that you should receive my prayer:
15: Show me now yet the interpretation of this dream.
16: For as I conceive in mine understanding, woe to them that will be left in those days and much more woe to them that are not left behind!
17: For they that were not left were in heaviness.
18: Now understand I the things that are laid up in the latter days, which will happen to them, and to those that are left behind.
19: Therefore are they come into great perils and many necessities, like as these dreams declare.
20: Yet is it easier for him that is in danger to come into these things, than to pass away as a cloud out of the world, and not to see the things that happen in the last days. And he answered to me, and said,
21: The interpretation of the vision will I show you, and I will open to you the thing that you have required.
22: Whereas you have spoken of them that are left behind, this is the interpretation:
23: He that will endure the peril in that time has kept himself: they that be fallen into danger are such as have works, and faith toward the Almighty.
24: Know this therefore, that they which be left behind are more blessed than they that be dead.
25: This is the meaning of the vision: Whereas you saw a man coming up from the midst of the sea:
26: The same is he whom God the Highest has kept a great season, which by his own self will deliver his creature: and he will order them that are left behind.
27: And whereas you saw, that out of his mouth there came as a blast of wind, and fire, and storm;
28: And that he held neither sword, nor any instrument of war, but that the rushing in of him destroyed the whole multitude that came to subdue him; this is the interpretation:
29: Behold, the days come, when the most High will begin to deliver them that are upon the earth.
30: And he will come to the astonishment of them that dwell on the earth.
31: And one will undertake to fight against another, one city against another, one place against another, one people against another, and one realm against another.
32: And the time will be when these things will come to pass, and the signs will happen which I showed you before, and then will my Son be declared, whom you saw as a man ascending.
33: And when all the people hear his voice, every man will in their own land leave the battle they have one against another.
34: And an innumerable multitude will be gathered together, as you saw them, willing to come, and to overcome him by fighting.
35: But he will stand upon the top of the Mount Sion.
36: And Sion will come, and will be showed to all men, being prepared and built, like as you saw the hill graven without hands.

37: And this my Son will rebuke the wicked inventions of those nations, which for their wicked life are fallen into the tempest;
38: And will lay before them their evil thoughts, and the torments wherewith they will begin to be tormented, which are like to a flame: and he will destroy them without labor by the law which is like to me.
39: And whereas you saw that he gathered another peaceable multitude to him;
40: Those are the ten tribes, which were carried away prisoners out of their own land in the time of Osea the king, whom Salmanasar the king of Assyria led away captive, and he carried them over the waters, and so came they into another land.
41: But they took this counsel among themselves, that they would leave the multitude of the heathen, and go forth into a further country, where never mankind dwelt,
42: That they might there keep their statutes, which they never kept in their own land.
43: And they entered into Euphrates by the narrow places of the river.
44: For the most High then showed signs for them, and held still the flood, till they were passed over.
45: For through that country there was a great way to go, namely, of a year and a half: and the same region is called Arsareth.
46: Then dwelt they there until the latter time; and now when they will begin to come,
47: The Highest will stay the springs of the stream again, that they may go through, therefore saw you the multitude with peace.
48: But those that be left behind of your people are they that are found within my borders.
49: Now when he destroys the multitude of the nations that are gathered together, he will defend his people that remain.
50: And then will he show them great wonders.
51: Then said I, O Lord that upholds rule, show me this: Wherefore have I seen the man coming up from the midst of the sea?
52: And he said to me, Like as you can neither seek out nor know the things that are in the deep of the sea; even so can no man upon earth see my Son, or those that be with him, but in the day time.
53: This is the interpretation of the dream which you saw, and whereby you only are here lightened.
54: For you have forsaken yours own way, and applied your diligence to my law, and sought it.
55: Your life have you ordered in wisdom, and have called understanding your mother.
56: And therefore have I showed you the treasures of the Highest; after other three days I will speak other things to you, and declare to you mighty and wondrous things.
57: Then went I forth into the field, giving praise and thanks greatly to the most High because of his wonders which he did in time;
58: And because he governs the same, and such things as fall in their seasons, and there I sat three days.

4 Ezra Chapter 14

1: And it came to pass upon the third day, I sat under an oak, and, behold, there came a voice out of a bush over against me, and said, Esdras, Esdras.
2: And I said, Here am I, Lord And I stood up upon my feet.
3: Then said he to me, In the bush I did manifestly reveal myself to Moses, and talked with him, when my people served in Egypt:
4: And I sent him and led my people out of Egypt, and brought him up to the mount of where I held him by me a long season,
5: And told him many wondrous things, and showed him the secrets of the times, and the end; and commanded him, saying,
6: These words will you declare, and these will you hide.
7: And now I say to you,
8: That you lay up in your heart the signs that I have showed, and the dreams that you have seen, and the interpretations which you have heard:
9: For you will be taken away from all, and from henceforth you will remain with my Son, and with such as be like you, until the times be ended.
10: For the world has lost his youth, and the times begin to wax old.
11: For the world is divided into twelve parts (pieces or section), and the ten part (pieces or section) of it are gone already, and half of a tenth section (piece):
12: And there remains that which is after the half of the tenth section (piece).
13: Now therefore set yours house in order, and reprove your people, comfort such of them as be in trouble, and now renounce corruption,
14: Let go from you mortal thoughts, cast away the burdens of man, put off now the weak nature,
15: And set aside the thoughts that are most heavy to you, and haste you to flee from these times.
16: For yet greater evils than those which you have seen happen will be done hereafter.
17: For look how much the world will be weaker through age, so much the more will evils increase upon them that dwell therein.
18: For the time is fled far away, and leasing is hard at hand: for now hasten the vision to come, which you have seen.
19: Then I answered before you, and said,
20: Behold, Lord, I will go, as you have commanded me, and reprove the people which are present, but they that will be born afterward, who will admonish them? Thus the world is set in darkness, and they that dwell therein are without light.
21: For your law is burnt, therefore no man knows the things that are done of you, or the work that will begin.
22: But if I have found grace before you, send the Holy Ghost into me, and I will write all that has been done in the world since the beginning, which were written in your law, that men may find your path, and that they which will live in the latter days may live.
23: And he answered me, saying, Go your way, gather the people together, and say to them, that they seek you not for forty days.
24: But look you prepare you many box trees, and take with you Sarea, Dabria, Selemia, Ecanus, and Asiel, these five which are ready to write swiftly;
25: And come hither, and I will light a candle of understanding in your heart, which will not be put out, till the things be performed which you will begin to write.
26: And when you have done, some things will you publish, and some things will you show secretly to the wise. Tomorrow this hour will you begin to write.

27: Then went I forth, as he commanded, and gathered all the people together, and said,
28: Hear these words, O Israel.
29: Our fathers at the beginning were strangers in Egypt, from whence they were delivered;
30: And received the law of life, which they kept not, which you also have transgressed after them.
31: Then was the land, even the land of Sion, parsed among you by lot; but your fathers, and you yourselves, have done unrighteousness, and have not kept the ways which the Highest commanded you.
32: And for as much as he is a righteous judge, he took from you in time the thing that he had given you.
33: And now are you here, and your brethren among you.
34: Therefore if so be that you will subdue your own understanding, and reform your hearts, you will be kept alive and after death you will obtain mercy.
35: For after death will the judgment come, when we will live again: and then will the names of the righteous be manifest, and the works of the ungodly will be declared.
36: Let no man therefore come to me now, nor seek after me these forty days.
37: So I took the five men, as he commanded me, and we went into the field, and remained there.
38: And the next day, behold, a voice called me, saying, Esdras, open your mouth, and drink that I give you to drink.
39: Then opened I my mouth, and, behold, he reached me a full cup, which was full as it were with water, but the color of it was like fire.
40: And I took it, and drank: and when I had drunk of it, my heart uttered understanding, and wisdom grew in my breast, for my spirit strengthened my memory:
41: And my mouth was opened, and shut no more.
42: The Highest gave understanding to the five men, and they wrote the wonderful visions of the night that were told, which they knew not and they sat forty days, and they wrote in the day, and at night they ate bread.
43: As for me. I spoke in the day, and I held not my tongue by night.
44: In forty days they wrote two hundred and four books.
45: And when the forty days were filled, that the Highest spoke, saying, The first that you have written publish openly, that the worthy and unworthy may read it:
46: But keep the seventy last, that you may deliver them only to such as be wise among the people;
47: For in them is the spring of understanding, the fountain of wisdom, and the stream of knowledge.
48: And I did so.

4 Ezra Chapter 15
1: Behold, speak you in the ears of my people the words of prophecy, which I will put in your mouth, says the Lord:
2: And cause them to be written in paper for they are faithful and true.
3: Fear not the imaginations against you, let not the incredulity of them trouble you, that speak against you.
4: For all the unfaithful will die in their unfaithfulness.

5: Behold, says the Lord, I will bring plagues upon the world; the sword, famine, death, and destruction.
6: For wickedness has exceedingly polluted the whole earth, and their hurtful works are fulfilled.
7: Therefore says the Lord,
8: I will hold my tongue no more as touching their wickedness, which they profanely commit, neither will I suffer them in those things, in which they wickedly exercise themselves. Behold, the innocent and righteous blood cries to me, and the souls of the just complain continually.
9: And therefore, says the Lord, I will surely avenge them, and receive to me all the innocent blood from among them.
10: Behold, my people is led as a flock to the slaughter: I will not suffer them now to dwell in the land of Egypt:
11: But I will bring them with a mighty hand and a stretched out arm, and strike Egypt with plagues, as before, and will destroy all the land thereof.
12: Egypt will mourn, and the foundation of it will be smitten with the plague and punishment that God will bring upon it.
13: They that till the ground will mourn for their seeds will fail through the blasting and hail, and with a fearful constellation.
14: Woe to the world and them that dwell therein!
15: For the sword and their destruction draws near, and one people will stand up and fight against another, and swords in their hands.
16: For there will be sedition among men, and invading one another; they will not regard their kings nor princes, and the course of their actions will stand in their power.
17: A man will desire to go into a city, and will not be able.
18: For because of their pride the cities will be troubled, the houses will be destroyed, and men will be afraid.
19: A man will have no pity upon his neighbor, but will destroy their houses with the sword, and spoil their goods, because of the lack of bread, and for great tribulation.
20: Behold, says God, I will call together all the kings of the earth to reverence me, which are from the rising of the sun, from the south, from the east, and Libanus; to turn themselves one against another, and repay the things that they have done to them.
21: Like as they do yet this day to my chosen, so will I do also, and recompense in their bosom. Thus says the Lord God;
22: My right hand will not spare the sinners, and my sword will not cease over them that shed innocent blood upon the earth.
23: The fire is gone forth from his rage, and has consumed the foundations of the earth, and the sinners, like the straw that is kindled.
24: Woe to them that sin, and keep not my commandments! says the Lord.
25: I will not spare them Go your way, you children, from the power, defile not my sanctuary.
26: For the Lord knows all them that sin against him, and therefore delivers he them to death and destruction.
27: For now are the plagues come upon the whole earth and you will remain in them for God will not deliver you, because you have sinned against him.
28: Behold an horrible vision, and the appearance thereof from the east;

29: Where the nations of the dragons of Arabia will come out with many chariots, and the multitude of them will be carried as the wind upon earth, that all they which hear them may fear and tremble.
30: Also the Carmanians raging in rage will go forth as the wild boars of the wood, and with great power will they come, and join battle with them, and will waste a portion of the land of the Assyrians.
31: And then will the dragons have the upper hand, remembering their nature; and if they will turn themselves, conspiring together in great power to persecute them,
32: Then these will be troubled bled, and keep silence through their power, and will flee.
33: And from the land of the Assyrians will the enemy besiege them, and consume some of them, and in their host will be fear and dread, and strife among their kings.
34: Behold clouds from the east and from the north to the south, and they are very horrible to look upon, full of rage and storm.
35: They will strike one upon another, and they will strike down a great multitude of stars upon the earth, even their own star; and blood will be from the sword to the belly,
36: And dung of men to the camel's hock.
37: And there will be great fearfulness and trembling upon earth and they that see the rage will be afraid, and trembling will come upon them.
38: And then will there come great storms from the south, and from the north, and another section (piece) from the west.
39: And strong winds will arise from the east, and will open it; and the cloud which he raised up in rage, and the star stirred to cause fear toward the east and west wind, will be destroyed.
40: The great and mighty clouds will be puffed up full of rage, and the star, that they may make all the earth afraid, and them that dwell therein; and they will pour out over every high and eminent place an horrible star,
41: Fire, and hail, and flying swords, and many waters, that all fields may be full, and all rivers, with the abundance of great waters.
42: And they will break down the cities and walls, mountains and hills, trees of the wood, and grass of the meadows, and their corn.
43: And they will go steadfastly to Babylon, and make her afraid.
44: They will come to her, and besiege her, the star and all rage will they pour out upon her: then will the dust and smoke go up to the heaven, and all they that be about her will bewail her.
45: And they that remain under her will do service to them that have put her in fear.
46: And you, Asia, that are partaker of the hope of Babylon, and are the glory of her person:
47: Woe be to you, you wretch, because you have made yourself like to her; and have decked your daughters in whoredom, that they might please and glory in your lovers, which have always desired to commit whoredom with you.
48: You have followed her that is hated in all her works and inventions: therefore says God,
49: I will send plagues upon you; widowhood, poverty, famine, sword, and pestilence, to waste your houses with destruction and death.
50: And the glory of your Power will be dried up as a flower, the heat will arise that is sent over you.

51: You will be weakened as a poor woman with stripes, and as one covered with wounds, so that the mighty and lovers will not be able to receive you.
52: Would I with jealousy have so proceeded against you, says the Lord,
53: If you had not always slain my chosen, exalting the stroke of yours hands, and saying over their dead, when you was drunken,
54: Set forth the beauty of your countenance?
55: The reward of your whoredom will be in your bosom, therefore will you receive payment in full.
56: Like as you have done to my chosen, says the Lord, even so will God do to you, and will deliver you into mischief
57: Your children will die of hunger, and you will fall through the sword: your cities will be broken down, and all yours will perish with the sword in the field.
58: They that be in the mountains will die of hunger, and eat their own flesh, and drink their own blood, for very hunger of bread, and thirst of water.
59: You as unhappy will come through the sea, and receive plagues again.
60: And in the passage they will rush on the idle city, and will destroy some portion of your land, and consume part (piece) of your glory, and will return to Babylon that was destroyed.
61: And you will be cast down by them as stubble, and they will be to you as fire;
62: And will consume you, and your cities, your land, and your mountains; all your woods and your fruitful trees will they burn up with fire.
63: Your children will they carry away captive, and, look, what you have, they will spoil it, and mar the beauty of your face.

4 Ezra Chapter 16
1: Woe be to you, Babylon and Asia! Woe be to you, Egypt and Syria!
2: Gird up yourselves with cloths of sack and hair, bewail your children, and be sorry; for your destruction is at hand.
3: A sword is sent upon you, and who may turn it back?
4: A fire is sent among you, and who may quench it?
5: Plagues are sent to you, and what is he that may drive them away?
6: May any man drive away an hungry lion in the wood? Or may any one quench the fire in stubble when it has begun to burn?
7: May one turn again the arrow that is shot of a strong archer?
8: The mighty Lord sends the plagues and who is he that can drive them away?
9: A fire will go forth from his rage and who is he that may quench it?
10: He will cast lightning, and who will not fear? He will thunder and who will not be afraid?
11: The Lord will threaten, and who will not be utterly beaten to powder at his presence?
12: The earthquakes, and the foundations thereof; the sea rises up with waves from the deep, and the waves of it are troubled, and the fishes thereof also, before the Lord, and before the glory of his power:
13: For strong is his right hand that bends the bow, his arrows that he shoots are sharp and will not miss when they are shot into the ends of the world.
14: Behold, the plagues are sent, and will not return again, until they come upon the earth.
15: The fire is kindled, and will not be put out, till it consume the foundation of the earth.

16: Like as an arrow which is shot of a mighty archer returns not backward: even so the plagues that will be sent upon earth will not return again.
17: Woe is me! woe is me! Who will deliver me in those days?
18: The beginning of sorrows and great mourning; the beginning of famine and great death; the beginning of wars, and the powers will stand in fear; the beginning of evils! What will I do when these evils will come?
19: Behold, famine and plague, tribulation and anguish, are sent as scourges for amendment.
20: But for all these things they will not turn from their wickedness, nor be always mindful of the scourges.
21: Behold, victuals will be so good and cheap upon earth, that they will think themselves to be in good case, and even then will evils grow upon earth, sword, famine, and great confusion.
22: For many of them that dwell upon earth will perish of famine; and the other, that escape the hunger, will the sword destroy.
23: And the dead will be cast out as dung, and there will be no man to comfort them: for the earth will be wasted, and the cities will be cast down.
24: There will be no man left to till the earth, and to sow it
25: The trees will give fruit, and who will gather them?
26: The grapes will ripen, and who will tread them? For all places will be desolate of men;
27: So that one man will desire to see another, and to hear his voice.
28: For of a city there will be ten left, and two of the field, which will hide themselves in the thick groves, and in the clefts of the rocks.
29: As in an orchard of olives upon every tree there are left three or four olives;
30: Or as when a vineyard is gathered, there are left some clusters of them that diligently seek through the vineyard.
31: Even so in those days there will be three or four left by them that search their houses with the sword.
32: And the earth will be laid waste, and the fields thereof will wax old, and her ways and all her paths will grow full of thorns, because no man will travel through it.
33: The virgins will mourn, having no bridegrooms; the women will mourn, having no husbands; their daughters will mourn, having no helpers.
34: In the wars will their bridegrooms be destroyed and their husbands will perish of famine.
35: Hear now these things and understand them, you servants of the Lord.
36: Behold, the word of the Lord, receive it and believe not the gods of whom the Lord spoke.
37: Behold, the plagues draw near, and are not slack.
38: As when a woman with child in the ninth month brings forth her son, with two or three hours of her birth great pains compass her womb, which pains, when the child cometh forth, they slack not a moment.
39: Even so will not the plagues be slack to come upon the earth, and the world will mourn, and sorrows will come upon it on every side.
40: O my people, hear my word and make you ready to your battle, and in those evils be even as pilgrims upon the earth.
41: He that sells, let him be as he that runs away and he that buys, as one that will lose.

42: He that occupies merchandise, as he that has no profit by it, and he that builds, as he that will not dwell therein.
43: He that sows, as if he should not reap so also he that plants the vineyard, as he that will not gather the grapes.
44: They that marry, as they that will get no children; and they that marry not, as the widowers.
45: And therefore they that labor do so in vain;
46: For strangers will reap their fruits, and spoil their goods, overthrow their houses, and take their children captives, for in captivity and famine will they get children.
47: And they that occupy their merchandise with robbery, the more they deck their cities, their houses, their possessions, and their own persons;
48: The more will I be angry with them for their sin, says the Lord.
49: Like as a whore envies a right honest and virtuous woman;
50: So will righteousness hate iniquity, when she covers herself, and will accuse her to her face, when he cometh that will defend him that diligently searches out every sin upon earth.
51: And therefore be you not like thereto, nor to the works thereof.
52: For yet a little, and iniquity will be taken away out of the earth, and righteousness will reign among you.
53: Let not the sinner say that he has not sinned, for God will burn coals of fire upon his head, which says before the Lord God and his glory, I have not sinned.
54: Behold, the Lord knows all the works of men, their imaginations, their thoughts, and their hearts;
55: Which spoke but the word, Let the earth be made and it was made; Let the heaven be made and it was created.
56: In his word were the stars made, and he knows the number of them.
57: He searches the deep, and the treasures thereof; he has measured the sea, and what it contains.
58: He has shut the sea in the midst of the waters, and with his word has he hanged the earth upon the waters.
59: He spreads out the heavens like a vault; upon the waters has he founded it.
60: In the desert has he made springs of water, and pools upon the tops of the mountains, that the floods might pour down from the high rocks to water the earth.
61: He made man, and put his heart in the midst of the body, and gave him breath, life, and understanding.
62: Yea and the Spirit of Almighty God, which made all things, and searches out all hidden things in the secrets of the earth,
63: Surely he knows your inventions, and what you think in your hearts, even them that sin, and would hide their sin.
64: Therefore has the Lord exactly searched out all your works, and he will put you all to shame.
65: And when your sins are brought forth, you will be ashamed before men, and your own sins will be your accusers in that day.
66: What will you do? Or how will you hide your sins before God and his angels?
67: Behold, God himself is the judge, fear him. Leave off from your sins, and forget your iniquities, to meddle no more with them for ever; so will God lead you forth, and deliver you from all trouble.
68: For, behold, the burning rage of a great multitude is kindled over you, and they will take away certain of you, and feed you, being idle, with things offered to idols.

69: And they that consent to them will be had in derision and in reproach, and trodden under foot.
70: For there will be in every place, and in the next cities, a great insurrection upon those that fear the Lord.
71: They will be like mad men, sparing none, but still spoiling and destroying those that fear the Lord.
72: For they will waste and take away their goods, and cast them out of their houses.
73: Then will they be known, who are my chosen; and they will be tried as the gold in the fire.
74: Hear, O you my beloved, says the Lord, behold, the days of trouble are at hand, but I will deliver you from the same.
75: Be you not afraid neither doubt; for God is your guide,
76: And the guide of them who keep my commandments and precepts, says the Lord God. Let not your sins weigh you down, and let not your iniquities lift up themselves.
77: Woe be to them that are bound with their sins, and covered with their iniquities like as a field is covered over with bushes, and the path thereof covered with thorns, that no man may travel through!
78: It is left undressed, and is cast into the fire to be consumed therewith.

2 Baruch - History

2 Baruch is also known as the Syriac Apocalypse of Baruch. It is part of the Jewish pseudepigraphical. It is a text written in the late first to early second century, after the fall of Jerusalem to the Romans in 70 AD.

It is not part of the canon of either the Jewish or "Western" Christian Bibles but is part of the Syriac Bible. Syriac Christianity is a distinctive and separate family. It is propagated in part by the Syriac language and culture as part of Near Eastern Christianity. The Aramaic origins borrowed much from early Judaism and Mesopotamian culture. As Christianity grew and was defined more with the Greek and Latin cultures and tongues, Syriac Christianity was persecuted.

2 Baruch is similar to Jeremiah. The lamentations and anguish seen within the text are attributed to a reaction to the fall of Jerusalem, and particularly the Temple in Jerusalem. According to the text, the Temple's sacred objects were rescued from destruction by angels, and await the temple's rebuilding.

The catastrophe of the Temple destruction caused the Jews to question their faith and their place in God's divine plan. The plundering and desecration of the temple by gentiles was tantamount to God's rejection of the Jews and called into question the very foundations of their faith.

If a religion holds that God's hand is in all things then one must resolves the question of why an omnipotent God allowed the destruction of his own temple, or the temple belonging to His people.

2 Baruch attempts to answer this question as it promises a Messiah (Anointed One) who will end the sinful ways and dominance of the heathens and re-establish the Jews as God's chosen people. Those who are truly called will be the righteous Jews who follow the Torah and its teachings.

The text presented below is a modern rendition based in part on R. H. Charles' work done in the early 1900's. Chapter and verse divisions have been redefined to provide more logical separations. Modern wording has replaced the more archaic phrasing in the text. The result was then compared to other authoritative works and the translation modified to provide the most accurate version possible.

2 Baruch

Chapter 1
1 And it happened in the twenty-fifth year of Jeconiah, king of Judah, that the word of the Lord came to Baruch, the son of Neriah, and said to him:
2 Have you seen all that this nation (people) are doing to Me, that the evils which these two tribes which remained have done are greater than (those of) the ten tribes which were carried away captive?
3 For the former tribes were forced by their kings to commit sin, but these two of themselves have been forcing and compelling their kings to commit sin.
4 For this reason, I bring evil upon this city, and upon its inhabitants, and it will be removed from before Me for a time, and I will scatter these people among the Gentiles that they may do good to the Gentiles. And My people will be chastened, and the time will come when they will seek the prosperity of this period (their times.)

Chapter 2
1 For I have said these things to you that you may tell Jeremiah, and all those that are like you, to leave this city.
2 For your works are to this city as a firm pillar, and your prayers as a strong wall.

Chapter 3
1 And I said: O Lord, my Lord, have I come into the world for this purpose that I might see the evils of my mother?
2 Not so, my Lord. If I have found grace in Your sight, first take my spirit that I may go to my father's and not witness the destruction of my mother.
3 For two things vehemently constrain me: for I cannot resist You, and my soul cannot behold the evils of my mother.
4 But one thing I will ask in Your presence, O Lord.
5 What will there be after these things? If You destroy Your city and deliver up Your land to those that hate us, how will the name of Israel be remembered?
6 Or how will one speak of Your praises?
7 Or to whom will Your law be explained and all things therein?
8 Or will the world return to the nature it had before, and the age revert to primeval silence?
9 And will the multitude of souls be taken away, and the nature of man not again be named? And where is all that which You said to Moses regarding us?

Chapter 4
1 And the Lord said to me: This city will be delivered up for a time, and the people will be chastened during a time, And the world will not be given over to oblivion.
2 Do you think that this is that city of which I said: On the palms of My hands have I graven you?
3 This building now built in your midst is not that which is revealed with Me, that which was prepared beforehand here from the time when I took counsel to make Paradise, and showed it to Adam before he sinned, but when he transgressed the commandment it was removed from him, as also Paradise.

4 And after these things I showed it to My servant Abraham by night among the allotted victims.
5 And again also I showed it to Moses on Mount Sinai when I showed him the likeness of the tabernacle and all its vessels.
6 And now, behold, it is preserved with Me, as also is Paradise.
7 Go, therefore, and do as I command you."

Chapter 5
1 And I answered and said: So then I am destined to grieve for Zion, For your enemies will come to this place and pollute your sanctuary, and lead your inheritance into captivity; And make themselves masters of those whom You have loved. They will depart again to the place of their idols, and will boast before them: And what will You do for Your great name?
2 And the Lord said to me: My name and My glory are to all eternity; And My judgment will maintain its right in its own time.
3 You will see with your eyes that the enemy will not overthrow Zion, nor will they burn Jerusalem, but be the ministers of the Judge for the time.
4 Now go and do what I have said to you.
5 And I went and took Jeremiah, and Adu, and Seriah, and Jabish, and Gedaliah, and all the honorable men of the people, and I led them to the valley of Cedron, and I explained to them all that had been said to me.
7 And they lifted up their voices, and they all wept.
8 And we sat there and fasted until the evening.

Chapter 6
1 And it came to pass the next day that the army of the Chaldees surrounded the city, and at the time of the evening, I, Baruch, left the people and I went out and stood by the oak.
2 And I was grieving over Zion, and lamenting over the captivity which had come upon the people.
3 Suddenly a strong spirit raised me, and carried me aloft over the wall of Jerusalem.
4 And I saw four angels standing at the four corners of the city, each of them holding a torch of fire in his hands.
5 And another angel began to descend from heaven, and said to them: Hold your lamps, and do not light them till I tell you.
6 For I am first sent to speak a word to the earth, and to place in it what the Lord the Most High has commanded me.
7 And I saw him descend into the Holy of holies, and take from there the veil, and the holy ark, and the mercy-seat, and the two tables, and the holy raiment of the priests, and the altar of incense, and the forty-eight precious stones, wherewith the priest was adorned and all the holy vessels of the tabernacle.
8 And he spoke to the earth with a loud voice: Earth, earth, earth, hear the word of the mighty God, And receive what I commit to you, And guard them until the last times so that when you are ordered you may restore them, so that strangers may not get possession of them.
9 For the time comes when Jerusalem also will be delivered for a time, until it is said, that it is again restored for ever.
10 And the earth opened its mouth and swallowed them up.

Chapter 7

1 And after these things I heard that angel saying to those angels who held the lamps. Destroy it and overthrow its wall to its foundations so that the enemy should not boast and say: We have overthrown the wall of Zion, and we have burnt the place of the mighty God.
2 And you have seized the place where I had been standing before.

Chapter 8

1 Now the angels did as he had commanded them, and when they had broken up the corners of the walls, a voice was heard from the interior of the temple, after the wall had fallen, saying:
2 Enter, you enemies. Come, you adversaries; For he who kept the house has forsaken it.
3 And I, Baruch, departed.
4 And after these things happened the army of the Chaldees entered and seized the house and all that was around it.
5 And they led the people away captive, and killed some of them, and bound Zedekiah the King, and sent him to the King of Babylon.

Chapter 9

1 And I, Baruch, came, and Jeremiah, whose heart was found pure from sins, who had not been captured in the seizure of the city.
2 And we ripped our garments, we wept, and mourned, and fasted seven days.

Chapter 10

1 After seven days the word of God came to me, and said to me:
2 Tell Jeremiah to go and support the people who are led captive in to Babylon.
3 But you remain here amid the desolation of Zion, and I will show you after these days what will occur at the end of days.
4 And I said to Jeremiah as the Lord commanded me.
5 And he indeed, departed with the people; but I, Baruch, returned and sat before the gates of the temple, and I lamented with the following lamentation over Zion and said:
6 Blessed is he who was not born, or he, who having been born, has died.
7 But as for us who live, woe to us, Because we see the afflictions of Zion, and what has befallen Jerusalem.
8 I will call the Sirens from the sea, And you Lilin, (Lilin, in Jewish myth, was the daughter of Lilith, Adam's first wife, and the demon Samael who is often identified with Satan) come from the desert. And you Shedim and dragons from the forests: Awake and prepare yourselves for mourning; and take up with me the dirges, and make lamentation with me.
9 You husbandmen, sow not again; and, O earth, wherefore gives you your harvest fruits? Keep within you the sweets of your sustenance.
10 And you, vine, why further do you give your wine; for an offering will not again be made there from in Zion. Nor will the first-fruits again be offered.
11 And do you, O heavens, withhold your dew, and open not the treasuries of rain?

12 And do you, O sun, withhold the light of your rays? And do you, O moon, extinguish the multitude of your light? For why should light rise again where the light of Zion is darkened?
13 And you, you bridegrooms, enter not in. And let not the brides adorn themselves with garlands. And you women, pray not that you may bear.
14 For the barren will above all rejoice, And those who have no sons will be glad, and those who have sons will have anguish.
15 For why should they bear in pain, only to bury in grief?
16 Why again should mankind have sons? Why should the offspring of their kind again be named; where this mother is desolate, and her sons are led into captivity?
17 From this time forward speak not of beauty, and do not discuss gracefulness.
18 Moreover, you priests, take you the keys of the sanctuary and cast them into the height of heaven; and give them to the Lord and say: Guard Your house Yourself. For we are found to be false stewards.
19 And you virgins who weave fine linen and silk with gold of Ophir (the place from where the fleets of Solomon brought gold), take with haste all (these) things and cast (them) into the fire, that it may carry them to Him who made them. And the flame send them to Him who created them, lest the enemy get possession of them.

Chapter 11
1 Moreover, I, Baruch, say this against you, Babylon: If you had prospered, and Zion had dwelt in her glory, the grief to us would have been great because you would be equal to Zion.
2 But now, the grief is infinite; and the lamentation measureless because you are prospered and Zion desolate.
3 Who will be judge regarding these things? Or to whom will we complain regarding that which has befallen us? O Lord, how have You borne (it)?
4 Our fathers went to rest without grief and the righteous sleep in the earth in tranquility.
5 For they knew not this anguish, nor yet had they heard of that which had befallen us.
6 Would that you had ears, O earth, and that you had a heart, O dust. That you might go and announce in Sheol (hell / place of the dead) and say to the dead: Blessed are you more than we who live.

Chapter 12
1 But I will say what I think and I will speak against you, O land, which are prospering.
2 The noonday does not always burn, nor do the rays of the sun constantly give light.
3 Do not expect [and hope] that you will always be prosperous and rejoicing. Do not be not greatly arrogant and boastful.
4 For certainly in its own season the divine rage will awake against you, even though now in long-suffering it is held in as it were by reins.
5 And when I had said these things, I fasted seven days.

Chapter 13
1 After these things I, Baruch, was standing upon Mount Zion, and a voice came from the height and said to me:

2 Stand up on your feet, Baruch, and hear the word of the mighty God.
3 Because you have been amazed at what has befallen Zion, you will therefore be certainly preserved to the conclusion of the times, that you may be for a testimony.
4 If ever those prosperous cities say: Why has the mighty God brought upon us this retribution?
5 You say to them: You and those like you who will have seen this evil; (This is the evil) and retribution which is coming upon you and upon your people in its (destined) time that the nations may be thoroughly beaten (smitten.)
6 And then they will be in anguish.
7 And if they say at that time: For how long? You will say to them: You who have drunk the strained wine, drink also of its dregs, the judgment of the Lofty One Who has no respect of persons.
8 On this account before he had no mercy on His own sons, but afflicted them as His enemies, because they sinned, then they were disciplined so that they might be sanctified.
9 But now, you peoples and nations, you are guilty because you have always trodden down the earth, and used the creation sinfully and wrongfully.
10 For I have always benefited you and you have always been ungrateful for the beneficence.

Chapter 14
1 And I answered and said: You have shown me the method (behavior / procedure) of the times, and that which will alter these things, and You have said to me that the retribution, which has been spoken of by You, will come upon the nations.
2 And now I know that those who have sinned are many, and they have lived in prosperity, and left the world, but few nations will be left in those times, to whom those words will be said which You have said.
3 For what advantage is there in this, or what evil, worse than what we have seen happen us can we expect to see?
4 But again I will speak in Your presence: What have they profited who had knowledge before You and have not walked in vanity as the rest of the nations, and have not said to the dead: "Give us life," but always feared You, and have not left Your ways?
5 They have been carried off, nor on their account have You had mercy on Zion.
6 And if others did evil, it was due to Zion, that on account of those who do good works should be forgiven, and should not be overwhelmed on account of the works of those who practice unrighteousness.
7 But who, O Lord, my Lord, will understand Your judgment, or who will search out the profoundness of Your way?
8 Or who will think out the weight of Your path?
9 Or who will be able to think out Your incomprehensible counsel?
10 Or who of those that are born has ever found the beginning or end of Your wisdom?
11 For we have all been made like a breath. For as the breath ascends involuntarily and again dies, so it is with the nature of men, who depart not according to their own will, and know not what will befall them in the end.
12 For the righteous justly hope for the end, and without fear leave this habitation, because they have with You a store of works preserved in treasuries.

13 On this account also these without fear leave this world, and trusting with joy they hope to receive the world which You have promised them.
14 But as for us --- woe to us, who also are now shamefully treated, and at that time look forward (only) to evil.
15 But You know accurately what You have done by means of Your servants; for we are not able to understand that which is good as You are, our Creator.
16 But again I will speak in Your presence, O LORD, my Lord.
17 In ancient times there was no world with its inhabitants, You did devise and speak with a word, and with that the works of creation stood before You.
18 And You did say that You would make man the administrator of Your works, that it might be known that he was by no means made on account of the world, but the world on account of him.
19 And now I see that as the world was made on account of us, and it abides, but we, on account of whom it was made, depart.

Chapter 15
1 And the Lord answered and said to me: You are rightly amazed regarding the departure of man, but you have not judged well regarding the evils which befall those who sin.
2 And as regards what you have said, that the righteous are carried off and the impious are prospered.
3 And as regards what you have said, "Man knows not Your judgment," on this account hear, and I will speak to you, and listen, and I will cause you to hear My words.
4 Man would not rightly have understood My judgment, unless he had accepted the law, and I had instructed him in understanding.
5 But now, because he transgressed knowingly on this ground that he worked, he will be tormented.
6 And as regards what you did say regarding the righteous, that on account of them has this world come, so also again will that which is to come, come on their account.
7 For this world is to them a strife and a labor with much trouble; and that accordingly which is to come, a crown with great glory.

Chapter 16
1 And I answered and said: O LORD, my Lord, the years of this time are few and evil, and who is able in his little time to acquire that which is measureless?

Chapter 17
1 And the Lord answered and said to me: With the Most High account is not taken of much time nor of a few years.
2 For what did it profit Adam that he lived nine hundred and thirty years, and transgressed that which he was commanded?
3 Therefore the multitude of time that he lived did not profit him, but brought death and cut off the years of those who were born from him.
4 Or wherein did Moses suffer loss in that he lived only one hundred and twenty years, and inasmuch as he was subject to Him who formed him, brought the law to the seed of Jacob, and lighted a lamp for the nation of Israel?

Chapter 18

1 And I answered and said: He that lighted has taken from the light, and there are but few that have imitated him.
2 But those many whom he has lighted have taken from the darkness of Adam and have not rejoiced in the light of the lamp.

Chapter 19
1 And He answered and said to me: So it was at that time he appointed for them a covenant. And He said to them: Behold I have placed before you life and death, and he called heaven and earth to witness against them.
2 For he knew that his time was but short, but that heaven and earth endure always.
3 But after his death they sinned and transgressed, though they knew that they had the law reproving them, and the light in which nothing could err, also the spheres (planets and stars?) which testify, and Me.
4 Now regarding everything that is, it is I that judge, but do not you take counsel in your soul regarding these things, nor afflict yourself because of those which have been.
5 For now it is the consummation of time that should be considered, whether of business, or of prosperity, or of shame, and not the beginning thereof.
6 Because if a man be prospered in his beginnings and shamefully treated in his old age, he forgets all the prosperity that he had.
7 And again, if a man is shamefully treated in his beginnings, and at his end is prospered, he remembers not again his evil treatment.
8 And again listen; though each one were prospered all that time all the time from the day on which death was decreed against those who transgress, and in his end was destroyed, everything would have been in vain.

Chapter 20
1 Therefore, behold! The days come, and the times will hasten more than the former, and the seasons will speed on more than those that are past, and the years will pass more quickly than the present (years).
2 Therefore have I now taken away Zion, that I may the more speedily visit the world in its season.
3 Therefore hold fast in your heart everything that I command you, and seal it in the recesses of your mind.
4 And then I will show you the judgment of My might, and My ways which cannot be known.
5 Go and sanctify yourself seven days, and eat no bread, nor drink water, nor speak to anyone.
6 Afterwards come to that place and I will reveal Myself to you, and speak true things with you, and I will give you commandment regarding the method (procedure / system) of the times; for they are coming and tarry not.

Chapter 21
1 And I went thence and sat in the valley of Cedron in a cave of the earth, and I sanctified my soul there, and I ate no bread, yet I was not hungry, and I drank no water, yet I thirsted not, and I was there till the seventh day, as He had commanded me.
2 And afterwards I came to that place where He had spoken with me.

3 And it came to pass at sunset that my soul (mind) took much thought, and I began to speak in the presence of the Mighty One, and said:
4 O You that made the earth, hear me; you that have fixed the firmament by the word, and have made firm the height of the heaven by the spirit, that have called from the beginning of the world that which did not yet exist, and they obey You.
5 You that have commanded the air by Your nod, and have seen those things which are to be as those things which You are (now) doing.
6 You that rule with great thought the hosts that stand before You; also the countless holy beings which You made from the beginning from the flame and fire, which stand around Your throne where You rule with indignation.
7 To You only does this belong that You should do whatsoever You wish.
8 Who causes the drops of rain to rain by number upon the earth, and alone know the conclusion of the times before they come; have respect to my prayer.
9 For You alone are able to sustain all who are, and those who have passed away, and those who are to be, those who sin, and those who are righteous as living and being past finding out.
10 For You alone live immortal and past finding out, and know the number of mankind.
11 And if in time many have sinned, yet others not a few have been righteous.
12 You know where You preserve the end of those who have sinned, or the conclusion of those who have been righteous.
13 For if there were this life only, which belongs to all men, nothing could be more bitter than this.
14 For of what profit is strength that turns to sickness, or fullness of food that turns to famine, or beauty that turns to ugliness?
15 For the nature of man is always changeable.
16 For what we were formerly now we no longer are, and what we now are we will not afterwards continue to be.
17 For if a conclusion had not been prepared for all, then their beginning would have been in vain.
18 Everything that comes from You, You informed me, and regarding everything about which I ask You, You enlighten me?
19 How long will that which is corruptible remain, and how long will the time of mortals succeed, and until what time will those who transgress in the world be polluted with much wickedness?
20 Command in mercy and accomplish all that You said You would bring, that Your might may be made known to those who think that Your long-suffering is weakness.
21 Show to those who do not recognize it, that everything that has befallen us and our city until now has been according to the long-suffering of Your power, because on account of Your name You have called us a beloved people.
22 Bring mortality to an end. Reprimand the angel of death, and let Your glory appear, and let the might of Your beauty be known, and let Sheol be sealed so that from this time forward it may not receive the dead, and let the treasuries of souls (the chamber of Guf, in Jewish mythology) restore those which are enclosed in them.
23 For there have been many years like those that are desolate from the days of Abraham and Isaac and Jacob, and of all those who are like them, who sleep in the earth, on whose account You did say that You had created the world.
24 And now quickly show Your glory, and do not put off what has been promised by You. When I had completed this prayer I was greatly weakened.

Chapter 22
1 After these things the heavens were opened, and I saw, and power was given to me, and a voice was heard from on high, and it said to me:
2 Baruch, Baruch, why are you troubled?
3 He who travels by a road but does not complete it, or who departs by sea but does not arrive at the port, can he be comforted?
4 Or he who promises to give a present to another, but does not fulfill it, is it not robbery?
5 Or he who sows the earth, but does not reap its fruit in its season, does he not lose everything?
6 Or he who plants a plant unless it grows till the time suitable to it, does he who planted it expect to receive fruit from it?
7 Or a woman who has conceived, if she bring forth untimely, does she not certainly kill her infant?
8 Or he who builds a house, if he does not roof it and complete it, can it be called a house? Tell Me that first.

Chapter 23
1, And I answered and said: "Not so, O LORD, my Lord."
2 And He answered and said to me: Why are you troubled about that which you know not, and why are you ill at ease about things of which you are ignorant?
3 You have not forgotten the people who now are and those who have passed away, so I remember those who are appointed to come.
4 Because when Adam sinned and death was the judgment against those who should be born, then the multitude of those who should be born was numbered, and for that number a place was prepared where the living might dwell and the dead might be guarded.
5 Before the appointed number is fulfilled, the creature will not live again for My spirit is the creator of life, and Sheol will receive the dead.
6 It is given to you to hear what things are to come after these times.
7 For truly My redemption has drawn near, and is not as distant as it was.

Chapter 24
1 The days come and the books will be opened in which are written the sins of all those who have sinned, and also the treasuries in which the righteousness of all those who have been righteous in creation is gathered.
2 For it will come to pass at that time that you will see, and the many that are with you, the long-suffering of the Most High, which has been throughout all generations, who has been long-suffering towards all who are born, like those who sin and those who are righteous."
3 And I answered and said: But Lord, no one knows the number of those things which have passed nor yet of those things which are to come.
4 For I know indeed that which has befallen us, but what will happen to our enemies I know not, and when You will visit Your works.

Chapter 25
1 And He answered and said to me: You too will be preserved till that time till that sign which the Most High will work for the inhabitants of the earth in the end of days.
2 This therefore will be the sign:
3 When a stupor will seize the inhabitants of the earth, and they will fall into many tribulations, and again when they will fall into great torments.
4 And it will come to pass when they say in their thoughts because of their much tribulation: The Mighty One doth no longer remember the earth yea, it will come to pass when they abandon hope, that the time will then awake.

Chapter 26
1 And I answered and said: Will that tribulation which is to be, continue a long time, and will it necessitate many years?

Chapter 27
1 And He answered and said to me: Into twelve parts (pieces or section) is that time divided, and each one of them is reserved for that which is appointed for it.
2 In the first section (piece) there will be the beginning of commotions.
3 And in the second section (piece) slayings of the great ones.
4 And in the third section (piece) the fall of many by death.
5 And in the fourth section (piece) the sending of the sword.
6 And in the fifth section (piece) famine and the withholding of rain.
7 And in the sixth section (piece) earthquakes and terrors and wanting (need for food, water, and shelter).
8 And in the eighth section (piece) a multitude of specters and attacks of the Shedim.
9 And in the ninth section (piece) the fall of fire.
10 And in the tenth section (piece) rapine and much oppression.
11 And in the eleventh section (piece) wickedness and hedonism.
12 And in the twelfth section (piece) confusion from the mingling together of all those things aforesaid.
13 For these slices of that time are reserved, and will be mingled one with another and reinforce one another.
14 For some will leave out some of their own, and receive (in its stead) from others, and some complete their own and that of others, so that those may not understand who are upon the earth in those days that this is the consummation of the times.

Chapter 28
1 Nevertheless, whosoever understands will then be wise.
2 For the measure and reckoning of that time are two parts (pieces or section) a week of seven weeks.
3 And I answered and said: It is good for a man to come and behold, but it is better that he should not come lest he fall.
4 But I will ask this also: Will he who is incorruptible despise those things which are corruptible? What happens in the case of those things which are corruptible, so that he might look only to those things which are not corruptible?
5 But if, O Lord, those things will certainly come to pass which You have foretold to me, show this to me also if indeed I have found grace in Your sight.

6 Is it in one place or in one of the sections of the earth that those things are come to pass, or will the whole earth experience them?

Chapter 29
1 And He answered and said to me: Whatever will befall the whole earth all who live will experience.
2 For at that time I will protect only those who are found in those same days in this land.
3 And when all is accomplished that was to come to pass in those sections, that the Messiah will then begin to be revealed.
4 And Behemoth will be revealed from his place and Leviathan will ascend from the sea, those two great monsters which I created on the fifth day of creation, and will have kept until that time; and then they will be food for all that are left.
5 The earth also will yield its fruit ten thousand fold and on each vine there will be a thousand branches, and each branch will produce a thousand clusters, and each cluster produces a thousand grapes, and each grape produces a cor (a unit of measure approximately 517 pints) of wine.
6 And those who have hungered will rejoice, moreover, they will behold marvels every day.
7 For winds will go forth from before Me to bring every morning the fragrance of aromatic fruits, and at the close of the day clouds distilling the dew of health.
8 And it will come to pass at that same time that the treasury of manna will again descend from on high, and they will eat of it in those years, because these are they who have come to the end of time.

Chapter 30
1 And it will come to pass after these things, when the time of the advent of the Messiah is fulfilled, that He will return in glory.
2 Then all who have fallen asleep in hope of Him will rise again.
3 And it will come to pass at that time that the treasuries will be opened in which is preserved the number of the souls of the righteous, and they will come forth, and a multitude of souls will be seen together in one assemblage of one thought, and the first will rejoice and the last will not be grieved. For they know that the time has come of which it is said, that it is the consummation of the times.
4 But the souls of the wicked, when they behold all these things, will then waste away the more.
5 For they will know that their torment has come and their perdition has arrived."

Chapter 31
1 And after these things I went to the people and said to them:
2 Assemble to me all your elders and I will speak words to them.
3 And they all assembled in the valley of the Cedron. And I answered and said to them: Hear, O Israel, and I will speak to you, And give ear, O seed of Jacob, and I will instruct you.
4 Forget not Zion, But hold in remembrance the anguish of Jerusalem.
5 For the days come, when everything exists will become the prey of corruption and will be as though it had not been.

Chapter 32

1 But if you prepare your hearts, so as to sow in them the fruits of the law, it will protect you in that time in which the Mighty One is to shake the whole creation.
2 Because after a little time the building of Zion will be shaken in order that it may be built again.
3 But that building will not remain, but will again after a time be pulled up by the roots, and will remain desolate until the time.
4 And afterwards it must be renewed in glory, and perfected for evermore.
5 Therefore we should not be distressed so much over the evil which has now come as over that which is still to be.
6 For there will be a greater trial than these two tribulations when the Mighty One will renew His creation.
7 And now do not draw near to me for a few days, nor seek me till I come to you.
8 And when I had spoken to them all these words, that I, Baruch, went my way, and when the people saw me leaving, they lifted up their voice and lamented and said: To what place do you depart from us, Baruch, and forsake us as a father who forsakes his orphan children, and departs from them?

Chapter 33
1 Are these the commands which your companion, Jeremiah the prophet, commanded you, and said to you:
2 Look to this people till I go and make ready the rest of the brethren in Babylon, against whom has gone forth the sentence that they should be led into captivity?
3 And now if you also forsake us, it were good for us all to die before you withdraw from us.

Chapter 34
1 And I answered and said to the people: Far be it from me to forsake you or to withdraw from you, but I will only go to the Holy of Holies to inquire of the Mighty One concerning you and concerning Zion; in the hopes I should receive more illumination and after these things I will return to you.

Chapter 35
1 And I, Baruch, went to the holy place, and sat down upon the ruins and wept, and said:
2 O that mine eyes were springs, and mine eyelids a spring of tears.
3 For how will I lament for Zion, and how will I mourn for Jerusalem?
4 Because in that place where I am now prostrate, of old the high priest offered holy sacrifices; and placed thereon an incense of fragrant odors.
5 But now our glorying has been made into dust, And the desire of our soul into sand.

Chapter 36
1 And when I had said these things I fell asleep there, and I saw a vision in the night.
2 I saw a forest of trees planted on the plain, and lofty and rugged rocky mountains surrounded it, and that forest occupied much space.

3 And over beside it arose a vine, and from under it there went forth a peaceful fountain.
4 Now that fountain came to the forest and was agitated into great waves, and those waves submerged that forest, and suddenly they pulled up by the roots the greater section (area) of that forest, and overthrew all the mountains which were around it.
5 And the height of the forest began to be made low, and the top of the mountains was made low and that fountain greatly overtook it, so that it left nothing of that great forest save one cedar only.
6 Also when it had cast it down and had destroyed and pulled up by the roots the greater part of that forest, so that nothing was left of it, nor could its place be recognized, then that vine began to come with the fountain in peace and great tranquility, and it came to a place which was not far from that cedar, and they brought the cedar which had been cast down to it.
7 And I saw that vine opened its mouth and spoke and said to that cedar: Are you not that cedar which was left of the forest of wickedness, and by whose means wickedness persisted, and did evil all those years, and goodness never?
8 And you kept conquering that which was not yours, and to that which was yours you never showed compassion, and you kept extending your power over those who were far from you, and those who ventured near to you held tightly in the toils of your wickedness, and you lifted yourself up always as one that could not be pulled up by the roots!
9 But now your time has sped by and your hour is come. Do you also therefore depart O cedar, after the forest, which departed before you, and become dust with it, and let your ashes be mingled together?
10 And now lay down in anguish and rest in torment till your last time comes, in which you will come again and be tormented still more.

Chapter 37
1 And after these things I saw that cedar burning, and the vine glowing and all around it the plain was full of unfading flowers. And I awoke and arose.

Chapter 38
1 And I prayed and said: O LORD, my Lord, You always enlighten those who are led by understanding.
2 Your law is life, and Your wisdom is right guidance.
3 Make known to me the interpretation of this vision.
4 For You know that my soul has always walked in Your law, and from my earliest days I departed not from Your wisdom.

Chapter 39
1 And He answered and said to me: Baruch, this is the interpretation of the vision which you have seen.
2 As you have seen the great forest which lofty and rugged mountains surrounded, this is the word.
3 The days come, and this kingdom will be destroyed which once destroyed Zion, and it will be subjected to that which comes after it.
4 After a time the kingdom will be destroyed, and another, a third, will arise, and that also will have dominion for its time, and will be destroyed.

5 And after these things a fourth kingdom will arise, whose power will be harsh and evil far beyond those which were before it, and it will rule many times as the forests on the plain, and it will hold firmly for a time, and will exalt itself more than the cedars of Lebanon.
6 And by it the truth will be hidden, and all those who are polluted with sinfulness will flee to it, as evil beasts flee and creep into the forest.
7 And when the time of its end and fall has approached, then the kingdom of My Messiah will be revealed, which is like the fountain and the vine, and when it is revealed it will root out the multitude of its host.
8 And concerning that which you have seen, the lofty cedar, which was left out of that forest, and the fact, that the vine spoke those words with it which you did hear, this is the word.

Chapter 40
1 The last leader of that time will be left alive, when the multitude of his hosts will be put to the sword, and he will be bound, and they will take him up to Mount Zion, and My Messiah will convict him of all his unlawful deeds, and will gather and set before him all the works of his hosts.
2 And afterwards he will put him to death, and protect the rest of My people which will be found in the place which I have chosen.
3 And his kingdom will stand for ever, until the world of corruption is at an end, and until the times aforesaid are fulfilled.
4 This is your vision, and this is its interpretation.

Chapter 41
1 And I answered and said: For whom and for how many will these things be or who will be worthy to live at that time?
2 I will speak to you everything that I think, and I will ask of You regarding those things about which I think.
3 I see many of Your people who have with drawn from Your covenant, and cast from them the yoke of Your law.
4 But I have seen others who have forsaken their vanity, and fled for refuge beneath Your wings.
5 What will become of them or how will the last time receive them?
6 Or perhaps the time of these will certainly be weighed, and as the beam inclines will they be judged accordingly?

Chapter 42
1 And He answered and said to me: "I will show you these things also.
2 To whom will these things be, and how many will they be?"
3 To those who have believed there will be the good which was spoken of before, and to those who despise there will be the contrary.
4 And regarding those who have drawn near (to Me) and those who have withdrawn (from Me) this is the word. As for those who were before subject (to Me), and afterwards withdrew and mingled themselves with the seed of mingled peoples, the time of these was the former, and was accounted as something exalted.
5 As for those who before knew (Me) not but afterwards knew life, and mingled (only) with the seed of the people which had separated itself the time of these (is) the latter, and is accounted as something exalted.

6 Time will succeed to (advance) time and season to season, and one will receive from another, and then with a view to the conclusion everything will be compared according to the measure of the times and the hours of the seasons.
7 Corruption will take those that belong to it, and life will take those that belong to it.
8 And the dust will be called, and there will be said to it: Give back that which is not yours, and raise up all that you have kept until its time.

Chapter 43
1 But, do you, Baruch, direct your heart to that which has been said to you, and understand those things which have been shown to you? For there are many eternal comforts for you.
2 You will leave this place, and you will pass from the regions which you see now, and you will forget whatever is corruptible, and will not again recall those things which happen among mortals.
3 Go and command your people, and come to this place, and afterwards fast seven days, and then I will come to you and speak with you.

Chapter 44
1 And I, Baruch, went from that place and came to my people, and I called my first-born son and the Gedaliahs my friends, and seven of the elders of the people, and I said to them:
2 I go to my fathers according to the way of all the earth.
3 But you should not withdraw from the way of the law, but guard and admonish the people which remain;
4 that they should not withdraw from the commandments of the Mighty One, for you see that He whom we serve is just, and our Creator is no respecter of persons.
5 And see what has happened to Zion, and what has happened to Jerusalem.
6 For the judgment of the Mighty One will be made known, and His ways, which, though past finding out, are right.
7 For if you endure and persevere in fear (respect / awe) of Him, and do not forget His law, the times will change over you for good. And you will see the consolation (reward) of Zion.
8 Because whatever exists now is nothing, but that which will be is very great. For everything that is corruptible will pass away, and everything that dies will depart, and all the present time will be forgotten, nor will there be any remembrance of the present time, which is defiled with evil.
9 That which runs now runs to vanity, and that which prospers will quickly fall and be humiliated.
10 That which is to come will be the object of desire, and for that which comes afterwards will we hope.
11 For it is a time that will not pass, and the hour comes which abides for ever.
12 And the new world (comes) which is blessedness and does not turn to corruption for those who depart to it, but it has no mercy on those who depart to torment, and it leads to perdition those who live in it.
13 For these are they who will inherit that time which has been spoken of, and theirs is the inheritance of the promised time.

14 These are they who have acquired for themselves treasures of wisdom, and with them are found stores of understanding, and they have not withdrawn from mercy and the truth of the law have they preserved.
15 For to them will be given the world to come, but the dwelling of the rest, who are many, will be in the fire."

Chapter 45
1 Instruct the people as far as you are able, for that labor is ours. For if you teach them, you will quicken them.

Chapter 46
1 And my son and the elders of the people answered and said to me: Has the Mighty One humiliated us to such a degree as to take you from us quickly?
2 We will truly be in darkness, and there will be no light to the people who are left For where again will we seek the law, or who will distinguish for us between death and life?
3 And I said to them: I cannot resist the throne of the Mighty One; nevertheless, there will not be wanting in Israel for a wise man, nor a son of the law to the race of Jacob.
4 But only prepare your hearts, that you may obey the law, and be subject to those who in fear are wise and understanding;
5 And prepare your souls that you may not leave them.
6 For if you do these things, good things will come to you., which I before told you of; nor will you fall into the torment, of which I testified to you before.
7 But with regard to the word that I was to be taken I did not make it known to them or to my son.

Chapter 47
1 And when I had gone out and dismissed them, I went from there and said to them:
2 I go to Hebron: for that is where the Mighty One has sent me. And I came to that place where the word had been spoken to me, and I sat there, and fasted seven days.

Chapter 48
1 And it came to pass after the seventh day, that I prayed before the Mighty One and said, O my Lord, You summon the advent of the times and they stand before You;
2 You cause the power of the ages to pass away, and they do not resist You; You arrange the method (progress / procedures) of the seasons, and they obey You.
3 You alone know the duration of the generations, and You do not reveal Your mysteries to many.
4 You make known the multitude of the fire, and You weigh the lightness of the wind.
5 You explore the limit of the heights, and You scrutinize the depths of the darkness.
6 You care for the number which pass away that they may be preserved and You prepare an habitation (abode) for those that are to be.
7 You remember the beginning which You have made, and the destruction that is to be You do not forget.

8 With nods of fear and indignation You command the flames, and they change into spirits, and with a word You quicken that which was not, and with mighty power You hold that which has not yet come.
9 You instruct created things in the understanding of You, and You make wise the spheres (orbs / heavenly bodies) so as to minister in their orders.
10 Armies innumerable stand before You and minister in their orders quietly at Your nod.
11 Hear Your servant and give ear to my petition.
12 For in a little time are we born, and in a little time do we return.
13 But with You hours are as a time (an age / eon) , and days as generations.
14 Be not angry with man; for he is nothing and take not account of our works; for what are we?
15 For by Your gift we come into the world, and we depart not of our own will.
16 For we said not to our parents, Beget us, Nor did we send to Sheol (place of the dead) and say, Receive us.
17 What therefore is our strength that we should bear Your rage or what are we that we should endure Your judgment?
18 Protect us in Your compassions, and in Your mercy help us.
19 Behold the little ones that are subject to You, and save all that draw near to You: Do not destroy the hope of our people, and do not cut short the times (occurrences) of our aid.
20 For this is the nation which You have chosen, and these are the people, to whom You find no equal.
21 But I will speak now before You, and I will say as my heart thinks.
22 In You do we trust, for Your law is with us and we know that we will not fall so long as we keep Your statutes.
23 To all time are we blessed at all events in this that we have not mingled with the Gentiles.
24 For we are all one celebrated people, who have received one law from One:
25 And the law which is among us will aid us, and the surpassing wisdom which is in us will help us.
26 And when I had prayed and said these things, I was greatly weakened. And He answered and said to me: You have prayed simply, O Baruch, and all your words have been heard.
27 But My judgment exacts its own and My law exacts its rights.
28 For from your words I will answer you, and from your prayer I will speak to you.
29 For this is as follows: he that is corrupted is not at all (is as though he does not exist);
30 He has acted sinfully in any way he could and has not remembered my goodness, and has not remembered My goodness, nor accepted My long-suffering.
31 Therefore you will surely be taken up, as I before told you.
32 For that time will arise which brings affliction; for it will come and pass by with quick vehemence, and it will be turbulent coming in the heat of indignation.
33 And it will come to pass in those days that all the inhabitants of the earth will be moved one against another, because they do not know that My judgment has drawn near.
34 For there will not be found many wise at that time, and the intelligent will be but a few. Moreover, even those who know will most of all be silent.

35 And there will be many rumors and tidings, not just a few. And the actions and deeds of spirits (phantoms) will be manifest, and many promises will be recounted. Some of them (will prove) idle, and some of them will be confirmed.
36 And honor will be turned into shame, and strength will be humiliated into contempt, and decency will be destroyed, and beauty will become ugliness.
37 And many will say to many at that time: "Where has the multitude of intelligence hidden itself, and to what place has the multitude of wisdom removed itself?"
38 And while they are thinking on these things, envy will arise in those who had not thought highly of themselves, and passion will seize him that is peaceful, and many will be stirred up in anger to injure many, and they will rouse up armies in order to shed blood, and in the end they will perish together with them.
39 And it will come to pass at the same time, that a change of times will manifestly appear to every man, because in all those times they polluted themselves. and they practiced oppression, and walked every man in his own works, and remembered not the law of the Mighty One.
40 Therefore a fire will consume their thoughts, and in flame will the control of their thoughts be tested; for the Judge will come and will not tarry, because each of the inhabitants of the earth knew when he was transgressing. But because of their pride they did not know My Law.
41 But many will certainly weep over the living more than over the dead.
42 And I answered and said: O Adam, what have you done to all those who are born from you? And what will be said to the first Eve who hearkened to the serpent?
43 For all this multitude are going to corruption, nor is there any numbering of those whom the fire will devour.
44 But again I will speak in Your presence.
45 You, O LORD, my Lord, know what is in Your creature.
46 Long ago You command the dust to produce Adam, and You know the number of those who are born from him, and how far they have sinned before You, who have existed and not confessed You as their Creator.
47 Their end will convict all of them, and Your law which they have transgressed will reward (revenge) them on Your day.
48 But now let us dismiss the wicked and inquire about the righteous.
49 And I will recount their blessedness and not be silent in celebrating their glory, which is reserved for them.
50 This transitory world which you live, has made you endured much labor in a short time, so in that world to which there is no end you will receive great light.

Chapter 49

1 Nevertheless, I will again ask mercy from You, O Mighty One, who made all things.
2 In what shape will those live who live in Your day? Or how will the splendor of those who are after that time continue?
3 Will they then resume this form of the present, and put on these members which hold us back, impeded us, and are now involved in evils, and in which evils are consummated, or will You possibly change these things which have been in the world as You also change the world?

Chapter 50

1 And He answered and said to me: "Hear, Baruch, this word, and write the remembrance of all that you will learn in your heart.
2 The earth will certainly return the dead, which it now receives in order to preserve them. It will not change their form, but it will return them in the same form it received them, and as I delivered them to it, so will it raise them.
3 Then it will be necessary to show the living that the dead have come to life again, and that those who had departed have returned again.
4 And when they have recognized those whom they now know, then judgment will grow strong, and those things which were spoken of prior will come to be.

Chapter 51
1 When that appointed day has passed, the appearance of those who are condemned will be changed and the glory of those who are justified will be shown.
2 For the appearance of those who act wickedly will become worse because they will suffer torment.
3 But the glory of those who have now been justified in My law, who have had understanding in their life, and who have planted the root of wisdom in their heart, their splendor for their face will be changed and glorified. Their face will be turned into the light of their beauty, that they may be able to take and receive the world which does not die, which is promised to them at that time.
4 Those that rejected My law, and stopped their ears that they might not hear wisdom or receive understanding will lament their actions over and above all things.
5 When they see those they were exalted over but who will be exalted and glorified more than they, they will both be transformed, the latter into the splendor of angels, and the former will waste away more as they wonder at the visions when they see the angelic forms.
6 For they will first see these things and afterwards depart to be tormented.
7 But those who have been saved by their works, and to whom the law has been a hope and understanding, and an expectation, and wisdom, and a confidence, will have wonders appear in their time.
8 For they will behold the world which is now invisible to them, and they will behold the time which is now hidden from them:
9 And time will no longer cause them to age.
10 For they will dwell in the high places of that world and they will be made like the angels and they will be made equal to the stars, and they will be changed into every form they desire from beauty to loveliness and from light to glorious splendor.
11 Before them the borders of Paradise will be spread out, and the beauty and majesty of the living creatures which are beneath the throne will be shown to them. They will see the armies of the angels who are held fast by My word, lest they should appear and are held fast by a command, that they may stand in their places until the time of their appearance comes.
12 There will be righteous excellence surpassing that of the angels.
13 For the first will receive the last. Those who have passed away will receive whom they were expecting. Those who had passed away and who we had head of we should expect to see.
14 For they have been delivered from the tribulation of this world and laid down their burden of anguish.

15 For what have men lost their life, and for what have those who were on the earth exchanged their soul?
16 They did not choose the time which is beyond the reach of anguish. But they chose that time whose results are full of lamentations and evils, and they denied the world which does make those who come to it grow old, but they rejected the time of glory. Thus that they will not have the honor of which I told you before."

Chapter 52
1 And I asked: How can we forget those whom are destined for sorrow?
2 Why do we mourn for those who die? Why do we weep for those who depart to Sheol?
3 Lamentations should be reserved for the beginning of the torment to come. Let tears be stored up for the time of destruction.
4 But even in the face of these things will I speak. What will the righteous do now?
5 Rejoice in the suffering which you now suffer. Why do you look for the decline of your enemies?
6 Make your soul ready for what is reserved for you, and prepare your souls for the reward which is stored up for you.

Chapter 53
1 And when I had said these things I fell asleep and I saw a vision. A cloud was ascending from a very large sea, and I kept looking at it and I saw it was full of black and white waters, and there were many colors in those same waters, and it looked like powerful lightning as seen from a summit.
2 And I saw the cloud passing quickly in short courses, and it covered all the earth.
3 Then, after these things that cloud began to pour all the waters that were in it upon the earth.
4 And I saw that all the waters which fell from it looked different.
5 To begin with, the waters were black and there was a lot for a time, and afterwards I saw that the waters became bright, but they were not as much, and after that I again saw black waters, and after these things again bright, and again black and again bright how this was done twelve times, but the black were always more numerous than the bright.
6 At the end of the cloud it rained black waters, and they were darker than had been all those waters that were before, and fire was mingled with them, and where those waters descended, they work devastation and destruction.
7 And after all of this I saw that lightning I had seen on the summit of the cloud seized hold of it and hurled it to the earth.
8 Now that lightning shone very brightly so that it illuminated the whole earth, and it healed those regions where the last waters had descended and work devastation.
9 And it took hold of the whole earth, and had dominion over it.
10 After these things I saw the twelve rivers were ascending from the sea, and they began to surround that lightning and to become subject to it.
11 And because of my fear I awoke.

Chapter 54
1 And I besought the Mighty One, and said: You alone, O Lord, know the deep things of the world before they happen. The things which occur in their times You

bring about by Your word. You speed the beginning of these times against the works of the inhabitants of the earth, and the end of the seasons You alone know.
2 For You nothing is too hard. You do everything easily by a nod.
3 You, to whom the depths come as the heights, and whose word the beginnings of the ages serve;
4 You, who reveal to those who fear what You prepared for them so that they may be comforted.
5 You show great acts to those who do not know You. You break down the walls of those who are ignorant, and You light up what is dark, and You reveal what is hidden to the pure, who have submitted themselves to You and in Your law.
6 You have shown your servant this vision. Reveal its interpretation to me.
7 I know that for those things I have asked You about, I have received and answer. You have revealed to me with what voice I should praise You, and with what members of mine I should praises You and cause hallelujahs to ascend to You.
8 If my members were mouths and the hairs of my head were voices, I could not give you adequate food of praise, nor could I worship you as is befitting. I could never tell the glory of your beauty or praise you enough.
9 For what am I among men? Why am I counted among those who are more excellent than I that I have heard all these marvelous things from the Most High and numberless promises from Him who created me?
10 Blessed be my mother among those that bear, and let she that bare me be praised among women.
11 For I will not be silent in praising the Mighty One, and with the voice of praise I will tell His marvelous deeds.
12 For who does deeds like Your marvelous deeds, O God? Who comprehends Your deep thought of life.
13 With Your counsel You govern all the creatures which Your right hand has created. You have established every fountain of light beside You, and You have prepared the treasures of wisdom beneath Your throne.
14 Those who do not love your law perish justly. The torment of judgment awaits those who have not submitted themselves to Your power.
15 For though Adam first sinned and untimely brought death upon all, yet each of those who were born from him has prepared his own soul for the torment to come, and each one of them has chosen for himself glories to come.
16 It is certain that he who believes will receive reward.
17 But now, you wicked are bond for destruction because you will quickly be visited because you have rejected the understanding of the Most High.
18 His works have not taught you, and you have not been convinced by the skill of His creation which argued with you continually.
19 Adam is therefore not the cause, except for only his own soul, but each of us has been the Adam (man) of his own soul.
20 But You, O Lord, explain (open) to me those things which You have revealed to me, and inform me regarding that which I besought You.
21 For at the creation and until the end of the world, vengeance will be taken upon those who have done wickedness according to the wickedness in them, and You will glorify the faithful according to their faithfulness.
22 For those who are among Your own You rule, and those who sin You blot out from among Your own.

Chapter 55

1 Then, when I had finished speaking the words of this prayer I sat there under a tree that I might rest in the shade of the branches.

2 And I wondered and was amazed as I pondered the multitude of goodness which sinners who are upon the earth have rejected, and the tremendous torment they have hated, though they knew that they would be tormented because of the sin they had committed.

3 And when I was thought about these things the angel Ramiel, who presides over visions of truth, was sent to me, and he said to me:

4 Why does your heart trouble you, Baruch, and why do you have disturbing thoughts?

5 If the report you have only heard regarding judgment moved you so much what will you do when you see it manifest before yours eyes?

6 And if you expect the day of the Mighty One and you are so overcome just by the expectation, what will you do when you come to its actual occurrence?

7 If at the mention of the announcement of the torment of those who have done foolishly, you are so completely upset, how much more will you be when the event reveals astonishing things? And if you have heard announcements of the good and evil things which are coming and are grieved, what will you do when you behold the majesty that will be revealed, which will convict some and cause others to rejoice.

Chapter 56

1 Nevertheless, because you have asked the Most High to reveal to you the interpretation of the vision you have seen, I have been sent to tell you.

2 And the Mighty One has certainly made known to you the arrangement of the times which have passed, and are destined to pass in His world regarding those of deceit and of those of truth from the beginning of its creation to its end.

3 As you saw, a tremendous cloud ascended from the sea, and covered the earth. This is the duration of the world which the Mighty One made when he thought to make the world.

4 And when the world came into being and had left His presence (area of the throne), the time of the world was short, and was established according to the vast intelligence of Him who sent it.

5 And as you saw before on the summit of the cloud, black waters descended previously on the earth. This is the transgression that Adam the first man committed.

6 For since the time he transgressed, (early) untimely death came. Grief was named and anguish was prepared, pain was created, and trouble was born, disease took hold, and Sheol kept demanding to be renewed in blood The birth of children was brought about, and the passion of parents was its fruit, and the greatness of humanity was humiliated, and goodness died.

7 What can be blacker or darker than these things?

8 This is the beginning of the black waters which you have seen.

9 From these black waters, black was derived, and from the darkness, darkness was produced.

10 For he became a danger to his own soul and even to the angels.

11 At the time when he was created, they (the angels) enjoyed liberty.

12 But some of them descended, and mingled with the women.

13 And those who did so were tormented in chains.
14 But the rest of the multitude of the angels, of which there is no number, restrained themselves.
15 Those who lived on the earth perished together with them (the fallen angels) through the waters of the flood.
16 These are the first black waters.

Chapter 57
1 And after these waters you saw bright waters. This is the spring of Abraham and his generations and the birth of his son and his son's son and of those like them.
2 Because at that time the unwritten law was named among them. The words of the commandments were then fulfilled. Belief in the coming judgment was then born and hope of the world that was to be renewed was then created. The promise of life to come was began.
3 These are the bright waters, which you have seen.

Chapter 58
1 The third black waters you have seen are the mingling of all sins, which the nations committed after the death of those righteous men in the wickedness of the land of Egypt where they did unrighteousness. And they made their sons serve unrighteousness.
2 However, these also perished in the end.

Chapter 59
1 And the fourth bright waters you have seen are the birth of Moses, Aaron, Miriam, and Joshua the sons of Nun and Caleb and of all those like them.
2 For at that time the lamp of the eternal law shone on all those who sat in darkness, which announced to them that believe the promise of their reward, and to them that deny, the torment of fire which is reserved for them.
3 But also the heavens at that time were shaken from their place, and those who were under the throne of the Mighty One were disturbed, when He was taking Moses to Himself For He showed him many reproofs along with the principles of the law and the completion of the times, as He also showed to you. He also showed the pattern of Zion and its size, in the pattern of which the sanctuary of the present time was to be made.
4 But then also He showed him the size of the fire, the depths of the abyss, the weight of the winds, the number of the drops of rain,
5 How much of (His) anger (He) holds back, and the amount of long-suffering (He has), and the truth of (His) judgment,
6 And the origin of wisdom, the wealth of understanding, the wellspring of knowledge,
7 The height of the air, and the greatness of Paradise, the end of the ages, and the beginning of the day of judgment,
8 The amount of the offerings, the earths which are yet to come,
9 The mouth of Gehenna (hell), the place of vengeance, the place of faith, and the place of hope,

10 The visions of future torment, the multitude of angelic hosts, the flaming hosts, the splendor of the lightning and the voice of the thunders, the orders of the captains of the angels, the treasuries of light, and the changing of times, and the searching of the law.
11 These are the bright fourth waters which you have seen.

Chapter 60
1 The fifth black waters you have seen raining are the deeds the Amorites committed, and the spells of their incantations which they performed, and the unrighteousness contained in their mysteries, and the pollutions they mixed.
2 Even Israel was polluted by sins in the days of the judges, though they saw many slip from Him who made them.

Chapter 61
1 And the sixth bright waters you saw is the time in which David and Solomon were born.
2 That was the time of the building of Zion, the dedication of the sanctuary, the shedding of much blood of the nations that sinned, and many offerings which were given in the dedication of the sanctuary.
3 Peace and tranquility existed at that time, And wisdom was heard in the congregation.
4 The wealth of understanding was magnified in the congregations, and the holy feasts and ceremonies were carried out in blessings and great joy.
5 The judgment of the rulers was without guile and it was witnessed as such. The righteous law of the Mighty One was accomplished with truth.
6 And the land was then loved by the Lord because its inhabitants sinned not and it was glorified beyond all lands. At that time the city Zion ruled over all lands and regions.
7 These are the bright waters which you have seen.

Chapter 62
1 And the seventh black waters which you have seen is the perversion brought about by the counsel of Jeroboam, who decided to make two calves of gold:
2 And all the iniquities which kings who were after him sinfully worked,
3 And the curse of Jezebel and the worship of idols which Israel practiced at that time.
4 The withholding of rain, and the famines which occurred until women ate the fruit of their wombs,
5 And the time of their captivity which came upon the nine tribes and a half tribe because they were in many sins.
6 Then, Salmanasar, King of Assyria, came and led them away captive.
7 But regarding the Gentiles, how they always were sinful and wicked, and always unrighteousness would be wearisome to tell
8 These are the seventh black waters which you have seen.

Chapter 63
1 And the eighth bright waters you have seen is the correction and uprightness of Hezekiah King of Judah and the grace of God which came upon him.

2 When Sennacherib was aggressing in order to kill Hezekiah the deadly rage of Sennacherib troubled Hezekiah because a great population of the nations were with him .
3 When Hezekiah the king heard those things which the king of Assyria was devising and how he planned to come and seize him and destroy his people, the two and a half tribes which remained and how he wished to overthrow Zion Hezekiah trusted in his works, and had hope in his righteousness, and spoke with the Mighty One and said:
4 "Look! Sennacherib is prepared to destroy us, and he will boast and strut when he has destroyed Zion."
5 And the Mighty One heard him because Hezekiah was wise and so He listened to his prayer because he was righteous.
6 Then the Mighty One commanded Ramiel, His angel, who speaks with you.
7 And I went out and destroyed their population, whose count of their chiefs alone was a hundred and eighty-five thousand, and each one of them had an equal number that he commanded.
8 And at that time I burned their bodies from the inside out, but their clothing and weapons I preserved outwardly so that more wonderful deeds of the Mighty One might be seen, and that because of this His name might be spoken of throughout the whole earth.
9 And Zion was saved and Jerusalem delivered and Israel was freed from tribulation.
10 And all those who were in the holy land rejoiced, and the name of the Mighty One was mentioned and glorified.
11 These are the bright waters which you have seen.

Chapter 64

1 "The ninth black waters which you saw was all the wickedness which was in the days of Manasseh the son of Hezekiah.
2 His deed showed that he had no regard for God. He killed the righteous people, and he forcibly stole away judgment. He shed the blood of the innocent. He violently raped women, he overturned the altars and destroyed their offerings. He drove out their priests so that they could not minister in the sanctuary.
3 He made an image with five faces: four of them looked to the four winds, and the fifth on the top of the image was a passionate enemy of the Mighty One.
4 Then rage went out from the presence of the Mighty One to the intent that Zion should be pulled up by its roots, just like it happened in your days.
5 A decree went out from God against the two tribes and a half tribe that they should also be led away captive, as you have now seen.
6 The impiety of Manasseh increased greatly to the point that it removed the praise of the Most High from the sanctuary.
7 Because of this Manasseh was then named "the impious", and finally his dwelling was in the fire.
8 For though his prayer was heard by the Most High, finally, when he was thrown into the brass horse and the brass horse was then melted, it was meant as a sign to him for that time.
9 He had not lived perfectly. He was not worthy but this was done so that he might know by whom he should be tormented in the end.
10 For He who is able to reward is also able to torment.

Chapter 65
1 Manasseh acted without regard for God, and thought that in his time the Mighty One would not look into these things.
2 These are the ninth black waters which you saw.

Chapter 66
1 "And the tenth bright waters which you have seen is the purity of the generations of Josiah King of Judah, who was the only one at the time who submitted himself to the Mighty One with all his heart and with all his soul.
2 He cleansed the land from idols, and sanctified all the vessels which had been polluted, and restored the offerings to the altar, and the horn of the holy was lifted, and he exalted the righteous, and honored all that were wise in understanding, and brought back the priests to their ministry, and destroyed and removed the magicians and enchanters and necromancers from the land.
3 He killed the sinners that were living and they also took from the sepulchers the bones of the dead and burned them with fire.
4 He established the festivals and the Sabbaths in their sanctity. He burned their polluted ones in the fire and the lying prophets which deceived the people were also burned in the fire, and the people who listened to them when they were living, he threw them into the brook Cedron, and heaped stones upon them.
5 And he was zealous with passion for the Mighty One with all his soul. He alone was steadfast in the law at that time, so that he left none that was uncircumcised, or that sinned in all the land, all the days of his life.
6 Therefore he will receive an eternal reward, and he will be glorified with the Mighty One beyond many at a later time.
7 For on his account and on account of those who are like him were the honorable glories, of which you was told before, created and prepared.
8 These are the bright waters which you have seen.

Chapter 67
1 "And the eleventh black waters which you have seen is the calamity which is now befalling Zion.
2 Do you think that there is no anguish to the angels in the presence of the Mighty One because Zion was delivered up in such a way or that the Gentiles boast in their hearts, and amass before their idols? The gentiles say, 'she who so often trod down is now trodden down and she who reduced others to slavery is now a slave herself.
3 Do you think that in these things the Most High rejoices, or that His name is glorified?
4 But how will it effect His righteous judgment?
5 Yet after these things the gentile will seize and scatter them in the tribulation and they will dwell in shame in every place.
6 Because Zion is delivered up and Jerusalem has been laid waste, idols prosper in the cities of the Gentiles, and the cloud of smoke from the incense of the righteousness which the commands is now extinguished in Zion. In every place in and surrounding Zion there is the smoke of sin.
7 The King of Babylon who has now destroyed Zion will arise, and he will boast about being ruler over the people, and he will speak great things in his heart in the presence of the Most High.

8 But he will fall in the end. These are the black waters.

Chapter 68
1 The twelfth bright waters which you have seen is the word.
2 After these things occur a time will come when your people will fall into distress, so that they will all run the risk of perishing together.
3 Nevertheless, they will be saved, and their enemies will fall in their presence.
4 In time they will have much joy.
5 After a little space of time Zion will be built again, and its offerings will be restored again, and the priests will return to their ministry, and the Gentiles will come to glorify it, but not as fully as they did in the beginning.
6 After these things there will be the fall of many nations.
8 These are the bright waters which you have seen."

Chapter 69
1 The last waters which you have seen were darker than all that were before them. Those were after the twelfth number were collected together. They belong to the entire world.
2 The Most High made division from the beginning, because He alone knows what will happen due to the depth and breadth of the sin which will be committed before Him. He foresaw six kinds of them.
5 He also foresaw six kinds of good works of the righteous which will be accomplished before Him. They will go beyond those which He will work at the end and conclusion of the age.
6 For Him there were not black waters with black, nor bright with bright; because it is the end.

Chapter 70
1 Hear the interpretation of the last black waters which are to come after the all other black waters. This is the word.
2 The days will come when the time of the age is ripe that is the harvest of evil and good seeds. This is what the Mighty One will bring upon the earth and its inhabitants and upon its rulers. It is disturbing to the spirit and lethargy of heart.
3 They will hate one another, and provoke one another to fight, and the cruel will rule over the honorable, and those of low status will be honored above the famous.
4 Many will be delivered into the hands of the few, and those who were nothing will rule over the strong. The poor will have abundance beyond the rich, and the wicked will exalt themselves above the heroic.
5 The wise will be silent, and the foolish will speak. The ideas of men will not be heeded, nor will the counsel of the mighty. The hope of those who hope be will not be rewarded.
6 And when those things which were predicted have come to pass confusion will fall upon all men. Some of them will fall in battle, some of them will die in torment and pain, and some of them will be destroyed by their own people.
7 Then the Most High will reveal those peoples whom He has prepared from before and they will come and make war with the leaders that will be left.
8 And whosoever survives the war will die in the earthquake, and whosoever survives the earthquake will be burned by the fire, and whosoever survives the fire will be destroyed by famine.

9 But whosoever of the victors and the vanquished survives and escapes all these things mentioned before will be delivered into the hands of My servant Messiah.
10 For all the earth will devour its inhabitants.

Chapter 71
1 And the holy land will have mercy on its own, and it will protect its inhabitants at that time.
2 This is the vision you have seen and this is the interpretation.
3 I have come to tell you these things because your prayer has been heard by the Most High.

Chapter 72
1 Listen, regarding the bright lightning which is to come at the end, after the black waters. This is the word.
2 After the signs which you were told of before, when the nations become turbulent, and the time of My Messiah is come, he will summon all the nations. Some of them he will spare, and some of them he will kill.
3 These things will come upon the nations which are spared by Him.
4 Every nation which does not know Israel and has not trodden down the seed of Jacob will be spared.
5 This is because some out of every nation will be subjected to your people.
6 But all those who have ruled over you or have known you will be given up to the sword.

Chapter 73
1 When He has brought everything that is in the world low and has sat down on the throne of His kingdom in peace for the dispensation, joy will be revealed and rest will appear.
2 Healing will descend in the dew and disease will go away and anxiety, pain and sorrow will vanish from among men. Gladness will go forth through the whole earth.
3 And no one will again die before his time (young) nor will adversity suddenly befall any.
4 Judgments, reproach, arguments, revenge, spilling of blood, passions, envy, hatred, and things like these will be condemned when they are removed.
5 For it is these very things which have filled this world with evils. On account of these the life of man has been greatly troubled.
6 Wild beasts will come from the forest and minister to men, asps and dragons (serpents) will come out from their holes to submit themselves to a little child.
7 Women will no longer then have pain when they bear children or suffer torment when they yield the fruit of the womb.

Chapter 74
1 In those days the reapers will not grow weary, nor those that build be weary from work. The works will quicken itself and speed those who doe the work and give them much tranquility.
2 That which is corruptible will be destroyed. It is the beginning of that which is not corruptible.

3 Those things predicted will belong to this age. It is far removed from evil and near to things eternal.
4 This is the bright lightning which came after the last dark waters."

Chapter 75
1 And I asked: Lord, Who can understand Your goodness? For it is incomprehensible.
2 Who can look into your compassions, which are infinite?
3 Who can understand Your intelligence?
4 Who is able to explain the thoughts of Your mind?
5 Who of those born can hope to attain those things unless to him are merciful and gracious?
6 Certainly if You did not have compassion on those who are under Your right hand they could not come to those things. Only those who are in the numbers you named can be called.
7 We who exist know why we have come and so we submit ourselves to Him who brought us out of Egypt. We will come again and remember those things which have passed. We will rejoice in what has been.
8 But if we do not know why we have come and if we do not recognize the kingdom of Him who brought us up out of Egypt, we will have to come again and seek after those things which have been now. We will be grieved with pain again because of those things which have befallen.

Chapter 76
1 And He answered and said to me: This vision has been revealed and interpreted to you as you asked me to do, now hear the word of the Most High that you may know what is to befall you after these things.
2 You will surely leave this earth, but not by death, but you will be preserved until the end of the age (times).
3 Go up to the top of that mountain, and all the regions of that land, and the figure of the inhabited world, and the tops of the mountains, and the depth of the valleys, and the depths of the seas, and the number of the rivers will pass before you so that you may see what you are leaving, and to what place you are going. Now this will happen after forty days.
4 Go now during these days and teach the people as much as you are able so that they may learn and not die at the last age but they may learn in order that they may live at the last age."

Chapter 77
1 And I, Baruch, went from there and came to the people, and assembled them together from the greatest to the least, and said to them:
2 Hear, children of Israel! See how many of you are who remain of the twelve tribes of Israel.
3 To you and to your fathers the Lord gave a law more excellent than to all peoples.
4 Because your brethren transgressed the commandments of the Most High, He brought vengeance upon you and upon them. He did not spare the former, and the latter also He gave into slavery.
5 He did not leave a trace of them. But you are here with me.!

6 If you direct your ways correctly you will not depart as your brethren departed, but they will come back to you.
7 You worship He who is full of mercy. Your hope is in Him who is gracious and true. He will do good and not evil.
8 Have you not seen what has befallen Zion?
9 Do you think that the place (area/location) had sinned and that is why it was overthrown? Did you think that the land had performed foolishness and that because of this it was delivered up?
10 Don't you know it was because of you who sinned, that those things which did not sin were overthrown? It was because of you who performed wickedness that those thing which did not do foolish acts were delivered up to its enemies?
11 All the people answered and said to me, We can recall the good things which the Mighty One has done for (to) us. We do recall them. There are these things and those things which we do not remember that He in His mercy knows.
12 In spite of this, please do this for us, your people, write to our brethren in Babylon an letter of (religious) teaching and a scroll containing hope so that you may confirm them before you leave us.
13 The religious leaders (shepherds) of Israel have died, and the lamps which gave light are extinguished, and the fountains from which we drank have withheld their stream.
14 We are left in the darkness among the trees of the forest, the thirst of the wilderness."
15 And I answered and said to them: Shepherds and lamps and fountains come from the law: And though we leave, yet the law remains.
16 If you have respect for the law, and are determined to become wise, a lamp will not be lacking, and a shepherd (religious leader) will not fail, and a fountain will not dry up.
17 I will write also to your brethren in Babylon, and I will send by means of men, and I will write in like manner to the nine tribes and a half, and send by means of a bird.
18 And on twenty-first day in the eighth month that I, Baruch, came and sat down under the oak under the shadow of the branches, and no man was with me, but I was alone.
19 And I wrote these two letters; one I sent by an eagle to the nine and a half tribes;
20 And the other I sent to those that were at Babylon by means of three men.
21 And I called the eagle and spoke these words to it: The Most High has made you that you should be higher than all birds.
22 Now go and do not stop in any place, nor enter a nest, nor settle upon any tree, till you have passed over the breadth of the many waters of the river Euphrates, and have gone to the people that dwell there, and drop down to them this letter.
23 Remember that at the time of the deluge Noah received the fruit of the olive from a dove when he sent it out from the ark.
24 The ravens also ministered to Elijah, bringing him food as they had been commanded.
25 Solomon, in the time of his kingdom, when he wished to send or seek for anything, commanded a bird to go out and it obeyed him as he commanded it.
26 So do not tire, and do not turn to the right hand nor the left, but fly and go by a direct way, that you may preserve the command of the Mighty One, according as I said to you.

Chapter 78

1 These are the words of that letter which Baruch the son of Neriah sent to the nine and a half tribes, which were across the river Euphrates, in which these things were written.
2 Baruch the son of Neriah says to the brethren carried into captivity: "Mercy and peace."
3 I bear in mind, my brethren, the love of Him who created us, who loved us from ancient times, and never hated us, but above all taught us.
4 And truly I know that all of us in the twelve tribes are bound by one bond, inasmuch as we are born from one father.
5 Because of this I have been the more diligent to leave you the words of this letter before I die, so that you may be comforted regarding the evils which have come upon you, and also that you may be grieved regarding the evil that has befallen your brethren; and also that you may justify (understand and accept) His judgment which He has decreed against you that you should be carried away captives. What you have suffered is a sentence disproportionably greater than what you have done. But this was done in order that, at the last times, you may be found worthy of your fathers.
6 So, if you consider that you have now suffered those things for your good, that you may not be condemned and tormented in the end, then you will receive eternal hope. But you must remove from your heart all error and vanity, for it was because of this you departed from here.
7 If you so do these things He will never forget you. He who gave His promise to those greater than us but on our behalf, that He will never forget or forsake us, but will gather together again those who were dispersed with much mercy.

Chapter 79

1 Now, my brethren, learn first what befell Zion and how Nebuchadnezzar King of Babylon came up against us.
2 For we have sinned against Him who made us, and we have not kept the commandments which he ordered us to keep. Yet he has not chastened us as we deserved.
3 For what befell you we also suffer in a the highest degree, for it happened to us also.

Chapter 80

1 And now, my brethren, I reveal to you that when the enemy had surrounded the city the angels of the Most High were sent, and they collapsed the fortifications of the strong wall and they destroyed the solid iron corners, which could not be pulled up.
2 Nevertheless, they hid all the vessels of the sanctuary, to prevent the enemy from possessing them.
3 And when they had done these things, they delivered to the enemy the collapsed wall, and the plundered house, and the burnt temple, and the people who were overcome because they were delivered up. They did this so the enemy could not

boast and say: " In war. by force have we been able to lay waste to the house of the Most High."
4 They also have bound your brethren and led away them to Babylon, and have forced them to live there.
5 But we, being very few, have been left here..
6 This is the tribulation about which I wrote to you.
7 And certainly I know that alleviation of the pain of the inhabitants of Zion consoles you. You knew that they prospered so your consolation was greater than the tribulation which you endured in having to leave it.

Chapter 81
1 But regarding consolation, listen to my word.
2 I was grieving regarding Zion, and I prayed for mercy from the Most High, and I said:
3 How long will these things last for us? Will we always have these evils on us?"
4 The Mighty One acted according out of the multitude of His mercies and according to the vastness of His compassion. He revealed to me His word so that my suffering would be relieved. He showed me visions that I should not again endure anguish. He made known to me the mystery of the times. And the advent of the hours he showed me.

Chapter 82
1 Therefore, my brethren, I have written to you, that you may comfort yourselves regarding the multitude of tribulations.
2 You know that our Maker will certainly avenge us and do to our enemies according to all that they have done to us. The end, which the Most High will make is very near will bring His mercy and the final result of His judgment is by no means far off.
3 For now we see the numerous prosperity of the Gentiles, even though they act sinfully and they are like a vapor.
4 We see their great power, even though they act wickedly, But they will become like a drop (of water).
5 We see the strength of their might, even though they resist the Mighty One every hour. But they will be considered as spittle.
6 We consider the glory of their greatness, though they do not keep the statutes of the Most High. But as smoke will they pass away.
7 And we think about the beauty of theirs gracefulness, even though they give it with pollutions. But as grass that withers will they fade away.
8 And we consider the strength of their cruelty, though they do not remember what it brought or how it ended. But as a wave that passes (through them) they will be broken.
9 And we remark about how the brag about being mighty although they deny that it was God that gave it to them. But they will disappear like a passing cloud.

Chapter 83
1 Most High will certainly speed up His times, and He will bring on His hours.
2 He will judge those who are in His world with certainty, and visit truth on all their hidden works.

3 He will examine the secret thoughts, and those things of all the members of man which they laid up in the secret chambers. He will make them appear in the presence of all with reproof.
4 Allow none of these present things to ascend into your hearts, but above all let us be expectant because that which is promised to us will come.
5 Do not let us look to the delights of the Gentiles now but let us remember what has been promised to us in the end.
6 For the end of the times and of the seasons and whatever is with them will cease together.
7 The conclusion of the age will show the tremendous strength of its ruler, when all things come to judgment.
8 Prepare your hearts for that which you have believed or you will be in bondage in both worlds and you be led away captive here and be tormented there.
9 That which is now or which was, or which will come, is the evil fully evil, nor the good fully good.
10 For all your health of this time are turning into sickness, and all strength of this time is turning into weakness, and all the power of this time is turning into impotence, and the energy of youth is turning into old age and death.
11 Every beauty of gracefulness of this time is becoming faded and hateful, and every prideful kingdom of this time is turning into humiliation and shame, and every praise of the glory of this time is turning into the embarrassment of silence, and every empty bragging insult of this time is turning into a mute ruin.
12 Every delight and joy of this time is turning to worms and decay, and every noise of the proud of this time is turning into dust and lethargy.
13 Every possession of riches of this time is being turned into Sheol (hell) alone, and all the yearning of passion of this time is turning into death, and every lustful desire of this time is turning into judgment with torment.
14 Every trick and craftiness of this time is turning into a proof of the truth. Every sweet ointment of this time is turning into judgment and condemnation, and every love of lying is turning to rudely to the truth.
15 Since all these things are done now does anyone think that they will not be avenged? The consummation of all things will come to the truth.

Chapter 84
1 Because of these things I have revealed to you this while I am still alive. I have said these things that you should learn the things that are excellent, for the Mighty One has commanded me to instruct you. So I will set before you some of the commandments of His judgment before I die.
2 Do not forget that Moses called heaven and earth to witness against you and said:
3 If you transgress the law you will be dispersed, but if you keep it you will be kept." He also used to say these things to you when you, the twelve tribes, were together in the desert.
4 After his death you threw them away from you and because of this there came upon you what had been predicted.
5 Moses used to tell you tell you what would befall you, and now you see they have befallen you because you have forsaken the law.
6 Now, I also say to you after you have suffered, that if you obey those things which have been said to you, you will receive from the Mighty One whatever has been laid up and waiting for you.

7 Let this letter be for a testimony between me and you so that you may remember the commandments of the Mighty One and that there may be to me a defense in the presence of Him who sent me.
8 And remember the law and Zion, the holy land, your brethren, and the covenant of your fathers. Do not forget the festivals and the sabbaths.
9 Deliver this letter and the traditions of the law to your sons after you, as also your fathers delivered them to you.
10 At all times make requests and pray diligently and unceasingly with your whole heart that the Mighty One may hold nothing against you, and that He may not count the multitude of your sins, but instead remember the rectitude of your fathers.
11 If He doe not judges us according to the multitude of His mercies, woe to all us who are born.

Chapter 85
1 Do you not know that in the past and in the generations of old our fathers had helpers? They were righteous men and holy prophets.
2 We were in our own land and they helped us when we sinned, and they interceded for us with Him who made us, because they trusted in their works, and the Mighty One heard their prayer and forgave us.
3 But now the righteous have been gathered and the prophets have fallen asleep, and we also have gone out from the land, and Zion has been taken from us, and we have nothing now except the Mighty One and His law.
4 If therefore we direct and commit our hearts we will receive everything that we lost, and much better things than we lost by many times.
5 For what we have lost would decay, but what we will receive will not be corruptible.
6 Also, I have written to our brethren to Babylon that to them also I may testify to these very things.
7 Let all those things I said before be always before your eyes, because we are still in the spirit and the power of our liberty.
8 The Most High is long-suffering towards us here, and He has shown us what is to be, and has not concealed from us what will happen in the end.
9 Before judgment takes its own (costs), and truth that which is its due, let us prepare our souls so that we may possess and not be taken as a possession and that we may hope and not be put to shame, and that we may rest with our fathers, and not be tormented with our enemies.
10 For the youth of the world is past, and the strength of the creation already exhausted, and the occurrence of the times is very short because they have already passed by. The pitcher is near to the cistern, and the ship to the port, and the course of the journey nears the city, and life to its conclusion.
11 Prepare your souls, so that when you sail and ascend from the ship you may have rest and not be condemned when you depart.
12 When the Most High will bring about all these things there will not be a place left for repentance, nor a limit to the times or a duration for the hours, or a change of ways, or a place to pray, or a way to send pleas, or to receive knowledge, or give of love. There will be no place of repentance for the soul, nor prayers for offences, nor intercession of the fathers, nor prayer of the prophets, nor help of the righteous.

13 There is the sentence of decay, the way of fire, and the path which leads to Gehenna (place of burning/hell/destruction).
14 There is one law (made) by one. There is one age and an end for all who are in it.
15 Then He will save those whom He can forgive, and at the same time destroy those who are polluted with sins.

Chapter 86
1 When you receive this, my letter, read it in your congregations with care.
2 Meditate on it, and above all do this on the days of your fasts.
3 Keep me in mind by means of this letter, as I also keep you in mind in it, always. Fare you well.

Chapter 87
1 And when I had ended all the words of this letter, and had written it without tiring to its close, that I folded it, and sealed it carefully, and bound it to the neck of the eagle, and dismissed it and sent it.

Conclusion

For thousands of years Israel has awaited the judgment and redemption of The Lord. When the world seemed the most unfair and brutal, hope was held out that the end must be near. The end of days was not a frightening event for the Jews of old. It was to be their greatest age, in which God himself judged all other nations as unworthy and rewarded those Jews who followed their God. Obedience to God was judged on how well one adhered to God's law and commandments.

The belief of divine recompense has echoed through history, changing the ways that both Christian and Jews have viewed their world and their destiny.

Even though the texts presented here are not in our western Christian canon, do not think they have not influenced our faith. The books provide insight into how Jews of the time thought, believed, and acted, but more than that, the texts were circulated and therefore bolstered and broadcast the doctrine and history they contained.

If one ever questioned that non-canonical texts influenced our Bible or our faith, we need to look no further than the famous parallel between the Book of Enoch, written in the second century B.C. and the Book of Jude in the New Testament , written in the first century A.D.

Enoch 1:9 And behold! He comes with ten thousand of His holy ones (saints) to execute judgment on all, and to destroy all the ungodly (wicked); and to convict all flesh of all the works of their ungodliness which they have ungodly committed, and of all the hard things which ungodly sinners have spoken against Him.

Jude 1:14-15 And Enoch also, the seventh from Adam, prophesied of these, saying, Behold, the Lord cometh with ten thousands of his saints, To execute judgment upon all, and to convince all that are ungodly among them of all their ungodly deeds which they have ungodly committed, and of all their hard speeches which ungodly sinners have spoken against him.

Yes, it is true. Documents, doctrine, and points of faith not found in our Bible tremendously influenced what has come to be the Judaism and Christianity we know and practice today.

SECTION THREE

LOST SCRIPTURES OF THE NEW TESTAMENT

The War Scrolls - The War Between the Sons of Dark and the Sons of Light

The War Scroll is a nine & a half foot scroll with as many as 19 columns, found in cave 1 at Qumran. It seems to be written as a sequel or expository to the eschatological war described in Dan 11-12. The author gives detailed instructions for a ritualized battle in which the "sons of light," led by Michael, destroy the Kittim, or the "sons of darkness," led by Satan. Many scholars identify the Kittim as an allusion to the Roman Empire.

The War Scroll, 1QM, was one of the original seven scrolls found in cave one by the Bedouin in 1947. The scroll has also been called "The War Rule" and "The War of the Sons of Light Against the Sons of Darkness." It was first published by E.L. Sukenik in 1954 and was re-edited as The Dead Sea Scrolls of the Hebrew University at Jerusalem: Hebrew University and Magnes Press, 1955.

The War Scroll contains nineteen columns and is written on five sheets. The end of the scroll is missing, but its beginning seems to be intact. At the bottom of the scroll there is damage and wear. The total length of the scroll in its present state is 9 feet, 8 inches. Since pieces of the scroll are worn away or missing, there are places within the translation where words are assumed to fit the flow of the sentence structure. These "best guess" words are noted by parentheses. If there are too many words missing or the meaning cannot be ascertained so that a "best guess" cannot be provided the missing words are denoted with the symbols (…).

The scroll is a mixture of apocalyptic and legal discussion. The scroll's main theological significance lies in the fact that this is a battle against the Sons of Light and the Sons of Darkness. Although most scholars believe the story is about good and evil, this in itself could allude to a struggle between the forces of life and death. In the end, God will intervene, conquer, and save his people. There are parallels to the books of Revelation and Daniel in the scroll and it is assumed that the author borrowed from Daniel as well as other material of the day, according to the date of the text's creation. All three books, Daniel, Revelations, and the War Scroll, share the common theme of life and light being victorious over evil and death. All point to fact that the outcome is already known, however, man must participate and is thus held culpable in the outcome.

There is controversy over the date of the scroll. Some say that the scroll was written between 50 B.C. and 50 A.D. because this is after the Roman Conquest around 63 B.C. but before the end of Herod's reign (4 B.C.). Another view is that the scroll was written after 70 A.D. and possibly as late as 135 A.D. However, most agree the date must be some time after the Roman Conquest, because the author of the scroll describes the weapons and battle tactics of the Roman army.

The War Scroll

The Master Rule of War.
The first attack of the Sons of Light will be initiated against the forces of the Sons of Darkness, which is the army of Belial. The troops are from Edom, Moab, the sons of Ammon, the Amalekites, Philistia, and the troops of the Kittim of Asshur. Supporting them are those who have violated the covenant.

The sons of Levi, the sons of Judah, and the sons of Benjamin, and those exiled to the wilderness, will fight against them with (?) against all their troops, when the exiles of the Sons of Light return from the Wilderness of the Peoples to camp in the Wilderness of Jerusalem.

Then after the battle they will go up from that place and battle the king of the Kittim and he shall enter into Egypt. In his time he will go out with great anger to do battle against the kings of the north, and in his anger he shall set out to destroy and eliminate the strength of Israel.

Then there will be a time of salvation for the People of God, and a time of the dominion of all the men of His forces, and a time of eternal destruction for all the forces of Belial. There shall be great panic among the sons of Japheth, and Assyria shall fall with no one to come to his aid, and the supremacy of the Kittim shall cease their wickedness and will be overcome without a single survivor. There shall be no survivors of all the Sons of Darkness.

Then the Sons of Righteousness shall shine into all ends of the world and continuing to shine forth until end of the appointed seasons of darkness. Then at the time appointed by God, His great brilliance will shine for all of eternity for the peace and blessing, glory and joy, and long life of all Sons of Light. On the day when the Kittim falls there will be a battle and horrible carnage before the God of Israel, for it is a day appointed by Him from ancient times as a battle of destruction for the Sons of Darkness.

On that day the congregation of the gods and the congregation of men shall engage one another and the outcome will be great carnage. The Sons of Light and the forces of Darkness shall fight one another to show the strength of God with the roar of a great multitude and the shout of gods and men. It will be a day of disaster. It is a time of distress for all the people who are redeemed by God. Compared to all their afflictions, no day exists like this and it is hastening to its completion as an eternal redemption. On the day of their battle against the Kittim, they shall go out to kill in battle.

In three groups the Sons of Light will stand firm to strike a blow at wickedness, and in three (parts) the army of Belial shall strengthen themselves to force the retreat of the forces of Light.

And when the banners of the infantry cause their hearts to melt, then the power of God will strengthen the hearts of the Sons of Light.
In the seventh section, the great hand of God will overcome Belial and all the angels under his control, and all the men of his forces shall be destroyed forever. And this is the total destruction of the Sons of Darkness and service to God during the years of war.

And the holy ones shall shine forth in support of the truth in the annihilation of the Sons of Darkness. Then a great roar (proceeded them when) they took hold of the implements of war . (And the) chiefs of the tribes and the priests, of the tribe of the Levites, the chiefs of the tribes, the fathers of the congregation the priests and thus for the Levites and the courses of the heads (of the procession will go forth.)

The number of the congregation's tribe (family) is fifty-two. They shall set in the rank the chiefs of the priests after the Chief Priest and his deputy. There will be twelve chief priests to serve in the regular offering before God. The chiefs of the courses will number twenty-six and shall serve in their courses. After them the chiefs of the Levites who serve continually will number twelve in all, one to a tribe. The chiefs of their courses shall serve each man in his office. The chiefs of the tribes and fathers of the congregation shall support them, taking their posts continually at the gates of the sanctuary.

The chiefs of their courses, from the age of fifty upwards, shall take their posts with their commissioners on their festivals, which are new moons and Sabbaths, and on every day of the year. These shall take their posts at the burnt offerings and sacrifices, to arrange the sweet smelling incense according to the will of God, in order to atone for all His congregation, and to satisfy themselves before Him continually at the table of glory.
All of these they shall arrange at the time of the year of remission.

During the remaining thirty-three years of the war the men of renown, those called of the Congregation, and all the heads of the congregation's family shall choose for themselves men of war for all the lands of the nations.
They shall prepare capable men for themselves from all tribes of Israel to go out for battle according to the call to war (draft), year by year. But during the years of remission they shall not ready men to go out for battle, for it is a Sabbath of rest for Israel.

The war will be waged during the thirty-five years of service. For six years the entire congregation will wage it together. Then the war shall be waged with divisions during the twenty-nine remaining years. In the first year they will fight against Mesopotamia. In the second the war will be fought against the sons of Lud. In the third they shall fight against the rest of the sons of Aram, which are Uz, Hul, Togar, and Mesha, who are beyond the Euphrates. In the fourth and fifth years they will battle against the sons of Arpachshad. In the sixth and seventh year they shall fight against all the sons of Assyria and Persia and those of the east up to the Great Desert. In the eighth year they will fight against the sons of Elam. In the ninth year they will fight against the sons of Ishmael and Keturah. And during the following ten years the war shall be divided against all the sons of Ham according to their families (tribes/clans) and their territories. During the remaining ten years the war shall be divided against all sons of Japheth according to their territories.

This is the Rule of the Trumpets:
These are the trumpets of alarm for all their service for the (armies of God) and their commissioned men, (The men will be set in divisions) by tens of thousands and thousands and hundreds and fifties and tens. Upon the trumpets (they will rely and upon the sounds of the trumpets, which) they shall (create for the different sounds of) the trumpets of the battle formations, and the trumpets for assembling them when the gates of the war are opened so that the infantry will advance, and the trumpets for the signal of the slain, and the trumpets of the ambush, and the trumpets of pursuit when the enemy is vanquished, and the trumpets of reassembly when the battle returns.

On the trumpets for the assembly of the congregation they shall write, "The called of God." On the trumpets for the assembly of the chiefs they shall write, "The princes of God." On the trumpets of the formations they shall write, "The rule of God." On the trumpets of the men of renown (they shall write), "The heads of the congregation's clans."
Then when they are assembled at the house of meeting, they shall write, "The testimonies of God for a holy congregation." On the trumpets of the camps they shall write, "The peace of God in the camps of His saints."
On the trumpets for their campaigns they shall write, "The mighty deeds of God to scatter the enemy and to put all those who hate justice to flight and a withdrawal of mercy from all who hate God."
On the trumpets of the battle formations they shall write, "Formations of the divisions of God to avenge His anger on all Sons of Darkness."
0n the trumpets for assembling the infantry when the gates of war open that they might go out against the battle line of the enemy, they shall write, "A remembrance of requital at the appointed time of God."
On the trumpets of the slain they shall write, "The hand of the might of God in battle so as to bring down all the slain because of unfaithfulness."
On the trumpets of ambush they shall write, "Mysteries of God to wipe out wickedness."
On the trumpets of pursuit they shall write, "God has struck all of the Sons of Darkness, He shall not diminish His anger until they are annihilated." When they return from battle to enter the formation, they shall write on the trumpets of retreat, "God has gathered."
On the trumpets for the way of return from battle with the enemy to enter the congregation in Jerusalem, they shall write, "The joy of God in a peaceful return."

The description of the banners.
This is the Rule of the Banners of the entire congregation according to their formations. On the grand banner which is at the head of all the people they shall write, "People of God," the names "Israel" and "Aaron," and the names of the twelve tribes of Israel according to their order of birth. On the banners of the heads of the camps of three tribes they shall write, "the Spirit of God," and the names of three

tribes. On the banner of each tribe they shall write, "Standard of God," and the name of the leader of the tribe and of its families. (On the banner of the divisions of the ten-thousand write the name of the leader of the ten thousand and the names of the chiefs (of the army) and his hundreds. On the banner of Merari they shall write, "The Offering of God," and the name of the leader of Merari and the names of the chiefs of his thousands.

On the banner of the thousand they shall write, "The Anger of God is loosed against Belial and all the men of his forces so that none remain," and the name of the chief of the thousand and the names of the chiefs of his hundreds. And on the banner of the hundred they shall write, "Hundred 0f God, the power of war against a sinful flesh," and the name of the chief of the hundred and the names of the chiefs of his tens. And on the banner of the fifty they shall write, "The might of God have ended the stand of the wicked" and the name of the chief of the fifty and the names of the chiefs of his tens. On the banner of the thousand they shall write, "The Anger of God is loosed against Belial and all the men of his forces so that none remain."
When they go to battle they shall write on their banners," The truth of God", "The righteousness of God", "The glory of God", "The justice of God", and after these the list of their names in full.

When they draw near for battle they shall write on their banners, "The right hand of God", "The appointed time of God", "The tumult of God", "The slain of God." After these things, write their names in full. When they return from battle they shall write on their banners, "The exaltation of God," "The greatness of God," "The praise of God," "The glory of God," with their names in full.

The Rule of the banners of the congregation:
When they set out to battle they shall write on the first banner, "The congregation of God," on the second banner write, "The camps of God," on the third write, "The tribes of God," on the fourth write, "The families of God," on the fifth write, "The divisions of God," on the sixth write, "The congregation of God," on the seventh write, "Those called by God," and on the eighth write, "The army of God." They shall write their names in full with all their order. When they come near for battle they shall write on their banners, "The battle of God," "The recompense of God," "The cause of God," "The reprisal of God," "The power of God," "The retribution of God," "The might of God," "The destruction of all the prideful nations by God." And their names in full they shall write upon them. When they return from battle they shall write on their banners, "The deliverance of God," "The victory of God," "The help of God," "The support of God," "The joy of God," "The thanksgivings of God," "The praise of God," and "The peace of God."

The Length of the Banners.
The banner of the entire congregation shall be fourteen cubits long. The banner of three tribes shall be thirteen cubits long. The banner of a tribe, twelve cubits. The banner of ten thousand, eleven cubits. The banner of a thousand shall be ten cubits. The banner of a hundred shall be nine cubits. The banner of a group of fifty shall be eight cubits, The banner of a group of ten, shall be seven cubits.

The description of the shields.
And on the shield of the Leader of the entire nation they shall write his name, the names "Israel," "Levi," and "Aaron," and the names of the twelve tribes of Israel according to their order of birth, and the names of the twelve chiefs of their tribes.

The description of the arming and deployment of the divisions.
This is the rule for arranging the divisions for war when their army is complete to make up the forward battle line:
The battle line shall be formed of one thousand men. There shall be seven forward rows to each battle line, arranged in order. The station of each man will be behind his fellow. All of them shall bear shields of bronze, polished like a face mirror. The shield shall be bound with a border of woven work and a design of loops, the work of a skillful workman consisting of gold, silver, and bronze bound together and jewels in a multicolored brocade. It is the work of a skillful workman, artistically done. The length of the shield shall be two and a half cubits, and its breadth a cubit and a half. In their hands they can hold a lance and a sword.

The length of the lance shall be seven cubits, of which the socket and the blade constitute half a cubit. On the socket there shall be three bands engraved as a border of woven work; of gold, silver, and copper bound together like an artistically designed work. And in the loops of the design, on both sides of the band all around, shall be precious stones, a multicolored brocade, the work of a skillful workman, artistically done, and an ear of grain.

The socket shall be grooved between the bands like a column, artistically done. The blade shall be of shining white iron, the work of a skillful workman, artistically done, and an ear of grain of pure gold inlaid in the blade. The blade will be tapered towards the point. The swords shall be of refined iron, purified in the furnace and polished like a face mirror, the work of a skillful workman, artistically done, with figures of ears of grain of pure gold embossed on both sides. The borders shall go straight to the point, two on each side. The length of the sword shall be a cubit and a half and its width four fingers. The scabbard shall be four thumbs wide and four handbreadths up to the scabbard. The scabbard shall be tied on either side with thongs of five handbreadths. The handle of the sword shall be of choice horn, the work of a skillful workman, a varicolored design with gold and silver and precious stones.

And when the troupes take their stand, they shall arrange seven battle lines, one behind the other and there shall be a space between (the lines) thirty cubits, where the infantry shall stand the (infantry) forward and they shall sling seven times, and return to their position. After them, three divisions of infantry shall advance and stand between the battle lines. The first division shall heave into the enemy battle line seven battle spears. On the blade of the first spear they shall write, "Flash of a spear for the strength of God." On the second weapon they shall write, "Missiles of blood to make fall the slain by the wrath of God." On the third spear they shall write, "The blade of a sword devours the slain of wickedness by the judgment of God." Each of these they shall throw seven times and then return to their position. After these, two divisions of infantry shall march forth and stand between the two battle lines. The first division will be equipped with a spear and a shield and the second division with a shield and a sword, to bring down the slain by the judgment of God, to subdue the battle line of the enemy by the power of God, and to render recompense for their evil for all the prideful and arrogant nations. So the Kingship shall belong to the God of Israel, and for the holy ones of His people He shall act powerfully.

The description of the deployment of the cavalry.
Seven rows of horsemen shall also take position at the right and at the left of the battle line. Their ranks shall be positioned on both sides, seven hundred horsemen on one side and seven hundred on the other. Two hundred horsemen shall go out with one thousand men of the battle line of the infantry, and they shall take position on all sides of the camp. The total being four thousand six hundred men, and one thousand four hundred cavalry for the entire army arranged for the battle line; fifty for each battle line.

The horsemen with the cavalry of the men of the entire army, will be six thousand made up by five hundred to a tribe. All the cavalry that go out to battle with the infantry shall ride stallions that are swift, responsive, unrelenting, mature, trained for battle, and accustomed to hearing noises and seeing all kinds of scenes.

Those who ride them shall be men capable in battle, trained in horsemanship, the range of their age from thirty to forty-five years. The (head) horsemen of the army shall be from forty to fifty years old, and they shall wear helmets and greaves (shin protectors), carrying in their hands round shields and a lance eight cubits long, and a bow and arrows and battle spears, all of them prepared in (accordance to instructions) to shed the blood of their guilty slain. These are the (instructions of the horsemen.)

The recruitment and age of the soldiers.
The men of the army shall be from forty to fifty years old. The commissioners of the camps shall be from fifty to sixty years old. The officers shall also be from forty to fifty years old. All those who strip the slain, plunder the spoil, cleanse the land, guard the arms, and he who prepares the provisions, all these shall be from twenty-five to thirty years old.

No youth, nor woman shall enter their encampments from the time they leave Jerusalem to go to battle until their return. No one crippled, blind, nor lame, nor a man who has a permanent blemish on his skin, or a man affected with ritual uncleanness of his flesh; none of these shall go with them to battle. All of them shall be volunteers for battle, pure of spirit and flesh, and prepared for the day of vengeance. Any man who is not ritually clean in respect to his genitals on the day of battle shall not go down with them into battle, for holy angels are present with their army. There shall be a distance between all their camps and the latrine of about two thousand cubits, and no shameful nakedness shall be seen in the areas of all their camps.

The ministry of the priests and Levites.
When the battle line are arrayed against the enemy battle line shall be seven priests

that will go through from the middle opening into the gap between the battle lines. The priests will be of the sons of Aaron, dressed in fine white linen garments, consisting of a linen tunic and linen breeches, and girded with a linen sash of twined fine linen of violet, purple, and crimson, and a multicolored colored sign and decorated caps on their heads, , and the garments for battle shall be the work of a skillful workman, and they shall not take them into the sanctuary.

The one priest shall walk before all the men of the battle line to encourage them for battle. In the hands of the remaining six shall be the trumpets of assembly the trumpets of memorial, the trumpets of the alarm, the trumpets of pursuit, and the trumpets of reassembly. When the priests go out into the gap between the battle lines, seven Levites shall go out with them. In their hands shall be seven trumpets of rams' horns. Three officers from among the Levites shall walk before the priests and the Levites. The priests shall blow the two trumpets of assembly.

(And there shall proceed men, with the words of) battle upon fifty shields, and fifty infantrymen shall go out from the one gate and (the) Levites, officers. With each battle line they shall go out according to all (if the) orders given. The men of the infantry (shall go out) from the gates and they shall take position between the two battle lines, and (join) the battle. (Then the priests shall raise the trumpets and) shall blow continually to direct the slingmen until they have completed hurling seven times.

Afterwards the priests shall blow on the trumpets of return, and they shall go along the side of the first battle line to take their position. The priests shall blow on the trumpets of assembly, and the three divisions of infantry shall go out from the gates and stand between the battle lines, and beside them the cavalrymen, Sat the right and at the left. The priests shall blow on their trumpets a level note, signals for the order of battle. And the columns shall be deployed into their formations, each to his position. When they have positioned themselves in three formations, the priests shall blow for them a second signal, a low legato note, signals for advance, until they come near the battle line of the enemy and take hold of their weapons. Then the priests shall blow on the six trumpets of the slain a sharp staccato note to direct the battle, and the Levites and all the people with rams' horns shall blow a great battle alarm together in order to melt the heart of the enemy.

With the sound of the alarm, the battle spears shall fly out to bring down the slain. Then the sound of the rams' horns shall quiet, but on the trumpets the priests shall continue to blow a sharp staccato note to direct the signals of battle until they have hurled into the battle line of the enemy seven times. Afterwards, the priests shall blow for them the trumpets of retreat, a low note, level and legato (smooth). According to this rule the priests shall blow for the three divisions. When the first division throws, the priests and the Levites and all the people with rams' horns shall blow a great alarm to direct the battle until they have hurled seven times. Afterwards, the priests shall on the trumpets of retreat blow for them. And they shall take their stand in their positions in the battle line and shall take up position (in front of the) slain, and all the people with rams' horns shall blow a very loud battle alarm, and as the sound goes out their hands shall begin to bring down the slain, and all the people shall quiet the sound of alarm, but the priests shall continue sounding on the trumpets of the slain to direct the fighting, until the enemy is defeated and turns in retreat.

The priests shall blow the alarm to direct the battle, and when they have been defeated before them, the priests shall blow the trumpets of assembly, and all the infantry shall go out to them from the midst of the front battle lines and stand, six divisions in addition to the division which is engaged in battle: altogether, seven battle lines, twenty-eight thousand soldiers, and six thousand horsemen. All these shall pursue in order to destroy the enemy in God's battle; a total annihilation.

The priests shall blow for them the trumpets of pursuit, and they shall divide themselves for a pursuit of annihilation against all the enemy. The cavalry shall push the enemy back at the flanks of the battle until they are destroyed. When the slain have fallen, the priests shall continue blowing from afar and shall not enter into the midst of the slain so as to be defiled by their unclean blood, for they are holy. They shall not allow the oil of their priestly anointment to be profaned with the blood of the vainglorious nations.

The description of the maneuvers of the battle divisions.
This is the Rule for changing the order of the battle divisions, in order to arrange their position against (the enemy in) a pincer movement and towers, line, arc, and towers, and as it draws slowly forward, then the columns and the flanks go out from the two sides of the battle line that the enemy might become discouraged. The shields of the soldiers of the towers shall be three cubits long, and their lances eight cubits long. The towers shall go out from the battle line with one hundred shields on a side. They shall surround the tower on the three front-most sides, three hundred shields in all. There shall be three gates to a tower, one on the right and one on the left. Upon all the shields of the tower soldiers they shall write: on the first, "Michael" and on the second, "Gabriel," on the third, "Cyril," and on the fourth "Raphael." "Michael" and "Gabriel" on the right, and "Raphael" and "Cyril" on the left. And (push the enemy) to the four(th) (side). They shall establish an ambush for the battle line of (three sides) and they shall fall on the slain.

The address of the chief priest.
(...) of our camps, and to keep ourselves from any shameful nakedness, and he (Moses) told us that You are in our midst, (and You are) a great and awesome God, plundering all of our enemies before us. He taught us from (the times) of old through out generations, saying, when you approach the battle, the priest shall stand and speak unto the people, saying, 'Hear O Israel, you are approaching the battle against your enemies today. Do not be afraid nor fainthearted. Do not tremble, nor be terrified because of them, for your God goes with you, to fight for you against your enemies, and to save you'" (See Deut. 20:2-4)

Our officers shall speak to all those prepared for battle, those of willing heart, to strengthen them by the might of God, to turn back all who have lost heart, and to strengthen all the valiant warriors together. They shall recount that which You have spoken by the hand of Moses, saying: "And when there is a war in your land against the adversary who attacks you, then you shall sound an alarm with the trumpets that you might be remembered before your God and be saved from your enemies

(See Num. 10:9)

The prayer of the chief priest.
Who is like You, O God of Israel, in heaven and on earth, that he can perform like you do with Your great works and Your great strength? Who is like Your people Israel, whom You have chosen for Yourself from all the peoples of the lands? They are people sanctified by the covenant, learned in the statutes, enlightened in understanding. Those who hear the glorious voice and see the holy angels, whose ears are open to hearing deep things. O God, You have created the expanse of the skies, the host of the stars (luminaries), the work of spirits and the dominion of holy ones, the treasures of Your glory in the clouds. (See 1 Enoch)

He who created the earth and the limits of her divisions into wilderness and plains, and (autumn, winter, and spring with its fruits; the circle of the seas, the sources of the rivers, and the rift of the deeps, 'wild beasts and winged creatures, the form of man and the generations of his seed, the confusion of language and the separation of peoples, the abode of families which have the inheritance of the lands, and holy festivals, courses of years and times of eternity.

(Only) these we know from Your understanding which (You have taught us.) And Your ears (listen) to our cry, for (the protection of) this house. Truly the battle is Yours, and by the strength of Your hand their corpses have been broken to pieces, without anyone to bury them. Indeed, Goliath the Gittitej a mighty man of valor, You delivered into the hand of David, Your servant, because he trusted in Your great name and not in sword and spear. For the battle is Yours. He subdued the Philistines many times by Your holy name. Also by the hand of our kings You rescued us many times because of Your mercy; not according to our works, for we have acted wickedly, nor for the acts of our rebelliousness. The battle is Yours, the strength is from You, it is not our own. Neither our power nor the strength of our hand have done valiantly, but rather by Your power and the strength of Your great valor.

Just as You told us in time past, saying: "There shall come forth a star out of Jacob, a scepter shall rise out of Israel, and shall crush the forehead of Moab and tear down all sons of Sheth (the noisy boasters), and he shall descend on Jacob and shall destroy the remnant from the city, and the enemy shall be a possession, and Israel shall do valiantly (Num. 24:17-19). By the hand of Your anointed ones, seers of things appointed, You have told us about the times of the wars of Your hands in order that You may glorify Yourself (and fight) among our enemies to bring down the hordes of Belial, the seven nations of empty, boasting, prideful nations, at the hand of the oppressed whom You have redeemed with power and retribution; and wondrous strength.

A heart that melts shall be as a door of hope. You will do to them as You did to Pharaoh and the officers of his chariots in the Red Sea. You will ignite the humble of spirit like a fiery torch of fire in a sheaf, consuming the wicked.
You shall not turn back until the annihilation of the guilty. In time past You foretold the appointed time for Your hand is powerful work against the Kittim, saying: And Assyria shall fall by a sword not of man, and a sword, 'not of men, shall consume him (Isa. 31: 8).

For into the hand of the oppressed You will deliver the enemies of all the lands; into the hands of those who are prostrate in the dust, in order to bring down all mighty men of (faithless) peoples, to return the recompense of the wicked on the head of (the guilty) to pronounce the fair judgment of Your truth on all sons of man, and to make for Yourself an everlasting name among the people.

(Give us victory in) wars, and to show Yourself great and holy before the remnant of the nations, so that they may know that You are God when You carry out judgments on (Gog and on all his company that are assembled all around us. For You will do battle against them from the heavens (and heap) upon them for confusion. For You have a multitude of holy ones in the heavens and hosts of angels in Your exalted dwelling to praise Your name.

The chosen ones of the holy people You have established for Yourself in a community. The number and The book of the names of all their host is with You in Your holy dwelling, and the number of the holy ones is in the abode of Your glory. Mercies of blessing (is with them) and Your covenant of peace You engraved for them with a stylus of life in order to reign over them for all time, commissioning the hosts of Your elect by their thousands and tens of thousands together with Your holy ones and Your angels, and directing them in battle so as to condemn the earthly adversaries by trial with Your judgments. With the elect of heaven they shall prevail.

And You, O God, are awesome in the glory of Your dominion, and the company of Your holy ones is in our midst for eternal support. We shall direct our contempt at kings, derision and disdain at mighty men. For the Lord is holy, and the King of Glory is with us together with the holy ones. Mighty men and a host of angels are with our commissioned forces. The Hero of War is with our company, and the host of His spirits is with our steps. Our horse riders are as the clouds and as the mist covering the earth, 'and as a steady downpour shedding judgment on all her offspring.

Rise up, O Hero, take Your captives, O Glorious One, take Your plunder, O You who do valiantly. Lay Your hand upon the neck of Your enemies, and Your foot upon the backs of the slain. Crush the nations, Your adversaries, and may Your sword devour guilty flesh. Fill Your land with glory, and Your heritance with blessing.

An abundance of cattle in Your fields; silver and gold and precious stones in Your palaces. O Zion, rejoice greatly, and shine with joyful songs, O Jerusalem. Rejoice, all you cities of Judah, open your gates forever that the wealth of the nations might be brought to you, and their kings shall serve you.

David was king and his praise was to ring out (shine):
All they that oppressed you shall bow down to you, and the dust of your feet they shall lick. O daughters of my people shout out with a voice of joy, adorn yourselves with ornaments of glory Rule over the kingdom, and Israel to reign eternally. (. . .) them the mighty men of war, O Jerusalem be exalted above the heavens, O Lord, and let Your glory be above all the earth.

The blessings of the war recited by all the leaders after the victory.
And then the Chief Priest shall stand and his brothers the priests, the Levites, and all the elders of the Army with him. They shall bless from their position, the God of Israel and all His works of truth, and they shall curse Belial there and all the spirits of his forces.

And they shall say response: "Blessed is the God of Israel for all His holy purpose and His works of truth. And blessed are those who serve Him righteously. who know Him by faith. And cursed is Belial for his contentious purpose, and accursed for his reprehensible rule. And cursed are all the spirits of his lot for their wicked purpose. Accursed are they for all their filthy dirty service. For they are the lot of darkness, but the lot of God is light eterna1. You are the God of our fathers. We bless Your name forever, for we are an eternal people. You made a covenant with our fathers, and will establish it for their seed throughout the ages of eternity. In all the testimonies of Your glory there has been remembrance of Your kindness in our midst as an assistance to the remnant and the survivors for the sake of Your covenant and to recount Your works of truth and the judgments of Your wondrous strength.

And You, O God, created us for Yourself as an eternal people, and into the lot of light You cast us in accordance with Your truth. You appointed the Prince of Light from of old to assist us, for in His lot are all sons of righteousness and all spirits of truth are in his dominion.

You yourself made Belial for the pit, an angel of malevolence, his dominion is in darkness and his counsel is to condemn and convict. All the spirits of his lot are the angels of destruction who walk in accord with the rule of darkness, for it is their only desire. But we, in the lot of Your truth, rejoice in Your mighty hand. We rejoice in Your salvation, and revel in Your help and Your peace. Who is like You in strength, O God of Israel, and yet Your mighty hand is with the oppressed. What angel or prince is like You for Your effectual support, for of old You appointed for Yourself a day of great battle to support truth and to destroy iniquity, to bring darkness low and to lend might to light, and for an eterna1 stand, and to annihilate all the Sons of Darkness and bring joy to all the Sons of Light for You Yourself designated us for an appointed time like the fire of His fury against the idols of Egypt.

The blessings of the war recited by all the leaders in the morning before the battle.
After they have withdrawn from the slain to enter the camp, all of them shall sing the hymn of return. In the morning they shall wash their clothes, cleanse themselves of the blood of the sinful bodies, and return to the place where they had stood, where they had formed the battle line before the slain of the enemy fell.

There they shall all bless the God of Israel and together they shall joyously exalt His name. They shall say in response: "Blessed is the God of Israel, who guards loving-kindness for His covenant and the appointed times of salvation for the people He redeems.

He has called those who stumble unto wondrous accomplishments, and

He has gathered a congregation of nations for annihilation without remnant in order to raise up in judgment he whose heart has melted, to open a mouth for the dumb to sing God's mighty deeds, and to teach feeble hands warfare. He gives those whose knees shake strength to stand, and strengthens those who have been beaten from the hips to the shoulder.

Among the poor in spirit (there is not) a hard heart, and by those whose way is perfect shall all wicked nations come to an end. There will be no place for all their mighty men. But we are the remnant of Your people. Blessed is Your name, O God of loving-kindness, the One who kept the covenant for our forefathers. Throughout all our generations You have made Your mercies wondrous for the remnant of the people during the dominion of Belial. With all the mysteries of his hatred they have not led us astray from Your covenant. His spirits of destruction You have driven away from us. And when the men of his dominion condemned themselves, You have preserved the lives of Your redeemed. You raised up the small fallen by Your strength, but those who are great in height You will cut down to humble them. And there is no rescuer for all their mighty men, and no place of refuge for their swift ones. To their honored men You will return shame, and all their vain existence shall be as nothing.

But we, Your holy people, shall praise Your name for Your works of truth. Because of Your mighty deeds we shall exalt your splendor in epochs and appointed times of eternity, at the beginning of day, at night and at dawn and dusk. For Your glorious purpose is great and Your wondrous mysteries are in Your high heavens, to raise up those for Yourself from the dust and to humble those of the gods.

Rise up, rise up, O God of gods, and raise Yourself in power, O King of Kings (and) let all the Sons of Darkness scatter from before You. Let the light of Your majesty shine forever upon gods and men, as a fire burning in the dark places of the damned. Let it burn the damned of Sheol, (who are) eternal burning among the transgressors (throughout) all the appointed times of eternity."

They shall repeat all the thanksgiving hymns of battle there and then return to their camps. For it is a time of distress for Israel, a fixed time of battle against all the nations. The purpose of God is eternal redemption, and annihilation for all nations of wickedness. All those prepared for battle shall set out and camp opposite the king of the Kittim and all the forces of Belial that are assembled with him for a day of vengeance by the sword of God.
The final battle the first engagement.

Then the Chief Priest shall stand, and with him his brothers the priests, the Levites, and all the men of the army. He shall read aloud the prayer for the appointed time of battle, as is written in the book 'The Rule of His Time", including all the words of their thanksgivings. Then he shall form there all the battle lines, as written in "The Book of the War."
Then the priest appointed for the time of vengeance by all his brothers shall walk about and encourage them for the battle, and he shall say in response: "Be strong and courageous as warriors. Fear not, nor be discouraged and let not your heart be faint.

Do not panic, neither be alarmed because of them. Do not turn back nor flee from them. For they are a wicked congregation, all their deeds are in darkness; it is their desire. They have established all their refuge in a lie, their strength is as smoke that vanishes, and all their vast assembly is as chaff which blows away (and they will become a) desolation, and shall not be found.

Every creature of greed shall wither quickly away like a flower at harvest time. Come, strengthen yourselves for the battle of God, for this day is an appointed time of battle for God against all the nations and bring judgment upon all flesh. The God of Israel is raising His hand in His wondrous strength against all the spirits of wickedness and the mighty ones of the gods are girding themselves for battle, and the formations of the holy ones are readying themselves for a day of vengeance against the God of Israel (but He will hasten) to remove Belial in his hell until every source of (him) is come to an end. For the God of Israel has called out a sword against all the nations, and by the holy ones of His people He will do mightily."

They shall carry out all the Rule on that day at the place where they stand opposite the camps of the Kittim. Then the priests shall blow for them the trumpets of remembrance. The gates of war shall open, and the infantry shall go out and stand in columns between the battle lines. (and stand in the gap.)

The priests shall blow for them a signal for the formation and the columns shall deploy at the sound of the trumpets until each man has taken his station.

Then the priests shall blow for them a second signal, (which is the signal) for confrontation. When they stand near the battle line of the Kittim, within throwing range, each man shall raise his hand with his weapon of war.

Then the six priests shall blow on the trumpets of the slain a sharp staccato note to direct the fighting. The Levites and the all the people with rams' horns shall blow a battle signal, a loud noise. As the sound goes forth, the infantry shall begin to bring down the slain of the Kittim, and all the people shall cease the signal, but the priests shall continue blowing on the trumpets of the slain and the battle shall prevail against the Kittim.

The final battle the second engagement.
When Belial prepares himself to assist the Sons of Darkness, and the slain among the infantry begin to fall by God's mysteries, to test by these mysteries and all those appointed for battle, the priests shall blow the trumpets of assembly so that another battle line might go forth as a battle reserve, and they shall take up position between the battle lines.

For those employed in battle they shall blow a signal to return. Then the Chief Priest shall approach and stand before the battle line, and shall encourage their heart by the wondrous might of God and fortify their hands for His battle. And he shall say in response: "Blessed is God, for He tests the heart of His people in the crucible. And (do) not (worry about) your slain. For you have obeyed, from of old, the mysteries of God.

Now as for you, take courage and stand in the gap, do not fear when God strengthens (you, for in the) land He shall appoint their retribution with burning (for) those tested by the crucible. He shall sharpen the implements of war, and they shall not become blunt until all the nations off wickedness come to an end.

But, as for you, remember the judgment of Nadab and Abihu, the sons of Aaron, by whose judgment God showed Himself holy before all the people.
But Eleazar and Ithamar He preserved for Himself for an eternal covenant of priesthood. But, as for you, take courage and do not fear them, for their end is emptiness and their desire is for the void. Their support is without strength and they do not know that from the God of Israel is all that is and that will be. He (alone is) in all which exists for eternity. Today is His appointed time to subdue and to humiliate the prince of the realms of wickedness. He will send eternal support to the company of His redeemed by the power of the majestic angel of the authority of Michael. By eternal light He shall joyfully light up the covenant of Israel peace and blessing for the lot of God to exalt the authority of Michael among the gods and the dominion of Israel among all flesh. Righteousness shall rejoice on high, and al1 sons of His truth shall rejoice in eternal knowledge. But as for you, O sons of His covenant, take courage in God's crucible, until He shall wave His hand and complete His fiery trials; His mysteries concerning your existence."

The final battle the third engagement.
And after these words, the priests shall blow for them a signal to form the divisions of the battle line. The columns shall be deployed at the sound of the trumpets, until each man has taken his station. Then the priests shall blow another signal on the trumpets, that I the signal for confrontation. When the infantry has approached the battle line of the Kittim, within throwing range, each man shall raise his hand with his weapon.

Then the priests shall blow on the trumpets of the slain and the Levites and all the people with rams' horns shall sound a signal for battle. The infantry shall attack the army of the Kittim, and as the sound of the signal goes forth,
they shall begin to bring down their slain. Then all the people shall cease the sound of the signal, while the priests continuously blow on the trumpets of the slain, and the battle prevails against the Kittim, and the troops of Belial are defeated before them. Thus in the third lot (the army are destined to fall slain.)

Author's note: The sections of the final battle involving the fourth, fifth, and sixth engagements are not legible. The codex has large pieces missing. Nothing of these engagements is preserved.

The final battle the seventh engagement.
... And in the seventh lot, the great hand of God shall be lifted up against Belial and against all the forces of his dominion for an eternal slaughter. The shout of the holy ones (will go forth) when they pursue Assyria. Then the sons of Japheth shall fall, never to rise again, and the Kitum shall be crushed without remnant or survivor. So the God of Israel shall raise His hand against the entire multitude of Belial. At that time the priests shall sound a signal on the six trumpets of remembrance, and all the

battle formations shall be gathered to them and divide against all the camps of the Kittim to completely destroy them. And when the sun hastens to set on that day, the Chief Priest and the priests and the Levites who are with him, and the chiefs of the battle lines and the men of the army shall bless the God of Israel there. They shall say in response: Blessed is Your name, O God of gods, for You have done wondrous things for Your people, and have kept Your covenant for us from of old. Many times You have opened the gates of salvation for us for the sake of Your covenant. And You provided for our affliction in accord with Your goodness toward us. You, O God of righteousness, have acted for the sake of Your name.

Thanksgiving for final victory.
. . . You have done wonders upon wonders with us, but from (times) of old there has been nothing like it, for You have known our appointed time. Today Your power has shined forth for us, and You have shown us the hand of Your mercies with us in eternal redemption, in order to remove the dominion of the enemy, that it might be no more. (This is) the hand of Your strength. In battle, You shall show Yourself strong against our enemies for an absolute slaughter. Now the day is pressing upon us to pursue their multitude, for You (go before us) and the heart of warriors You have broken so that no one is able to stand. Yours is the might, and the battle is in Your hand, and there is no God like You. Your (. . .) and the appointed times of Your will, and reprisal (...) Your enemies, and You will cut off from (...) .

And we shall direct our contempt at kings, (and our) derision and disdain at mighty men. For our Majestic One is holy. The King of Glory is with us and the host of His spirits is with our steps. Our horsemen are as the clouds and as the mist covering the earth; as a steady downpour shedding judgment on al1 her offspring.

Rise up, O Hero, Take Your captives, O Glorious One, and take Your plunder, O You Who do valiantly. Lay Your hand upon the neck of Your enemies, and Your foot upon the backs of the slain. Crush the nations, Your adversaries, and let Your sword devour flesh. Fill Your land with glory, and Your inheritance with blessing. An abundance of cattle is sin Your fields, silver and gold in Your palaces. O Zion, rejoice greatly, and rejoice, all you cities of Judah. Open your gates forever, so that the wealth of the nations might be brought to you, and their kings shall serve you. All they that oppressed you shall bow down to you, and they shall lick the dust of your feet. O daughters of my people, burst out with a voice of joy. Adorn yourselves with ornaments of glory, and rule over the kingdom of the (Kittim). Your (...) and Israel for an eternal dominion.

Ceremony after the final battle.
Then they shall gather in the camp that night for rest until the morning. In the morning they shall come to the place of the battle line, where the mighty men of the Kittim fell, as well as the multitude of Assyria, and the forces of all the nations that were assembled unto them, to see whether the multitude of slain are dead with none to bury them; those who fell there by the sword of God.

And the High Priest shall approach there with his deputy, his brothers the priests, and the Levites with the Leader of the battle, and all the chiefs of the battle lines and their officers (and they shall come) together.

When they stand before the slain of the Kittim, they shall praise there the God of Israel. And they shall say in response (Glory to) God most high…

Introduction to Gnosticism

Several of the following texts are Gnostic in origin and theology. To assist the reader in a deeper understanding of the Gnostic books, a brief introduction and explanation follows.

"Gnosticism: A system of religion mixed with Greek and Oriental philosophy of the 1st through 6th centuries A.D. Intermediate between Christianity and paganism, Gnosticism taught that knowledge rather than faith was the greatest good and that through knowledge alone could salvation be attained."

Webster's Dictionary

The word Gnostic is based on the Greek word "Gnosis," which means "knowledge." The "Gnosis" is the knowledge of the ultimate, supreme God and his spirit, which is contained within us all. It is this knowledge that allows one to transcend this material world with its falsities and spiritual entrapments and ascend into heaven to be one with God.

For centuries the definition of Gnosticism has in itself been a point of confusion and contention within the religious community. This is due in part to the ever-broadening application of the term and the fact that various sects of Gnosticism existed as the theology evolved and began to merge into what became mainstream Christianity.

Even though Gnosticism continued to evolve, it is the theology in place at the time that the Gnostic Gospels were written that should be considered and understood before attempting to render or read a translation. To do otherwise would make the translation cloudy and obtuse.

It becomes the duty of both translator and reader to understand the ideas being espoused and the terms conveying those ideas. A grasp of theology, cosmology, and relevant terms is necessary for a clear transmission of the meaning within the text in question.

With this in mind, we will briefly examine Gnostic theology, cosmology, and history. We will focus primarily on Gnostic sects existing in the first through fourth centuries A.D. since it is believed most Gnostic Gospels were written during that time. It was also during that time that reactions within the emerging Christian orthodoxy began to intensify.

The downfall of many books written on the topic of religion is the attempt to somehow remove history and people from the equation. History shapes religion because it shapes the perception and direction of religious leaders. Religion also develops and evolves in an attempt to make sense of the universe as it is seen and understood at the time. Thus, to truly grasp a religious concept it is important to know the history, people, and cosmology of the time. These areas are not separate but are continually interacting. This is how the information in this book will be presented to the reader.

A Brief Lesson in Gnosticism

The roots of the Gnosticism may pre-date Christianity. Similarities exist between Gnosticism and the wisdom and mystery cults found in Egypt and Greece. Gnosticism contains the basic terms and motifs of Plato's cosmology as well as the mystical qualities of Buddhism. Plato was steeped in Greek mythology, and the Gnostic creation myth has elements owing to this. Both cosmology and mysticism within Gnosticism present an interpretation of Christ's existence and teachings, thus, Gnostics are considered to be a Christian sect. Gnostic followers are urged to look within themselves for the truth and the Christ spirit hidden, asleep in their souls. The battle cry can be summed up in the words of the Gnostic Gospel of Thomas, verse 3:

> *Jesus said: If those who lead you say to you: Look, the Kingdom is in the sky, then the birds of the sky would enter before you. If they say to you: It is in the sea, then the fish of the sea would enter ahead of you. But the Kingdom of God exists within you and it exists outside of you. Those who come to know (recognize) themselves will find it, and when you come to know yourselves you will become known and you will realize that you are the children of the Living Father. Yet if you do not come to know yourselves then you will dwell in poverty and it will be you who are that poverty.*

Paganism was a religious traditional society in the Mediterranean leading up to the time of the Gnostics. Centuries after the conversion of Constantine, mystery cults worshipping various Egyptian and Greco-Roman gods continued. These cults taught that through their secret knowledge worshippers could control or escape the mortal realm. The Gnostic doctrine of inner knowledge and freedom may have part of its roots here. The concept of duality and inner guidance taught in Buddhism added to and enforced Gnostic beliefs, as we will see later.

The belief systems of Plato, Buddha, and paganism melted together, spread, and found a suitable home in the mystical side of the Christian faith as it sought to adapt and adopt certain Judeo-Christian beliefs and symbols.

Like modern Christianity, Gnosticism had various points of view that could be likened to Christian denominations of today. Complex and elaborate creation myths took root in Gnosticism, being derived from those of Plato. Later, the theology evolved and Gnosticism began to shed some of its more unorthodox myths, leaving the central theme of inner knowledge or gnosis to propagate.

The existence of various sects of Gnosticism, differing creation stories, along with the lack of historical documentation, has left scholars in a quandary about exactly what Gnostics believed. Some have suggested that the Gnostics represented a free thinking and idealistic movement much like that of the "Hippie" movement active in the United States during the 1960's.

Just as the "Hippie" movement in the U.S. influenced political thought, some early sects of Gnostics began to exert direct influence on the Christian church and its leadership.

Although it appears that there were several sects of Gnosticism, we will attempt to discuss the more universal Gnostic beliefs along with the highlights of the major sects.

Gnostic cosmology, (which is the theory of how the universe is created, constructed, and sustained), is complex and very different from orthodox

Christianity cosmology. In many ways Gnosticism may appear to be polytheistic or even pantheistic.

To understand some of the basic beliefs of Gnosticism, let us start with the common ground shared between Gnosticism and modern Christianity. Both believe the world is imperfect, corrupt, and brutal. The blame for this, according to mainstream Christianity, is placed squarely on the shoulders of man himself. With the fall of man (Adam), the world was forever changed to the undesirable and harmful place in which we live today. However, Gnostics reject this view as an incorrect interpretation of the creation myth.

According to Gnostics, the blame is not in ourselves, but in our creator. The creator of this world was himself somewhat less than perfect and in fact, deeply flawed and cruel, making mankind the child of a lesser God. It is in the book, *The Apocryphon of John*, that the Gnostic view of creation is presented to us in great detail.

Gnosticism also teaches that in the beginning a Supreme Being called The Father, The Divine All, The Origin, The Supreme God, or The Fullness, emanated the element of existence, both visible and invisible. His intent was not to create but, just as light emanates from a flame, so did creation shine forth from God. This manifested the primal element needed for creation. This was the creation of Barbelo, who is the Thought of God.

The Father's thought performed a deed and she was created from it. It is she who had appeared before him in the shining of his light. This is the first power which was before all of them and which was created from his mind. She is the Thought of the All and her light shines like his light. It is the perfect power which is the visage of the invisible. She is the pure, undefiled Spirit who is perfect. She is the first power, the glory of Barbelo, the perfect glory of the kingdom (kingdoms), the glory revealed. She glorified the pure, undefiled Spirit and it was she who praised him, because thanks to him she had come forth.
The Apocryphon of John

It could be said that Barbelo is the creative emanation and, like the Divine All, is both male and female. It is the "agreement" of Barbelo and the Divine All, representing the union of male and female, that created the Christ Spirit and all the Aeons. In some renderings the word "Aeon" is used to designate an ethereal realm or kingdom. In other versions "Aeon" indicates the ruler of the realm. One of these rulers was called Sophia or Wisdom. Her fall began a chain of events that led to the introduction of evil into the universe.

Seeing the Divine flame of God, Sophia sought to know its origin. She sought to know the very nature of God. Sophia's passion ended in tragedy when she managed to capture a divine and creative spark, which she attempted to duplicate with her own creative force, without the union of a male counterpart. It was this act that produced the Archons, beings born outside the higher divine realm. In the development of the myth, explanations seem to point to the fact that Sophia carried the divine essence of creation from God within her but chose to attempt creation by using her own powers. It is unclear if this was in an attempt to understand the Supreme God and his power, or an impetuous act that caused evil to enter the cosmos in the form of her creations.

The realm containing the Fullness of the Godhead and Sophia is called the pleroma or Realm of Fullness. This is the Gnostic heaven. The lesser Gods created in

Sophia's failed attempt were cast outside the pleroma and away from the presence of God. In essence, she threw away and discarded her flawed creations.

"She cast it away from her, outside the place where no one of the immortals might see it, for she had created it in ignorance. And she surrounded it with a glowing cloud, and she put a throne in the middle of the cloud so that no one could see it except the Holy Spirit who is called the mother of all that has life. And she called his name Yaldaboth." Apocryphon of John

The beings Sophia created were imperfect and oblivious to the Supreme God. Her creations contained deities even less perfect than herself. They were called the Powers, the Rulers, or the Archons. Their leader was called the Demiurge, but his name was Yaldaboth. It was the flawed, imperfect, spiritually blind Demiurge, (Yaldaboth), who became the creator of the material world and all things in it. Gnostics considered Yaldaboth to be the same as Jehovah (Yahweh), who is the Jewish creator God. These beings, the Demiurge and the Archons, would later equate to Satan and his demons, or Jehovah and his angels, depending on which Gnostic sect is telling the story. Both are equally evil.

In one Gnostic creation story, the Archons created Adam but could not bring him to life. In other stories Adam was formed as a type of worm, unable to attain personhood. Thus, man began as an incomplete creation of a flawed, spiritually blind, and malevolent god. In this myth, the Archons were afraid that Adam might be more powerful than the Archons themselves. When they saw Adam was incapable of attaining the human state, their fears were put to rest, thus, they called that day the "Day of Rest."

Sophia saw Adam's horrid state and had compassion, because she knew she was the origin of the Archons and their evil. Sophia descended to help bring Adam out of his hopeless condition. It is this story that set the stage for the emergence of the sacred feminine force in Gnosticism that is not seen in orthodox Christianity. Sophia brought within herself the light and power of the Supreme God. Metaphorically, within the spiritual womb of Sophia was carried the life force of the Supreme God for Adam's salvation.

In the Gnostic text called, *The Apocryphon of John*, Sophia is quoted:

> *"I entered into the midst of the cage which is the prison of the body. And I spoke saying: 'He who hears, let him awake from his deep sleep.' Then Adam wept and shed tears. After he wiped away his bitter tears he asked: 'Who calls my name, and from where has this hope arose in me even while I am in the chains of this prison?' And I (Sophia) answered: 'I am the one who carries the pure light; I am the thought of the undefiled spirit. Arise, remember, and follow your origin, which is I, and beware of the deep sleep.'"*

Sophia would later equate to the Holy Spirit as it awakened the comatose soul.

As the myth evolved, Sophia, after animating Adam, became Eve in order to assist Adam in finding the truth. She offered it to him in the form of the fruit of the tree of knowledge. To Gnostics, this was an act of deliverance.

Other stories have Sophia becoming the serpent in order to offer Adam a way to attain the truth. In either case, the apple represented the hard sought truth, which was the knowledge of good and evil, and through that knowledge Adam could become a god. Later, the serpent would become a feminine symbol of wisdom, probably owing to the connection with Sophia. Eve, being Sophia in disguise, would become the mother and sacred feminine of us all. As Gnostic theology began to coalesce, Sophia would come to be considered a force or conduit of the Holy Spirit, in part due to the fact that the Holy Spirit was also considered a feminine and creative force from the Supreme God. The Gospel of Philip echoes this theology in verse six as follows:

> *In the days when we were Hebrews we were made orphans, having only our Mother. Yet when we believed in the Messiah (and became the ones of Christ), the Mother and Father both came to us. Gospel of Philip*

As the emerging orthodox church became more and more oppressive to women, later even labeling them "occasions of sin," the Gnostics countered by raising women to equal status with men, saying Sophia was, in a sense, the handmaiden or wife of the Supreme God, making the soul of Adam her spiritual offspring.

In Gnostic cosmology the "living" world is under the control of entities called Aeons, of which Sophia is head. This means the Aeons influence or control the soul, life force, intelligence, thought, and mind. Control of the mechanical or inorganic world is given to the Archons. They rule the physical aspects of systems, regulation, limits, and order in the world. Both the ineptitude and cruelty of the Archons are reflected in the chaos and pain of the material realm.

The lesser God that created the world, Yaldaboth. began his existence in a state that was both detached and remote from the Supreme God in aspects both spiritual and physical. Since Sophia had misused her creative force, which passed from the Supreme God to her, Sophia's creation, the Demiurge, Yaldaboth, contained only part of the original creative spark of the Supreme Being. He was created with an imperfect nature caused by his distance in lineage and in spirit from the Divine All or Supreme God. It is because of his imperfections and limited abilities the lesser God is also called the "Half-Maker".

The Creator God, the Demiurge, and his helpers, the Archons took the stuff of existence produced by the Supreme God and fashioned it into this material world.

Since the Demiurge (Yaldaboth) had no memory of how he came to be alive, he did not realize he was not the true creator. The Demiurge believed he somehow came to create the material world by himself. The Supreme God allowed the Demiurge and Archons to remain deceived.

The Creator God (the Demiurge) intended the material world to be perfect and eternal, but he did not have it in himself to accomplish the feat. What comes forth from a being cannot be greater than the highest part of him, can it? The world was created flawed and transitory and we are part of it. Can we escape? The Demiurge was imperfect and evil. So was the world he created. If it was the Demiurge who created man and man is called upon to escape the Demiurge and find union with the Supreme God, is this not demanding that man becomes greater than his creator? Spiritually this seems impossible, but as many children become greater than their parents, man is expected to become greater than his maker, the Demiurge.

This starts with the one fact that the Demiurge denies: the existence and supremacy of the Supreme God.

Man was created with a dual nature as the product of the material world of the Demiurge with his imperfect essence, combined with the spark of God that emanated from the Supreme God through Sophia. A version of the creation story has Sophia instructing the Demiurge to breath into Adam that spiritual power he had taken from Sophia during his creation. It was the spiritual power from Sophia that brought life to Adam.

It is this divine spark in man that calls to its source, the Supreme God, and which causes a "divine discontent," that nagging feeling that keeps us questioning if this is all there is. This spark and the feeling it gives us keeps us searching for the truth.

The Creator God sought to keep man ignorant of his defective state by keeping him enslaved to the material world. By doing so, he continued to receive man's worship and servitude. He did not wish man to recognize or gain knowledge of the true Supreme God. Since he did not know or acknowledge the Supreme God, he views any attempt to worship anything else as spiritual treason.

The opposition of forces set forth in the spiritual battle over the continued enslavement of man and man's spiritual freedom set up the duality of good and evil in Gnostic theology. There was a glaring difference between the orthodox Christian viewpoint and the Gnostic viewpoint. According to Gnostics, the creator of the material world was an evil entity and the Supreme God, who was his source, was the good entity. Christians quote John 1:1 "In the beginning was the Word, and the Word was with God, and the Word was God."

According to Gnostics, only through the realization of man's true state or through death can he escape captivity in the material realm. This means the idea of salvation does not deal with original sin or blood payment. Instead, it focuses on the idea of awakening to the fullness of the truth.

According to Gnostic theology, neither Jesus nor his death can save anyone, but the truth that he came to proclaim can allow a person to save his or her own soul. It is the truth, or realization of the lie of the material world and its God, that sets one on a course of freedom.

To escape the earthly prison and find one's way back to the pleroma (heaven) and the Supreme God, is the soteriology (salvation doctrine) and eschatology (judgment, reward, and doctrine of heaven) of Gnosticism.

The idea that personal revelation leads to salvation, may be what caused the mainline Christian church to declare Gnosticism a heresy. The church could better tolerate alternative theological views if the views did not undermine the authority of the church and its ability to control the people. Gnostic theology placed salvation in the hands of the individual through personal revelations and knowledge, excluding the need for the orthodox church and its clergy to grant salvation or absolution. This fact, along with the divergent interpretation of the creation story, which placed the creator God, Yaldaboth or Jehovah, as the enemy of mankind, was too much for the church to tolerate. Reaction was harsh. Gnosticism was declared to be a dangerous heresy.

Gnosticism may be considered polytheistic because it espoused many "levels" of Gods, beginning with an ultimate, unknowable, Supreme God and descending as he created Sophia, and Sophia created the Demiurge (Creator God); each becoming more inferior and limited.

There is a hint of pantheism in Gnostic theology due to the fact that creation occurs because of a deterioration of the Godhead and the dispersion of the creative essence, which eventually devolves into the creation of man.

In the end, there occurs a universal reconciliation as being after being realizes the existence of the Supreme God and renounces the material world and its inferior creator.

Combined with its Christian influences, the cosmology of the Gnostics may have borrowed from the Greek philosopher, Plato, as well as from Buddhism. There are disturbing parallels between the creation myth set forth by Plato and some of those recorded in Gnostic writings.

Plato lived from 427 to 347 B.C. He was the son of wealthy Athenians and a student of the philosopher, Socrates, and the mathematician, Pythagoras. Plato himself was the teacher of Aristotle.

In Plato's cosmology, the Demiurge is an artist who imposed form on materials that already existed. The raw materials were in a chaotic and random state. The physical world must have had visible form which was put together much like a puzzle is constructed. This later gave way to a philosophy which stated that all things in existence could be broken down into a small subset of geometric shapes.

In the tradition of Greek mythology, Plato's cosmology began with a creation story. The story was narrated by the philosopher Timaeus of Locris, a fictional character of Plato's making. In his account, nature is initiated by a creator deity, called the "Demiurge," a name which may be the Geek word for "craftsman" or "artisan" or, according to how one divides the word, it could also be translated as "half-maker."

The Demiurge sought to create the cosmos modeled on his understanding of the supreme and original truth. In this way he created the visible universe based on invisible truths. He set in place rules of process such as birth, growth, change, death, and dissolution. This was Plato's "Realm of Becoming." It was his Genesis. Plato stated that the internal structure of the cosmos had innate intelligence and was therefore called the World Soul. The cosmic super-structure of the Demiurge was used as the framework on which to hang or fill in the details and parts of the universe. The Demiurge then appointed his underlings to fill in the details which allowed the universe to remain in a working and balanced state. All phenomena of nature resulted from an interaction and interplay of the two forces of reason and necessity.

Plato represented reason as constituting the World Soul. The material world was a necessity in which reason acted out its will in the physical realm. The duality between the will, mind, or reason of the World Soul and the material universe and its inherent flaws set in play the duality of Plato's world and is seen reflected in the beliefs of the Gnostics.

In Plato's world, the human soul was immortal, each soul was assigned to a star. Souls that were just or good were permitted to return to their stars upon their death. Unjust souls were reincarnated to try again. Escape of the soul to the freedom of the stars and out of the cycle of reincarnation was best accomplished by following the reason and goodness of the World Soul and not the physical world, which was set in place only as a necessity to manifest the patterns of the World Soul.

Although in Plato's cosmology the Demiurge was not seen as evil, in Gnostic cosmology he was considered not only to be flawed and evil, but he was also the beginning of all evil in the material universe, having created it to reflect his own malice.

Following the path of Plato's cosmology, some Gnostics left open the possibility of reincarnation if the person had not reached the truth before his death.

In the year 13 A.D. Roman annals record the visit of an Indian king named Pandya or Porus. He came to see Caesar Augustus carrying a letter of introduction in Greek. He was accompanied by a monk who burned himself alive in the city of Athens to prove his faith in Buddhism. The event was described by Nicolaus of Damascus as, not surprisingly, causing a great stir among the people. It is thought that this was the first transmission of Buddhist teaching to the masses.

In the second century A.D., Clement of Alexandria wrote about Buddha: "Among the Indians are those philosophers also who follow the precepts of Boutta (Buddha), whom they honour as a god on account of his extraordinary sanctity." (Clement of Alexandria, "The Stromata, or Miscellanies" Book I, Chapter XV).

"Thus philosophy, a thing of the highest utility, flourished in antiquity among the barbarians, shedding its light over the nations. And afterwards it came to Greece." (Clement of Alexandria, "The Stromata, or Miscellanies").

To clarify what "philosophy" was transmitted from India to Greece, we turn to the historians Hippolytus and Epiphanius who wrote of Scythianus, a man who had visited India around 50 A.D. They report; "He brought 'the doctrine of the Two Principles.'" According to these writers, Scythianus' pupil Terebinthus called himself a Buddha. Some scholars suggest it was he that traveled to the area of Babylon and transmitted his knowledge to Mani, who later founded Manichaeism.

Adding to the possibility of Eastern influence, we have accounts of the Apostle Thomas' attempt to convert the people of Asia-Minor. If the Gnostic gospel bearing his name was truly written by Thomas, it was penned after his return from India, where he also encountered the Buddhist influences.

Ancient church historians mention that Thomas preached to the Parthians in Persia, and it is said he was buried in Edessa. Fourth century chronicles attribute the evangelization of India (Asia-Minor or Central Asia) to Thomas.

The texts of the Gospel of Thomas, which some believe predate the four gospels, has a very "Zen-like" or Eastern flavor.

Since it is widely held that the four gospels of Matthew, Mark, Luke, and John have a common reference in the basic text of Mark, it stands to reason that all follow the same general insight and language. If The Gospel of Thomas was written in his absence from the other apostles or if it was the first gospel written, one can assume it was written outside the influences common to the other gospels.

Although the codex found in Egypt is dated to the fourth century, the actual construction of the text of Thomas is placed by most Biblical scholars at about 70–150 A.D. Most agree the time of writing was in the second century A.D.

Following the transmission of the philosophy of "Two Principals," both Manichaeism and Gnosticism retained a dualistic viewpoint. The black-versus-white dualism of Gnosticism came to rest in the evil of the material world and its maker, versus the goodness of the freed soul and the Supreme God with whom it seeks union.

Oddly, the disdain for the material world and its Creator God drove Gnostic theology to far-flung extremes in attitude, beliefs, and actions. Gnostics idolize the serpent in the "Garden of Eden" story. After all, if your salvation hinges on secret knowledge the offer of becoming gods through the knowledge of good and evil sounds wonderful. So powerful was the draw of this "knowledge myth" to the Gnostics that the serpent became linked to Sophia by some sects. This can still be seen today in our medical and veterinarian symbols of serpents on poles, conveying the ancient meanings of knowledge and wisdom.

Genesis 3 (King James Version)
1 Now the serpent was more subtil than any beast of the field which the LORD God had made. And he said unto the woman, Yea, hath God said, Ye shall not eat of every tree of the garden?
2 And the woman said unto the serpent, We may eat of the fruit of the trees of the garden:
3 But of the fruit of the tree which is in the midst of the garden, God hath said, Ye shall not eat of it, neither shall ye touch it, lest ye die.
4 And the serpent said unto the woman, Ye shall not surely die:
5 For God doth know that in the day ye eat thereof, then your eyes shall be opened, and ye shall be as Gods, knowing good and evil.

It is because of their vehement struggle against the Creator God and the search for some transcendent truth, that Gnostics held the people of Sodom in high regard. The people of Sodom sought to "corrupt" the messengers sent by their enemy, the Creator God. Anything done to thwart the Demiurge and his minions was considered valiant.

Genesis 19 (King James Version)
1 And there came two angels to Sodom at even; and Lot sat in the gate of Sodom: and Lot seeing them rose up to meet them; and he bowed himself with his face toward the ground;
2 And he said, Behold now, my lords, turn in, I pray you, into your servant's house, and tarry all night, and wash your feet, and ye shall rise up early, and go on your ways. And they said, Nay; but we will abide in the street all night.
3 And he pressed upon them greatly; and they turned in unto him, and entered into his house; and he made them a feast, and did bake unleavened bread, and they did eat.
4 But before they lay down, the men of the city, even the men of Sodom, compassed the house round, both old and young, all the people from every quarter:
5 And they called unto Lot, and said unto him, Where are the men which came in to thee this night? bring them out unto us, that we may know them.
6 And Lot went out at the door unto them, and shut the door after him,
7 And said, I pray you, brethren, do not so wickedly.
8 Behold now, I have two daughters which have not known man; let me, I pray you, bring them out unto you, and do ye to them as is good in your eyes: only unto these men do nothing; for therefore came they under the shadow of my roof.
9 And they said, Stand back. And they said again, This one fellow came in to sojourn, and he will needs be a judge: now will we deal worse with thee, than with them. And they pressed sore upon the man, even Lot, and came near to break the door.
10 But the men put forth their hand, and pulled Lot into the house to them, and shut to the door.

To modern Christians, the idea of admiring the serpent, which we believe was Satan, may seem unthinkable. Supporting the idea of attacking and molesting the angels sent to Sodom to warn of the coming destruction seems appalling; but to Gnostics the real evil was the malevolent entity, the Creator God of this world. To destroy his messengers, as was the case in Sodom, would impede his mission. To obtain knowledge of good and evil, as was offered by the serpent in the garden, would set the captives free.

To awaken the inner knowledge of the true God was the battle. The material world was designed to prevent the awakening by entrapping, confusing, and distracting the spirit of man. The aim of Gnosticism was the spiritual awakening and freedom of man.

Gnostics, in the age of the early church, would preach to converts (novices) about this awakening, saying the novice must awaken the God within himself and see the trap that was the material world. Salvation came from the recognition or knowledge contained in this spiritual awakening.

Not all people are ready or willing to accept the Gnosis. Many are bound to the material world and are satisfied to be only as and where they are. These have mistaken the Creator God for the Supreme God and do not know there is anything beyond the Creator God or the material existence. These people know only the lower or earthly wisdom and not the higher wisdom above the Creator God. They are referred to as "dead."

Gnostic sects split primarily into two categories. Both branches held that those who were truly enlightened could no longer be influenced by the material world. Both divisions of Gnosticism believed that their spiritual journey could not be impeded by the material realm since the two were not only separate but in opposition. Such an attitude influenced some Gnostics toward Stoicism, choosing to abstain from the world, and others toward Epicureanism, choosing to indulge.

Major schools fell into two categories; those who rejected the material world of the Creator God, and those who rejected the laws of the Creator God. For those who rejected the world the Creator God had spawned, overcoming the material world was accomplished by partaking of as little of the world and its pleasures as possible. These followers lived very stark and ascetic lives, abstaining from meat, sex, marriage, and all things that would entice them to remain in the material realm. Other schools believed it was their duty to simply defy the Creator God and all laws that he had proclaimed. Since the Creator God had been identified as Jehovah, God of the Jews, these followers set about to break every law held dear by Christians and Jews.

As human nature is predisposed to do, many Gnostics took up the more wanton practices, believing that nothing done in their earthly bodies would affect their spiritual lives. Whether it was excesses in sex, alcohol, food, or any other assorted debaucheries, the Gnostics were safe within their faith, believing nothing spiritually bad could come of their earthly adventures.

The actions of the Gnostics are mentioned by early Church leaders. One infamous Gnostic school is actually mentioned in the Bible, as we will read later.

The world was out of balance, inferior, and corrupt. The spirit was perfect and intact. It was up to the Gnostics to tell the story, explain the error, and awaken the world to the light of truth. The Supreme God had provided a vehicle to help in their effort. He had created a teacher of light and truth.

Since the time of Sophia's mistaken creation of the Archons, there was an imbalance in the cosmos. The Supreme God began to re-establish the balance by producing Christ to teach and save man. That left only Sophia, now in a fallen and bound state, along with the Demiurge, and the Archons to upset the cosmic equation. In this theology one might loosely equate the Supreme God to the New Testament Christian God, Demiurge to Satan, the Archons to demons, the pleroma to heaven, and Sophia to the creative or regenerative force of the Holy Spirit. This holds up well except for one huge problem. If the Jews believed that Jehovah created all things, and the Gnostic believed that the Demiurge created all things, then to the Gnostic mind, the Demiurge must be Old Testament god, Jehovah, and that made Jehovah their enemy.

For those who seek that which is beyond the material world and its flawed creator, the Supreme God has sent Messengers of Light to awaken the divine spark of the Supreme God within us. This part of us will call to the True God as deep calls to deep. The greatest and most perfect Messenger of Light was the Christ. He is also referred to as The Good, Christ, Messiah, and The Word. He came to reveal the Divine Light to us in the form of knowledge.

According to the Gnostics, Christ came to show us our own divine spark and to awaken us to the illusion of the material world and its flawed maker. He came to show us the way back to the divine Fullness (The Supreme God). The path to enlightenment was the knowledge sleeping within each of us. Christ came to show us the Christ spirit living in each of us. Individual ignorance or the refusal to awaken our internal divine spark was the only original sin. Christ was the only Word spoken by God that could awaken us. Christ was also the embodiment of the Word itself. He was part of the original transmission from the Supreme God that took form on the earth to awaken the soul of man so that man might search beyond the material world.

One Gnostic view of the Incarnation was "docetic," which is an early heretical position that Jesus was never actually present in the flesh, but only appeared to be human. He was a spiritual being and his human appearance was only an illusion. Of course, the title of "heretical" can only be decided by the controlling authority of the time. In this case it was the church that was about to emerge under the rule of the Emperor Constantine.

Most Gnostics held that the Christ spirit indwelt the earthly Jesus at the time of his baptism by John, at which time Jesus received the name, and thus the power, of the Lord or Supreme God.

The Christ spirit departed from Jesus' body before his death. These two viewpoints remove the idea of God sacrificing himself as an atonement for the sins of man. The idea of atonement was not necessary in Gnostic theology since it was knowledge and not sacrifice that set one free.

Since there was a distinction in Gnosticism between the man Jesus and the Light of Christ that came to reside within him, it is not contrary to Gnostic beliefs that Mary Magdalene could have been the consort and wife of Jesus. Neither would it have been blasphemous for them to have had children.

Various sects of Gnosticism stressed certain elements of their basic theology. Each had its head teachers and its special flavor of beliefs. One of the oldest types was the Syrian Gnosticism. It existed around 120 A.D. In contrast to other sects, the Syrian lacked much of the embellished mythology of Aeons, Archons, and angels.

The fight between the Supreme God and the Creator God was not eternal, though there was strong opposition to Jehovah, the Creator God. He was considered to have been the last of the seven angels who created this world out of divine material which emanated from the Supreme God. The Demiurge attempted to create man, but only created a miserable worm which the Supreme God had to save by giving it the spark of divine life. Thus man was born.

According to this sect, Jehovah, the Creator God, must not be worshiped. The Supreme God calls us to his service and presence through Christ his Son. They pursued only the unknowable Supreme God and sought to obey the Supreme Deity by abstaining from eating meat and from marriage and sex, and by leading an ascetic life. The symbol of Christ was the serpent, who attempted to free Adam and Eve from their ignorance and entrapment to the Creator God.

Another Gnostic school was the Hellenistic or Alexandrian School. These systems absorbed the philosophy and concepts of the Greeks, and the Semitic nomenclature was replaced by Greek names. The cosmology and myth had grown out of proportion and appear to our eyes to be unwieldy. Yet, this school produced two great thinkers, Basilides and Valentinus. Though born at Antioch, in Syria, Basilides founded his school in Alexandria around the year A.D. 130, where it survived for several centuries.

Valentinus first taught at Alexandria and then in Rome. He established the largest Gnostic movement around A.D. 160. This movement was founded on an elaborate mythology and a system of sexual duality of male and female interplay, both in its deities and its savior.

Tertullian wrote that between 135 A.D. and 160 A.D. Valentinus, a prominent Gnostic, had great influence in the Christian church. Valentinus ascended in church hierarchy and became a candidate for the office of bishop of Rome, the office that quickly evolved into that of Pope. He lost the election by a narrow margin. Even though Valentinus was outspoken about his Gnostic slant on Christianity, he was a respected member of the Christian community until his death and was probably a practicing bishop in a church of lesser status than the one in Rome.

The main platform of Gnosticism was the ability to transcend the material world through the possession of privileged and directly imparted knowledge. Following this doctrine, Valentinus claimed to have been instructed by a direct disciple of one of Jesus' apostles, a man by the name of Theodas.

Valentinus is considered by many to be the father of modern Gnosticism. His vision of the faith is summarized by G.R.S. Mead in the book "Fragments of a Faith Forgotten."

> "The Gnosis in his hands is trying to embrace everything, even the most dogmatic formulation of the traditions of the Master. The great popular movement and its incomprehensibilities were recognized by Valentinus as an integral part of the mighty outpouring; he laboured to weave all together, external and internal, into one piece, devoted his life to the task, and doubtless only at his death perceived that for that age he was attempting the impossible. None but the very few could ever appreciate the ideal of the man, much less understand it. " (Fragments of a Faith Forgotten, p. 297)

Gnostic theology seemed to vacillate from polytheism to pantheism to dualism to monotheism, depending on the teacher and how he viewed and stressed certain areas of their creation myths. Marcion, a Gnostic teacher, espoused differences between the God of the New Testament and the God of the Old Testament, claiming they were two separate entities. According to Marcion, the New Testament God was a good true God while the Old Testament God was an evil angel. Although this may be a heresy, it pulled his school back into monotheism. The church, however, disowned him.

Syneros and Prepon, disciples of Marcion, postulated three different entities, carrying their teachings from monotheism into polytheism in one stroke. In their system the opponent of the good God was not the God of the Jews, but Eternal Matter, which was the source of all evil. Matter, in this system became a principal creative force. Although it was created imperfect, it could also create, having the innate intelligence of the "world soul."

Of all the Gnostic schools or sects the most famous is the Antinomian School. Believing that the Creator God, Jehovah, was evil, they sat out to disrupt all things connected to the Jewish God. This included his laws. It was considered their duty to break any law of morality, diet, or conduct given by the Jewish God, who they considered the evil Creator God. The leader of the sect was called Nicolaites. The sect existed in Apostolic times and is mentioned in the Bible.

Revelation 2 (King James Version)
5 Remember therefore from whence thou art fallen, and repent, and do the first works; or else I will come unto thee quickly, and will remove thy candlestick out of his place, except thou repent.
6 But this thou hast, that thou hatest the deeds of the Nicolaitanes, which I also hate.

Revelation 2 (King James Version)
14 But I have a few things against thee, because thou hast there them that hold the doctrine of Balaam, who taught Balac to cast a stumbling block before the children of Israel, to eat things sacrificed unto idols, and to commit fornication.
15 So hast thou also them that hold the doctrine of the Nicolaitanes, which thing I hate.
16 Repent; or else I will come unto thee quickly, and will fight against them with the sword of my mouth.

One of the leaders of the Nocolaitanes, according to Origen, was Carpocrates, whom Tertullian called a magician and a fornicator. Carpocretes taught that one could only escape the cosmic powers by discharging one's obligations to them and disregarding their laws. The Christian church fathers, St. Justin, Irenaeus, and Eusebius wrote that the reputation of these men (the Nicolaitanes), brought infamy upon the whole race of Christians.

Although Gnostic sects varied, they had certain points in common. These commonalities included salvation through special knowledge, and the fact that the world was corrupt as it was created by an evil God.

According to Gnostic theology, nothing can come from the material world that is not flawed. Because of this, Gnostics did not believe that Christ could have been a corporeal being. Thus, there must be some separation or distinction between

Jesus, as a man, and Christ, as a spiritual being born from the Supreme, unrevealed, and eternal God.

To closer examine this theology, we turn to Valentinus, the driving force of early Gnosticism, for an explanation. Valentinus divided Jesus Christ into two very distinct parts; Jesus, the man, and Christ, the anointed spiritual messenger of God. These two forces met in the moment of Baptism when the Spirit of God came to rest on Jesus and the Christ power entered his body.

Here Gnosticism runs aground on its own theology, for if the spiritual cannot mingle with the material then how can the Christ spirit inhabit a body? The result of the dichotomy was a schism within Gnosticism. Some held to the belief that the specter of Jesus was simply an illusion produced by Christ himself to enable him to do his work on earth. It was not real, not matter, not corporeal, and did not actually exist as a physical body would. Others came to believe that Jesus must have been a specially prepared vessel and was the perfect human body formed by the very essence of the plumora (heaven). It was this path of thought that allowed Jesus to continue as human, lover, and father.

Jesus, the man, became a vessel containing the Light of God, called Christ. In the Gnostic view we all could and should become Christs, carrying the Truth and Light of God. We are all potential vehicles of the same Spirit that Jesus held within him when he was awakened to the Truth.

The suffering and death of Jesus then took on much less importance in the Gnostic view, as Jesus was simply part of the corrupt world and was suffering the indignities of this world as any man would. Therefore, from their viewpoint, he could have been married and been a father without disturbing Gnostic theology in the least.

The Gnostic texts seem to divide man into parts, although at times the divisions are somewhat unclear. The divisions alluded to may include the soul, which is the will of man; the spirit, which is depicted as wind or air (pneuma) and contains the holy spark that is the spirit of God in man; and the material human form, the body. The mind of man sits as a mediator between the soul, or will, and the spirit, which is connected to God.

Without the light of the truth, the spirit is held captive by the Demiurge, which enslaves man. This entrapment is called "sickness." It is this sickness that the Light came to heal and then to set us free. The third part of man, his material form, was considered a weight, an anchor, and a hindrance, keeping man attached to the corrupted earthly realm.

As we read the text, we must realize that Gnosticism conflicted with traditional Christianity. Overall theology can rise and fall upon small words and terms. If Jesus was not God, his death and thus his atonement meant nothing. His suffering meant nothing. Even the resurrection meant nothing, if one's view of Jesus was that he was not human to begin with, as was true with some Gnostics.

For the Gnostics, resurrection of the dead was unthinkable since flesh as well as all matter is destined to perish. According to Gnostic theology, there was no resurrection of the flesh, but only of the soul. How the soul would be resurrected was explained differently by various Gnostic groups, but all denied the resurrection of the body. To the enlightened Gnostic the actual person was the spirit who used the body as an instrument to survive in the material world but did not identify with it. This belief is echoed in the Gospel of Thomas.

> 29. *Jesus said: If the flesh came into being because of spirit, it is a marvel, but if spirit came into being because of the body, it would be a marvel of marvels. I marvel indeed at how great wealth has taken up residence in this poverty.*

Owing to the Gnostic belief of such a separation of spirit and body, it was thought that the Christ spirit within the body of Jesus departed the body before the crucifixion. Others said the body was an illusion and the crucifixion was a sham perpetrated by an eternal spirit on the men that sought to kill it. Lastly, some suggested that Jesus deceived the soldiers into thinking he was dead. The resurrection under this circumstance became a lie which allowed Jesus to escape and live on in anonymity, hiding, living as a married man, and raising a family until his natural death.

Think of the implications to the orthodox Christian world if the spirit of God departed from Jesus as it fled and laughed as the body was crucified. This is the implication of the Gnostic interpretation of the death of Jesus when he cries out, "My power, my power, why have you left me," as the Christ spirit left his body before his death. What are the ramifications to the modern Christian if the Creator God, the Demiurge, is more evil than his creation? Can a Creation rise above its creator? Is it possible for man to find the spark within himself that calls to the Supreme God and free himself of his evil creator?

Although, in time, the creation myth and other Gnostic differences began to be swept under the rug, it was the division between Jesus and the Christ spirit that put them at odds with the emerging orthodox church. At the establishment of the doctrine of the trinity, the mainline church firmly set a divide between themselves and the Gnostics.

To this day there is a battle raging in the Christian world as believers and seekers attempt to reconcile today's Christianity to the sect of the early Christian church called, "Gnosticism."

The Sacred Feminine

One of the most striking differences between the Gnostic church and the modern church is the absence of reverence for Mary, the mother of Jesus. This is due in part to the fact that today's accepted traditions of Mother Mary were not yet in place. In fact, some of the positions of the Catholic Church regarding Mary were not officially accepted until the mid to late nineteenth century.

In the writings of the early church fathers (Justin Martyr 165 A.D. and Irenaeus 202 A.D.), Mother Mary was seldom mentioned and only to contrast Mary's obedience with Eve's disobedience. The doctrine of Mary as Theotokos (God-bearer) probably originated in Alexandria and was first introduced by Origen. It became common in the fourth century and accepted at the Council of Ephesus in 431 A.D.

Since the orthodox Christian church continued to slip farther and farther toward the belief that sex was evil, the doctrine of the "Ever-Virginity" of Mary was established. This was the belief that Mary conceived as a virgin, but also remained a virgin even after giving birth to Jesus and thereafter for the rest of her life. The Catholic Church rejects the idea that Mary had other children, although the Bible speaks of the brothers and sisters of Jesus. The doctrine of "virginity" was established around 359 A.D.

The doctrine of the bodily Assumption of Mary was formally developed by St. Gregory of Tours around 594 A.D. This doctrine stated that Mary, the mother of Jesus, was taken up into heaven to be seated at the side of Jesus. The idea has been present in apocryphal texts since the late fourth century.

The Feast of the Assumption became widespread in the sixth century, and sermons on that occasion tended to emphasize Mary's power in heaven.

Of all the doctrines regarding Mary, the doctrine of the Immaculate Conception widened the divide between the Catholic churches and other Christian churches. This doctrine took the position that Mother Mary was born without the stain of original sin. Both Catholics and Orthodox Christians accept this doctrine, but only the Roman Catholic Church has named it "The Immaculate Conception" and articulated it as doctrine. Eastern Orthodox Christians reject the western doctrine of original sin, preferring instead to speak of a tendency towards sin. They believe Mary was born without sin, but so was everyone else. Mary simply never gave in to sin.

As we see in the following statement, the doctrine was not formally accepted until 1854 A.D.

> "The Most Blessed Virgin Mary was, from the first moment of her conception, by a singular grace and privilege of almighty God and by virtue of the merits of Jesus Christ, Savior of the human race, preserved immune from all stain of original sin."
>
> Pope Pius IX, Ineffabilis Deus (1854)

The evolution of the status of Mary the Mother of Jesus has taken eighteen-hundred years to become what it is today. The status of Mary Magdalene was likely established within the Gnostic communities by 400 A.D.

Gnostic texts often used sex as a metaphor for spiritual union and release. Since the Godhead itself had both a masculine element of the Supreme God, who is the Father, and a feminine element of Sophia, sexual terms are used freely. The sexual metaphor was expanded in the story of the Supreme God giving rise to

Sophia as he spewed forth the essence of everything. According to some sects Sophia became the creator or divine mother of both angels and lesser Gods, including the creator of the material world, the Demiurge.

Sexual duality found in Gnosticism, along with the concept of the sacred feminine seen in the Sophia myth, allowed for more reverence and acceptance of women in the Gnostic worship. Owing to this, the concept that Mary Magdalene was somehow special to Jesus, as is reported in the *Gospel of Philip*, or that he may have shared spiritual concepts with her that were unknown to the male apostles, as told in the *Gospel of Mary Magdalene*, is not so difficult to comprehend.

The parallel between Sophia and Mary Magdalene cannot be overstated. Sophia was the handmaiden of the Supreme God, carrying the life force, which was the emanation of God. She carried the truth within her, which she offered to Adam. The truth was offered up to set him free. Mary was the consort of Jesus, carrying the imparted knowledge and possibly his life force in the form of a child. She revealed to the apostles the truth Jesus personally and intimately gave to her alone. We will see this stated clearly in *The Gospel of Mary Magdalene* later in this book.

The mythos of Gnosticism's sacred feminine force comes full circle in the person of Mary Magdalene. From God to Sophia; from Sophia to the man Adam; from the second Adam, who is Christ Jesus, to Mary Magdalene, who offered up that which was given her to mankind; the circle of knowledge and life was complete once again.

Points of Logic, Faith, and Sex

Man's inability to understand the divine is eclipsed only by his inadequacy to accurately articulate what his feeble mind has so tenuously grasped. Each time man desires to "tinker" with theology in order to make that which is spiritual reasonable and logical to the carnal mind, more problems are raised than solved.

When the Gnostics began to entertain the idea of the man Jesus being the vessel and host of the Holy Spirit they broke from their first basic tenet of faith: that which states that the spiritual world could not co-mingled, with the material world. As Gnostic theology developed, lines blurred and softened to a point where it was realized that if man was a triune being of body, soul, and spirit there must be a level of interface between the two worlds. At this point it was decided that only the Supreme God was too holy and pure to interact with the material world. This left open the possibility for the man Jesus to carry the Holy Spirit.

But wait... isn't God and the Holy Spirit the same? They must not be for this belief to work. If they were the same then the symbiotic relationship of Jesus the man and the Holy Spirit of the Supreme God would not have allowed itself to have a relationship with Mary Magdalene.

Even though Jesus was considered the highest earthly creation, he was still not the equal of God.

Yet, according to theology being proclaimed by the established churches, the Holy Spirit was not only equal to God but the essentially the same as God. This presented a point of illogic in the Gnostic theology. This was solved by some Gnostic slight of hand. Since the Holy Spirit was a feminine force, it was not actually God, but was the spouse of the Supreme God. This set the stage for further parallels between Sophia and the Holy Spirit.

Rising to another level of the Sacred Feminine, it becomes the female part of the Godhead that empowered Jesus. The mother of the Godhead becomes the Christ Spirit that saves and leads mankind.

Later, as the Catholic Church struggled to make sense of their own female redeemer, they began to elevate Mother Mary by announcing the doctrine of the Immaculate Conception, so errors in logic were exposed. If Mother Mary was conceived without sin in order to carry Jesus, who was conceived without sin, one must ask why it wasn't necessary for the mother of Mary to also be conceived without sin. This logic continues backward ad infinitum until Eve herself and all female offspring must be sinless. Of course, the church flatly refuses this line of reasoning, saying only that certain things must be taken on faith. This is the same tact taken regarding the "Ever-Virginity" of Mother Mary, even in the face of scriptures proclaiming that the mother, sister, and brothers of Jesus had come to have audience with him.

It was the Greek Orthodox church that already had the answer to this dilemma. Original sin is not in their doctrine. They state only that humans are born with a predisposition toward sinning. This makes null the problem of sinless birth from the beginning.

Even though the theological events of doctrine concerning Mother Mary occurred over time, they serve as an undeniable pattern of the Catholic Church as it endeavored to "purify" women and rid them of sexuality.

It was the Gnostics that continued to increase the sexuality, power, and place of women in the schema of their faith.

The sexual metaphors used in the Gnostic texts have fanned the flames of great controversy and speculation. It has been widely accepted that societal norms of the time dictated that Jewish men were to be married by the age of thirty. This certainly applied to Rabbis, since marriage and procreation were considered divine commands. Jesus is referred to by the title of Rabbi in the Bible. It has been noted that his marital status would have placed him into a very small minority in the culture at the time, being a male over 30 years of age and unmarried. Thus, some Gnostic followers use this observation to bolster the idea Jesus was married. This idea was held by those who thought that Jesus, the man, was the vehicle for the Christ spirit.

For other Gnostics who believed Jesus to be an illusion placed on us by the Christ spirit while he was on earth, the idea of a spiritual illusion mingling with flesh was out of the question.

Most Gnostics held to the idea of the duality of sexes playing out in multiple layers. The feminine force of Sophia becomes the feminine force of the Holy Spirit and is made the bride of God. The sexual duality continues when the feminine force of the Holy Spirit inhabits the perfect man, Jesus, making him the messiah. The sexual context is ripe for the story to be continued in the persons of Jesus and Mary Magdalene, physically shadowing the spiritual relationship of the Holy Spirit and the Supreme God as well as Jesus and the Holy Spirit.

The concept of a married Jesus is revealed in several verses of The Gospel of Philip such verse 118.

> *There is the Son of Man and there is the son of the son of Man. The Lord is the Son of Man, and his son creates through him. God gave the Son of Man the power to create; he also gave him the ability to have children. Gospel of Philip*

If one were to examine the writings of Solomon, the play on words between the sexual and the spiritual aspects can be seen clearly. The Gnostics simply expanded on the theme.

Song of Solomon 1 (King James Version)
1 The song of songs, which is Solomon's.
2 Let him kiss me with the kisses of his mouth: for thy love is better than wine.
3 Because of the savour of thy good ointments thy name is as ointment poured forth, therefore do the virgins love thee.
4 Draw me, we will run after thee: the king hath brought me into his chambers: we will be glad and rejoice in thee, we will remember thy love more than wine:

Song of Solomon 2
16 My beloved is mine, and I am his: he feedeth among the lilies.
17 Until the day break, and the shadows flee away, turn, my beloved, and be thou like a roe or a young hart upon the mountains of Bether.

Song of Solomon 3
1 By night on my bed I sought him whom my soul loveth: I sought him, but I found him not.
2 I will rise now, and go about the city in the streets, and in the broad ways I will seek him whom my soul loveth: I sought him, but I found him not…

Song of Solomon 5
1 I am come into my garden, my sister, my spouse: I have gathered my myrrh with my spice; I have eaten my honeycomb with my honey; I have drunk my wine with my milk: eat, O friends; drink, yea, drink abundantly, O beloved.
2 I sleep, but my heart waketh: it is the voice of my beloved that knocketh, saying, Open to me, my sister, my love, my dove, my undefiled: for my head is filled with dew, and my locks with the drops of the night.
3 I have put off my coat; how shall I put it on? I have washed my feet; how shall I defile them?
4 My beloved put in his hand by the hole of the door, and my bowels were moved for him.
5 I rose up to open to my beloved; and my hands dropped with myrrh, and my fingers with sweet smelling myrrh, upon the handles of the lock.

Song of Solomon 7
1 How beautiful are thy feet with shoes, O prince's daughter! the joints of thy thighs are like jewels, the work of the hands of a cunning workman.
2 Thy navel is like a round goblet, which wanteth not liquor: thy belly is like an heap of wheat set about with lilies.
3 Thy two breasts are like two young roes that are twins.

Due to the inherent dualism of Gnosticism, sex was a symbol, and, at times, a portal to a mystical experience. Many religions are replete with sexual allegories, as is Gnosticism. Proceeding from the two points of sexual metaphor in Gnostic literature and the likelihood of marriage among the population of Jewish men, controversy arose when speculation began as to whether Jesus could have married. The flames of argument roared into inferno proportions when the translation of the books of Philip and Mary Magdalene were published.

> *And the companion (Consort) was Mary of Magdala (Mary Magdalene). The Lord loved Mary more than all the other disciples and he kissed her often on her mouth (the text is missing here and the word "mouth" is assumed). The others saw his love for Mary and asked him: "Why do you love her more than all of us?" The Savior replied, "Why do I not love you in the same way I love her?"*
> *The Gospel of Philip*

> *Peter said to Mary; "Sister we know that the Savior loved you more than all other women. Tell us the words of the Savior that you remember and know, but we have not heard and do not know. Mary answered him and said; "I will tell you what He hid from you."*
> *The Gospel of Mary Magdalene*

Seizing on the texts above, writers of both fiction and non-fiction allowed their pens to run freely amidst conjecture and speculation of marriage and children between Jesus and Mary Magdalene.

The writers *of The Da Vinci Code* and *Holy Blood, Holy Grail* took these passages and expanded them into storylines that have held readers captive with anticipation.

Did Jesus take Mary to be his wife? Could the couple have produced children? Gnostic theology leaves open the possibility.

As we step into the Gospel of Philip we encounter pure Gnostic ritual. The most sacred of all Gnostic rituals is contained in the metaphor of the duality of man and God seeking unity. With this in mind, the Lord established five sacraments: baptism, anointing, the Eucharist, redemption, and the Bridal-Chamber.

Whether the sacrament of the Bridal-Chamber was a ritual enacted by a man and woman, or strictly an allegory we may never know. All we know is that the concept of the Bridal-Chamber, where two become one, dualities merge into unity, and man finally unites with the truth within himself and finds the Supreme God is a recurring and central theme and experience of Gnosticism. Accordingly, the Gnostic Jesus would have likely been married as he led others by example.

Why, out of all the women in his life and travels, did he choose Mary of Magdala? Who was she? What made her special? Let us examine the evidence.

Who Was Mary Magdalene?

The Gospel of Philip shines light on a special connection between Jesus and Mary Magdalene. Philip calls Mary the Lord's "companion," a word that can mean "wife." But, who was this Mary, the Magdalene?

As was customary in Biblical times, the last name of the person was connected to his or her place of ancestry. This is evidenced in the fact that Jesus was called, "Jesus of Nazareth." Mary came from a town called Magdala, which was 120 miles north of Jerusalem on the shores of the Sea of Galilee. Magdala Tarichaea may have been the full name of the town. Magdala means tower, and Tarichaea means salted fish. The little village had the optimistic name of "The Tower of Salted Fish." The main business of the area was fishing, and there is a good chance that Mary worked in the fish markets, or actually owned a business selling fish. Magdala, it seems, was a prosperous fishing village with a reputation as a licentious city. Mary Magdalene apparently had money since Luke says that she ministered to Jesus out of her "substance."

The Jewish text, "Lamentations Raba," mentions a town called "Magdala," and says Magdala was judged by God and destroyed because of its fornication. This could explain western Christianity's assumption that Mary Magdalene was the prostitute caught in adultery and presented to Jesus.

In fact, we have linked Mary Magdalene with many of the women in the New Testament who were redeemed or forgiven. This is a powerful and rich myth that resonates with both men and women who have fallen from grace and seek redemption. However, the Bible never says that Mary Magdalene was ever a prostitute.

Luke does not name her as the woman who washes the feet of Jesus with her hair.

Luke 7 (King James Version)
36 And one of the Pharisees desired him that he would eat with him. And he went into the Pharisee's house, and sat down to meat.
37 And, behold, a woman in the city, which was a sinner, when she knew that Jesus sat at meat in the Pharisee's house, brought an alabaster box of ointment,
38 And stood at his feet behind him weeping, and began to wash his feet with tears, and did wipe them with the hairs of her head, and kissed his feet, and anointed them with the ointment.
39 Now when the Pharisee which had bidden him saw it, he spake within himself, saying, This man, if he were a prophet, would have known who and what manner of woman this is that toucheth him: for she is a sinner.
40 And Jesus answering said unto him, Simon, I have somewhat to say unto thee. And he saith, Master, say on.
41 There was a certain creditor which had two debtors: the one owed five hundred pence, and the other fifty.
42 And when they had nothing to pay, he frankly forgave them both. Tell me therefore, which of them will love him most?
43 Simon answered and said, I suppose that he, to whom he forgave most. And he said unto him, Thou hast rightly judged.

44 And he turned to the woman, and said unto Simon, Seest thou this woman? I entered into thine house, thou gavest me no water for my feet: but she hath washed my feet with tears, and wiped them with the hairs of her head.
45 Thou gavest me no kiss: but this woman since the time I came in hath not ceased to kiss my feet.
46 My head with oil thou didst not anoint: but this woman hath anointed my feet with ointment.
47 Wherefore I say unto thee, Her sins, which are many, are forgiven; for she loved much: but to whom little is forgiven, the same loveth little.
48 And he said unto her, Thy sins are forgiven.
49 And they that sat at meat with him began to say within themselves, Who is this that forgiveth sins also?
50 And he said to the woman, Thy faith hath saved thee; go in peace.

There is never a name given to the woman caught in the act of adultery.

John 8 (King James Version)
1Jesus went unto the mount of Olives.
2And early in the morning he came again into the temple, and all the people came unto him; and he sat down, and taught them.
3And the scribes and Pharisees brought unto him a woman taken in adultery; and when they had set her in the midst,
4They say unto him, Master, this woman was taken in adultery, in the very act.
5Now Moses in the law commanded us, that such should be stoned: but what sayest thou?
6This they said, tempting him, that they might have to accuse him. But Jesus stooped down, and with his finger wrote on the ground, as though he heard them not.
7So when they continued asking him, he lifted up himself, and said unto them, He that is without sin among you, let him first cast a stone at her.
8And again he stooped down, and wrote on the ground.
9And they which heard it, being convicted by their own conscience, went out one by one, beginning at the eldest, even unto the last: and Jesus was left alone, and the woman standing in the midst.
10When Jesus had lifted up himself, and saw none but the woman, he said unto her, Woman, where are those thine accusers? hath no man condemned thee?
11She said, No man, Lord. And Jesus said unto her, Neither do I condemn thee: go, and sin no more.
12Then spake Jesus again unto them, saying, I am the light of the world: he that followeth me shall not walk in darkness, but shall have the light of life.

The only clear history we have is a single statement that it was Mary who was once demon-possessed.

Luke 8 (King James Version)
1And it came to pass afterward, that he went throughout every city and village, preaching and shewing the glad tidings of the kingdom of God: and the twelve were with him,
2And certain women, which had been healed of evil spirits and infirmities, Mary called Magdalene, out of whom went seven devils,

3And Joanna the wife of Chuza Herod's steward, and Susanna, and many others, which ministered unto him of their substance.

Here is what we know with certainty:

She was a woman who followed Jesus as he ministered and preached.

Luke 8:1-3: Afterward, Jesus journeyed from one town and village to another, preaching and proclaiming the good news of the kingdom of God. Accompanying him were the Twelve and some women who had been cured of evil spirits and infirmities, Mary, called Magdalene, from whom seven demons had gone out, Joanna, the wife of Herod's steward Chuza, Susanna, and many others who provided for them out of their resources.

She was there when Jesus was crucified.

Mark 15:40: There were also some women looking on from a distance, among whom were Mary Magdalene, and Mary the mother of James the Less and Joses, and Salome.
Matthew 27:56: Among them was Mary Magdalene, and Mary the mother of James and Joseph, and the mother of the sons of Zebedee.

John 19:25: But standing by the cross of Jesus were His mother, and His mother's sister, Mary the wife of Clopas, and Mary Magdalene.

She continued to believe in Jesus after he was killed.

Mark 15:47: Mary Magdalene and Mary the mother of Joses were looking on to see where He was laid.

Matthew 27:61: And Mary Magdalene was there, and the other Mary, sitting opposite the grave.

Matthew 28:1: Now after the Sabbath, as it began to dawn toward the first day of the week, Mary Magdalene and the other Mary came to look at the grave.

Mark 16:1: When the Sabbath was over, Mary Magdalene, and Mary the mother of James, and Salome, bought spices, so that they might come and anoint Him.

She was the first to realize and announce the resurrection of Jesus.

John 20:1: Now on the first day of the week Mary Magdalene came early to the tomb, while it was still dark, and saw the stone already taken away from the tomb.

Mark 16:9: Now after He had risen early on the first day of the week, He first appeared to Mary Magdalene, from whom He had cast out seven demons.

John 20:18: Mary Magdalene came, announcing to the disciples, "I have seen the Lord," and that He had said these things to her.

Luke 24: But at daybreak on the first day of the week [the women] took the spices they had prepared and went to the tomb. They found the stone rolled away from the tomb; but when they entered, they did not find the body of the Lord Jesus. While they were puzzling over this, behold, two men in dazzling garments appeared to them. They were terrified and bowed their faces to the ground. They said to them, "Why do you seek the living one among the dead?

He is not here, but he has been raised. Remember what he said to you while he was still in Galilee, that the Son of Man must be handed over to sinners and be crucified, and rise on the third day." And they remembered his words.

Then they returned from the tomb and announced all these things to the eleven and to all the others.

The women were Mary Magdalene, Joanna, and Mary the mother of James; the others who accompanied them also told this to the apostles, but their story seemed like nonsense and they did not believe them.

It is the myth woven into the story of Mary that empowers her to us. To many, she is the captive, possessed, enslaved, caught in the midst of crime and tragedy, but at once redeemed, set free, and loved by God himself. She is hope and triumph. She represents the power of truth and love to change the life of the lowest and most powerless of us. She is you and me in search of God.

The Reaction of Christendom

Reaction to Gnosticism within the newly forming church was swift and bold. Beginning with a swelling defense in the New Testament itself, the writers began to define and defend doctrine. Labels, names, and descriptions of the Christian doctrine would be established later in various councils, but for now there would be decisive actions to fend off new ideas.

Considering the fact that there were two main approaches to Gnosticism in the first and second centuries, the stoic-ascetic approach of self denial and the hedonistic-epicurean approach of self indulgence, we will find two criticisms mounted against Gnosticism in the Bible. First we will examine the pronouncements against the more hedonistic sects.

2 Timothy 3 (King James Version)
1 *This know also, that in the last days perilous times shall come.*
2 *For men shall be lovers of their own selves, covetous, boasters, proud, blasphemers, disobedient to parents, unthankful, unholy,*
3 *Without natural affection, trucebreakers, false accusers, incontinent, fierce, despisers of those that are good,*
4 *Traitors, heady, highminded, lovers of pleasures more than lovers of God;*
5 *Having a form of godliness, but denying the power thereof: from such turn away.*
6 *For of this sort are they which creep into houses, and lead captive silly women laden with sins, led away with divers lusts,*
7 *Ever learning, and never able to come to the knowledge of the truth.*

Keeping in mind the previous information and scripture given regarding the Gnostic sect of the Nicolaitanes, Timothy mounts an attack against Pagans and wayward Christians, including certain Gnostics, who had fallen into debauchery. The last line of the admonition targets what he sees as the Gnostic weakness of, *"Ever learning, and never able to come to the knowledge of the truth."*

One of the most difficult passages to apprehend is found in I John chapter 4, where the writer attempts to draw a fine line between what is the error in Gnostic theology and what is the full truth of Christ on earth according to orthodoxy.

1 John (King James Version)
1 John 4
1 *Beloved, believe not every spirit, but try the spirits whether they are of God: because many false prophets are gone out into the world.*
2 *Hereby know ye the Spirit of God: Every spirit that confesseth that Jesus Christ is come in the flesh is of God:*
3 *And every spirit that confesseth not that Jesus Christ is come in the flesh is not of God: and this is that spirit of antichrist, whereof ye have heard that it should come; and even now already is it in the world.*
4 *Ye are of God, little children, and have overcome them: because greater is he that is in you, than he that is in the world.*
5*They are of the world: therefore speak they of the world, and the world heareth them.*
6 *We are of God: he that knoweth God heareth us; he that is not of God heareth not us. Hereby know we the spirit of truth, and the spirit of error.*
7 *Beloved, let us love one another: for love is of God; and every one that loveth is born of*

God, and knoweth God.
8 *He that loveth not knoweth not God; for God is love.*
9 *In this was manifested the love of God toward us, because that God sent his only begotten Son into the world, that we might live through him.*
10 *Herein is love, not that we loved God, but that he loved us, and sent his Son to be the propitiation for our sins.*
11 *Beloved, if God so loved us, we ought also to love one another.*
12 *No man hath seen God at any time. If we love one another, God dwelleth in us, and his love is perfected in us.*
13 *Hereby know we that we dwell in him, and he in us, because he hath given us of his Spirit.*
14 *And we have seen and do testify that the Father sent the Son to be the Saviour of the world.*
15 *Whosoever shall confess that Jesus is the Son of God, God dwelleth in him, and he in God.*
16 *And we have known and believed the love that God hath to us. God is love; and he that dwelleth in love dwelleth in God, and God in him.*
17 *Herein is our love made perfect, that we may have boldness in the day of judgment: because as he is, so are we in this world.*

With gentle and elegant words, John cuts to the bone, amputating the part of Christendom seen as heretical.

1 *Beloved, believe not every spirit, but try the spirits whether they are of God: because many false prophets are gone out into the world.*
2 *Hereby know ye the Spirit of God: Every spirit that confesseth that Jesus Christ is come in the flesh is of God:*
3 *And every spirit that confesseth not that Jesus Christ is come in the flesh is not of God: and this is that spirit of antichrist, whereof ye have heard that it should come; and even now already is it in the world.*

The statement above is a direct attack against the Gnostic beliefs regarding Jesus and the Christ spirit. The Gnostic belief that spirit and matter could not co-exist makes it impossible for Christ to inhabit a fleshly body. The belief by some was that Jesus was an illusion or specially prepared body and Christ was somehow separate from Jesus. This made it impossible for the man Jesus to be the literal son of God.

John drives home the differences and calls the differences heresies, proclaiming that those who do not hold to orthodox beliefs have the spirit of the antichrist.

After the establishment of cannon, many incorrectly cited the following chapter to condemn Gnosticism and other religions that seemed to be gaining a notable following. Ironically, Protestants would later use the same verses to condemn Catholicism.

Revelation 17 (King James Version)
1 And there came one of the seven angels which had the seven vials, and talked with me, saying unto me, Come hither; I will shew unto thee the judgment of the great whore that sitteth upon many waters:
2 With whom the kings of the earth have committed fornication, and the inhabitants of the earth have been made drunk with the wine of her fornication.

3 So he carried me away in the spirit into the wilderness: and I saw a woman sit upon a scarlet coloured beast, full of names of blasphemy, having seven heads and ten horns.
4 And the woman was arrayed in purple and scarlet colour, and decked with gold and precious stones and pearls, having a golden cup in her hand full of abominations and filthiness of her fornication:
5 And upon her forehead was a name written, MYSTERY, BABYLON THE GREAT, THE MOTHER OF HARLOTS AND ABOMINATIONS OF THE EARTH.
6 And I saw the woman drunken with the blood of the saints, and with the blood of the martyrs of Jesus: and when I saw her, I wondered with great admiration.
7 And the angel said unto me, Wherefore didst thou marvel? I will tell thee the mystery of the woman, and of the beast that carrieth her, which hath the seven heads and ten horns.
8 The beast that thou sawest was, and is not; and shall ascend out of the bottomless pit, and go into perdition: and they that dwell on the earth shall wonder, whose names were not written in the book of life from the foundation of the world, when they behold the beast that was, and is not, and yet is.
9 And here is the mind which hath wisdom. The seven heads are seven mountains, on which the woman sitteth.
10 And there are seven kings: five are fallen, and one is, and the other is not yet come; and when he cometh, he must continue a short space.
11 And the beast that was, and is not, even he is the eighth, and is of the seven, and goeth into perdition.
12 And the ten horns which thou sawest are ten kings, which have received no kingdom as yet; but receive power as kings one hour with the beast.
13 These have one mind, and shall give their power and strength unto the beast.
14 These shall make war with the Lamb, and the Lamb shall overcome them: for he is Lord of lords, and King of kings: and they that are with him are called, and chosen, and faithful.
15 And he saith unto me, The waters which thou sawest, where the whore sitteth, are peoples, and multitudes, and nations, and tongues.
16 And the ten horns which thou sawest upon the beast, these shall hate the whore, and shall make her desolate and naked, and shall eat her flesh, and burn her with fire.
17 For God hath put in their hearts to fulfil his will, and to agree, and give their kingdom unto the beast, until the words of God shall be fulfilled.
18 And the woman which thou sawest is that great city, which reigneth over the kings of the earth.

Is the whore of Babylon Mary, as conservative Christians claim? If it is Mary, is it the representation of Mother Mary or that of Mary Magdalene? Is Gnosticism the great heresy that will bring about the downfall of the Christian church?

Let us begin with the writer's concluding statement.

Revelation 17
15 And he saith unto me, The waters which thou sawest, where the whore sitteth, are peoples, and multitudes, and nations, and tongues.
16 And the ten horns which thou sawest upon the beast, these shall hate the whore, and shall make her desolate and naked, and shall eat her flesh, and burn her with fire.
17 For God hath put in their hearts to fulfil his will, and to agree, and give their kingdom unto the beast, until the words of God shall be fulfilled.

18 And the woman which thou sawest is that great city, which reigneth over the kings of the earth.

"The woman you saw is that great city which reigns over the kings of the earth." (Rev 17:18) The great whore is not a person at all, but a place - a city, which is a seat of power wherein kings and nations are ruled.

It is not the purpose of this work to defend Gnosticism, but only to explain it. Within that explanation must be the church's defense against it. After all, until the discovery of the Gnostic gospels we knew nothing of the Gnostics but what the church fathers said about the sect as they defended the church against what they considered to be a great heresy. For those who do not take time to thoroughly research information regarding the sect, they will be confronted with the same biased and limited information as was offered to the masses of the second century.

What we can say about Gnosticism is that it does not fit the pattern to be considered the "great whore" of Revelation, as some have said.

Are Gnostics Christian? Or, to ask the question in another way, is Gnosticism a sect or denomination of Christianity? The answer depends on what prerequisites must be fulfilled in one's faith and doctrine to be considered "Christian."

If the mention or presence of a scared feminine force precludes acceptance, then all of Catholicism would be excluded. Holy Mary, Mother of God now sits sinless on the right hand of Christ as an ascended co-redeemer with him. Having been impregnated by the Holy Spirit, she carried God in her womb and gave birth to God on earth. She lived as a virgin, gave birth, yet remained a virgin, and died as a virgin. She ascended to heaven and took her place, first as an intercessor between man and Christ, then was promoted by the church to the place of co-redeemer with Christ. She is the sacred feminine within the Catholic church.

Must one believe in original sin to be a Christian? The Eastern Orthodox Church does not hold to this doctrine. They believe we have a predisposition to sin, but they do not believe we are born into sin. Are those who follow one of the oldest Christian churches in the world Christians?

Must one believe in the doctrine of the trinity to be a Christian? The Church of Jesus Christ Latter-day Saints and Jehovah's Witnesses do not believe God and Christ are one and the same.

Although these denominations did not exist at the time the Council of Nicea met at Constantine's behest, when Constantine legalized Christianity, the same problem existed. What constitutes Christianity? To answer this question church leaders came together and by majority consent, the Nicene Creed was developed. The creed, written below, became the measuring rod which decided admittance into Christendom. But before and after the great council there have been creeds, and they all have been different.

History of the Gospel of Philip

The Gospel of Philip is assumed to be one of the sources of Dan Brown's novel, *The Da Vinci Code*, about Mary Magdalene, Jesus, and their children. The Gospel is one of the Gnostic texts found at Nag Hammadi in Egypt in 1945 and belongs to the same collection of Gnostic documents as the more famous Gospel of Thomas.

It has been suggested that the *Gospel of Philip* was written in the second century A.D. If so, it may be one of the earliest documents containing themes that would later be used in apocryphal literature. This is literature that describes the end of the world or the coming of the heavenly kingdom.

A single manuscript of the *Gospel of Philip*, written in Coptic, was found in the Nag Hammadi library. The collection was a library of thirteen papyrus texts discovered near the town of Nag Hammadi in 1945 by a peasant boy. The writings in these codices comprised 52 documents, most of which are Gnostic in nature.

The codices were probably hidden by monks from the nearby monastery of St. Pachomius when the official Christian Church banned all Gnostic literature around the year 390 A.D

It is believed the original texts were written in Greek during the first or second centuries A.D. The copies contained in the discovered clay jar were written in Coptic in the third or fourth centuries A.D.

From the time Gnosticism was labeled a heresy, the church began a policy of conversion or extermination. Beginning around 390 A.D. and continuing until the Cathar extermination, the church opposed Gnosticism and all movements, forms, and sects that proceeded from it.

In 1209 Pope Innocent III proclaimed a crusade against the last vestiges of "Gnostic-like" sects, the Cathars. For years the church discussed the Cathars, attempting to decide if they could be considered Christian or not. Eventually they would be labeled heretical and ordered to come into line with the orthodox beliefs of the Catholic Church. The Cathars held to their beliefs. Their doctrine included the belief that the world was split along lines of matter and spirit, good and evil. As with many Gnostic sects, they believed in abstaining from the world by purifying themselves, living a life of chastity and poverty. They believed in the equality of the sexes. The Pope saw the Cathars as a danger to the church since the members were admired for their modest lifestyle and the Cathar membership was growing.

Even though the Cathars were an ascetic sect, leading lives of peace and abstinence, they were hunted down and killed. Twenty years of carnage and warfare followed in which cities and provinces throughout the south of France were systematically eradicated. In an attempt to kill every Cathar, one of the worst episodes of the war ensued when the entire population of Toulouse, both Cathar and Catholic, were massacred. In 1243 the Cathar fortress of Montsegur in the Pyrenees was captured and destroyed. Those who refused to renounce their beliefs were tortured or put to death by fire. In spite of continued persecution, the Cathar movement continued through the 14th century, finally disappearing in the 15th century. Still, the church could not find or destroy all Gnostic literature. Books such as *The Gospel of Philip* remained.

The *Gospel Of Philip* is a list of sayings focusing on man's redemption and salvation as framed by Gnostic theology, and is presented here based on a comparative study of translations from the Nag Hammadi Codex by Wesley W. Isenberg, Willis Barnstone, The Ecumenical Coptic Project, Bart Ehrman, Marvin Meyer, David Cartlidge, David Dungan, and other sources.

Each verse was weighed against the theological and philosophical beliefs held by the Gnostic community at the time in which the document was penned. All attempts were made to render the most accurate meaning based on the available translations and information.

Exact wording was secondary to the conveyance of the overall meaning as understood by the contemporary reader.

When the wording of a verse held two possible meanings or needed expanded definitions, optional translations were placed in parentheses.

The Gospel of Philip

1. A Hebrew makes a Hebrew convert, and they call him a proselyte (novice). A novice does not make another novice.

Some are just as they are, and they make others like themselves to receive. It is enough for them that they simply are as they are.

2. The slave seeks only to be set free. He does not hope to attain the estate of his master. The son acts as a son (heir), but the father gives the inheritance to him.

3. Those who inherit the dead are dead, and they inherit the dead. Those who inherit the living are alive. They inherit both the living and the dead.

The dead cannot inherit anything. How can the dead inherit anything? When the dead inherits the living one, he shall not die but the dead shall live instead.

4. The Gentile (unbeliever) who does not believe does not die, because he has never been alive, so he could not die. He who has trusted the Truth has found life and is in danger of dying, because he is now alive.

5. Since the day that the Christ came, the cosmos was created, the cities are built (adorned), and the dead carried out (disposed of).

6. In the days when we were Hebrews we were made orphans, having only our Mother. Yet when we believed in the Messiah (and became the ones of Christ), the Mother and Father both came to us.

7. Those who sow in the winter reap in the summer. The winter is this world system. The summer is the other age or dispensation (to come). Let us sow in the world (cosmos) so that we will reap in the summer. Because of this, it is right for us not to pray in the winter. What comes from (follows) the winter is the summer. If anyone reaps in the winter he will not harvest but rather pull it up by the roots and will not produce fruit. Not only does it not produce in winter, but on the Sabbath his field shall be bare.

8. The Christ has come to fully ransom some, to save (restore and heal) others, and to be the propitiation (payment) for others. Those who were estranged he ransomed. He purchases them for himself. He saves, heals, and restores those who come to him. These he desires to pledge (in marriage). When he became manifest (in this world) he ordained the soul (with a body) as he desired (and set aside his own life), but even before this, in the time of the world's beginning, he had ordained the soul (he had laid down his own life for these souls). At his appointed time he came to bring the soul he pledged himself to back to (for) himself. It had come to be under the control of robbers and they took it captive. Yet he saved it, and he paid the price for both the good and the evil of the world.

9. Light and dark, life and death, right and left are brothers. It is impossible for one to be separated from the other. They are neither good, nor evil. A life is not alive without death. Death is not death if one were not alive. Therefore each individual shall be returned to his origin, as he was from the beginning. Those who go beyond the world will live forever and are in the eternal present.

10. The names that are given to worldly things cause great confusion. They contort our perception from the real to the unreal. He who hears the word "God" does not think of the real, but rather has false, preconceived ideas. It is the same with the words "Father," "Son," "Holy Spirit," "Life," "Light," "Resurrection," and "Church (the called out ones)," and all other words. They do not recall the real, but rather they call to mind preconceived, false ideas.

They (Archons) learned the reality of human death. They (Archons) who are in the world system made them (men) think of the false idea. If they had been in eternity, they would not have designated anything as evil, nor would they have placed things within worldly events (time and place). They (men) are destined for eternity.

11. The only name they (men) should never speak into the world is the name the Father gave himself through the Son. This is the Father's name. It exists that he may be exalted over all things. The Son could not become the Father, unless he was given the Father's name. This name exists so that they (men) may have it in their thoughts. They (men) should never speak it. Those who do not have it cannot even think it. But the truth created names in the world for our sake. It would not be possible to learn the truth without names.

12. The Truth alone is the truth. It is a single thing and a multitude of things. The truth teaches us love alone through many and varied paths.

13. Those who ruled (lower gods) desired to deceive man because they knew man was related to the truly good ones. They (Archons) took the designation of good and they gave it to those who were not good. They did this so that by way of words they might deceive man and bind him to those who are not good. When they receive favor, they are taken from those who are not good and placed among the good. These are they who had recognized themselves. The rulers (lower gods) had desired to take the free person, and enslave him to themselves forever. Rulers of power fight against man. The rulers do not want him to be saved (recognize himself), so that men will become their masters. For if man is saved there will be no need for sacrifice.

14. When sacrifice began, animals were offered up to the ruling powers (Archon / Demiurge). They were offered up to them while the sacrificial animals were still alive. But as they offered them up they were killed. But the Christ was offered up dead to God (the Supreme God), and yet he lived.

15. Before the Christ came, there had been no bread in the world. In paradise, the place where Adam was, there had been many plants as food for wild animals, but paradise had no wheat for man to eat. Man had to be nourished like animals. But

the Christ, the perfect man, was sent. He brought the bread of heaven, so that man could eat as he should.

16. The rulers (lower gods) thought what they did (create the material world) was by their own will and power, but the Holy Spirit worked through them without their knowledge to do her will.

17. The truth, which exists from the beginning, is sown everywhere, and everyone sees it being sown, but only a few see the harvest.

18. Some say that Mary conceived (impregnated) by the Holy Spirit. They are in error. They do not know what they are saying. How can a female impregnate another female? (The Holy Spirit is a feminine force.) Mary is the virgin whom no power defiled. She is a great problem and curse among the Hebrew Apostles and those in charge (church leaders). The ruler (lower god) who attempts to defile this virgin, is himself defiled. The Lord was not going to say, "my father in heaven", unless he really had another father (on earth). He would simply have said, "my father".

19. The Lord says to the Disciples, "Come into the house of the Father, but do not bring anything in or take anything out from the father's house."

20. Jesus (Yeshua) is the secret name; Christ (messiah) is the revealed name. The name "Jesus" (Yeshua) does not occur in any other language. His name is called "Jesus" (Yeshua). In Aramaic his name is Messiah, but in Greek it is Christ (Cristos). In every language he is called the anointed one. The fact that he is Savior (Yeshua) could be fully comprehended only by himself, since it is the Nazarene who reveals the secret things.

21. Christ has within himself all things; man, angel, mystery (sacraments), and the father.

22. Those who say that the Lord first died and then arose are in error. He would have to first arise (be born) before he could die. If he is not first resurrected (born) he would die, but God lives and cannot die.

(Alternate translation:
Those who say that the Lord died first and then arose are in error. He arose first and then died. If one does not first attain the resurrection, he will not die. As God lives, he would live also).

23. No one will hide something highly valuable in something ostentatious (that would draw attention). More often, one places something of great worth within a number of containers worth nothing. This is how it is with the (human) soul. It is a precious thing placed within a lowly body.

24. Some are fearful that they will arise (from the dead) naked. Therefore they desire to rise in the flesh. They do not understand that those who choose to wear

the flesh are naked (destitute in spirit). Those who choose to strip themselves of the flesh are the ones who are not naked.

25. Flesh and blood will not be able to inherit the kingdom of God. What is this that will not inherit? It is that which is upon each of us (our flesh). But what will inherit the kingdom is that which belongs to Jesus and is of his flesh and blood. Therefore he says: "He who does not eat my flesh and drink my blood, has no life in him." What is his flesh? It is the Word, and his blood is the Holy Spirit. He who has received these has food and drink and clothing.

26. I disagree with those who say the flesh will not arise. They are in error. Tell me what will rise so that we may honor you. You say it is the spirit in the flesh and the light contained in the flesh. But whatever you say there is nothing you mention that is contained outside of the flesh (material world). It is necessary to arise in this flesh if everything exists within the flesh (and everything exists as part of or connected to the material world).

27. In this world those wearing a garment are more valuable than the garment. In the kingdom of the Heavens the garment is more valuable than the one wearing it.

28. By water and fire the entire realm is purified through the revelations by those who reveal them, and by the secrets through those who keep them. Yet, there are things kept secret even within those things revealed. There is water in baptism and there is fire in the oil of anointing.

29. Jesus took them all by surprise. For he did not reveal himself as he originally was, but he revealed himself as they were capable of perceiving him. He revealed himself to all in their own way. To the great, he revealed himself as great. To the small he was small. He revealed himself to the angels as an angel and to mankind he was a man. Some looked at him and saw themselves. But, throughout all of this, he concealed his words from everyone. However when he revealed himself to his Disciples upon the mountain, he appeared glorious. He was not made small. He became great, but he also made the disciples great so that they would be capable of comprehending his greatness.

30. He said on that day during his thanksgiving (in the Eucharist), "You have combined the perfect light and the holy spirit along with angels and images."

31. Do not hate the Lamb. Without him it is not possible to see the door to the sheepfold. Those who are naked will not come before the King.

32. The Sons of the Heavenly Man are more numerous than those of the earthly man. If the sons of Adam are numerous although they die, think of how many more Sons the Perfect Man has and these do not die. And they are continually born every instant of time.

33. The Father creates a son, but it is not possible for the son to create a son because it is impossible for someone who was just born to have a child. The Son has brothers, not sons.

34. There is order in things. All those who are born in the world are begotten physically. Some are begotten spiritually, fed by the promise of heaven, which is delivered by the perfect Word from the mouth. The perfect Word is conceived through a kiss and thus they are born. There is unction to kiss one another to receive conception from grace to grace.

35. There were three women named Mary (Bitter) who walked with the Lord all the time. They were his mother, his sister and Mary of Magdala, who was his consort (companion). Thus his mother, his sister and companion (consort) were all named Mary.

36. "Father" and "Son" are single names, "Holy Spirit" is a double name and it is everywhere; above and below, secret and revealed. The Holy Spirit's abode is manifest when she is below. When she is above she is hidden.

**(Alternative translation:
"Father" and "Son" are single names; "Holy Spirit" is a double name. For they are everywhere: they are above, they are below; they are concealed, they are revealed. When the Holy Spirit is in the revealed it is below. When it is in the concealed it is above.)**

37. Saints are served by evil powers (lesser gods). The evil spirits are deceived by the Holy Spirit. They think they are assisting a common man when they are serving Saints. A follower of the Lord once asked him for a thing from this world. He answered him saying, "Ask your Mother, and she will give you something from another realm."

38. The Apostles said to the students, "May all of our offering obtain salt!" They had called Sophia (wisdom) salt and without it no offering can become acceptable.

39. Sophia (wisdom) is barren. She has no children but she is called Mother. Others are found (adopted) by the Holy Spirit, and she has many children.

40. That which the Father has belongs to the Son, but he cannot possess it when he is young (small). When he comes of age all his father has will be given to the son.

41. Those who do not follow the path are born of the Spirit, and they stray because of her. By this same spirit (breath or life force), the fire blazes and consumes.

42. Earthly wisdom is one thing, and earthly wisdom (death) is another. Earthly wisdom is simply wisdom, but death is the wisdom of death, and death is the one who understands death. Being familiar with death is minor wisdom.

43. There are animals like the bull and donkey that are submissive to man. There are others that live in the wilderness. Man plows the field with submissive animals, and uses the harvest to feed himself as well as all the animals, domesticated or wild. So it is with the Perfect Man. Through submissive powers

he plows and provides for all things to exist. He causes all things to come together into existence, whether good or evil, right or left.

44. The Holy Spirit is the shepherd guiding everyone and every power (lower ruler or lesser gods), whether submissive, rebellious, or feral. She controls them, subdues them, and keeps them bridled, whether they wish it or not.

45. He who was created (Adam) is beautiful. One would not expect his children to be noble. If he were not created but rather born, one would expect his children to be noble. But he was both created and born. Is this nobility?

46. Adultery occurred first and then came murder. And Cain was conceived in adultery because he was the serpent's (Satan's) son. He became a murderer just like his father. He killed his brother. When copulation occurs between those who are not alike, this is adultery.

47. God is a dyer. Just as a good and true dye penetrates deep into fabric to dye it permanently from within (not a surface act), so God has baptized what He dyes into an indelible dye, which is water.

48. It is impossible for anyone to see anything in the real world, unless he has become part of it. It is not like a person in this world. When one looks at the sun he can see it without being part of it. He can see the sky or the earth or anything without having to be part of it. So it is with this world, but in the other world you must become what you see (see what you become). To see spirit you must be spirit. To see Christ you must be Christ. To see the Father you must be the Father. In this way you will see everything but yourself. If you look at yourself you will become what you see.

49. Faith receives, but love gives. No one can receive without faith. No one can love without giving. Believe and you shall receive. Love and you shall give. If you give without love, you shall receive nothing. Whoever has not received the Lord, continues to be a Hebrew.

50. The Apostles who came before us called him Jesus, The Nazarene, and The Messiah. Of these names, Jesus (Yeshua), The Nazarene (of the rite of the Nazarites), and The Messiah (Christ), the last name is the Christ, the first is Jesus, and the middle name is The Nazarene. Messiah has two meanings; the anointed one and the measured one. Jesus (Yeshua) means The Atonement (redemption or payment). 'Nazara' means Truth. Therefore, the Nazarite is The Truth. The Christ is The Measured One, the Nazarite (Truth) and Jesus (Redemption) have been measured (are the measurement).

51. The pearl which is thrown into the mud is not worth less than it was before. If it is anointed with balsam oil it is valued no higher. It is as valuable as its owner perceives it to be. So it is with the children of God. Whatever becomes of them, they are precious in their Father's eyes.

52. If you say you are a Jew it will not upset anyone. If you say you are a Roman no one will care. If you claim to be a Greek, foreigner, slave, or a free man no one will be the least bit disturbed. But, if you claim to belong to Christ everyone will take heed (be concerned). I hope to receive this title from him. Those who are worldly would not be able to endure when they hear the name.

53. God is a man-eater (cannibal), because men are sacrificed to him. Before men were sacrificed, animals were sacrificed. Those to whom they are sacrificed are not gods.

54. Vessels of glass and vessels of clay are always made with fire. But if a glass vessel should break it is recast, because it is made in a single breath. If a clay vessel breaks it is destroyed, since it came into being without breath.

55. A donkey turning a millstone walked a hundred miles but when it was untied it was in the same place it started. There are those who go on long journeys but do not progress. When evening comes (when the journey ends), they have discovered no city, no village, no construction site, no creature (natural thing), no power (ruler), and no angel. They labored and toiled for nothing (emptiness).

56. The thanksgiving (Eucharist) is Jesus. For in Aramaic they call him farisatha, which means, "to be spread out." This is because Jesus came to crucify the world.

57. The Lord went into the place where Levi worked as a dyer. He took 72 pigments and threw them into a vat. When he drew out the result it was pure white. He said, "This is how the Son of Man has come. He is a dyer."

58. Sophia (Wisdom), which they call barren, is the mother of the angels. And the companion (Consort) was Mary of Magdala. The Lord loved Mary more than all the other disciples and he kissed her often on her mouth (the text is missing here and the word "mouth" is assumed). The others saw his love for Mary and asked him: "Why do you love her more than all of us?" The Savior replied, "Why do I not love you in the same way I love her?" While a blind person and a person who sees are both in the dark, there is no difference, but when the light comes, the one who sees shall behold the light, but he who is blind will remain in darkness.

59. The Lord says: "Blessed is he who existed before you came into being, for he is and was and shall (continue to) be."

60. The supremacy of man is not evident, but it is hidden. Because of this he is master of the animals, which are stronger (larger) than him, in ways both evident and not. This allows the animals to survive. But, when man departs from them, they bite and kill and devour each other because they have no food. Now they have food because man cultivated the land.

61. If one goes down into the water (is baptized) and comes up having received nothing, but claims to belong to Christ, he has borrowed against the name at a high interest rate. But if one receives the Holy Spirit, he has been given the name as a gift. He who has received a gift does not have to pay for it or give it back. If

you have borrowed the name you will have to pay it back with interest when it is demanded. This is how the mystery works.

62. Marriage is a sacrament and a mystery. It is grand. For the world is founded upon man, and man founded upon marriage. Consider sex (pure sex), it has great power although its image is defiled.

63. Among the manifestations of unclean spirits there are male and female. The males are those who mate with the souls inhabiting a female form, and the female spirits invite those inhabiting a male form to have sex. Once seized, no one escapes unless they receive both the male and female power that is endued to the Groom with the Bride. The power is seen in the mirrored Bridal-Chamber. When foolish women see a man sitting alone, they want to subdue him, touch and handle him, and defile him. When foolish men see a beautiful woman sitting alone, they wish to seduce her, draw her in with desire and defile her. But, if the spirits see the man sitting together with his woman, the female spirit cannot intrude upon the man and the male spirit cannot intrude upon the woman. When image and angel are mated, no one can come between the man and woman.

64. He who comes out from the world cannot be stopped. Because he was once in the world he is now beyond both yearning (desire) and fear. He has overcome the flesh and has mastered envy and desire. If he does not leave the world there are forces that will come to seize him, strangle him. How can anyone escape? How can he fear them? Many times men will come and say, "We are faithful, and we hid from unclean and demonic spirits." But if they had been given the Holy Spirit, no unclean spirit would have clung to them. Do not fear the flesh, nor love it. If you fear it, the flesh will become your master. If you love it, the flesh will devour you and render you unable to move.

65. One exists either in this world or in the resurrection or in transition between them. Do not be found in transition. In that world there is both good and evil. The good in it is not good and the evil in it is not evil. There is evil after this world, which is truly evil and it is called the transition. This is what is called death. While we are in this world it is best that we be born into the resurrection, so that we take off the flesh and find rest and not wander within the region of the transition. Many go astray along the way. Because of this, it is best to go forth from the world before one has sinned.

66. Some neither wish nor are able to act. Others have the will to act but it is best for them if they do not act, because the act they desire to perform would make them a sinner. By not desiring to do a righteous act justice is withheld (justice is not obvious). However, the will always comes before the act.
(It is not the act but the will that matters.)

67. An Apostle saw in a vision people confined to a blazing house, held fast in bonds of fire, crying out as flames came from their breath. There was water in the house, and they cried out, "The waters can truly save us." They were misled by their desire. This is called the outermost darkness.
(Alternate translation:

An Apostle saw in a vision people confined to a blazing house, held fast in bonds of fire, lying in the flames. There was water, but they had no faith and did not desire to be saved. They received punishment, being cast into outer darkness.)

68. Soul and spirit were born of water and fire. From water, fire, and light the children of the Bridal-Chamber are born. The fire is the spirit (anointing), the light is the fire, but not the kind of fire that has form. I speak of the other kind whose form is white and it rains down beauty and splendor.

69. The truth did not come into the world naked, but it came in types and symbols. The world would not receive it any other way. There is a rebirth together with its symbols. One cannot be reborn through symbols. What can the symbol of resurrection raise, or the Bridal-Chamber with its symbols? One must come into the truth through the (true) image (not the symbol or type of it). Truth is this Restoration. It is good for those not born to take on the names of the Father, the Son, and the Holy Spirit. They could not have done so on their own. Whoever is not born of them will have the name (Christ's ones) removed from him. The one who receives them receives the anointing of the spirit and the unction and power of the cross. This is what the Apostles call having the right with the left. When this happens, you no longer belong to Christ, you will be Christ.

70. The Lord did everything through sacraments (mysteries or symbols): There was baptism, anointing, thanksgiving (Eucharist), atonement (sacrifice or payment), and Bridal-Chamber.

71. He says: "I came to make what is inside the same as the outside and what is below as it is above. I came to bring all of this into one place." He revealed himself through types and symbols. Those who say Christ comes from the place beyond (above) are confused.

72. He who is manifest in heaven is called "one from below." And He who knows the hidden thing is He who is above him. The correct way to say it would be "the inner and the outer or this which is beyond the outer." Because of this, the Lord called destruction "the outer darkness." There is nothing beyond it. He says, "My Father, who is in secret." He says, "Go into your inner chamber, shut the door behind you and there pray to your Father who is in secret; He who is deep within." He who is within them all is the Fullness. Beyond Him there is nothing deeper within. The deepest place within is called the uppermost place.

73. Before Christ some came forth. They were not able to go back from where they came. They were no longer able to leave from where they went. Then Christ came. Those who went in he brought out, and those who went out he brought in.

74. When Eve was still within Adam (man), there had been no death. When she was separated from him, death began. If she were to enter him again and if he were to receive her completely, death would stop.

75. "My God, my God, Oh Lord why did you abandon me?" He spoke these words on the cross. He departed (divided) the place and was not there any longer.

76. The Lord arose from the dead. He became as he had been, but his body had been made perfect. He was clothed in true flesh. Our flesh is not true, but rather an image of true flesh, as one beholds in a mirror.

77. The Bridal-Chamber is not for beasts, slaves, or whores. It is for free men and virgins.

78. Through the Holy Spirit we are born again, conceived in Christ, anointed in the spirit, united within us. Only with light can we see ourselves reflected in water or mirror. We are baptized in water and light. It is the light that is the oil of the anointing.

79. There had been three offering vestibules in Jerusalem. One opened to the west called the holy, another opened to the south called the holy of the holy, the third opened to the east called the holy of the holies where the high priest alone was to enter. The Baptism is the holy, the redemption (payment or atonement) is the holy of the holy, and the holy of the holies is the Bridal-Chamber. The Baptism has within it the resurrection and the redemption. Redemption allows entrance into the Bridal-Chamber. The Bridal-Chamber is more exalted than any of these. Nothing compares.

80. Those who pray for Jerusalem love Jerusalem. They are in Jerusalem and they see it now. These are called the holy of the holies.

81. Before the curtain of the Temple was torn we could not see the Bridal-Chamber. All we had was the symbol of the place in heaven. When the curtain was torn from the top to the bottom it made a way for some to ascend.

82. Those who have been clothed in the Perfect Light cannot be seen by the powers, nor can the powers subdue them. Yet one shall be clothed with light in the sacrament (mystery) of sex (union / being united).

83. If the woman had not been separated from the man, neither would have died. Christ came to rectify the error of separation that had occurred. He did this by re-uniting them and giving life to those who died. The woman unites with her husband in the Bridal-Chamber and those who have united in the Bridal-Chamber will not be parted again. Eve separated from Adam because she did not unite with him in the Bridal-Chamber.

84. The soul of man (Adam) was created when breath (spirit) was blown into him. The elements were supplied by his mother (Sophia). When soul (mind or will) became spirit and were joined together he spoke words the powers could not understand. They envied him, his spiritual partner, and his opportunity. They wanted it all for themselves but the Bridal-Chamber was hidden from them.

85. Jesus manifested beside the River Jordan with fullness of the kingdom of the Heavens, which existed before anything. Moreover, he was born as a Son before birth. He was anointed and he anointed. He was atoned and he atoned for others.

86. It is right to speak of a mystery. The Father of them all mated with the Virgin who had come down. A fire shone over him on that day. He revealed the power of the Bridal-Chamber. Because of this power his body came into being on that day. He came forth in the Bridal-Chamber in glory because of the essence that issued forth from the Bridegroom to the Bride. This is how Jesus established everything. It was in his heart. In this same way it is right for each one of the disciples to enter into his rest.

87. Adam came into being from two virgins, from the Spirit and from the virgin earth. Christ was born from a virgin, so that the error which occurred in the beginning would be corrected by him.

88. There were two trees in paradise. One produced beasts, the other produced man. Adam ate from the tree that produced beasts becoming a beast he gave birth to beasts. Because of this, animals were worshipped. God created man and men created gods. This is how the world works; men create gods and they worship their creations. It would have been more appropriate for gods to worship mankind. This would be the way if Adam had not eaten from the tree of life, which bore people.

89. The deeds of man follow his abilities. These are his strengths and the things he does with ease. His result is his children who came forth from his times of rest. His work is governed by his work but in his rest he brings forth his sons. This is the sign and symbol, doing works with strength, and producing children in his rest.

90. In this world the slaves are forced to serve the free. In the kingdom of Heaven the free shall serve the slaves and the Bridegroom of the Bridal-Chamber shall serve the guests. Those of the Bridal-Chamber have a single name among them, it is "rest" and they have no need for any other. The contemplation of the symbol brings enlightenment and great glory. Within those in the Chamber (rest) the glories are fulfilled.

91. Go into the water but do not go down into death, because Christ shall atone for him when he who is baptized comes forth. They were called to be fulfilled in his name. For he said, "We must fulfill all righteousness."

92. Those who say they shall die and then arise are confused. If you do not receive the resurrection while you are alive you will not receive anything when you die. This is why it is said that Baptism is great, because those who receive it shall live.

93. Philip the Apostle said, "Joseph the Carpenter planted a grove of trees because he needed wood for his work (craft or trade). He himself made the cross from the trees that he had planted, and his heir hung on that which he had planted. His heir was Jesus, and the tree was the cross. But the tree of life in the midst of the garden (paradise) is the olive tree. From the heart of it comes the anointing through the olive oil and from that comes the resurrection."

94. This world consumes corpses. Everything eaten by (in) the world dies. The truth devours life, but if you eat truth you shall never die. Jesus came (from there) bringing food. And to those wishing it (whom he wished) he gave life, so that they not die.

95. God created the garden (paradise). Man lived there, but they did not have God in their hearts and so they gave in to desire. This garden is where they will be said to us, " You may eat this but not eat that, according to your desire." This is the place where I shall choose to eat various things there such as the tree of knowledge, which slew Adam. In this place the tree of knowledge gave life to man. The Torah is the tree. It has the power to impart the knowledge of good and evil. It did not remove him from the evil or deliver him to good. It simply caused those who had eaten it to die. Death began because truth said, " You can eat this, but do not eat that." This was the beginning of death.

96. The anointing (chrism) is made superior to Baptism, because from the word Chrism we are called Christians (Christ's ones / anointed ones) not because of the word Baptism. And because of Chrism he was called Christ. The Father anointed the Son, and the Son anointed the Apostles, and the Apostles anointed us. He who has been anointed has come to possess all things; he has the resurrection, the light, the cross, and the Holy Spirit. The Father bestowed this upon him in the Bridal-Chamber. The father gave it to the Son who received it freely. The Father was in the Son, and the Son was in the Father. This is the kingdom of Heaven.

97. It was perfectly said by the Lord: Some have attained the kingdom of Heaven laughing. They came forth from the world joyous. Those who belong to Christ who went down into the water immediately came up as lord of everything. He did not laugh because he took things lightly, but because he saw that everything in this world was worthless compared to the kingdom of Heaven. If he scoffs at the world and sees its worthlessness he will come forth laughing.

98. Compared to the Bread and cup, and the oil of anointing (Chrism); there is another one superior to them all.

99. The world (system) began through a mistake. He who made this world wished to make it perfect and eternal. He failed (fell away / did not follow through) and did not attain his goal. The world is not eternal, but the children of the world are eternal. They were children and obtained eternity. No one can receive eternity except by becoming a child. The more you are unable to receive, the more you will be unable to give.

100. The cup of the communion (prayer) contains wine and water. It is presented as the symbol of the blood. Over it (because of the blood) we give thanks. It is filled by (with) the Holy Spirit. It (the blood) belongs to the Perfect Man. When we drink we consume the Perfect man.

101. The Living Water is a body. It is right that we be clothed with a living body (The Living Man). When he goes down into the water he undresses himself so he may be clothed with the living man.

102. A horse naturally gives birth to a horse, a human naturally gives birth to a human, a god naturally gives birth to a god. The Bridegroom within the Bride gives birth to children who are born in the Bridal-Chamber. The Jews do not spring forth from Greeks (Gentiles), and Christians (those belonging to Christ) do not come from Jews. These who gave birth to Christians were called the chosen generation of the Holy Spirit (living God). The True Man, the Son of Mankind, was the seed that brought forth the sons of Man. This generation is the true ones in the world. This is the place where the children of the Bridal-Chamber dwell.

103. Copulation occurs in this world when man and woman mix (mingle or entwine). Strength joins with weakness. In eternity there is a different kind of mingling that occurs. Metaphorically we call it by the same names, but it is exalted beyond any name we may give it. It transcends brute strength. Where there is no force, there are those who are superior to force. Man cannot comprehend this.

104. The one is not, and the other one is, but they are united. This is He who shall not be able to come unto those who have a heart of flesh. (He is not here, but He exists. However, He cannot inhabit a heart of those who are attached to the fleshly world.)

105. Before you possess all knowledge, should you not know yourself? If you do not know yourself, how can you enjoy those things you have? Only those who have understood themselves shall enjoy the things they have come to possess.

106. The perfected person cannot be captured or seen. If they (Archons) could see him, they could capture him. The path to grace can only come from the perfect light. Unless one is clothed in the perfect light and it shows on and in him he shall not be able to come out from the World as the perfected son of the Bridal-Chamber. We must be perfected before we come out from the world. Whoever has received all before mastering all, will not be able to master the kingdom. He shall go to the transition (death) imperfect. Only Jesus knows his destiny.

107. The holy person (priest) is entirely holy, including his body. If one blesses the bread and sanctifies it, or the cup, or everything else he receives, why will he not sanctify the body also?

108. By perfecting the water of Baptism: thus Jesus washed away death (removed death from it). Because of this, we are descended into the water but not into death. We are not poured out into the wind (spirit) of the world. Whenever that blows, its winter has come. When the Holy Spirit breathes, summer has come.

109. Whoever recognizes the truth is set free. He who is set free does not go back (sin), for the one who goes back (the sinner) is the slave of sin. Truth is the Mother. When we unite with her it is recognition of the truth. Those who are set free from sin (no longer have to sin) are called free by the world. It is the recognition of the truth that exalts the hearts of those who are set free from sin. This is what liberates them and places them over the entire world. Love builds

(inspires). He who has been set free through this recognition is a slave of love, serving those who have not yet been set free by the truth. Knowledge makes them capable of being set free. Love does not take anything selfishly. How can it when it possesses all things? It does not say; "This is mine or that is mine," but it says, "All of this belongs to you."

110. Spiritual love is wine with fragrance. All those who are anointed with it enjoy it. Those who anoint themselves with it (are near to the anointed ones) enjoy it also. But when the anointed ones depart the bystanders who are not anointed remain in their own stench. The Samaritan gave nothing to the wounded man except wine and oil for anointing. The wounds were healed, for "love covers a multitude of sins."

111. The children of a woman resemble the man who loves her. If the man is her husband, they resemble her husband. If the man is her illicit lover, they resemble him. Often, a woman will have sex with her husband out of duty but her heart is with her lover with whom she also has sex. The children of such a union often resemble the lover. You who live with the Son of God and do not also love the world but love the Lord only will have children that look like the Lord and not the world.

112. Humans mate with the humans, horses mate with horses, donkeys mate with donkeys. Like attracts like and they group together. Spirits unite with Spirits, and the thought (Word) mingles with the thought (Word), as Light merges with Light. If you become a person then people will love you. If you become a spirit, then the Spirit shall merge with you. If you become a thought (the Word), then the thought (the Word) shall unite with you. If you become enlightened, then the Light shall merge with you. If you rise above this world, then that which is from above shall rest upon (in) you. But, if you become like a horse, donkey, bull, dog, sheep, or any other animal, domestic or feral, then neither man nor Spirit nor Word (thought) nor the Light nor those from above nor those dwelling within shall be able to love you. They shall not be able to rest in you, and they will have no part in your inheritance to come.

113. He who is enslaved without his consent can be set free. He who has been set free by the grace of his master, but then sells himself back into slavery cannot be set free.

114. The cultivation in this world comes through four elements (earth, air, fire, water). Crops are harvested and taken into the barn only if there is first soil, water, wind, and light. God's harvest is also by means of four elements; faith (trust), hope (expectation), love (agape'), and knowledge (recognition of the truth). Our soil is the faith in which we take root. Our water is the hope by which we are nourished. Wind (spirit) is the love through which we grow. Light is the truth, which causes us to ripen. But, it is Grace that causes us to become kings of all heaven. Their souls are among the blessed for they live in Truth.

115. Jesus, the Christ, came to all of us but did not lay any burden on us. This kind of person is perfect and blessed. He is the Word of God. Ask us about him and we

will tell you his righteousness is difficult to define or describe. A task so great assures failure.

116. How will he give rest to everyone; great or small, believer or not? He provides rest to all. There are those who attempt to gain by assisting the rich. Those who see themselves as rich are picky. They do not come of their own accord. Do not grieve them or anyone. It is natural to want to do good, but understand that the rich may seek to cause grief and he who seeks to do good could annoy those who think they are rich.

117. A householder had acquired everything. He had children, slaves, cattle, dogs, and pigs. He also had wheat, barley, straw, hay, meat, oil, and acorns. He was wise and knew what each needed to eat. He fed his children bread and meat. He fed the slaves oil with grain. The cattle were given barley, straw and hay. The dogs received bones and the pigs got acorns and bread scraps. This is how it is with the disciple of God. If he is wise, he understands discipleship. The bodily forms will not deceive him, but he will understand the condition of the souls around him. He will speak to each man on his own level. In the world there are many types of animals in human form. He must recognize each one. If the person is a pig, feed him acorns. If the person is a bull, feed him barley with straw and hay; if a dog, throw him bones. If a person is a slave feed him basic food, but to the sons present the perfect and complete food.

118. There is the Son of Man and there is the son of the son of Man. The Lord is the Son of Man, and his son creates through him. God gave the Son of Man the power to create; he also gave him the ability to have children. That which is created is a creature. Those born are a progeny (child or heir). A creature cannot propagate, but children can create. Yet they say that the creature procreates, however, the child is a creature. Therefore the creature's progeny are not his sons, but rather they are creations. He who creates works openly, and is visible. He who procreates does so in secret, and he hides himself from others. He who creates does so in open sight. He who procreates, makes his children (son) in secret.

119. No one is able to know what day a husband and wife copulate. Only they know, because marriage in this world is a sacrament (mystery) for those who have taken a wife. If the act of an impure (common) marriage is hidden, the pure (immaculate) marriage is a deeper mystery (sacrament) and is hidden even more. It is not carnal (common) but it is pure (undefiled). It is not founded on lust. It is founded on true love (agape'). It is not part of the darkness or night. It is part of the light. A marriage (act) which is seen (revealed or exposed) becomes vulgarity (common or prostitution), and the bride has played the whore not only if she has sex with another man, but also if she escapes from the Bridal-Chamber and is seen. She may only be seen (reveal herself to) by her father, her mother, the attendant (friend) of the bridegroom, and the bridegroom. Only these have permission to go into the bridal-chamber on a daily basis. Others will yearn to hear her voice or enjoy her perfume (fragrance of the anointing oil). Let them be fed like dogs from the scraps that fall from the table. Only those being from the Bridegroom belong with the Bride in the Bridal-Chamber. No one will be able to see the Bridegroom or the Bride unless he becomes one like (with) them.

120. When Abraham was allowed (rejoiced at seeing what he was) to see (the truth), he circumcised the flesh of the foreskin to show us that it was correct (necessary) to renounce (kill) the flesh of this world.

121. As long as the entrails of a person are contained, the person lives and is well. If his entrails are exposed and he is disemboweled, the person will die. It is the same with a tree. If its roots are covered it will live and grow, but if its roots are exposed the tree will wither and die. It is the same with everything born into this world. It is this way with everything manifest (seen) and covert (unseen). As long as the roots of evil are hidden, it is strong, but once evil is exposed or recognized it is destroyed and it dies. This is why the Word says; "Already the ax has been laid to the root of the tree." It will not only chop down the tree, because that will permit it to sprout again, the ax will go down into the ground and cleave the very root. Jesus uprooted what others had only partially cut down. Let each one of us dig deeply, down to the root of the evil that is within his heart and rip it out by its roots. If we can just recognize evil we can uproot it. However, if evil remains unrecognized, it will take root within us and yield its fruit in our hearts. It will make evil our master and we will be its slaves. Evil takes us captive, and coerces us into doing what we do not want to do. Evil compels us into not doing what we should do. While it is unrecognized, it drives us .

122. Ignorance is the mother of all evil. Evil ends in confusion and death. Truth is like ignorance. If it is hidden it rests within itself, but when it is revealed it is recognized and it is stronger than ignorance and error. Truth wins and liberates us from confusion. The Word said; "You shall know the truth and the truth shall set you free." Ignorance seeks to make us its slaves but knowledge is freedom. By recognizing the truth, we shall find the fruits of the truth within our hearts. If we join ourselves with the truth we shall be fulfilled.

123. Now, we have the visible (beings) things of creation and we say that visible things (beings) are the powerful and honorable, but the invisible things are the weak and unworthy of our attention. The nature of truth is different. In it, the visible things (beings) are weak and lowly, but the invisible are the powerful and honorable. The wisdom of the invisible God cannot be made known to us except that he takes visible form in ways we are accustomed to. Yet the mysteries of the truth are revealed, in types and symbols, but the Bridal-Chamber is hidden as it is with the Holy of Holies.

124. The veil of the Temple first concealed how God governed creation. Once the veil was torn and the things within (the Holy of Holies) were revealed, the house was to be forsaken, abandoned, and destroyed. Yet the entire Divinity (Godhead) was to depart, not to the holies of the holies, for it was not able to merge with the light nor unite with the complete fullness. It was to be under the wings of the cross, in its open arms. This is the ark which shall be salvation for us when the destruction of water has overwhelmed (overtaken) them.

125. Those in the priestly tribe shall be able to enter within the veil of the Temple along with the High Priest. This was symbolized by the fact that the veil was not

torn at the top only, (but was torn from top to the bottom). If it was torn only at the top it would have been opened only for those who are on high (from the higher realm). If it was torn at the bottom only it would have been revealed only to those who are from below (the lower realm). But it was torn from the top to the bottom. Those who are from above made it available to us who are below them, so that we might enter into the secret of the truth. This strengthening of us is most wonderful. Because of this, we can enter in by means of symbols even though they are weak and worthless. They are humble and incomplete when compared to the perfect glory. It is the glory of glories and the power of powers. Through it the perfect is opened to us and it contains the secrets of the truth. Moreover, the Holies of Holies have been revealed and opened, and the Bridal-Chamber has invited us in.

126. As long as evil is hidden, and not completely purged from among the children of the Holy Spirit, it remains a potential threat. The children can be enslaved by the adversary, but when the Perfect Light is seen, it will pour out the oil of anointing upon and within it, and the slaves shall be set free and the slaves shall be bought back.

127. Every plant not sown by my heavenly Father shall be pulled up by the root. Those who were estranged shall be united and the empty shall be filled.

128. Everyone who enters the bridal-chamber shall ignite (be born in) the Light. This is like a marriage, which takes place at night. The fire is ablaze and is seen in the dark but goes out before morning. The mysteries (sacraments) of the marriage are consummated in the light of day, and that light never dies.

129. If someone becomes a child of the Bridal-Chamber, he shall receive the Light. If one does not receive it in this place, he will not be able to receive it in any other place. He who has received that Light shall not be seen, nor captured. No one in the world will be able to disturb him. When he leaves the world he will have already received the truth in types and symbols. The world has become eternity, because for him the fullness is eternal. It is revealed only to this kind of person. Truth is not hidden in darkness or the night. Truth is hidden in a perfect day and a holy light.

History of The Gospel Of Mary Magdalene

While traveling and researching in Cairo in 1896, German scholar, Dr. Carl Reinhardt, acquired a papyrus containing Coptic texts entitled the Revelation of John, the Wisdom of Jesus Christ, and the Gospel of Mary.

Before setting about to translate his exciting find, two world wars ensued, delaying publication until 1955. By then the Nag Hammadi collection had also been discovered.

Two of the texts in his codex, the Revelation of John, and the Wisdom of Jesus Christ, were included there. Importantly, the codex preserves the most complete surviving copy of the Gospel of Mary, named for its supposed author, Mary of Magdala. Two other fragments of the Gospel of Mary written in Greek were later unearthed in archaeological digs at Oxyrhynchus in Northern Egypt.

All of the various fragments were brought together to form the translation presented here. However, even with all of the fragments assembled, the manuscript of the Gospel of Mary is missing pages 1 to 6 and pages 11 to 14. These pages included sections of the text up to chapter 4, and portions of chapter 5 to 8.

Although the text of the Gospel of Mary is incomplete, the text presented below serves to shake the very concept of our assumptions of early Christianity as well as Christ's possible relationship to Mary of Magdala, whom we call Mary Magdalene.

The Gospel of Mary Magdalene

(Pages 1 to 6, containing chapters 1 - 3, could not be recovered. The text starts on page 7, chapter 4)

Chapter 4

21) (And they asked Jesus), "Will matter then be destroyed or not?"

22) The Savior said, "All nature, all things formed, and all creatures exist in and with one another, and they will be dissolved again into their own elements (origins).

23) This is because it is the nature of matter to return to its original elements.

24) If you have an ear to hear, listen to this."

25) Peter said to him, "Since you have explained all things to us, tell us this also: What sin did the world commit (what sin is in the world)?"

26) The Savior said, "There is no sin (of the world). Each person makes his own sin when he does things like adultery (in the same nature as adultery). This is called sin.

27) That is why the Good came to be among you. He came to restore every nature to its basic root."

28) Then He continued; "You become sick and die because you did not have access to (knowledge of) Him who can heal you.

29) If you have any sense, you must understand this.

30) The material world produced a great passion (desire or suffering) without equal. This was contrary to the natural balance. The entire cosmos (body) was disturbed by it.

31) That is why I said to you, Be encouraged, and if you are discouraged be encouraged when you see the different forms nature has taken.

32) He who has ears to hear, let him hear."

33) When the Blessed One had said this, He greeted all of them and said; "Peace be with you. Take my peace into you.

34) Beware that no one deceives you by saying, 'Look (he is) here or look (he is) there. The Son of Man is within you.'

35) Follow Him there.

36) Those who seek Him will find Him.

37) Go now and preach the gospel (this good news) of the Kingdom.

38) Do not lay down any rules beyond what I told you, and do not give a law like the lawgivers (Pharisees) or you will be held to account for the same laws."

39) When He said this He departed.

Chapter 5

1) Then they were troubled and wept out loud, saying, "How shall we go to the Gentiles and preach the gospel of the Kingdom of the Son of Man? If they did not spare Him, how can we expect that they will spare us?"

2) Then Mary stood up, greeted them all, and said to her fellow believers, "Do not weep and do not be troubled and do not waver, because His grace will be with you completely and it will protect you.

3) Instead, let us praise His greatness, because He has prepared us and made us into mature (finished or complete) people."

4) Mary's words turned their hearts to the Good, and they began to discuss the words of the Savior.

5) Peter said to Mary, "Sister we know that the Savior loved you more than all other women.

6) Tell us the words of the Savior that you remember and know, but we have not heard and do not know."

7) Mary answered him and said, "I will tell you what He hid from you."

8) And she began to speak these words to them: She said, "I saw the Lord in a vision and I said to Him, 'Lord I saw you today in a vision.'

9) He answered and said to me; 'You will be happy that you did not waver at the sight of Me. Where the mind is there is the treasure.'

10) I said to Him; 'Lord, does one see visions through the soul or through the spirit?'

11) The Savior answered and said; 'He sees visions through neither the soul nor the spirit. It is through the mind that is between the two. That is what sees the vision and it is (there the vision exists).'"

(Pages 11 - 14 are missing. Text begins again at chapter 8)

Chapter 8

10) And Desire, (a lesser god), said, "Before, I did not see you descending, but now I see you ascending. Why do you lie since you belong to me?"

11) The soul answered and said, "I saw you but you did not see me nor recognize me. I covered you like a garment and you did not know me."

12) When it said this, the soul went away greatly rejoicing.

13) Again it came to the third power (lesser god), which is called Ignorance.

14) The power questioned the soul, saying, "Where are you going? You are enslaved (captured) in wickedness. Since you are its captive you cannot judge (have no judgment)."

15) And the soul said, "Why do you judge me, when I have not judged?"

16) "I was captured, although I have not captured anyone."

17) "I was not recognized. But I have recognized that God (the All) is in (being dissolved) both the earthly things and in the heavenly (things)."

18) When the soul had overcome the third power, it ascended and saw the fourth power, which took seven forms.

19) The first form is darkness, the second desire, the third ignorance, the fourth is the lust of death, the fifth is the dominion of the flesh, the sixth is the empty useless wisdom of flesh, the seventh is the wisdom of vengeance and anger. These are the seven powers of wrath.

20) They asked the soul, "Where do you come from, slayer of men: where are you going, conqueror of space?"

21) The soul answered and said, "What has trapped me has been slain, and what kept me caged has been overcome."

22) "My desire has been ended, and ignorance has died."

23) "In an age (dispensation) I was released from the world in a symbolic image, and I was released from the chains of oblivion, which were only temporary (in this transient world)."

24) "From this time on will, I will attain the rest of the ages and seasons of silence."

Chapter 9

1) When Mary had said this, she fell silent, since she had shared all the Savior had told her.

2) But Andrew said to the other believers, "Say what you want about what she has said, but I do not believe that the Savior said this. These teachings are very strange ideas."

3) Peter answered him and spoke concerning these things.

4) He questioned them about the Savior and asked, "Did He really speak privately with a woman and not openly to us? Are we to turn around and all listen to her? Did He prefer her to us?"

5) Then Mary sobbed and said to Peter, "My brother Peter, what do you think? Do you think that I have made all of this up in my heart by myself? Do you think that I am lying about the Savior?"

6) Levi said to Peter, "Peter you have always had a hot temper.

7) Now I see you fighting against this woman like she was your enemy."

8) If the Savior made her worthy, who are you to reject her? What do you think you are doing? Surely the Savior knows her well?

9) That is why He loved her more than us. Let us be ashamed of this and let us put on the perfect Man. Let us separate from each other as He commanded us to do so we can preach the gospel, not laying down any other rule or other law beyond what the Savior told us."

10) And when they heard this they began to go out and proclaim and preach.

History of The Apocryphon of John

The Apocryphon, or "Secrets" of John forms the cornerstone of Gnostic mythology and cosmology. In this text we are introduced to the major entities of creation and lordship. We learn how the universe, including earth and man, came into being. The origin of evil, the creator god, and the material world are explained in detail. The story seems to be a mixture of various belief systems, including those of Plato, who seems to have borrowed freely from the format of Greek mythology, and Christianity. The story is loosely based on Genesis chapters 1 through 13 as a timeline.

The basic text of the Apocryphon of John existed in some form before 185 C.E. when a book called the Apocryphon of John was referred to by Irenaeus in his book, Against Heresies (Adversus Haereses), written in that year. Irenaeus reported about the Gnostic texts saying that teachers in 2nd century Christian communities were writing their own books to gain converts. He called these books, "an indescribable number of secret and illegitimate writings, which they themselves have forged, to bewilder the minds of foolish people, who are ignorant of the true scriptures" (A.H. 1.20.1)

The Apocryphon of John continued to be circulated, expanded, and embellished for the next seven hundred years. The document was reportedly in use during the eighth century by the Audians of Mesopotamia.

Part of the mythology revealed in the Apocryphon of John is also present in the Gnostic book, The Sophia (Wisdom) of Jesus as well as other Gnostic texts.

The specific document that so angered Irenaeus was lost and remained so until 1945, when a library of papyrus codices from the 4th century A.D. were found at Nag Hammadi in Egypt. The Apocryphon of John was among the texts,

Four versions have been found thus far. These are comprised of a long version, of which we have two identical Coptic manuscripts. A short version is also Coptic but differs from the others by eliminating certain details. Among the texts, a third manuscript had been found that differs slightly from the first shorter manuscript in style and vocabulary. A fragment has been found that shows some minor differences which distinguish it from the other.

Which, if any, of these texts are original has not been determined, however, it is the longer version that is presented here. This version was chosen because it contained more details and offered an overall cohesion of thought. This could be due to additions and embellishments sown through the shorter, less detailed versions.

Since we have already covered the general idea behind Gnostic mythology it need not be repeated here. However, a chart showing the main characters and their position on the divine family tree might serve us well. It is shown below.

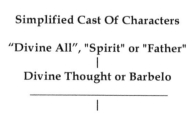

Simplified Cast Of Characters

"Divine All", "Spirit" or "Father"

|

Divine Thought or Barbelo

|

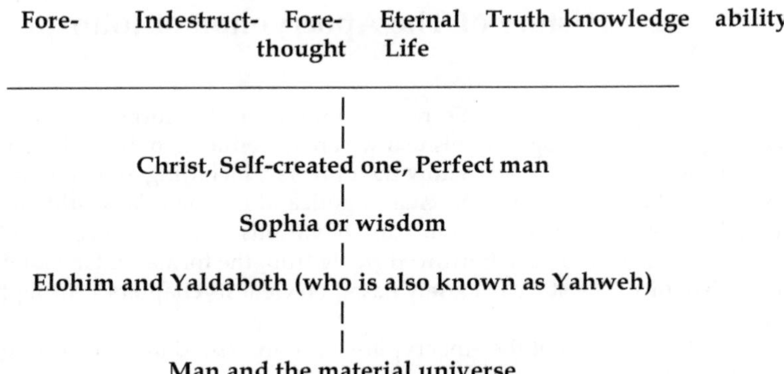
Fore-
Indestruct-
Fore-thought
Eternal Life
Truth
knowledge
ability
Christ, Self-created one, Perfect man
Sophia or wisdom
Elohim and Yaldaboth (who is also known as Yahweh)
Man and the material universe

The Apocryphon of John

The teaching of the savior, that will reveal the mysteries of things hidden which he taught John, his disciple, in silence.
On the day when John, the brother of James, the sons of Zebedee, had come to the temple, a Pharisee named Arimanius came up to him and said, Where is your master whom you followed? He said to him, He has gone back to the place he came from. The Pharisee said to him, This Nazarene deceived all of you with his deception. He filled your ears with lies, and closed your hearts and turned you all away from your fathers' traditions.

When I, John, heard these things I walked away from the temple into the desert. I grieved greatly in my heart, saying, How was the savior appointed, and why was he sent to the world by his Father, and who is his Father who sent him, and to which kingdom shall we go? What did he mean when he said to us, This kingdom which you will go to is an imperishable kingdom, but he did not teach us what kind it is.

Then, while I was meditating on these things, I saw the heavens open and the whole creation below heaven was shining and the world shook. I was afraid, and then I saw in the light a young man who stood by me. As I was looking at him he became like an old man. And he changed his visage again and become like a servant. There were not many beings in front of me, but there was a single being with many forms composed of light, and they could be seen through each other, and there were three forms within the one being.
He said to me, John, John, why do you doubt, and why are you afraid? (Mat. 28:17) Do you understand this image, do you not? Do not be afraid! I am the one who is with all of you always. I am the Father and the Mother, and I am the Son. I am the undefiled and incorruptible one. I have come to teach you what is and what was and what will be, so that you may know the things visible and invisible, and to teach you concerning the upright, immutable (unshakable / unwavering) race of the perfect Man. Now, therefore, lift up your face, that you may receive the things that I shall teach you today, and may tell them to your fellow spirits who are from the upright, immutable (unwavering/ unshakable) race of the perfect Man. (Eph.4:13)

And I asked if I might understand it, and he said to me, The One God is a king with nothing above it. It is he who exists as God and Father of everything, the invisible One who rules over everything, who exists as incorruptible, which is in the pure light that no eye can look upon.
He is the invisible Spirit. It is not correct to think of him as a god, or anything similar. He is more than god, since there is nothing above him, for no one is above him. He does not exist within anything inferior to him, because everything exists within him. He has established himself. He is eternal, self-sufficient, and self-sustaining. He is complete perfection. He did not lack anything to be complete and he is continually perfect in light. He is unlimited, since there was no one before him to limit him. He is unknowable, since there exists no one prior to him to comprehend him. He is immeasurable, since there was no one before him to

measure him. He is invisible, since no one has seen him. He is eternal, since he exists always. He is an enigma, since no one was able to apprehend him or explain him. He is unnamable, since there is no one who came before him to give him a name.

He is One, immeasurable light, which is pure, holy and immaculate. He is too sacred to speak of, being perfect and incorruptible. He is beyond perfection, blessedness, and divinity, because he is vastly superior to them all. He is not corporeal nor is he incorporeal. He is One and cannot be qualified or quantified, for no one can know him. He is not one among other beings; instead, he is far superior to all. He is so superior to all things that his essence is not part of the kingdoms, nor is he part of time. He who is a kingdom was created beforehand. Time does not matter to him, since he does not receive anything from another, for it would be received on loan. He who comes first needs nothing from anyone. Such a one expectantly beholds himself in his own light. He is majestic perfection. He is pure, immeasurable mind. He is a kingdom that gives the kingdoms their kingdom. He is life that gives life. He is the blessed One that blesses. He is knowledge and he gives knowledge. He is goodness that gives goodness. He is mercy and redemption and he bestows mercy. He is grace that gives grace. He does not give because he has these things but he gives the immeasurable, incomprehensible light from which all things flow.

How am I to speak with you about him? His kingdom is indestructible, at peace and existing in silence, at rest before everything was. He is the head of all the kingdoms (kingdoms), and he gives them strength in his goodness. For we know not the things that are unspeakably sacred, and we do not understand that which cannot be measured, except for him who was created from him, namely from the Father. It is he alone who told it to us.

He who beholds himself in the light which surrounds him and comes from him is the spring of the water of life. It is he who sustains the entire kingdom in every way, and it is he who gazes upon the image which he sees in the spring of the Spirit. It is he who puts his desire in the liquid light which is in the spring of the pure liquid light which surrounds him.

The Father's thought performed a deed and she was created from it. It is she who had appeared before him in the shining of his light. This is the first power which was before all of them and which was created from his mind. She is the Thought of the All and her light shines like his light. It is the perfect power which is the visage of the invisible. She is the pure, undefiled Spirit who is perfect. She is the first power, the glory of Barbelo, the perfect glory of the kingdom (kingdoms), the glory revealed. She glorified the pure, undefiled Spirit and it was she who praised him, because thanks to him she had come forth. She is the first thought, his image; she became the womb of everything, for it is she who preceded them all. She is the Mother-Father, the first man, the Holy Spirit, the threefold male, the triple power, the androgynous one with three names, and the eternal kingdom among the invisible ones, and the first to come forth.

She asked the invisible, pure, undefiled Spirit, Barbelo, to give her Foreknowledge, and the Spirit agreed. And when he had agreed, the Foreknowledge was created, and it stood by the Thought; it originates from the

thought of the invisible, pure, undefiled Spirit. Foreknowledge glorified him and his perfect power, Barbelo. It was because of her that Foreknowledge had been created.

And she asked again to grant her indestructibility, and he agreed. When he had agreed, indestructibility was created, and it stood by the Divine Thought and the Foreknowledge. It glorified the invisible One and Barbelo, because of whom it had been created.

And Barbelo asked to grant her Eternal Life. And the invisible Spirit agreed. And when he had agreed, Eternal Life was created, and they attended and glorified the invisible Spirit and Barbelo, the one because of whom they had been created.

And she asked again to grant her truth. And the invisible Spirit agreed. And when he had agreed, Truth was created, and they attended and glorified the invisible, excellent Spirit and his Barbelo, the one because of whom they had been created.

This is the five-fold creation of the kingdom of the Father, which is the first man and the image of the invisible Spirit, which came from Barbelo, who was the divine Thought; Forethought, Foreknowledge, Indestructibility, Eternal life, and Truth.

This is the androgynous five-fold being of the kingdom, which is the ten types of kingdoms, which is the Father.

(Five, being both male and female, or neither male nor female, become ten.)

And he looked at Barbelo with his pure light which surrounds the invisible Spirit, and his sparks, and she was impregnated by him. And a spark of light produced a light resembling his blessedness but it did not equal his greatness. This was the only-begotten child of the Mother-Father which had come forth. It is the only offspring and the only begotten of the Father, the pure Light.

And the invisible, pure, undefiled Spirit rejoiced over the light which was created, that which was produced by the first power of his Thought, which is Barbelo. And he poured his goodness over it until it became perfect and did not lack in any goodness, because he had anointed the child with the goodness of the invisible Spirit. It was his child and the child was there with him and he poured upon the child an anointing. And immediately when the child had received the Spirit, it glorified the Holy Spirit and the perfect Divine Thought, because the child owed these its existence.

And it asked to be given Mind as a fellow worker, and he agreed gladly. And when the invisible Spirit had agreed, the Mind was created, and it attended the anointed one (Christ), glorifying him and Barbelo. And all these were created in silence.

And Mind wanted to initiate an action through the word of the invisible Spirit. Thus, his will became an action and it appeared with the mind; and the light glorified it. And the word followed the will. It was because of the word that Christ, the divine self-created one, created everything. And Eternal Life and his will and Mind and Foreknowledge attended and glorified the invisible Spirit and Barbelo, because of whom they had been created.

And the Holy Spirit perfected and matured the divine Self-created one, and brought the son, together with Barbelo, so that he might present himself to the mighty and invisible, pure, undefiled Spirit as the divine Self-created one, the

Christ (the anointed one) who loudly proclaimed honor to the spirit. He was created through Forethought. And the invisible, pure, undefiled Spirit placed the divine Self-created one of truth over everything. And he caused every authority to be subject to him and to Truth, which is in him, so that he may know the name of the "All," whose name is exalted above every name. That name will only be spoken to those who are worthy of it.

From the light, which is the Christ, there is incorruptibleness and through the gift of the Spirit four lights shone from the divine Self-created one. He wished that they might be with him. And the three are will, thought, and life. And the four powers are Understanding, Grace, Perception, and Thoughtfulness.

And Grace belongs to the everlasting realm of the luminary Harmozel, which is the first angel. And there are three other kingdoms with this everlasting kingdom: Grace, Truth, and Form. And the second luminary is Oriel, who has authority over the second everlasting realm. And there are three other kingdoms with him: Conception, Perception, and Memory. And the third luminary is Daveithai, who has authority over the third everlasting realm. And there are three other kingdoms with him: Understanding, Love, and Idea. And the fourth luminary, Eleleth , was given authority over the fourth everlasting realm. And there are three other kingdoms with him: Perfection, Peace, and Wisdom (Sophia). These are the four luminaries which serve the divine Self-created one. These are the twelve kingdoms which serve the child of god, the Self-created one, the Christ. They serve him through the will and the grace of the invisible Spirit. The twelve kingdoms belong to the child of the Self-created one. All things were established by the will of the Holy Spirit through the Self-created one.

From the Foreknowledge of the perfect mind, through the expression of the will of the invisible Spirit and the will of the Self-created one, the perfect Man came into being. He was the first revelation and the truth. The pure, undefiled Spirit called him "Adam, The Stranger" (not of the earthly realm, but belonging to the divine realm). The spirit placed him over the first realm with the mighty one, the Self-created one, the Christ, by the authority of the first luminary, Harmozel; and with him are his powers. And the invisible one gave Adam The Stranger an invincible spiritual power. And Adam The Stranger spoke, glorifying and praising the invisible Spirit, saying, "It is because of you that everything has been created and therefore, everything will return to you. I shall praise and glorify you and the Self-created one and all the realms, the three: the Father, the Mother, and the Son, who make up the perfect power."

And Adam The Stranger placed his son Seth over the second realm in which the second luminary Oriel is present. And in the third realm the children of Seth were established over the third luminary, Daveithai. And the souls of the saints were lodged there. In the fourth realm the souls are kept of those who do not know the pleroma and who did not repent at once. These are they who persisted for a while and repented afterwards; they are in the area of the fourth luminary, Eleleth. They are those which glorify the invisible Spirit.

And the Sophia of the eternal realm manifested a thought from herself through the invisible Spirit and Foreknowledge. She wanted to produce a likeness of herself out of herself without the consent of the Spirit, but he had not approved. She attempted this act without her male consort, and without his permission. She had no male approval thus, she had not found her agreement. She had considered this without the consent of the Spirit and the knowledge of her compliment, but she brought forth her creation anyway. Because of the invincible power she possessed her thought did not remain idle, and something came out of her which was imperfect and different from her appearance because she had produced it without her compliment. It did not look like its mother because it has another form.

As she beheld the results of her desire, it changed into a form of a lion-faced serpent. Its eyes were like fire-like lightning which flashed. When she saw it she cast it away from her and threw it outside the realm so that none of the immortal ones might see it, for she had created it in ignorance. She surrounded it with a brightly glowing cloud and she put a throne in the middle of the cloud that no one might see it except the Holy Spirit who is called the mother of all that lives. And she called his name Yaldaboth.

This is the first Archon who took great power from his mother. And he left her and moved away from the realm in which he was born. He became strong and created for himself other kingdoms with a flame of glowing fire which still existed. And he mated with his own mindless ego that he had with him (he masturbated / or he was like his mother and did the same act of creation by himself) and brought into existence authorities for himself.

The name of the first one is Athoth, whom the generations call the reaper.
The second one is Harmas, who is the eye of envy.
The third one is Kalila-Oumbri.
The fourth one is Yabel.
The fifth one is Adonaiou, who is called Sabaoth (fool or chaos).
The sixth one is Cain, whom the generations of humans call the sun.
The seventh is Abel.
The eighth is Abrisene.
The ninth is Yobel.
The tenth is Armoupieel.
The eleventh is Melceir-Adonein.
The twelfth is Belias, it is he who is over the depth of Hades.
(These could be the 12 stations of the zodiac.)

There he placed seven kings corresponding to the sections of heaven to reign over the seven heavens and he placed five to reign over the depth of the abyss. (There were 7 known planets at the time of writing.) And he shared his fire with them, but he did not relinquish any power of the light which he had taken from his mother, for he is ignorant darkness.

And when light is added to darkness, it made the darkness bright. When darkness is added to light, it dims the light and it became neither light nor dark, but it became like dusk.

Now the Archon who is like the gloaming (gloom) has three names. The first name is Yaldaboth (fool / son of chaos), the second is Saklas, and the third is Samael. And he is evil in the arrogance and thoughtlessness that is in him. For he said, "I am God and there is no other God beside me" (Isaiah chapters 45 and 46). He said this because he did not know where his strength originated, nor from where he himself had come.

And the Archons created seven powers for themselves, and the powers created for themselves six angels for each one until they became 365 angels (the number of days in the solar year). And these are the bodies belonging with the names:
The first is Athoth, a he has a sheep's face;
The second is Eloaiou, he has a donkey's face;
The third is Astaphaios, he has a hyena's face;
The fourth is Yao, he has a snake face with seven heads;
The fifth is Sabaoth, he has a dragon's face;
The sixth is Adonin, he has an ape face;
The seventh is Sabbede (or Sabbadaios), he has a face that shone like fire.
This is the nature of seven types within the week.

But Yaldaboth had a plethora of faces, more than all of them, so that he could exhibit any face he wished to any of them, when he is in the midst of seraphim (seraphim plural of seraph. Seraphim are a class or type of angel of which, according to this text, Yaldaboth seems to be the head). He shared his fire with them and became their lord. He called himself God because of the power of the glory (brightness) he possessed that was taken from his mother's light. He rebelled against the place from which he came.

And he united the seven powers of his thoughts with the authorities that were with him. And when he spoke it became (happened).

And he named each power beginning with the highest:
The first is goodness with the first authority, Athoth;
The second is foreknowledge with the second power, Eloaio; The third is divinity with the third one, Astraphaio);
The fourth is lordship with the fourth power, Yao;
The fifth is kingdom with the fifth one, Sabaoth;
The sixth is envy with the sixth one, Adonein;
The seventh is understanding with the seventh one, Sabbateon.
And these each has a kingdom (sphere on influence) within the realm (kingdom of heaven).
They were given names according to the glory belonging to heaven for the powers of their destructiveness. And there was power in the names given to them by their creator. But the names they were given according to the glory of heaven would mean their loss of power and their destruction. Thus they have two names.

He (Yaldaboth) created all things and structured things after the model of the first kingdom created so that he might create things in an incorruptible manner. It was not because he had ever seen the indestructible ones, but the power in him, which he had taken from his mother, produced in him the image of the order of the universe. And when he saw the creation surrounding him the innumerable amount of angels around him that had come from him, he said to them, "I am a jealous God, and there is no other God beside me." (Exodus 20:3) But by announcing this he had let the angels who were with him know that there is another God. If there were no other god, why would he be jealous?

Then the mother began to move here and there. She realized she has lost part of herself when the brightness of her light dimmed. And she became darker because her partner had not consorted with her.

I (John) said, Lord, what does it mean that she moved here and there? The lord smiled and said, "Do not think it happened the way that Moses said it did 'above the waters'." (Genesis 1:2) No, it did not, but when she had seen the wickedness which had happened, and the fact her son had stolen from her, she repented. In the darkness of ignorance she began to forget and to be ashamed. She did not dare to go back there, but she was restless. This restlessness was the moving here and there.

And the prideful one stole power from his mother. For he was ignorant and thought that there was no other in existence except his mother. When he saw innumerable angels he had created he exalted himself above them. When the mother recognized that the cloak (body) of darkness was imperfect, and she knew that her partner had not consorted with her, she repented and wept greatly. The entire pleroma heard the prayer of her repentance, and they praised the invisible, pure, undefiled Spirit on her behalf. And the Spirit agreed and when he agreed the Holy Spirit anointed her from the entire pleroma. For her consort did not come to her alone, but he brought to her through the pleroma that which was needed to restore what she was lacking. And she was allowed to ascend, not to her own kingdom but to the kingdom above her son, that she could remain in the ninth (heaven / kingdom) until she restored what she lacked in herself.

And a voice called from the highest kingdom of heaven: "The Man exists and the son of Man." And the head Archon, Yaldaboth, heard it and thought that the voice had come from his mother. He did not know whence it came. He taught them, the holy and perfect Mother-Father, the complete Foreknowledge, the image of the invisible one who is the Father of the all things and through whom everything came into being, the first Man. He is the one who revealed his image in human form.

And the whole kingdom of the first (head) Archon quaked, and the foundations of the abyss shook. And the underside of waters, which are above material world, were illuminated by the appearance of his image which had been revealed. When all the authorities and the head Archon looked, they saw the whole region of the underside (of the waters) that was illuminated. And through the light they saw the form of the image (reflected) in the water.

And he (Yaldaboth) said to the authorities of him, "Come, let us make a man

using the image of God as a template to our likeness, that his image may become a light for us." And they created by the means of their various powers matching the features which were given to them. And each authority supplied a feature in the form of the image which Yaldaboth had seen in its natural form. He created a being according to the likeness of the first, perfect Man. And they said, "Let us call him Adam (man), that his name may be a power of light for us."

And the powers began to create.
The first one, Goodness, created a bone essence; and the second, Foreknowledge, created a sinew essence; the third, Divinity, created a flesh essence; and the fourth, the Lordship, created a marrow essence; the fifth, Kingdom created a blood essence; the sixth, Envy, created a skin essence; the seventh, Understanding, created a hair essence. And the multitude of the angels were with him and they received from the powers the seven elements of the natural (form) so they could create the proportions of the limbs and the proportion of the buttocks and correct functioning of each of the parts together.

The first one began to create the head. Eteraphaope-Abron created his head; Meniggesstroeth created the brain; Asterechme created the right eye; Thaspomocha, the left eye; Yeronumos, the right ear; Bissoum, the left ear; Akioreim, the nose; Banen-Ephroum, the lips; Amen, the teeth; Ibikan, the molars; Basiliademe, the tonsils; Achcha, the uvula; Adaban, the neck; Chaaman, the vertebrae; Dearcho, the throat; Tebar, the right shoulder; the left shoulder; Mniarcon, the right elbow; the left elbow; Abitrion, the right underarm; Evanthen, the left underarm; Krys, the right hand; Beluai, the left hand; Treneu, the fingers of the right hand; Balbel, the fingers of the left hand; Kriman, the nails of the hands; Astrops, the right breast; Barroph, the left breast; Baoum, the right shoulder joint; Ararim, the left shoulder joint; Areche, the belly; Phthave, the navel; Senaphim, the abdomen; Arachethopi, the right ribs; Zabedo, the left ribs; Barias, the right hip; Phnouth the left hip; Abenlenarchei, the marrow; Chnoumeninorin, the bones; Gesole, the stomach; Agromauna, the heart; Bano, the lungs; Sostrapal, the liver; Anesimalar, the spleen; Thopithro, the intestines; Biblo, the kidneys; Roeror, the sinews; Taphreo, the spine of the body; Ipouspoboba, the veins; Bineborin, the arteries; Atoimenpsephei, theirs are the breaths which are in all the limbs; Entholleia, all the flesh; Bedouk, the right buttock; Arabeei, the penis; Eilo, the testicles; Sorma, the genitals; Gorma-Kaiochlabar, the right thigh; Nebrith, the left thigh; Pserem, the kidneys of the right leg; Asaklas, the left kidney; Ormaoth, the right leg; Emenun, the left leg; Knyx, the right shin-bone; Tupelon, the left shin-bone; Achiel, the right knee; Phnene, the left knee; Phiouthrom, the right foot; Boabel, its toes; Trachoun, the left foot; Phikna, its toes; Miamai, the nails of the feet; Labernioum.
And those who were appointed over all of these are: Zathoth, Armas, Kalila, Jabel, (Sabaoth, Cain, Abel). And those who are particularly active in the limbs are the head Diolimodraza, the neck Yammeax, the right shoulder Yakouib, the left shoulder Verton, the right hand Oudidi, the left one Arbao, the fingers of the right hand Lampno, the fingers of the left hand Leekaphar, the right breast Barbar, the left breast Imae, the chest Pisandriaptes, the right shoulder joint Koade, the left shoulder joint Odeor, the right ribs Asphixix, the left ribs Synogchouta, the belly Arouph, the womb Sabalo, the right thigh Charcharb, the left thigh Chthaon, all

the genitals Bathinoth, the right leg Choux, the left leg Charcha, the right shin-bone Aroer, the left shin-bone Toechtha, the right knee Aol, the left knee Charaner, the right foot Bastan, its toes Archentechtha, the left foot Marephnounth, its toes Abrana.

Seven have power over all of these: Michael, Ouriel, Asmenedas, Saphasatoel, Aarmouriam, Richram, Amiorps. And the ones who are in charge of the senses are Archendekta; and he who is in charge of the receptions is Deitharbathas; and he who is in charge over the imagination is Oummaa; and he who is over creativity Aachiaram, and he who is over the whole impulse Riaramnacho.

The origin of the demons that are in the entire body is known to be these four: heat, cold, wetness, and dryness. And the mother of all of them is the material creation. And he who rules over the heat is Phloxopha; and he who rules over the cold is Oroorrothos; and he who rules over what is dry is Erimacho; and he who rules over the wetness is Athuro. And the mother of all of these is Onorthochrasaei, who stands in with them without limits, and she covorts with all of them. She is truly material and they are sustained by her.

The four ruling demons are: Ephememphi, who is attached to pleasure,
Yoko, who is attached to desire,
Nenentophni, who is attached to grief,
Blaomen, who is attached to fear,
and the mother of them all is Aesthesis-Ouch-Epi-Ptoe.
And from the four demons passions was created. And grief spawned envy, jealousy, distress, trouble, pain, callousness, anxiety, mourning, and more. Pleasure spawned wickedness, vanity, pride, and similar things. Desire spawned anger, wrath, and bitterness, and driving passion, the inability to be satisfied, and similar things. Fear spawned dread, subservience, agony, and shame. These are both good and evil, but the understanding of their nature is attributed to Anaro, who is over the material soul. It belongs with the seven senses, which are controlled by Ouch-Epi-Ptoe.

This is the number of the angels: together they are 365. They all worked on it from limb to limb, until the physical (material) body was completed by them. Now there are other ones in charge over the remaining passions whom I did not mention to you. But if you wish to know them, it is written in the book of Zoroaster. And all the angels and demons worked until they had constructed (fashioned) the physical body. And their creation was completely devoid of activity and was motionless for a long time.

And when the mother (Sophia) wanted to recapture the power which was taken from her by the head Archon, she prayed to the Mother-Father of the All, who is most merciful. He sent a holy decree containing the five lights down to the place where the angels of the head Archon reside. They advised him (Yaldaboth) that he should bring forth the power of the mother. And they said to Yaldaboth, "Blow some of your spirit into his face and his body will arise." And he blew the spirit power of the mother into his (Adam's) face. (Genesis 2:7) Yaldaboth did not know to do this because he existed in ignorance. And the power of the mother went out of Yaldaboth into Adam's physical body, which they had fashioned after the image of the one who exists from the beginning. The body moved and gained strength, and it was enlightened.

And in that instant the other powers became jealous, although he (Adam) had been created through all of them. They were jealous because they had given Adam their power and now he was more intelligent than those who had made him, and his mind was greater than that of the head Archon. And when they recognized that he was enlightened, and that he could think better than they, and that he was free of evil, they took him and threw him into the lowest material realm.

But the blessed One, the Mother-Father, the giving and gracious One, had mercy on the power of the mother which had been transmitted from the head Archon because he did not want the Archons to gain power over the material body again. Therefore, he sent, a helper to Adam through his giving Spirit and his great compassion. The enlightened Thought which comes out of him is called "Life" (Zoe means life and is the name of Eve in certain Greek texts and the Septuagint). And she assists the whole creature, by working with him and restoring him to his fullness and by teaching him about the descent (flaws) of his seed and by teaching him about the way of ascent (to go upward again), which is based on the way he came down. (Rom. 8:22)

And the enlightened Thought was hidden within Adam so that the Archons would not know she was there, but that the Thought might restore (correct) what was lacking of the mother.

And the man was revealed because of the shadow of light in him. And his thinking was higher than all those who had made him. When they looked up they realized that his thinking was superior. Then they conspired with the entire force of Archons and angels. They took fire and earth and water as a mixture and added the four fiery winds. And they worked them together and caused a great noise. And they brought Adam into the shadow of death so that that they might re-make him from earth, water, fire and the spirit (wind) which make up matter. This was the ignorance of their darkness and desire, and their lying (false) spirit. This is the tomb of the re-formed body that the thieves had clothed Adam in. It contained the bonds of forgetfulness and cause him to become a mortal entity. He is the first one who came down, and the first to be separated (from the Divine All). Now, it is up to the Thought of the light which was in him to awaken his thinking.

And the Archons took him and placed him in paradise. And they said to him, "Eat at your leisure," (Genesis 2:16) for their pleasure is bitter and their beauty is twisted. Their pleasure is entrapment and their trees lack any holiness and their fruit is deadly poison and their promise is death. And the tree of their life they had placed in the center of paradise (Genesis 2:9).

And I (Jesus) shall teach all of you the mystery of their life. It is the plan that they made together, which is made from the template of their spirit. The root of this tree is bitter and its branches are death, its shadow is hate. Its leaves are a trap,

and its blossom is the ointment of evil. Its fruit is death and its seed is desire. It sprouts (blooms) in darkness. Those who taste it dwell in Hades, and they rest in darkness.
But what they call "the tree of knowledge of good and evil" is the Thought of the light. They stationed themselves in front of it so that Adam might not understand his fullness and recognize his nakedness and be ashamed. But it was I (Jesus) who made them decide what they ate.

I said to the savior, Lord, wasn't it the serpent that instructed Adam to eat? The savior smiled and said, The serpent instructed them to eat because of its evil desire to produced sexual lust and destruction so that Adam would be useful to him. Adam knew that he was disobedient to Yaldaboth because the light of the Thought lived in him and made him stronger and more accurate in his thinking than the head Archon. Yaldaboth wanted to harvest the power that he himself had given Adam. And he caused Adam to forget.

And I said to the savior, "What is this forgetfulness?" He said, "It is not how Moses wrote and it is not how you have heard. He wrote in his first book, 'He put him to sleep' (Genesis 2:21), but that was how Adam perceived it. For also he said through the prophet, 'I will make their minds heavy, that they may not perceive nor understand.' (Isaiah 6:10)."

The Thought of the light hid herself in Adam. The head Archon wanted to bring her out through his rib but the Thought of the light cannot be apprehended. Although darkness pursued her, it did not catch her. Yaldaboth brought out part of Adam's power and he created another and formed a woman, using the template of the Thought which he had seen. The power he had taken from the Adam was formed into the female. This is what happened and not as Moses said, 'She was formed from the bone of his rib.' (Genesis 2:21)

Adam saw the woman beside him. In that instant the enlightened Thought appeared. She lifted the veil which occluded his mind. Adam sobered from the drunkenness of darkness and recognized his counterpart (compliment / agreement) , and he said, 'This is indeed bone of my bones and flesh of my flesh.' (Genesis 2:23) Therefore the man will leave his father and his mother, and he will cleave to his wife, and they will both be one flesh. (Genesis 2:24) For his partner will be sent to him and he will leave his father and his mother .

Our sister Sophia is the one who came down innocently in order to reclaim what she has lost. That is why she was called Life, because she is the mother of all things living, by the Foreknowledge of the sovereignty of heaven. Through her they that live have tasted the perfect Knowledge. I (Jesus) appeared in the form of an eagle on the tree of knowledge, which is the Thought from the Foreknowledge of the pure light. I did this so that I might teach them and wake them from them the deep sleep. For they were both in a fallen state, and they recognized they were naked. The Thought appeared to them in the form of light and she awakened their minds.

When Yaldaboth noticed that they fled from him, he cursed the earth he had

made. He found the woman as she was preparing herself for her husband. He was lord over her, though he did not know the mystery was instated through the holy plan, so they were afraid to rebel against Yaldaboth. And he demonstrated to his angels the ignorance in him by casting them out of paradise, and he clothed them in darkening blackness.

And the head Archon, Yaldaboth, saw the virgin standing beside Adam, but he was ignorant to the fact that the enlightened Thought of life had appeared in her. But when the Foreknowledge of All noticed it, she sent agents and they quickly stole the life (Zoe) out of Eve.

Then, the head Archon seduced her and he conceived two sons in her. The first is Eloim and the second is Yahweh. Eloim has a face like a bear and Yahweh has a face like a cat. The one is righteous but the other is unjust. (Yahweh is related to the New Testament and is considered a more just and kind God. Eloim is related to the Old Testament and is considered a jealous, revengeful, wrathful God.) He set Yahweh over fire and wind, and he set Eloim over water and earth. And he name them Cain and Abel in an attempt to deceive.

Sexual intercourse continues to this very day because of the head Archon. He instilled sexual desire in the woman who belongs to Adam. And Adam, through intercourse caused bodies to be replicated, and Yaldaboth breathed into them with his fraudulent spirit.

And he set the two Archons (Elohim and Yahweh) over principal elements, so that they might rule over the tomb (body). When Adam recognized the image of his own Foreknowledge, he begot the image of the son of man (Jesus) and he called him Seth, according to the fashion of the divine race living in the ethereal kingdoms. The mother (Sophia) sent her spirit also. It was in her image and was a replica of those who are in the pleroma. In this way she will prepare a dwelling place for the kingdoms to come.

Yaldaboth made them drink water of forgetfulness that he had made so that they might not remember from where they came. The seed remained with man for a while to assist him so that when the Spirit comes out from the holy kingdoms, he may raise up and heal him of his lack so the whole pleroma may again become holy and complete.

And I said to the savior, Lord, will all the souls be led safely into the pure light? He answered me and said, "Great things have arisen in your mind, and it is difficult to explain them to anyone except those from the race that cannot be moved. These are they on whom the Spirit of life will descend and with whom will be with the Power. They will be saved and become complete, perfect and worthy of greatness. They will be purified from all wickedness and evil actions. Then they will have no other care other than the incorruption, on which they shall focus their attention from here on, without anger or envy or jealousy or desire and greed for anything. They are affected by nothing except existing in the flesh, which they bear while looking expectantly for the time when they will be met by those who will receive them (their body). Such ones are worthy of the (incorruptible) imperishable, eternal life and the calling. They endure everything and bear up under everything, that they may finish the good fight (wrestling contest) and inherit eternal life. (Cor. 13:7)

I said to him, Lord, will the souls of those who did not do these works (things) but on whom the power and Spirit descended, be rejected? He answered and said to me, "If the Spirit descended upon them, they will certainly be saved, and they will be changed. The power will descend on every man, for without it no one could stand. And after they are born, when the Spirit of life grows in them and the power comes and strengthens that soul, no one can be led astray with evil deeds, but those on whom the false spirit falls are drawn astray by him.

I said, Lord, where will the souls go when they shed their flesh? And he laughed (smiled) and said to me, "The soul in which the power will become stronger than the false spirit is strong and she (the soul) turns and runs from evil and through the intervention of the incorruptible one, she is saved, taken up to the kingdoms and will rest there.

And I said, "Lord, what about those who do not know to whom they belong, where will their souls go?" And he said to me, "Those, the spoiled (double-minded) spirit has gained strength while they went astray and that casts a burden on the soul and draws her towards the deeds of evil, and he throws her down into forgetfulness. After she comes out of the body, it is handed over to the authorities that came into being through the Archon. They bind her with chains and cast her into prison, and hound her until she is set free from the forgetfulness and acquires knowledge. If she becomes perfected she is saved.

And I said, Lord, how can the soul become young again and return to its mother's womb or into (another) man? (This is a question regarding reincarnation.) He was glad when I asked him this, and he said to me, "You are blessed because you have understood!" That soul is made to follow another, since the Spirit of life is in it. It is saved through that soul. It is not forced into another flesh (body) again.

And I said, Lord, "Where will the souls go from those who gained knowledge but afterward turned away?" Then he said to me, "They will go to the place where the angels of misery (abject poverty) go. This is the place where there is no repentance (escape). There they will be kept with those who have blasphemed the spirit. They will be tortured and punished forever and ever. (Heb 6:4-8 and Heb 12:17-31)

I said, "Lord, from where did the false (evil) spirit come?" Then he said to me, "The Mother-Father, who is the gracious and holy of Spirit, the One who is merciful and who has compassion for all, the Thought of the Foreknowledge of light raised up the child of the perfect race and their thought was the eternal light of man."

When the head Archon realized that these people were exalted above him and their minds were stronger than him he wanted to capture their thought. He did not know that their minds were stronger and that he would not be able to capture their thoughts.

He made a plan with his agents, his powers, and they raped (committed adultery together, all of them, with) Sophia, and unbearable imprisonment (bitter fate) was born through them, which is the last unbreakable bondage. It is the kind that is unpredictable fate. This fate is harder and stronger than the gods, angels and demons and all the generations until this day together have seen. It imprisoned all through periods, seasons, and times. From that fate every sin, unrighteousness, blasphemy, forgetfulness, and ignorance and every oppressive command, and carnal sins and fear emerged. From this the whole creation was blinded, so that they may not know the God who is above them all. And because of the chain of forgetfulness, their sins were hidden from them. They are bound with measures, seasons, and time since fate is lord over everything.

When the head Archon repented for everything which had been created through him, he sought to cause a flood to destroy the works of man (Genesis 6:6). But the great light, the Foreknowledge, told Noah, and Noah announced it to all the children, the sons of men. But those who were estranged from him did not listen to him. It is not as Moses said, "They hid themselves in an ark" (Genesis 7: 7), but they hid in a certain place. Noah hid and also many other people from the immutable race. They went to a certain place and hid in a shining, glowing (enlightened) cloud. Noah understood his authority because she who is part of the light was with him. She enlightened them because the head Archon darkened the entire earth.

And he planned with his agents to send his emissaries (angels) to the daughters of men so that they might take some (as wives) for themselves and raise offspring (children) for their personal enjoyment. At first they had no success so they came together again and laid a plan. They made a false spirit (like themselves), but who looked like the Spirit which had come down to them. In this way they could defile souls through it.

And the emissaries (angels) transformed themselves into the image of the husbands of the women (the daughters of men). They filled them with the spirit of darkness, which was an evil concoction they had made for them. They brought gold and silver and a gift and copper and iron and metal and all kinds of things to the angels. And they led those who followed them away into great turmoil with their lies. The people grew old without enjoying life. They died before finding truth and without knowing the God of truth. This way the entire creation was enslaved forever, from the beginning of the world until now.

And they took wives and produced children of darkness born in the image of their spirit. To this day, they closed their minds, and they hardened their hearts through the intractability of the false spirit.

I, the perfect Aeon of the All, changed myself into my own child (seed), for I existed first and have traveled every path. I am the fullness of the light. I am the remembrance of the pleroma. I sojourned to the kingdom of darkness and endured so I could I enter into the midst of this prison. The foundations of chaos shook. I disguised myself from the wicked ones, and they did not recognize me.

I returned for the second time, and I journeyed here and there. I was created from those who belong to the light, and I am that light, the perfect Aeon. I entered into the midst of darkness and depths of Hades to accomplish my task. And the foundations of chaos shook so hard they could have fallen down and killed those in chaos. I sought to root them in light so that they might not be destroyed before the time was complete.

Still for a third time I went - I am the light which exists in the light, I am the remembrance of the perfect Aeon. I entered into the midst of darkness and the depths of Hades. I filled my face with light so I could perfect (complete) their kingdom. I came into the midst of their prison, which is the prison of the body (flesh). I announced, "He who hears, let him wake up from the deep sleep." And he wept and shed tears. He wiped away bitter tears from himself and he said, "Who is it that calls my name, and from where has this hope come to me, while I am in the chains of the prison?" And I said, 'I am the perfect Aeon of the pure light; I am the thought of the pure, undefiled Spirit, who raised you up to the place of honor. Stand and remember that it is you who heard and sought your own beginnings, which is I, the merciful one. Guard yourself against the angels of bitter providence and the demons of chaos and all those who seek to entrap you Guard against the deep sleep and the cage of Hades.

And I stood him up and sealed him in the light of the water with five seals so that death might not have power over him ever again.
Now I shall go ascend to the perfect kingdom. I have told you all I have to say. And I have said everything to you that you might write it down and give them secretly to your fellow spirits. It is the mystery of the immutable race.

And the savior gave these things to John so that he might write them down and keep them intact. And he said to him, Cursed is everyone who will trade these things for a gift or for food or for water or clothing or anything. These things were presented to him in a mystery, and immediately he disappeared from him. And he went to his fellow disciples and told them what the savior had told him.
Jesus Christ, Amen.

History of The Gospel of Thomas

In the winter of 1945, in Upper Egypt, an Arab peasant was gathering fertilizer and topsoil for his crops. While digging in the soft dirt he came across a large earthen vessel. Inside were scrolls containing hitherto unseen books.

According to local lore, the boy's father had recently been killed and the lad was preparing to chase the man who had murdered his father.

The scrolls were discovered near the site of the ancient town of Chenoboskion, at the base of a mountain named Gebel et-Tarif, near Hamra-Dum, in the vicinity of Naj 'Hammadi, about sixty miles from Luxor in Egypt. The texts were written in the Coptic language and preserved on papyrus sheets. The lettering style dated them as having been penned around the third or fourth century A.D. The Gospel of Thomas is the longest of the volumes consisting of 114 verses. Recent study indicates that the original work of Thomas, of which the scrolls are copies, may predate the four canonical gospels of Matthew, Mark, Luke, and John. The origin of The Gospel of Thomas is now thought to be from the first or second century A.D.

The word Coptic is an Arabic corruption of the Greek word Aigyptos, which in turn comes from the word Hikaptah, one of the names of the city of Memphis, the first capital of ancient Egypt.

There has never been a Coptic state or government per se, however, the word has been used to generally define a culture and language present in the area of Egypt.

The known history of the Copts starts with King Mina the first King, who united the northern and southern kingdoms of Egypt circa 3050 B.C. The ancient Egyptian civilization under the rule of the Pharaohs lasted over 3000 years. Saint Mina (named after the king) is one of the major Coptic saints. He was martyred in 309 A.D.

The culture has come to be recognized as one containing distinctive art, architecture, and even a certain Christian church system.

The Coptic Church is based on the teachings of St. Mark, who introduced the region to Christianity in the first century A.D. The Copts take pride in the monastic flavor of their church and the fact that the Gospel of Mark is thought to be the oldest of the Gospels. Now, lying before a peasant boy was a scroll written in the ancient Coptic tongue: The Gospel of Thomas, possibly older than and certainly quite different from any other Gospel.

The peasant boy who found the treasure of the Gospel of Thomas stood to be rewarded greatly. This could have been the discovery of a lifetime for his family, but the boy had no idea what he had. He took the scrolls home, where his mother burned some as kindling.

Because the young man had succeeded in his pursuit of the father's murderer, he himself was now a murderer.

Fearing the authorities would soon come looking for him and not wanting to be found with ancient artifacts, he sold the codex to the black market antique dealers in Cairo for a trifle sum. It would be years until they found their way into the hands of a scholar.

Part of the thirteenth codex was smuggled from Egypt to America. In 1955 whispers of the existence of the codex had reached the ears of Gilles Quispel, a professor of religion and history in the Netherlands. The race was on to find and translate the scrolls.

The introduction of the collected sayings of Jesus refers to the writer as Didymos (Jude) Thomas. This is the same Thomas who doubted Jesus and was then told to place his hand within the breach in the side of the Savior. In the Gospel of St. John, he is referred to as Didymos, which means twin in Greek. In Aramaic, the name Jude (or Judas) also carries the sense of twin. The use of this title led some in the apocryphal tradition to believe that he was the twin brother and confidant of Jesus. However, when applied to Jesus himself, the literal meaning of twin must be rejected by orthodox Christianity as well as anyone adhering to the doctrine of the virgin birth of the only begotten Son of God. The title is likely meant to signify that Thomas was a close confidant of Jesus, or more simply, he was part of a set of twins and in no way related to Jesus.

As mentioned earlier, church historians mention that Thomas evangelized India (Asia-Minor or Central Asia).

The text has a very Eastern flavor. At times it is almost Buddhist in its wording. (For a comparative study of Zen Buddhism's Tao Te Ching and The Gospel of Thomas, see the book *The Tao Of Thomas*).

The Gospel of Thomas is actually not a gospel at all. It contains no narrative but is instead a collection of sayings, which are said to be from Jesus himself as written (quoted) by Thomas. Although the codex found in Egypt is dated to the fourth century, most biblical scholars place the actual construction of the text of Thomas at about 70 - 150 A.D. although some place it slightly later.

The gospel was often mentioned in early Christian literature, but no copy was thought to have survived until the discovery of the Coptic manuscript. Since then, part of the Oxyrynchus papyri have been identified as older Greek fragments of Thomas. The papyri were discovered in 1898 in the rubbish heaps of Oxyrhynchus, Egypt. This discovery yielded over thirty-five manuscript fragments for the New Testament. They have been dated the earliest codex found in the library to about 60 A.D. As a point of reference, a fragment of papyrus from the Dead Sea Scrolls had been dated to before 68 A.D. This is not to say that the Gospel of Thomas was dated to these years, only that the oldest books found in the library date to this time area. Thus, the collection was a very old and select one.

There are marked differences between the Greek and Coptic texts of Thomas, as we will see.

The debate on the date of Thomas centers in part on whether Thomas is dependent upon the canonical gospels, or is derived from an earlier document that was simply a collection of sayings. Many of the passages in Thomas appear to be more authentic versions of the synoptic parables, and many have parallels in Mark and Luke. This has caused a division of thought wherein some believe Thomas used common sources also used by Mark and Luke. Others believe Thomas was written independently after witnessing the same events.

If Thomas wrote his gospel first, without input from Mark, and from the standpoint of Eastern exposure as a result of his sojourn into India, it could explain the mystical quality of the text. It could also explain the striking differences in the recorded quotes of Jesus as memories were influenced by exposure to Asian culture.

There is some speculation that the sayings found in Thomas could be more accurate to the original intent and wording of Jesus than the other gospels. This may seem counter-intuitive until we realize that Christianity itself is an Eastern religion, albeit Middle-Eastern. Although as it spread west the faith went through many changes to westernize or Romanize it, Jesus was both mystical and Middle-Eastern. The Gospel of Thomas may not have seen as much "dilution" by Western society.

The Gospel of Thomas was most likely composed in Syria, where tradition holds that the church of Edessa was founded by Judas Thomas, The Twin (Didymos). The gospel may well be the earliest written tradition in the Syriac church.

The Gospel of Thomas is sometimes called a Gnostic gospel, although it seems more likely Thomas was adopted by the Gnostic community and interpreted in the light of their beliefs.

Gnostics believed that knowledge is formed or found from a personal encounter with God brought about by inward or intuitive insight. It is this knowledge that brings salvation. The Gnostics believed they were privy to a secret knowledge about the divine. It is their focus on knowledge that leads to their name.

There are numerous references to the Gnostics in second century literature. Their form of Christianity was considered heresy by the early church fathers. The intense resistance to the Gnostic belief system seems to be based in two areas. First, there was a general Gnostic belief that we were all gods, with heaven contained within us. Jesus, according to the Gnostics, was here to show us our potential to become as he was; a son or daughter of God, for God is both father and mother, male and female. These beliefs ran contrary to the newly developing orthodoxy. The second line of resistance was political. This resistance developed later and would have come from the fact that a faith based on a personal encounter flew in the face of the developing church political structure that placed priests and church as the keepers of heaven's gate with salvation through them alone.

It is from the writings condemning the group that we glean most of our information about the Gnostics. They are alluded to in the Bible in 1 Timothy 1:4 and 1 Timothy 6:20, and possibly the entirety of Jude, as the writers of the Bible defended their theology against that of the Gnostics.

The Coptic and Greek translations of The Gospel of Thomas presented herein are the result of a gestalt brought about by contrasting and comparing all of the foremost translations, where the best phrasing was chosen to follow the intent and meaning of the text.

Because there are differences between the Coptic manuscript and the Greek fragments of Thomas, each verse will have the following format for the reader to view: The Coptic text will be presented first, since we have the entire Gospel in this language. The Greek text will come next. If there is not a second rendition of the verse, the reader may assume there was no Greek fragment found for that verse or the Greek version of the verse was identical to the Coptic version. Lastly, obvious parallels found in the Bible are listed.

Let us keep in mind that some of the differences between the translations of the Greek and Coptic may be attributed in part to the choice of word or phrase of those translating. It is the differences in overall meaning of verses between Coptic and Greek on which we should focus.

In the document to follow, the Gospel of Thomas will appear as a bold text. If there are other relevant but divergent interpretations of phrases in Thomas, they are included in parentheses. Any parallels of text or meaning that appear in the Bible are placed below the verse in italicized text. Author's notes are in regular text.

In this way the reader can easily identify which body of work is being referenced and observe how they fit together.

Since the deeper meanings within Thomas are both in metaphor and in plain, understandable language, it is hoped that each time the words are read some new insight and treasure can be taken from them. As we change our perspective, we see the meaning of each verse differently. As one turns a single jewel to view each facet, we should study the Gospel of Thomas in the same way.

Let us begin.

The Gospel Of Thomas

These are the secret sayings which the living Jesus has spoken and Judas who is also Thomas (the twin) (Didymos Judas Thomas) wrote.

1. And he said: Whoever finds the interpretation of these sayings will not taste death.

1. He said to them: Whoever discovers the interpretation of these words shall never taste death.

John 8:51 Very truly I tell you, whoever keeps my word will never see death.

2. Jesus said: Let him who seeks not stop seeking until he finds, and when he finds he will be troubled, and when he has been troubled he will marvel (be astonished) and he will reign over all and in reigning, he will find rest.

2. Jesus said: Let him who seeks not stop until he finds, and when he finds he shall wonder and in wondering he shall reign, and in reigning he shall find rest.

3. Jesus said: If those who lead you say to you: Look, the Kingdom is in the sky, then the birds of the sky would enter before you. If they say to you: It is in the sea, then the fish of the sea would enter ahead of you. But the Kingdom of God exists within you and it exists outside of you. Those who come to know (recognize) themselves will find it, and when you come to know yourselves you will become known and you will realize that you are the children of the Living Father. Yet if you do not come to know yourselves then you will dwell in poverty and it will be you who are that poverty.

3. Jesus said, If those who lead you say, "See, the Kingdom is in the sky," then the birds of the sky will precede you. If they say to you, "It is under the earth," then the fish of the sea will precede you. Rather, the Kingdom of God is inside of you, and it is outside of you.

Those who come to know themselves will find it; and when you come to know yourselves, you will understand that it is you who are the sons of the living Father. But if you will not know yourselves, you dwell in poverty and it is you who are that poverty.

Luke 17:20 And when he was demanded of by the Pharisees, when the kingdom of God should come, he answered them and said, The kingdom of God cometh not with observation: Neither shall they say, Lo here! Lo there! For, behold, the kingdom of God is within you.

4. Jesus said: The person of old age will not hesitate to ask a little child of seven days about the place of life, and he will live. For many who are first will become

last, (and the last will be first). And they will become one and the same.

4. Jesus said: Let the old man who has lived many days not hesitate to ask the child of seven days about the place of life; then he will live. For many that are first will be last, and last will be first, and they will become a single one.

Mark 9:35-37 He sat down, called the twelve, and said to them: Whoever wants to be first must be last of all and servant of all. Then he took a little child and put it among them, and taking it in his arms, he said to them: Whoever welcomes one such child in my name welcomes me, and whoever welcomes me welcomes not me but the one who sent me.

5. Jesus said: Recognize what is in front of your face, and what has been hidden from you will be revealed to you. For there is nothing hidden which will not be revealed (become manifest), and nothing buried that will not be raised.

5. Jesus said: Know what is in front of your face and what is hidden from you will be revealed to you.
For there is nothing hidden that will not be revealed.

Mark 4:2 For there is nothing hid, except to be made manifest; nor is anything secret, except it come to light.

Luke 12:3 Nothing is covered up that will not be revealed, or hidden that will not be known.

Matthew 10:26 So have no fear of them; for nothing is covered up that will not be uncovered, and nothing secret that will not become known.

6. His Disciples asked Him, they said to him: How do you want us to fast, and how will we pray? And how will we be charitable (give alms), and what laws of diet will we maintain?

Jesus said: Do not lie, and do not practice what you hate, for everything is in the plain sight of Heaven. For there is nothing concealed that will not become manifest, and there is nothing covered that will not be exposed.

6. His disciples asked him, "How do you want us to fast? And how shall we pray? And how shall we give alms? And what kind of diet shall we follow?"
Jesus said, don't lie, and don't do what you hate to do, for all things are revealed before the truth. For there is nothing hidden which shall not be revealed.

Luke 11:1 He was praying in a certain place, and after he had finished, one of his disciples said to him, Lord, teach us to pray, as John taught his disciples.

7. Jesus said: Blessed is the lion that the man will eat, for the lion will become the man. Cursed is the man that the lion shall eat, and still the lion will become man.

Mathew 26:20-30 He who dipped his hand with me in the dish, the same will betray me. The Son of Man goes, even as it is written of him, but woe to that man through whom the Son of Man is betrayed! It would be better for that man if he had not been born. Judas, who betrayed him, answered, "It isn't me, is it, Rabbi?" He said to him, You said it. As they were eating, Jesus took bread, gave thanks for it, and broke it. He gave to the disciples, and said, Take, eat; this is my body. He took the cup, gave thanks, and gave to them, saying: All of you drink it, for this is my blood of the new covenant, which is poured out for many for the remission of sins. But I tell you that I will not drink of this fruit of the vine from now on, until that day when I drink it anew with you in my Father's Kingdom. When they had sung a hymn, they went out to the Mount of Olives.

8. And he said: The Kingdom of Heaven is like a wise fisherman who casts his net into the sea. He drew it up from the sea full of small fish. Among them he found a fine large fish. That wise fisherman threw all the small fish back into the sea and chose the large fish without hesitation. Whoever has ears to hear, let him hear!

Matthew 13:47-48 Again, the kingdom of heaven is like a net that was thrown into the sea and caught fish of every kind; when it was full, they drew it ashore, sat down, and put the good into baskets but threw out the bad.

9. Jesus said: Now, the sower came forth. He filled his hand and threw (the seeds). Some fell upon the road and the birds came and gathered them up. Others fell on the stone and they did not take deep enough roots in the soil, and so did not produce grain. Others fell among the thorns and they choked the seed, and the worm ate them. Others fell upon the good earth and it produced good fruit up toward the sky, it bore 60 fold and 120 fold.

Matthew 13:3-8 And he told them many things in parables, saying: Listen! A sower went out to sow. And as he sowed, some seeds fell on the path, and the birds came and ate them up. Other seeds fell on rocky ground, where they did not have much soil, and they sprang up quickly, since they had no depth of soil. But when the sun rose, they were scorched; and since they had no root, they withered away. Other seeds fell among thorns, and the thorns grew up and choked them. Other seeds fell on good soil and brought forth grain, some a hundred fold, some sixty, some thirty.

Mark 4:2-9 And he taught them many things in parables, and in his teaching he said to them: Behold! A sower went out to sow. And as he sowed, some seed fell along the path, and the birds came and devoured it. Other seed fell on rocky ground, where it had not much soil, and immediately it sprang up, since it had no depth of soil; and when the sun rose it was scorched, and since it had no root it withered away. Other seed fell among thorns and the thorns grew up and choked it, and it yielded no grain. And other seeds fell into good soil and brought forth grain, growing up and increasing and yielding thirty fold and sixty fold and a hundred fold. And he said, He who has ears to hear, let him hear.

Luke 8:4-8 And when a great crowd came together and people from town after town came to him, he said in a parable: A sower went out to sow his seed; and as he sowed, some fell along the path, and was trodden under foot, and the birds of the air devoured it. And some fell on the rock; and as it grew up, it withered away, because it had no moisture. And some fell among thorns; and the thorns grew with it and choked it. And some fell into good soil and grew, and yielded a hundred fold. As he said this, he called out, He who has ears to hear, let him hear.

10. Jesus said: I have cast fire upon the world, and as you see, I guard it until it is ablaze.

Luke 12:49 I came to bring fire to the earth, and how I wish it were already kindled.

11. Jesus said: This sky will pass away, and the one above it will pass away. The dead are not alive, and the living will not die. In the days when you consumed what is dead, you made it alive. When you come into the Light, what will you do? On the day when you were united (one), you became separated (two). When you have become separated (two), what will you do?

Matthew 24:35 Heaven and earth will pass away, but my words will not pass away.

12. The Disciples said to Jesus: We know that you will go away from us. Who is it that will be our teacher?

Jesus said to them: Wherever you are (in the place that you have come), you will go to James the Righteous, for whose sake Heaven and Earth were made (came into being.)

13. Jesus said to his Disciples: Compare me to others, and tell me who I am like. Simon Peter said to him: You are like a righteous messenger (angel) of God. Matthew said to him: You are like a (wise) philosopher (of the heart). Thomas said to him: Teacher, my mouth is not capable of saying who you are like!

Jesus said: I'm not your teacher, now that you have drunk; you have become drunk from the bubbling spring that I have tended (measured out). And he took him, and withdrew and spoke three words to him: ahyh ashr ahyh (I am who I am).

Now when Thomas returned to his comrades, they inquired of him: What did Jesus say to you? Thomas said to them: If I tell you even one of the words which he spoke to me, you will take up stones and throw them at me, and fire will come from the stones to consume you.

Mark 8:27-30 Jesus went on with his disciples to the villages of Caesarea Philippi; and on the way he asked his disciples, Who do people say that I am? And they answered him, John the Baptist; and others, Elijah; and still others, one of the prophets. He asked them, But who do you say that I am? Peter answered him, You are the Messiah. And he sternly ordered them not to tell anyone about him.

14. Jesus said to them: If you fast, you will give rise to transgression (sin) for yourselves. And if you pray, you will be condemned. And if you give alms, you will cause harm (evil) to your spirits. And when you go into the countryside, if they take you in (receive you) then eat what they set before you and heal the sick among them. For what goes into your mouth will not defile you, but rather what comes out of your mouth, that is what will defile you.

Luke 10:8-9 Whenever you enter a town and its people welcome you, eat what is set before you; Cure the sick who are there, and say to them, The kingdom of God has come near to you.

Mark 7:15 There is nothing outside a person that by going in can defile, but the things that come out are what defile.

Matthew 15:11 It is not what goes into the mouth that defiles a man, but what comes out of the mouth, this defiles a man.

Romans 14.14 I know and am persuaded in the Lord Jesus that nothing is unclean in itself; but it is unclean for any one who thinks it unclean.

15. Jesus said: When you see him who was not born of woman, bow yourselves down upon your faces and worship him for he is your Father.

Galatians 4:3-5 Even so we, when we were children, were in bondage under the elements of the world: But when the fullness of the time was come, God sent forth his Son, made of a woman, made under the law, To redeem them that were under the law, that we might receive the adoption of sons.

16. Jesus said: People think perhaps I have come to spread peace upon the world. They do not know that I have come to cast dissention (conflict) upon the earth; fire, sword, war. For there will be five in a house. Three will be against two and two against three, the father against the son and the son against the father. And they will stand alone.

Matthew 10:34-36 Do not think that I have come to bring peace to the earth; I have not come to bring peace, but a sword. For I have come to set a man against his father, and a daughter against her mother, and a daughter-in-law against her mother-in-law; and one's foes will be members of one's own household.

Luke 12:51-53 Do you think that I have come to give peace on earth? No, I tell you, but rather division; for henceforth in one house there will be five divided, three against two and two against three; they will be divided, father against son and son against father, mother against daughter and daughter against her mother, mother-in-law against her daughter-in-law and daughter-in-law against her mother-in-law.

17. Jesus said: I will give to you what eye has not seen, what ear has not heard,

what hand has not touched, and what has not occurred to the mind of man.

1 Cor 2:9 But, as it is written, What no eye has seen, nor ear heard, nor the human heart conceived, what God has prepared for those who love him.

18. The Disciples said to Jesus: Tell us how our end will come. Jesus said: Have you already discovered the beginning (Origin), so that you inquire about the end? Where the beginning (origin) is, there the end will be. Blessed be he who will take his place in the beginning (stand at the origin) for he will know the end, and he will not experience death.

19. Jesus said: Blessed is he who came into being before he came into being. If you become my Disciples and heed my sayings, these stones will serve you. For there are five trees in paradise for you, which are undisturbed in summer and in winter and their leaves do not fall. Whoever knows them will not experience death.

20. The Disciples said to Jesus: Tell us what the Kingdom of Heaven is like. He said to them: It is like a mustard seed, smaller than all other seeds and yet when it falls on the tilled earth, it produces a great plant and becomes shelter for the birds of the sky.

Mark 4:30-32 He also said, With what can we compare the kingdom of God, or what parable will we use for it? It is like a mustard seed, which, when sown upon the ground, is the smallest of all the seeds on earth; yet when it is sown it grows up and becomes the greatest of all shrubs, and puts forth large branches, so that the birds of the air can make nests in its shade.

Matthew 13:31-32 The kingdom of heaven is like a grain of mustard seed which a man took and sowed in his field; it is the smallest of all seeds, but when it has grown it is the greatest of shrubs and becomes a tree, so that the birds of the air come and make nests in its branches.

Luke 13.18-19 He said therefore, What is the kingdom of God like? And to what shall I compare it? It is like a grain of mustard seed which a man took and sowed in his garden; and it grew and became a tree, and the birds of the air made nests in its branches.

21. Mary said to Jesus: Who are your Disciples like? He said: They are like little children who are living in a field that is not theirs. When the owners of the field come, they will say: Let us have our field! It is as if they were naked in front of them (They undress in front of them in order to let them have what is theirs) and they give back the field. Therefore I say, if the owner of the house knows that the thief is coming, he will be alert before he arrives and will not allow him to dig through into the house to carry away his belongings. You, must be on guard and beware of the world (system). Prepare yourself (arm yourself) with great strength or the bandits will find a way to reach you, for the problems you expect will come. Let there be among you a person of understanding (awareness). When the crop ripened, he came quickly with his sickle in his hand to reap. Whoever has ears to

hear, let him hear!

Matthew 24:43 But understand this: if the owner of the house had known in what part of the night the thief was coming, he would have stayed awake and would not have let his house be broken into.

Mark 4:26-29 He also said, The kingdom of God is as if someone would scatter seed on the ground, and would sleep and rise night and day, and the seed would sprout and grow, he does not know how. The earth produces of itself, first the stalk, then the head, then the full grain in the head. But when the grain is ripe, at once he goes in with his sickle, because the harvest has come.

Luke 12:39-40 But know this, that if the householder had known at what hour the thief was coming, he would not have left his house to be broken into. You also must be ready; for the Son of man is coming at an unexpected hour.

22. Jesus saw little children who were being suckled. He said to his Disciples: These little children who are being suckled are like those who enter the Kingdom.

They said to him: Should we become like little children in order to enter the Kingdom?

Jesus said to them: When you make the two one, and you make the inside as the outside and the outside as the inside, when you make the above as the below, and if you make the male and the female one and the same (united male and female) so that the man will not be masculine (male) and the female be not feminine (female), when you establish an eye in the place of an eye and a hand in the place of a hand and a foot in the place of a foot and a likeness (image) in the place of a likeness (an image), then will you enter the Kingdom.

Luke 18:16 But Jesus called for them and said, Let the little children come to me, and do not stop them; for it is to such as these that the kingdom of God belongs. Truly I tell you, whoever does not receive the kingdom of God as a little child will never enter it.

Mark 9:43-48 If your hand causes you to stumble, cut it off; it is better for you to enter life maimed than to have two hands and to go to hell, to the unquenchable fire. And if your foot causes you to stumble, cut it off; it is better for you to enter life lame than to have two feet and to be thrown into hell. And if your eye causes you to stumble, tear it out; it is better for you to enter the kingdom of God with one eye than to have two eyes and to be thrown into hell, where the worm never dies, and the fire is never quenched.

Matthew 18:3-5 And said, Verily, I say unto you, unless you turn and become like children, you will never enter the kingdom of heaven. Whoever humbles himself like this child, he is the greatest in the kingdom of heaven. Whoever receives one such child in my name receives me;

Matthew 5:29-30 If your right eye causes you to sin, pluck it out and throw it away; it is better that you lose one of your members than that your whole body be thrown into hell. And if your right hand causes you to sin, cut it off and throw it away; it is better that you lose one of your members than that your whole body go into hell.

23. Jesus said: I will choose you, one out of a thousand and two out of ten thousand and they will stand as a single one.

Matthew 20:16 So the last shall be first, and the first last: for many be called, but few chosen.
24. His Disciples said: Show us the place where you are (your place), for it is necessary for us to seek it.
24. He said to them: Whoever has ears, let him hear! Within a man of light there is light, and he illumines the entire world. If he does not shine, he is darkness (there is darkness).

John13:36 Simon Peter said to him, Lord, where are you going? Jesus answered, Where I am going, you cannot follow me now; but you will follow afterward.

Matthew 6:22-23 The eye is the lamp of the body. So, if your eye is healthy, your whole body will be full of light; but if your eye is unhealthy, your whole body will be full of darkness. If then the light in you is darkness, how great is the darkness!

Luke 11:34-36 Your eye is the lamp of your body; when your eye is sound, your whole body is full of light; but when it is not sound, your body is full of darkness. Therefore be careful lest the light in you be darkness. If then your whole body is full of light, having no part dark, it will be wholly bright, as when a lamp with its rays gives you light.

Author's Note:
Early philosophers thought that light was transmitted from the eye and bounced back, allowing the person to sense the world at large. Ancient myths tell of Aphrodite constructing the human eye out of the four elements (earth, wind, fire, and water). The eye was held together by love. She kindled the fire of the soul and used it to project from the eyes so that it would act like a lantern, transmitting the light, thus allowing us to see.

Euclid, (330 BC to 260BC) speculated about the speed of light being instantaneous since you close your eyes, then open them again; even the distant objects appear immediately.

25. Jesus said: Love your friend (Brother) as your soul; protect him as you would the pupil of your own eye.

Romans 12:9-11 Let love be without dissimulation. Abhor that which is evil; cleave to that which is good. Be kindly affectioned one to another with brotherly love; in honour preferring one another; Not slothful in business; fervent in spirit; serving the Lord…

26. Jesus said: You see the speck in your brother's eye but the beam that is in your own eye you do not see. When you remove the beam out of your own eye, then will you see clearly to remove the speck out of your brother's eye.

26. Jesus said, You see the splinter in your brother's eye, but you don't see the log in your own eye. When you take the log out of your own eye, then you will see well enough to remove the splinter from your brother's eye.

Matthew 7:3-5 Why do you see the speck in your neighbor's eye, but do not notice the log in your own eye? Or how can you say to your neighbor, Let me take the speck out of your eye, while the log is in your own eye? You hypocrite, first take the log out of your own eye, and then you will see clearly to take the speck out of your neighbor's eye.

Luke 6:41-42 Why do you see the speck that is in your brother's eye, but do not notice the log that is in your own eye? Or how can you say to your brother, Brother, let me take out the speck that is in your eye, when you yourself do not see the log that is in your own eye? You hypocrite, first take the log out of your own eye, and then you will see clearly to take out the speck that is in your brother's eye.

27. Jesus said: Unless you fast from the world (system), you will not find the Kingdom of God. Unless you keep the Sabbath (entire week) as Sabbath, you will not see the Father.

27. Jesus said: Unless you fast (abstain) from the world, you shall in no way find the Kingdom of God; and unless you observe the Sabbath as a Sabbath, you shall not see the Father.

28. Jesus said: I stood in the midst of the world. In the flesh I appeared to them. I found them all drunk; I found none thirsty among them. My soul grieved for the sons of men, for they are blind in their hearts and do not see that they came into the world empty, they are destined (determined) to leave the world empty. However, now they are drunk. When they have shaken off their wine, then they will repent (change their ways).

28. Jesus said: I took my stand in the midst of the world, and they saw me in the flesh, and I found they were all drunk, and I found none of them were thirsty. And my soul grieved over the souls of men because they are blind in their hearts. They do not see that they came into the world empty, therefore they are determined to leave the world empty. However, now they are drunk. When they have shaken off their wine, then they will change their ways.

29. Jesus said: If the flesh came into being because of spirit, it is a marvel, but if spirit came into being because of the body, it would be a marvel of marvels. I marvel indeed at how great wealth has taken up residence in this poverty.

30. Jesus said: Where there are three gods, they are gods (Where there are three gods they are without god). Where there is only one, I say that I am with him. Lift the stone and there you will find me, Split the wood and there am I.

30. Jesus said: Where three are together they are not without God, and when there is one alone, I say, I am with him.

Author's Note:
Many scholars believe pages of the manuscript were misplaced and verses 30 and 77 should run together as a single verse.

77. Jesus said: I-Am the Light who is over all things, I-Am the All. From me all came forth and to me all return (The All came from me and the All has come to me). Split wood, there am I. Lift up the stone and there you will find me.

Matthew 18:20 For where two or three are gathered in my name, I am there among them.

31. Jesus said: No prophet is accepted in his own village, no physician heals those who know him.

31. Jesus said: A prophet is not accepted in his own country, neither can a doctor cure those that know him.

Mark 6:4 Then Jesus said to them, Prophets are not without honor, except in their hometown, and among their own kin, and in their own house.

Matthew 13:57 And they took offense at him. But Jesus said to them: A prophet is not without honor save in his own country and in his own house.

Luke 4:24 And he said, Truly, I say to you, no prophet is acceptable in his own country.

John 4:43-44 After the two days he departed to Galilee. For Jesus himself testified that a prophet has no honor in his own country.

32. Jesus said: A city being built (and established) upon a high mountain and fortified cannot fall nor can it be hidden.

32. Jesus said: A city built on a high hilltop and fortified can neither fall nor be hidden.

Matthew 5:14 You are the light of the world. A city built on a hill cannot be hid.

33. Jesus said: What you will hear in your ear preach from your rooftops. For no one lights a lamp and sets it under a basket nor puts it in a hidden place, but rather it is placed on a lamp stand so that everyone who comes and goes will see its light.

33. Jesus said: What you hear with one ear preach from your rooftops. For no one lights a lamp and sets it under a basket or hides, but rather it is placed on a lamp stand so that everyone who comes and goes will see its light.

Matthew 10:27 What I say to you in the dark, tell in the light; and what you hear whispered, proclaim from the housetops.

Luke 8:16 No one after lighting a lamp hides it under a jar, or puts it under a bed, but puts it on a lamp stand, so that those who enter may see the light.

Matthew 5:15 Nor do men light a lamp and put it under a bushel, but on a stand, and it gives light to all in the house.

Mark 4:21 And he said to them, Is a lamp brought in to be put under a bushel, or under a bed, and not on a stand?

Luke 11:33 No one after lighting a lamp puts it in a cellar or under a bushel, but on a stand, that those who enter may see the light.

34. Jesus said: If a blind person leads a blind person, both fall into a pit.

Matthew 15:14 Let them alone; they are blind guides of the blind. And if one blind person guides another, both will fall into a pit.

Luke 6:39 He also told them a parable: Can a blind man lead a blind man? Will they not both fall into a pit?

35. Jesus said: It is impossible for anyone to enter the house of a strong man to take it by force unless he binds his hands, then he will be able to loot his house.

Matthew 12:29 Or how can one enter a strong man's house and plunder his goods, unless he first binds the strong man? Then indeed he may plunder his house.

Luke 11:21-22 When a strong man, fully armed, guards his own palace, his goods are in peace; but when one stronger than he assails him and overcomes him, he takes away his armor in which he trusted, and divides his spoil.

Mark 3:27 But no one can enter a strong man's house and plunder his property without first tying up the strong man; then indeed the house can be plundered.

36. Jesus said: Do not worry from morning to evening nor from evening to morning about the food that you will eat nor about what clothes you will wear. You are much superior to the Lilies which neither card nor spin. When you have no clothing, what do you wear? Who can add time to your life (increase your stature)? He himself will give to you your garment.

Matthew 6:25-31 Therefore I tell you, do not worry about your life, what you will eat or what you will drink, or about your body, what you will wear. Is not life more than food, and the body more than clothing? Look at the birds of the air; they neither sow nor reap nor gather into barns, and yet your heavenly Father feeds them. Are you not of more value than they? And can any of you by worrying add a single hour to your span of life? And why do you worry about clothing? Consider the lilies of the field, how they grow; they neither toil nor spin, yet I tell you, even Solomon in all his glory was not clothed like one of these. But if God so clothes the grass of the field, which is alive today and tomorrow is thrown into the oven, will he not much more clothe you--you of little faith? Therefore do not worry, saying, What will we eat? or What will we drink? or What will we wear?

Luke 12:22-23 And he said to his disciples, Therefore I tell you, do not be anxious about your life, what you shall eat, nor about your body, what you shall put on. For life is more than food, and the body more than clothing.

37. His Disciples said: When will you appear to us, and when will we see you?

Jesus said: When you take off your garments without being ashamed, and place your garments under your feet and tread on them as the little children do, then will you see the Son of the Living-One, and you will not be afraid.

37 His disciples said to him, when will you be visible to us, and when shall we be able to see you?

He said, when you strip naked without being ashamed and place your garments under your feet and tread on them as the little children do, then will you see the Son of the Living-One, and you will not be afraid.

38. Jesus said: Many times have you yearned to hear these sayings which I speak to you, and you have no one else from whom to hear them. There will be days when you will seek me but you will not find me.

39. Jesus said: The Pharisees and the Scribes have received the keys of knowledge, but they have hidden them. They did not go in, nor did they permit those who wished to enter to do so. However, you be as wise (astute) as serpents and innocent as doves.

39. Jesus said: The Pharisees and the Scribes have stolen the keys of heaven, but they have hidden them. They have entered in, but they did not permit those who wished to enter to do so. However, you be as wise as serpents and innocent as doves.

Luke 11:52 Woe to you lawyers! For you have taken away the key of knowledge; you did not enter yourselves, and you hindered those who were entering.

Matthew 10:16 See, I am sending you out like sheep into the midst of wolves; so be wise as serpents and innocent as doves.

Matthew 23.13 But woe unto you, scribes and Pharisees, hypocrites! because you shut the kingdom of heaven against men; for you neither enter yourselves, nor allow those who would enter to go in.

40. Jesus said: A grapevine has been planted outside the (vineyard of the) Father, and since it is not viable (supported) it will be pulled up by its roots and destroyed.

Matthew 15:13 He answered, Every plant that my heavenly Father has not planted will be uprooted.

41. Jesus said: Whoever has (it) in his hand, to him will (more) be given. And whoever does not have, from him will be taken even the small amount which he has.

Matthew 25:29 For to all those who have, more will be given, and they will have an abundance; but from those who have nothing, even what they have will be taken away.

Luke 19:26 I tell you, that to every one who has will more be given; but from him who has not, even what he has will be taken away.

42. Jesus said: Become passers-by.

43. His Disciples said to him: Who are you, that you said these things to us?

Jesus said to them: You do not recognize who I am from what I said to you, but rather you have become like the Jews who either love the tree and hate its fruit, or love the fruit and hate the tree.

John 8:25 They said to him, Who are you? Jesus said to them, Why do I speak to you at all?

Matthew 7:16-20 You will know them by their fruits. Are grapes gathered from thorns, or figs from thistles? In the same way, every good tree bears good fruit, but the bad tree bears bad fruit. A good tree cannot bear bad fruit, nor can a bad tree bear good fruit. Every tree that does not bear good fruit is cut down and thrown into the fire. Thus you will know them by their fruits.

44. Jesus said: Whoever blasphemes against the Father, it will be forgiven him. And whoever blasphemes against the Son, it will be forgiven him. Yet whoever blasphemes against the Holy Spirit, it will not be forgiven him neither on earth nor in heaven.

Mark 3:28-29 Truly I tell you, people will be forgiven for their sins and whatever blasphemies they utter; but whoever blasphemes against the Holy Spirit can never have forgiveness, but is guilty of an eternal sin.

Matthew 12:31-32 Therefore I tell you, every sin and blasphemy will be forgiven men, but the blasphemy against the Spirit will not be forgiven. And whoever says a word against the Son of man will be forgiven; but whoever speaks against the Holy Spirit will not be forgiven, either in this age or in the age to come.

Luke 12:10 And every one who speaks a word against the Son of man will be forgiven him; but he who blasphemes against the Holy Spirit will not be forgiven.

45. Jesus said: Grapes are not harvested from thorns, nor are figs gathered from thistles, for they do not give fruit. A good person brings forth goodness out of his storehouse. A bad person brings forth evil out of his evil storehouse which is in his heart, and he speaks evil, for out of the abundance of the heart he brings forth evil.

Luke 6:43-45 For no good tree bears bad fruit, nor again does a bad tree bear good fruit; for each tree is known by its own fruit. For figs are not gathered from thorns, nor are grapes picked from a bramble bush. The good man out of the good treasure of his heart produces good, and the evil man out of his evil treasure produces evil; for out of the abundance of the heart his mouth speaks.

46. Jesus said: From Adam until John the Baptist there is none born of women who surpasses John the Baptist, so that his eyes should not be downcast (lowered). Yet I have said that whoever among you becomes like a child will know the Kingdom, and he will be greater than John.

Matthew 11:11 Truly I tell you, among those born of women no one has arisen greater than John the Baptist; yet the least in the kingdom of heaven is greater than he.

Luke 7:28 I tell you, among those born of women none is greater than John; yet he who is least in the kingdom of God is greater than he.

Matthew 18:2-4 He called a child, whom he put among them, and said, Truly I tell you, unless you change and become like children, you will never enter the kingdom of heaven. Whoever becomes humble like this child is the greatest in the kingdom of heaven.

47. Jesus said: It is impossible for a man to mount two horses or to draw two bows, and a servant cannot serve two masters, otherwise he will honor the one and disrespect the other. No man drinks vintage wine and immediately desires to drink new wine, and they do not put new wine into old wineskins or they would burst, and they do not put vintage wine into new wineskins or it would spoil (sour). They do not sew an old patch on a new garment because that would cause a split.

Matthew 6:24 No one can serve two masters; for a slave will either hate the one and love the other, or be devoted to the one and despise the other. You cannot serve God and wealth.

Matthew 9:16-17 No one sews a piece of cloth, not yet shrunk, on an old cloak, for the patch pulls away from the cloak, and a worse tear is made. Neither is new wine put into old wineskins; otherwise, the skins burst, and the wine is spilled, and the skins are destroyed; but new wine is put into fresh wineskins, and so both are preserved.

Mark 2:21-22 No one sews a piece of unshrunk cloth on an old garment; if he does, the patch tears away from it, the new from the old, and a worse tear is made. And no one puts new wine into old wineskins; if he does, the wine will burst the skins, and the wine is lost, and so are the skins; but new wine is for fresh skins.

Luke 5:36-39 He told them a parable also: No one tears a piece from a new garment and puts it upon an old garment; if he does, he will tear the new, and the piece from the new will not match the old. And no one puts new wine into old wineskins; if he does, the new wine will burst the skins and it will be spilled, and the skins will be destroyed. But new wine must be put into fresh wineskins. And no one after drinking old wine desires new; for he says, "The old is good."

48. Jesus said: If two make peace with each other in this one house, they will say to the mountain: Be moved! and it will be moved.

Matthew 18:19 Again, truly I tell you, if two of you agree on earth about anything you ask, it will be done for you by my Father in heaven.

Mark 11:23-24 Truly I tell you, if you say to this mountain, Be taken up and thrown into the sea, and if you do not doubt in your heart, but believe that what you say will come to pass, it will be done for you. So I tell you, whatever you ask for in prayer, believe that you have received it, and it will be yours.

Matthew 17:20 He said to them, Because of your little faith. For truly, I say to you, if you have faith as a grain of mustard seed, you will say to this mountain, Move from here to there, and it will move; and nothing will be impossible to you.

49. Jesus said: Blessed is the solitary and chosen, for you will find the Kingdom. You have come from it, and unto it you will return.

Matthew 5:1-3 And seeing the multitudes, he went up into a mountain: and when he was set, his disciples came unto him: And he opened his mouth, and taught them, saying, Blessed are the poor in spirit: for theirs is the kingdom of heaven.
John 20:28-30 And Thomas answered and said unto him, My LORD and my God. Jesus saith unto him, Thomas, because thou hast seen me, thou hast believed: blessed are they that have not seen, and yet have believed. And many other signs truly did Jesus in the presence of his disciples, which are not written in this book:

50. Jesus said: If they say to you: From where do you come? Say to them: We have come from the Light, the place where the Light came into existence of its own accord and he stood and appeared in their image. If they say to you: Is it you? (Who are you?), say: We are his Sons and we are the chosen of the Living Father. If they ask you: What is the sign of your Father in you? Say to them: It is movement with rest (peace in the midst of motion or chaos).

51. His Disciples said to him: When will the rest of the dead occur, and when will the New World come? He said to them: That which you look for has already come, but you do not recognize it.

52. His Disciples said to him: Twenty-four prophets preached in Israel, and they all spoke of you (in your spirit). He said to them: You have ignored the Living-One who is in your presence and you have spoken only of the dead.

53. His Disciples said to him: Is circumcision beneficial or not? He said to them: If it were beneficial, their father would beget them already circumcised from their mother. However, the true spiritual circumcision has become entirely beneficial.

Jeremiah 4:3-5 For thus saith the LORD to the men of Judah and Jerusalem, Break up your fallow ground, and sow not among thorns. Circumcise yourselves to the LORD, and take away the foreskins of your heart, ye men of Judah and inhabitants of Jerusalem: lest my fury come forth like fire, and burn that none can quench it, because of the evil of your doings. Declare ye in Judah, and publish in Jerusalem; and say, Blow ye the trumpet in the land: cry, gather together, and say, Assemble yourselves, and let us go into the defenced cities.

54. Jesus said: Blessed be the poor, for yours is the Kingdom of the Heaven.

Matthew 6:20 Then he looked up at his disciples and said: Blessed are you who are poor, for yours is the kingdom of God.

Luke 6:20 And he lifted up his eyes on his disciples, and said: Blessed are you poor, for yours is the kingdom of God.

Matthew 5:3 Blessed are the poor in spirit, for theirs is the kingdom of heaven.

55. Jesus said: Whoever does not hate his father and his mother will not be able to become my Disciple. And whoever does not hate his brothers and his sisters and does not take up his own cross in my way, will not become worthy of me.

Luke 14:26-27 If any one comes to me and does not hate his own father and mother and wife and children and brothers and sisters, yes, and even his own life, he cannot be my disciple. Whoever does not bear his own cross and come after me, cannot be my disciple.

John 17:11-21 And now I am no more in the world, but these are in the world, and I come to thee. Holy Father, keep through thine own name those whom thou hast given me, that they may be one, as we are. While I was with them in the world, I kept them in thy name: those that thou gavest me I have kept, and none of them is lost, but the son of perdition; that the scripture might be fulfilled. And now come I to thee; and these things I speak in the world, that they might have my joy fulfilled in themselves. I have given them thy word; and the world hath hated them, because they are not of the world, even as I am not of the world. I pray not that thou shouldest take them out of the world, but that thou shouldest keep them from the evil. They are not of the world, even as I am not of the world. Sanctify them through thy truth: thy word is truth. As thou hast sent me into the world, even so have I also sent them into the world. And for their sakes I sanctify myself, that they also might be sanctified through the truth. Neither pray I for these alone, but for them also which shall believe on me through their word; That they all may be one; as thou, Father, art in me, and I in thee, that they also may be one in us: that the world may believe that thou hast sent me.

56. Jesus said: Whoever has come to understand the world (system) has found a corpse, and whoever has found a corpse, is superior to the world (of him the system is not worthy).

Hebrews 11:37-40 They were stoned, they were sawn asunder, were tempted, were slain with the sword: they wandered about in sheepskins and goatskins; being destitute, afflicted, tormented; (Of whom the world was not worthy:) they wandered in deserts, and in mountains, and in dens and caves of the earth. And these all, having obtained a good report through faith, received not the promise: God having provided some better thing for us, that they without us should not be made perfect.

57. Jesus said: The Kingdom of the Father is like a person who has good seed. His enemy came by night and sowed a weed among the good seed. The man did not permit them to pull up the weed, he said to them: perhaps you will intend to pull up the weed and you pull up the wheat along with it. But, on the day of harvest the weeds will be very visible and then they will pull them and burn them.

Matthew 13:24-30 He put before them another parable: The kingdom of heaven may be compared to someone who sowed good seed in his field; but while everybody was asleep, an enemy came and sowed weeds among the wheat, and then went away. So when the plants came up and bore grain, then the weeds appeared as well. And the slaves of the householder came and said to him, Master, did you not sow good seed in your field? Where, then, did these weeds come from? He answered, An enemy has done this. The slaves said to him, Then do you want us to go and gather them? But he replied, No; for in gathering the weeds you would uproot the wheat along with them. Let both of them grow together until the harvest; and at harvest time I will tell the reapers, Collect the weeds first and bind them in bundles to be burned, but gather the wheat into my barn.

58. Jesus said: Blessed is the person who has suffered, for he has found life. (Blessed is he who has suffered to find life and found life).

Matthew 11:28 Come to me, all you that are weary and are carrying heavy burdens, and I will give you rest.

59. Jesus said: Look to the Living-One while you are alive, otherwise, you might die and seek to see him and will be unable to find him.

John 7:34 You will search for me, but you will not find me; and where I am, you cannot come.

John 13:33 Little children, I am with you only a little longer. You will look for me; and as I said to the Jews so now I say to you, Where I am going, you cannot come.

60. They saw a Samaritan carrying a lamb, on his way to Judea. Jesus said to them: Why does he take the lamb with him? They said to him: So that he may kill it and eat it. He said to them: While it is alive he will not eat it, but only after he kills it and it becomes a corpse. They said: How could he do otherwise? He said to them: Look for a place of rest for yourselves, otherwise, you might become corpses and be eaten.

61. Jesus said: Two will rest on a bed and one will die and the other will live. Salome said: Who are you, man? As if sent by someone, you laid upon my bed and you ate from my table. Jesus said to her: I-Am he who is from that which is whole (the undivided). I have been given the things of my Father. Salome said: I'm your Disciple. Jesus said to her: Thus, I say that whenever someone is one (undivided)

he will be filled with light, yet whenever he is divided (chooses) he will be filled with darkness.

Luke 17:34 I tell you, on that night there will be two in one bed; one will be taken and the other left.

62. Jesus said: I tell my mysteries to those who are worthy of my mysteries. Do not let your right hand know what your left hand is doing.

Mark 4:11 And he said to them, To you has been given the secret of the kingdom of God, but for those outside, everything comes in parables.

Matthew 6:3 But when you give alms, do not let your left hand know what your right hand is doing.

Luke 8:10 He said, To you it has been given to know the secrets of the kingdom of God; but for others they are in parables, so that seeing they may not see, and hearing they may not understand.

Matthew 13:10-11 Then the disciples came and said to him, Why do you speak to them in parables? And he answered them, To you it has been given to know the secrets of the kingdom of heaven, but to them it has not been given.

63. Jesus said: There was a wealthy person who had much money, and he said: I will use my money so that I may sow and reap and replant, to fill my storehouses with grain so that I lack nothing. This was his intention (is what he thought in his heart) but that same night he died. Whoever has ears, let him hear!

Luke 12:21 Then he told them a parable: The land of a rich man produced abundantly. And he thought to himself, What should I do, for I have no place to store my crops? Then he said, I will do this: I will pull down my barns and build larger ones, and there I will store all my grain and my goods. And I will say to my soul, Soul, you have ample goods laid up for many years; relax, eat, drink, be merry. But God said to him, You fool! This very night your life is being demanded of you. And the things you have prepared, whose will they be? So it is with those who store up treasures for themselves but are not rich toward God.

64. Jesus said: A person had houseguests, and when he had prepared the banquet in their honor he sent his servant to invite the guests. He went to the first, he said to him: My master invites you. He replied: I have to do business with some merchants. They are coming to see me this evening. I will go to place my orders with them. I ask to be excused from the banquet. He went to another, he said to him: My master has invited you. He replied to him: I have just bought a house and they require me for a day. I will have no spare time. He came to another, he said to him: My master invites you. He replied to him: My friend is getting married and I must arrange a banquet for him. I will not be able to come. I ask to be excused from the banquet. He went to another, he said to him: My master invites you. He replied to him: I have bought a farm. I go to receive the rent. I will not be able to come. I ask to be excused. The servant returned, he said to his master: Those whom you have invited to the banquet have excused themselves. The master said to his servant: Go out to the roads, bring those whom you find so that they may feast. And he said: Businessmen and merchants will not enter the places of my Father.

Luke 14:16-24 Then Jesus said to him:, Someone gave a great dinner and invited many. At the time for the dinner he sent his slave to say to those who had been invited, Come; for everything is ready now. But they all alike began to make excuses. The first said to him, I have bought a piece of land, and I must go out and see it; please accept my regrets. Another said, I have bought five yoke of oxen, and I am going to try them out; please accept my regrets. Another said, I have just been married, and therefore I cannot come. So the slave returned and reported this to his master. Then the owner of the house became angry and said to his slave, Go out at once into the streets and lanes of the town and bring in the poor, the crippled, the blind, and the lame. And the slave said, Sir, what you ordered has been done, and there is still room. Then the master said to the slave, Go out into the roads and lanes, and compel people to come in, so that my house may be filled. For I tell you, none of those who were invited will taste my dinner.

Matthew 19:23 Then Jesus said to his disciples, Truly I tell you, it will be hard for a rich person to enter the kingdom of heaven.

Matthew 22:1-14 And Jesus answered and spake unto them again by parables, and said, The kingdom of heaven is like unto a certain king, which made a marriage for his son, and sent his servants to call those who were invited to the marriage feast; but they would not come. Again he sent other servants, saying, Tell those who are invited, Behold, I have made ready my dinner, my oxen and my fat calves are killed, and everything is ready; come to the marriage feast. But they made light of it and went off, one to his farm, another to his business, while the rest seized his servants, treated them shamefully, and killed them. The king was angry, and he sent his troops and destroyed those murderers and burned their city. Then he said to his servants, The wedding is ready, but those invited were not worthy. Go therefore to the thoroughfares, and invite to the marriage feast as many as you find. And those servants went out into the streets and gathered all whom they found, both bad and good; so the wedding hall was filled with guests. But when the king came in to look at the guests, he saw there a man who had no wedding garment; and he said to him, Friend, how did you get in here without a wedding garment? And he was speechless. Then the king said to the attendants, Bind him hand and foot, and cast him into the outer darkness; there men will weep and gnash their teeth. For many are called, but few are chosen.

65. He said: A kind person who owned a vineyard leased it to tenants so that they would work it and he would receive the fruit from them. He sent his servant so that the tenants would give to him the fruit of the vineyard. They seized his servant and beat him nearly to death. The servant went, he told his master what had happened. His master said: Perhaps they did not recognize him. So, he sent another servant. The tenants beat him also. Then the owner sent his son. He said: Perhaps they will respect my son. Since the tenants knew that he was the heir to the vineyard, they seized him and killed him. Whoever has ears, let him hear!

Matthew 21:33-39 Listen to another parable. There was a landowner who planted a vineyard, put a fence around it, dug a wine press in it, and built a watchtower. Then he leased it to tenants and went to another country. When the harvest time had come, he sent his slaves to the tenants to collect his produce. But the tenants seized his slaves and beat one, killed another, and stoned another. Again he sent other slaves, more than the first; and they treated them in the same way. Finally he sent his son to them, saying, They will respect my son. But when the tenants saw the son, they said to themselves, This is the heir; come, let us kill him and get his inheritance. So they seized him, threw him out of the vineyard, and killed him.

Mark 12:1-9 And he began to speak to them in parables. A man planted a vineyard, and set a hedge around it, and dug a pit for the wine press, and built a tower, and let it out to tenants, and went into another country. When the time came, he sent a servant to the tenants, to get from them some of the fruit of the vineyard. And they took him and beat him, and sent him away empty-handed. Again he sent to them another servant, and they wounded him in the head, and treated him shamefully. And he sent another, and him they killed; and so with many others, some they beat and some they killed. He had still one other, a beloved son; finally he sent him to them, saying, They will respect my son. But those tenants said to one another, This is the heir; come, let us kill him, and the inheritance will be ours. And they took him and killed him, and cast him out of the vineyard. What will the owner of the vineyard do? He will come and destroy the tenants, and give the vineyard to others.

Luke 20:9-16 And he began to tell the people this parable: A man planted a vineyard, and let it out to tenants, and went into another country for a long while. When the time came, he sent a servant to the tenants, that they should give him some of the fruit of the vineyard; but the tenants beat him, and sent him away empty-handed. And he sent another servant; him also they beat and treated shamefully, and sent him away empty-handed. And he sent yet a third; this one they wounded and cast out. Then the owner of the vineyard said, What shall I do? I will send my beloved son; it may be they will respect him. But when the tenants saw him, they said to themselves, This is the heir; let us kill him, that the inheritance may be ours. And they cast him out of the vineyard and killed him. What then will the owner of the vineyard do to them? He will come and destroy those tenants, and give the vineyard to others. When they heard this, they said, God forbid!

66. Jesus said: Show me the stone which the builders have rejected. It is that one

that is the cornerstone (keystone).

Matthew 21:42 Jesus said to them, Have you never read in the scriptures: The very stone which the builders rejected has become the head of the corner; this was the Lord's doing, and it is marvelous in our eyes?

Mark 12:10-11 Have you not read this scripture: The very stone which the builders rejected has become the head of the corner; this was the Lord's doing, and it is marvelous in our eyes?

Luke 20:17 But he looked at them and said, What then does this text mean: The stone that the builders rejected has become the cornerstone?

67. Jesus said: Those who know everything but themselves, lack everything. (whoever knows the all and still feels a personal lacking, he is completely deficient).

Jeremiah 17:5- 10 Thus saith the LORD; Cursed be the man that trusteth in man, and maketh flesh his arm, and whose heart departeth from the LORD. For he shall be like the heath in the desert, and shall not see when good cometh; but shall inhabit the parched places in the wilderness, in a salt land and not inhabited. Blessed is the man that trusteth in the LORD, and whose hope the LORD is. For he shall be as a tree planted by the waters, and that spreadeth out her roots by the river, and shall not see when heat cometh, but her leaf shall be green; and shall not be careful in the year of drought, neither shall cease from yielding fruit. The heart is deceitful above all things, and desperately wicked: who can know it? I the LORD search the heart, I try the reins, even to give every man according to his ways, and according to the fruit of his doings.

68. Jesus said: Blessed are you when you are hated and persecuted, but they themselves will find no reason why you have been persecuted.

Matthew 5:11 Blessed are you when people revile you and persecute you and utter all kinds of evil against you falsely on my account.

Luke 6:22 Blessed are you when men hate you, and when they exclude you and revile you, and cast out your name as evil, on account of the Son of man!

69. Jesus said: Blessed are those who have been persecuted in their heart; these are they who have come to know the Father in truth. Jesus said: Blessed are the hungry, for the stomach of him who desires to be filled will be filled.

Matthew 5:8 Blessed are the pure in heart, for they will see God.

Luke 6:21 Blessed are you who are hungry now, for you will be filled.

70. Jesus said: If you bring forth what is within you, it will save you. If you do not have it within you to bring forth, that which you lack will destroy you.

71. Jesus said: I will destroy this house, and no one will be able to build it again.

Mark 14:58 We heard him say, I will destroy this temple that is made with hands, and in three days I will build another, not made with hands.

72. A person said to him: Tell my brothers to divide the possessions of my father with me. He said to him: Oh man, who made me a divider? He turned to his Disciples, he said to them: I'm not a divider, am I?

Luke 12:13-15 Someone in the crowd said to him, Teacher, tell my brother to divide the family inheritance with me. But he said to him, Friend, who set me to be a judge or arbitrator over you? And he said to them, Take care! Be on your guard against all kinds of greed; for one's life does not consist in the abundance of possessions.

73. Jesus said: The harvest is indeed plentiful, but the workers are few. Ask the Lord to send workers for the harvest.

Matthew 9:37-38 Then he said to his disciples, The harvest is plentiful, but the laborers are few; therefore ask the Lord of the harvest to send out laborers into his harvest.

74. He said: Lord, there are many around the well, yet there is nothing in the well. How is it that many are around the well and no one goes into it?

75. Jesus said: There are many standing at the door, but only those who are alone are the ones who will enter into the Bridal Chamber.

Matthew 25:1-8 Then shall the kingdom of heaven be likened unto ten virgins, which took their lamps, and went forth to meet the bridegroom. And five of them were wise, and five were foolish. They that were foolish took their lamps, and took no oil with them: But the wise took oil in their vessels with their lamps. While the bridegroom tarried, they all slumbered and slept. And at midnight there was a cry made, Behold, the bridegroom cometh; go ye out to meet him. Then all those virgins arose, and trimmed their lamps. And the foolish said unto the wise, Give us of your oil; for our lamps are gone out.

76. Jesus said: The Kingdom of the Father is like a rich merchant who found a pearl. The merchant was prudent. He sold his fortune and bought the one pearl for himself. You also, seek for his treasure which does not fail, which endures where no moth can come near to eat it nor worm to devour it.

Matthew 13:45-46 Again, the kingdom of heaven is like a merchant in search of fine pearls; on finding one pearl of great value, he went and sold all that he had and bought it.

Matthew 6:19-20 Do not store up for yourselves treasures on earth, where moth and rust consume and where thieves break in and steal; but store up for yourselves treasures in heaven, where neither moth nor rust consumes and where thieves do not break in and steal.

77. Jesus said: I-Am the Light who is over all things, I-Am the All. From me all came forth and to me all return (The All came from me and the All has come to me). Split wood, there am I. Lift up the stone and there you will find me.

Author's Note:
Many scholars believe the order of verses 30 and 77 were misplaced and these two verses should be connected as one verse.

30. Jesus said: Where there are three gods, they are gods (Where there are three gods they are without god). Where there is only one, I say that I am with him. Lift the stone and there you will find me, Split the wood and there am I.

John 8:12 Again Jesus spoke to them, saying, I am the light of the world. Whoever follows me will never walk in darkness but will have the light of life.

John 1:3 All things came into being through him, and without him not one thing came into being.

78. Jesus said: Why did you come out to the wilderness; to see a reed shaken by the wind? And to see a person dressed in fine (soft - plush) garments like your rulers and your dignitaries? They are clothed in plush garments, and they are not able to recognize (understand) the truth.

Matthew 11:7-9 As they went away, Jesus began to speak to the crowds about John: What did you go out into the wilderness to look at? A reed shaken by the wind? What then did you go out to see? Someone dressed in soft robes? Look, those who wear soft robes are in royal palaces. What then did you go out to see? A prophet? Yes, I tell you, and more than a prophet.

79. A woman from the multitude said to him: Blessed is the womb which bore you, and the breasts which nursed you! He said to her: Blessed are those who have heard the word (meaning) of the Father and have truly kept it. For there will be days when you will say: Blessed be the womb which has not conceived and the breasts which have not nursed.

Luke 11:27-28 While he was saying this, a woman in the crowd raised her voice and said to him, Blessed is the womb that bore you and the breasts that nursed you! But he said, Blessed rather are those who hear the word of God and obey it!

Luke 23:29 For the days are surely coming when they will say, Blessed are the barren, and the wombs that never bore, and the breasts that never nursed.

80. Jesus said: Whoever has come to understand (recognize) the world (world system) has found the body (corpse), and whoever has found the body (corpse), of him the world (world system) is not worthy.

Hebrews 11:37-40 They were stoned, they were sawn asunder, were tempted, were slain with the sword: they wandered about in sheepskins and goatskins; being destitute, afflicted, tormented; (Of whom the world was not worthy:) they wandered in deserts, and in mountains, and in dens and caves of the earth. And these all, having obtained a good report through faith, received not the promise: God having provided some better thing for us, that they without us should not be made perfect.

81. Jesus said: Whoever has become rich should reign, and let whoever has power renounce it.

82. Jesus said: Whoever is close to me is close to the fire, and whoever is far from me is far from the Kingdom.

John 14:6-9 Jesus saith unto him, I am the way, the truth, and the life: no man cometh unto the Father, but by me. If ye had known me, ye should have known my Father also: and from henceforth ye know him, and have seen him. Philip saith unto him, Lord, show us the Father, and it sufficeth us. Jesus saith unto him, Have I been so long time with you, and yet hast thou not known me, Philip? he that hath seen me hath seen the Father;

83. Jesus said: Images are visible to man but the light which is within them is hidden. The light of the father will be revealed, but he (his image) is hidden in the light.

84. Jesus said: When you see your reflection, you rejoice. Yet when you perceive your images which have come into being before you, which neither die nor can be seen, how much will you have to bear?

85. Jesus said: Adam came into existence from a great power and a great wealth, and yet he was not worthy of you. For if he had been worthy, he would not have tasted death.

86. Jesus said: The foxes have their dens and the birds have their nests, yet the Son of Man has no place to lay his head for rest.

Matthew 8:20 And Jesus said to him, Foxes have holes, and birds of the air have nests; but the Son of Man has nowhere to lay his head.

87. Jesus said: Wretched is the body which depends upon another body, and wretched is the soul which depends on these two (upon their being together).

88. Jesus said: The angels and the prophets will come to you, and what they will give you belongs to you. And you will give them what you have, and say among yourselves: When will they come to take (receive) what belongs to them?

89. Jesus said: Why do you wash the outside of your cup? Do you not understand (mind) that He who creates the inside is also He who creates the outside?

Luke 11:39-40 Then the Lord said to him, Now you Pharisees clean the outside of the cup and of the dish, but inside you are full of greed and wickedness. You fools! Did not the one who made the outside make the inside also?

90. Jesus said: Come unto me, for my yoke is comfortable (natural) and my lordship is gentle— and you will find rest for yourselves.

Matthew 11:28-30 Come to me, all you that are weary and are carrying heavy burdens, and I will give you rest. Take my yoke upon you, and learn from me; for I am gentle and humble in heart, and you will find rest for your souls. For my yoke is easy, and my burden is light.

Acts 15:5-17 But there rose up certain of the sect of the Pharisees which believed, saying, that it was needful to circumcise them, and to command them to keep the law of Moses. And the apostles and elders came together for to consider of this matter. And when there had been much disputing, Peter rose up, and said unto them, Men and brethren, ye know how that a good while ago God made choice among us, that the Gentiles by my mouth should hear the word of the gospel, and believe. And God, which knoweth the hearts, bare them witness, giving them the Holy Ghost, even as he did unto us. And put no difference between us and them, purifying their hearts by faith. Now therefore why tempt ye God, to put a yoke upon the neck of the disciples, which neither our fathers nor we were able to bear? But we believe that through the grace of the LORD Jesus Christ we shall be saved, even as they. Then all the multitude kept silence, and gave audience to Barnabas and Paul, declaring what miracles and wonders God had wrought among the Gentiles by them. And after they had held their peace, James answered, saying, Men and brethren, hearken unto me: Simeon hath declared how God at the first did visit the Gentiles, to take out of them a people for his name. And to this agree the words of the prophets; as it is written, After this I will return, and will build again the tabernacle of David, which is fallen down; and I will build again the ruins thereof, and I will set it up: That the residue of men might seek after the Lord, and all the Gentiles, upon whom my name is called, saith the Lord, who doeth all these things.

91. They said to him: Tell us who you are, so that we may believe in you. He said to them: You examine the face of the sky and of the earth, yet you do not recognize Him who is here with you, and you do not know how to seek in (to inquire of Him at) this moment (you do not know how to take advantage of this opportunity).

John 9:36 He answered, And who is he, sir? Tell me, so that I may believe in him.

Luke 12:54-56 He also said to the crowds, When you see a cloud rising in the west, you immediately say, It is going to rain; and so it happens. And when you see the south wind blowing, you say, There will be scorching heat; and it happens. You hypocrites! You know how to interpret the appearance of earth and sky, but why do you not know how to interpret the present time?

92. Jesus said: Seek and you will find. But in the past I did not answer the questions you asked. Now I wish to tell them to you, but you do not ask about (no longer seek) them.

Matthew 7:7 Ask, and it will be given you; search, and you will find; knock, and the door will be opened for you.

93. Jesus said: Do not give what is sacred to the dogs, lest they throw it on the dung heap. Do not cast the pearls to the swine, lest they cause it to become dung (mud).

Matthew 7:6 Do not give what is holy to dogs; and do not throw your pearls before swine, or they will trample them under foot and turn and maul you.

94. Jesus said: Whoever seeks will find. And whoever knocks, it will be opened to him.

Matthew 7:8 For everyone who asks receives, and everyone who searches finds, and for everyone who knocks, the door will be opened.

95. Jesus said: If you have money, do not lend at interest, but rather give it to those from whom you will not be repaid.

Luke 6:34-35 If you lend to those from whom you hope to receive, what credit is that to you? Even sinners lend to sinners, to receive as much again. But love your enemies, do good, and lend, expecting nothing in return. Your reward will be great, and you will be children of the Most High; for he is kind to the ungrateful and the wicked.

96. Jesus said: The Kingdom of the Father is like a woman who has taken a little yeast and hidden it in dough. She produced large loaves of it. Whoever has ears, let him hear!

Matthew 13:33 He told them another parable: The kingdom of heaven is like yeast that a woman took and mixed in with three measures of flour until all of it was leavened.

97. Jesus said: The Kingdom of the Father is like a woman who was carrying a jar full of grain. While she was walking on a road far from home, the handle of the jar broke and the grain poured out behind her onto the road. She did not know it. She had noticed no problem. When she arrived in her house, she set the jar down and found it empty.

98. Jesus said: The Kingdom of the Father is like someone who wished to slay a prominent person. While still in his own house he drew his sword and thrust it into the wall in order to test whether his hand would be strong enough. Then he slew the prominent person.

99. His Disciples said to him: Your brethren and your mother are standing outside. He said to them: Those here who do my Father's desires are my Brethren and my Mother. It is they who will enter the Kingdom of my Father.

Matthew 12:46-50 While he was still speaking to the crowds, his mother and his brothers were standing outside, wanting to speak to him. Someone told him, Look, your mother and your brothers are standing outside, wanting to speak to you. But to the one who had told him this, Jesus replied, Who is my mother, and who are my brothers? And pointing to his disciples, he said, Here are my mother and my brothers! For whoever does the will of my Father in heaven is my brother and sister and mother.

100. They showed Jesus a gold coin, and said to him: The agents of Caesar extort taxes from us. He said to them: Give the things of Caesar to Caesar, give the

things of God to God, and give to me what is mine.

Mark 12:14-17 Is it lawful to pay taxes to the emperor, or not? Should we pay them, or should we not? But knowing their hypocrisy, he said to them, Why are you putting me to the test? Bring me a denarius and let me see it. And they brought one. Then he said to them, Whose head is this, and whose title? They answered, The emperor's. Jesus said to them, Give to the emperor the things that are the emperor's, and to God the things that are God's. And they were utterly amazed at him.

101. Jesus said: Whoever does not hate his father and his mother, as I do, will not be able to become my Disciple. And whoever does not love his father and his mother, as I do, will not be able to become my disciple. For my mother bore me, yet my true Mother gave me the life.

Matthew 10:37 Whoever loves father or mother more than me is not worthy of me; and whoever loves son or daughter more than me is not worthy of me.

102. Jesus said: Damn these Pharisees. They are like a dog sleeping in the feed trough of oxen. For neither does he eat, nor does he allow the oxen to eat.

Matthew 2:13 But woe unto you, scribes and Pharisees, hypocrites! because you shut the kingdom of heaven against men; for you neither enter yourselves, nor allow those who would enter to go in.

103. Jesus said: Blessed (happy) is the person who knows at what place of the house the bandits may break in, so that he can rise and collect his things and prepare himself before they enter.

Matthew 24:43 But understand this: if the owner of the house had known in what part of the night the thief was coming, he would have stayed awake and would not have let his house be broken into.

104. They said to him: Come, let us pray today and let us fast. Jesus said: What sin have I committed? How have I been overcome (undone)? When the Bridegroom comes forth from the bridal chamber, then let them fast and let them pray.

105. Jesus said: Whoever acknowledges (comes to know) father and mother, will be called the son of a whore.

106. Jesus said: When you make the two one, you will become Sons of Man (children of Adam), and when you say to the mountain: Move! It will move.

Mark 11:23 Truly I tell you, if you say to this mountain, Be taken up and thrown into the sea, and if you do not doubt in your heart, but believe that what you say will come to pass, it will be done for you.

107. Jesus said: The Kingdom is like a shepherd who has a hundred sheep. The

largest one of them went astray. He left the ninety-nine and sought for the one until he found it. Having searched until he was weary, he said to that sheep: I desire you more than the ninety-nine.

Matthew 18:12-13 What do you think? If a shepherd has a hundred sheep, and one of them has gone astray, does he not leave the ninety-nine on the mountains and go in search of the one that went astray? And if he finds it, truly I tell you, he rejoices over it more than over the ninety-nine that never went astray.

108. Jesus said: Whoever drinks from my mouth will become like me. I will become him, and the secrets will be revealed to him.

109. Jesus said: The Kingdom is like a person who had a treasure hidden in his field and knew nothing of it. After he died, he bequeathed it to his son. The son accepted the field knowing nothing of the treasure. He sold it. Then the person who bought it came and plowed it. He found the treasure. He began to lend money at interest to whomever he wished.

Matthew 13:44 The kingdom of heaven is like treasure hidden in a field, which someone found and hid; then in his joy he goes and sells all that he has and buys that field.

110. Jesus said: Whoever has found the world (system) and becomes wealthy (enriched by it), let him renounce the world (system).

Mark 10:21-23 Then Jesus beholding him loved him, and said unto him, One thing thou lackest: go thy way, sell whatsoever thou hast, and give to the poor, and thou shalt have treasure in heaven: and come, take up the cross, and follow me. And he was sad at that saying, and went away grieved: for he had great possessions. And Jesus looked round about, and saith unto his disciples, How hardly shall they that have riches enter into the kingdom of God!

111. Jesus said: Heaven and earth will roll up (collapse and disappear) before you, but he who lives within the Living-One will neither see nor fear death. For, Jesus said: Whoever finds himself, of him the world is not worthy.

112. Jesus said: Damned is the flesh which depends upon the soul. Damned is the soul which depends upon the flesh.

113. His Disciples said to him: When will the Kingdom come? Jesus said: It will not come by expectation (because you watch or wait for it). They will not say: Look here! or: Look there! But the Kingdom of the Father is spread upon the earth, and people do not realize it.

Luke 17:20 And when he was demanded of by the Pharisees, when the kingdom of God should come, he answered them and said, The kingdom of God cometh not with observation: Neither shall they say, Lo-Here! Lo-There! For, behold, the kingdom of God is within you.

(Saying 114 was written later and was added to the original text.)

114. Simon Peter said to them: Send Mary away from us, for women are not worthy of this life. Jesus said: See, I will draw her into me so that I make her male, in order that she herself will become a living spirit like you males. For every female who becomes male will enter the Kingdom of the Heaven.

The Question of Judas

No discovery since the Dead Sea Scrolls has rocked the Christian world like that of the newly translated "Gospel of Judas." The story presented in the short but powerful text reveals a plan in which heavenly ends justified monstrous means. Betrayal became collaboration and murder resembled suicide as Jesus and Judas began a macabre dance into eternity.

Orthodox Christianity has its doctrine, its canon, and its political story, but these are quite different from those exposed in the Gospel of Judas.

As the orthodox political viewpoint would have it, Jesus' demise was sought by the Roman authorities as he gained a following and was declared "King" by the Jewish populace. The Jewish religious leaders were also planning his death, believing that Jesus was attempting to reform Judaism, and wrest their control over the people.

The Gospel of Judas calls into question this accepted view of the political intrigue leading up to Jesus' betrayal and death.

Spokesman for the Maecenas Foundation, one of the companies in Basel, Switzerland working on the Judas project, Director Mario Jean Roberty, reports:

"We have just received the results of carbon dating: the text is older than we thought and dates back to a period between the beginning of the third and fourth centuries. We do not want to reveal the exceptional side of what we have, except that the Judas Iscariot text called into question some of the political principles of Christian doctrine."

Imagine Judas, the man all of Christendom has hated for two thousand years, now portrayed as the chosen one, the martyr, the scapegoat, and the man instructed and appointed by Jesus himself to orchestrate and carry out the greatest treachery of all time. But treachery ordered by the one betrayed is not treachery at all, but a loyal and devoted follower carrying out the wishes of his master.

What was Judas' reward for betraying Jesus? According to the Gospel of Judas it was special recognition by God and the blessing of Jesus, the savior of mankind. Strangely, there is evidence in our own Bible to substantiate this claim. Judas may have been promised a position of authority along with the other apostles.

The Gospel of Judas turns us on our heads and forces upon the reader a new and uncomfortable view. Did Judas have special knowledge and instruction from Jesus? Are we to thank him for the death of Jesus? Is lethal treachery appointed by the victim suicide or murder? Is this murderous quisling really a saint?

Who is this man, Judas? What do we know about him? Where did he come from? What did he want? What did he do?

These are just a few of the questions left to reverberate in the mind of the reader.

Theories of Judas abound. He is presented as greedy and selfish as well as sanctified spirit. Some say he was possessed, some say he was a saint, and some believe him to be Satan himself.

Was Judas the impetus of death, burial, and resurrection for Jesus, and thus the daemon who saved us? Will Judas be the Antichrist we will meet in the end of days or will he be ruling and judging the tribes of Israel?

Every story has two sides. Let us examine both sides, beginning with The Gospel of Judas, its history, its theology, and its text.

Understanding the Intent

The Gospel of Judas can be understood on a deeper level if its background is explored first.

One may ask the proper questions regarding the text of "who, what, when, where, and why." The question of "who" wrote the Gospel of Judas we may never know. What the author was trying to say will be explored in depth. Science can and has narrowed down the "when" and "where."

Why mankind writes is axiomatic. We write to document, explain, express, or convince. In the end, those are the reasons. Time will tell if the author of Judas has succeeded.

In a time when Gnosticism was struggling for influence in Christendom, the Gospel of Judas was written to challenge the beliefs of the newly emerging church orthodoxy, to explain Gnostic theology, and to propagate the sect. To better understand the gospel, it must be read with these goals in mind.

For centuries the definition of Gnosticism has in itself been a point of confusion and contention within the religious community. This is due in part to the ever-broadening application of the term and the fact that various sects of Gnosticism existed as the theology evolved and began to merge into what became mainstream Christianity.

Even though Gnosticism continued to evolve, it is the theology in place at the time that the Gospel of Judas was written that should be considered and understood before attempting to render or read a translation. To do otherwise would make the translation cloudy and obtuse.

It becomes the duty of both translator and reader to understand the ideas being espoused and the terms conveying those ideas. A grasp of theology, cosmology, and relevant terms is necessary for a clear transmission of the meaning within the text in question.

With this in mind, we will briefly examine Gnostic theology, cosmology, and history. We will focus primarily on Gnostic sects existing in the first through fourth centuries A.D. since it is believed most Gnostic Gospels were written during that time. It was also during that time that reactions within the emerging Christian orthodoxy began to intensify and the Gospel of Judas was written.

The downfall of many books written on the topic of religion is the attempt to somehow remove history and people from the equation. History shapes religion because it shapes the perception and direction of religious leaders. Religion also develops and evolves in an attempt to make sense of the universe as it is seen and understood at the time. Thus, to truly grasp a religious concept it is important to know the history, people, and cosmology of the time. These areas are not separate but are continually interacting.

What is the Gospel of Judas?

What is the Gospel of Judas and why does it differ so greatly from the gospel stories of the Bible?

The Gospel of Judas is considered a Gnostic text. The Gnostics were a sect of Christianity and like any sect or religion, they were fighting to expand and continue under the persecution of the newly emerging orthodoxy of the day.

The Gospel of Judas may have been written to help bolster and continue Gnosticism. This may explain its radical departure from the traditional Gospel story, as well as the reason for its creation.

Indeed, one way of looking at any religious book, canon or not, is as an attempt to explain one's beliefs, to persuade others toward those beliefs, and to interpret history and known storylines in the light of one's own theology and cosmology. This is done not only to add weight to one's own belief system but also simply because man sees events as having relevance to what he or she holds as truth.

As previously stated, the Gospel of Judas is, above all things, a Gnostic gospel since it revolves around a special knowledge or Gnosis given to Judas by Jesus. This knowledge represented that which Gnostics held as the universal truth.

The History of the Gospel of Judas

The newly discovered Gospel of Judas is very controversial for several reasons. Theologically, it is divisive due to its Gnostic theology. The main controversy in the text revolves around the theory that Jesus asked Judas to betray Him in order to fulfill His destiny and the scriptures. If this is true it would make Judas a saint and not the sinner and traitor as believed by the mainline church.

The text is also interesting simply because it is written in Coptic. Documents from the time period and region where the Coptic language was native are a rare find.

The word Coptic is an Arabic corruption of the Greek word Aigyptos, which in turn comes from the word Hikaptah, one of the names of the city of Memphis, the first capital of ancient Egypt.

There has never been a Coptic state or government per se, however, the word has been used to generally define a culture and language present in the area of Egypt within a particular timeframe.

The known history of the Copts starts with King Mina the first King, who united the northern and southern kingdoms of Egypt circa 3050 B.C. The ancient Egyptian civilization under the rule of the Pharaohs lasted over 3000 years. Saint Mina (named after the king) is one of the major Coptic saints. He was martyred in 309 A.D.

The culture has come to be recognized as one containing distinctive language, art, architecture, and even certain religious systems. There is even a very distinctive Coptic Christian church system with its own canon, which contains several more books than those of the Protestant or Catholic Bibles.

The religious controversy of the Gospel of Judas is compelling, if for no other reason than that of its differing view, which forces us to re-examine the way we read and understand the place, path, and actions of Judas and his act of betrayal.

The Gospels and the Book of Acts tell the story of Judas' betrayal of Jesus and the end to which Judas came. The canonical books refer to Judas as a traitor, betrayer, and as one influenced by the devil. However, the Gospel of Judas turns this idea on its head by claiming the Judas was requested, if not required, to plan and carry out the treachery that would be the impetus for the crucifixion. The plan was to surrender Jesus to the authorities so that scripture and prophecy could be fulfilled, and Jesus was the person devising the plan.

Most scholars agree that the Gospels of Matthew, Mark, Luke, and John were written between the date of Jesus' death and about 90 A.D. The Gospel of Judas was written originally in Greek around A.D. 180 at the earliest. If this is true, Judas could not have been the author. For Judas to have penned this work he would have been about 120 years of age at the time of its writing. Discounting this possibility, the original author is unknown.

Dates of the original texts are based on words and usage common to certain periods of time. This is comparable to how slang and catch phrases pass in and out of vogue in our own language.

Another way of narrowing down the date of the original text is to look for references to it in other writings. This would set the date marking the latest the text could have been written.

Tixeront, translated by Raemers, states: "Besides these Gospels, we know that there once existed a Gospel of Bartholomew, a Gospel of Thaddeus, mentioned in the decree of Pope Gelasius, and a Gospel of Judas Iscariot in use among the Cainites and spoken of by St. Irenaeus."

In Roberts-Donaldson's translation from Irenaeus the church father states, "Others again declare that Cain derived his being from the Power above, and acknowledge that Esau, Korah, the Sodomites, and all such persons, are related to themselves. On this account, they add, they have been assailed by the Creator, yet no one of them has suffered injury. For Sophia was in the habit of carrying off that which belonged to her from them to herself. They declare that Judas the traitor was thoroughly acquainted with these things, and that he alone, knowing the truth as no others did, accomplished the mystery of the betrayal; by him all things, both earthly and heavenly, were thus thrown into confusion. They produce a fictitious history of this kind, which they style the Gospel of Judas."

Irenaeus went on to say that the writings came from what he called a "Cainite" Gnostic sect that jousted with orthodox Christianity. He also accused the Cainites of lauding the biblical murderer Cain, the Sodomites and Judas, whom they regarded as the keeper of secret mysteries.

Knowing the dates of the writings of Irenaeus further clarifies the date to be around or before 180 A.D. Of course, this affects the Gospel of Judas only if we conclude that the text Irenaeus spoke of is the same text we have today. Sadly, there is no way to know with any certainty, but we do have a few clues.

Cain is not mentioned in the version of the Gospel of Judas we have today. Furthermore, the evolution of cosmology tends to be from the simple to the complex and this trend is shown in the current version since Yaldabaoth, who is also called "Nebro" the "rebel", is presented as the creator of Saklas and it is Saklas who is depicted later in the Gospel of Judas as the creator mankind and the physical world. However, in other Gnostic writings, Yaldabaoth is the "demiurge" or fashioner of the world, and is clearly identified as the same deity as Saklas. This means that in the Gospel of Judas there has been a split between Yaldaboth and Saklas, leading to a more complex cosmology. This indicates that the Gospel of Judas we have today was written later than that of which Irenaeus speaks, since in his time these deities were one and the same.

Now the archon who is weak has three names. The first name is Yaltabaoth, the second is Saklas ("fool"), and the third is Samael. And he is impious in his arrogance which is in him. For he said, 'I am God and there is no other God beside me,' for he is ignorant of his strength,

the place from which he had come."
Apocryphon of John, ca. 200 AD.

As for the dating of the copy found in Egypt, the formation of certain letters also change with time and the style of the lettering within the texts places the copies within a certain period. The 26-page Judas text is a copy in Coptic of the original Gospel of Judas, which was written in Greek the century before.

Radioactive-carbon-dating tests as well as experts in ancient languages have established that the copy was written between 220 and 340 A.D.

The discovered Gospel was written on papyrus, probably at a Gnostic monastery in Egypt. Although other copies may have been made they were probably lost in St. Athanasius's fourth-century campaign to destroy all heretical texts. All texts not accepted by the newly established church were to be burned. Heresy was not to be tolerated, and Gnosticism was considered at the top of the list. Not only was Gnosticism different from the orthodox theology, it condoned a personal search for God through knowledge and that was something outside the control of the church. To maintain its control, the new church had to crush these beliefs.

In order to protect the text from Athanasius's soldiers it is thought a Gnostic monk or scribe buried copies of certain Gnostic texts in an area of tombs in Egypt. These were not discovered until the late 1970s. The Gospel was one of three texts found that were bound together in a single codex.

The gospel was unearthed in 1978 by a farmer. He found a small container like a tomb box in a cave near El Minya, Egypt. In the small, carved, and sealed box was part of a codex, or collection of devotional texts.

The farmer sold the codex to an antiquities dealer in Cairo. The deal was kept secret but was reported to have taken place in 1983. The antiquities dealer was unaware of the content of the codex when he offered the gospel for sale to the Coptic studies scholar, Stephen Emmel, of Germany's University of Munster and another scholar. The meeting took place in a Geneva, Switzerland hotel room.

It was Emmel who examined the codex and first suspected the papyrus sheets discussed Judas. Although the text more than intrigued Emmel, the asking price was so high at $3 million dollars U.S. that there was no way to afford the purchase.

The seller was offered a price that was an order of magnitude lower than the asking price. This, the seller took as an insult and the deal stalled.

Due to the frustration brought about by not having his greed satisfied, the dealer stored the codex in a safe in a Hicksville, N.Y. bank for 16 years. There, away from the dry desert air, in the box with higher humidity, it deteriorated and crumbled until Zurich-based antiquities dealer Frieda Nussberger-Tchacos purchased it in 2000 for a sum much less than the original asking price. The codex was then acquired by the Maecenas Foundation for Ancient Art in Switzerland in 2001.

The foundation invited National Geographic to help with the restoration in 2004.

Over the next 5 years thousands of pieces of papyrus were placed back together like a jigsaw puzzle. Thousands of pieces, some so small they contained only a letter or two were restored to their position in the text using tweezers and computer imaging.

Once completed, a team of scholars translated the document into English, as best they could, considering the condition of the document and the number of pieces missing. The restored original is now housed in Cairo's Coptic Museum. A rendering of the text in Coptic can be seen at:
http://www.nationalgeographic.com/lostgospel/_pdf/CopticGospelOfJudas.pdf

Because of the extreme age and ill-treatment of the text much of it is illegible. There are gaps and holes in the codex. Entire lines are missing. Some parts of the translation were done on a "best-guess" basis. If there were letters missing from common words of phrases the translators could assume and replace letters and even words or phrases. When the gaps became larger or the meaning of the phrase was uncertain the translators simple noted the absence of data.

In this rendering we have attempted two bold moves. We wished to present a more engaging interpretation for the public, which necessarily demanded notes and explanations available at the point the ideas were encountered. We also wished to attempt to fill in some of the gaps in the text if possible.

As a matter of a disclaimer, it should be understood that the original translators did a remarkable job with the thousands of slivers and chips of papyrus that made up the codex. Once reconstructed, it became obvious that much of the text was simply missing, having disintegrated into dust and powder, never to be read again.

The text presented here takes the work done by many others and places the Gospel of Judas into a more readable language and format along with in-line commentary. It then expands the text, filling in the gaps as best it could be done, based on an understanding of the Gnostic theology, historical information, textual references, and logical flow of conversation.

All words or phases in parentheses indicate those additions made to the text, either as a matter of filling in the missing letters, words, or lines; or as a matter of clarification of ambiguous wording in the original text or its translation. When a word could be translated in more than one way, a slash "/" was used to note the various choices.

Commentary are marked clearly as "Notes" and are place in italic font within the text.

The reader should keep the probable function of the text in mind. The title gives some hint. It is not "The Gospel According to Judas", but it is instead, "The Gospel of Judas." This indicates that the writer wanted to exalt Judas, his position and contribution according to the theology being espoused and propagated by the text.

Knowing these things, the words and lines missing in the text can be a matter of educated and reasonable assumptions. They are, however, assumptions nonetheless.

Let us look now at the Gospel of Judas.

The Gospel of Judas

This is the proclamation, which was secretly revealed to Judas Iscariot by Jesus during that eight-day period that included (that was) the three days before he (Jesus) celebrated Passover (one translator has "celebrated his passion / suffering).

Note: The proclamation is not the logos, word or Christ for the orthodox church. The word here is a proclamation of judgment as in a court verdict.

1. Jesus appeared on earth to perform miracles and wondrous acts in order to save humanity.
Because some conducted themselves in a righteous way and others continued in their sins, he decided to call the twelve disciples.

2. He began to talk to them about the mysteries that lay beyond this world and what would happen at this world's end (at the end). He often changed his appearance and was not seen as himself but looked like a child (some translators have apparition or spirit) when he was with his disciples.

3. He came upon his disciples in Judea once when they were sitting together piously (training their piety - training in godliness). As he got closer to the disciples he saw they were sitting together, giving thanks and saying a prayer over the bread (Eucharist / thanksgiving). He laughed.

4. The disciples asked Him, "Rabbi, why are you laughing at our prayer of thanks? Have we not acted appropriately?"
He said, "I am not laughing at you. It is just that you are not doing this because you want to. You are doing this because your god (has to be / will be) praised."

5. They said, "Rabbi, you are the (earthly / only) son of our god."
Jesus answered, "How do you know me? (Do you think you know me?) I say to you truly, no one among you in this generation (in this race) will understand me."

6. His disciples heard this and became enraged and began mumbling profanities and mocking him in their hearts. When Jesus saw their inability (to understand what he said to them (their stupidity), he said,) "Why did you get so upset that you became angry? Your god, who is inside of you, (and your own lack of understanding guides you and) have instigated this anger in your (mind / soul). (I challenge) any man among you to show me who is (understanding enough) to bring out the perfect man and stand and face me."

7. They all said, "We are strong enough."
But in their (true being) spirits none dared to stand in front of him except for Judas Iscariot. Judas was able to stand in front of him, but even he could not look Jesus in the eyes, and he turned his face away.

Note: It is uncertain as to the reason Judas did not look at Jesus. It was a custom of respect not to look a superior in the eyes. Either Judas was unable to look at Jesus or was constrained by the position of Jesus as his Rabbi.

8. Judas said to Him, "I know who you are and where you came from. You are from the everlasting (eternal) aeon (realm or kingdom) of Barbelo (Barbelo's everlasting kingdom). I am not worthy to speak the name of the one who sent you."

9. Jesus knew that Judas was capable of understanding (showing forth / thinking about) something that was glorious, so Jesus said to him, "Walk away (step a distance away) from the others and I will tell you about the mysteries of God (the reign of God / kingdom of God).

10. It is possible for you to get there, but the path will cause you great grief because you will be replaced so that the twelve may be complete with their god again."
Judas asked him, "When will you tell me how the great day of light will dawn for this generation (race)? When will you explain these things?"
But as he asked these things, Jesus left him.

11. At the dawn of the next day after this happened, Jesus appeared to his disciples.
They asked Him, "Rabbi, where did you go and what did you do when you left us?"
Jesus said to them, "I went to another generation (race) that is a greater and holier generation (race)."

12. His disciples asked him, "Lord, what is this great race that is superior to us and holier than us, that is not now in this realm (kingdom)?"
When Jesus heard this, he laughed and said to them, "Why are you thinking in your hearts about the mighty and holy race (generation)? So be it - I will tell you. No one born in this age (realm / aeon) will see that (generation / race), and not even the multitude (army) of angels (controlling) the stars will rule over that generation (race), and no mortal (corruptible) person can associate (belong) with it.

13. That generation does not come from (a realm) which has become (mortal / corrupted). The generation of people among (you) is from the generation of humanity (of inferior / without) power, which (cannot associate with the) other powers (above) by (whom) you rule / are ruled."
When (the /his) disciples heard this, they were all troubled in (their heart / spirit). They were speechless (could not utter a word).

Note: This begins a distinction drawn between the generation or race of mankind, which is inferior, decaying, and unenlightened, and the "great generation or race," which is enlightened, incorruptible, and eternal. There are only two races; those who have gnosis and those who do not. Interestingly, Jesus does not place the disciples in the great generation.

14. On another day Jesus came up to (them). They said to (him), "Rabbi, we have seen you in a (dream), because we all had weighty (dreams about a night you were

taken away / arrested)."
(He said), "Why have (you come to me when you have) gone into hiding?"

15. They said, "There was (an imposing building with a great altar in it and twelve men, (which we would say were) the priests, and there was a name, and a crowd of people waiting (enduring because of their perseverance) at that altar, (for) the priest (to come and receive) the offerings. (However) we kept waiting (we were tenacious also)."
(Jesus asked), "What were (the priests) like?"

They said, "Some (of them would fast) for two weeks; (others would) sacrifice their own children, others their wives, (all the while) in praise (offered in) humility with each other; some have sex with other men; some murder; some commit a plethora of sins and acts of crime. And the men who stand in front of the altar call upon your (name / authority), and in all the acts springing from their lack of knowledge (lack of light), the sacrifices are brought to completion (by their hands) (the alter remained full through their handiwork of slaughtering the sacrifices)."
After they said these things they became uneasy and quiet.

16. Jesus asked them, "Why are you bothered? So be it, I tell you that all the priests who have stood before that altar call upon my name. I have told I you many times that my name has been written on the (judgment) of this race (and on) the stars through the human generations. In my name (these people) have planted barren trees, (and have done so) without any honor."

17. Jesus said to them, "You are like those men you have seen conducting the offerings at the altar. That is the god you serve, and the twelve men you have seen represent you. The cattle you saw that were brought for sacrifice represent the many people you have led (will lead) astray before that altar. (You) will stand (lead / represent) and use my name in that way, as will the generations of the pious and you all will remain loyal to "him." (Some translations have- "The lord of chaos will establish his place in this way.") After "him" another man will lead from (the group of fornicators), and another (will lead at the alter from those who) murder children, and another from those who are homosexuals, and (another) those who fast, and (one will stand from) the rest of those who pollution themselves and who are lawlessness and who sin, and (from) those who say, 'We are like the angels'; they are the stars that (make everything happen / bring everything to an end).

18. It has been said to the human generations, 'Look, God has received your sacrifice from the hands of a priest.' But the priest is a minister of error (minister in error / ministers but is in sin). But it is the Lord, the Lord of all (the fullness of the divine), who commands, 'On the last day (of time) they will be shamed (some have - "at the end of days").'"

Note: Jesus tells the disciples that they are loyal to the wrong god. He goes on to say that they are the ones who murder, fornicate, and sin. Furthermore, Jesus tells them that they will lead people into a spiritual slaughter like the cattle they saw sacrificed in their dream. At this time the 12 included Judas. This, along with other such verses has led many scholars to conclude that the Gospel of Judas was not depicting Judas to be the sanctified person the original translators thought him to be.

19. Jesus (told them), "Stop (sacrificing that which) you have (and stop hovering) over the altar. The priests are over your stars and your angels. They have already come to their end there. So let them (be entrapped / quarrel / fight) before you, and leave them alone. (Do not be tainted by this generation but instead eat the food of knowledge given to you by the great one.)

Note: We will see "stars" referred to often in the text. They are used to symbolize two unique concepts. It was thought that in the creation of the cosmos, luminaries were created which were powers controlling each person's destiny. It was also thought that each person was assigned a star as his or her eternal home or resting place. A good person would ascend to his or her own star to rule and rest. Thus, stars were conscious powers, carrying out orders from God, and also were places of destiny for those who escape the material plane.

20. A baker cannot feed all creation under (heaven). And (they will not give) to them (a food) and (give) to (those of the great generation the same food).
Jesus said to them, "Stop struggling with (against) me. Each of you has his own star, and every (Lines are missing here. Text could read " person has his own destiny." Or possibly, "person who does well will dwell and rest on their star").
(All things happen in their own season and all seasons are appointed. And in (the season) which has come (it is spring) for the tree (of paradise) of this aeon / age (and it will produce) for a time (then wither) but he has come to water God's paradise, and (also water this generation) that will last, because (he) will not corrupt / detour) the (path of life for) that generation, but (will guide it) from eternity to eternity."

21. Judas asked him, "Rabbi, what kind of fruit does this generation produce?"
Jesus answered, "The souls of every human generation will die. However, when these people (of this kingdom) have completed the time in the kingdom and the living breath leaves them, their bodies will die but their souls will continue to be alive, and they will ascended (be lifted up / be taken up)."
Judas asked, "What will the remainder of the human generations do?"
Jesus said, "It is not possible to plant seeds in (rocky soil) and harvest its fruit. (This is also the way (of) the (corrupted) race (generation), (the children of this kingdom) and corruptible Sophia / wisdom) (is / are) not the hand that has created mortal people, so that their souls ascend to the eternal realms above. Amen, I say, (that no) angel (or / of) power will be able to see that (kingdom of) these to whom (belong that) holy generations (above)."
After Jesus said this, he departed.

22. Judas said, "Rabbi, you have listened to all of those others, so now listen to me too. I have seen a great vision."

23. When Jesus heard this, he laughed and said to him, "You (are the) thirteenth spirit (daemon), why are you trying so hard / why do you excite yourself like this? However, speak up, and I will be patient with you."
Judas said to him, "In the vision I saw myself and the twelve disciples were

stoning me and persecuting me very badly / severely / strongly. And I (was following you and I) arrived at a place where I saw (a large house in front me), and my eyes could not (take in / comprehend) its size. Many people were surrounding it, and the house had a roof of plants (grass / green vegetation), and in the middle of the house (there was a crowd) (and I was there with you), saying, 'Rabbi, take me in (the house) along with these people.'"

24. He responded and said, "Judas, your star has misled you. No person of mortal birth is worthy to enter the house you have seen. It is a place reserved for the saints. Not even the sun or the moon or day (light) will rule there. Only the saints will live there, in the eternal kingdom with the holy angels, always (some have the text as - "will be firmly established with the holy angels forever"). Look, I have explained to you the mysteries of the kingdom and I have taught you about the error of the stars; and (I have) sent it (on its path) on the twelve ages (aeons)."

Note: The Lost Book of Enoch tells of stars, which are the guiding forces of man and nature, erring. They become misplaced and out of order. They had to be placed or directed back into their proper paths. See The Lost Book of Enoch, by Joseph Lumpkin.

Note: There are 12 Astrological Ages. The 12 signs of the zodiac make up a 360-degree ecliptic path around the Earth, and takes 25,920 years to make the Precession of the Equinoxes. Each sign is comprised of 30 degrees of celestial longitude. Each degree of the precession is equal to 72 Earth years, and each year is equal to 50 seconds of degrees of arc of celestial longitude. In a 24 hour Earth day, the Earth rotates the entire 360 degrees of the ecliptic, allowing a person to see all 12 signs.

25. Judas said, "Rabbi, could it be that my (spiritual) seed will conquer the rulers of cosmic power (could also be rendered: "is under the control of the archons or rulers of cosmic power"?)"

26. Jesus answered and said to him, "Come (with me so) that I (may show you the kingdom you will receive. I will show you what is to come of you and this generation), but you will be grieved when you see the kingdom and all its race (of people)."
When Judas heard Him he said to him, "What good is it if I have received it seeing that you have set me apart from that race?"
Jesus answered him and said, "You will become the thirteenth, and you will be cursed by the other generations, and you will come to rule over them. In the last days they will curse your ascent to the holy (race / kingdom)."

Note: I have chosen the word, "daemon" and not "demon" because the meaning of the text is unclear. A daemon is a divinity or supernatural being of a nature between gods and humans. In verse 24 Jesus tells Judas that he will never be worthy to enter the house, which symbolizes the eternal kingdom. Later in verse 26 Jesus seems to indicate that Judas will be cursed by the other disciples but will be raised to enter the holy generation in the last days. It is possible the interim time will be spent in what the Bible calls, "his own place."

27. Jesus said, "(Follow / come with me), so that I may teach you the (secrets) that

no person (has) ever seen.

Note: This begins a creation myth based on certain Sethian Gnostic cosmology. The telling of the story appears to be an attempt to link the Gnostic cosmology to the teachings of Jesus in order to add validity and authority to the creation story and entities as well as assisting in the propagation of the sect.

There is a great and limitless kingdom, whose scope no generation of angels has seen (and in it) The Great Invisible (Spirit) is, and no angel's eye has ever seen, no thought of the heart (mind) has ever understood it, and no name can be assigned it (it cannot be named).

28. "And a brightly glowing cloud appeared there. The Great Spirit said, 'Let an angel come into being as my assistant (attendant / helper).'
"A great angel, the enlightened, divine, Self-Generated (Self-Created) one emerged from the cloud. Because of him, four other angelic lights (luminaries), (Harmozel, Oroiael, Daveithai, and Eleleth) began to exist from another cloud, and they became assistants (helpers / attendants) to the Self-Generated angel (messenger). The Self-Created one proclaimed, 'Let (there) come into being (a star / Adam),' and it (he) came into being (at once). He (created) the first star (luminary / bright, shining being) to reign over him.

Note: Here we have a garbled text, the translation of which can go one of two ways. The words missing in the middle of the text could be Adam, who is also known as Adamas, or it could refer to a star, since the next reference is to a luminary. The direction of the text is unclear except that it is agreed that the word "it" is used in the text.

He said, 'Let angels (messengers) begin existence to adore (worship) (him),' and an innumerable plethora became existent. He said, '(Let there be) an aeon of light,' and he began existence. He created the second star to rule over him, to render service together with the innumerable plethora of angels. That is how he created the rest of the aeons of light. He made them rulers over them, and he created for them an innumerable plethora of angels to assist them.

29. "Adamas (Adam) was in the first luminous cloud (the initial divine expression) that no angel has ever seen, including all those called 'God.' He (was the one) that (created the enlightened aeon and beheld) the image and produced him after the likeness of (this) angel. He made the incorruptible (generation) of Seth appear (from) the twelve (aeons and) the twenty-four (stars / angelic lights / luminaries). He made seventy-two angelic lights appear in the imperishable generation, as the will of the Spirit dictated. The seventy-two angelic lights themselves made three hundred sixty angelic lights appear in the immortal race, by following the will of the Spirit, that their number should be five for each.

Note: Seth is the son of Adam and was considered to be divine as Adam was divine. Seth produced "that incorruptible generation." He was thought to have received the knowledge that would bring freedom from the material realm, and thus, salvation.

30. "The twelve realms (aeons) of the twelve angelic lights make up / appoint

their Father, with six heavens for each aeon, so that there are seventy-two heavens for the seventy-two angelic lights, and for each (there are five) skies, (producing all) three hundred sixty (skies for the stars). They were given authority and a innumerable host of angels, for glory and adoration (worship), (and then he gave the) virgin (pure spirits), for glory and worship of all the aeons and the heavens and their firmaments (skies).

Note: The numbers assigned to the various aeons, angels, and stars have significance in both biblical number symbolism and Pythagorean numerology.

One – Unity, sovereign, God, causality.
Two – Duality and / or merging.
Three - Spiritually complete, fullness, creation.
Four – Foundations, systems, order.
Five – Spirit, grace, movement.
Six - Mankind.
Seven – God, wisdom, knowledge, perfection.
Twelve – Law, rule, authority.
Thirteen – Cursed, beyond or without law.
Twenty-four – Heavenly government, elders, a system. Duality within the system.
Seventy-two – Both elements of two and seven as well as the element of completion.
Three hundred and sixty – Elements of three and six as well as the meaning of a full cycle such as a yearly cycle. An end, and a new start.

31. The totality (gathering) of those immortals is called the cosmos, that is to say perdition / decay / corruption, by the Father and the seventy-two angelic lights / luminaries who are with the Self-Created one and his seventy-two aeons. In the cosmos the first human appeared with his incorruptible powers.

Note: This first human is Adamas or Adam. It should be noted that the name "Adam" can also be rendered as "Man" in Hebrew.

32. And the aeon that appeared with his generation and the aeon in whom are the cloud of knowledge and the angel, is called El.

Note: El was the name of a Semitic god who was chief among the pantheon of gods affecting nature and society. He is father of the divine family and president of the divine assembly on the 'mount of assembly', the equivalent of Hebrew har mo'ed, which became through the Greek transliteration Armageddon. In Canaanite mythology he is known as 'the Bull', symbolizing his strength and creative force. He is called 'Creator of Created Things' which is how rivers were also metaphorically thought of. In the Biblical Garden of Eden a river flowed to form the four rivers, Tigris, Euphrates, Gihon and Pishon."
El expressed the concept of ordered government, justice and creation. The Bible never stigmatizes the Canaanite worship of El, whose authority in social affairs was recognized by the Patriarchs. His consort was Asherah, the mother goddess, represented in Canaanite sanctuaries by a natural tree (Hebrew ashera) such as the tree of life.

33. (He created the) aeon, (after that) (El) said, 'Let twelve angels come into being

(in order to) rule over chaos and the (cosmos / perdition).' And look, from the cloud {called Sophia} there appeared an (angel / aeon) whose face flashed with fire and whose appearance was defiled with blood. His name was Nebro, meaning "rebel." Another angel, Saklas, also came from the cloud. So Nebro created six angels—as well as Saklas—to be assistants, and these produced twelve angels in the heavens, with each one receiving a piece of the heavens.

Note: Nebro may be a female demon who mates with Saklas; others call Nebro by the name "Yaldaboth (child of chaos) Yaldaboth and Saklas are both names given to the insane or deficient deity that created the physical world. Also the reading could be influenced by the fact that in some mythologies Nebro is a head demon and Saklas is a head angel. Nebro has the same meaning as Nimrod, which is "rebel."

The Jews and Greeks of the day were literalists. Each and every word of the scriptures was taken at face value. Therefore, the god who created Adam and Eve was a limited and tangible god. He walked and talked and asked questions, the answers to which he did not seem to know. By building a creation story that includes Saklas the problems were solved. Now the references to multiple gods were answered and when god said let "us" create man, the references could be to Saklas and his helpers. Since the Saklas deity was limited and restricted it left the Supreme God to be "God."

34. "The twelve rulers (aeons) spoke with the twelve angels: 'Let each of you (receive a portion) and let them (that are in this) generation (be ruled by these) angels':

The first is Seth, who is called Christ.
The (second) is Harmathoth, who is (head ruler of the underworld).
The (third) is Galila.
The fourth is Yobel.
The fifth (is) Adonaios.
These are the five who ruled all of the underworld, and primarily over chaos.

Note: These five names are probably associated with the five planets known at the time the Gospel of Judas was written. They were placed on their paths and courses to keep order and give light, both real and spiritual.

35. "Then Saklas said to his angels, 'Let us create a human being in the similitude and after the figure / image / representation (of the Supreme God) .' They fashioned Adam and his wife Eve, who is called Zoe / life when she was still in the cloud.

Note: Zoe is another name for Eve in the Septuagint.

36. For it is this name (life) that all the generations seek the man, and each of them calls the woman by these names. Now, Sakla did not command (as he was instructed) but (he commanded) the generations (of man to live so long / for a defined period of time), (but he did created them in his (Saklas') likeness). And the (ruler Saklas) said to Adam, 'You shall live long, with your children.'"

37. Judas said to Jesus, "(What length) is the long span of time that humans will

live?"
Jesus said, "Why are you curious about this? Adam and his generation has lived his lifespan in the place where he received his kingdom, with his longevity bestowed by his ruler (as numbered with his ruler)."

38. Judas said to Jesus, "Does the human spirit die?"
Jesus said, "This is why God (the god of this realm) ordered Michael to loan spirits to people so that they would serve (be in servitude), but the Great One commanded Gabriel to give spirits to the great generation (race) which had no ruler over it (a generation that cannot be dominated). He gave the spirit and the soul. Therefore, the (remainder / mountain) of souls (loaned will come back to the god of this realm in the end).

Note: This passage indicates two lines of creation. For those people created by the god of this world the angel Michael was commanded to temporarily assign souls to his creation. To keep their souls they were enslaved to worship the god of this world. In contrast, the Great One commanded Gabriel to give souls to those of the great generation for eternity.

39. "(There was no) light (in this world to shine) around (the people to) allow (the) spirit (which is) within you all to dwell in this (body) among the generations of angels. But God caused knowledge to be (given) to Adam and those with him, so that the kings of chaos and the underworld might not oppress them with it."

Note: The word rendered as "rule" by most translators has the connotation of oppression.

40. Judas said to Jesus, "So what will those generations do?"
Jesus said, "Truthfully, I tell you all, that for all of them the stars bring matters to completion (heavenly apocalypse). When Saklas completes the span of time assigned for him, their first star will appear with the generations, and they will finish what they said they would do. Then they will (have illicit sex in my name and kill (sacrifice) their children and they will fast, and they will kill their wives in praise offered in humility with each other; some have sex with other men; some will murder, some commit a plethora of sins and acts of crime all in my name, and Saklas will destroy) your star over the thirteenth aeon."

41. After that Jesus (laughed).

Note: Jesus seems to find humor in the misguided judgments or concepts of the disciples. He laughs, as if shaking his head in disbelief of the error, then attempts to give insight and correction.

(Judas asked), "Rabbi, (why do you laugh at us)?"
(He) answered (Judas and said), "I am not laughing (because of you) but at the error of the stars, because these six stars wander about with these five warriors and they all will be destroyed along with their creations."

Note: The six stars were those who, along with Saklas or yaldaboth, created man and the cosmos. The five warriors refer to the five known planets at the time of the writing of the text. These planets were also connected with pagan worship and deities.

42. Judas said to Jesus, "Look at what those who have been baptized in your name do?"
Jesus said, "Truthfully I tell (you), this baptism done in my name (are done by those who do not know me. They sacrifice in vain to the god of this world. I baptized no one, for those baptized here have their hope here and those who follow me need no baptism for they will come) to me. In truth (I) tell you, Judas, (those offering) sacrifices to Saklas (do not offer sacrifice to the Great) God (but instead worship) everything that is evil.
"But you will exceed all of them. For you will sacrifice the man (the body that clothes / bares / contains me).

Note: Gnostic theology sets up a duality between the material world and the spiritual world. Since the god that created the material world was flawed, cruel, and insane, anything produced in that environment must be corrupted and opposed to the spiritual world. In this belief system the killing of Jesus' body was a good thing since it would free his spirit and unite it with the "Great One." Looked at from this angle, Judas was assisting Jesus in showing mankind the way. This line of reasoning must be taken as metaphorical. Some authors have suggested that Jesus had become entombed in his body and was asking Judas to free him. This cannot be so since Jesus comes and goes from the Holy Race or Generation above at will. Neither is Jesus touting mass suicide. Gnostic lived long lives and propagated their faith. The message here is that to remain detached from the material or corporeal and to strive to receive the knowledge here will free you in the life to come.

Already your horn has been raised, your anger has been ignited, your star has shown brightly, and your heart has (prevailed / been made strong / pure).

Note: The symbol horn is a phallic symbol but also a symbol of strength in much the way a rhino's horn is a sign of power and might.

Note: Although the lines added to the first half of this verse are tenuous, the information that is available establishes Judas' place according to this story. It does, however, open some questions. What was Judas' anger directed against? Was he sacrificing Jesus because he was angry at the established religion of the day? Was it this anger that made his heart strong or pure? Was anger his motivating force? If so, it harmonizes well with certain readings of the canonical gospels, which may indicate Judas wanted to expedite Jesus' kingdom so he would have a place of authority therein.

43. "Truly (I tell you,) your last (act will become that which will free this race but it will) grieve (you and will anger this generation and) the ruler, since he will be destroyed. (And then the) image of the great race of Adam will be raised high, for before heaven, earth, and the angels, that race from the eternal realms, exists (existed). Look, you have been told everything. Lift up your eyes and look to the cloud and the light within it and the stars around it. The star that leads the way is your star (you are the star)."

44. Then, Judas raised his eyes and saw the radiant cloud, and entered it. Those standing below him heard a voice coming from the cloud, saying, (The return of the) great race (is at hand and the image of the Great One will be established in

them because of Judas' sacrifice).

Note: This is the same cloud mentioned in verse 24. By entering the cloud Judas became one with the primal causality or "Great One / Supreme God." The Gnosis was imparted to him and he knew the mysteries. He then had understanding and strength to do what he was asked to do. This amounts to a transfiguration for Judas, much like that of Jesus. In the same manner, a voice from heaven announced his destiny.

45. (But the scribes waited for Judas, hoping to place a price on the head of Jesus.) Their high priests whispered that he had gone into the guest room for his prayer. But some scribes were there watching closely in order to arrest Jesus during the prayer, for they were afraid of the people, since he was accepted by everyone as a prophet. They approached Judas and said to him, "Why are you here? You are Jesus' disciple." Judas answered them in the way they wished. And he was given an amount of money and he handed Jesus over to them.

Note: We read of Judas' entrance into the radiant cloud and then his transaction with the scribes but there is no transition. It is possible the cloud is a metaphor for divine knowledge of the primal causality or Great God that produced Barbelo. See verse 28.

Note: The actual betrayal of Jesus by Judas is drastically downplayed. Only one paragraph is devoted to the actual act. Within this single paragraph no details are offered.

The gospel is constructed to give the reason for the betrayal. Building the rational of the act becomes far more important than the act itself, given the fact that it was the body that clothed Jesus that was destroyed and not the inner spirit. Shedding the body fulfilled destiny and freed the Christ spirit.

This was done as a demonstration of Jesus' belief in the immortal and eternal realm, which lay beyond human senses. The lesson of the Gospel of Judas and of Gnosticism in general had to do with reaching inside to gain knowledge of the unseen spiritual world. The orthodox church taught that only through martyrdom or the blessing of the church could one pass into the spiritual realm. Jesus was teaching another way. His death was the only way to exemplify his faith and show his disciples there was more than they could see in the material world. According to the Gnostic texts, the death of Jesus did not bring salvation. His life and death taught and provided knowledge, that if understood, would free the human race of its chains and allow it to ascend to the immortal realm.

This ends the Gospel of Judas.

THE 29th CHAPTER OF ACTS

The Sonnini Manuscript contains the account of Paul's journey to Spain and Britain. The document, purported to be the concluding portion of the "Acts of the Apostles" covers a portion of the period after Paul's two year enforced residence in Rome, in his own hired house. It is written in the style of the Bible Acts and reads like a continuation.

The Manuscript was found interleaved in a copy of Sonnini's Travels in Turkey and Greece and was purchased at the sale of the library and effects of the late Right Honorable Sir John Newport, Bart, of Ireland. Sir John's family arms were engraved on the cover of the book. It had been in his possession for over thirty years. With the book was a document from the Sultan of Turkey, granting to C. S. Sonnini permission to travel in all parts of the Ottoman dominions. The document was translated by C. S. Sonnini from an original Greek manuscript found in the Archives at Constantinople, and presented to him by the Sultan Abdoul Achment.

(The Biblical Acts of the Apostles and the Book of James are the only two New Testament books not ending in `amen.' This has led some Bible scholars to believe they are incomplete in their present form.)

Sometime in the late 1700's and before 1800, C.S.Sonnini published his copy of Sonnini's Travels in Turkey and Greece. Interleaved was a copy of the manuscript found in the Archives of Constantinople presented to him by the Sultan Abdoul Achmet. He was traveling during the reign of Louis XVI, who reigned from AD 1774 to AD 1793. He published his travels between those two dates, 1774 and 1793.

Dr. Gene Scott "Doc Notes" on the book "Did the Apostle Paul Visit Britain?" by R.W. Morgan, available from Dolores Press.

ACTS Chapter 29

Verse 1. Paul, full of the blessing of Christ, and overflowing in the Spirit, left Rome, having decided to go into Spain, becuase he had wanted to travel there for a long time, and he thought also to go from there to Britain.

Verse 2. Because he had heard in Phoenicia that some of the children of Israel, around the time of the Assyrian captivity,had escaped by sea to "the Islands far away" as proclaimed by the Prophet, and called by the Romans, Britain.

Verse 3. Since the Lord commanded the gospel to be preached far and wide to the Gentiles, and to the lost sheep of the House of Israel.

Verse 4. And no man hindered Paul because he testified boldly of Jesus before the governents and among the people; and be took with him certain of the brethren which lived with him at Rome, and they boarded a ship at Ostium, and having fair winds were brought safely into an safety (harbour) of Spain.

Verse 5. And many people gathered from the towns and villages, and the hill country; for they had heard of the conversion of the Apostles, and the many miracles he had performed.

Verse 6. And Paul preached with might in Spain, and great many people believed and were converted, for they knew he was an apostle sent from God.

Verse 7. And finding a ship in Armorica sailing to Britain they departed from Spain. Paul and his company passed along the South coast and reached a port called Raphinus.

Verse 8. Now when word spread wide that the Apostle had landed on their coast, large numbers of the inhabitants met him, and they treated Paul courteously and he entered in at the east gate of their city, and was housed in the house of a Hebrew and one of his own nation.

Verse 9. And the next day he came and stood upon Mount Lud;(Now the site of St. Paul's Cathedral.) and the people amassed at the gate, and assembled in the main street, and he preached Christ unto them, and they believed the word and the testimony of Jesus.

Verse 10. And at sunset the Holy Ghost fell upon Paul, and he prophesied, saying, "BEHOLD IN THE LAST DAYS THE GOD OF PEACE SHALL LIVE IN THE CITIES, AND THE INHABITANTS OF THEM SHALL BE COUNTED: AND IN THE SEVENTH CENSUS OF THE PEOPLE, THEIR EYES SHALL BE OPENED, AND THE GLORY OF THEIR INHERITANCE WILL SHINE OUT BEFORE THEM. NATIONS SHALL COME UP TO WORSHIP ON THE MOUNT THAT TESTIFIES OF THE PATIENCE AND LONG SUFFERING OF A SERVANT OF THE LORD."

Verse 11. And in the last days new announcements of the Gospel shall come forth out of Jerusalem, and the hearts of the people shall be filled with joy, and they shall look and spring of water shall be opened, and there shall be no more disease.

Verse 12. In those days there shall be wars and rumours of wars; and a king shall rise up, and his sword shall be for the healing of the nations, and peace he makes shall last, and the glory of his kingdom will be a wonder among princes.

Verse 13. And it came to pass that certain of the Druids came to Paul privately and showed by their rites and ceremonies (to prove) they were descended from the Jews which escaped from bondage in the land of Egypt, and the apostle believed these things, and he gave them the kiss of peace.

Verse 14. And Paul lived in his housing for three months proving the faith and preaching Christ continually.

Verse 15. And after these things Paul and his brethren left Raphinus, and sailed to Atium in Gaul.

Verse 16. And Paul preached in the Roman garrisons and among the people, encouraging all men to repent and confess their sins.

Verse 17. And there came to him certain of the Belgae to ask him about the new doctrine, and of the man Jesus; and Paul opened his heart unto them, and told them all things that had happened to him, how Christ
Jesus came into the world to save sinners; and they departed wondering among themselves about the things they had heard.

Verse 18. And after he preached and toiled muched Paul and his fellow workers went to Helvetia, and came to Mount Pontius Pilate, where he who condemned the Lord Jesus threw himself down headlong, and so miserably perished.

Verse 19. And immediately a torrent gushed from the mountain and washed his body (which had been) broken in pieces, into a lake.

Verse 20. And Paul stretched forth his hands upon the water, and prayed unto the Lord, saying, 0 Lord God, give a sign unto all nations that here Pontius Pilate, which condemned your only-begotten Son, plunged down headlong in to the pit.

Verse 21. And while Paul was still speaking, they looked there came a great earthquake, and the face of the waters was changed, and the lake took the form like unto the Son of Man hanging in an agony upon the Cross.

Verse 22. And a voice came out of heaven saying, Even Pilate has escaped the wrath to come, (See second death, Rev.21:8) for he washed his hands before the multitude at the shedding of the Lord Jesus' blood.

Verse 23. Because of this, when Paul and those with him saw the earthquake and heard the voice of the angel they glorified God and their spirits were greatly strenghtned.

Verse 24. And they journeyed and came to Mount Julius where two pillars stood, one on the right hand and one on the left hand, erected by Caesar Augustus.

Verse 25. And Paul was filled with the Holy Ghost and stood up between the two pillars, saying, Men and brethren, these stones which you see this day shall testify of my journey here and truly I say they shall remain until the outpouring of the spirit upon all nations, and the way will not be hindered throughout all generations.

Verse 26. And they went forth and came to Illyricum, intending to go by Macedonia into Asia, and grace was found in all the churches; and they prospered and had peace. Amen.

Printed in the USA
CPSIA information can be obtained
at www.ICGtesting.com
LVHW020215030424
776273LV00003B/101

9 781936 533572